ANCIENT MEXICO &
CENTRAL AMERICA

ANCIENT MEXICO & CENTRAL AMERICA

ARCHAEOLOGY AND CULTURE HISTORY

SUSAN TOBY EVANS

with 459 illustrations, 80 in color

To my husband, David Webster,
with many thanks

Frontispiece: At the Maya site of Tikal, the pyramids of the North Acropolis loom above the tropical forest.

First published in the
United States of America in 2004 by
Thames & Hudson Inc.
500 Fifth Avenue
New York, New York 10110

thamesandhudsonusa.com

This paperback edition 2004

Library of Congress Catalog Card Number
2003108922
ISBN 0-500-28440-7

Printed and bound in China by Midas

CONTENTS

PREFACE

FIVE HUNDRED YEARS AGO, news was reaching the Aztec emperor that alien forces were contacting his world. He was unnerved by evidence of strangers from the unknown, and omens of disaster. These unsettling bits of information formed the backdrop to his decisions as commander-in-chief of military forces controlling an empire of millions of tribute payers, to his life as the head of Mexico's most powerful dynasty, owner of palaces and pleasure parks, and to his role as his culture's chief priest and mediator of his world with the spiritual one, wielding the sacrificial knife on thousands of victims in the temple overlooking his palace.

The Aztec emperor was a fatalist, convinced that his overthrow by the aliens was inevitable. While it is tempting to wonder about the course of global history had a tougher-minded emperor led the Aztecs and resisted the Spaniards, our Western perspective on this situation views the overthrow of the Aztec empire as part of larger world historical forces. Modern times were being born out of the Middle Ages in Europe, and the Age of Discovery was revealing a whole world of wonders. Foremost among these marvels were two massive continents, North and South America, and their respective vast and complicated empires, those of the Aztec and Inca. The Europeans had a fairly small edge in military technology and an unexpected ally of conquest in the diseases they brought, that not only immobilized the population but conveniently killed off millions of them.

These discoveries and conquests added to the wealth and complexity of European life, and furthered the transformation of Western culture from its narrow medieval confines to its modern intellectual breadth. But the transformation for native cultures of the Americas was not one of their choosing. The Aztec empire became the cornerstone of a newly imperial Spain. Wealth that had flowed up to the Aztec capital, Tenochtitlan, still came into the same city, New Spain's capital of Mexico City, only it continued flowing on across the Atlantic to Spain. More significantly, the conquerors demanded the destruction of indigenous life ways and customs of the native populations that survived the Colonial-era plagues of disease and forced labor. Temple-pyramids were leveled and churches built atop them. Palaces were taken over and rebuilt for the conquistadores. Precious metal objects were melted into ingots and shipped to Spain. Carvings on stone and jade were shattered, their iconographic symbols an unwelcome reminder of the conquered past. Thousands of native books were burned, destroying a repository of knowledge and history.

Today we live in a new Age of Discovery, and are uncovering not just the wealth of Aztec culture, but the riches of all the cultures of ancient Mexico and Central America. The last fifty years have been especially productive for the recovery of archaeological evidence and the decipherment of ancient scripts and symbols. All of this information is made meaningful by our understanding of how cultures operate, and the conditions under which they change. "Culture history" once meant a recitation of events in chronological order, and even this was impossible, for the ancient Americas, until the revolution in dating techniques and the massive research efforts of the past fifty years. The culture history of ancient Mexico and Central America can now be recounted with a richness of detail and within a framework of evolutionary theory that makes this fascinating story understandable and compelling.

In this book, I try to tell the culture-historical story so that it will be clear to those with little or no knowledge of the ancient past of these regions – the general reader seeking a good introduction, the college student taking a course in the subject – as well as interesting to those who are already knowledgeable, such as avocational historians, and scholars in this field. Few of us who are professionals are true generalists Mesoamerican archaeology and ethnohistory comprise many fascinating subfields and in writing an overview I have attempted to cover all regions and time periods so that readers will have a framework of information and interpretation that encompasses many particular interests. The time range that the book covers begins with the peopling of the New World, perhaps 20,000 years ago, and continues through the contact period of the early 16th century AD, and the emergence of modern Mexican and Central American cultures. Chronology is the backbone of the book's structure, and the culture historical story is enlivened with numerous box features on cultural practices (e.g. child-raising) or valued materials (e.g. jade, metals). In order to maintain a generalist approach, I have minimized discussion of phase names and technical matters. These subjects are readily accessible through the time-lines and extensive bibliography and index. Known sites in Mesoamerica are so numerous that only a few could be discussed, relative to the total number. However, many sites appear in the 21 regional reference maps at the end of the volume, so that interested readers will know how to find out more information.

As the story-teller, I have been privileged to have had advice, suggestions, and corrections from many of my colleagues. I am particularly grateful to those who read the whole manuscript and gave me extensive comments, my colleagues Deborah Nichols and John M.D. Pohl, and my developmental editor at Thames & Hudson, Colin Ridler. Other colleagues who read much of the text and made welcome suggestions for improvement are Michael Coe, Richard Diehl, Jeremy Sabloff, and David Webster. Particular sections were enhanced by comments from Anthony Aveni (site orientations), David Grove (Formative-period cultural interactions), Joyce Marcus (Zapotec culture and Valley of Oaxaca), Simon Martin (Maya culture), and Payson Sheets (volcanic eruptions, especially Xitle and Ilopango). At times I asked questions and favors of many scholars, and I appreciate help and ideas from Christopher Beekman, Sue Bergh, Elizabeth Boone, Beatriz Braniff, Richard Cavallin-Cosma, Diane Chase, Napoleon Chagnon, John E. Clark, George Cowgill, Boyd Dixon, James Fitzsimmons, Kent Flannery, Bridget Gazzo, Gerardo Gutiérrez, Norman Hammond, Marion Hatch, Dan Healan, Kenneth Hirth, Dorothy Hosler, Stephen Houston, Bryan Just, Rex Koontz, Leonardo López Luján, René Millon, Mary Miller, Virginia Miller, Claire Milner, Patricia Plunket, Helen Pollard, Jeffrey Quilter, William Sanders, Nicholas Saunders, Harry Shafer, Virginia Smith, Dean Snow, Barbara Stark, Rebecca Storey, Mike Tarkanian, Carolyn Tate, Richard Townsend, Javier Urcid, Randolph Widmer, S. Jeffrey K. Wilkerson, and Eduardo Williams. Of course, I am responsible for the accuracy and sense of the narrative, and accept the inevitable changes in fact and interpretation that continue to flow from Mesoamericanist research.

Glancing through this book, you will notice its superb layout – wonderful illustrations placed within the text in a manner both intellectually meaningful and aesthetically pleasing – a signature of the publishers, Thames & Hudson. From the time I first thought of writing this book, I hoped that my narrative would have the best fate: being published by Thames & Hudson. The book was developed by Thames & Hudson editor Colin Ridler, whom Michael Coe has rightly called "the very best archaeology editor in the world" and I am indebted to Colin for his sponsorship of the book. My good fortune has also included working with Susan Crouch, the book's production editor, who has capably overseen complicated matters of logistics and accuracy, and Wendy Gay, tireless and gifted illustration maven. Rowena Alsey is responsible for the book's excellent design, and Celia Falconer for its production – to both of them my sincere thanks. Other Thames & Hudson staff who assisted on this project are Melissa Danny, Silvia Crompton, Susan Dwyer, Drazen Tomic, and the sales and marketing team.

This has been a substantial project, and I appreciate the support of my friends and family. My husband, David Webster, has always been enthusiastic about this book, and has been an invaluable resource of information and sounding board for ideas. I also thank Gene Davis Reese, Joanne Pillsbury, Ethel Medhurst Toby, and Elizabeth Toby Sagehorn for their encouragement.

Susan Toby Evans
Pine Grove Mills, Pennsylvania

PART 1 MESOAMERICA, MIDDLE AMERICA, AND ITS PEOPLES

Paleoindian through Initial Formative Periods (first populations–1200 BC)

	Paleoindian		Archaic	Initial Formative
	8000	5000	2000	1200 BC
Northern Arid Zone	Malpais, San Dieguito, Big Bend, Desert tradition, Coahuila complex, Cochise tradition *Frightful Cave*			
SE: Sierra Madre Oriental	Diablo Lerma	Infiernillo	Ocampo	Flacco/Guerra/Mesa de Guaje
SE: Tamaulipas	Diablo Lerma *Cave sites*	Nogales	La Perra	Almagre
Northwestern Frontier				*El Calón shell mound*
West Mexico				Matanchén, El Opeño Capacha complex Machalilla phase
Michoacán				
Guerrero			Ostiones ph./Initial Ceramic per./Xochipalpa complex *2400 BC: Puerto Marques, "Pox" pottery, earliest in Mesoamerica*	
Morelos				Amate phase
Basin of Mexico		*Santa Isabel Iztapan Mammoth Kill Site*	Playa, Zohapilco phases *2300 BC: earliest figurine*	Ixtapaluca phase Coapexco, Ayotla subphase *Tlatilco, Cuicuilco*
Tula region				
Toluca				
Puebla				Tzompantepec
Tlaxcala				Tzompantepec
Gulf Lowlands, north			Palo Hueco phase	
Gulf Lowlands, north-central		*Santa Luisa, La Conchita*		
Gulf Lowlands, south-central				
Tehuacán Valley	Ajuereado, El Riego		Coxcatlán Abejas Purrón	Ajalpan
Mixteca Alta				Early Cruz
Oaxaca		Naquitz phase *Guilá Naquitz Cave*	Jicaras, Blanca, Martinez, Espiridión, Tierras Largas *Gheo-Shih site; 4250 BC: maize at Guilá Naquitz*	*San José Mogote*
Tehuantepec				Lagunita
Gulf Lowlands, south				Ojochí, Bajío
Chiapas Interior Plateau			Santa Marta	Cotorra
Chiapas and Guatemala Coast			Chantuto A, B phases *Chantuto sites*	Barra, Locona, Ocós *Mokaya culture, Paso de la Amada*
Guatemala Highlands				Arévalo
Maya Lowlands, north	*Loltun Cave*			
Belize		Sand Hill Orange Walk	Melinda Progreso *Betz Landing*	
Maya Lowlands, south				
Southeastern Mesoamerica				
Intermediate Area	Period I		Period II	Period III
			Monagrillo shell mound, 2500 BC: earliest pottery in Middle America	

Selected phase names; *sites* and *events* are in *italic* type

1 ANCIENT MESOAMERICA

THE CIVILIZATION AND ITS ANTECEDENTS

IN NOVEMBER 1519, the Aztec king Motecuzoma (Montezuma) met his honored Spanish guest, Hernan Cortés, in Tenochtitlan, the Aztec capital that would later become Mexico City. The city, with its huge pyramids, plazas, and palaces, was arrayed around them [1.1]. Vast and busy, it was thickly settled with twice as many people as lived in any of the great cities of Spain at that time. And in contrast to the dusty dryness of so many Spanish towns, Tenochtitlan, surrounded by a lake, was a verdant green island crosscut by glittering canals and plastered roads. Thick stands of tall, willowy trees framed handsome mansions adorned with flowers and fragrant garlands. The city's center was dominated by the pyramids of the Great Temple precinct, and, just to the south, the city's main plaza, an expansive open square. Motecuzoma's grand palace filled another

1.1 *Tenochtitlan, view of the Great Temple precinct, looking to the southeast, with the mountains Iztaccihuatl and Popocatépetl in the distance.*

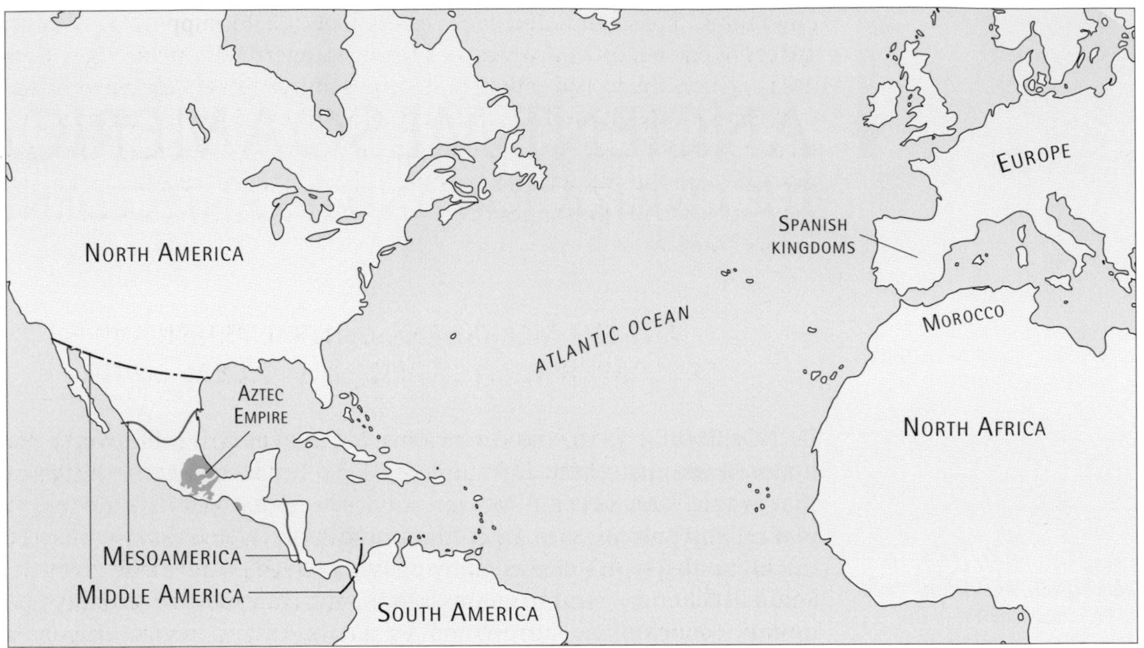

1.2 *Part of the Western world in* AD *1519, with emphasis on Middle America and Spain. The limits of the geographical subcontinent, Middle America, are shown with a dashed line. The limits of the culture area, Mesoamerica, are shown with a colored line. The Aztec empire, a political construct, covers the area that is shaded.*

whole block and opened onto the east side of the plaza. A second palace covered another block just west of the Great Temple precinct, and there Cortés and his company were quartered.

Motecuzoma's city was a fitting capital for his realm, which was substantially larger than the area controlled by any of the Spanish kingdoms [**1.2**]. This situation would persist for another year or so, then Spain would conquer and annex this Mexican domain. The Spanish-Mexican geopolitical situation was unusual, if not unique in human history: never before had there been such a collision of great empires completely unknown to each other. Here were two complex societies, Western European and Middle American, each with kings and peasants, and each was the product of a long course of cultural development completely uninfluenced by and separate from the other's history, dramatic proof of the independent operation of the forces of cultural evolution in the Old and New Worlds.

The subject of this book is the culture history of ancient Mexico and Central America, regions that extend over the geographical subcontinent Middle America, and whose cultures evolved over thousands of years. The cultures that arose there are now called "Mesoamerican" (meaning "of Middle America") and in AD 1519 their long period of independent development was coming to a close. In this book, the events and processes that shaped Mesoamerican cultural evolution are described and interpreted. Like all other human societies since the end of the most recent Ice Age about 10,000–12,000 years ago, those of Middle America changed from roving bands of hunter-foragers to, by AD 1500, a complex mosaic of many kinds of societies, from the Aztec tribute empire, a network of nation-states and chiefdoms that dominated land fertile enough to support agriculture, to independent bands and tribes of hunter-foragers who made their living in areas where food production was impossible. Village agriculture was the mainstay of Mesoamerican life in AD 1500, but since the time of the first farmers, about 2000 BC, the productive surplus had been increasingly diverted into the support of elite political and ritual specialists, with societal inequalities made permanent in a social class system and the political apparatus of the state.

ANCIENT MEXICO AND CENTRAL AMERICA IN GEOGRAPHICAL, CULTURAL, AND GLOBAL CONTEXT

These cultural changes took place over many centuries, in diverse regions that together span thousands of miles. To describe them in sufficient detail so that the processes of change are understandable will take the rest of this book. We begin now with a brief discussion of the geographical setting of Mesoamerica, and then a comparison of this setting with those of other great cradles of world civilization. Because culture history is so strongly affected by the dynamics of change in food procurement strategies, in population size, in basic technology, and in political, social, and ideological transformations, these factors are of critical importance and I discuss their interactions in detail below.

Mesoamerica and Middle America: Culture and Geography

While *Middle America* is a geographical zone encompassing the region from the Isthmus of Panama in the south through the Sonoran and Chihuahuan deserts of northern Mexico and the U.S. Southwest, *Mesoamerica* is a culture area, defined by shared features of indigenous cultural adaptation. As the map shows [**1.3**], Mesoamerica only extends over part of Middle America, covering that contiguous area where cultivation of maize (corn) brought reliable harvests. Over time, the boundaries of the culture area shifted somewhat, with changes in climate that determined whether or not maize cultivation was possible in the borderlands.

From the Formative period (beginning about 2000 BC) on, Mesoamerican culture developed and thrived wherever maize, beans, and squash were staple crops, the most important foods in a varied and nutritious diet that also included many vegetables and fruits. The few domestic animals – small hairless dogs and turkeys – were important sources of dietary protein, as were wild game and fish. Food was sufficiently abundant to support villages of farmer-artisans, who not only raised crops, but also made pottery and stone tools, items of basketry, textiles, and skins, using materials that were locally available, and some from other regions.

Exchange of raw materials and finished goods over long distances was stimulated by the marked environmental variation over Middle America,

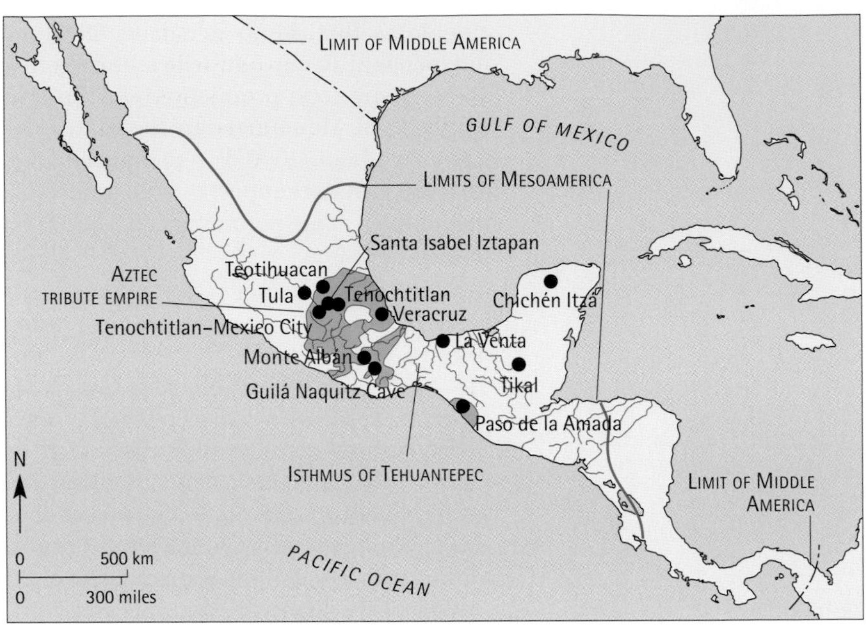

1.3 *Middle America and Mesoamerica. Motecuzoma and the other great lords collected tribute from an area that covered much of modern Mexico. The map shows the boundaries of this tribute empire, as well as those of the cultural area called Mesoamerica. As a distinct cultural region, Mesoamerica comprised the area inhabited by a large set of loosely related ethnic groups who shared important cultural practices, such as the set of crops they depended upon, the spiritual principles they venerated, the way they farmed and built their houses. Although not all of the 12–15 million people living in Mesoamerica in 1519 sent tribute to the Mexica Aztecs, they would have recognized familiar features found over a huge area.*

where several impressive mountain ranges crowd into a tropical zone bounded by two vast oceans. In few other areas of the world are so many contrasting environments so closely juxtaposed: tropical coast is only a few hundred miles from peaks that are permanently capped with snow. In addition to these sharp distinctions in habitat, Middle America was frequently subjected to such transforming effects as hurricanes, volcanic eruptions, and earthquakes. This rugged and dynamic terrain created many environments, many valleys where local populations flourished. In every region, people established distinctive ethnic identities that integrated subsistence and artisanal practices with veneration of the powerful features of the local landscape, and of the sacred ancestors of their leaders.

The early years of the Formative period saw the establishment of village agriculturalists all over Mesoamerica. As the centuries passed, in some regions there developed chiefdoms that unified several villages under the direction of one lineage, and later, states that legitimized the right of the few to the labor and products of the many. The state as a political construct typifies the most complex kinds of societies in the world. In Aztec Mexico, Cortés encountered a state headed by Motecuzoma that managed a tribute empire, in many respects similar contemporaneous states in Europe. Aztec society had a class system similar to those of Catholic Spain and Islamic North Africa. Cortés was not surprised to find a great empire, because since long before Columbus's time, European explorers had expected to find China if they traveled far enough west. The astonishing thing about Cortés's intrusion into the Aztec world, from the European perspective, was comprehending that there was a completely unknown, completely independent empire in the world: civilizations and empires are very rare and complex forms of human society. When the Spaniards later pushed into the South American Andes they found yet another, that of the Incas. These discoveries, of the Aztec and Inca empires, were two of the greatest events of the Age of Discovery; no other societies contacted during that time, or since, compared to these in terms of complexity, size, and wealth.

How Societal Complexity Develops

Cortés and his contemporary explorers did not set out with the goal of proving the independent existence of the two previously unknown cradles of civilization, nor did they see these great states as important social scientific evidence showing the presence of broadly similar patterns of human cultural evolution in different parts of the world. Yet the Mesoamerican and Andean civilizations document such global patterns for us today, and provide strong evidence of broad similarities in development, from the hunter-forager societies that covered the globe 12,000 years ago, to states like those of 16th-century Spain and Mexico.

The major question – how did the Aztec empire, in particular, and Mesoamerican culture, in general, develop – is encompassed within the larger story of humankind. Although the Aztec empire had consolidated a far greater area than had any previous polity in the whole culture history of Mesoamerica, theirs was not a "primary state," the first ever in Mesoamerica. The Aztec state was a variation upon earlier Mesoamerican states, going back centuries; the first were rising strongly as Rome was establishing its imperial power over Europe. When Cortés contacted the Aztec empire, he was discovering the most recent manifestation of Mesoamerican complex society (for a discussion of types of societies, see box overleaf).

Complex Societies and Civilizations A society is "complex" when the people within it differ significantly from each other in such measures as their social station, wealth, and degree of political influence. Complex societies have richer and poorer people, and very complex societies have very wealthy people ruling over a mass of lower-class producers. In ancient farming cultures, like that of the Aztecs, the wealth and surplus generated by the producers – mostly farmer-artisans – permitted the wealthy to develop and enjoy the finer things of life, "civilized life." "Civilization" is a meaningful term, and is fully discussed in the box on pp. 136–137. Briefly, for our purposes here, civilization is the set of cultural traits that develops as society becomes complex: mature art style, monumental architecture, and intellectual achievements such as writing and astronomy.

The two great civilizations of the Americas, those of Mesoamerica and the South American Andean region, were among the six primary civilizations in the history of the world [**1.4**], the others arising in Southwest Asia (Mesopotamia), Egypt, the Indian subcontinent, and East Asia (China). In these six broadly productive regions of the world, the first states arose, matured, and gave rise to secondary states, there and elsewhere, part of a

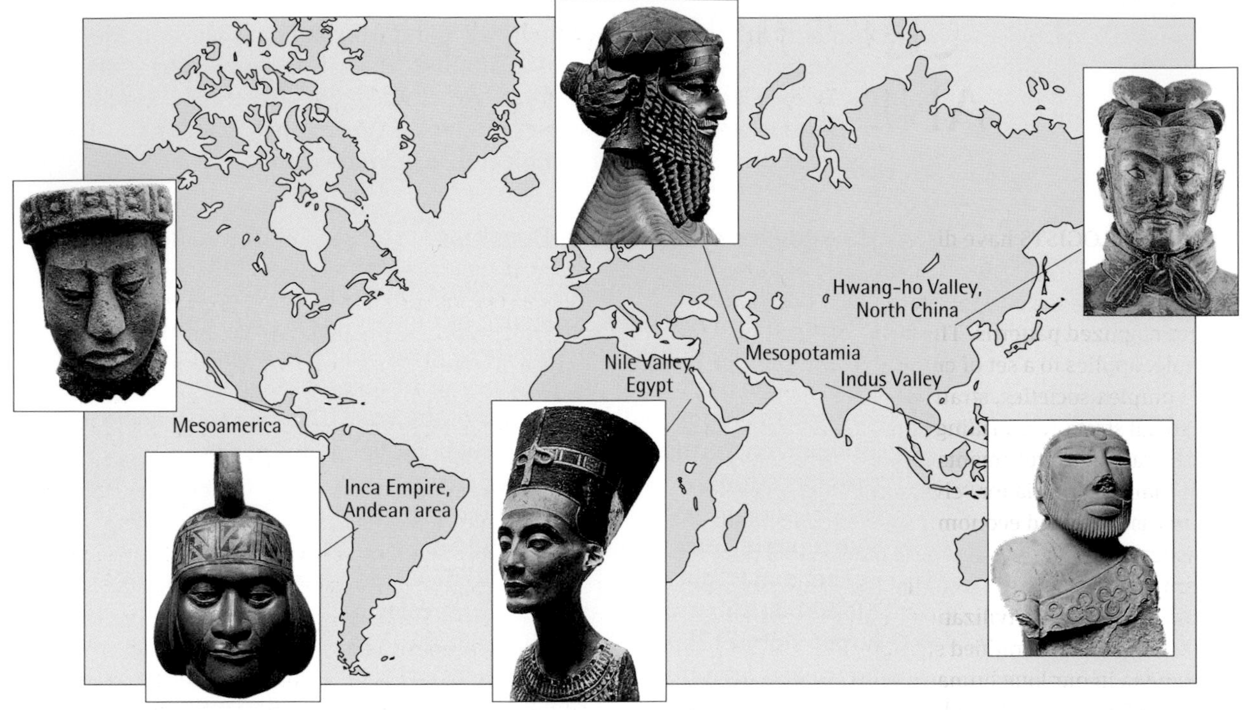

1.4 *The world's "cradles of civilization" are those six areas where civilization developed independently of outside influence. This map of the world shows the locations of Mesoamerica, the Inca Empire/Andean area, Mesopotamia, the Nile Valley in Egypt, the Indus Valley, and the Hwang-ho Valley in North China. Accompanying figures exemplify both high-status individuals in these societies, and the sophisticated art styles associated with them.*

long process that we call cultural evolution. It has brought us to our present situation of complex nation-states, supra-national organizations (e.g. the United Nations, the European Union) and a global economy.

Culture and Earliest Humans Human culture is defined, at a very basic level, as adaptive behavior patterns that our species has used to try to enhance our ability to survive and prosper. The oldest physical evidence of human culture consists of very simple stone tools made by our ancestors about 2.5 million years ago in East Africa. Fully modern humans developed in Africa by about 100,000 years ago, and from Africa, modern humans moved into all parts of Eurasia, their expanding populations supported by hunting and foraging as they continued to exploit new frontiers of unoccupied territory.

The timing of pioneering episodes is still under debate, but areas significantly detached from Africa and Eurasia, such as Australia and New Guinea, were inhabited by about 50,000 years ago. The Americas began to be populated toward the end of the Pleistocene epoch (last Ice Age), as eastern Siberia and northernmost North America were joined by a land bridge that was exposed as glacial episodes resulted in declining sea levels. Herd animals such as bison and deer moved out across the new areas of tundra, and foragers followed them, migrating to a new continent without knowing it. This occurred at least 15,000 years ago, and perhaps 30,000 years ago or more.

CULTURAL EVOLUTION AND TYPES OF SOCIETIES

ANTHROPOLOGISTS have discerned broad patterns of sociocultural integration that apply to all human societies, and have developed terms that designate these recognized patterns. The term "civilization," for example, applies to a set of cultural features found in the most complex societies, stratified states that have distinct social strata (e.g., ruling elite, commoners, slaves) and centralized governments (see box, pp. 136–137). Given that the criteria for "civilization" include such features as cities and economic specialization and sophisticated art styles [**1.5**], we can agree that the modern world in general is dominated by several "civilizations," "Western Civilization" among them. However, civilization and the stratified state are relatively recent phenomena in our long human history, arising only about 5,000 years ago. Long before that, and persisting into the 20th century, were other forms of social order, such as egalitarian bands of hunter-foragers who comprised all of the world's population until about 10,000–12,000 years ago, the end of the most recent Ice Age.

World culture history presents a rich array of societal types, and in any region, different types of societies have been tried, changed, abandoned, elaborated – there is no evidence for "unilinear" evolution in the sense that in each region, mobile hunter-foragers "evolved" into village-dwelling farmer-foragers who then developed chiefdoms that later became states. Such a simplified sequence of general events violates the reality, the messy course of human events. However, no one can deny the broad transformation of society that has occurred since the end of the Pleistocene, when all of our ancestors were hunter-foragers, to the present, when virtually all lives are shaped, if not dominated, by huge nation-states and global corporations guiding the world's economic system. And recognizing this, it is useful to categorize the several basic kinds of societies that comprise our collective cultural history.

Societal typologies can be based upon many features, and here, economic organization is fundamental, because how people make a living determines whether or not a surplus of wealth can be produced – and controlled – by some segment of society. That surplus is essential to other kinds of societal elaboration, such as whether different social ranks or classes exist, and what kind of government determines policy, because if someone is to spend their time in ways other than food-getting, someone else must provide the food to support that individual. Thus the basic distinction is made between three kinds of society: *egalitarian*, in which there is virtually no accumulation of individual wealth, and social relations are all family-based, *ranked*, in which some families enjoy certain material advantages over others, and *stratified*, in which whole classes of people are distinguished by marked differences in wealth and power [**1.6**].

Recognizing these patterns in the archaeological record relies strongly on several important types of evidence, such as the size and complexity of archaeological sites, and the number and size of sites in a particular region at a particular time period.

1.5 *The arch at Labná, a Maya site, drawn by Frederick Catherwood (c. 1840).*

1.6 *(Overleaf) Table outlining features of different kinds of societies.*

Modes of Sociocultural Integration in Pre-Industrial Societies (1.6)*			
	Egalitarian	**Ranked**	**Stratified**
Type of society	Bands (mobile foragers) and tribes (village horticulturalist-foragers)	Chiefdoms (village agriculturalists)	States (archaic agrarian, non-industrial)
Subsistence	Hunting, foraging, and/or simple horticulture	Usually food production (farming, intensive collecting), supplemented by hunting, foraging	Intensive food production which produces dependable food surpluses
Economy	No accumulation of personal property, no differential access to key resources; generalized sharing within the group; little occupational specialization; division of labor is based on age and sex; distribution of goods is limited to sharing among and between families	Limited but significant differential access to key resources, depending upon family; farmer-artisans produce food, goods, in the households, kin groups setting; trade is common, particularly for prestige goods, produced under the clientage of the rulers	Marked differential access to, and distribution of key resources, depending upon class and family; food surpluses support many specialized artisanal and administrative occupations; complex trade relations often involve dedicated market places and established currencies
Territory	Related groups, sharing a common ethnic identity and language, exploit a known region and have mutually recognized use rights	Region is exploited and claimed by a polity comprising many communities, sharing ethnicity and language	Region has well-defined boundaries, defended by military action of organized armies
Population and settlement pattern	Coresiding group or community (temporary camp or permanent farming/intensive collecting village) numbers several dozen to several hundred, and may maximize distance between groups in order to maximize resource catchment zone. Some communities may be specialized in seasonal or resource exploitation use. Density: low, < 1/km^2	Settlement types in the region include a central community, larger and more functionally diverse than the many surrounding villages of several hundred people each (two-tiered settlement pattern is a diagnostic of ranked societies in the archaeological record). Population in the region claimed by the central capital may number several thousand. Density varies greatly depending on food availability; may be as high as several hundred people/km^2	Settlement types in the region include cities as well as smaller centers and villages, a hierarchy of site types encompassing at least three tiers (a diagnostic of state-level societies in the archaeological record). Settlement system integrated as a single polity can encompass thousands, even millions of people. Population density is very high in core areas
Community	Campsite of mobile hunter-foragers, or permanent village; in any region, communities will be similar in size and range of functions	Central community has special administrative and economic functions, larger population than the many surrounding villages of	Cities are functionally, socially, and even ethnically diverse, small centers serve local administrative and economic needs, villages of farmer-

*based on Webster, Evans, and Sanders 1993: 160–161

Modes of Sociocultural Integration in Pre-Industrial Societies			
	Egalitarian	**Ranked**	**Stratified**
		farmer-artisans. Most communities are permanently occupied	artisans are most common community type
Society	Order is maintained by familial authority and face-to-face interaction. Prestige is conferred by ability and age; social cohesion is promoted through descent groups and sodalities	Kinship, face-to-face interaction continue to facilitate societal integration. Kin groups include large descent groups; these vary in prestige, and provide the basis for social ranks that distinguish individuals	Whole groups are ranked as social strata, with associated features of access to wealth and privilege. In local residential groups, kinship and face-to-face controls still maintain social harmony, but overall, social control is maintained by enforcement of codified laws established by ruling elites
Politics	No community is ruled by another: each is autonomous. There are few or no formal offices; leadership is situational, leadership positions are achieved by seniority and merit; leaders use authority and charisma, but have no recognized right to enforce policy through coercion. Feuding is common, resolved by community fissioning	Communities acknowledge centralized rule by chief and the chief's descent group. Formal offices include several kinds of chiefs, recruited to office from highest ranking descent groups (ascribed rather than achieved status). Leadership depends on individual authority and charisma, with little recourse to coercive force. Conflict resolution includes fissioning of the polity, particularly if the leader is weak	The state as a political system is dominated by hereditary elite, with complex hierarchies of administrative officials, most of whom had authority ascribed to them because of social rank; some lesser officials may have achieved position through merit. Power is enforced through physical coercion
Religion, ideology	Belief system venerates the natural world as sacred, infused with spiritual power; individual, community well-being is insured by intercession by shamans who communicate with the spirit world. Community rituals mark rites of passage for individuals, group, natural world	Belief system may venerate ethnic deities as well as natural spirits; special buildings, rites may unite whole community, rites of passage and increase continue to orient individual, family life, and shaman remains important as spiritual intercessor and curer	Belief system is codified, with organized religion emerging as an institution associated with the state, with professional priests as officials in charge of ceremonies in monumental ceremonial buildings. Priests may serve shamanic functions, and shamans may continue to serve communities
Examples in Mesoamerican culture history	Paleoindian- and Archaic-period groups	Formative agrarian sedentary villagers	Terminal Formative, Classic, and Postclassic centers and their supporting populations

Hunting, Foraging, and Food Production All over the world, archaeologists have observed the same general patterns of behavior by these ancient mobile foragers. In some regions, the resources for hunting and foraging were rich, and populations could grow large and relatively dense, even establishing year-round permanent settlements. Furthermore, some of the wild plant and animal foods that our ancestors came to depend upon most heavily were also those that flourished under human care. The development of agriculture as a set of cultivation and stock-raising techniques, applied to a particular group of plants and animals, was not a unique invention but rather was repeated many times in many places: a set of gradual, mutually adaptive changes in human practices and the lives of the plants and animals they needed for survival. This slowly evolving process of increasing dependency upon food production as an alternative to collecting wild food and hunting, repeated in different parts of the globe, gave rise to countless regional patterns of subsistence, most of them "mixed strategies" combining some food production with continued foraging and hunting for wild resources.

Many environments were rich enough to support mixed strategies without requiring changes to insure crop security, but in others, productive agriculture demanded substantial investments of labor and materials in order to guarantee a harvest. The world's earliest civilization arose in Mesopotamia, which was the flat plain between the Tigris and Euphrates Rivers, where the earliest cities and states appeared. It was not nearly as rich an environment in terms of its resources as were the surrounding ranges of hills – the Fertile Crescent – where food production had begun, and where plants and animals still essential to our diets were first domesticated. Pioneering populations in Mesopotamia brought these domesticates with them, but had to work much harder than their mixed-strategist ancestors in the Fertile Crescent, in order to secure a stable food supply. However, once irrigation canals and levees were built in Mesopotamia, the harvests of cultivated crops were large enough to support many more people than could a mixed strategy.

Group Size, Resources, and Conflicts Large and dense populations present challenges to human ingenuity, with regard to social organization as well as food production. Anthropologists know that human groups face certain size limits, no matter how sophisticated our technology becomes. At the most basic materialist level, there is a limit on how much food any region can provide, and this was a genuine constraint until modern transport technology assured the provisioning of even the least productive and most remote zones. But other constraints on a group's population size are social, and seem to derive from very ancient patterns of human life. For example, despite our daily modern interaction with thousands of people, whether in person or through information media, in any period of our lives each of us can only develop strong emotional bonds with about a dozen people at most, what we might call a "sympathy group" (Dunbar 1996). Coincidentally, this would be an effective size for a band of mobile foragers.

Furthermore, the maximum number of people with whom we can develop workable relations of trust, regulated by face-to-face interaction and the presence of a mutually respected leader, during any time, is several hundred people. With the advent of laws and police forces, many hundreds of people could live peaceably together, but for family ties to be sufficient to keep order, there is a definite limit on the size of the group. In fact, a group of several hundred people is a standard "company," and many instances in human history evidence the effective utility of a group of this size – military companies, religious congregations, groups of pioneering colonists. Perhaps the most compelling evidence that this "company" is an optimum size for relations based on trust is the ethnographic observation that groups of several hundred, be they encampments or permanent settlements, represent the largest communities that can be effectively regulated by kinship ties of custom and respect, with individuals voluntarily bowing to the authority of the senior members of their group.

When local circumstances permit or require community populations to rise above this size, then conflicts arise within the community, and they cannot be resolved by traditional means; they can only be resolved by one of two radical solutions. The first, and most common solution in our human past, was that the group would split along its lines of conflict, fissioning into two smaller groups, at least one of which establishes a new community elsewhere.

The second solution to community conflict is much more dramatic, because it requires a serious change in social organization: the establishment (or imposition) of an authority beyond one's kin lineage leader. This amounts to adding a level of social control that transcends the kinship-regulated village, and transforms a single-level social system into a hierarchy, or the simplest form of complex society. At the same time, the new leaders, having taken on the responsibility of keeping order in a group too large to govern by traditional familial means, would be in a position to demand concrete demonstrations of loyalty and support, such as tributes of food, labor, and/or materials. That some individuals would then have to produce food surpluses would permit the rulers and also other individuals to be freed from subsistence pursuits. Those who could make a living as specialists in such fields as curing, craft production, ritual practices, or administration, could trade their products and services for the food surpluses of others.

Cradles of Food Surplus and Authority Figures This relation between a dependable, surplus-producing food supply and the emergence of impersonal – or suprakin – authority figures and specialists in various occupations is the basis for societal complexity throughout the world. The first agrarian states of the Old World were in the great river valleys of Mesopotamia, Egypt, China, and India. The New World was settled much later, and its earliest states developed in fertile lowlands and the more agriculturally challenging highlands.

The cultural sequences in all six regions follow the same general pattern:

- the key region was used repeatedly or periodically for hunting and foraging;
- animal and crop domestication gradually occurred as a co-adaptive process, possibly in adjacent areas, from which it spread to the key region;
- agricultural intensification in the key region resulted in highly productive landscape; which
- spurred further population growth; and
- permitted the development of larger settlements, which, in turn, stimulated the development of a complex social and political hierarchy and complex division of labor.

Culture History and Chronology

These sequences are the bases of historical development in the cradles of civilization. We often think of history as a narrative derived from documents, but the world is full of regions where documents reveal only a small part of the culture's history. Any culture area's history can only be told through the use of various kinds of evidence: documents that describe events and customs, oral traditions of myth and epic, material culture remains ranging from small personal possessions to networks of towns and cities across a landscape. Working with all available sources to establish the correct chronological order of events and materials is essential in order to reconstruct meaningful history.

Chronology and chronometric (time-measured) ordering of cultures and events is the backbone of interpretation of causes and effects in history; this is how we determine the processes that comprise cultural evolution. Today we modern people take accurate historical chronology for granted because so much of recent history is thoroughly documented. Also, a scientific revolution in archaeological dating techniques occurred in the last few decades, with the development of an array of methods, for example radiocarbon dating, that permits the reconstruction of histories even for ancient cultures lacking written records. Chronology is the basic structure which unites data – sites, artifacts, and documents – and theory – identifying and interpreting the processes of change.

Periods in Mesoamerican Culture History In this book, we use a set of chronological terms that have become standard for putting Mesoamerican cultures in sequential order. Readers should note that this is a commonly-used sequence, but that different authors may use slightly differing dates. The *Paleoindian period* refers to the time beginning with the first migrations of northern Asian peoples into the New World. During this time, all New World people were mobile hunter-foragers, and they hunted the great Ice Age animals – mammoths, for example – that ranged over the broad plains of the Americas. The climate began to change about 12,000 years ago, and by about 8000 BC we see a transformation of the landscape as the climate assumed modern patterns, and many Ice Age animals had become extinct. The *Archaic period* begins with these changes, because they demanded that hunter-foragers change their patterns of adaptation, and concentrate on the plants and animals that came to characterize specific regions.

By about 5000 BC, local patterns of adaptation had become so specialized that, in some places, people had begun to manipulate the growing patterns of wild plants – had begun to domesticate them to assure a more stable food supply. By about 2000 BC, these changes ushered in the *Formative period* (sometimes referred to as the Pre-classic period), so-called because the first steps had been taken in the formation of mature Mesoamerican society. In fact, because Mesoamerican culture could only exist where cultivation could be practiced, the Formative period is when Mesoamerican culture really begins to take shape within the geographical limits defined in Figure **1.3**. The Formative period encompasses 2000 BC–*c.* AD 300, and within this period Mesoamerican societies were transformed from bands of mobile hunter-foragers, to village-based farmers, to groups of villages under the leadership of one chief, to states ruled by hereditary elites controlling the wealth produced by many commoners.

The *Classic period* dates from *c.* AD 250 or 300 to 900, and witnessed the development of many states and proto-states, particularly in the Central Highlands of Mexico and the Maya lowlands. The *Postclassic period* extends from AD 900 to *c.* 1521, the year of the conquest of Mexico by Spain, and encompassed further state development, culminating in the establishment of the great tribute empire of the Aztecs, a political entity that covered much of modern Mexico. From the time of European intrusion until the early 1800s, Middle America was ruled by Spain, in a *Colonial period* that saw the suppression of religious and artistic elements of indigenous culture. Beginning in the early 1800s, the *Republican period* brought independence to Mexico and to the emerging nations of Central America. It also brought a renewed interest in prehispanic history, and by the end of the 19th century, important archaeological and ethnohistorical research was under way.

This brief summary of these broad periods masks considerable variation within Mesoamerica, and even more variability when we consider societies beyond Mesoamerica, but still within Middle America. Even at the time of the Spanish intrusion, there were many peoples living as hunter-foragers, especially in the northern Mexican deserts, and there were many chiefdoms, particularly in Panama and other regions south of the Mesoamerican culture area.

While the period names and their associated dates, as outlined above, have a strong cultural evolutionary basis, they will be used in this book as chronological markers rather than as developmental terms, and readers should note this distinction, as well as the slightly different use of these period names, and dates, in other sources. The theoretically-informed culture-historical approach followed here will survey all of the geographical area, Middle America, during each of these periods, in an effort to capture the dynamic nature of cultural evolution within the whole subcontinent.

Horizons, Traditions, and Diffusion The broad period names sometimes refer to *horizons*, which are very widespread manifestations of the same kinds of traits over a very large area (Willey and Phillips 1958: 33). In the Early and Middle Formative period, for example, traits identified with Olmec culture, Mesoamerica's first great cultural tradition, are found from West Mexico and the Central Highlands down into Southeastern Mesoamerica. Such Olmec-style traits – building styles, art styles – can be termed a *horizon style*. Horizons, and the styles associated with them, help archaeologists to extend chronological markers to areas that display such styles but which may lack other means of establishing the timing of their appearance.

Of course, diffusion of styles is assumed to take time, and the rate of diffusion may be poorly understood. In fact, the direction of diffusion may be poorly understood, as well, which is why each advance in chronometric dating, or new discoveries in particular regions, may bring revisions in our understanding of the pace and direction of trends in culture history. *Tradition* is also used to describe certain constellations of tool types or other traits that are broadly distributed and assumed to be contemporaneous. For example, the "Fluted Point tradition" was the technological adaptation to hunting used by Paleoindian hunter-foragers all over the Americas.

Phase Names and Culture History Within each region, archaeological research has established a set of phases with regionally distinct, and sometimes even site-specific phase names, such as Monte Albán I, II, III, etc., pertaining to the great Oaxacan capital. These identify the widespread occurrence of similar traits within a region (or within a site), and serve as a chronological control, maintaining the chronological order of the appearance of traits within a region, no matter what changes in actual dating may occur. We may learn, from more advanced radiocarbon dating, that a phase is earlier or later than we had previously thought, but we still know that Phase Y falls between Phase X and Phase Z, and includes particular kinds of materials and a particular subsistence strategy.

Phase names are invaluable, but to the novice they can be distracting. Professional archaeologists sometimes use phase names to convey information in a kind of shorthand, assuming that everyone knows what traits embody a particular phase at a particular site. Sometimes phase names are used without any clue to chronometric dates, which reduces the usefulness of phase names when comparing one region to another. In fact, this avoidance of assigning dates to a phase name often occurs because there may be no means to do so authoritatively. In this book, phase names are, wherever possible, linked to dates that represent our best current information. Because of the abundance of phase names in use in Mesoamerica, not all can be included in the book's discussion of regions and sites. Readers should also note that phase names are often used as "culture" names, referring to the set of behavioral patterns and material remains that are characteristic of an area during a particular period.

The remainder of this chapter will provide a brief introduction to

Mesoamerica's whole culture history – a cognitive map of the rest of the book. We will begin with a general survey of the culture history of the Paleoindian, Archaic, Formative, Classic, and Postclassic periods, concluding in Tenochtitlan, where we began. Chapter 2 takes up the topics of cultural ecology and the regions of the geographical area, Middle America, concluding with an in-depth look at the earliest Middle Americans. Chapter 3 will deal with the Archaic period in greater depth, Chapters 4 through 9 will cover the Formative period, Chapters 10 through 13, the Classic period, Chapters 14 through 19, the Postclassic and the period of European contact. In the final chapter, we shall see how Mesoamerican culture has survived, and how it was rediscovered, particularly in the last century, by the efforts of archaeologists, ethnohistorians, and epigraphers. Now, let us begin the journey.

MIDDLE AMERICAN AND MESOAMERICAN CULTURE HISTORY

The distinction between Middle America, the geographical region, and Mesoamerica, the cultural region, is an effective device for understanding the basic difference between the lives of hunter-foragers, who must follow their food sources, and those of farmers, who produce their food. Middle America as a resource zone for wild food is a far larger region than is Mesoamerica, the area wherein maize could dependably support farming villages.

Middle America: Hunter-Foragers of the Paleoindian and Archaic Periods

During the last Ice Age, Siberian hunter-foraging bands pushed east over the land bridge between Siberia and Alaska, following herds of Pleistocene animals as they moved into this new territory, and into the Americas beyond. These were the first human inhabitants of the Americas, and they left behind very little evidence of their lives. This would be expected, given the modest material culture repertoire of mobile hunting-foraging peoples, the low density and numbers of these bands of foragers, and the millennia that have elapsed.

The most dramatic evidence we have for Paleoindian Middle America comes from Santa Isabel Iztapan, not far from present-day Mexico City [**2.11**]. There, about 10,000 years ago, mammoth hunters brought down their prey by driving the creatures into the swampy shores of an ancient lake. With the climate changes and attendant extinctions that marked the end of the Pleistocene Ice Ages, the distinctive regions of Middle America evolved geophysically, and became the distinctive set of habitation zones we know today. Early Archaic peoples made a living by hunting small game and by gathering wild plants. Early Archaic hunter-foragers no doubt camped on open ground, but the best-preserved sites from this period are caves, like Guilá Naquitz in the Valley of Oaxaca [1.7].

1.7 *Early Archaic peoples used caves as seasonal campsites. Here we see Guilá Naquitz Cave, occupied sporadically between 8000 and 6500* BC *by just a few people at a time – probably a nuclear family.*

As foragers became more expert at collecting – and even nurturing– certain plants, the plants became more dependent upon the foragers, a relationship that is the first step towards domestication. Specialized collection was also an important feature of groups living close to aquatic resources, either along the seacoasts or by the shorelines of fresh-water lakes and rivers. Along the Pacific Coast, some groups specialized in collecting fish and shellfish, and drying this seafood for long-term storage – perhaps even trade – on platforms constructed out of sea shells. Some of the platforms reached several hundred feet in length. And at about 2400 BC, along the coast, the first pottery appeared.

Food Production and Sedentism The trends of the Middle and Late Archaic combine increased specialization at exploiting food sources with changes in some of the plant foods themselves, as the plants most suited to provide dietary sustenance were manipulated toward greater and more stable productivity. In short, plant domestication was taking place. In world culture history, such food-producing experiments are often associated with sedentism, but the relationship between farming and settling down isn't a simple one. For many peoples, living year-round at a particular campsite was made possible not by farming but by proximity to particularly productive concentrations of wild resources, and domestication of crops is a separate process. Thus domestication may be closely related to the establishment of permanent villages, but it is not a prerequisite for their establishment.

Sedentism is seductive to humans: once the possibility of staying in one place and the promise of living in greater comfort appeared on the horizons of human culture, group after group gave up mobile foraging and established permanent settlements. And in time, human procreation resulted in larger populations which required expanded food production, and eventually entailed the emergence of leaders who commanded the resources – labor and tributes – of a broad area. Later Mesoamericans would see the origin of domesticated maize – corn – as tantamount to the creation of their world.

Mesoamerica: Villagers and Urbanites of the Formative, Classic, and Postclassic Periods

These trends, their culmination so dramatically expressed at Tenochtitlan, were just beginning as the Late Archaic became the Initial Formative period. It is from evidence dating to this time that we can begin to discern the Mesoamerican culture area and distinctive patterns of Mesoamerican culture. For example, by about 1500 BC, civic-ceremonial architecture was in evidence, with two important types of building, the ball court and elite residence, that would be found in virtually every subsequent important Mesoamerican site. The earliest known examples come from the village of Paso de la Amada, on the Pacific coastal plain southeast of the Isthmus of Tehuantepec. Figure 1.8 shows what the village headman's house probably looked like. Adjacent to the headman's house, the ball court at this village

1.8 *On the Pacific Coast of Chiapas, Paso de la Amada's elite residence was among the New World's earliest houses of rulers. Much larger than other houses at this village, it was rebuilt several times. This artist's reconstruction shows the roof being thatched.*

RELIGION AND CREATION

OUR BEST modern scientific information reveals that the present universe is 13.7 billion years old, and that the earth came into being about 4.5 billion years ago in a process of consolidation of gases and matter. Pre-modern cultures approached the problem of explaining the creation of the known world quite differently, from the perspective of their understanding of how the natural world worked, and how humans acted within the realm they inhabited. For all peoples of Mesoamerica, the world around them was vital and living, and had spiritual substance, a perspective sometimes referred to as *animism*. The spiritual power that enlivened the mountains, rivers, and trees needed to be acknowledged and propitiated, and the earth itself was perceived as a living being, its caves and springs were orifices to another world, the realm of beginnings and endings. Thus explanations of the origin and structure of the earth and the universe were derived from spiritual and sacred premises, from what we would call religion.

Anthropologists recognize that religion is an essential component of all cultures, and it evolved along with other components of culture. For hunter-foragers, the co-residing group is sacred, and so are the plants and animals upon which life depends, and important features in the local landscape. As sedentism and food production paved the way for important societal changes, the focus of sacredness shifted as well. The most important food crops received more ritual attention than did other useful plants and animals. The most important family in the tribal village or chiefdom claimed a special and more direct relationship to supernatural powers. With the development of the state, the public practice of religion became an institution, with a set of specified dogmas and rules, requiring the loyalty of all members of society. In many ancient agrarian states, religion encompassed not only the deities and precepts of the rulers, but also the more traditional household ritual practices, which retained their focus upon the family and its concerns.

This cultural evolutionary background helps put into perspective the ancient Mesoamerican creation myths that we know from the Aztecs and the Maya. Their religions were mature, state-level doctrines with a wide array of rituals, liturgy, and personifications of spiritual power. There were deities – gods and goddesses – among the spiritual forces, but their human-like form was but one aspect of a range of guises that a deity could assume. Deities and culture heroes figure importantly in creation accounts designed to answer the essential existential questions about how the world and the deities came into being, and what purpose humans serve.

Mesoamerican creation myths have in common the idea that the present world is one in a series, that previous worlds were destroyed, along with their inhabitants. Note the essential assumption that time is cyclical, because this premise explains much about Mesoamerican attitudes toward human and cosmological history.

For the Aztecs, the present age is the fifth world, product of the fifth creation of the life-giving sun [**1.10**]. Each of the five worlds has had a patron deity and a human – or nearly-human – population [**1.9**]. The four previous worlds were catastrophically destroyed, and the present world is scheduled to have a cataclysmic end (the Maya predicted that the present world would end on the date equivalent to our 23 December 2012). Note that while different deities ruled each of these Aztec ages, there is a certain evolutionary progress to the inhabitants and what they subsist upon. In fact, food is one of the critical elements of each age: the two original Aztec deities, self-created and the source of the other gods and of humans and the five ages, were Tonacatecuhtli and Tonacacihuatl ("nourishment lord" and "nourishment lady"). Maize defines the present age, being its most important sustenance, and various legends recount how the gods obtained maize for use by humans. Because of this, and the act of creating humans, which the gods accomplished by grinding up the bones of extinct humans and mixing them with blood of the gods, humans owed to the gods a debt that was repaid with the blood of sacrifice – either autosacrifice, drawing one's own blood, or the sacrificial killing of an animal or a human being.

Aztec Creations of the World, or "Ages" or "Suns" (1.9)*

"Sun" or "age"	Ruling deity	Earth inhabited by	Earth destroyed by
Ocelotonatiuh	Tezcatlipoca (all-knowing, all-powerful, patron of shamans)	Giants living on acorns	Jaguars, which devoured the giants
Ehecatonatiuh	Quetzalcoatl (god of wind and life, and Tezcatlipoca's adversary)	Humans living on pine nuts	Windstorms, after which humans became monkeys
Tletonatiuh or Quiauhtonatiuh	Tlaloc (god of storms and rain)	Humans living on wild plants	Rain of fire, after which humans became turkeys, dogs, butterflies
Atonatiuh	Chalchihuitlicue (goddess of water)	Humans living on precursor to maize	Deluge, after which humans became fish
Ollintonatiuh	Tonatiuh (sun god)	Humans living on maize	Earthquake

Sustenance also figures importantly in creation myths of the Maya. Our best source is the *Popol Vuh*, a 16th-century highland Maya document, whose accounts of sacred events echo the paintings found on ceramic vessels of the Classic Maya. In the *Popol Vuh*, the era before the present one saw the exploits of two sets of twins who battled tricky gods in the underworld. The creator couple gave birth to the first set of twins, which included Hun Hunahpu, an avatar of the Maize God. After his decapitation, he miraculously conceived twin sons, the Hero Twins, who themselves battled scheming gods and died in the underworld, but were reborn. These cyclical patterns of death and regeneration are typical of the myths of ancient agrarian peoples over the world, and mirror the cultivation cycle of the year's seasons, and the growth patterns of annual crops, like the all-important maize.

1.9 *(Above) Table describing the Aztec view of creations of the world.*

1.10 *(Left) Known as the "Aztec Sun Stone" or "Aztec Calendar Stone," this monument features what is probably an earth monster, not a sun god, and is not a true calendar. It commemorates the five creations, with the date of the most recent featured in the square cartouche at the top of the stone, and the dates of the four previous creations in the square cartouches surrounding the central figure.*

* based on Nicholson 1971 and Ortiz de Montellano 1990: 40–41

1.11 *Mesoamericans used polished stone axes to clear the land for planting. The Kunz Axe, shown here, was a ceremonial representation of the utilitarian tool, and one of the largest Mesoamerican pieces of sculpted jade. The face shows the snarling mouth and almond-shaped eyes typical of Olmec representations of what scholars have called a man-jaguar, or "were-jaguar."*

was well-built and sizable, even by standards of much later and more complex Mesoamerican societies. We assume that the large villages along this coastal plain were led by headmen who served as war leaders and also as hosts for feasts that may have involved sporting events with strong ritual overtones. Such leaders may in fact have been chiefs, and their villages the focal points for the political integration of surrounding villages into local chiefdoms.

In the Early and Middle Formative, Olmec society arose in the marshy lowlands of the Isthmus of Tehuantepec. Here the Olmecs built great ceremonial centers that are recognized today as the first major monumental sites of Mesoamerica. They also created sculptures from stone, jade, and ceramics that are, today, recognized worldwide as superb art objects [**1.11, 1.12**]. The earliest Olmec site, San Lorenzo, in the southern coastal lowlands of the Gulf of Mexico, now remains as a huge platform upon which the Olmecs erected – then buried – some of their "colossal heads," which were portraits of their rulers (see box, pp. 142–143). The second important Olmec site, La Venta, shows the type of architecture that we associate with great civilizations: a massive pyramid towers over its surroundings, and was the cornerstone of an extensive and elaborate group of platforms and plazas. As we shall see in Chapters 5 and 6, there

1.12 *The sculpture popularly known as "The Wrestler" was found in the Olmec heartland, the southern Gulf lowlands. The mastery exhibited by the figure's form and execution demonstrate the maturity of Olmec art.*

1.13 *Monte Albán occupies the summit of an isolated ridge in the middle of the Valley of Oaxaca. It was first built during the Late Formative period, and includes a pyramid at the south end of the site (top of photo), a palace at the north end, and temple platforms ranged around the sides, and forming a kind of "ridge" in the middle, reminiscent of the site's topography amidst valleys ringed by mountains.*

are impressive Olmec-era sites in other parts of Mesoamerica, and while none achieves the drama of La Venta, all display several of the hallmarks of civilization (see box, pp. 136–137).

Urban Life in the Late Formative and Terminal Formative Periods One hallmark of civilization, the city, was probably not a feature of Olmec society. Even though Olmec sites were large and impressive by any pre-Columbian standards, *city* is a term that requires specific conditions of size and density of habitation (at least 5,000 people in one compact community), and a diverse population in terms of its social statuses, occupational specializations, and range of ethnic affiliations. During the Late Formative period, beginning about 500 BC, Mesoamerican cities came into being.

Our best evidence for the development of cities comes from the highlands west of the Olmec heartland. In the Valley of Oaxaca, at Monte Albán [**1.13**], a planned community came into being at around 500 BC, and by 200 BC, 17,000 people lived on or near this precipice crowned by the civic-ceremonial center. Monte Albán seems to have served as a political capital for an extensive region, and to have aggressively – sometimes violently – extended its territory. The growing complexity of Mesoamerican society is made apparent by such strategies for expanding what was surely state-level political organization.

As Monte Albán was reaching its peak size and influence, Teotihuacan, in the Basin of Mexico, was being built [**1.14**]. One of the only cities of the ancient world to be laid out on a gridded system of streets, its orientation reflected the conviction of its planners and architects that Teotihuacan was the place where the gods had started the movement of time. Teotihuacan's faith in its own importance was confirmed by tens of thousands of migrants to the city, who swelled its numbers to over 100,000 by AD 300, making it the New World's largest city until Aztec Tenochtitlan [**1.15**]. Only a few hundred years later, the pyramids would fall into disrepair and the city would be reduced to a set of villages ringing them.

States of the Classic Period While Teotihuacan was still in its heyday, it sent traders, envoys, and colonists all over Mesoamerica. One cadre of Teotihuacanos, possibly sent by the city's ruler himself, reached the Maya region in AD 378, and at Tikal these foreigners installed

1.14 *(Opposite) Teotihuacan's Pyramid of the Sun is at the center of this photo, its shape echoing the slope of the Patlachique Mountains in the distance, a demonstration of the Mesoamerican idea that pyramids were effigies of mountains. The processional avenue, the Street of the Dead, runs in front of the Sun Pyramid, stretching from the Moon Pyramid, lower left, to the Ciudadela, upper right, and beyond.*

1.15 *(Opposite below) Teotihuacan masks express an austere calm, a clue to behavioral ideals in this huge but enigmatic ancient city.*

1.16 *Tikal's North Acropolis shows the effects of many episodes of rebuilding, over hundreds of years.*

one of their own as the new king. This brief intrusion created no real long-term changes in Maya culture, yet, centuries later, Teotihuacan emblems and accoutrements were still being used by the Maya to indicate very high status.

What is more telling about this interesting incident is that it is known to us because the Maya documented their history with the New World's most expressive written language, a hieroglyphic script that they inscribed into stone, and painted into books and onto ceramic vessels and plastered walls. This practice, plus the Maya refinement of the Mesoamerican calendric system, lasted for over 600 years, starting at about AD 250–300. Thus monuments at Tikal [1.16] and other Maya sites defined the Classic period for pioneering scholars in the field of Mesoamerican studies, and because of their writing and beautiful ceremonial centers, the Maya have remained the best-known of Mesoamerican cultures.

"Mysterious Maya" has such euphonious alliteration that even as scholars have peeled away more and more of the mysteries – with surveys, excavations, breakthroughs in decipherment – one hesitates to lose all the glamour of a culture whose remains are so beautiful but enigmatic. In fact, one of the biggest and most enduring mysteries was the reason for the apparent

1.17 *The Temple of the Warriors at Chichén Itzá is from the later, Mexicanized part of the site. The many columns once supported a roof.*

collapse of Maya civilization. The 600-year spate of inscribing and raising monuments to Maya rulers ended rather suddenly, as if centers were all abandoned within a few years of AD 900. And, in fact, when Cortés journeyed through the southern Maya lowlands in 1524, after having conquered Tenochtitlan, his expedition nearly starved because the landscape was virtually deserted, and there were no farming villages to supply food. Recent research shows that the collapse of Maya civilization in the lowlands was a more gradual process, beginning with environmental degradation that undercut the authority of Maya kings, and ending with the tropical forest reclaiming the farmlands within a few centuries.

Postclassic Period Empire Building Another reason not to mourn Maya culture is that it continued to thrive in the central and northern Yucatán lowlands, where great centers were rising in the Late Classic and Early Postclassic. The most famous of these is probably Chichén Itzá [**1.17**]. Chichén is itself something of a mystery, because it combines pure Maya architecture with buildings that are clearly in the style of the Central Highlands of Mexico. In fact, there are striking parallels between the architecture of Chichén and that of Tula, its contemporary and a dominant site in the Central Highlands, 1,000 km (*c.* 600 miles) to the west. At both Chichén and Tula [**1.18**], warfare and sacrifice pervade the imagery on carved stone monuments. Scholars traditionally have regarded the Early Postclassic era as a time when militarism came to control political interactions, yet recent research has shown that the Classic period – and the Formative – have a rich corpus of evidence of conflicts and bloodshed, and also that during the Postclassic, far-reaching trading networks bound together distant regions.

These important features are critical to understanding how these societies operated, and how each society inherited some of its cultural patterns from those that went before. Great ruined pyramids are impressive, and most professional archaeologists trace their lifelong interest in ancient societies to their first sense of being dazzled by the past – by reading about, or seeing an archaeological site or an ancient artifact that made the lives of ancient people seem vivid and immediate. At the same time, archaeological cultures present puzzles that are fascinating to try to solve.

1.18 *These massive statues of Toltec warriors, called "Atlantean figures," served as columns for a structure atop Tula's Pyramid B, which was very similar to Chichén's Temple of the Warriors.*

Tula and Chichén Itzá faded, like the others, but as always, new cities arose. Tula's successor was Tenochtitlan, which in 1521 was not a ruin, until Cortés's siege and conquest of the Aztec capital leveled most of it. From 1492 to 1517, the Spaniards who explored and colonized the Caribbean region had only encountered groups of foragers and village-dwelling farmers, and had easily overrun and destroyed these people and their modest villages. But Mexico presented them with a very different cultural situation. It was thickly settled by farmer-artisans governed by nobles and priests and was the indigenous heartland of a civilization. From the time that he landed on the coast of Mexico, Cortés perceived that life in the Aztec empire shared many features with contemporaneous Spain and north Africa. Down on the Gulf Coast, hundreds of kilometers from Tenochtitlan, Cortés had seen Aztec tribute collectors making much-feared visits to sizable towns ruled by petty noble lords. The tribute collectors, imperious in their colorful and dramatic uniforms, arrogantly reviewed account books and tribute goods and coldly snubbed the Spaniards.

Aztec pride was short-lived. In the first place, millions of people, "allies" and enemies alike, had suffered under Aztec oppression. They hated the Aztecs and enthusiastically made new alliances with the Spaniards. Thus the few hundred Spaniards rather suddenly were backed up by tens of thousands of seasoned warriors who shared their intent to unseat Motecuzoma and his regime. The Spaniards also had other advantages. Firearms and metal armor were, in the long run, technologically superior to obsidian blades and padded cotton warrior costumes. Spanish horses and war dogs also baffled and terrified the Mesoamericans. Even more potent were the diseases that the Europeans brought, which fell upon a population utterly lacking resistance to them (Diamond 1999). The combined forces of these and other factors meant that once contact was made, conquest was virtually inevitable.

New Spain: The Colonial Period

The Aztec empire was conquered but the Spaniards maintained its governmental structure for at least a century: they installed themselves at the top of the great societal and economic hierarchy, maintaining Aztec tribute arrangements for decades into the Colonial period, as they transformed the farmlands into cattle ranches and plantations for cash crops. In an effort to stamp out all vestiges of devil worship, thousands of native books – and some Aztecs accused of idolatry – were burned, images of deities were destroyed, temples leveled and upon their platform bases, Catholic churches arose. The Great Temple of the Aztecs began to be leveled during the siege of 1521, but maintained such bulk that for decades it loomed over Mexico City's Cathedral, built next to it in the old temple's ritual precinct.

In fact, many survivals showed that the past had shaped much of the transformation to a new Mexico: Tenochtitlan remained the capital, and became Mexico City, and the ritual precinct of the Aztecs remained the city's most sacred area, site of the new Cathedral [**1.19–1.21**]. The Aztec plaza it faced

1.19 *In the heart of modern Mexico City lies the heart of ancient Aztec Tenochtitlan: the Great Temple (Templo Mayor), its successive staircases exposed by archaeological excavation.*

became – and still is – Mexico City's main square, the Zócalo. The palace of the viceroys of New Spain was built on top of the ruins of Motecuzoma's palace. The conquistadores squabbled over claims to the old pleasure parks and game reserves of the Aztec kings. The very names of Mexico and Mexico City are derived from the ethnic name of the Aztecs of Tenochtitlan: the Mexica.

Mexico and Central America: The Republican Period and the Rise of Modern Archaeology

During the 1600s and 1700s, Spain was so protective of its New World empire that foreigners were seldom allowed to visit, and so conservative in intellectual attitude that no curiosity about the old ways was permitted. But in the 19th century, European scholars and philosophers began to show an enormous interest in the other cultures of the world, and Mexicans and Central Americans – the native peoples and those of Spanish descent – grew weary of being governed from afar. In the early 19th century, independence from Spain was declared, and scholars from Mexico, Central America, Europe, and North America began to record, and attempt to recover and preserve, what remained of the ancient past of Mesoamerica.

At the same time, archaeology was evolving from an interest in antiquities as curiosities to a serious and systematic study of the cultures of the past (Willey and Sabloff 1974; Bernal 1980). In North America and in Mexico, archaeology was conceptualized as a part of the larger discipline, anthropology, the study of human physical and cultural similarities and variation, over the whole world and throughout all our human history. Archaeology of Mesoamerica, then, is basically a branch of cultural anthropology (*ethnology*), focusing on the cultures of the past (*ethnography* is the study of cultures in the present). Archaeologists are also sometimes biological anthropologists – study of human skeletal remains from many sites tells us much about the health and diet of ancient populations, as well as their patterns of relatedness, while demographic studies, focusing upon population size and structure in terms of age and sex, also reveal much about patterns of societal growth and decline.

Archaeological research done in the late 19th century continues to provide an essential body of basic information about the sites and artifacts that were studied then. But the 20th century brought revolutions in methods and techniques, with discoveries such as radiocarbon dating and remote sensing permitting a huge new body of data, which in turn has inspired dramatic changes in interpretations, and reconstructions of culture history and processes. Field techniques such as regional surveys disclosed settlement patterns, opening up a much more sophisticated perspective upon the populations of commoners living around the great ceremonial centers and cities, and also upon the domains governed by the elites in these central places.

Ethnohistorical and art historical research has also recovered and interpreted the iconographic and documentary records of ancient Mesoamerica, and has traced the strong survival of pre-Columbian ways of life as they were expressed in the Colonial period. So many codices and chronicles have been published in the last few decades that anyone can possess, in these facsimile editions, a library that would have been prized by a 16th-century Spanish king.

The Aztec poet, King Nezahualcoyotl of Texcoco, composed an elegy to the inevitability of change and death: "even jade must shatter" he wrote in a poem about how all things eventually are lost to time's relentless course. Nonetheless, we are enriched by our knowledge of cultures that are, in many ways, so unlike those of the modern world, and in their rise and fall we may trace the general patterns of the changes that occur in all civilizations, even our own.

1.20 *Excavations at Mexico City's Templo Mayor revealed Aztec ritual sculpture. Above, the Aztec god Xiuhtecuhtli ("Turquoise Lord") was one of the fire deities, as well as being a patron of rulership and of time. The disk motifs in his headdress represent preciousness and time, an expression of the Mesoamerican preoccupation with the sanctity of calendrics.*

1.21 *This reclining figure is a form known as a "chacmool." It served as a sacrificial altar at the temple of the storm god, Tlaloc, atop the first enlargement of the Templo Mayor (Stage II,* *see box, pp. 452–453**).*

2 ECOLOGY AND CULTURE: MESOAMERICAN BEGINNINGS

VIEWING THE CONTINENTS from on high is a commonplace modern experience. No need to board a space shuttle or even an airplane, you can get an all-encompassing picture from a map [**2.1**]. Ancient Mesoamericans had no such perspectives, except limited vistas from the heights of mountains, but with their commonly-held view that the world they lived on was the rugged back of an earth monster (sometimes depicted as a partially submerged crocodilian creature or a turtle), they would have enjoyed seeing our view of the subcontinent of Middle America as spiny, with jagged mountain ranges running down the east and west sides of the great funnel shape of Mexico.

MESOAMERICA'S MAJOR GEOPHYSICAL AND BIOTIC FEATURES

The mountain ranges – Sierra Madre Occidental ("west") and Oriental ("east") – join together at the east–west *Neovolcanic Axis*, with peaks over 5,500 m (*c.* 18,000 ft), many of them active volcanoes. The mountains end at the western limits of the Isthmus of Tehuantepec, a broad, relatively flat plain linking the lowlands of the Gulf of Mexico with the coastal plains along the Pacific Ocean. The Isthmus, with its juxtaposition of mountain escarpment and plain, is the most important geographical and cultural division within Mesoamerica, and we shall be returning to it, as a point of orientation, throughout the book. East of the Isthmus the mountain spines appear again and continue, rising and falling through southeastern Mexico, Guatemala, Honduras, Nicaragua, and Costa Rica, with alluvial plains fanning out toward the Caribbean coasts of Belize and Nicaragua. The mountains continue down to Panama, the narrow neck of land connecting Middle America and South America.

From the top of the funnel to the bottom of Panama is a distance of about 5,000 km (*c.* 3,000 miles) and a north–south difference of over 20 degrees of latitude, and much of the area lies south of the Tropic of Cancer. The close conjunction of tropical zones of radically different altitude has resulted in environmental diversity virtually unparalleled on earth. Desert and humid tropics exist side by side and there is a strong north-to-south trend from arid

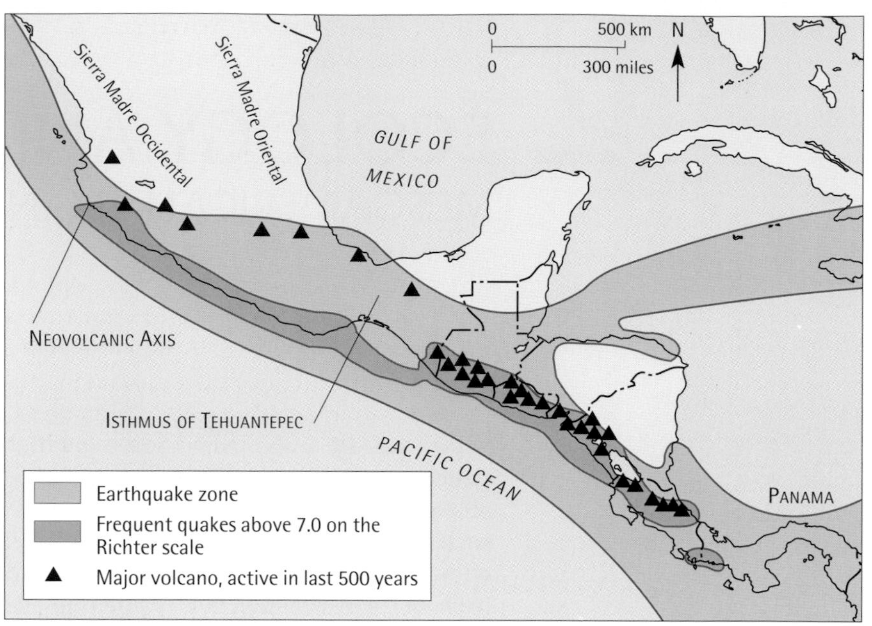

2.1 *The earth is alive in Middle America. The map shows major geological hazards besetting various regions. The most intense region of earthquake and volcanic activity is in southeastern Mexico and southern Guatemala.*

environments to sub-humid (semi-humid) zones, to humid "tropical" ones. Northern Mexico's central portion is dominated by dryland desert and steppe, except where mountains form temperate intrusions. Further south, the mountains of southeastern Mexico and Guatemala form temperate zones within the humid tropical climate of the surrounding lowlands.

Topography and climate have together shaped regional development of Mesoamerican culture by determining where maize can be grown. The boundaries of some cultural regions have shifted over time, as climate has changed with regard to critical minimums of rainfall for cultivation. In general, the northern limit of Mesoamerica falls somewhat south of the northern rainfall isohyets marking precipitation of 500–800 mm (20–30 in) annually.

The southern boundary of Mesoamerica is less clearly defined. Here, aridity is seldom a problem, but there is another hazard, very broken topography and very limited expanses of habitable land. Thus the localized regions that could sustain substantial cultivation are separate from each other and were somewhat isolated from Mesoamerican culture, and no region was large enough to sustain the dense, large populations that characterized Mesoamerica. The most southerly valley system that consistently sustained Mesoamerican cultural presence is the Motagua River Drainage, which links the Guatemala highlands with the Caribbean Sea, and unites a series of smaller tributary valleys (such as the Copán Valley in western Honduras). But east of this drainage, the landscape is more heavily dissected, and while Mesoamerican traits were found, in different periods, at sites all the way down to Panama, the continuity of cultural traditions is broken up by the mountains of central Honduras on the north and east. Along the Pacific Coast, Mesoamerican sites are found as far south as northern Costa Rica.

Native Vegetation: Neotropical and Nearctic Environments, Dry Lands and Wetlands

Middle America is biotically rich because it is the overlap region of the Americas, two continents that were brought together by continental drift less than 100 million years ago. North America's *Nearctic* plants and animals were adapted to cooler and drier conditions than were the *Neotropical* plants and animals native to humid Central and South America. Much of the Mesoamerican culture area, particularly the tropical lowlands, is Neotropical habitat, but the Central and Southern Highlands of Mexico and regions to the north support Nearctic biota (Emery 2001).

Each of these biotic regions overlaps significantly with two very different types of environment in Post-Pleistocene Middle America: arid lands (dry lands) and aquatic lands (humid lands, or wetlands). First, the dry lands region characterizes the deserts of the U.S. Southwest and northern Mexico, and from there it extends south and eastward through the various highland regions, to the escarpment at the western edge of the Gulf lowlands and southeast to the Isthmus of Tehuantepec.

There, the wetlands begin with the lowlands along the Gulf of Mexico, and extend eastward across the great swath of the Isthmus of Tehuantepec, which separates dry highland zones such as Oaxaca and Tehuacán on the west from the steamy, humid-tropical set of habitats that extend along both coasts and continue east and south. The distinction between Nearctic dry lands and Neotropical wetlands determined the kinds of resources that could be used as wild food and could be manipulated into domestication by their resident populations. The western dry lands provided resources such as seeded and fruiting plants and small animals, while the Isthmian and eastern tropical lowlands held extensive lacustrine and riverine as well as coastal resources. The dry lands adaptation provided the basis for cultivated plants that became staples for all of Mesoamerica, while in the Isthmian zone, intensive collecting of rich aquatic resources permitted the beginnings of sedentism.

However, given the adaptive radiation of plant and animal species through the microenvironments of many adjacent regions, whether or not aided by humans, Middle Americans had a wide range of food choices. Dry lands encompassed many aquatic habitats, because all over the arid highlands, swampy environments developed in the bottomlands of valleys, particularly in geophysical drainage basins with no hydrological outlet. The Basin of Mexico, for example, became an enclosed basin as its ring of volcanoes grew in the Pleistocene. It became a valley – the Valley of Mexico – only about 400 years ago, after the arrival of the Spaniards, who dug a canal through the mountains and drained the Basin's lakes and swamps. Now, Mexico City "is slowly sinking into the maw of the earth" (Wolf 1959: 6), after having been established – as Tenochtitlan – on swampy islands in the middle of a set of lakes [**2.2**]. The rich and varied ancient Basin of Mexico presented a mosaic of habitats, reminding us that cultural adaptations to dry

2.2 *Tenochtitlan was built on islands in Lake Texcoco, part of the lake system that developed at the bottom of the Basin of Mexico. In the distance, the southeastern rim of the basin is defined by two of Mexico's highest peaks: Iztaccihuatl and the active volcano Popocatépetl, right.*

lands and to aquatic resources are not necessarily mutually exclusive in Middle America's many regions.

The Big Divide: West of the Isthmus vs. Isthmus and East

The region of greatest overlap between the two great habitat types, Neotropical and Nearctic, would have been on the border between the Isthmus of Tehuantepec and the highlands to its west. This formed a significant divide as cultures developed: as we shall see, when ceramics were first developed, the two earliest types overlapped in the Isthmus. The Isthmus became the most important locus of Mesoamerica's first complex society, that of the Olmecs. In this book, the geographical division between the area west of the Isthmus, and the area of the Isthmus and east, will be used repeatedly because within Mesoamerica, this provides a workable, empirically-based division, whose roots lie in the native life forms – plants and animals – that each region originally supported.

The definition of major regions as culture areas depends on the nature of the exploiting culture. In the Paleoindian and Early Archaic periods, when all were hunter-foragers, the whole area of Middle America shows only relatively minor variation in the material culture repertoire. Culturally coherent regions begin to emerge with Archaic-period subsistence specializations, and these occurred, at first, over very broad zones. This process of cultural regionalization first occurred through the development of tools and skills related to exploiting intensively the particular plant and small animal resources of a particular environment. This is a topic for the next chapter, but here we need to understand that since the end of the last Ice Age, around 10,000 years ago, basic climate and vegetative zones remained reasonably stable until the European intrusion. "Reasonably stable" points to several important pre-Columbian cases of human-caused environmental instability

– severe deforestation causing extensive erosion, for example, or the widespread diffusion of an important plant food that originated in one region – that will be discussed later, in the course of particular regional culture histories.

Climate and Crops

With all the microenvironmental variation in Middle America, we need to establish a few broad categories of environment. There are three – arid, subhumid, and humid – and they are based on a combination of factors (Vivó Escoto 1964). These are latitude, altitude, temperature, and rainfall, plus the traditional Middle American criterion of what crops can be grown [**2.3**]. This pragmatic farming perspective encompasses three main categories by terms that are widely used in Middle America today, by agronomers as well as archaeologists, and they will be used in this book to characterize regions. The categories are: *tierra caliente*, or hot lands, *tierra templada*, or temperate lands, and *tierra fría*, cool lands.

Temperature affects how much rainfall is needed to secure crops. Above 1,000-m (3,281-ft) elevation, in temperate and cool *tierra templada* and *tierra fría*, an annual rainfall of at least 500 mm (20 in) is the approximate minimum for cultivation of maize without irrigation, while in *tierra caliente*, rainfall levels must exceed 800 mm (31 in) because of the hot lands' higher evapotranspiration rate. And note that these are minimums, not averages. Unfortunately for farmers, much of Middle America's annual

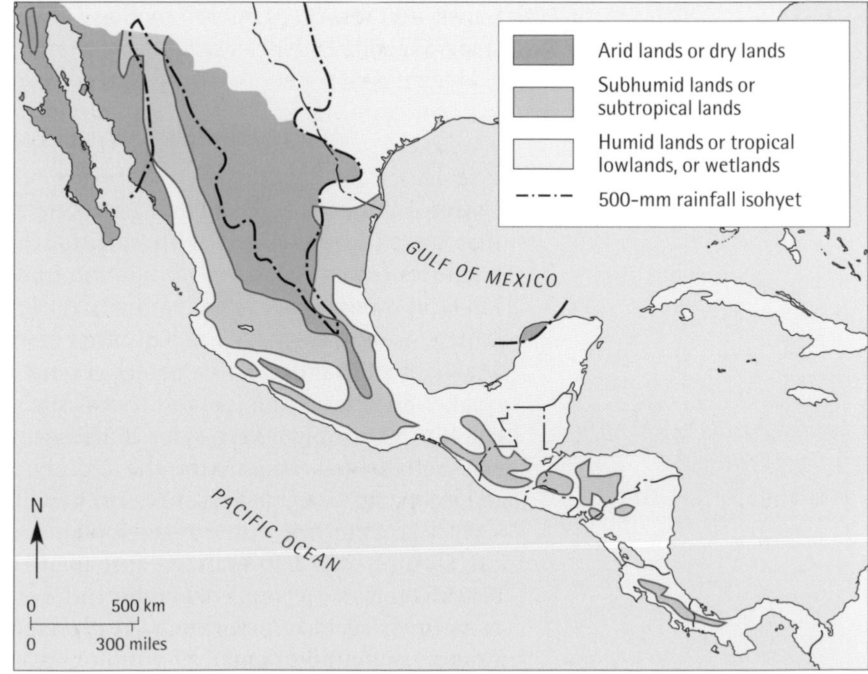

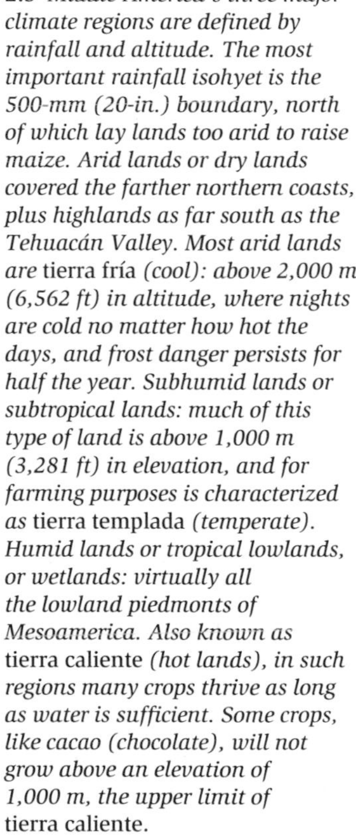

2.3 *Middle America's three major climate regions are defined by rainfall and altitude. The most important rainfall isohyet is the 500-mm (20-in.) boundary, north of which lay lands too arid to raise maize. Arid lands or dry lands covered the farther northern coasts, plus highlands as far south as the Tehuacán Valley. Most arid lands are* tierra fría *(cool): above 2,000 m (6,562 ft) in altitude, where nights are cold no matter how hot the days, and frost danger persists for half the year. Subhumid lands or subtropical lands: much of this type of land is above 1,000 m (3,281 ft) in elevation, and for farming purposes is characterized as* tierra templada *(temperate). Humid lands or tropical lowlands, or wetlands: virtually all the lowland piedmonts of Mesoamerica. Also known as* tierra caliente *(hot lands), in such regions many crops thrive as long as water is sufficient. Some crops, like cacao (chocolate), will not grow above an elevation of 1,000 m, the upper limit of* tierra caliente.

rainfall shows considerable variation from year to year, so the average must be considerably higher to encompass such perturbations and insure year to year productivity. This challenge was met in many regions by irrigation systems and other projects of landscape alteration in order to secure reliable harvests, and such projects of intensification of labor and land were significant investments that could increase the value of some land, making those who owned it even wealthier and exacerbating tendencies toward societal ranking and economic inequality.

This Cradle, Compared with Other Cradles

How does Middle America compare with the natural environments of other cradles of civilization? The Old World's earliest civilizations lay in great valleys with major rivers: the Nile River of Egypt, the Euphrates and Tigris Rivers of Sumer, the Indus River of Harappa and Mohenjo-Daro, and the Hwang-ho River of China. These immense drainage systems helped to unify the regions, providing ready avenues of communication and exchange. Middle America's spines of mountains and centrifugal drainage patterns provided no single broad region of enduring centrality for the whole culture area.

This lack of central focus did not hamper the development of complex society, but rather may have served, in the long run, to promote such development. Regional cultures worked within their distinctive contexts, exploiting and venerating the physical resources locally available, while they also freely borrowed neighboring regional cultures' technological advances, crop domestication, and social innovations. The particular challenges and resources offered by these closely juxtaposed regions stimulated trade of goods and ideas as well as migration.

MESOAMERICANS AND CULTURAL ECOLOGY

Native Americans believed that the world around them was created by spiritual forces and charged with spiritual power: the landscape and living creatures within it shared animation and potency. Such a belief, known today as "animism," is well-suited to the Middle American subcontinent, which, as we have seen, has a number of impressively lively characteristics. Much of the landscape is young, being formed even now, as the earth quakes and clashes along fault lines, volcanoes smoke and erupt, and tropical storms bring gushing skies that cause rivers to flood. Furthermore, all this activity has heightened the closely juxtaposed contrasts in climate, landscape features, and resources in this highly diverse area.

As Mesoamerican culture developed, some geophysical and meteorological features were formalized into deities, but in a distinctively Native American way. Accounts from the 16th century, often written by Spaniards, sometimes seem to describe a set of deities like those of ancient Rome or Greece, humanlike "gods" of wind or lightning. Indeed, the Mesoamerican concept of godliness encompassed superheroes, but as expressions of a motivating force of a certain kind that inhabits different forms. Yes, there were "mountain gods" but the mountains themselves were "gods" in the sense that they were infused with the sacred and powerful mountain spirit. The same lambent force was thought to live in the active volcano, Popocatépetl, for example, as in the little seed-candy mountain models that were featured at feasts and ceremonies honoring the mountain spirits – and also in larger mountain models, the pyramids.

Thus ancient Mesoamericans would have regarded their surroundings with a constant alert interest, reading the moods of the spirits and anticipating their needs. They saw themselves, living within a vital landscape, as in a reciprocal relationship with the spiritually alive natural world, and believed that their actions prompted a response from the web of spiritual forces around them, just as they had acted in response to the spiritually alive world's needs.

Enculturing the Ecological Context

The principle that people live within, are affected by, and act upon a highly responsive natural environment has a familiar ring, because it is a basic premise of our modern understanding of how the world works. The modern principle is called *cultural ecology*, the notion that human culture and the biophysical environment are linked in a dynamic feedback relationship, such that a change originating in one part of this interactive system will prompt a response in another, and so on. Today we humans have such a strong impact on the environment that we can almost immediately notice profound global effects of our most intrusive actions – nuclear power plant meltdowns, for example – but we should note that our interest in short-term gains often spawns a reluctance to take responsibility for our actions – witness a lack of resolve on how to address global warming, even though it is certainly in our long-term interests to do so.

Cultural ecology takes into account human attitudes (such as refusal to forego short-term profits), because the belief system of any culture plays an important role in shaping events and processes. The foundation of cultural ecology, like that of any strong framework, is rooted in the ground: how does any particular environment shape the food quest? The way we get our food is directly linked to how many people a region can support. Complex society develops and is sustained when large and dense populations can be provided for.

Note that for any given subsistence strategy, a particular landscape will have a productive potential, measuring how much food can be supplied. Of course, there are other factors besides food which limit the number of people a region can sustain – potable water and safe habitation sites are just two of these. Cultural ecological analysis of a region considers such factors, and also social relations and spiritual expressions of these broadly adaptive patterns. The key features of a culture are called the *culture core* [**2.4**].

IDEOLOGY ↓
↑ ORGANIZATION
economy, polity, society ↓
↑ TECHNOLOGY
resource exploitation,
subsistence, settlement pattern ↓
↑ environment

2.4 *Cultural ecology posits that culture and the environment interact dynamically: each sets limits upon the other, and exploits the possibilities presented by the other. The culture core consists of those technological, organizational, and ideological features most directly related to meeting the most important material needs of a society (adapted from Steward 1955). In the model shown above, the relationships among major features of the culture core are indicated by their placement and by arrows that show the direction of the effect. Thus we assume that a culture's ideology affects how it exploits the environment, but that ideological effects are operationalized by working through cultural organization (economy. polity, and society) and also through the constraints and possibilities offered by technology. The pivotal juncture of this human-environmental relationship has to do with* subsistence practices *(and the* settlement pattern *that is determined by those subsistence practices in any particular region), that is, how people make a living, but most specifically how a culture derives its food (e.g. hunting and foraging, modern industrial megafarming).*

Because cultural ecology considers the mutually integrated roles of all aspects of culture – subsistence strategy, social organization, economy, politics, and ideology – it is holistic in scope and empirical in its perspective, giving greatest weight to evidence rather than to attitudes. Of necessity, this kind of cultural analysis is immensely attractive to archaeologists, because ancient peoples leave behind their broken tools and ruined buildings, but not always a record of their attitudes.

Ideology: What We Say We Do

Trash doesn't tell lies. It may leave some important things out of the picture, and thus mislead us into biased interpretations, but trash reflects actual life. If we rely too much on official accounts of history, we may accept a biased or idealized perspective, but material remains are compelling evidence. Studies of modern trash heaps and interviews with their contributors show disparities between what people do, and say they do. For example, far more empty alcoholic beverage containers are dumped than would be indicated by reported usage rates (Rathje 1974). Similarly, the Aztecs claimed that they were very abstemious, and mostly eschewed alcohol. However, fermented alcoholic beverages were widely available, and potential for abuse was widespread. The Aztecs invoked the death penalty for certain instances of public drunkenness, a rather severe response to a non-problem.

Cultural ecology doesn't ignore such attitudes ("we voluntarily lead sober lives") but incorporates them into the explanatory framework, because they identify social norms and motivators: what society reveres and will tolerate. But subsistence and other material features must take precedence in any general reconstruction of a regional culture, modern or ancient, because unless we eat and can find shelter, we die. When archaeologists understand how ancient people made their living, then one of the most basic issues of how a regional culture develops has been addressed. Cultural ecology has been widely influential, and is accepted by most Mesoamericanist archaeologists today as the best general means of broadly understanding culture and its relation to the environment. Cultural ecology lays a foundation for more detailed exploration of specialized research topics.

Subsistence: What We Really Do

Subsistence, the food-getting system, is a fundamental element of the culture core. As we saw in Chapter 1, the first inhabitants of Middle America hunted big game and foraged for other food and materials, and when the big game died off, there ensued a long period of dependence on other, less dramatic wild resources. These resources were encouraged to adapt to human needs, and those plants and animals that cooperated became increasingly dependent upon humans, and humans upon them. Finally, as the mutual bonding of human and domesticated species was complete, foraging as a subsistence strategy virtually disappeared in many areas. People and maize

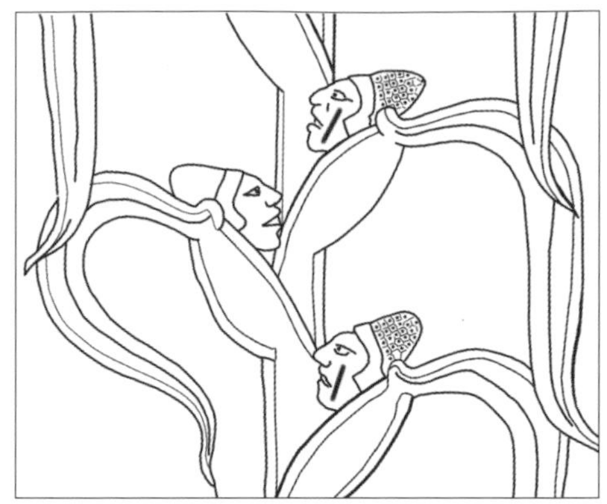

2.5 *For Mesoamericans, the integration of the environment, spiritual values, and human culture was not an intellectual exercise but their own deeply ingrained way of life. Here, a maize plant sprouts human heads instead of corn cobs. Maize is the food that humans eat, thus it is what humans are made of. Maize is also a gift of the gods, and, in grateful reciprocity, humans should offer themselves as sacrificial victims – maize for the gods. Note that in this mural from Late Classic Cacaxtla (Tlaxcala), the human heads are elongated. This is not just artistic license, in order to emphasize the analogy between the ears of maize and heads of humans, but also a realistic depiction of the results of cranial remodeling, a practice widespread in Mesoamerica that involved constraining an infant's head between boards until the soft bones had assumed a cone-like or wedge-like shape. This caused no damage to the brain, and was regarded as a mark of beauty and refinement.*

lived through each other, and complex societies grew up in areas where crops could support dense stands of human beings [**2.5**]. Surplus production, and the long-term storage of surpluses, permits some people in a society to devote their time to other matters beside the food quest. But because wild resources are intermittently distributed, they can usually only support small scattered groups. Hunter-foragers remain mobile, changing their residence several times a year and lacking any permanent storage facilities that permit accumulation of food and goods.

Sedentism and Its Consequences

This mobile life, though strenuous and spartan, was relatively healthy; when our ancestors settled down and depended upon farming, they began to show signs of nutritional stress, reduced stature, and more disease, even as overall population size rose. Yet, as a species, we are strongly drawn toward sedentism, and have almost invariably settled down in one place when resource availability permitted. Sedentism marks a major turning point, beyond which a society can begin to become more elaborate, to develop status differences beyond those basic ones determined by age, sex, and skills. The nuclear family that was the basic element of mobile forager camps remained the building block of all more complex Mesoamerican societies, a component part of larger and more complex social, political, and economic structures: the egalitarian tribe, the ranked chiefdom, and the stratified state.

Sedentism permits the storage of food and accumulation of goods, two powerful elements of social ranking, economic organization, and political power in complex societies. Control of resources is an important basis for the ascendance of the few over the many, the ability of certain individuals or families to compel the others to work for them. That power may also draw upon ideological features, traditional aspects of a belief system that links some families more strongly to powerful forces and that justifies the social and economic divisions between them and the rest of society.

As the culture history presented in Chapter 1 shows, Mesoamericans started as egalitarian hunter-foragers, and over millennia of adaptation to their varied environments, developed many strategies for food production and maintaining social order. Overall, the trend is most certainly toward the elaboration of more complexly stratified societies, with highly specialized economies, autocratic political organization, and ideology institutionalized into state-supported religious cults. This trend is general, however, and in some areas, increasing cultural complexity was followed by a transformation into simpler subsistence strategies and cultural patterns, in some ways a regression to earlier patterns of societal organization.

Action and Agency: The Individual's Role

What was the individual's role in these broad processes? History often promotes a particular person as an agent of change, a pivotal actor – how does a strong focus on broad trends account for, and take into consideration such agency and action? This issue is particularly pertinent for those periods of Mesoamerican culture for which we have documentation of named persons (usually rulers) and their activities.

For example, recent advances in the decipherment of Maya hieroglyphics have greatly increased our knowledge of dynastic histories, and even of particular individuals. The result is a far richer culture history than could ever be achieved by archaeological evidence of artifacts and architecture alone. Archaeology may reveal that a Maya city was burned and looted, but decipherment of monuments extolling the conquest permits us to understand the political integration of the region at that time, and the interactions leading to the disaster. The Maya king's text may be propagandistic and self-aggrandizing, but it is a priceless message from him that has reached us.

Pivotal individuals in history humanize the culture for us, literally embody it and sometimes caricature it. Focus on the individual's role evokes the hoary "Great Man" theory of history – that important individuals motivate events. Thus we can ask, for example, whether World War II would have taken place without Hitler, or if computers would have taken over our lives without Bill Gates, or if particular Maya rulers were individually responsible for widespread warfare in the Classic period. From a holistic, systemic perspective of cultural development, it would seem that individuals act within the constraints, and under the impulses of their times. Individuals can affect, and sometimes effect significant cultural developments, and delineation of the role of individuals provides welcome detail, enlivening the great flow of events.

The relation between an individual's actions and larger general processes was aptly characterized by the French historian Fernand Braudel in his study of the cultures around the Mediterranean Sea. He used the sea itself as his model, finding that at the most general level, the human-environmental relationship was like the slow but vast seasonal changes of the sea, while the social history of particular groups represented "swelling currents." The third level, "traditional history ... on the scale ... of individual men" represents "surface disturbances, crests of foam" (Braudel 1972: 20–21).

Cultural Evolution and What it is Not

All these levels show change over time, but changes signifying ongoing important processes, that is, cultural evolution, take place on the more general levels. Note that cultural evolution does not mean "progress" toward complexity, any more than societal complexity always spells improvement in the lives of the mass of the people. It merely means change over time, but cultural evolution is so often assumed to move toward greater complexity (and this has certainly been the overall trend in our human history) that anthropologists sometimes speak of "devolution" when describing reversals in the trend, localized "collapses" of complex cultures.

Mesoamerican culture history has several striking examples of this phenomenon, such as the near-disappearance of Maya civilization in the southern lowlands of Yucatán 1,000 years ago. As we shall see, the Maya in this region failed to maintain a stable relation with the sacred earth, and created an imbalance in the cultural-ecological system by growing too many humans who needed too much corn, and starved the earth in the process. This is a striking example of the importance of understanding Middle American regions as habitats for Mesoamerican cultures.

CULTURAL REGIONS

Throughout this book, cultures are described as developing within particular regions, and in many chapters, the cultures and sites of the dry lands west of the Isthmus of Tehuantepec are grouped together, while those of the Isthmus and east are also grouped together. To understand these regions and how they relate to each other, we will here survey them, adopting a somewhat standardized north to south perspective, grouping together adjacent areas into zones of broad environmental consistency and cultural integration [**2.6**]. More information on each region is provided, in the form of a map and some basic facts, in the Reference Maps section at the back of the book (pp. 551–572), and this section will serve as a reference for the rest of the book. The basic facts, such as "Terrain and natural vegetation" (see Wagner 1964: 221–263), "Climate for cultivation," and "Hazards" help to explain the landscape features most economically significant, and most venerated, in any region. The maps show many archaeological sites that are not mentioned elsewhere in the text; these sites are also cited in the index, providing a means of locating minor sites in order to research them further in regional summary books and articles. We start this survey north of Mesoamerica proper, in the southwestern U.S., the "Northern Arid Zone" of Mesoamerican cultural influence, and move south and east.

Northern Arid Zone

The northern limit of continuous expression of Mesoamerican cultural traits is roughly the limit of maize cultivation dependent upon rainfall (see Map 1, p. 552). North of this limit village farming occurred only intermittently in terms of time and space; some ranked societies emerged and showed Mesoamerican influence, but these were not sustained. The Aztecs called this region "Chichimeca" after the mobile hunter-forager peoples, Chichimecs, who lived there in the 15th century AD, and who continued the Desert tradition lifeways begun in the Early Archaic period (see Chapter 3). Along the coastal plains and slopes, wetter and milder conditions favored sedentism.

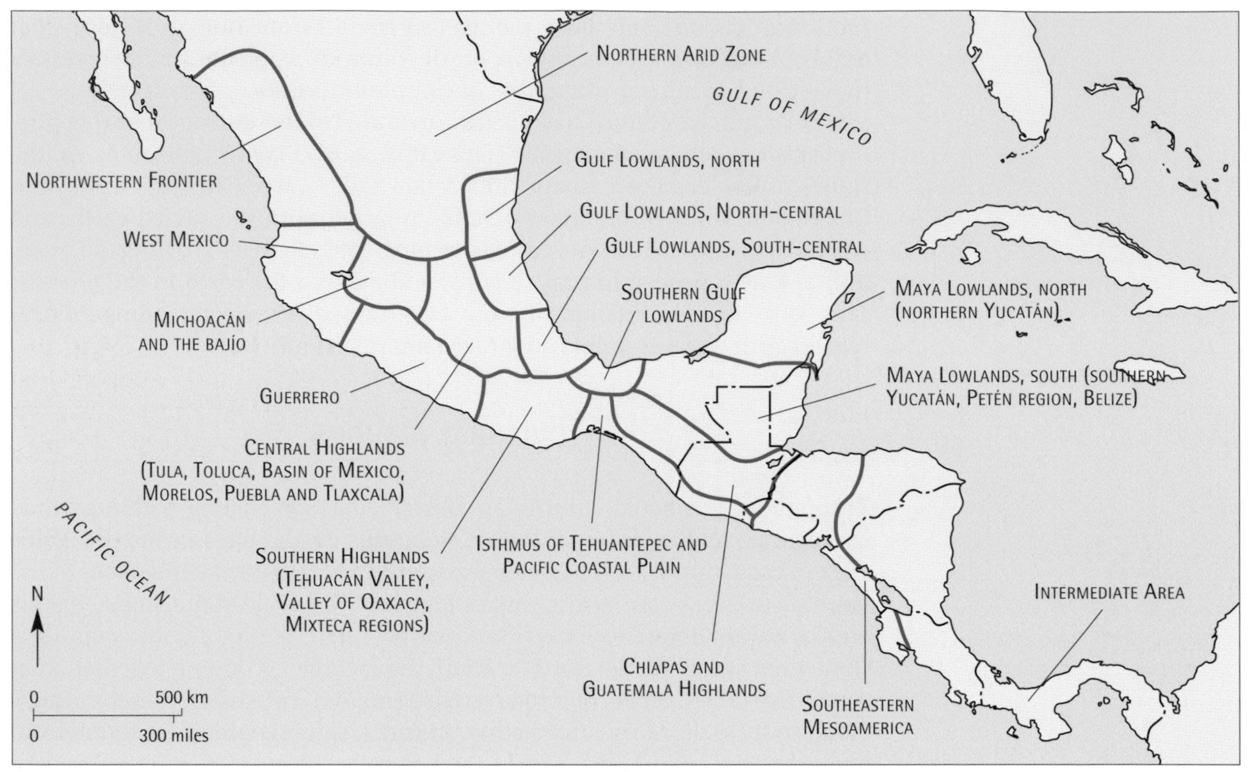

2.6 *Middle America, showing major cultural regions.*

Northwestern Frontier

Mesoamerica's Northwestern Frontier extended along the Pacific Coast lowlands and mountains (see Map 2, p. 553), its earliest occupation dating to the Paleoindian period, with Formative-period shell mounds, and sizable towns in the Classic period. At that time, an important mining center, Alta Vista, was developed in the mountains.

West Mexico

At about the 20th parallel, the Sierra Madre Occidental breaks into a series of broad valleys, draining into the Pacific (see Map 3, p. 554). This region's mountains are at the west end of the Neovolcanic Axis, a string of volcanoes extending over to the Gulf Coast. Late Formative and Early Classic cultures in these valleys shared the tradition of placing their dead in shaft tombs.

Michoacán and the Bajío

In the broad valleys east of West Mexico, the Postclassic Tarascan tribute state arose. Just to the north of Michoacán is a region now known as the Bajío (flatlands), a highland plain forming the northern borderland of Mesoamerica (see Map 4, p. 555). Climate shifts toward greater aridity put the region outside Mesoamerica and into the Northern Arid Zone; during the Formative and Postclassic eras, it sustained cultivation and significant settlement, becoming part of Mesoamerica, what scholars call "Northern Mesoamerica" (Spanish, "Mesoamerica Septentrional"). With the introduction of European plows and crops, the Bajío became a productive wheat-raising region.

Guerrero

Southern Michoacán borders rugged terrain which surrounds the Balsas Depression, a massive valley system based on the Balsas River (originating in the Central Highlands) and the Tepalcatepec River (originating in West Mexico and Michoacán). This river system provided important routes for migration and trade, but the region's broken topography discouraged both political integration and outside conquest (see Map 5, p. 556). Guerrero's important role in the development of complex society is shown in Teopantecuanitlán, whose formal "Olmec" architecture dates from the Middle Formative.

Central Highlands

Mexico City/Tenochtitlan stands in the center of a set of high-altitude valleys, the Central Highlands of Mexico [**2.7**]. Though this region is at about the same latitude as the humid central Maya lowlands of the Yucatán Peninsula, which is *tierra caliente*, the elevation of these highland valleys makes them cold and fairly arid *tierra fría*. Yet despite these challenges, whenever Mesoamerica has experienced significant unification, its focus has been in the Basin of Mexico, the central region of the Central Highlands.

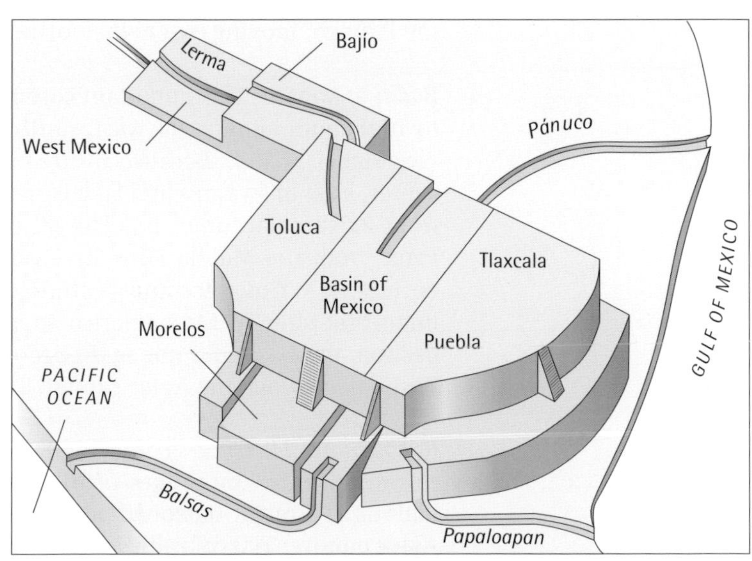

2.7 *Central Highlands: "In shape, this mountain mass resembles one of the pyramids built by its early inhabitants: massive walls, an eastern and a western escarpment, thrust upward from narrow coasts into a great tableland" (Wolf 1959: 3). The schematic diagram shows how this platform was drained by four of Mexico's most important rivers, the Pacific-bound Lerma (downstream, called the Santiago) and Balsas, and the Pánuco and Papaloapan, providing routes of contact with the Gulf of Mexico.*

The Basin of Mexico and its surrounding regions (Tula, Toluca, Morelos, Puebla, Tlaxcala) formed a culture area that has been termed the "Central Mexican Symbiotic Region," consisting of adjacent basins and valleys that enjoyed fairly high levels of interaction, exchanging raw materials, finished goods, and ideas. A more common expression in referring to this region is simply "Central Mexico" which refers in general to the cultures of this area, without specifying a precise region or time period. Because "Central Mexican" is a more accurate descriptive term than "Aztec," which refers to the dominant culture of the Basin of Mexico during the Late Postclassic, or "Tlahuican" (cultures of Postclassic Morelos), etc., it is in common use and readers should note that this is the region to which the term refers.

Morelos The Valley of Morelos is the southern component of the Central Highlands, and it is significantly warmer and more humid than the rest of the highlands (see Map 6, p. 557). This milder climate and greater proximity to the early complex societies of the Isthmus and Southern Highlands made it much more culturally precocious than the Basin of Mexico. Chalcatzingo was an important Middle Formative-period ceremonial center, and the Late Classic site of Xochicalco was one of the successors to Teotihuacan.

Toluca and Tula Northwest of Morelos, Mexico's highest valley, Toluca, was an ethnically diverse region in the Postclassic period, dominated by the Matlatzincas, speakers of a language related to Otomí, who had their capitals at Calixtlahuaca and Toluca. The region served as a buffer between the Tarascans and the Aztecs (see Map 7, p. 558). The Tula region, to its north, was an arid, hilly plateau transected by important rivers. It was most densely settled in the Postclassic period, when Tula, one of the important successors to Teotihuacan, developed at the upper reaches of two of Middle America's great rivers: the Lerma/Santiago, flowing west to the Pacific, and the Pánuco, moving east to the northern Gulf lowlands.

Basin of Mexico This important core region was a hydrological basin ringed by high mountains on the west, south, and east, and by low hills to the north (see Map 6, p. 557). Because all streams within the Basin drained toward the center, a set of swamps and lakes formed which were an important resource from Paleoindian times on. The alluvial plain around the lakes was cultivated from the Middle Formative on, and important Late Formative sites developed at Cuicuilco and Teotihuacan. Teotihuacan was one of the most important sites in Mesoamerica in the Early Classic period, but after its decline, the Basin did not again become culturally dominant until the Late Postclassic, when the Aztec capital, Tenochtitlan, achieved prominence.

Puebla and Tlaxcala These highland plains are broad valleys separated from each other by ranges of hills (see Map 8, p. 559). Tlaxcala became famous as a major independent area surrounded by regions tributary to the Aztec empire; Tlaxcala allied itself with Cortés in the war against the Aztecs, and Tlaxcalan troops were essential to that victory. Puebla was a well-populated region throughout Mesoamerican culture history. Its great capital, Cholula, was occupied from the Formative period into the present, and its pyramid was the largest pre-Columbian structure in Mesoamerica.

Gulf Lowlands, Northern and Central Regions

Extending for over 500 miles along the Gulf of Mexico, Mesoamerica's Gulf lowlands have four culturally distinct regions. Three are discussed immediately below; the southernmost region will be described as part of the Isthmian area.

Gulf Lowlands, North East of the Bajío, the mountainous Sierra Madre Oriental formed a kind of Northeastern Frontier which was also the southeasternmost Northern Arid Zone, another mosaic of subsistence strategies and sedentism, depending on climate and influence of adjacent regions. The mountainous region drops off to the northern plain of the Gulf lowlands, wetland traversed by rivers and with tropical climates. The northernmost Gulf lowlands region (see Map 9, p. 560) was known at the time of contact as the Huasteca, after the Mayan-speaking Huastecs, who first arrived there in the Formative period.

Gulf Lowlands, North-central Just to the south lie the north-central Gulf lowlands, where El Tajín became one of Mesoamerica's premier centers in the Late Classic and Early Postclassic (see Map 10, p. 561). Northern and north-central Gulf lowlands were culturally related to tropical lowlands immediately to the south, as well as adjacent dry lands to the west.

Gulf Lowlands, South-central In this region Cortés made his first base of operations in Mexico by establishing the town of Veracruz. Nearby Zempoala was a regional capital in the Aztec empire. Long densely settled, the area's important sites included Tres Zapotes, a Formative center, and Early Classic Matacapan in the Tuxtla Mountains, with strong ties to Teotihuacan (see Map 12, p. 562).

Southern Highlands

Another great highlands region of Mexico is the Sierra Madre del Sur, an extension of the Sierra Madre Occidental south of the Neovolcanic Axis. Guerrero, discussed above, is its western component; east of Guerrero lay the mountains of Oaxaca, with the Valley of Oaxaca and the Mixteca regions, and east of that, the Tehuacán Valley, itself a southern extension of the Valley of Puebla.

Tehuacán Valley Rugged and arid, this Valley's caves document the early stages of plant domestication, though extensive cultivation and dense settlement was inhibited by the dryness of the climate (see Map 12, p. 563). As the climate map shows [2.3], this valley was a southernmost extension of habitats like those of the Northern Arid Zone. At the northern end of the valley, at the site of permanent springs, settlement began in the Archaic and extends into the present with the town of Tehuacán.

Mixteca Moving west, we come to a broad region that was, and is, home to Mixtec-speakers. There are three Mixteca zones: the Mixteca Alta, closest to the Tehuacán Valley, is mountainous, Mixteca Baja is a hilly area to its west, and the Mixteca de la Costa is a narrow stretch of Pacific Coast (see Map 13, p. 564). The Río Verde drains this mountain zone, and significant settlement began there in the Formative period, though the Mixteca is best known for its Postclassic city-states in the Mixteca Alta, which produced some of Mesoamerica's finest historical documents.

Valley of Oaxaca East of these Mixteca zones is the y-shaped Valley of Oaxaca (see Map 14, p. 565), an early hearth of domestication, sedentism, and complex society, with Monte Albán as Mesoamerica's first true city.

Isthmus of Tehuantepec, Pacific Coastal Plain and the Southern Gulf Lowlands

Middle America's major internal division lies at the border between these arid regions and the humid lowlands of the southern Gulf region and the Isthmus of Tehuantepec. These lowlands are steamy and tropical in climate, heavily influenced by the meandering, repeatedly flooding rivers draining the highlands regions. The Isthmus links the Gulf lowlands with the coastal and piedmont zone extending down the Pacific Coast of Chiapas (Mexico), Guatemala, and El Salvador.

Gulf Lowlands, South The Coatzacoalcos River and its many tributaries weave through the swampy lowlands of the southern Gulf Coast (see Map 15, p. 566). This region was the heartland of Olmec culture, Mesoamerica's first great complex society, with centers at San Lorenzo and La Venta.

Isthmus and Pacific Coastal Plain The Isthmus of Tehuantepec comprised the whole area from the Gulf of Mexico to the Pacific, a relatively level stretch, north to south, of less than 120 km (200 miles). The northern section is the southern Gulf lowlands, and it extends south to a set of hills close to the Pacific. South of this, the coastal plain zone along the Pacific stretched down to El Salvador (see Map 16, p. 567). It was an area of vigorous cultural development from the Early Formative period on, with very early developments toward ranking and centralization of political power. At Paso de la Amada, Mesoamerica's earliest known ball court was found.

Chiapas and Guatemala Highlands

Upslope and north of this coastal zone lay the highland zones: the western inland plateau of Chiapas and the eastern, Guatemala highlands (see Map 17, p. 568). This region's culture history encompassed Middle Formative communities through the Postclassic city-states still fighting the Spaniards in the mid 1520s. Important centers include Chiapa de Corzo, continuously occupied since 1400 BC, and Kaminaljuyú, with a later start, at 1000 BC, but now part of Guatemala City, that nation's modern capital.

Maya Lowlands, North and South

The Chiapas plateau grades to the north down to the Gulf lowlands, and east of La Venta begin the Maya lowlands, which extend over the Yucatán Peninsula, a limestone shelf pocked with sinkholes, but almost lacking rivers. Here arose the great Maya cities of the Terminal Formative, Classic, and Postclassic periods. Maya city-states like Uxmal and Chichén Itzá continued to thrive in the north (see Map 18, p. 569) after great centers like Tikal and Palenque in the southern lowlands (see Map 19, p. 570) were abandoned at the end of the Classic period. The easternmost Maya lived in the Motagua Valley and its tributaries: Copán was the most important center.

Southeastern Mesoamerica

East and south of the Maya regions was a frontier area influenced by the Mesoamerican cultures – by the Olmecs in the Formative, by the Maya during the Classic, and by Central Mexican cultures in the Postclassic (see Map 20, p. 571). Yet its linguistic and other ethnic affiliations were non-Mesoamerican, and complex societies flourished there during periods of isolation from Mesoamerican influence. Cerén, an Early Classic-period farming village in El Salvador, was preserved under a volcanic ash fall, offering detailed evidence of the lives of farmer-artisans there, and by extension, in countless other Mesoamerican farming villages.

Intermediate Area

Beyond Mesoamerica, to the south, lay Middle America's southernmost region, which had many cultural affinities with South America (see Map 21, p. 572). Mesoamerica shared certain basic traits with the Chibcha-speakers who lived there – cultivation of maize and use of cotton, for example, but there is little evidence of significant cultural interchange. Monagrillo, in Panama, evidenced the earliest use of ceramics in Middle America, about 5,000 years ago.

MESOAMERICA'S FIRST INHABITANTS: HUNTER-FORAGERS, TO 8000 BC

The outline of regions has stressed their distinctiveness, and as this Mesoamerican culture history unfolds, these distinctions are found to be undeniably important in shaping local cultural adaptations and regional ethnic identities. These regional descriptions pertain to the last few thousand years, well past the end of the most recent glacial period of the Pleistocene, the great epoch of the Ice Ages that began about 2 million years ago, and ended about 10,000–12,000 years ago, and during which humans evolved in Africa, Europe, and Asia.

But it was not until nearly the end of the Pleistocene that humans reached the New World. By about 30,000 years ago in the Old World, fully modern humans had pushed into even the most extreme habitats of Africa, Asia, and Europe. In the far north, they hunted and foraged for their food, occasionally bringing down one of the huge beasts, such as mammoths, so characteristic of Late Pleistocene steppes and forests. These animals were "megafauna" – mammoths, giant ground sloths, sabre-toothed tigers, and others that became extinct as Pleistocene climatic conditions ended, and also because some of these life forms were hunted into extinction by humans. Most of the human diet was from less massive sources, consisting of available edible plants and small animals. Small groups camped close to the resources exploited at the moment, and, because any region's wild resources could only support a relatively low population for a limited period, campsite groups were small, probably a few related nuclear families, and temporary, a few days or weeks. Groups camped in caves or rock shelters, or on open ground under brush or skins draped over a simple framework of branches – or even mammoth bones. They had simple stone tools and could control the use of fire.

Our species has long excelled at adaptive radiation into new habitats, and like all other living creatures, we follow the Law of Biotic Potential, consistently producing more offspring than necessary to replace each generation, because, given life's many perils, this insured that some would survive to perpetuate the species. When the size of the population exceeded the ability of a particular region to support it (the region's "carrying capacity"), there was a tendency for some people to seek a better life elsewhere. This helped people avoid the other, more dismal consequences of overcrowding – environmental degradation, more work to increase food production, plus the inevitable conflicts and social inequalities – but these will be considered in later chapters. Of greater interest in this Late Pleistocene part of the human story is the tendency of some of these hunter-foragers to keep pushing into increasingly remote regions. They moved into and beyond northeastern Asia, pushing north up into the Siberian Peninsula, moving east on foot and along the coast in small, simple water craft, following their various food sources into new territory, into the Americas (see table, opposite).

Middle America's Early Paleoindian Sites (2.8)

Northern Arid Zone

San Isidro Cave Earliest levels date to the Malpais tradition, a pre-Clovis occupation of the Sonoran and Chihuahuan deserts

Diablo Cave Estimated date, 30,000 years ago

Rancho la Amapola Kill site at a late Pleistocene spring; megafauna bones, bone and stone tools, hearth; radiocarbon dated to more than 15,000 years ago, possibly 33,000 years ago

Basin of Mexico

Tlapacoya-Zohapilco site (Basin of Mexico) 2,500 stone tools, plus fossil remains, cooking areas, dating to Tlapacoya phase, possibly over 20,000 years ago

Puebla

Caulapan and other sites in the Valsequillo region (Puebla) Five sites had stone tools and the remains of Pleistocene fauna. The Caulapan locus has a possible radiocarbon date of 21,000 years ago and other Valsequillo dates may be even older, but there has been vocal criticism of recovery methods

Maya Lowlands, North

Loltun Cave Probably pre-Clovis late Pleistocene mastodon and horse, and stone and bone tools; no radiocarbon dates are yet available

2.8 *Middle America's Early Paleoindian sites. See Reference Maps (pp. 552–572) for site locations.*

The pattern was not so much one of a continuous frontier being constantly advanced by pioneers, but of a mosaic of human occupation as successive regions were occupied [**2.8**]. Hunter-foragers are mobile in the sense that they must move from one campsite to another throughout the year in order to follow the productive seasons of the resources they exploit. But note that successful hunter-foragers must know a particular territory very well, and thus their yearly round of shifting campsites takes place within a fixed region, fiercely protected from encroachment by other hunting-foraging groups.

The lives of Paleoindian Mesoamericans were structured by their food quest, and while the largest resources were megafauna, there were also legions of other useful smaller animals and plants; these probably formed the basic subsistence foods and goods for these hunter-foragers. Lacking the means of storing large quantities of food for extended periods, their daily occupation was hunting and foraging for food, along with the artisanal activities that produced and maintained the group's household and hunting equipment, a modest assemblage of material goods, because mobile foragers can only own what they can carry on their backs as they move from campsite to campsite throughout the year.

Asian Origins

Scholars generally agree that "natives of both North and South America ... came from northeastern Asiatic stock ... [and thus] the only reasonable migration route must be via Beringia [the exposed land bridge of the Bering Strait] and thence western North America" (Wright 1991: 113). Native Americans and Asians share certain physical traits such as blood groups, distinctively "shovel-shaped" incisors, and the epicanthic fold above the eye.

They also share some cultural practices and beliefs that may have common roots: while Euro-Americans look at the full moon and see a face, Asians and Native Americans perceive in the rising full moon's surface patterns the figure of a rabbit, a creature whose fertility is echoed in the synchronicity of the phases of the moon and those of the human menstrual cycle. There are a few parallels between Mesoamerican and Asian divinatory calendars and astronomical techniques, and between how Mesoamericans and Asians saw the structure of the universe (Coe 1999: 57). In northeast Asia and Native America we find that certain individuals with strong divinatory and spiritual power – shamanic power – become leaders. In Asian and Native American cultures, shamans mediated between the living and the dead, between humans and the rest of the landscape [**2.9**] and throughout Mesoamerican culture history, great leaders also were great shamans. For Paleoindian-period foragers, food and physical well-being were priorities, so the group's ritual life, guided by its shaman, would have focused on seeking integration with the spirits of the natural world, particularly through the *rites of passage* that celebrate an individual's major life transitions, *rites of increase* to mark seasonal and annual changes, and *rites of propitiation* to avert or survive a crisis for the group or one of its members.

Note that Asian "migrants" were not intentionally leaving Siberia for a better life in the Americas. Instead, this great migration took place as a gradual push along Asia's eastern frontier, pioneers moving across a continuous strip of land, or along a rugged but continuous coastline. The earliest Americans, whose children would be the first Native Americans, were simply hunting and foraging, moving away from where established populations of Siberians were already hunting the mammoths and other big game, and finding good campsites and kill sites as they moved east and south. Successive generations adapted to various regions and then radiated beyond them, through North America, into Middle America. This marks the onset of the "Paleoindian" period, a term that combines the sense of contemporaneity with Paleolithic populations of the Old World, with the traditional term for Native Americans.

2.9 *(Opposite) This carved stone figure from the Middle Formative period, about 46 cm (18 in) high, is in a posture called the "transformation pose," commonly found in Olmec culture sculpture and thought to depict the shaman's change from human to animal form. The jaguar features indicate the shaman's transformation to the alter ego jaguar.*

SHAMANISM

SHAMANISM is a belief system focusing on spiritual mediation by gifted individuals who purport to move between the profane everyday world of human life, and the spirit world (Vitebsky 1995). Serving the spiritual needs of their communities, shamans allay anxieties and intervene in crises of health, social harmony, and prosperous relations with the natural world. On a more sinister note, in their position of trust they can also cause anxiety through psychological manipulation. Shamans are believed by their adherents to be able to divine future events or diagnose the cause of illness, and they hone these alleged skills by seeking enlightenment through a transformational experience such as an ecstatic trance induced by dreaming, drugs, rhythmic drumming and dancing, or physical stress (self-induced hunger or pain). In an altered state of consciousness, the shaman hallucinates a transformation into an animal spirit in order to learn the cause of the crisis.

"Shaman" is a Siberian word, and there the shamanic tradition has ancient roots; the term has been applied to community spiritual leaders throughout the world, particularly where organized, institutionalized religion has little influence in comparison with local practices designed to keep the group in a harmonious relationship with the natural environment. The Siberian shaman was a healer, spiritual medium, and hunting and raiding leader for hunter-forager groups. In egalitarian societies, the shaman would have been a most influential group member.

Shamans may be men or women, called to their role by a life crisis that reveals the individual's sensitivity to emotional and social ambience, and ability to gain the confidence of their followers through convincing displays of psychic and extrasensory power, often based on mastery of magic (sleight-of-hand). The shaman masters the "'dialectic of hierophanies' – the radical separation between profane and sacred and the resultant splitting of the world" (Eliade 1964: xii).

Shamanism is still practiced among traditional peoples of present-day Mexico and Central America, and was part of the spiritual bedrock of ancient Mesoamerica, a "base religion" (La Barre 1970). Descended from northeast Asia's Late Pleistocene hunter-foragers, Native Americans carried on ancestral spiritual practices. Shamans in the Americas have traditionally used hallucinogens to connect with the spirit world, and this practice goes back to Paleoindian times. The oldest evidence in the world of hallucinogenic plants in an archaeological context comes from Desert Culture sites of the Northern Arid Zone, where caches of seeds of the plant *Sophora secundiflora* have been found, dating to between 8440 and 8120 BC (Furst 2001). The seeds are highly toxic but will, in controlled doses, induce ecstatic trances. Peyote, a hallucinogenic cactus found in the Northern Arid Zone, was in use as early as 5000 BC, and was traded widely throughout Mesoamerica.

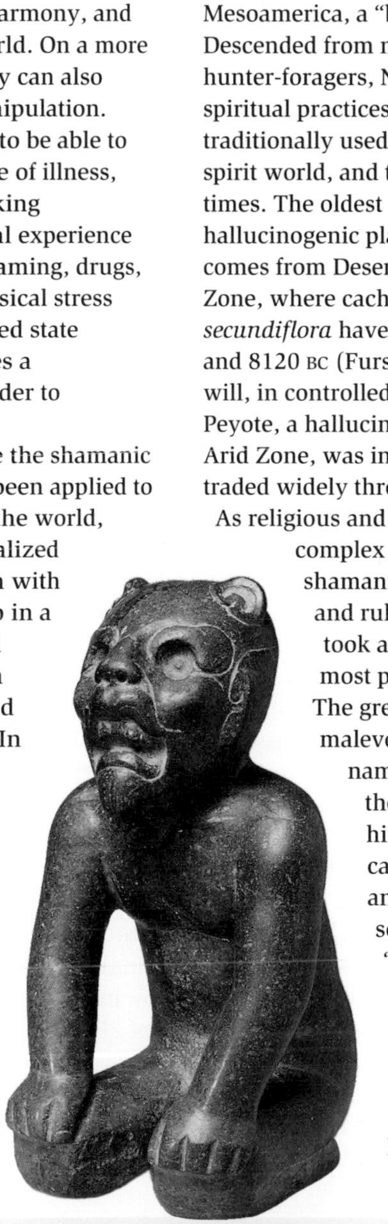

As religious and social institutions became more complex in the Formative and Classic periods, shamanic practices lent strength to leaders and rulers. By Classic times, powerful kings took as their animal familiar the jaguar, most powerful of Middle American beasts. The great god of the Late Postclassic was the malevolent trickster Tezcatlipoca, whose name means "Smoking Mirror." He was the patron deity of shamans, and was, himself, "the eternal shaman – capricious, clever, ever changing shape and form" (Day 1991: 246). Scholars sometimes disagree whether or not "shaman" can be applied to powerful diviners in complex societies (Klein *et al.* 2002), but as we shall see, this deeply rooted tradition is expressed through important key figures throughout Mesoamerican culture history.

Paleoindian Periods

The Paleoindian period is also known as the *Lithic Stage*, because chipped stone tools constitute most of what little material culture evidence exists from these millennia. Most of these artifacts could be laid out on several card tables, and most of their archaeological contexts are uncertain and difficult to date. It would be impossible to reconstruct the culture on the basis of these stone tools and kill sites alone. Important evidence also comes from paleoenvironmental studies, archaeological evidence from neighboring culture areas, general patterns of behavior common among hunting-foraging peoples, and comparison of DNA of Siberians and Native Americans.

When did Native Americans become established in the New World? This issue is still debated by archaeologists: the evidence for Paleoindian-period occupation is extremely sparse, as would be expected, given the modest material culture repertoire of mobile hunting-foraging peoples, the low density and numbers of these bands of foragers, and the length of time elapsed. Some estimates date human arrival in the Americas to over 200,000 years ago, based on such evidence as dating of geological strata bearing crude stone objects identified as possible artifacts. However, this time period is well before the emergence of fully modern humans, and there is no evidence in the New World of any hominids except for fully modern *Homo sapiens*. Furthermore, there is no evidence for occupation of Siberia at this time. At present, scholars agree that there is no convincing evidence of human occupation of the New World at this early time.

2.10 *Paleoindian-period chipped stone tools. Middle Paleoindian projectile points: top, Clovis point from North America; the bottom three points were found in association with mammoths at Santa Isabel Iztapan.*

*Early Paleoindian, or Pre-Clovis Cultures (30,000 ± 10,000 years ago–*c. *11,000* BC*)* Recently many scholars have come to accept the possibility that human arrival and dispersion may have begun 20,000, or even as much as 50,000 years ago (Hester 2001) – many millennia before distinctive fluted "Clovis" spear points came into use (see below). Evidence for human occupation in the period around 20,000 years ago has collected along many lines – geophysical, human genotypes and phenotypes, timing of linguistic differentiation – and while some lines of evidence are more convincing than others, the overall weight of argument favors this perspective. Sites identified as Early Paleoindian are listed in the table on p. 63.

A great boost in the credibility of this position came from recent scholarly consensus over the age of Monte Verde, a southern South American site dated to 13,000 years ago, with a possible earlier occupation at 33,000 years ago (Dillehay 2000). Monte Verde's carefully documented age convinced many scholars that original populations coming into the Americas must have predated this site by many millennia, and thus strengthened the credence of claims of dates of 20,000 years ago, and earlier, at other sites. Still, there is no scholarly consensus over just when the first humans arrived in the Americas: "no one doubts the possibility of a pre-Clovis occupation of the Americas, but few would want to go to court with the evidence as it is presently constituted" (Beaton 1991: 212).

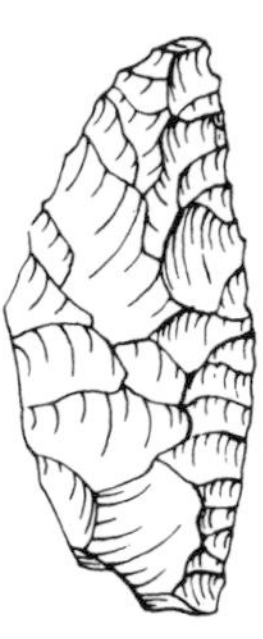

Late Paleoindian, or Clovis Culture and Other Fluted Point Traditions (c. 11,000–8200 BC) For many years, scholars used a particular chipped stone tool, the Clovis point [**2.10**], as a diagnostic of the earliest well-documented cultural complex known for North and Middle America. Regardless of whether other cultures predate Clovis, this complex marks the first appearance of fluted projectile points in the New World's archaeological record. Clovis points are native to the New World, and when found in good archaeological contexts they provide convincing evidence of a widespread generalized hunting-foraging culture in the Americas by 12,000 years ago, and imply a pre-Clovis process of dispersal from Asia for at least several thousand years before Clovis points appeared.

The chipped stone tools of the Clovis complex included "skillfully-made, bifacially-flaked spear and dart points" – the point was hafted to a thrusting spear or perhaps to a shaft used with a spear thrower (often called by its name in Nahuatl, the Aztec language: *atlatl*) – and these "would have made formidable weapons" (Zeitlin and Zeitlin 2000: 63). Points vary in size, and no doubt had multiple uses beyond killing megafauna, but our image of Clovis culture-bearers has been influenced by the presence of such tools at mammoth-kill sites in the U.S. and Mexico, and some of these weapons have been found embedded in the bones of the hunted animals. The chert and obsidian from which they were made sometimes originated hundreds of miles away, indicating travel over great distances; a biface found at a Clovis site in Texas was made of obsidian from a source in the Northern Arid Zone, 1,600 km (1,000 miles) away (Hester 2001).

Clovis points are most commonly found in North and Middle America. Another important point type in the late Pleistocene Americas was the fish-tail point, found in southern Middle America and, more commonly, in South America, including Fell's Cave in Tierra del Fuego at the southern end of South America. These continent-wide shared patterns of material culture provide evidence that even 12,000 years ago, certain traits were specific to certain regions.

Big Game Hunters

Regardless of arrival times, Pleistocene Native Americans were hunters, and prey species, especially big game like mammoths, would have loomed large in any group's cognitive perception of the local environment, even if mammoth meat represented a minuscule contribution to the annual diet. The prestige of hunting, particularly of men as hunters, in descriptions of hunting-foraging societies has long annoyed those fair-minded individuals who point out that foragers – including countless women – provided the bulk of the diet, with necessary and nutritious foods of greater overall survival value to the band than were the very occasional rewards of a successful hunt.

What accounts for the hunting mystique, and the greater prestige of meat? For one thing, our view of these early cultures is biased because most of the material remains preserved from this period are hunting tools made of stone. Myriad other devices made of perishable materials, such as foraging nets and baskets, would not have outlasted their users. Another reason for the bias pertains to all human populations, and lies in our evolutionarily-derived predisposition to enjoy the flavor of animal meat and fat, a preference that helped insure our survival through lean times. Another factor may be the pleasure and value of the hunt as a social bonding experience. At times, hunting may be a starkly individual pursuit, but it often may involve many or all of the group's able-bodied adults, particularly males, in a mutual effort requiring courage, cunning, discipline, and trust. Yet another factor is the social solidarity engendered by sharing out the meat from a substantial kill. The distribution is made with great care by the hunters, based on kinship and friendship ties and existing debts of reciprocity, and forms another set of bonds in the network of generalized reciprocity.

A further compelling social reason is the barbecue feast to roast the beast, a rare occasion for celebration and satiation. In fact, some regular campsites, visited at particularly lush seasons of food availability, would have brought together several bands into one "macroband" for a time of reunion, feasting, rituals, and mate choice. Feasting has a social value far beyond the caloric value of the foods offered, with meat as the central part of the meal, and prestige accruing to the hunters and the shaman.

Mammoth Kill and Dead Human Sites: Santa Isabel Iztapan and Tepexpan (Basin of Mexico) It's a heroic image: a puny human, armed only with a spear, brings down a thick-skinned mammoth, weighing over 8 tons and capable of charging at 30 miles an hour. However, the odds were equalized by human ingenuity, as demonstrated by mammoth kill sites all over the world, showing that hunters were crafty about stalking these beasts and took advantage of conditions that increased the chance of a kill. Hunter-foraging groups drove herds of panicked animals over cliffs or into swamps, immobilizing their prey.

Such was the case at the ancient lakeshore underlying Iztapan and Tepexpan, adjacent modern villages a few kilometers apart, about 35 km (22 miles) northeast of modern Mexico City. Here at least eight mammoths (*Mammuthus imperator*) met their death during the Late Pleistocene, perhaps as early as 9000 BC, or as late as 7000 BC – within the fluted point period [**2.11**]. These mammoth bones were first exposed in Tepexpan in the mid 1940s, showing up in the excavation of an irrigation ditch, in a sealed Late Pleistocene stratum. "The huge beast had become stuck fast with its forelegs in the bog, and thus rendered helpless, had met its death without being able to extricate itself" (DeTerra 1957: 161).

When the mammoths lived, the local area would have been a swampy lagoon, and other remains were found in the vicinity. One human skeleton, known as "Tepexpan Man," was discovered in 1945 and was thought to be contemporaneous with the mammoths. Controversy has dogged this find, and recent analyses determined that it was actually "Tepexpan Woman,"

2.11 *It was man – or, possibly, woman – against mammoth at Santa Isabel Iztapan about 10,000 years ago. The doomed mammoths, mired in muck, were killed by Paleoindian hunters. The hunters probably used the* atlatl, *a spear-throwing device.*

and that it is possible that she died only 2,000 years ago (García Barcena 1994). Despite this specimen's problems, it is clear that hunters were bringing down the mammoths, and that meeting doom by becoming mired in the muck was an occupational hazard for humans as well as for their prey.

Further excavations at Iztapan recovered, from the same stratum, a complete mammoth associated with three chipped stone artifacts: two points and a knife [**2.10**]. These stone tools cast strong light on the Clovis-era toolkit. First, there are no Clovis points at Tepexpan/Iztapan, though other fluted points occur. Second, the tools resemble several distinct types not usually found together at Late Pleistocene sites in the U.S., and this may indicate that the toolkit of hunter-foragers was more varied than some archaeological assemblages indicate. In addition to tools, Paleoindian peoples of the Basin of Mexico seem to have also created representational art [**2.12**].

Global Warming, Varied Toolkits and Mixed Strategies: The End of the Paleoindian Period and Beginning of the Archaic Period

About 10,000 years ago, the earth's climates shifted away from Ice Age patterns, toward the warmer, moister climate that has largely prevailed since. Global warming at the end of the Pleistocene was probably slower than recent warming due to human-induced changes; how and if this recent trend can be reversed are serious problems we face in our immediate future. If nothing else, we should view such changes as another testing ground for cultural ecology, as we witness the cultural responses to shifting habitat patterns of plants and animals moving into regions previously too cold for them. The world's deserts will gain in area, accelerating a trend that began at the end of the Pleistocene.

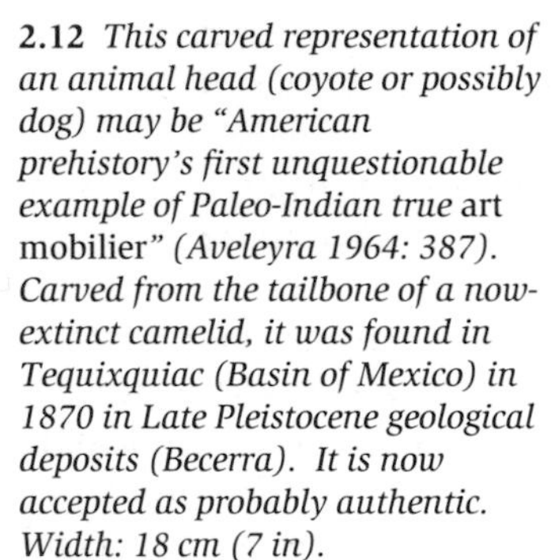

2.12 *This carved representation of an animal head (coyote or possibly dog) may be "American prehistory's first unquestionable example of Paleo-Indian true* art mobilier*" (Aveleyra 1964: 387). Carved from the tailbone of a now-extinct camelid, it was found in Tequixquiac (Basin of Mexico) in 1870 in Late Pleistocene geological deposits (Becerra). It is now accepted as probably authentic. Width: 18 cm (7 in).*

Paleoindian big-game hunting traditions depended on herds whose preferred habitat was grassy plains. The North American bison survived in great numbers up to the time of European contact (they were hunted nearly to extinction at the end of the 19th century by Euro-American hunters) because the vast expanses of the Great Plains provided refuge for the herds. In contrast, Middle America's mountainous topography confined grasslands to the valley bottoms, which eventually served as traps for hunting large animals into extinction. Note that in contrast to other cradles of civilization, terminal Pleistocene Middle America provided its human population with no animals that could be domesticated for bearing burdens or pulling loads. The potential consequences of this lack are enormous, because it cost Mesoamericans the eventual development of transport technology based on beasts of burden, which, in the Old World, had spurred the development of simple machines – such as wheeled carts – that were the foundation of more complex technology.

3 ARCHAIC FORAGERS, COLLECTORS, AND FARMERS (8000–2000 BC)

THE END OF THE PLEISTOCENE would have been imperceptible to any single generation of Middle Americans 10,000 years ago. Small changes in climate accumulated over the centuries, bringing changes in local topography and flora and fauna. Middle America's climate became wetter and warmer, and, perhaps more important, seasons became more pronounced. Summer was the rainy season, and winter was cold and dry, a pattern that persists to this day. This seasonality of sometimes severe weather produces conditions that can sculpt landscapes. Flat plains became riddled with canyons as weeks of dry weather turn soil to dust, then weeks of torrential rain wash the soil away.

Mammoth, bison, and other megafauna dependent upon the cool grassy steppe so extensive during the late Pleistocene retreated north to the Great Plains of North America, and became extinct in Middle America. The open plain was a good environment for megafauna herds and their hunters, but the new, more dissected landscape had more microenvironments, and supported different kinds of plant and animal resources, whose abundance varied, by seasons.

Paleoindian-period hunters of big game may have always depended largely on other food sources, but with Middle America's climate changes and the extinction of big game, the food quest of necessity shifted definitively toward smaller game (deer, rabbits), fruits like cactus prickly-pears, and seeds from grasses and seed pods [**3.1**]. Processing these foods required new kinds of tools, and ground stone milling tools were added to the Paleoindian toolkit of flaked and fluted points, knives, and scrapers. These milling stones were made by grinding down fine-grained stone like basalt into crude bowls that served as mortars, used with "pestles" – the earliest were hand-sized cobbles – to pulverize seeds like those from foxtail grass. Ground stone tools [**3.2**] represent a technological revolution for emerging Mesoamerican culture, new devices for a new job: getting calories and protein from small plants.

The Archaic period lasted about 6,000 years, roughly from 8000 to 2000 BC. During this time, Middle American foragers became increasingly adept at securing food from plants, ultimately developing a basic triad of plant

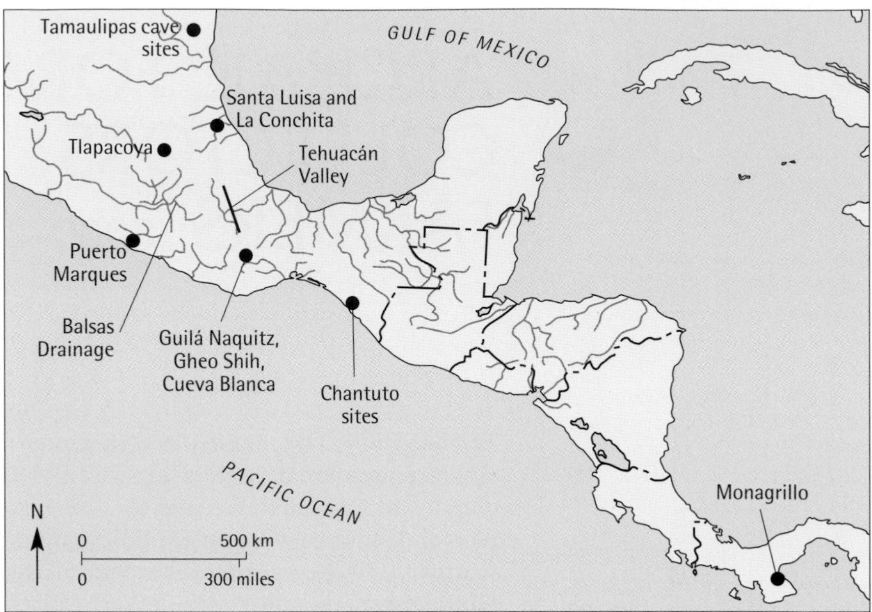

3.1 *Middle America, showing Archaic regions and sites mentioned in Chapter 3.*

crops – maize (corn), beans, and squash – that still serves as the broad base of the food pyramid for modern peoples of Mexico and Central America. The Archaic began with a foraged diet that was balanced but would have been exotic to modern palates (antelope meat, seeds from mesquite pods), and ended with foods familiar to all of us, grown by farmers living in villages.

How these changes took place, and when and where they took place, are important matters, because farming underwrote all later cultural evolutionary processes. These changes are also matters of keen debate among scholars, and readers should be aware of two important factors affecting our knowledge of the Archaic period. First, available data for this long period are scarce, indeed. Second, these data lay out a chronology of plant domestication that has been revised recently (1989 and after, discussed in greater

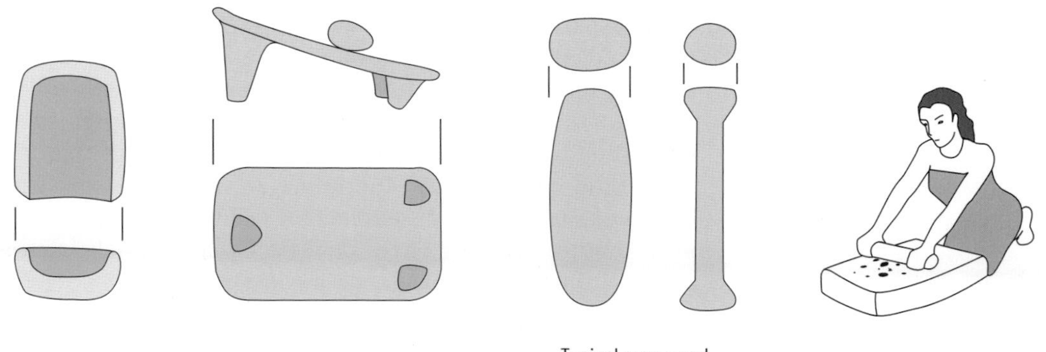

Legless basin-style metate and legged flat metate

Typical mano and "dog-bone" mano

Mano and metate in use

detail below), somewhat transforming our understanding of the rate at which the domestication process took place, but not the nature of the process itself. In this chapter we examine the closely linked processes of domestication of plants and establishment of sedentary village life, and discuss chronological revisions, concluding with a look at the early Mesoamerican village, bedrock of all later Mesoamerican cultural developments.

3.2 *(Opposite and below) "Ground stone tools" were used for much more than grinding other materials. Ground – and polished – stone tools were manufactured, by hand, by grinding stones down with other stones or sand, until they were of the desired shape to perform the needed function. Preferred materials were "andesite, basalt, chert, fossil coral, granite, gneiss, limestone, quartzite, rhyolite, sandstone, and schist" (Garber 2001: 300). Ground and polished stone tools in use in the Formative, Classic, and Postclassic periods show the repertoire of utilitarian forms that developed from Archaic-period beginnings. "Donut stones" may have been used as net-sinkers or mace heads. Even today in Mexico, where ready-made masa (ground maize) products like tortillas are widely available, no traditional household is without a mano and metate so that for special occasions, traditional foods can be properly made. These modern milling stones have a venerable history going back 8,000 years.*

ARCHAIC TRANSFORMATIONS: CHANGES TOWARD DOMESTICATION OF PLANTS, AND SETTLED LIFE

By 2000 BC, the end of the period under discussion in this chapter, the Mesoamerican culture area had been established in Middle America, with permanent villages and domesticated crops. The sequence of adaptive changes that led foragers toward increased stability in food sources – and in residence – is fairly well understood, thanks to the efforts over the last 50 years by scholars who charted whole regions of Middle America, identifying early sites and resources. Several regions were targeted by archaeologists as likely to hold evidence of domestication experiments: the Northern Arid Zone (Tamaulipas and associated cave sites), the Basin of Mexico, Tehuacán Valley, Valley of Oaxaca, Chiapas and Guatemala highlands cave sites, and the southern Maya lowlands of Belize. Long-term interdisciplinary studies in these regions combined geographical information (including biota) with archaeological surveys and excavations, often in caves where bands had camped repeatedly.

The greatest strides in understanding domestication of Middle American plants have been made in research done in arid lands not only because these are the natural habitats of these plants, but because archaeological preservation of materials is much better in dry climates than the wet tropics, and sea levels have risen since the end of the Pleistocene, inundating shoreline sites. However, the precocity of Isthmian culture in the Late Archaic and Early Formative periods would indicate that although the Early Archaic period is

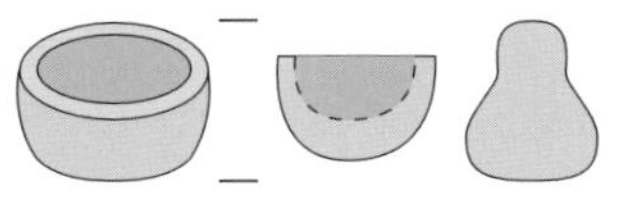

Bowl-style mortar and pestle

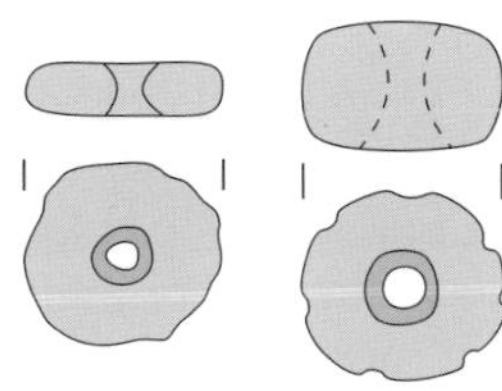

"Donut stones"

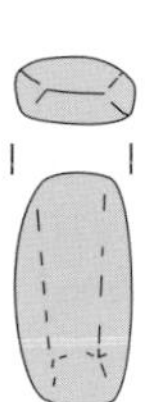

Axe

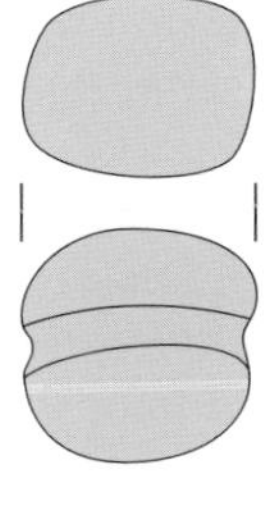

Maul with groove for hafting

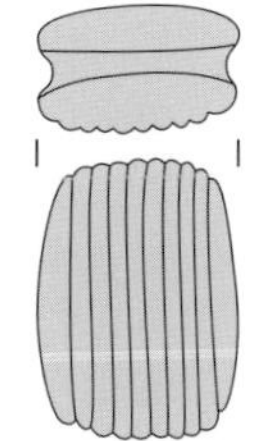

Bark beater used to process fig tree bark into paper and bark cloth

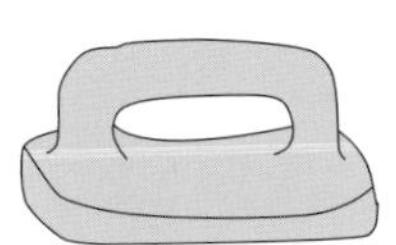

Plastering tool for finishing walls and floors

poorly documented there, it must have encompassed important changes in the social patterns accompanying sedentism and the increasingly intensive exploitation of localized resources.

That said, we turn to regions where data from the Early Archaic have been found. Most famous among them were those focused on the Tehuacán Valley, the Valley of Oaxaca, and the mountains of southern Tamaulipas.

Domestication of Plants and Sedentism, in the Dry Lands West of the Isthmus of Tehuantepec

The Desert Tradition "The roots of the Mesoamerican cultural tradition are imbedded in the North American Desert Tradition" (Willey 1966: 78). The Desert tradition arose in the North American west in the Early Archaic, and persisted for nearly 10,000 years, into the 19th century AD among Native American Shoshone and Paiute peoples of the North American Great Basin and among some peoples such as the Seri of the Northern Arid Zone of Mexico. Subsistence consisted of small-game hunting (using weapons as well as techniques such as rabbit drives and traps) and foraging for plant foods.

Seeds and nuts, good sources of protein, became important to the diet, and remains of these plant and animal foods have been found in dry caves, along with tools such as milling stones, baskets, and nets. Use of grinding stones long predates formal ground stone tools. To pulverize something – reduce it to powder – one need only apply pressure on it, rubbing it between two hard surfaces. Paleoindian peoples may have pulverized materials such as seeds, medicinal herbs or mineral ores by placing them in a handy concave rock, and rubbing them with a cobble. In the Early Archaic, grinding stones became more formal, though many deliberately made grinding tools were quite crude, perhaps mostly finished by being rubbed together as they pulverized the substance being worked. We recognize these as prototypes of later mortars and pestles and of manos and metates, the latter set being the "hand" and base stones used to grind corn in traditional Mesoamerican households to this day.

In the Northern Arid Zone, at Frightful Cave, the Desert tradition is expressed in the earliest remains, dated from 6900 to 5300 BC. These included milling stones and perishable items such as baskets and sandals. Spear throwers and spear shafts were also found, documenting that this implement was in use at this time; dart points from the Paleoindian period were probably used with spear throwers, as well, though no direct evidence has been found.

The Archaic toolkit was varied, with ground milling stones and flaked-stone points, knives, and scrapers, as well as bone tools such as awl-like punches for making holes in leather and for weaving and basketry. Archaic mobile foragers were handy at providing themselves with necessary tools and carrying devices, and seem to have harvested a broad variety of materials and foods, collecting more intensively as they understood and manipulated the growth habits of the plant materials they sought, thus providing themselves with an even greater supply with each successive year. Stability in resources was vital to insure that campsites would sustain habitation, and the more extended the period of resource availability, the longer the stay.

Think Like an Archaic Forager Archaeological reconstruction of past lifeways challenges the cultural historian to think like the culture-bearer. Strictly speaking, this is impossible, as misunderstanding arises chronically among living members of the same culture, so to presume a psychic oneness with a forager in the Tehuacán Valley 8,000 years ago is absurd. However, much can be achieved by understanding something of how individuals coped with their environments and provided for basic needs.

Food is a basic feature in all such equations. Involuntary hunger is very rare in the modern developed world, but was common in antiquity. And such hunger, unlike other shortages, cannot be overlooked. The average person needs something like 2,000–2,500 calories a day, and about 30–60 grams of protein, and vitamins and minerals, as well. As noted above, our common craving for fats and sweets was probably an evolutionary adaptation to induce overeating and fat-production, to see us through lean times.

The densest sources of protein and fat are meat and related foods like insects, larvae and other eggs of all kinds (from fish roe to fowl eggs), and even some plant foods, especially seeds and nuts. Figure **3.3** shows how foods compare. The values have been standardized to a 100-gram "serving" – an amount just about equal to the meat in a "quarter-pounder" hamburger. The foods have been arranged in order of protein value, and it's easy to see that a diet consisting entirely of leafy greens and raw fruit may be ideal spa cuisine for modern couch potatoes, but foragers required denser, richer food. Thus while Archaic foragers turned increasingly to plants, they paid attention to those plants that delivered protein, and eventually built their subsistence strategy around them.

Foods sought by foragers thrived in wild habitats, and the forager's food quest was somewhat like that of other animals that graze in a particular habitat, because even when humans mediated the harshness of the environment with the comforts of the hearth and sandals, or improved their hunting and gathering success with nets and spear throwers, they, like the deer, had to follow the food from one part of a region to another. We should also note that while the transformation from the wild forebear to the domesticate did not significantly alter food values, per gram of edible material, the domestication process delivered the food more efficiently. Farmers, worldwide, were the world's first practical evolutionists, creating domesticated plants that depended on humans, many to the point that without human nurturing they would fail to reproduce. Farmers selected those plants bearing more and larger fruiting bodies, coming into fruition sooner, holding the ripe fruit or seeds on the plant for an effective harvest, and having an extended season of harvest. Seeds of plants with desirable features were selected for the next planting season.

3.3 *The Archaic diet probably consisted of a wide range of foraged foods. The nutritional values given here are for edible portions only of a few foods representing a sample of the total – thus the edible seeds of wild progenitors of domesticated maize may have provided similar nutrition, ounce for ounce, as their domesticated descendants, but the seeds were smaller and on smaller cobs, and more difficult to harvest.*

Food Values for Foragers (3.3)

Food	Calories (kilocalories)	Protein, grams
	per 100 grams = c. 3.5 oz	
MEAT		
Caterpillar larvae, dried	430	52.9
Rabbit	175	30.9
Armadillo	175	29
Deer meat (venison)	150	30
Beetles, raw	192	27.1
Egg, fish (caviar)	250	27
Snail, raw	100	16
Crickets, raw	117	13.7
Egg, quail	150	13
Caterpillar larvae, raw	81	10.6
GRAIN/SEED, DRIED		
Squash or pumpkin seed	550	30
Beans, common	340	22
Teosinte	334	21.6
Chenopodium	327	14.2
Acorns	547	13.8
Amaranth seed	350	13
Maize	350	10
TREE LEGUME		
Mesquite seeds	300	6
VEGETABLE		
Amaranth leaves, raw	86	3.7
Nopal cactus leaves	29	0.1
FRUIT		
Papaya	125	2
Nopal (prickly pear, tuna)	65	1.5
Blackberries, raw	50	1
TUBER		
Manioc, Sweet (dried)	125	1.0
PLANT SAP & HONEY		
Maguey sap	50	< 1
Honey	306	< 1

Food, Sex, Demography, and Settled Life: The Laws We Live By

Deer, humans, and all other living things follow the Law of Biotic Potential, we noted in the last chapter, tending to produce more offspring than the environment can support, as nature's way of insuring that enough members of any species survive to carry on the line. The law is enforced through the sex drive. By responding to the deeply-rooted urge to seek pleasure and company, people mate and reproduce with the potential to expand their families enormously, a disaster for a foraging band or for any group with no uninhabited territory available for expansion.

Modern contraception permits many people to enjoy sex without necessarily engendering offspring; birth control is widely available and highly reliable for the first time in human history. Without contraception, every sexual encounter could have extremely expensive consequences, particularly in situations of limited resources. For foragers, resources included not only food and water, but also the adult strength to carry a baby or toddler on the trek from one campsite to another (while also carrying all worldly goods). Modern hunter-foragers generally space their children about four years apart, using abstinence or infanticide, in order not to tax these various resources, because when the food or water runs out at a campsite, the group has to move on, or die. If parents are burdened by too many small children on a trek, they become exhausted and cannot move to new sources of food and water.

Such circumstances also call forth another biological "law," Leibig's Law of the Minimum: the necessary resource in least supply will limit the operation of a living being. Thus, abundance of food is irrelevant if there is too little drinkable water. Or too few adult shoulders on which babies can be carried during the next trek. The allocation of limited resources among potentially burgeoning needs created pressure to make food sources and other resources more secure.

Responding to this pressure, humans – foragers as well as the rest of us – have constantly tinkered with the flow of resources, trying to improve productivity in order to maintain a particular lifestyle, while minimizing the necessary labor. Thus we humans follow several basic principles relating to cultural choices: the Law of Least Effort (minimize labor) and Romer's Rule, which holds that many cultural innovations originate as ways of maintaining a lifestyle, not necessarily intending to change it. Thus, a century ago, horse-drawn carriages were replaced by horseless carriages, early automobiles that looked just like the carriages and were to function in the same way, but with less effort than it took to maintain a horse. Some visionaries may have foreseen the impact of the automobile and all of its vehicular kin, but most people adopted the automobile for conservative reasons: to continue in the same lifestyle, more efficiently.

The transition from mobile foraging to sedentism and domestication results from a long series of mostly minor choices and innovations designed to increase efficiency and minimize risk in exploiting, or even controlling food sources. In Chapter 1 the point was made that in ancient Southwest Asia, the world's first known permanent settlements were established near highly productive stands of wild emmer wheat, and thus sedentism was found to precede domestication of plant and animal food crops: people settled down when they could intensively collect the right high-protein grains. The original commitment to extend the encampment to a year-round occupation may have seemed like a situational choice at the time, a decision to put off leaving for just a few weeks – perhaps this year the plants nurtured at the site over several years would produce enough food to support the group through one more season.

These small choices and adjustments add up, over time, to enormous consequences for demographic trends toward larger, denser populations, and cultural evolutionary trends toward greater complexity. In Chapter 1, the discussion of societal types laid out the strong correlation between the size of the autonomous co-residing group and the complexity of society, including social hierarchies and economic status. In this and subsequent chapters, we see the changes as they accumulate – gradually at first, but then building toward civilization and the state-level social institutions that underwrite it.

Early Archaic Band Society: Social Organization, Economic Organization, Political Control, Ideology

Social organization – the mobile band – would have remained much the same in Archaic times as it was during the Paleoindian period: small groups, very dispersed over the landscape they exploited. There was a general trend in the Archaic toward larger and more enduring campsites, with the early Archaic witnessing the smallest – microband – occupations.

We understand the microband to include five to 10 people, perhaps one or two nuclear families. Yearly periods of food abundance would have brought several microbands together, and this larger group – the macroband – may have together conceptualized itself as the rightful possessor of a certain territory. Egalitarian ethics of sharing do not extend to those groups outside the mating pool of related microbands, and outsiders – other egalitarian bands – may have been fiercely discouraged from moving into an occupied region. This sense of territoriality is pivotal to the trend toward regionalization of culture that began in the Archaic, and matured in the Formative period with clear-cut markers of ethnicity, the hallmarks of Mesoamerica's regional civilizations.

In band societies, a person's status is earned by skill, and because effective knowledge changed so little from one generation to the next, a knowledgeable older person was a vital repository of information critical for survival, and of the lore defining the group's culture. We assume that among men and women, the labor needed to survive was somewhat divided along gender lines, with each adult knowing a general range of tasks but specializing in certain activities. The only accumulation of property was the individual's personal tool kit and important amulets, so no one had preferential access to basic resources, and there was little potential for social ascendancy. Yet there would have been powerful individuals, such as the group's shaman. Others with considerable authority were the exceptionally successful hunters, foragers, healers, and artisans.

Seasonality and Scheduling

Responding to the emergence of seasons and attendant environmental changes, foragers in the arid highlands of Central and South-central Mexico pursued a subsistence strategy of adapting their own habits to those of important food resources, and they scheduled the shift from one campsite to another based on the seasonal availability of food (Flannery 1968). Seasons broke the year into broad resource-exploitation time periods.

Dry Season Subsistence The dry season lasted from fall into late spring. Resources were relatively scarce, and encampments were smaller, indicating that the foraging band was at minimum size, a "microband." Two important foods during the dry season were game (including snakes, lizards, insects, grubs, larvae) and sap from the *Agave* plant, or maguey.

Dry season camps may be thought of as hunting camps, with maguey sap as the staple food ensuring survival even when there was no game. In the Early Archaic, the sap and pulp of the fibrous leaves and heart of the plant would have provided calories and vitamins, as well as thirst-slaking liquid, while the fibers were useful for making string, nets, snares, carrying baskets, and other vital artifacts of the string industry. Maguey had a critical role in Mesoamerican culture history, from the Archaic through the Postclassic and into the present (see box, overleaf).

The daily need for potable liquid – juicy plants, if not water – may have inspired the domestication of a kind of squash, the bottle gourd, the first plant domesticated in Middle America, early in the Archaic. Dried gourds served as canteens for carrying water, and were readily cut into other shapes such as bowls. The seeds from squashes like gourds were high in protein and calories [**3.3**].

Rainy Season Subsistence The summer rainy season brought greater abundance of foods and water, and larger, "macroband" groups could be supported, at rainy season campsites, for longer periods. The season opened with the ripening of cactus fruit, and progressed as other fruits became ripe, tree legumes like mesquite, whose pods bore sweet seeds. Wild forebears of avocados were sought for the oil in their seeds, not for their flesh. Grass seeds, as well other foods like nuts, acorns, and fruit, became available during and at the end of the rainy season. In autumn and winter, rainfall diminished and foragers continued to snare small game like rabbit and get nourishment and moisture from fruits and leaves of edible cacti and maguey.

Early Archaic Foragers at Guilá Naquitz Cave, Valley of Oaxaca

The Valley of Oaxaca has been studied as an Early Archaic habitat for human foragers. The human population of the Valley was low, perhaps 75–150 in all, judging from known sites such as surface scatters of stone tools, isolated projectile point finds, and, most important, caves and rock

MAGUEY

MAGUEY (pron. mah*gay*) plants are of the genus *Agave*, which means "admirable," an apt name for the unfailingly reliable source of so many useful products: "in most *tierra fría* contexts maguey was as productive of energy and nutrients as any of the standard prehispanic Mesoamerican seed crops" (Parsons and Parsons 1990: 6). In some arid years, maguey "is the only crop that does not fail" (Flannery 1968: 83) [**3.4**]. The plants in the photo [**3.5**] are growing in the Teotihuacan Valley of the Basin of Mexico. The plant is extremely hardy, thriving above 1,800 m (5,900 ft) above sea level, tolerating frost and drought, growing slowly to a large size, and transplanting readily from offshoots that survive, uprooted, for months, so foragers may have carried small immature plants along and established them at all their regular campsites. The drawing [**3.6**] is from the 16th-century encyclopedia, the *Florentine Codex* (Sahagún 1963 [1569]), and shows an Aztec farmer carrying young maguey plants in a basket whose weight is balanced against the farmer's forehead by a tumpline, probably woven of maguey fiber. He wears a loincloth woven from slightly finer maguey thread than the tumpline. In his right hand is his *coa*, or digging stick.

Young magueys will take eight to 10 years to mature, and then send up a central flowering stalk, after which the plant dies. The base of this stalk, in the center of the rosette of huge, tough leaves, is the heart of the plant. When removed before the plant flowers, this heart of the plant could be baked and chewed for its oozing, jelly-like sap, similar to that of okra or aloe. That seems to have been the extent of its Archaic-period use as food – maguey quids were the most common Archaic dry cave campsite food remains. A few ounces of pulp a day would have provided some calories and a significant proportion of minerals and B vitamins to the diet, and slaked thirst.

From the Formative period on, techniques were developed to process the plant more efficiently. Removing the heart of the plant before it flowers causes it to release its juices into that central cavity, and if the plant is carefully tended, this flow of sap will go on for months. A farming family with 100 plants in various stages of growth, interplanted among maize, beans, and squash, can harvest, year-round, 12 liters of sap a day, a food energy contribution of over 5,000 calories a day (Evans 1990). Furthermore, by planting maguey they can establish that farm where

3.4–3.6 *(Left) The Aztecs honored only two food plants with deification, maize and maguey. This is the maguey goddess, Mayahuel, as shown in the* Codex Magliabechiano. *(Opposite above) Maguey growing in the Teotihuacan Valley. (Opposite below) An Aztec maguey farmer in his fields.*

no potable water is available, and use maguey sap as their drink. This flavorful sap is now called *aguamiel* (water-honey), and it can be drunk fresh or readily fermented into a mildly alcoholic beer, *pulque* (pron. *pull*kay), that was a widely drunk beverage in pre-Columbian times.

The plant's fibers were also an important product; they were extracted from the leaves and twined into thread, string, and rope. After the development of weaving, probably by 1500 BC, maguey thread was woven into textiles that had a wide variety of uses, including clothing and household furnishings.

Evidence for maguey domestication consists of species developed for particular functions, as fiber production or sap production, and is not found until the Middle Formative period. Maguey is still known as survival food to the traditional peoples of Mexico, and innovations to maguey cultivation and processing

during the Formative and Classic periods made the plant indispensable for extending settlement over arid piedmont zones. Today, maguey sap is distilled into the alcoholic beverage tequila, but distillation was not known in the New World until the Spaniards introduced it in the AD 1500s.

shelters (Marcus and Flannery 1996). These were camping places for very small groups, perhaps half a dozen people, probably a one-family microband. The low population and small size of the co-residing group may be related to changes in the animal populations. Climate shifts resulted in a decline in animal species that could be communally hunted (antelope, jackrabbits), and an increase in species taken by traps or snares, or by solitary hunters (white-tailed deer, cottontail rabbits).

Several important Archaic caves have yielded evidence of repeated occupation. Guilá Naquitz [**3.7, 3.8**] near Mitla in the Valley of Oaxaca was occupied on at least six separate occasions between *c.* 8000 and 6500 BC. Guilá Naquitz's food remains, tools, and activity areas have been recovered. This information, particularly pertaining to Levels D and B1 of the site, provides a portrait of an Early Archaic camping group. This was a microband, numbering around five people, foragers who began

3.7, 3.8 *Guilá Naquitz Cave, in the Valley of Oaxaca, sheltered an Archaic-period family. In the photo (above), a more distant view than that shown in Figure 1.7, the cave is in the center, with a person standing in the opening. The vegetation is thorny scrub forest, and the cave's situation offers protection and light and warmth. The plan (right) shows the path leading into the cave, which is roughly 9 m (about 30 ft) across. There were several hearths on the north side, and behind them was an area of food preparation debris. On the south side another concentration of debris marked an area where the remains of deer, rabbit, and turtle were processed. Foraging groups maintain a basic gender-based division of labor, and these debris zones may represent areas within the cave where women and men performed those tasks common for people of their age and sex (Marcus and Flannery 1996).*

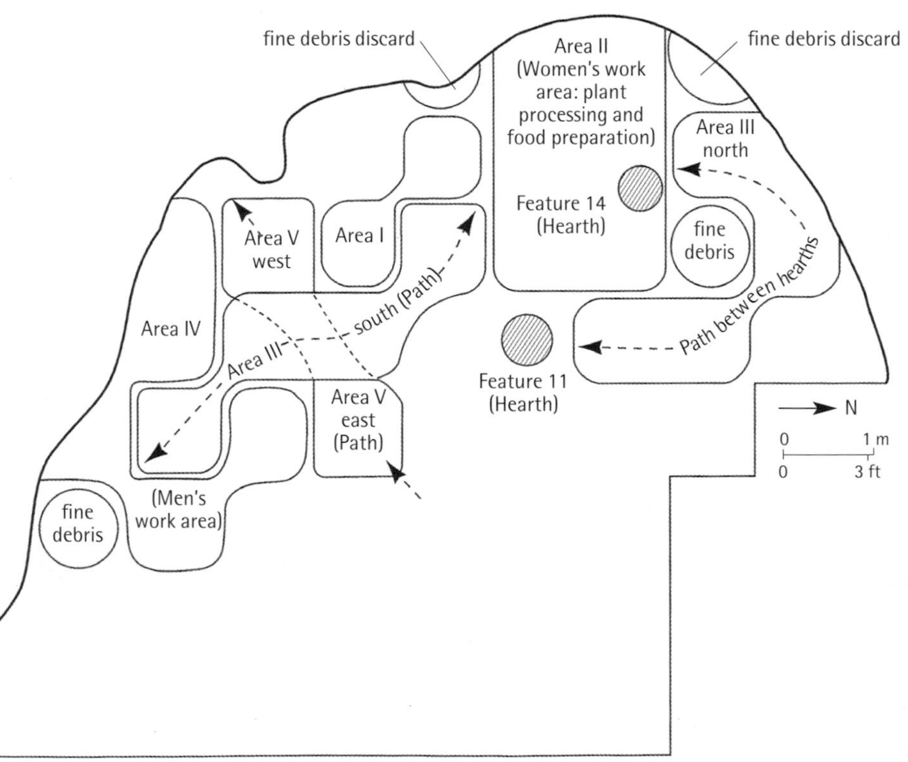

camping at the cave in summer and left before the following February, judging from the foods they ate. Maguey quids, the remains of thoroughly chewed maguey hearts, indicate reliance on the plant for food, and the fibers from maguey leaves provided raw materials for string and nets.

Meals at the rock shelter featured lots of acorn pulp, fruits of various kinds, the fleshy parts of succulent plants like maguey and cactus leaves, plus meat from deer and rabbits. Acorns, the most important starch component of their diet, were ground into flour on milling stones. The acorn harvest was a critical resource for this part of their yearly round – the group dug two storage pits for them, and had so many acorns that they could leave behind 3,000 when they moved on. Sweet foods were also attractive; mesquite pods were also stored in pits, and other fruits like prickly pears from cactus were gathered, as well.

Fires were started by twirling a stick into a prepared hole in a larger stick until sparks flew and ignited tinder, an arrangement known as a "fire drill," also found at Early Archaic sites in Tamaulipas. At nightfall, the group settled into a thick layer of oak leaves near their hearths. This pattern persisted for months, and then the band left the cave for another campsite. "We do not know where the family went, but we suspect that they ascended to the more humid forests of the higher mountains, just as the deer do during the dry season ... they evidently left their campfire smoldering, since it later ignited many of the oak leaves they had used as bedding" (Marcus and Flannery 1996: 57).

FROM EARLY ARCHAIC TO MIDDLE ARCHAIC AND BEYOND

Guilá Naquitz Cave's story could be repeated all over the highlands of Middle America, where other caves and rock shelters protected foragers while they pursued the food quest among sparsely distributed resources. The northern end of the Valley of Oaxaca connects to the southern end of the Tehuacán Valley, another region where Archaic-period lifeways have been a particular focus of archaeological interest.

The Tehuacán Valley

The Tehuacán Valley is more arid than Oaxaca – in Chapter 2 it was noted that this southernmost extension of the Valley of Puebla is also the southernmost extension of the climate regime of the Northern Arid Zone, with only about 400 mm (15 in) of annual rainfall, and none between November and April. The valley's alluvial plain and slopes provide various habitats for plants and animals [**3.9**]. The slopes are also peppered with caves, and the valley bottom is watered by several springs. Those at the north end of the valley, at the modern town of Tehuacán, have been in use for over 10,000 years; water from these springs is now so widely sold that, throughout Mexico, bottled mineral water is often simply referred to as "Tehuacán."

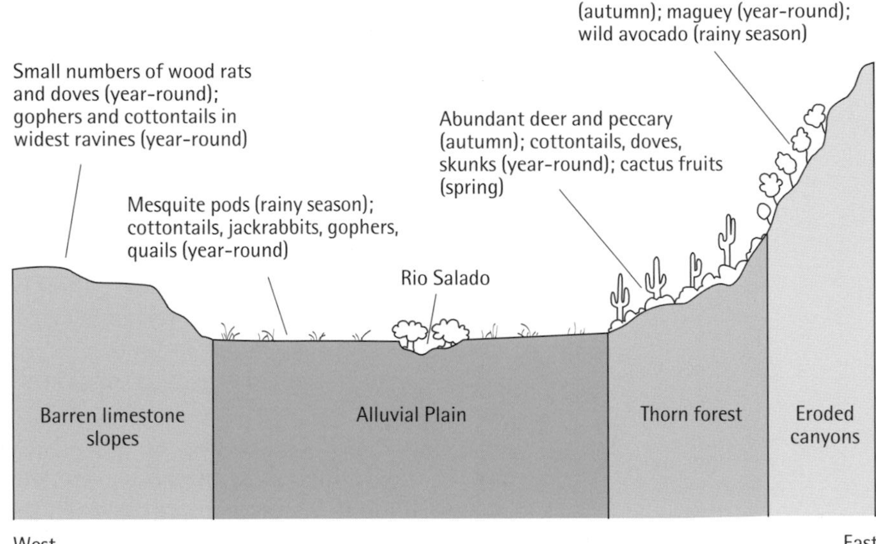

3.9 *This cross-section of the microenvironments of the Tehuacán Valley, encompassing about 20 km (12 miles), illustrates how localized resources drew mobile foragers from one area to the next. Small game was available year-round, as was maguey; other plant foods ripened in the spring and summer (Coe and Flannery 1964). While the Tehuacán Valley's climate is extreme in its harshness, the distribution of resources over a particular region is typical. Foragers "must exploit a wide variety of small ecological niches in a seasonal pattern" but farmers "concentrate on one or on only a few microenvironments which lie relatively close at hand" (Coe and Flannery 1964: 654).*

One of these sources is El Riego spring; close by is El Riego Cave, occupied repeatedly during the Archaic period. Research there and at other Tehuacán Valley sites used by foragers has revealed a sequence of cultural phases [**3.10**]. In Chapter 1, the distinction was made between major periods (such as the Paleoindian and the Archaic) and regional phases, describing time spans when sites in the region shared particular cultural features. In contrast to the Paleoindian period, with its fairly homogeneous cultural adaptation for very long stretches of time, the Archaic period had definite and perceptible phases, and these are distinct over broad regions, and are the roots of later regional ethnic elaborations of Mesoamerican culture.

Even more impressive, from the perspective of interpreting Archaic belief systems, was evidence of ritual activities. Two sets of burials were found, the remains wrapped with blankets and nets. This in itself indicates respect for the dead and the earliest known Middle American observance of a rite of passage honoring the dead, a general practice that has been part of human culture since Neanderthal times.

But what was even more interesting was the strong indication that another Middle American practice had begun: human sacrifice. One of the El Riego phase burial groups held the remains of two children; one had been cremated. "The head of the other child had been severed and roasted, the brains had been removed, and the head had been placed in a basket on the child's chest" (MacNeish 1964). Whether these were sacrificial victims or simply unfortunate individuals who died of natural causes and were given funerary rites of a rather elaborate nature, this evidence tells us that in the Early Archaic, the belief was held that the newly dead were regarded as worthy of veneration.

Human sacrifice might seem to a modern individual an odd way of expressing such respect – we take lives either in homicidal rage or madness, or in retribution for heinous crimes. Indeed, even in ancient times – in Mesoamerica and other cradles of civilization – ritual human sacrifice was often carried out to inspire political terror, or dispatch an antisocial individual. However, the rituals of sacrifice were designed to capture and use the vital spirit of the individual, a means of contacting the spirit world. Later in Mesoamerican culture, human sacrifice was thought of as repayment to the gods of the debt owed them for creating humankind and providing maize. In general, veneration for the dead and ritual observance of the event of passage from life to death typifies all later Mesoamerican culture. Evidence here, in Archaic Tehuacán, of such observance points to the potential power held by individuals who mediated between the worlds of living and dead – the shamans.

Regionalization of Culture: "Traditions" of the Early Archaic Period

The Tehuacán sequence exemplifies how particular regional phases can typify broader cultural adaptations, called *traditions*. The whole Paleoindian period can be divided into two major traditions: the earlier Pre-fluted Projectile Point tradition, and later Fluted Point tradition, extending over two basic kinds of Middle American environment: arid lands and aquatic lands. In the later Paleoindian period, some cultural differentiation was shown in the overlapping distribution of fluted points and "fish-tail" points, which were characteristic of South America but occurred as far north as Belize. When end-of-Pleistocene climate changes created distinctive regional environments (and microenvironments), foragers carefully adapted to the resources of particular regions and developed tools and skills related to intensive exploitation, and this paid off in securing adequate food and good campsites.

When, in the Middle and Late Archaic periods, experimentation with cultivation resulted in increasing commitment to food production, a major geographical division in Middle American cultures was established on the basis of the differences between the Nearctic biota of the arid lands west of the Isthmus of Tehuantepec, shared with the North American west, and the Neotropical biota characteristic of the wetter, hotter lands of the Isthmus and east, shared with South America. Regional traditions – the precursors of later regional cultures – multiplied during the Archaic, and on the basis of similarities among Early Archaic sites [**3.1**], several broad traditions have been defined.

In the far north, the Desert tradition was shared among several related offspring traditions: Cochise and Big Bend traditions extended far into North America. In the Sierra Madre Oriental of Tamaulipas, in northeastern Mexico, the Infiernillo tradition was characterized by adaptive patterns similar to El Riego-phase Tehuacán, and cave sites in this region yielded some of the earliest evidence of use of bottle gourds and other precursors of domesticated plants.

TEHUACÁN VALLEY SEQUENCE

FOR MANY REGIONS, the Archaic period is poorly understood because so few sites are known. Archaeological survey of the Tehuacán Valley mapped sites from its whole history of occupation, and the maps show important changes from the Early Archaic to the Early Formative [**3.10**]. From this survey, and excavation at selected sites, the valley's sequence of phases was developed. It has become one of the most famous phase sequences for any region in Mesoamerica, because it provided the first broad perspective on the important transformation from foraging to village farming (MacNeish 1967–1972). Thus the Tehuacán sequence tells an evolutionary story, showing the order in which various traits entered the complex of material goods and practices that characterize any culture, and in particular, the changes in relative dependence on wild and domesticated foods. Readers should note that the dates for transition from one phase to another have been subject to revision, and two sets of dates are provided: dates as estimated by Richard MacNeish, the Project's general director, in a recent summary (MacNeish 2001), and, in square brackets, the dates from the project report (Johnson and MacNeish 1972). These are but two of several published alternative sets of dates for these phases, mostly converging on the time frame outlined below.

Paleoindian Period

Ajuereado phase initial occupation of the Tehuacán Valley during the Paleoindian period, beginning 30,000 (± 10,000 years) years ago, and extending to 8650 BC [> 10,000 years ago–6800 BC]. Microband camps of foragers who hunted Pleistocene fauna using chipped and flaked stone tools. Site: Coxcatlán Cave.

Archaic Period

Early Archaic *El Riego phase*, 8650–5700 BC [6800–5000 BC], two kinds of camps: dry season microband, wet season macroband; subsistence heavily depended on wild animals and wild plants. Plants were increasingly important to the diet and included several later domesticates (squash, chile, avocado); some purposeful planting may have occurred. Material culture includes ground stone tools, early evidence of weaving (blankets, mats, coiled baskets) and woodworking (dart shafts, and traps). Earliest evidence of deliberate burial, including possible evidence of human sacrifice. The El Riego tradition, regions sharing this general set of cultural traits and adaptations, extended throughout the Central Highlands, 7600 to 5000 BC. Sites: Caves (north to south): El Riego, Tecorral, Coxcatlán, Purrón, and Abejas; open site near Chilac.

Middle Archaic *Coxcatlán phase*, 5700–3825 BC [5000–3400 BC], microband-macroband pattern continues, with a possible increase in size of macrobands. Coxcatlán phase has long signified the onset of use of domesticated plants at Tehuacán, but with reanalysis and revised radiocarbon dating of some specimens, greater emphasis has been placed on the plants of the Coxcatlán phase as examples of incipient rather than mature domestication of maize, chile, avocado, beans, bottle gourd, squash. Sites: Caves: El Riego, San Marcos, Coxcatlán, Purrón, and Abejas.

Late Archaic *Abejas phase*, 3825–2600 BC [3400–*c.* 2300 BC], most habitations were campsites, but some permanent settlements may have been established on river terraces. Steadily decreasing reliance on wild foods, increasing nutritional reliance on plants being domesticated, especially maize, beans, and squash. Material culture innovations in split-stitch basketry, stone bowls and jars. Sites: mainly Coxcatlán Cave, with further evidence from San Marcos, Abejas, and Purrón Caves and a pit-house site near Chilac.

Transition, Late Archaic to Formative Period

Purrón phase, 2600–1600 BC [*c.* 2300–1500 BC], a poorly understood transition from sedentary village horticulture to more complex society. Domesticated plants account for *c.* 35 percent of the diet. Material culture remains include some of Mesoamerica's earliest evidence for tempered pottery, from early Purrón, in shapes mimicking ground stone vessel forms.

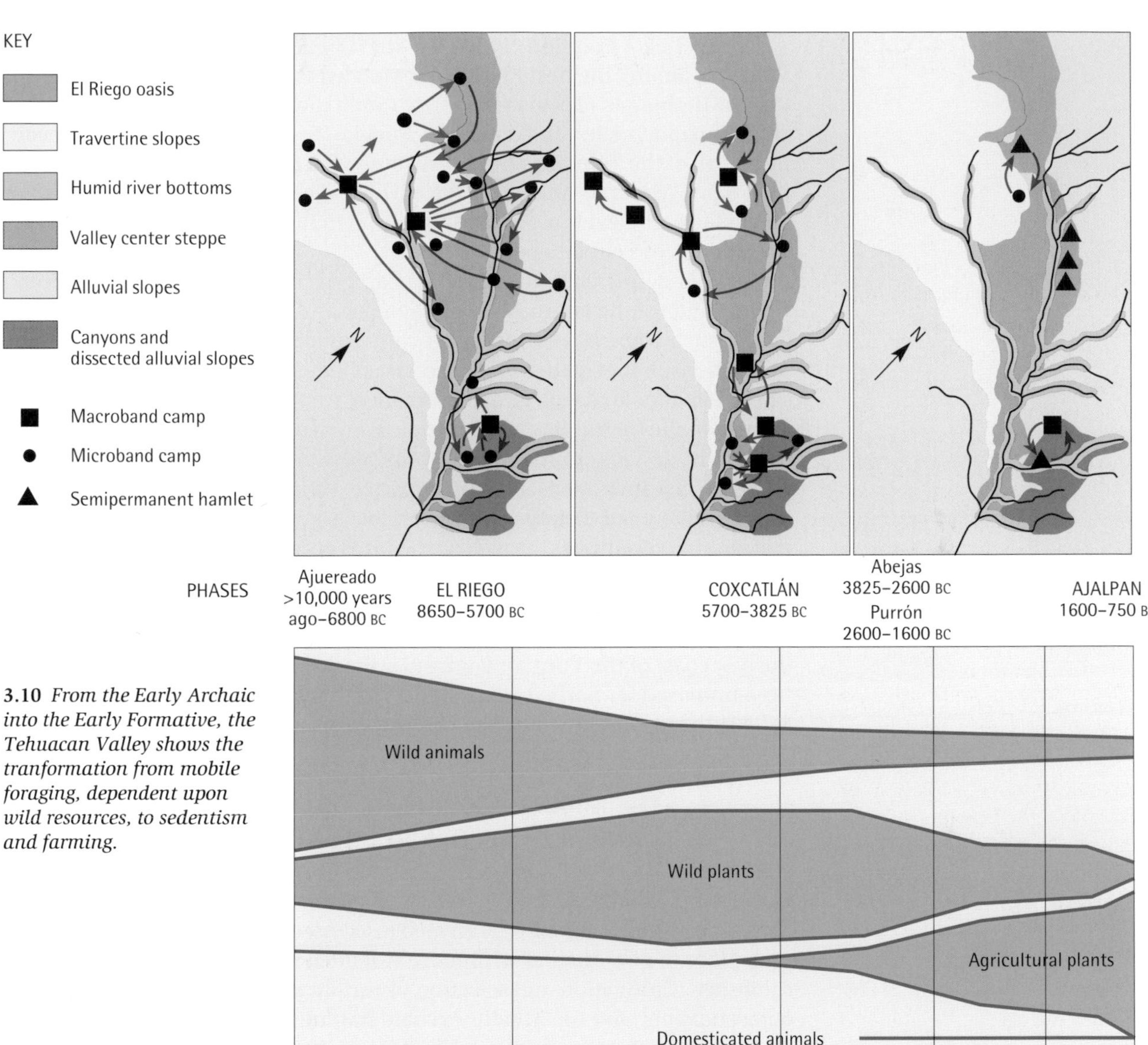

3.10 *From the Early Archaic into the Early Formative, the Tehuacan Valley shows the tranformation from mobile foraging, dependent upon wild resources, to sedentism and farming.*

Early-Middle Formative *Ajalpan phase*, 1600–750 BC, Tehuacán residents were full-time agriculturalists, still getting some foods from wild plants and animals. Remains of dog, first noted for the Abejas phase (3825–2600 BC) are much more common, indicating an important addition to the diet. The typical farming village had 100 to 300 people, families in wattle-and-daub houses. Material culture remains include a variety of stone tools and well-made pottery.

Subsequent phases of the Tehuacán sequence, to be discussed later in the book: Santa María phase, 750–150 BC, Purrón Dam, first stage; Palo Blanco phase, 150 BC–AD 750; Venta Salada phase, AD 750–1520.

The El Riego tradition, based on the El Riego phase of the Tehuacán Valley, is among the best known. It extended from the northern edge of the Central Highlands (Tecolote Cave), through the Basin of Mexico (the Tlapacoya/Zohapilco site) and Valley of Puebla (El Texcal Cave, lowest level), just north of the Tehuacán Valley. A somewhat different Early Archaic tradition, Santa Marta, is shared by the early levels of Guilá Naquitz in Oaxaca, and in the early levels of Santa Marta Cave, in the hills of Chiapas just east of the Isthmus of Tehuantepec.

Less well-defined are hypothesized Early Archaic adaptations in the tropical lowlands of the Isthmus of Tehuantepec and many regions to its east. No doubt, such tropical environments were exploited by Early Archaic-period populations, but evidence of foragers is ephemeral under the best of circumstances, and for archaeological preservation, tropical environments are among the worst. Furthermore, interior tropical environments such as dense tropical forests, in spite of their aura of lushness, are actually poor choices for foraging, because foods rich in nutritive value are scarce. Along watercourses, lakes, and the ocean, however, food sources are many – fish, shellfish and other invertebrates, as well as the birds attracted to aquatic habitats.

Some tropical environments have yielded promising archaeological results. In the north-central Gulf lowlands, Santa Luisa and La Conchita are sites whose long span of occupation begins with the Early Archaic. Along the east coast of the Yucatán Peninsula, the Southern Maritime tradition has been proposed for Early Archaic Belize, with two poorly understood phases, Sand Hill and Orange Walk, the latter with some ground stone tools.

THE MIDDLE ARCHAIC, *c.* 5500–3500 BC, AND LATE ARCHAIC, *c.* 3500–2000 BC

During the Middle Archaic, some wild plants were increasingly used as food, and were nurtured – cultivated – to increase their productivity. This took place in conjunction with more extended stays at summer wet-season campsites. Cultivation and selection of certain plants eventually resulted in domestication, and the Middle Archaic has long been regarded as the time when maize was domesticated. The Middle Archaic phase of the Tehuacán sequence – Coxcatlán – was long considered the "type phase" for the debut of domesticated maize.

However, recent advances in analyzing maize, particularly through the use of AMS (accelerator mass spectrometry) to determine radiocarbon dates, have brought new interpretations of chronology and origins, and this has caused considerable controversy and confusion. Readers should be aware that in the published scholarly literature on these topics there is now a wide range of dates applied to the same set of stages of the evolutionary process. New dates are published regularly, but revisions are typically slow to percolate through the literature on the subject. That noted, let us return to maize: when was it domesticated, where did it happen, and why?

Maize Domestication

Maize domestication is now thought to have taken place by 4000 BC in the highlands of Oaxaca and the Balsas Drainage area west of Oaxaca. Evidence supporting this southwest Mexico birthplace comes from direct dating (AMS) of domesticated maize found in Guilá Naquitz Cave to 4250 BC (Piperno and Flannery 2001), and the abundance in the Balsas area of undomesticated forms of teosinte, a grassy plant now regarded as the wild progenitor of modern maize (Beadle 1939; Bennetzen *et al.* 2001). Balsas drainage wild teosinte subspecies *Zea mays mexicana* and *Zea mays parviglumis* are, biochemically, the closest relatives to domesticated *Zea mays mays*, and the next closest *Zea mays* kin are found in the valleys of West Mexico (Doebley *et al.* 1990).

The early maize found in deep levels of Tehuacán's San Marcos and Coxcatlán Caves was already domesticated (Benz and Iltis 1990), and was once thought to date from about 5000 BC. In 1989, a reanalysis of radiocarbon dates using the direct AMS technique revised the date of Tehuacán's earliest fully domesticated maize to 2700–2600 BC at most (Long et al. 1989). Tehuacán maize represents the diffusion of this crop from regions far to the west, testimony to ancient roots of interregional contacts throughout Mesoamerica. Fully domesticated maize appeared "on the southern Pacific and Gulf coasts of Mexico by about 3400 BP [before present, thus approximately 1400 BC], and ... in South America and the southwestern United States by 3200 BP [approximately 1200 BC]" (Smith 1995: 159).

By 2000 BC Mesoamericans in all kinds of habitats had chosen village horticulture as their subsistence strategy, an "explosion" of plant cultivation (Willey 1966) that had coincided with a climate shift, the Medithermal, toward cooler, moister conditions at about 2500 BC. To be sure, foraging was still a major component of a Late Archaic/Early Formative "mixed economy" that depended upon cultivated and natural resources. Over the course of Mesoamerican culture history, the economy remained mixed in many areas, but the proportion of food and materials derived from collecting declined as that from intensive production increased. At the time of European contact, millions of Mesoamericans depended on well-organized farming and exchange systems to supply their needs. Foraging remained the subsistence strategy of choice in more marginal habitats, particularly those with a long dry season; foragers still occupied parts of the northern arid lands long after the arrival of the Spaniards.

Once maize was domesticated, it spread rapidly and was grown wherever conditions permitted: the maize-growing area is the foundation for settled life in the culture area, Mesoamerica [**1.3**]. Domesticated forms of the set of foods eaten by Archaic foragers did not appear all at once: domesticated maize became widespread in the Late Archaic but domesticated beans were not widely cultivated until the Late Formative period (*c.* 250 BC). Domesticated amaranth seed is very difficult to distinguish from wild, but has traditionally been regarded as appearing at Tehuacán in the Coxcatlán phase.

3.11 *Maize from the Tehuacán Valley, ranging from the Early Archaic cob just over 3 cm (1 in) long, to the modern-looking example from c. AD 1500.*

It should be emphasized that wild and semi-domesticated forms of many of these plants were being cultivated as long as there was a decent return on the investment of time and labor. As the plants evolved toward greater productivity, cultivation became the most effective subsistence strategy. Once productive forms are developed, they spread rapidly because people are eager to adopt such innovations, the Law of Least Effort and Romer's Rule prompting us to take advantage of higher productivity (and the promise of less work to gain it) in order to keep our food supply secure. New maize seed obtained from the Balsas would have been enthusiastically received by forager-farmers in Tehuacán, where the new larger cobs of dried maize would have been recognized as a big improvement over semi-domesticated plants then under cultivation [**3.11**]. Early use of maize may have focused on consumption of the kernels when unripe, or consuming it as gruel (known as *atole*) or fermenting maize into a potable beverage.

Forager-farmers on the margins of as yet unsettled areas, like the lowlands of Yucatán, could use maize as their tool of colonization. Once maize reached a certain size and degree of domestication, its potential productivity threw into disarray the established strategy of foraging with some cultivation. The return on the investment of time and labor into maize was too great, relative to pursuing other foods, and maize and other cultivated foods accounted for more and more of the time spent on subsistence, until, by the Early Formative period, a new equilibrium was achieved all over Mesoamerica with the establishment of village farming. The increasing dependability of maize would have resulted in larger populations, which would have required new farmlands devoted to more maize cultivation.

Despite chronometric revisions, the broad general sequence of ongoing processes of plant cultivation and longer stays at wet-season campsites remains, for the present, as stated in widely-published phase descriptions, but the timing of these events in some regions may be considerably more recent than traditionally assumed. "Even if it turns out that the Coxcatlán phase dated to 3500–2500 BC rather than 5000–3500 BC, it would not change the context of early agriculture" (Marcus and Flannery 1996: 69), nor will it change the context of other cultural processes such as sedentism, occupational specialization, or the emergence of social inequality as these developed toward the end of the Archaic period and the beginning of the Formative.

Other Middle Archaic Evidence, West of the Isthmus

Central Highlands: Zohapilco, at Tlapacoya, c. *5500–3500* BC From Paleoindian times into the Initial Formative, the marshy shores of the Basin of Mexico's central lake system attracted foragers, but their ephemeral campsites are now covered by alluvium, layers of soil borne off the surrounding hill slopes in the rainy season. Interpreting the depth and complexity of lacustrine sediments and the few traces left by foragers are minor problems compared with that of penetrating the surface layer, which consists of Mexico City.

Given the small chance of detecting forager settlements, we are fortunate that the Initial Formative living site Zohapilco, at Tlapacoya Hill on the edge of ancient Lake Chalco, was revealed by an archaeological excavation consisting of a long, deep trench (Niederberger 1987). Similar investigations around the edge of the Basin of Mexico's central lake system would, no doubt, uncover other, similar sites.

3.12 *From Tlapacoya/Zohapilco, this 4,300-year-old depiction of a pregnant woman is only 5.7 cm (2.25 in) long. This locally-made ceramic figurine is broken just below the torso – the abstract figure, shown facing forward, has indentations for eyes, a small protuberance for a nose, and most distinctive, the swollen belly. Like Old World "Venus figurines," the function of this image is unclear, but the meaning seems to pertain rather obviously to fertility.*

In Zohapilco's earliest phases, called Playa (Playa 1 and 2, *c.* 5500–3500 BC), residents used chipped stone tools and had a diet based on wild foods. While occupation of the site extended throughout wet and dry seasons, suggesting the possibility of permanent, year-round settlement, the archaeological evidence is not sufficient to prove permanent sedentism.

The Middle Archaic occupation of Zohapilco was interrupted by a volcanic eruption that occurred sometime before 3000 BC. The site was reoccupied in the Late Archaic, and from a hearth dated to 2300 BC has come the oldest Middle American example of a ceramic figurine [**3.12**]. Figurines are abundant in Mesoamerica, in all periods – though not in all regions – from the Initial Formative through the Postclassic and they even persisted in the Colonial period. Generally of a comfortable size to fit in the hand, and usually made of fired clay, figurines commonly depict a person, or deity in human form, though many represent animals and some are even models of buildings such as temple-pyramids. Their function is generally understood to be related to rituals, though the details of how they were used, even by the Aztecs, are not completely clear. That so many have been found broken seems to suggest dedication of the figurine to a particular event, perhaps a life crisis, and then destruction of the figurine after the event, or ritual pertaining to it, was over.

Southwestern Highlands: Gheo-Shih, c. *5000–3000* BC Zohapilco was an open-air site, not a rock shelter, and such encampments were precursors of Late Archaic villages. Another Middle Archaic open-air site was Gheo-Shih, not far from Guilá Naquitz in the Valley of Oaxaca (Flannery and Spores 1983). The site seems to have been occupied several times during the summer wet season, a time when macroband groups could camp, eating newly ripe mesquite pods and other wild foods. Gheo-Shih's activity areas included some oval rings of stones on the ground that may have been bases for walls of huts, also areas of chipped stone tool manufacturing and

3.13 *At Gheo-Shih, an open-air site, two lines of boulders outlined a space which "was swept clean and contained virtually no artifacts. To either side ... artifacts were abundant" (Flannery and Spores 1983: 23).*

lapidary work or fine stone working for decorative purposes. Here, lapidary work involved drilling through flat river pebbles, apparently so they could be worn as pendants. Personal adornment such as jewelry can reveal social customs and the individual's place in society, and becomes more elaborate, and better documented, with further cultural development. We mark here an early example of a practice that in later periods would signify rank, wealth, and access to spiritual power.

Gheo-Shih's most famous feature is a much larger construction, a prepared field lined by boulders and cleared of all debris [**3.13**]. This area measures 7 by 20 m (23 by 66 ft), and its function is unknown. However, two possible uses of this area were as a dance ground and as a ball court. Dancing is among cultural universals, and was essential to the ceremonies of later periods, so we can safely assume its importance to Archaic and Paleoindian peoples, as well. The ball game is one of Mesoamerica's defining traits, and formal ball courts are known from the earliest Formative period, implying yet-undocumented antecedents in the Archaic period. Regardless of its functions, this construction is one of Mesoamerica's earliest examples of community-focus structures: the plazas, temple-pyramids, and palaces of the Formative and later periods that we call civic-ceremonial architecture.

Southwestern Highlands: Cueva Blanca, c. *3300–2000* BC Late Archaic occupations at Cueva Blanca, a cave near Gheo-Shih and Guilá Naquitz, illustrate the continued use of caves and rock shelters, but with more specialized functions. The remains from C and D levels of Cueva Blanca – deer and rabbit bones, projectile points and bifacially-flaked knives – reflect its use as a hunting camp, probably by a group of men on a winter hunting trip, away from their long-term base camp.

Foraging and Collecting With regard to the pursuit of wild food as a subsistence strategy, there is a distinction between "foraging," a generalized food-and-materials quest that involves the larger camping group, and "collecting," the more specialized pursuit of a particular resource by a small group of individuals with particular skills. The emergence of collecting as a set of specialized efforts takes Middle Americans another step toward a division of labor more complex than the simple age-and-gender distinctions of mobile foragers. A hunting party of a few men, sent out to secure game animals for food and materials, frees the time of those in the base camp to further specialize in other skilled occupations, and more extended encampments encourage dependence on a wider array of material goods (and specialized tools) because with fewer moves, more material possessions can accumulate.

Gulf Lowlands Sites Along the north-central Gulf Coast, Santa Luisa, in the Tecolutla River delta, was close to rich aquatic resources and also to forested and savannah environments (Wilkerson 1973). Santa Luisa's history is thought to extend back 8,000 years, and during the Formative it was the most important site in the region. Its Archaic role may have been as a central base camp from which specialized hunting or collecting groups would go out, living at smaller, more temporary camps, such as represented by the La Conchita site.

By the Late Archaic Palo Hueco phase (*c.* 3200–2400 BC), permanent settlements in the Gulf lowlands were supported by intensive collection of shellfish and other aquatic resources, and possibly also from cultivation of manioc, a starchy root crop, source of modern tapioca. This general preceramic settlement and subsistence pattern is called the Palo Hueco tradition and is typical of Isthmian adaptations of the Late Archaic.

A Note on the Term "Preceramic"

The term "preceramic" becomes significant in the Middle to Late Archaic, because ceramic use is an important indicator of other aspects of lifestyle. This period is transitional, introducing new traits that will characterize the rest of Mesoamerican culture history, like ceramic use, sedentism, intensive collecting, and farming. However, these traits don't come in neat packages, but appear in shifting constellations over different regions. "Preceramic" designates those sites lacking the clay-firing industry and its earliest ceramic products, pottery vessels and representational figurines. Later, the Mesoamerican ceramic industry would extend to production of other items, tools like small weights for spinning thread ("spindle whorls"), and building materials such as bricks and drains. However, the first products were modest: bowls mimicking the size and shape of gourd bowls, and figurines depicting well-nutritioned women.

Middle and Late Archaic: Isthmus and East

Pacific Coastal Plain The Isthmian region included the humid lowlands of the Pacific Coast, extending northwest and southeast from the Isthmus. The Pacific lowlands were much narrower than those of the Gulf of Mexico. Along the Pacific northwest of the Isthmus, the rugged mountains of Sierra Madre del Sur often meet the shoreline, with a maximum of 20 km (*c.* 12 miles) between the sea and the 1,000-m (3,281-ft) elevation mark. In contrast, along the Gulf of Mexico, the gentle plain of the Gulf lowlands gradually extends up to 100 km (60 miles) from the shoreline to the 1,000 m elevation mark. The Pacific Coast's much steeper rise leaves much less reasonably level room for farming villages. North of the Isthmus, the longest stretch of continuous alluvial or piedmont areas is in the Mixteca de la Costa region, and it runs for about 300 km (180 miles) along the coast and ends at the modern town of Acapulco.

However, from the Isthmus south, the coastal plain is about 600 km (360 miles) long, and 50 km (30 miles) wide at 1,000 m elevation. Part of this long coastal plain, extending from the Sierra Madre of Chiapas down to the sea, was called the Soconusco region in Postclassic times, and the name is often applied to the whole coastal plain southeast of the Isthmus. This broad band of humid tropical shoreline is riddled with lagoons, the teeming habitats of mangrove oysters and other aquatic creatures. The warm, wet coastal plain was also an excellent environment for plant cultivation, and the juxtaposition of these two productive zones provided another setting for the specialized collecting of the Middle and Late Archaic.

Perhaps as early as 4000 BC, people living around Laguna Chantuto and adjacent swamps and estuaries began to pile up huge numbers of shells into massive mounds [**3.14**]. We might think that such a monumental pile of shells was a trash heap, a midden consisting of detritus from countless meals, but the clams inside these shells had not been eaten. These shells were not discarded, but were being used as building material to construct this mound in a swampy environment lacking other alternatives such as stone (Michaels and Voorhies 1999; Voorhies 1989). The mounds probably functioned as drying platforms for processing other fish and shellfish, dried fish being a valuable local product because it provided an important adjunct to the diet, adding food energy, protein, flavor, and salt in a long-lasting easily transportable form.

The Chantuto shell platforms are an example of an emerging industry, a specialized food-processing pursuit that seems to transcend the efforts of a single foraging microband. The shell platforms' purpose was to facilitate mass production of larger quantities of a type of food product from a locally abundant resource. This is an early example of the broad pattern of economic specialization, a necessary precursor to the development of complex societies.

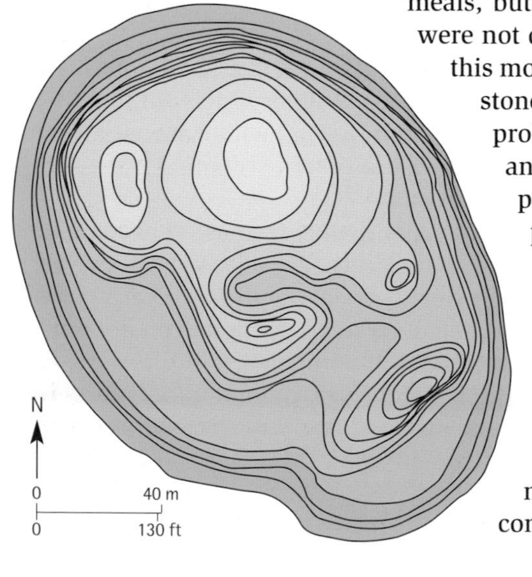

3.14 *The Chantuto sites, along the coast of Chiapas, were "massive piles of tiny shells capped with a mantle of soil. Shaped basically like truncated cones, they form islands within the mangrove forest swamp" (Michaels and Voorhies 1999: 41). The shell mound at Tlacuachero ultimately was over 7 m high and 175 m across (c. 23 ft high, 570 ft across). The contour intervals in this diagram represent 0.5 m (1.6 ft).*

Chantuto region sites seem to have formed a two-tiered settlement hierarchy by the end of the Archaic, with numerous shell-mound sites serving the needs of larger inland sites such as Vuelta Limón, whose artifact repertoire included heavy forest-clearing tools, presumably for slash-and-burn cultivation, a technique that entails felling vegetation, including trees, and then burning off the plot to clear it. Note should be made of the fact that Vuelta Limón was a preceramic site, because early in the Formative period Soconusco would become a key region for the production of Mesoamerica's most elegant and sophisticated pottery.

Maya lowlands, c. *3000–2000 BC* Archaeological evidence of settlement of the Maya lowlands in the Late Archaic is extremely scarce. On the east side of the Yucatán Peninsula, in Belize, the Betz Landing site (*c.* 4200–3000 BC) showed occupation over a long period, possibly year-round. Stone tools included ground stone milling stones as well as net sinkers, evidence of how aquatic resources were collected.

While inland tropical zones are not rich habitats for foraging, cultivators could clear the forests and plant crops. Sediment cores from the Yucatán interior reveal that maize pollen was in the air – and had settled into swamps and lakes – after 3000 BC. Thus forest clearing had begun, and the ground stone axe would have been an essential tool. Felling a mature tree with a sharp steel axe is a very big job; the job would have been much bigger with the stone axe, even though it was much more effective than any other felling tool in the Archaic toolkit. This is an important point to consider: that in spite of the high costs of slash-and-burn cultivation, colonizing the interior had become possible because maize was sufficiently productive, and perhaps necessary because growing populations demanded new land.

Intermediate Area, Late Archaic, Period III, 4000–1000 BC Well south of the Mesoamerican culture area, the southern Intermediate Area's unique position between Middle and South America gave it precocious status in the Late Archaic. The narrow strip of land comprising modern Panama and southern Costa Rica is mountainous and coastal, with tropical forest pressing against the shorelines, Pacific and Atlantic. While the broken, heavily forested terrain resisted overland interaction between the many small valleys, travel along the coast by rafts would have taken place in the Late Archaic.

The argument for such means of travel rests on the emergence of a whole new industry – ceramics (Rice 1996). The New World's earliest known pottery came from the Atlantic Coast of northern South America, at the site of Puerto Hormiga (Colombia), dated to about 3000 BC. However, it would be wrong to assume that ceramic technology was invented in one single place, and spread to other places by a simple diffusionary process. History is full of cases of independent, nearly contemporaneous inventions, because over broad areas, conditions are ripe to put together the pieces of the process: the production technique and the functional use of the products, in this case, the idea that a durable vessel could be produced by baking a piece of clay.

Ceramics and Sedentism, Ceramics and Cultivation Ceramics and sedentism have traditionally been linked in cultural evolutionary sequences, partly because ceramic vessels represent an investment in heavy materials and facilities that would have been inappropriate for mobile foragers. Another reason is that the products – pottery vessels – are usually larger and heavier than analogous vessels made of gourds, more cumbersome to transport in the mobile foraging round. Given the same function – bowl, canteen – a gourd is a better choice for a mobile forager, even if the forager has figured out that baked clay will permanently retain its shape. It makes sense to assume that this technique was known to mobile foragers, because baskets are often lined with mud to make them waterproof, and there must have been many occasions when such baskets burned, leaving a crude pottery vessel as an inner shell.

Ceramics and agriculture have also been linked as a Mesoamerican "package" of traits that seem to have been adopted together in some areas. Large vessels are good for storage of grains, for storage of the family water supply in the now-permanent residence, for softening and cooking dried maize, and fermenting beverages made of mashed grains or ripening maguey sap. Such beverages had an alcohol level similar to that of beer and were generally safer to drink than available water sources. Large vessels for their storage have an important role in Early Formative Soconusco.

3.15 *Monagrillo pottery, the earliest known in Middle America, is crude, with simple incised decoration.*

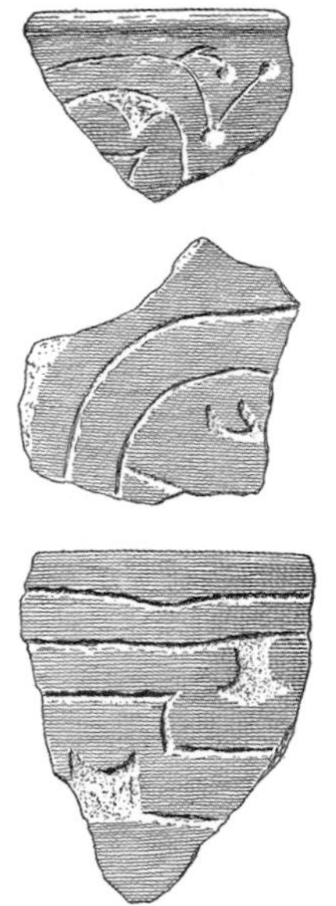

Monagrillo, Middle America's First Ceramics In spite of this strong link between maize agriculture and pottery use in Mesoamerica, the earliest pottery in Middle America is found in the Intermediate Area among Late Archaic/Early Formative peoples who pursued a mixed strategy of collection and cultivation of resources. The Monagrillo ceramic complex dated to about 2500 BC [**3.15**]. Monagrillo ceramic complex sites are found on the south (Pacific) coast of Panama, the Chiriqui Peninsula and Parita Bay. Monagrillo, the type site, is a shell mound on the bay, and other sites with Monagrillo pottery are Momoztli, another shell midden, and Aguadulce Shelter and Cueva Ladrones (see Map 21, p. 572). By 1000 BC, pottery appeared in eastern Panama. Earlier than that, pottery vessels were made in the Greater Nicoya area, appearing at such Nicaraguan sites as Ometepe Island and Los Angeles, both dating to the mid-Dinarte phase (*c.* 2000 BC).

The patterns of mixed subsistence and sedentism seem to have been exceptionally workable in the Intermediate Area, because they persisted throughout all pre-Columbian time periods. Studies of skeletons there show no changes in bone chemistry from period to period that would indicate increased reliance on maize or other staples. There were settled villages throughout the area by 1000 BC, and scholars regard Intermediate Area sedentism and pottery as local developments emerging from widespread knowledge of these traits.

Guerrero: Pacific Coast, Late Archaic

Soon after the appearance of ceramics at Monagrillo, pottery vessels occurred along the Pacific Coast of Mesoamerica. Our earliest known evidence of pottery in Mesoamerica is from Puerto Marques, just south of modern Acapulco, and ceramics there date from perhaps as long ago as 2400 BC. Puerto Marques was at the northern end of the coastal plain extending north of the Isthmus, and it was another shell midden site. Its earliest level, sampled in a small (0.8 cubic m/1.05 cubic yd) excavation, had no ceramics, but in the next level up appeared "Pox pottery," so called because of the pockmarks on its interior surface where bits of fiber temper burned away in the firing process. Temper is material added to raw clay to increase the clay vessel's durability, and the kind of temper (fiber, grit, shell, etc.) is a diagnostic trait that may indicate shared knowledge of the technology. The exterior of Pox pottery bears a red slip, similar to Initial Formative ceramics from coastal Soconusco, and also to pottery found in Ecuador and dating even earlier (Grove 1981).

Y2K: The Archaic Ends, and the Formative Period Begins

Village agriculture settled over Middle America by 2000 BC, the turning point into the Initial Formative. These earliest Mesoamericans adapted to their regions with a coherent package of techniques that worked together to secure a stable existence. The Mesoamerican culture area emerged out of the landscape where maize could be grown as a staple crop and would become the cornerstone of a basic repertoire of dependable foods. Mesoamericans lived in huts clustered into villages and hamlets, and used vessels of clay as well as gourd, stone, and basketry. The Initial Formative period was a time of emergence of a few signs of status differentiation among families in villages – some had larger houses, more elaborate burials. Subsequent periods show increasing differentials of wealth and power, lifting a small number of people into elite status while obligating the rest to support the ruling few.

Much of this process of increasing social complexity depended upon sedentism, which permits the accumulation of property and provides the crop security upon which population growth depends. Dependence on food production may encourage population growth because of the "peak load of labor during field preparation, planting, and harvesting, which makes the help of older children and close kin desirable; ... a positive incentive for offspring" (Stark 1981: 367).

Worldwide, our distant ancestors who were mobile foragers enjoyed a spartan but generally healthy existence, living in small groups governed by the egalitarian ethic of sharing and cooperation within the group. Sedentism radically changed the balance of social relations. Even in an egalitarian tribal village, some enjoy greater prestige and can disproportionately influence the group's fate, but sedentism also brought ownership of things and use rights to land, strong attachments that emphasized the needs and interests of the individual, or family lineage faction, at the cost of the good of the whole society.

So, why settle down? First, the costs of frequent moves are eliminated; food and goods can be accumulated against lean times. The weak and infirm are not subjected to the stress of dislocations. Labor that is invested in establishing or improving living facilities and croplands is repaid over the years.

What are the costs of sedentism? Prime locations for permanent settlements are rare. The community site must have nearby, abundant, and permanent resources such as water and food and fuel. In Mesoamerica, except in those places where navigable waterways provided efficient transport routes, all goods and food were carried by human porters, not beasts of burden or carts, a situation which prevailed until European contact brought wheeled carts and oxen and horses to pull them. In addition to a stable flow of supplies, the settlement needs to be kept clean and maintained, and the site must be defensible from others who want it, be they humans or animals.

Sedentism is less healthy than mobile foraging: a more monotonous diet is likelier to bring forth nutritional deficiency disease (such as anemia), and closer contact with more people increases chances that communicable diseases will become established. On the other hand, New World peoples were remarkably free of communicable disease until European contact, possibly because the trek across the Bering Strait acted as a cold filter, selecting out the unhealthy, while small group size could not sustain vectors of communicable disease (Dillehay 1991). Another advantage Mesoamericans had against infectious disease was the relatively low population of Mesoamerican domesticated animals, which curbed the opportunity for animal diseases to find new hosts in human populations. A major source of disease in the world's agrarian communities is farm animals – in the Old World, diseases such as smallpox were a human expression of bovine cowpox (Diamond 1999). Nonetheless, even with these advantages in New World health, any population concentration will increase the chance of problems such as polluted water, poor sanitation, and inadequate food supply.

The perils of sedentism also include the destructive power of human rage. As noted in Chapter 1, a population of several hundred people constituted a kind of maximum size for independent sedentary villages. Larger populations than that cannot be controlled by simple ethics of respect for family elders and fear of shame before the community. Factionalism can develop, and quarrels between factions can only be resolved by acceding to the judgment of a higher authority, or by violent contest. In the latter case, the losers leave the village and go off to establish another autonomous village. With the former, which involves acceptance of the binding power of mediation, villages are maintained at a larger size, but conflict resolution will almost inevitably alienate some of the residents, or make the losers into second-class citizens. Equally important, the establishment of a paramount authority will give rise to permanent administrative officers who hold authority over the whole community and are in a position to enjoy a disproportionate share of the community's wealth.

4 THE INITIAL FORMATIVE (*c.* 2000–1200 BC)

THE FORMATIVE PERIOD, 2000 BC–AD 300, witnessed the crystallization of the Mesoamerican culture complex as a set of distinctive traits and behavioral patterns. At the start of the Formative [**4.1**] we find small autonomous agricultural villages, typical of tribal peoples, established in certain key regions. There, in the centuries around 1500 BC, a transformation begins, moving the social order away from the egalitarian ethic of autonomous tribal villagers. By AD 300, all Mesoamericans lived in societies based on differential ranking of individuals and whole groups, and lived under political formats of chiefdoms and states, where the few ruled over the many, and extracted goods and services from them.

During the Formative period, villages and agriculture spread across the Isthmus of Tehuantepec and through the highlands. Then, in the Isthmus and other regions, Olmec ceremonial centers and distinctive art developed.

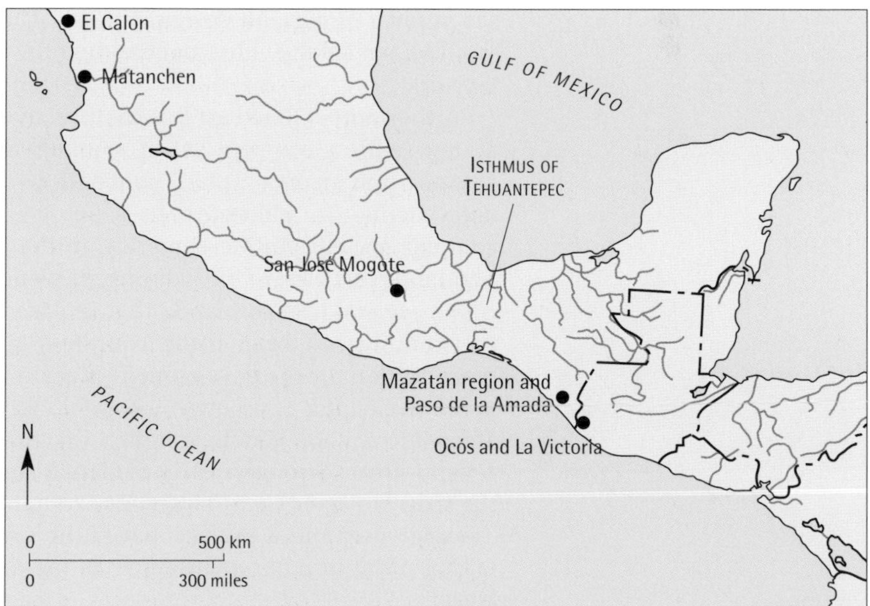

4.1 *Middle America showing Initial Formative-period regions and sites mentioned in Chapter 4.*

This was followed, in the Oaxaca Valley and the Basin of Mexico, by the establishment of states, with cities dominating and drawing tributes from hinterlands of agricultural villages. The Formative period, by scholarly convention, covers several important developmental stages, vividly expressed over broad regions. Thus it is the subject of the next six chapters (4 through 9). This chapter covers the earliest Formative, the era sometimes called "Initial period," from about 2000 BC to 1200 BC.

CULTURAL TRENDS OF THE FORMATIVE PERIOD

Throughout the Formative, cultural evolutionary forces created complex societies with mature artistic expressions of power and wealth, iconographically rich with the symbols related to a well-developed belief system. Although the related regional cultures are distinctive, in each, all cultural aspects were highly integrated – the belief system anchored the society within its natural environment by spiritualizing the landscape and weather, while time was transcended by ancestor veneration and measured by the interworking of two calendars, keeping track of the seasons of the earth and the seasons of human life.

Precursors to the Olmecs

Olmec culture, the focus of the next chapter, was the earliest in Mesoamerica to establish visually impressive ceremonial centers, which signal to us some important features of complex society. We intuitively recognize in great Olmec (and later) sites a considerable investment of labor and materials, in the service of a grand design. Whose? Olmec art depicts individuals who would have led the elite, commanding the lives of workers and the crops of farmers.

Furthermore, Olmec art is a mature style, and seems to convey a belief system with a coherent set of symbols and ideas. Where did the belief system and iconographic conventions come from? What were its antecedents? To address these issues we look to the earliest evidence of complex societies in Mesoamerica, in the Isthmus of Tehuantepec and the highlands just west of the Isthmus, particularly in the Valley of Oaxaca.

The societal transformation that replaced egalitarianism with sociopolitical ranking has been made countless times in human history. It is a precondition for the development of state-level organization, which, as we noted in Chapter 1, occurred independently in six world regions, including Mesoamerica. In Middle America the first pulses of change occurred in several areas. Strongest early evidence comes from the Soconusco region, the strip of Pacific Coast piedmont extending southeast from the Isthmus of Tehuantepec, and it is clear that at the same time, the same processes are taking place in other areas, such as the adjacent Oaxaca highlands to the west.

Recognizing Social Inequality in the Archaeological Record

In ancient societies that lack documentary records, archaeologists recognize the presence of social inequalities through material evidence. Within egalitarian societies, there is little to differentiate one family, or campsite, or village from another on the basis of occupational specialization, material goods, type of housing. Even when mobile foragers settle into village agriculture, there are few distinctions among families, and, over a region, tribal villages are much like each other. Each is autonomous, and none is an administrative or economic central place, relative to the others.

When we find a settlement system comprised of villages clustered around a central village that has some civic or ceremonial structure of more imposing dimensions and position, and has a population larger than several hundred people, we take it as evidence that village autonomy has been transcended, replaced by central authority, and that social inequality and disparities of wealth have been established, even at a modest level. Note that such differences may be subtle, but that clearly, some people or families are emerging as focal points of power in a society evolving away from egalitarian tribalism. Modest examples of civic-ceremonial architecture represent – and sometimes literally are – the foundations of later monumental efforts involving massive earth-moving and construction.

Social and economic inequalities show up in the artifact repertoire, and in grave goods and differences among houses, revealing that some people live more comfortably, have more and better possessions, and are buried with some of it. Late Archaic-period development of settled agricultural villages opened the possibility of accumulation of goods in permanent settlements. Not constrained by the need to limit permanent possessions to those which could be carried along in the yearly round of mobile foraging, villagers could store things.

Consider the ramifying effects of this change upon craft production and artisanship. With sedentism, regional craft specialization flourished, as succeeding – and increasing – generations of artisans gained skill in exploiting local resources and in working various kinds of materials. Of course there had been exchange of materials and goods between regions in Paleoindian and Archaic times, but the Formative period marks a huge increase in the scale and kinds of exchange, with many more materials in circulation, including raw materials and finished products, and even luxury goods.

Archaeologists use the term "luxury goods" – and also "elite crafts," "preciosities" – to denote items that are not utilitarian tools, for subsistence or other basic purpose, but that are costly and have important social functions. It should be emphasized that the modern Western perspective on luxury goods is strongly shaped by our own values, which view the physical and social world radically differently from all ancient peoples. "Luxury goods" is an understandable term for ancient finely-crafted items, insofar as it draws our attention to their heightened economic value: we expect that ancient – and modern – luxury goods will be made of fine materials, made by master artisans in a sophisticated style, and be affordable to few people.

The modern definition often stops there, because economic value of personal possessions is our shorthand code for the owner's socioeconomic rank. Today, we often place less emphasis upon other features of material goods, such as the ideological power of symbols, the kinship or other social linkages represented by the item's design, material composition, artisanship, or availability – while in ancient societies these were essential to the item's value. These differences in meaning challenge our ability to understand the contextual significance of luxury goods from such societies.

Smoke and Mirrors

Archaeologists sometimes come upon artifacts, including luxury goods, whose function can only be guessed at. An inside joke among archaeologists is that the default category of mystifying objects is "ritual item." Nonetheless, there is a kernel of truth in this tendency to see spiritual function in odd things. Ideologically significant symbols and forms are less bound by functional constraints shaping basic tool design. For example, manos and metates used to grind corn today are the same general size, shape, and material as the ancestral forms made millennia ago. However, ritually important goods have taken many forms in ancient and modern times, including representational and abstract expressions of things and forces.

What would you guess was the function of the item pictured in Figure **4.2**? It is made of a very hard impervious stone, and its shape, which includes a plane surface and concave indentation, was achieved by grinding and polishing. The object shows the development of lapidary techniques, achieving highly refined effects by grinding the stone with another stone and polishing with sand and a slurry of grit. Careful attention to finishing is revealed in balanced form and high surface polish. Trying to infer function from similar items known from other cultures, in terms of its shape and material, we might think that the object resembles a palette for preparing ink or paint or cosmetics. Context, of course, provides clues to function, but none of these Formative items has been recovered from a context of use, except as grave goods, or depicted on figurines.

As the figurine indicates [**4.3**], these items were worn high on the forehead, like miner's lights, often by substantially built adult males. They were also worn as pendants or other pectoral devices, as indicated by male and female figurines. From this evidence we might think of the item as adornment, as jewelry, yet it also may be part of the insignia or regalia of an official important person. In sum, we readily recognize it as a luxury good, finely crafted from unusual materials, and infer that its use was apparently restricted to certain privileged members of the social order.

Fortunately, we know more about the function of this item from later examples, and from modern experimentation that confirmed its capabilities. The polished concavity is a type of reflective lens, a mirror (Carlson 1981). Initial Formative-period mirrors were not the straightforward image reflectors of modern times, though they had some reflective capacity. Like

modern mirrors, they could cast glints of light, and even, under proper conditions, cause tinder to smolder and burn. Recall that two very basic and ancient and potent themes in Mesoamerica were shamanism and the spiritual force of the natural environment. The shaman's power to appear to be controlling or engaging in a dialogue with the natural world would be greatly enhanced by a device to bring forth smoke and fire, two lively elements whose movement identified them as vectors of the life spirit.

The shaman's actual power to control the universe was, of course, subject to the same limitations that apply to all humans. We know, from modern scientific information, that no single human can use thought control to change weather patterns, or exist physically in two locations at the same time, or change into another species. There are many diseases whose course is untouched by any mental concentration or medicine, traditional or modern. All these disclaimers notwithstanding, the shaman's power is real in the sense that a willing suspension of disbelief is induced in clients and onlookers, who maintain respect for the shaman's reputation for capabilities such as shape-changing and time travel. The shaman's genuine intuitive skills and charisma were extended by magical tricks involving sleight-of-hand and appropriate props. These props sometimes also served as powerful amulets and insignia of rank. Glinting light into the eyes of dazzled onlookers, the shaman's mirror could also make smoke and fire appear, enhancing the shaman's prestige enormously. This type of mirror is the earliest known example of a mirror-using tradition that continued to the time of the conquest.

4.2, 4.3 *The Initial Formative period marks the first appearance of the Mesoamerican mirror, a polished concavity in fine-grained stone. While modern mirrors function mostly to enhance good grooming and cater to narcissism, mirrors in ancient Mesoamerica were dazzlers, flashing light at onlookers and causing smoke and fire. The upper photo shows one of these mirrors; the figurine is typical of grave goods in the El Vivero burial in the Mazatán area of the southern Pacific Coast, showing how concave mirrors were used as adornment.*

More than Smoke and Mirrors The smoke-and-mirrors, shamans-and-power discussion served to focus our attention on the inception of some key features of what will become the mature Mesoamerican cultural tradition. While power in shamanism and exchange in luxury goods (of which the mirror is one example) are only two elements in a complex story, they serve as an intellectual motif for understanding the Mesoamerican cultural trait complex, as it develops. Now let us turn to broader patterns.

Mesoamerica's "New Stone Age"

In the Old World, particularly in Mesopotamia and Europe, the transition to settled village agriculture was called the "Neolithic" (new stone) revolution. New kinds of stone tools appeared – ground stone tools were added to a basic flaked stone repertoire. In Archaic-period Mesoamerica, the same set of far-reaching changes marked the emergence of a "Neolithic" lifestyle: dependence upon grain as the staple food, and important new tools and traits, like ceramics, prismatic blades [**4.4**], and development of fiber crafts like weaving.

The broad similarities between the Neolithic of Southwest Asia and Late Archaic/Early Formative of Mesoamerica nicely illustrate that the same forces of cultural evolution operated in these two utterly independent regions, and even more aptly demonstrate how evolutionary paths diverge. In both regions, complex, state-level societies ruled by hereditary elites would later arise. Both would have cities, intensive agriculture, large, dense populations, complex economies with many kinds of finished goods, actively traded. But in Southwest Asia, tool technology development continued into the Bronze and Iron Ages, as metal outstripped stone for many technological applications, including tools to manufacture other tools. Simple machines of stone and iron parts, like water-driven mills, were the ancestral forms of the complex machines of the Industrial Revolution.

In Mesoamerica in general, metal never became an important tool material, and in AD 1520 the tool repertoire was still basically the same "Neolithic" assemblage that had emerged by the end of the Formative. Metals were valued for other qualities – brilliance and malleability, for example – and precious metals were artfully crafted into elaborate representational designs. As for the wheel, its best known Mesoamerican application was as part of ceramic dog figurines, reminiscent of pull-toys, though probably having spiritual significance in that they were readily enlivened into movement. Spindle whorls for twining fiber into thread and bow-drills for stone-working were among the only mechanisms that could be regarded as wheel-based tools.

Regionalism: Ceramics and Other Features Even within Mesoamerica, different broad regions showed variation in the application of "Neolithic" traits, ceramics, for example. We recognized the beginnings of regionalization as occurring at the end of the Pleistocene. Paleoindian hunters followed herds moving across vast grass steppes, but when climate change made seasons and regions distinct, success in foraging and hunting depended upon knowing one region very well. With sedentism, regionalism became necessarily much more pronounced, and in the Initial Formative, with earliest ceramics, two broad interaction spheres can be perceived: the Isthmian cultures, where the Olmecs would emerge as Mesoamerica's first great monument builders, and the highlands to the west, where even more sophisticated cultures follow those of the Olmecs [**4.5–4.7**].

Pottery designs shared over a large area are indicators of other shared traits, and we find that for the Initial Formative period, the Isthmian region and the highlands region to its west have distinctive sets of features, summarized in the table [**4.8**]. Differences begin with that most basic resource, the food supply. While both regions use the Mesoamerican crop triad (maize, beans, squash), Isthmian aquatic and forest resources are rich and dependable, thus encouraging a more mixed subsistence economy than could be sustained in the more arid highlands.

The Isthmian mixed subsistence economy may have given rise to a more varied, yet centralized settlement pattern, permitting a relatively high population density, with central villages as home bases for various campsites and hamlets used by special-purpose foragers. Isthmian peoples traded, and we

PRISMATIC BLADES

MASS PRODUCTION OF GOODS is fundamental to modern capitalism, and is integral to global trade and industrial innovation. Non-industrial societies have far more conservative rates of innovation, production, and consumption, but still reveal instances of innovation toward streamlined and regularized production of goods. In Mesoamerica, prismatic blade production was a new tool production process, resulting in a new kind of tool. This innovation first occurred at about 1500 BC; during the Formative period prismatic blades came to predominate over flake tools in many areas (e.g. Awe and Healy 1994).

Technique Straight-sided blades are struck from a prepared core, usually of obsidian, each blow against the prepared end of the core resulting in a complete, usable tool whose regular, faceted shape resembles a prism – hence, "prismatic blade" [**4.4**]. The core is a cobble with an end removed to provide a flat platform for striking off the blades. After this core has been prepared, there is no production waste, as there is no retouch – each blade's cutting edges are razor-sharp, and all the blades could be reassembled, puzzle fashion, to recreate the original form of the core.

Material In order to manufacture flawless blades from a core, the material must be extremely fine-grained. The best prismatic blades are made from the best obsidian, though blades can be struck from obsidian with internal irregularities, and even from fine-grained stone like chert.

Advantages and Socioeconomic Consequences Each flake is a complete blade requiring no further input of time or effort, and no waste of materials as debitage from further flaking (needed to produce a sharp serrated edge on Clovis and other points). More important, prismatic blades were so useful that they were a basic component of the Mesoamerican toolkit from the Initial Formative to well after European contact. They were found as part of domestic tool assemblages throughout Mesoamerica, regardless of economic status of the householders. The blades were also used in composite tools, for example inserted into grooves in a wooden handle to make a highly effective slashing weapon – it could decapitate a horse, the Spaniards found in pitched battles with the Aztecs during the conquest.

While an experienced blade-maker could easily punch blades from a prepared core, this was not an easy technique to master, and excellent obsidian was not cheap, so core-blade production was a specialized occupation, and prismatic blades were obtained by the average farmer-artisan through trade rather than by attempting the technique at home (Parry 2001). Thus the advent of prismatic blades represented also an important step toward increasing reliance on exchange of goods, both finished products and raw materials. The importance of prismatic blades as markers of long-distance exchange reached a peak with the rise of Teotihuacan's influence. Just north of Teotihuacan was the Pachuca obsidian source, which produced obsidian that was not only of excellent quality, but was green, the noblest and most revered color in Mesoamerica. In the Terminal Formative and Early Classic periods, Pachuca green prismatic blades found their way all across Mesoamerica, the calling cards of the Teotihuacan trading network.

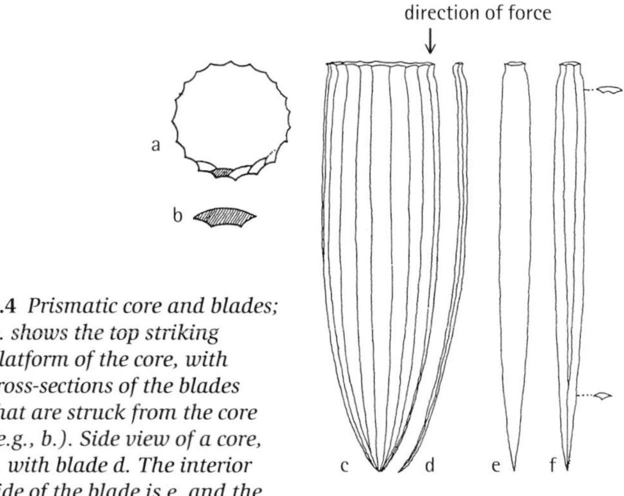

4.4 *Prismatic core and blades; a. shows the top striking platform of the core, with cross-sections of the blades that are struck from the core (e.g., b.). Side view of a core, c. with blade d. The interior side of the blade is e. and the exterior is shown in f.*

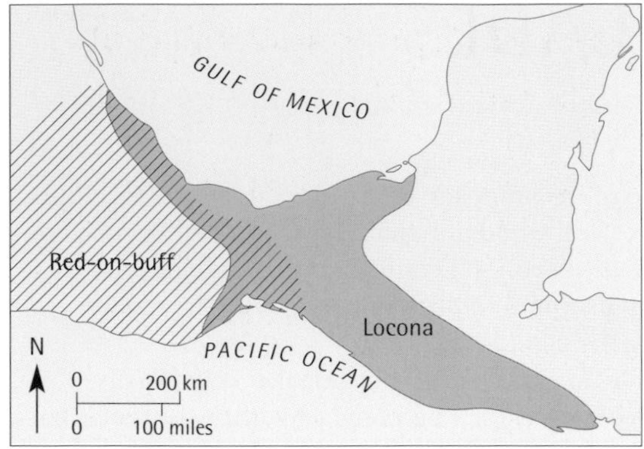

can trace the distribution of such materials as obsidian as they moved from their volcanic sources to their contexts of use. But highland regions were more active in exchanging materials and goods over long distance, both among various ecozones of the highlands, and in obtaining materials from the Isthmian tropics, exotic things like jade and other lapidary stones, brilliantly colored feathers. In fact, luxury goods are common in both regions, though the roster of materials varies slightly. The distribution of these goods seems far more concentrated in the hands of a few people in the Isthmian region, and there is other clear evidence of social ranking in monumental architecture such as elite residences and ball courts.

Social ranking implies the emergence of another trait common to complex societies, the political economy. A political economy is the whole set of materials and practices comprising production, distribution, and consumption of goods as these are controlled or influenced by the decisions of a society's rulers. Egalitarian societies operate with subsistence economies: differential access to key resources is very limited and there is no surplus of important materials for any one person to control. More complex societies also have subsistence economies operating at local levels – individual farming families provide for their own subsistence and needs, for example – but their surpluses support the rulers and the growing cadre of specialized artisans. Thus luxury goods and trade tell us not only about increasingly refined tastes and social contexts for sumptuary display, but also that the subsistence economy has become the foundation for a more complex set of relations of applying limited means to various ends, under the control of the rulers.

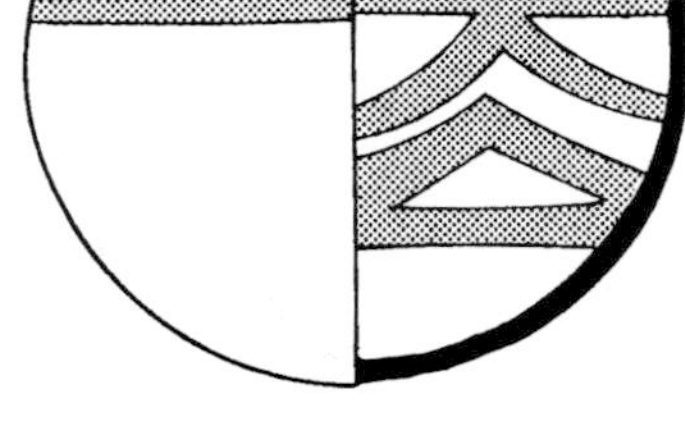

4.5–4.7 *Pottery came into use all over Mesoamerica in the Initial and Early Formative, but west of the Isthmus, the vessels were simple shapes (as above), simply decorated with red designs on the natural buff color of the ceramics. In contrast, even early Isthmian vessels (at right, from the Mazatán area) transcend mere utilitarian forms and functions, and include finely-made, elaborately decorated vessels that seem fit for feasts – big, beautiful jars that would have been perfect for serving beer to an assembled group of honored guests. Some motifs and surface treatments seem to reflect the influence of contemporaneous ceramics of the northwest coast of South America (present-day Ecuador), but these vessels are locally made.*

4.8 *The differences between the Isthmian zone and the highlands to the west went far beyond pottery styles. The table shows a series of characteristics about which the cultural patterns of the two broad regions were distinctive (based on Clark 2001b).*

Early Village Agricultural Societies of Mesoamerica (4.8)

Supra-region	Highlands West of the Isthmus	Tropical Lowlands, Isthmus and East
Subsistence	Maize agriculture	Mixed economy: agriculture significant, with root crops and maize, continued use of wild resources, fish, turtle, deer
Settlement pattern	Small villages, dispersed	Larger villages, loosely clustered
Pottery	Simple, utilitarian	Vessel forms varied, with many elite vessels for feasting, rituals
Interregional interaction	Common, as evidenced by non-local goods, common ceramic and figurine styles over whole region	None
Luxury materials and goods	Common, in addition to obsidian, trade in iron-ore mirrors, jade and greenstone, bird feathers, marine shells, cacao	Common, in addition to elaborate vessels, trade in carved jade, greenstone, and mica
Social complexity	None	Yes, ranked societies by 1400 BC, with shaman-chiefs, as represented in figurines, differential distribution of goods
Monumental architecture	None	Elite residences, ball courts

ISTHMIAN REGION

While the Late Archaic Chantuto region had developed a two-tiered settlement pattern, there are no indications that any one village was central to, or outranked other, similar villages. In the Initial Formative, a true site hierarchy can be detected in the adjacent Mazatán region, also along the coast. This is one of many Mazatán traits that signal the transformation from egalitarian to ranked society, from tribes to chiefdoms.

The Rise of the Chiefdom

"The rise of the chiefdom may well have been the single most important step ever taken in political evolution" (Carneiro 1998: 37). The chiefdom is a political format entailing the aggregation of a set of villages into a kind of permanent alliance under the control of the headman of one of the villages, who becomes chief of them all. This office of authority usually becomes hereditary, and is usually inherited in the male line. The overall increase in societal complexity means that village autonomy has been lost, and social ranking has become established, with the chief's family having the highest rank and other families taking their positions in the ranking hierarchy according to how closely related they are to the chief. The subsistence economy becomes the basis for surplus production, controlled by the rulers.

This evolutionary transformation from egalitarian to hierarchical society has taken place many times in human history, and almost as many times, these chiefdoms soon unraveled into a set of autonomous tribal villages. However, the process of developing a chiefdom out of a tribal village would recur each time circumstances were ripe for it, and once the general trend toward greater social complexity had become well-established in a region, it would tend to persist. Eventually, a chiefdom would gain relative permanency, and the centralized hierarchy of villages around the chiefly village was accompanied by a social hierarchy in which individuals, and whole groups, occupied different statuses relative to each other.

4.9 *Yanamamo men display their weapons, as well as their party finery, at the start of a feast.*

The idea that independent groups gave up autonomy willingly, and rationally entered into social contracts with their prospective rulers, was popularized in the 18th century by the French philosopher Rousseau. The idea is still widely accepted and, as pertaining to the transformation from egalitarian tribes to ranked chiefdoms, seems to be utterly false. In fact, village autonomy (and tribal egalitarianism) seems to be lost through coercion, and if contracts establishing social hierarchies can be said to exist, they stipulate that the stronger village (or faction) establishes a practice of bullying and extortion upon the weaker. The best bully wins the top position in an emerging chiefdom, and the chief is almost always a war leader.

Consider the Yanomamo headman as a potential chief [4.9]. A charismatic headman in a large, crowded, centrally located village demonstrates strong leadership in certain situations – raiding, feasting, alliances. Between such times, the village operates more like other simpler, more marginal villages. But as other central villages get

YANOMAMO

TO UNDERSTAND HOW the dynamics of power shift away from egalitarianism, and how chiefdoms emerge, we turn to the Yanomamo, a well-known tribal culture in tropical southern Venezuela. While they have had very limited contact with modern Western culture for decades, in the early 1960s they were still living according to their indigenous cultural patterns except for the presence of a few metal trade items. The present tense used in this description refers to this "ethnographic present" of the Yanomamo in a virtually uncontacted state (Chagnon 1997).

Egalitarian tribal agriculturalists, they live in dozens of villages, each with fewer than 200 people belonging to two or three lineages. These kin groups provide the basis for Yanomamo social and political organization, and the senior adult male in the most powerful (or largest) lineage serves the village as headman. He has no real power – he cannot force his followers to obey his directives. But a good headman has great authority, and people generally follow his lead, partly because of his personal charisma, and also because he has many kinsmen and so can lead raiding parties to intimidate or destroy neighboring villages. He is also a practiced shaman, calling his personal spirits in trances induced by hallucinogenic drugs, and by this means is able to convince his followers that he can see the future, or cure an ailing villager. The transcendent state induced by drug use by all adult men helps them to develop an attitude of fierceness as warriors, and killing others enhances this spiritual strength.

A good Yanomamo headman can administer a village of 100 or even 200 people. If a village grows beyond several hundred, the limited authority of the headman and of kin-based means of social control cannot maintain order. If intravillage hostilities erupt, a common Yanomamo pattern is for the village to fission, with the smaller faction leaving the local area to found a village further away. As long as there is uncontested habitable land, this pioneering strategy alleviates social tensions, but villages in the center have few convenient areas to pioneer. In fact, central villages tend to become larger, and their headmen tend to have greater authority than those of small peripheral villages. Villagers are intimidated into accepting the headman's authority, because they belong to a lower-ranking faction or because of the difficulty of starting a new village elsewhere.

The strength of a Yanomamo headman's authority depends on the number of allies he can muster, and having many wives (polygyny) not only provides many children but also links the headman's lineage with those of his in-laws. Headmen tend to have the most wives, and wives spell wealth to the Yanomamo: women do the farming and much of the other work, bear sons who will become members of their father's raiding parties and daughters who can be promised to potential allies. Negotiations for these marriage and raiding alliances often take place at feasts, which open with the men displaying their finery and preparedness for warfare [**4.9**]. A man rich in wives can host a large feast, because they can provide so much food from their farm plots.

Subsistence farmers, the Yanomamo have technologically simple material goods, locally made from local resources. Little distinguishes the headman from others in this regard. Yanomamo are well aware of the value of trade as a basis for non-violent relations among villages, and villagers will claim inability to produce a common item (string, puppies to raise as hunting dogs) in order to maintain trading relations. Insofar as there is a "luxury goods" component to their trade, it may entail materials for personal adornment (feathers, cosmetics), special food items or drugs.

These patterns of tribal life help us to understand the transformation from the earliest farming villages of Mesoamerica to the patterns consistent with chiefdoms. The Yanomamo illustrate how group dynamics operate within certain limits, particularly relating to village size, village location, and the means by which these factors influence social crises and their resolution. We also see how patterns of feasting and alliance building quickly shift to enmity and deadly raids.

larger, tensions between villages increase, and the headman may have new opportunities to serve as chief, extending the situational powers inherent in war leadership for his own village and its allies into a position of permanent control over all.

Chief as Office: Achievement and Ascription

Permanent control extends beyond the lifetime of a single powerful charismatic individual: the position of chief is a permanent *institution*. Thus succession to office becomes an important issue, because if each generation's leader achieved that status by competition with other candidates, say, among each lineage's strongest man, then internal divisiveness would be costly to heal.

Anthropologists distinguish between two means by which individuals assume particular statuses: *achievement* and *ascription*. Being born male, and born into a high-ranking lineage are "ascribed" conditions – the bearer of these traits is passive with regard to acquiring them: they are ascribed to him. In contrast, accomplished deployment of terror and diplomacy are skills "achieved" by study and practice. "Achievement" and "ascription" are fairly self-explanatory terms, though human relations are never so simply rational as to reward achievement in a strict meritocracy, and, conversely, even when authority and honors are ascribed to an individual solely on the basis of heredity, societies can protect themselves from being victimized by the accession of a high-born dolt by means such as assassination. Hereditary, ascribed qualifications for leadership may have the benefit of enhancing social stability, but unless a would-be leader can demonstrate aptitude, another close kinsman (or, occasionally, kinswoman) is likely to take over.

Engendered Political Evolution

The language of the discussion of headmen and chiefs has made no concession to gender neutrality – were there headwomen? Did women lead war parties or host drunken feasts? Initial Formative-period attitudes about the appropriate roles of men and women are difficult to reconstruct; some clues lie in ethnographic analogues, as well as archaeological evidence, and in Mesoamerican traditions of later periods. Extrapolating a historically known trend back into the past is an interpretive method called "the direct historical approach" because it follows a direct line of cultural descent back from what we do know, to an earlier, less-well-known era. As might be expected, this approach must be cautiously applied even to temporally and spatially adjacent cultures, and becomes extremely chancy when applied over great distances of time and space. Furthermore, attribution of attitudes is far trickier than attribution of tool functions; it's difficult to understand the mind set of the very well-documented Aztecs, much less the cultures 3,000 years earlier and hundreds of miles away.

However, we recognize deep cultural roots for many features of Mesoamerican society, and while Mesoamerica's diverse regions encompass many variants of culture patterns, it is definitely the case that some traits are found throughout all regions and time periods. Shamanism, for example, is widespread and apparently very deeply rooted. It is also an important basis for political power. Shamanism and skilled curing have always involved both men and women, and traditions of the Initial Formative no doubt included positions of respect for its knowledgeable mature women. Yet it is also true that ethnographic case examples of chiefdom formation point strongly to warfare and raiding as venues for grabbing political power, and these almost universally involve men.

Women did serve important political roles in later Mesoamerican cultures. Aztec women owned property, had extensive political rights and occupied many respected public positions in skilled craft production and civic administration, occasionally even ruling over city-states. However, the evidence of Mesoamerican emergent leadership seems to emphasize men, as does our best-documented ethnographically known cases of the transition from egalitarian, autonomous villages to social ranking within and among a diverse set of communities, led by a chief.

Mokaya of Mazatán

These concepts help us to understand processes ongoing on the Soconusco Coast and elsewhere in the Initial Formative, when chiefdoms were emerging out of egalitarian tribal organization. Archaeologists have called this coastal culture "Mokaya" meaning "people of the corn" in the Mixe-Zoque language spoken in the region today. The first Mokaya phase, Barra, occurred early in the Initial Formative, and calibrated radiocarbon dates generally range around 1800–1650 BC (Clark 1991). Barra phase saw the first widespread settlement over this area, and also its first pottery; as we noted above, it was, from the beginning, of sophisticated design and included large jars suitable for storing and serving beverages.

For the "people of the corn" and other Initial Formative Isthmians, maize was, in fact, only a small part of the subsistence economy. At that time, maize was long domesticated, but the inch-long ears yielded little edible food from a significant investment of energy in cultivation. Mokaya maize may have been a specialty food, grown, for example, because its juices made flavorful beer. Growing staple grains to provide for protein and calorie needs was not important to the Mokaya and other Isthmus folk. Living alongside swamps, these people always had a range of resources.

During the Locona phase (1650–1500 BC [Clark 1991]), a two-tiered settlement pattern involved central villages, each covering 20–75 hectares (50–190 acres) and hamlets, 1–5 hectares (2+ to 12 acres) [**4.10**]. The central villages may each have had 1,000 residents, a community size far exceeding the maximum limit for simple social controls based on kinship. The settlement pattern and large size of central villages indicate a need for

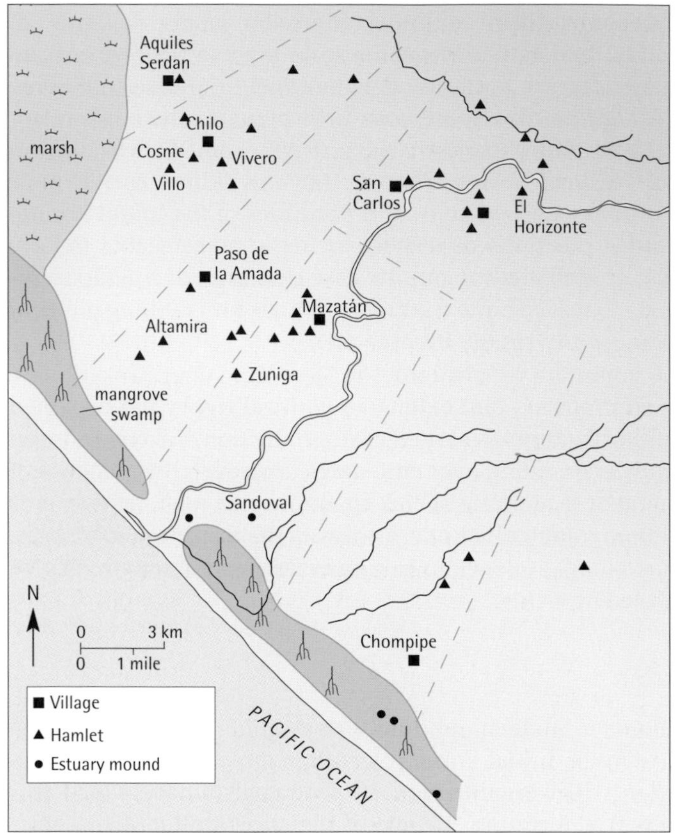

4.10 *In the Mazatán area at about 1500 BC, a two-tiered settlement pattern indicated that larger villages may have been administrative central places for the hamlets that surrounded them, site spacing that implies a chiefdom level of political organization.*

chiefs rather than headmen, and this is supported by other evidence, such as the mirrors and figurines indicative of differences in social rank, and large-scale architecture entailing the cooperative labor of many people.

Each central village had a local surrounding area with a range of resources, and, judging from the kinds of obsidian found at each, these central villages were independently trading for obsidian with suppliers from three different sources in the Guatemala highlands (Clark and Salcedo 1989). The rich coastal and estuarine resources of Mazatán supported these chiefdoms, and trade items produced there included salt. The Soconusco region in later times was famed as one of Mesoamerica's premier sources of cacao beans, from which chocolate is made. At present our earliest evidence of cacao use comes from the Middle Formative Maya lowlands (Powis *et al.* 2002). Evidence from the Classic period includes a glyph for cacao in the Maya writing system, and a screw-top chocolate jar found in the Classic Maya site of Río Azul (Hall *et al.* 1990). There is little doubt that cacao production extended back into the early part of the Formative period, when chocolate was drunk and cacao trees were nurtured in tropical regions to produce this valuable, readily traded crop.

Paso de la Amada: Earliest Ball Court and Other Elite Features Of all Locona-phase sites, Paso de la Amada is the best known, with several monumental structures, pioneering examples of well-known and widely distributed later civic-ceremonial building types, the palace and ball court [**4.11**]. Paso's elite residence was much larger and better-finished than other houses, and its ball court was the earliest formal court in all Mesoamerica (Blake 1991).

For the rest of Mesoamerican culture history, the ball game played a key role in community life, and probably in mediating relations among communities (Hill and Clark 2001). The ball game was played by two individuals or two teams, with action much like soccer in moving a rubber ball around a court. Formal ball courts were long rectangles, averaging about 40 m (130 ft) long, though many were less than 20 m (66 ft) long, and Chichén Itzá's measured 150 m (*c.* 490 ft). Paso de la Amada's was 80 m long and 7 m wide (260 by 23 ft), bounded by long parallel platforms *c.* 2 m (*c.* 7 ft) high. Formal ball courts were enclosed by sloping walls, but pick-up games could be played on any level surface (recall Gheo-Shih's "dance ground").

That the action centers on the movement of the rubber ball arouses no surprise in the modern reader, because the most popular modern sports center upon rubber balls. Yet we are witnessing the dawn of a sports phenomenon that didn't hit Europe until about 500 years ago, when Aztec teams touring Europe in the 16th century AD demonstrated the rubber ball-centered game. This bit of sports trivia helps to personalize the Mesoamericans of the Initial Formative, and a modern sports fan would find the action of their games engrossing. Here, however, is another phenomenon, like "luxury goods," which is seemingly familiar but in cultural context is laden with meanings quite different, and more finely nuanced than modern ball games. The Mesoamerican ball game as a drama of sacrifice and renewal is well-known from later periods, and we will return to this topic in later chapters.

Rubber has became a crucial industrial material in the modern global economy. Mesoamericans also developed practical as well as recreational and ritual uses for it. Aztec sources cite its various medicinal applications, the Maya used it to haft weapons, and Aztecs and Maya both waterproofed clothing with it (Stone 2002). However, Mesoamericans valued it for its sacred essence, associating the flow of latex with the flow of blood, and the rubber ball in motion expressed the vitality common to all things that move. Mesoamericans, as we know, occupied a living landscape, believing that spiritual forces inhabited both physical geography and biota, as well. They revered things that exhibited signs of life – reflecting mirrors, featherwork banners that ruffled in the breeze, shining metal that cast glints of brilliance. The rubber ball, set into play, would have represented a potent life force.

This was an important spiritual dimension, yet it is obvious that rubber's economic value was also significant. Materials displaying such vitality would be highly valued and widely traded [4.12]. The best rubber comes from tropical gum trees (*Castilla elastica*), which grow at elevations lower than 600–700 m (2,000–2,300 ft), and thus latex would have been another important Isthmian product to trade into the highlands (Tarkanian and Hosler 2000). Lower quality rubber is derived from another plant (*Parthenium argentatum*) native to the Northern Arid Zone and Northwestern Frontier of Mesoamerica.

4.11 *Paso de la Amada's plan shows a pattern of dispersed housemounds over high ground. Unusual for this period are Mounds 6 and 7, the elite residence and the ball court. While Mound 6's structure was a substantial residence, it is dwarfed by the size of the ball court.*

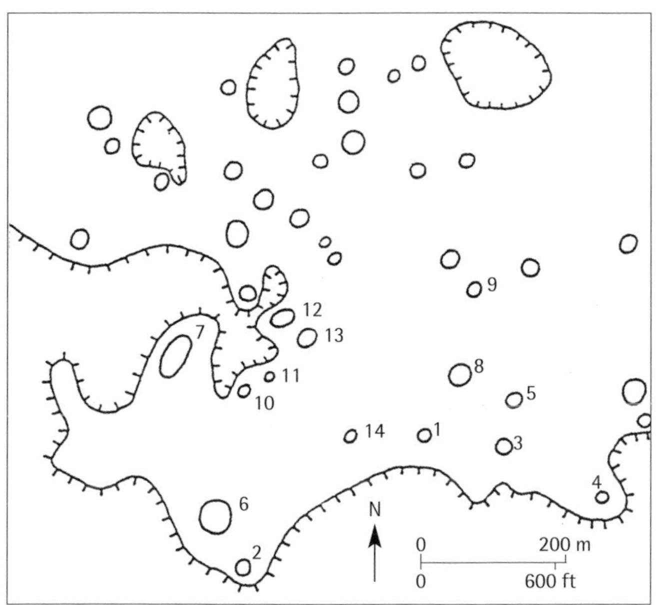

The Initial Formative ball court at Paso de la Amada is important evidence of the great time depth of ball game traditions. There were probably similar courts in the other large villages of the region, and "emerging elites within villages may have sponsored the construction of ball courts in order to enhance their status and prestige both locally and regionally" (Hill, Blake, and Clark 1998: 878). In later communities, as at

4.12 *Rubber products were known in Mesoamerica for at least 3,000 years before the material was introduced to the rest of the world. Because it is an organic material, rubber preserves poorly in most archaeological contexts. The best preserved organic materials are those that have been perpetually waterlogged, and these rubber balls were deposited as an offering in a sacred spring at El Manatí, near the Olmec center, San Lorenzo, over 3,000 years ago (Ortíz and Rodríguez 2000). Rubber balls of this type were undoubtedly used in the ball game, and rubber may have been another tropical luxury good traded locally and over long distances.*

Paso, there was a strong spatial association of the ball court with another important type of civic-ceremonial building: the elite residence.

Ethnographic and archaeological studies confirm our common sense notion that privileged people enjoy better and more impressive housing than commoners of the same culture. Our modern values are clear: impressive housing is an elite perquisite and insignia of status in our society. In traditional societies, the ruling family is generally larger, particularly where polygyny is practiced, and the household includes servants and retainers. The family needs a larger house for the ruler's administrative and communal responsibilities, such as hospitality and largesse. The house must demonstrate command of resources and attention to detail. Signs of disrepair or stint signal to allies and underlings a loss of power and prestige, making them more inclined to shift their loyalties (and tribute offerings) to another ruler.

At Paso de la Amada, Mound 6 was found to be the remains of a residence several times larger than average [**1.8**]. The mound was built up of at least six superimposed layers, indicating rebuildings of the platform and the structure on top of it. Associated artifacts and trash indicated a residential function, rather than a communal purpose such as a "young men's house." One rebuilding episode in the sequence, Structure 4, measured 10 m wide and 22 m long (33 by 72 ft). Such large buildings required considerable effort: a later Mound 6 structure, Structure 2, would have taken 488 person-days of labor, or the work of 20 persons for about 25 days (Blake 1991:36). An effort of this magnitude benefits from help outside the immediate resident family, perhaps another measure of the growing power of community leaders in the earliest Formative.

Another indicator of social inequality is the treatment of the dead. In most egalitarian communities graves and grave goods are simple, but as social relations become more differentiated and hierarchical, the power of wealth extends into the afterlife. One might expect that some adult men and women would be buried with luxury goods to demonstrate their high status, but when children's grave goods are luxurious, it indicates the exalted position of even the smallest members of powerful families. An elaborate child burial at Paso de la Amada is further evidence of ranking.

The Mokaya in Decline

By the Ocós phase (*c.* 1500–1350 BC [Clark 1991]), communities of 400 to 1,000 people had been established. The type site, Ocós, is further south along the coastal piedmont, and it is near La Victoria, the small site whose excavation provided the initial identification of Mokaya culture (Coe 1961). Sometime during Ocós phase, there may have occurred a shift in Mesoamerican climate, with cooler and drier conditions along the Pacific piedmont. Cushioned by its mixed subsistence economy, the people of the region may not have suffered, but cultural disruptions are indicated by the decline of Paso de la Amada, whose ball court was filling in with silt by the end of Locona phase.

Elsewhere Along the Isthmus in the Initial Formative

By Cherla (or Late Ocós) phase (1350–1200 BC [Clark 1991]), new styles of ceramics and figurines indicated that other regional cultures were growing more complex and sophisticated. The rise of San Lorenzo Tenochtitlan as the Isthmus's – and Mesoamerica's – most important community by 1200 BC will be discussed in the next chapter, but here let us note that extensive settlement took place in the San Lorenzo area during the Initial Formative. In the Isthmus and adjacent areas at this time, groups were migrating, colonizing uninhabited (or uncultivated) areas and sometimes pushing aside the village-farmers already established and causing them to extend settled village life into new areas.

Language as a Chronological Marker

Evidence for such movements comes from linguistics. Language is among the most significant markers of ethnic identification, and by studying the kinds of words and speech construction that make up various languages in different regions, linguists can trace the movements of speakers of certain languages. We know that the Americas were peopled in several great migratory episodes lasting many years, and we assume that each episode included hunter-foragers speaking dialects more closely related to others at the time of their migration than to those spoken in previous, or subsequent episodes (Greenberg, Turner, and Zegura 1986). Furthermore, the mobile lifestyle and low population densities during the Paleoindian period and much of the Archaic may have put a premium on maintaining a single language or set of mutually intelligible dialects over very extensive areas.

This may have been the case in the Early Archaic, but with later Archaic intensive exploitation of particular regions, and the development of sedentism, more localized languages developed. Linguists sometimes trace the time elapsed since languages diverged from their rootstock by a method known as *glottochronology*. This method assumes that certain basic terms – sun, moon, terms for close family members, for body parts – are learned so early and are so conservatively maintained that they will remain more constant than other terms. Languages which share basic terms, and are relatively more similar, are thought to have diverged more recently than languages with few or no terms in common. The proportion of common terms is scaled chronologically, and the hypothesis is that after 1,000 years, two diverging languages share 75–80 percent of their basic vocabulary. After another 1,000 years, they would share about 60 percent (75–80 percent of 75–80 percent [Hymes 1960]). While error rates can be quite high, "[i]n Mesoamerica, it appears that glottochronology provides a rather reliable guide for cultural chronologies" (Carmack, Gasco, and Gossen 1996: 405).

Language as an Ethnic Marker

The relation between ethnicity and language is strong but complex – language is a major component of group identification, yet speakers of the same language may not necessarily share religious beliefs, customs, costume. Thus caution must be exercised in applying simple, linguistically based timetables of ethnic divergence. However, with multiple lines of evidence, scholars can use language similarities to substantiate (or cast doubt on) theories about ancient ethnicity and migration patterns.

Scholars believe that the language spoken in the Isthmus during the Initial Formative may have been proto-Mixe-Zoque, a forerunner of the Soconusco region's present-day native language (Campbell and Kaufman 1976). Proto-Mixe-Zoque was thus probably the language of Olmec culture, of the northern Isthmus and southern Gulf lowlands, though the protean Olmec area, well settled by 1500 BC, was a melting pot of several cultures.

To the east of the Isthmus, the Maya highlands of Guatemala were the area of origin of the Mayan language, whose speakers then moved north into the lowlands of the Yucatán Peninsula, and later also pushed west into the northern Gulf lowlands, a region called the "Huasteca" after the Huastec Mayan dialect they spoke. They may have made this rather long migration (several hundred miles) because of population pressure caused by migrations of Mokaya peoples into the central and southern Gulf lowlands. Even further to the east, along the Caribbean Coast in northwestern Honduras, Puerto Escondido was an established village by 1600 BC, with sophisticated pottery (Joyce and Henderson 2001) and probably maize cultivation, judging from maize pollen detected in sediments in Lake Yojoa, just 65 km (40 miles) to the south, in this early period (Rue 1989).

HIGHLANDS WEST OF THE ISTHMUS

The Isthmus and adjacent coastal plains were full of varied subsistence resources. In contrast, life in the highlands west of the Isthmus was harsher; the foraged food from their mixed economy was less varied and dependable. Furthermore, early cultivation of maize in the highlands was usually a simple horticultural project, depending on summer rains to water the crop to fruition. But as we noted in Chapter 2, wherever dependable rainfall is less than 500 mm (20 in), rainfall-dependent farming is risky. Given that Late Archaic/Initial Formative maize cobs were very small, the yield for a whole hectare of land (2.5 acres) was only about 70 kg (*c.* 150 lb). Thus mixed strategists of the highlands would have looked for ways to secure and increase their yield.

The Valley of Oaxaca is a good focus for highland developments in the Initial Formative, because, relative to other parts of the highlands, it is somewhat precocious in terms of cultivation techniques and settlement hierarchies. The valley floor represents the largest expanse of agricultural

4.13 *The* coa, *a digging stick with a fire-hardened, shaped end, functioned in the same way as the modern hoe, shovel, and rake. Unlike those tools, it was not a composite tool – no blade was hafted onto the digging end. These 16th-century illustrations from the encyclopedic survey of Mesoamerican life, Sahagún's* Florentine Codex *(*The General History of the Things of New Spain*) show Aztec farmers, but their garb, and the techniques in use would no doubt pertain to much earlier times as well. Above, a farmer plants seeds taken from the bag tied around his neck. Below, The farmer uses the* coa *to tend young maize plants. See also Figure 3.6, showing a farmer using a* coa *to tend maguey.*

land in the highlands – 1,500 sq. km (600 sq. miles) – and while it lies at 1,500 m (4,922 ft) above sea level, frost is rare. Thus food production had great potential here, and in time compensated for the relative dearth of other resources (Blanton, Kowalewski, Feinman, and Finsten 1993).

The earliest villages in the Valley of Oaxaca date from 1700 to 1400 BC, and were situated on the alluvial plain along rivers, where the water table is exceptionally high. Farming was made secure by dipping water from shallow wells dug right in the fields, down to the level of the water table. This technique, called "pot irrigation," was highly effective but very small scale, in that no supra-familial organization was needed, as would be by a massive canal irrigation system (Flannery *et al.* 1967).

Crops were also secured by planting seeds deep enough so that the developing root system could feed upon the water table, through capillary action. Mesoamerican farming traditions depend upon a wooden digging stick that the Aztecs called a *coa* [**4.13**]. Unlike a hoe or a plow, which makes (and then covers) a furrow, the *coa* is used to make a single depression that reaches into the damp subsoil, and into this a seed is dropped. While this method is labor intensive, it is also highly productive, because the farmer monitors the soil's moisture content and insures that each seed has a maximum chance of germinating. Furthermore, each hill of loosened soil can grow several plants simultaneously, with the famed Mesoamerican crop triad making optimum use of space: beans twining around maize stalks, and squash covering the ground. The plants even boost each other's productivity, with beans fixing nitrogen in the soil, and squash conserving soil moisture by shading the ground. This dietary triad – maize, beans, and squash – also delivers good nutritional balance, a problem with largely vegetarian diets lacking dairy products.

Using a *coa*, a single Oaxacan farmer can cultivate a maximum area of about 2 hectares (Kirkby 1973) – a hectare covers an area a little larger than two football fields. This working capacity is important to know, because it sets a baseline energetic limit on nuclear family farming in Mesoamerica: in order to support a nuclear family by farming, crops grown on 2 hectares (or less) must be able to supply many basic needs.

Let us assume that the average person needs 2,000 kilocalories each day, a generous estimate because children need much less than this, and few adults need much more. Further assuming that the mixed strategist/early farmer's diet will be largely carbohydrate and protein, and little fat, 2,000 kcals amounts to a little less than half a kilogram (less than a pound) of food per person. Assuming that the co-residing family group consists of the nuclear family plus occasional other relatives, about five people, then they consume daily about 2 kg of food (about 4.4 lb), and yearly the household needs at least 730 kg (*c.* 1,600 lb). More is needed to cover loss from crop damage and to maintain supplies of seed for the next planting season.

We know that Oaxaca Valley foragers ate a wide range of foods and emphasized a few key resources. Among them was wild mesquite, which bears sweet edible beans in pods gathered from the shrubby trees. Wild mesquite yields about 170 kg (375 lb) of pods per hectare, a good value for mixed-strategists. A 2-hectare field planted in Late Archaic/Initial Formative inch-long maize cobs would yield 140 kg (*c*. 300 lb). A cost-benefit analysis of maize domestication has shown that not until domesticated maize yields reach 200–250 kg (441–551 lb) per hectare – three or four times the yield of the earliest domesticates – does it make good energetic sense to clear the land of wild resources and cultivate maize and other staple crops (Kirkby 1973). Archaeologists believe that maize had achieved this level of productivity by *c*. 1700–1500 BC, when village farming appeared in the Valley of Oaxaca (Marcus and Flannery 1996).

The actual direct evidence for these early permanent villages is scarce, because pioneering sites underlie later, larger settlements. Choice locations were, consistently, along the alluvial plain adjacent to major rivers, where the water table is high and *coa*-planting could secure an adequate crop. The houses had pine posts, with walls of wattle-and-daub (woven reeds heavily plastered with mud) and thatched roofs. "Near the house, each family dug storage pits for its harvested maize ... [each] held up to a metric ton [2,205 lb] of shelled corn, or a year's supply for a family of 4–5" (Marcus and Flannery 1996: 73).

Earliest Highland Ceramics

During this Initial Formative period, the first pottery appeared in the Oaxaca Valley and in the neighboring Tehuacán Valley. The close relationship of ceramics and sedentism has already been discussed; we should here note how fortuitous this is for archaeological recovery of information. Ceramic vessels are excellent markers of the time and place of their origin, as revealed by their style and material [**4.14**]. Fired clay has the permanence of stone – it may be broken into smaller and smaller sherds, but it does not biodegrade or dissolve. In Mesoamerican archaeology, our knowledge of cultural occupations is very much based on field surveys of materials on the surface of the soil. Such surveys identify sherds from various periods, even including, at times, the earliest materials known for a region.

This seems somewhat contradictory: archaeology assumes superposition of layers, oldest at the bottom, so how can early materials end up on top? This occurs, to a limited degree, for several reasons: sherds, like other soil inclusions, have a tendency to work their way to the surface, heaved up by the compaction of smaller particles under them, or by plowing. Furthermore, Mesoamerica's dramatic climate and topography make erosion a widespread pattern, and archaeologists sometimes see sherds representing a whole range of time periods, lying on a ground surface from which all soil has eroded away, leaving exposed the ancient substrate of compacted volcanic ash (a substance called *tepetate*, Nahuatl for "stone-mat").

In Tehuacán's Purrón phase and Oaxaca's Espiridión phase, both around 1500 BC, ceramic vessels were used in the highlands for the first time. These were undecorated, simple brown or buff bowls and tecomates, mimicking the shapes of gourd bowls and jars so long in use. These early highland wares are known from a few hundred sherds.

POTTERY VESSEL FORMS

POTTERY FORMS and surface treatments are essential for archaeologists to understand Mesoamerican cultures and culture history, because in addition to serving as markers of particular phases and places and interchange between them, pottery types reveal the lives of their users – what was cooking, and being served, which symbols had important meaning, which forms were coveted for their elegance or became classics of functionality.

Pottery classification is based on characteristics of: material composition (clay, temper, surface treatments like slip or stucco), form (morphology), function, provenience (site or culture of origin), chronology (period of original use, also periods during which examples were treasured as heirlooms – "curated"). The *type-variety* approach to pottery analysis (Gifford 1960) has been used to standardize classification, particularly in the Maya regions, by defining broad types that would be found in use in a particular site, and the varieties within each type that would represent the individualized work of small groups of potters.

Below [**4.14**] are the most basic forms in use in Mesoamerica, as based on morphology and (secondarily) function. The morphological categories are based on the proportion of width to height, from the flattest (plates and griddles) to the tallest (jars, vases, bottles). A separate category, ritual vessels, is functionally distinct from the other vessels, which are generally used in culinary and social contexts, for cooking and serving. These forms occur from the Initial Formative period on into the present. Note that there is no scale for the drawings; they simply depict form. Definitions use both morphological and functional distinctions. Composite forms combine several morphological patterns and thus are subject to a variety of categories: "composite bowl," "composite jar," "composite vase" may be used by different ceramists to describe the same vessel.

Pottery Vessel Forms (4.14)

Culinary, Social Vessels, Sometimes with Ritual Functions

PLATE

Shallow vessel, height is $< 1/5$ of diameter. Cooking and serving.

Comal

Large heavy griddle, for cooking tortillas.

DISH

Moderately shallow vessel, height $= 1/5$ to $1/3$ of diameter. Cooking and serving. *Tamale* dishes are of this type. A *cazuela* is a large dish for serving.

BOWL

Plain bowls

Wide-mouthed vessel, height is $1/3$ to equal to diameter; many shapes; some are effigy vessels. Cooking and serving. The *molcajete* is a "grater bowl" – its striated interior bottom is a grinding surface for pulverizing chiles and other ingredients.

Pottery Vessel Forms *continued*

Bowl *continued*

Tecomate

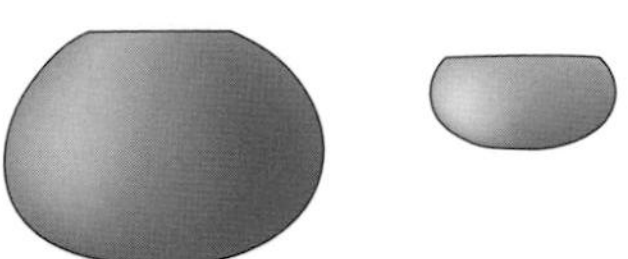

Round bowl with incurving rim or jar lacking a neck; shaped like a round gourd, which was probably the prototype.

Tripod, tetrapod bowl

Bowl on three or four supports, ranging from "nubbins" to "spider-legs."

Spider-leg tripods

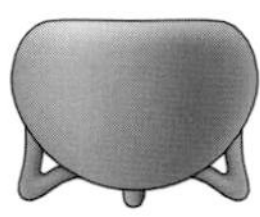

Tecomate tripod

Globular tripod

Cylinder

Straight-sided bowl. "Tripod cylinder" is particularly associated with Teotihuacan tripod cylinders.

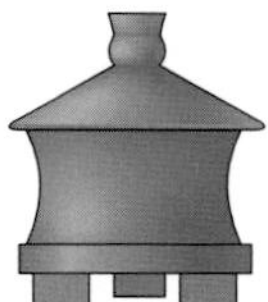

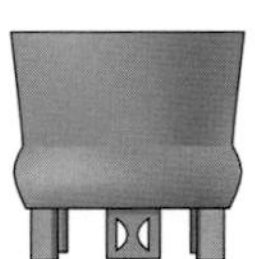

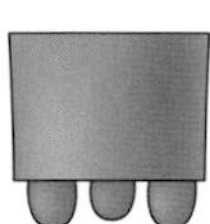

Tripod cylinders

Composite bowl

Bowl with silhouette combining several different forms; see also composite vase.

Basal-break bowls

Body-break bowl

Rim shoulder bowl

Basin

Very large bowl used for cooking.

Cup, Vase, Jar

Containers, higher than they are wide, often with a neck. Bottles, vases, cups are often decorated and used for serving.

Cup

Goblet used for drinking.

Spouted chocolate vessel

Pulque cup

Pottery Vessel Forms *continued*

VASE (and composite vase)

Decorative vessel higher than it is wide; used in rituals, social settings as a serving, drinking vessel, perhaps even used as a vase for flowers.

JAR

Jars are large, for cooking and serving.

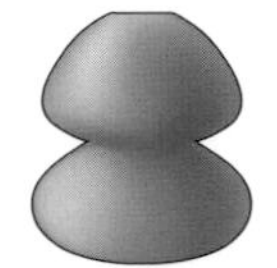
Bule: nipped-in waist

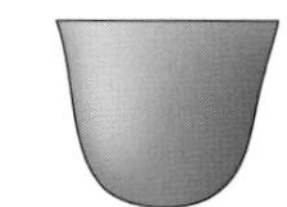
Crater: round bottom, wide mouth

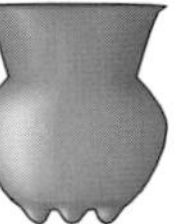

Olla

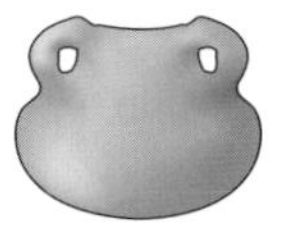

Large wide-mouth jar for collection and storage of liquids; handles facilitate carrying.

Shoe-shape or 'patojo'

Small jar, sometimes ovoid; designed to rest on its side and thus make efficient use of cooking fires by slipping under the side of a larger jar on the fire.

Ritual Vessels

MINIATURE VESSELS

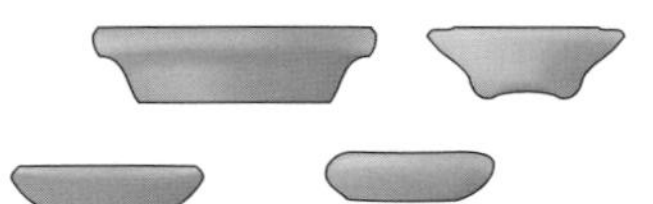

Small versions of vases, jars, etc., used as offerings at shrines and as grave goods.

BRAZIER ***BRAZERO***

Large heavy vessel for burning incense and fires for heating; some are effigy vessels: deities, ancestors.

CENSER ***INCENSARIO***

'Flower pot' censer

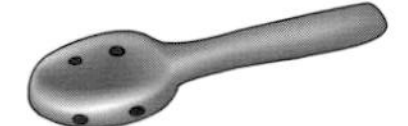
Ladle censer

Incense burner, freestanding or handheld; forms vary, some are small bowls with perforations and long handles; composite censers include many parts.

CANDELERO

Incense burner with 1 or 2 indentations.

Ancestor Cults and Oaxaca in Tierras Largas Phase

Much of what we reconstruct about Oaxaca's earliest settled phase, Espiridión, is extrapolated back from the much-better-known and more recent Tierras Largas phase (1400–1150 BC), and subsequent San José phase (1150–850 BC), when the village of San José Mogote, centrally located in the Etla arm of the valley, became the largest site in the region [**4.15–4.17**]. Tierras Largas-phase San José Mogote consisted of 15–30 houses, and the smaller community of Tierras Largas had 10 households (Winter 1976: 228). Until the Late Formative, when Monte Albán became the capital of the Oaxaca Valley system, San José Mogote continued to grow, while Tierras Largas remained a hamlet with fewer than a dozen households.

As was the case in the Soconusco region, social complexity in Oaxaca found expression through architecture. At Paso de la Amada "monumental" or "civic-ceremonial" buildings were the ball court and elite residence. At

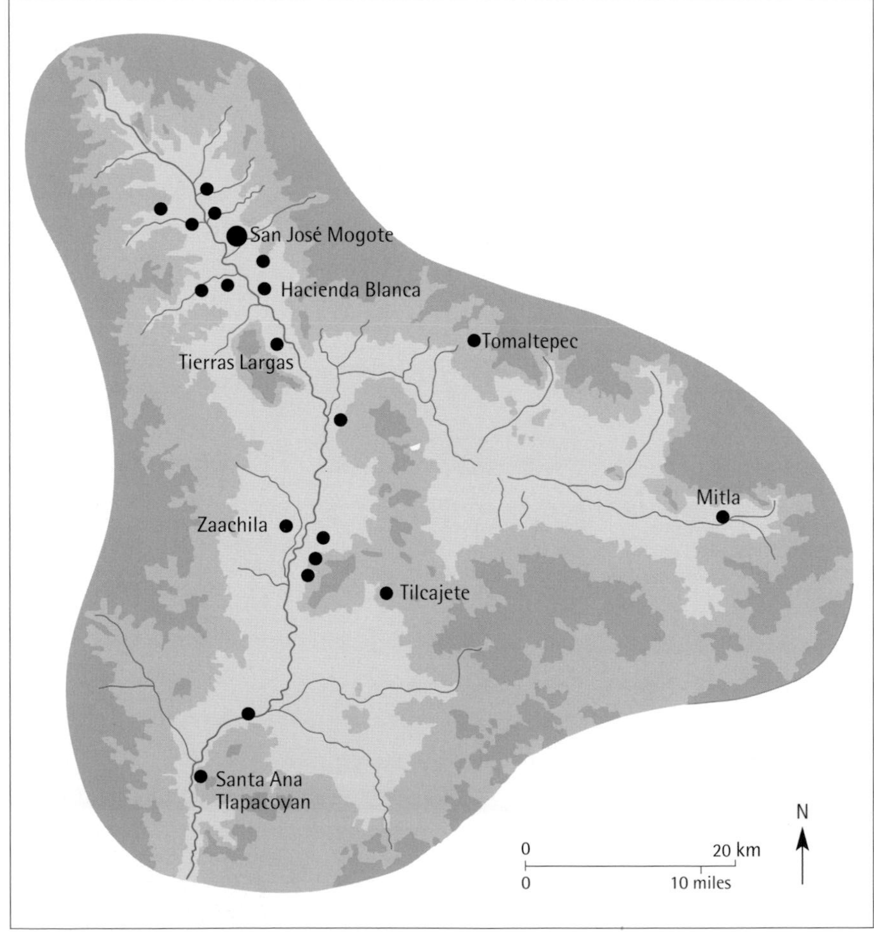

4.15 *The Valley of Oaxaca stretches out in three directions, with first-class agricultural land extensive in the northern, Etla arm of the valley, which also has the most settlement, early on. Two types of communities are present in the Tierras Largas phase: several hamlets with a few dozen residents, and a village, San José Mogote.*

4.16, 4.17 *(Opposite) The reconstruction drawing and photo are of a structure in San José Mogote which is thought to have had community-wide functions as a "men's house" where the adult males of the village would convene. The step-like construction along the south wall may have been an altar. A pit in the center of the floor was filled with powdered limestone, "perhaps stored for use with a ritual plant such as wild tobacco ... jimson weed ... or morning glory" (Marcus and Flannery 1996: 87).*

San José Mogote, a different kind of civic-ceremonial building occurs: the community house, or "men's house." This functional interpretation is an extrapolation, based on later such buildings, and on ethnographic analogues. Another clue as to the significance of this building in ritual was its orientation: 8° west of north, which was the orientation of La Venta, the Olmec capital that achieved prominence in the Middle Formative. Orientations of monumental buildings and whole sites indicate the importance of alignments as mastery of astronomical and calendric knowledge was gained.

Elsewhere in the Highlands: Basin of Mexico, Morelos, Tehuacán Valley

There is some evidence of volcanic activity in the mountains at the southern edge of the Basin of Mexico at around 1500 BC. While volcanism varies in effects from a picturesque smoke plume persisting for many peaceful years to red hot lava flows that sterilize a landscape for decades, any volcanic activity involving ash fall or worse would have sent foragers on a trek toward calmer ground. It would also impress all witnesses with the living power of a region's mountains. The period from about 1400 to 1000 BC may have brought increased rainfall to the Central Highlands (Messenger 1990), offering an attendant increase in security of crops and extension of areas cultivable without irrigation. The implication is that if farming populations in core areas were increasing, this period would have been ideal for relieving demographic pressure on available land through the colonization of adjacent areas.

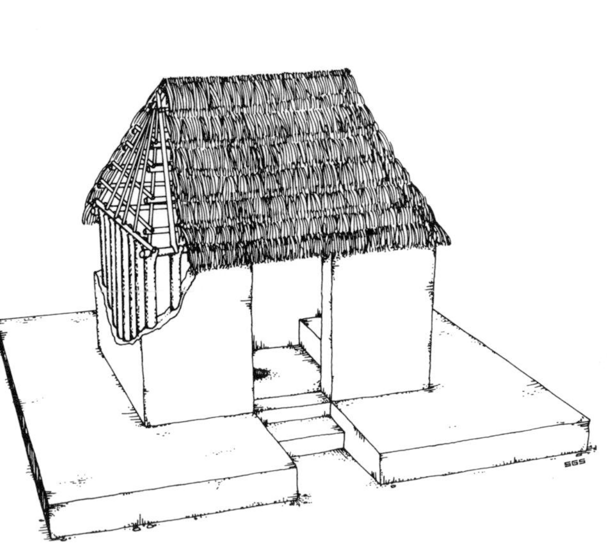

All over the highlands, pottery-using farmers established villages. Tehuacán Valley's Ajalpan phase, which followed upon the poorly understood initial ceramic Purrón phase, showed evidence of a strong dependence upon domesticated food. In the Mixteca Alta region, Early Cruz-phase (1500–1200 BC) settlements were established at Etlatongo and Yucuita (Winter 1984), sites that became important in later phases. Archaeological surveys in the Nochixtlán Valley (Spores 1984) and Tamazulapan Valley (Byland and Pohl 1994) revealed a widespread pattern of small farming settlements, with simple buff-colored pottery.

Similar patterns are detected for Morelos in the Amate phase (1500–1000 BC) and for Puebla and Tlaxcala's Tzompantepec phase (? to 1200 BC), with pottery like that used in the Tehuacán Valley. Some of these small farming hamlets were on piedmont slopes, and apparently used agricultural terracing in order to secure their crops by harnessing erosion to deepen the soil on terraces. This innovation would remain an important element of cultivation technology in Middle America into modern times. Maguey was – and is – often planted on the outer edge of the terrace to secure the soil and enhance productivity of the plot.

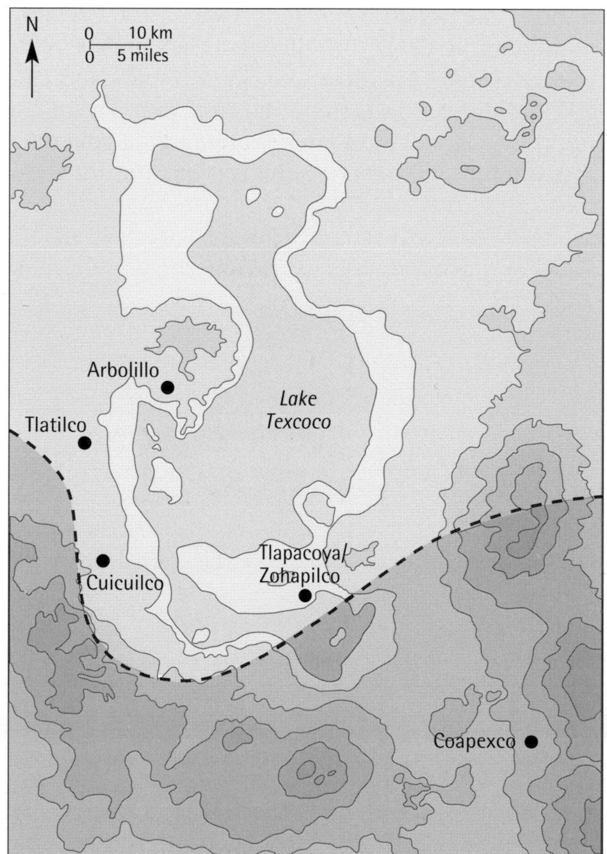

Basin of Mexico Widespread use of ceramics in the Basin of Mexico began around 1500 BC. Initial Formative sites occurred over the southern Basin [**4.18**], a distribution characteristic of a "horizon." Some scholars have used the term Early Horizon to refer to the widespread distribution of pottery-using village farmers in the period 1500–1000 BC, particularly in the Basin of Mexico. While logically sound, the terminology did not replace the more common usage, Initial Formative.

The map shows sites along the lakeshore and on the adjacent alluvial plain. We see the earliest occupations at Tlatilco and Cuicuilco. At the bottom right of the map, there is a pass that connects with the Valley of Morelos, which had a warmer climate and earlier settlements than were found in the Basin – though ceramics from this period from both regions are very similar, "it is tempting to view ... initial colonization of the Basin by sedentary farmers from Morelos" (Sanders, Parsons, and Santley 1979: 95).

Regardless of whether the Basin was colonized by pottery-using farmers from Morelos, or settled by its own foragers as they adopted the cultural patterns of their neighbors, the Basin developed a two-tiered settlement system of the same general type as found in the Mazatán region and in the Oaxaca Valley. This consisted of central villages of several hundred people and much smaller communities of a few families. This is consistent with tribal settlement patterns, and indicates a growing complexity of organization. The critical size of the larger villages would demand the emergence of more powerful central authorities.

West Mexico

Western Mexico's Formative period development did not follow the pattern shared by Central Highlands regions, but instead demonstrated its own unusual traditions. The earliest of these is the construction of monumental shell mounds along the coast. Later in the Initial Formative and further inland, shaft tombs were dug in many areas, but we know little of the populations responsible for this practice, which continued into the Classic period, and will be discussed in Chapters 9 and 10.

West Mexican Coast Initial Formative Pacific coastal traditions in general are known from shell mounds, similar to those made by the Chantuto people of Late Archaic/Initial Formative Soconusco. Some of the most impressive mounds were constructed on the West Mexican coast.

The Matanchén shell mound site (Nayarit) consists of a huge mound, 3,600 sq. m (*c.* 38,750 sq. ft) in area and over 3 m (*c.* 10 ft) high (Mountjoy, Taylor, and Feldman 1972). Uncalibrated radiocarbon dates cluster around 2000 BC, and a few net sinkers and other stone tools were found among the remains of conchs, mollusks, and other shellfish. The tools were characteristic of Archaic adaptations, and Matanchén is regarded as an Archaic-style complex, with no ceramics in evidence.

About 100 km (60 miles) up the coast, the huge shell mound at El Calón (Sinaloa) was constructed in the swampy coastal region now known as Marismas Nacionales sometime in the Initial Formative, and is among the largest of the 600 + shell mounds there. This pyramidal structure measured at least 25 m (82 ft) high with an area 7 by 10 m (23 by 33 ft) at the top, rising from a base roughly 80 by 100 m (c. 260 by 330 ft). It is entirely made of shell, including large blocks of unopened shellfish. Some scholars believe that El Calón was a trash midden; to others, its size, shape, and material indicate monumental architecture. As with the shell mounds of the Chantuto region, such shells were not trash but rather served as tough, durable building material. El Calón may date from before 1500 BC, but the Opeño phase, 1500–1000 BC, is more likely. If El Calón is a deliberately constructed pyramid, it is one of the earliest truly monumental structures in the New World, contemporaneous with North America's early monumental site, Poverty Point (Louisiana), and similar in size to its largest mound, "A."

4.18 *Basin of Mexico, 1500–1150* BC. *During wet years, the whole basin is temperate* tierra templada, *but in dry years, everywhere north of the dashed line becomes arid* tierra fría. *While the Initial Formative period was probably fairly temperate in terms of rainfall, the early development of settlement in the southern Basin owes much to the more moderate climate there, as well as proximity to Morelos, via the Amecameca Pass, in the southeast corner of the Basin. In this period the Basin had two kinds of sites: villages of several hundred people (as many as four such villages have been identified), and small hamlets.*

Initial Formative: The Mesoamerican Culture Area

By the end of the Initial Formative period, 2000–1200 BC, key elements defining the Mesoamerican cultural tradition were in place, and would spread and undergo further elaboration. Mesoamerican culture was based on maize agriculture, and the farm plot (*milpa* in Nahuatl) was widely seen among later peoples as the essence of cosmic identity, the nexus of the relationship between people and their gods (Miller and Taube 1993:114). The earth was the *milpa* of the gods, and outside the *milpa*, chaos reigned. For individual Mesoamericans, their *milpa* was the means by which they sustained themselves and their gods.

Much of the tool technology that would be in use during the coming 3,000 years of Mesoamerican culture was in place, and most of the cultigens had been domesticated. From region to region, and within the regions that farmers settled, land varied in productivity. When populations were small, community social relations were family relations, and there were fewer people competing for the best land.

Only in a few areas did village sizes achieve a critical maximum at which tribal organization could not sustain community harmony. This is one piece of evidence that indicates that chiefdoms were developing. The chief's capacity for capitalizing on the labor of others may be evidenced by some of the monumental construction reviewed above, but note that there are many ethnographic examples of substantial platforms and buildings being constructed by small numbers of people. Imported goods and luxury goods also indicate that long-distance trade routes had been established, and that skilled artisans had mastered the problems of working lapidary materials, and were producing fine goods for a small segment of the population. Belief systems are difficult to reconstruct at this remove, yet we see the establishment of figurine traditions indicating household rituals, and perceive that some of the monumental construction had a ritual component. With these basic elements in place, the Mesoamerican world was ready for Olmec culture to flower.

PART 2 COMPLEX SOCIETIES OF THE FORMATIVE

Early Formative through Terminal Formative Periods (1200 BC–AD 300)

	Early Formative	Middle Formative		Late Formative	Terminal Formative
	1200	900	600	300	BC AD 300
Northern Arid Zone		Coyote tradition, Cochise tradition			Chihuahua tradition
SE: Sierra Madre Oriental	Laguna				
SE: Tamaulipas		Laguna	La Florida phase		Eslabones phase
Northwestern Frontier	Bolanos Period I				Loma San Gabriel culture
West Mexico	San Felipe phase *El Opeño, Capacha cultures*		Chupícuaro phase *Bajío, Chupícuaro*	El Arenal phase *Shaft-tomb complex, Huitzilapa*	Ortices phase Comala phase
Michoacán			Infiernillo complex	Loma Alta phase	
Guerrero	Initial Ceramic per., Xochipalpa complex *Teopantecuanitlán*				*Cuetlajuchitlan*
Morelos	Barranca phase *Chalcatzingo*	Cerro Tepaltepec	Cantera phase		
Basin of Mexico	Ixtapaluca, Zacateno phases *Tlatilco, Cuicuilco*		Ticoman phase Tlapacoya phase *Cuicuilco, Loma Torremote*	Patlachique, Tzacualli, Miccaotli phases Tlamimilolpa phase *Cuicuilco, Teotihuacan*	
Puebla	Tlatempa phase	Texoloc phase		Tezoquipan phase *Amulucan, Tlalancaleca*	*Tetimpa region sites, Cholula*
Tlaxcala	Tlatempa phase	Texoloc phase		Tezoquipan phase	
Gulf Lowlands, north	Pavón phase	Ponce phase *Panuco*	Aguilar phase Chila phase	El Prisco phase	*San Antonio Nogalar Tancanhuitz*
Gulf Lowlands, north-central					Tajín I *El Pital*
Gulf Lowlands, south-central	Trapiche phase		Lower Remojadas phase	Upper Remojadas phase *Tres Zapotes*	
Tehuacán Valley		Santa María	*Purrón Dam*	*Quachilco, Quiotepec*	Palo Blanco phase
Mixteca Alta	Middle Cruz phase	Late Cruz phase *Yucuita, Etlatongo*	Ramos phase *Yucuita, Monte Negro*		
Mixteca Baja			Ñudée phase		
Oaxaca	San José phase *San José Mogote, Huitzo*	Guadalupe phase	Rosario phase *San José Mogote, Monte Albán*	Monte Albán I phase	Monte Albán II phase *Monte Albán, Dainzú*
Tehuantepec		*Laguna Zope*			
Gulf Lowlands, south	Early Olmec Chicharras phase *San Lorenzo*	Nacaste phase, Palangana phase *La Venta*			*La Mojarra and early writing*
Chiapas Interior Plateau	Dili phase, Escalera phase *San Isidro, Chiapa de Corzo*		Francesca phase *Chiapa de Corzo, La Libertad*	Guanacaste phase *Chiapa de Corzo*	Horcones phase Istmo phase Jiquipilas phase *Chiapa de Corzo*
Chiapas and Guatemala Coast	Cuadros and Jocotal phases, Conchas phase	Frontea, Escalon, Duende phases *Tzutzuculi, La Blanca, El Mesak Izapa*		Hato, Crucero, Guillen phases Crucero phase Izapa	Izapa phase
Guatemala Highlands	Arévalo	Las Charcas, Providencia, Arevelo, Miraflores-Arenal *Kaminaljuyú*		Arenal phase *Kaminaljuyú*	Santa Clara phase *Kaminaljuyú*
Maya Lowlands, north	Ecab phase, Cupul phase		Tihosuco phase *Edzná*		Chakan phase *Becán, Komchén*
Maya Lowlands, south	Xe complex, Swasey-Bladen complex, Mamon, Chicanel phases *Cuello Nakbé, El Mirador, Cerros*				Holmul phase *Uaxactún*
Southeastern Mesoamerica		*Chalchuapa, Playa de los Muertos, Yarumela*	Uapala ceramic sphere *Chalchuapa*		
Intermediate Area	Period IV				

Selected phase names; *sites* and *events* are in *italic* type

5 THE OLMECS: EARLY FORMATIVE (*c.* 1200–900/800 BC)

OLMEC CULTURE EMERGED as Mesoamerica's first highly complex cultural system at about 1200 BC, and flourished until 500 BC or later, with its most important sites being San Lorenzo during the first period (Early Formative or Initial Olmec period, 1200–900/800 BC), and La Venta during its second (Middle Formative period, 900/800–500/400 BC). At the same time, other complex societies were developing in the Valley of Oaxaca, Morelos, the Basin of Mexico, West Mexico, and Guerrero. In general, these two periods are covered by Chapters 5 and 6, respectively, but overview sections in each chapter address themes and archaeological evidence from both [**5.1**].

EARLY FORMATIVE AND INITIAL OLMEC

A Jade-Green World

Mesoamerica at 1200 BC was a world of tribal horticultural villages. Its peoples did some farming in the well-watered bottomlands of valleys, and, in the highlands, even had begun to increase yields by using terracing and irrigation techniques, as well as by using improved domesticated crops. Foraging still played an important role; people continued to hunt and trap

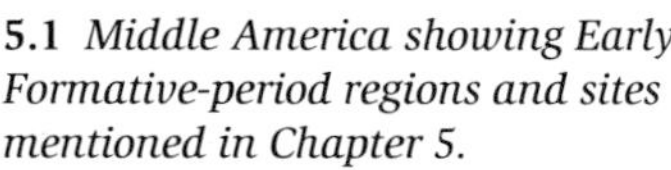

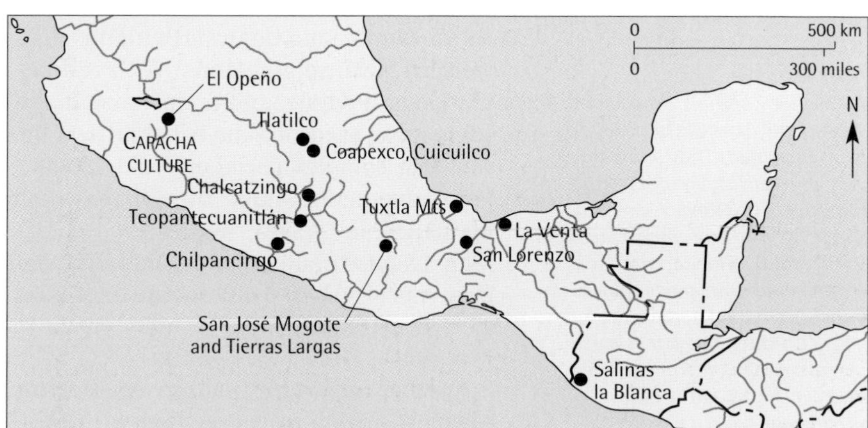

5.1 *Middle America showing Early Formative-period regions and sites mentioned in Chapter 5.*

and collect important plants. The landscape became clearly divided between cultivated land and the wilderness beyond it, and in Middle America's highly dissected terrain this inevitably meant the balanced symmetry of *milpas* near water, against a backdrop of wooded mountains.

The farming village and its *milpas*, green with crops, would represent to Mesoamericans a connection point between heaven and earth, the fruitful union of water and mountains, prosperity springing from the proper regulation of the agricultural year, and effective mediation with controlling spiritual forces. Green, the potent sign of the life force, represented essential sanctity to Mesoamericans: their most treasured gem stone was jade, and iridescent blue-green quetzal feathers became the ultimate symbol of lordly power. In fact, all bundles of blue and green stalks represented preciousness, be they feathers, or stalks of fresh corn, or *tules* (marsh grasses). For example, bundles of green stalks were an icon for Mesoamerica's most sacred and important cities, those given the name "Tollán" or "Tula" – place of the tules. Blue-green jade was also a metaphor for water, in raindrops or in the expanse of a lagoon, and a blue-green circle or disk became an icon for water as well as for jade, for preciousness in general, and for royalty and the power held by royal and sacred persons.

The disk also symbolized, to Mesoamericans, life's quotidian measure, the day. That a unit of time should share in the sacred and precious associations of the other meanings should not surprise us, because measurement and veneration of time in its various rhythms was a major focus of Mesoamerican culture, from the Formative on. Note how these different essences are linked through a highly flexible system of metaphorical meaning, such that the occurrence of any one of them carries along some sense of the others. It is important for us to become aware of this, because this system differs substantially from our modern cognitive categorizations of inorganic/organic, ritual/secular.

5.2–5.4 *Jade was crafted by artists throughout Mesoamerican culture history, its handling reflecting the aesthetics of different cultures. The three masks are (from left to right) Middle Formative Olmec, probably from Veracruz, Terminal Formative Zapotecs from Monte Albán, and Late Classic Maya, from Palenque. They show three very different styles of working the material. The Olmec mask is a single carved piece, incised with scroll motifs. The Zapotec mask is crafted of distinct parts, like a puppet face, and depicts the bat god. The Maya mask is a mosaic portrait of King Pakal the Great, and was found within his sarcophagus.*

It is clear that by the Early Formative, the cultivable valleys of Middle America were strewn with farming villages and that the Mesoamerican culture area had reached a significant proportion of its ultimate extent. The two major waves of sedentism occurred around 1500 BC (Isthmus, Southern, South-central, and Central Highlands) and around 1000 BC (Maya lowlands, western Mexican highlands). This reflects an increase in the size of the population as a whole, and an increase in the size of certain villages, which in some areas exceeded the tribal critical limit of several hundred people. We saw that complex societies – chiefdoms – probably emerged in the Initial Formative period along the Chiapas-Guatemala Coast and perhaps in the highlands, in Oaxaca. Impressive public structures were being raised, and long-distance trade in luxury materials and finished goods was brisk. Strong elements of a shared culture are expressed in these phenomena, and we are alerted to themes that strongly mark the rest of Mesoamerican culture history.

Another important trend in this culture history is the shift of focus from region to region in succeeding periods. Chapter 1 reviewed this changing

JADE

MORE PRECIOUS to the Mesoamericans than gold, or any other substance, were the green and bluegreen gemstones commonly called "jade." However, true mineralogical jade, nephrite, does not occur in the New World. Instead, other green-to-blue hard stones were valued for lapidary work, and most important among them was jadeite, a sodium aluminum silicate given its greenish color by inclusions of iron and copper. Other hard stones also valued for jade-like qualities were serpentine, albite, quartz, and hornblende, which were more widely distributed. The Aztec term for precious green-blue stone, "chalchihuitl" (chahl-*chi*-hweet), referred not only to jadeite, but also to certain minerals found in the Northern Arid Zone and Northwestern Frontier: turquoise and chrysocolla (copper silicate), the green-blue stone prized in the mining area known as Chalchihuites, exploited particularly in the Classic period. The nearby site of Alta Vista de Chalchihuites showed the influence of Teotihuacan trading interests.

The only known sources of jadeite in Middle America are along the Motagua River in Guatemala (Bishop and Lange 1993), though neutron activation analysis indicates that there are other, yet unknown sources (Bishop 2001:384). Recent explorations in the Motagua region have yielded the previously unknown location of "Olmec blue jade" (Seitz *et al.* 2001).

Jade-like stone (hereafter, jade or greenstone) was first worked by Olmec artisans, who mastered the techniques of shaping this hard stone with tools made from other hard stone – jade itself – and abrading it with sand made of quartz or jade. Artistic projects ranged in scale from single beads to carvings of single large pieces of jade, such as the 4.42 kg (nearly 10 lb), 14.9-cm (nearly 6-in) high full-round head of the Maya sun god, from Altún Ha (Pendergast 1979–1990). Jade was fashioned into depictions of deities, persons, shamanic transformations, animals, plants, and abstract forms. Jade objects, even the simplest and smallest, were luxury goods, made from rare material and with masterful artisanship. Perhaps because of its color, shared with water and vegetation, it was associated with the life force, and jade beads were put in the mouths of the dead.

pattern, and while archaeological evidence from all periods and all regions reveals that fascinating sites and events characterize local culture histories, the focal points change. "Rise and fall" of regions and culture areas is an engrossing theme, and inherent in such historical study is the search for causes underlying florescence and decline, perhaps even for the cure for cultural superannuation.

Things That Move Cultures

The Mokaya peoples of the Chiapas-Guatemala Coast, politically precocious during the Initial Formative, experienced a decline in power during the Early Formative. They continued to maintain contacts with neighboring regions, getting obsidian from the Guatemala highlands (Clark and Salcedo 1989; Clark 1991) and using ceramics similar to those found in the Gulf lowlands, Chiapas highlands, and Oaxaca. But over time, and especially after 1000 BC, these contacts seemed to indicate increasing power of external influence – probably from the Olmecs, dominating the Gulf lowlands from San Lorenzo (Blake 2001). Imagery on ceramic vessels changes to include complex Olmec motifs, with iconography that may have required the interpretation of Olmec ritual specialists or members of the Olmec elite (Lesure 2000).

The Decline of Paso de la Amada This trend is visible at Paso de la Amada, where the ball court was abandoned, though the site was not. Having seen the ball court as a diagnostic clue to chiefly power, we can only assume that power had been lost, that hosting ball games on an impressive formal court was a practice that no longer enhanced the prestige of Paso de la Amada and its ruling lineage – or that Paso's leadership had "lost the team franchise" and the community could no longer afford such displays of affluence and authority.

However, population in the region remained high, with many small centers and surrounding hamlets. Salinas la Blanca, for example, was a small site in a coastal estuary environment; local inhabitants lived in wattle-and-daub houses and raised maize as well as gathering mollusks and other sea creatures. They also hunted deer and collected local fruit (Coe and Flannery 1967). This pattern was typical along the coast, as far south as western El Salvador, where settlement was beginning in the Chalchuapa area.

East and South of the Pacific Coastal Plain

Up from the coastal plain, in the highlands of Chiapas and Guatemala, farming villages spread along the river valleys and around the lakes. Large villages developed in the Chiapan interior at Chiapa de Corzo, Acala, and Plumajillo, the latter specializing in the production of small cubes of polished ilmenite iron-ore, ornaments that were exported to San Lorenzo.

Pollen cores from the Maya lowlands indicate the presence of slash-and-burn agriculturalists, the early Maya who, from language studies, are presumed to have moved out of the Chiapas and Guatemala highlands, radiating north and east to settle the lowlands of Yucatán and the river valleys to the east.

Southern Gulf Lowlands

Meanwhile, in the southern Gulf lowlands, the pace of complexity was picking up. Monumental architecture seems to appear rather suddenly there, but our perception may result from biased archaeological evidence. The region's swampy environment makes preserving and retrieving the early archaeological record very difficult. Limited archaeological evidence indicates that villages dotted the region throughout the Initial Formative. It is around 1200 BC that this region becomes the most architecturally and artistically (and, by extension, socially) complex in all of Mesoamerica.

What caused this shift in cultural equilibrium? Historians look for answers first in the most obvious place: inevitable changes in human-environmental relations caused by instability in some component of the food-producing equation. Was there a shift in the weather pattern? In fact, a broad El Niño or La Niña change seems to have taken place, with cooler temperatures between 1400 and 1000 BC. If the overall climate of ancient cool spells follows the same patterns prevalent today, then this would have been accompanied by a decrease of up to 50 percent in rainfall along the Chiapas-Guatemala Coast (Messenger 1990). Evidence there points to a mixed subsistence economy not wholly dependent upon maize as a staple crop, and thus seemingly less affected by such changes than would have been the case with heavy dependence on a few crops well-adapted to a particular climatic regime. However, even in the Initial Formative this coastal region may have specialized in the production of cacao or some other valuable crop, and climate disruption would have undercut local prosperity.

In contrast, the southern Gulf lowlands would have been less affected by cooler weather: there would have been less change in annual rainfall in this region, coupled with a drought-indifferent cultivation program along riverbanks, tapping deep, moist soils. They may also have been using an improved, tropical-adapted hard kernel maize (Grove 1981), which, by the subsequent Middle Formative period, was passed along to the Chiapas-Guatemala Coast (see Chapter 6). As we noted in Chapter 4, Initial Formative maize in some areas may have been a specialty food, eaten green or fermented into beer – the lack of manos and metates as grinding tools on the coast before the Middle Formative does not mean maize was not being cultivated, but does suggest that it was not a staple crop.

The Formative-period peoples of the southern Gulf lowlands are known to us as the Olmecs, their name at the time of European contact. In the Nahuatl language it meant something like "'citizen of Olman,' the rubber country, the tropical lowlands in general, and more specifically the southern Gulf coast, from where the best rubber came" (Covarrubias 1986 [1946]: 82). The

5.5 *The Olmecs were among Mesoamerica's finest sculptors, particularly of large works in hard stone, and they often worked in the round, finishing all sides of a sculpture. "The human form is the focus of Olmec art. ... [but] Olmec sculptures often portray composite beings that are biologically impossible, mingling human traits with characteristics of various animals" (Joralemon 1996: 51).*

A single piece of greenstone, the Las Limas figure weighs 60 kg (132 lb). The figure is a youth, male or of indeterminate sex, holding a seemingly lifeless representation of "the Olmec supernatural" – sometimes called a were-jaguar, or the Olmec rain god, or the Olmec maize deity, whose characteristics include a cleft head, almond-shaped eyes, "snarling" mouth. The seated figure wears and holds insignia of shamanic powers (Tate 1999: 183).

highland Aztecs had to import rubber, and sought it through tribute and trade, using it to make balls for the ball game and also as an important ceremonial accoutrement – ritual costumes were dotted with rubber. We know that rubber was also prized in Formative times, and in the last chapter we discussed how the ball game harnessed rubber's intrinsic vitality.

Olmec culture has such distinctive features, as we shall see in this and the next chapter, that the Early and Middle Formative periods are sometimes referred to as Early and Middle Olmec periods. While traits characteristic of the southern Gulf lowlands are found throughout Mesoamerica, it should be emphasized that a few sherds of Olmec-style vessels found, say, at a site in the Basin of Mexico, do not mean that an Olmec "empire" extended over a vast area. Furthermore, other regions were also actively developing their own trappings of complex society, and the patterns of interchange among such regions as Morelos, Oaxaca Valley, and the Gulf lowlands are themselves complex. That said, let us first examine the signature features of the most distinctive of these regional cultures: the Olmecs of the southern Gulf lowlands.

The Olmecs: First Florescence of Mesoamerican Complex Culture

Olmec culture produced Mesoamerica's first mature complex societies, and Olmec art is Mesoamerica's first great art style that modern sensibilities recognize: Olmec themes, most significantly expressed in sculpture, are the refined, mature dialect of a widespread aesthetic language of form and line, played out regionally with distinctive features and modes of expression. We identify the Olmec florescence, beginning around 1200 BC, as the earliest in a succession of distinctive Mesoamerican artistic traditions and their associated complex cultures [5.5].

Olmec art reflects these themes in dramatic ways, and to divorce art from social meaning violates an essential ancient unity, though it is important to establish the modern limits of understanding. Olmec art is enormously valuable on today's "art market" because of its antiquity and rarity, but also because in its balance, execution, and scale it is a mature artistic tradition, demonstrating grand themes through aesthetically satisfying forms [5.6].

With Olmec culture, Mesoamerica joined other emergent civilizations in other parts of the world, where massive architecture and imposing graphic and plastic works expressed the fusion of spiritual and social power (see box, overleaf). Public expressions of secular and sacred strength are common in complex societies. Think of the pyramids of ancient Egypt, or a more recent example, the Capitol of the United States. This is a huge Neo-Classical building situated on a low hill dominating the capital city of the world's most powerful country. In executing this design on a massive scale and in a commanding place, Americans appropriated the ideals of Greek building design and democracy while showing off America's growing wealth and influence.

Living with such iconic architectural and artistic measures of societal complexity, we use them as shorthand for understanding other aspects of the society, features we may have no way of measuring, such as the extent and nature of political power and interregional interactions. Important Mesoamerican archaeological traits signalling complexity, beginning with the Olmecs, were also monumental constructions, often focused on plazas, and accompanied by "monumental and portable art which served ritual, dynastic, or other functions; ceramics bearing iconographic motifs; figurines; and the use of jade and greenstone as precious, status items" (Grove 1981: 374). We will return to the types and meanings of Olmec art after looking at the larger cultural context: landscape and sites.

5.6 *These jade ear spools, their incised designs highlighted with cinnabar, are a pair found under the floor of Tomb C at La Venta. Although no trace of a body remained, the ear spools were found 15 cm (c. 6 in) apart, suggesting that they were part of the ornaments of a high-status individual buried in the tomb.*

EARLY OLMECS AND THEIR NEIGHBORS

Subsistence in the Isthmus

Communities in the southern Gulf lowlands region of the Isthmus were along rivers. Farmers used ground-stone axes to clear the tropical forest along the rivers by slash-and-burn techniques; soil would be annually replenished by river flooding, resulting in high agricultural productivity. Maize was apparently cultivated from the time of earliest occupations at Gulf lowlands sites, and improved maize varieties may have been traded from the Central Highlands through the Gulf lowlands and then onto the Soconusco-Pacific Coast, where the appearance of grinding tools is accompanied by ceramics of Gulf lowlands style (Grove 1981: 389). The trade for seeds of highland maize may have accompanied trade in obsidian, which, for the Gulf lowlands, was oriented toward Central Highlands sources, further securing cultural interactions between those adjacent regions. Obsidian chips have been found at some sites; they may have been embedded into pieces of wood, making graters to process manioc, a starchy edible root crop.

Spiritually Charged Landscape

The Early Formative period also witnessed the crystallization of several generalized landscape features as crucial to Mesoamerican spiritual well-being: mountains, caves, and water sources (particularly springs). In Aztec times, the term denoting "city-state" was composed of the words "water" and "mountain" to express the convergence of water, the precious essence of life, with the mountain around which powerful spiritual forces gather. These traditions of veneration have very ancient roots, and we see artistic and ritual expression of such beliefs in the early Olmecs.

The Aztecs also held caves to be sacred, apparently for the same reasons as did the Olmecs and other Mesoamericans: caves represent passageways to the interior of the living earth, and are orifices of the earth as a living being. In caves, oracular powers could be actualized by spiritual practitioners – including secular rulers with shamanic powers.

WHAT IS CIVILIZATION?

CIVILIZATION IS NOT one of the basic societal types discussed in Chapter 1, but rather, is a set of features that accompany the more complex types, the ranked chiefdom and especially the stratified state. A civilization may be named for a region, an ethnic group, or, less often, a site ("Teotihuacan civilization"), and it describes an unapologetically elite-oriented view, focusing on the showiest monuments of conspicuous consumption by the powerful, expressed in an unmistakable style. "Maya civilization" calls to mind distinctive and sophisticated architectural and artistic styles, expressed in temple-pyramids and carved stelae. These are instantly recognizable both as characteristically Maya, and also as well-known types of elite wealth display that are similar in form and function to the temples and pyramids and sculpted monuments of ancient Egypt and Sumer.

These monuments glorify the power of one stratum of a stratified state, the rulers, over the rest of the strata, the farmer-artisans and even slaves whose surplus food and goods support the rulers and their entourage. However, the surplus produced by those peasants and slaves is another, less showy, essential part of civilization. A civilization's monumental art and architecture, buildings serving civic and ceremonial functions, are usually at the centers of cities. Here, "civilization" is stripped down to a checklist in order to understand the organizational signatures of archaeological societies. We look for:

Subsistence

• *Food surpluses* are produced by agriculture, which may feature intensive cultivation and emphasis on staple crops. Surpluses are claimed from farmers as taxes or tribute offerings by administrative institutions that distribute the surpluses to those who do not farm, the elites and specialized workers.

Settlement pattern

• Has at least *three levels* (e.g. cities, towns, and villages) indicating regionally-administered complex political organization.

• Has *cities*: large (at least 5,000 people), densely populated settlements with different and more complex functions than rural settlements, and neighborhoods that are distinguished by artisanal specialization or ethnicity.

Economic organization

• Marked *differential access to key resources.*

• *Complex division of labor*: specialized goods and services are provided by specially trained individuals, *occupational specialists*, in contrast to the majority of the population making a living as farmer-artisans. Occupational specialists include ritual and administrative specialists, merchants, full-time artisans.

• *Long-distance trade and commerce*: regularized and conducted for profit, often involving luxury goods.

Political organization

• Permanent formal institutions used by rulers to maintain the structure of the *state*, and to maintain internal order and external relations. Rulers hold legitimized *power* to inflict damage on those opposing their will.

Social organization

• *Stratified* socially, with sharply delineated, usually endogamous *social classes*, headed by an economically and socially dominant ruling class (elites).

• Overall increased importance of *economic status* and *place of residence* as integrating mechanisms in society, with importance of kinship limited to intra-class integration.

Ideological principles, intellectual traditions

• *State religion* coexists with and may demand precedence over older folk traditions like family ancestor veneration, promoting instead reverence centralized toward a hierarchy of authorities who are usually members of the elite class by reason of birth or from the material wealth they control by virtue of wealth of the formal religion. *Public ceremonies* and *festivals* focus attention on state cults and rulership, while demonstrating wealth and occasionally sharing its effects with commoners.

• Use of *writing* and/or other record-keeping, and other intellectual achievements such as *arithmetic, astronomy, calendrics*, developed and used by trained intellectual practitioners in the service of the elite class, sometimes including members of the elite working as scribes etc.

• *Monumental public architecture* for use by elites in civic and ceremonial duties and as residences.

• *Distinctive and sophisticated art styles* used by elites to express their power to command resources, particularly luxury goods of all kinds (from palaces to gem stones). Such art styles are sometimes called "Great Traditions," the singular, readily recognizable forms and designs that we associate with a mature complex society.

As we shall see, Mesoamerican societies offer a range of expressions of these traits. The Olmecs, for example, had sophisticated artistic styles and monumental structures, but their largest centers seem not to have been true cities, occupational specialization was not elaborate, and achievements such as writing and calendrics were in a nascent state. From this we can infer that Olmec society supported an influential elite group, but its social organization was probably characterized by ranking rather than stratification, and it was probably not governed as a state. Thus Olmec civilization would be termed emergent rather than fully developed.

Colossal Heads and Buried Drains: Monumental Display at San Lorenzo Tenochtitlán

San Lorenzo is the most important Early Formative site in Mesoamerica. Occupation of the area around San Lorenzo had begun by the Initial Formative (Ojochí phase, 1500–1350 BC), as village farming spread throughout the Isthmus. Early ceramics bear similarities to the very elegant contemporaneous material from the Soconusco and adjacent regions (see Chapter 4), but were simpler, "a kind of country cousin of that more spectacular culture" (Coe 1981:123). The next phase (Bajío, 1350–1250 BC) literally set the stage for Olmec culture: construction of the massive (1,200 m by 600 m; 3,937 by 1,969 ft) platform, rising 50 m (164 ft) above the surrounding landscape [5.7]. This was "largely a natural eminence consisting of Tertiary clays and bentonites, but covered with up to 7 m of artificial fill" (ibid.: 119), and upon its summit, the Olmec center we know as San Lorenzo would be built. This was the earliest monumental project of its size, and demonstrated that the rulers of the site could command and organize very large labor parties, representing "far more a 'quantum jump' than many of the innovations a century or more later which initiated the San Lorenzo (Olmec) phase" (Grove 1981: 377).

The site's plan shows the platform's deeply fissured edges, which its earliest excavators thought resulted from erosion. Later investigation showed that these were deliberate landscape modifications, perhaps in certain cases serving the same purpose as modern shipping piers or docks, to facilitate receipt of building and sculpture materials and trade goods destined for the center's elite, who lived along the top of these fingers of land extending out from the platform on the west side. The entire platform has certain symmetrical features – several sets of mirror-image ridges – but the shape has defied interpretation as an effigy.

Beyond the platform itself, San Lorenzo offers few clues as to Early Formative architecture. Only the North, Central, and South Plazas/Courtyards have been identified as features of Initial Olmec-period San Lorenzo. Quite possibly, Olmec-era civic-ceremonial structures extended along this axis, but their presence, size, orientation, and layout must remain conjectural.

After the Chicharras phase (1250–1150 BC) during which monumental sculptures began to be carved, the center's apogee was achieved in the San Lorenzo phase (1150–900 BC), during which most of its monuments were created, such as the "colossal heads" diagnostic of Olmec culture of the southern Gulf lowlands, and "[u]nusual engineering projects were carried out, such as the system of stone drains ... and the complex of artificial ponds which seem to have been controlled by such drains" (Coe 1981: 128).

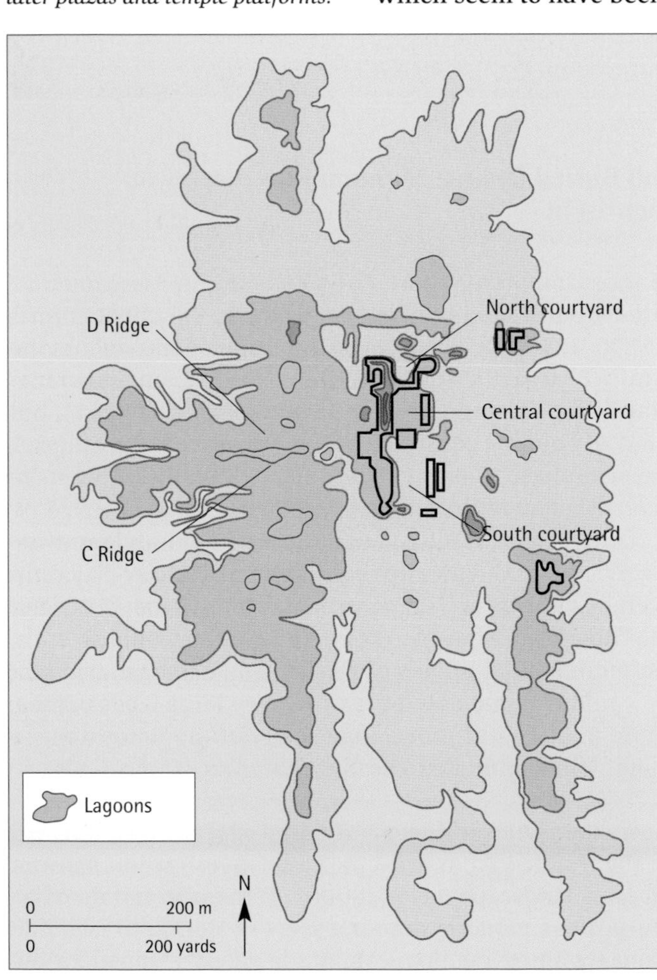

5.7 *San Lorenzo was built atop a plateau that the Olmecs modified by "constructing six outwardly projecting, artificial ridges" (Diehl and Coe 1996: 14) of which only "D Ridge" has been investigated. D Ridge itself measures about 200 m long by 50 m wide by 6.5 m high, an earthmoving project involving 67,000 cubic m of soil. The Early Formative modifications to the plateau as a whole were very impressive, but it should be noted that the "North," "Central," and "South" courts shown on the plan are but vestiges of the ceremonial architecture of this early period. They were covered over by much later plazas and temple platforms.*

Much of this monumental sculpting and landscaping used basalt, but the area around San Lorenzo lacks native stone. Basalt was brought from Cerro Cintepec in the Tuxtla Mountains, about 50 km (31 miles) to the northwest. The stones were transported mostly by raft, taking advantage of the myriad waterways in this marshy region. This was no small feat, as some of the monuments weighed over 20 tons, and "would have to have been pulled on rollers through a vertical distance of some 50 m. Almost certainly this involved the coerced or inveigled labor of hundreds or perhaps even thousands of laborers" (Coe 1981: 141).

Again, let us note that monumental construction in all its phases uses lots of labor, and that people in egalitarian societies do not, as a rule, produce such monuments because there are no effective means for organizing and marshaling a large labor force. Each time- and labor-consuming step of the process is further evidence that San Lorenzo's rulers held considerable power.

For example, not only was stone imported to be used for sculpture glorifying the rulers, but it was also imported to be used for construction of elite residences, such as the "Red Palace" [**5.8**]. Near this residence, one of several "scattered across the central upper portion of the site, where most of the sculptures are found"

5.8 *At San Lorenzo, excavations at the "Red Palace" offer a rare look inside residential architecture at this site. It "shows the ostentatious use of stone elements such as columns, aqueducts, and step coverings" (Cyphers 1996: 65) – all of which were expensive to build, using imported stone. The curved drain and massive columns express, in a domestic context, Olmec aesthetic emphases upon monumentality and appealing curvilinear form.*

(Cyphers 1996: 65) were the Basalt Workshop and Monument Reworking Workshop, the locations indicating that these materials and their execution into monuments were under elite control. Despite the paucity of architectural remains of civic-ceremonial structures at San Lorenzo, important features have been recovered, such as floors of a quality far beyond the usual layer of packed brown clay. Some had a layer of red ochre or white clay (bentonite), and this practice signals an Olmec penchant for care devoted to pavements.

Commoner neighborhoods were located on the sides of and around the plateau, yet at present there is no comprehensive reconstruction of the size of the commoner population or their lifeways. Given the terrain, vegetative cover, and ephemeral nature of vernacular architecture, such evidence may never be recovered, and San Lorenzo's commoners – lifeways and extent of population – may only be understood by extrapolation from other evidence [**5.9**].

The top of the plateau is pocked with ponds (called *lagunas* by the site's excavators) which probably were dug to provide some of the materials to build platforms and pyramidal structures. However, some of these were stone-lined, using expensive imported material, and connected to stone-lined drains. Stone-lined drains run through the "Red Palace," and the modified ponds may have had ritual uses, in ceremonies venerating water or demonstrating control over the flow of water, as well as the utilitarian purpose of providing readily accessible water for cleaning and bathing.

5.9 *The seated figure, San Lorenzo Monument 10, is nearly 119 cm (4 ft) high. It was recovered from a ravine on the San Lorenzo plateau. Bearing the familiar cleft head and snarling mouth, this individual's hands are encased in "knuckle-dusters," a term Olmec scholars use to describe these implements, depicted in art but not found as artifacts at Olmec sites. Their function is not known; scholars have suggested that they might be wood-working tools, or even "knuckle-dusters" – paraphernalia for fighting.*

Other Nearby Olmec sites: Potrero Nuevo and El Azuzul

The area surrounding San Lorenzo included smaller communities and special purpose sites (Symonds 2000). "San Lorenzo" is often called "San Lorenzo Tenochtitlán" because of the proximity of another site a few kilometers to its north, Tenochtitlán (not to be confused with the Aztec capital), which is also known as Río Chiquito because it lies along the banks of the river Chiquito. Tenochtitlán has large mounds arranged in groups of long platforms that delineate plazas, with pyramidal structures at the ends, but like the civic-ceremonial architecture often shown on plans of San Lorenzo itself, Tenochtitlán's civic-ceremonial focus was of later date, and "much of the site had been rebuilt in the Villa Alta phase [AD 900–1200]" (Coe 1981: 119).

Potrero Nuevo, a few kilometers east of San Lorenzo, is another site largely occupied in the Early Postclassic, but some scholars have associated it with Olmec culture because several Olmec-style monumental sculptures were found there. The San Lorenzo-phase site was very modest, and the monuments probably all originated in San Lorenzo (ibid.: 121).

More clearly contemporaneous with Early Formative San Lorenzo is a site a few kilometers to its south. El Azuzul is on a hill called Loma del Zapote and overlooks the juncture of two rivers, "an ideal strategic location from which San Lorenzo's rulers could have controlled river traffic" (Diehl and Coe 1995: 15). Here monumental sculptures were arranged in a tableau: twin young men face jaguars [5.10]. This scene, interpreted with our

5.10 *Atop Loma del Zapote, a ceremonial complex called El Azuzul overlooked approaches to San Lorenzo, greeting visitors with the sight of sculptures of twins in a ceremonial, perhaps transformational posture, facing sculptures of jaguars. This is a staged scene, and such grouped arrangements of sculptures are characteristic of the Olmecs. In this case, the scene calls to mind "later period myths about twins and jaguars, the most notable of which is the [Maya]* Popol Vuh*'s tale of the Hero Twins" (Cyphers 1996: 68).*

present knowledge of Olmec iconography, offers the powerful images of duality and shamanic transformation, as indicated by the postures of the figures and the juxtaposition of men and felines. Its setting, on a highly visible strategic point, and its monumental scale would have announced to all who approached San Lorenzo from the highlands that they were entering a realm ruled by humans who could command the labor of master artisans, and whose supernatural alter egos possessed great power.

El Manatí

One of the landscape features seen from San Lorenzo is El Manatí, a hill with freshwater springs at its base, about 20 km (12 miles) to the southeast. Thus the site combined two essential elements of the sacred landscape, mountain and water. At these springs, rituals were held during the Initial Olmec period, perhaps as early as 1500 BC. Offerings were made there, and consisted of carved stone items (figures and a palette-like carved footprint), dozens of carved wooden statues in Olmec style [**5.11**], rubber balls, and the bones of children (Ortíz and Rodríguez 2000). In Aztec times it was the practice in the Central Highlands to sacrifice children to water gods at springs and whirlpools, and the tears of the panicked children were regarded as a sympathetic magic to encourage the flow of natural water. El Manatí is not only important as a ritual site from this early period, but its unusual conditions of preservation have protected from decay many artifacts made of organic materials.

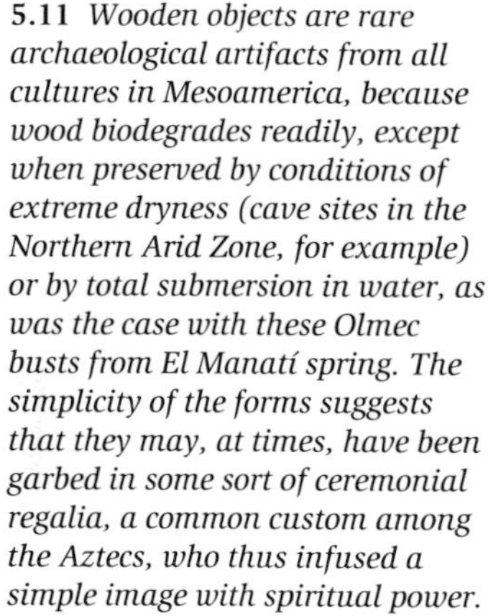

5.11 *Wooden objects are rare archaeological artifacts from all cultures in Mesoamerica, because wood biodegrades readily, except when preserved by conditions of extreme dryness (cave sites in the Northern Arid Zone, for example) or by total submersion in water, as was the case with these Olmec busts from El Manatí spring. The simplicity of the forms suggests that they may, at times, have been garbed in some sort of ceremonial regalia, a common custom among the Aztecs, who thus infused a simple image with spiritual power.*

COLOSSAL HEADS

THE OLMECS have gained fame as sculptors in various media, at all scales from statuettes hardly larger than a man's thumb to massive thrones/altars weighing more than 50 tons. Their most famous sculptures are colossal heads. The first to be discovered was found in the mid-19th century; the top, just visible, was thought to be the base of a huge kettle. Since then, 17 in all have come to light.

They have long been recognized as the portraits of men in their prime, probably the rulers of the sites where they were found – San Lorenzo, La Venta, Tres Zapotes and neaby Cobata. They wear helmetlike headgear, possibly the protective garb of ball players. Some also wear ear spools or earflares, which were polished stone ornaments, fitted into enlarged holes in the ear lobes. The faces are fairly flat, and the features, worked in bas-relief, are large. The backs of the heads are flatter than the fronts.

Realistic portraiture is never easy, because great skill is required to express vivid individuality without crude stylistic simplifications. Some of the colossal head portraits succeed better than others in this task, with the least masterly (and one of the largest, about 2.7 m, or 9 ft tall) being the Cobata monument, and the most sensitive portraits being San Lorenzo Heads 1 and 2.

We know little about the life cycle of a colossal head. Scholars have noted that they may have been reworked from the large sculpted blocks long called altars that actually may have served as the thrones of particular rulers. La Venta's "Altar 4" for example was large enough for such reworking, and a head may have been sculpted from the throne to commemorate a rite of passage in the ruler's life, or to commemorate his death.

The mode of display is not clear, nor is it even clear that they were displayed. Some have been found buried: in San Lorenzo the heads perhaps formed a linear buried arrangement, but the nature of this deposition is difficult to interpret. At La Venta a head was found at the base of the pyramid, and given the Olmec predilection for using sculptures as combined elements in dramatic scenarios (see La Venta discussion, Chapter 6),

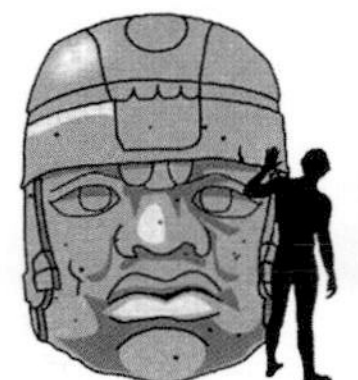

San Lorenzo

1 2 3 4 5 6 7 8 9

we would expect that the heads may have advertised the power of a community's ruling lineage to produce a strong sequence of rulers. The pockmarks that indicate mutilation of these sculptures may have been made in the course of ritual desanctification. Or they may have been the marks of disrespect, made by outsiders – enemies of the community – or by members of a rival faction within the community, grasping power from the established rulers. In time, some colossal heads were probably broken up, serving as raw materials for smaller sculptures or for tools such as grinding stones.

5.12–5.14 *The 17 known Olmec colossal heads date from the Early Formative period. Included here are examples from La Venta, which will be discussed in Chapter 6. The colossal heads were made from basalt, the source of the San Lorenzo heads being Cerro Cintepec in the Tuxtla Mountains. The materials were probably transported to the Olmec centers via the network of rivers in the southern Gulf lowlands, and the reconstruction drawing shows a colossal head and an altar (or throne) being moved on rafts by cadres of farmers recruited for public service when their seasonal agricultural duties are completed. The portrait bust, from San Lorenzo, is of one of that center's rulers – his helmet may be ball game regalia.*

10

Tres Zapotes

1

2

Cobata

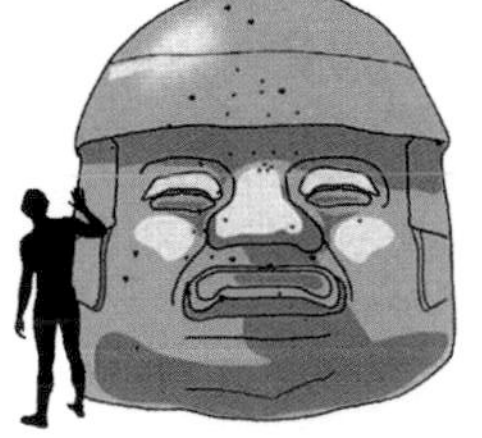

1

La Venta

1

2

3

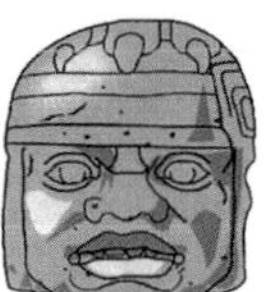

4

Themes and Modes in Olmec Art

Having gained some familiarity with San Lorenzo and its neighbors, let us return to a more general discussion of Olmec art. Certain themes recur and intertwine, some are already apparent in the Early Formative, and many have been related to veneration of maize. Among the most important of these themes are:

- monumental architectural format: immense constructed platforms, topped by platform mounds that flank plazas;
- monumental sculpture, depicting sacralized secular power, for example, the colossal heads, and "altars" that are thought to have functioned as thrones;
- curvilinear sculptural style, often depicting humans or human-beast hybrids, with facial features that may include: pudgy face with snarling, fanged mouth, almond-shaped eyes, flame eyebrows, and cleft forehead;
- transformation/reworking of monuments, for example, "altars" that were reworked into colossal heads;
- spatial arrangement of sculptural elements into a tableau, for example, colossal heads, the El Azuzul twins;
- transformation/shamanic transformation, including postures of transformation, for example, the El Azuzul twins in feline pose, facing a jaguar;
- veneration of twins and duality, for example, the El Azuzul twins;
- veneration through offerings and sacrifice: autosacrifice, human sacrifice, as at El Manatí; offering of limp creature [**5.5**]; and
- infants and children as agents of sacred power: child sacrifices as at El Manatí, children depicted in sculpted, hollow figurines (there are widespread examples of these, for example as found at Las Bocas [Puebla], Etlatongo [Mixteca Alta; Blomster 1998]).

Shamans and Transformation

Important related themes in Olmec art are power and transformation, particularly the power gained through the transformation of an individual into a supernatural alter ego, a "co-essence" known to Mesoamericanist scholars as a *nagual*, from the Aztec term for this phenomenon, *nahualli*. The Maya term, *uay* (pron. *why*), is also used. The *nagual* could move in two worlds, that of everyday events and that of spiritual forces. Archaeologically speaking, we seek evidence of effective claims to such power in the massive monumental architecture and sculpture that the Olmecs brought into Mesoamerican culture, and we seek that power's basis through artistic depictions of powerful beings, be they sculptured portraits of mature men in high-status garb, or of were-beings seeming to fuse the traits of jaguars and humans. Scholars believe that the political power expressed in civic-ceremonial complexes and luxury goods is based in the effective expression of shamanic powers, perhaps the power to control agricultural fertility.

HIGHLAND DEVELOPMENTS, WEST OF THE ISTHMUS

Settlement Patterns and Settlement Systems

The distribution of archaeological sites over a landscape tells us much about the society that produced it. First, because ancient farming peoples with limited transportation usually lived close to their fields, we can study differences in agricultural productivity as a rough measure of access to key resources by different communities. Second, because societal complexity is reflected in community size, the pattern of site sizes reveals the mode of sociopolitical complexity. As we have noted, egalitarian tribal villages are generally all the same size, and distributed over the landscape so as to maximize each village's usable land while maintaining autonomy from the other villages (see table, p. 24). When a much larger community emerges, in a central place among smaller farming villages, we take it as evidence of political ranking, and that the site is a "capital" ruled by a lineage which has firmly established its hereditary right to draw upon the resources of its region.

Oaxaca: San José Phase (1150–850 BC)

The size and monumentality of San Lorenzo in the southern Gulf lowlands indicate that it served as a capital for its region, yet we know little about the surrounding communities that supported it, or the process by which San Lorenzo assumed ascendancy. The picture is much clearer in the Valley of Oaxaca, where that region's emergent Zapotec civilization experienced a "defining moment" at the start of the San José phase (1150–850 BC) (Marcus and Flannery 1996: 93). The settlement system focusing on San José Mogote is one of the most important indicators of the emergence of ranking here [**5.15**]. Furthermore, archaeologists believe that crop productivity may have been increased with the initiation of two simple irrigation methods that are still in use in this region: "pot irrigation" which involves digging many shallow wells and scooping up the water for use on the surrounding plants, and also irrigation ditches, small-scale systems tapping water from streams to flow over the fields.

San José Mogote and Tierras Largas Over the course of the San José phase, the population of the Oaxaca Valley tripled, with 2,000 people living in about 40 communities, twice as many as in the previous phase. Even more impressive was the concentration of half the Valley's population into San José Mogote, a village covering 20 hectares (c. 50 acres), with outlying *barrios* (neighborhoods) covering another 40 to 50 hectares (100–125 acres). In contrast, the village of Tierras Largas, only slightly smaller than San José Mogote at the start of this period, remained the same size, a community of about 10 households or fewer (Winter 1976). We would assume that the center of political decision-making for the Valley was at San José

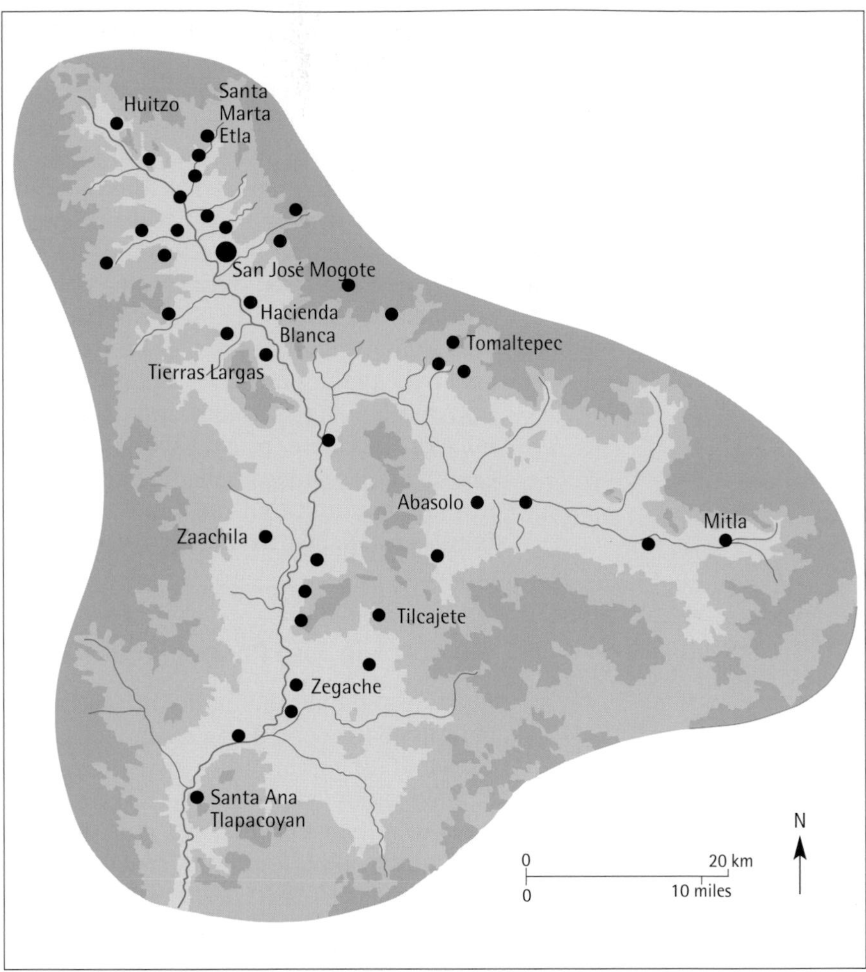

5.15 *Settlements in the Valley of Oaxaca, San José phase (1150–850 BC) were larger and more numerous than before, and they continued to cluster around the best land in the valley: three-quarters of the Oaxaca Valley's other settlements were on or adjacent to first class land (Marcus and Flannery 1996: 106).*

Mogote, with many small villages like Tierras Largas receiving orders and carrying them out.

The archaeological record is biased in favor of the largest sites. San José Mogote is a modest place in comparison with San Lorenzo, and especially in comparison with later central places, real cities. Yet it draws our attention because of its relative significance. However, we must keep in mind that smaller sites like Tierras Largas are also important, and underrepresented in the archaeological record. Tierras Largas shows another basic feature of the foundation of Mesoamerican civilization: the small community that was tributary to the larger, more impressive central community in its region. Elites and their accoutrements depended utterly on the contributions of food, materials, and labor from farmer-artisans in countless small villages. The kinds of houses found in Tierras Largas [**5.16, 5.17**] are much like residences of farming households throughout Mesoamerica, even, in remote rural areas, today.

In each of these houses, the activities range from those which are common to all houses of Mesoamerican farmer-artisans to some which are particular to certain houses within a community where specialists live. Even more unusual are specializations in the production of rare or precious goods, which occurred in a few houses in the larger communities. The activity area of the house consisted not just of the physical structure but also of its surroundings. Within the house's adjacent area, the houselot, were found other features such as ovens, burials, refuse middens, and bell-shaped storage pits, many capable of holding a ton of dried maize, which is enough to support a family of five for a year.

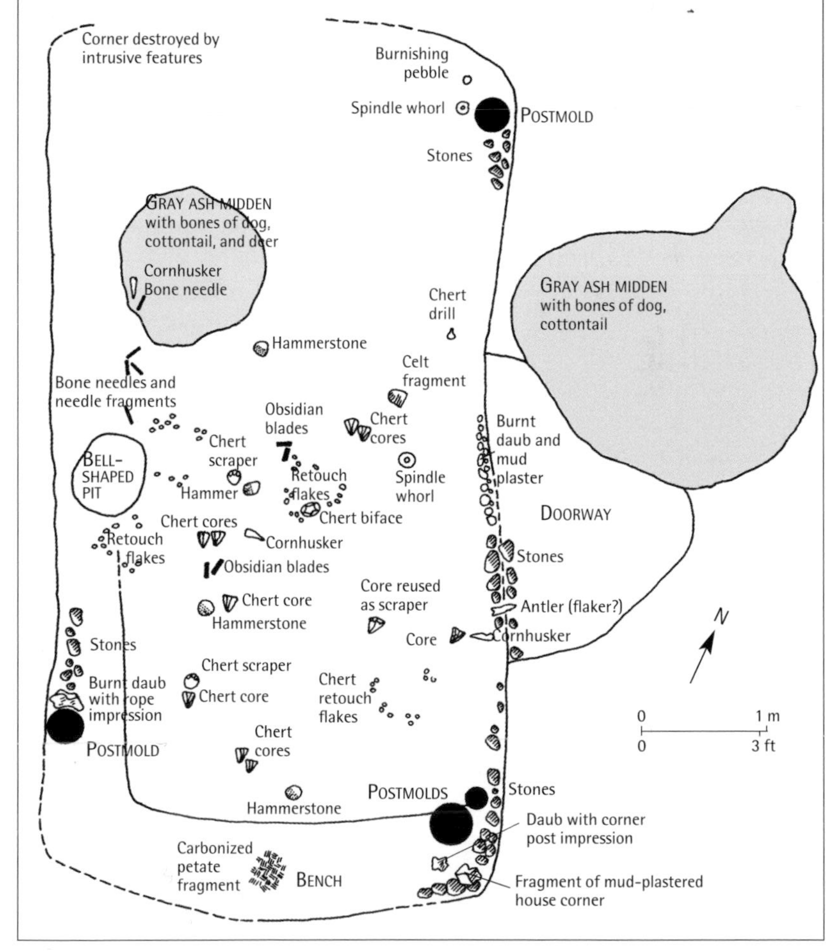

5.16, 5.17 *Tierras Largas, Structure 1, is a modest one-room house, roughly 4 by 8 m (13 by 26 ft), a family's living and working space. The photo shows the house before excavation, but after the overburden of soil had been removed. Stone and bone tools and ceramic remains were recovered, showing activity patterns as revealed in the plan. Universal activities for farmer-artisans include food procurement, preparation and storage, and preparation and retouching of certain tools. Some households in a community may specialize in the production of stone or bone tools, leatherworking, or pottery.*

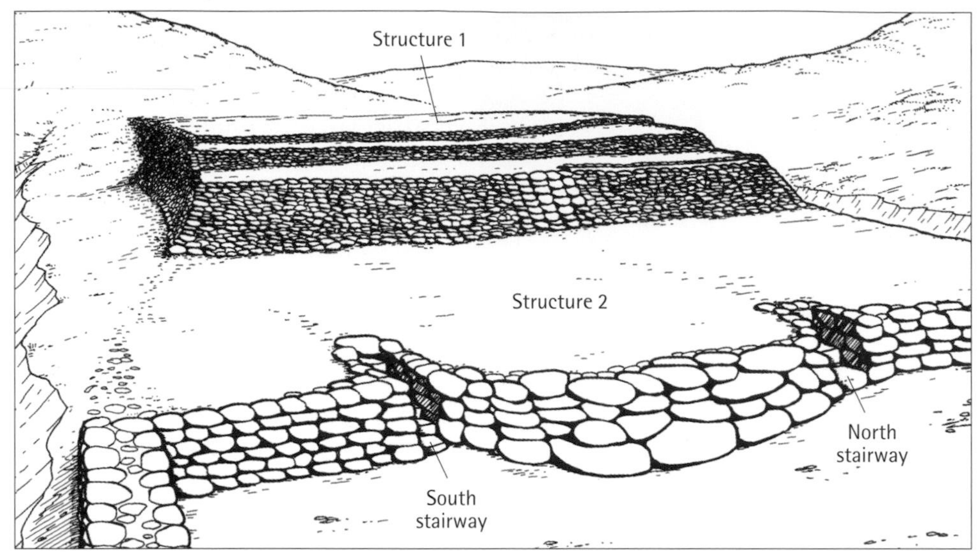

5.18 *San José Mogote, Structures 1 and 2 together form an impressive monumental structure. The platforms supported public-scale buildings that have been destroyed; they were made of wattle-and-daub with the innovation of bun-shaped adobe bricks. Public-scale buildings can serve as a united focus for an ethnically diverse community.*

5.19 *(Opposite left) Motifs on pottery vessels in the Oaxaca Valley during the San José phase draw upon Olmec icons of lightning (as a fire-serpent, top) and earthquake (as an Olmec supernatural with cleft head, fourth from top). Many smaller communities had one motif or the other on their pots, but only the central community, San José Mogote, had significant proportions of pottery of both types.*

Other Indicators of Ranking: Substance and Symbols San José Mogote also had many small houses of the kind excavated at Tierras Largas. San José was not only large and internally diverse, with neighborhoods of differing density, but its houses varied as to size and quality of finishing. Men of the community had at least one special meeting hall, rebuilt over the years. Even more impressive, a multi-level construction, Structures 1 and 2, rose several meters in height, with a platform 18 m (*c.* 60 ft) across [**5.18**]. The structure was faced with cobbles and boulders, some brought from 5 km (*c.* 3 miles) away. The scale of the building and importation of the building materials implies that San José Mogote's leaders were able to command the cooperation of people in the surrounding countryside (Marcus and Flannery 1996: 109–110).

The means by which the mass of people come to carry out the will of the few operates differently in different societies, but all known cases in the history of humankind seem to involve some degree of coercion – psychological and/or physical. As we noted earlier, sometimes this occurs because growing population densities no longer permit bickering factions within a tribal village to simply part ways and seek new land to cultivate. The weaker faction submits to the will of the stronger.

The stronger faction may have developed its strength through a combination of factors: canny choices of farm plots, good alliance-building tactics, sheer luck, healthy offspring of both sexes – boys to serve as the next generation's leaders, girls to give in marriage to strong allies. Also, as we have seen evidenced at Paso de la Amada and San Lorenzo, power is gained by association with potent natural and supernatural forces. Throughout the volatile landscape of Mesoamerica, the forces controlling earth and sky controlled human destiny as well. Motifs used on pottery vessels in the Valley of Oaxaca in the Early Formative may indicate that identification with the

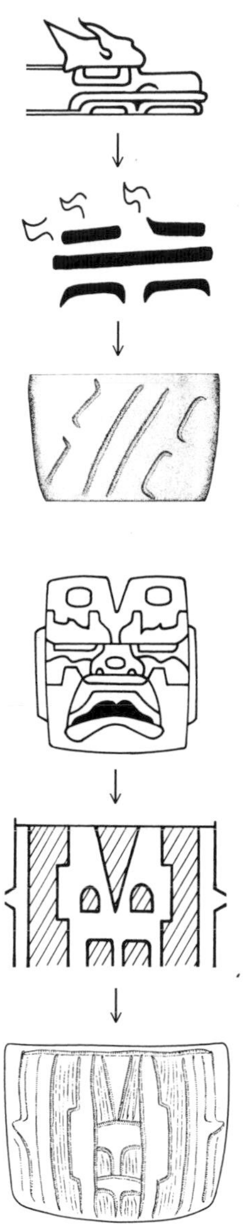

forces of earth and sky by different factions served as a kind of nascent ethnic consciousness [**5.19**]. The two different pottery motifs were stylized versions of earthquakes and lightning. "These two motifs were almost mutually exclusive in their distribution" across the landscape (Marcus and Flannery 1996: 96), with small villages tending to have the vessels with lightning motifs, Tierras Largas having pottery that heavily favored the earthquake motif, and San José Mogote having both, and materials from "the burials and the household refuse reflect this dichotomy of ancestral 'celestial spirits.'" (ibid.).

The motifs seem to demonstrate shared ideology with Olmec culture of the Gulf lowlands. What motivated contact between these regions? Propinquity of these two regions with their distinctive resources would account for contact; the Valley of Oaxaca was the highland region closest to the southern Gulf lowlands. Early Formative exchange networks linked many regions: the map [**5.20**] shows the area over which items were traded in the Early Formative (Niederberger 1987: 727; Wheeler 1976: 326).

Obsidian and pottery moved over these distances. One Oaxacan product that found its way east was the polished stone mirror. Iron ores were a local Oaxacan product, and San José Mogote was a center of production for mirrors, several of which have been found in San Lorenzo. We have no direct evidence documenting how long-distance movement of goods took place in the Early Formative. Possibly, itinerant traders carried small, high-quality items such as polished mirrors from Oaxaca or shell from the Pacific Coast. Imagine the scene: the lords of San Lorenzo eagerly watch the traders unload their pack, perhaps hoping for the perfect mirror in which to find the perfect transcendent vision of the supernatural world.

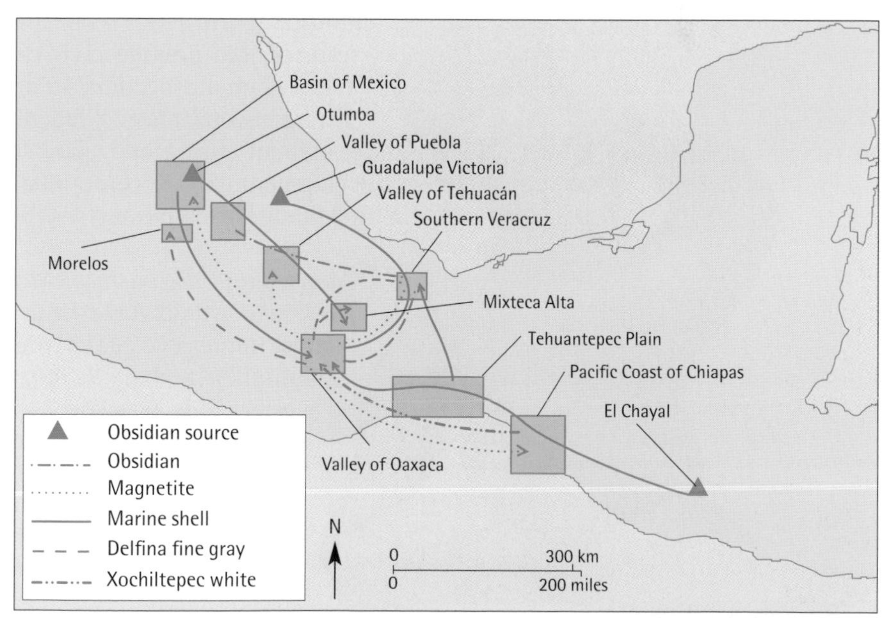

5.20 *(Right) Early Formative trade networks linked most of Mesoamerica. Obsidian procurement was one of the major motivating factors, and this established routes along which other goods, such as pottery vessels, traveled. In addition to raw materials and finished products, ideas and iconography moved over great distances.*

Elsewhere in the Central Highlands: Puebla, Morelos, and the Basin of Mexico

Traders moved up between the Gulf lowlands and the Central Highlands over several main routes. One ran west, then north through the Tehuacán Valley into the broad plain of southern Puebla and eastern Morelos. From there, the Basin of Mexico was reached by the Amecameca Pass.

These highland valleys and basins were experiencing the same kinds of population growth and settlement expansion as the Valley of Oaxaca, a phenomenon possibly related to a cooler, wetter interval in the climate cycle of the Central Highlands *c.* 900–800 BC (Messenger 1990). Larger communities served as centers for clusters of small villages. *Milpas* surrounded the villages, and terrace systems made hill slopes productive, channeling rainfall runoff as soils deepened.

Puebla In the Tlatempa phase (1200–800 BC), southern Puebla's hills were dotted with villages where farmers had built up farm plots behind low stone terraces, using simple irrigation canals to water these fields. Several sites emerged as pivotal to exchange between the highlands and Gulf lowlands. Las Bocas was in a strategic location on this route, but this small site is poorly understood, in part because it has been so thoroughly looted, in modern times, for its ceramic sculptures [5.21].

Morelos In the Early Formative period, Morelos was settled by sedentary farmers. Amate-phase (1500–1100 BC) villages were small, with only 100–200 inhabitants, but in the Barranca phase (1100–700 BC), Chalcatzingo became the largest site in its region, with a population of several hundred (Hirth 1987: 353), and modifications to the hill slope, terraces that presage civic-ceremonial architecture. This site had a dramatic location, 40 km (*c.* 25 miles) west of Las Bocas, where several steep-sided hills punctuate the plain, with a permanent spring and good land for farming. Chalcatzingo's development of civic-ceremonial architecture reached its apogee in the Middle Formative and will be discussed in detail in Chapter 6.

Morelos and the Basin of Mexico The view north from Chalcatzingo would have been dominated by one of Mexico's most impressive peaks, the active volcano Popocatépetl, its summit less than 50 km (*c.* 31 miles) away. At Popo's western side was the Amecameca Pass, linking Morelos, with its more tropical climate, with the high-altitude Basin of Mexico (see below). In the last chapter, we noted that village agriculture came later to the Basin than it did to Morelos, and in fact the complex of pottery-using sedentary farming may have been introduced to the Basin from Morelos.

5.21 *Las Bocas, a small site on the trade route between the southern Gulf lowlands and the Central Highlands, became famous in modern times as a source of Olmec-style ceramic sculptures. These hollow figurines, many with infantile features, may possibly have been ritually important, recalling the infant sacrifices at the El Manatí shrine to water deities. Las Bocas has been a victim of the modern art market's voracious appetite for looted antiquities; there is some small consolation to be had in realizing that many more "Las Bocas" figures have been sold than can ever have been associated with the site.*

Coapexco Coapexco, located in the Amecameca Pass, was one of the oldest villages in the Basin, but apparently was only occupied for about 100 years around 1150 BC. In spite of this brief period, it may have had a sizable population, perhaps 1,000, living in several dozen houses extending over 44 hectares (109 acres) (Tolstoy 1989; Tolstoy and Fish 1975). Coapexco was far from the lake around which settlements like Zohapilco/Tlapacoya flourished. It was, however, on the main route linking the Basin with the southern Gulf Lowlands, via the Valley of Morelos. While there is no evidence of civic-ceremonial architecture, differences among households are indicated by house size and quality of artifacts, and the San Lorenzo Olmec tradition is reflected in ceramics and figurines.

The Basin of Mexico in the Early Formative The period from about 1200 to 800 BC comprises the Ixtapaluca, Ayotla (1250–1000 BC), and Manatial (1000–800 BC) phases (with some overlap among them) and also part of what has been termed Phase 1 of the Basin's First Intermediate period. During this time, the Basin had experienced considerable population growth, with the south having over 90 percent of the population. In the more arid north, the only settlements were tiny, while the south, its climate more amenable to rainfall cultivation, saw the growth of villages, some having over 1,000 people. As population size and community size increased, the spacing between sites decreased, yet no communities seem to have assumed the role of regional center, and none had civic-ceremonial architecture. Close to the lake are several small Early Formative sites. At El Terremote and Santa Catarina, remains of houses, storage pits, and other domestic refuse have been found, along with remains of maize (Tolstoy *et al.* 1977).

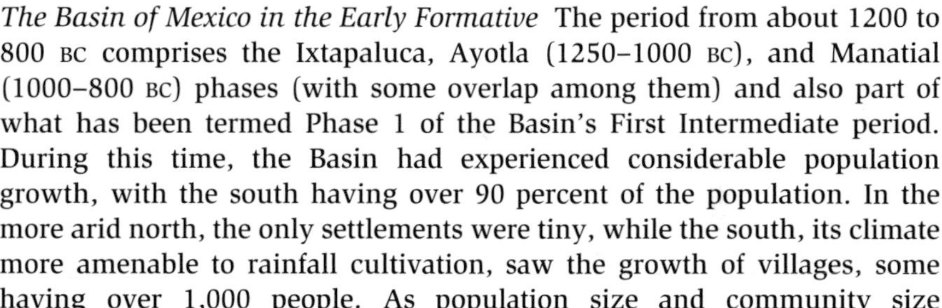

5.22 *Tlatilco's cemetery was used repeatedly as indicated by the photo of skeletal remains which overlie each other. Note that there is no single preferred orientation for interment of these bodies; these are "extended burials" in the sense that the skeletons are stretched out in a supine position ("flexed burials" occur when the body is interred in a fetal position). Ceramic vessels were among the mortuary goods buried with the dead.*

Two important Early Formative centers in the Basin were Tlatilco and Cuicuilco. The latter site is famous as the Late-Formative-period rival of Teotihuacan, a rivalry lost as the volcano Xitle covered Cuicuilco with a thick coat of lava and ash. This dramatic story is featured in Chapter 8; our knowledge of Cuicuilco prior to its apogee and demise is extrapolated from the bits of evidence jack-hammered out of one of the toughest excavation venues in all archaeology. About Tlatilco's Early Formative career, somewhat more is known.

Tlatilco Tlatilco, in the western Basin, was on the piedmont slope above the lake system. The site comprises as many as three small villages and an extensive cemetery [**5.22**]. The site's importance is due more to the rich Early Formative materials it has supplied than to its political position among its Early Formative neighbors.

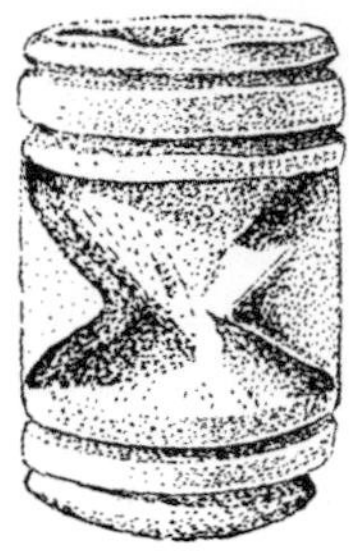

5.23 *(Above) Tlatilco's ceramics included stamps as well as pots and figurines. Stamps were usually made of clay – sometimes of stone – and were used from the Early Formative through the Late Postclassic. These roller stamp examples are reminiscent of roller seals from ancient Mesopotamia, which were used to impress into wet clay a mark of ownership. Roller seals in Mesoamerica are not known to have had that function; their distribution at Tlatilco indicates use by all members of society, not just the more affluent. They, and flat stamps, may have been used to apply paint or ink to the skin or to cloth. Roller stamps seem to "occur in greatest quantity in Central Mexico (Valley of Mexico, Morelos, Puebla) in the Early Formative (to* c. *900* BC*)" (Grove 1987: 274). Thereafter, flat stamps predominate.*

Tlatilco was first excavated by brick workers in the early 20th century, who mined its soil for building materials. The whole vessels and jade pieces they encountered quickly drew the attention of collectors of pre-Columbian antiquities. Miguel Covarrubias, an artist and visionary ethnologist of ancient Mesoamerican life, recognized that the vessels and figurines were similar to artifacts from other "Archaic" sites (as Formative-period sites were then called). Years before absolute dating methods confirmed his interpretations, Covarrubias recognized that Olmec culture was the first of the great Mesoamerican cultural horizons, predating Maya culture. Covarrubias became one of the directors of the first controlled excavations at Tlatilco, in the 1940s (Porter [Weaver] 1953).

In all, of an estimated 500 burials in the Tlatilco cemetery, about 375 were documented. An analysis of the sex of interred individuals and the associated grave goods indicated that vessels with Olmec-style motifs were more likely to be buried with women (Tolstoy 1989), a correlation that suggests differential acculturation, if not enculturation, of women into Olmec customs, but this has not been substantiated. Tlatilco potters were sophisticated in their concepts and execution. Other ceramic artifacts included stamps for impressing designs [**5.23**]. In addition to the burials, the site had many bell-shaped storage pits, and some house platforms were also discerned.

Tlatilco's pottery vessels covered a wide range of types, with many effigy vessels of animals, and many composite and inventive shapes [**5.24–5.27**]. The acrobat form is a common theme in Olmec art, and their depiction on effigy vessels illustrates the ancient Mesoamerican preoccupation with shape-changing, as expressed in acrobatic skill. Aztec acrobats so dazzled the Spaniards that they were sent on tour through Europe in AD 1528–1529; Pope Clement VII was so impressed that he thanked God he lived in an age to see such things (Honour 1975: 61). The more subtle, metaphorical meaning of shape-changing relates back to shamanic capabilities and *nagualism*, transformation into the body of an animal alter ego. Sleight-of-hand refers to just one bodily aspect of the magical power to transform one's self; "techniques of shamanic transformation may account for at least some

5.24–5.26 *(Opposite below) Two different examples of Tlatilco's pottery – and* **5.27** *below – reveal great mastery of form and execution. (Opposite left and center) The bottle (c. 17 cm/6.5 in) also has a black slip with a motif of a monster (rollout opposite left) with "flame eyebrows" like the "lightning" motifs on Oaxaca Valley vessels. (Opposite right) The effigy vessel depicts a fish whose open mouth is the vessel's spout (c. 13 cm/5 in). The glossy black finish is not a true glaze – glazes were introduced to the New World after European contact – but is instead a polished slip (clay and pigment in a slurry, a pourable solution, applied to the surface of a vessel).*

of the tumbling figurines and yogalike poses in the art of both the Olmec and the West Mexican shaft tomb people" (Furst 1995: 71).

Tlatilco's Olmec affinities have been strongly emphasized, but, in fact only a small proportion of the vessels recovered are in Gulf lowlands style. Many more show similarities to West Mexican ceramic assemblages, with stirrup-spouted vessels, for example. This points to the diversity of cultural influences characterizing Early Formative Mesoamerica. While Coapexco, at the Basin's southeastern border, seems to have more strongly shared in the collective symbolic system and material culture characterizing Chalcatzingo to the south, and Teopantecuanitlán and San Lorenzo, far beyond, to the southwest and southeast, the western Basin of Mexico's materials resemble West Mexico's and also those of sites such as Gualupita, in northwestern Morelos (in present-day Cuernavaca). Gualupita was another brickyard, notable because its earliest occupation represented the first Early Formative site to be systematically studied (Vaillant and Vaillant 1934).

5.27 *(Below left) The "acrobat" from Tlatilco was among the grave goods of a man whose other funerary offerings suggested that he might be a shaman; the vessel's spout is the opening on the left knee (25 cm/c. 10 in high).*

5.28 *(Below right) Tlatilco's figurines were so abundant that they have become a distinguishing trait of the site. They included Olmec hollow "Las Bocas" types and, more commonly, the "pretty lady" type shown here.*

Northern Arid Zone

In these regions, the harsh aridity of the overall environment favored a continuation of mobile hunter-forager subsistence patterns, even into the Colonial period. Yet people will generally adopt any innovation that makes life easier, and thus it was that maize spread north. There is evidence that maize was being cultivated in the U.S. Southwest, a northern extension of Middle America's Northern Arid Zone, as early as 1200 BC (Smith 1995). This is a good example of the complexity of the mixed strategy: mobile foragers cultivated maize as an additional component of their subsistence strategy, apparently having acquired it from Mesoamerica by down-the-line trade across many hundreds of miles.

West Mexico

There are few Archaic or Initial Formative remains in western Mexico. The earliest occurrence of ceramics, indicating widespread farming villages, seems to date from the Early Formative period, and village farmers apparently entered the region from the southeast, moving west along two routes, establishing the El Opeño culture in the north and the Capacha culture in the south (Mountjoy 1999: 253).

We know about both cultures largely from their burial patterns, and from their grave goods such as ceramic vessels buried with the dead. Of habitation sites, the pioneering farming villages themselves, there is no direct evidence from either region. Perhaps the houses were ephemeral, or are now buried beneath alluvial sediments or later towns. However, both El Opeño and Capacha left distinctive ceramics, the earliest from this region.

El Opeño Culture This culture derives its name from El Opeño and other funerary sites. Beginning around 1500 BC, Opeño peoples cut shaft tombs into the subsoil [**5.29**]. These Opeño-style shaft tombs possibly were antecedents of the Late Formative shaft-tomb tradition in West Mexico (Chapter 7).

In spite of the lack of habitational remains, the tombs have yielded insights into the lives of the earliest settlers of West Mexico (Oliveros 1989). Some of the simple jars and bowls found in the tombs have "incised motifs similar to those commonly found at Olmec sites" and figurines display Olmec-like traits such as cranial deformation (Mountjoy 1998: 254, 253). Some of the human crania themselves have been deformed, a practice common among later Mesoamerican cultures. One cranium had been trepanned. Trepanation – cutting away part of the skull bone around the brain to alleviate discomfort – is a risky business in any cultural setting, but this Opeño individual survived; the cut edges of bone show the signs of having healed.

5.29 *El Opeño culture offered the first manifestation of West Mexico's most famous cultural feature, the shaft tomb. This diagram of Tomb 4 from the Citala area shows the characteristic "short, stepped entryway leading into a single mortuary chamber" (Weigand and Beekman 1998: 36).*

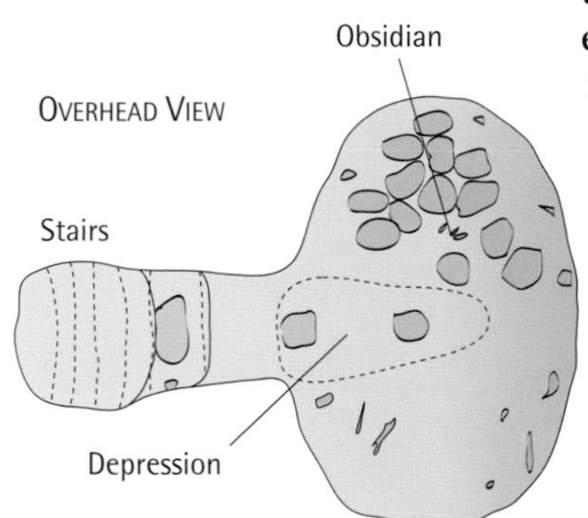

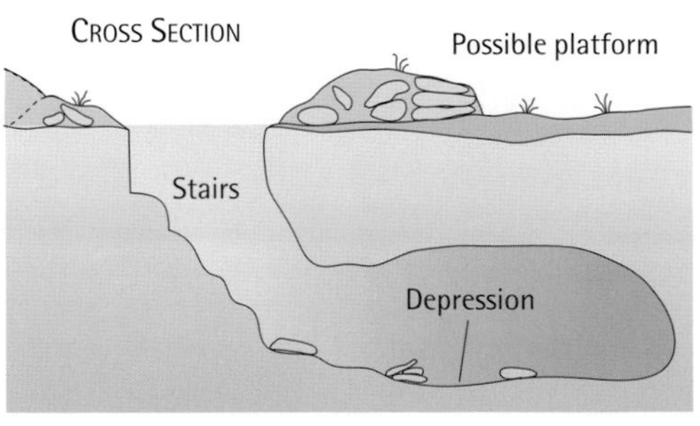

5.30 *These figurines from an El Opeño tomb provide evidence that the ball game was being played in West Mexico, despite the apparent lack of formal ball courts. The original group of 16 figurines, male and female, probably formed a vignette of ball game play among the males, while the female spectators reclined. The males shown here wear leg or knee protectors and hold paddles or "large, heavily padded gloves for hitting the ball" (Day 1998: 153).*

One of the tombs also yielded figurines of ball players [**5.30**], found in association with a miniature piece of ball game equipment. The oldest structural remains of ball courts in West Mexico date from 600 BC, although the game was no doubt played on any cleared level field of the appropriate size. Far away from tropical lowland sources of rubber, West Mexicans may have made balls from a latex-like substance derived from local plants. This material was inferior in its resilience in play to Gulf lowlands rubber; given the Mesoamerican propensity to see the vital spirit in all materials, it is understandable that Isthmian products like rubber would have been avidly sought after all over Mesoamerica.

Capacha Culture About 100 km (*c.* 60 miles) southwest of El Opeño, the Capacha complex of ceramics appeared in Colima in the Early or even Middle Formative, perhaps as early as the Initial Formative. Capacha diagnostic ceramics are from burials, and consist of ceramic vessels with distinctive forms and elaborate surface treatments. Many are gourd-shaped, such as the "bule" (see box, pp. 119–121), while others are complex composites of several chambers linked by tubes, the unusual "trifid" form. The burials themselves are sometimes assumed to have been shaft-and-chamber tombs, but are, rather, simple pits (Kelly 1980).

That graves have been the only source of archaeological materials has of course biased our perception of the extent of Capacha culture. Fine vessels are rare and treasured, that is why they are appropriate grave goods for highly respected individuals. Habitation sites will have some fine wares and then large numbers of plain ware, or utility ware vessels, the everyday cooking and serving and storage vessels used around the house. The lack of good contexts limits archaeological inference concerning proper phases of plain ware sherds found extensively over this region, but probably they represent the utility vessels of the Capacha complex (Mountjoy 2001).

The origin of Capacha materials has been the subject of debate. Based on similarities of some Capacha motifs with those of contemporaneous Machalilla culture of the Pacific Coast of Ecuador, influence from South America has been posited (Kelly 1980), but Capacha materials have more in common with Olmec motifs (Mountjoy 2001). Capacha materials have been found along the Jalisco and Nayarit coasts, dating from the Early, Middle, and Late Formative (*c.* 1200–300 BC).

Guerrero

If one were to retrace the probable origins of the Capacha peoples back to Guerrero, increasing proximity to Guerrero would show increasing evidence of cultural traits shared with the Olmecs of the Gulf lowlands. In spite of Guerrero's broken terrain, this huge region is unified by the drainage systems of the Balsas-Mezcala River, and was a magnet for trading interests as a source of hot climate resources (cotton, cacao, rubber), maritime products like shell, and minerals – metals (silver, gold, copper, and tin), as well as lapidary stones (including varieties of jade-type stones) and finished products like Mezcala masks and figures.

Guerrero's rugged terrain has, throughout Mesoamerican culture history, made access to this region perilous. Portable Olmec-style art objects such as polished stone masks were long known to have come from Guerrero, but because these items were looted, little was known of their provenience. Sedentary village life seems to have begun by 1400 BC (Paradis 2001), but the region's Early Formative mode of social organization was very poorly understood until the recent discovery of the impressive center in eastern Guerrero, Teopantecuanitlán (Martínez Donjuán 1995), which shattered the notion that Guerrero was marginal when compared with other regions of the Olmec world.

Teopantecuanitlán Olmec interaction with Guerrero is apparent at Teopantecuanitlán, which had affiliations with Chalcatzingo (Jiménez García *et al.* 1998: 37), about 80 km (*c.* 50 miles) to the northeast. Teopantecuanitlán lies about 5 miles (8 km) from the confluence of the Amacuzac and Mezcala Rivers, in a mountain valley. Remains cover about 160 hectares (c. 400 acres), only a small part of which has been explored. Evidence includes buildings of various types and also agricultural terraces. The site was occupied between 1400 and 600 or 500 BC, with its apogee around 1000–800 BC (Martínez Donjuán 1995). During that phase, the residential architecture in Teopantecuanitlán's Lomerios residential quarter, including the Tlacozotitlán locale, consisted of groups of several stone-based rectangular houses clustered around courtyards. Residents made shell and obsidian ornaments, both materials imported to the site (Reilly 2001).

Teopantecuanitlán's importance lies not only in its location in Guerrero, but in the precocity of its monumental architecture, particularly the ritual precinct called the Enclosure, which is the first known occurrence of a civic-ceremonial precinct centered upon a sunken patio, surrounded by rooms and platforms [5.31]. The building's orientation and special features indicate time-reckoning functions.

The Enclosure's cut-stone masonry work is of high quality, and the symmetrically placed monumental sculptures are decorated with figures in pure Olmec style, their almond-shaped eyes and snarling mouths revealing a close kinship with sculptures in the Gulf lowlands. One of the monoliths bears a flower and two bars, possibly the day-sign "10 Flower" (Jiménez García *et al.* 1998: 40); if so, it is one of Mesoamerica's earliest symbolic representations of an abstract calendrical concept, each bar equal to five. The sculptures are placed so that on the spring equinox, the shadows cast by two of them by the rising and setting sun pass through the Enclosure's center.

5.31 *Teopantecuanitlán's Sunken Patio complex, with northern and southern platforms at the top and bottom of the plan. They enclose a sunken courtyard which features a miniature ball court. Within this ball court were four nearly identical Olmec-style sculptures, yet unlike those in the southern Gulf lowlands, these were bas-reliefs, the features carved into massive flat pieces, each about 1 m (3 ft) high.*

The Enclosure centers upon what appears to be a miniature ball court; elsewhere at the site there is a full-sized I-shaped (78-m/256-ft long) court. At one end of this court is an adobe structure that functioned as a sweat bath. The ball game we have already encountered in other contexts; the Teopantecuanitlán sweat bath is one of the oldest examples of what became an important feature of Mesoamerican culture. In fact, sweat baths were common to Native American life, found in North, Middle, and South America, which invites speculation that the practice was extremely ancient, perhaps brought from the Old World. Formal sweat baths – permanent structures built for the purpose of steam-cleaning individuals for reasons of hygiene and health – were common at Mesoamerican sites from the Late Formative through the Late Postclassic. After the European intrusion, the Spanish conquistadores suppressed sweat baths because in Spain bathhouses had served as houses of prostitution. But in the New World there was no such scandalous association, and the sweat bath has persisted, gaining new adherents today as a New Age health regime.

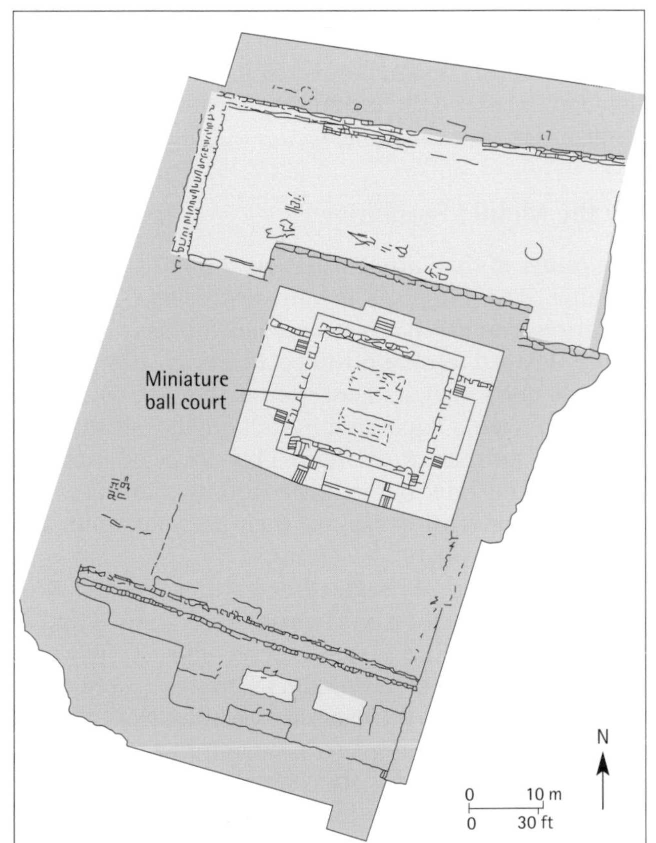

Just as we have noted that the ball game could be played on any level field, and no doubt long antedates the occurrence of formal ball courts, the sweat bath could be enjoyed in any improvised enclosed space – a framework of branches covered with animal skins could produce the desired effect. The physical evidence of a formal sweat bath signals that such bathing may have taken on the formal associations of other elite practices in the Formative period. Like the ball game, like feasting, the sweat bath may have been a means of bonding between members of Mesoamerica's developing elite class.

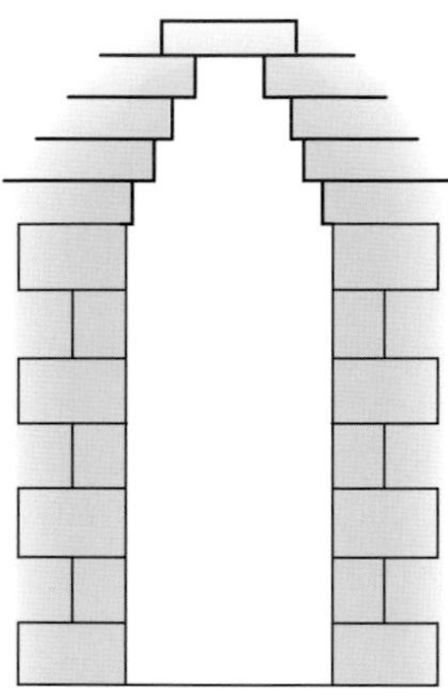

Corbeled vault (New World)

True arch (Old World)

5.32 *Corbeled vault compared with true arch. The overlapping stones used to achieve the vaulted ceiling could only span a limited space, so the vaulted chamber would have a high ceiling, but the chamber itself would be very narrow.*

Teopantecuanitlán's builders and sculptors achieved impressive results, and here again we find buried drains and at least one colossal head (1 m high, 1 m wide). The drainage channels were used to bring water to agricultural fields; one seems to have functioned as a sewer. About 100 m (328 ft) of the irrigation channel have been excavated; "the walls are covered by enormous stone blocks. The interior space, 70–90 cm (28–36 in) wide by 90–150 cm (35–60 in) high, could move or store almost one cubic m (35 cubic ft) of water per linear meter" (Martínez Donjuán 1995: 66).

Another important architectural feature has its oldest Mesoamerican manifestation at Teopantecuanitlán: the corbeled vault, sometimes called the "false arch" because it permits a high vaulted ceiling without the use of the interlocking trapezoidal arch stones, as found in the Old World [**5.32**]. The corbeled vault is most notable in architecture of the Maya lowlands, becoming widespread by the end of the Formative and during the Classic period. Here at Teopantecuanitlán the corbeled vault was used to create the roofs of tombs for high-status burials. In one tomb were found remains "of small mosaics and bone fragments coated with a thin layer of red pigment" (Martínez Donjuán 1994: 160).

Such corbel-vaulted tombs were also found elsewhere in the region, such as at Coovisur in the Chilpancingo area. During its apogee at the end of the Early Formative, Teopantecuanitlán is thought to have been the capital of its local region; some of the sites in this region flourished in the Middle Formative, and will be discussed in Chapter 6. By the end of the Middle Formative, about 600 BC, Teopantecuanitlán was abandoned.

Setting the Stage for the Middle Formative

San Lorenzo, impressive center of the Early Formative, did not survive this period as an Olmec capital. The impulses toward developing solidarity among elite lineages at various centers in a system of chiefdoms is balanced by the centrifugal tendency toward mutual hostility. Power is, after all, the ability to coerce others to do one's will, and coercion is the use, or serious threat, of force. Upstart leaders would have gathered adherents and allies for raids and skirmishes, with the promise of wealth readily collected from the storehouses of their victims. And how did it come to pass that the once-strong rulers of, say, San Lorenzo fell from grace, their portraits mutilated and their great monumental site in ruins?

We have seen the close association, through Olmec art, of the elite with supernatural powers controlling vegetation and climate. Only a small fluctuation in the weather, or in the agricultural cycle, can be sufficient to cause commoners to lose faith in the *mana* of their rulers (Drennan 1976). But while any one chiefdom may be fragile, the general institutions of complex society and differentials of access to key resources are not. In a situation of steadily increasing populations, it is virtually inevitable that one set of elites will be replaced by another.

6 THE OLMECS: MIDDLE FORMATIVE (*c.* 900–600 BC)

THE MIDDLE FORMATIVE PERIOD marks the second and last major florescence of Olmec cultures of the Gulf lowlands and adjacent areas. After this period, the southern Gulf lowlands never again assume cultural hegemony in Mesoamerica. During this period, other regions were gaining in size and complexity, and important developments took place in the highlands to the west and north, as well as in the Chiapas interior plateau, the Guatemala highlands, the Maya lowlands, and Southeastern Mesoamerica [**6.1**].

DEVELOPMENTS IN THE SOUTHWESTERN HIGHLANDS

Guerrero: Teopantecuanitlán and Cave Sites

Eastern Guerrero's precocity in the Olmec world is an intriguing puzzle, with some very solid pieces of evidence and many lacunae. The solid evidence consists of: a small number of known archaeological sites, a

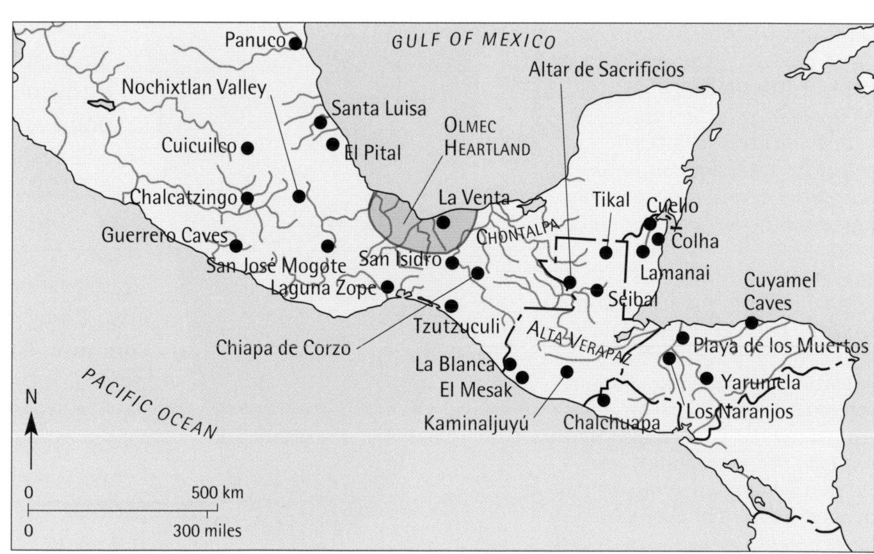

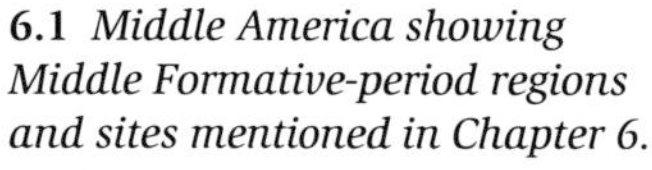
6.1 *Middle America showing Middle Formative-period regions and sites mentioned in Chapter 6.*

substantial corpus of portable art such as carved jade objects, and a few monumental carvings and cave paintings. The major site evidence was discussed in Chapter 5. Teopantecuanitlán continued to flourish in the Middle Formative period, and it seems clear that it was a regional capital for communities in the area, as attested by the contemporaneous Coovisur and Temixco II cemetery sites around Chilpancingo.

6.2–6.4 *Formative-period Guerrero produced remarkable works of art. (Right) The polished jadeite celt (28 cm/11 in) is a formalized, ritual version of polished stone axes that cleared the forests for Early Formative slash-and-burn farmers all over Mesoamerica. Incised upon it is an elaborately garbed figure wearing a mask and carrying a bundle and staff, and standing or striding. (Opposite left) From the Xochipala area, this kneeling figure in clay (14.4 cm/5.7 in) illustrates an ancient Mesoamerican preoccupation, achieving a transcendent state through ingesting, smoking, or snuffing an intoxicant or hallucinogen. This pipe dates to the Early Formative (1500–1200* BC*), and is "the earliest, sculpturally and symbolically the most spectacular snuffing pipe" (Furst 1995: 77). (Opposite right) Worked in emerald green jade, the standing figure (8.3 cm/3.25 in) has the features of the Olmec supernatural, but is in the pose of a peasant farmer, holding the tumpline that bears the weight of the sack or basket on his back.*

Portable art from Guerrero is more difficult to analyze with regard to its temporal significance, because so much of it was brought to light from looting, not systematic excavation, and thus its context is unknown and has been destroyed by the looting process. Accompanying the looting-and-destruction cycle is a lesser but important subspecialization: faking antiquities of the type popular enough to be looted. While there is a certain grim satisfaction in the thought that wealthy but unscrupulous art collectors are buying fakes and being defrauded out of substantial sums of money, the practice of faking further complicates our understanding of Olmec culture, its iconography, and the chronology of cultural trends. In spite of the repugnance that looting inspires, scholars cannot ignore looted objects; they are often among the most beautiful and richest in imagery, particularly for a poorly understood area like Guerrero.

Several Guerrero objects are shown [**6.2–6.4**]. These illustrate a small part of the range of materials and themes important to Olmec elite life, and clearly demonstrate Guerrero's important place in the Early to Middle Formative cultural complex. The Guerrero snuffing pipe offers insight into trends toward greater societal complexity. As societies evolved toward ranking, substances like peyote, mushrooms, and even tobacco may have become controlled, in the sense that they would have been reserved for those who were trained to understand and interpret the visions these hallucinogens produced. In Aztec times, the use of such substances by commoners was regarded as extremely dangerous, if not life-threatening. This class-based prohibition may have been established along with other means of distinguishing the elite. Privileged access to intoxicants and hallucinogens would have created a bond among members of an elite group who could demonstrate their strong ties to the supernatural – by seeming to change their shape, by achieving enlightenment from the gods, and by garbing themselves in iconographically rich regalia.

Non-Portable Art from Guerrero

Olmec-Guerrero style was expressed in non-portable materials as well as in clay and greenstone. The stela from San Miguel Amuco [**6.5**] presents us with two strong icons: the bundle (probably of feathers) and the avian serpent. The bundle represents yet another kind of blue-green preciousness, the feathers of the quetzal bird which adorned the headdresses of Mesoamerican royalty up to the time of the Spanish conquest. In a manner now familiar to us, other stalk-like green things (tules, corn stalks) were metaphorically suggested by the bundle, which thus took on the complex

6.5 *The individual incised into a stela (standing monument) at San Miguel Amuco (Guerrero) struck a pose similar to that of the striding figure on the celt [**6.2**]. They are both richly costumed, masked and standing facing left, legs and head in profile, torso facing front. The Amuco stela has two bundles and two avian serpent motifs: in the figure's arms he holds a bundle, and "a glyphic version of the same bundle occurs near the head of the figure" (Taube 1995: 88). He wears a bird mask, and near his shoulder is the head of a bird. The bundle and the bird are a shorthand message that signifies sacred and secular power (85 cm/33 in).*

meanings of agricultural fertility, the moisture of marshlands, the density of populations in complex societies – all as burdens and perquisites of rulership.

The bird is a hybrid, a bird-snake, an "Avian Serpent" which is the more accurate scholarly name for a familiar Mesoamerican icon, the "Feathered Serpent" which is also known by the Nahuatl term, Quetzalcoatl, combining the meanings of quetzal bird and snake (*coatl*). Those familiar with the most popular Mesoamerican myths will recognize Quetzalcoatl as both a deity and a culture hero, an actual ruler of 11th-century AD Tula, whose disappearance into the east was said (by the Spaniards) to have its resolution in the arrival of Cortés, a reincarnated Quetzalcoatl, in AD 1519.

Thus the appearance of the Avian Serpent in the iconographic scene of the Early and Middle Formative is worth noting. Imagine a shimmering iridescent blue-green flying dragon, combining the characteristics of valued and powerful animals of the Mesoamerican world, including those of the rulers themselves, and representing the sky as source of the sacred rain and backdrop for the time-keeping motions of sun, moon, and stars.

6.6 *(Opposite) Watching from a tree in the Calakmul Biosphere Reserve (Mexico), this young female jaguar is one of a small surviving population whose range has been reduced to one-third of its former size, crowded out by destruction of the rainforest as the human population increases.*

Other impressive figures are illustrated in paintings found on cave walls in Guerrero. Caves, oracles, rulers of sacred and secular domains – these are by now familar associations to us. While the Guerrero caves, Juxtlahuaca, Oxtotitlán, Cacahuaziziqui, and Texayac, are often located in remote canyons, their paintings were cosmopolitan rather than provincial in subject, and the renderings presage the mural painting tradition that matured in Classic-period sites like Teotihuacan. Oxtotitlan's Mural C-1 [**6.7**] shows yet another regally costumed figure, this time seated on a bench. An even more interesting individual, in Oxtotitlan's Painting 1-d [**6.8**], is hardly clothed at all, wearing only a headdress and linked to a jaguar.

JAGUARS

Most of us live in places where the only animals that cause real distress are microorganisms of disease. The pre-modern world, however, offered many kinds of big fierce beasts, and they figured importantly not only in regional mythologies but also in the organization of civil defense: marauding predators are bad for business – threatening isolated households, farmers working in their *milpas*, traders exchanging not only goods but information over long distances.

In Mesoamerica, the fiercest of all wild animals was the jaguar (*Panthera onca* or *Felis onca*, Nahuatl *ocelotl*, Mayan *balam*). It is the largest and most aggressive of New World big wild cats (there were no domesticated New World cats). Besides the jaguar, other cats native to Middle America are the ocelot (*F. pardalis*), the puma or mountain lion (*F. concolor*), the margay (*F. wiedii*), and the jaguarundi (*F. yagouaroundi*). The oncilla (*F. tigrina*) is limited to Costa Rica and south, and the lynx (*L. rufus*), to the mountains of the Northern Arid Zone and north.

The jaguar weighs over 100 lb (over 40 kg), is *c.* 2 m (6 ft) long from its nose to the end of its tail, with strong jaws, impressive fangs, and razor-sharp claws, its pelt is an explosion of black rosettes over tawny buff – or, more rarely, all black – an embodiment of beauty and danger. It lives in the tropical rain forest, though no doubt ranged much further before hunted out of more open terrain.

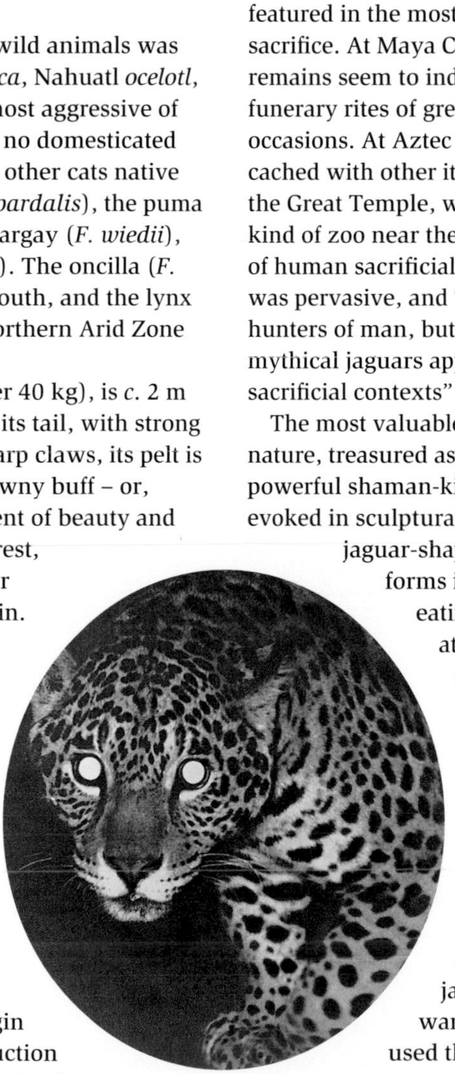

The jaguar is a night hunter, often from the heights of trees, and is one of the few cats truly comfortable in the water. It preys on the larger mammals of the tropical forest – monkeys, deer, tapir – and other cats such as the ocelot. It hunts "all creatures – land-bound, arboreal, aquatic, carnivore, and herbivore" (Saunders 1998: 21). Thus its range of habits and habitats evoke respect as much as its size and strength. Mesoamerican origin myths attributed to jaguars the destruction of the first world. In spite of its reputation for fierceness, it was slow to attack humans, and in fact "is virtually undocumented as a man-eater" (Rabinowitz 1986: 201). However, the same is true of the North American wolf, another animal widely perceived as a deadly enemy of humankind.

In contrast, the jaguar had good reason to be wary of humans; pre-Columbian peoples hunted jaguars for a variety of purposes. Taken live, the animals would be featured in the most crucial ceremonies involving sacrifice. At Maya Copán and at Teotihuacan, jaguar remains seem to indicate that the animals were killed in funerary rites of great rulers and on other ritual occasions. At Aztec Tenochtitlan, jaguar remains were cached with other items of great value in the pyramid of the Great Temple, while live big cats were caged in a kind of zoo near the temple precinct, and fed the torsos of human sacrificial victims. In art, jaguar symbolism was pervasive, and "jaguars are rarely portrayed as hunters of man, but jaguars, jaguar impersonators, or mythical jaguars appear – sometimes actively – in sacrificial contexts" (Benson 1998: 62).

The most valuable part of the jaguar was its essential nature, treasured as a worthy alter ego of the most powerful shaman-kings. This essential nature was evoked in sculptural depictions of the whole animal – jaguar-shaped thrones, for example, or jaguar forms in the murals of Teotihuacan or eating human hearts in the bas-reliefs at Tula and Chichén Itzá. Or, a few crucial parts would suggest the whole: the fangs and mouth so integral to Olmec iconography, or the spots from the pelt that mark one of the Hero Twins of the Maya epic, *Popol Vuh*. The next most valuable part was the pelt itself, used all over Mesoamerica to adorn rulers and deities. Kings sat on thrones upholstered with jaguar pelts, and the Aztec elite warrior battalion, the Jaguar Knights, used the pelts in their costumes.

6.7, 6.8 *Guerrero's cave paintings presage Mesoamerica's great mural tradition. (Above) The figure in Oxtotitlan's Mural C-1 is yet another person in a bird mask, "once physically connected to a feather cape and backrack" and the figure has adopted a swooping posture as he sits atop a bench or throne whose crossed eye-bands and sky band between its fangs identify it as an Olmec sky dragon (Reilly 1995: 39–40). (Right) In Oxtotitlan painting 1-d, man and beast are positioned "to suggest a sexual union between them" with the jaguar's tail a seeming extension of the man's genitals. Perhaps this is meant to convey the idea that "human semen possesses a vital feline power and potency, sharing with it the life force" (Jiménez García* et al. *1998: 45). The image may also visually propose the conjunction of the sacred jaguar's special relationship with rulers – at least one Maya ruler was named "Penis Jaguar."*

We shall return to the topic of elite appropriation of feline power in a discussion of the Middle Formative Olmecs of the Gulf lowlands, below. As elite power pertains to eastern Guerrero, it is clear that it was an important Early and Middle Formative region, and while eastern Guerrero became marginal in subsequent eras, it was central, during these periods, to the trade in luxury goods that brought greenstones, Pacific Coast shell, and jaguar pelts to more inland sites. Along one such well-traveled route, Teopantecuanitlán was only about 100 km (61 miles) south of Chalcatzingo, its contemporary and successor.

Morelos: Chalcatzingo's Apogee

Chalcatzingo was well-positioned at a kind of trade-route crossroads, interconnecting the routes down to Guerrero, up to the Basin of Mexico, and east and south to Oaxaca and the Gulf lowlands. Chalcatzingo was located at the foot of imposing hills looming up from a fertile plain, and the spring at the base of these hills gave the site and its supporting population the water necessary to farm and to flourish [6.9]. Chalcatzingo reached its greatest extent in the Cantera phase (700–500 BC) when it had a population of 500–1,000, civic-ceremonial architecture and monumental art. Exotic raw materials like greenstone were imported for redistribution and local craft activities, and social differentials were clearly demonstrated in contrasts in housing and in the treatment of the dead. The end of the Cantera phase marked a

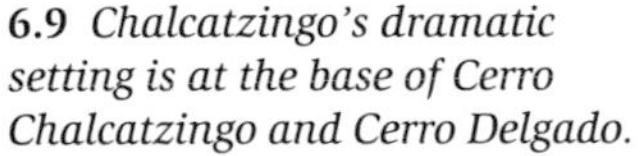

6.9 *Chalcatzingo's dramatic setting is at the base of Cerro Chalcatzingo and Cerro Delgado.*

sharp decline in Chalcatzingo, with abandonment of public and residential buildings.

Chalcatzingo's Cantera-phase public architecture is dominated by broad terraces extending away from its hills, downslope and to the north. On the terraces are positioned structures that include an elite residence, uphill from the "Plaza Central," Terrace 1. On Terrace 25, a sunken patio recalls another sunken patio, found at Teopantecuanitlán, but not in the Gulf lowlands . This architectural feature may represent a kind of opening to the otherworld, an earth-monster mouth. Centered in the sunken patio is a tabletop altar, a style known from San Lorenzo and La Venta, but otherwise not found outside the Gulf lowlands (Grove 2001).

Chalcatzingo's largest construction, Structure 4, is a platform about 70 m (230 ft) long and almost as wide. Several high-status burials were found there, with jade ornaments and an iron ore mirror (Grove and Cyphers 1987: 29–31). Chalcatzingo's many burials represented all social statuses, and were often found under the floors of houses. Chemical analysis of the bones, compared with the quality of grave goods, revealed that the richest burials were of individuals who had eaten meat, while the simplest interments were of those with a more vegetarian diet (Schoeninger 1979: 53).

6.10 *Chalcatzingo's Monument 21 is a stela, 2.4 m (7.9 ft) high, which was erected in front of a platform. It shows a woman, dressed in skirt, sandals, and head covering, facing and holding a bundle tied with bands; the woman and bundle stand on a stylized earth monster (Angulo 1987: 150–151).*

This implies, of course, differential access to high-quality, high-protein food, but it also points to the fact that the diet of farmers, while more secure than that of foragers, became less varied, in part because habitats for wildlife were more limited. Similarly, it recalls the ancient role of meat in feasting, and how, among egalitarian hunters, sharing the kill was a means of confirming social solidarity. The lives of headmen and chiefs focused upon securing their special privileges, especially through alliances with other powerful individuals, as celebrated in feasts.

What was the role of women in these burgeoning chiefdoms? Chalcatzingo offers a clue in what may be the earliest depiction of a woman in Mesoamerican monumental art [**6.10**]. The iconography of Monument 21 has been analyzed for insights into the woman's role, the contents of the bundle, and the locational intimations as to the woman's status and origin, as offered by the earth monster mask. Drawing from widespread Mesoamerican practices, we can hypothesize that the woman was a person, not a deity, a noble foreigner who was a partner in a marriage alliance, and the bundle represented her dowry, possibly indicating the continuing tributes that her dowry would bring to the Chalcatzingo lord who would become her husband (Cyphers 1984).

Chalcatzingo's stone carvings are justly famous, and the most remarkable are not stelae, but bas-reliefs carved into the surrounding cliff faces. Consider, for example, Monument 1, popularly known as El Rey, The King [**6.11**]. It depicts a life-sized figure seated inside a niche or cave (the niche opening is *c.* 1.5 m [57 in] high),

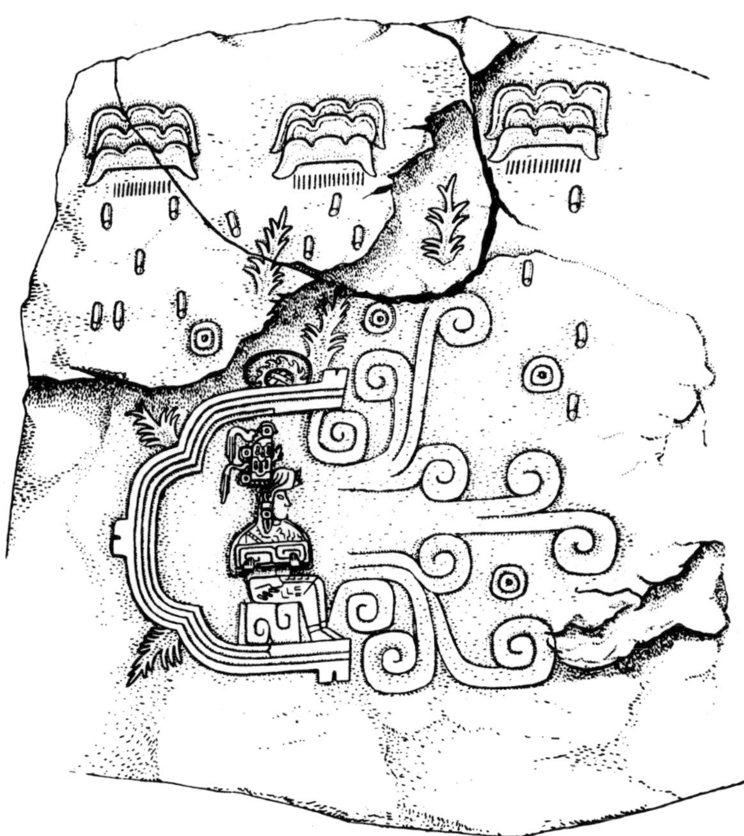

6.11 *Bas-relief of "The King," Chalcatzingo. Another important Mesoamerican tradition that was initiated during the Early Olmec period is rock art. This bas-relief depicts a richly dressed human figure seated in a cave-like niche, surrounded by swirling images of rain and wind, possibly a hurricane (Oliveros 1995). In motif and execution it is typical of Mesoamerican rock art: it deals with rain or rain-making, and it is a* petroglyph, *a design pecked into a rock face (Mountjoy 2001). In Mesoamerica, petroglyphs on rock faces are far more common than are painted designs, called* pictographs.

with scroll volutes issuing from the niche, and above this scene are other stylized objects, "three elaborate rain clouds from which !-shaped raindrops fall" (Grove and Angulo 1987). There are also four pairs of concentric circles, discussed above as symbols of preciousness, of water, of royalty; three more such circles decorate the headdress of the figure in the niche. Water is clearly important in this scene: the bas-relief is positioned on the hillside right above the major drainage channel for the slopes of Cerro Chalcatzingo. A closer look at the design reveals that the niche is topped by an eye, and thus the niche could be interpreted as a cave, the mouth of the earth monster. Thus the individual in this scene has appropriated three sacred locational elements: hill, water, and cave.

The figure itself is impressively garbed, sitting on an elaborate stool and holding a richly decorated object. Iconographers have interpreted the figure as a ruler, and the object being held as a ceremonial bar, a symbol of office (Angulo 1987: 136–137). The scroll symbols within and outside the niche are an age-old Mesoamerican motif for rain clouds (Taube 1995: 97). Even with such elementary decipherment of the symbols involved, we sense that a powerful individual, positioned in a sacred place, is the locus from which life-giving water is dispersed.

Basin of Mexico: Occupation at Tlatilco, Zacatenco, and Cuicuilco

6.12 *This white-slipped jar from the Basin of Mexico illustrates Olmec motifs, featuring an open-mouthed jaguar with a cleft head and flame eyebrows.*

The Middle Formative Basin of Mexico was a thriving land; population during this period increased from about 6,000 to about 20,000, still almost entirely in the southern half of the Basin (Sanders 1981: 165) [**6.12**]. Several villages became quite large: Cuicuilco, Cuautlalpan, and Chimalhuacan. But several other much smaller sites are much better known from the Middle Formative Basin of Mexico: El Arbolillo and Zacatenco. They lie on the southern flanks of the Sierra de Guadalupe, a range of hills in the western Basin that is today famous as the location of the shrine of the Virgin of Guadalupe, just north of Mexico City. The villages were close to the lakeshore, and the villagers would have lived off farming as well as foraging for lacustrine resources. El Arbolillo, about 8 hectares (20 acres), was occupied from 900 to 500 BC. Zacatenco was about twice as large, and continued to be occupied until about 50 BC. At both sites, figurines were found in abundance in trash deposits, suggesting that they were used in rituals and then discarded (Tolstoy *et al.* 1977).

In the same general area, a different kind of archaeological evidence was brought to light. Near Santa Clara Coatitlán, deeply buried Middle Formative irrigation canals were uncovered in deep trenches dug for road fill in the 1970s. These extensive canal systems were built, at considerable cost of energetic investment, by farmers dependent upon rainfall to water their crops, and wishing to reduce the effects of year-to-year fluctuations in the amount of rainfall (Nichols 1987). In fact, the period from 900 to 800 BC may have brought significantly higher rainfall to the Basin of Mexico, encouraging expansion of field systems and populations, while the subsequent climate phase, 800–550 BC, saw a return to drier conditions (Messenger 1990).

Puebla: The Amalucan Irrigation System

The same general climate regime affected the Puebla region, to the east. There, during the Texoloc phase (800–300 BC), a system of drainage and irrigation canals was developed at Cerro Amalucan. As was the case in the Basin of Mexico, Puebla during this period saw the growth of large villages with special features. Moyotzingo, for example, had modest public architecture, along with differentiated residential districts. Higher-status houses were built on higher ground, and made of adobes, while in lower-lying areas, wattle-and-daub huts provided housing for farmers and artisans.

Tlaxcala

In Tlaxcala, the northern part of the Puebla-Tlaxcala region, conditions were somewhat cooler and drier than in Puebla, like the contrast between the warmer and wetter southern Basin of Mexico and the more challenging climate of the northern Basin. During Texoloc times a new ground-stone artifact appears, usually made of tabular basalt and shaped almost identically to the blades of modern garden hoes (Garcia Cook 1981: 249). This resemblance is so striking that a "hoe" function was imputed to these tools, and it was assumed that they were used to cultivate fields, or perhaps muck out irrigation canals. In fact, the "hoes" were used to scrape pulp from the fibers of the long leaves of the maguey plant. Maguey was, at some point, discovered to be an excellent terrace border plant, and while its nutritional value had long been recognized, the scrapers indicate that its fibers were being processed in an efficient way, with a special tool developed for this purpose.

Gulf Lowlands North, North-central, and South-central

East from Puebla and Tlaxcala, on the Gulf of Mexico side of the Sierra Madre Oriental, were the regions of the Gulf lowlands that were north of the Olmec heartland, and showed a few signs of contact with Olmec culture, but no outright influence by Olmec centers. The northernmost of the two regions is dominated by the drainage of the Tamesi and Pánuco Rivers, and settlements of the Formative period grew up along these watercourses, their inhabitants pursuing a mixed strategy of exploiting riverine resources and farming. At the site of Pánuco, occupation stretched along the river for several kilometers, with wattle-and-daub houses of apsidal shape; evidence of cotton spinning and weaving is found in spindle whorls made from potsherds ground into circular shapes and perforated, and from fabric impressions onto pottery (Wilkerson 2001).

To the south the north-central Gulf lowlands stretch for about 200 km (*c.* 125 miles), draining four major rivers. In the Early Formative this region shared the general cultural characteristics of the more northerly area, but in the Middle Formative it followed a more distinctive trajectory, with some Olmec portable objects finding their way to several sites.

Two north-central Gulf lowlands centers, Santa Luisa and El Pital, had very long occupations, and were becoming substantial communities in the Middle Formative. Santa Luisa, on the Tecolutla River, boasts the longest chronology of any site along the Gulf Coast, 8,000 years of continuous occupation, into the present. By the Early Formative, Santa Luisa was a farming village growing maize and perhaps cotton. Local ceramics include imitations of Olmec motifs, and architecture rests on platform mounds. The Middle Formative here runs from 1000 to 300 BC, and is characterized by larger villages, some with very large hearths that may have served multiple households (Wilkerson 1983).

El Pital's trajectory of occupation, while shorter, is more dramatic, beginning in the Middle Formative, growing explosively in the Late Formative, and flourishing from AD 100 to 600. It will be discussed in Chapters 8, 9, and 10.

Occupation of the south-central Gulf lowlands is scattered during this period, though isolated occurrences of Olmec-style sculpture have been found, the northernmost being at Los Idolos near Misantla, and El Viejón, at the far north, along the coast, where a slab stela was found.

Valley of Oaxaca and the Mixteca Region

In the Southwestern Highlands, the Oaxaca Valley's northern Etla arm continued to demonstrate new levels of cultural complexity, with the Middle Formative development of a three-tiered settlement system, including two types of administrative sites. This is understood archaeologically by site size, location, and the presence of civic-ceremonial architecture. San José Mogote continued to be the largest site in the entire Oaxaca Valley, but other sites also had public architecture, assumed to mark the administrative functions of resident elite populations over smaller sites in their surrounding hinterlands.

Such political hinterlands are inferred from several lines of evidence, and relative size and complexity of adjacent contemporaneous settlements is an important indicator. Another is similarity of the material culture repertoire. Ceramic styles, in particular, signal shared culture. In the period from 850 to 700 BC, the sherds of the Oaxaca Valley that characterized the diagnostic pottery of the Guadalupe phase in the Etla subvalley "can be recognized from Huitzo in the north to Tierras Largas in the south" – further south and east, in the Tlacolula and Valle Grande subvalleys, a distinct pottery style emerges, and "this regional diversity tells us that dynamic changes were underway, with competing centers arising in different areas of the valley" (Marcus and Flannery 1996: 111).

The whole Valley of Oaxaca had a population of 2,000–2,500, in about 45 communities, half of them in the Etla subvalley, about half the Oaxaca Valley population in San José Mogote's 60–70 hectare (*c.* 150–175 acre) extent. San José's Structure 8 was a substantial platform for a large, now-destroyed building; the platform made of dirt fill and loaf-shaped adobes, covered with a facing of stone.

A nearby site, Fábrica San José, specialized in the production of salt (from its saline springs) and building stone, and was much smaller – fewer than a dozen houses and no civic-ceremonial architecture – but even in this tiny community, status differences were apparent through patterns in architecture, material culture repertoire, and mortuary treatment. Fábrica San José may have been linked to San José Mogote through marriage ties (Drennan 1976). Analysis of burials showed that the richest were those of adult women, indicating that these women held the highest status in the community.

This is consistent with a very widespread practice in Mesoamerica, called "elite hypergyny." "Hypergyny" is a word like "polygyny"; the latter means "many women" and is used to describe marital situations in which many wives share one husband. "Hypergyny" means "higher woman" and refers to a relatively higher status of the wife. In Mesoamerica, marriage ties bound together political territories, and typically, the lord of a lower-order center would marry the daughter of his overlord, thus a woman of higher status than his own. Aztec kings made certain that their royal daughters were the primary or principal wives of their allies. Their offspring would

6.13 *Huitzo, Valley of Oaxaca. Reconstruction drawing of Structure 3, probably a one-roomed temple, sitting atop Structure 4, a platform about 2 m high and 15 m wide (6.5 ft, 49 ft). The whole building was coated with lime plaster and had a thatched roof.*

rule the lower-order center and be closely bound to the higher-order center by family ties as well as political treaties, a situation that eventually created family solidarity among elites that extended over a huge area and transcended elite loyalties to their own peoples. The idea is simple and effective, and may well have developed in the early part of the Formative period.

However, in spite of its dominant demographic status, San José Mogote had its rivals. At the northern end of the Etla subvalley, less than 20 km (12 miles) away, Huitzo was a much smaller site but with impressive public architecture that rivaled San José's [**6.13**]. While San José's location in the subvalley is central, Huitzo's is marginal to the Oaxaca Valley system, yet pivotal as a contact point between the Oaxaca Valley and the Cuicatlán Cañada (Canyon) that connects it to the Tehuacán Valley and Puebla, and also between the Oaxaca Valley and the Mixteca Alta, a system of small valleys to the northwest.

Mixtecs and Mixtecas "Mixtec" is a term that brings together geography, ethnicity, linguistics, and art and writing styles in a rather messy package. "Mixteca" refers to a group of people who speak Mixtec languages, which began to be distinguished from other Otomanguean languages by 1000 BC in the mountain valleys northwest of the Valley of Oaxaca (Monaghan 2001). This region is the Mixteca Alta, and from there, Mixtec-speakers moved down the river valleys to the sea, settling the region called "Mixteca de la Costa." From the Mixteca Alta they also moved west into the lower, more arid lands bordering eastern Guerrero, the "Mixteca Baja." Eventually, in the Classic period, Mixtec speakers would move into the Oaxaca Valley and establish kingdoms among the Zapotecs.

Even in the Initial Formative period, peoples of the Mixteca Alta had shell and obsidian obtained by long-distance trade, and by the Early Formative the exchange patterns were even more diverse, with more obsidian from more sources, shell from both the Pacific and Atlantic Coasts (Winter 1984: 208). The Middle Formative saw an increase in the amount of jade and other greenstones imported into the region.

In the Nochixtlán Valley, two early settlements were Yucuita and Etlatongo. Yucuita was large during the Middle Formative. Stylistic similarities between materials found at Yucuita and Huitzo point to interactions between these two sites during this period, and by the Late Formative, markets were being established, including at Yucuita.

ISTHMUS AND EAST

The Pacific Coast of the Isthmus of Tehuantepec and Adjacent Areas to the South

Southeast of the Oaxaca Valley, the Pacific Coast of the Isthmus of Tehuantepec shared developmental trends of the coastal plains of Soconusco and more southeasterly regions. The coastal plain formed a continuous culture area from the western side of the Isthmus of Tehuantepec in the north, where the mountains of southeastern Oaxaca meet the seas, southeast to western El Salvador, where another range interrupted the plain – a distance of nearly 700 km (about 400 miles).

At the far western end, the site of Laguna Zope grew to 90 hectares (222 acres) in size with a population of 1,000 by 500 BC, becoming a major trading center in the Middle Formative (Ríos phase, 800–400 BC). Laguna Zope specialized in the export of sea shell for lapidary work. At the same time, it served as a trading entrepôt for other materials, such as obsidian moving from the Central Highlands and highland Guatemala, and its material culture repertoire showed Maya influence during this phase (Zeitlin 1993).

Further down the coast, Tzutzuculi became an important Middle Formative center, with Olmec-related sculpture and ceramics, and several dozen mounds in plaza groups, covering an area of 35 hectares (86 acres). Izapa, established in about 1500 BC, was also developing public-scale architecture. La Blanca, further southeast in the coastal zone, was a small community that boomed in the Middle Formative Conchas phase to over 100 hectares (247 acres) in area, one of the largest Middle Formative settlements. This growth took place amidst a general increase in the number and size of sites in its immediate area [**6.14**].

La Blanca was one of three sites (the others were La Zarca and El Infierno) with massive earthen mounds over 20 m (66 ft) high. La Blanca had over 40 residential platforms, but they were not formally arranged into plaza groups. Mound 1 was more than 25 m (82 ft) high with a base measuring about 140 by 120 m (460 by 394 ft), while other mounds were less than 10 m (33 ft) high, and not laid out in a formal arrangement. Thus Mound 1 was "among the largest constructions of Middle Formative Mesoamerica, only slightly smaller in volume than the Great Mound at La Venta" (Love 1991: 57). The comparative architectural and settlement size evidence would

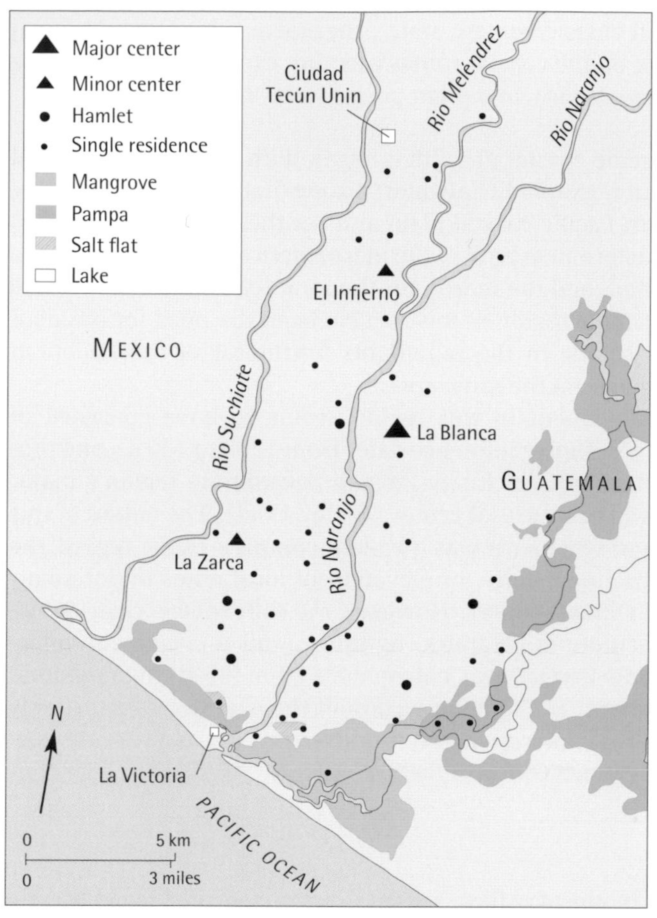

6.14 *Río Naranjo region, on the southern Pacific coast at the presentday boundary of Mexico and Guatemala, had a three-tiered site hierarchy in the Conchas phase, with El Infierno and La Blanca as regional centers.*

argue strongly that La Blanca was the chiefly center of its region. Other evidence came from fine pottery, jade and greenstone items, and other lapidary materials, which occurred in much larger quantities at La Blanca than at other sites.

El Mesak: Small Village, Fancy Stuff How should we weight these different lines of evidence? How much do the sherds of Olmec vessels matter in determining the extent of ranking among individuals and families in Formative-period communities? At archaeological sites, the presence of precious goods is a popular measure of status: among house mounds, those with the fanciest sherds could be presumed to house the highest-status residents. This makes logical sense because it draws upon our common experience that wealthy people tend to have nicer things, and more of them, than poor people. But we have to remember that even modest households, ancient or modern, may possess a few high-quality items, and also that fashions change, and some styles dubbed classics by posterity are rejected as old-fashioned by their possessors when a new fashion arrives, even if the quality of material and finishing has declined. Thus the residents of the biggest house may have adopted a new style while their lesser-status neighbors still use old-fashioned wares that are handsome and graceful.

Keeping that in mind, we consider El Mesak, a "small village on the outer coast" of Guatemala, a swampy environment well-suited to a mixed strategy involving foraging for coastal resources as well as farming (Pye and Demarest 1991). First occupied in the Initial Formative, El Mesak's earliest levels show a heavy reliance upon shellfish. In time, El Mesak came to specialize in salt production, and the uppermost excavation layers date from the Middle Formative. Ceramics from this period of occupation have Olmec motifs, and jade has been found, as well.

But El Mesak seems to have had a simple subsistence economy, and if these are elite goods, then "[w]hy would a small village on the outer coast maintain a group of elites? ... little would seem to justify the existence of an elite presence" (Pye and Demarest 1991: 96). Yet the process of change at this village, from the Initial Formative over 1,000 years to the end of the Middle Formative, indicates that this local community absorbed and modified outside influences, undergoing changes because of external contacts. As this happened, "local elites emerged, and ... the site acquired an additional function as a portage on the coastal routes carrying exotics to the emerging chiefdoms in Chiapas, Oaxaca, and other points west" (ibid.: 97).

Chalchuapa The Pacific coastal plain that began with Laguna Zope ended with the Ahuachapan region in El Salvador, a zone that forms the boundary between the southern Pacific coastal plain and Southeastern Mesoamerica. This was the southeasternmost limit of the Mesoamerican culture area in the Early Formative period, and the reason for the long reach of Olmec culture into this relatively remote region seems to have been the need for obsidian from the Ixtepeque source in the mountains northwest of the Zapotitan Valley, and greenstone from the same area.

Early Formative settlement in this region seems to have consisted of simple farming villages; Olmec influence dates from 1200 to 400 BC, and provoked the development of Chalchuapa, which became the region's major political, religious, and commercial center (Willey 1984). The nature of this influence is unknown, whether it was a violent conquest of the region, the establishment of a trading colony, or elevation of local elites by intermarriage with imported Olmec spouses. However, the influence is clear on the material culture – sculpture, ceramics, figurines, and especially architecture. During the Middle Formative, Chalchuapa's 20-m (66-ft) high pyramid was built at the northern, El Trapiche section of the site; the structure was one of the largest in Mesoamerica at that time. Nearby, at Las Victorias, bas-reliefs depict four costumed Olmec-style figures [**7.2**].

Olmec Influences

Sites bearing Olmec motifs may have shared in a sophisticated iconographic and even sociopolitical system. Moreover, they all had in common a basic economic role, that of supplying the larger centers with such goods as cacao, salt, and shell. Such trade would account for "the scattered examples of Olmec-style bas-reliefs in Mesoamerica (San Miguel Amuco, Xoc, Chalchuapa, etc.), including those at Chalcatzingo and the coastal Chiapas examples [Pijijiapan, Padre Piedra, Tzutzulculi]" (Grove 1981: 387). Furthermore, ambitious elites would appropriate Olmec ritual practices as a means of enhancing their own authority and prestige. In subsequent periods, local development would give these motifs and practices importance in their own regional context.

Intermediate Olmec and La Venta

While San Lorenzo's huge platform hinted at vast expenditures of labor in a truly monumental design, it gave very few clues as to the architecture of the Initial Olmec period. La Venta, the most important Mesoamerican site of the Middle Formative, offers a clear perspective on monumental architecture and its relation to sculpture.

La Venta In spite of partial destruction by 20th-century construction, the site's civic-ceremonial features, extent, and major features comprise a community so large (200 hectares, about 500 acres) and complex that La Venta has at least some characteristics of a true city (González Lauck 1996: 75).

La Venta is located amidst Middle America's greatest expanse of alluvial coastal plain, a region channeled by rivers draining the spine of the Sierra Madre Oriental and fed by 2 m (*c.* 80 in) of rainfall annually. The rivers served as highways, and riverbanks, their soil renewed by floodwaters, could produce three crops a year. La Venta's immediate area shows signs of occupation as early as the Initial Formative period (1750 BC), and La Venta itself was occupied by about 1200 BC. Construction of its major structures began soon afterward. La Venta was not subject to flooding, having been built upon a salt dome, a geological feature that is still slowly rising.

At La Venta we see the first monumental expression of a site orientation shared with other sites: 8° west of north, found as well at San José Mogote. This orientation at La Venta has been interpreted as coinciding with that of the north-south orientation of the Milky Way on 13 August, the second zenith of the sun in the tropics (Freidel *et al.* 1993). In the Terminal Formative, at Teotihuacan and among the Maya, 13 August would be marked as the day of the creation of the present world, in 3114 BC. While it is provocative to think that this idea had such a long germination, another, more immediate reason for La Venta's orientation may be that the site may have been a model of the Isthmus itself: La Ventans traveled far for construction materials and trade goods, and as "they explored the physical space and the cultural cognitive realms of the Isthmus, they imitated, on a small scale, the topography of their known world" (Tate 1999: 173).

Overall, the site's layout expresses a pattern that would become common at many sites in later time periods, with a pyramid facing upon a plaza whose sides are demarcated by lower structures [**6.15**]. The main pyramid was often at the northern end of this layout, and the flanking platforms were usually the bases for lower and more complex ceremonial and administrative structures – temples, priestly quarters, the palace of the local lord. The pyramid itself was often topped by a temple. As we shall see, Mesoamerican sites played many variations on this theme.

Pyramid C-1 dominates the site, and has traditionally been thought to date to the Middle Formative period. It formed the southern end of Complex A, a ceremonial precinct to which access would have been restricted. A line of monolithic basalt columns ended with Mound A-2 [**6.18**], which held the Tomb of the Monolithic Columns, containing the remains of two or three young people, carved jade figures [**6.19**] and other jade objects, and a headdress made of stingray spines, prized among New World elites (Pillsbury 1996). These and other mortuary offerings were mingled with abundant "traces of organic material. The red cinnabar lay in a fashion which gave the impression that it had been inside of wrapped bundles. Probably the bodies had been thus wrapped before interment" (Stirling and Stirling 1942: 642).

Tomb offerings are known from many sites and many cultures, but La Venta is most unusual, even in Mesoamerica, for the number and grandeur

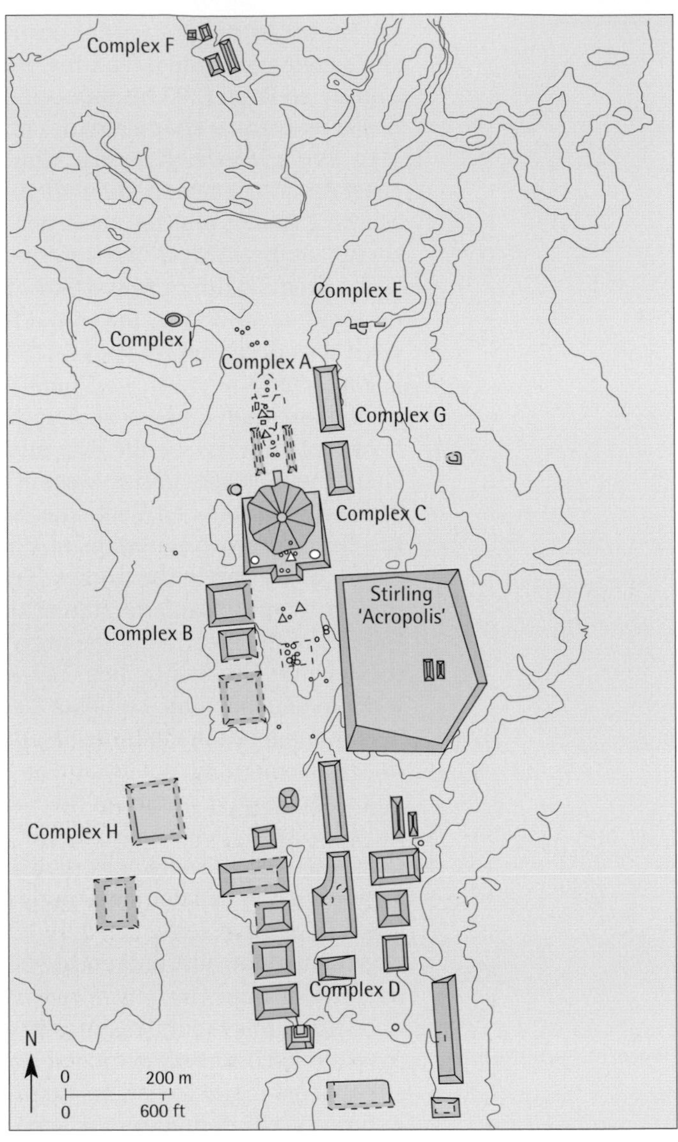

6.15 *The La Venta site plan centers upon Complex C, including the pyramid C-1 on its platform. The pyramid, about 30 m (98 ft) high and with a volume of about 100,000 sq. m (130,800 sq. yd), is today in the shape of an eroded cone and scholars have speculated as to whether this is its original design, a deliberate representation of a volcanic mountain, such as one of the Tuxtla mountains about 60 km (37 miles) to the west. "The architectural remains found ... on the south side ... indicate a pyramidal structure with a series of stepped volumes and inset corners" (González Lauck 1996: 75), and steps up to the summit.*

6.18 *(Opposite far right) At La Venta, just north of Pyramid C, was located Complex A, with Structure A-2 and the Mosaic Pavement, a massive offering of serpentine blocks composed of over 400 cut stone blocks and measuring roughly 4.5 by 4.5 m (c. 15 by 15 ft), created when "workers dug a pit 23 feet deep in a courtyard, spread a base of sticky tar from petroleum seeps, and laid out blue-green serpentine blocks. They bordered the image with yellow clay, tamped blue clay in central openings, then covered it all with layers of colored clay" (Stuart 1993: 107).*

of its buried offerings, many of them not associated with tombs. Complex A had more than 50 offerings, including some of the most spectacular Olmec materials ever found. Many consisted of fine ceramic vessels, polished iron ore mirrors, and ceremonial stone celts and axes. For the most part, these were not associated with tombs, but represented the dedication of rare materials and significant investment of labor toward the execution of an iconographically rich design; the completed offering was then buried. Perhaps the most famous example [**6.16, 6.18**] is the "jaguar mask" mosaic, which may be a tree of life, or a cosmogram diagramming the relationship between La Venta and the underword (Reilly 1995).

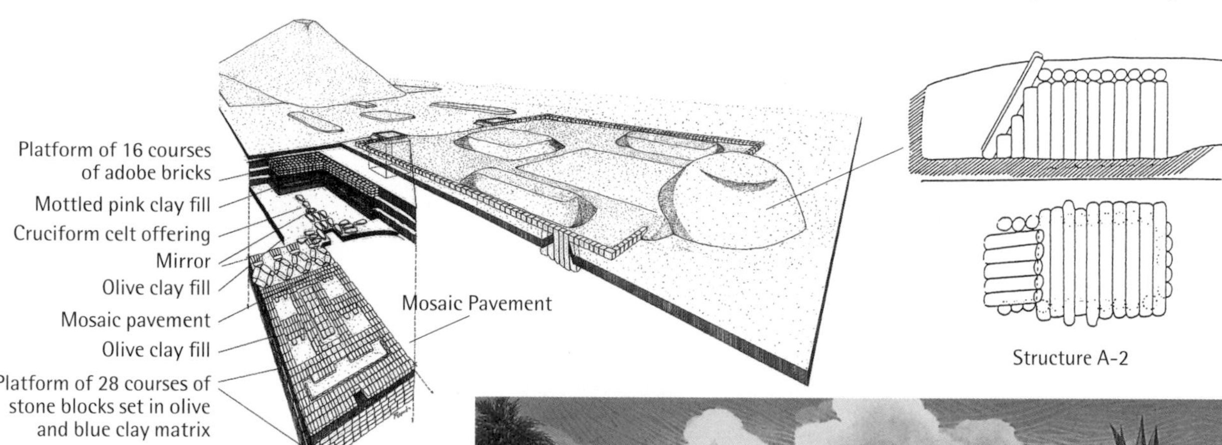

6.16, 6.17 *(Above) La Venta, Structure A-2 tomb and a sculpture found within it. The tomb was built of basalt columns. After interment of the deceased and their funerary offerings, the entire structure was buried.*

6.19 *(Below) The seated woman (7.5 cm/3 in) is worked in jade, and wears a pendant of hematite – a mirror, indicating that Olmec women had authority in their own right.*

6.20 *La Venta, the buried offering of figurines (about 18 cm/7 in tall) and celts (about 24 cm/9.5 in tall) typifies the Olmec propensity to arrange objects in meaningful scenes. All the figures and celts are carved from fine-grained jade and serpentine, except for the single sandstone figure with his back to the "wall" of celts.*

At the other end of the size spectrum is Offering 4, a scene comprising 16 figurines, in jade, serpentine, and sandstone, and six polished stone celts, slightly larger [**6.20**]. The figurines are male and all are depicted as having cranial reshaping. They are positioned so that most of them form a semicircle around four, who seem to parade in front of the single sandstone figure, standing with his back to the celts.

There were many other monuments at the site: stelae, colossal heads, "altars" such as the tabletop "Altar 4" that was probably a throne for the ruler depicted on its front façade [**5.14**]. La Venta not only has provided the single largest assemblage of Olmec sculpture, but it has, more importantly, yielded the contexts for these sculptures, demonstrating how they were associated with particular structures, embedded in ritual contexts, and grouped to provide scenarios that are clearly meaningful, although their meaning is not always clear to us.

The Chontalpa Region La Venta's hinterland included the Chontalpa zone at the eastern edge of the Olmec culture area in the southern lowlands. Chontalpa is the swampy delta of the Grijalva and Usumacinta river systems, as they merge with the Gulf of Mexico. Here, the earth is given living vitality (or made unstable, depending on one's perspective) by another kind of geomorphological activity besides volcanism and earthquakes. Rivers repeatedly flood their levees and reposition themselves into new channels; habitable land sinks below the water like a submerging caiman, and rises up somewhere else. In spite of this instability, human occupation of the Chontalpa began in the Initial Formative and became heavy in the Early Formative.

Surveys along the Pajonal channel system revealed that by La Venta's apogee (late La Venta phase, 800–500 BC), "settlement along the Pajonal channel complex included at least two, perhaps three centers with large earthen platforms" (von Nagy 1997: 267). These sites, Zapata and La Encrucijada, are comparable to the second-order centers around La Venta, showing the distance-decay function that applies to settlement systems in peripheral areas, where the biggest sites, representing the regional administrative centers, are only as large as secondary sites in the core area. The collapse of La Venta had its repercussions here, with the abandonment of settlements along the Pajonal channel system.

Chiapas Highlands and Chiapa de Corzo

The Chiapas interior plateau, adjacent to the southern Gulf lowlands, was culturally sophisticated because of influences from the Pacific coastal plain in the Initial Formative period, and from the Olmec culture in the Early and Middle Formative. The period from 900 to 500 BC was one of the most dynamic in the history of the Chiapas interior plateau, with a series of communities with ceremonial centers that were laid out in a pattern similar to that of La Venta: the tallest pyramid at one end of a long plaza flanked by platform mounds.

One important site was San Isidro, established on a trade route between the Chiapas interior and the Gulf lowlands. Its Early Formative ceremonial remains included pyramids and offerings of polished stone celts; unlike the jade celt offerings at La Venta, celt offerings at San Isidro and other Middle Grijalva sites were mostly "hurriedly made of a very soft greenish-grey silt stone" (Lee 1974: 8). San Isidro, which continued to be occupied into the Classic period, now lies beneath the waters of the Malpaso Reservoir (Lowe 1981).

Modern Chiapa de Corzo continues an occupation on this site that dates back roughly 3,000 years. Formal civic-ceremonial architecture was laid out in about 700 BC, following the pattern set at La Venta, and at this time the community was the most important chiefdom in Chiapas. While the Grijalva was not passable for canoe traffic from Chiapa de Corzo downstream to San Isidro, the upstream stretch to Mirador was passable. Mirador's civic-ceremonial center followed the La Venta (and Chiapa de Corzo) pattern, and was established about the same time as Chiapa de Corzo's, though occupation at Mirador began about 1400 BC.

The most southerly of these Chiapan centers was La Libertad, founded in about 750 BC, apparently to control trade between the Guatemala highlands, further to the southeast, and the Chiapas interior and Gulf lowlands beyond it. Its civic-ceremonial architecture dates from about 700 BC and covers 45 hectares. A cruciform mound 100 m (328 ft) long is flanked by two pyramids, each about 20 m (66 ft) high, which contain elite burials.

Guatemala Highlands

In the Initial Formative period, farming villages dotted the Guatemala highlands, and by the Early Formative (Las Charcas phase, 1000–750 BC) in the largest of the valleys of the southern Maya highlands, the community of Kaminaljuyú, established around 1000 BC, had become more complex, with platforms supporting wattle-and-daub buildings. These structures and the fine ceramics found associated with them indicate that the town had become an administrative center, probably for trade in items sought by the Olmecs. Kaminaljuyú is not far from Mesoamerica's best known – and only documented – jade source, in the Motagua Valley to the northeast.

Maya Culture

The Chiapas interior and the Guatemala highlands are thought to have been the original homeland of Maya cultures, those shared among speakers of Mayan languages. Note that the adjective referring to the language is "Mayan" rather than "Maya," which refers to the people and their culture. Like the Mixtec speakers, Mayan speakers encompass a wide variety of cultural traits, but also share a basic ethnic pattern of which language forms an elementary component. At the time of contact, the various Mayan languages were spoken over the Yucatán Peninsula and in the highlands of Chiapas and Guatemala, and were about as closely related as Romance languages are today. The region of greatest Mayan language diversity is the highlands of Chiapas and Guatemala, and many scholars believe that this was the original homeland of the Maya, with migrations to the lowlands taking place throughout the Formative period.

The Southern Maya Lowlands

There were people living north of the Chiapas-Guatemala highlands in the Archaic period; pollen evidence indicates that during the Late Archaic, the tropical forest was being cleared and maize was grown as early as 2500 BC (Pohl *et al.* 1996). While there are some traces of ceramics, and even of the presence of regional ceramics traditions at this time, it is in the Early Formative period, about 1200–1000 BC, that sedentary, ceramics-using populations settled in the Yucatán Peninsula (Houston 2001).

Much of the evidence for the earliest of these communities lies buried under later occupations at the same sites. For example, ceramics represent-

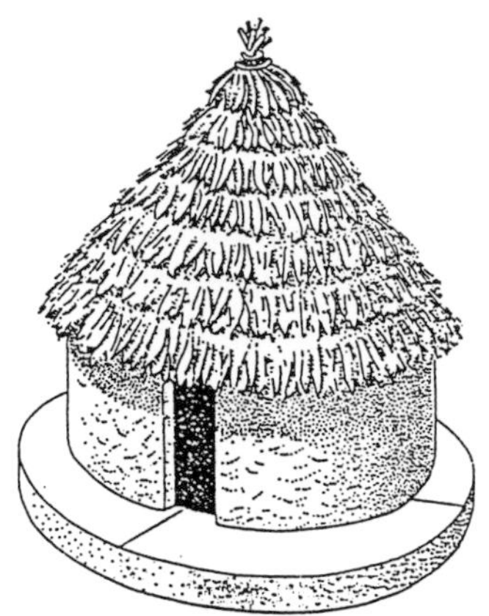

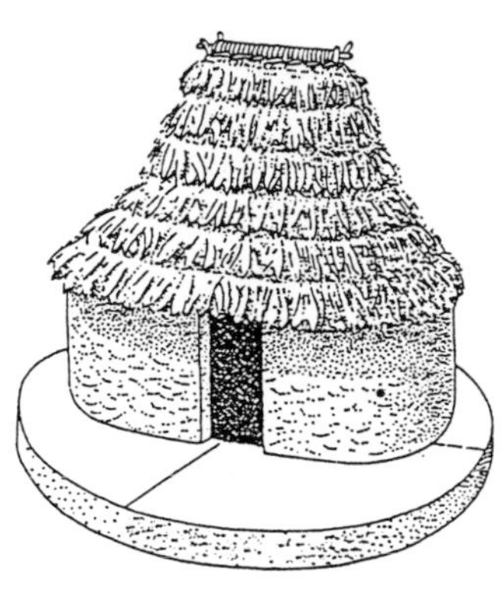

6.21 *Cuello's Middle Formative houses, shown in reconstruction drawings, are of a type still built by traditional Maya farmers. House posts were a framework for smaller branches, forming a "wattle" structure that would then be "daubed" with mud. In many areas, this was further sealed with a coating of plaster. The roof was often thatched with palm fronds.*

ing the Xe complex and dating from 900 to 750 BC comprised the earliest materials at Altar de Sacrificios and Seibal, sites in the southwestern Petén. These sites may have been peopled by migrants from the regions just to the south, the Chiapas highlands and the northern, Alta Verapaz highlands of Guatemala, where population levels were high and ceramics similar to Xe were in use (Andrews, V. 1990). Yet Isthmian contacts with the southwestern Petén were also evidenced: "at Seibal ... [were] found a cache of jade celts and a jade perforating instrument of probable La Venta manufacture" (Coe 1999: 54).

The Swasey and Bladen ceramic phases are more widespread, occurring as far east as Belize, where Cuello's Swasey/Bladen occupation may have begun as early as 1200, and continued to 600 BC. At that time, low earthen platforms were constructed, upon which pole-and-thatch houses about 6 m (20 ft) in diameter were built, either circular or apsidal in shape [**6.21**]. Cuello was occupied throughout the Formative and Classic periods, when it was a lower-order ceremonial center. Its archaeological importance rests upon its status as one of the earliest known Maya villages whose early phases have been well-investigated, providing information about the establishment of maize-based subsistence, along with pottery. During Bladen phase (900–600 BC), jade and obsidian were imported to the site, and jade accompanied child burials, evidence of ascribed rank. Meanwhile, houses increased substantially, from about 4 by 8 m (13 by 26 ft) to 6 by 12 m (20 by 40 ft) by 600 BC (Hammond 1991). One Middle Formative structure has been identified as a sweat bath, one of the earliest known (Hammond and Bauer 2001).

Other sites in the Belize area with very early occupations are Colhá and Lamanai. At Pulltrouser Swamp pollen evidence showed the presence of maize and manioc as early as the Late Archaic period, and at San Antonio and Cob Swamp, rising water levels at about 1000 BC caused farmers to drain their fields, an intensification measure that indicates a willingness to invest extra effort in order not to relocate.

Early and Middle Formative periods were times of pioneering occupation at other sites in Belize (Altún Ha, Santa Rita Corozal and Nohmul), in the western Petén, closest to the Chiapas highlands (Altar de Sacrificios, Seibal, Piedras Negras, and in cave deposits in the Petexbatun region), and at sites in the northern and central part of the Petén (e.g. Tikal, Río Azul, Yaxhá, Tayasal). Mamom-phase (*c.* 700–400 BC) developments in the northern Petén demonstrate that Middle Formative Maya lowlands sites were not all modest farming villages. Nakbé by 750 BC had some structures nearly 20 m (66 ft) tall.

The Northern Maya Lowlands

The northern Yucatán Peninsula experienced its first continuous settlement beginning in the Middle Formative period. Pioneers took two different routes, slashing and burning forests for cultivation as they went. The earlier migrants came from the southern Petén up the west side of the peninsula, initiating settlement at Dzibilnocac, Dzibilchaltún, and Komchen. Another set of migrants pushed upward somewhat later on the east side, moving out of northeastern Petén and Belize.

The Maya of the Motagua

Small farming villages were scattered throughout the Motagua region, but there were some indications of social ranking in differential treatment of the dead, with precious grave goods such as jade and Olmec-like motifs on ceramics. In the Copán Valley, occupation began as early as 1400 BC, according remains in Gordon's Caves and in deeply buried deposits in the valley floor, and may have begun much earlier. Middle Formative burials were found under later deposits, but there were probably only a few hundred people living in the vicinity of what would become Maya Copán.

Southeastern Mesoamerica

East of the tributaries to the Motagua, the mountainous countryside stretched down South America, broken by the alluvial plains of a few river valleys, the stretch of swampy, mosquito-infested lands of eastern Honduras and Nicaragua, and a few Pacific coastal plains that were, from time to time, touched by Mesoamerican culture. As a rule, from the Middle Formative through the Postclassic, the regions closest to the Motagua and Pacific coastal plain of Chiapas, Guatemala, and western El Salvador were most likely to share traits with Mesoamerica, and during many periods the southeastern border of Mesoamerica moved to encompass these regions. Thus the Middle Formative Ahuachapan region is the southeasternmost extension of the Pacific coastal plain, but in the Late Formative period its development becomes more local, and in the Classic period, it again joined the Mesoamerican culture area. Similarly, the site of Copán was settled and developed long before an influx of Maya brought it firmly into the Mesoamerican cultural sphere.

Middle Formative developments east of the Motagua Valley center on a north-south area that runs from the Bay of Honduras in the Caribbean, along the Sula-Ulua drainages to Lake Yojoa and then south to the Gulf of Fonseca on the Pacific. Middle Formative settlements at Puerto Escondido and Playa de los Muertos along the Ulua River have house floors that supported pole-and-thatch structures. At Puerto Escondido, one structure was significantly larger than the others, possibly having a public or community-wide function (Joyce and Henderson 2001).

6.22 *Few Playa de los Muertos figurines have been found whole, which is almost universally true of Mesoamerican figurines, because they were probably used for particular rituals, rites of passage or rites of crisis, and then destroyed by being snapped in two. As we have seen, figurines are the oldest ceramic artifacts, and each region has a distinctive tradition. Playa de los Muertos figurines stand out for their personality; "almost every one has individual characteristics.... Each ... has its own expression and needs no torso to aid the portrayal of feeling" (Stone 1972: 61), though the torsos are themselves expressive, showing a variety of female figures, nude and in many different postures.*

Playa de los Muertos is best known for its cemetery, where burials reflected clear differences in rank, as evidenced by the elaborate burial of a child, "adorned with a necklace of white shell beads with a carved shell in the center flanked by two small jadeite pendants. A beaded belt or girdle of more than ninety jadeite beads was around the waist. By contrast, the excavation of an adult grave at the same site yielded only skeletal remains" (Stone 1972: 58).

The characteristic ranking found in chiefly societies is rarely more clearly demonstrated than in this comparison of the richly garbed child and the unadorned adult. Despite the site's lack of imposing architecture, the graves at Playa de los Muertos revealed Olmec influence in the use of jade and some Olmec-related motifs on pottery vessels. The graves also yielded many figurines of a highly distinctive type [**6.22**]: "unpainted, highly polished, solid figurines modeled by hand" (ibid.: 61).

South along the Ulua River on a well-traveled route to the Gulf of Fonseca on the Pacific Ocean, Lake Yojoa is Honduras's largest (22 km long by 14 wide, 13.6 by 8.7 miles), and at its northern end is the site of Los Naranjos. Pollen cores indicate that in this tropical mountainous region, maize cultivation may have occurred as early as the Late Archaic period (Rue 1989). Los Naranjos grew up as a trading center as evidenced by shell, obsidian, jadeite, and exotic ceramics. Middle Formative Olmec influence, probably related the movement of precious materials, is evidenced in sculptured monuments. These are unprovenienced but probably date to the Jaral phase (800–400 BC), the first occupation at the site, which continued to be occupied until AD 1200. Los Naranjos was a substantial center even in the Middle Formative, its central plaza having two mounds nearly 20 m (66 ft) tall dating to the Middle and Late Formative periods. Another imposing construction is a ditch 1.3 km (0.8 miles) long and 15–20 m (50–66 ft) wide; this seems to have been a fortification, perhaps against local marauders on this frontier of Mesoamerica. Seven km (4.3 miles) northwest of Los Naranjos, the site of Lo de Vaca also began to be occupied during the Middle Formative period.

Sixty km (37 miles) south of Los Naranjos, Yarumela was another imposing Middle Formative center for trade in precious commodities and was occupied between 1000 BC and AD 200. Like Los Naranjos, Yarumela was protected by its location, bounded on the west by a substantial ditch and on the east by the Humuya River, a tributary of the Ulua [**6.23**]. Also like Los Naranjos, Yarumela had numerous large mounds, including the 19-m (62-ft) high "El Cerrito" (Dixon *et al.* 1994). The site's occupation lasted until AD 200.

The Intermediate Area: Caves of Eastern Honduras

In eastern Honduras, river systems run toward the northeast, bounded by mountain systems running southwest to northeast. In these mountains, caves provided sacred ground for burials in the Middle Formative. The Cuyamel Caves, 300 m (984 ft) above the Aguan River Drainage, had skeletal remains interred with fine ceramics, including one bearing Olmec motifs (Joyce and Brady 2000). This is one of the remotest examples of Olmec influence, and this period is probably this region's closest association with Mesoamerican culture. The motivation may possibly have been cultivation of cacao in this tropical environment, but no associated habitation remains have been located to clarify this issue.

Talgua Cave, in the Olancho Valley, is associated with a habitation site about a kilometer away, and the cave "may be a lineage burial site" (Brady *et al.* 1995: 40). The settlement has dozens of structural platforms, some over 3 m high and 30 m long (10 ft, 98 ft). The people were farmers, but stable carbon isotope analysis of bone found in the cave revealed that maize was not their crop; possibly they were living on manioc. The burial remains in the cave were well-concealed, reached through a fissure over 600 m (*c.* 2,000 ft) past the cave entrance. Some individuals had been buried with offerings, their disarticulated skeletons carefully "stacked and placed in a niche some ten feet above the floor level, along with a broken ceramic vessel and two broken pieces of finely worked jade" (Brady *et al.* 1995: 39).

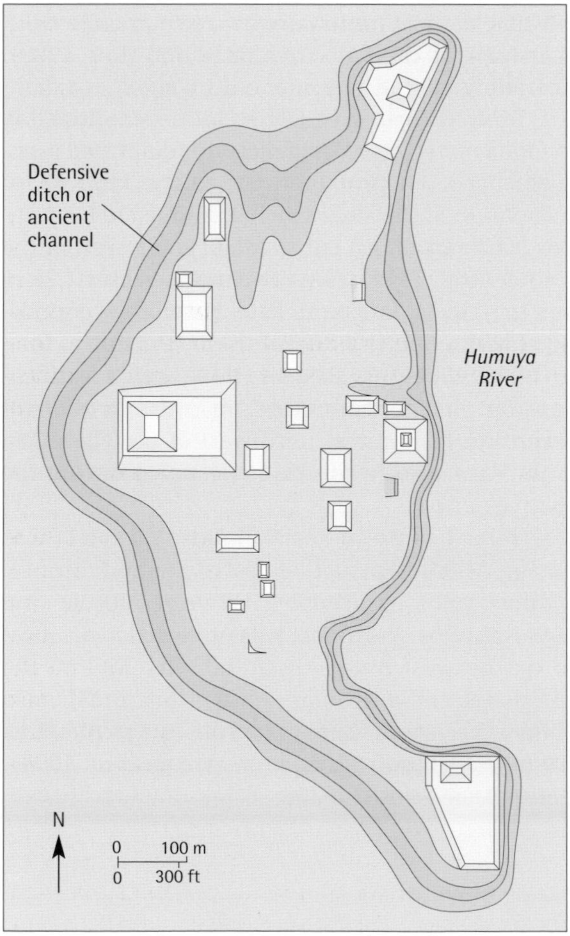

6.23 *Yarumela covered more than 30 hectares (74 acres) and featured a formal arrangement of monumental structures, as shown in the plan. The site's location in the middle of the Comayagua Valley exploited a major corridor, a north–south trade route between the Pacific Ocean and the Caribbean Sea, and this is evidenced at the site by shell ornaments from both coasts, as well as Guatemalan jade and other exotics. The main mound, El Cerrito (at left), was visible all over the valley.*

Transition to the Post-Olmec Era

At about 600/500 BC, several regions were on the verge of significant changes. The Olmec heartland, the southern Gulf lowlands, ceased to be a major source of ideas for regions elsewhere, and began to receive strong external influences, as from the southern Pacific Coast. In Oaxaca, the continuous pattern of settlement throughout the valley was disrupted by the development of a centrally important zone – in the area where Monte Albán would arise.

7 MIDDLE TO LATE FORMATIVE CULTURES (*c.* 600/500–300 BC)

THE REPEATED PATTERN of culture history throughout the world is one of the growth, florescence, and decline of a particular region, and as one region declines another flourishes. Perhaps it is more accurate to say that another is flourishing because of the decline of the center of power, or even that the upstart is the reason for the decline of the established center of power. Issues of causality become easier to address as archaeological and historical documentation becomes more complete.

The Olmecs presented us with the first Mesoamerican culture to have a strong impact over a huge area, and with the first Mesoamerican mystery: how and why did their culture decline, and how and why did the southern Gulf lowlands, heartland of vibrant culture since the Early Formative, become almost uninhabited by 400 BC, and remain so for nearly 600 years (Clark 2001b)? To be sure, the site of Tres Zapotes became important, but although it has sometimes been touted as the third major Olmec capital (after San Lorenzo and La Venta), its cultural trajectory belongs more to the strong regional developments of the Late Formative (Pool 2000), and its location is in the south-central Gulf lowlands, west of the Olmec heartland in the Early to Middle Formative.

The period from about 600 to about 300 BC covers the transition from a time when Mesoamerica had one strong cultural influence over a huge region – a cultural horizon – to a period of widespread regional developments [7.3]. "Olmec influence" is a vague term, because the nature of San Lorenzo's and La Venta's interactions with areas like Chalcatzingo and Chalchuapa is difficult to define: military conquest is highly unlikely, but artistic representations of armed and costumed Olmec-like figures indicate that the idea of formal militarism may have been exported along with Olmec iconography [7.1, 7.2]. Commercial ties were probably the motivating factor, with high-ranking Olmec individuals encouraging local leaders in various regions to adopt Olmec practices and styles – co-opting local political structures and incorporating them into Olmec trade networks.

It is important not to conceptualize Olmec influence as grandiose "empire formation," because this term denotes far more complex organization than was evidenced during the Formative period. It is even debatable whether or not Olmec culture was a "Mother Culture" from which other regions drew inspiration for their own indigenous developments, as Miguel Covarrubias argued in 1942 (Diehl and Coe 1996; Flannery and Marcus 2000; Arnold 2000). Yet it is indisputable that while Olmec iconography that is diagnostic of the culture of the southern Gulf lowlands is found as far north as Tlatilco in the Basin of Mexico, south and east to Los Naranjos and Yarumela and Chalchuapa, west to San José Mogote and Teopantecuanitlán, the reverse is not true. There was not a simultaneous dispersal of locally developed motifs from any of these regions, over a similarly broad area, during the Early and Middle Formative.

Whether we interpret Olmec cultures as seeding Mesoamerican regions for localized further developments, or only as incidentally supplying some interesting artistic motifs to regions already vigorously developing their own complex societies, the shift in focus from the first great cultural horizon to more regional concerns becomes apparent after 600 BC, as the southern Gulf lowlands were apparently abandoned, and new centers of complex society rose elsewhere. During the period from 600 to 300 BC, the most important of these developments took place in the Valley of Oaxaca.

7.1, 7.2 *Militarism in the Middle Formative is evidenced by depictions of armed and "uniformed" individuals. The spear-carriers carved into Cerro Chalcatzingo, Morelos (below) have the same posture and costume elements as those carved at Las Victorias, near Chalchuapa, El Salvador (upper image). The direct distance between the two sites is over 1,000 km (more than 620 miles), and the southern Gulf lowlands lie between them, but, of course, Olmec-style traits are found in even more distant parts of Mesoamerica.*

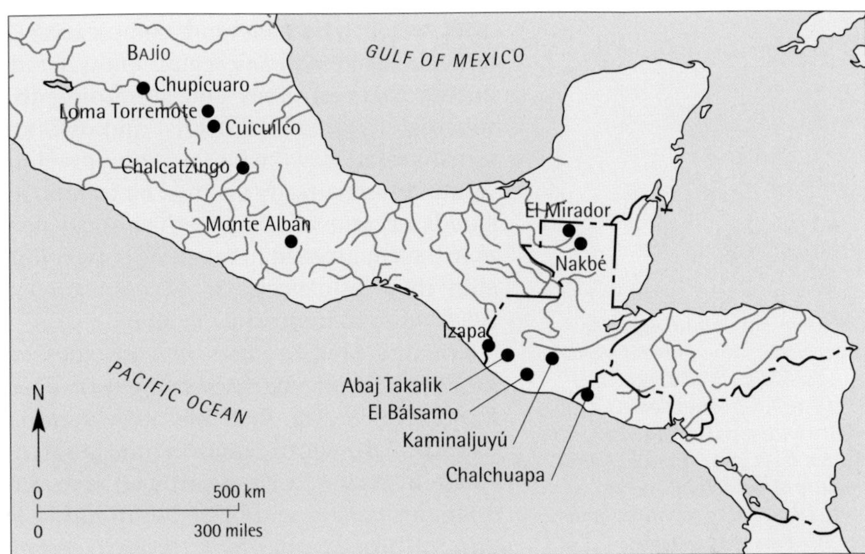

7.3 *Middle America showing Middle to Late Formative-period regions and sites mentioned in Chapter 7.*

WEST OF THE ISTHMUS: RISE OF MONTE ALBÁN

The Valley of Oaxaca: San José Mogote, Eclipsed by Monte Albán

San José Mogote's size and hegemony over other sites seems to have peaked during the Rosario phase (700–500 BC). During this time San José was the central community in the Etla arm of the Valley of Oaxaca, surrounded by smaller villages. To the south lay a considerable area in the very center of the valley with no habitation at all. The eastern or Tlacolula arm of the Valley was witnessing increasing settlement, centered upon Yegüih, with Mitla at the eastern end of that subvalley. Settlement in the southern Zaachila arm seems to have followed the same pattern as that of the other two subvalleys, with Tilcajete as central community (Spencer and Redmond 2001).

San José was the largest settlement in the whole Oaxaca region (total population in Rosario phase, at least 3,500), with a population of about 1,000 living over an area measuring 60–65 hectares (*c.* 150 acres). "Within that sprawl were seven areas of elite residence as defined by decorated fine gray ware. ... The 'downtown' area of public buildings and elite residences alone covered at least 42 ha" (Marcus and Flannery 1996: 125).

As population in the Oaxaca Valley grew, and new chiefdoms came to be established in the subvalleys, competition among them was likely to take the characteristic form for chiefdoms: raids and marauding. Terror tactics are not the exclusive preserve of "civilized" societies: in human history, torture and murder have long pedigrees. Egalitarian societies could little afford to sustain hostile relations within the group, but competition with another group for any critical resource called upon the society's keenest use of cutting-edge technology and intimidation tactics.

As societies became more complex, so did the resources they defined as critical. Farmers in any region know what plots of land are capable of producing the best crops and sustaining that production. Chiefs know the sources of precious minerals, and also know the best artisans capable of transforming raw materials into precious ornaments. Sometimes these resources are already claimed by others, and thus acquiring access to them entails accommodating the reciprocal needs of the controlling parties, as may have happened in relations between the Olmecs and the chiefdom societies they influenced. Or, access may entail mayhem and murder, plus celebration of successful exploits.

7.4 *How can painful death be expressed in monumental fashion? San José Mogote's Monument 3 (1.45 m/4.8 ft long) depicts a figure with a puffy, slitted eye, lips drawn back in a grimace, overall posture of vulnerability, the stylized bloom of rounded elements on the chest and abdomen suggesting the guts after disembowelment. In addition, the monument is inscribed with what may be very early glyphs. These symbols, combining a circle and triangle, "are stylized drops of blood. In later periods, the same motif would be carved on the stairways of temples where sacrifices were performed" (Marcus and Flannery 1996: 130).*

San José Mogote offers several clues to the means by which societally sanctioned violence was being practiced in Middle to Late Formative Mesoamerica. The first line of evidence is the Oaxaca Valley settlement pattern [7.5], which seems to indicate that each arm of the Valley formed a coherent region, each region well separated from the others by the central no-man's land extending 10 km (6 miles) and more.

In San José Mogote itself, the civic-ceremonial center provides evidence of victory and defeat. On Mound 1, the well-modified natural rise dominating the site, a large wattle-and-daub temple atop Structure 28 had been burned in a conflagration so intense it was unlikely to have been accidental. Burning a community's temple was a common raiding target in Mesoamerican culture history. In Aztec glyph language, "conquest" was denoted by a drawing of a temple with flames coming out of its roof. Structure 28's temple may have met such a fate in a raid.

Even more compelling evidence of warfare was found on Mound 1. Structures 14 and 19 are joined by a corridor, and embedded in the threshold was a carved monument [7.4] depicting a naked, contorted male figure, apparently "a slain or sacrificed captive. The monument was positioned at the threshold of a corridor running between two large public buildings, so that anyone passing through the structure would tread on it" (Blanton *et al.* 1993: 69).

As a permanent memorial, Monument 3 leaves no doubt about the high value placed on bloodshed. Throughout Mesoamerica, blood was the gift of humans to the spirit world. Sharp devices used in autosacrifice – drawing one's own blood – included stingray spines, imitation stingray spines made of obsidian and jade, and maguey thorns, and they were the treasured personal goods of individuals who regularly sanctified themselves in that way. In contrast, Monument 3 demonstrates sacrifice on a societal level: acquiring the victim through special effort (raiding or other tactic of terrorizing), then ritually rendering that person lifeless.

Monument 3 has another important element: a glyph message between the feet of the victim. The lower element has been interpreted as meaning "one" and the upper element as "earthquake," together forming one of the day-names in the Zapotec ritual calendar. Possibly, "this is the victim's personal day-name – "1 Earthquake" – taken from the 260-day calendar" (Marcus and Flannery 1996: 130).

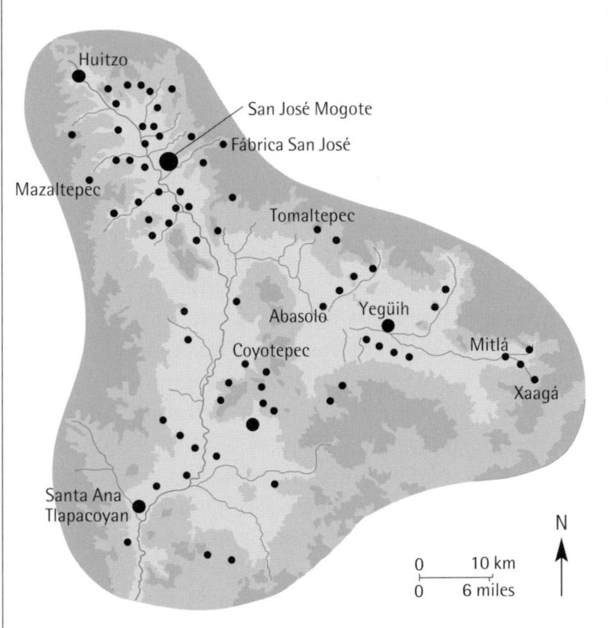

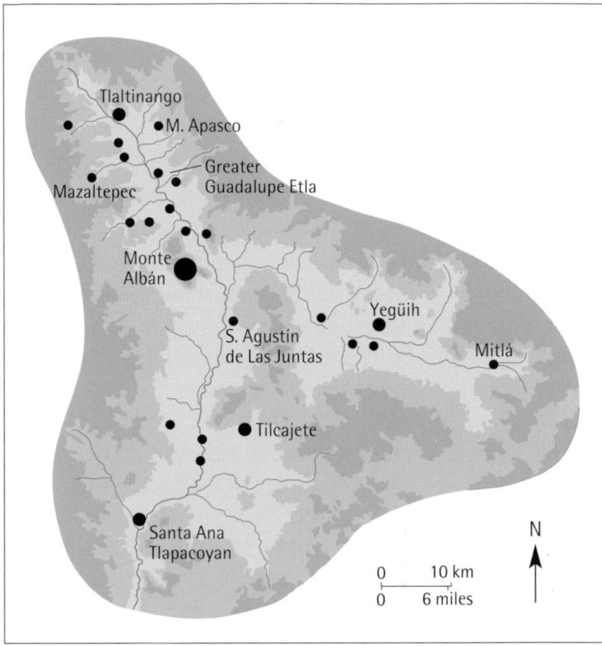

7.5 *(Above left) During the Rosario phase, 700–500 BC, San José Mogote became the largest site in the Valley of Oaxaca. Each of the valley's three arms had extensive settlement, but there is a significant central area where no communities were established during this phase, presumably to avoid conflict.*

7.6 *(Above right) The Monte Albán Early I (or Monte Albán Ia) phase, 500–300 BC, shows Monte Albán established at the central place of the valley. San José Mogote was vastly reduced.*

The unfortunate "1 Earthquake" was probably not the first individual to have a name from the 260-day calendar – this practice was no doubt much older than the Middle to Late Formative, possibly even a trait brought from northeastern Asia. Because this monument's age has been established by radiocarbon dating of an overlying stratum, it is one of the oldest known occurrences of the use of a name glyph, and also the first known occurrence of a Zapotec hieroglyph. The Zapotec writing system would become one of Mesoamerica's most important (Urcid 2001).

While important cultural features like formalized names and glyphic representations were appearing, the various signs of political competition in the Oaxaca Valley – the settlement pattern, the evidence of raiding and destruction – indicate a situation moving toward change.

Monte Albán

At around 500 BC, the settlement system of the Oaxaca Valley was dramatically altered, with the establishment of the political capital, Monte Albán, in the center of the three-armed valley [7.6]. Situated atop a 400-m (1,312-ft) high ridge in the center of the previously uninhabited buffer zone, Monte Albán had about 5,000 inhabitants by 400 BC; this represented over half the Oaxaca Valley's population, and most of the other 260 communities were villages of fewer than 100 inhabitants. The trend toward population aggregation was just beginning: by 200 BC, Monte Albán's population would be over 17,000 (Marcus and Flannery 1996: 139).

DIVINATORY ALMANAC

THE 260-DAY CALENDAR moves through a sequence of 13 numbers meshed with 20 named days [7.7]; unique number-and-day name combinations are exhausted after 260 days. If our calendar were slightly altered, dropping out the month names but retaining a sequence of 30 numbered dates running against seven named days, we would have a 210-day calendar of unique dates – "Monday the 1st, Tuesday the 2nd, ... Tuesday the 30th, Wednesday the 1st, ..."

Each set of 13 numbers, running against the list of day names, forms what scholars call a trecena, and these shared many divinatory characteristics. Thus, for the Aztecs, the initial trecena of 1 Crocodile, 2 Wind, 3 House, 4 Lizard, 5 Serpent, 6 Death, 7 Deer, 8 Rabbit, 9 Water, 10 Dog, 11 Monkey, 12 Grass, and 13 Reed, "all were good. He who was then born ... would prosper ... And if a woman were then born, she would also prosper and be rich" (Sahagún 1979 [1569]: 2). The second group begins with 1 Jaguar, and by the eighth day of that cycle, the 20 day names have been used up and the ninth day of the second group is 9 Crocodile, starting again at the top of the list of day names.

The 260-day divinatory almanac was found throughout Mesoamerica, though the names of days and the timing of their occurrence did not always correspond from region to region. The Aztecs knew it as the *tonalpohualli*, and it is sometimes referred to by Mayanists as the *tzolkin*, a modern Mayan word. While the span of 260 days has been linked to various natural phenomena, such as the length of the maize-growing season in some regions, its most basic correspondence is with human pregnancy. In traditional societies,

Day Names (7.7)*

Order	Aztec of Tenochtitlan	Zapotec	Lowland Maya
1st	Cipactli (crocodile)	Chilla (crocodile)	Imix (earth monster)
2nd	Ehecatl (wind)	Quiy (wind)	Ik (wind)
3rd	Calli (house)	Guela (night)	Akbal (darkness)
4th	Cuetzpallin (lizard)	Achi (lizard)	Kan (ripe maize)
5th	Coatl (serpent)	Zee (serpent)	Chicchan (serpent)
6th	Miquiztl (death)	Lana (black)	Cimi (death)
7th	Mazatl (deer)	China (deer)	Manik (hand)
8th	Tochtli (rabbit)	Lapa (rabbit)	Lamat (planet Venus)
9th	Atl (water)	Niça (water)	Muluc (water)
10th	Escuintli (dog)	Tella (dog)	Oc (dog)
11th	Ozomatli (monkey)	Loo (monkey)	Chuen (monkey)
12th	Malinalli (grass)	Piya (drought)	Eb (bad rain)
13th	Acatl (reed)	Quiy (reed)	Ben (growing maize)
14th	Ocelotl (jaguar)	Gueche (jaguar)	Ix (jaguar)
15th	Cuauhtli (eagle)	Naa (eagle)	Men (moon/eagle)
16th	Cozcaquauhtil (vulture)	Loo (crow)	Cib (wax)
17th	Ollin (earthquake)	Guiloo (earthquake)	Caban (earth)
18th	Tecpatl (knife)	Opa (cold)	Etz'nab (knife)
19th	Quiauitl (rain)	Ape (cloudy)	Cauac (storm)
20th	Xochitl (flower)	Lao (flower)	Ahau (lord)

*based on Adams 1977: 302, Marcus and Flannery 1996: 20

where childbearing secures the future, all aspects of gestation are important. It is understandable that the span of time encompassed by synchronizing the day of conception and the day of birth would seem an essential period.

In all Mesoamerican regions, the days of the 260-day calendar were associated with good, bad, and indifferent omens and traits, and these, in turn, marked the individuals born (and presumably, conceived) upon those days. The first trecena dates for the Aztecs were all good. Certain fudge factors were employed to correct inauspicious birthdays. In Aztec times, the exact date of birth could be concealed by the parents and midwife, and the day of the naming ceremony could take place within a few days of the birth (Sahagún 1979 [1569]: 3). While only ritual specialists could make the most sophisticated prognostications from such almanacs, the lucky and unlucky days were common knowledge. Those born on "Two Rabbit," for example, "did nothing but drink wine" (ibid.: 11) and Sahagún's informants devoted a whole chapter of the Book of Omens to the different kinds of drunkards. Poor Two Rabbit – there would be no hiding from fate.

Monte Albán's large initial population suggests that its founding families came "from a number of valley communities" (Blanton *et al.* 1993: 69). Of course, there was considerable expense in establishing a new center vertically distant from agricultural land and significant supplies of potable water. Provisioning the center's residents required substantial labor, and the valley's earliest permanent irrigation systems, presumably to increase crop yields, date to Monte Albán Early I. Other Early I changes, such as those in the ceramic repertoire, indicate larger societal transformations. Pottery types seem to reflect that wares that were produced in large numbers by highly specialized artisans were supplying the needs of regional exchange systems that were developing (see box, pp. 194–195).

The New Shape of Maize: The Tortilla

Another aspect of provisioning was the kind of foods that were eaten. Maize had been the most important staple crop for many centuries, and its value in part depended on how readily it could be dried and stored. To prepare for eating, the dried maize kernels were soaked in water to which ground limestone was added. This process, called "nixtamalization" (after the Nahuatl word for lime-soaked maize, *nixtamal*), softened the maize kernels. An added benefit was that it fortified the maize with protein, niacin, and calcium, a mineral scarce in the Mesoamerican diet, which lacked not only large herd animals like cattle, but cattle byproducts like milk and cheese.

Once soaked, the maize kernels could be ground into a dough, and then prepared in various ways. Probably the most "instant" ground maize dish was gruel (*atole*); more elaborate to prepare were tamales, which are made by adding other ingredients – bits of meat, beans, seasonings – to the maize dough, wrapping the concoction in corn husks or leaves, and steaming the

7.7 *The use of a sequence of 20 named days was widely shared in Mesoamerica, and as the lists show, many shared names were in the same position, from one sequence to another.*

bundles. The form of cooked maize dough that people today find most familiar is the tortilla, a flat pancake cooked on a griddle and then used as a wrapper for other foods (like beans), or as a dipper for sauces like guacamole (which is a Nahuatl-derived word meaning "avocado sauce"), or simply eaten plain, even when old and stale. Tortillas last for days; they become lighter as they dry out and yet are still edible.

Tortillas were apparently first prepared in this period, judging from the initial appearance of comals, flat griddles of a type still in use to cook them. Tortillas, lightweight and durable, are ideal for provisioning laborers and warriors who must spend considerable time away from their homes. The changes in social and economic arrangements that resulted in the sudden eruption of a huge political center and depopulation of other communities in the valley must have called for new innovations in keeping laborers fed. Tortillas may have been part of the solution.

Monte Albán's Neighborhoods and Early Monuments

There were three distinct neighborhoods, or *barrios*, in Early I Monte Albán, perhaps representing emigrants from separate regions of the Valley of Oaxaca. In the Main Plaza itself, virtually all of the great monumental structures date to later periods, but the Main Plaza itself seems to have been established as a level open space from the beginning.

One monumental construction that may possibly have been established in Monte Albán Early I phase is a collection of bas-relief portraits, the *danzantes*, called "dancers" because of their unusual postures [**7.8–7.10**]. To date, over 300 danzante sculptures have been recovered, many of them reused as steps in later buildings. Many scholars believe that these are portraits of sacrificial victims, following the same reasoning outlined above for the similar figure recovered from San José Mogote, but an alternative view presents them as figures undergoing age-set rituals (Piña Chan 1992).

Urbanism and Settlement Models

Was Monte Albán Early I a city? With 5,000 inhabitants, it fulfills one of the most basic urban definitions: a large and densely settled community. Another of the criteria is heterogeneity of the population, in terms of economic status and occupational specialization, social class, ethnicity, and political power. These basic definitional features appeal to archaeologists because they are quantifiable: population size and density and evidence of socioeconomic and even ethnic heterogeneity can be estimated (Sanders and Webster 1988: 521–522).

In addition to measuring these features of the community itself, we look at the larger settlement pattern, to determine whether the community played a centralized role in its region, whether or not it was a "central place" in geographical terms. The geographical

7.8–7.10 *Monte Albán Early I remains were largely obliterated by later construction, but surviving from this period is a gallery of bas-relief sculptures, found at the base of Mound M (a structure which dates from the Classic period). The* danzante *sculptures are all of the same style and type, but each expresses death – or ritual trance – in an individualized manner. Like the eviscerated corpse shown in San José Mogote Monument 3, Monte Albán's* danzantes *seem lifelessly collapsed, with mouths open and eyes closed, their splayed postures often revealing mutilation, especially of the genitals. Many are identified by glyphs on their bodies or close to their heads; these may be the names of the individuals. They are nearly life-size; the examples shown opposite are 1.17 and 1.4 m (3.8 and 4.6 ft) tall.*

models described in the box on pp. 198–199 are useful in archaeological interpretation of settlement patterns because from them we can infer the dominant societal processes. The Oaxaca Valley maps have shown how San José Mogote, centrally located in the Etla arm, adjacent to first-rate agricultural land, was the largest site – and no doubt a regional capital, or central place – for centuries. In the Rosario-phase Valley of Oaxaca, sites seem to cluster around central places, a pattern that implies the importance of administration of each separate region.

What kind of process created the settlement pattern of Monte Albán Early I? In a sense, we are seeing another kind of administrative central place pattern, but now it fills a hypertrophied variant pattern called the "primate center" pattern, meaning that one community has achieved such primacy over its region that it completely dominates the settlement pattern. Geographers calculate that a primate center pattern is one in which the dominant center is at least twice as large as the next largest center; in other words, the parity among central places in any of the three central-place theory models is completely blown away.

Monte Albán exploded onto the landscape, a ready-made urbanized community. While it may not have fulfilled all the definitional requirements of the term "city," it certainly pioneered the city form in Mesoamerica, and served as a primate center for the Oaxaca Valley until about AD 200.

EXCHANGE AND MARKETPLACE SYSTEMS

ANTHROPOLOGISTS RECOGNIZE that materials circulate within and beyond any society by a variety of exchange mechanisms, such as gifts, tributes, taxes, barter, and sale. These exchanges are effected by a range of mechanisms, from gestures of generosity within the nuclear family to modern stock exchange transactions, and more formalized and institutionalized means of exchange depend upon general social complexity (Hirth 1984a). In ancient Mesoamerica, marketplace systems were among the most sophisticated forms of exchange, and over time they developed into elaborate networks of periodically held markets which convened at towns throughout various regions. By the Postclassic period and probably well before it, larger towns supported daily markets. Typically, food and goods were bartered; such exchanges were as closely matched in value as possible. Eventually formalized exchange media came into use, setting a standard of value that could be calculated in specific numbers of standardized items. Aztec exchange media included woven textiles, cacao beans, and sheets of hammered copper.

Long-distance trade was a very old practice in Mesoamerica, and local exchanges were intrinsic to the development of settled farming. However, it is a major revolution to standardize exchange practices into a specific setting and a specific time interval. This may have happened in Monte Albán I (Feinman, Blanton, and Kowalewski 1984) and in the adjacent Mixteca Alta region, where a marketplace flourished at Yucuita (Winter 1984: 209). These developments have clear implications for social complexity. For example, laws of supply and demand govern economic behavior for all kinds of societies; before someone invests time and labor into supplying a certain commodity to exchange for something else, there must be some assurance that some other individuals will want it, in part because they, in turn, have invested their time and labor into producing some other needed good. However, even though such exchanges would have taken place in egalitarian forager societies, marketplaces represent a much more formalized institutionalization of these principles. And "marketplace exchange," an aspect of Mesoamerican economic organization that began in the Middle to Late Formative and endured into the present in traditional town markets, is very different from the "market economy" as a capitalistic system characteristic of the modern Western world (Heilbroner 1975).

Marketplace Administration Marketplaces function largely on informal expectations of supply and demand, and on reasonable goodwill among the participants. Yet there are responsibilities. Someone must maintain the plaza, allocate the spaces fairly and clean it after the market closes. Accusations of cheating or thievery must be arbitrated. The great marketplace of Aztec Tlatelolco, in Tenochtitlan, was attended by 60,000 buyers and sellers daily, and was administered by a whole set of specialist bureaucrats. Other city markets also had full-time administrators. In smaller towns and villages, local lords carried out these responsibilities, levying small taxes on marketplace transactions, and claiming the right to convene a market as an important dynastic privilege. How early such trends were apparent in the life of markets is impossible to say, but noble administration of marketplaces is consistent with the Middle Formative period's other features of chiefly privilege.

Marketplace Systems and Calendars A regional marketplace system, with many small periodically held markets, must establish regular successive timing of these markets, such as every five days, or every 20 days. While most buyers and sellers would be local people, some specialized sellers were itinerant traders moving throughout the region and attending each market as it convened, carrying special goods from market to market. Clearly, a regionally shared calendar, even a short one of 20 named days, would regulate the actions of buyers and sellers. There is good practical reason to suspect that the divinatory almanac also regularized economic transactions.

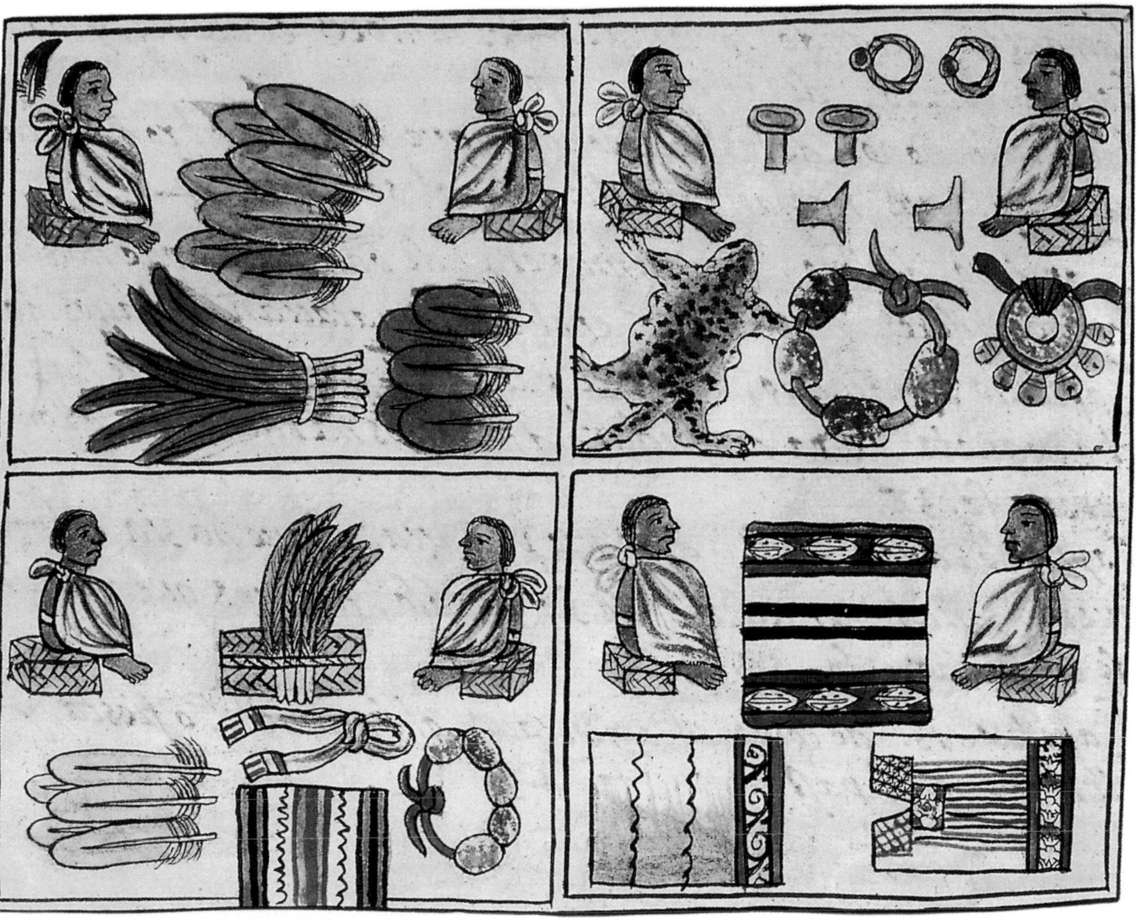

7.11, 7.12 *By the Late Postclassic, marketplace trade and long-distance trade had both become highly elaborated, and were closely related, in that rulers controlled the markets and the lucrative long-distance trading guild, the* pochteca. *Many* pochteca *trading items were precious elite goods that rulers sent to each other as gifts, while other commodities were destined for trade in big city marketplaces. Illustrations from the* Florentine Codex *(Sahagún 1961 [1569]) depict Aztec merchants. (Above) Four images of merchants and their goods, including feathers, textiles, strings of jade beads, metal and lapidary jewelry, such as ear and lip ornaments and bells, and a jaguar pelt. (Left) Merchants (who had their own guild) – or their porters– on the road. Porters could carry loads of up to 23 kg (50 lb) (Hassig 1988: 64).*

ELSEWHERE IN THE HIGHLANDS AND WEST MEXICO

Further to the north and to the west in the Highlands, the decline of Chalcatzingo in Morelos and Teopantecuanitlán in Guerrero indicate the waning power of Olmec culture. In both regions, farming villages thrived throughout, but no major political centers dominated the landscape. In Puebla, farming villages were centered upon larger towns with civic-ceremonial architecture in the Texoloc phase (800–400 BC), such as Tlalancaleca (see Chapter 8). Toward the end of this phase, fortified sites were established.

East of the Sierra Madre Oriental, the northern stretches of the Gulf lowlands also experienced continued expansion of settlements and agricultural intensification, with the larger communities of El Pital, Santa Luisa, and Las Higueras evidencing a complex site hierarchy.

The Basin of Mexico

In the Basin of Mexico, too, population growth continued, with farming villages such as Zacatenco filling in around the lake, and several large centers in the southern Basin: Chimalhuacan, Cuautlalpan, and, most important, Cuicuilco, the subject of further discussion in Chapter 8. In the Teotihuacan Valley, the northeastern and most arid arm of the Basin, settlement was established at Teotihuacan. The Basin's larger sites cover 40–50 hectares (*c.* 100–125 acres), and Cuicuilco may have had a population of 10,000 at this time (Sanders 1981: 165), clearly serving as the focal central place for communities of the many surrounding villages, which covered about 10 hectares each (*c.* 25 acres). The Ticoman site (500–50 BC) covered about 20 hectares (*c.* 50 acres); its 58 burials indicate ranking among the interred (Vaillant 1931; Tolstoy 1978).

We noted in the last chapter that irrigation was an early innovation in the Central Highlands, and that by the Middle Formative it was used in the Basin of Mexico and elsewhere to secure more substantial crops. As population pushed out of the rainier, more agriculturally secure southern Basin into the Basin's northern valleys, irrigation was an important means of pioneering more marginal areas (Nichols 1982). This represented an investment of labor into improving the land, an *intensification* of agricultural practices. Such intensification practices make land more valuable, increasing the stake of the landholders in maintaining their access to improved fields.

Patron-Client Relations at Loma Torremote The diversity of the Middle to Late Formative settlement pattern is demonstrated in Loma Torremote, a village in the Cuautitlán region in the northwestern Basin of Mexico. At its greatest extent, *c.* 650–550 BC, the site had a population of about 2,000 people, living in more than 400 walled residential compounds. Each of these compounds "contained one or more wattle-and-daub residences, a number of extramural activity areas, refuse dumps, and storage pits" (Santley 1993:

74). The compound's outer adobe wall also enclosed patio space, and under the patio were burials.

Compounds were clustered into groups, with little difference "in quality of house construction between compounds or clusters" (Santley 1993: 74). However, over time clear distinctions emerged within the compounds, with some households showing greater affluence. This may have resulted from the development of patron-client relations, a type of unbalanced reciprocal relationship in which the person needing a particular resource (the client) requests it from a more powerful individual (the patron), setting up a relationship of indebtedness and loyalty that may involve whole families and lineages, and persist from generation to generation, thus bearing the seeds of permanent social inequality within a community.

Say, for example, that the first pioneering families to farm the Cuautitlán region chose deep soil land near the river. Over time, as the best land was all claimed and population grew, other families – or related families not in the direct line of inheritance for the best lands – would have to farm in higher-risk zones. Given that rainfall fluctuates significantly in this semi-arid region, there would be years in which the poor-dirt farmers would starve without the patronage of their wealthy neighbors or distant kin, who regularly grew surpluses on lands whose value had been further intensified by labor investment in canal irrigation.

Studying traditional societies in the world today, anthropologists have found that when clients fall behind on paying a debt, especially if difficult conditions continue for several years, the patron-client relationship can become permanent, persisting "from generation to generation, [and involving] an increase in the patron's ability to acquire land, labor, and other resources, and finally a rise in the social and economic position of the provider and his household" (Santley 1993: 78).

The patron-client relationship offers a different perspective on the development of ranking within a community. A standard model of how a chiefdom operates is based on the centralized accumulation of goods by the chief, who then secures a following through redistribution of goods to loyal supporters. This enhances the chief's position of greater access to key resources like land and labor. Actual circumstances of establishment and maintenance of chiefly authority probably combined several strategies of aggrandizement.

West Mexico

The period 600–300 BC saw consistent population growth in the highland basins and valleys west of the Basin of Mexico: Toluca and Michoacán experienced steady increase in the numbers of sites, and some regional centers were developing. Farmers were also pushing north, into an area north of the Lerma River, known as the "Bajío."

The Bajío was a frontier area for Mesoamerica, part of "Mesoamerica Septentrional" or "Northern Mesoamerica" – a region that sometimes shared the characteristics of the larger Mesoamerican culture area to the south, and

CENTRAL PLACE MODELS

GEOGRAPHICAL MODELS describing conditions of community development posit three main types of settlement patterns, derived from three different processes by which population in pre-industrial societies comes to be distributed over a landscape: farmers' markets (the mercantile model), political administration, or transport (trade and travel considerations). While the drawings show purely ideal situations, such as never occur in real life, they demonstrate the action of the three most important reasons why communities occurred in some places and not others. Note that the hexagonal shape of the idealized patterns is, itself, the idealization of efficiency of packing any number of items into a particular area: soap bubbles, the cells in a beehive, and many other such hexagonal patterns occur in nature.

The first model, "the mercantile model," draws upon constraints on marketplace systems, such as those discussed in the box on pp. 194–195. In a landscape largely inhabited by farmers, farming villages are located so as to maximize the distance between them in order to maximize nearby farmland, while minimizing (insofar as possible) the distance between them and the central communities that emerge as marketplaces. Look at the patterns: the mercantile model is the only case where the sites are as widely spaced as possible, with every "lower-order" village able to choose between three "higher-order" towns as marketplaces for its goods. This maximizes the competitive advantage for producers; in a situation of perfect competition, each town would draw upon the area around itself, plus get a one-third share of each of the areas around six villages (1 + [1/3 x 6] = 3), three hinterlands per town. Market centers and farming villages function best when the landscape is evenly dotted with them, and this pattern appears in the absence of other constraints, such as no-man's-lands created by hostility, or forced aggregation by powerful towns, or landscape features that dictate an ideal spot for strategic or transport reasons.

In the transport variant of the model, villages may be located simply as resting points between towns, in regions where transport considerations are paramount. In Early Formative Morelos and Puebla, for example, Chalcatzingo and Las Bocas were established in part because of the importance of their locations at the ends of valleys. San Lorenzo overlooked the confluence of several river transport routes. The transport model posits that lower-order centers will be located to facilitate contact between higher-order centers, relating to two higher-order centers each, rather than to three in the mercantile model. In the transport-efficient landscape, the central place draws on half the resources of its six nearest villages (1 + [1/2 x 6] = 4), four hinterlands per town.

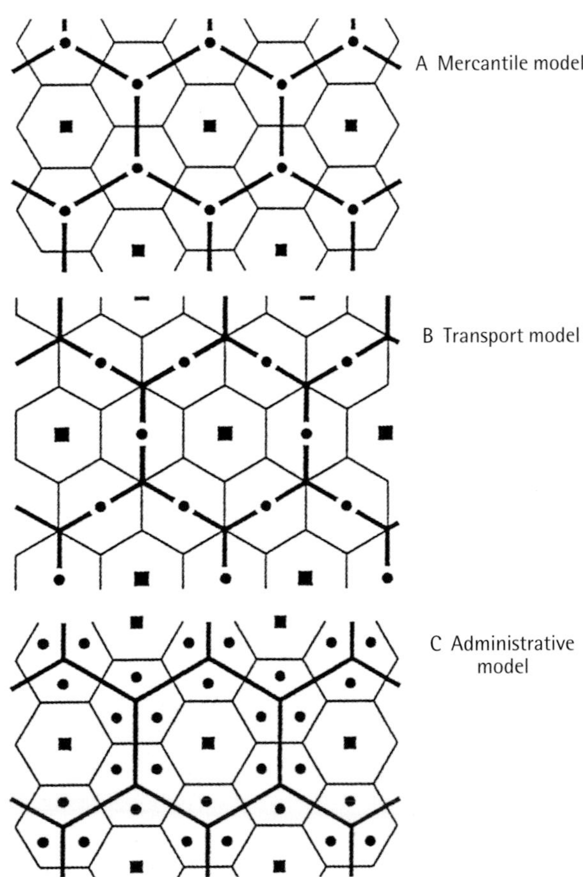

When political conditions in a region compel each higher-order central place to close its borders, protecting its hinterland against the others, the villages seem to crowd around the towns in a pattern that geographers call "the administrative model." If each model has the same number of higher-order towns, then the administrative model is the one that provides the most villages, and the most hinterlands per town (1 + 6 = 7), because the villages still try to maximize their spacing, within the constraints of the rigid political boundaries. An example of this kind of settlement system occurred in the Late Postclassic eastern Basin of Mexico, when each city-state capital was surrounded by its dependent settlements. When Nezahualcoyotl, ruler of the whole region, decided to break down the local loyalties of the city-state capitals, he assigned them tributary villages that were closer to other capitals, thus violating the "administrative principle" on the city-state level in order to insure coherence of the whole region (Evans and Gould 1982).

Given that landscapes are never featureless, but always have distinctive patterns of resources of all kinds and thus these patterns are never found in real life, what do central place models tell us? They offer insights into the cultural and geophysical determinants of settlement patterns derived from archaeological evidence (surveys and excavation) and from ethnohistorical documentation about political and commercial ties among communities. Thus central place models provide a whole new line of evidence in circumstances where knowledge of cultural processes is limited. A pattern of farming sites distributed evenly over a relatively homogeneous landscape would seem to be "normal" in the sense that we intuit the desire for people to want to maximize their hinterland of resources they can draw upon. Yet, given the constraints on this pattern and the others, deviations from the norm should alert us to special considerations such as the attractions of special resources, and the deterrence of hostile zones (like the buffer zone in the center of the Valley of Oaxaca, before the establishment of Monte Albán) or regions with few resources (the lack of settlement in most of the Northern Arid Zone).

at other times was the homeland of mobile foragers. The Bajío was first settled in the Middle to Late Formative, then depopulated at the end of the Classic period (*c.* AD 800), then repopulated at about AD 1300. During this earliest phase of settlement, the best-known site is Chupícuaro, a cemetery and community now inundated by a reservoir. Chupícuaro's period of florescence is thought to be 300 BC–AD 300; it will be discussed in greater detail in Chapter 8.

West Mexico's tombs of the Early to Middle Formative provided evidence of the El Opeño and Capacha cultures, discussed in Chapter 5. These cultures may be culturally ancestral to the shaft-tomb tradition prevalent in West Mexico from about 500 BC to AD 300. Shaft tombs are also known from the Pacific Coast of northern South America, beginning possibly as early as 500 BC (Foster 2001: 662). The beautiful ceramics – particularly figurines – found in West Mexican shaft tombs made them a popular target for modern looters, who have destroyed tombs and archaeological contexts and materials in order to retrieve the figurines to sell to collectors. Recently, several undamaged tombs have been found and systematically excavated; they and the Teuchitlán culture to which they pertain will be discussed in later chapters.

7.13 *(Opposite) The idealized patterns of the central place model produce hinterlands around each higher-order central place community. A mercantile model; B transport model; C administrative model.*

LAST YEARS OF THE OLMECS IN THE ISTHMUS AND EAST

Terminal Olmec Period, 600–300 BC

It was during this period, 600–300 BC, that Olmec culture slid into relative oblivion, as other regions grew vigorously. San Lorenzo and La Venta were both abandoned at about 400 BC. Tres Zapotes, in the south-central Gulf lowlands, is often called the third Olmec capital, as if it were completing the cultural development begun with San Lorenzo and florescent with La Venta. And, in fact, it was at Tres Zapotes that the first Olmec-style colossal head was discovered, and eventually another colossal head was found there. But Olmec art represented a small fraction of Tres Zapotes's sculptural corpus, and its Olmec-period occupation is poorly understood. We shall return to Tres Zapotes in the next chapter, noting here that the archaeological record for the southern Gulf lowlands, the true Olmec heartland, reveals little cultural activity there until the onset of the Classic period.

7.14 *(Opposite) Escuintla region, settlement system development. In the Early Middle Formative, substantial sites are ranged along the base of the foothills (from west to east, Cristobal, Bonampak [actually a second-order center], El Bálsamo, Monte Alto, and El Cerrito. Each first-order center in this region covered "at least 20 hectares, with at least 10 mounds, two of which are eight meters or over in height" (Bové 1989: 85). In the Late Middle Formative, more ecozones are occupied, and while, in general, the largest communities remain those of the previous period, new capitals are established nearer and on the coast, and third- and fourth-order sites fill in the coastal plain. During the Late Formative and Terminal Formative periods, the number and kinds of sites increase, mostly on the coastal plain below the original – and continuing – capitals. In terms of Central Place Theory, the pattern seems to express a combination of mercantile and administrative patterns, with the strongly localized marine resources (among other factors) causing distortions from the ideal.*

The Southern Pacific Coast: Izapa and Its Style

From the Initial Formative through the Early Formative/Initial Olmec and into the Middle Formative, the Isthmian region formed a broad band of closely-knit cultures, sharing ceramic styles and sculptural motifs, trading for raw materials and finished goods. The big Olmec centers of San Lorenzo and La Venta drew upon the established cultural practices of chiefdoms along the Soconusco Coast, and then, in turn, sparked the growth of trading and administrative centers from Laguna Zope in the northwest down to Chalchuapa in the southeast. As the great Olmec centers fell into ruins, so fell the impetus for trade in precious materials and goods, and secondarily in ideas and icons. The presence of Olmec motifs along the coast is almost exclusively a Middle Formative phenomenon. Yet in spite of the loss of Olmec trade, the centers along the Pacific coastal plain of the Isthmus of Tehuantepec and south to El Salvador were, by the Middle to Late Formative, sufficiently well-established to thrive.

At the west end of this continuum, Laguna Zope remained a sizable trading center, and until about 200 BC it would show more influence from contacts with cultures to the east, including that of the Maya, than from its nearer neighbor to the northwest, Monte Albán. Moving southeast down the coast, we find other Middle Formative sites still thriving: Tzutzuculi, Izapa, La Blanca, Abaj Takalik.

Further southeast, El Bálsamo's occupation dates from 500 to 200 BC. This was a large center, with mounds up to 10 m (33 ft) high in formal arrangements oriented to 16° E of N, forming long plazas (Heller and Stark 1989). El Bálsamo was a first-order community in the larger spatial context of the Late Middle Formative-period settlement system of the Escuintla region, which had three or four kinds of sites, indicating a fairly complex administrative hierarchy (Bové 1989: 75). Figure 7.14 shows the development of sites in

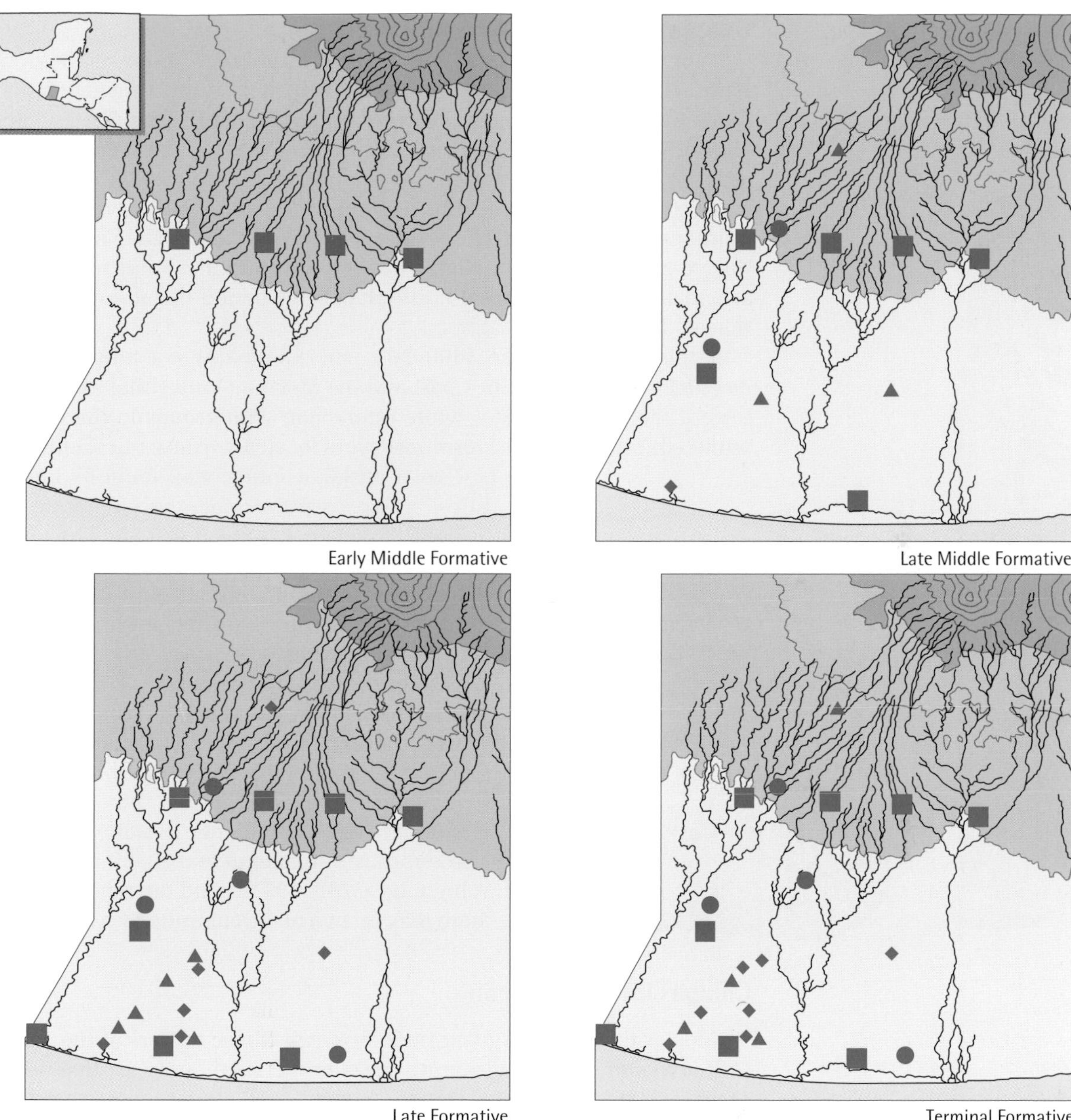

the region for nearly 1,000 years, from the Early Middle Formative through the Terminal Formative. Uphill and to the north of the Escuintla region, the area around the modern town of Santa Lucia Cotzumalguapa was also expanding in population from its Early Formative origins, and would flourish during the Classic period.

Guatemala Highlands: Kaminaljuyú

Kaminaljuyú's Majadas-phase (750–700 BC) and Providencia-phase (700–400 BC) developments included a doubling of the population (Brown 1984: 218) coinciding with agricultural innovations, drainage schemes to expand cultivation in marshy areas near the community, no doubt to support the growing population at Kaminaljuyú and the other smaller communities springing up in the Middle to Late Formative Valley of Guatemala. The ceramic repertoire includes flat comales (griddles) and figurines with articulated arms. Sculptural traditions of this period included sinuous bas-reliefs [**7.15, 7.16**].

In the Verbena phase (400–300 BC), Kaminaljuyú's affiliations were directed toward the Pacific Coast and the Motagua Valley that extended east toward the Caribbean Sea, while interaction with groups to the northwest withered. Two important resources were located northeast of Kaminaljuyú: the El Chayal obsidian source was about 35 km (*c.* 22 miles) away, and the Motagua jade source was about 75 km (*c.* 47 miles) distant. The obsidian source was important to Kaminaljuyú's trade network, but Kaminaljuyú may not have controlled access to the jade source during the Formative period.

Architecture at Kaminaljuyú consisted of formal linear plazas framed by platform mounds and conical mounds, which functioned as burial mounds. In fact, the site's largest mound, E-III-3, dates from this period, when Miraflores culture was dominant (Hatch 2001). The mound was 20 m high and 70–90 m wide (66 ft high, base 230–295 ft), and the remains interred here may be two of the community's rulers [**7.17**].

Chiapas Interior Plateau

As long as there was ongoing trade between Olmec centers of the southern Gulf lowlands, and provisioning areas to the south and east that supplied precious goods like cacao, jadeite, feathers, and jaguar pelts, as well as in utilitarian items like obsidian, Chiapas interior sites flourished. With the cessation of demand from San Lorenzo and especially La Venta, the Chiapas interior centers declined, and some were virtually abandoned (Clark 2001a). La Libertad, on the southernmost end of the northwest-to-southeast Grijalva River Valley trade route, was founded and monumentally built in the 700s BC, and did not survive beyond 300 BC. Other centers, like Chiapa de Corzo, San Isidro, and Mirador, continued to prosper, seeming to turn their attention to the rising powers of the Maya lowlands, such as Nakbé and El Mirador.

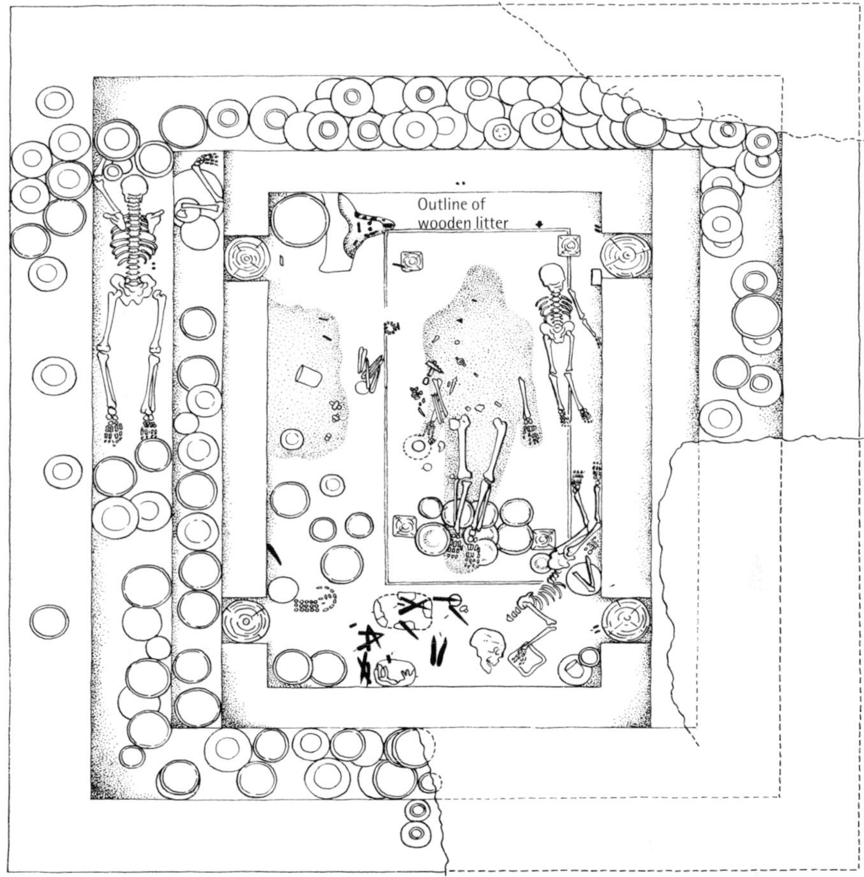

7.17 Kaminaljuyú, plan of Tomb II in Structure E-III-3. The central figure is the tomb's main occupant. His body was wrapped and then covered with cinnabar. The other skeletons represent sacrificial victims interred as part of the funerary rites. Four round posts held up the tomb's roof – the other circles represent the many pottery vessels included as mortuary offerings. Other grave goods included jade beads, tools of obsidian and soapstone and bone, quartz crystals, stingray spines, painted gourds, and sheets of mica.

7.15, 7.16 *(Opposite) Kaminaljuyú, Guatemala highlands, Middle to Late Formative sculptures are in a sinuous style bearing affinities to earlier Olmec art and later Maya stelae. (Opposite left) Majadas phase (750–700 BC) at Kaminaljuyú was defined on the basis of a cache found in Mound C-III-6; Stela 9 (1.45 m/4.75 ft high), also from Mound C-III-6, depicts a gesturing figure; the scroll emerging from his mouth is a symbol representing speech in Mesoamerican art. Among the Aztecs, the more elaborate the speech scroll, the more musical or poetic the discourse. (Opposite right) Stela 19 (1.09 m/3.9 ft high) depicts a man holding a serpent. The man and the serpent both seem to be wearing masks, possibly of sky and earth deities (Stone 1976: 72).*

Maya Lowlands, South and Central

The period from 600 to 300 BC offers much richer archaeological remains in the Maya lowlands than did the previous periods, both in terms of architecture and ceramics. Pottery includes Mamom "resist" wares, the name derived from the technique of painting designs on the pots with a waxy substance that resists the adherence of the slip of colored clay that gives the pot its permanent surface. With Mamom wares, the lines of resist design were often wavy.

Many sites experienced steady growth. At Altar de Sacrificios, residential platforms were built up, and in the San Felix Mamom phase (600–300 BC) Altar's first pyramid platform was erected. In the Petexbatun region, the period 500–200 BC brought the first substantial occupations at Punta de Chimino and Aguateca. Thirty km (19 miles) away, Itzan was developing from early Middle Formative origins.

Farther north, in the Petén region, dramatic changes at Nakbé and El Mirador signalled that complex societies were flourishing among the lowland Maya. Nakbé had established monumental architecture as early as the 8th century BC, with some platforms 18 m (59 ft) high. The Middle to Late Formative period also saw the foundations of monumental architecture at Uaxactún and Tikal. The rise of Maya monumental architecture in the Petén and elsewhere will be discussed in Chapter 8.

Round structures are rare in Mesoamerica (Pollock 1936), and during the Formative period in the Maya area may have served as the focus of public community events. Evidence of round structures from Cahal Pech (Belize) suggests that round structures were performance platforms as well as burial shrines (Aimers *et al.* 2000).

Maya Lowlands, North

The northern Maya lowlands were heavily settled later than the Petén and other southern Maya lowlands regions, and as we noted in the last chapter, populations pushed north along both sides of the Yucatán Peninsula. These early settlements continued to grow and develop important features – Dzibilchaltún in the 6th century had one of the earliest sweat baths in the Maya lowlands – and engaged in long-distance trade with the Guatemala highlands. Settlements established during the period 600–300 BC included Becán, Oxkintok, Komchen, Kabah, Uxmal, and Yaxuná.

Trends to Watch

During the period from 600 to 300 BC, developments in many regions presaged the monumental sites that would arise there. The Isthmus, nursery for nascent Mesoamerican civilization, gave way to the highlands to the west, where Monte Albán would continue to develop as a capital, and the southern Maya lowlands, to the east, where Nakbé and El Mirador would become the largest Maya sites ever.

8 THE EMERGENCE OF STATES IN THE LATE FORMATIVE (300 BC–AD 1)

THE TIME SPAN from 300 BC to AD 300 encompasses the end of the Formative period in Mesoamerica. The Late Formative (300 BC–AD 1) is the subject of this chapter [**8.1**], and the Terminal Formative (AD 1–300) is the subject of Chapter 9. It should be noted that some scholars, particularly Mayanists, do not distinguish a "Terminal Formative" period, and extend Late Formative (or Late Preclassic) to the beginning of the Classic period, to AD 250 or 300. For our purposes, using the more detailed terminology helps to distinguish important trends during this 600-year period, when Mesoamerican culture evolved from widespread chiefdoms to the emergence of some states among the chiefdoms.

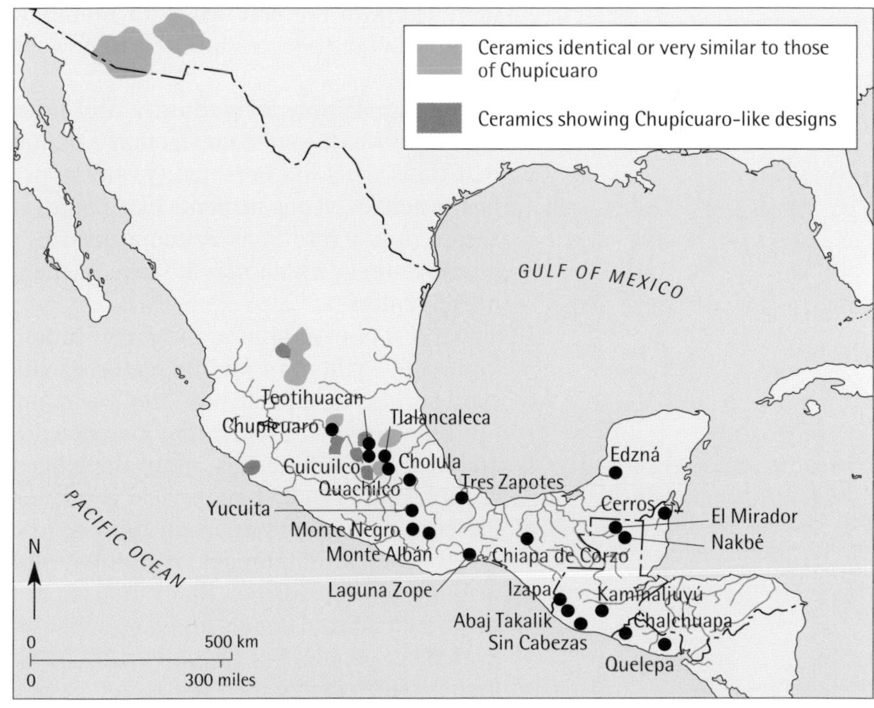

8.1 *Middle America showing Late Formative-period regions and sites. Late Formative mortuary complexes of western Mexico: Chupícuaro and shaft-tomb complexes in the north, in the Tepalcatepec River Valley (Chumbícuaro complex of Terminal Formative), and Balsas-Mezcala culture in the central valley of the Balsas River (Jiménez García* et al. *1998). All these regions had farming villages, but the cultures are poorly known except for ceramics from funerary complexes.*

Regions with ceramics (vessels, figurines) identical or very similar to those of Chupícuaro: Tula region sites: Tepeji del Río, Tula; Basin of Mexico sites: Cerro del Tepalcate, Cuanalan, Cuauhtitlan, Cuicuilco, Teotihuacan, Ticoman; Morelos site: Gualupita [Cuernavaca]; Michoacán site: Queréndaro area; West Mexico: Coahuayana Valley; Northwestern frontier: La Quemada.

Regions with ceramics showing Chupícuaro-like designs: Basin of Mexico sites: Tlapacoya, Zacatenco; Northern Arid Zone; Bajío: Morales-phase Guanajuato region; Northern Arid Zone, northeast site: Tulancingo; Northern Arid Zone, northwest Mexico, southwest U.S. Canutillo culture of Zacatecas and Durango; Aguascalientes looters' site of unknown location; Mogollon and Hohokam cultures.

Social Stratification

States are the most complex political organizations – all modern peoples are encompassed, to a greater or lesser degree, within the aegis of one state or another. The evolution of this form in the world's six cradles of civilization, including Mesoamerica, involved an important change in social relations. In chiefdoms, kinship ties still integrate all families into a society wherein each family is socially ranked by how closely it is related to the ruler. In contrast, in states, social strata emerge (hence the term *stratified society*) in which the whole stratum (or class) is ranked, vis-à-vis other classes. Kinship is still essential, but it provides social cohesion *within* strata – kinship does not provide a basis for relations between members of lower and higher ranking strata.

In stratified societies, the upper stratum or class has more access to political office, authority, and wealth than do the lower classes. In fact social stratification confers so many benefits upon those who control the resources that once the societal transformation begins, the power-holders will restructure political relations in order to preserve social stratification for future generations. Anthropologists use the term *institutionalization* to describe how political offices and hierarchies of power are permanently established. In modern common usage, "institutionalization" implies the commitment of someone to a mental or penal facility, but here the meaning is quite different: the establishment of formal offices (king, general) and administrative departments (revenue service, army) that endure from generation to generation. Think of the contrast with mobile hunter-foragers, whose "officers" consisted of the people most able to do a job when that particular job needed doing.

Making positions of authority and power into institutionalized, permanent offices of the state means that a political structure has been established that transcends the personality, skills, or lifetime of any individual. Also, institutionalized departments like armies and bureaucracies insure that elite access to key resources is guaranteed by law, even by legally sanctioned physical force, which may be deployed against external enemies and internal dissenters.

The cost of maintaining these institutionalized offices and departments is high, and egalitarian mobile bands or village farmers don't produce sufficient surplus to support non-producers like bureacrats and soldiers, or even full-time artisans, even if they perceived a need for them. With chiefdoms and their ranked lineages, some elements of complexity emerge: agriculture is sufficiently productive to yield a surplus that can support specialists like the chief and some important figures: priests, artisans. The chief's village may be larger and grander than other villages, and lineages may cooperate to build an impressive chiefly house, or a massive pyramid topped by a temple, or a set of canals and dams that yield even more crops, and sustain even more people. But the chief rules by charisma and by the prestige of his higher rank – essentially, the society is one extended family.

Demography and Stratification A large and dense population is no guarantee of the emergence of state-level institutions that secure social and economic inequities, but it is a necessary precondition for these institutions, because states, even more than chiefdoms, run on surplus, and more farmers and artisans produce more surplus. A large farming and craft-working population also creates its own complex web of economic dependencies, as we have seen with evidence of the emergence of marketplaces and market systems.

Central communities gather together thousands of residents, and the density and diversity of such urbanized populations further necessitate economic interdependence, and the regulation of complex economic and social relations. People and goods need to be protected from incursions by enemies, and a military force, paid by the ruler, owes its first loyalty to the ruling family and will serve to protect its interests. Evidence of the institutionalized power of force may be seen in fortifications and the development of political boundaries. Sometimes evidence of migrations may testify to political unrest in a region targeted for takeover by an expanding state.

Ideology and Stratification Finally, as features of sophisticated religious and dynastic iconography are refined by elite artisans and ritual specialists, the elements of a distinctive symbolic system emerge. In Mesoamerica, as in so many other agrarian societies, tracking the solar year was essential to the timing of cultivation activities. Formative-period sites show planning features that indicate the importance of marking seasonal changes; "horizon calendars" used landscape features or structures to keep track of – and predict – such important yearly events as the equinoxes and the solstices.

The solar calendar was meshed with the 260-day divinatory almanac, and these two became an effective means of keeping track of time. This power to calculate and position events in the past and in the future further enhanced the benefits of stratification enjoyed by the elite, because they could memorialize their own histories as well as interpret, to the masses, the supernatural events. Calendrics and writing were closely linked in Late and Terminal Formative Mesoamerica, and are expressed together in dynastic monuments such as stelae, and tomb paintings, and these became important public symbols of emerging states.

Pottery Style Zones and Elite Long-distance Exchange

The emergence of politically unified regions, representing complex chiefdoms and simple states, during the Late and Terminal Formative periods is perceptible archaeologically by several features. Among the most important is the advent at this time of distinctive regional "pottery style zones" wherein particular combinations of types of clay, vessel forms, and surface decoration create distinctive and localized types. In this chapter, several ceramic spheres are discussed: Chupícuaro wares in the Central Highlands around the Basin of Mexico, gray wares of the Oaxaca Valley, Miraflores ceramics of the Guatemala highlands, Chicanel wares widespread across the Maya lowlands, and Usulutan pottery, traded around Southeast Mesoamerica and into adjacent Maya regions.

Such pottery zones "involve a series of repeated contacts and alliances expressed through active imitation, movement of potters through intermarriage, gift-giving and trade, or some combination of these factors" (Stark 1997: 282). At certain times in Mesoamerica, style zones were very large: during the Early and Middle Formative periods, Olmec motifs were broadly shared. However, during the Late Formative, such style zones contracted, apparently as a result of population growth in the contexts of many regions where coherent political zones developed that were also areas of shared artistic traditions (ibid.: 283).

At the same time, distinctive pottery vessels were valued items in long-distance trade and elite gift exchange. Trade from one region to another in Mesoamerica necessarily moved smaller, more valuable items rather than staple food or bulky utilitarian goods that could be manufactured almost anywhere. There is little doubt that elites controlled long-distance trade in some direct way, perhaps sponsoring and/or accompanying trading expeditions, or collecting taxes from traders. The arrangement may have merged trade with gift-giving, in the sense that reciprocity of valuable goods between elite groups in different regions may have been an important feature of widespread trading networks. One may be honored by the receipt of a basket load of beautiful vessels from a trading partner far away, and one may pass some of these along to another trading partner without violating the rules of reciprocity. However, regardless of the formality of such arrangements, long-distance trade was conducted for the benefit of the rulers (as well as at their cost) because it provided the cacao beans, quetzal feathers, jade, and decorated serving vessels that elites used to advertise and affirm their status.

Decorated serving vessels function at the most basic level to serve food at feasts. From Early Formative times, such vessels were found in contexts that emphasized the close association of hospitality and chiefly power. Recall that even before maize was productive enough to serve as a staple crop, its cultivation may have been prompted by its usefulness as a basis for beer, enlivening social and political occasions with a mildly alcoholic drink to establish a festive mood.

Feast foods would have been important, as well. By the Late Formative, virtually all of Mesoamerica's food crops had been domesticated and widely shared, and we can assume that the foods of that time encompassed the same range of flavors that have come to typify Mesoamerican cuisine. A feast hosted by a chief for visiting traders, perhaps themselves members of other elite families, would have featured fragrant chile-spiced stews, steaming tamales, and chocolate drinks. The decorated serving vessels used to present the food would express, in a kind of stylistic code understandable to his guests, the chief's contacts with other important rulers over a considerable region.

PROTO-STATES IN THE HIGHLANDS WEST OF THE ISTHMUS

Basin of Mexico: Teotihuacan and Cuicuilco

Insights into the behavior of Late Formative rulers – feasting, trading – help us to understand cultural processes in regions where there is little direct evidence for particular feasts and alliances. In the Basin of Mexico, for example, the Late Formative period saw the rise of Teotihuacan, which in the Early Classic period would become the largest city in the New World, with a population of over 100,000. In fact, only Tenochtitlan, the Aztec capital in AD 1519, would achieve similar size in the pre-Columbian New World. However, while Teotihuacan was undoubtedly impressive, we know very little about its early rulers and how they achieved power. We do know that Teotihuacan was jolted to huge size by absorbing virtually all the population of the entire Basin of Mexico, and we can assume that in order to support this unprecedented demographic congregation, Teotihuacan had to have developed the proper resources, such as adequate supplies of food and water.

At the start of the Late Formative period, the Basin of Mexico's population was still solidly concentrated in the southern regions, as revealed in the Late Formative settlement pattern [8.2] which shows substantial sites on the lower piedmont around the lake, particularly in the south. Two changes from the previous period are notable: some new communities were established in the northern Basin, and, most dramatically, two very large sites had emerged as regional capitals at opposite ends of the Basin: Cuicuilco in

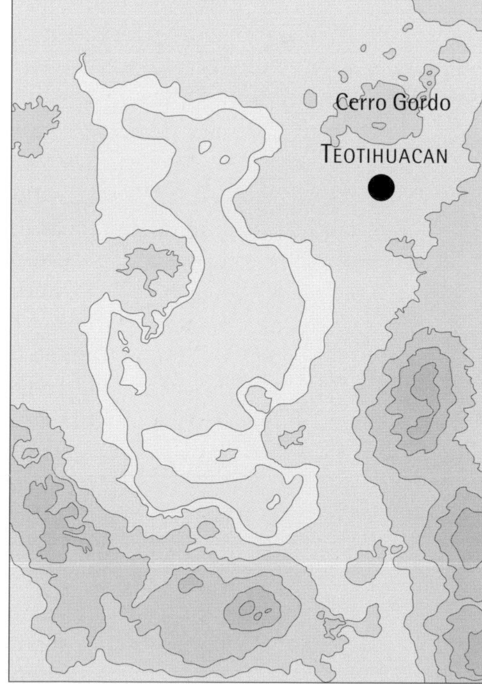

8.2 *Basin of Mexico, comparison of Late Formative (300 BC–AD 1) (left), and Terminal Formative (AD 1–300) (right), settlement patterns. After the demise of Cuicuilco, the smaller regional centers disappeared and Teotihuacan dominated the entire Basin.*

the southwest and Teotihuacan in the northeast. Cuicuilco eventually had 20,000 people or more; Teotihuacan in the Late Formative was at least that large, and growing fast (Sanders 1981: 165). The rivalry between Cuicuilco and Teotihuacan was resolved when Cuicuilco was devastated by volcanic eruption.

Cuicuilco and the Old God of Fire

Cuicuilco had been the Basin's first monumental civic-ceremonial center, and had the Basin's first major pyramid, a truncated stepped cone [**8.3**]. The site was probably founded at about the same time as Coapexco, in the Early Formative period, and its last pyramid-building episodes took place around 400–200 BC.

Many archaeological sites are buried, but few were so thoroughly entombed as Cuicuilco was by lava flows from Xitle, a nearby volcano. We don't know exactly when Xitle's erupted; possible dates range from 400 BC to AD 400. However, Popocatépetl was erupting from 250 BC to 50 AD (Seibe 2000), severely disrupting southern Basin communities. Cuicuilco was submerged by Xitle's eruptions: ash falls were followed by lava flows up to 10 m (33 ft) deep, extending over about 80 sq. km (32 sq. miles), sealing the archaeological context so thoroughly that excavation proceeds with jackhammers, hardly ideal for preserving detail or investigating settlement patterns or residential architecture. In fact, we know little about Cuicuilco beyond the main pyramid, but knowing how it declined helps to reconstruct the important historical processes of the period.

First, Cuicuilco's importance in the Middle Formative period was based upon agriculture and trade. As we have noted, at that time, 90 percent of the Basin's population lived in the middle and southern regions, with higher rainfall, more secure cultivation, and this productivity was enhanced by application of irrigation techniques. Trade, by the end of the Middle Formative, was indicated by ceramics from the Chupícuaro region (see below), Morelos, the Balsas region of Guerrero, and Monte Albán (Muller 1985: 256).

By 100 BC, the population in Cuicuilco and environs was about 20,000, the community's area perhaps 4–5 sq. km (about 2 sq. miles). In the background, Xitle would have been an active presence, issuing forth smoke plumes much like Popocatépetl does today. It makes perfect sense that the deity most strongly associated with Cuicuilco is the old fire god of the hearth, known to the Aztecs as Huehueteotl [**8.4**]. Huehueteotl's images appear in Cuicuilco's figurines, and on a 4-m (13-ft) high stele near the pyramid. Huehueteotl carved in stone, with smoke flowing upward from the disk of his hat, is echoed in the form of the conical pyramid itself, its summit crowned by an altar where the smoke of burning incense and sacrifices would rise to the heavens. This in turn echoed Xitle, the conical smoking pyramidal mountain. This is a good example of how Mesoamerican ritual practice tried to capture through replication the vital forces of the natural world.

By the time Xitle erupted, with spectacular and frightening displays of fire and smoke, its effects and those of Popocatépetl's would have caused Cuicuilcans and others to flee for their lives; several lines of evidence suggest that many of the refugees went to Teotihuacan. First, changing settlement patterns from the Late to Terminal Formative indicate a massive demographic shift from the rest of the Basin to Teotihuacan. Also, Huehueteotl braziers were found in Teotihuacan's household contexts but there was no great pyramid temple dedicated to this deity. This indicates the deity's importance as a family god, privately revered for his association with ancient ethnic roots, but in the volcanically inactive environment of the northern Basin of Mexico, this deity would not have been publicly venerated for his awful power to destroy. Cuicuilco itself became a pilgrimage site, visited for centuries after the disaster, but with little habitation until the Early Classic, when a village was established that continued to be occupied until the time of European contact (Muller 1985: 257–258).

Teotihuacan and the Sanctity of Flowing Water

At Teotihuacan, active volcanoes did not threaten survival, but the scarcity of water did. In the Teotihuacan Valley, where the average rainfall hovered around 500 mm (20 in), the critical minimum for cultivation, nothing could dependably grow without water flowing from springs seeping out from beneath Cerro Gordo, the mountain behind the site, and water drenching the land from storms sweeping over the valley. Thus it is understandable that Teotihuacanos revered the Storm God (probably an early version of the Maya Chac and Aztec Tlaloc) and the Great Goddess, who was associated with Cerro Gordo. Teotihuacan's preferential access to the water that guaranteed fertility depended, however, not upon their piety, but upon their skill at harnessing the irrigation potential of the springs.

8.3, 8.4 *(Opposite) Cuicuilco was located in the shadow of a volcano, and honored this chancy relationship in architecture and ritual. Its Late Formative pyramid (opposite above) is cone-shaped like a volcano, and was built in two stages. The final version, as shown, measured about 135 m across and 20 m high (443 ft, 66 ft). Representations of the old fire god, called Huehueteotl (pron. hway-hway-TAY-oht) by the Aztecs, were common. This deity was "... of great antiquity, with a standarized representation continuing with little change from the Middle Formative times on" (Miller and Taube 1993: 93). He is often depicted (opposite below) in stone (infrequently, in ceramics) as a seated figure with a flat round hat, which served as a brazier.*

Prior to the Late Formative, the Teotihuacan Valley had been an extremely marginal area for human settlement, and it is not surprising that there is little evidence of permanent habitation there, prior to the establishment and growth of Teotihuacan and its irrigation systems. With simple rainfall-dependent farming, a year or two of below-average rainfall could destroy the population. The springs that flowed from under the great basalt shelf formed by the lower reaches of the south slopes of Cerro Gordo would have made the lower Teotihuacan Valley (from the site of Teotihuacan down to Lake Texcoco) into something of a bog. The town of Teotihuacan was established in the middle valley, near the springs, and from this area down to Lake Texcoco, agricultural intensification during the Late Formative included canal irrigation and the development of drained fields (Sanders

1976: 117–119), probably using a technique of cutting canals through the bog and piling the excavated muck upon the raised parts, which creates rectilinear islands of highly productive farm land, served by an efficient system of canals. This technique created the *chinampas* (misnamed "floating gardens") around Tenochtitlan in the Late Postclassic.

Irrigation canals and drained fields are part of a larger pattern of intensification of agriculture occurring all over Mesoamerica throughout the Formative period, and also throughout the Classic and Postclassic periods, as well. It is part of the feedback relationship between growing populations and the need to support them by extending cultivation into agriculturally marginal areas, which prompted the development of innovations like terracing and irrigation that turned some marginal areas into very productive farmlands, which in turn permitted even more population growth.

At the same time, insofar as more productive land was controlled by some lineages, they would become wealthier and more powerful as the value of their holdings increased. Older Teotihuacan families would probably have had claims on the best land, and the newcomers, constituting a sudden demographic explosion, would have given the rulers of a city a huge increase in the labor pool to apply to intensification projects. Of course, this mass of refugees would have also required careful and diligent governance and social programs in order to maintain order and supply their basic needs. In Chapters 9 and 10 we shall look at how Teotihuacan dealt with these opportunities and problems.

8.5, 8.6 *Chupícuaro figurine (above, see Porter 1956: 617) and ceramics (below, see Braniff 1998: 76).*

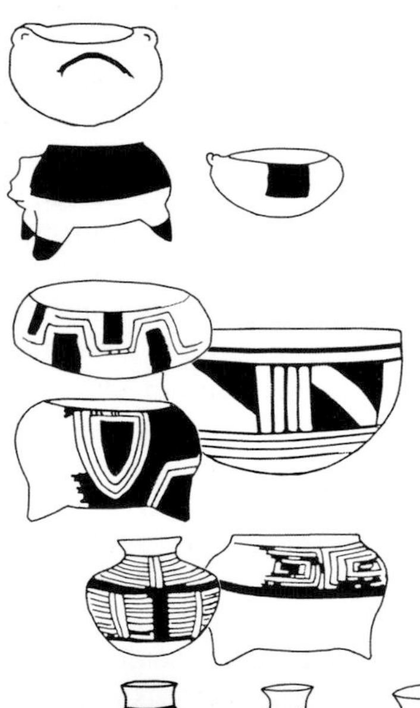

West Mexican Funerary Complexes: Shaft Tombs and Chupícuaro

Pre-Columbian cultures of western Mexico first gained the attention of the modern world in the early 20th century, when distinctive and sophisticated ceramic vessels and figures, looted from ancient graves, were offered for sale to art collectors in Mexico and the United States. So thoroughly were the graveyards and shaft tombs of West Mexico destroyed by looters that it is only very recently that a few sites have been found intact and systematically excavated. Two of the most important Late Formative cultures of western Mexico that are known largely from such looted materials – plus a few excavations – are the Chupícuaro complex and the shaft-tomb complex. The latter began in the Late Formative and was often associated with circular ceremonial sites of the Teuchitlán tradition. Because these features flourished in the Terminal Formative and Classic periods, they will be discussed in Chapters 9 and 10.

Chupícuaro Culture While the Chupícuaro complex is commonly grouped with West Mexican cultures, it is only 200 km (124 miles) distant from the Basin of Mexico, and twice as far from the West Mexican heartland of shaft-and-chamber tombs and Teuchitlán architecture (see below, and Ch. 9). Chupícuaro materials are found in the Bajío, that southernmost sector of the Northern Arid Zone

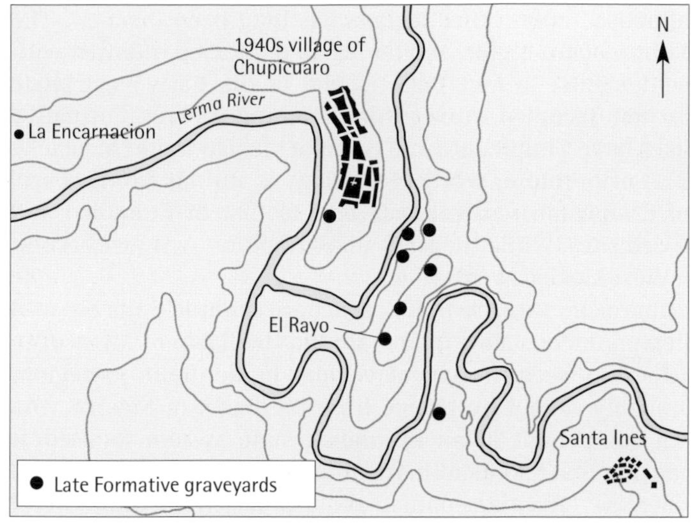

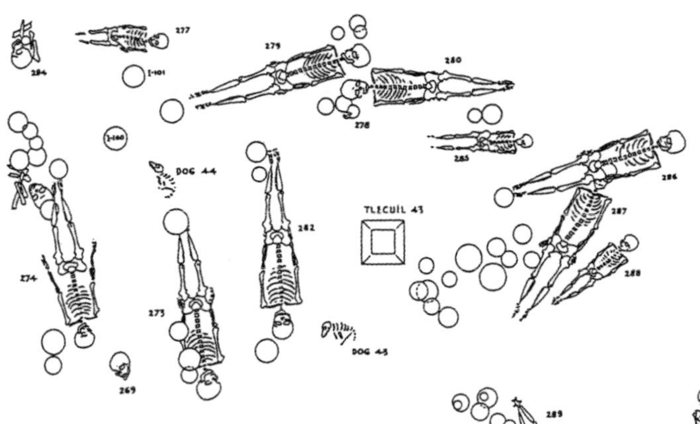

8.7, 8.8 *Late Formative archaeological sites surround the modern village of Chupícuaro. Darkened circles represent the Late Formative graveyards excavated in the 1940s. Bodies at excavation pit 111 at El Rayo cemetery were interred in simple pits, not in tombs. Extended upward-facing burials were most common (as at Tlatilco), but downward-facing and flexed burials also occurred. Grave goods included pottery vessels (circles) and dogs, sacrificed, no doubt, to accompany the dead to the underworld. Hearths (Nahuatl "tlecuil") were constructed among the graves, and in one case, on top of a grave.*

that was outside the boundaries of Mesoamerica except for during the Late Formative and Classic periods, and the Late Postclassic. These periods of cultural activity were probably the result of broad shifts in temperature and rainfall that created periodic changes in the overall productive potential of the region.

On the eastern reaches of the Bajío, along the Lerma River as it coursed north from the Toluca Valley and west toward Michoacán and western Mexico, Chupícuaro culture emerged in the Late Formative period. It is most famous for the decorated pottery and distinctive figurine types which originated in this area and were traded or copied across Mesoamerica [**8.5, 8.6**]. Unfortunately, most Chupícuaro materials known today are looted and bear little information about the context of their origin, while the Chupícuaro site itself, which consisted of several adjacent Late Formative cemeteries along the Lerma River, is now beneath the waters of the Solís Dam [**8.7, 8.8**]. Because of the fragmentary nature of the finds, it has been difficult to date Chupícuaro culture firmly. Recent reviews of Chupícuaro ceramics at various sites have provided a span from 650 to 100 BC (Braniff 1998: 102, also Gorenstein 1985: 45).

At Chupícuaro, inferences about societal complexity and practices have been derived from excavations of the graves and recovery of mortuary assemblages: the evidence consisted of about 400 skeletons including those of apparent sacrificial victims, about 50 dog skeletons, mortuary furniture in the form of hearths, grave goods including ceramic vessels and figurines of two distinct types, and musical instruments such as ceramic whistles and flutes, and rasps that were made from human femurs.

We know that Chupícuaro habitation sites were situated on hilltops around the confluence of the Lerma River and its various tributaries (Sánchez Correa 1993: 96), but we know almost nothing of their size and layout. The hilltop habitation pattern is of interest to archaeologists for various reasons, and important among them is that it suggests a defensive posture in response to endemic violence. There are, of course, other reasons, for example, the need to avoid flooding of nearby rivers, or to live adjacent to, but not directly upon, fertile agricultural fields.

Chupícuaro "influence" upon other regions has long been debated. The area between the Chupícuaro region and the Basin of Mexico is dotted with Late Formative settlements; in fact Tula, capital of the Early Postclassic Toltec realm, was first occupied during this time, and its Late Formative ceramic assemblages have Chupícuaro and Basin of Mexico traits (Mastache and Cobean 2001). Furthermore, while chronology is still far from secure, the florescence of Chupícuaro corresponds best to that of Cuicuilco and other Basin of Mexico sites, while the shaft-tomb tradition was just becoming established in West Mexico at this time.

Thus it should come as no surprise that Chupícuaro ceramic traits are well known from contemporaneous sites in and around the Basin of Mexico. In fact, Chupícuaro does not seem to have developed gradually in its region, but rather was probably settled by people from the Basin of Mexico, and may have been "a component of an expanding state system focused at Cuicuilco, an expansion that had its militaristic aspect" (Florance 1985: 45). With Cuicuilco's demise, "frontier populations such as Chupícuaro [were] more susceptible to acculturation by older West Mexican populations" (ibid.).

Elsewhere in the Central Highlands

While the Basin of Mexico is often the focus of attention upon Central Mexico by reason of its cultural dominance during the heydays of Teotihuacan (Terminal Formative to Middle Classic) and Tenochtitlan-Mexico City (Late Postclassic to the present), the surrounding regions had important centers and cultures, as well. There was considerable variation in the extent to which these regions established and maintained a strong cultural presence, and this variation seems to have had a close relationship to the security of cultivation. The Tula and Toluca regions, for example, cooler and more arid than areas to the south, had attendant higher risk for crops; settlements there were becoming well established in the Late Formative, later than more southerly regions.

Morelos Morelos lies southeast of Toluca, and in contrast to the regions just discussed, it has a lower elevation and a warmer, wetter climate for more secure cultivation, and, not surprisingly, it has a longer history of settlement complexity. Chalcatzingo's abandonment (by 500 BC) coincided with the widespread development of settlement clusters consisting of large regional centers with a few thousand people, each center surrounded by a hinterland of farming villages. In northern Morelos, Basin of Mexico influence was strong, and clusters of communities became drawn into spheres of influence dominated by Cuicuilco or Teotihuacan and shared their level of sociocultural development, the transition from chiefdom to state-level societies.

8.9 *(Opposite) The illustration from the* Florentine Codex *captures the general conformation of the Mesoamerican dog.*

Basin of Mexico obsidian predominates in Morelos, with that from the Otumba source, near Teotihuacan, accounting for half. Probably the importation of this essential tool material was another perquisite of the rulers,

BEST FRIENDS

"THE DOGS that they breed for food ... are quite tasty" (Hernan Cortés 1986 [1526]: 398).

Dog skeletons were found among the Chupícuaro burials, but this was not a pet cemetery. The dogs were no doubt sacrificed to accompany deceased humans into the afterlife: Mesoamericans, like some Old World peoples, believed that a perilous journey was involved, and canine companions could ease the way. Dogs seem well-suited to the underworld; "they walk with their noses to the ground ... dig in the earth ... eat carrion .... They have night vision ... [and sense] sounds and smells that are imperceptible to humans" (Benson 1997: 24).

The role of guide after death marked the end of a dog's lifetime of usefulness; its role combined the functions of family pet and farm animal raised for food. In a land short on sources of edible protein, the dog was a future meal on four paws, but dogs inspired affection and respect for their loyalty and service.

All dogs descend from wolves and belong to the species *Canis familiaris*. Worldwide, dogs were the first animals to be domesticated: they are sociable, tractable, have useful hunting skills, and are aggressive against interlopers of any species. The domestication process probably occurred more than once, but American dogs share descent with Old World dogs, and may have been brought to the New World by Paleoindian-period hunter-foragers. The oldest remains of domesticated dogs in Middle America are from about 5,000 years ago (Abejas-phase Tehuacán Valley); evidence of their presence elsewhere in the Americas dates back to Paleoindian times.

The increasing amount of dog in the diet at Tehuacán from the Early Archaic on (see p. 87) indicates that it was a vital source of protein as dependence on hunted food lessened. During different phases of the Formative period, dog remains accounted for 70 percent of mammal bones in refuse middens at San Lorenzo, and at Teotihuacan dog remains far outnumbered those of deer (Schwartz 1997: 65).

As dog became more widespread in the Formative-period diet, several different breeds were developed. Compared to the modern range of breeds they would all seem quite similar to each other, and would require their own modern "working breeds" category, perhaps called "culinary breeds." Ancient Mexican dogs resembled modern Chihuahuas, but were much larger, 45–60 cm (17.7–23.5 in) high to the top of the head (Valadez Azúa *et al.* 1999: 190, 192). Some were nearly hairless, some even shaggy-coated. The large hairless variety was nearly driven to extinction by the 16th-century Spaniards, who used it as pickled meat for their long ocean voyages (Coe 1994: 96).

Breeding and selling dogs for the food market was lucrative work; those born under the day sign of the dog were thought to be naturals for this profession, and would be lucky, never hungry, and, as the Aztecs put it, "all came to be capes [for him]" (Sahagún 1979 [1569]: 19–20) – the cape being a medium of exchange, this expression means "he was rolling in money."

Dogs are famed for their devotion and sympathy, and Mesoamericans appreciated these traits, as evidenced by the Aztec sentiment that a dog was "a constant companion ... happy, amusing" (Sahagún 1963 [1569]: 16), as well as by affectionate depictions of dogs in art, such as West Mexican figurines and some Maya vase paintings. Furthermore, the Central Mexicans revered Xolotl, a deity with canine attributes who was the companion – in some accounts the twin brother or alter ego – of Quetzalcoatl, the Feathered Serpent. He and Xolotl went to the underworld to retrieve the bones of ancestral humans, to create the present human race.

"elite groups who may have engaged in resource pooling and special exchange relationships with groups closer to the sources of supply" (Hirth 1984: 146). This would be beneficial for the elites of both northern Morelos and the Basin of Mexico, and enhance societal stratification, insofar as access to this key resource was dominated by the upper stratum. In southern Morelos, the pace of sociocultural change was not accelerated by Basin of Mexico influences; ceramics in the southwest show closer ties to Guerrero.

Puebla and Tlaxcala Northeast of Morelos, the same kind of settlement pattern was established, with ceremonial centers that would continue to develop into the Classic period and beyond, surrounded by farming villages. With its rich agricultural land, Puebla supported substantial populations from the Formative period on, and, like contemporaneous agriculturalists in the Basin of Mexico, experimented with methods of increasing productivity, for example, the irrigation canals at Amalucan [**8.10**]. These local terrace and irrigation systems bear watching for what they tell us about labor costs, and the potential for projects that are much more monumental. Just to establish Amalucan's system would have required excavation of a minimum of 80,000 cubic m (104,640 cubic yd) of soil, dug and moved with wooden *coas*, and hauled away in baskets. And that was just the beginning: canals silt up every year, so they require repeated episodes of digging and hauling.

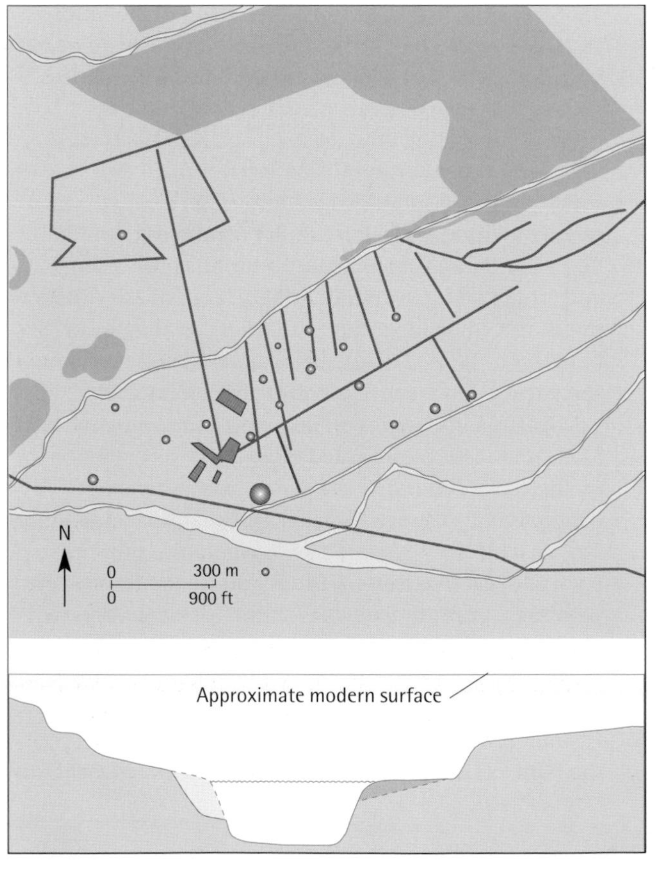

8.10 *Amalucan (Puebla) was occupied during Tezoquipan phase, when it measured 60–120 hectares (150–300 acres). The plan of the site, including its pyramids and its set of irrigation ditches, is worth examining, because it represents a trend common throughout Mesoamerica, and gives us an idea of the extent of irrigation systems that were installed and maintained by villagers. The scope of labor projects feasible with a population like Teotihuacan's would be enormously greater. Amalucan's irrigation system as mapped runs to nearly 8 km (5 miles) (Fowler 1968). The cross section of the excavated canal shows the extent of labor – the canal was dug to a depth of c. 2.5 m (8.2 ft) below soil surface and was about 4 m (13.1 ft) across at base.*

At some sites, labor effort was devoted to monumental structures. By Postclassic times, Cholula was Puebla's most important city – it was the first New World city the Spaniards saw that compared in size with European cities, and its Postclassic pyramid was the largest in the New World. Cholula had been established in the Early Formative and civic-ceremonial construction began in the Late Formative period. Like Teotihuacan, Cholula may have absorbed an influx of refugees fleeing the effects of Popocatépetl's eruptions (Plunket and Uruñela 1998a).

Civic-ceremonial centers with pyramids were also established at Xochitecatl and Totimehuacan, and architecture was elaborated at Tlalancaleca [**8.11, 8.12**], where population continued to grow from its Early Formative beginnings to a high of 10,000 by the Late Formative. Its dozens of ceremonial complexes displayed architectural traits that would later be identified with Teotihuacan: building façades featured long vertical panels surmounting sloping aprons, the "*talud-tablero*" style (see

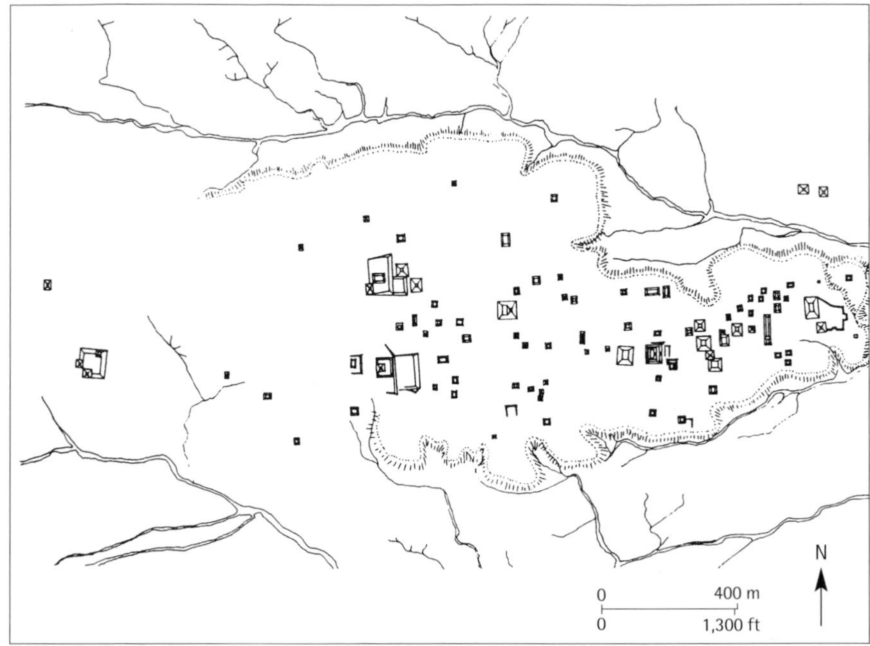

8.11, 8.12 *Tlalancaleca (Puebla). Occupied 1100* BC–AD *100, the site runs along the top of a volcanic ridge between two* barrancas *(gullies). The site plan (right) shows monumental architecture; some of the mounds measured at least 15 m (c. 50 ft) high. Habitation extended over this zone and out onto the plain to the northeast. (Below) The stela (Elemento 7) depicts a deity or person representing death. His mouth is defleshed and skull motifs adorn the sides and back of the stela. The spots on the figure's body may represent a jaguar component of the figure's nature (Aguilera 1974).*

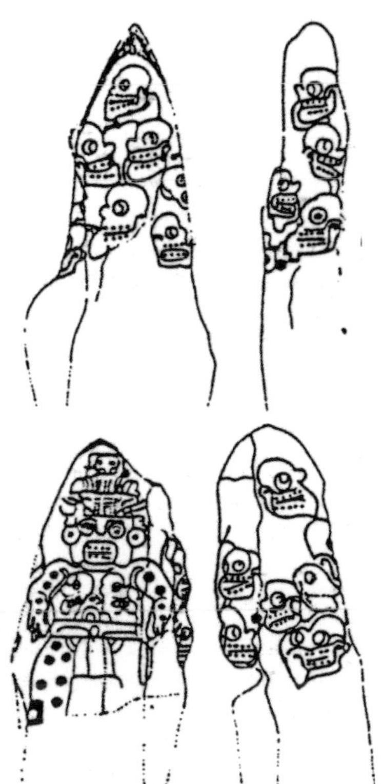

Chapter 9), which was also found elsewhere in Puebla, suggesting that it originated there and was adopted in the Basin of Mexico. Tlalancaleca lost much of its population by the end of the Late Formative, and was abandoned at the beginning of the Terminal Formative.

About 10 km (6.2 miles) due north of Tlalancaleca is Gualupita las Dalias, a site much smaller than Tlalancaleca but so similarly laid out that archaeologists nicknamed it "Tlalancalequita" or "Little Tlalancaleca" (García Cook and Rodriguez 1975). On a ridge running east, between two *barrancas* (gullies), pyramids and house platforms were distributed, with agricultural terraces running down the slopes of the ridge. Gualupita, like Tlalancaleca, shows evidence of interaction with distant cultures, in this case, its figurines and some of its ceramics resemble those of the Chupícuaro-Cuicuilco interaction sphere. Both Gualupita and Tlalancaleca were less than 100 km (62 miles) directly east of Cuicuilco.

Tehuacán In the Tehuacán region, Late Santa María and Early Palo Blanco phases (500–150 BC, 150 BC–AD 250) saw the development of Quachilco, the Tehuacán Valley's first substantial community: "It served as a primitive 'central place,'" for much of the valley (Drennan 1979: 169). As Figure **8.13** shows, the community had impressive civic-ceremonial architecture overlooking houselots that were also farm plots. Status differences are clear from the architecture. Around the central plaza, some houses were built on stone-faced platforms 1–2 m (3.3–6.6 ft) high, while others were "of simple wattle and daub construction, in some cases without even a stone wall foundation" (Drennan 1978: 78).

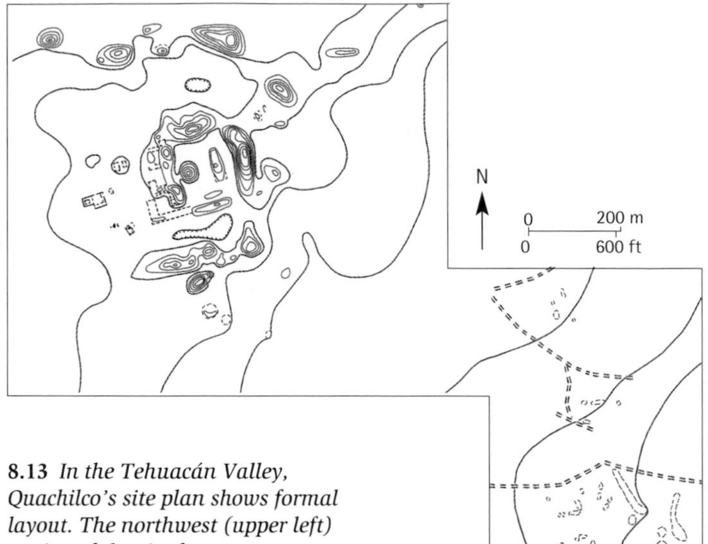

8.13 *In the Tehuacán Valley, Quachilco's site plan shows formal layout. The northwest (upper left) section of the site focuses upon a plaza,* c. *150 by 125 m (492 by 410 ft), surrounded by mounds "ranging from 2 to 9 m [6.6 to 29.5 ft] in height ... the remains of rather elaborate stone architecture" (Drennan 1978: 23). Quachilco reached maximum size (about 30 hectares [74 acres], and several hundred people) by 150 BC, and was abandoned some time around AD 1. Although the site was reoccupied in the Postclassic period, and mounds around the central plaza were enlarged then, the pattern of civic-ceremonial architecture was established in the Late Formative. The southeast (lower right) portion of the site plan shows a residential* barrio, *its house mounds interspersed among irrigation ditches. This underlines the basic fact of Tehuacán Valley life: no substantial permanent settlements were possible without irrigation.*

The reasons for Quachilco's decline are not clear, but part of the answer may lie in the growing population of the Tehuacán region. By AD 1, half a dozen other substantial settlements had grown up in the valley, and rather than having a single substantial site, the valley had competing sites, probably the seats of small chiefdoms. Moreover, the new centers were located on defensible hilltops, unlike Quachilco's vulnerable position on relatively low-lying ground. One of these new centers, Cuayucatepec, will be discussed in Chapter 9. The change in settlement pattern toward a more defensive posture is probably related to the growing power of Monte Albán, discussed below.

Further south in the Tehuacán Valley, about 25 km (15.5 miles) south of Quachilco, was a monumental construction that dwarfed any Late Formative-period civic-ceremonial structure in Mesoamerica. The Purrón Dam was built in four stages, beginning about 700 BC and ending in the Early Palo Blanco phase. The first dam could have been "built by cooperation within a single small village" as it required the work of 10 men for about 100 days, but with each successive level, "the volume of work greatly increased" and to accomplish Stage 4 required a labor force encompassing all 19 nearby settlements (Woodbury and Neely 1972: 98). Indeed, if this were a project to irrigate lands to grow crops for the region, then the estimated capacity of Stage 4, 2.64 million gallons, would have irrigated little more than 300 hectares (741 acres), not enough to meet local food needs.

The Arroyo Lencho Diego region and Purrón Dam were abandoned by about AD 250. Perhaps the next stage of labor investment was too daunting given the return, or the area became unsafe as the ambitions of larger polities created havoc for the small regional clusters of communities.

Cuicatlán Cañada

The canyon of Cuicatlán is a narrow southern extension of the Tehuacán Valley, north of the Valley of Oaxaca. It is on a natural route between the two valleys, and, like the Tehuacán Valley, showed evidence of Monte Albán's growing political strength in the Late and Terminal Formative periods. Evidence of this is the change in settlement distribution occurring at about 200 BC. This date marks the transition between the canyon's Perdido phase (600–200 BC) and Lomas phase (200 BC–AD 200), when small sites at the northern (Tehuacán) end of the canyon were replaced by fortified sites around Quiotepec (Spencer and Redmond 1997). Quiotepec was at

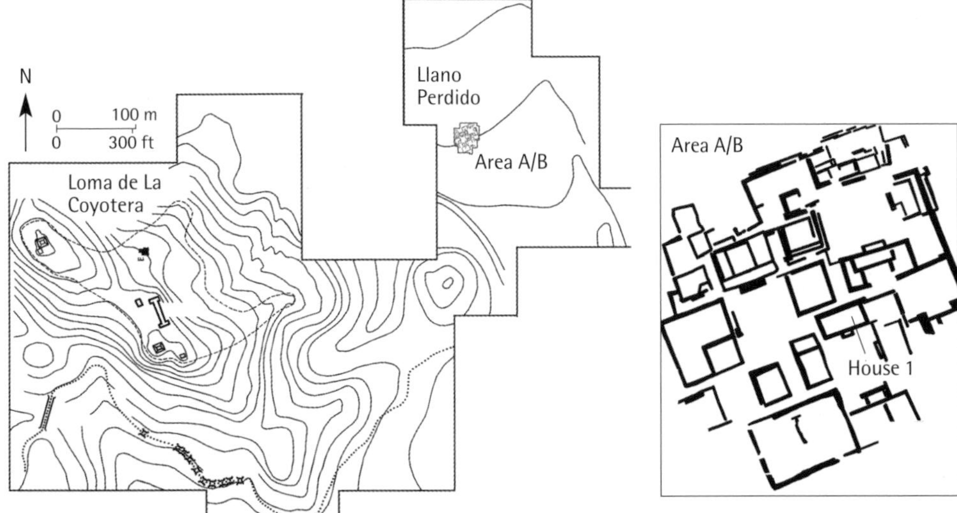

8.14, 8.15 *In the Cuicatlán Cañada at around 200 BC, Llano Perdido (upper right on the site plan) was destroyed by burning. The new settlement, atop Loma de La Coyotera, had far more formal architecture, with several pyramidal monuments and a ball court. Llano Perdido's houses, along with storage and ritual buildings, were grouped around patios, in four compounds, as shown in the plan of Area A/B (35 m/115 ft across, see upper right). Residential architecture consisted of small, single-family houses. The reconstruction drawing shows House 1 (at right of center on the plan), with its hearth in the corner.*

a point of confluence of rivers draining the Tehuacán Valley and northern reaches of the Oaxaca Valley, as they join to flow toward the south-central Gulf lowlands, thus an important link between these three regions.

Further south in the canyon, the transition from lower-lying sites to more defensible hilltop settings is shown at Llano Perdido and Loma de La Coyotera [8.14, 8.15]. The contrasts between Llano Perdido and Loma de La Coyotera nicely illustrate the processes taking place in many regions of the highlands west of the Isthmus, where farming villages on the plains were abandoned in favor of more defensible positions, hilltop sites.

The Mixteca

West of the Cuicatlán Cañada, the broken, mountainous terrain of the Mixteca Alta insured the necessary isolation for distinctive regional development of Mixtec culture, but the river valleys gave ready access to adjacent regions, so trade in ideas and goods was active. The Late Formative period began a long stretch of important cultural transformations in the Mixteca Alta, including social stratification and the rise of the state, a state religion, and a three-tiered settlement system (Spores 1984).

Yucuita continued as the most important community in the Nochixtlán Valley, an urbanized center with a population of about 6,500, nearly half the population of the valley, "the first center encountered by travelers or traders coming into the region from the Valley of Oaxaca, the [Cuicatlán] Cañada, or the Tehuacán Valley" (Winter 1984: 208). Perhaps because of its vulnerable position and Monte Albán's expansionism, Yucuita was abandoned at the end of the Late Formative, and remained unoccupied for a century or more.

Yucuita lies at the highest reaches of a vast drainage system that merges to become the Río Verde, which meets the Pacific Ocean 150 km (93 miles) to the south. For the last 30 or so km (*c.* 18 miles) the river crosses a coastal plain, part of the region known as Mixteca de la Costa. In a previous chapter the point was made that the Guerrero-Oaxaca Coast is not a continuous sweep of coastal plain, as is the Pacific coastal plain from the Isthmus toward the southeast. Instead, the mountains interrupt the continuity, and the Mixteca de la Costa, while isolated, is one of the relatively few stretches of coastal plain.

This isolation meant that the region was slower to have permanent settlement, but by the Late Formative period it had many communities, probably maintaining "a two-tiered settlement hierarchy [with] ascribed status differences, elite control of prestige goods, and large-scale construction activities" (Joyce 1993: 71). At two sites, Cerro de la Cruz and Río Viejo, decorated serving vessels were imported from the Oaxaca Valley and from another undetermined foreign location. Such imports testify to long-distance trading networks, and to the needs of local elites to validate and bolster their status by demonstrating contacts with foreign powers and the ability to amass and use precious goods.

Monte Albán

The same process of urbanization perceptible in the Basin of Mexico was taking place simultaneously in the Valley of Oaxaca, where Monte Albán reached a size of 17,000 by the end of Late Monte Albán I (300–100 BC), making it one of the largest New World centers at that time. While the Basin of Mexico saga of population aggregation was hastened by a natural disaster, the Valley of Oaxaca was the stage for an altogether more human drama, of one chiefdom achieving statehood by "*taking over its neighbors*, eventually turning them into subject provinces of a much larger polity" (Marcus and Flannery 1996: 157, emphasis theirs).

As we have seen, Monte Albán drew much of the population of the Oaxaca Valley into the center, beginning about 500 BC. This situation was less pronounced than the Basin of Mexico's much larger area of nearly complete abandonment, and the settlements outside Monte Albán are of various sizes, forming a site hierarchy of three, and perhaps four tiers, one strong indication of state-level organization. The site types include defensible hilltop centers. By 100 BC, the entire valley was under Monte Albán's control, and as the Cuicatlán Cañada region demonstrated, neighboring areas were affected as well.

We would look for direct demonstration of Monte Albán's growing affluence and power in the development of its monumental architecture, but of this phase, very little remains. In Chapter 7, we noted that the *danzante* sculptures attested to Monte Albán's power to intimidate its enemies. Probably the major project of clearing and leveling the hilltop plaza was under way by the last few centuries BC, and major components of the monumental architecture may have been laid out, but later building episodes have eliminated this evidence.

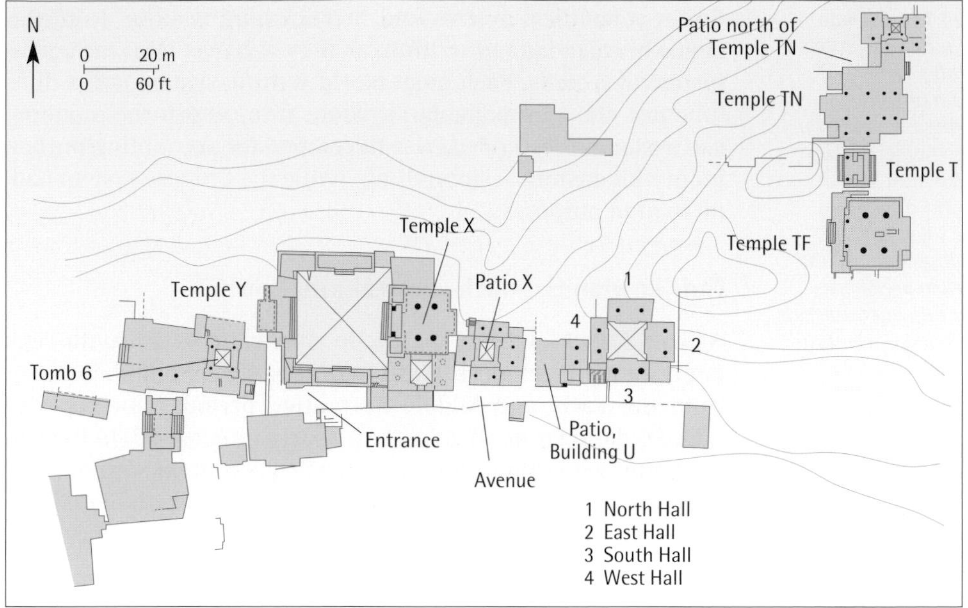

8.16 *Monte Negro lies atop a hill about 60 km (37 miles) west of Monte Albán. The site's overall plan shows its extended hilltop layout, while the detail reveals a pattern of linked plazas and buildings. Note that several architectural features will also characterize later civic-ceremonial buildings at Monte Albán and elsewhere, such as the pattern of four adjacent buildings around a patio, and the use of columns, which permitted the development of much larger enclosed rooms, as well as protecting inhabitants in this cold, high-altitude (2900 m/9,515 ft elevation) environment. Buildings 1–4 and 6 probably represent elite residences.*

Monte Negro

To understand what Monte Albán looked like at this time, a contemporaneous site, Monte Negro, serves as a good example [**8.16**]. Monte Negro is in the Mixteca Alta, but may have been founded by people from the Oaxaca Valley. In the Peñoles region, between Monte Albán and the Mixteca, substantial settlement that developed there in the Late and Terminal Formative bore ceramics of Monte Albán I and II styles (or local imitations), but Mixtec ceramics are rare, indicating that Peñoles functioned as Monte Albán's colonized western hinterland (Finsten 2001). Monte Negro, just west of Peñoles, may have been an outpost: its "defensible location hints that it may have been on or near the frontier between the Zapotec and hostile neighbors" (Marcus and Flannery 1996: 169). This frontier seems to have been pushing outward, from Monte Albán, which naturally would make their new neighbors somewhat hostile. The mountaintop situation of so many sites during this period provides strong evidence for the need for defensive posture, indicating that the larger, stronger, better-organized cultures were expanding in a bellicose fashion.

ISTHMUS AND EAST

While the greater Isthmian region had been the dynamic heartland of Olmec culture, by the Late Formative period other regions were pushing ahead with programs of political expansion undreamed-of by the rulers of San Lorenzo or La Venta. Still, the Isthmian region retained a kind of precocity: it is there that we find the oldest expressions in Mesoamerica of the Long

8.19 *(Opposite) The Calendar Round, best diagrammed as a set of three intermeshing gears. "A" represents the set of 13 day numbers that mesh with 20 named days ("B") to form the 260-day divinatory almanac. These in turn mesh with the 365 days of the calendar of the solar year ("C"). The names of days and months used here are from the Maya system, the bar and dot numerals used in cycles A and C count the day numbers.*

Count calendrical system and hieroglyphic writing. Note the interdependence of calendar and writing, as they serve as joint means of maintaining historical records. Each great world writing system had a different original function: the Mesopotamian system, from which the modern Euro-American system is descended, was developed for accounting purposes as well as for mythic-historical storytelling, while the Chinese system had its origins in divination purposes.

Gulf Lowlands, South-central and South

At Tres Zapotes, in the Papaloapan river plain of the south-central Gulf lowlands, two Olmec colossal head sculptures were found. Such sculptures date from the Early and Middle Formative periods, but occupations at Tres Zapotes dating from that time are poorly understood. In the Late and Terminal Formative periods, the site consisted of four clusters of large mounds, up to 18 m (59 ft) high, arrayed around plazas, three of them in an area extending over 2 sq. km (0.8 sq. miles), while the fourth group is 2 km (1.24 miles) northwest of the main set of mounds.

Most of the site's sculpture dates from the Late and Terminal Formative periods. Sculptural styles indicate continuity from those of the Olmec, while also expressing "features in common with the Pacific Coast of Chiapas and Guatemala [that] attest to the continued importance of elite communications across the trans-Isthmian lowlands" (Stark and Arnold 1997: 25). Examples of these similarities are shown in **8.17** and **8.18**, where a shared style of framing the narrative figures characterizes monuments erected about 500 km (*c.* 300 miles) apart. Presumably, the elites across the Isthmus shared in the Olmec linguistic tradition and spoke Mixe-Zoquean languages. Mixe-Zoquean glyphs may have been precursors to written Mayan.

8.17, 8.18 *The Trans-Isthmian region shared sculptural styles and iconography. Here, two scenes are being played out within the maw of a jaguar, on the left, at Izapa (Monument 2), and on the right at Tres Zapotes (Stela D), about 500 km (310 miles) distant.*

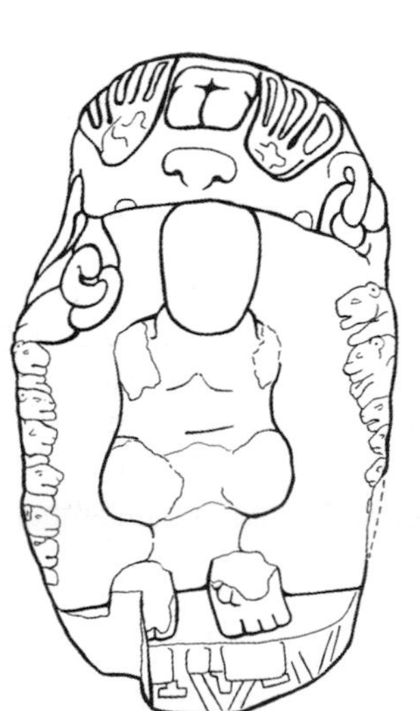

Chiapas Interior Plateau

A few centers of interior Chiapas survived what appears to have been major population restructuring in the period 400–200 BC, when La Venta's important influence on this region was dead, and Maya centers in the Petén were growing powerful. In fact, Maya peoples began to push into the northern part of interior Chiapas, and Zoque-culture communities that survived, such as "Santa Rosa, Chiapa de Corzo, and Mirador, show a strong presence of Maya trade wares and architectural styles" (Clark 2001: 126). Yet continued elite ties with other Mixe-Zoque peoples of the Isthmian region are indicated by the very early calendric monument, Chiapa de Corzo's Stela

CALENDRICS

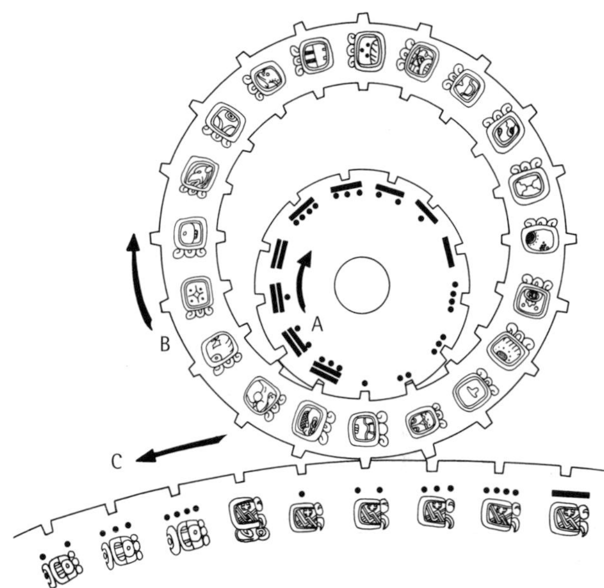

IN SEVERAL IMPORTANT SENSES, the rhythms of time inspired the Mesoamerican system of historical storytelling that combined writing with intermeshing calendars. The 260-day divinatory almanac, we have seen, joined 20 different day names with 13 numbers, and individuals were often known by the day name of their birth. The solar calendar (a 365-day "vague year" rather than the 365.25-day modern solar year), was the product of astronomical reckoning. It was also crucial to the lives of agriculturalists, and was formulated as a calendar more similar to our own, with 18 successive months, each with 20 days, with an additional period of five "unlucky" days at the end to complete the solar year.

When these divinatory almanac and solar calendars are meshed together [**8.19**], the result was a set of roughly 18,980 uniquely named days, a "Calendar Round of 52 solar years [that] was present among all the Mesoamericans ... and is presumably of very great age" (Coe 1999: 59). Thus the Calendar Round was highly serviceable for the purposes of keeping track of recent and ongoing events and their divinatory and/or dynastic significance, particularly when these were expressed through orations rather than more permanent written records. When you count time in this way, each cycle is repeated in sets of named days without reference to any uniquely numbered year, such as the common era's AD 2000.

However, a longer view is necessary when more control over time promises greater understanding of the cosmos and the deities that decide human fate, and when political fortunes of human families may rise (or fall) depending on the glory and depth of their histories. For these long-term purposes, a "Long Count" must be devised, one that fixes each date uniquely, in successive order.

Mesoamericans established the Long Count as an absolute dating system, that is, one in which each date is unique and occurred a certain number of years or days ago, by combining several important mathematical concepts. They expressed numbers in positional notation, similar to our own system, but where ours is decimal (10-base), theirs was vigesimal, with each place denoting a multiple of 20. Mesoamericans were also the first in the world to devise a mathematical system that used zero (Sharer 1994: 556-557). In virtually all Mesoamerican numerical notation systems, a dot represents one, and a bar represents 5, and where zero is used, it is indicated by a shell.

Numbers were used as calendric dates on monuments in the greater Isthmian region at the end of the Late Formative period. On monuments, dates were written as five numbers descending from top to bottom, with the top value representing multiples of 144,000 days (394 years, the Maya *baktun*). The second represented multiples of 7,200 days (about 20 years, the Maya *katun*), the third's units were 360 days (the Maya *tun*, the rough equivalent of a solar year), the fourth counted units of 20 days, and the last, the day. The earliest known examples include Stela 2 at Chiapa de Corzo, with 7.16.3.2.13, a date corresponding to December 9, 36 BC (Lee 1969: 105–106) and Stela C at Tres Zapotes, with 7.16.6.16.18, a date corresponding to a day in 32 BC (Stirling 1943: 14), counted from a beginning point calculated as about 13 August 3114 BC.

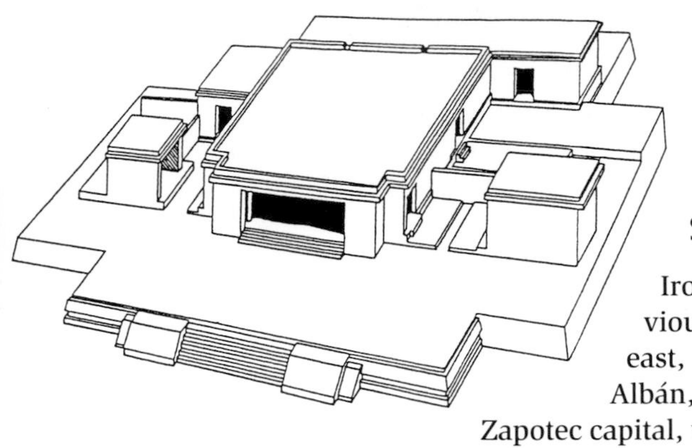

2, dated to 36 BC. Chiapa de Corzo is one of Mesoamerica's oldest continuously occupied communities, and in the Late Formative period it had one of Mesoamerica's earliest true palaces [8.20].

South Coast of the Isthmus, and Pacific Coastal Plain

Ironically, the important center of Laguna Zope, which in previous periods showed affinities with Isthmian cultures to the east, at around 200 BC showed a shift in focus toward Monte Albán, as evidenced by gray ware ceramics similar to those of the Zapotec capital, which was pushing its influence in all directions. But while Laguna Zope was drawn into the Oaxacan sphere of influence, cultures along the coastal plain to the south and east demonstrated lively local developments, with links north, to the upcoming Maya sites of the Guatemala highlands and the lowlands of the Yucatán Peninsula. The coastal plain sites most dramatically express their cultural coherence through related traditions of artistic style and architectural layout. The Chiapas Coast was among the best areas for cacao-growing, and was the source area for cacao and other tropical resources such as feathers and feline skins.

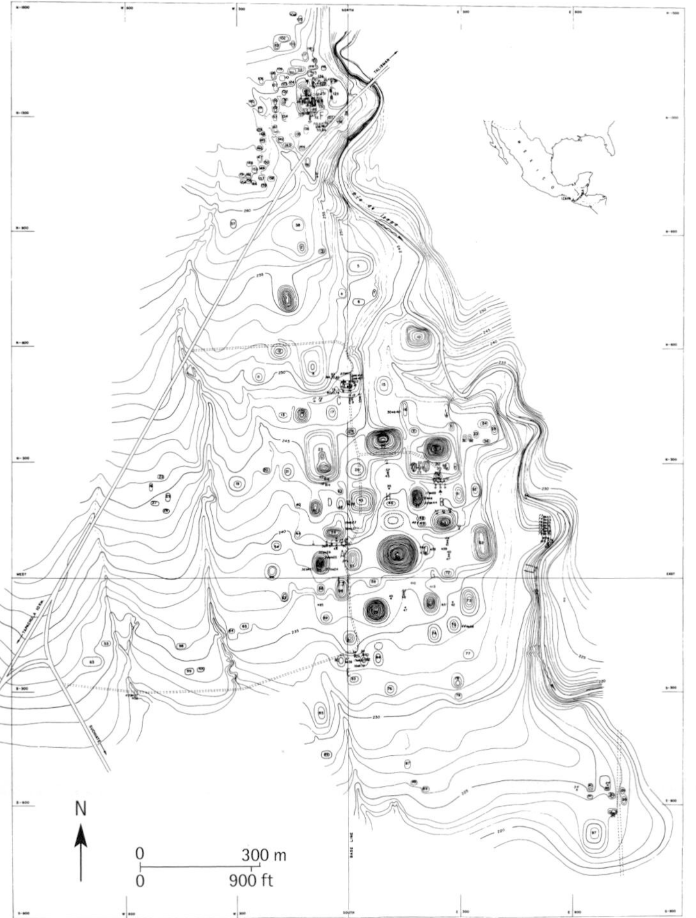

Izapa was the largest Late Formative site along the Chiapas coastal plain [8.21]. Izapa's occupation had begun in about 1500 BC, and continued to the time of the Spanish conquest. By the Middle Formative (900–600 BC) the site's Mound 30A (just southeast of the center of the site plan) was a stepped pyramid nearly 10 m (*c.* 33 ft) high (Ekholm 1969), but it was during the Late Formative and Early Classic periods that Izapa achieved florescence as a regional capital.

While Izapa's political control was probably limited to its local hinterland, its artistic influence seems to have been considerable. Izapa's known corpus of sculpture, mostly upright stelae and frog-shaped altars, now numbers over 250, and displays common features with earlier Olmec and later Maya styles, but "Izapa works are more site-specific in form, content, and technique than previously recognized. ... it was not a regional style, but a very localized one" (Smith 1984: 48). The subject matter draws heavily on flora and fauna of the coastal

8.20 *(Opposite above) Chiapa de Corzo's Mound 5 palace was one of Mesoamerica's earliest luxurious residences – not merely a much larger version of the typical wattle-and-daub structure with thatched roof, but built out of cut stone, roof beams, and finished with heavy plaster.*

8.21 *(Opposite below) Izapa extended over an area 2.3 km (1.4 miles) long, with 80 mounds in eight groups, each with pyramids centered around plazas. Positioned in front of the monumental platforms are stela-altar pairs, a combination common at Maya sites of the Terminal Formative and Classic periods. Volumetrically, the combined monumental architecture, including rebuildings, totaled about 250,000 cubic m (327,000 cubic yd) (Adams 1991: 91).*

estuary environment so important to the coastal plain. The Izapans also sculpted several deity figures, including a "Long-lipped God" who was "an ancestral form of Chac, the ubiquitous Maya patron of lightning and rain" (Coe 1999: 63–64). Izapa's deity representations are the "first public confirmation of certain gods" that become important to the Maya (Miller and Taube 1993: 17).

In the same coastal piedmont zone, about 50 km (31 miles) further down the coast is Abaj Takalik, with about 70 mounds in nine groups. Clearly this is another important center, and one on a route between the Guatemala highlands and the coast. In fact, Abaj Takalik seems to represent the northern edge of a Late Formative-Terminal Formative culture sphere centered at Kaminaljuyú and extending southeast to Chalchuapa. What is not clear, however, is the dating of Abaj Takalik's occupation, which makes interpreting the site's diverse sculptural corpus – some of it recarved in antiquity – more challenging, and it has variously been assigned to periods from Middle Formative to Late Classic (Bové 1989). Several monuments from Abaj Takalik bear early dates, from the Terminal Formative period.

Highly distinctive portrait sculptures appeared in the Late Formative along the southern Pacific coastal plain and adjacent highlands. These "potbellies" are as spherical as the Olmec colossal heads, if slightly smaller, but each represents a whole individual [**8.22**]. They date to the period from 400 to 100 BC, and seem to represent a local cult, unrelated to any Olmec influence, that was widely distributed but seemed to disappear quite suddenly, perhaps "evidence for a structural change of great magnitude occurring in Southern Mesoamerica, especially the coastal area and adjacent highlands, at the end of the Formative" (Bové 1989: 5). Potbelly sculptures may be another means of advertising the power of the chief to members of and visitors to the local coastal polities, or they may be a local variant of the "Fat God" – "without known functions but ubiquitous among the peoples of Mexico and the Northern Maya Area in Classic times" (Coe 1999: 66).

8.22 *This "potbelly" sculpture (Monte Alto, Monument 11) is typical of the genre. Such sculptures were found at various sites along the coast, as far to the southeast as the end of the coastal plain, at the ceremonial center of Santa Leticia (El Salvador).*

Several headless potbellies were found at a large village site about 60 km (37 miles) south of Abaj Takalik, and the site was thus named "Sin Cabezas" ("without heads"). Sin Cabezas had about 150 mounds, largely residential, arrayed over 300 hectares (741 acres), and centered upon a 200-m (656-ft) long platform with several much larger-than-average mounds on top of it and adjacent to it. One of these was Mound F4, clearly domestic in function, the high status of its residents evidenced not only by its larger size and proximity to the site's ceremonial core, but by the concentration of elite goods and burials. Not only that, F4 was the locus of a workshop that produced alabaster beads and pendants, virtually all of which were used by the residents of the mound.

This is an important early example of involvement of elites in elite craft production, possibly as high-status artisans working with luxury materials or as patrons of lower-status workers (Whitley and Beaudry 1989: 112). During the Classic and Postclassic periods, elite members of Maya and Aztec societies, for example, not only controlled precious materials, they themselves worked the materials to make ornaments which only the elite could wear. While this may possibly have had some basis in an ideological sense of appropriate sanctification of production through the exalted personage of a member of the ruling group, one practical reason, well known from Aztec society, was that elite polygyny produced far more offspring than could be supported by the few administrative positions available in every generation. Training the surplus offspring to be artisans working in precious goods saved the family dignity and maintained the important distinction between the lives of the commoners and the lives of the divinely-related rulers, while keeping a monopoly over precious materials and the ornaments made from them.

8.23 *(Opposite) The Kaminaljuyú sculptural tradition shows strong affinities with the sinuous designs and elaborate iconography of works from Izapa and other coastal plain sites, as well as being related to the Maya sculptural tradition. Stela 11's figure stands between smoking incense burners identical to those in use by Miraflores culture people, and similar to those on Izapa monuments. His grotesque face is actually a mask, surmounted by other masks including that of the Principal Bird Deity (Vucub Caquix), whose vulture-like visage was a widespread subject of sacred art in the Late and Terminal Formative, with examples from the Gulf lowlands, Maya lowlands, and even Oaxaca (Miller and Taube 1993: 137–138, 182).*

Southeastern Mesoamerica: Chalchuapa and Its Trading Partners

The southern Pacific Coast range of volcanic peaks in the Guatemala highlands continues on into El Salvador. While Kaminaljuyú was becoming an important center in the Guatemala highlands, Chalchuapa, about 150 km (93 miles) further southeast, was a well-established trade center in the El Salvador highlands not far from the present-day Guatemala border. From this position, Chalchuapa was a gateway between the Maya and Mixe-Zoque cultures of the Guatemala-Chiapas highlands and the Pacific coastal plain, and the farming communities and ceremonial centers that dotted the landscape of Late Formative Southeast Mesoamerica to the north and east, into Honduras and up to the Caribbean Sea.

Chalchuapa had been an important trade center in the Olmec era, and the end of the Middle Formative brought a cessation in construction activity, although it is clear from artifact evidence that occupation was continuous, and ceramics show affinities with Kaminaljuyú's Miraflores and other phases, and the Mamom ceramics of the Maya lowlands. From about 400 BC and continuing to about AD 500, the community's importance as a center of long-distance trade was re-established, and monumental construction resumed, with the rebuilding of the El Trapiche pyramid (Sharer 1978: 209–210). This was Chalchuapa's peak of activity and the civic-ceremonial center achieved its greatest extent. Politically independent, Chalchuapa seems to have been a focal point of trade in Usulutan ware, as well as continuing to distribute obsidian from the Ixtepeque mine.

Usulutan-style ceramics were widely distributed over Southeastern Mesoamerica, from Quelepa in the southeast (the easternmost site in Middle America with an oriented plan), north to Yarumela and further on to the Sula Plain in northern Honduras and Copán in western Honduras. Like the Miraflores ceramics of Kaminaljuyú and the Chicanel wares widespread among the Late Formative Maya, Usulutan pottery was found over a broad area (sometimes called the Uapala ceramic sphere) that was not integrated into one political system. Instead, the integrating mechanism seems to have been reciprocal feasting, with these serving vessels as a "material medium of commensality" that suggest "that forms and protocol of peaceful interaction were themselves being routinized and perhaps institutionalized" (Wonderley 1991: 164).

Guatemala Highlands

In the highlands above the coast, Kaminaljuyú during the Arenal phase (300 BC–AD 100) continued to direct more of its attention toward the coastal plain rather than toward the Chiapas highlands. During this period, the later part of Miraflores culture, population densities were greatest and the site underwent its most expansive program of monumental building and production of sculptures [**8.23**].

The sculptural traditions of the coast, best known from Izapa, were at first shared with Kaminaljuyú. However, by the turn of the millennium Kaminaljuyú was itself an important source of influence on sites ranging from Abaj Takalik to Chalchuapa. At the same time, Kaminaljuyú style would become "the major source of influence on the developing lowland Maya style in the monumental arts" (Parsons 1986: 45). For example, the tradition of erecting stelae with historical texts seems to have arisen in the area south of the Maya lowlands, particularly in the Guatemala highlands (Sharer 1994). Furthermore, Kaminaljuyú's monuments show important rulership ideals and practices dealing with sacrifice by decapitation and autosacrifice of bloodletting from the penis – traits that will later validate the rule of Maya kings (Kaplan 2002).

Kaminaljuyú had an important role in trading, and perhaps controlling obsidian from several highland sources – El Chayal and Jilotepeque. Evidence from the coast seems to indicate that obsidian as a raw material became more scarce, that the local production of prismatic blades from prepared cores was restricted, possibly because Kaminaljuyú was "controlling blade production and exportation for the south coast" (Bové 1989: 6). In addition to wealth from trade, Kaminaljuyú had rich resources in agriculture, intensively nurtured by complex irrigation systems. In spite of this strong position, Kaminaljuyú would decline in the Terminal Formative period, but become important once again in the Early Classic, under Teotihuacan's influence.

Maya Lowlands

Given the growing influence that the lowland Maya were exerting in the Chiapas plateau, it is not surprising that during the period 300 BC–AD 300, the Maya lowlands replaced the southern Gulf lowlands as the focus of cultural development in tropical Mesoamerica. During this time, the overall population of the Maya lowlands was distributed throughout the region, sometimes in such densities that overuse of the land caused environmental degradation, and intensive cultivation measures were used. Another indicator of population density is the appearance of fortification systems. The Chicanel phase (300 BC–AD 300) showed increasing commitment to elite enterprises: new monumental construction, new forms of public art.

Monumental buildings are a feature of important capitals today, and this was true in antiquity, as well. Elites publicly express their power by commissioning the construction of fancy shrines and palaces, raised up on substantial platforms to enhance their impressiveness. In a sense, the elite residence and ball court at Paso de La Amada in the Early Formative are the earliest known such expressions in Mesoamerica, and by the Late Formative, temple-pyramids were everywhere. After all, in spite of the visual dominance of these structures, they could be built with utilitarian materials – the fill could even be trash – and with modest amounts of labor, once communities reached sufficient size that commoners grew enough crops to support other enterprises in the off season.

8.24 *(Opposite) Nakbé's plan shows the relationship between major groups of pyramids and plazas, and the causeways that linked them. At the eastern end of the Kan Causeway is the East Group with an "E-Group" layout. An "E-Group" "consists of a large pyramidal structure on the western side of a plaza or platform; the eastern side of the plaza is dominated by an elevated, elongated structure on a north-south axis" (Hansen 1998: 64). If there are structures on the ends of this platform, they face west (in "triadic groups" they face each other). Other examples are widespread throughout the southern Maya lowlands, suggesting that this pattern was part of the shared ideology of Maya elites.*

In some areas, nature conspired to make monumental construction a regional specialty. The Yucatán Peninsula, heartland of the Maya, was a shelf of limestone, an excellent building material readily worked with tools made of flint, another local product (e.g., at Colhá [Shafer and Hester 1983]). Our best information about the development of these trends comes from the Mirador region, and the most precocious site is Nakbé.

Nakbé Occupation at Nakbé began in the Early Formative, by 1400 BC. By 800 BC, Nakbé extended over 50 hectares (124 acres), with unimpressive low platforms of rough stones surmounted by wattle-and-daub structures. Yet the site had an elite component, evidenced by imported goods and by reshaping of the teeth of higher-status individuals, a bit of cosmetic dentistry that advertised the bearer's ability to afford such luxury. With the passing centuries, Nakbé's architecture grew as low platforms were rebuilt into higher ones, covered liberally with plaster.

The ancient Olmec custom of placing standing stone monuments (stelae) in front of particular buildings has already been seen in various other contexts throughout Mesoamerica; it would achieve spectacular expression at Classic-period Maya sites, and appears at Nakbé at around 500 BC. This period, the Late Middle Formative, is a transition for the Nakbé-El Mirador region: ceramics continue to typify established Mamom types, but there are new styles of site planning, literally establishing a basis for a great leap forward toward monumentality, with modest villages leveled and filled to serve as platform foundations for huge new buildings, the whole effort "indicating that the platform construction and erection of monumental architecture were planned, simultaneous events" (Hansen 1998: 63)

Late Formative Maya Architecture At Nakbé we see developing the grammar of Maya architecture, which included buildings grouped in regular patterns, such as "E-Group" complexes [**8.24**], and architectural devices such as "apron moldings" – a course of tenon stones which slightly overhung the bottom courses of stone work in a wall, and secured cut-stone façades onto the increasingly steep sides of pyramids. Other Late Middle Formative site features at Nakbé were a ball court and a causeway. Causeways would become important at many Maya sites. They linked important architectural features within a site, and later, linked sites with each other.

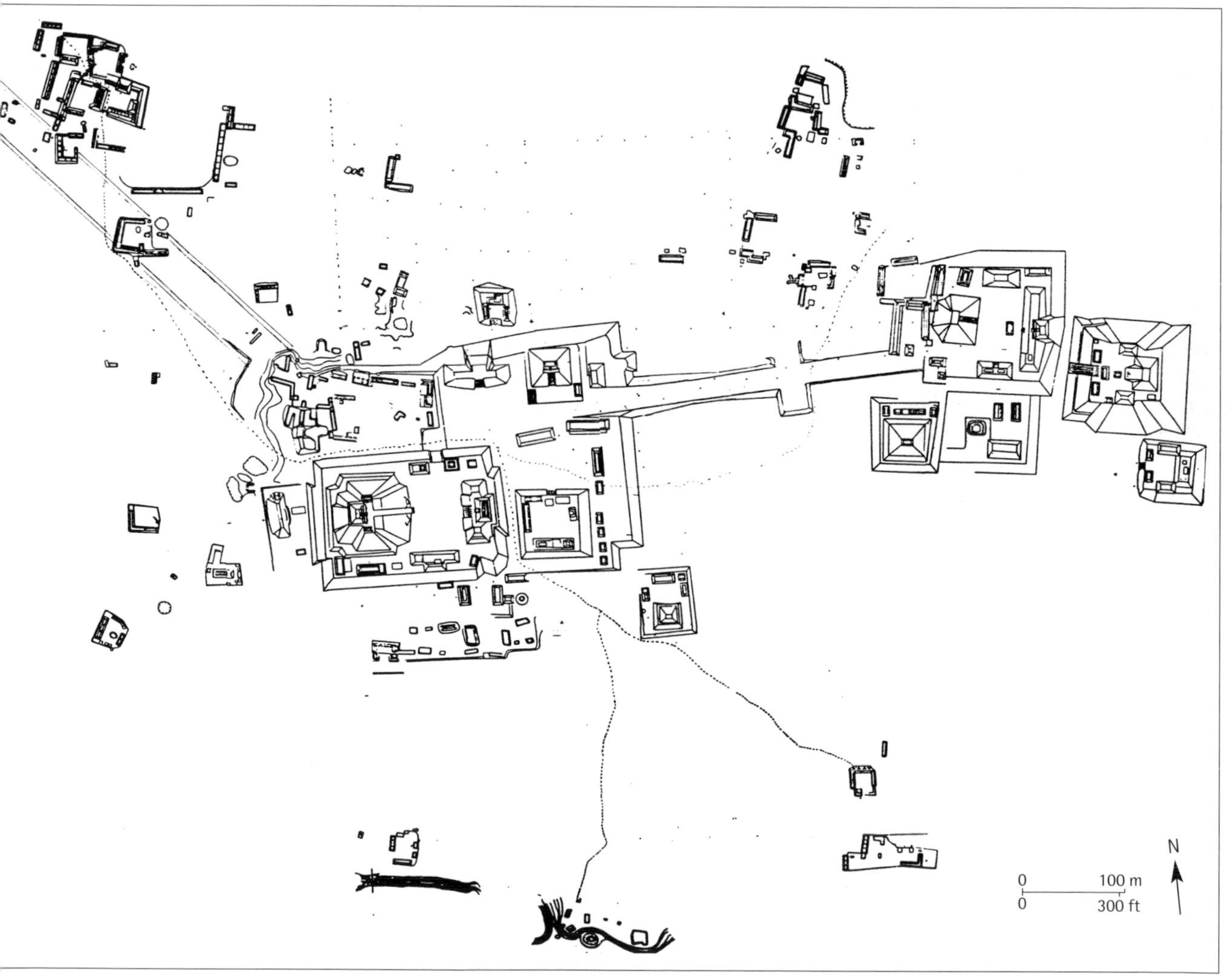

They were often raised well above ground level – the Kan Causeway at Nakbé was 4 m (13 ft) above adjacent ground level in some places – and were paved with crushed white stone, which inspired their Mayan name, *sacbe* ("white way").

The Late Formative was a dynamic period in the Maya lowlands, with population increases adding to the number of sites and making existing sites larger. This is accompanied by the widespread Chicanel ceramic tradition, whose most characteristic vessels are red or dark monochrome wares with waxy surface treatment. However, the trend that dominates all others in the material culture record is the crystallization of the Maya civic-ceremonial center pattern, characterized by monumentality in architectural form, with pyramids achieving heights up to 70 m (230 ft – roughly as tall as a 23-story building), as at El Mirador, even before the Classic period. Each site's concentration of temples and palaces, grouped on raised platforms, created an acropolis. Another important feature was architectural embellishment: building façades served as panels for depictions of deities [**8.25**], usually carved stucco masks that were brightly painted.

In the Petén region, Nakbé was replaced by El Mirador as the premier site, with one of the most impressive displays of ceremonial architecture known for all Maya sites, even to the end of the Classic period [**8.26, 8.27**]. Connected to Nakbé, 13 km (8 miles) away, by a *sacbe* that crossed the swampy bogs that are now called *bajos*, El Mirador is "the oldest Maya capital city" (Coe 1999: 76). Its construction took place over several centuries, ending about AD 100. On the periphery of the civic-ceremonial center were the residences of the commoners, their house groups consisting, in typical Mesoamerican fashion, of three or four one-room structures, each on a low platform, surrounding a small central plaza that served as a patio. The *bajos* on the periphery of El Mirador may have been intensively cultivated, as they were at other sites (see discussion of Cerros, below). El Mirador's contacts with other centers are documented by the presence of Usulutan wares imported from the Guatemala highlands. All this activity took place within a few centuries, because El Mirador was abandoned soon after AD 150, and never sustained substantial occupation again.

8.25 *Uaxactún, Group H. This Late Formative compound exemplifies the triadic arrangement of a dominant structure flanked by two smaller structures that face each other. Huge masks decorate the space between the stairways. These depict the deities that ruling dynasties called upon to validate their position of authority.*

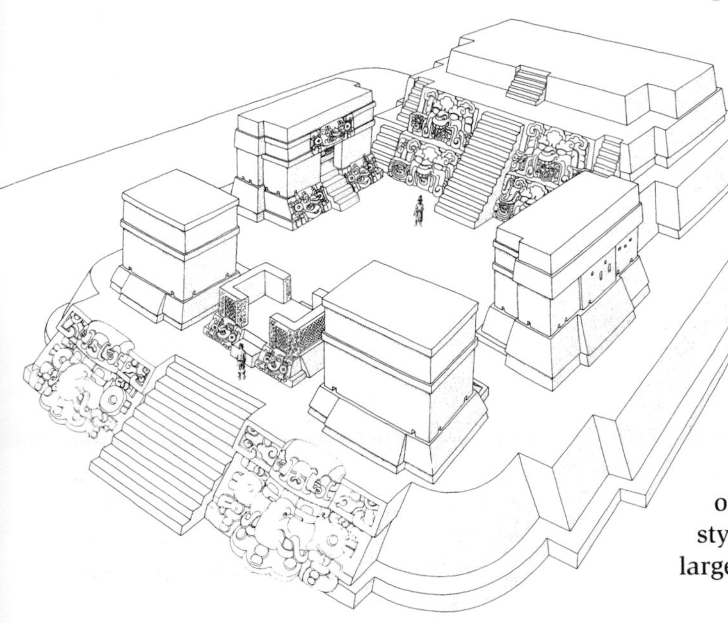

Architecture as History Much can be learned about culture history from architectural history. Architecture is the most imposing category of material culture remains, and, like other artifacts, bears the stamp of its time and ethnic origins, so we tend to use changing architectural style as a shorthand for processual change in the larger culture. But while it is tempting to use monumentality as a measure of elite control over labor, and look for cosmology in patterns of site layout, we must consider that the site layouts we see are often "not designed systems of architecture so much as historical accretions, with all of the noise and sloppiness that characterize evolved, as opposed to engineered systems.... [such accretions] of many structures built at different times cannot easily be read as texts ... because they are so garbled by historical contingency" (Webster 1998: 18).

Thus we should try to distinguish between the ceremonial centers that manifest a planning program, and those that present us with the accumulated results of centuries of change. The commencement of a building program is a historical event, as happened in Late Middle Formative Nakbé, or when existing structures were dramatically reconfigured, as archaeological research has documented for the lowland Maya and other Mesoamerican cultures from the Formative period on. By the end of the Late Formative, many of the centers that figure importantly in the continuing history of indigenous cultural development had been founded and their civic-ceremonial architectural signatures had been established. Some, like El Mirador, would be abandoned altogether, while others, like Tikal, grew and changed.

Monumental Agriculture, Architecture, and Rulership: Edzná and Cerros As the Purrón Dam demonstrated, not all monumental projects are temple-pyramids. Many Maya sites display significant reconfiguration of the landscape for the purposes of agriculture and water supply, at the same time that monumental architecture is being built.

At Edzná on the west side of the Yucatán Peninsula, more than 2 million cubic m (2.4 million cubic yd) of earth were moved to create 27 reservoirs and a set of canals, 31 km (19 miles) in all, radiating out from a monumental platform. The system drained areas that had too much water, brought it to fields needing it, and stored it for the use of the town's residents. The water control system was largely completed by 150 BC (Matheny *et al.* 1980–1983).

On a peninsula on Chetumal Bay on the coast of Belize, the small Late Formative community of Cerros [**8.28, 8.29**] demonstrates that the construction of massive ceremonial architecture was just one part of a program of landscape modification in which the Maya "were able to remove >200,000 m^3 [>239,000 cubic yd] of limestone fill, establish a catchment runoff surface, and produce an engineered landscape that included civic architecture as well as raised fields" (Scarborough 1994: 190–191).

These massive public works projects and resulting monumental civic-ceremonial architecture show how Maya society was stratifying, how the rulers (Maya *ajaw* [sing.]) were able to direct the labor of the many, the farmer-artisans. What lends cohesion to chiefdoms – the ability for everyone to trace their kinship ties to the chief and also to the (possibly fictional) ancestor who founded the whole society – becomes cumbersome when population size increases to the point that kin-based social controls no longer function effectively. And such family ties become inconvenient when chiefs are convinced of their own distinctive, if not sacred ancestry, and that the single

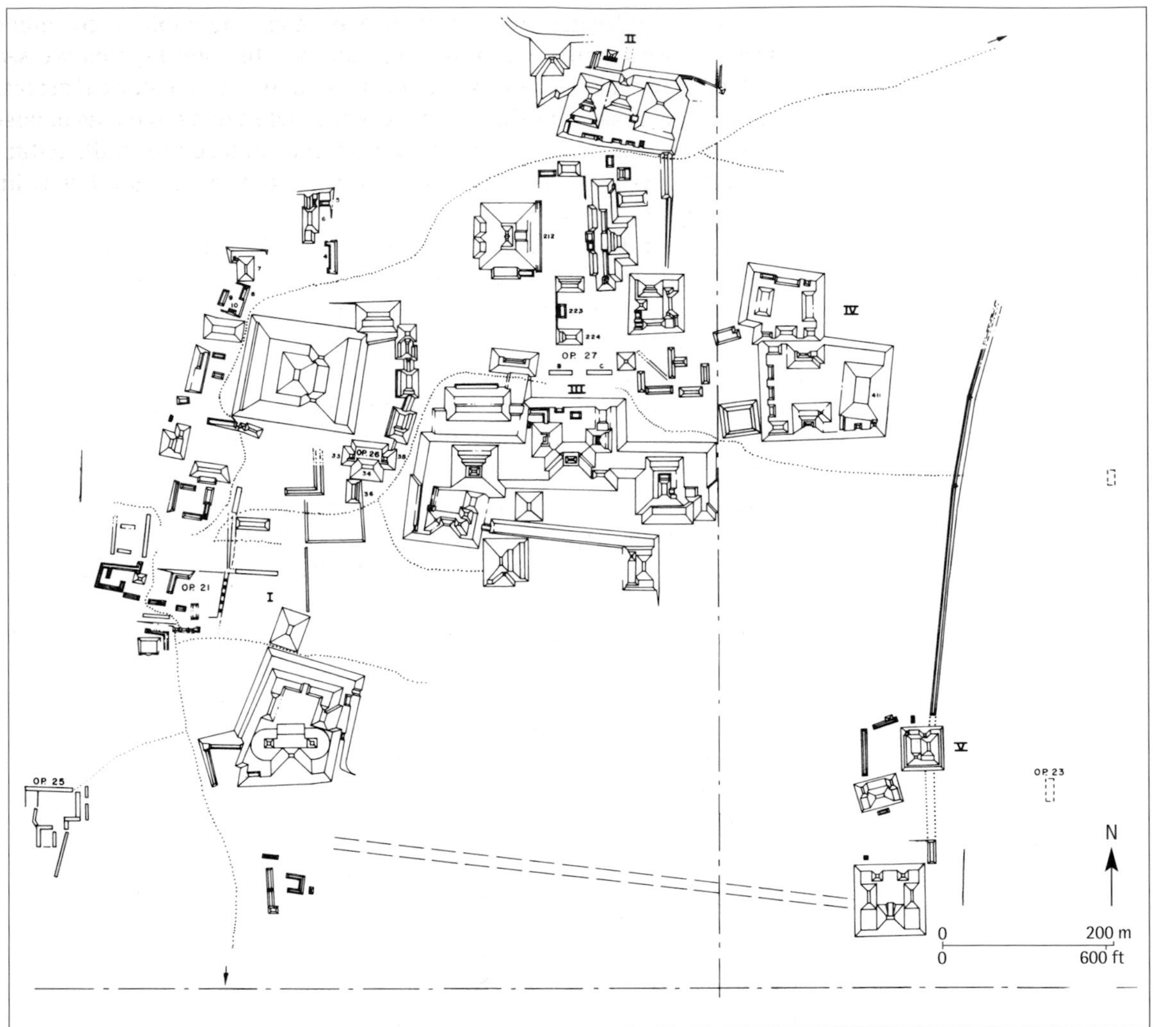

family tree uniting all is, rather, a great noble tree surrounded by the maize plants of the commoners.

All over Mesoamerica, Late Formative elites were distancing themselves from their subjects by directing those same subjects to build impressive temple-and-palace complexes where the elites would live and commune with the gods, and where the commoners could occasionally visit to observe the exalted goings-on – or to perform menial labor. Long-distance exchange kept ideas and symbols, as well as materials, flowing from one region to another, and this exchange focused on elites – they were the ones who exchanged fine decorated pottery vessels and other preciosities, and they were probably the ones who controlled trade at the local marketplace level as well as being the contact points for long-distance traders. Some high-status individuals may have accompanied the trading expeditions.

8.26, 8.27 *(Opposite) El Mirador's Great Acropolis, in the center, has evidence of palace architecture. Not shown on this plan is the Danta complex, which lies 800 m (1/2 mile) east of El Mirador, and is the site's largest architectural complex, though much of its bulk and its height of 70 m (230 ft) is based upon a natural hill. (Below) The El Tigre complex, at the west side of the site, is shown in a reconstruction drawing. Note the triadic arrangement of temple pyramids atop the massive central pyramid, echoing the triadic arrangement of the central pyramid and the two that face each other across the front plaza. Also note the apron moldings visible at the base of the large pyramid, a treatment of sloping pyramid sides that will become common in the Maya lowlands. This complex "covers a surface area six times larger than Temple IV at Tikal, the greatest building at that mammoth Classic site" (Sharer 1994: 111). The El Tigre pyramid is 55 m (180 ft) high, with a volume of about 380,000 cubic m (497,040 cubic yd).*

Part of long-distance exchange were ideas about how rulers should behave and be treated. This is not to argue that the idea of, say, a ruler claiming to be descended from mythological god-like beings was thought up in one place and then spread around – simple diffusionism – but rather that societal changes were making many regions fertile ground for the adoption and innovation of new means of justifying and realizing the stratification process. Seeing himself increasingly distanced from his subjects, and needing those same subjects to cooperate with grand schemes of ditch-digging and pyramid-building, a ruler might hear of another ruler's ability to use descent from sacred ancestors toward directing public works, and feel justified in establishing the same program.

And we must never underestimate the human taste for conspicuous consumption (Veblen 1953) and one-upsmanship (Potter 1962), efforts to outshine one's peers which can produce tremendous effect, in substance and in style. Stelae, upright stone sculptures, were appearing in many regions, for example, but among the lowland Maya they became the ultimate memorial of the events in a ruler's life, combining portraiture, calendrics, divination, writing of historical and sacred texts, expression of local style, and the aesthetic expertise of individual sculptors.

So when we look at Cerros we can picture its ruler ascending Structure 5C between four huge masks of sculpted plaster which depict the Hero Twins (see pp. 34–35) and the Sun and planet Venus. The stairway represented cosmological levels that the ruler – *ajaw* – would ascend on ceremonial

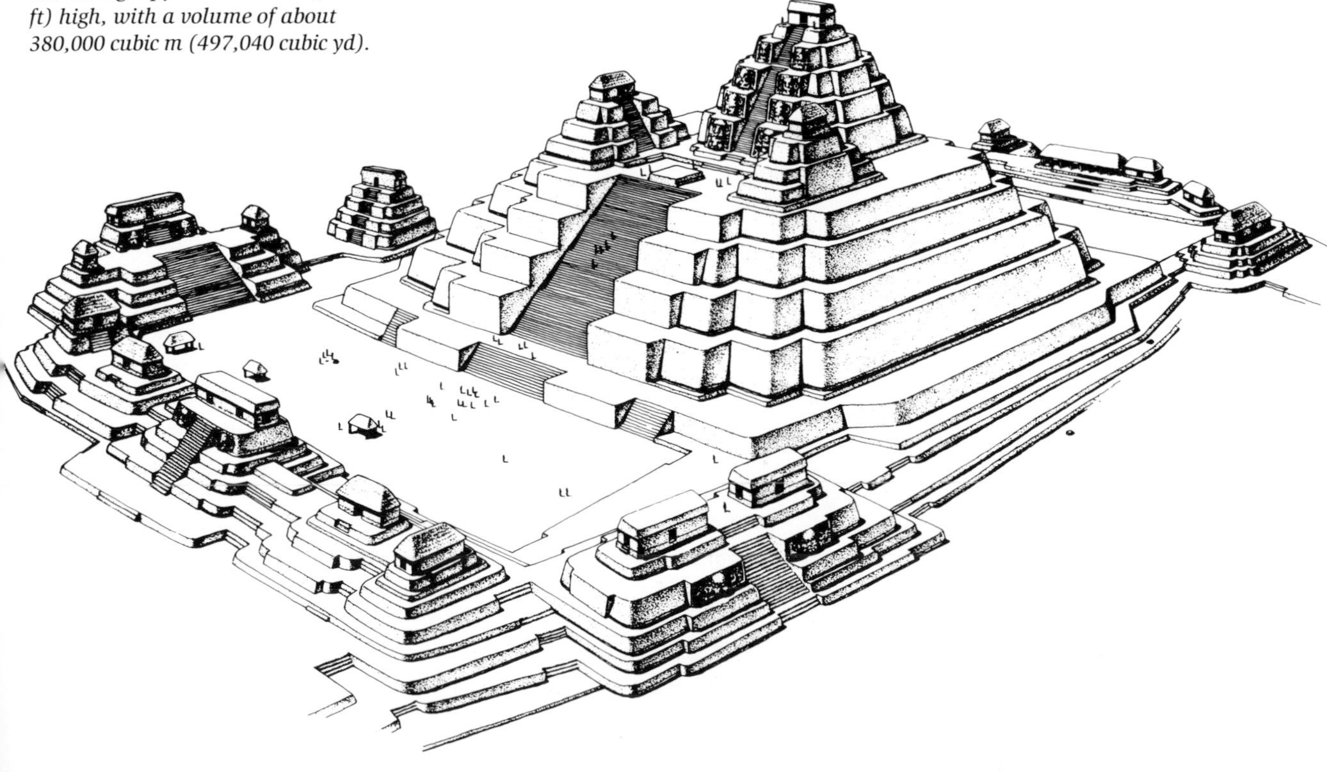

8.28, 8.29 *The ancient canal at Cerros (below) encompasses an area that is now about 31 hectares (77 acres), but was once larger before erosion of the site by the sea. The Cerros civic-ceremonial focus, at the north end of the site, included Structure 5C (at right), the first temple to be built at what was formerly an agricultural village. Note the huge masks flanking the staircase: they combine iconographic symbols representing the rising and setting sun and the planet Venus as morning and evening stars, along with insignia of the Hero Twins. In using the temple, ascending and descending the stairs, rulers would associate themselves with such cosmic forces.*

occasions, moving through fourfold quadrants of time and space that would become so important to Classic Maya ideology. We are witnessing this local *ajaw* making evident his association with the mythic Hero Twins, whose exploits in the underworld included rescuing their father, the Maize God and thus the source of life for all people. All humankind must owe a debt of gratitude to the Hero Twins, but because the rulers were more closely related to such deified characters, their debt would consist of glorification of the gods and rites of autosacrifice, while the debt of the commoners would consist of serving the needs of these human relatives of the most sacred spirits.

Chetumal Bay
Canal
N
0 200 m
0 600 ft

Maya rulership as an institution used the Hero Twins to leverage social stratification, successfully transforming the Hero Twins myth "from an ideological affirmation of ethnic brotherhood across a vast segmentary society into a celebration of hierarchical division of that society into living representatives of those ancestors [the elite] and their worshippers [the commoners]" (Freidel and Schele 1988: 549). As Chapter 9 will make clear, this social gap would only widen.

9 THE TERMINAL FORMATIVE (AD 1–300)

THE PERIOD FROM AD 1 to 300 reveals a Mesoamerica with a set of coherent cultural patterns and emerging states [9.1]. The subsistence base of productive agriculture was firmly established, with domesticated crops and strategies of intensification of land use. The repertoire of material items – artifacts such as pottery vessels and stone tools – had also been developed to a mature state, and local and long-distance exchange patterns had, by this time, deep traditions. Centralized, state level of political organization, characterized by the legitimized power of the elites to enforce their directives, is most graphically displayed at Monte Albán and Teotihuacan, while Maya centers also demonstrate the themes of the great divide between the strata of ruler and ruled. The growing population of commoners provided an important resource – labor – for the monumental projects by which the elites demonstrated their exalted status.

Cities are the dominant communities of most state-level polities; many Terminal Formative communities had urban features such as a large, dense population and a focal area of civic-ceremonial architecture, although few

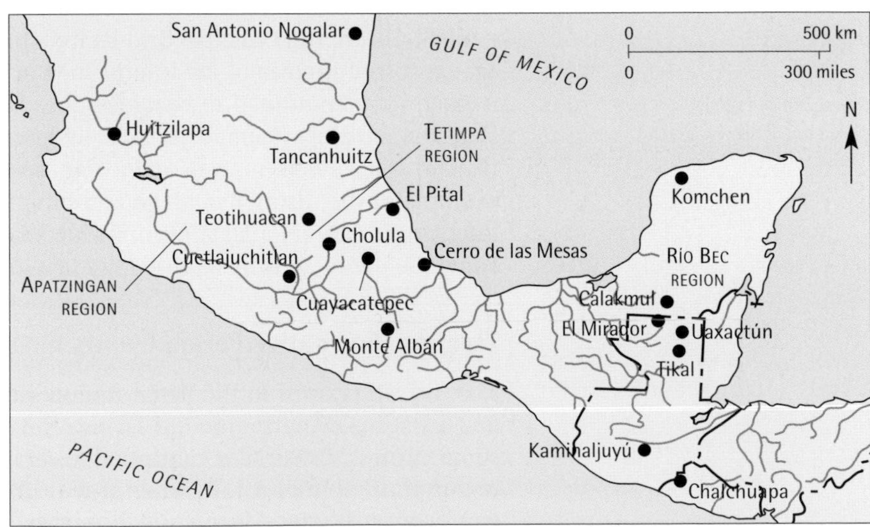

9.1 *Western Middle America showing Terminal Formative-period regions and sites mentioned in Chapter 9.*

approach the size and density of Teotihuacan. Its monumental structures are built in this period, but the gridded city plan and apartment compounds would not develop until the Classic period. At Teotihuacan, and at many other centers, the "Great Traditions" of artistic and intellectual achievement are evidenced in architecture, sculpture, painting, and symbolic systems. The belief systems of these regional cultures shared certain important features of explaining the cosmos and its origins, but the variation among regions reveals the special features intrinsic to the relationship of each regional culture with its particular environment, and the legacy of each regional culture from its own trajectory of development.

EARLY MAYA CENTERS

Maya Lowlands of the Yucatán Peninsula

In the Maya lowlands during the Terminal Formative period, some centers, like Nakbé and El Mirador, declined, but elsewhere in the southern lowlands, already-established centers like Uaxactún and Altar de Sacrificios grew larger and more impressive. Programs of public works that expressed the political power of increasingly visible rulers continued and elaborated trends established in the Middle and Late Formative periods. The larger pattern is of demographic growth, with the civic-ceremonial centers serving as flashpoints for conflict and alliance among dynasts.

The Terminal Formative lowland Maya shared not only Chicanel pottery, but also the other traits we have been examining: civic-ceremonial centers with standardized monumental architecture, intensive cultivation methods including, in a few places, drained fields and irrigation systems, an elite class comprising an interrelated set of dynasts whose ancestor cults were elaborated into religious institutions found over a huge area and recognized as the divine right to rule of Maya elites, and the emergence of formal deities – the Sun God, the Principal Bird Deity – to validate rulership. Monumental art expressed themes of the intertwined activities of deities and rulers, and iconography continued to become more formalized until it gained expression in a writing system, expressed by inscriptions on standing monuments (stelae) as well as in wall paintings and on vases. The earliest known example of the distinctive Maya combination of a portrait of a ruler with a long count date on a stela occurred at Tikal at AD 292 (Stela 29), and heralded the period of fully mature Maya civilization, the Classic period.

Terminal Formative Period Events in the Maya Lowlands

The overall pattern in the Petén region was of growth, with more centers, and existing centers growing larger and grander. There were, however, some failures. El Mirador continued to serve as the major center in the Petén region until about AD 150, when it was abandoned; thereafter, only squatters lived at the site. Meanwhile, however, Tikal, established by 800 BC, was

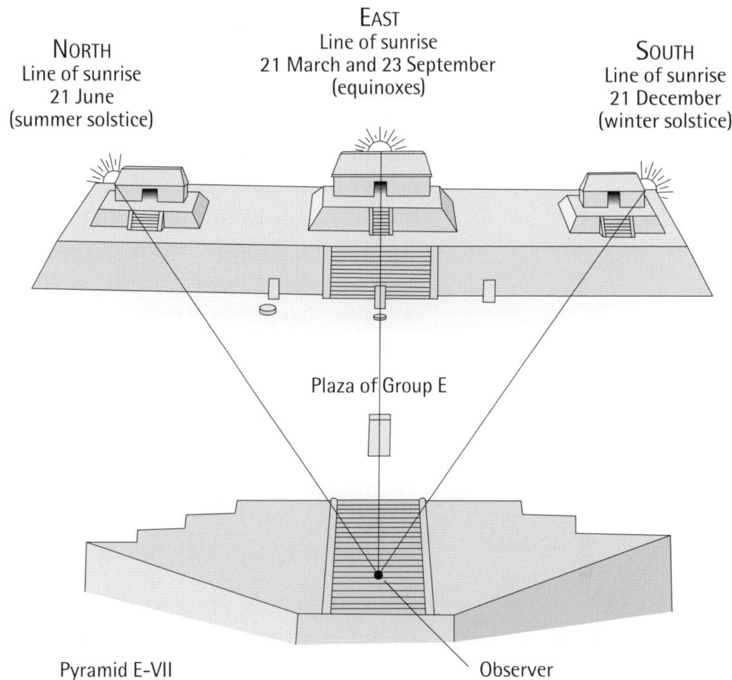

9.2 *Uaxactún, Group E, which was laid out by the end of the Terminal Formative. This was the first "E Group" ever identified at a Maya site (see Figure* 8.4 *for an older example), and it illustrates very well the orientation of the pyramid, and the group as a whole, toward the eastern horizon, and use of buildings as markers on an horizon calendar oriented to the east, which here appears at the top of the plan.*

In this book, most plans and maps have been laid out so that north is at the top, a modern Western convention based upon the earth's polar axis. However, for many ancient peoples, including those of Mesoamerica and Europe, the east-west axis dominates. The east – literally, the orient – as the place of the rising sun is the basis for "Our word orientation *... in some lexicons as ... that part of the church one looks at when viewing the altar from the nave. In many cases, east is the direction along which the rising sun's first light penetrates the church on the day of the patron saint after whom the church was named" (Aveni 1989: 263).*

developing civic-ceremonial architecture in its Great Plaza region. Tikal's nearest neighbor, Uaxactún, 24 km (15 miles) to the north, was developing its own monumental architecture [**9.2**].

Calakmul was another Petén site that was becoming important in the Terminal Formative period, having been occupied since the Middle Formative. In the Late Formative, it seems to have comprised a regional polity with Uaxactún and El Mirador, to which it was connected by a *sacbe* 38 km (24 miles) long. Calakmul's Structure 2 was the oldest Mesoamerican building with a vaulted roof (the previous examples of this architectural innovation had been tombs) (Carrasco Vargas 2000: 14).

Río Bec: Early Fortifications

In an ecological transition zone between the tropical environment of the Petén region of the southern Maya lowlands and the drier scrub forest of more northerly Yucatán, the Río Bec region began to be occupied some time after 1000 BC, and by the Late Classic period had many sites with distinctive architecture (see Chapter 12). At Becán, the largest of the Río Bec sites, the foundations for civic-ceremonial architecture were laid by the end of the Terminal Formative, but Becán's greatest source of fame lies in a ditch. The ditch and associated parapet, nearly 2 km (1.2 miles) long, formed a vertical barrier over 11 m (33 ft) high, and were part of a system of fortifications surrounding the site's central area of 19 hectares (47 acres) (Webster 1976). These features indicate that well before the Classic florescence of Maya sites, population densities in the Maya lowlands had reached sufficient size to warrant competition among centers for important resources like cultivable land.

Conflict is, of course, nothing new in Mesoamerica's culture history, but wherever substantial effort is committed to insuring continued survival in a potentially hostile environment, it stands as evidence of organizational power on the part of the rulers – military leaders accrue power, and use it to secure access to resources like land. Civic-ceremonial centers like Becán are, indeed, the focal points of ceremonies, which, for the Maya, often involved ancestor veneration, a useful ideological justification for territoriality. Such centers also serve for the coordination of economic activities, e.g. trade, investment of labor, redistribution of goods, and also as the administrative headquarters for political leaders maintaining, defending, and sometimes extending the boundaries of their polities (Webster 1977). From fortifications at Becán and other Maya sites, it is clear that conflicts and their resolution were very much a part of the evolution of Maya culture.

Northern Maya Lowlands

Other imposing sites in the Maya lowlands further to the north included Edzná on the western, Campeche, side of the Yucatán Peninsula, and Yaxuná, Aké, and Komchen on the northern plains. Komchen in the Terminal Formative covered 2 sq. km (0.8 sq. miles). At its center were five monumental platforms, two of them linked by a very early example of a *sacbe*. Surrounding the civic-ceremonial buildings were 900 to 1,000 other structures, most of them houses. The town was only 15 km (9.3 miles) from the coast, and its prosperity may have been based on trade along the coast, and trading salt produced there. Komchen declined by the end of the Terminal Formative, possibly because the kinds of conflict that inspired the Becán ditch and other fortifications became endemic among the Maya, and no region-wide political authority system arose to control them.

Southeastern Mesoamerica

During the Terminal Formative period, the ceremonial centers and farming villages of Southeastern Mesoamerica continued to flourish, though much of this region went into decline at the end of this period. The volcano Ilopango, in El Salvador, erupted with great force in about AD 420 (Dull *et al.* 2001). Its effect on the cultures of western El Salvador and Honduras was profound, but readers should be aware that the date of its eruption has long been interpreted as 200 years earlier, a fact that is incorporated into many culture histories now in print. Reinterpretation of Ilopango and its effects extends the vibrant Late-Terminal Formative period in this region to the early 5th century. After that, much of the area becomes more marginal to Mesoamerican cultural influence until the end of the Classic period and the Postclassic period, when it is once again drawn into Mesoamerica.

Guatemala Highlands

Southeast Mesoamerica during the Late and Terminal Formative periods looked to Chalchuapa as a kind of cultural capital, and Chalchuapa, in turn, seems to have looked to Kaminaljuyú, the only urbanized community in the southeastern highlands. Terminal Formative-period Kaminaljuyú was in transition. Before AD 100, there were population increases in the Valley of Guatemala, and Kaminaljuyú had 10 precincts, each with a civic-ceremonial group consisting of a temple-topped pyramidal funerary mound (as in previous periods) and an associated platform which served as the base for elite residences. Between AD 100 and 200 (Santa Clara phase), there was a sharp decline at Kaminaljuyú, and part of the site may even have been abandoned. This may have resulted from a climate trend toward drying out of the adjacent lake and canal systems (Hatch 2001). In any event, it was a time when no major construction projects were built, nor were monuments erected.

The city was revitalized in about AD 200 (Aurora phase, AD 200–400) by an incursion of Teotihuacanos, who made their mark on the local material culture, introducing Teotihuacan-style monumental architecture and ceramic vessels similar to those of the Central Highlands, and showing a lack of interest in erecting the standing sculptures common to Formative Kaminaljuyú and to Maya sites. The nature of Teotihuacan influence at Kaminaljuyú, whether it resulted from colonization or replacement of indigenous elites by foreigners, has long been debated by scholars. We will return to this topic in our discussion of the Early Classic period in the Guatemala highlands, after having evaluated Teotihuacan's own culture history, and its role in cultural trajectories elsewhere in Mesoamerica.

The Isthmus and Early Writing

With the Terminal Formative, cultural patterns across the Isthmus continued from those of the Late Formative period, showing continued interchange of ideas and goods throughout the greater Isthmian zone, from the south-central Gulf lowlands down to Izapa along the Pacific coastal plain. Cerro de las Mesas and Tres Zapotes were important sites, though the extent of Terminal Formative occupation is obscured by later, Classic-period construction. Cerro de las Mesas shows evidence of elaboration of its social hierarchy; a rich, centrally located burial attests to the wealth of the elite.

Among the cultural traits continuing from the Late Formative was the region's precocity in the development of symbolic systems. In Chapter 8, the earliest monuments with Long Count dates, products of the Isthmus, were described. Evidence from the Terminal Formative Isthmus includes the oldest extensive texts of Mesoamerican glyph writing, a script referred to as "Isthmian" (also "Epi-Olmec" or "Intermediate" or "Tuxtla" after the Tuxtla statuette, an important example of the script's use). The script is thought to be a written version of pre-proto-Zoquean, an ancestral form of modern Isthmian languages, Mixe and Zoque.

Unlike Maya hieroglyphs, the Isthmian inscriptions have not yet been substantially deciphered, and in fact, the decipherments attempted to this point (Justeson and Kaufman 1993, 1997) have used just 10 inscribed sources, the longest among them being that on La Mojarra Stela 1 [9.3].

9.3 *La Mojarra Stela 1 measures 1.42 by 2.34 m (4.7 by 7.7 ft). The site of La Mojarra is small, only about 1 sq. km (0.4 sq. mile), and is located on the Acula River. In the river shallows this stela was found. The text has not yet been definitively deciphered, but two dates occurring in the text can be interpreted as referring to 21 May* AD *143, and 13 July* AD *156. Parts of the inscription may refer to the individual shown, who may have been a ruler, and to the events in his life, but proper decipherment will depend upon better knowledge of the cultural context, and a larger corpus of recovered examples of texts (Houston 2000: 131).*

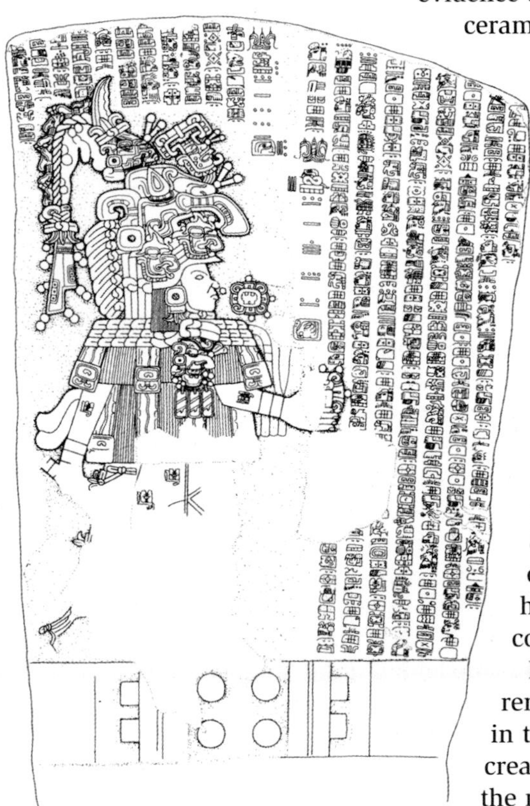

WEST OF THE ISTHMUS

Mesoamerica provides good evidence about how writing evolved in ancient civilizations, because we can see, by looking at various adjacent regions during the period of incipient writing, that the idea was widespread and that there were shared themes: calendrics, names of important individuals, names of important places. While the oldest long texts now known have come from the Isthmian region, the Oaxaca Valley had a very early tradition of using symbols, as we saw for Middle-Late Formative San José Mogote.

Monte Albán Period II (200/100 BC–AD 200/300) inspired a new kind of symbolic expression, place glyphs to keep track of and advertise the extent of the growing Monte Albán polity [9.4]. Back in Monte Albán I times, there were strong indications of Monte Albán's growing influence in adjacent regions such as the Mixteca Alta and the Cuicatlán Cañada. Judging from evidence such as striking changes in local ceramic styles, reflecting a new ceramic repertoire with Monte Albán gray wares and other products, it is clear that the center was the capital of a cultural sphere stretching to points 150 km (93 miles) away. Whether or not Monte Albán conquered these places and incorporated them into a formalized political relation is difficult to say, but the more than 40 place glyphs displayed on Building J indicate some sort of domination, "a textual claim that it had expanded well beyond the confines of its core physiographic zone, the Valley of Oaxaca" (Marcus and Flannery 1996: 198).

Also note the contrast between the personal portraiture of the *danzantes* and the far more abstract representation of the place glyphs [9.4]. "The numerous carvings dating to Early and Late [Monte Albán] I depict captured leaders who had been brought back to the capital to be humiliated and slain. In contrast, the fewer phase II [place glyph] slabs show the conquests of particular places or centers rather than individuals" (Blanton *et al.* 1993: 84). Such place glyphs, as representing tribute-paying polities, are commonly used in Aztec-period documents, and this tradition may have deep roots, and represent the formation of an extensive tribute confederation centered upon Monte Albán.

Building J, showcase of place glyphs, was part of a massive urban renewal project that took place in Monte Albán II times and resulted in the layout of the site as seen today [9.5]. This project began with creating a level area 300 m long and 200 m across (656 by 984 ft) on the ridge top for the Central Plaza between the North and South Plat-

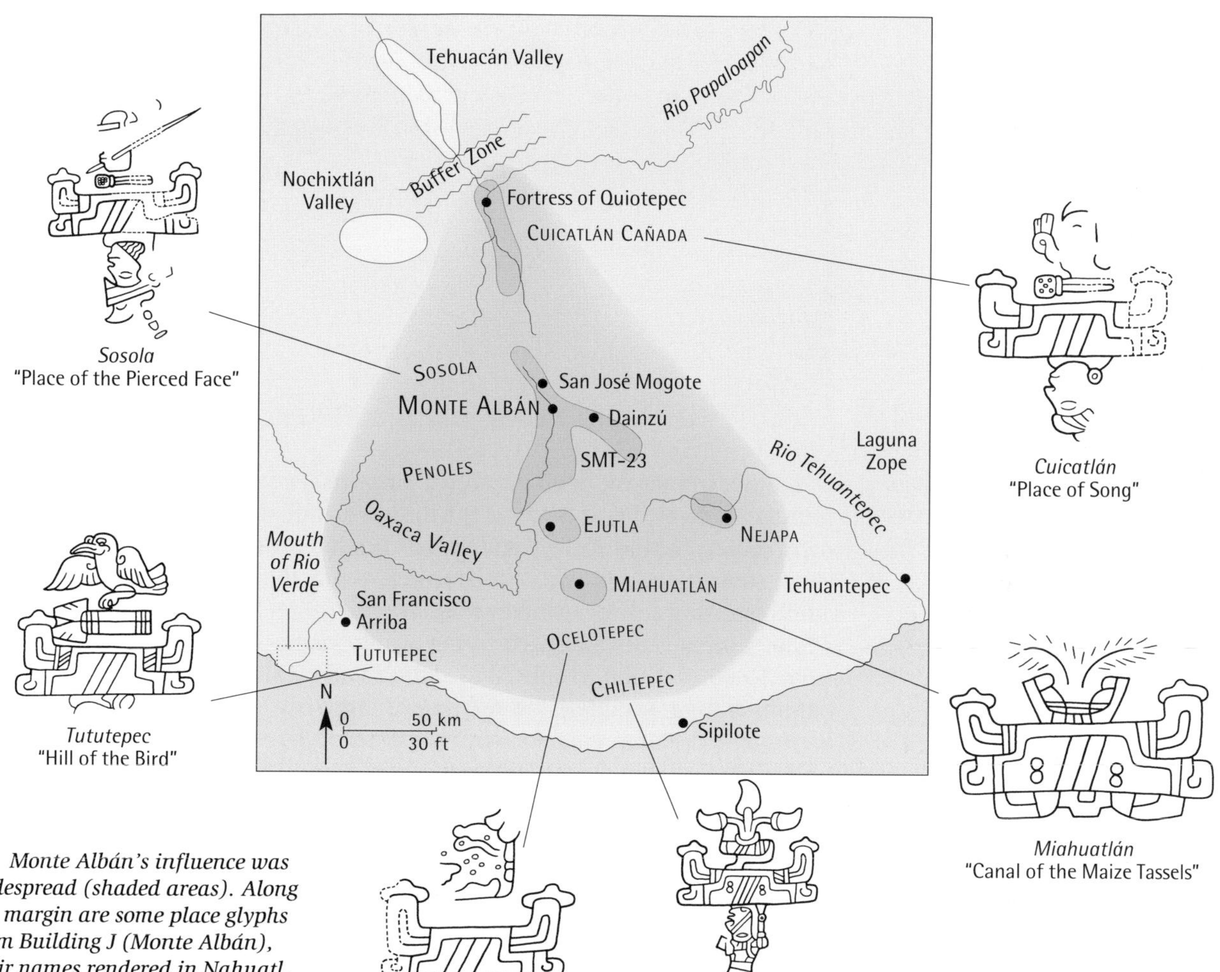

9.4 *Monte Albán's influence was widespread (shaded areas). Along the margin are some place glyphs from Building J (Monte Albán), their names rendered in Nahuatl, the* lingua franca *of the Aztec empire; the names were then adopted by the Spaniards in the 16th century. Each central motif means "hill of" or "place of," the upside-down head may be shorthand for conquest. Counterclockwise from top right, the glyphs are thought to represent Cuicatlán ("Place of Song", note the decorated speech scroll coming from the head above the hill), Miahuatlán ("Canal of the Maize Tassels"), Chiltepec ("Hill of the Chile Plants"), Ocelotepec ("Hill of the Jaguar"), Tututepec ("Hill of the Bird"), and Sosola ("Place of the Pierced Face") (Marcus and Flannery 1996: 197–198).*

forms, "a titanic feat which required the leveling of enormous rock outcrops and the filling of deep concavities. Intelligent advantage was taken of some of the outcrops by using them as nuclei for the great stone constructions which border the plaza on the north and south sides" (Acosta 1965: 818).

Another enormous public works project from this period was the construction of a defensive wall running for 2 km (1.2 miles) around the base of the hill on the northwestern side. Investment in fortifications, as we have seen, indicates endemic hostility sufficiently persistent to justify considerable expense. A center as ambitious as Monte Albán, with public art programs memorializing political terrorism, probably had enemies. And it may have felt vulnerable because of a loss of population in the valley as a whole: a 20 percent decline (from about 50,000 to about 40,000), possibly the result of efforts to expand the territorial base of the tribute polity by colonization.

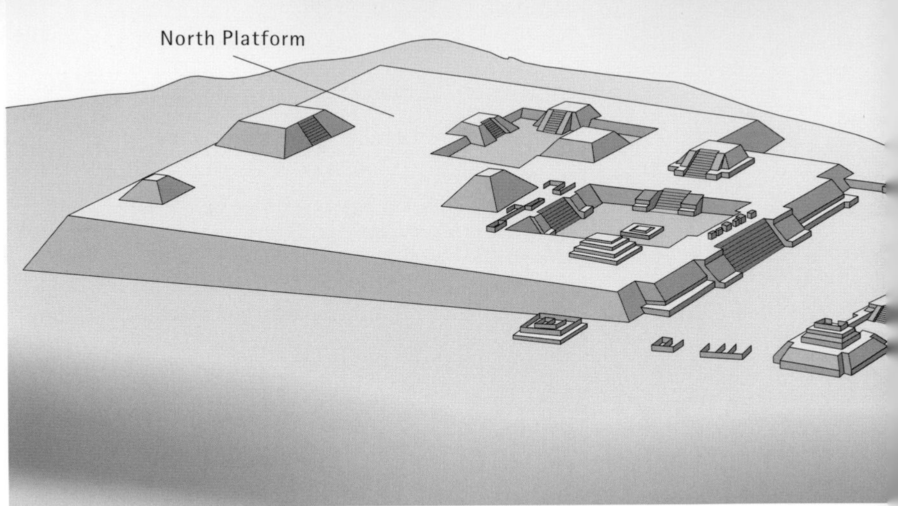

9.5 *Monte Albán, reconstruction view from the southwest, showing architecture of periods II and III. Many of the structures and platforms were erected upon natural outcroppings. Period II construction included Building J (the arrow-shaped building in the plaza, just north of the South Platform) and the center's first I-shaped formal ball court (not visible in this drawing, it was on the east side, just to the southeast of the North Platform).*

Another important demographic change in the valley was a decline in the number of sites, by about one third, down to just over 500. Yet the settlement pattern of the valley, which surrounded Monte Albán with dozens of small sites in period I, was transformed to one that was normal for a center administrating a three-armed valley. Monte Albán had a population of about 14,500 at this time, and each of the valley's arms had several sites ranging from 1,000 to 2,000 people, and which had public architecture indicating administrative functions. Interspersed between these secondary centers were about 30 large villages, with populations from 200 to 1,000 people and indications of modest public architecture, and filling out the rest of the pattern were over 400 small villages, consisting of several dozen houses but no public architecture.

This hierarchy of central places reveals integration of the valley into one political entity, administered from Monte Albán. Even more compelling are the Monte Albán-style architectural features that appear in the secondary centers that are surrounded by third-order sites. These are San José Mogote, reoccupied after a period of near-abandonment, Dainzú, and SMT-23, probably "major regional administrative centers for the Etla, Tlacolula, and Valle Grande regions, respectively" (Marcus and Flannery 1996: 175).

The architectural similarities include such features as the plaza itself. At newly rebuilt San José Mogote, the main plaza was the same size as that of Monte Albán itself, with similar kinds of buildings around and in the plaza. Each site's North Platform, for example, "supported a governmental structure reached by climbing a large stairway and passing through a colonnaded portico ... both sites had two-room temples along both sides of the plaza" (Marcus and Flannery 1996: 179) and both had I-shaped ball courts and palaces where the elite dwelled. In these features we see the signs of a regional class of elites developing, people who were no doubt related to each other through blood ties and marriage ties, and who administered Monte Albán's political and economic policies at the local level.

Dainzú's civic and ceremonial architecture was also much expanded during this period, with some traits echoing Monte Albán's monuments, but

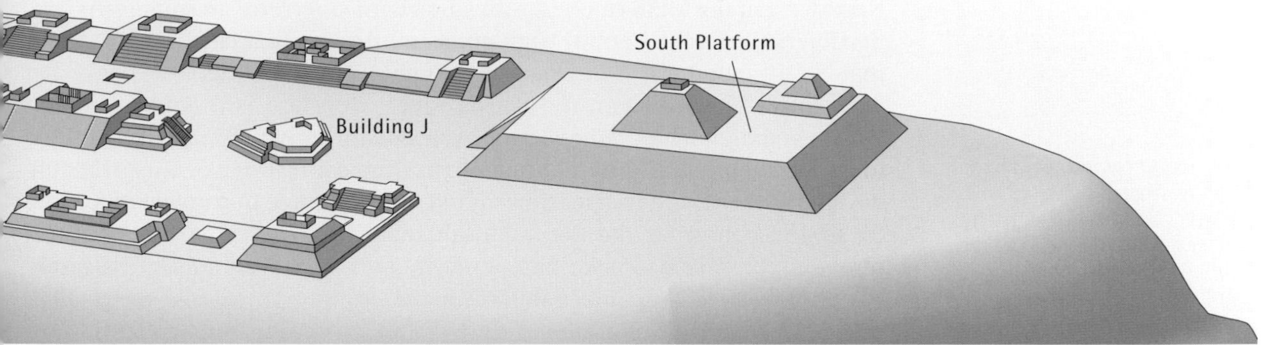

with a distinctive subregional style that was expressed as well through sculptures found not only at Dainzú but at neighboring sites like Abasolo and Macuilxóchitl (Bernal 1973). An important theme in the sculptures was the depiction of athletes. First occupied at about 600 BC, Dainzú continued to expand in the Classic period and was abandoned in about AD 1200.

Monte Albán's influence was found far to the south. Ejutla, for example, was on a route between Monte Albán and the Pacific Ocean, and quantities of shell found there were probably bound for Monte Albán (Feinman and Nicholas 1992). The shell was of the same type as that found at Laguna Zope, to the east. For the last period of its long existence, Laguna Zope was more closely linked to Monte Albán than to sites along the Isthmian coastal plain to the east and south. But at the same time that Monte Albán developed ties to Ejutla and Mixteca de la Costa regions, Laguna Zope languished, and was abandoned at about AD 300.

Some substantiating evidence of the growing importance of Mixteca de la Costa comes from Río Viejo, in the Río Verde Valley near the Pacific Coast. Occupied since the Middle to Late Formative period, the site boomed in the Terminal Formative, covering 150–200 hectares (*c.* 370–494 acres) and boasting large mounds. Furthermore, the regional settlement pattern comprised many new smaller sites, with Río Viejo as the central place. The reasons for the valley's growing population may have resulted from enhanced agricultural productivity due to the deposition of alluvium eroded from the Oaxaca and Nochixtlán Valleys upriver, "[c]hanges in highland land use that affected the hydrology and geomorphology of the lower Río Verde Valley" which in turn made the valley "more attractive as an exchange partner" in networks that included goods from Monte Albán (Joyce 1991: 145).

In the Mixteca Alta, Huamelulpan became an important site, and Yucuita continued to dominate the Nochixtlán Valley. Yucuita was the central place for this valley, eventually covering about 1.5 sq. km (0.6 sq. miles) and demonstrating social differentials in the variety of its architecture and other material culture remains, which included exotic goods indicative of the site's continued importance in long-distance trade.

Guerrero

Northwest of the Mixteca regions lies northern Guerrero, an important connection between the Central Highlands and the Pacific Coast, via the rivers that drain southern Morelos and Puebla: the Atoyac, Nexapa, and Amacuzac. These all join the Balsas River. Guerrero is a land of broken terrain and high temperatures, geophysical features which have contributed to its isolation but also to its productivity; the earliest maize was probably developed there, and in later times it was a rich source of tropical crops like cacao and cotton for the Central Highlands. Our understanding of Guerrero's importance has been hampered by lack of archaeological research. The discovery of Teopantecuanitlán, for example, transformed the perception of Guerrero during Olmec times from intriguing but marginal to a region at the forefront of important cultural trends.

Similarly, the recent uncovering of Terminal Formative Cuetlajuchitlán in northern Guerrero revealed a community built "on an urban-type grid, based on the intersection of two transverse axes oriented to the cardinal directions, joined to parallel passageways that delimited residential and ceremonial groups of rectangular plan and with sunken patios" (Manzanilla López and Talavera González 1993: 110) [9.6]. About 200 m (656 ft) away from the site center, residential architecture was found. Pottery at the site is mostly from Guerrero, with evidence of foreign contacts in Oaxaca gray wares, fine wares from Morelos and Puebla, and in vessels and figurines similar to those found at Ticomán in the Basin of Mexico. Other materials also indicate that Cuetlajuchitlán was an important trading center, drawing shell from the Pacific and green obsidian from the Pachuca mines north of Teotihuacan.

Elsewhere in the Balsas Drainage, distinctive local traditions of pottery were associated with various clusters of farming villages: in the central Balsas region was the Balsas/Mezcala culture, and further to the northwest, around Apatzingán, the Chumbícuaro culture. These cultures have been little investigated beyond a rough definition of ceramic types; phases are generally based upon stylistic changes in pottery and mortuary patterns rather than upon absolute dates derived from carbon samples or other materials. Cultural remains from around the Mezcala River include an arrestingly simple sculptural style much prized by modern collectors and made famous by 20th-century Mexican artist Miguel Covarrubias. Mezcala-style works probably began to be produced in the Late–Terminal Formative, and seem to have reached an apogee in the Classic period; they will be discussed in subsequent chapters. The Apatzingán area lies in the river valley of the Tepalcatepec, a tributary to the Balsas from the mountains of West Mexico, and this valley is the southeasternmost area wherein West Mexico's shaft tombs are found.

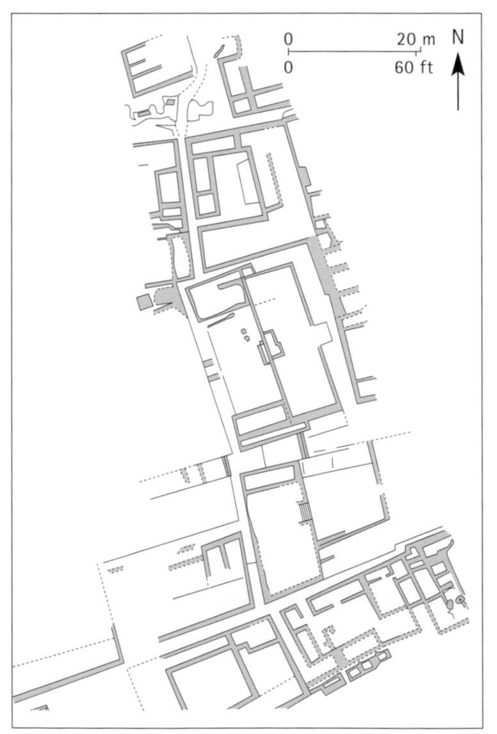

9.6 *Cuetlajuchitlán, Guerrero, occupied from c. 600 BC to AD 200. The site's architecture dates from the Terminal Formative period and buildings are densely packed in a gridded pattern, into which is incorporated a water-supply and drainage system. The central unit in this plan is a civic-ceremonial building. The odd shape of the excavation unit reflects the salvage nature of the archaeological project, which was part of cultural resource recovery in preparation for building a freeway between Cuernavaca, just south of Mexico City, and Acapulco, on the Pacific Coast.*

West Mexico: Shaft-Tomb Cultures and the Teuchitlán Tradition

As we have seen since the Archaic-period Tehuacán Valley, the treatment of the dead tells us much about society in general. During the Late and Terminal Formative burial customs in various regions have provided important evidence of the ability of elites to command rich materials, significant labor forces, even human sacrifices in order to provide society's leaders with lavishly provisioned eternal resting places, built into the community's most sacred architecture.

In West Mexico, the mortuary complex known as the shaft-tomb, or shaft-and-chamber tomb tradition, is possibly the most famous aspect of this region's pre-Columbian culture history, though by no means the most important. In fact, culture historians have sometimes unjustifiably marginalized this entire region because little was known of it beyond the shaft tombs, or rather, the beautiful hollow figurines buried with the deceased individuals for whom the tombs were constructed. Ironically, so great was the art market interest in the hollow figures that looters would destroy whole sites in order to secure them. Thus the grave goods interred to honor and accompany the dead served as the lure to vandals to destroy the larger record of ancient West Mexican life ways.

Fortunately, in recent years systematic techniques of survey and excavation have brought to light some of the communities associated with the burials. In fact, while the largest communities shared important Mesoamerican features such as ball courts and pyramids, they also have a unique type of site layout, a pattern of mounds arrayed in circles, with some of the mounds covering shafts leading to tombs. These sites, which are known as the Teuchitlán tradition, date from the beginning of the Late Formative to the end of the Late Classic [9.7]. The custom of digging and using shaft tombs also started at the beginning of the Late Formative, but it peaked early, in the Terminal Formative.

9.7 *West Mexico: relative frequencies of several related cultural features. There is considerable overlap between the largest Teuchitlán sites and monumental shaft tombs (those "with multiple chambers that open off shafts four m [13 ft] or more deep" [Weigand and Beekman 1998: 39]), but it is clear that the latter is a Terminal Formative phenomenon, tapering off at the same time that populations over a broad area concentrate in the zone around Teuchitlán, with defensive hilltop sites guarding the boundaries.*

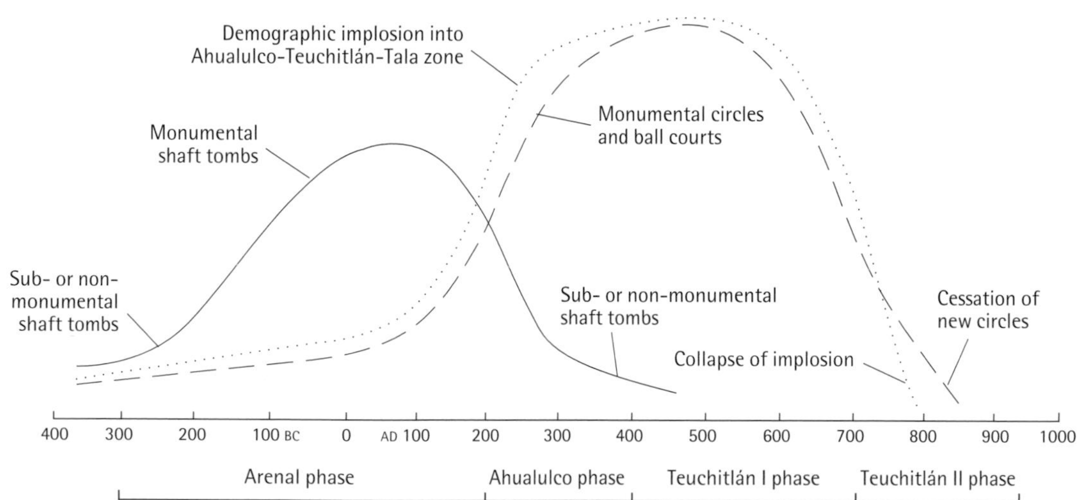

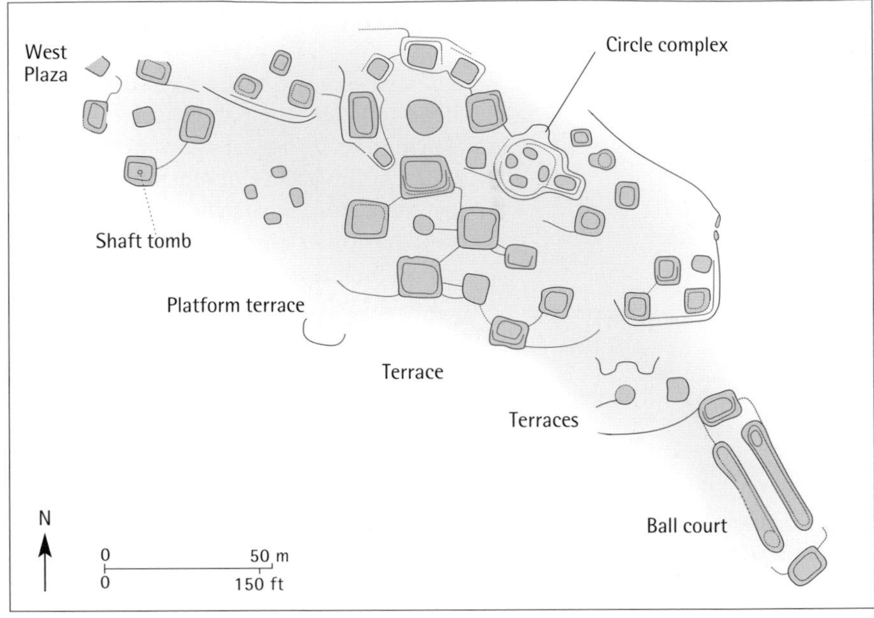

9.8 *Huitzilapa, a small Late Formative West Mexico ceremonial center, shows the relationship of circular Teuchitlán tradition architecture and the shaft tomb. Plan of central part of the site, with the circular arrangement of mounds in the center, and other, smaller mound groups surrounding it. Note the ball court in the southeast section of the plan; it is one of four at the Huitzilapa site. Some of the site's monuments are oriented 17° east of north, close to orientations of monumental architecture at Teotihuacan and sites in Puebla, and related to horizon calendars (Tichy 1976: 4).*

The Tomb at Huitzilapa Hundreds of shaft tombs have been found over a broad area in West Mexico. The tradition has its roots in the area, possibly deriving from El Opeño mortuary customs. By the Middle Formative, circular platforms averaging about 30 m (98 ft) across and 2 m (6.6 ft) high were found in the state of Jalisco, and the burials beneath them included simple graves and more complex shaft tombs.

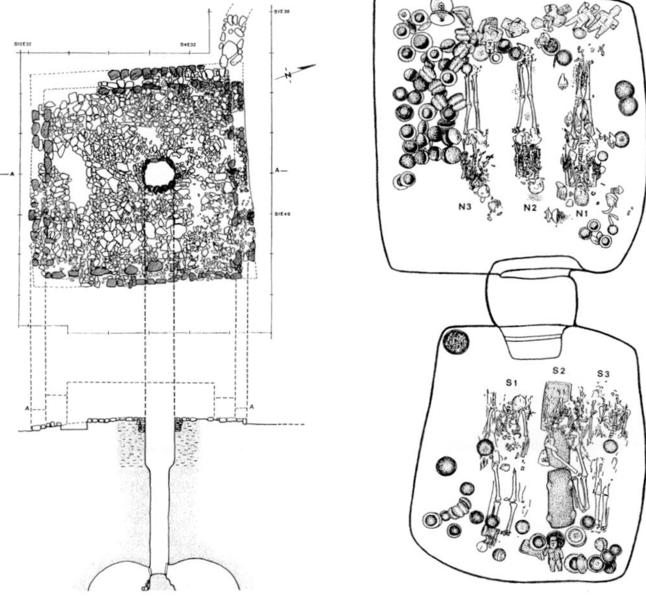

9.9–9.12 *In Huitzilapa's West Plaza, a single shaft provided access to two tombs. (Below left) The south platform, showing the shaft, 7.6 m (25 ft) deep, opening onto two chambers. (Below right) Each tomb has two men and a woman. Highest-ranking was a man in the north tomb, his arms covered with shell bracelets. Three conch shells rested below his groin, "placed to resemble a phallus ... The conch carries its own associations with fertility..." (López and Ramos 1998: 66) and in later Central Mexican cultures was associated with Quetzalcoatl, patron of rulership and creativity. (Opposite above) Excavations at the Guachimontón complex at Teuchitlán have revealed the stepped conical shape of this tradition's pyramids, a unique architectural form in Mesoamerica. (Opposite below) On the plan there is a skeleton labeled N1 and at his feet was this figure, an athlete holding a ball. The association of high-ranking N1 with ballplaying is another feature linking this culture with its own ancient traditions of ballplaying, and with the larger Mesoamerican association of ballplaying and rulership.*

In the Late and Terminal Formative periods, shaft tombs reached their greatest elaboration. The grave contexts varied, and included simple pit burials, bottle-shaped burial chambers, and three kinds of shaft-and-tomb arrangements: shallow shafts (up to 2 m/6.6 ft deep) with one tomb chamber, deep shafts (up to 10 m/33 ft deep) with one or two chamber tombs, and monumental shaft-tombs, some more than 20 m (66 ft) deep, and often having three tomb chambers. The last type is found only in the Teuchitlán tradition core area, and there, such tombs were part of Terminal Formative circular compounds that were modest versions of the monumental circular architecture of the Classic period.

Huitzilapa, a site in the Teuchitlán core area, nicely exemplifies the development of these sites during the Terminal Formative period, and even more important, provides a rare look at a pristine shaft tomb [**9.8–9.11**]. Huitzilapa also had a cemetery, so the shaft tomb in the West Plaza's residential Group F-4, the largest residential compound, represents the only such feature known for the site. The shaft was in the center of the South Platform, and thus the structure on this platform could have served as a kind of temple, "a place for contact with the forces of the universe.... an opening was made within the homogeneity of ordinary space, allowing a transition from the profane to the sacred zones above and below" (López Mestas C and Ramos de la Vega 1998: 57–58).

That the tombs beneath F-4 were those of one family was indicated by skeletal evidence: high-ranking N1 bore a congenital abnormality, the fusion of two vertebrae, and shared this condition with four of the other five individuals in this set of tombs, indicating that the tomb was one family's house of the dead.

West Mexican Architectural Models

The richness of West Mexico's Terminal Formative artistic and architectural traditions is further evidenced in a kind of "figurine" unique in Mesoamerican culture history: the ceramic model of a community activity taking place in its architectural context [**9.13**]. Sometimes the models only depict a dance or ceremony, sometimes a single house with its residents. There are models of ball courts framing the action of the game in play, and models like the one shown, where onlookers and performers share a ceremony. In terms of their vitality and detail, as visual records of pre-Columbian life the architectural models are only matched by Maya painted vases of the Classic period.

The models that depict Teuchitlán-style architecture reflect an archaeologically known feature, the post hole for the pole from which a man, attached to the top by a rope, would descend to earth as if flying. *Voladores* (flyers) still perform their acrobatic feat in modern Mexico, but in the ancient past the actor would have been a shaman, using this event to maintain "a special connection with the cosmos – [and] balances himself atop a pole and transforms himself magically and momentarily into an eagle for passage between levels of the cosmos and the spiritual worlds" (Witmore 1998: 144). With sweeping motions, the *volador* transcended the earthbound human state, inspiring awe and reverence in a ceremonial event that drew the community together.

9.13 *This West Mexican architectural model shows two buildings facing on a plaza. A festival is taking place, with musicians part of a throng of people surrounding a pole topped by a* volador*-type acrobat, an ancient depiction of a ceremony still performed in modern Mexico.*

The Teuchitlán Tradition

The diagram illustrating the sequential peaks of the shaft tombs and Teuchitlán architecture presented us with a case in which important cultural features characteristic of complex societies – monumental tombs, monumental architecture, and a shift in settlement pattern toward larger community size and higher population density – did not all co-vary. Would we not expect the great Teuchitlán sites to have the most monumental shaft tombs? This decline of monumental shaft tombs and their furnishing, at around AD 300, occurs at the same time that smaller tombs were installed beneath "large circular ritual precincts.... The shift from private family or lineage commemorative monuments to more inclusive public forms of ritual architecture suggests the need to incorporate diverse communities in an embracing civic order" (Weigand and Beekman 1998: 45). Teuchitlán-tradition monumental architecture – a large scale version of Huitzilapa's pattern – matures in the Early Classic period, and will be discussed in Chapter 10.

Northwestern Frontier and Northern Arid Zone

The Teuchitlán core area, around the Volcán de Tequila, lay northwest of Lake Chapala, between it and the Pacific coastal plain as it extended north along the Sea of Cortés, separating the Mexican mainland from Baja California. This coastal plain, occupied by shellfish collectors from the time of the Early Formative period, backed onto the Sierra Madre Occidental, and in the valleys running along the east side of the Sierra, farming villages were established in the Terminal Formative period. The Bolaños-Juchitlán Valley linked the Teuchitlán core area with the Northwestern Frontier of Mesoamerica, and there we find the northernmost extension of the shaft-tomb tradition and the Teuchitlán tradition, with the modest sites of Totoate and La Florida, over 200 km (124 miles) north of the core area.

But further north along the eastern foothills of the Sierra, the village traditions of Chalchihuites and Loma San Gabriel were just becoming established in the Terminal Formative period. These cultures were developing in a region long used as a trading route to the north, to what is now northwestern Mexico and the U.S. Southwest. In the Classic and Early Postclassic periods, the U.S. Southwest would become an important focus of trade, with Mesoamerican traders eager to exploit turquoise from sources there and in the Great Basin even further to the north.

Trading up to this region has a long history. We know that maize reached the U.S. Southwest by about 1200 BC. However, for many centuries maize had been cultivated as an adjunct to the diets of mobile collectors. It was not until the Late and Terminal Formative periods that there appeared the signs of incipient sedentism – houses and storage facilities in the U.S. Southwest. True sedentism and use of pottery were established in AD 200–300. But the Terminal Formative pattern "appears to be the northernmost extension of a Mesoamerican pattern that originates with the Chupícuaro tradition. Mesoamerican influences that archaeologists link to this economic and social change range from the basic (maize, pottery) to the subtle (highly stylized and altered iconographic elements)" (McGuire 2001: 525).

Central Highlands Surrounding the Basin of Mexico

Chupícuaro culture had its core area in the Bajío, and seems to have been linked to the southern Basin of Mexico center, Cuicuilco, which, by the Terminal Formative, was all but abandoned as Teotihuacan drew population into the Teotihuacan Valley of the northeastern Basin. West of the Basin, the Valley of Toluca had been well populated in the Middle Formative, but by the Late and Terminal Formative periods it was virtually abandoned, and, except for a few small sites in easily defended areas, would remain so until the Early Classic period (Sugiura 2000: 33).

Morelos To the south, Morelos, in contrast, experienced continued population growth, as well as differentiation of regional cultures, with western sites showing greater interaction with Guerrero and eastern sites being drawn into Teotihuacan's sphere of influence. Typically, population clusters focused on a central community, larger than the others and with more imposing public architecture, and established on higher ground, above the alluvial plain which supported it. One trend over the Late and Terminal Formative in Morelos is the decline in long-distance trade as trading relations among regions in Morelos intensified.

Puebla In recent years, western Puebla has been on civil defense alert in anticipation of the eruption of Popocatépetl, one of Mexico's most active volcanoes. Archaeologists now working in the Tetimpa region, just southeast of the volcano, keep their field vehicles pointed toward the exit roads as Popo's smoke plume drifts over them. Meanwhile, they excavate through a layer of volcanic pumice deposited about 1,000 years ago, uncovering the remains of settlements abruptly abandoned between AD 50 and 100, after habitation in this region that dated back to 700 BC, with a period of abandonment from 200 to 50 BC.

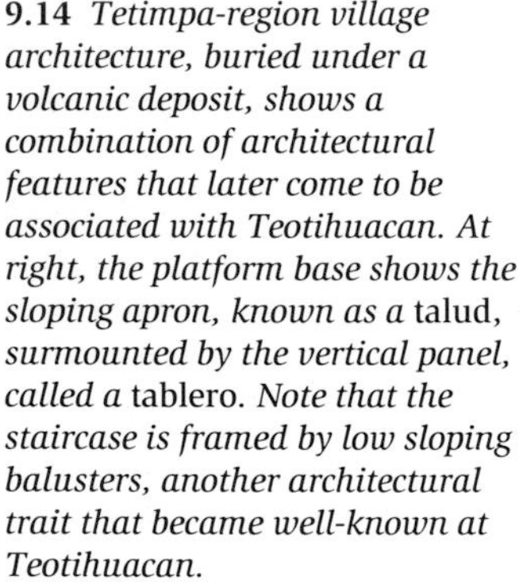

9.14 *Tetimpa-region village architecture, buried under a volcanic deposit, shows a combination of architectural features that later come to be associated with Teotihuacan. At right, the platform base shows the sloping apron, known as a* talud, *surmounted by the vertical panel, called a* tablero. *Note that the staircase is framed by low sloping balusters, another architectural trait that became well-known at Teotihuacan.*

Tetimpa's farming villages featured wattle-and-daub houses set upon elegant formal platforms [**9.14**]. Two or three of these would form the sides of a small plaza; at its center was a shrine (Plunket and Uruñela 1998). One of the shrines seems to have been a kind of effigy-volcano; like their near-contemporaries at Cuicuilco, the Tetimpans tried unsuccessfully to allay nature's power to destroy. Some other Pueblan centers lost population, as well. Tlalancaleca continued to be a substantial site, over 100 hectares and dozens of mounds and mound groups, until about AD 100. Xochitecatl occupation was interrupted: in Late and Terminal Formative times it was a major ritual center, its mountaintop location roughly equidistant from the massive

volcanoes La Malinche, to the east, and Iztaccihuatl and Popocatépetl, to the southwest. Some of Xochitecatl's ceremonial architecture dates from this period, but it was abandoned during the Terminal Formative, possibly as a result of volcanic activity. Substantially rebuilt in the Late Classic, it was a companion site to Cacaxtla and will be discussed in Chapter 13. Totimehuacan remained one of Puebla's important centers.

Cholula The lack of skeletal evidence beneath the pumice layer indicates that Tetimpans may have had time to flee from the volcano's rain of death. They may have gone to Cholula, over 20 km (12 miles) to the east. Cholula remained occupied throughout the Terminal Formative, when it covered about 2 sq. km (0.8 sq. miles) and had a population of 5,000–10,000, possibly swelled by refugees from Popo's range of damage, but we would not expect that the increase in population size would be as dramatic as that of Teotihuacan after the abandonment of Cuicuilco. For one thing, unlike the Basin of Mexico with its peculiar pattern of aggregating virtually all the Basin's population into one city, Puebla's settlement pattern remained a mix of larger civic-ceremonial centers surrounded by hinterlands of farming villages.

In the Terminal Formative period construction began on Cholula's Great Pyramid, which eventually became the largest structure, by volume, in the pre-Columbian New World [**9.15, 9.16**]. Today parts of its base are restored, but it mostly appears to be a green hill topped by a large church in the middle of the modern town. Cholula's location guaranteed it long-term stability of occupation, because it was at the intersection of major routes connecting the Basin of Mexico with the Gulf lowlands and with Oaxaca, via the Tehuacán Valley.

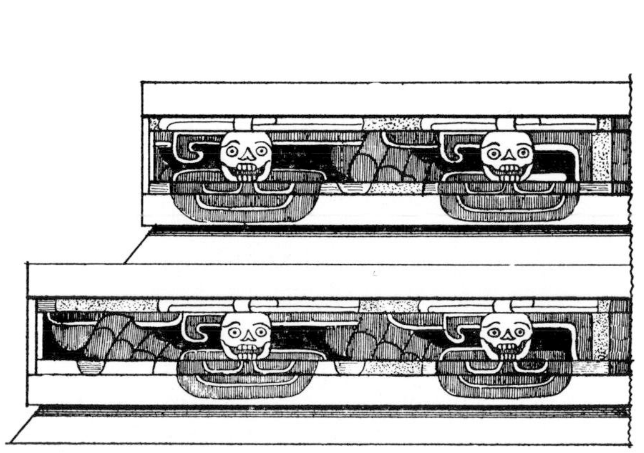

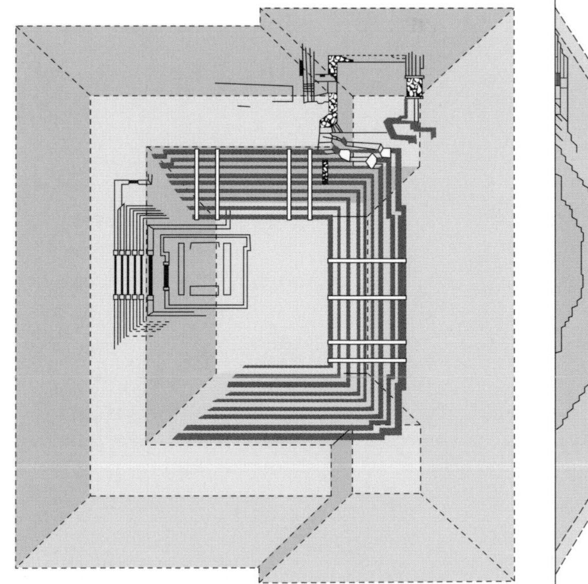

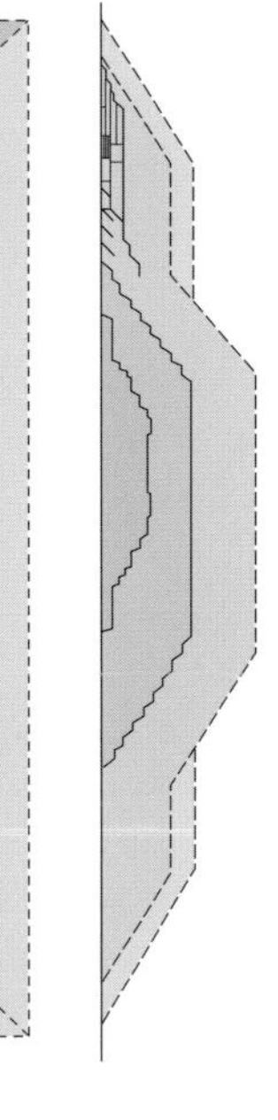

9.15, 9.16 *The Great Pyramid of Cholula would, by the end of the Late Postclassic period, become the largest structure, by volume, in the pre-Columbian New World. It was built in four major stages, each one covering and enlarging the one before it. Structure I, the first, established the orientation for later rebuildings at 17° east of north, about the same as the orientation of the Pyramid of the Sun at Teotihuacan. Structure I was a substantial 120 m (394 ft) on a side and 17 m (56 ft) high – thus its base was longer than a football field, and it rose to a height of five stories. Its flat top, 43 m (141 ft) on a side, held temples that were later destroyed as the pyramid was enlarged. (Marquina 1999 [1951]: 119, Lám. 36) (Below left) The first pyramid was remodeled to include a talud-and-tablero façade. On the tableros a frieze of mural painting depicts the repeated motifs of insect heads and bodies. (Marquina 1999 [1951]: 121, Fig. 5)*

Tehuacán Valley Evidence is strong that by the end of the Late Formative, Monte Albán had extended its sphere of influence all the way up through the Cuicatlán Cañada, to the southern end of the Tehuacán Valley. Up at the northern end, where the valley meets the southeastern Pueblan Plain, the mountains constrict slightly. On a ridge overlooking the valley from the east side is Cuayucatépec, a site occupied between 150 BC and AD 250, with a population of about 1,000. This was one of the half-dozen sites that sprang up as Quachilco was declining into abandonment (see Chapter 8), and the newer sites shared features of defensibility. Cuayucatépec had "substantial walls blocking access to all or part of the site" (Drennan 1979: 171). It overlooked an area of good soils that could have been readily irrigated, and while the principal concentration of public-scale architecture was on the ridge top, the site extended to an area on the alluvial plain, where there was a ball court.

9.17 *El Pital, in the north-central Gulf lowlands, has a site core covering about 1.75 sq. km (0.7 sq. miles), with over 100 buildings "ranging from a few meters high to about 35 m [115 ft], the largest known structures of the eastern lowlands. These include small constructions, elongated platforms, numerous ball courts, and massive temples, practically all focused on plazas" (Wilkerson 1994: 60).*

The Northern Gulf Region

Along the north-central and northern Gulf coastal lowlands, as elsewhere, there was a pattern of central places with civic-ceremonial architecture, surrounded by hinterlands. Out of this emerged a major center in the north-central lowlands, El Pital, on the Nautla River about 15 km (9 miles) inland from the sea [**9.17**]. While Postclassic-period sherds litter the surface, materials from the end of the Formative and the Early Classic periods predominate, particularly around major architecture. In fact, the community may have drawn population from sites such as Las Higueras, a coastal site over 30 km (19 miles) southeast of El Pital, which was mostly abandoned by the end of the Terminal Formative. Santa Luisa, on the other hand, nearly 40 km (25 miles) to the north, continued to thrive, and showed evidence of El Pital interactions in its pottery.

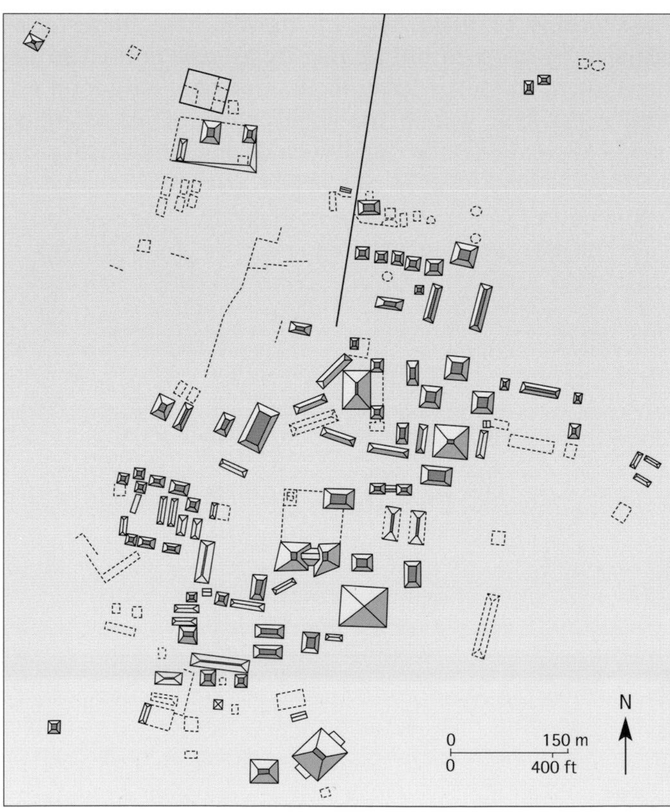

Around El Pital, a region of over 100 sq. km (40 sq. miles) was intensively cultivated and settled, with hundreds of house mounds distributed around a system of raised fields, "among the largest earth-moving projects of their time in ancient Mesoamerica" (Wilkerson 1994: 63). Such efforts converted swampy areas to fertile croplands, growing food and important tropical trade crops, cotton and cacao. Thus the Nautla River provided the rich alluvium for intensive cultivation, and the watercourse for a trade route. El Pital may have been a trading partner with Teotihuacan; its chronology is a much better match with Teotihuacan's period of outreach than is El Tajín's, and El Pital faded at the end of the Early Classic, when Teotihuacan lost interest in enterprises far from home. El Tajín, a small settlement in the Terminal Formative, became a powerful Late Classic city.

In the northern Gulf lowlands, important centers developed in the Late and Terminal Formative, and round temple-platforms are found at sites like Tancanhuitz. Some scholars have found this feature an indication of some sort of interaction involving Cuicuilco, while others have pointed to the possibility that the Gulf lowlands was experiencing ethnic diversity, as evidenced by the coexistence of round and square building plans. It is unfortunate that the archaeological record of this area is so poorly understood. Several better-known sites help illuminate cultural developments in the Terminal Formative and Early Classic periods. The Pánuco sites, though damaged by Colonial-period and modern settlements, offer evidence of occupation of this area from the Early Formative through the time of European intrusion. Further north, San Antonio Nogalar's distinctive architecture reflects a local tradition, and its artifacts also are drawn from Tamaulipas traditions to the north, and from Pánuco to the south. Note, however, that Mesoamerican traits such as the ball game are characteristic of this region, which serves as a kind of borderland to the eastern side of the Northern Arid Zone.

TEOTIHUACAN, THE PLACE WHERE TIME BEGAN

The Terminal Formative was a time when most regions of Mesoamerica developed large, complex civic-ceremonial centers, as this review has shown. From Chalchuapa to San Antonio Nogalar, towns boasted ball courts and pyramids, and many ruling families showed off their fine trade goods brought from far away. However, all these relatively impressive central places seem small compared with Teotihuacan, which, in the Terminal Formative period, developed a ceremonial boulevard 1.5 km (*c.* 1 mile) long, with massive pyramids and smaller three-temple complexes grouped along it [**9.18**].

Teotihuacan's rulers clearly had pretentions of grandeur, and they seem to have been based on a belief that their city was the place where time began. Over 1,500 years later, the Spanish cleric Fray Bernardino de Sahagún recorded an Aztec legend:

"How the gods had their beginning ... that there in Teotihuacan, they say, is the place; the time was when there still was darkness. There all the gods assembled and consulted among themselves who would bear upon his back the burden of rule, who would be the sun" (Sahagún 1978 [1569]: 1).

Whether the Teotihuacanos themselves understood their role in cosmic history in precisely this way is uncertain – the site's name is an Aztec term

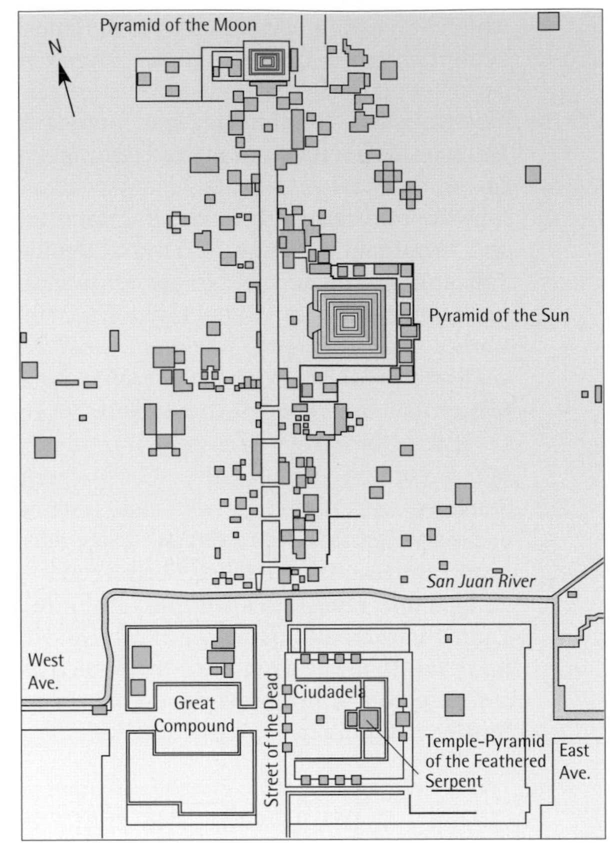

9.18, 9.19 *Teotihuacan's ceremonial core in the Terminal Formative period. The Pyramids of the Moon and Sun were probably built by AD 150, while the Ciudadela ('Citadel') and Temple-Pyramid of the Feathered Serpent were constructed by AD 250. The plan shows the main ceremonial buildings along the Street of the Dead; the alignment is 15.25° east of north. There would have been considerable residential architecture dating from this period, but it is buried beneath the site's famous apartment compounds and city grid, which date from the Early Classic period [**10.2**].*

meaning something like "Place of the Gods," and the names of its major features are all Nahuatl words. Scholars disagree as to whether or not Formative- and Classic-period Teotihuacanos spoke Nahuatl (see Chapter 16); Nahuatl was the language most widely used at Teotihuacan in the Postclassic period, and the Classic-period glyph language is consistent with Postclassic Nahuatl glyphs.

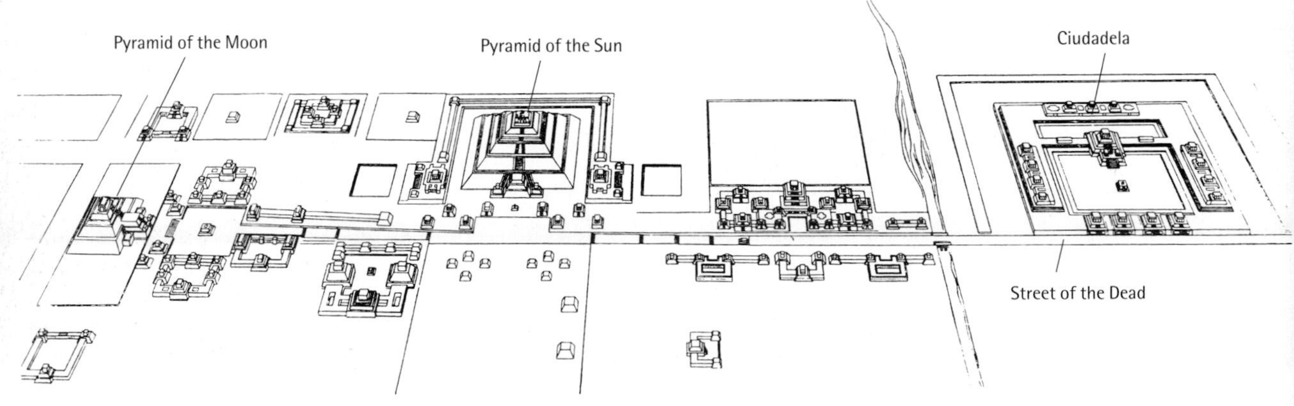

9.20 *(Opposite) The visual power in the alignment and positioning of Cerro Gordo and the two pyramids is obvious to anyone looking north along the Street of the Dead. The proportional similarity of the pyramids of the Sun (right) and Moon (center) leads the eye to expect that they are at least the same size, and the Moon Pyramid's position at the end of the causeway suggests that it is even the larger of the two. "That it is, in fact, smaller, brings the massive mountain behind it telescoping forward, magnifying its visual impact" (Evans and Berlo 1992: 9).*

The Magic of Location: Place of the Gods

Teotihuacan's layout as an alignment with their cosmos has been deciphered by means of archaeoastronomy and measurements of the landscape. Perhaps the pivotal feature is the Pyramid of the Sun. It was built over a cave to which access was gained by a tunnel to the west. The cave, "undoubtedly a center of worship as caves in Mexico have been over the centuries, actually determined the site of the Pyramid of the Sun" (Heyden and Gendrop 1980: 20).

The pyramid was oriented slightly north of west (about 15.5°) toward the horizon point of the setting sun on two days a year: around 13 August and 29 April – about one 260-day divinatory almanac count apart. Other astronomical horizon events viewed from this perspective were also meaningful in terms of the agricultural year and the belief system (Millon 1993: 35, Note 7).

Thus the cave was the sighting point for a very important horizon calendar, and the alignment of the cave entrance and the setting sun was crosscut, at right angles, by the sacred causeway we know as the Street of the Dead, at whose northern terminus was built "Teotihuacan's first great pyramid – the earliest, innermost Moon Pyramid" (Millon 1992: 384). Above the cave was built the Pyramid of the Sun, first as a modest adobe brick shrine, faced with cobbles.

But diligent efforts toward architectural magnificence quickly transformed Teotihuacan. By early Terminal Formative times, the city's population neared 100,000, and the Pyramid of the Sun was constructed over the cave to immortalize its significance and dramatize the power of the city's rulers (Millon 1993). While we know nothing of the individuals who planned the city, the plan itself reveals precise measurements using a standard measurement unit of 0.83 m (32 in). This is about the same as a traditional folk measure in use in many parts of the world, the distance from an adult's fingertip to the center of the chest (in Spain, it is called the "vara"). Applying this unit of measurement to Teotihuacan, one finds that the distances between many of the principal monuments, measured by this standard, are numbers that have ritual significance, as if "a master plan forming a representation of the universe existed from the beginning of the city's configuration" (Sugiyama 1993: 104).

For example, the original base of the Pyramid of the Sun measured 260 varas, the sacred number of the days of the divination almanac which was an ancient calendar shared over Mesoamerica. Other sacred numbers are found in the dimensions and spacings of major monuments over the city. The importance of this is the insight it provides into ancient Mesoamerican urban planning. Serious civil engineering problems were challenging the architects of Teotihuacan and other sites, and they were solved in practical ways. Yet, working within the limits of practical solutions, designers honored the forces of creation and destruction that they perceived as controlling their universe.

The first great building effort, at about AD 100, brought the Sun Pyramid to nearly the size we see today, while the second construction resulted in the completed structure, 225 m on a side along the base, and about 75 m high (738 ft across, 246 ft high), including the now-destroyed temple (or twin temples) on top. Its volume is roughly 1 million cubic m (1,308,000 cubic yd), and because it was built virtually as a single construction effort, the Sun Pyramid stands as the largest single-phase structure in the pre-Columbian New World. One million cubic meters amounts to roughly 30 million basket loads of dirt and rubble fill, much of it apparently excavated out from the complex cave system running under the city. If a worker could haul five loads a day, then 6 million work-days were necessary to complete the bulk of the pyramid. A labor force of only 6,000 workers, a fraction of the city's population, could have done it in 10 years, working only 100 days a year.

A huge pile of dirt, however pyramidally shaped, is not an impressive civic monument. Finishing consisted of a layer of mud and volcanic gravel, and then lime plaster, imported from adjacent valleys, and finally, brilliantly colored murals. Harvesting the needed timber for construction projects deforested the Teotihuacan Valley, and this triggered sheet erosion that scoured off the topsoil, an effect still visible throughout the valley. Today, the Pyramid of the Sun is bereft of its plaster and bright paint, and yet it still strikes the observer as a stylized mountain. The creation of mountain effigies was clearly the intent of the pyramid builders, who saw the landscape as living, and each pyramid as a living portrait of the mountains around it.

What Gods did the Pyramids Honor? The pyramids were funerary monuments (Millon 1993: 37, Note 19), and certainly dedicated to deities, but, to date, there is no definitive evidence as to the identity of these gods, or the nature of their relationship to deity principles known from elsewhere in Mesoamerica. From art that dates to the Classic period, two major Teotihuacan deities have been identified: a male Storm God, with clear relation to the later deity Tlaloc, and a female whom scholars call the Goddess or the Great Goddess. Teotihuacan was unusual in Mesoamerican culture history in venerating a major female deity, and she may be the deity of the Sun Pyramid, in fact, "perhaps the Goddess was *literally* the cave and temple" (Pasztory 1997: 91), in the strong sense in which Mesoamericans animated all of the landscape, including the built environment of artificial mountains. However, very little hard evidence – artistic representations, for example – exists that could substantiate this particular association of deities and pyramids. "Equally good arguments have been presented the other way around, and neither may be true" (Pasztory 1993: 50).

The Temple-Pyramid of the Feathered Serpent and the Ciudadela Adornment of the great pyramids continued. In about AD 175, the Pyramid of the Sun was enhanced with a platform whose sides were finished in *talud-tablero*, that is, with a "*tablero*" panel above a sloping apron, the "*talud*." This represented an early use of an architectonic motif that would become a signature of the city. The last of the city's great architectural structures to be built was the Temple-Pyramid of the Feathered Serpent, much smaller than the two other pyramids, a seven-tiered extravaganza of bas-relief serpents, interpreted as fire serpents, representing war [**9.21**].

The Feathered Serpent, called Quetzalcoatl by the Aztecs, was a patron of rulership, creativity, and fertility, as well as being associated with the celestial body we call Venus. To the ancient Mesoamericans, who carefully followed its 584-day cycles as the Morning and Evening Star, it was associated with warfare, and Venus cults were known among peoples of the Central Highlands as well as among the Maya and peoples of the Gulf lowlands, and among the Zapotecs of Oaxaca. "In addition to military conquest, the Venus cult was concerned with the symbolic transformation of blood into water and fertility through the ritual execution of captives" (Carlson 1993: 61).

The Temple-Pyramid of the Feathered Serpent faced onto a huge square precinct called the Ciudadela, built at about the same time as the temple-pyramid, by between AD 150 and 200. The pyramid was apparently the tomb of an important early leader, and of the probably 260 individuals who were sacrificed at the building's dedication and at the time of the leader's interment (Cabrera Castro 1993: 106) [**9.22, 9.23**].

The Magic of Location: Place of the Food and Tools

9.21 *(Above) A group of nine skeletons, male sacrificial victims (note their hands secured behind their backs) interred wearing U-shaped shell necklaces representing human jaws. In several cases, the necklaces consisted of actual human jaws. The circular objects were disks representing mirrors worn at the backs of their costumes.*

9.22 *(Opposite above) The façade of the Temple-Pyramid of the Feathered Serpent, in alternating motifs showing his head emerging through the feathered rim of a mirror (Taube 1992: 197) and wearing a blocky headdress as a symbol of rulership which combines the Feathered Serpent's associations of militarism, sacrifice, and authority (Sugiyama 1992: 213–215, 219).*

9.23 *(Opposite below) A reconstruction of the Temple-Pyramid of the Feathered Serpent, with cutaway showing the location of the central burial and peripheral groups of sacrificial victims.*

City-sized cosmograms are impressive expressions of the belief systems of complex societies, and the power of their rulers to command labor and materials on a truly monumental scale. However, all this complexity and monumentality had to be paid for. In Chapter 8 Teotihuacan's subsistence base was discussed: it was clear that the city's population could have been supported by surrounding productive areas. Most important was the tract of drained fields (*chinampas*) that extended through the lower Teotihuacan Valley, from the city down to the lake. The middle and upper valleys also had broad areas of productive alluvial soil, but the lower valley raised-bed and canal system not only yielded several crops a year that could be easily delivered, by canoe, to the western edge of the city, but also had implications for increasing the stratification inherent in Teotihuacan's multi-ethnic social order of old Teotihuacano families, enclaves of foreigners like the residents from Monte Albán, Cuicuilcan refugees, and immigrants from other communities around the Basin of Mexico, abandoned during the Late Formative period. Establishing the grid of excavated canals and their associated deep-soil islands was a labor-intensive effort that would have made the *chinampa* region very valuable land. It also is much more characteristic of intensification directed from a central authority than it is of collective efforts of individual families acting independently, and thus would suggest that the city's rulers controlled the means of production.

In the Terminal Formative and Classic periods, Teotihuacan established contacts with, and influenced the development of communities 1,000 km (621 miles) away. What were the Teotihuacanos bringing to these places that was so impressive, that made them so influential? First of all, another

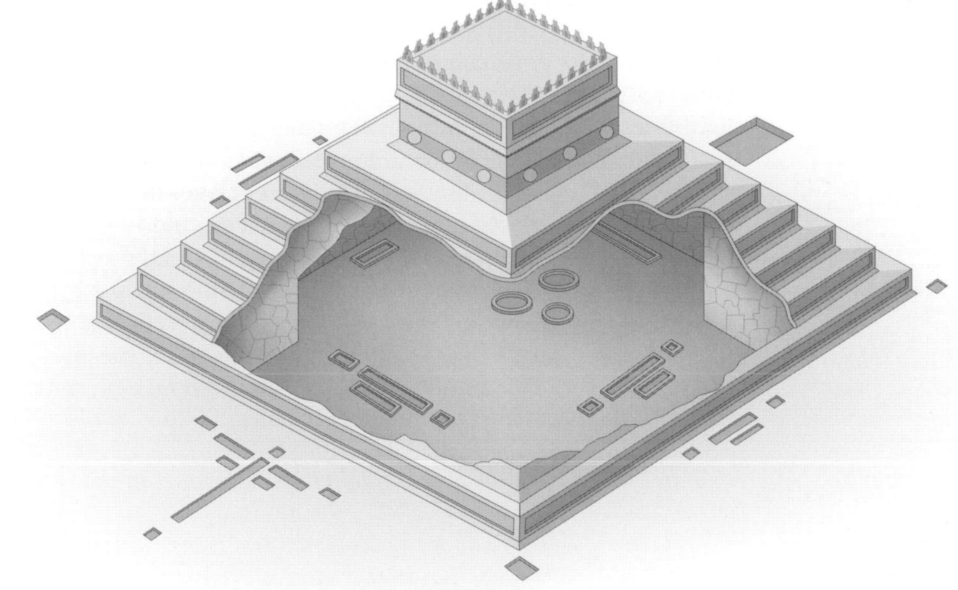

9.24 *This richly costumed jaguar walks along a causeway-aqueduct that emerges from a sacred building. Irrigated fields form the background. This scene is from a mural at Tetitla, one of thousands of apartment compounds built in the Early Classic period. At the same time, a vast network of canals channeled the water of the city's springs. The jaguar, symbol of the earth and water from it, became as important as the Feathered Serpent, associated with water from the sky.*

feature of Teotihuacan's locational magic was its proximity to several of the most important obsidian sources in Mesoamerica. The upper valley Otumba source of gray and black obsidian had long been exploited and its products traded for hundreds of kilometers. An even better grade of obsidian was found at Pachuca, just northeast of the Teotihuacan Valley. It possessed a perfectly even texture, making it the finest grade of material for pre-Columbian Mesoamerica's cutting tools. And probably equally important for its popularity was its range of colors: clear green to greenish-gold. Greenstones of all types – jadeite, turquoise – were more highly valued than gold itself by the Mesoamericans, and Pachuca obsidian was a greenstone that could be used to make the finest knives. Trading expeditions from Teotihuacan would have carried basket loads of obsidian blades along with other fine goods – pottery, figurines.

In addition to carrying such precious goods, the traders carried the charisma of the great center itself, which we cannot discount as a powerful factor [**9.24**]. Over a huge area, regional cultures shared the notion that spiritual forces were inherent in sentient beings and natural phenomena. When strangers arrived, full of confidence about their place in the cosmos and privileged knowledge about other regions of Mesoamerica, provincial elites would have eagerly sought a means to secure these exalted emissaries as trading partners, anxious to share in arcane lore and precious goods.

By the end of the Terminal Formative, Teotihuacan's impressive monuments were built and the basis for its economy well-established. However, the cost of this grandeur was apparently too high for the people who bore it, because after AD 250 a radical shift in policies occurred, which will be discussed at the beginning of the next chapter.

PART 3 CULTURES OF THE EARLY CLASSIC

Early Classic Period (AD 250/300–600)

Region	Early Classic (300 – 400 – 500 – 600)
Northern Arid Zone	
NW Mexico, U.S. SW	Hohokam tradition
Northern Deserts	Coyote tradition
SE: Sierra Madre Oriental	La Salta, Eslabones phases
SE: Tamaulipas	Eslabones, Palmillas phases
Northern Mesoamerica	*Bajío region occupation*
Northwestern Frontier	Cañutillo phase, Loma San Gabriel culture *Alta Vista*; *Alta Vista*
West Mexico	Ahualulco phase; Chametla phase; Teuchitlan phase *Teuchitlán tradition*
Michoacán	Chumbícuaro phase *El Otero, Tingambato*
Guerrero	*Mezcala style*
Basin of Mexico	Tlamimilopa phase; Xolalpan phase *Teotihuacan*
Tula region	*Chingú*
Puebla	*Cholula*; Tenanyecac
Gulf Lowlands, north	Pithaya phase; Zoquil phase *San Antonio Nolagar*
Gulf Lowlands, north-central	*El Pital*; Tajín II
Gulf Lowlands, south-central	Upper Remojadas I phase; Upper Remojadas II phase *Cerro de las Mesas, Matacapan*
Tehuacán Valley	Palo Blanco phase
Mixteca Alta	Las Flores phase
Mixteca Baja	Ñuiñe phase
Oaxaca and Tehuantepec	Monte Albán III phase *Monte Albán, Jalieza, Dainzú*
Chiapas Interior Plateau	Laguna phase; Tsah phase *Chiapa de Corzo, Lagartero, Laguna Francesca*
Chiapas and Guatemala Coast	Jaritos phase; Kato phase *Izapa, Abaj Takalik, Balberta*
Guatemala Highlands	Aurora phase *Kaminaljuyú*; Esperanza phase *Kaminaljuyú*
Maya Lowlands, north	Cochuah
Maya Lowlands, south	Tzak'ol phase *Tikal, Uaxactún, Palenque, Yaxchilán, Calakmul, Copán, Caracol*
Southeastern Mesoamerica	*Chalchuapa, Cerén, Gualjoquito, Quelepa*

Selected phase names; *sites* and *events* are in *italic* type

10 TEOTIHUACAN AND ITS INTERNATIONAL INFLUENCE (AD 250/300–600)

THE CLASSIC PERIOD in Mesoamerica was first defined by scholars as the time of florescence of Maya centers. Noting that the dates on monumental stelae at Maya sites ranged from about AD 250 or 300 to about AD 900, scholars argued that this period must constitute a sort of Mesoamerican "golden age" when art, society, and technology had achieved a maturity on a par with that of ancient Greece, and thus Mesoamerica, like the ancient Mediterranean world, had "Classic" features.

The designation of this 600+ year span as the Classic period has been remarkably serviceable for much of Mesoamerica, and readily subdivides into "Early" and "Late" phases of roughly 300 years each. Of course, as local and regional culture histories have become more refined, these simple designations have undergone almost as many modifications as the Maya pyramids. Many scholars use AD 200, or even earlier, as a starting point for the Classic period, and many apply such refinements as the "protoclassic" (the period immediately preceding the Classic), "Middle Classic" (*c.* AD 500–700), and "Epiclassic" (AD 800–1000). In this book, period designations are used as chronological markers for the whole culture area, a practice that reflects a general trend toward this kind of usage; readers should be aware that some scholars use the "Classic" period to designate a developmental phase in a particular region, whose timing may or may not correspond to that of the AD 250/300–900 range.

What Happened in the Classic

Whether by foresight or chance, the pioneering scholars who designated AD 300–600 as the Classic period marked out an era of flourishing cities and ceremonial centers, ruling over true states and vast territories. Some of Mesoamerica's most important archaeological sites had their florescence during the Classic period: Teotihuacan, Cholula, El Tajín, Monte Albán, Palenque, Tikal, Copán. These centers represent some of the great regional cultures that maintained a high degree of complexity during the Classic and even persisted into the Postclassic period, and there are yet others that have recently become better known, such as the Teuchitlán tradition.

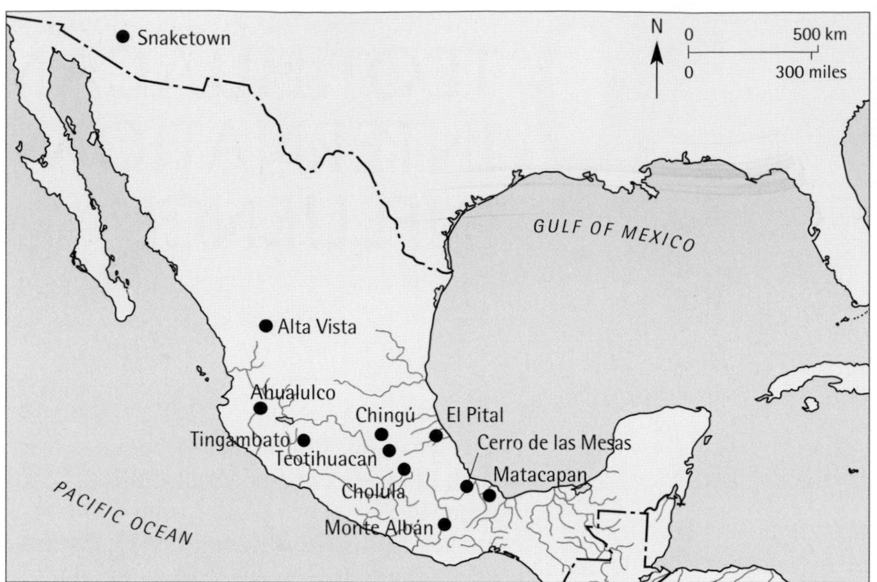

10.1 *Middle America , showing Early Classic-period regions and sites mentioned in Chapter 10.*

All over Mesoamerica in the Terminal Formative period, monumental centers were being built as populations aggregated into communities of unprecedented size and density. Teotihuacan, unparalleled in this regard, may have had 80,000 people in the first centuries AD. Maya centers were more dispersed, but still encompassed tens of thousands of farmer-artisans living on house-plots clustered around impressive ceremonial and palatial-administrative buildings. Some important Terminal Formative sites declined, but the overall Early Classic trend was toward more numerous centers, larger and more complex in terms of ethnic diversity and socioeconomic organization. In the next four chapters, we will follow Classic era trends across Mesoamerica, continuing now with Teotihuacan and other developments west of the Isthmus [**10.1**], then turning in Chapters 11 and 12 to the Early and Late Classic in the Maya region and adjacent areas, then returning to the west in Chapter 13.

TEOTIHUACAN: PYRAMIDS AND PALACES

At AD 300, Teotihuacan was more massive than ever, with a population topping 100,000, yet the nature of its societal organization is still an enigma to us today. In strong contrast to the Classic Maya, whose dynastic histories are becoming very well known, Teotihuacan's traditions of rulership can only be speculated about, along with the nature of its internal organization, and the nature of its external relations with lands over which it held strong influence, and foreign powers in which Teotihuacan diplomatic missions can be seen to have meddled significantly. We do know that, more than any other Mesoamerican center prior to Tenochtitlan, Teotihuacan maintained strong ties with other centers, and may have even established colonies. Teotihuacanos traded in goods and ideas, particularly in ritual concepts related to war and sacrifice.

The Evolution of Teotihuacan's Plan

In the Early Classic period, the city achieved its greatest spatial extent [**10.2**], the result of a vast urban redevelopment project that swept over the insubstantial residences housing its huge population and laid out a grid which took its orientation from the north–south ceremonial avenue we call the Street of the Dead. Upon this grid were built about 2,200 apartment compounds. They varied in size and interior layout, but all were roughly square, averaging around 50–60 m (31 to 37 ft) on a side, and housing extended families consisting of about 60–100 people who were related to each other in patrilineages. The windowless exterior walls of these apartment compounds made the city's residences private, and each typically featured sets of rooms around interior courtyards that opened the building interiors to light and air. The courtyards usually centered upon altars which are thought to have been monuments to the founding ancestors of the lineage occupying the compound. Limited archaeological evidence indicates that such ancestors were buried under the altars.

Teotihuacan's pattern of gridded streets and apartment compounds seem familiar to us, because so many modern cities, particularly in the U.S.A., are laid out on a grid. Yet in the ancient world, cities tend to have grown by accretion, and

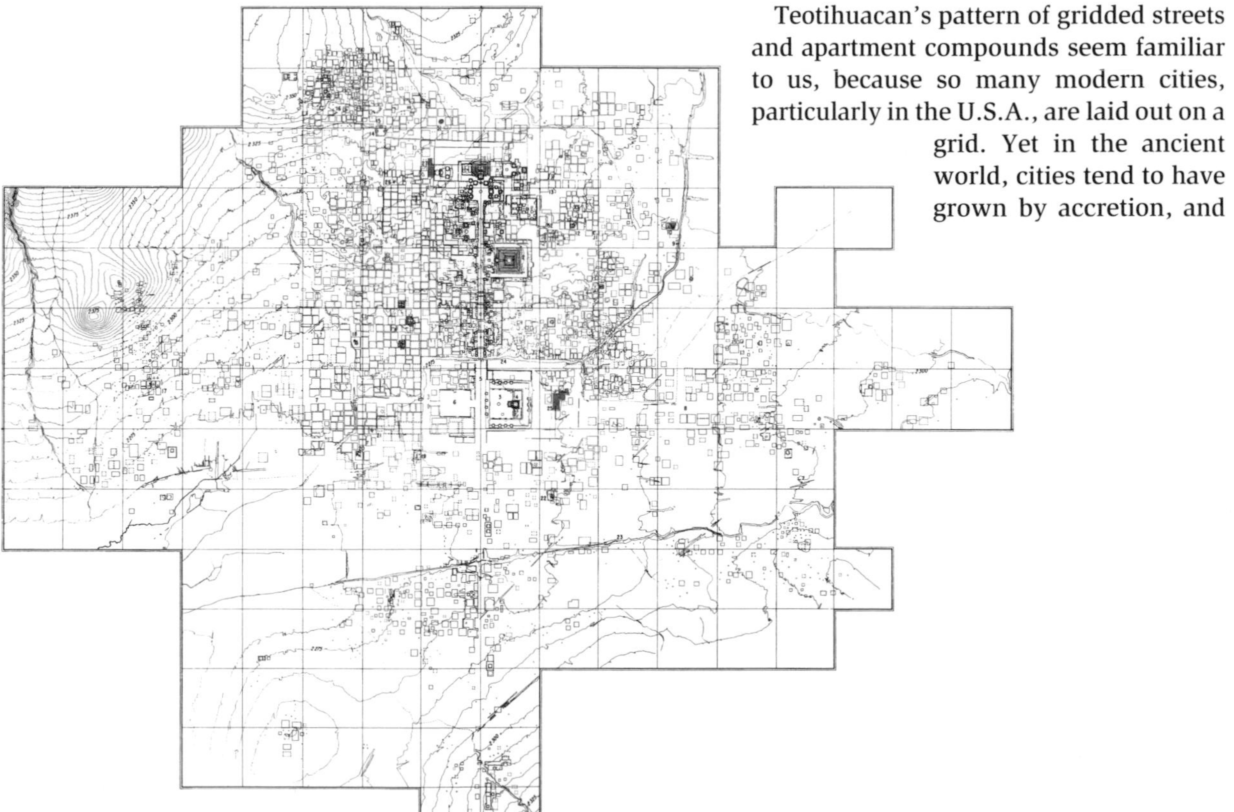

10.2 *Teotihuacan, map of the Early Classic city, when it achieved its greatest extent, about 20 sq. km (8 sq. miles). The "Street of the Dead" forms a north–south axis and runs for more than 5 km (3 miles), starting at the Pyramid of the Moon and running past the Pyramid of the Sun, and the southern limit of civic-ceremonial architecture, the Ciudadela.*

the streets may be crooked and definitely neither parallel not perpendicular in relation to other streets. This gridded pattern, elaborated to its present size sometime after AD 250, is nearly unique in Mesoamerica, and was definitely unique at this scale anywhere in the ancient world. The grid, and apartment compounds, seem to have resulted from a true social revolution, and while the details – even many of the key facts – of this revolution may never be known, we can see, in the evolution of the city itself, the trend toward strong personalized leadership and then the antagonistic response to it.

Late and Terminal Formative Teotihuacan had gone from a modest regional capital to one of the world's largest cities almost instantly. The heart of the old city seems to have been the Oztoyahualco area, northwest of the Pyramid of the Moon, whose earliest phases were low platforms. The huge structural masses of the Pyramids of the Sun and Moon, built around AD 1, seem to have been, in part, the dedicatory funeral monuments of early rulers, as well as being effigy mountains honoring the Storm God and the Goddess. At the time the pyramids were built, it is likely that a palatial residence for the city's rulers had also been established.

Three Teotihuacan Palaces

10.3 *The necklace below was worn by one of the sacrificial victims buried beneath the Temple-Pyramid of the Feathered Serpent. Beads carved in the form of teeth were fashioned into U-shaped representations of human jaws. Other necklaces found in these contexts were actually made of human jaws.*

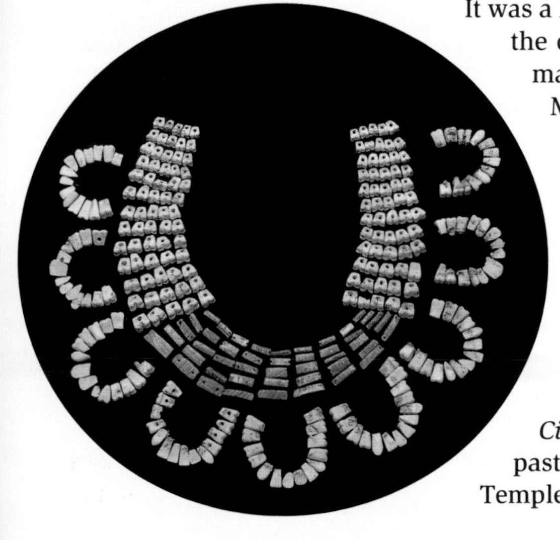

Teotihuacan's enigmatic social and political history is clarified by a look at how rulership may have changed over the course of the Terminal Formative and Early Classic. Our best archaeological evidence for this evolution of rulership comes from what may have been the possible evolution of palaces in the city. The last, the Early Classic-period Street of the Dead Complex, is the candidate for which there is by far the best documentation.

Palace of the Early Rulers Teotihuacan's oldest district was its northern section, and this was also the focus of its first monumental construction. Xalla, a large compound in this region, may date to the Terminal Formative. It was a huge square complex, 400 m (1,312 ft) on a side. Like so many of the city's structures, its location was significant. Looking at the city map, one can discern that the southern edge of the Pyramid of the Moon, northern edge of the Pyramid of the Sun and the western front of Xalla compound form three boundaries of a huge square. This may have been a monumental plaza amidst the first major civic-ceremonial architecture of the city. The square is now bisected by the Street of the Dead and filled with other buildings, particularly the three-temple complexes around the southern base of the Pyramid of the Moon. However, these complexes are in *talud-tablero* style, which did not become popular at Teotihuacan until the end of the Terminal Formative.

Ciudadela Palaces The focus of civic-ceremonial life shifted south, past the Sun Pyramid, with construction of the Feathered Serpent Temple-Pyramid in the 3rd century AD [10.3]. There, rulership became

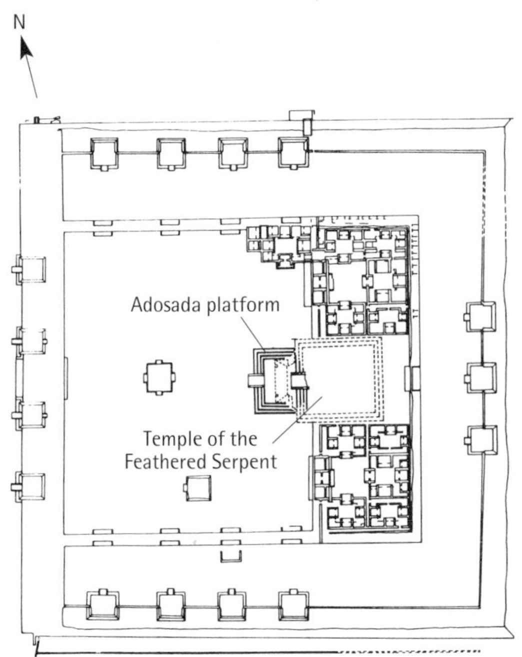

10.4, 10.5 *Teotihuacan. (Above right) Aerial view looking north, showing (from rear) Cerro Gordo with the Pyramid of the Moon at its base, the Street of the Dead extending south from it, with the Pyramid of the Sun along its east side, and the Ciudadela in the foreground of the photograph. The Temple-Pyramid of the Feathered Serpent is in the right foreground, the Adosada platform built in front of it and room complexes on either side. (Above) Ciudadela, plan, showing the layout of the apartment compounds.*

more personalized, lavishly demonstrated in the sacrifices attendant upon the construction of the pyramid as a funerary monument for its central burial. As remarkable as the temple-pyramid is its vast enclosure wall, establishing this complex as the Ciudadela ("citadel") with a huge interior space (4.4 hectares/10.8 acres) setting off the Pyramid, framed by identical apartment compounds, each with five sets of rooms around a small patio [**10.4, 10.5**]. These may have been the residential palaces for rulers at the time of the Feathered Serpent Temple-Pyramid's use. The Ciudadela's interior space was sufficient to hold "up to 100,000 persons... In other words, at least the entire active adult population of the city" (Cowgill 1983: 322).

The Feathered Serpent Temple-Pyramid's façade is laden with symbols of militarism. That and the sacrifice of hundreds of people in the course of its construction must have presented to the inhabitants of the city (still living in "temporary" housing) a bloody spectacle of political theater: many lives brutally cut short for the greater glory of a single individual. It is at this point that Teotihuacan's social history radically changed, and the marked evidence comes from the Feathered Serpent Temple-Pyramid itself, which was not only defaced, but covered over with another building, the Adosada, which sits in front of it and was built in the 4th century. This was a very expensive act of ritual termination of the original use of the Pyramid, and while the Ciudadela continued in active use after this termination ritual, the "event reflects internal political conflicts... *official* looting or exploitation of symbols by newly raised ruling groups..." (Sugiyama 1998: 148). The apartment complexes of the Ciudadela may then have been dedicated to use as priestly quarters, or perhaps as a school for elite youth, such as the calmecac schools of the Aztecs.

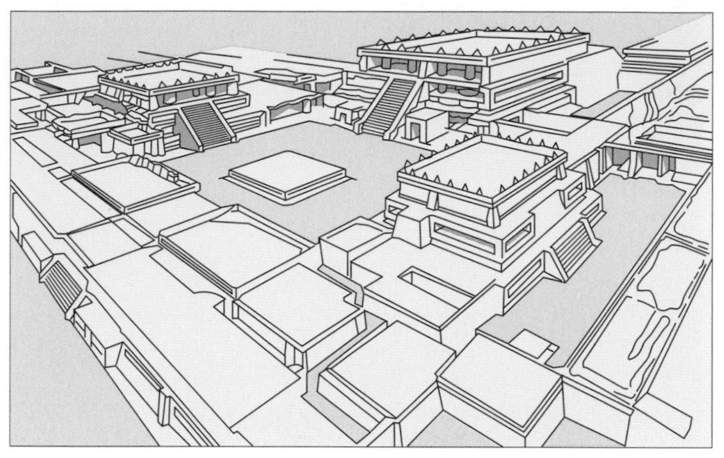

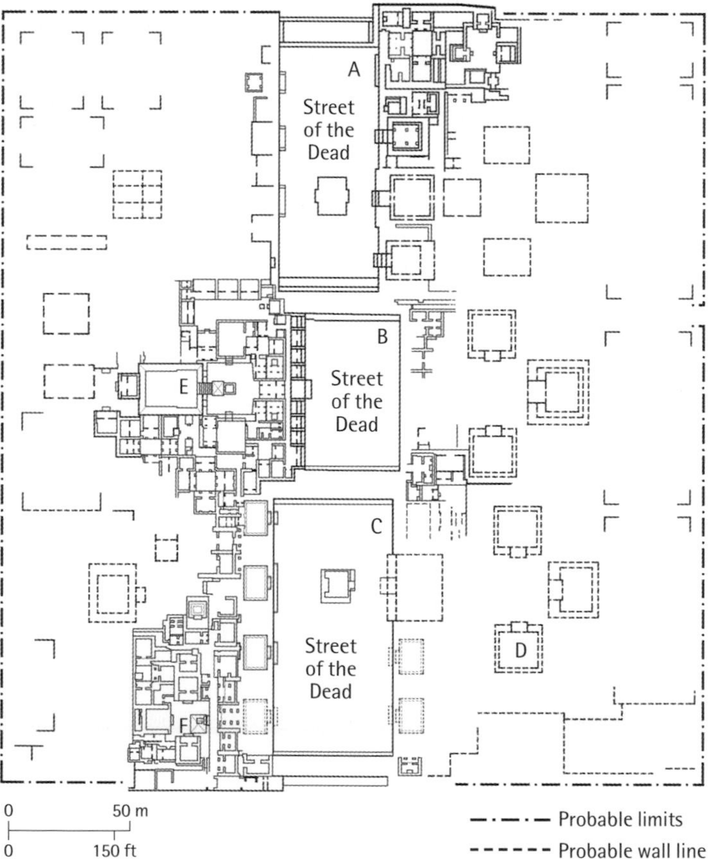

The Street of the Dead Complex After these acts of destruction, the construction of the apartment compounds began on a massive scale. The city's new rulers built a huge new palace, the Street of the Dead Complex, but they literally kept a low profile. The new administrative-residential compound for the rulers is smack in the middle of the city: look at the city center map and find the massive, nearly square expanse of architecture between the Ciudadela and the Pyramid of the Sun. It is bisected by the Street of the Dead [**10.7**, see also **10.8**]. On the map it has been outlined with a dashed line because without such a marker, it is difficult to distinguish it from the other apartment compounds. Far from being a monument raised to the heavens, this was, if anything, an effigy of the average apartment compound [**10.6**]. It made no architectural statement through obtrusive height, but its size and location reveal its importance, as does the quality of its construction and decor, indicated by its interior rooms and courtyards.

This third tradition of rulership seems to have lasted several hundred years, until at least the AD 500s. During this time, Teotihuacan was Mesoamerica's most powerful and influential city. Its sphere of immediate influence extended west into Toluca and northwest into the Tula region, where limestone was exploited from the Teotihuacan-controlled town, Chingú. In the Valley of Morelos, Teotihuacan had a source of cotton, which could not be grown in the colder climate of the Basin of Mexico. These adjacent areas seem to have

10.8 *(Right) Teotihuacan, the central part of the city, showing the locations of major monuments and excavated apartment compounds. The Street of the Dead Compound is highlighted with a colored line.*

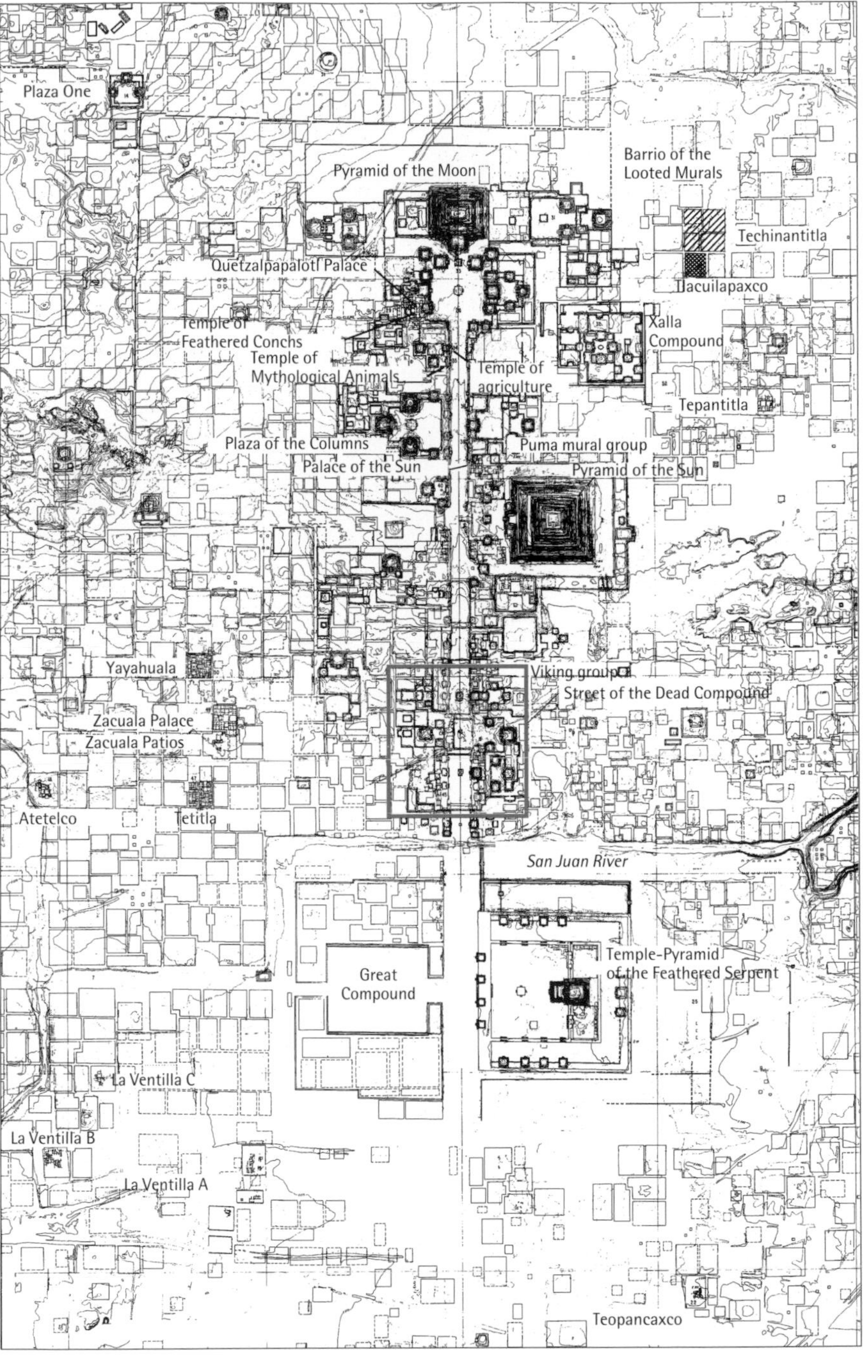

10.6, 10.7 *(Opposite) Teotihuacan, Street of the Dead Complex. The plan of the Complex shows that only about one-fourth of its area has been excavated, with the most important residential focus being the West Plaza Group (Morelos García 1993), illustrated in the reconstruction drawing, which shows the main plaza, with access to the Street of the Dead (shown along the lower left). The plaza, of modest dimensions given the vast size of the complex, features the central altar common to Teotihuacan's apartment compounds. While the rest of the Complex has not been excavated, surface survey has shown that it was covered by buildings and plazas, warrens of rooms suitable for many functions, and contrasting with the Ciudadela buildings in plan and extent.*

A *Viking Group*
B *Plaza East habitations*
C *Escaleras Superpuestos*
D *Excavations of 1917*
E *West Place (Plaza Oueste) Compound*
F *Edificios Superpuestos*

10.9 *Teotihuacan's greatest art forms were architecture and mural paintings. From the Tepantitla compound, this mural's central figure is an elaborately garbed female with water dripping from her hands. She may represent the Goddess, one of Teotihuacan's major deities. Note that her face is not the harpy eagle headdress (with quetzal plumes), but is the masked visage below that. The plant extending above her is a morning glory, prized in Mesoamerica as an intoxicant. To the Aztecs it "was more than just the agent of communication with the supernatural. It was itself supernatural, indeed a god" (Furst 1973: 203) and its presence in this mural suggests that the Teotihuacanos offered it similar reverence.*

10.10 *From the Techinantitla compound, a lord's speech scroll is full of symbols of preciousness. He wears the goggles that came to be associated with Tlaloc, the storm god.*

been under Teotihuacan control for the purpose of securing specific resources, but Teotihuacan did not administer an "empire." Much more distant from Teotihuacan were areas that seem to have been taken over by Teotihuacanos, such Matacapan along the Gulf Coast and Kaminaljuyú in the Guatemala highlands. At Maya Tikal, Teotihuacan interfered heavily in local politics in the late 4th century, and Teotihuacan materials and designs figure importantly in some regions, such as the coastal plain of Chiapas and Guatemala, an important source of elite materials such as cacao and jaguar pelts.

Indeed, Teotihuacan's ruling class decked themselves out lavishly. Mural paintings show ranks of individuals garbed in elaborate costumes, including an important Central Mexican symbol of rulership, quetzal feathers imported from Guatemala [**10.9**, **10.10**].

10.11 *Even after Teotihuacan's precipitous decline at the end of the Early Classic, the urban area still retained a large population, though it lacked the social coherence provided by centralized rulership. This ceramic statue of Xipe Totec, the Flayed Skin God, was found near the Xolalpan* barrio *(Linné 2003 [1934]) and probably dates to the 8th century (Scott 1993). The obvious theme of human sacrifice expressed in the costume of the victim's skin may relate to a rise in militarism in the Late Classic.*

It is the costumes that catch the eye, not any hint of individual personalities. Comparisons among figures in many murals – including depictions of mythological beasts as well as humans – fail to reveal any individuality, but show that the costumes are uniforms, sets of garments and headdresses that unambiguously present the figures as office-holders, not as individuals. As we shall see, this is in sharp contrast to Maya traditions of strong interest in the ruler as a person. At Teotihuacan, the rulers hid behind costumes but did not deny themselves the elegant perquisites of their rank.

The Apartment Compounds: Social Strata Within and Among the Residences

In its day, the Early Classic city of Teotihuacan was Mesoamerica's purest expression of social stratification. It is not that other Mesoamerican cities did not demonstrate contrasts between rich and poor, between the privileged descendants of the gods and the peasant-farmers who served them, not to mention the enslaved who were merely property. But at Teotihuacan we see the contrasts etched over a very large population, and see many gradations of wealth. These were spatially distributed in the city's neighborhoods, which scholars, using the modern term for neighborhoods in Mexico, call *barrios*.

Within each *barrio*, compounds varied as to wealth, but there were even greater differences among *barrios*, "abrupt distinctions ... rather than ... any simple gradient in status from highest in the city center to lowest on the periphery" (Millon 1981: 211). These neighborhoods included ethnic enclaves – the Oaxacans lived in a *barrio* in the northwest part of the city, and may have been plaster-working specialists, from the preponderance of stuccoing tools in this area (Crespo and Mastache 1981). The "Merchant's Barrio" might have been inhabited by people from the Gulf lowlands; houses in this area are round, typical of Huastec buildings in the north Gulf lowlands (Rattray 1987).

Social strata are often defined in similar terms as biological species are defined, by who can mate with whom. In archaic states, social strata were generally endogamous: the ruling elite lineages traded marriage partners, even with rulers of other cities. In many archaic states, polygyny was practiced, and wives of lesser rank were drawn from non-aristocratic social strata, but the principal wives were almost always of high rank, and it was their children who would inherit the power and privileges of the highest class.

The next highest social statuses may be the elite military officers, priests, elite artisans, and even traders in elite goods, and their families. Then, below these "upper middle class" groups is the much larger societal segment of farmer artisans who also chose mates from their own class. Slaves in Mesoamerican society seldom seem to have constituted a large class, as they did in ancient Rome, but rather were individuals brought low by war, misfortune or crime.

10.13, 10.14 *(Opposite) Tlajinga 33 was home to an extended family that produced plain, cheap storage and cooking vessels, a type of pottery called San Martín Orange (opposite above). (Opposite below) Its plan shows the compound's irregularity, in contrast to elite and middle-class residences. Occupied* AD *250–700, it was rebuilt piecemeal and often, of adobe, the cheapest building material. Over time the focus of the building shifted south; the earliest central courtyard was the dark square at the top of the plan, but by the end of the compound's occupation, the courtyard was the large square on the west side, just below center.*

In ancient and modern societies, marriage is an important life choice not only for the couple but for their families. In all traditional societies it is a means of maintaining status – and achieving higher position, if possible – and thus most cultures have made mate choice a matter of negotiation between families, not of romantic attachment between individuals. At Teotihuacan, we know from studies of skeletons buried within apartment compounds that the extended families living there were related along male lines, with brides marrying into the compound (Spence 1974). We also know, from the variety of material remains and quality of room finishing within compounds, that there were internal variations in wealth. This is fully understandable in the context of traditional society. A co-residing group consisting of related families will always comprise some that are of higher status than others. Very often the oldest males have the highest status, and their wives and children have higher status than the other wives and children of younger men. Often there will be relatives reduced to dependency by bad luck; they are taken in and supported in return for service. There may be hired servants as well, and if the family can afford it, slaves.

The highest stratum of Teotihuacan society lived in the palaces discussed above. Elite males may, at times, have lived in compounds that seem to have been devoted to priestly or military cadres. The Quetzalpapalotl compound just southwest of the Pyramid of the Moon may have housed priests, and as noted above, the Ciudadela "palaces" may have been used for religious purposes after the Terminal Formative, perhaps becoming priestly schools.

Apartment compounds were typically built on raised platforms, made of gravel in mud mortar. Lower walls were built of cut and uncut stone, and upper walls were of adobes, all mortared with mud. Walls were coated with lime plaster, and then painted, often with murals. There were many apartment compounds that were well-finished and bore extensive murals, as shown for Tepantitla [10.9]. These compounds form a kind of "middle class" of residential architecture, even though some have long been called "palaces," such as the "Zacuala Palace" shown in **10.12**.

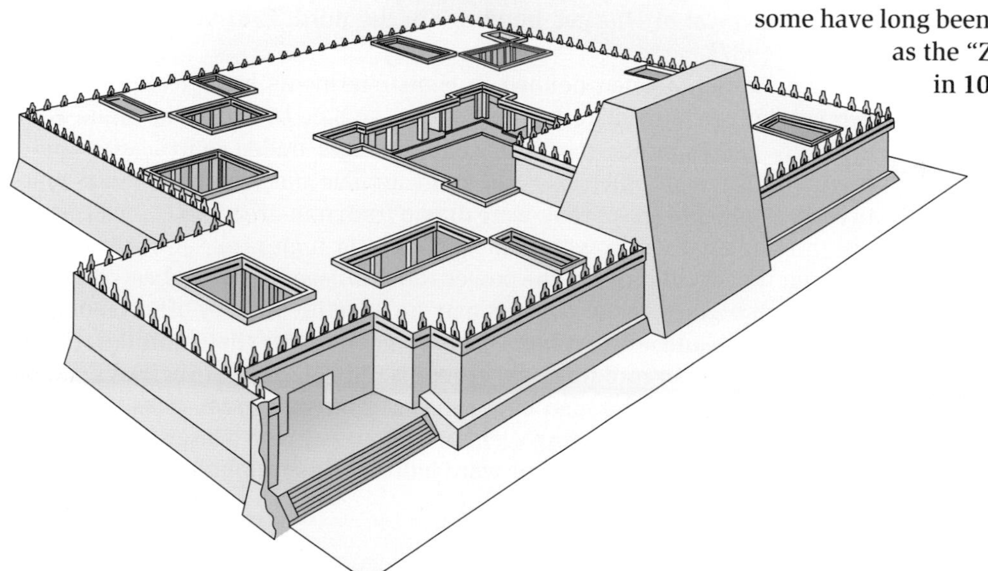

10.12 *Teotihuacan, Zacuala compound, located about 400 m (1,310 ft) west of the Street of the Dead compound. It measures about 60 by 75 m (197 by 246 ft), and features six patios in addition to the central patio, perhaps housing six or more nuclear family groups. This reconstruction drawing shows the building's entrance, on the southeast side, windowless exterior wall, and pattern of patios within.*

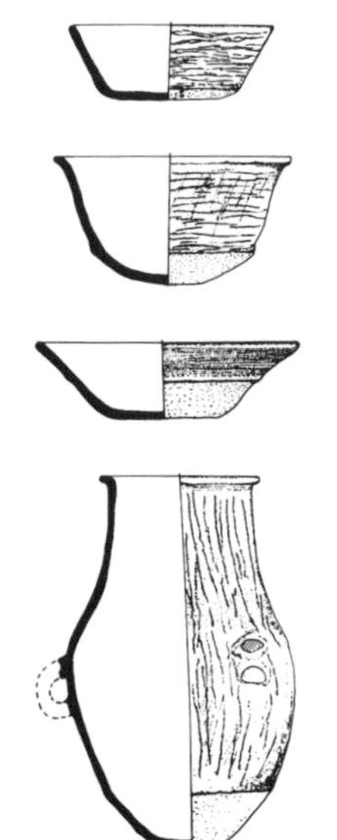

Economy: Food and Basic Goods We know that Teotihuacan's economic basis was agriculture and craft production. Intensification of the landscape created extremely valuable permanently irrigated acreage which was probably held by wealthy families. This productive zone was so close to the city that it may have been worked by virtually all lower- or working-class residents, the overwhelming majority of the population. These people also worked at various trades and crafts as the seasonality of agricultural labor permitted. Construction is one obvious example, given the sheer volume of buildings put up over the city's half-millennium of greatest growth. And construction would include a range of jobs from hauling stone and lime plaster to fine masonry work and plastering to felling trees and shaping timber for posts and beams, and bringing them to the city.

Every compound probably produced some of its own durable goods, such as woven cloth, as well as a surplus to be traded. All around the city, about one-third of the compounds included workshops making a variety of utilitarian goods for domestic consumption, and some elite goods to be traded over great distances. Two major obsidian sources nearby figured importantly in the city's productive potential; gray and black obsidian from Otumba was widely traded since the Early Formative, and green obsidian from Pachuca was made into fine prismatic blades. Not only was obsidian processed for export, but it was also essential for the manufacture of other tools and goods, such as those made from perishable materials such as wood, of which little trace remains in the archaeological record. Weaving would have been a major occupation of Teotihuacan's women, and thus there would have been tens of thousands of wooden looms, but not one has survived.

Ceramics are almost as durable as stone, and thus we have evidence of the production and consumption of pottery vessels and other ceramic artifacts within Teotihuacan and beyond it. The city's more than 2,000 households needed utility vessels, and some of the lower-class compounds specialized in such production, such as the San Martín Orange *ollas* and basins produced at Tlajinga 33 compound [**10.13**, **10.14**]. Futhermore, city potters produced fancy vessels and figurines, rich with the Teotihuacan

10.15–10.17 *(Right) Life-size stone masks, a signature of Teotihuacan, may have been attached to the bundled mummified remains of important deceased individuals, perhaps serving as oracles (Headrick 1999). (Below left) A "theater" censer shows elaborate staging of a scene with many appliquéd design elements surrounding a central face whose mouth is covered by a butterfly mask. Butterflies connote fertility as well as spirits of the dead. These censers may have served as oracle vessels through which the spirits of the dead could be contacted. (Below right) A Thin Orange ware vessel in the shape of a dog. Made in the Valley of Puebla, it is thin-walled and elegant in varied forms, used at Teotihuacan and distributed along its trade routes (Rattray 1990).*

symbolism, for local use and for export as trade items or as gifts. All over Mesoamerica, the cylindrical vessel with tripod supports was a signature for Teotihuacan contact. The surfaces of these vessels were decorated with incised designs, or given a surface finish of stucco and painted with the same glowing colors as were used in Teotihuacan's murals. Other ceramic items were small crude incense burners called *"candeleros"* because most have two adjacent holes, the right size for modern candles. Figurines were found throughout the city, and show an evolution in technology of production, the earliest being hand-modeled by women working in their residences; later on in the city's development, figurines were shaped in molds, by men working in workshops, a trend toward mass production (Barbour 1976). The forum for exchange of both local and long-distance goods [**10.15–10.17**] may have been the Great Compound, a vast expanse facing the Ciudadela.

Considering the export of Teotihuacan's lexicon of symbols brings us to the subject of Teotihuacan's level of

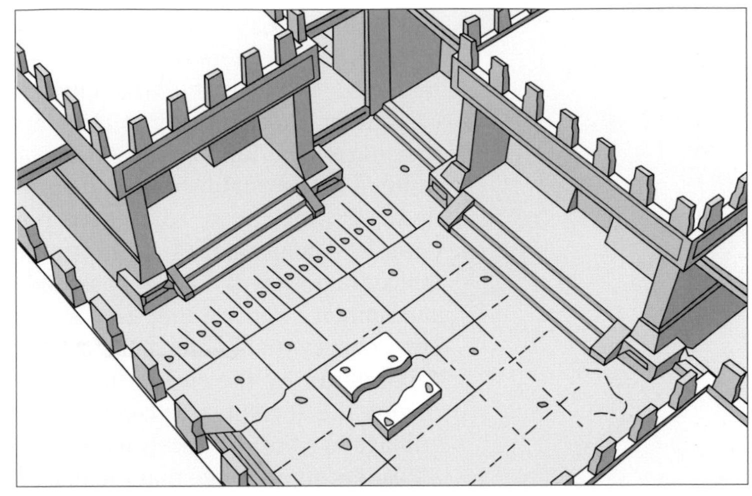

10.18, 10.19 *Teotihuacan, La Ventilla compound, dating from the Early Classic period; "the signs appearing in the Plaza de los Glifos appear in other Teotihuacan texts, not only at Teotihuacan, but in regions as distant as the Escuintla area of Guatemala" (Taube 2000: 15). (Right) Plaza of the Glyphs, where Teotihuacan writing was found painted onto the floor, the glyphs and glyph compounds separated by red lines. (Below) Glyphs found at Plaza of the Glyphs.*

literacy. We know that by the Early Classic period, both Oaxaca and the Maya had developed systems of abstract notation, including writing – and in fact, evidence of these scripts is even found at Teotihuacan (Taube 2000). Teotihuacanos used a bar-and-dot notation for numbers that was essentially the same as those used in Oaxaca and the Maya area, but beyond that had its own extended system of glyphs [**10.18, 10.19**]. The glyphs must also be read contextually, their meaning derived from their placement within a larger graphic framework. For example, in **10.9** and **10.10**, all of the individuals have things flowing from their hands. The items within the flow design are various symbols for preciousness, while the action, "hand scattering," has a larger meaning, possibly as a political or religious statement expressing "the active participation of gods and humans in the support and maintenance of the Teotihuacan worlds through the showering of water, jade, or other precious materials upon its earthly domain" (Taube 2000: 27).

How the End Began

Around AD 500, another backlash occurred, perhaps precipitated by the failure of the rulers to bring forth enough fertility and riches. Buildings all along the Street of the Dead were torched (Wolfman 1990), extensive and deliberate acts of destruction which seem to have been perpetrated by the city's inhabitants, and which triggered a final period in the Classic city's life. Teotihuacan did not become a deserted wasteland; its surviving elite families may have departed to live in still-friendly towns elsewhere, places that were perhaps ruled by their relatives, but many people remained. It was still a large city in terms of its population, but after this event it lacked the power to influence life beyond its own confines. By the Late Classic period, a process of population dispersal out of the city had resulted in the establishment and growth of communities in and beyond the Basin of Mexico. In adjacent regions, new cities grew powerful: Tula, Cholula, Xochicalco, El Tajín. Another probable immediate effect was the rapid emigration of the highly skilled artisans who created the fine paintings and lapidary and ceramic wares so prized by the city's wealthy. Then as now, purveyors of elite goods need to go where their affluent patrons live. Teotihuacan by the end of the Classic period was a set of sizable villages ringing the ancient civic-ceremonial center, which remained a place of pilgrimage in spite of its destruction as the core of a vital city.

Readers should note that the dates of destruction of the city's center have long been debated, and that many scholarly writings on Teotihuacan use a chronology developed before absolute dating techniques were applied to Teotihuacan materials. Within the traditional chronology, the timing of the burning along the Street of the Dead was thought to have occurred as late as AD 650 or 750, some scholars even using the traditional end of the Classic period, AD 900, as the end of Teotihuacan's power, as well. However, these late dates clash with other evidence from Teotihuacan and elsewhere.

The direct dating of burned materials to about AD 500 puts the great city's steep decline toward the end of the Early Classic period, and in fact makes this event pivotal for the timing of the "Middle Classic," a distinctive culture historical phase comprising the 500s and 600s, significant in several important parts of Mesoamerica, including the Maya area and West Mexico. Events in those parts make much more sense in the light of a rather radical power vacuum after centuries of strong influence from the Basin of Mexico.

What Caused the Uprising?

Ancient cities, worldwide, were costly to maintain and stressful to inhabit. Political stability depended upon the peoples' perception that their needs were being met, and that the rulers were powerful (or at least adequate) intermediaries between them and the spiritual forces controlling continued fertility of the earth. Teotihuacan's rulers seem to have been reformed at least once, when they turned away from building massive funerary monuments and toward the construction of extensive good-quality housing for the city's populace, but they were on a collision course with long-term effects of urban growth, the rise of other powerful centers after a lack of competitors in the city's early centuries, and global climate forces.

Among the long-term effects were inevitable decline in the quality of life of a large, dense population. Until the advent of modern medicine, inhabitants of cities were more diseased, and lived shorter lives than rural people. A demographic rule of thumb is that before the advent of modern medicine, only half the population survived beyond age five. The conditions that contribute to infant mortality, such as shortages of critical resources, are particularly grueling for city-dwellers. In fact, pre-industrial cities depended upon a constant influx of rural migrants in order to maintain population size, and because cities offer economic opportunities attractive to those rural folk who lack direct access to their own farm plots, in many parts of the world there is a fairly constant movement of population from the countryside to the city, in spite of the perils. But while a rural family working a farm plot and doing a little hunting can support itself and garner an adequate and even slightly varied diet, once people live in cities they become part of a complex urban web of economic specialization, and their resources for independence are limited. Even the affluent become vulnerable to stresses such as scarcity of water, or scarcity of certain kinds of food, or overabundance of sewage or garbage.

We know that many of the Old World's endemic infectious diseases were unknown in the pre-Columbian New World, but Mesoamericans were not immune to the effects of parasites and malnutrition, and Teotihuacan's population felt these stresses. However, unlike many of the world's cities, Teotihuacan could not readily replenish its demographic losses by drawing from a large rural hinterland population, because the city had been created out of depopulation of that hinterland in the first place. The city maintained a high population level for centuries on the basis of its initial immigration and intrinsic increase, and then, after the Street of the Dead destruction, dropped down to 20,000–30,000 by the end of the Classic period.

One cause was malnutrition. It affected the lower classes and probably took a significant but less painful toll across the city, from rich and poor. The Mesoamerican diet, with a strong focus on maize, beans, and squash, provides adequate nutrition, especially with the addition of calcium from the ground limestone required to soften dried maize. But here we see where the rural farmers would have had a slight advantage, because of their ability to hunt or trap animals to add protein to the diet. In the lower-class compound, Tlajinga 33, many burials were excavated and studied for the effects of disease and nutrition stress on the development of bones and teeth (Widmer and Storey 1993). There, "stress in the form of infection and undernutrition was common, if not chronic, among the residents" (Storey 1992: 266).

Tlajinga's population was worse off, in terms of health and wealth, than any other Teotihuacan skeletal populations yet studied, which, admittedly, are few. Oztoyahualco, a slightly more affluent compound in the old part of town, is freer of disease (Manzanilla 1993a). However, while Teotihuacan's lowest-status inhabitants in general constituted the largest proportion of the population, they are the least well studied – the civic-ceremonial architecture and better-finished compounds have long attracted the most scholarly attention.

Another long-term problem was environmental degradation. Agricultural productivity had been improved by ditching and grading the boggy lower Teotihuacan Valley, but other problems were arising, such as erosion in the middle and upper valley, and deforestation on the surrounding slopes.

10.20 *(Right) The Feathered Serpent motifs that adorned the façade of the Temple-Pyramid of the Feathered Serpent were, at the beginning of the Early Classic period, defaced or covered over, with the construction of the Adosada in front of the original pyramid.*

10.21 *(Above) From the Pyramid of the Moon looking south down the Street of the Dead, the Pyramid of the Sun's sloping angles echo those of Cerro Patlachique, in the distance behind it. The horizontal "barricades" across the Street of the Dead in the distance mark the city's main palace, the Street of the Dead Complex.*

10.22 *(Right) The Pyramid of the Moon is the result of several rebuilding episodes. Its original platform structure, now deeply buried, was one of the oldest monumental constructions at Teotihuacan. Recent excavations have located a tomb, dated to about* AD *150 and containing a sacrificial victim and offerings such as greenstone carvings, raptorial birds, and jaguars.*

Building and maintaining Teotihuacan required wood for construction timbers, for tools, to reduce to charcoal for cooking and heating fires. Plaster is manufactured from limestone by burning, again requiring wood. While much of the plaster that coated the walls and floors of all but the lowliest residences in this splendid, shining city was processed in the Tula region, this was another strain on the diminishing timber supply. The Teotihuacan Valley's relatively pristine environment in the Middle Formative would have had forests all over the hills, but in this cool semi-arid highland valley, once the trees were cut, regrowth would have been very slow even if human populations had been absent.

Semi-arid, of course, refers to overall rainfall; though limited to winter and early spring, the violent rainstorms are capable of washing away freshly exposed soil. This not only erodes the soil from the deforested areas and from farm plots on the rainfall-dependent slopes, but the mud also clogs the watercourses all the way down to the lake, increasing the labor required to keep canals open.

In addition to these environmental and demographic trends, Teotihuacan's troubles may have been part of a much larger pattern, "a period of worldwide cold around AD 530 to 590" (Gill 2000: 293), possibly precipitated by the eruption in about AD 535 of the volcano preceding the present one known as Krakatoa, which plunged the world into a kind of "nuclear winter" for years (Keys 1999). Colder climatic spells are characteristically associated with drought, and any drought affecting the Central Highlands would make many marginal areas, like the Teotihuacan Valley, especially vulnerable to desertification. Thus, in the early 500s, the effects of this trend might have already been being felt in this region.

The fertility of the land would have been compromised by anthropogenic effects as well as global cooling. The fertility of at least some of the people would have been affected by poor sanitation and shortages of essential materials like food and firewood. One can easily imagine that many Teotihuacanos might have perceived a breakdown in their relationship with supernatural forces, and the fault would lie with their rulers, the intermediaries who had failed in their most important task. Time had been created at Teotihuacan when a minor deity threw himself into a huge bed of coals and became the sun. For reasons unfathomable to the Teotihuacanos and certainly unalterable by their rulers, the solar deity withdrew from their sight.

Teotihuacan's Political Economy: Selling an Ideological Package

This rise-and-fall story provides the framework by which we can understand Teotihuacan's position of prestige in Mesoamerican culture history. While much about Teotihuacan remains an enigma, much has been demystified by evidence for the material basis for the society, including its complex iconographic system. Teotihuacan, the place where time began, used that legendary primacy to claim ascendancy in lands far from Central Mexico, especially where precious goods could be obtained. However, cultures elsewhere in Mesoamerica had their own complex regional histories, and continued on their own developmental trajectories when Teotihuacan influence was withdrawn.

TEOTIHUACAN PRESENCE WEST OF THE ISTHMUS

Teotihuacan's Influence Elsewhere in the Central Highlands, to the North and West

In the Toluca region, just west of the Basin of Mexico, the process of depopulation that had begun in the Late Formative and continued into the Terminal Formative, when the whole area was virtually uninhabited, was reversed in the period AD 200–450, with several dozen small sites, mostly on the alluvial plain and along the natural corridor connecting Toluca with the Basin. The material remains at these sites, including architecture, indicate settlement from Teotihuacan (Sugiura 2001).

North from Toluca, beyond low hills, lies the Tula region, which is also separated from the Basin of Mexico by rolling hills so low that the divide marking the Basin's drainage from that of the Tula region is barely perceptible. Thus there was little transport "friction" (in the geographer's sense of that word) between Teotihuacan and the Tula region, and the strong lure of limestone for plaster drew Teotihuacan interest to the northwest. Chingú was one of several sites Teotihuacan seems to have established near this resource, in about AD 200; while the site is quite small, less than one square kilometer, its plan is gridded, with small square residences (15–40 m on a side, 50–131 ft) similar to Teotihuacan's apartment compounds, and Teotihuacan figurines have been found in the houses (Díaz 1981). Also at Chingú are sherds from Oaxacan wares, especially in houses near the town's ceremonial center, and at the workshops. Chingú declined after AD 400. Its short existence coincided exactly with Teotihuacan's greatest need for finishing plaster for its construction programs.

Other Tula-region sites contemporaneous with Chingú were El Tesoro and Acoculco, near Tepeji del Río. This area was also rich in limestone, and had a long period of occupation, extending up through the Aztec period into the present. Its Early Classic material remains are even more notable for the abundance (over 50 percent) of Monte Albán-related ceramics, in proportions similar to those of the Oaxaca *barrio* at Teotihuacan (Crespo and Mastache 1981). The Oaxacan presence in this area, over 800 km (*c.* 500 miles) north of Monte Albán, testifies to several strong trends in Mesoamerican culture history: the ethnic mosaic that was part of so many regions and also the strong association of ethnicity with particular trades and crafts, in this case, limestone processing. By AD 400, the Tula region showed a decline in Teotihuacan influence, and also by that time a new, hybrid settlement pattern was established: hilltop centers (such as Magoni) were built, and their material repertoire differed from the continuing, Teotihuacan-related settlements on the plain.

10.23 *Guachimontón complex, Teuchitlán. "Ancestral temples belonging to leading family lineages surround circular pyramids marking the tomb of a great leader" (Witmore 1998: 139). The reconstruction drawing illustrates how Guachimontón's rings of buildings spill westward, downslope toward irrigated fields. Each of the central pyramids had staircases in four directions leading to a platform that served as a temple base, or as a stage for the volador ceremony. The site's main ball court lay between the two largest circles.*

Teotihuacan and the Bajío and Northwestern Frontier

The Bajío region continued to be occupied, with some sites showing the presence of Teotihuacan-related populations, in small numbers. Teotihuacan influence was more marked further to the northwest. Between AD 200 and 400, along the eastern slope of the Sierra Madre Occidental, the first villages were settled, and at the same time, the minerals in this region began to be exploited. These were especially prevalent in the southern "Chalchihuites" region (the northern section is known as Loma San Gabriel), *chalchihuitl* being the Aztec name for semi-precious greenstone. In the Chalchihuites area, varieties of malachite, azurite, and turquoise-like stones were found (Cabrero 1989: 310).

In the Early Classic, the sites of Alta Vista and Cerro Moctehuma were established, the former becoming important in the Late Classic. Yet evidence seems clear that Teotihuacan belief systems were influencing the establishment of these sites; Alta Vista's plan and architecture owe much to Teotihuacan, and the importance of calendrics here is manifested in a horizon calendar.

Another intriguing cultural development, from the perspective of the widening ripples of impact from Teotihuacan, is the early roots of the major traditions of the U.S. Southwest. During this period, Anasazi, Mogollon, and Hohokam cultures may have begun to differentiate themselves, with Hohokam being in the Sonoran Desert that forms part of the Northern Arid Zone, north of the Mesoamerican culture area. Throughout this zone, the Early Classic period is the time when sedentism begins to be found in certain areas. Snaketown, in southern Arizona, was established in about AD 450.

The U.S. Southwest is a major source of true turquoise, and contacts over this vast area to secure *chalchihuitl* for Central Mexico may have begun as early as the Early Classic period.

West Mexico

During the Terminal Formative, the Teuchitlán tradition was developing a unique form of monumental architecture, while the shaft-tomb tradition, over a somewhat larger area, was peaking. The Teuchitlán tradition would reach its greatest complexity between AD 200 and 700, perhaps spurred by Teotihuacan's apogee. These developments toward complexity were affecting the Bajío and the Northwestern Frontier as well as West Mexico, and perhaps elite status rivalry was one impetus for "this intensification of social systems" including, in West Mexico, "entirely local competitive pressures for both rare and strategic resources" (Weigand and Beekman 1998: 41).

The major Teuchitlán centers were not just aggregates of circular buildings and ball courts, impressive though these were [**10.23**]. Ahualulco, one of the most important of these sites, was situated above a marshy lake area where *chinampa* agriculture was practiced, and the region possessed important obsidian resources. That competition for such resources existed is evidenced by the changing settlement pattern throughout the Early and Middle Classic, during which hilltop sites were established above passes connecting the valleys. Over time, the low-lying sites near them were abandoned in favor of the more defensible locations.

Michoacán, Guerrero, Morelos

In Michoacán, the effects of Teotihuacan influence were somewhat less ambiguous. To the well-established local settlement systems of large and small villages, the Early Classic period brought a whole new type of site, ceremonial centers, which appeared at El Otero, Tres Cerritos, and Tingambato. These and similar sites featured "architectural forms and artifacts indicating direct contact with the Teotihuacan culture of the Basin of Mexico" (Pollard 2001: 460).

Not only do these sites have pyramids, plazas and ball courts, but they also have such Teotihuacan signatures as Thin Orange pottery and the use of *talud-tablero*-style architecture [**10.24**]. However, a problem in interpreting the interaction between Michoacán and Teotihuacan is the dating of these remains. At Tingambato, for example, the two construction periods cor-

10.24 *Tingambato, Michoacán. The site had two periods of construction:* AD *450–600 marked the initial ceremonial buildings, pyramidal bases with Teotihuacan-style* taluds *and stairway balusters. These were topped by perishable temple structures. The pyramids surround a plaza, as shown below, and the orientation of these structures varies between 12° and 17° East of North. In the second stage,* AD *600–950, the ball court was built and even more Teotihuacan elements were incorporated into the site's architecture, as flimsy houses were replaced with square structures with central patios focused upon altars (Siller 1984). One tomb held the remains of over 30 people; six of the men had teeth that had been cosmetically altered ("dental mutilation"), a trait common elsewhere in Mesoamerica that had its first appearance here.*

respond roughly with Teotihuacan's apogee, and with the period after the destruction of the site's center. Possibly, the early remains represent a diffusion of traits, carried by traders or ritual-calendric proselytizers, while the second phase may have been the result of a genuine diaspora, part of the dispersal of elites leaving Teotihuacan to seek a better life elsewhere. Tingambato was abandoned after AD 900.

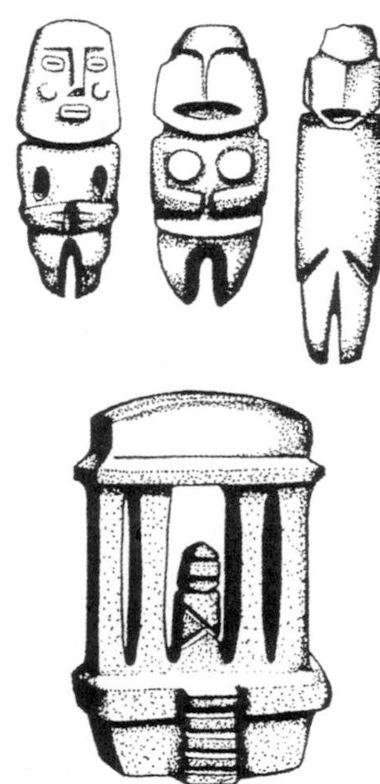

10.25 *Mezcala lapidary-style figures such as these have rarely been found in context, but excavations at such sites as Ahuináhuac, Cuetlajuchitlán, La Organera-Mezcala and La Organera Xochipala have confirmed that the style originated in Guerrero, probably in the Late Formative. Production may have continued through the Classic period into the Postclassic.*

Guerrero Like Michoacán, Guerrero shows widespread evidence of interaction with Oaxaca and with Teotihuacan. From the latter, Guerrero borrowed *talud-tablero* architecture, Thin Orange and cylindrical tripod vessels, even Teotihuacan-style figurines and sculpted depictions of deities with Tlaloc characteristics, while Oaxacan influences were manifested in pottery and stelae with Zapotec iconography.

The interchange was not all one way, however. Guerrero exported to Teotihuacan and other places some of the most famous stone carvings in all Mesoamerica: lapidary works in "Mezcala style," as it was termed by Miguel Covarrubias in the 1940s [**10.25**]. As striking in their simple elegance as Greek Cycladic figures, Mezcala works have a blurred chronology because of being treasured by Mesoamerican peoples, "curated" as heirlooms up to the time of Spanish contact. The Mezcala-Balsas region is Guerrero's best documented, archaeologically, for this period, and featured large, densely settled sites such as Ahuináhuac and Apantipan, surrounded by smaller communities, with workshops where the polished stone items were produced by working stone with string, sand, and water.

Morelos A spur of mountains extending south from Tepoztlán, near modern Cuernavaca, divides Morelos into two parts, west and east. On the west side, the Early Classic settlements were small and the population culturally related to Guerrero groups to the south. Warm, tropical eastern Morelos, however, was brought into the cultural orbit of the Basin of Mexico during several periods. In the Early Classic this region displayed many Teotihuacan traits that seem to have accompanied rather radical changes in settlement pattern, and, by extension, in cultural organization. Eastern Morelos seems to have become Teotihuacan's source for cotton. In the Amatzinac river valley, for example, populations grew during this time, with most people living in farms dispersed over the intensively cultivated rural landscape, rather than living in the regional center (Hirth 1980). The settlement system displays a strong hierarchical order.

Mixteca, Oaxaca

Mixteca Alta The Mixteca Alta was a region of localized city-states, never completely dominated by any one of them, and never conquered by outsiders. By the start of the Early Classic period, Monte Negro was abandoned; if this site was a Monte Albán outpost, this represents a cessation of Monte Albán's efforts to control or intimidate communities in the Mixteca Alta by planting a hilltop colony in their midst. However, Monte Albán's influence remains apparent in some places in local ceramic assemblages, where pottery typical of Monte Albán mass-produced wares, and local imitations, are found (Byland and Pohl 1994).

In contrast to the localized evidence of contact with Monte Albán, Mixteca Alta sites in general had significant amounts of Thin Orange, and local imitations of Thin Orange, though not in as great abundance as were the Monte Albán wares. The presence of Thin Orange types may indicate that Teotihuacan was trading in this area, but to date there is no firm evidence that the Mixteca Alta served as a zone of conflict between Teotihuacan and the Zapotec capital. However, during the Early Classic, Monte Albán's meddling may have been the impetus "that led local Mixtec centers to relocate to the tops of defensible hills" (Byland and Pohl 1994: 60). At Etlatongo, for example, the Formative component of the site lay on the alluvial plain, but in the Classic period, as population grew, the civic-ceremonial architecture, including a ball court, was situated on an adjacent hill.

Oaxaca The same defensive posture was seen in the Classic-period settlement pattern of the Valley of Oaxaca itself, with sites on hilltops. In the Early Classic, two-thirds of the population lived in sites that were defensible or had actually been fortified by walls and ditches. In fact, there was a reduction of population in the northern, Etla arm of the valley, long protected from incursion from Puebla by Monte Albán presence in the Cuicatlán Cañada, the southern extension of the Tehuacán Valley. A bigger threat might have been aggression by Mixtecans. In spite of these indicators of strife, or fear of the same, Monte Albán III (AD 200–700) represents the major florescence of Zapotec civilization, and in the Oaxaca Valley overall there was a population increase, to well over 100,000 people.

Demographic growth was accompanied by a shift southward. While San José Mogote, in the Etla subvalley, continued to serve as a central place for its local region, it was in sharp decline in Monte Albán IIIa (AD 200–500), and there were much larger communities developing in the southern and eastern subvalleys. In the south, Jalieza had over 10,000 people, and in the eastern subvalley a cluster of sites (Dainzú, Macuilxóchitl, Tlacochahuaya, and Guadalupe) comprised a population just as large. Monte Albán was still the major city in the valley, with more than 15,000 people in IIIa, with site expansion to the ridgetop to the north, Atzompa.

Activity in the building or rebuilding of Monte Albán's civic-ceremonial center during this time is presently a matter of debate by scholars. The restoration of the site many years ago has obscured evidence about fine chronology during the crucial period, Monte Albán III. Some scholars point to the completion of the North and South Platforms as evidence of continuing civic grandeur, while others believe that some construction efforts at Monte Albán itself were defensive, responses to genuine aggressive threats, possibly from Teotihuacan.

Keeping in mind that secure evidence of the latter may (or may not) be forthcoming, let us examine the material and epigraphic evidence for the heyday of Zapotec culture at its capital. The Early Classic brought the completion of Monte Albán's civic-ceremonial architecture as we see it today. The South Platform, a huge flattened pyramid, was dedicated during the reign of the ruler 12 Jaguar. The carved monuments that commemorate this ruler and the dedication are embedded in the northeast corner of the South Platform [**10.26–10.28**]. That the dedicatory cache and the depictions of the visitors are hidden from view seems odd to modern sensibilities – we well understand conspicuous consumption, but altogether hiding things of great value is foreign to our customs. However, the ancient Zapotecs, like other Mesoamericans, were engaged in an active dialogue with forces of the supernatural, and the "hidden" placement of these things meant that they would, in fact, be conspicuous to the living earth.

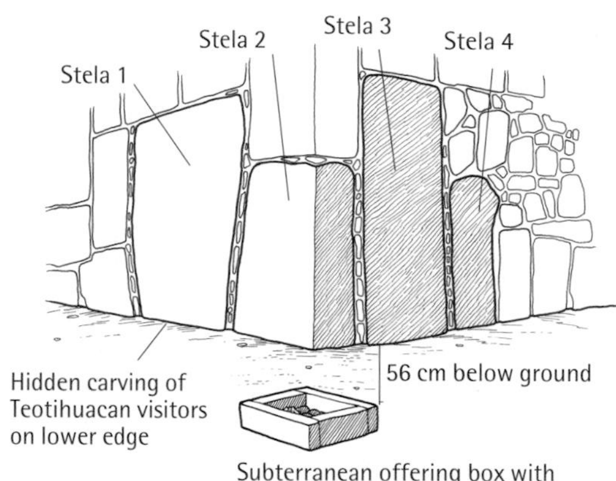

The North Platform was another massive truncated pyramid, considerably lower than the South Platform, and covered with residential compounds. This area seems to have been the location of palaces for Monte Albán's rulers. Zapotec nobles were regarded as the descendants of the gods, particularly "Cociyo" (Lightning), and while the nobility included many grades of nobles, from the rulers down to their distant and perhaps not very wealthy relatives, nobility formed a true social stratum in the sense that nobles were endogamous, and married each other rather than members of the commoner stratum. The commoners included peasant farmer-artisans, and also artisans and merchants whose wealth might surpass that of minor nobles, but they, too, could only marry within their class.

In Mesoamerica in general, people venerated their ancestors as active forces in their lives, but in few places was this practiced as enthusiastically as among the Zapotecs, and this belief goes far to explain the strength of class endogamy. To marry outside the nobility would mean that a noble's children would have ancient ancestors who were just human, a terrible degradation of family value. Ancestors were tended so carefully that they literally had their own rooms in Zapotec noble palaces, the tomb forming the foundation of the

10.26–10.28 *(Opposite) Monte Albán's South Platform was dedicated by a ruler 12 Jaguar, and into its northeast corner, carved stone monuments commemorate him and these events. (Opposite top) The placement of carved stone panels, and a cut stone cache buried half a meter below the surface. (Opposite center) 12 Jaguar, seated on a throne, as depicted on Stela 1. Much of the Zapotec glyph message he faces cannot, as yet, be deciphered. (Opposite below) Depictions of visitors from Teotihuacan who may have attended the dedication. This scene was carved along the lower edge of Stela 1, where it would not be visible. The headdresses, familiar to us from Teotihuacan's murals and other art, identify them as officials of the state. In their hands they carry pouches of incense, a precious and sacred gift for this ceremony.*

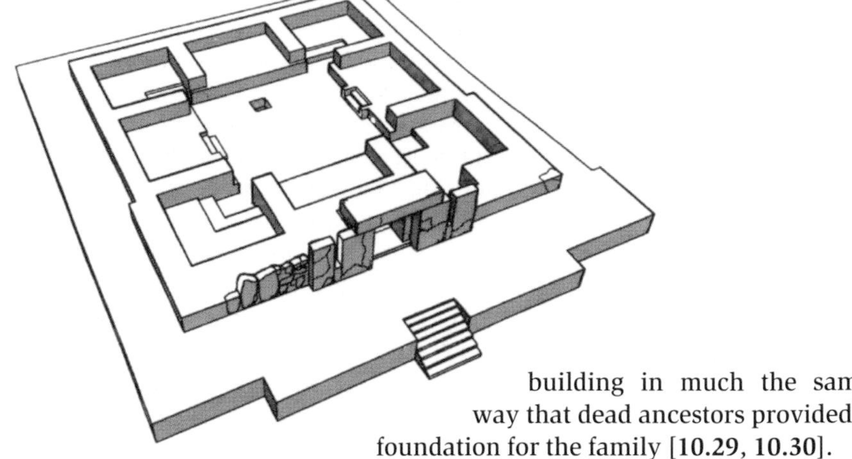

building in much the same way that dead ancestors provided a foundation for the family [**10.29, 10.30**].

In this way, the dead were made part of the living family. The funerary urns may have served as repositories for the life force of the departed (Marcus and Flannery 1996: 210). The Mesoamerican concept of the spiritual animation of many objects and phenomena regarded as "inorganic" by modern sensibilities was expressed by the Zapotec term *pee* (pronounced "pay"), meaning "wind," "breath," or "spirit." To the Zapotecs, movement expressed *pee*, and the rippling of a feather banner, or rising smoke, or clouds scudding on the wind would have all been examples of the sacred life force in action. "Even time was considered to be alive" (Marcus 2001: 846).

The vitality of Zapotec culture, however, was undergoing a transformation, as we shall see in Chapter 13. The demographic shifts begun in the Early Classic continued, and eventually the Mixtecs would enter the Valley of Oaxaca and add their settlements to those of the Zapotecs.

10.29, 10.30 *Zapotec tombs were built into their houses. In fact, construction of the family crypt was completed as a first step in house building. Tombs were decorated with wall murals and had niches in the walls for the display of pottery vessels and funerary sculpture. (Above) The palace associated with Tomb 105 on the North Platform has a plan typical of elite residences at Monte Albán: rooms arranged around a central courtyard which has a small entrance (towards the rear) to the tomb beneath the back room. Such buildings averaged 20–25 m (65–82 ft) on a side. (Right) A Zapotec funerary urn. This example depicts an individual in plumed feline headdress.*

Puebla and Tlaxcala

10.31 *These resist-painted drinking cups are from Teotihuacan; regarded as personal items, they were often included with an individual's grave goods. They were probably used to imbibe* pulque, *the intoxicating maguey-sap beer. While the nutritive qualities of maguey sap had been exploited since Archaic times (if not before), and knowledge of the sap's propensity for fermentation was probably equally old, the production of good party-grade* pulque *requires additives such as roots and herbs. Exactly when such refinements were introduced is unknown, but the use of drinking cups suggests that this occurred by the Early Classic, as does a Cholula mural depicting an elite social scene, "Los Bebedores" (The Drinkers). In the mural a rabbit holds a drinking cup like those shown, evidence of the early association of rabbits with* pulque. *The Aztec maguey goddess, Mayahuel, was the patroness of the day named "rabbit" in the 260-day calendar, and those born on day 2 Rabbit were fated to be drunkards; the association may link the legendary procreative capacity of rabbits with the societal reverence for fertility, and the use of drunkenness as a pathway to uninhibited sexual expression (Anawalt 1993).*

Cholula Moving north from the Valley of Oaxaca, the Tehuacán Valley during its long Palo Blanco phase (200 BC–AD 700) was influenced both by the Mixteca Alta and by Monte Albán. However, to its north, in the Valley of Puebla, the city of Cholula was becoming an important force in Mesoamerican culture history. During the Early Classic, Cholula dominated Puebla and Tlaxcala, even apparently drawing population in from Tlaxcala, though the overall effect was not as dramatic as had been Teotihuacan's Terminal Formative demographic vacuum-cleaning of the Basin of Mexico. The difficulty of interpreting ancient Cholula stems from its continuous occupation into the present. Mesoamerican pyramids, in general, are regarded as effigy mountains, but at Cholula this has become fact – the substantial Colonial-period church at the summit of the Great Pyramid appears to be a chapel on top of a forested hill. But excavations at the base of the hill reveal the bottom levels of the pyramid, and all around lies the busy modern city of Cholula. While Teotihuacan's remains, untouched for centuries, inspire the romantic sense of a city desolated in antiquity, Cholula is buried beneath the thriving present.

Ironically, the enigma of Teotihuacan's societal organization is an open book compared to that of Classic Cholula. Teotihuacan's apartment compounds, workshops, and palaces have revealed so much because after the Early Classic, the ceremonial center of Teotihuacan would never recover. In contrast, Cholula would become one of the great cities of the Central Highlands in the Late Classic and Postclassic, the major shrine for Quetzalcoatl, which drew many pilgrims, and a city that impressed Cortés and his entourage as they made their way to Tenochtitlan in 1519. However, we cannot even be certain of Cholula's Early Classic-period extent: scholarly estimates range between 5 and 10 sq. km (2 to 4 sq. miles), with a population minimum of 15,000.

During the Classic period, construction continued on the Great Pyramid of Cholula, taking place in many distinct stages (in contrast to Teotihuacan's pyramid construction) and eventually achieving a height of 60 m (197 ft), and 350 m (*c.* 1,150 ft) across at the base. Postclassic enlargements would bring the base dimension to 400 m (1,312 ft), and the height to 66 m (217 ft). Some façades are in *talud-tablero* style, but it should be recalled that the earliest incidence of this style was in Puebla, not Teotihuacan. Other of the Great Pyramid's façades "consisted of nine tiers completely made up of steps, in a unique architectural style that is distinctly non-Teotihuacanoid" (McCafferty 2001: 140).

In terms of architecture and other aspects of material culture, such as ceramics and ritual objects, Cholula demonstrates interaction with, but not domination by Teotihuacan. The figurines characteristic of household rituals share some features with those at Teotihuacan, but have a distinct local personality. Similarly, Thin Orange, manufactured south of Cholula and so popular at Teotihuacan, is rare at Cholula. One vessel type found at

Cholula and at Teotihuacan, the drinking cup, indicates the well-established popularity of *pulque*, a beer made from the sap of agave (maguey) plants [**10.31**].

By the end of the Early Classic Cholula may have gone into a decline. Some scholars link this to the decline of Teotihuacan, but given the grim climatic events of the 6th century, the two cities may have both suffered from the same environmental problems. In Tlaxcala the Early Classic was not a time of growth, with population in decline, perhaps drawn to Cholula. Teotihuacan presence in Tlaxcala was apparently motivated by the need to secure the area as a trade route to the Gulf lowlands, not to gain control of Tlaxcalan resources.

Gulf Lowlands

The lowlands – from the Huasteca in the north down to Matacapan in the south – were the source of tropical goods like cacao and cotton that the Teotihuacanos prized. The northern Gulf lowlands have Mesoamerica's highest concentration of circular buildings, but they are rare in the Central Highlands, which is one reason why the Teotihuacan "Merchant's Barrio" with its round structures has been linked to Huastec ethnicity. The Huasteca achieved prominence in the Late Classic, and will be discussed in Chapter 13.

In the north-central Gulf lowlands, El Pital continued to dominate the region, and at Santa Luisa an extensive canal system indicates continuing prosperity for this long-lived site. However, toward the end of the Early Classic, Santa Luisa went into a decline while El Pital was practically abandoned. These events may have been related to larger climate changes, but it is important to note that there was no cessation of cultural development here. Rather, it seems that cultural dominance was beginning to shift south within the region, to El Tajín, which would become one of the great cities of the Late Classic period.

In the south-central Gulf lowlands the Classic period brought "a proliferation of large centers, elaborate craft and architectural traditions, changing trade, and other activities that usually attest to complex social organization" (Stark and Arnold 1997: 26). Pottery styles in this region during the Classic period are highly varied, with little evidence in general of Teotihuacan diagnostics such as Thin Orange. This suggests a continuation of localized spheres of political – and economic – interaction in this region. The regional capital in the Mixtequilla region may have been Cerro de las Mesas, which was occupied until the end of the Classic period. Its ceremonial architecture, similar to La Venta's layout, featured monumental mounds (up to 24 m/79 ft high) around an artificial pond, a trait typical of the planning of Formative-period centers in the south and south-central Gulf lowlands (Stark 1991). One very minor site in the south-central Gulf lowlands that has become famous is Remojadas, because it has yielded such an array of distinctive figurines that its fame has outstripped its size [**10.32**].

Matacapan Further to the south and east lay the Tuxtla Mountains, a volcanic rise on the Gulf Coast, just northwest of Lake Catemaco. There, the site of Matacapan arose in the Early Formative; its apogee was as a Teotihuacan-related trading center in the later Early Classic. Matacapan's ceremonial core covered about 2.5 sq. km (1 sq. mile), with dispersed population in the surrounding 20 sq. km (8 sq. miles), with a population of perhaps 10,000.

Matacapan was not just another site showing Teotihuacan interaction or influence, but may have been a colony, because it bears traits indicative of immigration from Teotihuacan. In addition to architecture with *talud-tablero* façades, the ceramic component of household contexts includes cylindrical tripod vessels, incense burners and figurines in Teotihuacan style. The latter items would be used in household rituals – not just fancy wares brought out at feasts to impress visitors with such diagnostics of connections to the prestigious Central highlands, but essential parts of a Teotihuacano's life, transplanted to a community over 400 km (248 miles) away (Santley 1994). Some of these Teotihuacan-style items were actually made at Matacapan, as would be the case when migrants try to maintain their ethnicity. Teotihuacan's decline presaged that of Matacapan: in the Late Classic, the site dwindled and so did evidence of its relation to Teotihuacan.

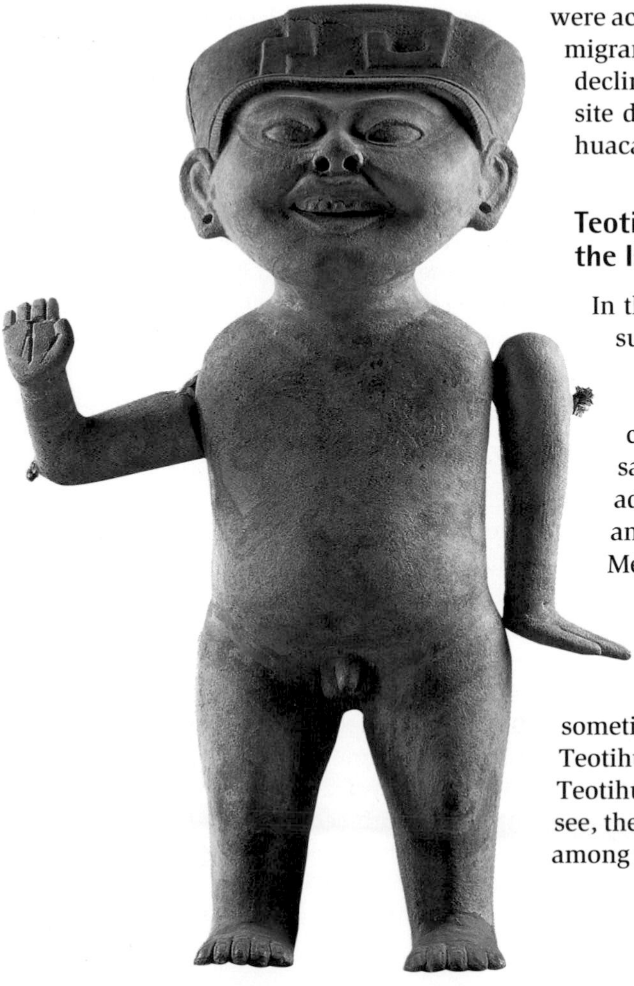

10.32 *This "Smiling Face,"* "Cara Souriente," *figurine from Remojadas in the south-central Gulf lowlands stands about 48 cm (18.75 in) high. Figurines of this type seem to be expressing friendly good will, but some scholars have interpreted the expression as deriving from intoxicants, or even as a grimace of pain.*

Teotihuacan's Important Partners South of the Isthmus

In this chapter, the story of Teotihuacan's greatness and subsequent decline has been told, along with the stories of its powerful contemporaries like Monte Albán, and rising powers like Cholula. In the next chapter, we look at the events unfolding during the same period, in the Maya lowlands, highlands, and adjacent regions. Teotihuacan's development as a huge and complex city was one of the great events in Mesoamerican culture history, and in a sense the cities of the Maya form a kind of cultural counterpoint to it. None of them resembled Teotihuacan in terms of urbanization; rather, they formed a mosaic of dynastically ruled civic-ceremonial centers, sometimes surrounded by tens of thousands of people. Teotihuacan's influence in this region was quite limited – Teotihuacan was not an "imperial" power – but as we shall see, the city where time was born made its presence felt even among the Maya.

11 THE MAYA IN THE EARLY CLASSIC (AD 250–600)

THE EARLY CLASSIC PERIOD among the lowland Maya was a major cultural florescence, with widespread programs of monumental architecture and dynastically related inscriptions, evidence of the sophisticated royal lineages ruling in scores of capitals. As we know, the Classic period was named after the time span during which the Maya erected monuments dated with their Long Count system. The cessation of dated monuments by around AD 900 signaled a dramatic collapse of the elaborate traditions of rulership and its accompanying material culture attributes, such as fine arts and architecture – centers were abandoned, and eventually, whole areas were almost entirely depopulated. In this and the following chapter, the story of the Classic-period Maya and their near neighbors shows how an early civilization rose and fell [11.1].

Late and Terminal Formative-period sites like El Mirador and Nakbé revealed that rulership and its impressive trappings had a long history in the Maya lowlands. We assume that by the 1st century AD, the Maya had hereditary kings ruling over domains centered upon their capitals, with

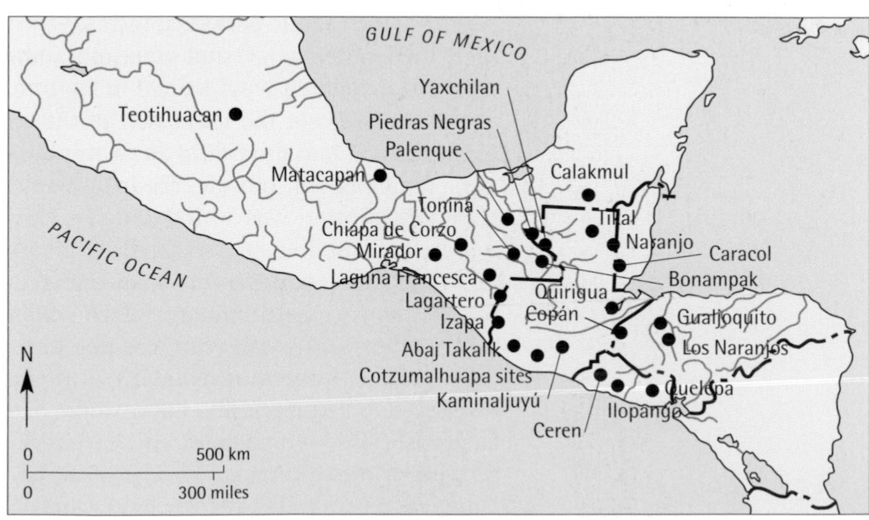

11.1 *Middle America showing Early Classic-period regions and sites mentioned in Chapter 11.*

productive work done by peasants administered by the king's noble relatives. Maya kings belonged to the Mesoamerican tradition of shamans as power-holders, securing the support of their people through the shared perception that the kings were adequately performing as intermediaries with supernatural forces: that natural cycles of agrarian fertility would be maintained, and that the sacred cycles of time would be properly overseen and events in the future would be perceptively divined and correctly foretold.

Kings also took the lead in reassuring their followers that cycles of time and regeneration would continue, through various practices of sacrifice. Offerings have been found in many Maya contexts, including caves, tombs, and *cenotes* (water-filled sinkholes). The "Cenote of Sacrifice" at Chichén Itzá has been explored and precious goods have been recovered which were, presumably, deposited there as offerings, particularly in the Postclassic period. In addition to goods of all kinds, living things – animals and humans – were sacrificed. Kings led sacrificial rites, and also practiced autosacrifice, undergoing the pain of drawing blood from their earlobes, tongues, and genitals. Kings themselves were sacrificed by other kings, if taken captive in battle.

The spiritual natures of Maya kings and their role as shamans were regarded as so powerful that kings were thought to be able to enlist the help of spiritual alter egos. Thus they shared in the ancient Mesoamerican tradition of the spirit companion (in Mayan, *way* [pron. why]), an animal alter ego of the ruler. Furthermore, death of the body was another kind of transformation of the soul, and the temple-pyramids at Maya sites were built as monuments to and dwellings of the spirits of deceased kings, sites of ancestor veneration that were part of the royal residential complex. This creation of a "domestic mausoleum in the residential complex itself" (McAnany 1995: 100) was a practice shared on a much more modest scale by Maya peasants as well, and, as we have seen, was common elsewhere in Mesoamerica.

During the Classic period, some Maya kings took great pains to document their own genealogies, and erect monuments to (possibly fictional) ancestors, actions which would serve to legitimize their own claims to rulership, as well as seeking the good will of the spirits of the departed to help the living family, and providing an example as to how they wished themselves to be remembered. In time, the idea would arise that a Maya ruler, particularly a dead ruler, was a kind of deity. However, the Maya clearly revered a whole range of deities associated with various domains. We have seen that at Monte Albán and Teotihuacan, and even extending back into the Olmec realm, there are anthropomorphized gods with particular powers and interests. To Mesoamericans, the cosmos had multiple levels. The Aztecs saw nine levels of underworld and 13 of the upperworld, with earth as the first level of each. Horizontally, the cardinal directions defined sacred quadrants, each associated with a color and part of the divinatory calendar. The center portion of this quincunx was also sacred, a vertical unifying *axis mundi*. Now, we return to the earthly landscape of the Maya heartland.

MAYA LOWLANDS

The Yucatán Peninsula is, by Middle American standards of topography, a relatively flat plain, though some relief is provided by low hills, escarpments, and swampy *bajos*, and even a few lakes. The change in vegetation from the northwestern corner of the peninsula, down to the southern lowlands, results from different rainfall patterns. In the northwest corner of the peninsula the annual rainfall is as little as 500 mm (*c.* 20 in), while a few parts of the southern lowlands receive over 4,000 mm (4 m, *c.* 160 in). The 1,500-mm limit (*c.* 60 in) divides the northern and southern lowlands, with the northern lowlands having a "tropical savannah" habitat, and the southern lowlands, the Petén region, having a "tropical monsoon" habitat, according to Koeppen classification of types of environments. While all the Maya regions are "in the tropics" as far as latitude is concerned, most of the vegetation of the northern Yucatán Peninsula is scrubby and dry for much of the year, with true tropical forest occurring in the south, where rainfall is heavier.

Thus climate and habitat distinguish the two major culture areas of the lowland Maya. We shall begin in the south, because the Early Classic-period history of the centers of this region is much better known, owing to the precocity of settlement as well as to the extensive and early documentation of rulers and traditions of rulership, through Maya writing. Yet we shall reserve most discussion of the architecture of the great sites of southern and northern lowlands until the next chapter. Sites such as Tikal and Calakmul dominated the Maya lowlands in both the Early and Late Classic, but the monumental architecture uncovered by modern archaeological research dates to the Late Classic. The occupations at these sites during the Early Classic, insofar as deep excavations have revealed their traces, made them the most substantial settlements in their region, but they were modest in comparison with their later selves, or in comparison with El Mirador and Nakbé at the end of the Formative period.

The Petén Region and Maya Politics

The southern Maya lowlands extend across the southern Yucatán Peninsula, from the Usumacinta River drainage in the west, through the Petén region in the central portion and Belize on the east, and even, according to some scholars, further southeast to embrace important Maya sites near the Motagua River. The Petén has a southern subregion, the Petexbatún area (Foias 2002), and borders upon the Northern Maya Lowlands with the Río Bec subregion. The Petén region has always been regarded as the heartland of Classic Maya culture, because early and important sites were located there, and because its sites most intensively bore the tradition of Maya inscriptions [**11.2**]. Early Classic culture in the Petén is known as Tzak'ol culture.

Across the Petén and into adjacent regions, Early Classic rulers jostled for power, setting up alliances and provoking mortal enmities. While Maya

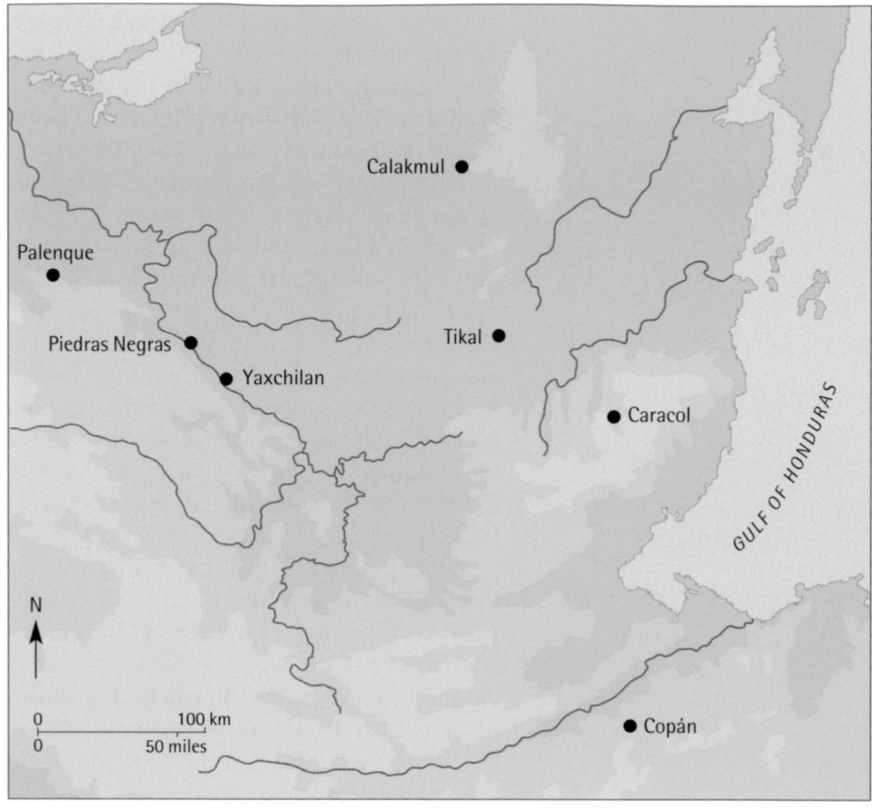

11.2 *Early Classic Maya sites of the Petén and adjacent regions.*

11.3, 11.4 *(Opposite) Tikal, Stela 29. The front side shows a ruling lord in full regalia, possibly "Foliated Jaguar," and bears the earliest Long Count date known from the Maya lowlands. The date, on the back side, appears as 8.12.14.13.15, the equivalent of* AD *292 in the modern calendar. It is calculated as the period elapsed since the date that the Maya believed marked the creation of the present universe: 13 August 3114* BC*. At present, interpretations of Classic Maya dates use the Goodman-Martinez-Thompson (GMT) correlation, plus two days, and the dates are given in the Julian calendar, contemporaneous with the dates, not the Gregorian calendar in modern use. Because the Stela 29 date falls in Bak'tun 8, scholars refer to it as a "Cycle 8" date, or one which occurs in the 9th Bak'tun (in the same sense that we live in the 21st century). The Long Count calendar was devised in the 8th* bak'tun.

peasants were tied to their *milpas* for all their lives, Maya elites played out their destinies on a larger landscape. Marriage alliances sent royal women hundreds of miles to marry into the lineages of distant centers; battles and raids were fought at distant sites, and the losers were taken off to be sacrificed at the capitals of the winners. Diplomatic missions to arrange these matters also sent royals and nobles traveling to each other's capitals, as did trading expeditions. These patterns are far more pronounced, and better documented, for the Late Classic period, but certainly had their origins in the Early Classic, if not before.

The documentation of these patterns comes from inscriptions and depictions on stelae and vases and wall paintings and bas-reliefs, but the evidence we have today, while an invaluable view of Maya life, records only a fraction of the lives of rulers and centers. Outside the southern lowlands, inscriptions are relatively rare, and at many sites within the southern lowlands, inscriptions were made on materials such as readily erodable stone that have not survived in a readable form. Or the inscriptions and depictions may have been looted or otherwise vandalized. Thus there are many gaps in the records – important reigns and events may be unknown to us because of the vagaries of survivability.

From a number of lines of evidence – inscriptions as well as architecture

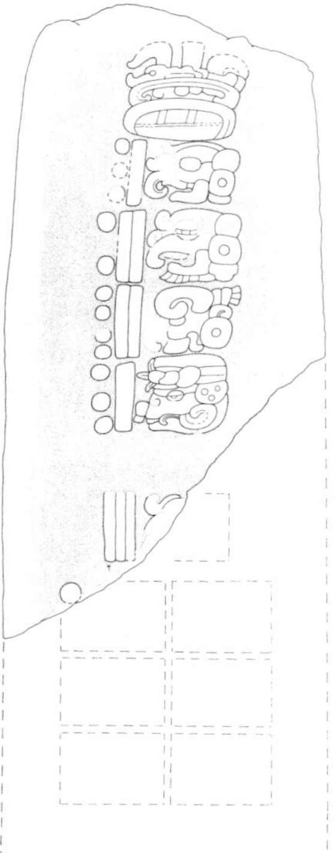

and depictions of events painted onto elite goods like pottery vessels or carved into stone – it has become clear that the pattern of Maya political interaction was not just a mess of seemingly random raids and marital unions, but rather was a deeply rooted system of allied sites centering on two great capitals, Tikal and Calakmul, that, from the Early Classic – probably from the end of the Formative period – were the powers that set policy for many of the other centers, and few sites were not caught up in the web of conflicts and alliances that had their origins in the competition between them.

Kings of Calendrics: Time and Early Classic Maya Rulers

Perhaps the best known of the Petén Maya sites, Tikal was occupied as early as the Middle Formative period, and its royal dynasty may have been established by the 1st century AD. This hypothesized dynastic foundation by King Yax Ehb' Xook is based on comments in later Classic inscriptions, plus a rich burial (Burial 85) in the early construction of the North Acropolis (Martin and Grube 2001). The early dynastic record is fragmentary, but Tikal's Stela 29 depicts a ruling lord (Mayan *ajaw*) and dates from AD 292 **[11.3, 11.4]**.

Maya dynasties, like those in Mesoamerica in general, were patrilineal, with many of the known linkages being father to son. Sometimes, when there was no son, rulership passed to an uncle or male cousin. Sometimes, when the king's son inherited the throne at a very young age, his mother would serve as regent until he achieved maturity. Very rarely, a royal woman was actually installed as a ruler, and this seems to have happened in Tikal on at least one occasion, during the 10th *bak'tun* (a 400-year cycle), in the year the Maya would have known as 9.4.0.0.0.

The turn of the *k'atun* was typically honored by ceremonies and monuments, and often our knowledge of rulers comes not from monuments commemorating their accession to office, or death, but from their names as appearing on monuments to time (Fitzsimmons 1998). This recalls the issue of rulers as shamans, as diviners, because time had many cyclical aspects, and lucky and unlucky days recurred. The Long Count, as a non-recurrent calendar, was used in conjunction with the 260-day divination calendar and the 365-day vague solar year. Monument dates began with an "Initial Series" that included, in addition to the Long Count date, the 260-day date

Maya Units of Time (11.4)

Date on Stela 29	Unit	Length in days	Length in years
8	*Bak'tun*	144,000	c. 400
12	*K'atun*	7,200	c. 20
14	*Tun*	360	c. 1
13	*Winal*	20	
15	*K'in*	1	

Tikal, Early Classic Partial King List (11.5)

	Ruler	Events
	Yax Ehb' Xook *c.* AD 90 or 219	Dynasty founded
	Foliated Jaguar AD ?	
	Animal Headdress AD ?	
AD 300	Siyaj Chan K'awiil I r. c. AD 307	
	Lady Unen B'alam *c.* 317	Break in male line of succession
	K'inich Muwaan Jol d. May 359?	
	Chak Tok Ich'aak I r. 360?-378	
		Break in male line of succession
	Yax Nuun Ayiin I r. 379-404?	Son of Spearthrower Owl; sponsored by Siyaj K'ak' ("Smoking Frog")
AD 400	Siyaj Chan K'awiil II r. 411-456	Dynastic foundations at Palenque, Copán, Quirigua
	K'an Chitam r. 458-486?	
	Chak Tok Ich'aak II r. 486-508	
AD 500	Lady of Tikal r. 511-527 >	
	Bird Claw ?	
	Wak Chan K'awiil r. 537-562	553: sponsored Caracol ruler, but by 556, war with Caracol and Calakmul; 562: Tikal defeated in "star war"
		562–592: hiatus: Tikal overrun, probably by Calakmul

All tables in this chapter based on Martin and Grube 2000. *Note* alternative forms of names are found in the Index, not in these lists.

11.5 *(Above) Tikal's Early Classic Rulers.*

11.7 *(Opposite below) A blackware vase found in Tikal shows, at far right, a Teotihuacan-style temple with* talud-tablero *platform, and at far left, a Maya temple. To its right, a Maya temple stands on a* talud-tablero *platform, on which rests a Maya figure greeting a delegation of Teotihuacanos. Four of them carry darts, and three of these carry spear throwers, identifiable by their hooked ends. To the right of the four figures in military garb are two wearing the tassled headdresses characteristic of Teotihuacan bureaucrats and bearing what might be decorated ceramic vessels, the gift characteristic of Mesoamerican alliance-building. To their right, two seated figures may represent Teotihuacan civilians.*

(from the divinatory almanac, the "tzolkin") and the deity patrons of various parts of the date, including the lunar cycle.

All of this, plus architectural constructs like E-groups and observatories, made powerful raw material for divination, in the hands of one of the few members of society trained to understand all the calendric cycles and their meanings. The yearly agrarian cycle of field preparation and planting and harvesting would have been of foremost concern to the common people, who would have looked to their ruler and his trained calendar priests for guidance as to the proper – and most auspicious – timing of these events. But beyond these undertakings lay others of more urgent concern to royals and nobles, matters such as the best time to make war, or offer sacrifices, or erect a building.

The Maya preoccupation with time long predated Maya contact with Teotihuacan, famed as "the place where time began," but the shared interest in the flow of time and its meaning must have created a powerful bond between the two cultures. After all, Teotihuacan's orientation was based on the same date in 3114 BC that the Maya believed established the present universe. Teotihuacanos had received this wisdom from other cultures, including those of the southern Pacific Coast that also influenced the Maya. However, at Teotihuacan the mechanics of time and its meaning seem to have become a religion, and one which they exported.

Tikal as an Early Classic Maya Center

Celebrating the *k'atun* ending of 8.17.0.0.0 (AD 376), Tikal's King Chak Tok Ich'aak I ("Jaguar Paw") must have enjoyed his position of prestige as ruler of the largest and most sophisticated kingdom in the Maya lowlands [11.5]. Two years later he disappeared: coincidentally, this happened in January, 378, just as strangers from "the west" arrived in Tikal [11.7]. A year later, a new king, Yax Nuun Ayiin ("Curl Snout") would be installed under the sponsorship not of the existing Tikal dynasty, but of one of the westerners, Siyaj K'ak ("Smoking Frog") [11.6]. This new king was of Teotihuacan descent, the son of Spearthrower Owl, an important ruler (r. 374–439), possibly of Teotihuacan itself (Stuart 2000: 483).

These interpretations are based on very recent translations of glyphs, as well as on the presence of Teotihuacan styles, symbols and even materials at Tikal. There is a strong indication that the power of the strangers was based on militarism. As we have seen for Teotihuacan, militaristic imagery dominated the last of the great pyramids, the Temple-Pyramid of the Feathered Serpent, and, in Maya art, Teotihuacan figures are distinguished by their warrior costumes and weaponry. The very name "Spearthrower Owl" combines the owl, a powerful Mesoamerican animal of prey, with a weapon, the spear thrower, that was well-suited to the open terrain of the Central Highlands, but one which was unsuited to the tropical forests of the southern Maya lowlands. In fact, this new weapon may have caused a stir, but did not become part of the weaponry used by Maya military forces (Hassig 1992).

Furthermore, Teotihuacan's exportation of its brand of militarism may have reflected the schism in Teotihuacan itself: the Temple-Pyramid of the Feathered Serpent was built over during this period to conceal its war-themed sculptures. Taking over the dynastic line of

11.6 *(Below) Tikal, Stela 31. The back panel (not shown) has an extensive historical text recording the events of the Teotihuacan intrusion. The front panel (center) shows Tikal's ruler Siyaj Chan K'awiil II. He holds aloft a headdress bearing a motif of his grandfather, Spearthrower Owl. On the stela's sides are two views of his father, Tikal ruler Yax Nuun Ayiin I, with a square Teotihuacan-style shield and a spear thrower. The left figure's headdress is like those on the façade of the Temple-Pyramid of the Feathered Serpent, while on the right figure's shield is a goggled face with a partial mask below his nose.*

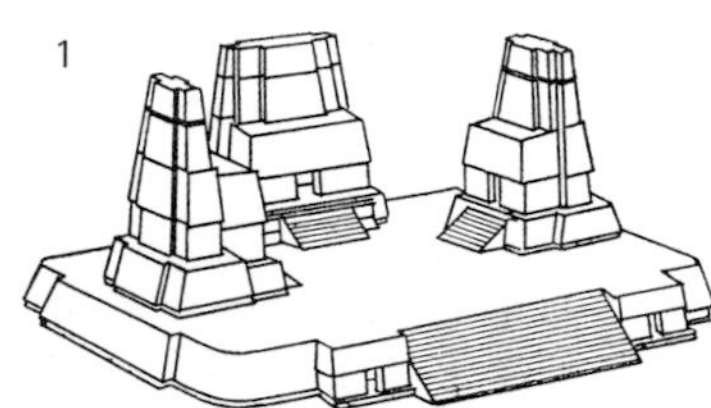

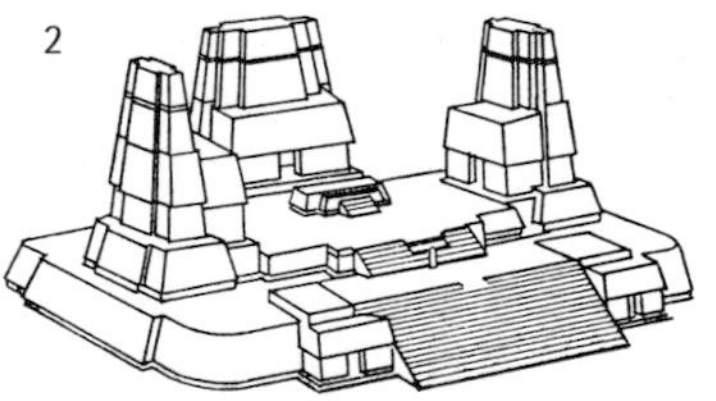

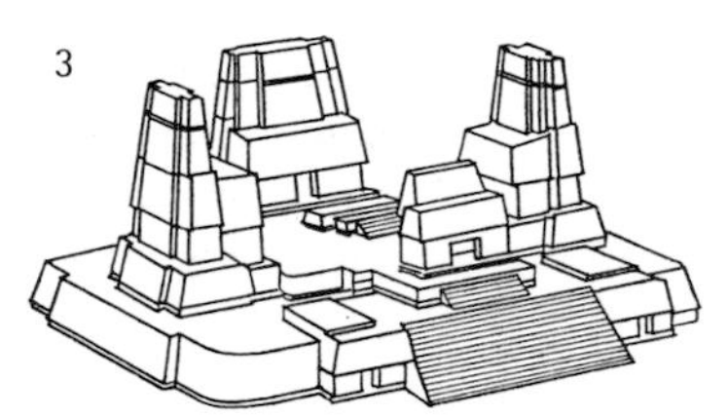

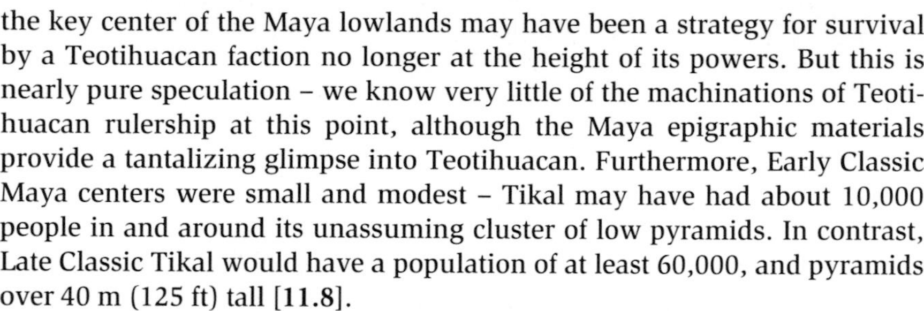

the key center of the Maya lowlands may have been a strategy for survival by a Teotihuacan faction no longer at the height of its powers. But this is nearly pure speculation – we know very little of the machinations of Teotihuacan rulership at this point, although the Maya epigraphic materials provide a tantalizing glimpse into Teotihuacan. Furthermore, Early Classic Maya centers were small and modest – Tikal may have had about 10,000 people in and around its unassuming cluster of low pyramids. In contrast, Late Classic Tikal would have a population of at least 60,000, and pyramids over 40 m (125 ft) tall [**11.8**].

What was the effect of Teotihuacan influence on the Maya? The Central Mexican interlopers who usurped the Tikal dynasty seem to have surrounded themselves with symbols and regalia typical of their homeland. However, *talud-tablero*-style architecture was introduced at Tikal in restricted contexts, for example, around Structure 5C-54, which was an E group, designed to mark the equinoxes and solstices of the solar calendar (Coggins 1993). Some of the burials were of Central Mexican style. For

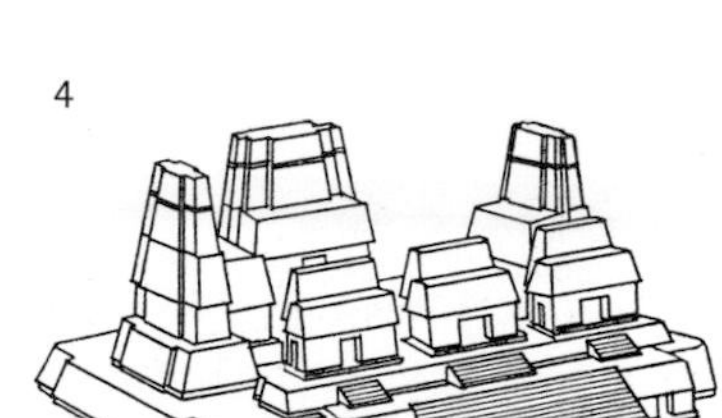

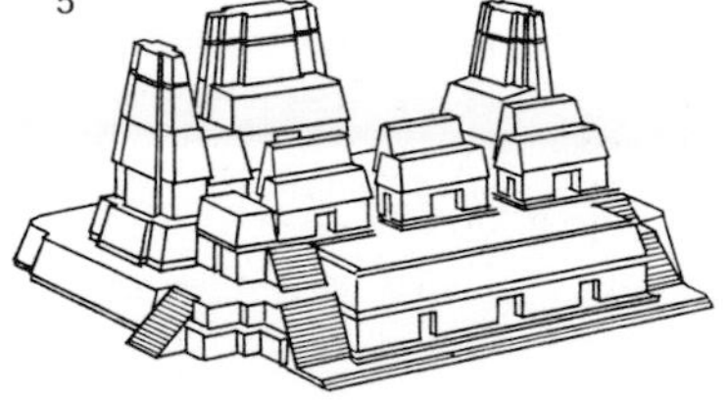

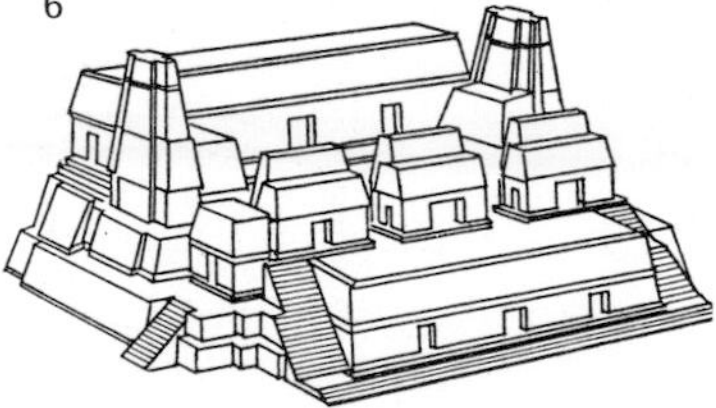

11.8 *(Opposite) Tikal's North Acropolis was built and rebuilt, from the Formative period through the Classic. It is the royal cemetery, where many of Tikal's kings are entombed. The placement of stelae in front of the monuments is a signature of Maya ceremonial center layout.*

example, Burial 10 in the North Acropolis seems to be that of Yax Nuun Ayiin, and the deceased was accompanied by pottery vessels with Teotihuacan motifs, and attended by nine sacrificial victims.

However, over time, these distinctive features became swamped by the indigenous Maya culture. The scholarly debate over whether Teotihuacan actively intervened in Maya life, or simply lent prestige through its iconographic motifs, may be resolved as affirming both positions (Stuart 2000). That is, the Early Classic shows evidence of Teotihuacan interference, probably by use of force, at Tikal, Copán, and elsewhere. However, by the Late Classic period, Maya royals were using motifs derived from Teotihuacan (by then a husk of its former self) as a way of demonstrating their preferential familiarity with ancient and highly valued symbols of power.

There are some indications that Teotihuacan influence may have contributed to the proliferation of the Maya rulership hierarchy. In the Early Classic, some rulers – *ajaws* – seemed to promote themselves into a kind of overlord position, acting as patrons or sponsors of lords at less important sites, calling themselves "divine lord" (*k'uhul ajaw*). The title *kaloomte'* distinguished the most powerful lords at a few sites such as Tikal, and some even claimed the more exalted title *ochk'in kaloomte'*, the first term meaning "west" as in, Teotihuacan-derived. Spearthrower Owl himself is described as a *kaloomte'*. Yet, long before Teotihuacanos meddled in their affairs, Maya centers were engaged in continuous shifting alliances and struggles, and, as we have seen from evidence of fortifications, warfare was not an imported idea. And while no Classic Maya capital forged an "empire" with itself as the controlling focus of a set of lesser states, by the early 6th century, Tikal and Calakmul were the most powerful centers, and others were drawn into the sphere of influence of one or the other (Martin and Grube 2000).

11.9 *(Opposite and below) Uaxactún's palace "A-V" (A-five) was rebuilt numerous times. Archaeological investigation revealed that the original platform group of three buildings facing onto a patio became increasingly restricted and private as it was expanded. The sequence of reconstruction drawings shows how the complex grew during the Classic period.*

Consider Uaxactún, about 20 km (12 miles) north of Tikal, and founded at about the same time in the Formative period. Early Classic Uaxactún, like other centers, already had monumental architecture – temple-pyramids and ball courts and elite residences – but these were to grow much larger over the next few hundred years [**11.9**]. Even while growing, Uaxactún was experiencing problems dealing with the aggression of external powers, possibly from Teotihuacan. Uaxactún and Tikal both experienced a Middle Classic decline, and Tikal's Late Classic reawakening was followed by a new burst of activity at Uaxactún.

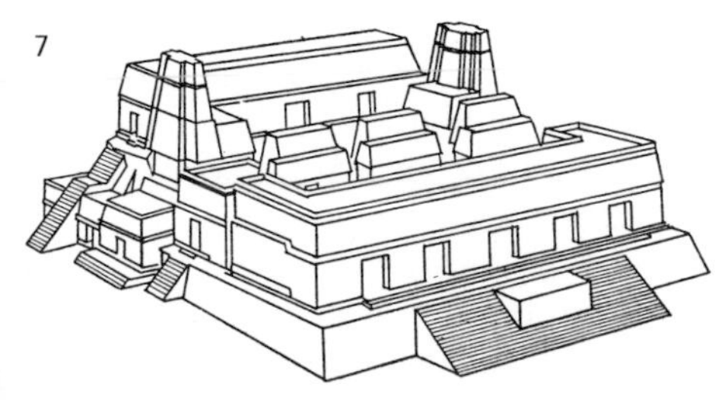

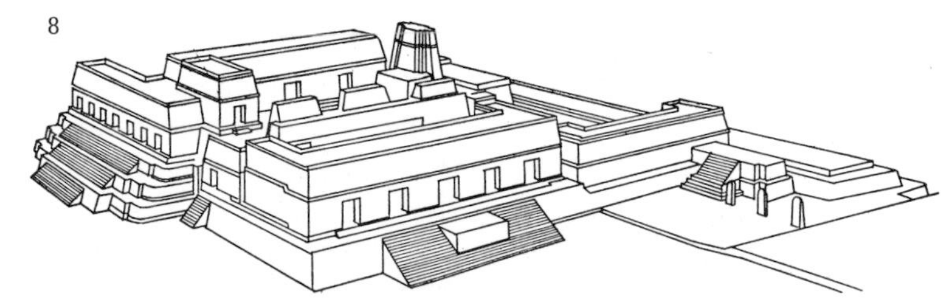

The Usumacinta Region

Tikal had important allies, and some enemies, to the west in the area drained by one of Mesoamerica's great rivers, the Usumacinta. This river winds northward toward the Gulf of Mexico, meandering through a vast marshy area in the southern Gulf lowlands. The Usumacinta's headwaters in the western highlands of Guatemala are merely 350 km (217 miles) away from the Gulf, as the crow flies, but calculated as the river and its tributaries flow, the distance is many times that. Though the courses of the Usumacinta and tributaries such as the Lacantún, Salinas/Chixoy, and Pasión were no doubt used as arteries of travel, it is most likely that trails near the rivers often provided the routes, because many stretches of the rivers around the Maya centers were not navigable by pre-hispanic craft.

Still, the Usumacinta and its tributaries provided a grand avenue of trade, and major Maya sites in the drainage of this system include (beginning downriver) Palenque, Pomona, Piedras Negras, Yaxchilan, Lacanhá and Bonampak. Farther to the west, in the hilly Chiapas Plateau, were sites such as Toniná that interacted most frequently with the Usumacinta sites. Along and near the Pasión River, we find the venerable site of Altar de Sacrificios, and Itzán, Seibal, and Cancuén. Clustered nearby are the Petexbatún sites, including Dos Pilas, colonized in the early 7th century by a disaffected faction from Tikal, and Aguateca, later a refuge for the Dos Pilas rulers as their polity collapsed.

Palenque The Usumacinta River system has formed a broad delta – it is about 100 km (60 miles) south of the Gulf of Mexico before the mountains of the Chiapas highlands begin to rise. In the first range, overlooking the coastal plain, Palenque was established at around AD 200. Major resources here were the travel routes along the rivers and the fertility of the plain, a rich environment for cacao cultivation. At the site, cascading waterfalls enliven the setting for temples and palaces, and Palenque's Classic-period name, Lakamha' – "Big Water" – reflects this resource.

Palenque's dynasty seems to have been established in AD 431 by a lord from another (yet unknown) center, contemporaneous with Tikal's period of greatest influence from Teotihuacan. One Palenque inscription even mentions Siyaj K'ak, suggesting that "the dynasty's foundation was linked to these developments" (Martin and Grube 2000: 156).

Fragmentary records of Early Classic Palenque indicate a fragmented succession from the late 5th century on: many rulers, most of them with short reigns [**11.10**]. From 583 to 604, there ruled Lady Yohl Ik'nal, one of the few women in all Mesoamerican culture history to hold power in her own right, rather than as a place-holder regent for a son or other male successor. Alas for Lady Yohl Ik'nal, her reign was a troubled one. It may have been in 599 that Palenque was "axed" – assaulted and perhaps even sacked by Calakmul, which again attacked in 611, during the reign of Lady Yohl Ik'nal's successor. After his death, in 612, Palenque's line of succession seems to

Palenque, Early Classic King List (11.10)

	Ruler	Events
	K'uk' B'alam I r. 431–435	Dynasty founded, contemporaneous with Teotihuacan influence at Tikal and perhaps reflecting those events
	Casper b. 422, r. 435–487	
	B'utz'aj Sak Chiik b. 459, r. 487–501	
AD 500	Ahkal Mo' Naab' I b. 465, r. 501–524	
	K'an Joy Chitam I b. 490, r. 529–565	
	Ahkal Mo' Naab' II b. 523, r. 565–570	
	Kan B'alam I b. 524, r. 572–583	1st Palenque ruler to use k'inich (Great Sun) name
	Lady Yohl Ik'nal r. 583–604	One of few Mesoamerican women rulers to serve in her own right. Palenque sacked by Calakmul in 599

break down, but as we shall see in Chapter 12, its architecture and monuments reached spectacular heights under the Late Classic-period leadership of K'inich Janaab' Pakal I ("Pacal").

Yaxchilan Situated on a bend in the Usumacinta, Yaxchilan's location also took advantage of the surrounding hills as a horizon calendar, and its early rulers no doubt substantiated their right to power by reading the interplay of astronomy and landscape, interpreted through the Maya calendar and the dynasty's genealogy (Tate 1992) [**11.12**]. Yaxchilan's Early Classic history, like that of other Maya sites, is obscured by its Late Classic-period development. However, later documents, such as a hieroglyphic stairway recapitulating the early years of its dynasty, indicate that the founder, in 359, was Yopaat B'alam I. Yaxchilan's inscriptions record a lively participation in the alliances and skirmishes of the day [**11.11**], with particular

11.10 *(Above) Palenque's Early Classic kings.*

11.11 *(Below) Yaxchilan's Early Classic kings.*

Yaxchilan, Early Classic King List (11.11)

	Ruler	Events
	Yopaat B'alam I 359–?	Dynasty founder
	Itzamnaaj B'alam I *c.* 370s?	
	Bird Jaguar I r. 378–389	
	Yax Deer-Antler Skull r. 389–402?	
AD 400	Ruler 5 r. 402?–?	
	Tatb'u Skull I r. 425??	
	Moon Skull r. > 454-467	7th in the dynastic line, conflicts with Piedras Negras
	Bird Jaguar II r. 467	Victory over Piedras Negras
AD 500	Knot-eye Jaguar I r. > 508–*c.* 518	9th king, captured nobles from Bonampak, Piedras Negras, Tikal
	Tatb'u Skull II r. 526–537 >	Captured lords of Bonampak and Calakmul
	Knot-eye Jaguar II r. > 564 >	Between 537 and 629 there were four known kings, but this is the only one that can be identified with certainty

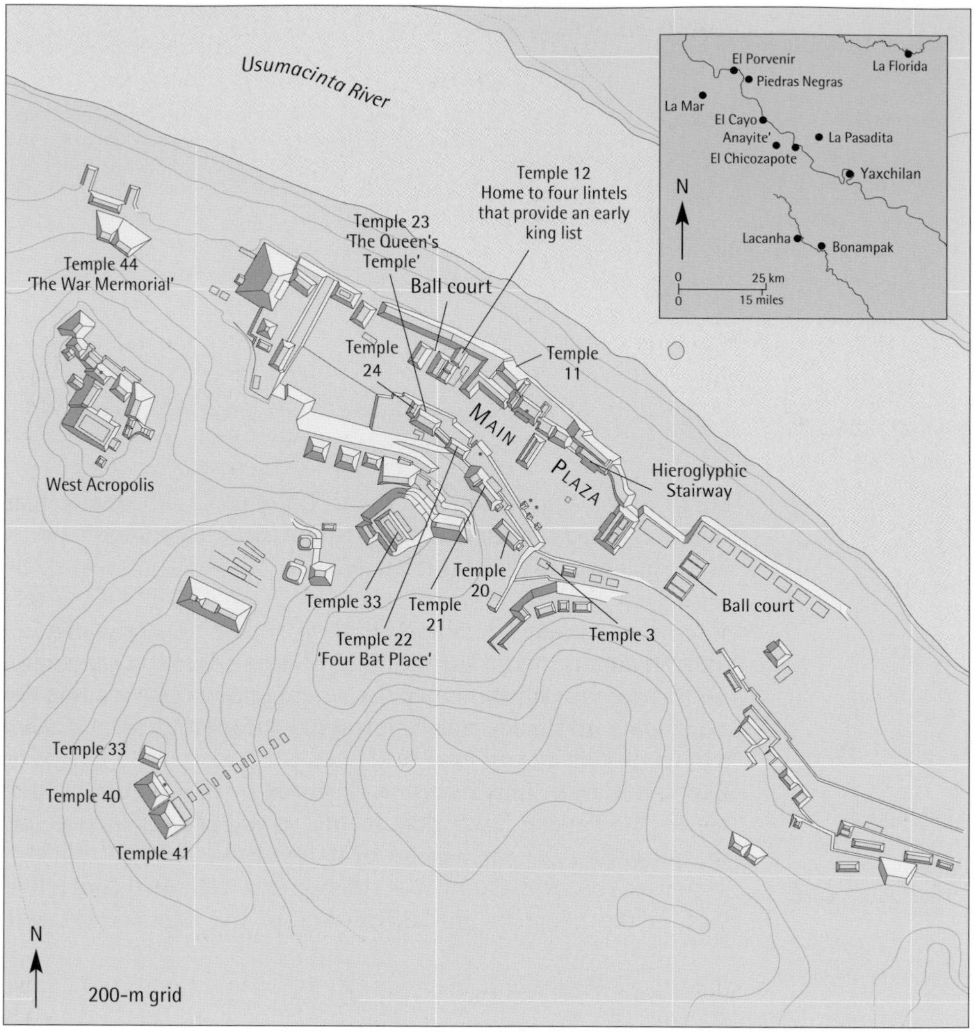

11.12 *Yaxchilan's layout, along the banks of the Usumacinta River, is a good example of how the Maya used the landscape in planning their ceremonial centers. The Main Plaza is a linear feature in front of linear monumental platforms, all running parallel to the river.*

regard to Piedras Negras (its nearest neighbor), Bonampak, and even Tikal and Calakmul. Even in the Early Classic period, Yaxchilan was rich in inscriptions, particularly on the underside of wooden lintels – those entering the center's temples must have adopted a heavenward gaze in order to acknowledge the messages of the images and words.

Calakmul and the Northern Maya Lowlands

If any one Classic Maya lowlands capital can be said to have established an overlord relation with many other centers, including, for a time, Tikal, it was Calakmul [11.13]. Located nearly 100 km (62 miles) north of Tikal, Calakmul was at the boundary between the Petén region of the southern Maya lowlands, and Río Bec region at the southern edge of the northern

Calakmul, Early Classic King List (11.13)

Ruler	Events
Yuknoon Ch'een I ? – before 520	
Tuun K'ab' Hix >520–546>	Presided over accession of Naranjo ruler in 546
Sky Witness >561–572	Displaced Tikal in influence (probably sacrificed Tikal's ruler in 562), subdued Caracol, attacked Palenque
First Axewielder 572–579	

11.13 *Calakmul's Early Classic kings.*

Maya lowlands. The northern Maya lowlands were considerably drier than the Petén, and bore their own distinct variations on the Maya cultural patterns. Unfortunately, our knowlege of the Early Classic in the northern lowlands is very incomplete, in part because that region produced so few Maya texts. We do know that there was ongoing occupation of Late and Terminal Formative-period sites, and a continuation of the material culture patterns – pottery styles, for example – of earlier times.

Calakmul would become the largest Classic Maya center, but as was the case with Tikal and other centers, the monumental architecture and site plans known today from archaeological research represent Late Classic construction. Like Tikal, Calakmul was established in the Formative period and by the 1st century AD was linked to El Mirador, Nakbé, and other sites by a system of *sacbes* extending dozens of kilometers away from the site. Our knowledge of its dynastic succession is limited to the 6th century and later. Coincidentally, this is when Calakmul's aggressions against Tikal effectively drove that center into a decline, a tale of political woe we will recount at the end of this chapter.

Maya of the Motagua: Copán and Quirigua

The Maya sites of the Usumacinta are among the westernmost examples of the culture. At the other, southeastern end of the culture area lie Copán and Quirigua, whose Early Classic histories show that they were part of the influences that were affecting Tikal and Palenque. There were communities at both Copán and Quirigua long before these centers were taken over by Maya ruling lineages. At both sites, the dynastic lines seem to have been established in AD 426, at a ceremony involving the two dynastic founders, K'inich Yax K'uk' Mo' of Copán [**11.16**] and Tok Casper of Quirigua.

Quirigua's location on the Motagua River made it an ideal trading post, linking the Guatemala highlands with the Caribbean Sea, but throughout nearly all of the Classic period, Copán was clearly the dominant partner and Quirigua its lucrative subsidiary. The Copán River, a southern tributary of the Motagua, flows through a broad fertile alluvial plain, the best agricultural land in the Copán Valley. Surrounding hills were covered with pine forests; by the end of the Late Classic these were cleared so that the hills could be cultivated along with the alluvial plain.

MAYA WRITING

NATIVE AMERICANS devised some remarkable systems of record-keeping, but only in Mesoamerica did true writing occur, and only the Maya developed a sophisticated writing system which could fully express narratives. That is, while Zapotec, Mixtec, and Aztec systems of writing succinctly conveyed politically important information through stylized expressions such as place names and sometimes personal names, and conventions for kinds and amounts of goods, the Maya writing system was much more flexible and expressive, capable of recording grammatical sentences, complete thoughts (Coe and van Stone 2001).

Maya texts have long been noteworthy because of the beauty of their form: each distinct, sinuous block forms an integral part of a whole design – Maya writing is one of the world's traditions of calligraphy in the true sense of "beautiful writing" (Coe and Kerr 1998). The ovoid blocks are "... grouped, and the groups disposed in rows..." (Rafinesque-Schmaltz, 2001 [1832]: 47). While the blocks were to be read from left to right, their organization was in pairs of columns, thus one would read Column A, Row 1, Column B, Row 1, Column A, Row 2, etc., until the block at the bottom of Column B, before proceeding to Column C. As we have seen on stelae, the blocks form part of the sculpted artistic composition, as well as conveying meaning, and this combination of aesthetic and information-bearing properties is expressed in all the media for Maya writing: stone and stucco sculpture, walls of buildings and caves, vase painting, screenfold books of deerskin or paper made from fig tree bark (*amatl* in Nahuatl).

Decipherment of Maya texts has been one of the most productive areas of Mesoamerican research in recent years, the culmination of centuries of effort, beginning with Fray Diego de Landa, the man who took it upon himself to burn all the Maya books he found. Landa, writing in 1566, interpreted Maya hierglyphs as an alphabet, in that each glyph was the equivalent of a

11.14, 11.15 *Maya writing was flexible in that the same concept – here, balam ("jaguar") – could be expressed in several different ways (right). The scribe below is focused upon his work, in which the roles of historian and artist were combined.*

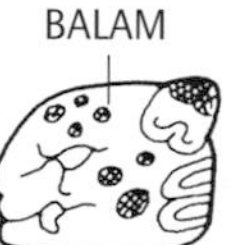

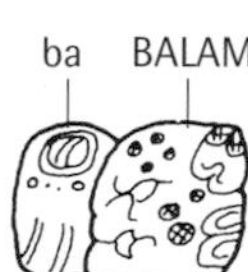

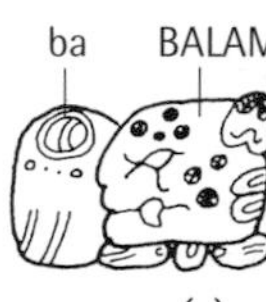

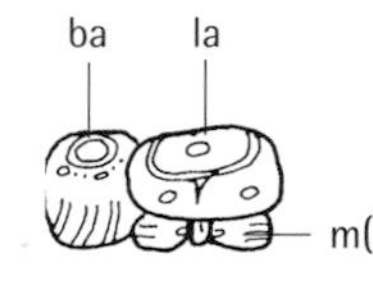

letter in the European alphabet. This was wrong, because written Maya is largely logosyllabic, "the phonetic glyphs always represent one syllable" (Knozorov 2001 [1956]: 146).

However, complicating the decipherment problem is the variability in expression. The illustration [11.14] shows five ways to write balam, the Mayan word for "jaguar." The far left example is a logograph, the far right example a combination of syllables, and those in between are logo-syllabic. As we alphabetically trained readers can imagine, this gave scope for the artist-scribe to compose in an aesthetically pleasing way, and complicated the job of becoming fully literate in both reading and writing Mayan.

While most Maya people could probably understand some of the texts they saw – even we illiterates can see that the figure on the left is a spotted cat – few commoners would own screenfold books or decorated vases, and commoners would have only rarely entered the sacred precincts of the ceremonial centers. Maya hieroglyphic writing was an elite enterprise, its topics the religious and political matters of greatest interest to the rulers and their families. In fact, many sculpted monuments record the interplay of the lives of the rulers and the Maya calendrical cycles (Proskouriakoff 1960). Furthermore, scribes themselves were members of elite families (Johnston 2001). In Mesoamerica, nobles often became skilled artisans, and scribal work called for a combination of literacy and training in the fine arts. The scribe depicted in a vase painting [11.15], is actually the Young Maize God, a patron of scribes, shown with pen in hand and stack of paper; in his left hand he holds his inkwell, a conch shell .

Copán, Early Classic King List (11.16)

	Ruler	Events
	Yax K'uk Mo' r. 426–437 *c.*	Dynasty founder; investiture in 426, along with Quirigua's 1st king, at an unknown location; 152 days later, YKM at Copán
	Popol Hol r. >437>	Son of YKM; established early architecture at Main Group, including ball court, in Maya style
	Ruler 3 r. *c.* 455	
	Ku Ix r. *c.* 465	
	Ruler 5 r. *c.* 475	
	Ruler 6 r. *c.* 485	
AD 500	Waterlily Jaguar r. >504–524>	Further development of the Main Group; WJ is mentioned in a text at Caracol
	Ruler 8 r. *c.* >551	
	Ruler 9 r. 551–553	
	Moon Jaguar r. 553–578	Son of Waterlily Jaguar

11.16 *Copán's Early Classic kings.*

In the early 400s, however, the local population was small and the region's potential for growth – and wealth – under Maya political control was large. It was as if Maya culture was expanding into new territory, finding an area with growth potential, some established population and infrastructure (modest buildings in the area that would become the Copán "Main Group"). Copán would be the only important Maya site on the western edge of Southeastern Mesoamerica; the Copán River leads toward

11.17, 11.18 *Yax K'uk' Mo' (right) was founder of the Copán dynasty, and his association with Teotihuacan was never forgotten, as revealed in this goggle-adorned portrait made 300 years after his accession in* AD *476. (Opposite) The elaborately adorned funerary shrine known as Rosalila was built* c. AD *571 over the earlier buildings shrouding Hunal, Yax K'uk' Mo''s original funerary monument. It would itself become deeply buried within Temple 16, but unlike other early buildings it was not dismantled, but entombed whole, its brightly-painted stucco decorations intact (Agurcia and Fash 1991). Thus Rosalila is a rare complete example of Early Classic Maya architecture, and of use of color (in this case, red, yellow, and green) in temple decoration. Our assumption that Mesoamerican architecture was austere in its surface treatment is a misperception largely derived from seeing buildings after time's erasure of their brilliant colors.*

the Maya region, but east of Copán, the topography is oriented away from the other Maya sites, and increasingly toward lower Central America.

Yax K'uk' Mo', Copán's dynastic founder, was not a local man. Late Classic depictions of him show him wearing round "goggles" [**11.17**], a Central Mexican fashion associated with the Storm God/Tlaloc, and shown, for example, on the Fire Serpent masks adorning the Temple-Pyramid of the Feathered Serpent [**9.22**]. Yet we know that by the Late Classic, the Maya used Teotihuacan traits as a means of appropriating the prestige of the past, and such embellishments were not necessarily intended to demonstrate literal Teotihuacan heritage. However, other lines of evidence support Yax K'uk' Mo''s association with Teotihuacan, if not his membership in Teotihuacan's royal lineage (or Tikal's branch of Teotihuacan's royal lineage). Bone chemistry studies of his skeleton, sumptuously buried in a crypt in the Teotihuacan-style building, Hunal (now deeply embedded within the subsequent pyramid, Temple 16), reveal that he was a foreigner to the Copán Valley (Sharer *et al.* 1999).

Yax K'uk' Mo''s wife may be the woman archaeologists call the "Lady in Red" because of the lavish use in her tomb of the reddish minerals cinnabar and hematite. Ancient peoples, worldwide, adorned deceased individuals with such minerals as a means of simulating the warm glow of living flesh. The "Lady"'s other mortuary offerings were consistent with a woman of very high status; among them was a Teotihuacan-style ceramic vessel whose decorative motifs include a *talud-tablero* building. The "Lady in Red" was a local woman; it would have been logical for the foreign newcomer to establish his new dynasty by taking a wife from the local elite lineage.

The descendants of Yax K'uk' Mo' devotedly kept alive his memory and presumed Teotihuacan heritage, as demonstrated in the rebuildings of his mortuary shrine, known as Rosalila [**11.18**]. Copán's second Maya ruler was Yax K'uk' Mo''s son Popol Hol ("Mat Head"), and he began the building program at the Main Group that, over the next 400 years, elevated this civic-ceremonial center far above its alluvial plain beginnings, and toward its prominence as an acropolis of elegant Late Classic buildings, and as one of the Maya world's greatest capitals. In the Early Classic, it was transformed by an infusion of Maya culture from a village into an international commu-

nity, and we can imagine that this involved reconnaissance missions to determine the fertility of the Copán Valley and tractability of its resident population, before the arrival, no doubt with great dignity, of a procession of Teotihuacan-influenced Maya lords, their retainers, servants, burden bearers, and the trappings and important ritual objects associated with sanctity and politics.

SOUTHEASTERN MESOAMERICA AND THE INTERMEDIATE AREA

The Gods Must be Angry: The Southern Coast and the Eruption of Ilopango

By definition, a lord must have underlings over whom to exert power. Arable land is useless for a royal personage unless there are peasants to work the land. Thus it was one of history's fine coincidences that there also arrived in the Copán Valley, in the early 5th century, refugees fleeing from the eruption of Ilopango, a volcano about 120 km (75 miles) south of Copán

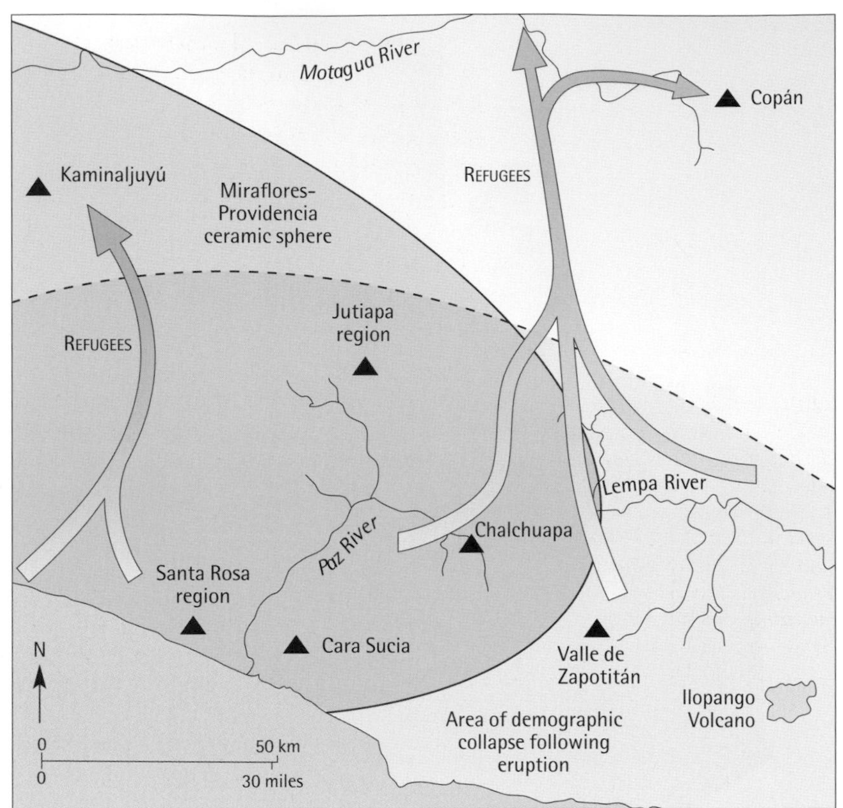

11.19 *Ilopango, a volcano in Southeastern Mesoamerica, sent refugees from what is now western El Salvador and southeastern Guatemala fleeing for their lives into the Guatemala highlands and the Motagua River Valley. Agricultural potential was destroyed for decades in the valleys around the volcano, and even after communities were reestablished, their cultural and economic orientation toward the southern Maya area was severed; Chalchuapa, for example, an important trading center between the Maya and the Southeastern Frontier since Middle Formative times, never recovered this role. Readers should note that the recently calculated early 5th century date (*AD *429 ± error factors; Dull* et al. *p. 25) is roughly two centuries more recent than Ilopango eruption dates cited in older sources, which dated the event to about* AD *200.*

[11.19]. In a situation somewhat analogous to that of Teotihuacan and the collapse of Cuicuilco, Copán – and many other places in the southeastern Maya realm – would have experienced instant population growth, in the form of desperate refugee farming families. Considering that the cultural ecology of Mesoamerica involved the interplay of environmental limits and potentialities with the cultural means of exploiting and controlling these, then it would have been cognitively correct for peasants and rulers alike to regard a volcanic eruption as mountain rage. A peaceful refuge like the Copán Valley would, by the definition of believers in this cultural-environment system, be evidence that the rulers were acting in harmony with the needs of the spiritually charged landscape.

From the perspective of any one individual's lifetime, an event like the eruption of Ilopango marks the total devastation of vast expanses of land, dealing death to countless people. But from the longer-term perspective of culture history, the gods never stay angry for long. Within months, the sky clears, within a few years, volcanic deposits begin to weather into fertile soil. Populations whose ancestors sought safety in adjacent regions may hear family lore, warnings of danger, but population pressure and the lure of a potentially productive vacant landscape would prompt settlers back to live in the shadow of past violence.

Cerén Ilopango had dropped 2 m (*c.* 7 ft) of ash on the Zapotitán Valley, to its west. Even San Andres, the valley's capital, was abandoned. But good locations re-emerge from the ruin – water courses usually resume their same general patterns, the ash can be farmed, the larger buildings cleaned off and rebuilt. So San Andres once again became the primary community in a hierarchy that included several kinds of smaller sites.

Many of these smaller sites were new, built upon Ilopango deposits. For example, the village of Cerén was first occupied after the Ilopango eruption. It was abandoned one summer day in about AD 590, when Loma Caldera, a nearby small volcano, spewed scalding water, ash, and gasses over a limited area. This event was too localized to change the course of culture history over a whole region, but did bury Cerén beneath 5 m (16 ft) of ash, turning it into a kind of Pompeii, a well-preserved community in which catastrophe had fossilized even small details of daily life. The volcanic activity was preceded by an earthquake, so villagers may have escaped with their lives – no bodies have been found (Sheets 1992; Sheets [ed.] 2002).

Cerén's buildings include houses and several public-scale buildings [**11.20**]. Structure 3, one of the public buildings, faced on a plaza, and may have been a meeting house, with long benches, and still in place, a vessel that may have contained a beverage, "ladled out with the polychrome hemispherical vessel found sitting on top of the wall above it" (Sheets 2001: 111). Across the plaza, Structure 13 was a sweat bath capable of seating a dozen people. One ceremonial building held curated ritual objects (Brown 2000).

11.20 *Cerén, plan of part of the site. The blank area in the upper right had been bulldozed to put up modern silos, an operation which exposed Structure 1, leading to the discovery of the site. Excavated buildings under the ash fall were first identified by ground-penetrating radar.*

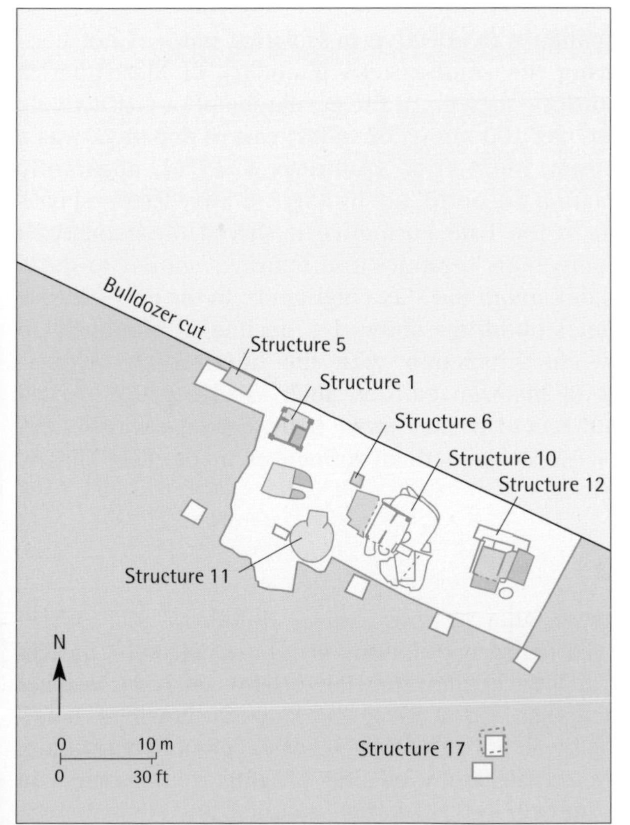

Household archaeology at Cerén showed that each household lived in and used a set of three single-room buildings: the residence, a storage building, and a kitchen. The remarkable preservation revealed that House 1's family had a wide range of ceramic vessels in use – 70 in all. Other implements included gourds and baskets, plus ground-stone and chipped-stone tools. Obsidian blades were found placed in the rafters of the house, probably to keep such sharp tools safely away from the family's children.

Cerén's remarkable preservation even retained evidence of its *milpas*, revealing the patterns of furrows where maize had been planted. The villagers also grew maguey, flowers, medicinal plants, and crops such as manioc and cacao. In its brief life span, Cerén was a modest place, like thousands of other contemporaneous farming villages. Its tremendous value to us is as a window onto the lives of countless peasant farmers all over Mesoamerica, tending their crops, relaxing in the sweat bath, worrying about their children injuring themselves on knives left lying about.

Elsewhere in Southeastern Mesoamerica

As was noted above, Copán represented the southeasternmost major Maya center, located along a river that flowed into the Motagua, and thus toward the Maya heartland. However, Copán's valley was connected with the major drainages of the Sula, Ulua, and Chamelecón Rivers, flowing north into the Caribbean Sea, and it is clear that Early Classic populations in those regions had contact with the Maya, but retained non-Maya cultures. There was considerable demographic growth in the Classic period, and towns with civic-ceremonial architecture served as central places for regions dotted with villages.

Gualjoquito, for example, located at a confluence of the banks of the Ulua River, had been occupied since the Late Formative period and was long a trading center, but it was completely rebuilt in the Early Classic. The arrangement of its plaza and surrounding substantial platform mounds seem to echo Copán's architecture, with a ball court and elite residence (Ashmore *et al.* 1987). Further south, Los Naranjos, on Lake Yojoa, evidenced contact with both the Maya region and with Central American cultures to the south. It remained occupied until about AD 1200. Maya materials even found their way into the Guanacaste region of central Costa Rica (Stone 1976).

Yet it is clear that Ilopango was effective in isolating parts of northern Central America – moving the southeastern boundary of Mesoamerica northwest for a few centuries – as seen in the development of distinctively local styles. Quelepa, just over 100 km (*c.* 62 miles) east of Ilopango, was a substantial site dating from 500/400 BC (Andrews V 1976), apparently settled by Lenca speakers from the north, not by Maya or Mixe-Zoque speakers from the west. Still, in the Late Formative it shared Mesoamerica's material culture, with indigenous ceramics and figurines similar to those found in western El Salvador and in the Maya highlands. In the Early Classic period, its civic-ceremonial buildings showed a decline in similarity to Mesoamerican styles, while interaction with the Intermediate Area is revealed by some items of material culture, such as elaborately carved metates on long legs, and sets of pecked stone balls. Quelepa would later show renewed contact with Mesoamerican influences in the Late Classic and Early Postclassic periods.

The Intermediate Area

The Caribbean lowlands of what is now eastern Honduras and eastern Nicaragua never supported dense populations of peasant farmers; indigenous peoples in these areas were egalitarian tribes (Helms 1976: 2). In what is now southwestern Nicaragua, Costa Rica, and Panama, however, small chiefdoms were emerging by AD 500. The Pacific coastal plain of Nicaragua, for example, had a regional hierarchy of sites ranging from hamlets to regional centers, some with over 100 habitation mounds, and some materials indicate trade with western Honduras (Fletcher 2001: 514). Ranking, as an organizational principle evidenced by differentials in access to local and imported elite goods, was prevalent in this region (Hoopes 1991).

ISTHMUS, COASTAL PLAIN, CHIAPAS, AND GUATEMALA HIGHLANDS

That the coastal regions of the Intermediate Area were, over many centuries, interacting with Mesoamerica was the result of trade along the Pacific Coast. Even though the mountains met the sea in western El Salvador, interrupting the coastal plain, this presented little barrier to trading parties. The Soconusco and south Pacific Coast of Mesoamerica had long been an avenue in the exchange of goods and ideas; in the Formative period it was part of the interaction sphere of the Isthmus of Tehuantepec.

Nonetheless, the Isthmus, once the proud heartland of Olmec culture, was, by the Early Classic, a backwater with few settlements. Farther east, the old Mixe-Zoque culture continued to thrive at sites such as Chiapa de Corzo and Mirador in the western portion of the Chiapas interior plateau. In this region almost no Teotihuacan influence was felt. Further to the east, in the region now along the Mexico-Guatemala border, ethnicity changed to Maya, and Early Classic Maya communities there were Lagartero and Laguna Francesca. Further to the north, along the Usumacinta and its tributaries, as we have discussed above, were the much larger Maya centers like Piedras Negras, Yaxchilan, Palenque, and Toniná that were drawn into the cultural sphere of the southern Maya lowlands.

Although the Isthmian region proper had declined by most measures of cultural vitality, the Pacific Coast continued to thrive. Communities there were not among the great civic-ceremonial centers of the Classic, but the region's importance as a supplier of tropical lowland valuables like cacao lent it lasting value. Abaj Takalik and Izapa remained important centers, and the growing power of the Santa Lucia Cotzumalhuapa sites would make itself felt in the Late Classic (Chapter 12).

The transition between the Terminal Formative and the Early Classic also brought cultural disruption, with a tendency toward strong localization. Many large communities, probably seats of chiefdoms during the Late and Terminal Formative, were abandoned by the Early Classic (Bové 1989). Another kind of evidence of loss of cultural unity is provided by fortifications at the site of Balberta, in the Escuintla region. Balberta grew up during the Terminal Formative and may have become a local capital for the coastal piedmont in the Early Classic. Teotihuacan-style ceramics found in this region, probably dating from AD 375 to 450, may reflect influences toward militarism in the service of protecting long-distance trade to the Central Highlands capital (Berlo 1989). However, this is not a Matacapan: Balberta's architecture, household pottery and ritual materials do not indicate the presence of Teotihuacan populations, yet features of elite iconography seem to borrow Teotihuacan's style of power.

Maya Highlands

In contrast to the relative homogeneity of the Yucatán plain, the landscape of the highlands of Guatemala and Chiapas was a mosaic of many rich valleys, surrounded by chains of extinct and live volcanoes. The tropical latitude and high altitude combined to make agriculture productive and yet provide ready access to tropical resources like quetzal feathers, jaguar pelts, and cacao. Continuing traditions of resource exploitation established in the Formative period, the highlands supplied jade from the Motagua River Valley and obsidian from several important sources. With such rich commodities distributed across broken topography, it is no wonder that political development in this region was shaped by competition among Formative-period chiefdoms, and later, among Postclassic-period states. In spite of a lack of political unity, central-place communities in the highlands during the Early Classic show little concern with defensibility, but rather are located in proximity to good agricultural land and water sources for irrigation systems.

11.21, 11.22 *Kaminaljuyú. (Below) A lidded tripod vase, also a form characteristic of Teotihuacan, from Mound 2, Tomb II. (Opposite) Structure A-7 in Mound Group A was built in typical Teotihuacan style in this compound, in which Teotihuacanos established themselves at Kaminaljuyú.*

Kaminaljuyú The largest site in the Guatemala highlands remained Kaminaljuyú. Kaminaljuyú's Aurora phase, AD 200–400, marked the intrusion of Teotihuacan influence, and the subsequent Esperanza phase, AD 400–550, saw this influence spread throughout the site, with widespread occurrence of Teotihuacan-style ceramics and architecture featuring *talud-tablero* façades (Hatch 2001). It should be noted that Kaminaljuyú, a large (5 sq. km, 2 sq. miles) and important site, is in the same location as Guatemala City, that nation's capital, and its many mound groups have been leveled and built over as the modern city has expanded. The site was identified and its study began while Guatemala City was still of relatively modest size (Kidder et al. 1946; Shook *et al.* 1953; Sanders 1974), and part of Kaminaljuyú has been preserved as a park, but less than 10 percent of the site remains intact (Kelly 1982: 410).

Kaminaljuyú's history, as reflected in its cultural materials, shows that, over time, it was culturally diverse to a far greater extent than other Mesoamerican capitals, in the sense that successive periods brought distinct changes in material culture. At Kaminaljuyú in the Late and Terminal Formative periods, features common to the Pacific Coast are found, and may in turn have been dispersed north to the Maya. In the Classic period, features of mature Maya culture and mature Teotihuacan culture are also present. Teotihuacanos seem to have established themselves at Kaminaljuyú at Mounds A and B, perhaps to gain access to, or control the nearby El Chayal obsidian source. They built in *talud-tablero* style and used vessels characteristic of Teotihuacan, though many vessels of this style found at Kaminaljuyú were locally made [**11.21**, **11.22**].

Kaminaljuyú's new residents made their presence forcefully felt. The site's acropolis, covering about 8 hectares (over 3 acres), included temples, ball courts, and elite residences, and was built in Teotihuacan style. Reli-

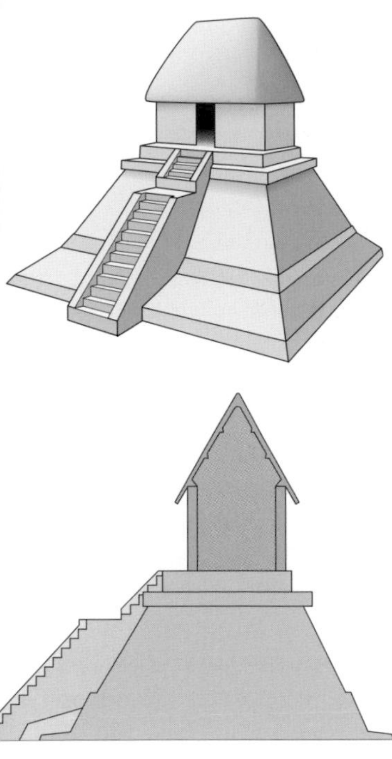

gious themes imported from the Central Highlands dominate, eclipsing the old Kaminaljuyú concentration upon veneration of individuals, with their elaborate, sacrifice-filled funerary monuments. Thus they brought "an end to the individualistic approach to the supernatural" (Borhegyi 1965: 28) and replaced it with "a focus on a high god-oriented religious system" (Sanders 1974: 107), with the Storm God/Tlaloc as its most important figure, accompanied by images of quetzal feathers, jaguars, serpents, butterflies, and owls.

The Long Shadow of Teotihuacan

Teotihuacan influence: it has been a recurring theme throughout this chapter, and the last. We have seen it at Matacapan, at Tikal, at Copán, and, of course, in regions around Teotihuacan itself, and to the north and west. It has manifested itself in various ways – symbols of prestige, architecture, household goods and figurines that indicate not just "influence" but lifeways borne by people raised in the culture. Kaminaljuyú was among the first sites to be identified as evidencing the presence of Teotihuacanos, and Teotihuacan features are far more pervasive there than at Tikal. Nonetheless, there seems to be a wide variety in the ways Teotihuacanos meddled in the cultural trajectories of other places.

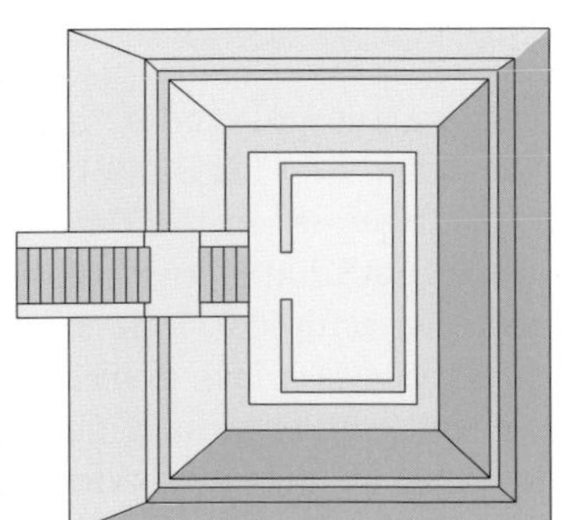

Matacapan appears to have been a colony of Teotihuacanos, a population of families who settled in the community. Tikal's (and possibly Copán's) Teotihuacanos may have been a cadre of elites who took advantage of a time of dynastic weakness to impose themselves as leaders over Tikal for a few generations, marrying into local elite lineages and in time becoming remembered through a system of motifs and symbols of their power. Kaminaljuyú seems to have experienced a takeover more profound than the incursions into the lowland Maya sites, yet probably not a full-scale colonization by many families traveling to, and settling in the Guatemala highlands. Instead, the colonists were probably members of the elite.

While it is clear that trends within Teotihuacan society encouraged or necessitated these excursions, it is not clear why. We recognize Teotihuacan presence from its material goods, and we know that Teotihuacan's elites valued jaguar pelts and quetzal feathers, probably also cotton and cacao, so the motivation of trade, or securing ready access to sources of exotic materials, is an obvious answer. Teotihuacan seems to have successfully exported important elements of its ideological system and also the technological means to secure local veneration of calendar changes: pecked crosses like those of Teotihuacan are found from the Northwestern Frontier to the Maya lowlands, and E-groups, the means of marking the important equinox and solstice transitions, may have been another Teotihuacan idea, passed south (Aveni, Dowd, and Vining 2003).

Meanwhile, back at Teotihuacan, political convulsions effaced the bloody rise of the Feathered Serpent cult, and, according to our most recent reckoning of dates, this occurred just before Spearthrower Owl's henchmen arrived

Caracol, Early Classic King List (11.23)		
	Ruler	**Events**
	Te' K'ab' Chaak r. 331–349 >	First ruler, known only from mentions in Late Classic texts
	K'ak' Ujol K'inich I r. c. 470	
AD 500	Yajaw Te' K'inich I r. 484–514 >	Caracol possibly attacked by Tikal and Calakmul
	K'an I r. 531–534	
	Yajaw Te' K'inich II r. 553–593 >	553: Caracol rites supervised by Tikal king, but by 556, conflict with Tikal, and Caracol moved from political sphere of Tikal to that of Calakmul

11.23 *Caracol's Early Classic kings.*

in Tikal. Were they Feathered Serpent partisans, sent away to work off their aggressions far from home? Were they part of the new administration, trained to control the warlike Feathered Serpent cult and now extending their cleanup operations throughout and beyond Teotihuacan's area of influence? At this point in our knowledge of Mesoamerican culture history, these and other speculations are equally unverifiable, but at least we have sufficient knowledge of trends ongoing in the Maya lowlands and Central Highlands to recognize the long reach of cultural interaction, and some of the possible motivating factors.

Looking Ahead: Mid-Classic Maya Upheavals

By the 6th century, Teotihuacan's emissaries, puppet governors, and colonists in the Maya lowlands had long been absorbed into local mythology and gene pools. Tikal, Teotihuacan's high-prestige ally in the Petén, was falling on hard times, its dynastic line broken, its tradition of memorializing the rhythmic passage of time and its rulers in sculpted stone was apparently broken, as well. This diminution of activity is a less dramatic "hiatus" than was once thought, but with the recent proliferation of decipherments we are able to see in greater detail the events that threw shadows over Tikal.

In the mid 500s, Calakmul began to challenge Tikal's authority, apparently subverting Tikal's relations with its clients such as Caracol [**11.23**], and, possibly, Naranjo. In 562, Tikal was the victim of a "star war" – so-called because these military campaigns were timed to patterns in the visible trajectory of the planet Venus. Calakmul was apparently the perpetrator, and Tikal's ruler Wak Chan K'awiil was killed. As we shall see in Chapter 12, Tikal would rise again, but Calakmul and other sites would share the power of the Maya realms.

PART 4

LATE CLASSIC, CLASSIC COLLAPSE, AND EPICLASSIC

Late Classic and Early Postclassic Periods (AD 600–1200)

	Late Classic		Epiclassic		Early Postclassic	
	600	700	800	900	1000	1100–1200
Northern Arid Zone						
NW Mexico, U.S. SW	Hohokam tradition				Hohokam, Mogollon traditions	
Baja California	Coyote tradition				Comondu tradition	
Casas Grandes region		Viejo period		Medio period *Casas Grandes*		
SE: Sierra Madre Oriental				San Lorenzo		
SW, Pacific Coast				Huitambo ceramic complex		
Northern Mesoamerica	Bajío region *Acambaro/Cerro el Chivo*					
Northwestern Frontier	Chalchihuites tradition *Alta Vista, La Quemada*			Culiacán phase *Aztatlán complex*		
West Mexico	Chametla phase, Teuchitlán II phase *Guachimontón, metal working*					
Michoacán				Chapala phase		
Morelos		*Xochicalco*				
Basin of Mexico	Metepec phase *Teotihuacán*	Coyotlatelco phase *Teotihuacan, Azcapotzalco*		Mazapan phase *Culhuacan, Xaltocan*		Aztec I, II
Tula region		Prado phase	Corral phase *Tula Chico*	Tollán phase *Tula*		
Toluca	*Teotenango*					
Puebla	Tecalac phase *Cantona, Cacaxtla, Cholula*			*Cholula*		Tlaxcala phase *Cholula*
Tlaxcala	Acopinalco complex		Tecalac phase	*Cuatro señorios*		Tlaxcala phase *Cuatro señorios*
Gulf Lowlands, north	*San Antonio Nolagar, Tamuín-Tantoc*			Las Flores phase		
Gulf Lowlands, north central	Tajín III *El Tajín, Yohualinchan*					
Gulf Lowlands, south central	Upper Remojadas II phase *Cerro de las Mesas*				Cempoala I phase	Cempoala II phase
Tehuacán Valley		Venta Salada phase, Early - *Cozcatlan, Teotitlan, Tehuacan Viejo*				
Mixteca Alta	Las Flores phase		Early Natividad phase *Tilantongo, Coixtlahuaca*			Late Natividad
Mixteca Baja	Ñuiñe phase					
Oaxaca and Tehuantepec	Monte Albán IIIb phase *Monte Albán, Jalieza*		Monte Albán IV phase *Jalieza, Mitla, Zaachila, Lambityeco*			
Gulf Lowlands, south	*Chontal-Putún*					
Chiapas Interior Plateau	Tsah phase, Paredon and Maravillas phase *Chiapa de Corzo, Tenam Rosario*			Ruiz *Chiapa de Corzo*	Suchiapa phase *Chiapa de Corzo*	
Chiapas Coast	Loros phase *Plumbate ware*		Metappa phase	Peistal phase	Remanso phase	
Guatemala Coast	Cotzumalhuapa phase *Cotzumalhuapa sites*					
Guatemala Highlands	Amatle phase *Kaminaljuyú*		Pamplona phase	Ayampuc phase		
Maya Lowlands, north	Motul ceramic phase *Río Bec, Chenes sites*		Cehpech phase *Cobá, Uxmal, Chichén Itzá, Kabah, Sayil, Labná*		Sotuta ceramic sphere	
Maya Lowlands, south	Tepeu phase *Tikal, Uaxactún, Palenque, Yaxchilán, Calakmul, Dos Pilas, Piedras Negras, Bonampak, Caracol, Copán*					
Southeastern Mesoamerica	*La Sierra, Chalchuapa, Cihuatán, Pipil migrations*					
Intermediate Area			*Rivas*	Chiriqui cultural phase		

12 THE LOWLAND MAYA: APOGEE AND COLLAPSE (AD 600–900)

DURING THE LATE CLASSIC PERIOD, events in the Maya lowlands dominated the culture history of eastern Mesoamerica [12.1]. Maya culture in the southern Maya lowlands represents one of the world's great early civilizations. Temple-pyramids formed dazzling aggregates of monumental architecture, and sculpture and inscriptions described royal families of proud descent and lofty ambitions. Paintings on vases and walls show charming scenes of palace life – and brutal torture to celebrate victory in war [12.5, 12.6, 12.7]. All this activity and display was underwritten by the work of a large population of farmer artisans, their *milpa*-houselots dispersed over the landscape surrounding the clusters of civic and ceremonial architecture. Populations in the immediate vicinity of some sites may have been as high as 70,000 or more, a demographic wealth of labor for elite-directed projects like construction of monumental buildings or the production of textiles on a large scale.

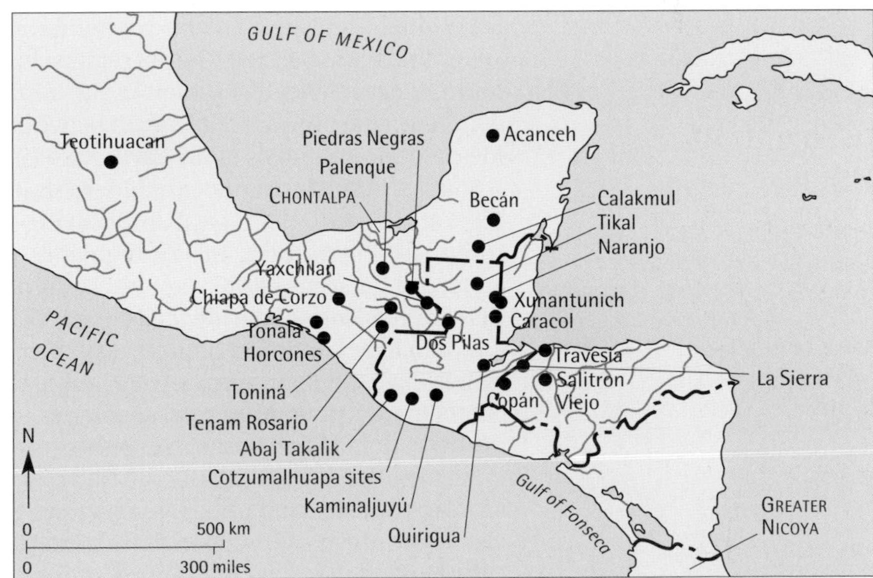

12.1 *Middle America, showing regions and sites mentioned in Chapter 12.*

As famous as the southern lowlands Maya have become for their art and architecture, they have gained even greater renown for the seeming suddenness of the fall of their civilization, a situation known as "the Maya Collapse." After centuries of reworking the landscape with hydrological projects and effigy mountains – pyramids and temples – dedicated to gods and dynasts, after countless skirmishes and sacrifices, marriage alliances and calendrical ceremonies, after raising a forest of king-effigies as stelae, Classic Maya rulers of the southern lowlands came to the end of their resources, and civilization there screeched to a halt in the 9th century. While the Maya collapse was first recognized in the sudden cessation of erection of dated monuments, this relatively ephemeral danger sign pointed to the larger disaster, that the productive basis for society withered and that the farmer-artisans lost their living.

This apparently rapid evaporation of a population of millions from the southern lowlands, with no ready explanation, fed the "myth of the mysterious Maya," a culture-historical conundrum that cast a glamorous glow over the ancient ruins. In fact, in recent years much harsh light of fact has been shed on the Maya collapse. As we shall see in this chapter, evidence from many sources indicates that the problems besetting the Maya were complex, overwhelming even, but the crux of their difficulties seems to have been an imbalance in the age-old relationship between humans and the maize-producing earth. With too many humans needing too much maize, it was the earth's fertility that collapsed, bringing the southern lowlands Maya down with it. As guardians of the relationship between people and the sacred powers of the natural world, Maya rulers had clearly failed at their task, and could no longer command the respect of their people.

However, Maya civilization continued to thrive outside the southern lowlands. In the northern Yucatán Peninsula a period of dazzling growth was beginning. The Late Classic saw the development of refined architectural styles in the Río Bec and Chenes regions just north of the Petén, and further north, great centers like Uxmal in the northwest and Cobá in the northeast dominated their regions. Chichén Itzá, which would become one of the major Mesoamerican capitals of the Early Postclassic period, was already thriving.

Southeastern Mesoamerica achieved its political and demographic peak in the Late Classic, with local lords vying for control over hinterlands of tribute-paying farmers. In the highlands of Guatemala and Chiapas, and along the adjacent coast, the culture historical picture is much less clear than for the Maya of the lowlands. Early Classic trends in settlement patterns and ethnicity continued, but a surge in long-distance migrations moved Nahua-speaking Pipil groups [16.3] through the Chiapas highland and coast on their way to Southeast Mesoamerica, where they established a strong presence in the Early Postclassic period.

So powerfully have the Classic Maya of the southern lowlands captured scholarly interest and public imagination that the available books and articles about them outnumber those pertaining to any other Mesoamerican culture of similar temporal and spatial extent. Given these resources, it is tempting to devote many pages to the exploits of kings, to their fabulous tombs and the stratigraphy of their acropolises. However, the goal of this book is to provide a balanced culture history, and to learn more about the Maya, the reader can consult the excellent Maya-oriented sources now available, many of which are cited herein.

In the first part of this chapter, we trace this southern lowland Maya golden age and its end, looking at the development and interaction of several major sites, and then at the collapse in greatest detail as it occurred at Copán and the Copán Valley. For Copán, we have not only spectacular remains from the center of elite activities, but also a comprehensive record of how commoners lived upon, used, and abandoned the surrounding valleys. However, other related culture areas have their own ongoing histories, and in the second half of this chapter we turn to the northern lowlands, Southeastern Mesoamerica, Guatemala and Chiapas highlands, and the southern Pacific Coast.

LATE CLASSIC MAYA CULTURE

Rising out of the jungle, Maya pyramids provide an image of ancient civilization almost as familiar, in modern popular culture, as do the pyramids of Egypt [**12.3, 12.4**]. Like Egyptian pyramids, many of those of the Maya represented funerary monuments of rulers. However, the highest Maya pyramids were topped by sanctified temples, and lower, broader pyramids provided the bases for multi-room palaces. In fact, a Maya capital typically consisted of a densely constructed regal-ritual center surrounded by hundreds, sometimes thousands of commoner houses dispersed among houselot gardens. The remains of the houses of the commoners, built on low platforms and of perishable materials, are now invisible to all but trained archaeological surveyors. It is the regal-ritual centers, the clusters of dramatic buildings around courtyards and plazas, that capture the modern imagination, and these are where the rulers and their families and retinue lived, worked, and worshipped (Sanders and Webster 1988).

Maya capitals may have been considerably more luxurious and civilized than many contemporaneous noble establishments in Europe. Life in the Maya regal ritual center was focused upon the ruler, and rulers seem to have identified themselves to an extraordinary degree with their centers. At each center, "[l]ike giant hermit crabs, successive rulers loaded themselves with solid accretions in the form of tombs, temples, ball courts, and carved monuments and with ... the associations with the great people and events of the past and, of course, with the gods and ancestors" (Webster 2001: 131–132).

While Maya rulers served their people as the putative intermediaries between heaven and earth, they had more immediate and pragmatic agendas, and the extent to which they connived and battled against each other was first indicated to archaeologists by massive earthworks thought to be defensive. More recently, this chronic belligerence has been confirmed

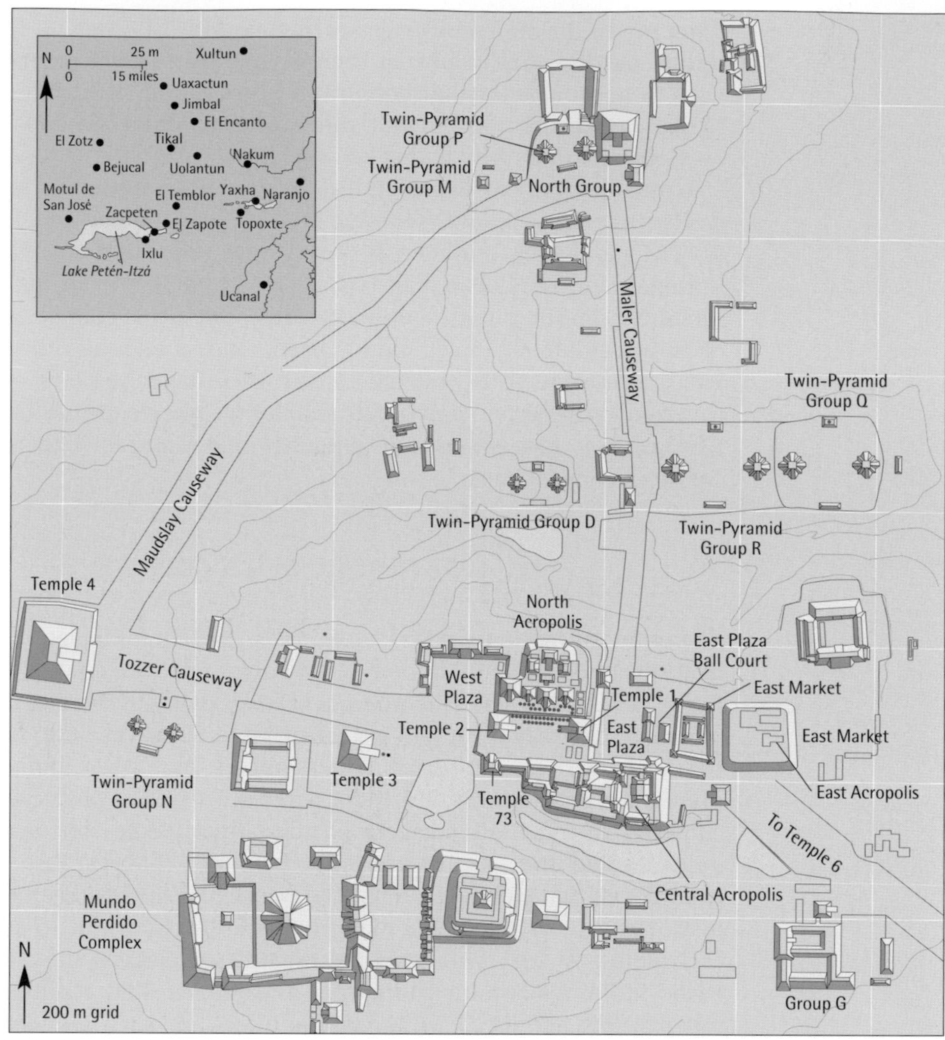

12.2 Tikal's Great Plaza was in front of the North Acropolis, and was framed by Temples I and II [12.3, 12.4]. This complex appears just below and right of center in the site plan, and shows how this main focus of the civic-ceremonial precinct was linked to outlying temples and palaces by a system of sacbes.

by epigraphers, who have translated many texts documenting the Maya preoccupation with political alliance and conflict.

By AD 900, these vain quarrels would be vanishing into the ever-encroaching past, but in AD 600, Maya multitudes followed the action with feelings of triumph or despair, depending on their loyalties and the outcome of the latest skirmish. Vanquished nobles would escape with their lives or be enslaved, perhaps sacrificed. Their kingdoms might be taken over by their rivals, with pretenders installed to rule and collect tributes in crops and labor from the farmer-artisan commoners, and taxes from marketplace and long-distance trade. Even peacetime dynastic successions could create an atmosphere of insecurity; in "hegemonic" political systems like these, with policy-making in the hands of the ruler, "the transition of authority from an established figure to an untried successor is a period of uncertainty, a junc-

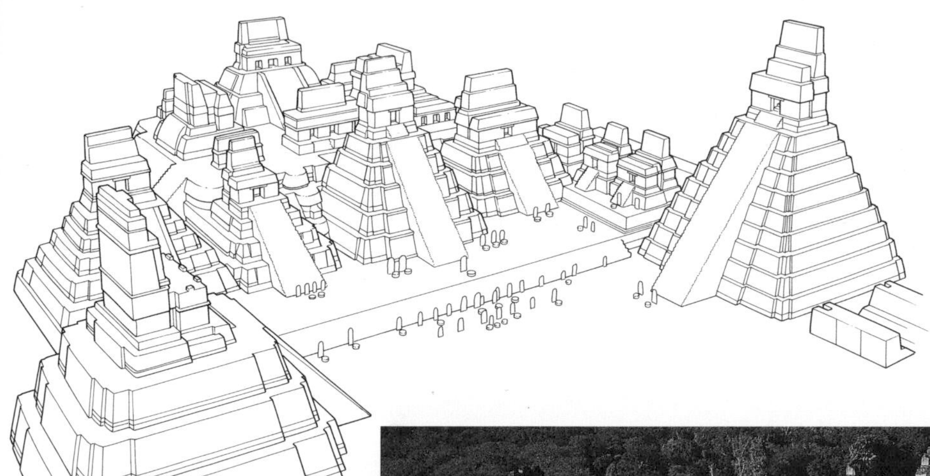

12.3, 12.4 *Tikal is perhaps the Classic Maya site best-known to the general public, and Temple I, at right in the photo (right, taken by Nicholas Hellmuth) and drawing (above), rises steeply to a height of about 52 m (170 ft), its summit and roofcomb topping the surrounding forest. Buildings of the North Acropolis dominate the background and frame the Central Plaza.*

ture at which old ties might be altered or repudiated entirely" (Martin and Grube 2000: 106). However, for the commoners, life would continue much as before the defeat or victory.

Eventually, the familiar patterns of royal wars and massive construction and commemorative monuments began to erode. One sign of the loss of power by the Maya rulers was evidence from several centers (Copán and Caracol, for example) that absolute rule was giving way to shared decision-making and revenues, between royals and non-royal nobles. Perhaps this was seen as an effective means to continue enforcement of tributary contributions in the face of declining crop yields and increasing ill health among people in all social statuses.

The "collapse," perceived at site after site between about 800 and 900 through a steep decline in the quality of monumental art and architecture, followed by cessation of such efforts to glorify rulers, was actually a dramatic manifestation of the loss of elite power. Our best evidence reveals that regions were not immediately abandoned, that commoners maintained substantial population for several generations. However, while the Law of Biotic Potential enables humans and other organisms to bounce back from demographic disasters relatively rapidly, given the availability of necessary resources, this rule does not apply to rebuilding the soil from which crops must grow. The earth itself had been starved, and the long centuries required for recovery of the topsoil and its fertility represented a calendric cycle far too long to help the dwindling Maya of the southern lowlands. With each generation, the villages grew smaller, and finally, a few hundred

12.5–12.7 *Bonampak was a relatively small site, subject to Piedras Negras and then to Yaxchilan, but its murals of Maya elite life are a unique treasure (Miller 1986). The murals are located in Structure 1, at right in the drawing (below) which shows the Bonampak acropolis. (Above) The scene from Room Two; at top the victorious ruler and other nobles, including several ladies of the court, at right. Lying and sitting on the stairs, in the painting, are naked defeated warriors – one pleads with the king, while the fellow below him is either unconscious or dead. To his left, prisoners benumbed by the pain of torture watch blood drip from their fingers – presumably their fingernails have been torn off. (Opposite) The lower scene shows musicians, while above them, lords in regalia form a procession.*

years after the elite collapse, the survivors drifted away to the very few remaining substantial communities, or into the forest, becoming hunter-foragers like their ancient ancestors.

Courtly Life at the Height of the Late Classic

The Maya recorded their history as a series of ceremonies, often celebrating victory in warfare and sacrifice of enemies, particularly captured lords. This emphasis upon conflicts stemmed from their importance as pivotal events – they often signaled a change in fortune for the capitals involved. Even if losing a battle did not cost a ruler his life, it might mean forfeiting tributes or profits from control of trade routes – the loss of income sources that had supported the rich life of the court and the expert sculptors, architects, plaster masons, painters, scribes, weavers, and embroiderers, and other artisans who depended upon times of peace and prosperity and whose efforts made Maya regal-ritual centers sophisticated, lively, and beautiful. Conversely, winners could entirely renovate their sites, and commission impressive monuments.

Looking beyond the ups and downs intrinsic to the fiercely competitive world of the Late Classic Maya, we find many parallels with courtly life in the ancient agrarian states of the Old World. Daily life in the center would have found the ruler engaged in the tasks of administering his kingdom while carrying out a continuous series of ceremonial obligations. The round of activities would be determined in large part by the seasons and by the stars, because the agrarian cycle would have its demands on the availability of labor for other purposes (like enlarging buildings, or getting started on that fancy new tomb) and would also bring harvest time, when the king's accountants would need to assess the yield. With the changing cycle of the planet Venus came threats of war and the necessity for local leaders to mobilize the cadres of farmer-soldiers. Throughout the year, craft production would continue and goods would be collected and marketed. Trading and diplomatic parties would be sent off, and would arrive from afar, and be entertained at feasts. Ritual events – calendar turnings, royal weddings and births, ball games, for example – might also be festivals [**12.10**], but many ceremonies would require the royals to pierce themselves painfully in order to give blood to the gods in return for having given life and maize to those on earth.

The people who were in a Maya regal-ritual center on a typical day ranged from the king and his family to the lowliest servants. There was, of course, a strong distinction between members of the court, the royal family and its close noble associates, and the commoners and slaves who waited on the royals and nobles. Such distinctions represented social strata, and this stratification, a characteristic of state-level societies, is an important indicator of the degree of societal complexity. Let us consider some of the key players among the nobles and affluent commoners who frequented a Maya regal-ritual center.

12.8, 12.9 *(Opposite) Dental remodeling covers a spectrum of shapes, as seen at right. On the left, an individual with tabular cranial remodeling, a shape achieved by binding this person's head between boards in infancy.*

COSMETIC ALTERATIONS

IDEAS OF BEAUTY are culture-bound. A generation ago, scholars described "dental mutilation" and "cranial deformation" among the ancient peoples of Mesoamerica (Romero 1970), whereas now we refer to "cosmetic alterations" of the face and body, because so many people today choose procedures like these – body piercing, tattooing – and even tooth adornment in order to enhance their personal style.

Body piercing was common in Mesoamerica, the simplest and most ubiquitous example probably being piercing the earlobes for ear spools, some quite large. The lower lip, about an inch below the mouth, was also commonly pierced for a piece of jewelry called a labret, and other ornaments were suspended from holes in the nose. We assume that tattooing was practiced, and temporary tattoos may have been stamped onto the skin using ceramic seals that could impress designs [**5.23**]. Body piercing and tattoos affect soft tissue, and except for depictions of these practices in graphic and plastic art forms, or descriptions in ethnohistoric sources, we have no direct, corporeal evidence.

There is abundant evidence for dental and cranial remodeling in ancient Mesoamerica, dating at least as far back as the Early Formative, and practiced through the time of the Spanish intrusion. Dental remodeling [**12.9**] consisted of reshaping the bottom of the tooth, filing patterns into the surface of the tooth, and/or embedding precious stones such as jadeite, pyrite, or turquoise into holes bored into the tooth. This practice seems to have reached its peak of popularity among the Maya of the Late Classic, and seems to have been done when the individual was a young adult. Skeletal evidence shows that it probably caused health problems such as dental abcesses.

Remodeling of the cranium was far more common. This procedure must be initiated when the individual is an infant, and the cranial bones are still soft. Bound between padded boards for a tabular effect, or by a band tightly wound around the head, for an annular effect, the top of the skull slowly – and permanently – assumes an elongated shape [**12.8**]. Like dental remodeling, cranial shaping is very ancient, and was practiced throughout Mesoamerica. Some scholars believe that it was a perquisite of elites, but skeletons from modest graves exhibit this, as well.

Among the Maya, crossed eyes were regarded as beautiful. This cosmetic alteration was deliberately induced by headgear that dangled an object in front of and between the wearer's eyes. Maya art offers good insights into culture-bound notions of beauty – the elongated head that emphasized a strong, prominent nose [**12.14**], close-set eyes with a convergent focus, a dazzling smile glinting color and unusual shape – in today's cultural climate of self expression through body art, the Maya would be a rich source of inspiration.

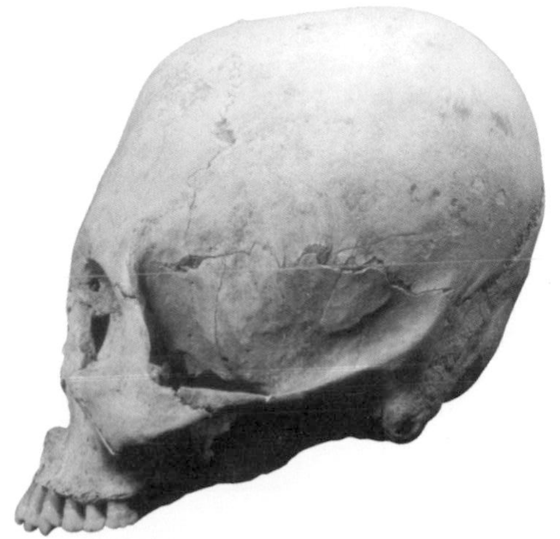

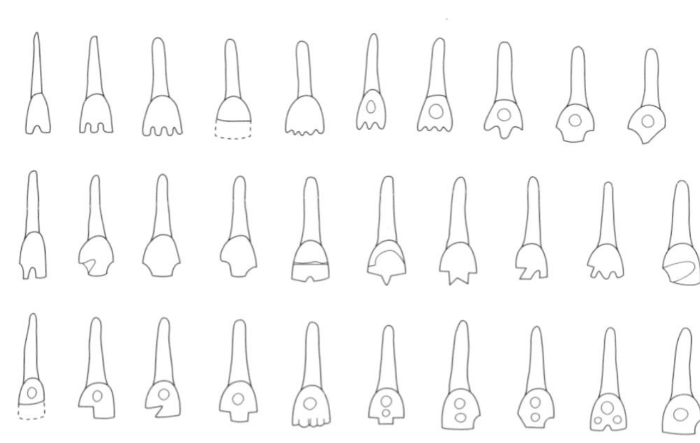

Maya Kings Kings were at the center of courts, in the sociological sense that courts were groups of people involved in maintaining the administrative and ritual functions of the state and the ruling family [**12.12**]. The court consisted of a ruler and his (or very occasionally, her) extended family, retainers such as non-royal nobles, and servants (Inomata and Houston 2001). Directed by the ruler, members of the court functioned as bureaucrats, directing and putting into effect public policy (setting taxation rates and collecting taxes, going to war, glorifying victories with carved monuments, and so forth). Within the court there would be factions competing amongst themselves for the attention and favors of the ruler, or perhaps, competing with the ruler, as happened in Tikal with the fissioning episode that resulted in the establishment of Dos Pilas. In such cases, the ruler's personality and good judgment must maintain the loyalty of all factions, or at least spearhead the survival of the loyal faction (Brumfiel 1986).

Royal Women Royal women were politically and economically important. Marriages between dynasties at different capitals secured alliances, and in some cases legitimated or energized a lineage fallen on hard times, as occurred with the arrival of "the Princess of Palenque" at Copán. We lack irrefutable evidence that these nobles were polygynous, having more than one wife; we assume so, based on the prevalence throughout Mesoamerica of this practice. By the Late Classic, royal wives were noted with greater frequency in texts, probably as a result of the proliferation of members of royal

12.10 *At Copán, a ball game brought crowds to the steps of the surrounding temple-pyramids. This scene, set in about* AD *800, shows the ruler Yax Pasaj and his family, watching from atop Temple 11. Nearby Temple 26 is thronged as well, with onlookers positioned on the terraces and on the Hieroglyphic Stairway, whose sculpted risers held the longest Maya text, with about 2,000 glyphs. This reconstruction painting shows the kinds of people one might find in a royal court, but consider, as well, all the secondary participants in this scene – the porters, cooks, cleaners, water-carriers and other servants who prepared for the festival and will clean up after the nobles when the celebration is over.*

and noble families, because of the many offspring produced by polygyny (Houston and Stuart 2001).

Polygyny was generally restricted to elite men because it was expensive to support a large household of women and children. However, it was also lucrative. Women produced not only the heirs and their siblings, who would be the progenitors of the succeeding generation, as well as serving as bureaucrats and elite artisans, but women of the palace were a vital work force in textile production. Textiles – from spinning thread to decorating the finished fabrics, and fashioning them into clothing and household wares – were the work of women of all statuses, but palace women produced items that had prestige and ideological value far beyond the labor and materials involved. Like decorated ceramic vessels, decorated textiles were distributed as gifts between nobles, and served to demonstrate exchange relations among powerful families. Decorated textiles, as clothing, were emblems of power and often used designs and materials that would have been restricted to elite use, by sumptuary laws.

12.11 *This large Late Classic plate shows Hunahpu, the father of the Hero Twins, as a scribe. In his left hand he supports a screenfold book covered in jaguar skin, and in his right, inscribes the book with a brush. The association of the scribal role with deities is a strong one among the Maya; Itsamná (God D) himself, "the supreme deity of the Maya pantheon" (Coe and Kerr 1998: 102) was the inventor of writing and the first scribe, and other deities also served as patrons of scribes and painters.*

Titled Officials, Wealthy Land-Owners, and Elite Artisans These people were also members of the court. Consider the grandeur of Maya architecture and monuments, elaborate jewels and ceramics preserved in burials, and the artistic representations of rich fabrics, screenfold books, feather banners and wooden goods – things that would not be preserved in the archaeological record. Not only did the Maya have a lot of fancy stuff, but all these buildings and elite gear represent the efforts of many people. Traders, diplomats, astronomers, designers, specialists in executing designs in different raw materials, calligrapher scribes, sculptors, painters, inventory overseers, work crew foremen – these people would have been in consultation with the ruler and nobles, and in many cases may have been nobles themselves.

12.12 *This rollout photo of a chocolate pot shows a Maya ruler (ajaw) seated on a bench-like throne, receiving another lord, who is seated on a litter (Reents-Budet 1994). Touches of jaguar pelt adorn the litter and cushion the throne, and advertise the high status of these lords, as do their quetzal feather headdresses. The palace setting is suggested by the throne, whose Mayan name meant not only "seat" but also the person in power, and the burden of authority that rulership conveyed (Noble 1998).*

12.13 *(Opposite) Late Classic Maya centers in the southern lowlands were named in texts by "emblem glyphs" that were titles of rulership of various kingdoms (Berlin 1958). In the map, the centers are identified by their modern names, while along the sides are arrayed emblem glyphs grouped according to the two main sets of allies – Tikal's and Calakmul's – and the third group, of centers whose loyalties fluctuated. Emblem glyphs seem to have been the property of legitimate dynasties; note how that of Dos Pilas, founded by Tikal dissidents, is the same as that of Tikal itself.*

After all, with or without polygyny, each generation of children of the ruler usually contains only one heir. The future of the girls was destined by biology as well as custom; royal daughters would become honored wives, running their own noble households in other Maya centers, and weaving and decorating their own palace textiles. For the king's sons who did not inherit the rulership there were prestigious positions of artisanship and administration of the realm. To become a skilled scribe or jeweler demanded years of training as well as some talent, so we can assume that in addition to other occupations, there were teachers, and that knowledge was systematized.

Many nobles, and members of the royal family, would have gotten a basic living from surpluses of fields cultivated by peasants, but considered the property of the elite. We have no idea of the extent to which this would have been considered ownership of land in the modern sense; property-holding was probably lineage-based, and our best evidence for elite differential access to the best land is the proximity of their compounds to it. In Copán, for example, the noble compounds, and the Acropolis itself, the residential compound of the ruling family, all adjoin the richest alluvial plain of the Copán Valley. Today this land is devoted to tobacco as a cash crop rather than to subsistence crops like maize. In the past, a similar pattern may have prevailed, with alluvial land planted intensively in cacao mostly destined for trade, leaving maize production to the less fertile sloping piedmont areas of the valley, where the peasant farmers actually lived.

These farming families also produced the basic utilitarian goods needed by everyone: grinding stones, textiles for everyday use, utility ware pottery. In seasons when crops and harvests did not require their attention, their labor would be drafted to work on construction and upkeep at the regal-ritual centers – building temple-pyramids and palaces, excavating vast reservoirs, maintaining canals and roads, doing housework and yardwork for elite households – and preparing for and participating in military raids and campaigns.

This brief overview has merely outlined courtly life, and the process of Maya cultural development in the southern lowlands, where hieroglyphic writing, and the recent revolution in its decipherment, have given us detailed histories of many regal-ritual centers. For the rest of the Maya lowlands and other regions east of the Isthmus, the paucity of texts has rendered culture history less exact. Yet for all regions, archaeological research – surveys, excavations, laboratory analyses – provides so much information that only a few key processes, and a few of the many important sites can be summarized in the space available here.

MAYA OF THE SOUTHERN LOWLANDS

The Late Classic brought new dimensions to diplomatic connections established in the Early Classic period. By the Late Classic, the political identities of the larger centers in the southern lowlands were well established [12.13]. The most essential rivalry was between the two largest sites, Tikal and

TIKAL AND ITS ALLIES
or Calakmul's enemies

Tikal

Palenque

Copán

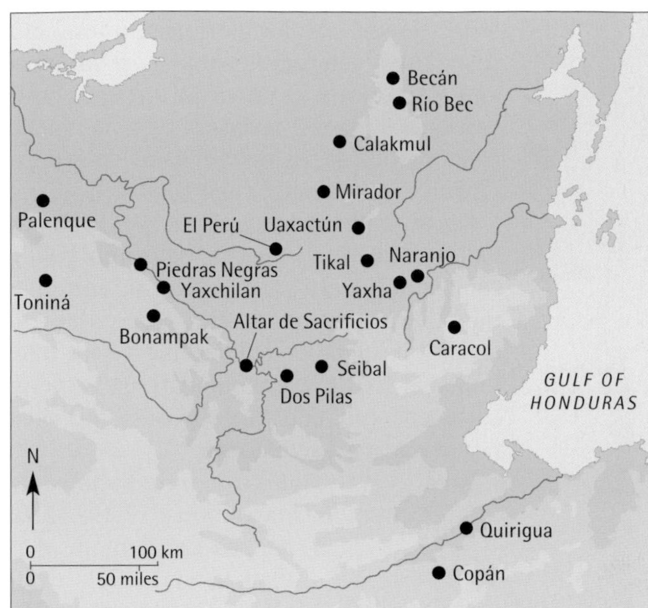

SITUATIONAL
ALLIES OR ENEMIES

Toniná

Piedras Negras

Naranjo

CALAKMUL AND ITS ALLIES
or Tikal's enemies

Calakmul

Caracol

Dos Pilas

El Perú

Yaxchilan

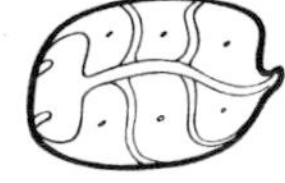
Quirigua

Calakmul. Upriver from Palenque [**12.20**], along the Usumacinta, Piedras Negras and Yaxchilan [**12.21**] seem to have fought each other throughout the Late Classic, with no clear pattern of permanent alliance to the larger powers. Calakmul had a loyal ally in Dos Pilas [**12.22**] and Caracol [**12.36**], itself in conflict with Naranjo, which was at times a vassal of Calakmul [**12.31**], showing that patterns of alliance could be complicated. Some of the smaller centers, such as Naranjo's client state, Xunantunich, rose and fell in the course of the Late Classic (LeCount *et al.* 2002). Copán [**12.26**] and Quirigua, somewhat removed from the southern Maya lowlands heartland, had their own ongoing rivalry; Copán seems to have cultivated long-term relations with Tikal [**12.30**] and Palenque, while Quirigua looked to Calakmul for help against Copán.

AD 600–700

As we left the story, in the last chapter, Tikal had fallen upon difficult times, and as the 7th century opened, Calakmul successfully attacked the major sites of Tikal and Palenque. The century ended with the decline of Calakmul itself.

Palenque and Pakal the Great

In 612 began the rule of Muwaan Mat – the same name as an ancestral deity of the site. Muwaan Mat's identity remains enigmatic, but may have been the mother of, and regent for, Palenque's most famous king, K'inich Janaab' Pakal I ("Pacal" or "Great Sun Shield"), who assumed power in 615 at age 12, and ruled until 683. Pakal is one of the best-known Mesoamerican

kings, famed for his mortuary monument [**12.16**]. Yet his reign was not easy. His kinship to Palenque's established dynasty was, at best, tenuous, and his realm was mired in foreign conflict. Yet Palenque's "greatest artworks and longest texts emerged as reactions to the defeat and breakdown of its royal line, as new dynasts strove to legitimize and consolidate their power" (Martin and Grube 2000: 155).

For example, the palace [**12.17, 12.18**] was built on an Early Classic foundation, a platform measuring roughly 58 by 79 m (190 by 259 ft). Pakal's rooms and courtyards created an administrative residence that dominated the central part of the site. The palace had facilities for ceremonies and receptions, plus amenities like sweat baths and latrines. The design also included architectural innovations to increase the span encompassed by the corbeled vault, and also to reduce the weight displaced to the walls, by the use of mansard-style roofs.

Pakal is even more strongly associated with his own funerary monument, the Temple of the Inscriptions [**12.14–12.16**]. The design of the sarcophagus and its cover made it possible to ready the tomb, and then, after Pakal's death, inter the body and slide the cover over it. Then, the coffin was connected to the temple atop the pyramid by a "psychoduct" or "spirit tube" – a pipe built into the stairway, by which Pakal's descendants could contact his spirit. The tomb was plastered shut, and in the anteroom, five captives were sacrificed to be Pakal's companions on his trip to the otherworld. These rites of passage completed, the mourners

12.14–12.16 (Opposite) Palenque's Temple of the Inscriptions (opposite, below right) was named for its three panels inscribed with 617 glyphs, the second-longest Maya text (the longest is Copán's Hieroglyphic Staircase). The panels are located within the temple, and were apparently commissioned by Kan B'alam II, Pakal's son. But the structure's greatest treasure lay deep within its pyramid: the sarcophagus of Pakal (portrait head, opposite, above left) containing the king's body, reddened with cinnabar and adorned with a treasure of jade jewelry. (Opposite, below left) Pakal's sarcophagus cover.

12.17 *(Above right) Palenque, East Court of the palace (at lower left in 12.18). Houses B (center) and C (at right) date to Pakal's reign.*

would ascend the stairs and emerge in the Temple of the Inscriptions, performing more rituals in sight of the assembled Palenqueans in the plaza below. Such rites, private and public, would assure a safe transition through the dangerous liminal state of passage from the world of the living to the realm of the dead, for Pakal's spirit and Palenque's political stability. However, Pakal's 7th-century reign was Palenque's time of greatness. The dynasty struggled along until around 800, but soon thereafter, Palenque was abandoned (Mathews and Schele 2001).

12.18 *(Right) Palenque, the central part of the site, as looking south and showing the palace, at center, and the Temple of the Inscriptions (Pakal's tomb) to its right. Palenque's palace is unusual for its mansard roofs and high tower. The photos provide a sense of the palace's complex interior. There were many additions from the time it was established in the Early Classic, on a platform 3 m (10 ft) high, until its abandonment at the end of the Classic period. The central building, E, just to the left of the tower, was the earliest of the many rooms atop the platform (Greene 1985: II: 7). Pakal made House E his throne room, and added C, B, and A to form the East Court. The tower was probably added in the late 8th century.*

12.19 *Palenque is built into a hillslope that extends down, toward the north, giving the site a spectacular view of the plain of the southern Gulf lowlands. The palace dominates the center of the site, with temples crowding up the slope to the south, behind it.*

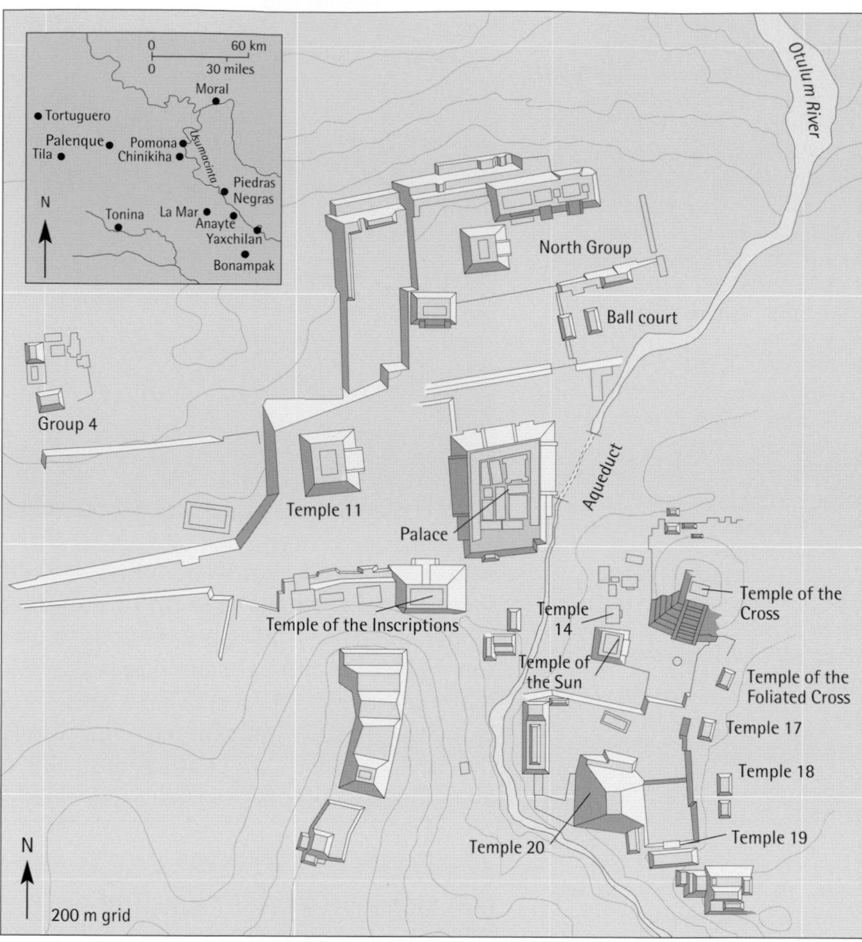

12.20 *Palenque's Late Classic rulers.*

Palenque, Late Classic King List (12.20)

	Ruler	Event
AD 600	Aj Ne' Ohl Mat r. 605–612	Palenque sacked by Calakmul in 611
	Muwaan Mat/Lady Sak K'uk' ("Lady Beastie") ?r. 612–615, d. 640	Muwaan Mat: mythical dynastic placeholder? Or Pakal's mother, Lady Sak K'uk', acting as regent
	Pakal the Great b. 603, r. 615–683	Palace and Temple of the Inscriptions built. Conflicts with Calakmul
AD 700	Kan B'alam II b. 635, r. 684–702	Group of the Cross dedicated in 690. Conflicts with Toniná
	K'an Joy Chitam II b. 644, r. 702–711	K'an Joy Chitam captured by Toniná in 711
	Ahkal Mo' Naab' III b. 678, r. 721–736	Palenque victorious vs. Piedras Negras
	Janaab' Pakal II r. > 742 >	740s: Palenque defeated by Toniná; Palenque princess sent to Copán, became mother to Yax Pasaj
	K'uk' B'alam II r. 764–783 >	
	Janaab' Pakal III r. 799–?	Janaab' Pakal III: Palenque's last ruler

All king lists based on Martin and Grube 2000. Alternative forms of names are found in the index, not in these lists.

Yaxchilan, Late Classic King List (12.21)

	Ruler	Event
AD 600	Bird Jaguar III r. 629–669 >	15th in dynasty, son of Knot Skull; scant history = possible submission to Piedras Negras, Palenque or Toniná
	Itzamnaaj B'alam II r. 681–742	Site expansion, sculpture progams
AD 700	742–752	Interregnum between reigns of Itzamnaaj B'alam II and Bird Jaguar IV
	Yopaat B'alam II ("Penis Jaguar") r. > 749 >	Evidence of this reign only from a Piedras Negras text
	Bird Jaguar IV b. 709, r. 752–768	Construction programs, aggression vs. other centers
	Itzamnaaj B'alam III b. 752? r. 769–800 >	Controlled Bonampak
AD 800	Tatb'u Skull III r. > 808 >	Last ruler of Yaxchilan; conflict with Piedras Negras

12.21 *Yaxchilan's Late Classic kings.*

Yaxchilan

It was Yaxchilan's growing strength that in part caused the decline of Palenque and Piedras Negras. In 681, just before the death of Palenque's Pakal, Yaxchilan's Itzamnaaj B'alam II ("Shield Jaguar the Great") began a 60-year reign, a period of increasing prosperity, probably based upon military victories which restored the center's control over trade along this stretch of the Usumacinta River. He had at least three wives, and his principal wife, Lady K'ab'al Xook ("Lady Xoc" [shark]) was very influential; Itzamnaaj B'alam II dedicated Temple 23, one of Yaxchilan's most important buildings, to her, and imported master sculptors to adorn it with panels depicting her performing various duties typical of a Maya royal consort [**12.23, 12.24**].

Calakmul in its Prime, Tikal Split in Two

It may have benefited Yaxchilan that its ally, Calakmul, was at the peak of its powers in the 7th century. Calakmul was probably the largest Classic Maya site, covering 30 sq. km (11 sq. miles), and had more inscribed monuments than any other Maya site, but unfortunately most were carved of poor quality limestone, which has eroded to indecipherability. Calakmul's rulers would have been disappointed, because they aggressively conquered, or at least seriously disrupted other polities – deeds that are the stuff of impressive commemorative texts.

Tikal's problems with maintaining dynastic succession around AD 600 were worsened by attacks from Calakmul. By AD 650, there were two kings claiming to be the true head of the lineage and rightful holder of the emblem glyph: one at Tikal, and the other, backed by Calakmul, attacked and established hegemony over Dos Pilas, over 100 km (over 60 miles) south of Tikal. Dos Pilas was occupied for not much over a century, its population never exceeding 5,000. Despite its small size and shallow history, Dos Pilas successfully harassed Tikal, no doubt coordinating attacks with its huge ally, Calakmul, and in fact fighting on after Calakmul began to decline, just before AD 700.

Dos Pilas, Late Classic King List (12.22)		
	Ruler	**Event**
	B'alaj Chan K'awiil *c.* 648–692 >	Founder, possibly son of Tikal's K'inich Muwaan Jol II; client of Calakmul; ongoing, mostly successful conflicts vs. Tikal
	Itzamnaaj B'alam *c.* 697	
AD 700	Itzamnaaj K'awiil b. 673, r. 698–726	Successful militarist vs. Tikal, built El Duende complex
	Ruler 3 r. 727–741	735: defeat of Seibal; Aguateca enlarged as a fortifiable 2nd capital
	K'awiil Chan K'inich 741–761 >	Successful militarist, but reign ended with his disappearance and the near abandonment of Dos Pilas

12.22 *Dos Pilas's Late Classic kings.*

AD 700–800

Tikal was revitalized by victory over Calakmul in 695, and Dos Pilas continued, for decades, to subjugate its Petexbatún region hinterland (Demarest *et al.* 1997). If only hinterlands had remained properly subdued, then Maya history would not have been so riven by conflict, but in AD 761, Dos Pilas's vassal, Tamarandito, drove out the king of Dos Pilas and prompted the construction of a set of defensive walls there before the nobles fled to take over an even smaller, more defensible capital at Aguateca [**12.25**].

At Yaxchilan, Itzamnaaj B'alam II's son, Bird Jaguar IV, expanded buildings, erected monuments, and harassed other centers. Bird Jaguar left

12.23, 12.24 *From Yaxchilan's Temple 23, Lintel 25 (below left) commemorates the accession of Itzamnaaj B'alam II in 681. It shows his wife Lady Xook in a trance, having conjured up a vision serpent from whose mouth appears the spirit of the 4th-century founder of the Yaxchilan dynasty. The vision serpent has some central Mexican characteristics – those visual references, plus the dynastic founder, are strong elements in legitimizing the rule of the new king. Lintel 24 (right) shows Lady Xook, kneeling, performing autosacrifice by pulling a thorn-spiked rope through her tongue, while her husband holds a torch. They are celebrating the birth of his son.*

12.25 The Maya collapse began early at smaller, more peripheral centers. These reconstruction drawings show how Dos Pilas went from a flourishing regal-ritual center to a fortified ruin in AD 761 (Demarest 1993: 103). On the left in the lower picture, the two stockades cut through the ravaged palace, while in the center, farmers set up their thatched houses in the central plaza after the nobles had decamped to found a smaller, more defensible capital at Aguateca. Occupation there lasted 50 years, and then the rival dynasty from Tikal disappeared.

Yaxchilan physically transformed, and cast himself as a hero in various dramatic sculptures. Like his father, he married – and immortalized in sculpture – several women, including at least one from a center that was Yaxchilan's enemy, using marriage as a powerful political tool to cement an alliance. Bird Jaguar's reign marked the last stretch of Yaxchilan's time of greatest prosperity. Bird Jaguar's son and grandson ruled into the early 9th century, and continued programs of building and inscribing, but artistic quality declined precipitously, an aesthetic barometer of far greater societal problems. The last inscribed date, 808, marked the capture of Ruler 7 of Piedras Negras. Soon thereafter, Yaxchilan was abandoned (García Moll 1996).

Tikal's ally, Palenque, was troubled by its rival Toniná – Palenque began the 7th century with a defeat by Calakmul, but with the accession of Pakal, enjoyed a period of growth that extended into the early 700s, when Toniná repeatedly defeated it. Palenque had some consolation in drubbing Piedras Negras, and sending a Palenque princess to marry into Copán's dynasty and give birth to Yax Pasaj, who would oversee Copán's late-8th-century greatness, and then feel Maya culture begin to collapse beneath his feet.

But let us go back to Copán long before Yax Pasaj's birth, to AD 700, early in the reign of Waxaklajuun Ub'aah K'awiil ("18 Rabbit"), who oversaw a period of brilliant artistic achievement. Today's visitors to Copán are impressed by the many stelae, carved in the round in a sinuous, sophisticated

Copán, Late Classic King List (12.26)

	Ruler	Event
AD 600	Butz' Chan 578–628	Population expansion throughout Copán region
	Smoke Imix b. *c.* 612, r. 628–695	Copán possibly controlled Quirigua
	Waxaklajuun Ub'aah K'awiil 695–738 ("18 Rabbit")	Copán at its cultural height, but this king was beheaded at Quirigua
AD 700	K'ak' Joplaj Chan K'awiil 738–749	Copán in decline, Quirigua may have taken over Motagua trade routes
	K'ak' Yipyaj Chan K'awiil 749–761 >	Expansion of the Hieroglyphic Stairway
AD 800	Yax Pasaj Chan Yopaat 763–810 >	Buildings, monuments emphasize Teotihuacan imagery and dynastic founder, as well as nobles with whom the ruler shared power; signs of decline abound
	Ukit Took' 822	

12.26 *Copán's Late Classic kings.*

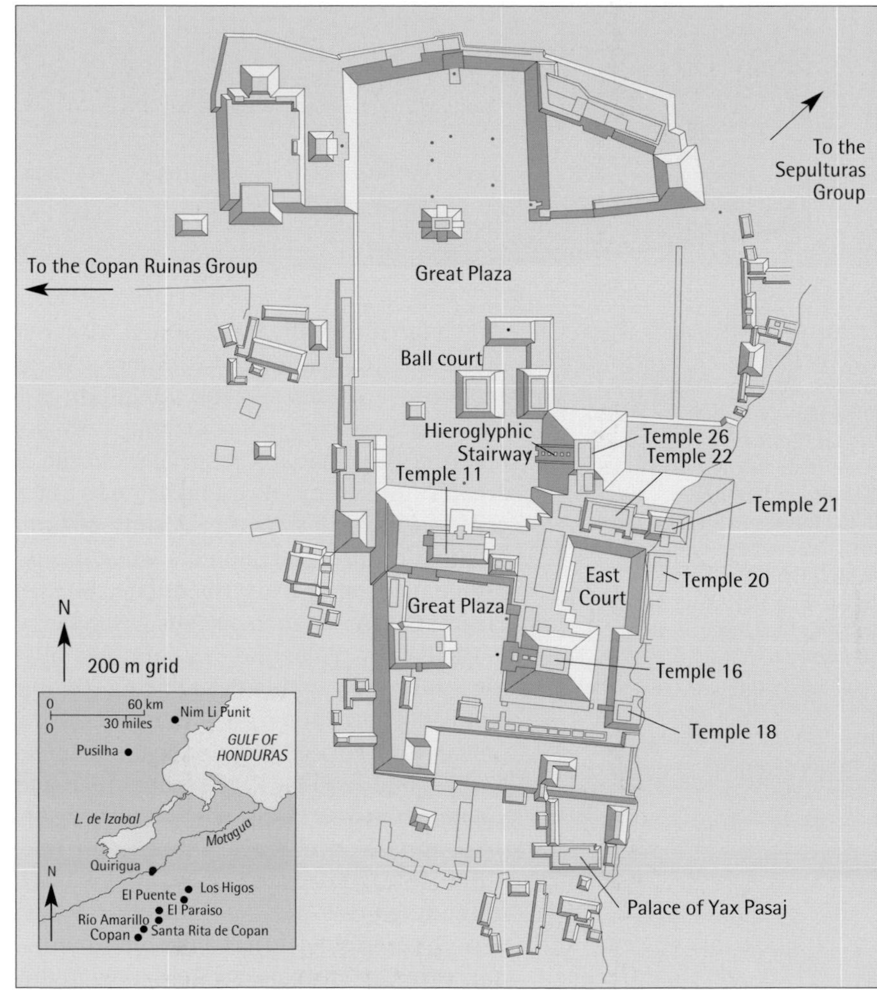

12.27, 12.28 *(Right; opposite above) Copán grew by accretion over many centuries, until, in its mature form, it consisted of a huge level "Great Plaza" overlooked by a towering Acropolis. Within the Acropolis, courtyards are rimmed by temples and palaces. The north end of the Acropolis looks down upon the ball court, shown opposite above (and also in* **12.10** *and* **14.19***).*

12.29 *(Opposite) Copán's Stela A is one of seven portrait stelae of Waxaklajuun Ub'aah K'awiil ("18 Rabbit"), who ruled between* AD *695 and 738. Erected in 731, this one declares Copán to be one of four great Maya capitals, the others being Tikal, Palenque, and Calakmul. These views were made by Frederick Catherwood, the artist who traveled with the writer John Lloyd Stephens to the Maya region in 1839 and 1840. Their works, still in print today, were largely responsible for first bringing the Maya to general public knowledge.*

style – many are portraits of 18 Rabbit [**12.29**]. In addition to erecting these monuments to himself, he continued the process of shaping Copán's Acropolis, giving the ball court its final form and beginning to install the dynastic history that was the Hieroglyphic Stairway. 18 Rabbit also continued the practice of exacting fealty from nearby Quirigua, but in AD 738, Quirigua shook off this burden by capturing and beheading 18 Rabbit. This apparently left Quirigua in control of the trade in obsidian and jade and other goods that flowed along the Motagua Valley. In the sincerest form of flattery, Quirigua rebuilt itself as a smaller version of Copán.

By the late 700s, a vigorous ruler, K'ak' Yipyaj Chan K'awiil ("Smoke Squirrel") was rebuilding Copán's pyramids and monuments, including the Hieroglyphic Stairway (Fash 1991). In an effort to lend prestige and credibility to this renaissance, Teotihuacan symbolism was incorporated into Copán's sculpture, including an inscription that juxtaposed Maya glyphs with a "translation" into Mexicanized glyphs as well. The Teotihuacan-looking script that is part of the message is, at present, undecipherable, and may in fact be meaningless gibberish in terms of its actual sense. However, such nonsense messages indicate an effort to appropriate the prestige of the symbols. Numerous texts on Maya vases and other sources include Maya glyphs that are nonsensical, as if the "scribe" had seen Maya writing and could not read it, but knew that the vase would have more prestige with a written message. Modern Western tourists in the Third World are sometimes startled to see people wearing tee-shirts saying, for example, "sexy Coca-Cola baby" – a message that has no real meaning, but reflects the wearers' desire to appropriate the powerful icons of Western culture as conveyed by our modern dominating texts, advertising, pop music and films.

Tikal, Late Classic Partial King List (12.30)

	Ruler	Event
AD 600	Animal Skull *c.* > 593–628 >	A.S. possibly not in patriline of succession; revived pre-Teotihuacan-intrusion king list
	23rd, 24th Rulers *c.* 640	One of these rulers may have been K'inich Muwaan Jol II, claimed as father of Dos Pilas 1st ruler, B'alaj Chan K'awiil; time of civil war, fissioning: the disaffected faction (backed by Calakmul) founded Dos Pilas
	Nuun Ujol Chaak *c.* > 657–679 >	Attacked Dos Pilas 672, lost it in 677, defeated in 679
	Jasaw Chan K'awiil I *c.* 682–734	Oversaw Tikal's turnaround. 695: defeated Calakmul; revived Teotihuacan symbolism
AD 700	Yik'in Chan K'awiil 734–746 >	Erected several stelae, altars and lintels; built/rebuilt temples, palaces, *sacbeob*
	28th Ruler > 766–768	
	Yax Nuun Ayiin II 768–794 >	Tikal's power over Caracol etc. ending
AD 800	Nuun Ujol K'inich *c.* 800?	
	Dark Sun > 810 >	
	Jewel K'awiil > 849 >	Known from a reference at Seibal
	Jasaw Chan K'awiil II > 869 >	Last ruler, attempt to re-establish rulership

Calakmul, Late Classic King List (12.31)

	Ruler	Event
AD 600	Scroll Serpent 579–611 >	Attacked Palenque
	Yuknoom Chan > 619 >	Supervised Caracol ruler in ritual of 619
	Tajoom Uk'ab' K'ak 622–630	623: 1st Late Classic monuments at Calakmul, Stela 28 and 29
	Yuknoom Head 630–636	Attacked Naranjo
	Yuknoom the Great b. 600, r. 636–686	Father, possibly: Scroll Serpent; supported Dos Pilas faction in Tikal split, conflicts with Tikal; meddled at Piedras Negras
	Yuknoom Yich'aak K'ak' b. 649, r. 686–695?	695: Calakmul's golden age came to a close
	Split Earth 695? >	May have been a Tikal-sponsored pretender
AD 700	Yuknoom Took' K'awiil > 702–731 >	An altar at Tikal, dated 733-36, shows a bound Calakmul captive, possibly this ruler
	Wamaw K'awiil > 736 >	Quirigua source dated 736 indicates Calakmul help vs. Copán
AD 800	Ruler Y > 741 >	Tikal victorious over Calakmul's client states
AD 900	Ruler Z > 751 >	
	B'olon K'awiil > 771–789? >	
	Chan Pet > 849 >	
	Aj Took' > 909? >	Stela 61 gave Calakmul's final inscribed date, 899, or, more probably, 909

12.30, 12.31 *(Opposite) Late Classic kings of Tikal and Calakmul.*

12.32, 12.33 *(Below) Altar Q is a vivid dynastic statement. Its use (at left) may have involved the sacrifice of 15 jaguars whose bones were cached nearby. The jaguar is the king's* way, *so they may represent Yax Pasaj's royal predecessors at Copán. They also may represent a huge tribute obligation: delivering 15 live jaguars to Copán. In Altar Q's front panel (at bottom in the diagram), Yax Pasaj receives the staff of office from the dynastic founder, Yax K'uk Mo', whose Teotihuacan-style goggles suggest Yax Pasaj's efforts to legitimize the basis of his rule. Compensatory over-achievement by a king with shaky credentials recurs not only in Maya history, but throughout human history: great deeds may be spurred by a sense of insecurity, while the fully legitimate and complacent inheritors of wealth and power may attain nothing.*

Borrowed prestige was even more important to the next Copán king, Yax Pasaj, son of the Palenque princess. Who his father was is uncertain, but he took great pains to honor the Copán dynasty, rebuilding existing structures embellished with imagery extolling the traditional lineage. His most famous monument, Altar Q (AD 776), was a portrait of himself and the 15 preceding Copán kings [**12.32, 12.33**].

AD 800–900

The end of Yax Pasaj's reign fades into the uncertainty of the period of general decline of elites in the southern Maya lowlands. The new *k'atun* cycle initiated in AD 790 seems to have been a turning point for the nature of political activity, in that in this year, more sites erected stelae than at any other time, suggesting a general climate of local declarations of dynastic importance (Martin and Grube 2000). However, the slide toward cessation of building programs and dated monuments had begun (Sharer 1994: 346).

Yax Pasaj's successor, in AD 822, was the last ruler of Copán; he managed to begin one sculpted monument, but its unfinished state speaks volumes for the curtain falling over this brilliant era of Maya culture. Quirigua faded out at about the same time; Caracol's final glyph date was AD 859; Tikal and Calakmul, substantial cities, maintained traditions of kingship into the late 800s and even perhaps early 900s. For many Maya regal-ritual centers, the end of their days of glory might have looked something like the view of Dos Pilas after AD 761, with defensive palisades flung up, using stone torn from the temple-pyramids and palaces, and stout poles cut from the forests.

CONSTRUCTION COSTS

MONUMENTAL ARCHITECTURE is designed to dazzle the spectator with its size and sumptuous quality, and is one criterion by which we judge societal complexity. Mesoamerican pyramids are, after all, effigies of mountains, and who could make mountains except the gods? Or, perhaps, a ruler with a huge supply of laborers? Archaeological exploration of monumental structures like temple-pyramids and palaces has led to an assessment of how they were built, and at what cost. Even the most extensive Mesoamerican buildings depended upon fairly simple methods of construction, with most platforms being solid, and roomed structures having thick walls and relatively small rooms. Building materials were usually local, though finishing materials, such as lime plaster, may have been imported. As with modern buildings, cost is correlated with size. But while modern buildings are usually completed in one construction episode, ancient monuments can involve repeated rebuildings and can also use natural promontories to enhance the illusion of large size. These considerations must be calculated into the estimate of construction cost.

Compare, for example, the Pyramid of the Sun at Teotihuacan and the Temple of the Inscriptions pyramid at Palenque [**12.34, 12.35**]. Volume provides a very rough measure of labor cost: moving the rubble and dirt to form the core of the pyramid is the basic task in creating the model-mountain, but it is also the least demanding in terms of skill. From designing the structure to applying the plaster on the cut-stone sheathing and decorating the plaster with paint or bas-reliefs, there are many specialized jobs involved in monumental construction. But estimating the cost of piling up a big mound of dirt allows us to begin to understand how a big effect was created with local resources.

At Teotihuacan, much of the material for the pyramids was mined from cave systems under the pyramids themselves. If we assume that workers hauled this fill in baskets, each holding about a cubic foot, then 35 million loads were required. If a worker can make six round trips a day from the nearby source to the construction site, then close to 6 million person-days of labor are required to build the pyramid. Daunting? A task requiring slaves groaning under their loads? Hardly. In fact, given that farmers can count on at least three months when their crops do not require attention, then about 70,000 workers could finish the job in one 90-day season. In fact, the pyramid was built over the course of several hundred years, so we would be more accurate in conceptualizing a labor force of about 7,000 working in the off-season for 10 years, or 700 working for 100 years. Either of these scenarios makes no dent in a population of 100,000. Similar calculations for Palenque would show that the pyramid of the Temple of Inscriptions was not a strain on labor resources.

A thorough analysis of the cost of construction requires a careful energetic approach, one which considers all the steps in the building and finishing process. Such an approach "provides a means of explicitly defining subjective assessments of scale and quality, or ... cost" (Abrams 1994: 38). Accounting for all costs involved in construction of residences of different statuses at Maya Copán revealed a range of labor value, from 25,000 person-days for the royal residence, to less than 100 person-days for rural farmhouses (Abrams 1994: 82–85). The costs tallied nicely with the labor pool available to the residents – the farming family could easily build its own house in part of the dry season, while the king (or his majordomo) could call upon workers from all over the region to provide the necessary labor. And, once again applying the 90-day "building season" schedule, only about 280 workers would be necessary in order to complete the palace structure in one season. These calculations should not detract from our admiration for ancient monuments, but rather provoke even greater respect, that such beauty and balance were achieved with fairly simple technology and a modest work force.

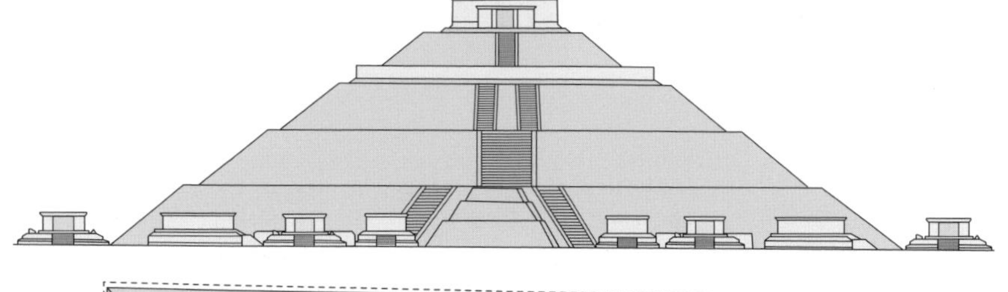

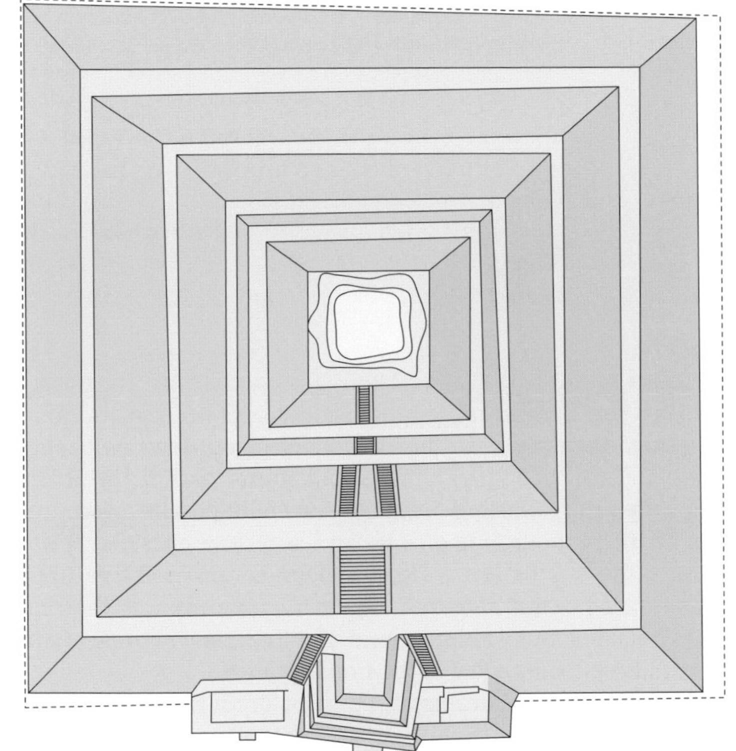

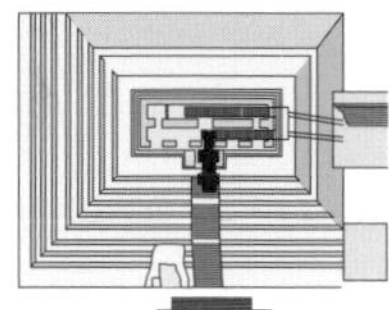

12.34 *The Pyramid of the Sun at Teotihuacan (left), compared with the Temple of the Inscriptions at Palenque (right), both to the same scale.*

12.35 *(Below) The comparitive construction costs of the Pyramid of the Sun and the Temple of the Inscriptions.*

Comparative Construction Costs (12.35)

	Teotihuacan Pyramid of the Sun	Palenque Temple of the Inscriptions
Substrate	Level	Hillside
Pyramid height	69 m (226 ft)	27.2 m (89.2 ft)
Pyramid base	*c.* 226 m (741.5 ft) on a side	42.5 by 60 m (139.4 by 197 ft)
Number of building episodes, timing	Probably three, 300 BC–AD 225	One, AD 675–*c.* 702
Local population at time of construction	*c.* 100,000 in AD 100	*c.* 10,000 in AD 700*
Volume	Over 1 million cu. m (over 35 million cu. ft), not including temple	32,500 cu. m (*c.* 1,150,000 cu.ft), including temple

*Palenque's hinterland has not been completely surveyed; this estimate is based on population densities at comparable Maya sites.

Caracol, Late Classic King List (12.36)		
	Ruler	**Event**
AD 600	Knot Ajaw b. 575, r. 599–613 >	
	K'an II b. 588, r. 618–658	Under one of its most successful rulers, Caracol grew, and grew rich, allied with Calakmul and attacking Naranjo in 626, 627, and 631
	K'ak' Ujol K'inich II r. 658–680 >	680: Caracol a victim of "star war" assault by Naranjo
AD 700	Ruler VII r. > 702 >	Caracol's hiatus, 680–798, Caracol and Calakmul declined while Naranjo and Tikal flourished
	Tum Yohl K'inich > 793? >	
	K'inich Joy K'awiil > 798 >	Restoration of royal traditions and regional influence; B-Group ball court
AD 800	K'inich Toob'il Yopaat 804–830 >	Renaissance continued
	K'an III > 835–849 >	Monuments erected in outlying residential group show need to appeal to non-royal nobles
	Ruler XIII > 859 >	Final glyph date = 859

12.36 *Late Classic kings of Caracol.*

This account of the Late Classic Maya has emphasized the elite, because Maya nobles wrote the texts about themselves, and because recent advances in decipherment of these texts has suddenly given new life to these vivid individuals and their complex rituals and brutal battles. We have noted, throughout, that the luxurious lives of Maya elite families were underwritten by the work of thousands of unrecorded farmer-artisans; perhaps over 90 percent of the population were not members of the Maya upper class. However, archaeological research in the regions around the regal-ritual centers has revealed much about commoner lives, and at present, the region that has been best documented is the Copán Valley.

At AD 800, this valley, the drainage of the Copán River, would have been Yax Pasaj's domain – an area of about 500 sq. km (200 sq. miles), with a population of over 25,000, nearly half living within a 10-minute walk of the Acropolis. Most of the best agricultural land was also near the Acropolis, and the hillier reaches of this region would have had small pockets of alluvium near the streams. But such was the level of the overall population, that the hillsides were in use for farming, too. Pollen cores show that the hillsides had been stripped of the pine forest native to this region, no doubt in part to provide construction materials and firewood, as well as clear land to extend cultivation.

Farming steep slopes that have thin soils is not an effective long-term strategy. The first few crops are an adequate return on the investment of time and effort, but then soil fertility drops, and rains wash the topsoil down into the valley. While, theoretically, such additions to the lower valley alluvium should enhance soil fertility there, in fact when these events took place in the Late Classic Copán Valley, there was devastating erosion, as told in the stratigraphy of archaeological trenches (Webster, Freter, and Gonlin 2000: 118–119). With a diet in which about 70 percent of the calories came from maize and there was little animal protein, it is not surprising that skeletal evidence revealed widespread serious nutritional stress affecting all age groups and social strata. So, while the population in AD 800 was high, it seems that the region's carrying capacity for intensive cultivation was being exceeded, because such intensive use had unleashed environmental degradation.

Did this result in demographic collapse? As Figure **12.37** shows, the high population levels in the Copán Valley were sustained for about 150 years. But after AD 900, a significant decline began, such that by AD 1200, about 1,000 people remained, and the numbers dwindled even further. No adjacent regions record a significant influx, so we must assume that over time, "fewer children were born to replace those who died, and every once in a while a family would move away ... a phased and extended collapse process, rather than an abrupt, cataclysmic event" (Webster 2002: 302).

Causes of Collapse at Copán and Elsewhere

At Copán there were few signs of the conflicts that seem to have played a role in the demise of other Maya sites, nor of a massive drought at about AD 800 that may have hastened the fall of kings at Calakmul and elsewhere

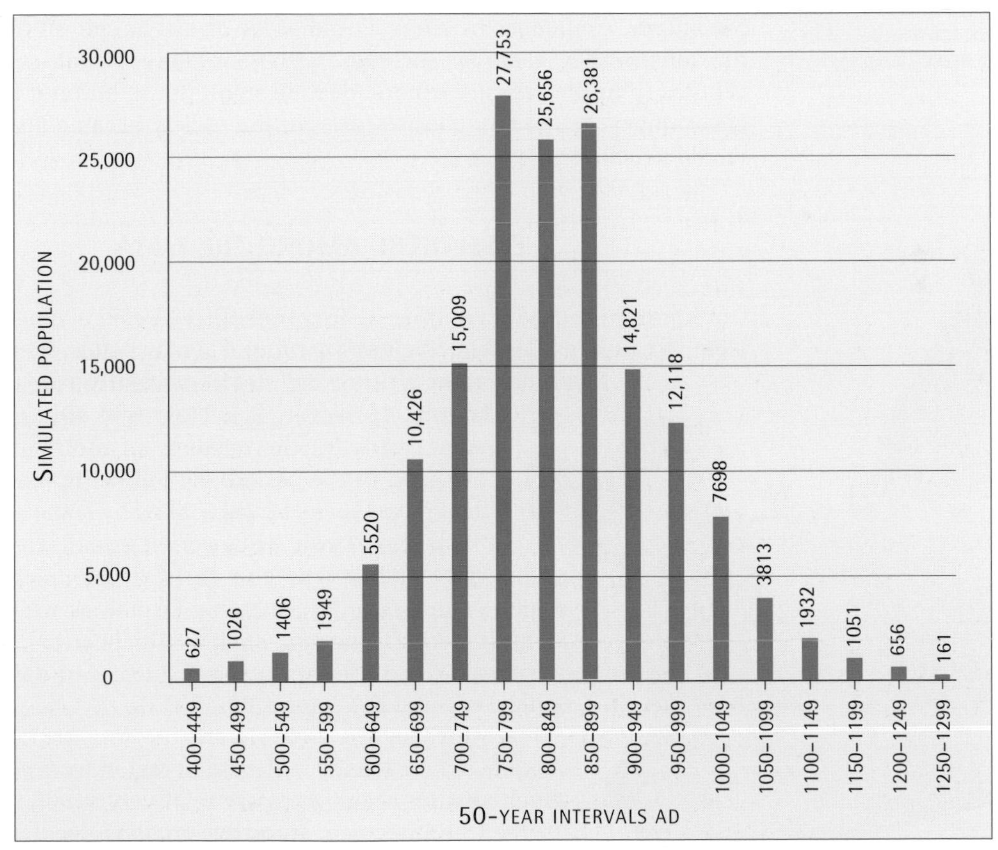

12.37 *Copán Valley settlements, including the Acropolis and the rich elite compounds around it, plus the small villages of farmers distant from the regal-ritual center, provided the population estimates plotted in this chart of the valley's population size, by 50-year intervals. The valley's population was tiny when the Maya dynasty was founded, in AD 476, but in 300 years had grown to over 25,000 people. Five hundred years later, only a handful of farmers remained.*

(Gill 2000). Nowhere in the southern Maya lowlands is there evidence of disease epidemics – though debilitating chronic conditions like tuberculosis and malnutrition would have culled the population and left the survivors weakened. Nor is there evidence of foreign invasions: after all, there was a collapse of royal power, followed by a demographic slide to virtual depopulation, and conquest generally involves subjugation of the population, not its elimination.

The seeds of the Maya collapse were sown during its time of greatest glory. With populations increasing, areas of cultivation were extended, including areas that could not sustain reasonable yields indefinitely. As crop yields declined, health problems, especially among the mass of the population, increased. Meanwhile, the elite class became more elaborate, with larger and more ambitious royal families who, perhaps reluctantly, shared power with other noble lineages. Factionalism and the increase in violent conflict that accompanied it flourished at the same time that populations became increasingly vulnerable to any perturbation in climate or agrarian productivity (see also Pyburn 1996; Lucero 2002).

Given the role of kings as exalted shamans, projecting an ability to contact and influence the spirit world, interpreting the workings of the heaven, it is no wonder that when the lives of the people began to degrade, along with the *milpas*, confidence in kings would erode as fast as soil off the slopes of the Copán Valley. Complex societies, with their many specialists and flow of tributes from the artisan-farmers, depend upon the stability of functioning government. As the foundation stones of the society became dislodged, the whole structure fell.

12.38 *This figurine of a Maya noblewoman weaving comes from Jaina, a cemetery island off the west coast of the Yucatán Peninsula. Jaina's graves have yielded a wealth of these portraits of the Maya. This western island was in the path of the setting sun, and thus alluded to the land of the dead. In contrast, the east, with its rising sun, gave life. Off Yucatán's east coast lay Cozumel, an island famous for its shrine to the Maya fertility goddess, Ixchel, visited by women hoping to become pregnant.*

ELSEWHERE AMONG THE MAYA

Our knowledge of Maya culture history outside the Petén is much less complete, because, while isolated glyphs are found at many sites, the tradition of Maya narrative writing did not consistently extend north of Calakmul. However, it is clear that after centuries of solid growth, the centers of northern Yucatán bloomed in the period just following the collapse of the Petén Maya [**12.38**]. Called by some scholars the "Terminal Classic," this period extends from 800 into the 900s and covers the early development of Puuc region centers, the largest being Uxmal, as well as centers in north-central Yucatán, such as Chichén Itzá, and, in the northeast, Cobá (these northern Yucatecan developments will be covered in Chapter 14).

Just north of the Petén were the Río Bec and Chenes regions, where trends in the Petén region were echoed, on a much smaller scale. Sites are relatively small, but famous for their architecture, featuring ornately decorated façades

[12.39]. This tradition peaked in the Late Classic; at Becán, the largest Río Bec site, the Early Postclassic seems to have brought some sort of militaristic intrusion from northern Yucatán that effectively ended the elite tradition, but population persisted in the Río Bec and Chenes regions to the end of the Early Postclassic, around AD 1200.

Farther north is Acanceh, a site so thoroughly overlain by a modern town that adequate archaeological research is impossible. However, the site's several imposing monuments survive, and testify to some kind of Teotihuacan intrusion in the northern plains of Yucatán. Acanceh's two remaining archaeological constructions are a Formative-period pyramid, 11 m (36 ft) high, and a high platform, the Acropolis, surmounted by the Palace of the Stuccoes [**12.40, 12.41**], which probably dated to the Early Classic (though this remains a problem, and some researchers put it as late as the last centuries of the Late Classic). The building had an elaborate molded frieze "unlike any other extant architectural relief in the Maya area ... motifs strongly recalling central Mexican iconography" (Miller 1991: 20).

How unfortunate that the introduction of these motifs cannot be assigned a secure date, because it would clarify not only Teotihuacan's role at Acanceh, but the timing and events of the decline of Teotihuacan, itself. By the Late Classic, Teotihuacan's core had been destroyed, and gone were the city's policies of international meddling. What was left of the colonies and outposts and networks of traders? Matacapan declined after Teotihuacan's decline, but there is some evidence that trade networks were kept alive by the middlemen, particularly along the Gulf Coast and coast of the Yucatán Peninsula, who had served Teotihuacan interests and then maintained the contacts they had established.

12.39 *In the Río Bec and Chenes regions, monster mask doorways dominated the fronts of buildings, while the concept of the temple-pyramid has been stylized into a vertical design element rather than a functioning ritual structure. This reconstructed view of Structure 1 at Xpuhil I, a Río Bec site, shows staircases that "hardly could have been designed for actual use .... Their sophisticated simulation of functional forms marks the style as derivative" (Proskouriakoff 1963: 52).*

These Late Classic and Early Postclassic-period trading peoples have been called by different names, confounding the problem of sorting out their ethnicity, history, and timing of their actions. They seem to have been Maya whose center of operations was the Chontalpa region (Scholes and Roys 1948; Thompson 1970), the marshy delta of the Usumacinta, along the Gulf Coast at the southwestern reaches of the Yucatán Peninsula. They have been called "Putun" or "Chontal" (the 16th-century name for the Maya of that region) and are one of several related groups known as the "Itzá" (Ball and Taschek 1989). Using a Maya language that incorporated Mexican names, they penetrated far inland into Maya territory, perhaps establishing themselves at some sites. Thus their activities merged trading, travel, and colonization, and extended from the Late Classic through the Postclassic. One Itzá faction took over a minor community in about AD 850 and made it into the great center we know as Chichén Itzá (Kowalski 1989). These stories come to maturity in the Postclassic period.

Southeastern Mesoamerica and the Intermediate Area

So vigorous was the growth of Maya culture during the Classic period that Maya appetites for exotic materials motivated trading contacts with Southeastern Mesoamerica and the Intermediate Area. The greatest evidence of contacts is found in the closest regions – the Sula-Ulua-Chamelecon valleys of western Honduras, and the Pacific coastal valleys of El Salvador and even Costa Rica. Mesoamerica's "Classic" period is expressed in Southeastern Mesoamerica and the Intermediate Area as a time of demographic expansion and cultural complexity – sites show signs of marked ranking in mortuary patterns and residences. These trends are particularly marked in the Pacific coastal regions such as the Gulf of Fonseca and Greater Nicoya, beginning at about AD 500. It should be noted that the archaeological record of regions east of Mesoamerica has not been well-documented, particularly in comparison to that of the Maya, but the general trends reveal that even after Ilopango caused cultural isolation in El Salvador, even after the Maya elites and their taste for foreign precious goods had faded into oblivion, the cultural trajectories in the Intermediate Area stayed the course, maintaining ranked societies where they were already established.

12.40, 12.41 *Acanceh, Structure 1, the Palace of the Stuccoes. (Below) Detail of stucco frieze, showing animal motifs superimposed on central Mexican mountain signs – the bowl-like forms interspersed between the upper row of "mountains" represent the Teotihuacan sign for Tollan (Taube 2000: 25–26). (Opposite, top) Reconstruction of the north façade of the "Palace" building; (Opposite, middle) plan of the palace. (Opposite, bottom) The cross section of rooms, showing the characteristic Maya corbeled vault roof construction.*

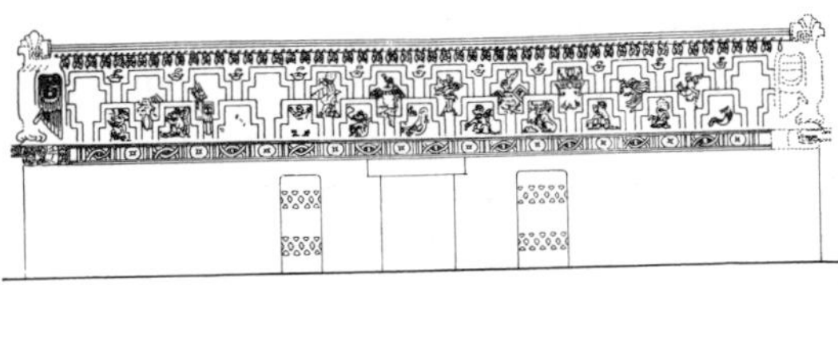

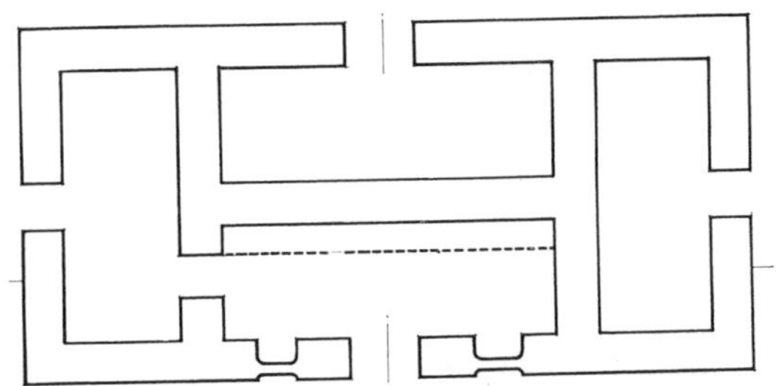

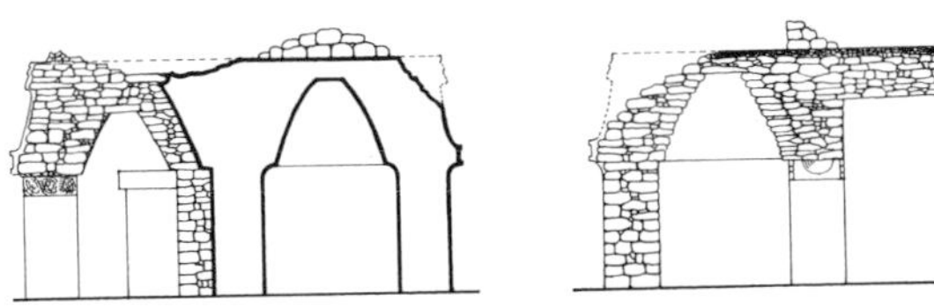

Closer to Mesoamerica, northwestern Honduras in the Late Classic period had several large sites with monumental architecture, including ball courts. Travesía was abandoned by about AD 950, while occupation at Cerro Palenque, which included hundreds of housemounds, lasted until AD 1050 (Joyce 1991). The Cajón region, linking western Honduras with the Caribbean coastal plain to the northeast, had long been occupied by farmers, and in the Late Classic reached its highest population level. The region's chiefdom centered upon Salitron Viejo, which had a population of 1,000 to 1,500, with a group of elite residences on a 2.5-m (8-ft) high platform, extending 75 by 120 m (246 by 394 ft). Shortly thereafter, by AD 1000, the whole region was abandoned (Hirth *et al.* 1989).

La Sierra Some regional capitals were sustained, however, even in a modest condition. In the Late Classic period, La Sierra, about halfway between Copán and the Caribbean Sea, had over 400 housemounds and a site core with temples, a ball court, and over a dozen platforms for elite residences. The site's artifact repertoire indicates that elites there made use of symbols and materials that secured their solidarity with the rulers of other realms, including the Maya, while also consolidating the loyalty of their subjects (Schortman *et al.* 2001). The core of the site seems to have been abandoned after AD 950, but residence around the core continued until about AD 1300.

The Pacific Coast

The coast of Guatemala enjoyed a Late Classic cultural boom, followed by a demographic bust of unknown cause. The boom was Cotzumalhuapa culture, centering upon several localities – El Baúl, El Castillo, and Bilbao – that made up one large (6 sq. km, or *c.* 2.5 sq. miles) settlement area. The three centers may have been built by the area's three successive rulers. We know that this region was one of Mesoamerica's premier cacao-producing zones, so its affluence was assured. What bloomed in the Late Classic was a distinctive style of artistic representation and writing that scholars call "Cotzumalhuapa style" [**12.42**].

A little farther to the northwest along the coastal plain, the area around Abaj Takalik produced Plumbate, a type of pottery whose name derives from its lustrous gray surface which resembles a lead glaze but is actually a slip with substantial amounts of alumina and iron. Plumbate was probably the most widely traded ware in pre-Columbian Mesoamerica, and has been found from West Mexico to the Intermediate Area, and particularly at the major Early Postclassic sites, Tula and Chichén Itzá.

The Guatemala and Chiapas Highlands

After Teotihuacan's decline, Kaminaljuyú remained a substantial site. In fact, considerable "building activity dates to the Late Classic period, including the construction of eleven ball courts" (Hatch 2001: 389). Population levels in the area remained substantial, and seem to have been sustained into the Postclassic in the region as a whole, but the end of the Late Classic brought the end of Kaminaljuyú.

Populations in the Chiapas interior plateau seem to have been in flux during the Late Classic. The Maya who had established themselves in the northeastern sector of the Chiapas Depression occupied a series of "tenams" – fortified hilltop sites. The largest of these was Tenam Rosario, whose founding population may have come from Yaxchilan in about AD 650 (de Montmollin 1995). These sites barely outlived the lowland Maya centers, and the region was abandoned in about AD 1000, possibly because of drought. In the western part of the Chiapas interior plateau, the ancient community of Chiapa de Corzo was taken over in about AD 800 by Manguean-speaking invaders who maintained control until the Spanish conquest in 1524. Down on the Chiapas Coast, sites at Tonalá and Horcones were occupied in the Middle Classic. Horcones has Teotihuacan-style stelae, while Tonalá seems to have been a northern outpost of Cotzumalhuapa style, with at least one such monument pertaining to the ball game.

12.42 *This Cotzumalhuapa-style stela, El Baúl Monument 27, is carved in bas-relief and "depicts a ballgame scene in which the victor wears a monkey mask" (Hatch 1989: 185). He is Ruler 3, and the flaming speech scroll emanating from his mouth probably indicates harsh words for the loser at his feet. On this and many of the other 150 or so known Cotzumalhuapa monuments are glyphs that have yet to be deciphered.*

The End of the Classic Period in the Isthmus and East

The period that marked the close of the Classic period among the Maya and their neighbors was a true, epoch-changing disruption. Abandonment of the great Maya cities of the southern lowlands may have proceeded far more slowly than previously thought, but the results of the process were the same. And all around the dying culture of the Petén swirled peoples on the move, some relocating as part of this cultural collapse, some taking advantage of lacunae of leadership that gave opportunities for the strong and ambitious. Now let us turn to Mesoamerica west of the Isthmus, the source of some of the migrants pushing into and through the Maya domains.

13 THE LATE CLASSIC AND EPICLASSIC IN THE WEST (AD 600–1000/1100)

THE PERIOD BETWEEN AD 600 and 1000/1100 saw radical changes throughout Mesoamerica, with a regionalization of cultures at the same time that a widespread cult flourished, emphasizing militarism and human sacrifice [13.1]. As this era opened, Teotihuacan had just undergone a shocking attack on its ceremonial center – the great city would remain a focus of substantial settlement, but its organizational heart had been stilled, and its continuing influence on other cultures would be as a mythic ancestor, not as a vital ally or foe. Soon afterwards, Monte Albán would also lose its position of dominance.

Flourishing past the decline of the great western cities, the Maya of the Southern Yucatecan lowlands achieved a brilliant cultural apotheosis and then collapsed, as we saw in the last chapter, while the Maya culture of northern Yucatán flourished (a topic to be continued in Chapters 14 and 15). Maya culture, of course, has survived, in many important ways, into the

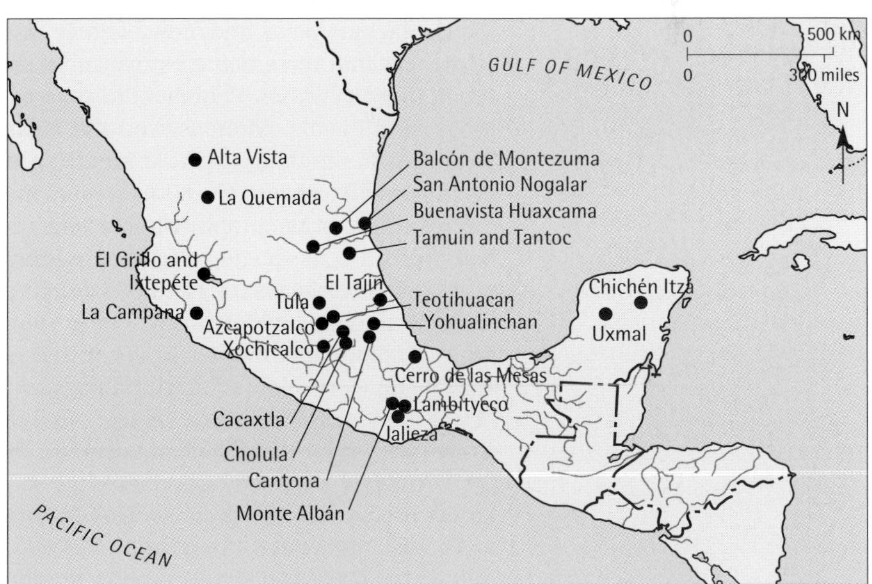

13.1 *Sites and regions of the Late Classic and Early Postclassic referred to in Chapter 13.*

13.2 *This sculpture from Chichén Itzá is a* chacmool, *a standardized figure depicting a reclining male with his head turned. The figure may represent "the recumbent and dying Maize God" (Miller and Samayoa 1998: 64) on whose stomach an impersonator of the young Maize God would be sacrificed, in order to secure the continuation of the earth's fertility.*

present. The Late Classic period saw the roots of a system of northern Yucatecan regional polities that was still vigorous when the Spaniards arrived just after AD 1500.

At the end of the Late Classic, important northern Yucatecan sites included Cobá in the northeast, Uxmal in the northwest, and, dominating the center, Chichén Itzá. Chichén's culture was deeply rooted in the ancient Maya traditions of that region. But Chichén was something else, as well: a hybrid of old Maya and new, nearly pan-Mesoamerican belief systems, influences that were being expressed at sites all across Mesoamerica, from the northern Yucatán Peninsula to regions to the west, along the Gulf lowlands, into Puebla, Morelos, and the Basin of Mexico, and beyond, to the Tula region, the Bajío, to West Mexico and the Northwestern Frontier and even, possibly, up into the Southwest of the present-day U.S.

Over this vast geographical area spread a constellation of shared traits, many of them associated with veneration of the Feathered Serpent deity, with various centers serving as this deity's pilgrimage sites. The 52-year Calendar Round was widely used. There were widespread architectural forms such as colonnaded halls and decorative friezes with human sacrifice and warfare imagery. New sculptural forms such as the *chacmool* sacrificial altar [**13.2**] – its form a reclining figure – and the *tzompantli* skull rack demonstrate that human sacrifice had become a major focus of ritual, transcending the Formative and Early Classic-period sacrificial practices of Teotihuacan, Monte Albán, and southern lowland Maya centers. These traits were distributed, and new centers became powerful, through the linked processes of militarism, trade and tribute, and migration.

Militarism A significant number of sites were built on fortified hilltops, and others had defensive walls. This indirect evidence of pervasive warfare is corroborated by strong indicators that the militarism of this period was professionalized, a trend toward occupational specialization that no doubt had roots in Teotihuacan and southern lowland Maya polities of the Early Classic. In later, Aztec times there were warrior societies, organizations of trained, combat-ready soldiers who shared distinctive uniforms and insignia – the two most famous were the Eagle Knights and the Jaguar Knights. These cadres of soldiers not only indicate a high level of military organization, and an emphasis on militarism in maintaining and advancing Aztec goals, but they also provided avenues for social and economic advancement for men of all ranks. Noble youths were trained to be officers, but an Aztec commoner who distinguished himself in war could win material rewards as well as advancement into quasi-noble status. In the Late Classic, figures in murals and on monuments, such as at Cacaxtla and Xochicalco, are consistent with the garb and emblems of these professional militarists (Hirth 2000: 258–63).

Trade and Merchants, Tribute and Lords The shared ideas that characterized Late Classic–Epiclassic pan-Mesoamericanism were carried along the extensive trade networks that linked Mesoamerican regions with each other and with zones beyond the borders of the larger culture area. Trade contacts reached the Northern Arid Zone, where turquoise was mined, and the northwest coast of South America, where metal-working techniques originated that were developed in West Mexico during this period. Several sites in the Central Highlands seem to have been production centers for obsidian blades, which were then widely distributed. In the Gulf lowlands and other tropical *tierra caliente* regions, cotton and cacao were important products for long-distance trade. Many sites had goods imported from great distances. The range of trade, and widespread presence of marketplace-like plazas at many communities, indicate that there may have been professional merchant groups, like the Aztec *pochteca* merchants, who controlled long-distance trade under the patronage of local lords. In Aztec society, the *pochteca* also served diplomatic and espionage functions, sometimes even engaging in military skirmishes.

The interchange of goods within the hinterlands surrounding each regional capital was no doubt organized as political tribute: materials and services accruing to the ruler. In Mesoamerica, where bulk transport technology was always limited to human porters on trails, and more rarely, canoes on waterways or coastal routes, local staple food provisioning was essential to the growth of any substantial community. Thus the most basic tribute item would be food. And because no community could become substantial and impressive without the work of organized construction crews – or remain a dazzling temple-and-palace complex without constant maintenance – labor service was also imperative. So populations in the hinterlands around capitals would supply food and labor, and also produce finished goods, such as ceramics and textiles, for local use and long-distance trade.

This tribute pattern, so well-known from the Late Postclassic Aztec empire, was already centuries old in the Late Classic, as indicated for example by Maya vase paintings showing what appear to be tribute bundles brought to Maya kings. At Late Classic Xochicalco, figures and glyphs on the Pyramid of the Plumed Serpents "illustrate tribute resulting from successful warfare" (Smith 2000: 80) in much the same format as would become familiar in Aztec tribute rolls.

Migrations Nature abhors a vacuum, and growing human populations have seldom failed to move into attractive vacant territory – or into regions inhabited by weaker groups who could be displaced or subjugated. Tracing migrations through the archaeological record is a sticky problem, as we have discussed in previous chapters. When does a new pottery style, for example, reveal the incursions of an incoming ethnic group, rather than the diffusion of a new trait? Does the spread of the Feathered Serpent cult reveal the actual movement of populations, or, instead, the movement of effective proselytizers?

Migration accounts are a key feature in the histories of many ethnic groups of the Late Postclassic – immigration and success in establishing a firm territorial hold over a new homeland was a major point of pride for the Aztecs, as it was for countless other Mesoamerican societies. Many of these Late Postclassic-period migration accounts, recorded in the Early Colonial period in native documents and by Spanish chroniclers, reach back into the Late Classic and Epiclassic. Coyotlatelco peoples, perhaps originating in west or northwestern Mexico, settled in the Central Highlands after AD 600. The Olmeca-Xicalanca are said to have moved into Puebla from the east and south in the Late Classic, followed by the Tolteca-Chichimeca from the northwest, in the Epiclassic. The Maya Huastecs had long had a strong presence in the northern Gulf lowlands, and became the dominant culture there in the Classic period.

The Feathered Serpent Cult Over all of Mesoamerica, militarism, trade, and migration were spreading a belief system focusing upon the Feathered Serpent. Thinking about humankind in general, what accounts for the rapid spread of a religious cult over a wide area? We know, for example, that Christianity was but one of many contemporaneous miracle cults extant in Southwest Asia 2,000 years ago. Its enduring popularity – its ability to outcompete other miracle cults – seems to have been generated by a combination of traits that no other belief system of the time offered: grounded in the ancient Judaic belief system, Christianity promised eternal life with the human sacrifice of its founder, while it also emphasized nonviolence and generosity as powerful counterpoints to the norms of dominant Roman culture. It had broad appeal, to both sexes and all ethnic groups and social classes.

Turning to the Feathered Serpent cult, we can see that it may have been perceived as a welcome positive influence at a time of cultural fatigue, appealing to those ambitious for power during this period of political opportunity. We see the roots of Feathered Serpent traits in Olmec iconography, and strong expression at Teotihuacan. But it is after Teotihuacan declines that the imagery of the cult appears as an essential motif at sites all over Mesoamerica.

The Feathered Serpent is associated with creativity, fertility, regeneration, and with ruling elites, elite goods, and trade. The emphasis upon human sacrifice found in the iconography at many sites, and particularly associated with the ball game, was justified as nourishment for the gods, reciprocity to those who had given their blood to create humankind. Human sacrifice served the needs of the elite by incorporating a terror tactic into militarism – the ghastly fate of the prisoner-of-war as sacrificial victim – while also underscoring the special relationship, even kinship, between rulers and their gods, which set elites apart from the commoners and justified the rights to dictate policy and accumulate wealth. The cult's spread, ultimately extending from the copper-mining region of the Northern Arid Zone to the cotton- and cacao-growing tropics of the Gulf and Maya lowlands, was a cultural regeneration, its adherents attracted by a set of compelling beliefs associated with the sumptuous expression of powerful motifs upon materials representing the best that traveling merchants could gather from all over Middle America.

Calendrics Among the shared beliefs was calendrics, the art of keeping track of time, and this was among the special skills of the rulers, who often oriented their ceremonial centers toward calendrical horizon landmarks, grounding their earthly locus of rulership in the changing patterns of the sun and stars, and thus placing themselves in a central position relative to the cycles of time. The Long Count, a defining feature of the Classic Maya of the southern lowlands, fell into disuse, with a few later examples limited to Maya monuments commemorating royal reigns. By and large, Maya dates were reduced to the Short Count, the 13 *k'atun* cycle of about 256 years. All over Mesoamerica, the 52-year Calendar Round was in use, and this combined the 260-day divinatory calendar with the 365-day vague year (see p. 223). The Feathered Serpent cult emphasized elite solidarity and legitimacy of sacred rulership over a broad area, and calendrics and the coordination of regional Calendar Rounds would have been a logical part of the privileged knowledge disseminated by the cult.

Which Came First? What is not clear, at present, is the timing of this sharing of traits, or the direction of its diffusion. Over a northeast to southwest span of over 2,000 km (over 1,200 miles), dozens of sites show these features, but determining when each region expresses them is a daunting problem. Like the dilemma of distinguishing migrating peoples from diffused traits, tracking the spread of ideas prompts the questions: where did they develop, and what was the timing of their spread into other areas?

WHAT WAS THE FEATHERED SERPENT?

"FEATHERED SERPENT" is a literal interpretation of a pair of iconographic motifs that were consistently linked from the Formative period on: a serpent bearing a crest of feathers, or whose scales were feathers, or who was found paired with one or more quetzal birds. The term is also a serviceable translation of "Quetzalcoatl," the Postclassic Nahuatl deity whose name combined the quetzal bird (its long iridescent feathers graced royal headdresses all over Mesoamerica) and the rattlesnake, potent symbol of fertility and regeneration as it sheds its skin and is renewed. Serpents are also associated with water and earth, and in Mayan, the "words for snake and sky are identical" (Miller and Taube 1993: 141). Quetzal feathers are associated with all things precious and verdant, from jade to clusters of maize leaves and tule reeds. Tules symbolized the dense stands of people who lived in the capitals, the greatest of which were called Tollan and were the earthly domains of rulers who claimed descendance from the Feathered Serpent deity.

"Feathered Serpent" encompasses "Quetzalcoatl" and other expressions of this principle ranging from Olmec depictions of an avian serpent [**13.4**] to the Postclassic culture hero, Topiltzin Quetzalcoatl. Given the facile way in which Mesoamerican metaphysical beings morphed into each other, cross-dressing in bits of deity costumes and bearing varied combinations of symbolic meaning and gear, a summary of the major variants and avatars is in order.

"Plumed Serpent" and "Serpent with Quetzal Birds" images are found among the Olmec. These clearly draw upon the powerful symbols of fertility and wealth, and their archaeological contexts place these attributes within the domains of ruling lords.

Feathered Serpent depictions become common during the Classic period, particularly in Central Mexico, with the most famous example being those embellishing the levels of the Temple-Pyramid of the Feathered Serpent at Teotihuacan [**13.3**]. In the Late Classic/Epiclassic, such motifs are also found at Xochicalco, Cacaxtla, and at Gulf lowlands sites such as Las Higueras and El Tajín.

In the Late Postclassic period, Quetzalcoatl was regarded in some parts of Central Mexico as one of the creators of humankind at the beginning of the fifth, present world, and as the deity who retrieved maize from the underworld for mankind. Quetzalcoatl was one of the patrons of rulers, priests, and merchants, an association which no doubt has deep roots and should color our intepretation of the Late Classic–Epiclassic spread of the cult. He is also known as Tlahuizcalpantecuhtli, the deity of the morning star (the planet Venus).

13.3 *At Teotihuacan, images of the Feathered Serpent abound. In this mural from the Techinantitla compound, water pours from the serpent's mouth, while flowers – one of Quetzalcoatl's blessings – flourish below.*

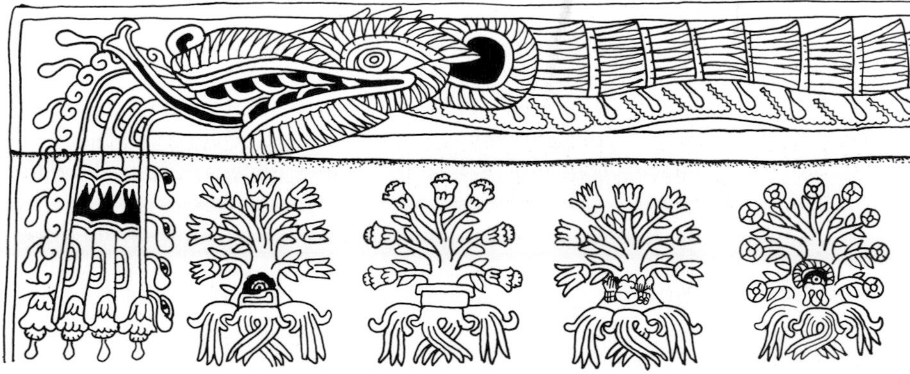

Topiltzin Quetzalcoatl (or Ce Acatl [One Reed, a day name] Topiltzin Quetzalcoatl) was a semi-historical, semi-mythical heroic figure who was said to have brought Tula to greatness (Nicholson 2001). "[T]he Tolteca, his vassals, were highly skilled ... they cut the green stone and cast gold ... these [crafts] ... proceeded from Quetzalcoatl – all the crafts work, the learning" (Sahagún 1978 [1569]: 13). He also emphasized autosacrifice rather than human sacrifice. Legend has it that he was undone by overindulgence in *pulque* – drunk through the connivance of the great trickster god Tezcatlipoca, he exposed himself, and retreated from Tula in disgrace. He departed toward the east, traveling to Yucatán on a raft made of serpents, and Yucatecan accounts record the arrival there of Kukulcan (Mayan for Feathered Serpent). His vow to return one day to reclaim his domain may have worsened the Aztec emperor Motecuzoma's crisis of confidence over the omens of doom besetting him when Cortés and his company arrived on the Gulf Coast on the day One Reed, 1519: "they thought it was Quetzalcoatl Topiltzin who had come to arrive" (Sahagún 1975 [1569]: 5).

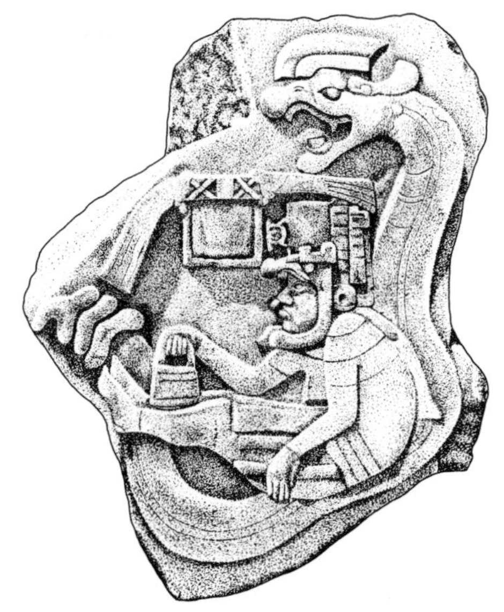

13.4 *La Venta's Monument 19 shows a crested serpent encompassing what is probably a ruling lord. Bundles of quetzal feathers frame either side of a crisscross sky band between the serpent's and human figure's heads.*

Quetzalcoatl as Ehécatl, or Ehécatl Quetzalcoatl, the Wind God, is a common Postclassic avatar of the deity. Here again, the strong sense of fertility pervades the deity, because the wind presages the life-giving rains. Yet, in Postclassic Cholula, he was patron of merchants (O'Mack 1991: 12–13). His costume [**13.5**] comprised a welter of symbolic details. The conical cap was typical of the Gulf lowlands, and perhaps indicates a region of origin for this version of the deity. He wore a spiral pectoral which is a cross-section of a conch shell, and a duckbill mask, and often carries an *atlatl*, the spear thrower which was so indelibly regarded as the symbol of Central Mexican militarism. Temples to this deity were often round, another symbolic nod to the sweep of the wind.

13.5 *In a native-style book compiled in the mid-16th century, soon after the conquest, Ehécatl-Quetzalcoatl bears his characteristic insignia, and is here associated with the creation of flowers.*

For many years, archaeologists assumed that the direction of spread of this Feathered Serpent-dominated pan-Mesoamerican style was from Tula (also known as Tula de Allende, or Tula de Hidalgo, in the modern state of Hidalgo) to Chichén Itzá, but recent radiocarbon dates from Chichén now seem to indicate that the traits may have occurred there before they were found at Tula. However, this conclusion can only be sustained if similar dating tests are applied to materials from Tula and confirm the present dating of phases, which is now largely based on the ceramic sequence – such revisionist information is not currently available.

And what of the other important sites that rise to power in the Late Classic and the Epiclassic (AD 700–900/1000)? Cholula is perhaps the most important site in Postclassic Mesoamerica that was associated with the Feathered Serpent cult, but it may have undergone a decline in the Late Classic, while Xochicalco, Cacaxtla, and El Tajín rose to prominence and with Feathered Serpent cult traits. How can one sort through the commonalities, without falsely attributing waves of influence from one center to another?

Carefully. In this chapter, we will start with Teotihuacan, which enters the Late Classic period as a shadow of its former self. This cultural black hole is a major factor in creating the many opportunities for aggression, conflict, migration, and usurpation that characterize this volatile period. Teotihuacan's symbols survive in new contexts, used to add prestige to the regimes of its old allies and enemies alike. Our overview will then turn to the northwestern Central Highlands and from there explore Mexico west of the Isthmus, reviewing the sites and cultures important to this period, with this set of traits in mind. The scholarly arguments for precedence of one site or region over another will be noted, but, out of respect to this interpretatively dynamic situation, the discussion will avoid conclusions that attribute trends of cultural primacy to one end of Mesoamerica or another.

THE BASIN OF MEXICO AND REGIONS TO ITS NORTH AND WEST

Basin of Mexico

The "fall of Teotihuacan" is still in chronological flux, in terms of scholarly agreement about when this happened, and readers are alerted to a wide range of dates still being touted. Some scholars still cling to a very conservative approach, based on guesstimates made before chronometric dating was widespread and placing the decline of the site in the 8th or even the 9th century. And, in fact, Teotihuacan's materials have not been subjected to dating tests on a scale appropriate to the site's size and importance. However, as was indicated in an earlier chapter, our best chronometric dates point to a 6th-century decline in Teotihuacan's power, and this fits in well with the culture history of Mesoamerica in general. Further chronometric dates may impel radical revisions of the interpretations presented here, or may substantiate them.

In the early part of the Late Classic period, Teotihuacan remained a large and important city, with a population in the tens of thousands, but trade and diplomacy are no longer evident. In fact, the Street of the Dead and its massive monuments, now vandalized, were to become one of the Late Postclassic period's most important pilgrimage sites, and this functional transformation would have begun at the start of the Late Classic. The population of the city's residential neighborhoods formed a ring of towns around its ruined core. Settlement in these towns has persisted into the present, with the most important, from Late Classic times on, being at the western edge of the ancient city – in the Postclassic it would be the capital of a regional city-state, and today it is known as San Juan Teotihuacan.

In the Terminal Formative period, the settlement pattern of the Basin of Mexico had been simplified, to gigantic Teotihuacan and very little else. Gradually, even during Teotihuacan's apogee, this pattern began to normalize – the alluvial plain around the lake system was dotted with farming hamlets, and some larger villages were established. In the eastern Basin, the site of Cerro Portezuelo was occupied from the Early Classic to the Late Postclassic, and exhibited a site layout that would become common in the Late Postclassic, of widely spaced house mounds in linear settlements that extended along the sloping piedmont (Nicholson and Hicks 1961). Across the lake was Azcapotzalco, destined to become one of the Basin's most important capitals in the Early Postclassic, and already a substantial settlement in Late Classic times. At the site, an area known as "Coyotlatelco" ("coyote hill") provided archaeologists with the first evidence of Coyotlatelco pottery (Tozzer 1921).

Coyotlatelco Pottery and Culture

Featuring buff-colored vessels with red designs, this pottery type was associated with a culture that extended from northwest and west Mexico and the Bajío to the Basin and adjacent Puebla/Tlaxcala areas, and seems to have become established in the Basin of Mexico as early as AD 600 (Cobean and Mastache 2001). These early Coyotlatelco communities are unprepossessing, sometimes just shacks in abandoned Teotihuacan apartment complexes. Other Coyotlatelco settlements show planning, and include platforms with modest civic and ceremonial buildings with built-in cut stone hearths (known as a *tlecuil*) and *temascal* sweat baths (Rattray 1996), both of which became standard features in the house compounds of the Central Highlands in Toltec and Aztec times. Coyotlatelco sites in the Tula region extended over terrace systems of farm plots around houses, the dispersed house mound settlement pattern that would blanket the Central Highlands during the Late Postclassic.

Still, their habitation sites are less the work of empire builders than of discrete groups of sedentary agriculturalists moving into lightly settled areas after Teotihuacan's decline. And moving in from where? The closest Early Classic cultural affinities with Coyotlatelco-style ceramics, lithics, and house types are found in arid regions to the north, west, and northeast of the

Basin of Mexico. Their ethnic affiliations may be mixed, derived from Otomí-speaking and Nahua-speaking peoples, an amorphous (and difficult to define) polyglot group known as "Chichimecs" – "people of the dog lineage" (Carrasco 1971: 461). This term often carried the connotation of hunter-forager, yet was used to describe many groups who were sedentary farmers. In fact, the huge arid area north of Mesoamerica proper is still called the "Gran Chichimeca" and was thought by the Aztecs to be "a place of dry rocks...of death from thirst...of starvation.... It is to the north" (Sahagún 1963 [1569]: 256).

The term Chichimec is important because during the Postclassic period, these groups forged strong confederations in the Basin of Mexico, merging with the more refined Toltecs, the cultural descendants of the Early Postclassic capital, Tula. Yet, just as "Tula" or "Tollán" was used not just for the site of Tula de Hidalgo, but as a name for several important Mesoamerican capitals, so "Toltec" came to have a broader meaning than "citizen of Tula de Hidalgo" – "Toltec" indicated a cultured person or a skilled artisan. These presumed names of ethnic groups are a bit like Mesoamerican deities – meanings merge and are transformed, with several entities sharing characteristics. For all their aura of semi-civilized crudeness, the Chichimecs brought a reputation for hardiness and aggression that nicely complemented the Toltecs with whom they became linked in as one of the important cultures moving over the Epiclassic landscape.

Tula Region

Coyotlatelco peoples were moving into the Tula region in the Late Classic, and their sites are quite distinct from those established in the Early Classic by Teotihuacanos, or Teotihuacan-related groups. The Coyotlatelco site of Tula Chico dates from the Prado and Corral phases (*c.* AD 700–900). Tula Chico is generally regarded as an embryo for the great Early Postclassic capital Tula, which was centered 1.5 km (*c.* 1 mile) to the southwest. Tula Chico's ceramics include Coyotlatelco wares as well as types similar to those of the Bajío, lending "credence to ethnohistorical accounts that associate Tula's founding with the intrusion of...peoples from the northwest" (Healan 2001: 776).

The Bajío

The Late Classic was a period of major occupation of this region, with hilltop settlements, including Acámbaro, along the drainage systems of major rivers (Brambila 2001). Clusters of sites around hilltop centers with civic-ceremonial architecture probably formed loose confederations. Late Classic Bajío sites shared the red-on-buff pottery traditions emerging in the northwestern part of the Central Highlands. The region is semi-arid, and the habitation pattern of houses distributed over terraces may indicate an erosion-control strategy of using maguey to edge terraced plots of maize and other plants, the maguey sap providing a potable beverage (readily fermented into *pulque*) in regions where fresh water sources are distant from residences. As Teotihuacan influence receded, the region seems not to have attracted the attention of any other major power until Tula's apogee in the Early Postclassic.

Northwestern Frontier

During the Middle and Late Classic period, several centers in the Northwestern Frontier grew to substantial dimensions. Before we knew that Teotihuacan's decline was a mid-Classic phenomenon, Alta Vista and La Quemada were characterized as colonial centers, established by Central Mexican interests. With our present understanding of the timing of political regionalization throughout Mesoamerica, it seems clear that Northwestern Frontier centers may have blossomed in the Late Classic because of Teotihuacan's decline: freed from a dependency relationship with the core state, growth in peripheral regions is stimulated "because resources previously being fed to the core can be allocated to local uses" (Nelson 1993: 177).

While it is clear that foreign cultures influenced Alta Vista (which flourished *c.* AD 400–850) and La Quemada (slightly later, *c.* AD 500–900), the Northwestern Frontier was itself innovative in the development of some key features of the Late Classic and Epiclassic. Colonnaded halls were important at both sites, and both sites show abundant skeletal remains reflecting a variety of mortuary situations, including human sacrifice. In this semi-arid region, maguey was cultivated along with maize, so *pulque* would have been readily available. At La Quemada, specialized scraping tools for the processing of maguey sap and fiber are like those commonly found in Postclassic Central Mexico, indicating that maguey-farming techniques were being perfected that would later be applied extensively on sloping piedmont lands in semi-arid zones.

The Northwestern Frontier was the trading gateway to the emerging Hohokam cultures farther north in what is now northwestern Mexico and the southwestern U.S. Clearly, the Chalchihuites culture of Alta Vista, named for the region's extraction and processing of precious local greenstone, also processed even more precious turquoise, which was especially prized in the Epiclassic and Postclassic. Stones such as hematite and cinnabar, as well as greenstones, were extracted from from the earth in hundreds of tunnels excavated in branching patterns several kilometers long (Schiavetti 1994).

Alta Vista and the First Skull Racks The heightened emphasis on display of human skeletal remains is evidenced here in two of the earliest known skull racks, wooden frameworks upon which crania were exhibited. The Aztecs called the skull rack *tzompantli*, and used it for the skulls of sacrificial victims; it became an important feature at sites all over Mesoamerica from the Late Classic period on. At Cerro de Huistle (*c.* 100 km/60 miles west of

13.6 *Chichén Itzá's* tzompantli *is a representational skull rack, a rendering in stone of the actual presentation of trophy skulls, strung like beads onto poles in a multi-level wooden framework.*

La Quemada), deposits of skull-rack posts had associated bones that were almost entirely from adult males (Hers 1989).

While impressive displays of stacked skulls, often sculpted in bas-relief, are well-known from other regions, such as the Classic Maya, the *tzompantli* tradition seems to have begun in the Northwestern Frontier, and spread in the Late Classic – Chichén Itzá would have the "largest, most complete, and most elaborate *tzompantli*" (Miller 1999: 350) – a four-level bas-relief of skulls in profile [**13.6**]. The actual display of perforated skulls on a free-standing wooden rack is an alternative expression of a whole series of skeletally-themed exhibitions, which involve either bones themselves, or depictions of bones, occurring in many regions of Mesoamerica, and throughout its culture history. There is a particularly strong association of the skull rack with closely related phenomena, the ball game and sacrificial death by decapitation (Gillespie 1991), traits that surged through Late Classic–Epiclassic Mesoamerica.

La Quemada This site (also known as Tuitlán, or Chicomoztoc) was a ceremonial center in the Northwestern Frontier that was occupied from AD 500–900. It was at the center of a road system extending toward satellite sites. La Quemada itself probably had only about 500 residents, and the population of the hinterland may have been a few thousand people. La Quemada's material culture shows dependence on local materials – obsidian is very rare, pottery is all local.

La Quemada's complex of public buildings and plazas and ball courts stretched over 0.5 sq. km of a hilltop and adjacent slopes, from a northern pyramid to the southern Hall of the Columns, a true colonnaded building. The site's mortuary remains were a very visible part of the lives of its people, with displays of skeletons of both the cherished and the hated. Temple 18, at the western edge of the site, seems to have been a charnel house for the community's revered dead (Nelson *et al.* 1992). Elsewhere at the site, human bones were treated less carefully. In the Hall of the Columns were the remains of hundreds of individuals, many of them adult males. Many of the bones were "mutilated, some were apparently displayed, and most ended up in huge discard piles that suggest little respect for the deceased" (Nelson 1995: 613; see also Pérez 2002).

West Mexico

Sites of the Teuchitlán tradition reached their greatest extent in the early part of the Late Classic period, with architectural rings of structures stretching to a diameter of 125 m (410 ft) and clustered in groups. At Guachimontón, as many as eight rings and two ball courts formed the site's center [**10.23**]. There are 55 ball courts (a few over 100 m long) known from sites in the Teuchitlán core area, indicating that they served to strengthen ties among members of the tradition's elite class, the rulers, rather than integrating the more densely settled core with the culture's peripheral hinterland (Weigand 1996). The Teuchitlán tradition collapsed in the Late Classic, in the period from AD 700–900. The circular architectural tradition was no longer being promoted; insofar as Teuchitlán sites were being remodeled, the additions were rectilinear buildings.

New cultural traditions arose in West Mexico. The Atemajac Valley, now home to Guadalajara, second largest city in Mexico, is on the southwestern edge of the Bajío. Most of the known sites in this region date to the period AD 550 to 850, possibly a bit earlier. These sites, such as El Grillo and Ixtépete, show influence from the Bajío, if not Central Mexico, with features related to Coyotlatelco culture. Earlier circular structures were replaced by U-shaped and rectangular architecture and new ceramic types and mortuary styles, such as the box tomb, were introduced. The subsequent Atemajac phase probably dates to AD 750–900, though it might be somewhat later. New ceramic styles indicate an intrusive population, probably from further south in West Mexico. The sites, many of them located on hilltops, are small and seem to lack public architecture (Galván Villegas and Beekman 2001).

13.7, 13.8 *La Campana (Colima) dates from* AD *700–900. Its central feature is this pyramid (right and below), with staircases centered on each of its four sides, and its corners oriented toward the cardinal directions, and the smoking mountain Volcán de Fuego, appropriated into the site's layout. Tomb 9 at the site yielded a ceremonial brazier featuring Quetzalcoatl in an act of autosacrifice, perforating his penis, as he did to provide the blood from which humankind was created.*

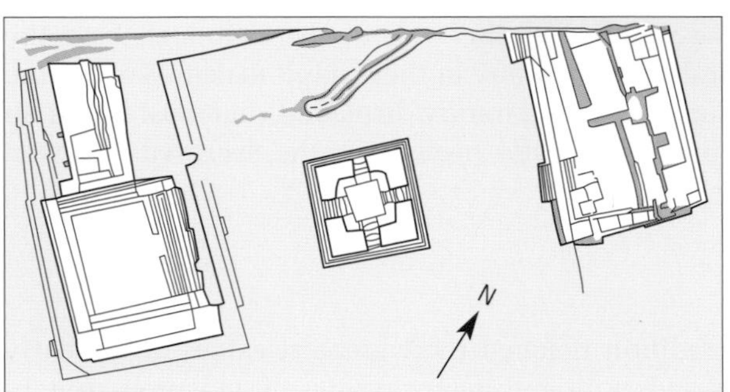

Well-excavated sites of the later Late Classic period in West Mexico are unusual, but La Campana, near the Pacific Coast, has monumental rectilinear architecture similar to that found in other sites elsewhere in Mesoamerica [**13.7, 13.8**].

West Mexico and Metalworking Mesoamerica enjoyed a technological revolution in the Late Classic: metalworking techniques were introduced from South America to West Mexico, and from there, during the period AD 600–800, metal objects began to disseminate over Mesoamerica and up into the Northern Arid Zone. The techniques are thought to have been brought from northwestern South America (now Ecuador) by the metalworkers themselves – the techniques are sufficiently complicated that it would have required the presence of skilled workers "to communicate information about extractive metallurgy as well as ... processing and manufacturing techniques" (Hosler 1994: 185). Metalworking in Mesoamerica, as we know, was not focused upon the development of cutting tool technology – tweezers and needles were the most common utilitarian metal artifacts – rather, valued properties of metal ornaments were color, brilliance, and sound (see box, pp. 364–365).

GULF LOWLANDS

Northern Gulf Lowlands: The Huasteca

During the Late Classic, the population of the northern Gulf lowlands and adjacent mountains of the Sierra Madre Oriental was settled in small polities centered upon such sites as San Antonio Nogalar, Buenavista Huaxcama, and Balcón de Montezuma. At all these places, many of the residential and ritual buildings were circular, an unusual trait in Mesoamerica, except for the Teuchitlán tradition of West Mexico. This northern Gulf region was, of course, on Mesoamerica's periphery, but periodically – as during the Late Classic and Postclassic periods – it was more closely integrated into the larger political trends of the Central Highlands, being situated nearly due north of the Basin of Mexico, with ready access to it through the Metztitlán Valley, along one of the tributaries of the Pánuco River. The Pánuco River system, one of Mesoamerica's major drainage systems, has its origins all along the west side of the Sierra Madre Oriental, thus connecting the northern lowlands with west and south – with the Bajío and the Tula region.

During the Classic period in the northern lowlands, we see the growing importance of the Huastecs, a Maya-speaking group that had moved into this region in the Formative period. By the Late Classic period, their lively culture was an integral part of the larger pattern of shared pan-Mesoamerican traits, and we can accurately call this region by its still-popular name, "the Huasteca" – land of the Huastecs.

Tamuín and Tantoc, two major sites of this region, lie about 100 km (*c.* 60 miles) inland from the Gulf of Mexico, on the Tampoán River, a tributary of the Pánuco. The sites are *c.* 7 km (*c.* 4 miles) apart – close enough so that their names are sometimes simply hyphenated, because they share a long (though poorly understood) culture history, with Tantoc having a somewhat longer occupation (beginning in the Formative period) and becoming the region's most important site in the Postclassic period. Tamuín, in the Late Classic, consisted of mounds and plazas extending over 106 hectares (262 acres), and its mural is one of the most important Huastec pictorial records [**13.9**].

Central Gulf Lowlands

The north-central and south-central Gulf lowlands occupied an important place in Late Classic–Epiclassic Mesoamerica. The central Gulf lowlands were not only the geographical midpoint between the great cultural poles of Chichén and Tula, but they contributed essential pieces to the shared constellation of traits, and its most imposing center, El Tajín, was a masterwork of architecture embellished with dazzling art, which will be discussed below.

13.9 *At Tamuín, a Huastec capital, a mural dating from the 9th or 10th century, and extending over 4.7 m (15.4 ft), shows what seem to be 12 elaborately costumed gods and warriors with "iconographic elements associated with Quetzalcoatl ... and other Mesoamerican deities" (Solís 1993: 52). As the detail of these two processional figures shows, the style of the art is clearly related to Mixteca-Puebla traditions (de la Fuente and Staines 2001).*

METALWORKING

WE HAVE NOTED in other contexts the value that Mesoamericans placed on any material that mimics the vibrancy of life – the movement of a rubber ball around a ball court, feather banners ruffling in a breeze. Metal objects expressed vitality through their reflective brilliance and warm color, and the tinkling sound made by bells and other multi-component ornaments.

Metalworking technology in Mesoamerica developed in West Mexico because it was the region in contact (presumably by sea) with the South American region which had already developed the techniques and was producing the bells and other objects that would become the repertoire of Mesoamerican metalworking. West Mexico was a natural recipient of such technology because of the presence there of readily available sources of the appropriate ores.

Mesoamerican metalworking had two phases of development (Hosler 1994). *Period 1* (AD 600–800 to 1200) involved copper-working. Copper is the easiest of metals to extract and work: some copper deposits are so pure that lumps of the raw material can be cold-hammered into shape. Yet even in this first phase, copper was extracted from minerals such as malachite and cuprite by smelting, which involves subjecting the ores to high heat. The metal was shaped into objects by melting it and pouring it into casts. These were either simple, producing blanks further shaped by hammering, or more complex, producing nearly-finished shapes from molds made with the lost-wax technique. This involves making a wax model of the finished object, producing a clay mold by encasing the wax model and then melting out the wax and filling the cavity with molten metal.

Most of the metal objects produced during this first period of Mesoamerican metallurgy were copper bells. These were small, usually spherical, and tinkling – the sound signified fertility and regeneration through its similarity to rainfall, thunder, and the rattle of rattlesnakes (consider, for example, the Temple-Pyramid of the Feathered Serpent at Teotihuacan, where the rattles of the serpents are an important and integral part of the repeated design). Manufactured originally in West Mexico in the Late Classic, by the Early Postclassic bells were found over a huge area, from what is now the U.S. Southwest down to Chichén Itzá, where hundreds were cast into the Cenote of Sacrifice. Their presence at many sites would seem to indicate that they were widely traded, but in fact the bells may evidence the presence, at these sites, of the traders themselves, who may have been wearing the bells while trading other products (Kelley 1995: 116).

Period 2 (AD 1200 to 1521) saw an elaboration of the technology, with more metals being worked and used, and an expansion of the range of products.

13.10–13.12 *Metalworkers were skilled artisans in ancient Mesoamerica. The illustration from the* Florentine Codex *(1569) shows the cold-hammering technique, here used to fashion "axes" (illustrated in the central drawings), which were actually used by the Aztecs as a medium of exchange. Cast copper bells were added to ear ornaments and pendants, and also worn in groups on the ankles and legs. In Aztec times they were markers of high status, part of deity and deity-impersonator costumes, and also worn by veteran long-distance merchants as part of the insignia of their high rank (Sahagún 1959 [Book 9]: 4).*

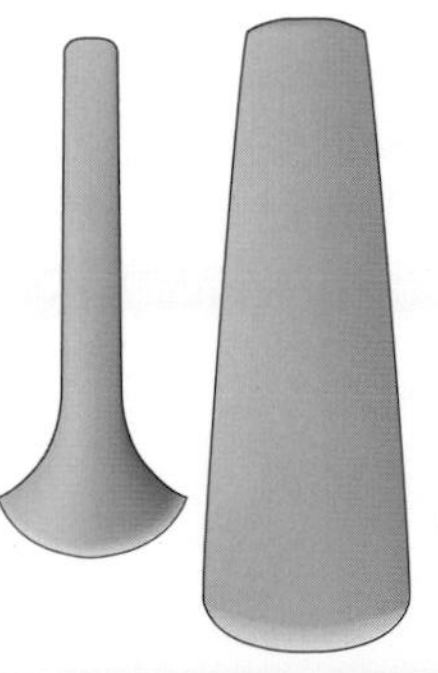

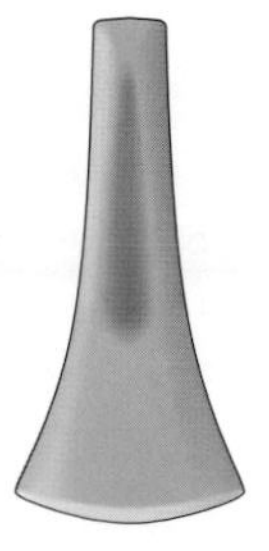

Mesoamerica can be said to have entered the Bronze Age in the sense that objects were made of alloys of copper and tin and copper and arsenic. These metals were superior to simple copper, in terms of strength and adaptability to more elaborate designs. Their production also involved a complicated process of locating and exploiting special sources as well as mastering a more complex smelting and casting procedure (Hosler and Macfarlane 1996).

The fascinating thing about bronze technology in Mesoamerica is that it wasn't used to make a wide range of cutting tools, as in the Old World, where bronze technology ushered in a whole new era of utilitarian and military applications, and ultimately led to the Iron Age as smelting techniques became even more refined. Some simple bronze tools and weapons were made in Mesoamerica, but the real focus of the use of the alloys was upon production of decorative items that looked like gold and silver, which were sacred materials. Gold and silver were apparently thought to have been the sacred excrement of the sun and moon. Gold and silver themselves were also found in West Mexico, and were also worked, but they were much softer metals. It was better to use the alloys that could be made to resemble them but could be adapted to a much wider range of shapes. The Spaniards were briefly dazzled by the brilliant jewelry and elaborate figures they were presented with, which looked so much like gold and silver, but quickly discarded them to search for the rarer items in precious metals.

The lush, swampy Gulf lowlands fascinated the Postclassic Aztecs, who saw the region as a land of food, and in famine times it was a place where Aztec rulers established enclaves, and commoners sold themselves into slavery in order to survive. The region was also a place of luxury – cacao, vanilla, and cotton grew there – products reserved, in the chilly Central Highlands, for the elite. These were important trade items in the Late Classic period, and distinctive cultural practices also bloomed in the Gulf lowlands. A death cult, focusing upon veneration of Mictlantecuhtli and Mictlancihuatl (underworld lord and lady) became a fixture of life. At El Zapotal, near Cerro de las Mesas, a skeletal representation of Mictlantecuhtli sat on a throne in a temple dedicated to him.

South-central Gulf Lowlands

In this region, small polities continued to dominate political geography. Teotihuacan's declining influence was echoed by Matacapan's declining size, but because there was no single capital controlling this region, there was limited opportunity for a takeover by a new set of dynasts bearing the attributes of the Feathered Serpent cult.

Cerro de las Mesas, occupied since the Middle Formative, had a final period of occupation in the Late Classic, when it was one of the region's largest capitals. Its prosperity may have been based upon cotton: the region produces cotton, and it was no doubt traded as a raw material, and was also spun into thread, and woven into cloth. Thus cotton could enter the economy at several levels – in fact, by the Late Postclassic, lengths of simple woven cotton cloth, called "mantas" by the Spanish, had become an accepted medium of exchange in the marketplaces.

13.13 *Mesoamerican women spent much of their lives in textile production, learning spinning and weaving at an early age and perfecting these skills as adults. In addition to supplying their own families with cloth, women produced the thread and lengths of cloth that were an important part of each family's tribute obligation. This drawing from the* Codex Mendoza *(c. 1541–1542) shows an Aztec woman spinning thread. In her left hand she holds a bundle of unspun fiber, and with her right hand she guides the filament onto the spinning spindle, a process which results in spun thread. The spindle is the straight stick weighted at the bottom (below the spooled thread) with a spindle whorl. The bottom end of the spindle rests in a small bowl placed on a straw mat. Cotton, a fine thread, called for a relatively light spindle whorl, while maguey thread required a much heavier whorl.*

Cotton While Mesoamericans spun and wove the fibers of many plants and animals, cotton was the only textile material that was widely produced (although only cultivable in *tierra caliente*) and widely used, and that consistently produced a fine, supple thread and fabric. Woven cotton was readily fashioned into simple garments and had other important uses: bedding and awnings for the house, ritual costumes and wrappings for the temple. Only maguey fiber equaled that of cotton in importance in everyday life and the larger economy, and in general maguey fiber was coarser, yielding a bast fabric more like linen, or even burlap.

Cotton was traded extensively as early as the Formative period, but during the Classic period a technological innovation in spinning was generally adopted, enhancing thread production (Stark *et al.* 1998). This was the development of the mold-made spindle whorl, a weight for the spindle that made the spinning process easier and the resulting thread more consistent [**13.13**]. We mentioned in a previous chapter that this was perhaps one of the only applications in Mesoamerica of the principle of the fly-wheel, a device that in the ancient Old World was applied on a much larger scale, to potters' wheels and other simple machines. In Mesoamerica, prior to the development of the standardized, mold-made spindle whorl, other whorls were used to regularize the motion of the spindle – archaeologists often find potsherds that have been carefully shaped into circles, and then drilled through the center, and these may have served this purpose. However, the mold-made whorl has a symmetry of form that is crucial to producing thread of consistently fine quality, as rapidly as possible.

North-central Gulf Lowlands and El Tajín

One of the great Mesoamerican centers of the Late Classic and Epiclassic periods, El Tajín probably controlled much of the north-central Gulf lowlands region. The great alluvial plain of this hot country region was ideal for such crops as cotton and cacao, and programs of agricultural intensification involved techniques to drain swampy areas (Diehl 2000: 179). First occupied in the Late or Terminal Formative, El Tajín grew rapidly in the mid-Classic, probably contributing to the decline of El Pital, Teotihuacan's Early Classic contact center in the north-central Gulf lowlands.

El Tajín achieved greatest size and power in the Late Classic and Epiclassic, possibly with a population of 20,000 and urban area of about 1 sq. km (0.4 sq. miles), after which it was all but abandoned until the Late Postclassic (Wilkerson 2001b). The site has distinctive traditions of art and architecture, such as extensive use of step-fret motif, and the use of the "flying cornice" as adornment on *talud-tablero* façades.

El Tajín had over a dozen ball courts, possibly each associated with a different ruler. Ball-game paraphernalia reveals the importance of cult and its strong ritualized relation to rulership, militarism, sacrifice, and the underworld. Sculptured panels of the South Ball Court show a sequence of scenes portraying festive preparations for the ball game, the game itself and the sacrifice of one of the players, his visit to the underworld to obtain *pulque*, and the autosacrifice of an underworld deity who pierces his penis "allowing the blood to enter the *pulque* vat, thus completing the cycle" (Diehl 2000: 178). *Pulque* is here related to ritual sacrifice and the ball game and integrated with imagery of the planet Venus in its 584-day cycle, and with *pulque* as a gift of the underworld gods (Wilkerson 2001b). While we know that *pulque* use in Mesoamerica long predates the Late Classic, intoxication in this context at El Tajín seems to have had a particular function in unleashing violence and putting it to ritual purpose.

The site's upper level is Tajín Chico, a huge platform with monumental structures probably used as palaces, thus seeming to have a secular rather than a ritual function [**13.14**]. Yet one of Tajín Chico's structures, Building A, was designed so that its interior corridors are shaped like miniature ball courts, and access to the building is through a tunnel-like stairway that seems to spatially mimic the passage between earth and underworld emphasized in the ball game and its associated rituals (Sarro 2001). The Tajín Chico area is dominated by the Building of the Columns, which may have been the palace of 13 Rabbit, one of the last rulers. The columns are decorated with figures, such as "Eagle Knight" (Marquina: 446–447).

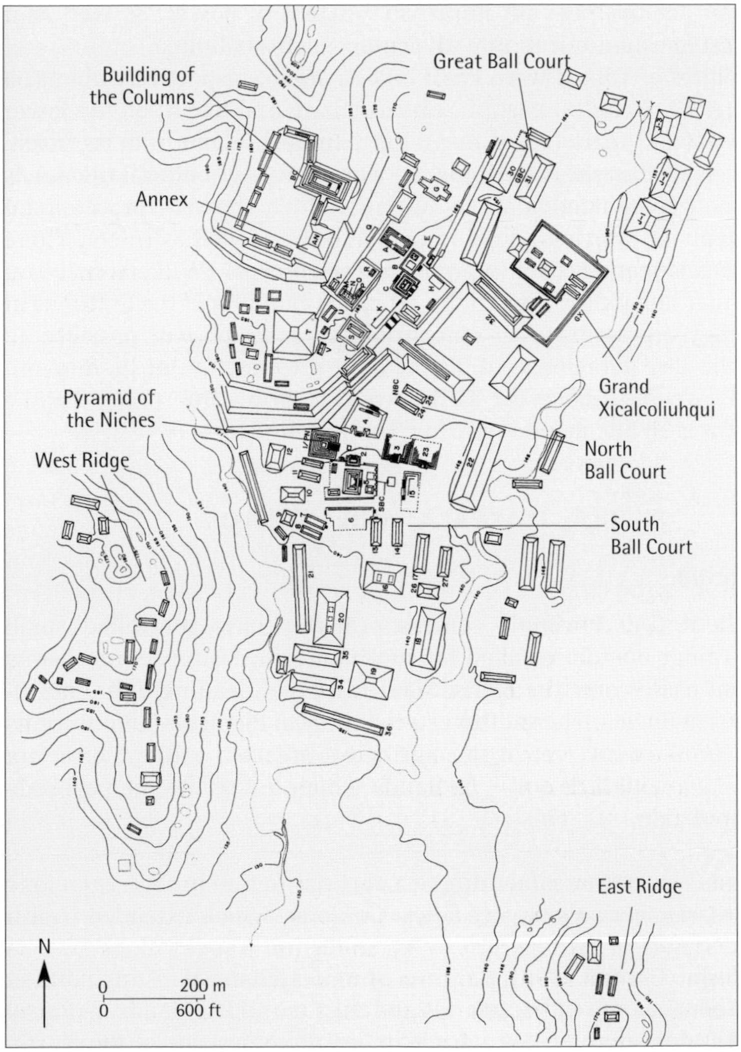

13.14 *El Tajín's plan, by Jeffrey K. Wilkerson, shows how the site spills down hillsides, with the newer section, the huge leveled platform of Tajín Chico, dominating the northwest sector. The Pyramid of the Niches with its 365 recesses (probably commemorating the days of the solar year), is at the center of the plan, with staircase on the east side. Note the many ball courts and their varying sizes and orientations.*

El Tajín's Hinterland and Secondary Capitals Determining the region controlled by a major capital is difficult in the absence of historical documentation. Archaeologists look to other indicators, such as the relative size of major centers, the distance between them, and stylistic similarities in architecture and other aspects of material culture. For example, Yohualinchan was a secondary center less than 50 km (*c.* 30 miles) south of Tajín. Its architecture mimics Tajín's in the use of flying cornices and niches, but on a smaller scale and with lower quality. Located on the lower slopes of the Sierra Madre Oriental at the edge of the plain of the north-central Gulf lowlands, Yohualinchan was a gateway community for

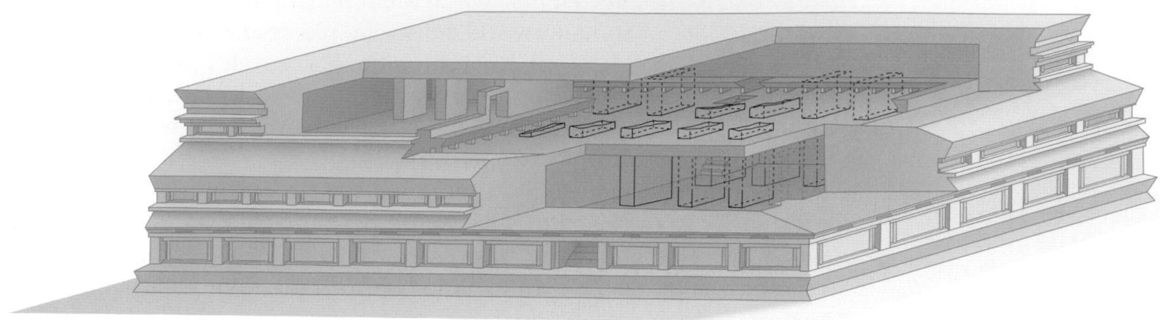

13.15 *The reconstruction drawing shows Building B, one of Tajín's palaces, which demonstrates several architectural features at El Tajín. The "flying cornice" adorns the top of the* talud-tablero *façade, and the* tablero *sections are niches. The cutaway section reveals interior stairways. These were used at other sites, but rarely do they link two extensive stories as shown here. Note, in the upper story, pillars support the ceiling and thus provide extensive open space, and the banquette (bench) lining the edges of the room. The structure's base is 30 by 105 m (98 by 348 ft).*

travel between this region and Puebla, to the southwest. Tajín's influence at Yohualinchan demonstrates an impressive extent of power, as well as a strong interest in communication with centers such as Cholula.

Other satellites of Tajín's were Paxil and Aparicio, respectively about 65 and 80 km (*c.* 40, 50 miles) east of Yohualinchan, and like it, on the lower slopes of the Sierra. Aparicio was just 8 km (5 miles) inland from the coast, where an even smaller site, Las Higueras, was a local agricultural town. Las Higueras has become famous for its murals, which showed "processional scenes ... involving warriors, deity impersonators, as well as rulers. There are ball game and maguey beer (*pulque*) cult references" (Wilkerson 2001a: 345). So similar in style are they to the art of the Building of the Columns at Tajín that they are assumed to date from the same period, possibly AD 900–1100, the last florescence of Tajín, and, presumably, of its domain. Santa Luisa, occupied since the Early Archaic, also came under Tajín's control, and was all but abandoned after Tajín declined.

PUEBLA, TLAXCALA, AND MORELOS

Eastern Puebla

While northern Gulf lowlands centers probably only controlled small regions, El Tajín's domain reached far south, encompassing approaches to the important passes over the Sierra Madre Oriental, leading to the northeastern plains of Puebla. The southwestern Valley of Puebla is famous for its agricultural productivity, yet in the northeast, adjacent to the Sierra, are expanses of lava with little soil – badlands which to this day support only scattered population.

Cantona Thus it comes as something of a surprise to find in this region one of the Late Classic-period's largest cities, Cantona, which extended over a densely settled area of 12.5 sq. km (5 sq. miles) on a rocky slope (García Cook and Merino Carrión 1998). Cantona occupies a natural resting point in trade routes between the Gulf lowlands and the Central Highlands, being 60 km (37 miles) due south of Yohualinchan, on the other side of the Sierra.

And while this proximity to the lush lowlands would have made it easy for Cantona to have imported food, they may have been supplying the lowlands with *pulque* – the maguey plant that provides the sap prefers the arid highlands (Cantona is at 2,500-m elevation – *c.* 8,200 ft – and its region has a rainfall of only about 700 mm/27 in). Given the importance of the *pulque* cult to El Tajín and its subsidiaries, a regular source of supply from the highlands would have been a valuable asset in a trading partner.

Occupied from the Formative period on, Cantona's apogee was in the Late Classic and Epiclassic, and it was abandoned after AD 1050. The city's residences surrounded its 100+ plazas, the foci of civic-ceremonial architecture, which included many ball courts – 24 have been located so far. Many of the human remains recovered from the city were sacrificial victims, and in some cases the bones show processing consistent with butchering and cooking. The city's layout was not like Teotihuacan's grid – circulation at Cantona was constrained, as was access to the ceremonial courtyards. Throughout the city were watchtowers, and fortifications seem to have been designed to repel foreign invaders and discourage internal unrest.

Cantona's material culture remains show some unusual patterns. There is an abundance of pottery, but it is of a local type – and in spite of a Classic-period occupation there is an almost total absence of Thin Orange, that ubiquitous marker of Teotihuacan contact. A few sherds indicate wares from the Gulf lowlands, the Central Highlands and the Bajío, the Mixteca Alta, and even West Mexico. There are no figurines, in spite of the proximity of the Gulf lowlands and the remarkable ceramic figurine traditions there. Sculpted items, mostly from the abundant local basalt, include a set of phallus-shaped stones, placed as an offering at the foot of the central plaza's pyramid.

Two very extensive plazas may have served as markets. The city was a major distribution center for obsidian from the nearby Oyameles-Zaragoza sources, which was traded to southern Puebla, the southern Gulf lowlands, and the Maya lowlands. Most of the lithic remains are prismatic blades of obsidian from these local sources, and there are many blade-producing workshops. Cantona may have grown to its very large size – some archaeologists speculate that its population may have been 80,000–90,000 – as an obsidian trading center that first competed with Teotihuacan's obsidian distribution network and then, with Teotihuacan's collapse, grew much more powerful in long-distance trade.

Western Puebla, Tlaxcala, and Morelos

The broad fertile plains that make up much of Puebla, Tlaxcala, and Morelos were ripe for the development of new capitals in the Late Classic. At around AD 600, the collapse of Teotihuacan's influence seemed to have left something of a power vacuum in the region, while volcanic eruptions from Popocatépetl in *c.* AD 650 and between 700 and 750 blanketed parts of western Puebla with a layer of ash, and must have provided a dramatic backdrop to life over a very broad region. Amidst this political and natural chaos, immigrants arrived to establish new centers and make trouble at old ones. The pan-Mesoamerican quality of these times that derived from the widespread sharing of traits can also be seen in the cosmopolitan mix of ethnic groups that resulted from migrants pushing – or being pushed – into adjacent territories. In Puebla, the Olmeca-Xicalanca were among the best-known of these incoming ethnic groups, but their origins are poorly understood. Their pottery, for example, combined wares related to those of the southern Gulf lowlands (heartland of the Postclassic Xicalanga long-distance merchants), the Central Highlands (Coyotlatelco tradition) and the Mixteca Alta (García Cook 2001).

The Olmeca-Xicalanca may have been responsible for a decline in the fortunes of Cholula (Plunket and Uruñela 2001). In fact, settlement patterns shifted toward defensible hilltops for 200 years (*c.* AD 650–850), and Cholulans sought a haven on Cerro Zapotecas, just 3 km (*c.* 2 miles) west of Cholula's Great Pyramid. This hill was terraced for farming and for the establishment of a small residential and ceremonial center (Mountjoy and Peterson 1973). Violence followed the Cholulans, however, and houses and temples show evidence of having been burned.

Cacaxtla The Olmeca-Xicalanca may have been the perpetrators of this destruction, but they were also engaged in impressive building programs of their own. Cacaxtla, *c.* 15 km (*c.* 10 miles) north of Cholula, was established soon after AD 600 and was occupied until AD 900. While it has been claimed by some archaeologists to have become the Valley of Puebla's new capital, it is an impressive but not an extensive site. Built on a slope less than a mile west of the already-established ceremonial site of Xochitecatl, Cacaxtla was well-fortified with moats and a wall. Its acropolis consists of several open plazas surrounded by multi-room structures that served elite residential and ritual functions. Its population may have been as large as 10,000.

Cacaxtla's spectacular murals are rendered in Maya style, but depict military scenes in which the figures with Maya costume elements are bested by those in Central Highlands garb [**13.16**, **13.17**]. The murals also feature imagery of the planet Venus, whose cycles governed the timing of warfare for the Maya and others, and glyphs of towns that may have been conquered by Cacaxtla. There are also more peaceful themes, such as a merchant and his trader's pack, called a cacaxtli in Nahuatl. Cacaxtla, "place of the

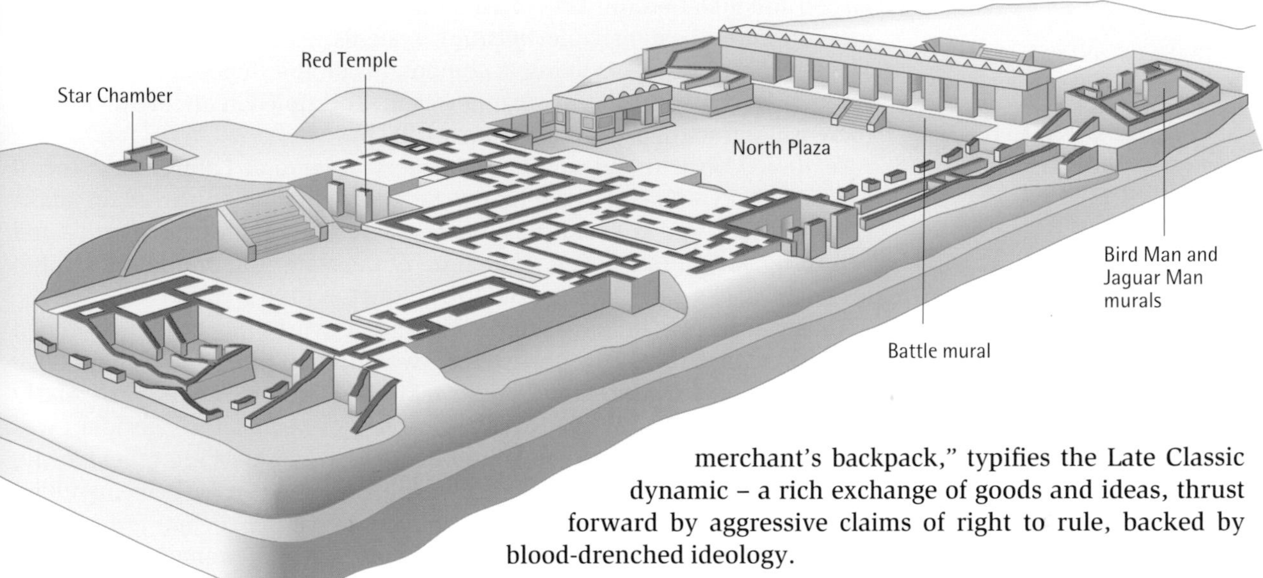

merchant's backpack," typifies the Late Classic dynamic – a rich exchange of goods and ideas, thrust forward by aggressive claims of right to rule, backed by blood-drenched ideology.

13.16, 13.17 *Cacaxtla's acropolis was colorfully adorned with murals, including the Bird Man (opposite), the first to be uncovered. Note the planet Venus symbols in the square motif at his right shoulder, and the feathered serpent upon which his taloned feet stand. The border has a blue background, a watery world where conchs and turtles live.*

Cholula On the great fertile plain of Puebla, Cholula became Mesoamerica's most important center of Ehécatl-Quetzalcoatl worship in the Postclassic period. As we have noted in previous chapters, Cholula the modern city overlies ancient Cholula, and sorting out the timing of historical events is difficult, but a cultural decline is perceptible. Some scholars believe that the decline from AD 650 to 850 involved abandonment, but cultural continuity is also perceived, nonetheless "with substantial change in material culture, probably as the result of changing ethnic composition and religious orientation" (McCafferty 2000: 350). Evidence from the Epiclassic period reveals a new episode of construction at the Great Pyramid, with the Patio of the Altars showing design motifs similar to those of El Tajín and the Mixteca Alta, and the first use of Quetzalcoatl imagery at Cholula. A large palace near the Great Pyramid was built at around AD 800, but whether it was used by priests of the temple or by secular rulers is unclear. It is clear, however, that by the Epiclassic, Cholula had returned to a role of prominence, and this more or less coincided with Cacaxtla's decline.

Morelos

Late Classic Morelos showed the signs of the power vacuum with a decline in population in the east, which had always been more influenced by Teotihuacan. However, nearly 1,000 years after Chalcatzingo's Middle Formative apogee, a small village developed there, with civic-ceremonial architecture including a circular pyramid and a ball court (Arana 1987). Western Morelos saw the rise of Xochicalco, the region's most famous archaeological site.

13.18–13.20 *Xochicalco's complex of civic and ceremonial buildings included five ball courts, and focused upon the Pyramid of the Plumed Serpents (below). This building's west-facing staircase (opposite above) was the only interruption in a sloping* talud *festooned with feathered serpents. (Opposite below) The detail is from the left side of the staircase, and shows a serpent entwined around two date glyphs, possibly day-names (Smith 2000: 65–67). In the* tablero *frieze , seated figures with quetzal headdresses face the front of the pyramid. Some are associated with glyphs that may be place names. Most hold knotted bags, some are speaking, as indicated by the speech scroll, and in front of each is a set of teeth appearing to bite a disk. This pair of motifs may refer to tribute-paying – in Nahuatl that verb is comprised of words meaning "to eat something precious" (Hirth 1989: 73).*

Xochicalco Built atop five adjacent hilltops, this center flourished between AD 650 and 900. Certainly the threat of violence was a factor in Xochicalco's location and its extensive fortification systems. At its height, the city had 10,000–15,000 residents living in compounds on the slopes below the civic-ceremonial center. The general area was first occupied at about 900 BC, and there was a trace of occupation from AD 900 to 1521.

Feathered serpent and sacrificial imagery abound at Late Classic Xochicalco. The Pyramid of the Plumed Serpents dominates the main plaza [**13.18–13.20**], and at Xochicalco, the Feathered Serpent "is more than a god of fertility and abundance; it is the head of the state cult, and ... the symbol for Xochicalco's elite" (Smith 2000: 79).

Xochicalco's role in long-distance trading networks has been determined from its architecture – the presence of two different plazas that could have served as marketplaces – and from its material culture remains, particularly obsidian (Hirth 2000). Most (over 75 percent) of Xochicalco's obsidian was imported from the Ucareo source in Michoacán, 200 km (124 miles) away. Twelve obsidian prismatic blade-producing workshops have been identified at the site, many of them domestic contexts involving several presumably related families. There were several workshops which seemed to serve the needs of craft specialists in whole neighborhoods, and one specialized facility with a very high concentration of obsidian, and no domestic artifacts at all.

Ucareo obsidian was probably brought in from western Mexico by a trade route through Teotenango, northwest of Xochicalco, in the Toluca Valley. Another trade route, linking Xochicalco with Guerrero, to the southwest, brought Mezcala-style carvings as well as some exotic pottery vessels, shell, and cacao. A third route, southeast to the Mixteca Baja, would have supplied other exotic ceramics and also some Gulf Coast-style carvings and Maya-style jade carvings. Note that there seem to have been no commercial ties with the Basin of Mexico – even decorated Coyotlatelco ceramics, so widely traded within the Basin of Mexico, and common at Late Classic Teotihuacan, are absent here (Cyphers 2000).

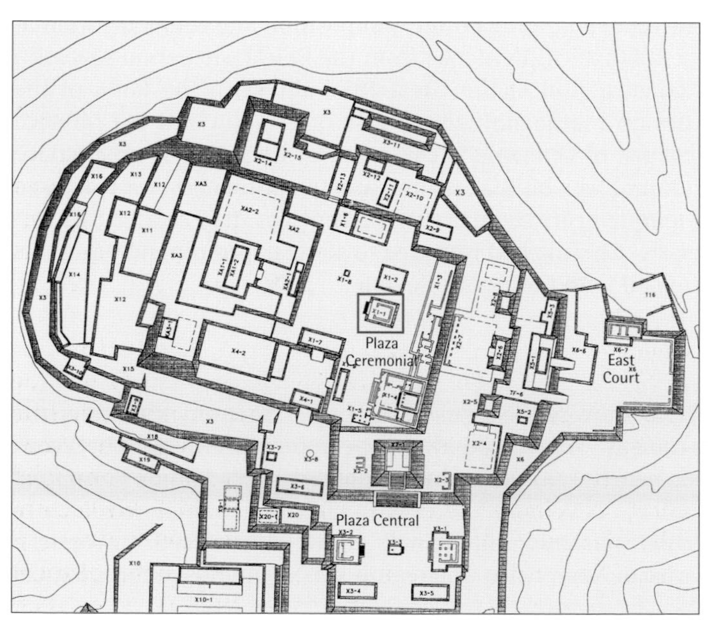

Xochicalco's motifs of conquest and tribute-extraction were mentioned at the beginning of this chapter. It would seem that this was not a satisfactory situation for those who became the underclass, the tribute-payers, because in AD 900 the ceremonial center and surrounding residential neighborhoods met a violent end, so thoroughly destroyed that subsequent occupation in the Postclassic is limited to traces of domestic debris. While Xochicalco may have been destroyed by aggressive newcomers to the area, such conquests are usually takeovers, and preserve a center and its tribute-payers. Utter desolation more commonly results from the ferocious rage of the oppressed; in other words, Xochicalco was probably destroyed by its own tributary population (Hirth 2000: 267–268).

MIXTEC REGIONS AND OAXACA

The Late Classic period in these regions is another story of a great city – Monte Albán – in rapid decline, and the expansion, into the void, of other peoples, other ethnic groups. In this case it was the Mixtec, whose rivalries with each other and with the Zapotecs effected a cultural mosaic in the Valley of Oaxaca, a pattern which began in the Classic period and extended through into the Postclassic.

Mixtec cities, while always modest in size, would become centers of commerce and culture in the Postclassic period. The Mixtec were to become famed, in the Postclassic period, for their skill in writing and other elite crafts. Their historical codices, written in the Mixtec script, recounted events and personages important to this era and the Postclassic period, and are among the oldest surviving pre-Columbian books. Much of the content of these books deals with dynastic alliances and conflicts, and the vigor of Mixtec cities is reflected in their push from the Mixteca Alta down into the Valley of Oaxaca. The Mixtec were not, however, empire builders – their interest was in establishing and maintaining city-states and their adjacent hinterlands. Mixteca Alta cities seem to have experienced a population decline in the Late Classic, with fortified hilltops being used as ritual centers while residences were built on valley floors (Marcus and Flannery 2001: 392). Mixteca Alta cities flourished in succeeding periods, and will be discussed in Chapters 14 and 16.

Oaxaca and Monte Albán

During the earliest centuries of the Late Classic period, Monte Albán increased to its largest size, and then, by AD 750, "the public buildings in its Main Plaza were crumbling" (Marcus and Flannery 2001: 390–391). Its elites fled to other Zapotec centers in the Oaxaca Valley, thereafter using the great city as a necropolis. The timing of abandonment of the Main Plaza is uncertain – Monte Albán IIIb, the period of largest size and then decline, is dated from AD 500 to 700/750. Thereafter, population at the site was limited to the families farming the 2,000+ terraces on the city's slopes.

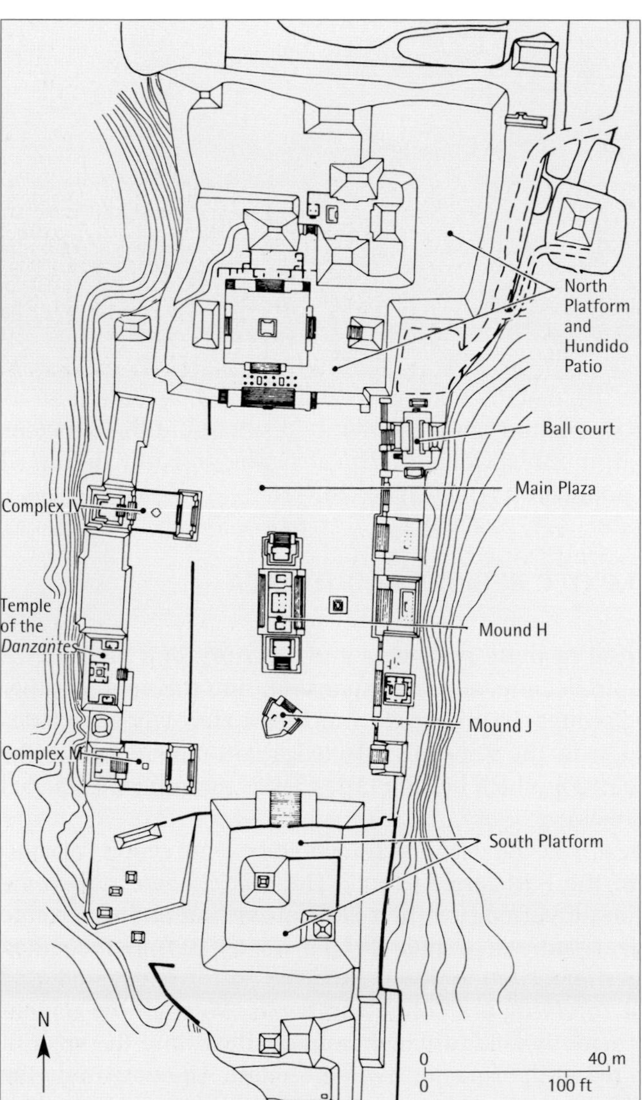

The overall Oaxaca Valley pattern in phase IIIb was of a collapse of Monte Albán's wide-ranging hegemony, causing population to concentrate at Monte Albán, which "reached its peak of urban development ... with a population estimated at 24,000" (Marcus and Flannery 1996: 234). It was at this time that the Main Plaza [**13.21, 13.22**] achieved its final form, with the array of buildings that we see today. It should be noted that Zapotec religion honored a supreme being, a self-creating creator, but "no images were made of him and no one could come into direct contact with him" (Marcus 2001: 846). Images were made of Lightning (Cociyo) and other elements so dramatically part of life on Monte Albán's ridge: Wind, Clouds, Hail, and Rain. However, the Feathered Serpent is absent from Monte Albán's Classic-period iconography – the city's powers were in decline as the cult was on the rise.

During Monte Albán IV (AD 700/750–1000), Jalieza became the largest community in the Oaxaca Valley, with a population of about 16,000, after which it declined to about 6,500 in the Late Postclassic. Mitlá and Zaachila also

13.21, 13.22 *Monte Albán's location on a hilltop in a valley surrounded by mountains is echoed in the site's layout, with the central buildings forming a set of promontories surrounded by a plaza and other monumental architecture. This view, towards the northeast, shows the central buildings "J," thought to be an astronomical observatory, with the "I"-"H"-"G" complex to its north, and behind that, the northern complex, probably the palace of the rulers. As the plan (opposite) shows, the South Platform was surmounted by a pyramid. Just northwest of it was System M, where the* danzante *bas-reliefs were installed in an earlier epoch.*

became more important, and Yagul flourished, with an acropolis of several buildings around patios, and a Zapotec-style ball court larger than that of Monte Albán. Late architecture shows a mixture of Mixtec and Zapotec styles, reflecting the mixed ethnicity of these times. Also a sign of the times, a fortress was built on the hilltop behind the site.

Lambityeco This was another of the Zapotec city-states that grew as Monte Albán was collapsing. Located in the middle of the eastern Tlacolula arm of the Oaxaca Valley, it probably had a population of about 4,000 in AD 800. Its residences show the Zapotec pattern of incorporating tombs into house construction, and the house of the town's ruler, the *coqui*, and its chief priest, the *bigaña*, are particularly elaborate examples of this pattern (Lind and Urcid 1983). The last occupants of the *coqui*'s house seem to have been Lord 8 Death and Lady 5 Reed, whose remains were the last to have been interred in the multi-occupant tomb. Plaster portraits of Lord 8 Death's grandparents and great-grandparents adorn the tomb's façade and reliefs on the altar complex just above it, in the south patio of the house [**13.23**]. North of the house is a sweat bath, the family's own place for hygiene, curing, and purification before rituals. The nearby house of the town's chief priest, the *bigaña*, is similar in size, slightly different in layout, and also features an ancestral tomb – but no femurs are missing. Lambityeco's florescence only outlasted Monte Albán's by a short while, and ended soon after AD 800.

13.23 *At Lambityeco, the ruler's house, a set of rooms around two patios, extended over 370 sq. m (1,329 sq. ft). Lord 8 Death's grandfather is shown in the altar frieze; he's grasping a human femur (thigh bone) in his hand, and this is "a symbol of his hereditary right to rule" (Lind and Urcid 1983: 80). In the tomb, many of the femurs were missing, removed by descendants as symbols of their authority.*

Tehuantepec Region During the Late Classic, Zapotec political interference did not extend southeast to the Pacific Coast, and there is little evidence of trade between the Oaxaca Valley and this part of the Isthmus of Tehuantepec (Zeitlin 2001: 544). Cultural affinities are with the northern side of the Isthmus, the Gulf of Mexico. Southern Tehuantepec's largest community, Saltillo, shared some of the traits of the ball game cult, with a cache of decapitated heads and considerable evidence of Tajín-style materials, including ball game paraphernalia, but no formal ball court has been identified.

Further Developments

The next chapter takes us to a ball court about which there is absolutely no doubt – it is Mesoamerica's largest and most imposing example, at Chichén Itzá. Departing from our format of examining stages of culture history as they occurred on either side of the great divide of the Isthmus of Tehuantepec, we focus upon Chichén in the east (Chapter 14) and Tula in the west (Chapter 15), at the end of the Classic period and beginning of the Postclassic.

14 THE MAYA IN THE TERMINAL CLASSIC AND EARLY POSTCLASSIC (AD 800–1200)

THE COLLAPSE OF MAYA CIVILIZATION in the southern lowlands was so spectacular a failure of human cultural adaptation that, in the modern popular imagination, it has sometimes eclipsed the important survival and success of Maya civilization elsewhere east of the Isthmus of Tehuantepec. Maya cultures thrived throughout the Late Classic, Terminal Classic and Epiclassic, and Postclassic periods, in the northern Yucatán Peninsula and in the highlands of Guatemala and the interior plateau of Chiapas [14.1]. Today, *c.* 7,500,000 Maya living in Mexico and Guatemala are the direct descendants of these peoples.

We saw, in Chapter 12, that after the failure of Petén Maya rulers to maintain their power and the failure of the earth to sustain crop production, demographic decline over several centuries gradually eroded populations down to numbers so small that it was no longer feasible to maintain defensible settlements. Presumably, survivors lived off the land, becoming hunter-foragers who used the ancient civic-ceremonial centers as shrines and campsites, much like the 19th- and early 20th-century Lacandon Maya of eastern Chiapas. Some survivors close to the borders of the southern lowlands culture area may have joined the flourishing Maya communities in the Chiapas and Guatemala highlands, or those in the north and east.

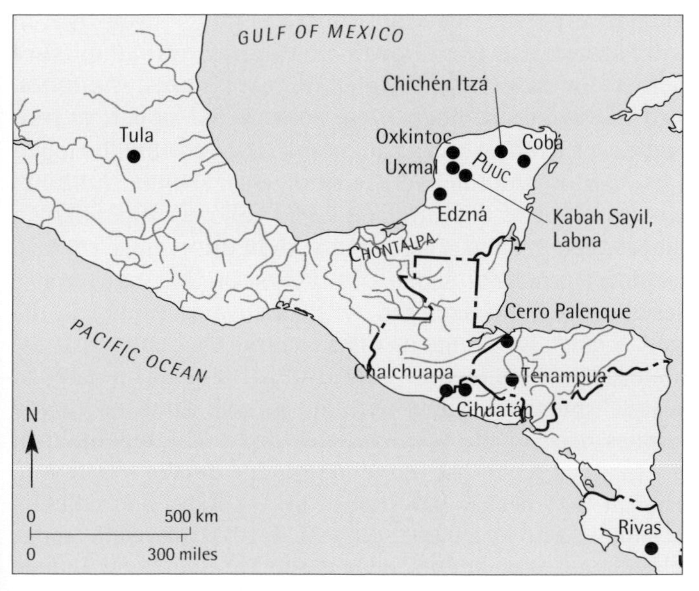

14.1 *Eastern Middle America, showing Early Postclassic-period regions and sites referred to in Chapter 14.*

As the world of the southern lowlands disintegrated, the northern lowlands became influenced by the expanding cultural horizon discussed in Chapter 13, that began in the wake of Teotihuacan's decline and extended into the Early Postclassic. In Chapter 12, the Río Bec sites just north of the Petén, and Chenes sites further to the northwest, were mentioned. Here we will discuss Maya culture further north: the Puuc sites in the

northwest, Cobá and its associates in the northeast, and in the center and ultimately dominating Yucatán in the Early Postclassic, Chichén Itzá. Themes of conflict involving communities and their dominant lineages continue; defensive city walls were a common feature, even at modest sites (Dahlin 2000; Palka 2001).

While the inscriptions whose decipherment has so illuminated the history of the Petén Maya are nearly absent in northern Yucatán, some light is shed on the developments of this period by the earliest reach of the Colonial era annals documenting the events unfolding at various sites. There are about a dozen books of Chilam Balam that are 18th- and 19th-century compilations of earlier writings, and they combine prophecy and divination with references to pre-Conquest events (Gibson and Glass 1975: 379–387), including those occurring in this Terminal Classic and Early Postclassic era.

Obviously, such faint echoes of earlier events are difficult to interpret, or even credit, but like any signals from a void they are worth considering, and as the gap of time is reduced, they become stronger and more interpretable. One political trend that was strongly manifested in the many city-states of Late Postclassic northern Yucatán was that of shared rule, in which a town would be governed by a council composed of the members of several powerful lineages. This tradition of joint rulership, sometimes called Mul Tepal, may extend back to the period we now consider.

NORTHWESTERN YUCATÁN: THE PUUC REGION

"Puuc" is a Mayan word for "ridge" and the Puuc Range is a low line of hills around a northwest–southeast running ridge, distinctive in the northern Yucatán Peninsula's otherwise rather flat and featureless plain. This part of the peninsula has relatively fertile soil, but rainfall is much lower than in the Petén and the dry season lasts from November through April. Puuc sites are famous for their many underground water storage cisterns, *chultunes*. These bottle-shaped, plastered chambers were constructed as part of residential house groups; each *chultun* had a catchment basin around the top to funnel rainfall to its interior, and the average storage capacity of *chultunes* in the Puuc region was about 36,000 liters (*c.* 9,500 gallons). If per person use is calculated at between 2.5 and 5 liters a day, then the average *chultun* could supply several dozen people throughout the dry season (McAnany 1990).

Another manifestation of Puuc concern with the water supply is the countless water god (*Chac,* also *Chaac* or *Chak*) masks that embellish the façades of their monumental architecture [**14.2, 14.3**]. These are rendered in distinctive "Puuc-style" mosaics rather than in carved stone or carved plaster, the techniques used in the southern lowlands. The repetition of motifs is on such a massive scale that the iconographic details recede into the overall pattern, but the effect is like that of prayer flags, an endlessly recurring litany of supplication to spiritual powers, here, rendered in stone.

The time of establishment of most Puuc sites is poorly understood, but we

14.4 *The regularity and elegance of Puuc architecture is demonstrated in the three-level Palace at Sayil, 84 m (275 ft) wide. Its 70 rooms open out onto terraces formed by the roofs of lower levels and the ground level patio. The columned doorways of the second level provide "a rhythmic alteration with simple rectangular openings [that] is one of the pleasing traits of the Puuc style" (Proskouriakoff 1963: 56).*

14.2, 14.3 *(Opposite) Like an architectural mantra, Puuc mosaics repeat the image of Chac, who represented water in all its modes: in* cenotes, *cisterns* (chultunes), *lakes, the sea, rivers, rain and clouds (de la Garza 1995). Long-nosed Chac masks decorate Uxmal's Nunnery. The drawing is from the* Dresden Codex, *the oldest (possibly 13th century) and most complete of four surviving Maya screenfold books (Miller 1996).*

know that the area was settled in the Formative period, and Puuc architecture is known from between AD 700 and 800 at Edzná and Oxkintoc, where this style began (Ball 2001). It is clearly related to the architectural style of the adjacent Chenes region. Furthermore, Puuc sites share the cultural heritage of the Petén Maya, though inscriptions are fairly rare. The Puuc sites also reflect the political turmoil further south – many Puuc sites have defensive features such as walls, and the demographic increases in the Puuc region during the period of southern Maya collapse no doubt represent migrations north. The best-known Puuc sites, flourishing *c.* AD 800–1000, are Kabah, Sayil, and Labna, and the largest and most elaborate, Uxmal.

Kabah, Sayil, and Labna

These three sites form a line about 20 km (12 miles) long, about 20 km south of Uxmal. They are contemporaneous with Uxmal, and their visible architecture dates to AD 800–1000 [**14.4**]. It is likely that these sites and Uxmal were political equals in the last centuries of the Classic period, and then Uxmal achieved some sort of regional ascendancy.

Intensive surveys around Sayil revealed a dense population, probably dating to after AD 700 (Tourtellot and Sabloff 1994; Smyth *et al.* 1995), an important labor resource for construction projects (Carmean 1991). A causeway 1.7 km (*c.* 1 mile) long leads from Sayil to the recently discovered site, Chac II, which dates to AD 600–800 (Smyth *et al.* 1998).

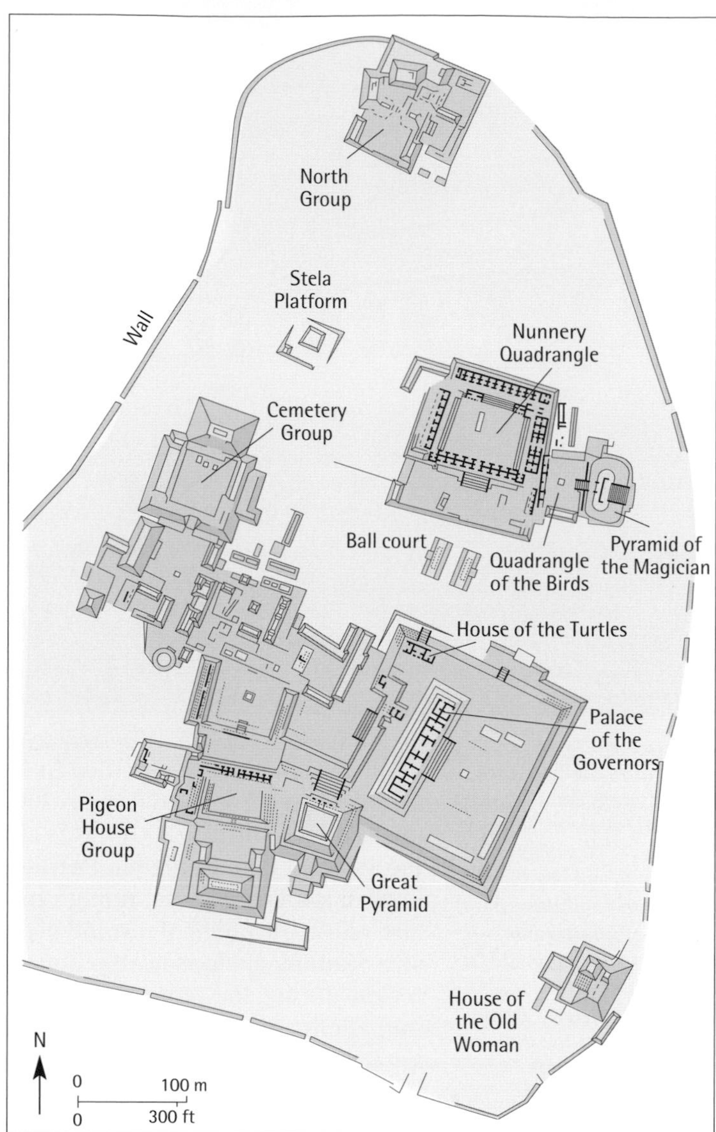

14.5 *(Below) Uxmal's Stela 14 is in the tradition of the southern lowlands. Lord Chac wears a huge necklace of precious stones, and a broad-brimmed hat with three tiers of feathers. The slightest movement would have created a riveting impression of resplendent undulation. Lord Chac stands on a jaguar throne, which itself presses down upon two nude males whose splayed posture and puffy eyes suggest that they are dead.*

Uxmal

One of ancient Mesoamerica's greatest sites, Uxmal was built on a grandiose scale. The site as a whole covered at least 10 sq. km (4 sq. miles) and its size and complexity, and the presence of causeways (*sacbeob*) heading off toward other sites would indicate that it may have served as some kind of central place for its region. However, in contrast to the situation of the Petén Maya, there is no epigraphic evidence touting victories over other polities. While inscriptions are few, we do know that Uxmal's greatest king, Lord Chac, lived around AD 900 [14.5] and that some of Uxmal's greatest monuments were built at the time of his reign.

Looking at the site plan [14.6], one's eye is drawn to the two great platform-based structures of the Nunnery Quadrangle and the Palace of Governors, respectively north and south of the central ball court. Note, however, the presence of several other quadrangular groups of buildings – linear structures arranged around large, squarish interior courtyards – the North Group and the Cemetery Group are prominent among them. These have been less well-explored, archaeologically, than the Nunnery Quadrangle and Palace of the Governors, but if Mul Tepal-style shared rule by several lineages was operating at Uxmal, these compounds may represent each lineage's residential and administrative palace (Pohl 1999).

The Palace of the Governors [14.7] may have served as an elite administrative and residential building. It dominates a 14-m (46-ft) high square platform, roughly 175 m (574 ft) on a side – the Palace, 95 m long, 11 m deep, and almost 9 m tall (312, 36, and 30 ft), is a good example of what archaeologists who study the Maya call a "range structure" – a linear building on a low platform with a set of side-by-side rooms. In fact, the term was developed to denote a building that was probably a palace, but for which there was no definite evidence of occupation as a noble or royal residence. While "range structure" admirably avoids falsely imputing a function in the

14.6 *(Opposite above) Uxmal's monumental architecture is encompassed by a defensive wall. In the center is the ball court, between the Nunnery Quadrangle and the Palace of the Governors, all three brought to their final stage of building, or rebuilding, about the time of the reign of Lord Chac. While the Great Pyramid is the largest structure at the site, the most visually dominating monument is the massive conical oval, the Pyramid of the Magician.*

14.7 *Uxmal's Palace of the Governors, with an intricate mosaic frieze adorning the façade.*

absence of, say, a dated inscription stating "this was Lord Chac's house," palace function can be inferred from a building's size, layout, and proximity to a community's other major monuments, as well as from the repertoire of material remains.

Nunnery Quadrangle This compound was given its name by the Spaniards, who saw a similarity between the convent architecture of their own culture, and this array of many nearly identical double cell-like rooms within an enclosed cloister-style space. Four "range structures" face in upon a squarish courtyard measuring *c.* 46 m by 61 m (151 by 200 ft). The orientation of these buildings, their levels, numbers of rooms, and ornamentation have been carefully analyzed and found to correspond to a Maya cosmogram (Kowalski 1987). The North Building may represent the northern, celestial component of the cosmos – 13 doorways may stand for the 13 levels of the heavens, and serpent motifs recall the Maya – and greater Mesoamerican – association of serpents and sky.

The wealth of meanings embedded in this compound does not preclude its practical functions as the residential and ritual headquarters of a powerful lineage. The rooms are similar in size to those of noble houses elsewhere in the Maya lowlands, and the expanse of the courtyard would have served as a daily workspace as well as the ideal setting for feasts and ceremonies. For more formal religious events, the adjacent Pyramid of the Magician might have been a more appropriate venue.

Pyramid of the Magician When Uxmal was first visited by John Lloyd Stephens and Frederick Catherwood, natives called this distinctive elliptical temple-pyramid, *c.* 35 m (115 ft) high, "the Pyramid of the Dwarf" after a legend in which it was built overnight by a dwarf with supernatural powers who bested Uxmal's ruler in a series of challenging tests, ending in the ruler's death and the dwarf's elevation to rulership (Stephens 1969 [1841]: II: 423–425). If the Pyramid of the Magician, as it is now called, was in fact built in one night, the tale is even more impressive than Stephens thought, because the present structure is the fifth building episode. The various rebuildings seem to reflect the maturation of Puuc style, as it emerged from its Chenes-style beginnings [**14.8, 14.9**].

14.8 *(Below) Uxmal's Pyramid of the Magician began as a range structure on the east side of the quadrangular platform now known as the Quadrangle of the Birds. This initial structure was built in about* AD *550 and featured the familiar Chac masks. Construction of north and south range buildings indicated conformance to standard Uxmal practice in palace design, but the original building sprouted a pyramidal superstructure 22 m (72 ft) high, with a main staircase draped over the range building at its base. The fourth range structure on the west side, with arched entryway, completed the quadrangle. Finally, the Pyramid of the Magician was built to its completed size and layout, and other buildings and their decoration indicated that the complex was Lord Chac's own residence (Huchim Herrera and Toscano Hernández 1999).*

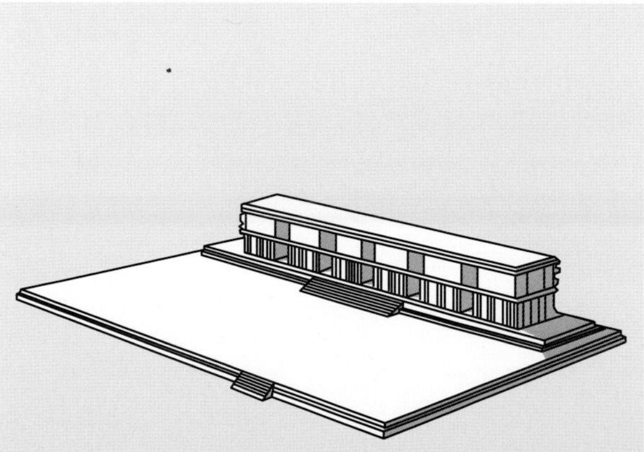

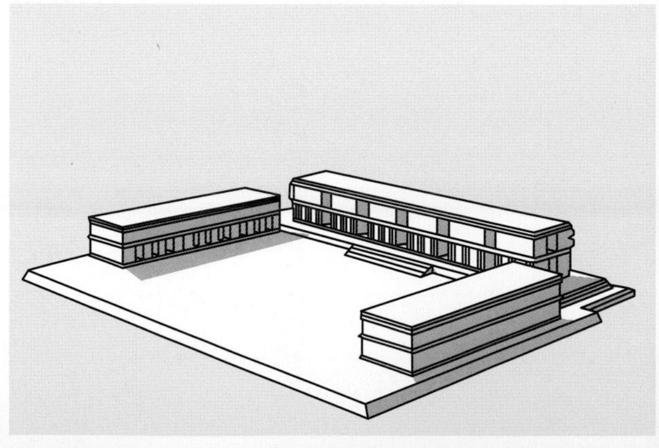

14.9 *(Above) Uxmal's Pyramid of the Magician, with its unusual oval shape, looms over the set of range structures that spawned it. The temples on the top of the pyramid are at two levels.*

Decline of the Puuc Sites Uxmal seems not to have flourished much beyond Lord Chac's reign, though the final years of the Puuc sites are poorly understood. Some scholars put Uxmal's decline at *c.* 925, while others assume that the site functioned throughout the 10th century. Occupations at Uxmal and Chichén Itzá overlapped somewhat in time, but there is no evidence that there were relations between the sites. Uxmal's contemporary, and counterpart site in the Yucatán Peninsula, was Cobá, *c.* 220 km (137 miles) nearly due east.

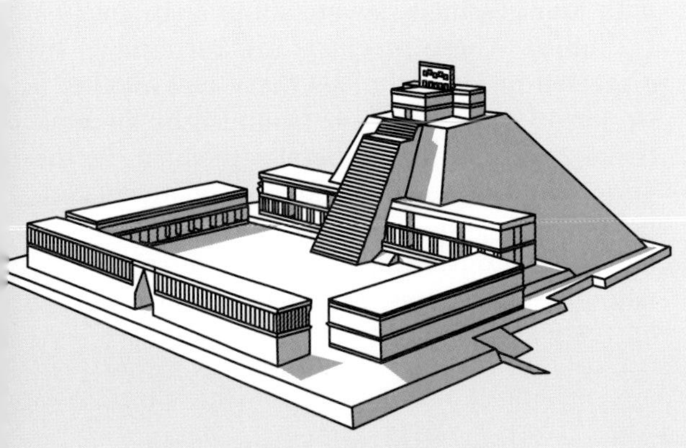

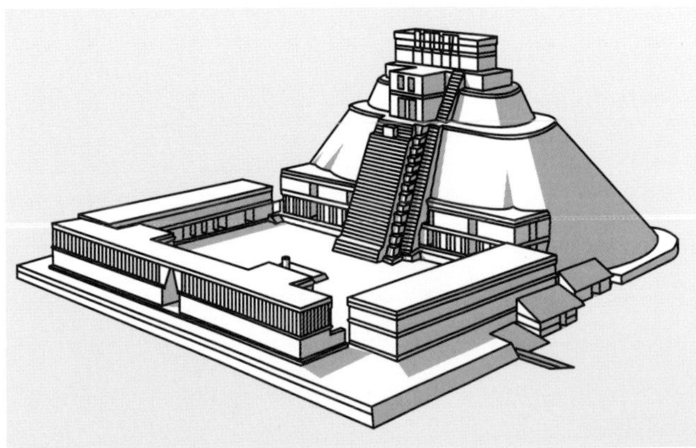

NORTHEASTERN YUCATÁN: COBÁ AND ITS REGION

The northeastern region of the Yucatán Peninsula had the same long history of occupation as did the other Maya areas. During the Classic period, sites in this area seem to have had a close relationship with the centers of the Petén; there is some evidence that in the early to middle Classic, Teotihuacan influenced developments in northeastern Yucatán. Then more local hegemony took hold, and in the Late Classic, Cobá asserted itself as the regional capital. There seems to have been contact, perhaps even alliances between Puuc sites and those in the northeast, judging from shared ceramics (Suhler *et al.* 1998). Cobá's attempts to maintain its power were manifested in a physical link, a *sacbe*, to Yaxuná, 100 km (62 miles) to the west. But Yaxuná was only 20 km (12 miles) from Chichén, the emerging great power in Yucatán in the Terminal Classic. Chichén's strength eventually overwhelmed the northeastern sites; conquest of Cobá may have occurred by AD 1100.

14.10 *Cobá's main precincts were located around a set of swampy lakes, and are joined by raised causeways. Thus Cobá had a highly unusual layout, with multiple aggregates of civic and residential architecture dispersed over a considerable area. The site's two ball courts were in the central area.*

Cobá Cobá offers a nice contrast to Uxmal: where Uxmal's many quadrangles (and a few impressive broad-based pyramids) were relatively crowded within its perimeter wall, in an environment where water is a precious resource for half the year (October to March), Cobá is a set of neighborhoods sprawled around a cluster of lakes, with internal *sacbeob* linking the precincts and also external causeways raying out in all directions, joining Cobá to other sites [14.10, 14.11].

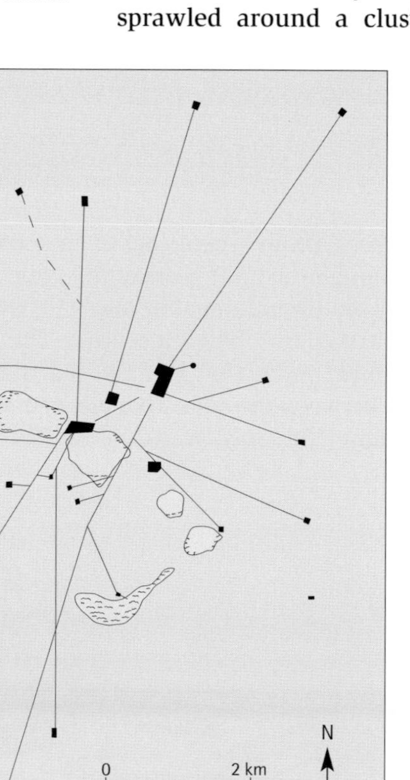

Visitors to Cobá's ruins are impressed by the precipitous height of those pyramids that have been cleared of vegetation. Their form and dimensions reveal close ties to the Maya of the Petén lowlands, and Stela 1, dating from AD 682, suggests that Cobá had ties with Dos Pilas and Naranjo (Ball 2001).

Cobá's distinctive settlement pattern is characterized by the dispersal of its major ceremonial precincts, which are separated by distances of up to 1 km (0.6 miles), with low density residential occupation between them. The site's core area, with four precincts, covers about 2 sq. km (0.8 sq. miles). These precincts are surrounded by dispersed residential areas that cover another 8 sq. km (3.2 sq. miles), surrounded by an additional 2 sq. km of peripheral settlement. By the Terminal Classic, Cobá's area of relatively contiguous habitation covered 70 sq. km (28 sq. miles), encompassing about 20,000 structures, with a population estimated at 55,000 (Folan *et al.* 1983; Manzanilla 2001).

14.11 *Cobá's Imoja temple structure, in the main precinct, dates to the Late and Terminal Classic periods, and is 24 m (79 ft) tall. The site's pyramids, are, individually, as impressively monumental as any elsewhere in the Maya lowlands, but they are dispersed among Cobá's several clusters of civic-ceremonial architecture.*

Cobá's Causeways The *sacbe* system based in Cobá was apparently an effort to consolidate a rather large territory. The labor involved in constructing these causeways was substantial. They were elevated above ground level in this area of considerable rainfall (over 1,500 mm/60 in per year) and standing water, ranging between 0.5 to 2.5 m in elevation (*c.* 1.6 to 8 ft), and averaging 4.5 m (15 ft) wide. Some were quite short, a kilometer or less, but others were impressively long. The *sacbe* from Cobá to Yaxuná was the longest in Mesoamerica. Evidence from Yaxuná indicates that the causeway was constructed during the Late Classic period, perhaps as Cobá was beginning to feel competition from Chichén and wanted to assert its authority as far to the west as possible.

VECTORS OF CHANGE: CHICHÉN ITZÁ AND THE PUTÚN MAYA

The centers of western and eastern Yucatán thrived until the increasing power of Chichén Itzá, in the center of the Yucatán Peninsula, eclipsed them. Chichén's rise to power is an enduring topic of speculation among scholars, because Chichén is Mesoamerica's most notable "fusion site" – it bears evidence of the coexistence of two important cultural elements: Maya, which is indigenous to its region, and "Toltec" – culture of the Central Mexican Highlands. Scholars have debated whether Tula influenced Chichén, or vice versa. Central Mexican architecture at Chichén is on a grand scale and dominates the center of the site. Themes of Central Mexican political, religious, and military power are expressed on monumental art and in portable sumptuary objects.

Thus it would seem logical to assume that bearers of Central Mexican culture played an important role at Chichén. At Tula, on the other hand,

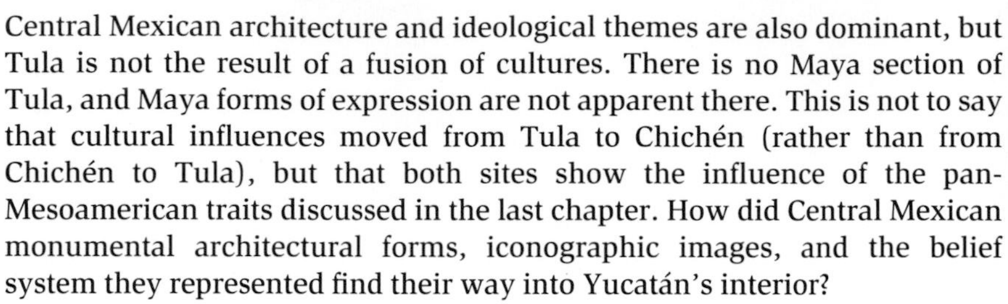

Central Mexican architecture and ideological themes are also dominant, but Tula is not the result of a fusion of cultures. There is no Maya section of Tula, and Maya forms of expression are not apparent there. This is not to say that cultural influences moved from Tula to Chichén (rather than from Chichén to Tula), but that both sites show the influence of the pan-Mesoamerican traits discussed in the last chapter. How did Central Mexican monumental architectural forms, iconographic images, and the belief system they represented find their way into Yucatán's interior?

14.12 *Warrior costumes (and textiles) were sought as tribute by the Late Postclassic Aztecs, as these illustrations from the* Codex Mendoza *show. The professionalization of warrior cadres, however, was a much older phenomenon, and was probably well-established by the Epiclassic period.*

Putún, Chontal, Itzá: Traders along the Gulf Coast

Throughout human history, the incursions of one culture into another have often stemmed from a few strong, compelling motivations. Migration, military conquest, religious proselytization, and long-distance trading are among the most important [**14.12**]. As we have seen, these factors seem to have acted in concert to spread ideas and material culture styles over a broad area of Central Mexico in the Late Classic and Early Postclassic. Turning to the central Yucatán Peninsula, the motivations for the intrusion of Central Mexican stylistic motifs are more difficult to recover. Large-scale migrations seem unlikely. Religious proselytization, in the form of an emphasis upon Central Mexican belief systems, may have been an important factor, but seems secondary to both military conquest and securing trade routes. In fact, militarized trade was critical to the expansion of the Late Postclassic Aztec empire – the "vanguard merchants" were long-distance *pochteca* traders who penetrated areas outside the empire in order to secure a pretext for further, more politically oriented interaction, while also spying for the Aztec emperor and bringing back information about the target polity's wealth and defenses.

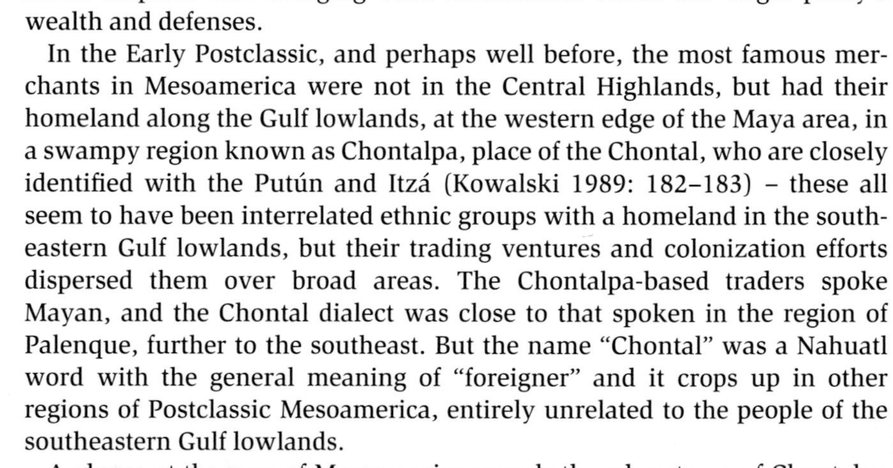

In the Early Postclassic, and perhaps well before, the most famous merchants in Mesoamerica were not in the Central Highlands, but had their homeland along the Gulf lowlands, at the western edge of the Maya area, in a swampy region known as Chontalpa, place of the Chontal, who are closely identified with the Putún and Itzá (Kowalski 1989: 182–183) – these all seem to have been interrelated ethnic groups with a homeland in the southeastern Gulf lowlands, but their trading ventures and colonization efforts dispersed them over broad areas. The Chontalpa-based traders spoke Mayan, and the Chontal dialect was close to that spoken in the region of Palenque, further to the southeast. But the name "Chontal" was a Nahuatl word with the general meaning of "foreigner" and it crops up in other regions of Postclassic Mesoamerica, entirely unrelated to the people of the southeastern Gulf lowlands.

A glance at the map of Mesoamerica reveals the advantages of Chontalpa as a central location for trading peoples. That part of the coastal lowlands is a web of watercourses, and terminus of several major rivers – the Grijalva, draining the Chiapas interior plateau, and the Usumacinta, with its headwaters in the Guatemala highlands. While the courses of these rivers were only

14.13 *The Maya traders that Columbus met in 1502 were traveling in a canoe carved of a single log. The vessel's width was about 2.4 m (8 ft), and its length at least 15 m (c. 50 ft). The illustration, showing the general style of such canoes, is from a wall mural in the Temple of the Warriors at Chichén Itzá, dating from the Early Postclassic. The AD 1502 canoe had 25 oarsmen, plus the traders and their families who sat under an awning in the middle of the canoe. Christopher Columbus's son, who accompanied this voyage and witnessed the canoe, described the goods carried by the trader: "cotton mantles ... wooden swords with ... flint knives that cut like steel; hatchets .. made of good copper; ... many of the almonds which the Indians of New Spain use as currency..." (Columbus 1984 [1502–1503]: 130). The almonds were, of course, cacao beans. It is ironic that Columbus recognized, from "the canoe and its contents ... the great wealth, civilization, and industry of the peoples of the western part of New Spain" (ibid.) but finding the passage to Asia was still his greatest priority, so rather than turning his ships west, toward the Aztec empire, he headed east, along the Caribbean Coast of Central America.*

partly navigable, trails along them and their tributaries made the drainage systems major arteries of communication. The southern Maya lowlands and the Maya highlands were accessible from Chontalpa by overland river course routes.

Contact with other groups to the west and east along the Gulf Coast was achieved by seagoing canoe. On Christopher Columbus's fourth voyage, in 1502, his ships traveled to the Bay of Honduras, just east of the southeastern coast of the Yucatán Peninsula. This occasioned the first encounter between Europeans and the peoples of Mesoamerica, when the Europeans came upon a Maya trading vessel [**14.13**]. The huge canoe's cargo reflected the riches of the lowlands – cotton, cacao – and goods traded from afar, such as obsidian and copper.

By the Late Postclassic period there were trading communities all along the coast of Yucatán. In the Late Classic and Early Postclassic, amidst general political disarray in the southern Maya lowlands and the decline of Teotihuacan, the Chontalpa traders seem to have thrived. A well-organized and adequately armed trading network could provide a certain institutional continuity, a preservation of orderly and established modes of interchange in periods of upheaval, and could also maintain avenues of access to luxuries for surviving elites and for the new rising elite class. River course and overland routes maintained contact with the Maya highlands and distributed the desirable lustrous gray Plumbate ceramics of the Chiapas Coast. Of course, the Chontalpa traders lived in the lowlands where cotton and cacao grew, traded along the Yucatán Coast where salt was processed (Kepecs 2003; McKillop 2002) and thus they could always supply materials that were coveted – and needed – by their trading partners (Scholes and Roys 1948).

The 16th-century Chontalpa traders known as the Putún have been called "the Phoenicians of the New World" (Thompson 1970), and were thought by some scholars to have been the same group as the Early Postclassic Chontalpa traders who were presumed to have ushered in a northern Yucatecan "New Empire" subsequent to the "Old Empire" of the Classic southern lowland Maya. While these "imperial" terms have fallen into disuse, the Chontalpa traders managed to breathe new life into some Late Classic Maya sites, introducing new, Central Mexico-related concepts and materials at those and other sites, including Chichén Itzá, changes which seem to have taken place after about AD 850.

While the transformation – or hybridization – of Maya culture toward greater sharing of traits from elsewhere in Mesoamerica is sometimes referred to as conquest by foreigners, it seems more probable that the "outsiders" were not marching grimly down from Tula, but rather that they were cosmopolitan, Mayan-speaking militarized traders from Chontalpa. They lived in a zone that bordered both sides of the Isthmus and this allowed them to penetrate neighboring regions, coming under far-flung cultural influences. In time, the Itzá of Chontalpa moved into the central part of northern Yucatán and influenced cultural development there.

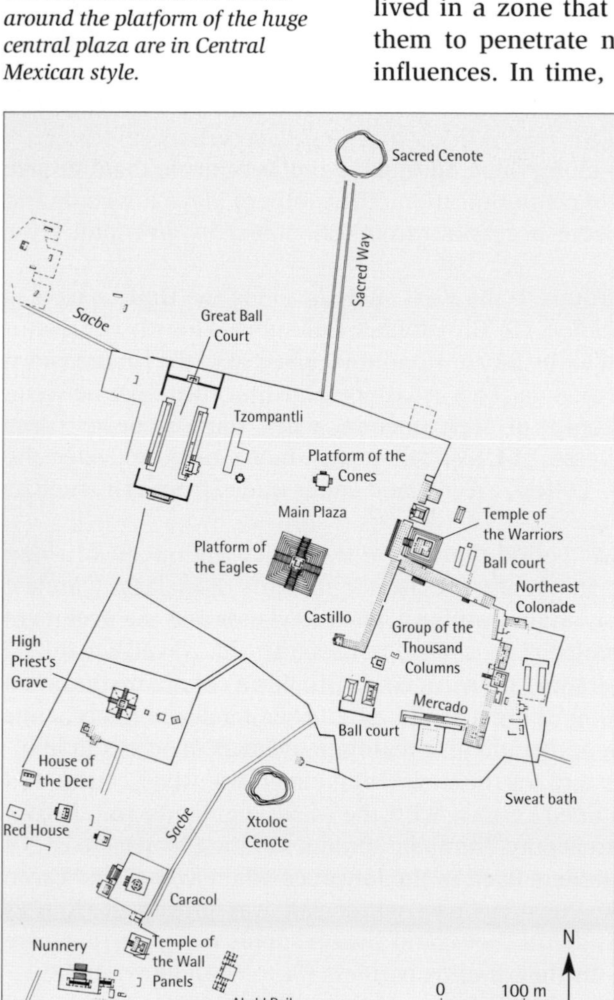

14.14 *Chichén Itzá's major architectural focus, the central part of the site, covers about 1 sq. km (0.4 sq. mile), from the Sacred Cenote in the north to Las Monjas and the Akab' Dzib in the south. South of this are more remains in the Maya tradition (the area north of the Sacred Cenote has not yet been systematically investigated). The massive structures in and around the platform of the huge central plaza are in Central Mexican style.*

Chichén Itzá

The Itzá seem to have been motivated by commercial interest as they moved in to take over "north coast salt beds and their related long-distance trade networks" (Andrews and Robles 1985). Establishing their capital at Chichén Itzá ("mouth of the well of the Itzá"), they transformed the community into the major center in northern Yucatán from AD 850–1150, extending over about 15 sq. km (*c.* 6 sq. miles). While the chronometric dating of Chichén is still being refined, most scholars believe that after about 1150, Chichén experienced near-total abandonment, followed by reoccupation and renewed importance as a Late Postclassic pilgrimage center and even serving briefly as an Early Colonial capital for the Spaniards.

Today, Chichén draws hundreds of thousands of tourists each year. They marvel at the monumental scale of its major structures, and puzzle over the mix of cultural styles represented there – even casual observers recognize the contrast between the modestly-scaled Puuc-style buildings at the southern end of the site, and the massive, blocky architecture, borrowed from Central Mexico, that dominates the broad plaza at the site's center. This juxtaposition of two very distinct cultures, Maya

14.15 Looking south from the Sacred Cenote, one would have seen Chichén Itzá at its height, as this painting by Tatiana Proskouriakoff shows. The Castillo pyramid dominated a huge platform, and was flanked by the Temple of the Warriors (to the left) and the ball court (at far right).

and Central Mexican, is more dramatically displayed at Chichén than at any other archaeological site in Mesoamerica (Cobos 2001).

The Maya buildings that share much in common with those of Uxmal and other Puuc sites probably date from the Puuc florescence. Mexican-influenced structures share proportions and features with the monumental architecture of Tula and other Late Classic–Epiclassic sites of the Central Highlands. For many years, it was thought that Chichén's different zones were occupied sequentially, with Toltec invaders imposing their will and architectural program, replacing the Maya rulers who established the site. While there is considerable evidence of militarism associated with the Central Mexican-style sculptures and murals, many scholars now believe that such foreign influences were indirect rather than involving armies from Tula, and that the two cultures coexisted at Chichén. At its height, Chichén may have been ruled by both factions (Kristan-Graham 2001).

Nonetheless, the most imposing architectural statement at Chichén is made by Mexican-style buildings [**14.15**]. The architectural group was built on a broad artificial terrace, and was surrounded by a now-destroyed wall. In addition to the massive structures, there are relatively small, low platforms with motifs of eagles and felines carrying human hearts. Their style is very similar to that of bas-reliefs found at Tula, and emphasizes the same sanguinary themes, an unveiled threat of violence. Other references, to the planet Venus whose celestial cycle set the rhythm for warfare, underscore the importance of militarism in the Itzá realm.

These themes, combined with widely spaced distribution of the huge buildings over the broad flat expanse of the North Terrace, seem designed to dwarf the human individual, to promote a sense of wary respect. Compared

14.16 *Chichén's Castillo pyramid is topped by a temple whose main entrance faces north, at right in this photo. While its form is commonly associated with Central Mexican architecture, there are some similar pyramids at Late Classic Maya sites, and some with nine terraced levels.*

with Xochicalco's cluster of structures on its hilltops, or Tajín's welter of ball courts and pyramids crowding down its slopes, Chichén's mass of monuments is balanced by the extent of vacant space.

The Castillo Centered upon the North Terrace, this is the consummate four-sided, four-staircased pyramid. So impressive are its size and proportions that all others that are of this type seem to be modest downscale copies. At *c.* 23 m (*c.* 75 ft) high, the last expansion of the Castillo encloses an earlier building, and it contains a jaguar-shaped throne associated with the Central Mexican-influenced faction at Chichén. As presently reconstructed, the Castillo is crowned by a temple whose main entrance, with feathered serpent supports, faces north. The north side's staircase is framed by serpent-headed balustrades, which, on the vernal and autumnal equinoxes, create a shadow against the pyramid's terraces that mimics the undulations of a descending serpent [**20.18**].

These feathered serpent images have given this structure its other name, the Temple-Pyramid of Kukulcan, a Mayan word for feathered serpent. Some modern sources recount a legend that the culture hero and king of Tula, Topiltzin Quetzalcoatl, arrived in Chichén Itzá after having been driven from Tula, and that it was he who brought Mexican cultural elements. While Topiltzin may have been an historical figure, as we shall discuss in Chapter 15, it is unlikely that he traveled to the Yucatán Peninsula (Kristan-Graham 2001).

The Great Ball Court West of the Castillo lay the largest ball court in all of Mesoamerica. There are 12 others at the site (Velázquez 2000), but this one dominates its side of the North Terrace, as well as the entire ball court repertoire. The playing alley is 146 m (479 ft) long, and 37 m (121 ft) wide – longer, though not wider, than a standard U.S. football field.

BALL COURTS AND THE BALL GAME

MODERN SPORTING EVENTS like soccer and American football pit two teams against each other with the goal of moving a rubber ball over a field. This activity captures the emotions and brings out the ethnic loyalties of countless fans. In a sense, the Mesoamerican ball game also functioned at this level, and, just like modern sporting events, it provided entertainment and bucked up the economy – think of the labor costs of building Chichén's great ball court, and the provisions and jobs that made up the service economy catering to the needs of the pilgrim-fans drawn by the ball games. However, as we have seen from the ball court at Paso de la Amada onward, the meaning of these "sporting events" was far more richly nuanced than sports in modern life: formal ball games were religious and political occasions, recreating sacred events related to fertility of the earth, and at the same time providing an opportunity for feasting and cementing alliances.

Ball Game

The idea of a formalized contest between two teams, centered upon the movement of a rubber ball, no doubt preceded the construction of formal ball courts, and may date from the Late Archaic (see Gheo-Shih, Chapter 3). By AD 1500, the rules had formalized, and there were regional variations on the rules of play of *tlachtli*, as the Aztecs called it, known to the Maya as *ulama*, a word that shares its roots with the words for rubber – "Olmec" for example, means of the Land of Rubber. Today there are more than 1,500 ball courts known from Mesoamerican archaeological sites, and 1,200 modern ball courts in use in Mexico and the U.S. Southwest and California (Taladoire 1994).

In the ancient game's best-known variant, players kept the ball aloft by hitting it with their hips, and scored if the ball touched the ground of the opposing team's end of the court. Some courts featured rings embedded in the walls at the center line, and passing the ball through these rings would have been extremely difficult but apparently high-scoring.

Teams consisted of one to seven players, who were equipped with body protectors made of leather and wood [14.17]. We know about these body protectors mostly from representations in stone: modern archaeologists call these items *yugos* ("yokes"), and many of them have been found in the Gulf lowlands. Other paraphernalia, also represented in stone, were *hachas* ("axes"), and *palmas* ("palm stones"), so-called because of their shapes.

The game was a spectacle enjoyed by commoners and aristocrats. The Aztec appetite for the game is evidenced by

14.17 *From Jaina, this figurine shows a ballplayer in costume, including a headdress in the shape of a deer head. He holds the ball in his right hand, possibly prepared to start the game.*

an annual tribute demand that brought 16,000 rubber balls to Tenochtitlan (Berdan 1992). Aztec kings ranked the ball game high as a leisure activity (Sahagún 1979 [1569]: 29) – we know that some kings sometimes played, and they certainly watched the action of the game, and gambled on the outcome. Kings wagered valuables like jewelry, slaves, land and houses, and quantities of cacao beans. The Aztec ruler also understood the entertainment value of the ball game, and staged such events when "the common folk and vassals were very fretful ... to animate the people and divert them. He commanded the majordomos to take out the rubber ball, and the girdles, and the leather hip guards, and the leather gloves with which the ruler's ball players were dressed" (Sahagún 1979 [1569]: 58). From the ruler's storehouses were brought the items to be wagered, and the challenging team had to match the wager.

Representations of sacrifice of individuals in assocation with the ball game have given rise to the notion that the losers were ritually dispatched at the end of each game. This would certainly have been the case in highly sacralized games, perhaps played by individuals already fated to such a death, but there is no evidence that this practice was common. Rather, it is likely that skilled players were valued, and this may have represented an avenue to social and economic advancement not unlike that of military service.

Ball Courts

By AD 1500, the ball game had been played on ball courts from the U.S. Southwest to the Amazon of South America, and even on Caribbean islands, where the largest known ball court, 135 by 250 m (443 by 820 ft),

14.18, 14.19 *(Below) Plans and profiles of some of Mesoamerica's most important ball courts show the variation in size and orientation. I-shaped courts are more common in the highlands west of the Isthmus, while open-ended courts typify the Maya lowlands. Chichén's court is thus in keeping with the Central Mexican architectural style of its construction. (Opposite) The photo shows a game being played on the central court at Copán.*

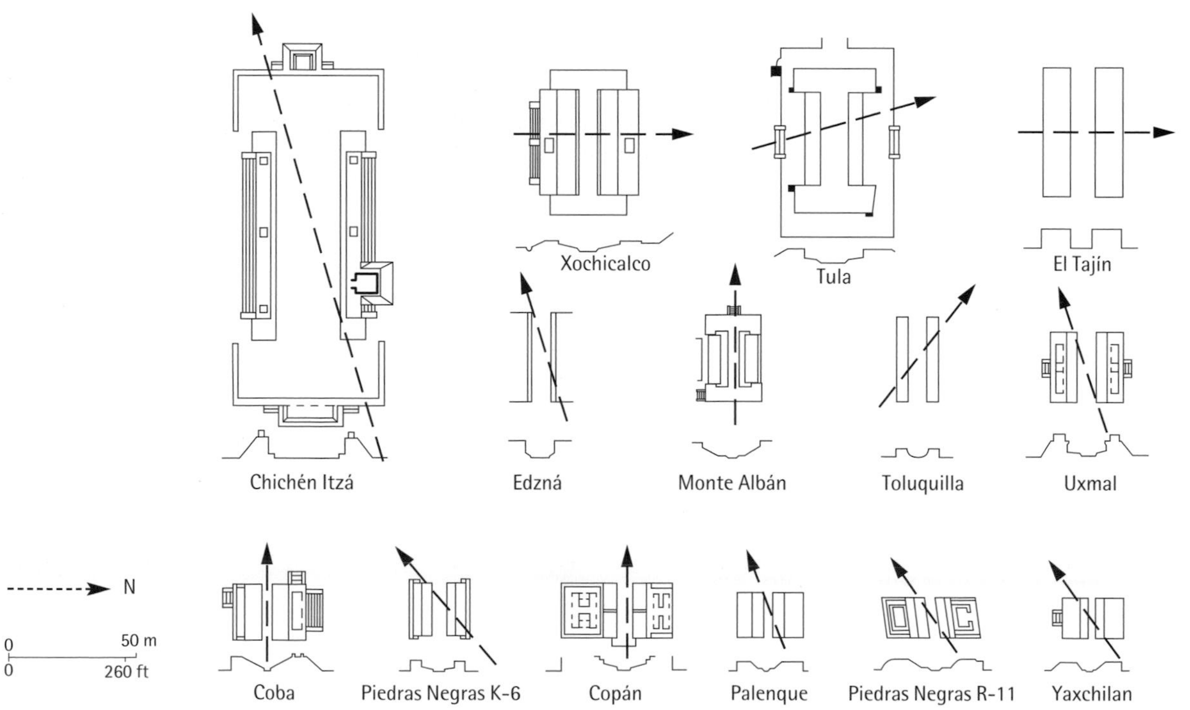

was found at Pueblo Viejo, Cuba. In all courts, the playing field is oblong or rectangular, sometimes with extended end-zones, resulting in an I-shape, such as the largest courts at Chichén and Xochicalco [**14.18, 14.19**].

Construction of the ball court was accompanied by a dedication ritual which involved the placement of a cache. Sometimes this buried treasure consisted of precious and sacred objects such as greenstone, which seemed to transform the ball court into a sacred space. Other caches contained fine pottery serving vessels, seeming to emphasize the ball game as an occasion for politically-motivated feasting (Fox 1996). The dedication ritual made the ball court into a sacred space, but it also brought it alive, "reflecting widespread Mesoamerican beliefs that buildings, in this case ballcourts, were animate entities subject to their own rites of passage" (Fox 1996: 487).

This perspective is entirely in keeping with what we know of the ancient Mesoamerican's perception of forces at work throughout their physical environment, living pulses of energy that must be propitiated and, if possible, used to advantage. While it is easy for the modern Western mind to understand this principle as applied to things that move – rubber balls, water in a stream – applying it to buildings requires a greater cognitive stretch. Nonetheless, in our own societies we ceremonially dedicate important buildings, including sports fields, and celebrate changes in our personal domestic arrangements with house warmings. In these ways we acknowledge the importance of the built environment and our hope that it may serve our needs.

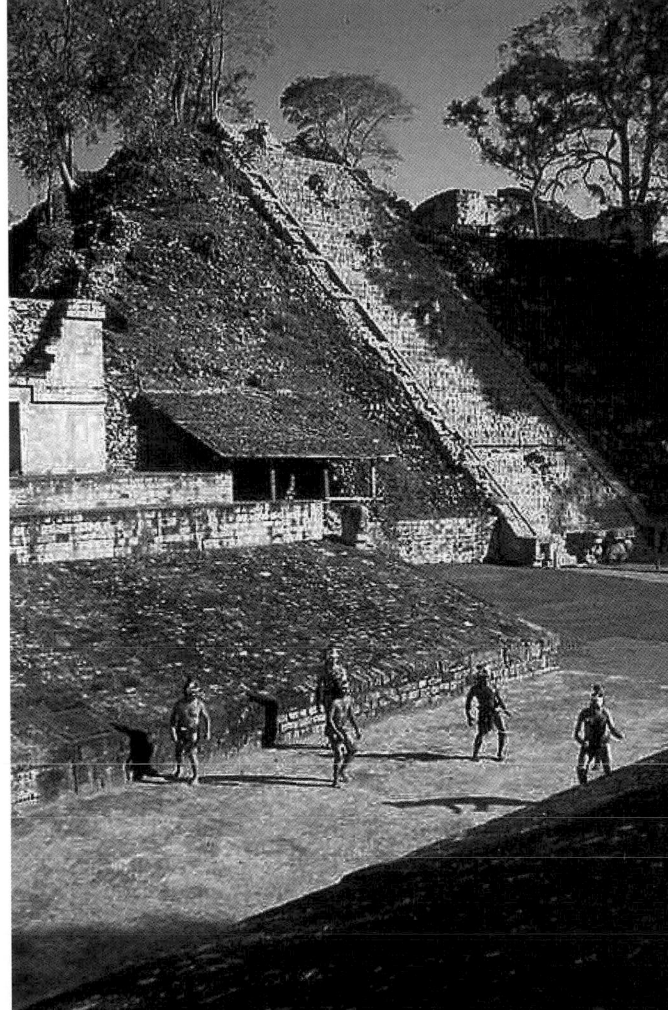

Ball Games, Ball Courts, and the Negotiation of Power

The themes of fertility, including sacrifice in the service of fertility, that permeate ball game iconography are rooted in the ruler's need to maintain the prosperity of his domain, to demonstrate his spiritual efficacy as a mediator with the powerful otherworld. Potential followers, and rival factions, are impressed by lavish spectacles and by bumper crops and adequate rainfall. The ball game not only drew together these themes in dramatic display, but also gave political rivals an arena for conflict resolution. The distribution of ball courts in the Central Highlands of Mexico (Santley *et al.* 1991) and in the Valley of Oaxaca (Kowalewski *et al.* 1991) indicates that during periods of political fragmentation, many sites had ball courts, while periods of centralization limited the number of courts to the larger capitals. The appearance, at Chichén, of a massive ball court, may have been one of the means by which the Itzás indicated their larger goals of making their capital the premier political center in northern Yucatán.

14.21, 14.22 *(Opposite) "Caracol" is Spanish for "snail shell" and Spanish explorers gave the building shown on the opposite page in the reconstruction drawing its name because of its round shape and interior spiral staircase. In cross-section, the Caracol reveals its function as an observatory, with sightlines oriented toward yearly passages of sun and moon, and also toward the most extreme horizon points achieved in the eight-year cycle of the planet Venus (Aveni 1989: 244).*

Sacred Cenote, or Well of Sacrifice The north-facing Castillo temple looked out upon a *sacbe* leading directly to what is perhaps the greatest of all Yucatecan cenotes. Cenotes were natural sinkholes in the limestone shelf of the Yucatán Peninsula, and in this region of limited rainfall and few rivers they were enormously important, and revered as apertures to the world of the spirits. Chichén has at least seven cenotes, and the largest is this Sacred Cenote. It was the focus of the earliest, Late Formative-period occupation of Chichén Itzá. Nearly circular in shape, it is *c.* 24 m (*c.* 80 ft) in diameter and the water level is an equal distance below the ground surface.

Archaeological dredging operations have yielded the largest known corpus of Maya carved jades (Miller and Samayoa 1998) as well as many offerings of copal incense, ceramics, wooden objects, textiles and spindle whorls, and skeletal remains of adults of both sexes and children (Coggins and Shane 1984). The colorful legend that only beautiful virgins were sacrificed by being tossed into the Sacred Cenote cannot, unfortunately, be substantiated by the existing evidence, but the materials committed to the cenote's depths are of high quality, bespeaking a concern with rendering unto the spiritual world fine gifts to mediate crises in human lives.

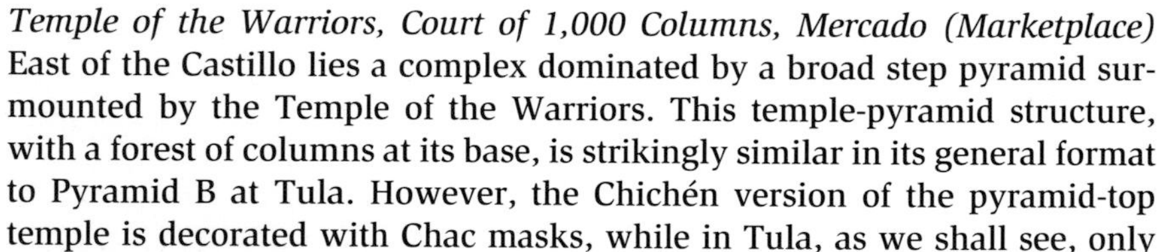

Temple of the Warriors, Court of 1,000 Columns, Mercado (Marketplace) East of the Castillo lies a complex dominated by a broad step pyramid surmounted by the Temple of the Warriors. This temple-pyramid structure, with a forest of columns at its base, is strikingly similar in its general format to Pyramid B at Tula. However, the Chichén version of the pyramid-top temple is decorated with Chac masks, while in Tula, as we shall see, only atlantean supports remain, and the temple is gone.

14.20 *Two icons of Epiclassic and Postclassic architectural and sculptural style, columns and the* chacmool, *come together atop the Temple of the Warriors at Chichén Itzá.*

The temple's exterior may nod to Puuc style, but the interior is all Central Mexican, with the architectural feature of a large enclosed space (the roof no longer exists) made possible by the lavish use of columns. As we saw in Chapter 13, this hall-of-columns style was much-used in northwestern Mexico in the Late Classic period.

The ranks of columns at the base of the Temple of the Warriors extend around the south side of that pyramid, and would have created an expansive roofed area. The counterpart space, at Tula, has been interpreted as a meeting hall that was also used for processionals, such as by merchants returning from their trading expeditions. The "Mercado" is another columned building in

A Moon sets at greatest northern declination along this line
B Due west. Sun sets along this line on 21 March, the vernal equinox
C Moon sets at greatest southern declination along this line
D Due south
E Observation chamber

this complex, but its marketplace function has yet to be substantiated. Also in this complex were two small ball courts, but they – and most other ball courts – are tiny in comparison with the Great Ball Court.

The Caracol This unusual structure [**14.21, 14.22**] functioned as an observatory, and bears architectural traits of both Central Mexico and the Puuc styles of the buildings that surround it. The building's function in keeping track of the solar and lunar years seems understandable given the importance of the agricultural cycle in most ancient states. The Caracol's capacity to track the cycle of the planet Venus pulls it into the realm of warfare – the Venus cycle seems to have been an important determinant of militarism – and of the Feathered Serpent, with whom the celestial body was associated.

The Caracol makes a fitting point of departure from our discussion of Chichén, because it unites militarism and calendrics, two crucial elements of the city's greatness in the several centuries when it was ruled by the Itzá. The central plaza drew together Feathered Serpent imagery with references to calendrics – the Castillo itself may have served as a gnomon of the solar year – and depictions of violent death through war and sacrifice. These features are themselves united in a cycle of warfare, and provide a strong basis for rulership and expansion of domination over a broad region. Commerce was another important prerogative of rulers, and the Itzá also controlled trade, from Chichén and from their port at Isla Cerritos, about 100 km (*c.* 62 miles) north of the city.

14.24 *(Opposite) Typical of wheeled figurines is this ceramic model of a dog, who has holes at the ends of his legs to accommodate the axle for the wheels.*

Chichén's period of major construction may have drawn to a close by AD 1000 (Ringle *et al.* 1998). The reasons for Chichén's decline in the late 12th century are poorly understood (Ball and Taschek 1989), and the city was abandoned as the Itzá established for themselves a new capital at Mayapan, to be discussed in Chapter 17.

SOUTHERN PACIFIC COAST AND SOUTHEASTERN MESOAMERICA

Chichén seems to have resulted from the incursions into northern Yucatán of Maya-speaking peoples along the southeastern Gulf lowlands. Can we also detect populations moving south across the Isthmus of Tehuantepec, influencing cultural developments along the Pacific Coast of Chiapas, Guatemala, and El Salvador? To some extent, the answer is yes, though the demographic shifts are of a different kind, and archaeological data from the path of migration, the Soconusco, are sparse for this period [**14.23**]. Rather than a movement of militaristic mercantile groups like the Itzá, the more southerly migrations seem to have involved farming families leaving the southern Gulf lowlands and moving to the region now comprising the Pacific coastal plains and adjacent valleys of southern Guatemala, El Salvador, Nicaragua, and northern Costa Rica.

These regions are part of a frontier zone that was at some times more heavily influenced by Mesoamerica, and at others, more oriented toward the Intermediate Area. For example, southern Costa Rica was part of the Intermediate Area's sphere of influence during this time, as the Rivas site attests (Quilter 2004). Architecture at Rivas was circular, as was common farther south, with stone foundations *c.* 10 m (33 ft) in diameter forming house complexes that surrounded patios. Subsistence was mixed, based on maize cultivation and hunting. Yet northern Costa Rica was oriented toward Mesoamerica. It and adjacent regions were settled by Nahuat-speaking Pipil and Nicarao settlers from about AD 800 to 1250/1350, and these groups brough with them not only a language closely related to Nahuatl, spoken by the Aztecs, but many other cultural traits derived from Central Mexico (Fowler 1989). They may have been inspired to leave their homeland because of excessive tribute demands by the ruling Olmeca-Xicalanca groups, and they may have been drawn to the Pacific coastal areas because of the ideal environment for growing cacao and cotton. At Chalchuapa, Mexicanized traits such as a ball court and circular pyramid appear in the site's ceremonial center in the Early Postclassic, indicating a probable Pipil presence (Sheets 2000), but the Pipil also founded sites, such as Cihuatán.

14.23 *Although archaeology of the Early Postclassic period has not been a strong focus of research along the Pacific Coast of Chiapas and Guatemala, materials analyses have revealed that this region is the origin point of one of Mesoamerica's most widely traded ceramic types during this period, called Plumbate (Neff and Bishop 1988). Plumbate is found at both Tula and Chichén Itzá, and countless other sites occupied in the Early Postclassic. "Plumbate" would indicate that lead is part of the vessel's composition, but it is not. Instead, the name refers to the vessel's lustrous deep gray surface finish, which resembles lead but does not contain that mineral (Shepard 1948).*

INVENTING THE WHEEL IN THE SERVICE OF THE GODS

COMPARISONS between ancient Mesoamerica and the great Archaic civilizations of the Old World generally include a discussion of technology, with Mesoamerica judged as having a "Stone Age technology," with far less sophisticated mastery of materials (such as metals) and engineering (such as use of the wheel). As we have seen with regard to metals, the assessment is true insofar as practical applications are concerned, but does not consider the value of metals and objects made from them in the proper cultural context. The same may be said of the wheel and axle, which seem to have been developed in the Late Classic period and spread widely through Mesoamerica on Toltec interaction networks during the Early Postclassic.

This might call forth images of creaking carts full of Toltec obsidian cores making their way to far away lands, returning to Tula laden with cacao and Plumbate vessels, but the wheeled "vehicles" were on a much smaller scale, most no larger than 15 cm (6 in) long, almost all in the shape of quadrupedal animals [**14.24**]. And in fact, the cart would have been useless in Mesoamerica, because what kind of beast would have pulled it? A team of hairless dogs? Human porters more efficiently carry individual packs over long distances, rather than pulling carts. Lacking the effective means to haul a wheeled vehicle eliminated the motivation to invent one.

The earliest known wheeled animal figure came from Classic-period levels at Pavón (northern Gulf lowlands; Ekholm 1946). This Huastec origin for a Tula-associated practice is one of several important cultural traits that were so derived, as we shall see in Chapter 15, and lends credence to native legends of a Gulf lowlands origin for some of the founders of Tula.

A few Late Classic wheeled figurines have been found, but most come from sites dating to the Postclassic. There are a few rare examples of platforms on wheels, but most are animals: dogs or coyotes, jaguars, monkeys, and deer. The typical example is a dog or coyote whose legs had been somewhat flattened and pierced, before firing, to accommodate the axle, which was probably a wooden stick. Some examples featured cylindrical axle housings. Wheels were flat clay disks that seem to have been made for this purpose. In fact, many clay disks that archaeologists have interpreted as spindle whorls may have served as figurine wheels, instead – proper spindle whorls are hemispherical, concentrating the fly-wheel mass near the spindle.

The resemblance of these figurines to pull-toys in the modern Western world has led some scholars to refer to them as "wheeled toys" but this functional attribution is almost certainly wrong. Rare examples of their discovery in archaeological context occurred in the Gulf lowlands, at Tres Zapotes and Nopiloa, where they "were found in dedicatory caches associated with mound-construction, a highly unlikely context for children's toys" (Diehl and Mandeville 1987: 243). At Tula, they were most often found in trash midden or construction fill, in or near houses, not in the civic-ceremonial center, which suggests a domestic setting for use. That these are animals also recalls the animal beings who were thought to serve as alter egos for certain individuals in transcendent states. The wheels would permit the semblance of movement, of vitality, so treasured in all its manifestations, and regarded as a allusion to life itself. Furthermore, dogs, one of the most popular subjects, were thought by the Aztecs to accompany the deceased on the journey to the underworld.

Cihuatán and Santa María

Insight into Pipil culture comes from two sites in western El Salvador. Cihuatán seems to have been its region's capital during its period of occupation, AD 900–1200. It features a planned civic-ceremonial plaza of 5–6 hectares (12–15 acres) featuring *talud-tablero* architecture, with a pyramid 18 m high (59 ft), two I-shaped ball courts, and at least one palace complex (Bruhns 1980). Central Mexican traits like Tlaloc braziers, *chacmool* figures, tubular pottery drain pipes, and wheeled figurines are found here, and are typical of Tula, as we shall see in the next chapter. The whole site, including residences of commoners, covered 375 hectares (926 acres).

Cihuatán was apparently the primary center for secondary regional centers such as nearby (16 km/10 miles) Santa María, which shared its architectural traits, having its own plaza complex with pyramid and ball court, surrounded by commoner residences. As at Cihuatán, the material culture showed affinities with Central Mexico in forms and iconography. These sites represented the earliest wave of the Pipil migrations southeastward, which continued into the 1300s.

Western Honduras

While population levels in regions along the Pacific increased due to the Pipil migrations, in the northern part of Southeastern Mesoamerica, a demographic decline took place. The decline of the southern lowlands Maya at the end of the Late Classic had local impact with Copán's eventual abandonment. One can imagine the domino effect of the loss of an important boundary community like Copán – it was not only the significant economic impact of the disappearance of this easternmost node of Maya production and consumption, including luxury consumerism, but also the political security of the presence of a major capital and its military forces. With that gone, the political landscape of western Honduras decentralized. A few local capitals, like Cerro Palenque (AD 850–1000) and Tenampua (AD 900–1100), enjoyed brief periods of florescence. However, the region still remained an important part of trading networks that ranged from the Intermediate Area up to Tula.

Tula has been, throughout this chapter, a shadowy presence, in part because of the structure of these regional discussions, and also because archaeologists are still so uncertain about the timing of events in Tula and Chichén Itzá at the end of the Classic period and beginning of the Postclassic. Let us now look at this great capital, which, for the Aztecs, became so legendarily magnificent that they thought it a kind of earthly paradise.

15 THE RISE OF TULA AND OTHER EPICLASSIC TRANSFORMATIONS (AD 900–1200)

"THERE AT TULA ... they were indeed rich. Of no value was food ... the varicolored cotton grew: chili-red, yellow, pink ... And there dwelt all ... birds of precious feather ... And all the green stones, the gold were not costly.... And also cacao grew ...

They lacked nothing in their homes. Never was there famine. The maize rejects they did not need; they only burned them [to heat] the sweat baths with them" (Sahagún 1978 [1569]: 13–14).

This description of paradise lost applied not to some tropical city, where, in fact, cotton and cacao could have been grown, but to Tula, a fallen kingdom in the Central Highlands, near the southern edge of the Chichimec desert [**15.1**]. Once upon a time, the story goes, this desert bloomed with the riches of far-off lands, and then Tula's king, Topiltzin Quetzalcoatl, was disgraced and went into exile, sending Tula, as well, into a tailspin of decline.

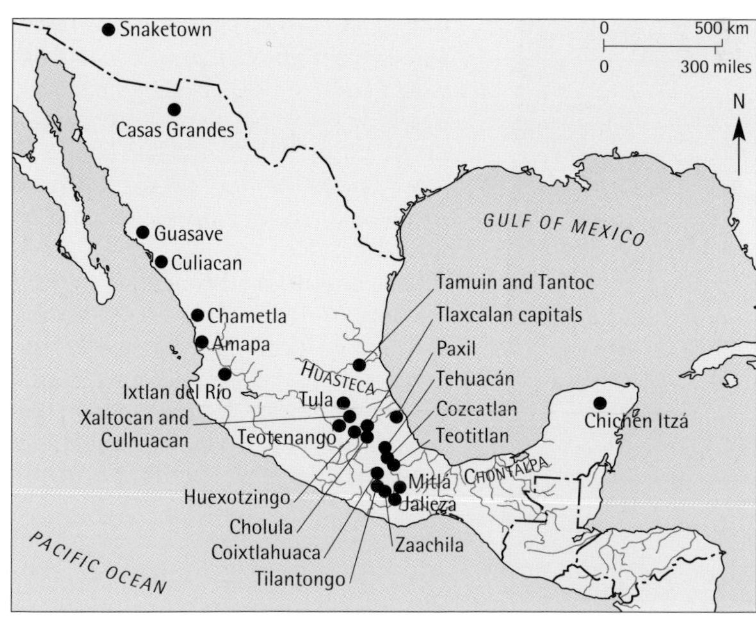

15.1 *Western Middle America showing Early Postclassic-period regions and sites referred to in Chapter 15.*

TULA AND TOLTEC CULTURE

Was there an actual environmental change that caused the blooming of the semi-arid Tula region (present average annual rainfall, 700 mm/28 in)? Circumstantial evidence for this comes from the settlement record itself: the Early Postclassic period is the era when farmers flocked to the Tula region, and also was the apogee of other arid areas far to the north, such as the U.S. Southwest. The hypothesis that this was due to a climatic humid period (Armillas 1964) has not been proven or disproven.

Nonetheless, even without exceptional rainfall, the Tula region has hydraulic resources in the several tributaries of the Tula River, which eventually flows into the Pánuco in the northern Gulf lowlands, the Huasteca region. While Tula's high altitude (*c.* 2,135 m/7,000 ft) would prohibit cacao and cotton from being grown there, careful use of available water would certainly provide adequately for a large population.

The population combined the Late Classic residents with newcomers. Much later sources refer to these immigrants as the Teochichimecs, originating in the

15.2 *(Below) The Aztecs looted Tula for sculptural pieces, and copied others. The atlantean figures typical of Tula were clearly the inspiration for this smaller version (1.15 m, just under 4 ft), which has many of the same costume elements, such as the butterfly-shaped pectoral. This sculpture and four others were found in the 1940s in Mexico City, in the area of the Templo Mayor precinct, and may have represented deified warriors associated with the cardinal directions and the center of the cosmos (Matos and Solís 2002).*

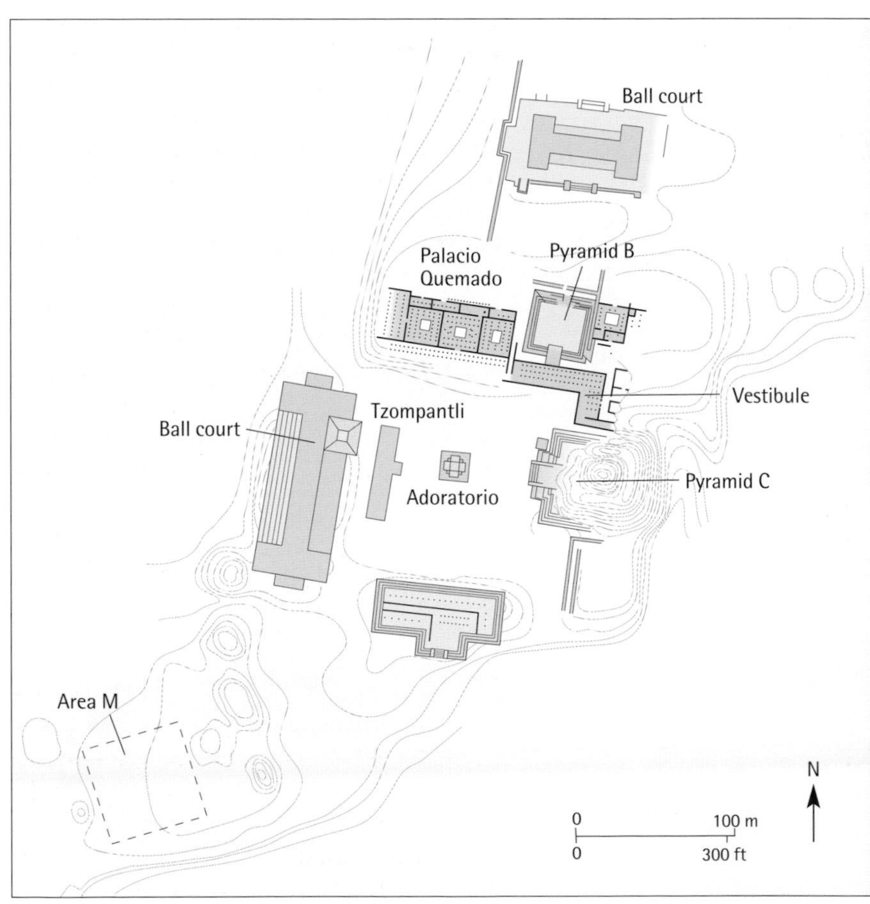

15.3, 15.4 *Tula's civic-ceremonial precinct (shown in the plan, opposite right) was the heart of the city. Pyramids B and C, in the northeast corner, dominate the quadrangle (above). The Palacio Quemado ("Burned Palace"), west of Pyramid B, is the largest segment of a vast colonnaded set of buildings. Area M, in the southwest corner, is the Palacio Tolteca excavated by Désiré Charnay in the 1880s.*

more arid lands to the north, and the Nonoalcos, who originated in the Chontalpa area (Davies 1977) but who may first have spent time in the Huasteca, a region which influenced Tula (Diehl 1983). There were also, no doubt, Teotihuacanos, skilled artisans and ambitious civil and religious functionaries who, upon the decline of their city, would have sought new urbanizing arenas for their talents, and Tula would have been a logical choice.

Tula: Setting, Layout, Functions At its height, AD 900–1150 (Tollan phase), Tula may have covered nearly 16 sq. km (*c.* 6.4 sq. miles) and had an urban population estimated at 60,000, with another 60,000 in the surrounding countryside. At its center was a ceremonial precinct which in important ways bore Teotihuacan's influence (Mastache and Cobean 2000). The grid of Tula was laid out *c.* 17° east of north, as characterizes one of the important orientations at Teotihuacan, and entirely obliterated the earlier grid upon which Tula Chico, the Coyotlatelco-era settlement, had been established. Unlike Teotihuacan's linear arrangement of major monuments along the Street of the Dead, Tula's ceremonial focus was built around a rectangular plaza *c.* 120 by 140 m (394 by 459 ft) [**15.3, 15.4**]. The platform comprising the base of the monuments and the plaza was itself a monumental effort, made of fill which is, in some places, 7 to 8 m (23 to 26 ft) deep.

Pyramids C and B Pyramid C is the largest structure at Tula, and its relation to Pyramid B echoes that of Teotihuacan's Pyramid of the Sun to the Pyramid of the Moon, both in relative placement and size, and in the orientation of the two monuments, suggesting a deliberate reference to the older Tollan, Teotihuacan (Mastache, Cobean, and Healan 2002). Pyramid C has only been partially excavated in modern times – the Aztecs damaged it extensively, digging for treasure.

As Figure 15.4 shows, Pyramid B is remarkably like Chichén Itzá's Temple Pyramid of the Warriors, which also is fronted by colonnaded halls. Pyramid B's sculptural corpus emphasizes themes of war and sacrifice. The most conspicuous features atop the pyramid are the atlantean warriors, huge statues of battle-garbed Toltecs bearing the spear throwers and back shields that were part of Central Mexican soldiers' uniforms. Behind them were four columns that seem to have depicted kings of Tula, and also depict attributes of Tlaloc, Quetzalcoatl, and Tezcatlipoca, the earliest known illustration of the god whose name meant "Smoking Mirror." Tezcatlipoca was "the dread, capricious god of gods" of the Aztecs, the archsorcerer and transformer, who moved on earth as a jaguar (Nicholson 1971: 444). He was also the patron of feasting and banquets, as well as of warriors and rulers.

Pyramid B's bas-relief panels depicted prowling jaguars and coyotes, birds of prey, and "a composite creature having human, reptile, and avian attributes" interpreted as "a representation of Tlahuizcalpantecuhtli, the god Quetzalcoatl in his embodiment as the planet Venus, the evening star" (Mastache and Cobean 2000: 105), another association with warfare. Tlahuizcalpantecuhtli may also be the "warrior" depicted in the atlantean columns.

Historical and Ecological Roots of Tula's Religion

The Early Postclassic period in the Central Highlands provided the basis for much of Aztec religion, which was very well documented. Thus it is possible to track certain patterns of ritual practice and the histories of some deities back to Tula, and from there back even further: the Huasteca seems to have been an important source for Tula's religion, perhaps lending credence to the legendary origin of one of the city's major ethnic components. Because of this, we will break into the discussion of Tula to review contemporaneous events in this region, and then return to the Toltecs.

The Northern and North-central Gulf Lowlands in Toltec Times

That the Gulf lowlands would be a source of cultural cross-fertilization at this time is evident because the region was densely settled, ethnically mixed, and politically decentralized into a series of small competing polities. After the fall of El Tajín in the south, no single state was as dominant; instead, several smaller centers occupied defensible locations. Typical of these is Paxil, near Misantla, whose architecture features Tajín-style flying cornices over sloping *taluds* (Ruiz Gordillo 1999). This modest ceremonial center, with a linear array of platforms and a ball court, is located on a ridge between two watercourses.

It was during this period that the north-central Gulf lowlands, just south of the northern Gulf lowlands "Huasteca," became known as "Totonacapan" because of the migration there of the Totonacs, who spoke a language related to Mayan. In the Late Postclassic, the name Totonacapan would come to mean "land of food" to the Aztecs, because of its unfailing fertility. In times of famine in the Central Highlands people would go to the land of the Totonacs and sell themselves as slaves in order to survive.

In the Huasteca, occupation continued at Tamuín and Tantoc and other large sites on the plain of the lowlands, such as Tancol, near modern Tampico. Modest sites like Buenavista Huaxcama and Balcón de Montezuma were occupied in the Sierra Madre Oriental, close to the southern Chichimec region and influenced by ongoing cultural development there and in areas further south and west.

The Huasteca has been identified as the region that Central Mexicans in the Late Postclassic referred to as Tamoanchan, "a mythical and paradisiacal place of origin" (Miller and Taube 1993: 160; see also López Austin 1997). There, according to one legend, the gods first created the present version of humankind, and there, the gods gave humans intoxicating *pulque*, the fermented sap of the maguey. For the Aztecs, the Huasteca represented abundance and licentiousness, and thus it was at once attractive and repellent to them, in much the same way that modern Americans demonize and imitate what they perceive to be the affluent and libidinous life ways of southern California. For the Toltecs, the Huasteca may have served something of the same function, lending strong cultural influences that would become part of the beliefs and practices of the Central Highlands.

Tula's Major Deities

The great monuments in Tula's city center bear evidence, from images and iconographic indicators, that major deities were venerated there. Tlaloc, the goggle-eyed successor to the Storm God of Teotihuacan, joined Quetzalcoatl and Tezcatlipoca as the most important subjects of rituals. Quetzalcoatl's manifestation as Ehécatl, the Wind God, is evidenced by a round temple in Tula's Corral locality. Ehécatl worship, and the round temples dedicated to him, are thought to have originated in the Huasteca. Four other deities known from Tula also had strong Huastec associations: Xipe Totec, the Flayed Skin God who represented agricultural renewal, and three important female deities, Tlazolteotl ("Filth God") and Xochiquetzal ("Flower Quetzal"), both concerned with sexuality, and Itzpapalotl (lit. "Obsidian Butterfly"), a Tamoanchan-based death goddess who made her first iconographic appearance at Tula.

Household Gods A small Late Archaic fired-clay figurine is Mesoamerica's oldest known ceramic artifact [**3.12**], and, since that time, figurines have been found in most cultural contexts. They were integral to rituals at the individual and household level, and surveys and excavations of domestic contexts find figurine fragments among the potsherds and obsidian blades that make up the surviving detritus of daily life. At Tula, the figurines were of a distinctive "gingerbread man" type [**15.6**], clearly mold-made, but

FEMALE DEITIES

WHILE MAJOR temple-pyramids in the central ritual precincts of Postclassic cities were dedicated to male deities, female deities were venerated at other important temples and shrines as well as in private homes. Because female deities watched over the important stages in a woman's life, and the activities women performed, they were particularly revered by women. Yet their powers extended over everyone's lives, and all people showed them respect, and turned to them for comfort or protection. In typical Mesoamerican fashion, these deities are distinct yet overlapping, blending into each other in much the same way as the different phases in a human life commingle, yet form clearly differentiated stages.

Xochiquetzal

Xochiquetzal, a major Postclassic Central Highlands patroness of women, has been seen as a counterpart to the Greco-Roman Aphrodite/Venus. In Xochiquetzal's care was active female sexuality in its various aspects: desireability and its logical biological outcome, fertility, as it was expressed in healthy pregnancy, safe delivery in childbirth, and caring motherhood. The menstrual cycle governing female fertility and the phases of the moon have a natural affinity, so it is not surprising that she was a moon goddess (Milbrath 2000). Her Maya counterpart, Ixchel, had a shrine on Cozumel Island that was much-visited by women wishing to become pregnant.

Xochiquetzal

Furthermore, various accounts name Xochiquetzal as the consort of several important deities: she was Tlaloc's partner in Tlalocan, his paradise, and, in Tamoanchan, she was linked to Tezcatlipoca. Sexual promiscuity on the part of women or men was not admired by the Aztecs, who saw it as one of the many ways that chaos and disaster could enter one's life. Thus the power of sexual pleasure was recognized as a force to be reckoned with, and Xochiquetzal was linked to some fearsome female deities – the Tzitzimime – who extracted painful vengeance on those who took enjoyment to excess.

In addition to being a love goddess, Xochiquetzal had a strong domestic side and was one of the patronesses of textile arts. The personal life of the typical Mesoamerican woman was divided among childbearing and rearing, spinning and weaving, and other household duties, so Xochiquetzal's auspices oversaw much of women's lives.

Tlazolteotl

Xochiquetzal was woman in her fertile prime, whereas Tlazolteotl was woman older and wiser, still spinning and weaving, but having a new role with regard to sexuality: confessor and curer. It was her role to "eat filth" – to absorb guilt and sin and their material expressions, excrement and disease – and absolve the sinner. While Xochiquetzal and Tlazolteotl were distinct in terms of cult rituals and the range of their responsibilities, as female overseers of sexuality and the textile arts, they may be thought of as different parts of the same deity complex (Sullivan 1982).

Also related to Tlazolteotl was *Toci* or *Teteo Innan*, an Aztec grandmother goddess who had power to cure, as a sweat bath deity, and comfort – her images bear the same black markings around the mouth that define Tlazolteotl as an eater of human corruption. Toci is sometimes erroneously conflated with *Tonantzin* ("Our Lady"), a maize deity whose Late Postclassic shrine on the hillside at Tepeyacac just north of Tenochtitlan is now the site of the Roman Catholic Basilica dedicated to the Virgin of Guadalupe, modern Mexico's patron saint.

Chicomecoatl and *Xilonen* were also maize goddesses, representing the mature ears and also green maize. *Mayahuel* was the goddess of the maguey plant (there were many *pulque* deities, honoring fermented maguey sap), and in the Central Highlands, maguey "was the only crop other than corn to be represented by its own deity" (Boone 1994: 79).

Cihuacoatl ("Woman Snake") was another of the goddesses who watched over childbirth. A patroness of midwives, she, like Xochiquetzal and Tlazolteotl, was regarded as a protector of the sweat bath, a place whose curative properties included easing labor pains. Childbirth was seen as a dangerous, potentially lethal part of women's lives, the analogue to men's battlefield experiences. In fact, Cihuacoatl was the special patroness of women who died in childbirth. They were deified, becoming the *Cihuateteo* ("Woman Gods") who accompanied the sun from noon to sunset, the morning solar transit having been escorted by the spirits of men who died in battle. They were feared as abductors of children, causes of insanity, and seductresses who lured men into adultery. The *Tzitzimime* were another set of celestial women-gods who also had sweat bath associations (Robelo 1980), but few of the other niceties attached to curing. They were regarded as demons of the night sky, celestial bodies gone bad who could attack the sun and destroy the earth.

These characterizations indicate an ambivalence, at least in Aztec society, about the powers of women, but we must recall that our view of these deities is somewhat colored by 16th-century Spanish clergy who recorded their myths, and who were also involved in rooting out heresies. These proselytizers for Catholicism regarded midwives as their worst enemies, because they encouraged women in the pain and uncertainty of labor and childbirth to turn to the old ways for comfort (Klein 2000). Thus it was in Spanish interests to conflate the fertility goddesses and the curers who invoked them with European pawns of the devil, witches and witchcraft.

15.5 *Female deities, from the* Codex Magliabechiano *(mid-1500s). Xochiquetzal encourages underage youths to drink* pulque *and then commit "abomination and fornications" as practiced in* tierra caliente – *"land where the sun is hot" (Codex Magliabechiano, Boone 1983: 197). Mayahuel and Xilonen oversaw maguey and maize, two crops that together supplied most of the calories for most people in the Central Highlands. Grandmotherly Toci, a broom in her right hand, has unspun cotton adorning the broom and her earplugs, and forming a base for her feather headdress. Cihuacoatl's snake skirt has been abstracted to a textile pattern. Two flint sacrificial knives are positioned over her skeletal face.*

detailed so that no two were identical. Also present at Tula were the distinctive wheeled animal figurines [14.24] that gained widespread popularity at this time. As was noted in Chapter 14, this trait may have originated in the Huasteca.

Apartment Compounds and House Groups Tula's rulers may have occupied the palace excavated by Charnay, or other compounds close to the civic-ceremonial center. Less exalted citizens of Tula were housed in several different kinds of residential complexes. Limited excavations indicate that close to the center, housing consisted of apartment compounds wherein several suites of rooms surrounded central courtyards. They were similar to those of Teotihuacan, but much smaller. These probably dated to early in Tollan phase, and seem to have housed higher-ranking families.

As the city grew in the latter part of the Tollan phase, residential construction further from the city center was less formalized than that of the apartment compounds. Houses were conjoined into "house groups" that were more flexible in size and layout. About 1.3 km (0.8 miles) northeast of the civic-ceremonial center was the Canal Locality [**15.7**, **15.8**], a set of three house groups (Healan 1977). Reasoning from similar domestic situations in the Late Postclassic and from ethnographic analogues, we can assume that these three may have accommodated an extended family.

This complex was built over a period of time, with the Central House Group being the oldest, and the West House Group a more recent addition. Furthermore, the houses, and rooms within them, varied as to quality and desirability as well as having functional differences. Concentrations of artifacts related to food storage and preparation identified some of the smaller rooms as kitchens, while corners of the courtyards were also used for food preparation as well as other tasks. In Mesoamerica, we have noted, much of life was lived out of doors, and a family's everyday tasks were largely accomplished in courtyards amidst residential rooms (typical of *tierra fría*), or plazas surrounded by small individual houses (as found in the tropical lowlands).

It is a universal truth that each member of a family occupies a distinctive status *vis-à-vis* other family members. Similarly, the different nuclear families that comprise an extended family household maintain graded positions relative to each other, based on birth order, achievements, luck, and other factors. Status differences within houses of extended families are perceptible to some degree by comparing the rooms as to size, quality of finishing, and orientation. In the chilly high altitude atmosphere of the Central Highlands, west-facing rooms were valued, because they captured the warmth of the afternoon sun. House VI, for example, just east of the Central House Group's courtyard, was clearly a superior room: large and well-finished, it had one of the only plastered floors in the compound (the others were packed earth), and faced west onto the courtyard. House X, in the East House Group, was another superior room.

In contrast, the Central Group's Houses IV and IX were small, with thin

15.6 *(Opposite) Tula's flat figurines had surface details of costume and jewelry, enhanced by paint surviving only as traces on most examples. These fragments are typical of what archaeologists find among household debris in Mesoamerica; whole figurines are more common in mortuary contexts, such as the shaft tombs of West Mexico, or the Maya cemetery at Jaina. Some figurines may have served as household guardians, placed in shrines within the house and venerated with incense. Others may have been acquired for a specific purpose, such as invoking a deity to bring rain, to protect a loved one, or safely guide someone through a difficult experience such as childbirth or war.*

walls, dirt floors, and out-of-the-way locations. They were added onto the Central Group after the other, larger rooms were built around the courtyard. We can imagine the most recently married couple in the extended family moving into one of these houses, and then perhaps moving up to a better location as space became available when senior members of the family died or were widowed and shifted to a shared living arrangement elsewhere in the House Group.

Militarists and Merchants Commoners like the Canal Group's residents worked as artisans or laborers in Tula's complex economy, which was administered by the elite, from the civic-ceremonial center. High-ranking individuals may have held their meetings, feasts, and processionals in the Palacio Quemado. This "Burned Palace" consists of large square rooms with benches, surrounded by wide passageways – the layout does not indicate spaces that would have served any of the normal domestic functions required by a true residential palace, but it would have been ideal for official events held by those in charge of the state and its economy.

Processions of jaguars and other beasts are a pervasive theme in Mesoamerican elite architecture. They are found in the murals of Teotihuacan (Atetelco and other apartment compounds), at Chichén Itzá (Mercado, Temple of the Eagles), here at Tula, and later at Tenochtitlan. They merge the menace of militarism with a processional theme that is also associated with the mercantilism that was so important to the economies of all four great

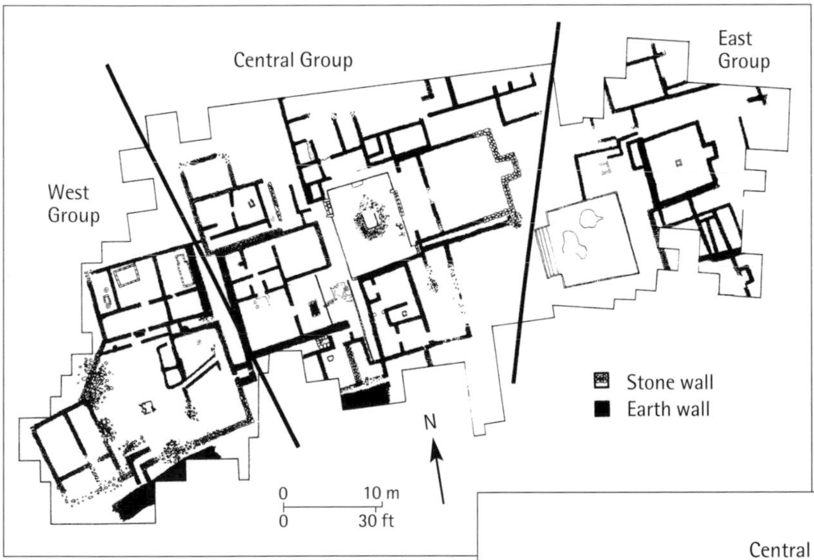

Central Group
East Group
West Group
Stone wall
Earth wall
N
0 10 m
0 30 ft

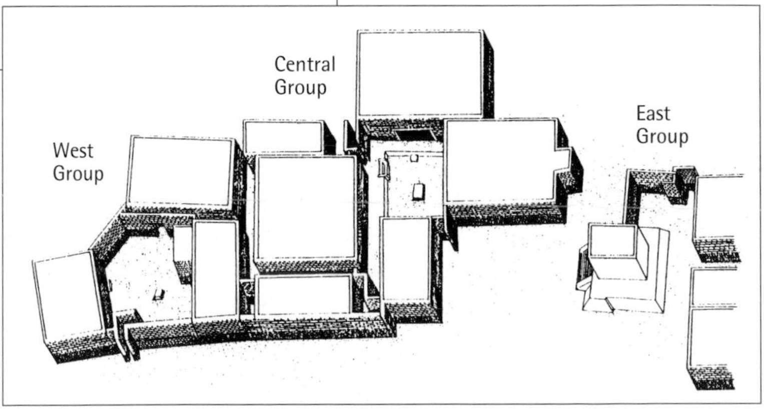

Central Group
East Group
West Group

15.7, 15.8 *The south wall of Tula's Canal Locality separated the compound from a city street; access through the baffled entrance into the courtyard of the West House Group maintained privacy. The temple between the Central House Group and the East House Group would have served the needs of the whole compound.*

centers. Both warriors and long-distance traders are known, from Aztec sources, to have celebrated their achievements in ritualized processions, and, as we have noted in previous discussions, armed merchant caravans not only maintained trading networks, they also established commercial and political alliances, serving as advance troops with diplomatic powers.

Important clues as to the function of this complex are provided not only by its layout, but by the bas-reliefs that decorated the fronts of the banquettes, and also the upper walls. Many of these sculpted pieces have been lost, looted by the Aztecs for use in their own ceremonial center. In fact, in their zeal to appropriate Tula's prestige by using its rich treasures in their own capital, the Aztecs degraded the site they venerated. "The Aztecs were so thorough and left Tula so impoverished that several scholars have maintained that it is not spectacular enough to have been the Toltec capital!" (Diehl 1983: 27). What remain of the bas-relief panels, however, tell a clear story of political power in the service of ideologically and economically motivated rituals (Klein 1987; Kristin-Graham 1993).

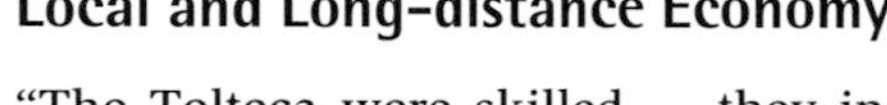

Local and Long-distance Economy

"The Tolteca were skilled ... they indeed formed works of art; they performed works of skill. In truth, they invented all the wonderful, precious, marvelous things which they made ... many of them were scribes, lapidaries, carpenters, stone cutters, masons, feather workers ... potters, spinners, weavers. They were very learned ... [and] very wise" (Sahagún 1961 [1569]: 167–168).

The Aztec view of the Toltecs, we have seen, cast them in a glamorous and no doubt highly idealized light, but even in its time-ravaged condition, Tula reveals that once upon a time, very talented and productive artisans lived there. Like the gradations within any complex society, there were higher and lower statuses of artisan, with the highest status being held by those who created luxury goods for the elite. As was true of the Maya, a scribe was a literate, learned individual to whom others turned as an authority and a source of documents. Lapidaries cut, polished, and set into jewelry or art works the imported precious stones such as turquoise and jadeite. Feather workers took fragile materials imported from hundreds of kilometers away and turned them into headdresses and banners that shimmered with color as they captured the breeze.

This luxury goods economy was the apex of a pyramid of materials procurement, production of goods, and distribution that involved much more than insignia of rank for society's most exalted members. Everyone needed food, and it was likely that most of the Tula region's population played some part in farming. Everyone needed housing – and the city needed its massive monuments – and thus building materials were another important component of production and consumption. Construction itself was probably a family matter for most commoner houses, but definitely involved skilled designers and artisans at the civic level.

15.9 *Feline symbolism at many Mesoamerican sites was associated with militarism. This carved tablet, 1.26 m (just over 4 ft) high, was found at Tula and shows a spotted cat.*

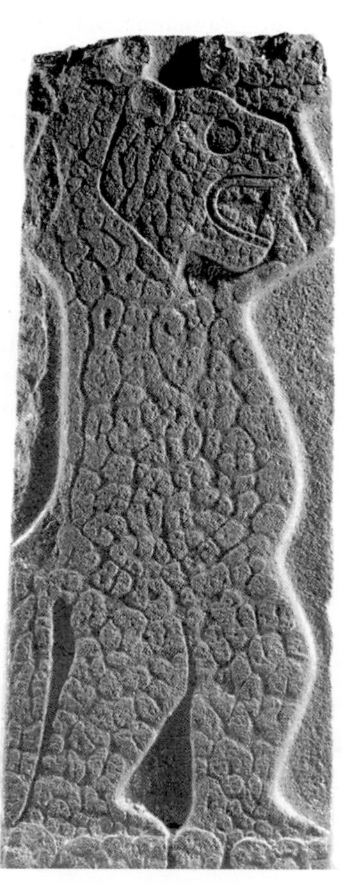

Some of the city's pottery was fine and imported, like Plumbate, but most of the vessels used at Tula were local, and Toltec potters procured clays that occurred in outcrops along the Tula River, and formed and fired these wares. Clay ritual objects were also produced: censers, braziers, and figurines. Green obsidian from the Pachuca source *c.* 65 km (40 miles) to the northwest was prized, accounting for 80 percent of the obsidian worked in the city, with Michoacán's Ucareo source providing about 10 percent. Prismatic blades were the commonest obsidian tool type, and a workshop on the east side of the city produced well-prepared cylindrical cores from which such blades could be struck.

15.10 *Feathered serpents decorate the background of the scene on this ceremonial vessel, thought to come from Tula. The figures at the bottom may be conducting a ritual: the one on the right is speaking or singing, and the figure at left holds a vessel like this one.*

Toltec Influence upon West Mexico, the Northwestern Frontier, and the Northern Arid Zone

Tula's trade networks took such goods – and Central Mexican lifestyles and belief systems – to peoples hundreds of kilometers away. In West Mexico, after the decline of its indigenous Teuchitlán tradition, architecture expressed the Mesoamerican pattern of rectangular platforms facing onto plazas. Interpretations of West Mexico suffer from a dearth of adequately excavated sites, but some of the most important trends can be identified from the evidence which has been gathered, both of sites and new traditions in that region, and the presence, in other areas, of metal objects originating in West Mexico and precious materials like turquoise that were traded through it. In fact, West Mexico's involvement in metalworking "undoubtedly introduced entirely new demands on the systems for obtaining scarce resources, and on distribution networks" (Weigand and Beekman 1998: 51), demands that may have overwhelmed the established order and favored the new Toltec-era trade networks.

Metalworking During the Early Postclassic, West Mexican metallurgy entered a new phase of technological development, with the production of bronze, made by smelting copper with tin, and copper with arsenic. Copper was also combined with silver, but it was the copper-tin and copper-arsenic bronzes that became standard materials. These processes not only represent advancements in technology, but also success in seeking out the necessary raw materials, which could be found in West Mexico, the Northwestern Frontier, and in Guerrero.

The development of bronze was linked, in the Old World, with advances in the design of tools and weapons. In Mesoamerica, such matters played a secondary role to aesthetic considerations – bronze permitted refinements in the design of bells and ornaments, and could be manipulated to create shimmering effects of brilliance, resembling gold and silver, which were structurally much weaker and thus unsuitable for the new designs. Furthermore, the alloys were developed to enhance the quality of sound that the bells made. To a very limited extent, alloys were applied to production of tools such as projectile points and sewing needles, but the greatest interest of

Mesoamerican metallurgists was in the aesthetic properties of metals, and their success in developing materials and products that appealed to elite consumers was evident in far-ranging trade in such items as bells (Hosler 1994).

Ixtlán del Río Ixtlán del Río (also known as Torrilas) had a very long period of occupation, probably beginning in the first centuries AD, and extending to the time of European intrusion. The site is now one of West Mexico's few archaeological parks, and most of the visible architecture dates from the Postclassic. Its platforms, columned buildings, cemeteries, and I-shaped ball court extend over an area of *c.* 1 sq. km (0.4 sq. mile) (Weigand 2001: 821). The site's most imposing and central structure is a circular pyramid 50 m (164 ft) in diameter. This pyramid was excavated in the 1940s and imaginatively reconstructed. At that time, the circular architecture dominating sites of the Teuchitlán tradition had not yet been discovered, so the lack of other cultural precedent gave rise to the idea that the shape indicated that it was dedicated to Quetzalcoatl as Ehécatl, the wind god. Given the site's long period of occupation, one could plausibly argue that this circular structure is either a remnant of the Teuchitlán tradition, or an intrusive Central Mexican feature.

Aztatlán Complex This term was applied in the Early Colonial period to the cultural complex found along the Pacific Coast of West Mexico and the Northwestern Frontier. Archaeological research has indicated that the sites in the Aztatlán complex emerged in the early Postclassic. The pottery that characterizes these sites is so similar to Mixtec codex style (see below) that some researchers once speculated that Aztatlán was the result of a colonization effort by Mixteca-Puebla peoples. These coastal and uplands regions were clearly part of the period's extensive trade networks, but Aztatlán sites were not just trading centers. They were the focal communities in river valleys along the coast, supported by local farming and by production of metal objects and obsidian as well as pottery.

The trading component of the Aztatlán complex [15.11, 15.12] tied Central Mexico with the Northern Arid Zone. Along the Pacific coastal plain, Amapa, Chametla, Culiacan, and Guasave were important links, while another route moved goods along the east side of the Sierra Madre. Aztatlán culture seems to have revitalized the interior after the decline of Chalchihuites centers such as Alta Vista and La Quemada.

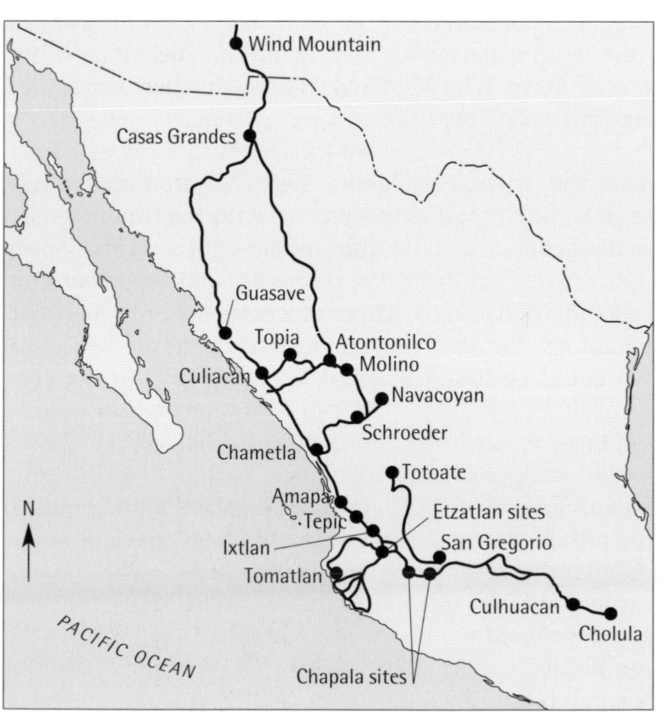

15.11 *The map shows the sites that were actively trading during this period and the hypothesized route linking them. The overland point to point distance between Guasave, the northernmost coastal site, and Cholula was about 1,500 km/932 miles (Kelley 1986: 85).*

15.12 *Designs on pottery from Aztatlán sites show affinities with the Central and South-central Highlands of Mexico. At bottom, design motifs in the Codex Style of Mixteca-Puebla decorate a vessel found at the Schroeder site (roll-out of motifs) and pottery found at Guasave: the three cartouches possibly show Central Mexican deities. The pair of designs contrasts Aztec I pottery, an Early Postclassic type from the Basin of Mexico (at top) with a design on a Guasave vessels.*

The Northern Arid Zone: Mesoamerica and the Puebloan or "Great House" Cultures

During the Early Postclassic, the Aztatlán trade route brought the Northwestern Frontier region into its closest relations with the core of Mesoamerica. In turn, Aztatlán channeled elements of the Mesoamerican belief system far to the north along with the precious materials and symbols so highly valued by Mesoamerican elites. Casas Grandes (Paquimé) was a major link between the Aztatlán system and the puebloan or "great house" cultures of southwestern North America, and is discussed below. Casas Grandes was the most important site in the Mogollon tradition, which extended through the mountains of southern Arizona and New Mexico, and into north-central Mexico.

West of the Mogollon, sites in the Hohokam tradition included Snaketown (AD 450–1150), with two oval ball courts and evidence of trade with Mesoamerica in copper bells and other items. Farther north, sites in the Anasazi tradition flourished in Chaco Canyon from about AD 950 to about 1200, when a series of severe droughts began that caused dispersal and relocation of the population. At its height, Chaco Canyon may have traded copper and turquoise, which occurs in copper deposits such as the still-viable mines at Cerillos, north of Albuquerque (New Mexico).

A recent study of cannibalism in the Chaco Canyon area posited that at around AD 900, Mesoamerican "warrior-cultists dedicated to gods of the Tezcatlipoca-Xipe Totec complex" moved to the Chaco Canyon area and terrorized the local population into "heavy payments of tribute, constructing the Chaco system of great houses and roads, and providing victims for ceremonial sacrifice" (Turner and Turner 1999: 463). This overstates Mesoamerican influence in this region, and undervalues the ability of peoples in all parts of the world to devise ways of subjugating their fellow human beings. Indeed, many scholars believe strongly that "Chaco Canyon was not at the north end of a high-volume long-distance exchange system, nor did its exchange relationships with the south hold transformative power" (Renfrew 2001: 16). Casas Grandes, as the major center in long-distance trade, focused upon exchange "with the Mogollon and passed few Mesoamerican goods on to the Anasazi" (McGuire 1989: 56).

Casas Grandes First occupied at around AD 1, its period of greatest development was between about 1100 and 1450. Casas Grandes was the largest pueblo (2,000 rooms) in the "Oasis America" region that comprised the pueblo dwelling sites of the present-day U.S. Southwest and northern Mexico (Di Peso *et al.* 1974; Schaafsma and Riley 1999). Unlike most other pueblos, Casas Grandes also had substantial monumental architecture, as well. The I-shaped ball court shown on the plan (**15.13**) was one of two at the site, and there were at least a dozen within 30 km (19 miles) of the site, possibly a means of local political integration (Whalen and Minnis 1996).

Casas Grandes is best known for facilities and materials related to trade, particularly feathers, shell, copper, and probably turquoise. The site had extensive cages for accommodating and breeding macaws and other colorful birds whose feathers were treasured for decorative and ritual purposes. The birds were often themselves used in rituals, as their decapitated remains attest. Another important trade item was shell. More than 20 species have been identified, and two storage rooms contained 4,000,000 pieces of Nassarius shell, a 10-mm (3/8-in) long specimen imported from the Gulf of California, 300 km (186 miles) distant. The precipitous decline of Casas Grandes after 1450 may have resulted from changes in long-distance trade networks (Brown 1994), or in reaction to political turmoil that marked the decline of the puebloan traditions to the north and the rise of the Aztec empire to the south.

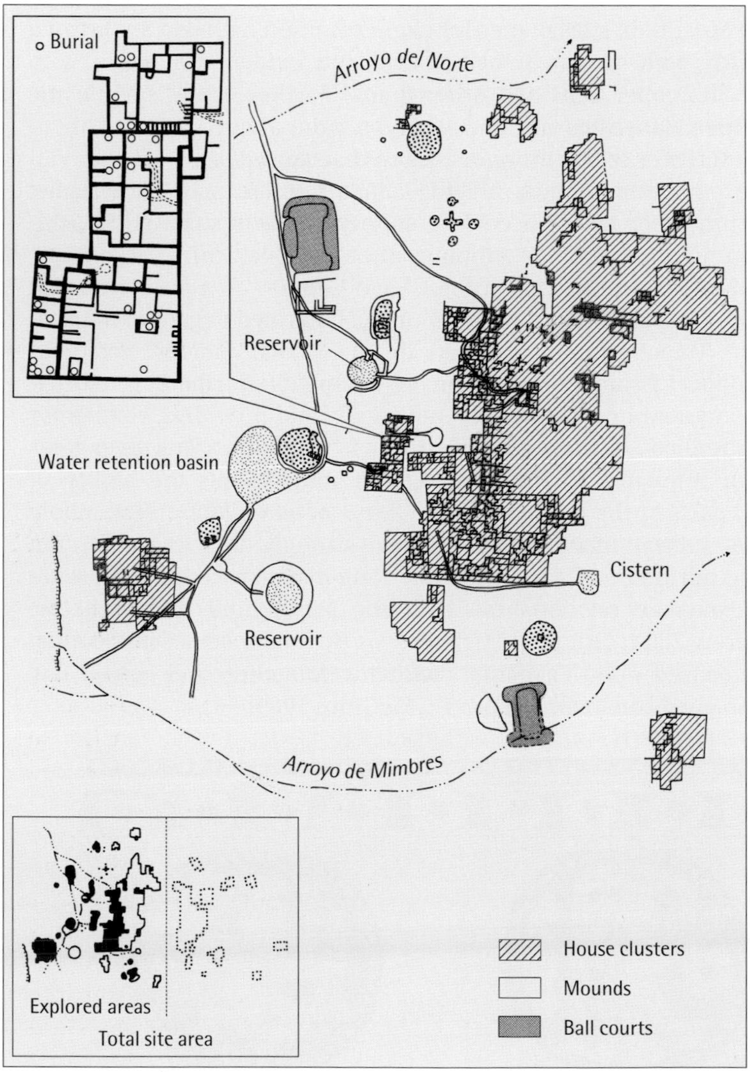

15.13 *Casas Grandes had a rectilinear plan of groups of rooms around extensive courtyards, with several eccentric features, such as the monumental Mound of the Cross. In this region of very low rainfall (300 mm/12 in), irrigation from mountain streams was essential to grow crops for the population. As the site plan shows, watercourses transected Casas Grandes and there were several ponds.*

Mesoamerican and Mississippian Cultures

Although Casas Grandes is far to the north of the boundary of the contiguous Mesoamerican culture area, even when the southern Chichimec desert was at its greenest, in many respects it represents the northernmost site which bore a significant number of Mesoamerican traits. As we have seen, during the Early Postclassic period Mesoamerican traits and materials reached into North America, but scholarly opinions have long been divided over the extent to which Mississippian cultures (*c.* AD 1100–1450) were contacted by Mesoamerican networks of trade and belief systems. Mississippian cultures were found throughout southeastern North America, and featured chiefdoms centered upon large sites with impressive platform mounds, the populations supported by maize agriculture.

To date, only one object at a Mississipian site has been irrefutably identified as originating in Mesoamerica. This is a scraper made of green Pachuca obsidian, and it was found at Spiro Mounds (Oklahoma). This fascinating example of the range of materials distribution cannot be regarded as evidence of direct contact, or even of cultural influence. Rather, the scraper probably came to Spiro Mounds through a complicated set of down-the-line trades and/or gift exchanges. By the time it reached Spiro Mounds the object may have been prized only for its unique green color, having lost all known association with Mesoamerica. It seems clear that Mississippian cultures were indigenous, their societal complexity and architectural monuments resulting from their own trajectory of cultural development.

It may have been the northwest Mexican Aztatlán trading network that started the Spiro Mounds scraper on its long journey. Aztatlán towns probably grew prosperous as Toltec or Chichimec trading parties followed a regular pattern of visits, moving according to a schedule set by both the solar and divinatory calendars. The commercial combination of desirable goods and an attractive belief system is familiar to us in the modern world – it is the appeal of free market capitalism – and the collapse of such commercial enterprises is also familiar, as when local people protest the imposition of foreign standards, or the foreigners themselves are beset by troubles at home. When confidence is lost, collapse begins.

Gods, Heroes, and Antiheroes

The collapse of Tula, late in the 12th century, is also the story of a fallen hero. Scholars have traditionally associated Tula with Quetzalcoatl, the Feathered Serpent. Not only was Tula once thought to have been the source of the Feathered Serpent cult that we have already seen evidenced so extensively, but it was also regarded as the seat of rulership for Topiltzin Quetzalcoatl, the culture hero of the Toltecs and one of Tula's last Early Postclassic rulers (Nicholson 2001). Some native chroniclers named him as Tula's first ruler, as well, but this may have been a retroactive designation to conform with the notion that time is strongly cyclical: that which ended with Topiltzin Quetzalcoatl must have begun with him, as well.

As we have seen, the Feathered Serpent is a very old sacred entity in Mesoamerica, with roots in Olmec culture and florescence at Teotihuacan. The apotheosis of the deity into a culture hero at Tula who is then disgraced is recounted in sometimes contradictory accounts, which have a basic structure. Topiltzin Quetzalcoatl is caused, by the trickery of Tezcatlipoca in human guise, to embarrass himself – in some versions of the story he became drunk on *pulque* and committed indecent sexual acts. He was ostracized, and in shame he abandoned his city. He traveled east, an iconic

15.14, 15.15 *(Opposite above) Teotenango's "Sistema del Norte" consisted of platforms built into a hillside, thus making the site defensible. The buildings include temples and residences, a market area and a ball court (just below and to the right of center in the photo). (Opposite below) The integration of Teotenango into the belief system so characteristic of other Late Classic–Early Postclassic sites is demonstrated by its architecture and artistic works, such as these bas-relief panels. Top, a necklace-wearing jaguar bears the date 2 Rabbit just above his back. Lower panel, a butterfly with a buzzard's head is dated 13 Reptile.*

black-garbed, bearded figure who was said to have appeared in various places: Cholula, Chichén Itzá (where he was called Kukulcan). Many thought that some day he would reappear to reclaim his realm, and when, in 1519, Hernán Cortés showed up on the Gulf Coast on Quetzalcoatl's name day, bearded and dressed in black, the Spaniard stepped into the perfect part for a conquistador.

The withdrawal of Topiltzin Quetzalcoatl's protection coincided with disaster for Tula. In fact, by AD 1200, it was no longer an important capital. Possibly, a far-reaching climate reversal brought cold weather to parts of Mesoamerica, adversely affecting areas already marginal for cultivation (Gill 2000). Even more certain was that the movements of peoples looking for a better life had not ended while Tula's culture thrived. Belligerent nomads from the borders of the Gran Chichimeca, ready to take advantage of weakened states, continued to migrate south, and among them were the Aztecs, moving toward their destiny.

Tula's influence, however, was far from over. Tula had consolidated trade routes extending from the U.S. Southwest down into Costa Rica, and along this system the Nahua-speaking world had expanded far beyond Central Mexico. Belief systems as well as goods had spread through this network of interaction, and the Feathered Serpent – deity and culture hero – had become part of the ideology of other groups in Mesoamerica. Tula's dynasty was established as the most prestigious in the Postclassic world. As long as there were native nobles in Central Mexico – even after the Spanish conquest – descent from Tula's kings would be the touchstone of legitimacy, and the most skilled artists and artisans would be called "tolteca."

TULA'S NEIGHBORING REGIONS

Tula's political domain is difficult to reconstruct. Clearly, the Tula region was the heartland of the polity, and Tula seems to have controlled at least the northern half of the adjacent Basin of Mexico. We would expect that Tula exerted military control and extracted tribute from a substantial area. The size of the city and monumentality of its core architecture indicate a large supporting population, steadily supplying raw materials, finished goods, labor and service, but there are no tribute lists that demonstrate what other realms were allied with Tula, voluntarily or not. Native histories from the Early Colonial period state that ancient Tula had been the capital of an "empire," and name the "cities" that were subordinate to it. Such documents were often written in the Colonial period with the purpose of glorifying a community or ethnic group that was fighting for its rights – or existence – in Spanish legal courts. The actual situation may have involved local villages and their chiefs rather than cities and kings.

Michoacán, Toluca, Morelos

Tula may have had no "empire" but it certainly had a powerful effect on adjacent regions. Michoacán between AD 800 and 1000 supplied Tula with Ucareo obsidian, and by AD 900 northeastern Michoacán was showing changes in settlement pattern as populations aggregated at defensible locations, a pattern that continued until the Late Postclassic emergence of the Tarascan state (Pollard 1993). East of Michoacán, the northern Valley of Toluca, with small regional centers surrounded by farming hamlets, would have been part of Tula's domain. The most important Tolucan site, Teotenango **[15.14, 15.15]**, was in the southern part of the Valley, and its interactions were oriented toward tropical *tierra caliente* further south, particularly with Xochicalco in the early part of Teotenango's occupation. But in the Valley of Morelos, Xochicalco's decline was accompanied by a generally sparse population in the region at the start of the Early Postclassic. This situation was reversed after a few centuries, with an influx of migrants from the north.

Teotenango had been occupied from the Late Classic; its civic-ceremonial center was first built in the Early Postclassic by an ethnically mixed population of native Teotenangans and Otomí-speaking Teochichimecs from the north, and Coyotlatelco pottery is abundant during these early periods (Piña Chan 2000). Teotenango flourished as Matlatzinca peoples settled there at the end of the Early Postclassic. The Feathered Serpent was revered here, and dated monuments evidence use of calendrics.

The monumental part of the site was surrounded by more dispersed settlement by commoners (Piña Chan 1975). They would have farmed the plain, and the abundance of maguey scrapers found at the site indicates their reliance on this durable product to protect against maize crop loss due to frosts. Teotenango's elevation is 2,745 m (9,000 ft) – the Toluca Valley's alluvial plain in general has the highest altitude of any in the Central Highlands.

The Basin of Mexico

Some native chroniclers claimed that Tula shared power with Culhuacan and "Otumba" – "place of the Otomí." Culhuacan was in the southwestern Basin of Mexico; in the northern Basin, Xaltocan became the capital for Otomí-speaking peoples, a minority in this Nahuatl-speaking region. The Teotihuacan Valley town now known as Otumba was only a small village in the Early Postclassic period, and only became an Otomí center in about 1400. Thus Xaltocan was probably "Otumba," Tula's ally. Culhuacan's political power was quickly diminished as new and aggressive groups settled the Basin of Mexico and established larger and stronger towns, but its relationship with Tula made it the heir to Toltec greatness. When, in the late 1300s, the Mexica Aztecs established their own dynasty, they chose a member of Culhuacan's ruling lineage as their own ruler, in order to capitalize on Tula's legendary prestige.

Early Postclassic Teotihuacan was virtually dead at the core, with only scattered settlement along the Street of the Dead and in its residential complexes. Its remnant population clustered into towns on the fringes of the old Classic city. The Postclassic town of Teotihuacan was on the southwest edge of the old city, and became a capital for the Teotihuacan Valley in the Late Postclassic and Colonial periods. Elsewhere in the valley, small farming communities were dispersed along the edge of the alluvial plain. These small villages would become settlement nodes as population increased in the Late Postclassic.

PUEBLA/TLAXCALA AND THE SOUTHWESTERN HIGHLANDS

Migration epics are so prevalent in the native histories dealing with the Early Postclassic that it is difficult not to credit a general trend, during this period, of a movement of small groups of peoples from the Chichimec regions (but see Price 1980), living off the land as they pushed toward the southeast (pp. 418–419). To describe such groups as hunter-foragers ignores their variability; it seems that many of them were displaced farmers, used to the customs of community life and looking for new places to resume them. When such groups moved into the Basin of Mexico or the Valley of Puebla, they may have settled on unoccupied territory, or usurped land from its inhabitants, or indentured themselves in some way to the lords of resident populations.

Cholula and the Valley of Puebla

In fact, the "Toltec" officers at the entrance to Chicomoztoc Cave in the *Historia Tolteca-Chichimeca* illustration were recruiting the Chichimecs to help oust the Olmeca-Xicalanca from Cholula. The resulting ethnic fusion, the Tolteca-Chichimeca, may have been responsible for the destruction of Cacaxtla, the Olmeca-Xicalanca capital. They are also credited with destruction at Cholula's Great Pyramid complex, including stelae-smashing at the Patio of the Altars on the south side of the Pyramid. The Patio of the Altars complex shows the eclectic styles that came together at Cholula: *talud-tablero* architecture, Gulf lowlands scrolls, and Mixtec codex-style motifs in murals. "It is during this Epiclassic/Early Postclassic period that Cholula became a crucible out of which evolved the Mixteca-Puebla stylistic tradition" (McCafferty 2001: 300).

Mixteca-Puebla Style From the 10th century on, centered on Puebla and the Mixteca Alta, but found hundreds of kilometers away, spread an art style that was attractive and distinctive, and was applied to visual expression in pottery, murals, jewelry, carvings, and, especially, codices. Mixteca-Puebla style [15.16], was also known as "International Style," because of the geographical extent of its expression. We have noted its appearance on pottery at Aztatlán sites, and it was also found far to the south, in the Guatemalan highlands, but it was the dominant style in its heartland, and it served as a standardized text form to depict deities, calendrics, and especially dynastic records. Being found in so many regions, it served as a *lingua franca*, "not linguistically based in the same way as Zapotec hieroglyphic writing" but rather "a highly developed figurative system of visual communication" (Pohl and Byland 1994: 197).

While the Mixtec codices were essential for documenting royal genealogies and important historical events for the various city-states of the Mixteca Alta, Cholula pottery, in Mixteca-Puebla style, had a wide distribution and was valued by elites all over the Central Highlands as the most prestigious dinnerware, as masses of sherds of this style found in excavations at Motecuzoma II's palace in Tenochtitlan attest.

Throughout Mesoamerican culture history, nobles exchanged fine pottery as gifts and probably used and displayed it to demonstrate their ties to important allies

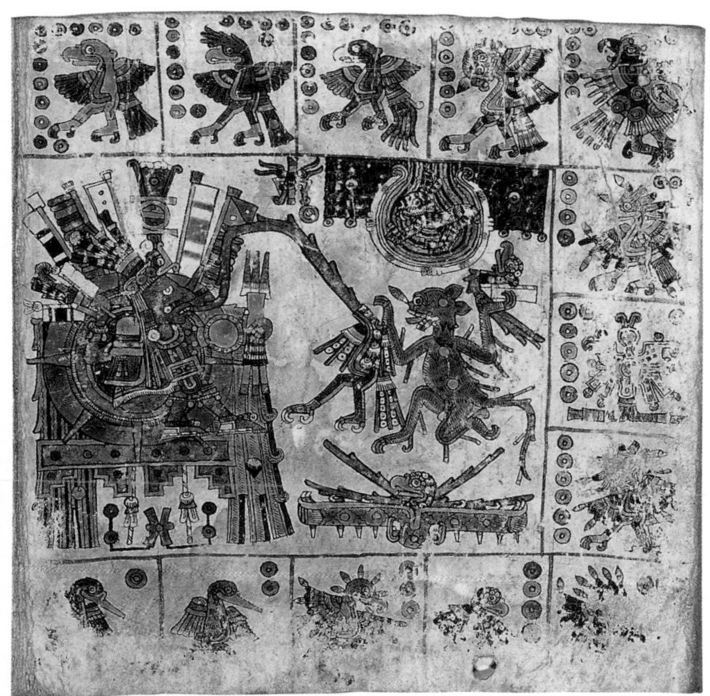

15.16 *Mixteca-Puebla style is recognizable by its highly stylized and conventionalized imagery, with bold, symbolically significant colors. Figures are drawn boldly, with formalized postures, outsized heads, and dramatic gestures in a manner "akin to modern caricature and cartooning of the Disney type" (Nicholson 1966: 260). The* Codex Borgia *(1993 [*c. 1500*]) typifies this style. This screenfold manuscript was painted on animal hide in southern Puebla or the Mixteca Alta. Its content is religious, featuring the 260-day divinatory almanac and depictions of deities. Here we see a central panel with the sun seated on the left, and up to the right, a rabbit-filled moon. Surrounding them are 13 celestial "birds" – actually 12 birds and a butterfly – that represent the levels of heaven (Byland 1993).*

MIGRANTS AND ORIGINS

LATE POSTCLASSIC ethnic groups of the Central Highlands described their ancestors as migrants, many of whom originated in a homeland far to the northwest during the Late Classic and Early Postclassic. Many sources name this homeland Aztlán ("White Place" or "Place of the White Heron"), and modern scholars developed the name "Aztec" to refer to Postclassic peoples who claimed this place of origin. "Aztec" has come to refer more to the groups in the Basin of Mexico, most specifically to the group who called themselves the Mexica and who founded Tenochtitlan-Tlatelolco.

The heart of this homeland was Chicomoztoc, a seven-lobed cave [15.17]. Caves were, of course, regarded as sacred places in Mesoamerica, and the cave under the Pyramid of the Sun was enlarged and configured in a several-lobed pattern. The illustration from the *Historia Tolteca-Chichimeca* (1989 [after 1544]) shows seven couples, the ancestral founders of important ruling lineages in the Late Postclassic. In fact, this Chicomoztoc-based descent line justified right to govern for Central Highlands rulers.

The two figures at the cave entrance are Toltecs recruiting Chichimecs to emigrate from Chicomoztoc. The figure on the right may be Quetzalteueyac (Quetzal Plume from the Lips) – his beard and black garb recall Topiltzin Quetzalcoatl. Depictions of Chicomoztoc name the Chichimec tribes. Not all sources name the same tribes, but among those noted are the Chichimeca (ancestral founders all over the Central Highlands), Mexica, Tepaneca, Xochimilca, Cuitlahuaca, Chalca, and Acolhua, all founders of city-states in the Basin of Mexico, Matlatzinca and Malinalca (settled in the southern Valley of Toluca), Tlahuica (settled in Morelos), and Tlaxcalteca and Huexotzinca (settled in Tlaxcala and Puebla). Mixtec origin accounts also refer to Chicomoztoc.

Where was Aztlán, and Chicomoztoc? Some scholars have entertained the possibility that the migration epics may have been myths, and that the fabled homeland of the Mexica, for example, may have been the islands where they eventually established Tenochtitlan-Tlatelolco (Seler 1991 [1894]). Other scholars regard the accounts as plausible, for several important reasons. Populations in the Tula region, West Mexico, and the Northwestern Frontier surged in the Late Classic and Early Postclassic, followed by abandonment of some areas and decline in others. Environmental stresses may have reduced arable portions of the landscape, causing farmers to seek lands to the south. We have noted that many diagnostic traits of the Late Classic and Early Postclassic – *chacmool* statues, skull racks, colonnaded halls, Coyotlatelco pottery – had their earliest expression in the regions north and west of the Central Highlands. It may have been that the decline of the Chalchihuites sites, Alta Vista and La Quemada, was the first dramatic stage of a long diaspora (Hers 2002).

15.17 *Chicomoztoc ("Seven Caves") was depicted in many native historical annals. This illustration from the* Historia Tolteca-Chichimeca *was drawn by an Early Colonial-period native artist in Puebla, and was part of an historical account of how Tolteca-Chichimeca ancestors migrated from the northwest, stopping at Tula and then moving on to conquer the Olmeca-Xicalanca at Cholula.*

15.18 *The* Codex Boturini *follows the Mexica Aztecs from Aztlán to Culhuacan, Tula's ally in the Basin of Mexico, where their leader is sacrificed. The first excerpt shows the beginning of the journey, when the four Mexica god-bearers seem to lead eight named ethnic groups. About 28 years later, the Mexica settled down for a 19-year stay at Tollan (Place of Reeds). Then, 116 years later, their long journey was almost over, as they lived for 20 years at Chapultepec (Grasshopper Hill).*

The *Codex Boturini* is one of the manuscripts in which the Mexica Aztecs depicted their journey from Aztlán, which took place in the Early Postclassic period. It was drawn in the Early Colonial period, but in native style and on a traditional screenfold strip of native fig-bark paper, and it was probably a copy of a pre-Columbian prototype. It was a continuing story of peregrination unfolding over nearly 200 years and 23 episodes of habitation, ranging from four to 28 years. Figure **15.18** shows one of these. At left, the first drawing shows the start of the long journey, beginning in year One Flint (square cartouche). "In the pictorial annals, Aztlán itself is always an island in the middle of a rectangular lake" (Boone 2000: 214), and we should note that this is not an encampment but a town, with pyramid and residences.

The first stop on the journey was a cave, where an oracle in a hummingbird mask gives much advice to the migrants, judging from the volume of speech scrolls. The hummingbird is significant: this is Huitzilopochtli, the special patron deity of the Mexica. Moving to the right, we see eight nearly identical motifs, combining house + name glyph + person talking. These are the ethnic groups that left Aztlán along with the Mexica. The use of the house is an interesting device, because it implies a larger meaning than just a physical residence. It suggests that the lineages might be conceptualized in similar terms to the noble "houses" of medieval Europe, which were generally based upon a family descent line, but which broadly incorporated relatives, fictive kin, and allies, and which had political and economic functions (Lévi-Strauss 1983). By the time this manuscript was drawn, the groups in question had been established as the rulers of various important Central Highlands cities for generations, and their dynasties and palace establishments both fulfilled the criteria of noble houses.

The Mexica, in turn, are represented by the four god-bearers still ahead. This being a Mexica story, they naturally give themselves pride of place at the head of the migrating group. Each of the god-bearers has a name glyph above the head. These ritual specialists – three men and a woman – carry on their backs the sacred bundle of Huitzilopochtli himself, and the accoutrements of his cult. The Mexica soon parted ways with the other ethnic groups, and the rest of the manuscript is a formulaic repetition of footprints leading to a place name and four seated figures in front of a set of year cartouches that tell us how long the Mexica stayed in each place. This chronometric exactitude is a nice touch, implying accuracy, but we must remember that much of each group's lore was carried in verbal accounts in which numeric values were often rounded off. When the various chronicles are compared with the archaeological record for establishment of the migrant populations, the dates "fall around AD 1200 for the Valley of Mexico groups and around 1220 for the groups in the surrounding valleys" (Smith 1996: 40). This would place the departures from homelands in the 11th century – the Mexica would have spent several decades in Tula when it was at its height, perhaps picking up jobs in construction and service industries as the civic-ceremonial center was being enlarged.

and in-laws. In the Postclassic Central Highlands, Cholula pottery signaled political coalition-building in a highly fragmented and fiercely competitive arena of city-state development (Pohl 1999). The various dynasties had a shared culture history, and also shared material culture attributes such as architecture and the types of goods in use. As competing factions, they built coalitions by expressing their legitimacy and strength through a common iconographic language (Brumfiel 1989).

The Mixtec City-states and Dynasties With the decline of Teotihuacan and Monte Albán, the settlement pattern in the Mixteca Alta shifted from hilltop sites to locations on the alluvial plain, where the city-states that dominated the Late Postclassic period in this region would develop. Conflict among several dynasties seems to have taken a severe turn with the "War of Heaven," a bloody dynastic struggle that began in AD 963 and lasted several decades, according to Mixtec accounts which combine myth and history, and legitimized dynastic rights to lands. Historical information in the codices stretches back to a little before this time.

Many Mesoamerican royal families claimed some sort of distant descent from godlike ancestors, but the Mixteca royals took this to an extreme. They were, in their language, iya – divine, and among themselves spoke a private Iya language (Monaghan 1995). Their ancestors emerged from sacred trees at Apoala, a town in the Mixteca Alta. Mixtec society was rigidly stratified, and each class was endogamous. A king might take commoner wives, but the mother of the heir had to be a member of a royal family. The preoccupation of royal dynasties with their own sacred legitimacy accounts for the space devoted in their codices to genealogy [**15.19**]. The marriages, investiture ceremonies, victories in the battlefield, etc. are reminiscent of the content of Maya writing on stelae.

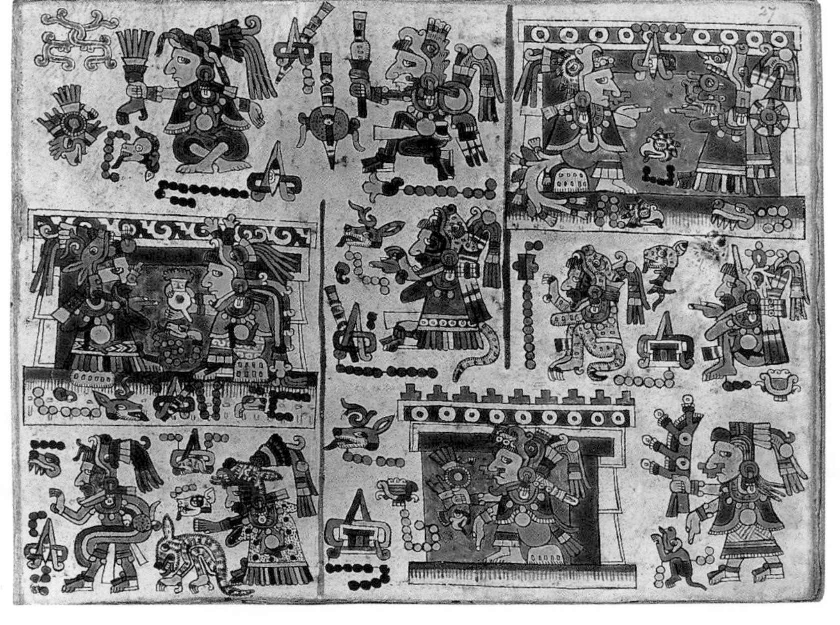

While Tilantongo was thought to have been the Mixteca Alta's most important capital during the reign of 8 Deer, the strength of the other city states is demonstrated by the emphasis on coalition building and ceremonies wherein fealty is promised by representatives of other dynasties. Another Mixtec capital, Coixtlahuaca, was located on the eastern border of the Mixteca Alta, near a major river leading to the northern Tehuacán Valley which itself opened onto the southern Puebla plain. Throughout the Postclassic Coixtlahuaca was a more cosmopolitan community than others in the Mixteca Alta, with various ties to distant regions. In the Early Postclassic, Coixtlahuaca was allied through marriage with Chichimec lineages in Cuauhtinchan, according to the *Historia Tolteca-Chichimeca*. In the Late Postclassic, it became a major trading town with a market "where much wealth flowed ... they traded in gold, feathers, cacao, finely worked gourds, clothing, cochineal..." (Durán 1994 [1581]: 182). But in 1458, after Aztec *pochteca* merchants were murdered there, Tenochtitlan sent an army of 200,000 to avenge this injustice. After that, Coixtlahuaca and the surrounding territory were absorbed into the Aztec empire and paid tribute to Tenochtitlan.

15.19 *Mixtec codices were read from right to left, in columns starting down a page to the bottom, then turning upward to the top, etc., a pattern called "boustrophedon" (meaning: as an ox turns while plowing a field). The story unfolding on page 26 of the* Codex Nuttall *(1975 [preconquest]) centers – literally – upon the Mixteca's most famous king, 8 Deer, who ruled Tilantongo. In the upper right, the scene is a palace, and the A-O year sign, a Mixtec convention (Smith 1973) is emblazoned with a flint knife, surmounted by six circles, telling us that the year is 6 Flint (*c. AD *1044). 8 Deer's father, 5 Alligator (wearing a goggle-eye Tlaloc mask) is marrying (Byland and Pohl 1994: 240). The story moves down the page, time passes, and the couple's three children are shown. At the turning point of the column is another palace with an A-O year sign at lower left – the year is 10 House (*c. *1061) and the woman is 5 Alligator's second wife. Above her are her three children, starting with 8 Deer who was born in 12 Reed (*c. *1063). Elsewhere in the codex 8 Deer is shown having his nose pierced in an investiture ceremony, possibly held at Cholula, and becoming ruler of Tilantongo in about 1097 or 1098. Returning to page 26, the palace scene at center left is set in 13 Reed (*c. AD *1103), and shows 8 Deer getting married; his bride offers him a foaming mug of chocolate. Below them are their two sons.*

Puebla, Tlaxcala, Tehuacán, and Oaxaca

This orientation toward Puebla reflected the growing importance of Postclassic Cholula. After experiencing something of a decline while the Olmeca-Xicalanca dominated its region at the end of the Classic period and beginning of the Postclassic, Cholula came back into its own in the 12th century. This resurgence was spearheaded by Tolteca-Chichimeca migrants who were adherents of the Quetzalcoatl cult, and who made Cholula into the Late Postclassic's greatest pilgrimage center for Quetzalcoatl veneration.

This shift in belief-system focus is reflected in the abandonment of the Great Pyramid and the construction of the Pyramid of Quetzalcoatl. Today, as we have noted, modern Cholula has blanketed the ancient city, leaving only the Great Pyramid as an island of pre-Columbian construction – surmounted by the Colonial-period church. Of the Pyramid of Quetzalcoatl, nothing remains except the fact that it was located on the east side of the town square.

Cholula may have been the largest city-state in the broad plains of Puebla, Tlaxcala and the northern section of the Tehuacán Valley, south of Puebla, but many other city-states were developing as a result of growing indigenous populations and the addition of migrants. In the Tlaxcala region the four best known were Tepeticpac, Ocotelulco, Tizatlan, and Quiahuiztlan. These are in the vicinity of the modern capital city, Tlaxcala, and their importance may have been exaggerated in the annals written in the Early Colonial period. Yet, in the Late Postclassic, the Tlaxcalan region was a critical gap in the extent of the Aztec empire: its position just east of the Basin of Mexico and its belligerence toward Aztec schemes of territorial expansion resulted in an important historical role once the Spaniards arrived and were lining up allies. Rulers of the Tlaxcalan capitals figured importantly in the Spanish conquest of Tenochtitlan.

Nahuatl expansion into the Tehuacán Valley transformed it from a backwater of small settlements to a region with three substantial towns – Tehuacán Viejo, Cozcatlan, and Teotitlan – that were part of the Tolteca-Chichimeca "alliance corridor" linking Tlaxcalan sites in the north with Huexotzingo and Cholula before extending southeast to reach the Tehuacán Valley and continuing over to Coixtlahuaca, at the edge of the Mixteca Alta

(Pohl and Byland 1994). From Coixtlahuaca, Mixtec-Zapotec alliances and trading partnerships extended west and south down into the Valley of Oaxaca [**15.20**].

Once-powerful Monte Albán was a small Postclassic community of no political significance. The Valley of Oaxaca was a patchwork of independent polities; some, like Zaachila, were Zapotec, while others, like Mitlá, were Mixtec. The largest Early Postclassic center was Jalieza, which had been one of the valley's two secondary centers during Monte Albán's apogee in the Early Classic period. Early Postclassic Jalieza sprawled over 8 sq. km (3.2 sq. miles) of hilltops and downslope terraces, having a population of about 16,000 (Finsten 1995).

In Conclusion

The Early Postclassic period was a time of continued movement of populations, localized population increases, and the growth of two great mercantile and military centers that did not last beyond AD 1200. The relations between Tula and Chichén Itzá seem obvious from similarities between the sites, but the nature of the interaction between them is as yet unknown. The Mesoamerican frontier advanced to the north, perhaps because of a climatic change that permitted the expansion of agriculture to regions previously too arid to sustain village farming. This new region was a staging ground for trade routes that extended farther north than at any other time in Mesoamerican culture history.

By the 1200s, the northern border had fallen back to its Early Classic-period limits, and contacts with the far north ended. The dislocations caused by cultural and environmental changes prompted migrations that added new demographic and cultural elements to the established ethnic groups and their settlement systems all over the Central Highlands and into the South-Central Highlands. These turbulent times brought forth hundreds of city-states all over Mesoamerica, and in the Late Postclassic, several of them gained sufficient strength to control most of the rest.

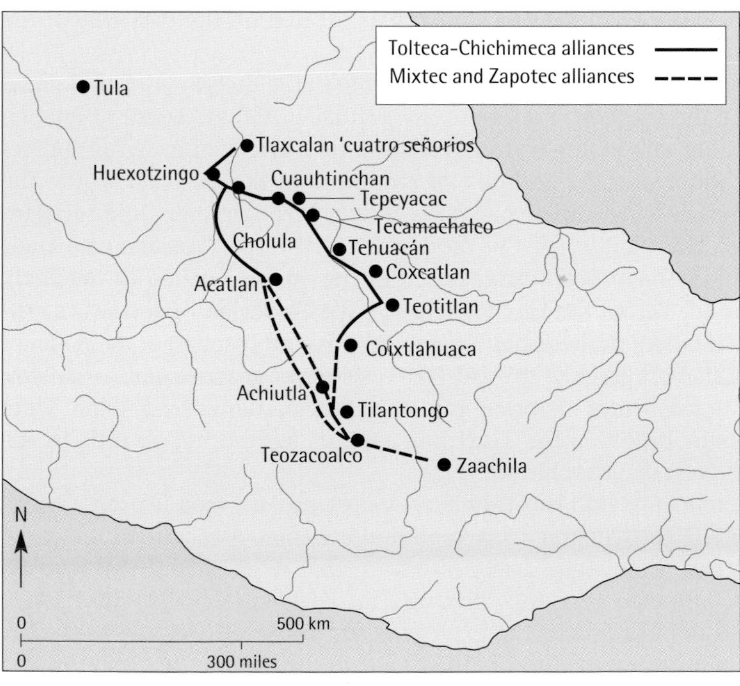

15.20 *Tolteca-Chichimeca of the Central Highlands were linked with Mixtecs and Zapotecs of the South-central Highlands along an "alliance corridor" that covered 300 km (186 miles) of territory. Marriage ties were the means by which these communities were joined as two sets of sites, and Coixtlahuaca was the pivot point for the two systems.*

PART 5

THE POSTCLASSIC AND THE RISE OF THE AZTECS

Middle Postclassic through Early Colonial Periods (AD 1200–1600)				
	Middle Postclassic		Late Postclassic	Early Colonial
	1200	1300	1400	1500 1600
Northern Arid Zone				
SE: Sierra Madre Oriental	San Antonio-Los Angeles			
SE: Tamaulipas			Los Angeles phase	
Northwestern Frontier	Chalchihuites tradition	Aztatlán complex		
Michoacán	Tzintzuntzan phase *Zacapu, Uayameo, Pátzcuaro*		*Tzintzuntzan*	*Tzintzuntzan*
Guerrero		*Tlaxhxo, Tlapan, Cihuatlán*		
Morelos		*Cuauhnáhuac, Huaxtépec, Yautépec*		*Cuernavaca*
Basin of Mexico		Aztec III (Chimalpa phase) *Texcoco, Tenayuca, Tacuba (Tlacopán), Tenochtitlan-Tlatelolco, Xaltocan, Culhuacan, Coyoacan, Cuitláhuac, Mixquic, Xochimilco, Chalco*		Aztec IV *Tenochtitlan-Mexico City*
Tula region	Fuego phase	Palcio phase		
Toluca		Matlatzinca *Toluca, Teotenango, Calixtlahuaca, Tenancingo*		
Puebla		Tlaxcala phase - *Cholula*		
Tlaxcala		Tlaxcala phase - *Cuatro señorios*		
Gulf Lowlands, north		Pánuco phase		
Gulf Lowlands, north-central		Teayo *Zempoala, Castillo de Teayo*		
Gulf Lowlands, south-central		Cempoala III phase *Tochtepec, Cotaxtla, Huatusco, Isla de Sacrificios*	Cempoala IV phase	
Tehuacán Valley		Venta Salada phase, Late		
Mixteca regions		Late Natividad phase		
Oaxaca and Tehuantepec	*Monte Albán, Zaachila, Mitla*			
Gulf Lowlands, south		*Xicalanco, Coatzacoalco*		
Chiapas Interior Plateau	Suchiapa phase	Tuxtla phase *Canajaste, Chiapa de Corzo*	Urbina phase	Villa Flores phase
Chiapas and Guatemala Coast		Proto-historic phase *Soconusco*		
Guatemala Highlands		Chinautla phase *Iximché, Zaculeu, Mixco Viejo, Utatlán*		
Maya Lowlands, north	Hocaba phase *Mayapán*	Tases phase	Chikinchel phase *Cozumel, Tulum*	Chauaca phase
Maya Lowlands, south	*Tayasal (Flores)*		*Nito*	
Southeastern Mesoamerica			*Naco*	
Intermediate Area				*Darien*

Selected phase names; *sites* and *events* are in *italic* type

16 THE MIDDLE POSTCLASSIC (1200s–1430)

AMONG THE THOUSANDS of peoples migrating south at the end of the Early Postclassic period was Huemac, one of the last kings of Tula. In the Basin of Mexico, he found refuge on Chapultepec Hill, overlooking the lake where Tenochtitlan – and Mexico City – would later rise [**16.1**]. There, legend says, his despair overtook him and he committed suicide in a cave in the hillside in 1168. A few years after this event, Chapultepec Hill also became a refuge for a small group of Aztecs, the Mexica [**15.18**]. They were driven off the hill by better-established groups, but by 1420 they had returned to the area, founded Tenochtitlan, and were making Chapultepec into a refuge of a much more sophisticated kind, a recreational resort for their kings, for relaxation after the responsibilities of ruling their growing capital. A century later, just before the Aztec empire was conquered by Spain, king Motecuzoma came despondently to Huemac's cave. Seeing omens of doom, he appeared at the cave entrance to gain access to paradise. Huemac's spirit, guardian of the cave, turned him back to meet his fate.

Motecuzoma's premonitions were correct and the Spaniards conquered the Aztecs. Then the Spaniards lost no time in squabbling amongst them-

16.1 *Mesoamerica showing sites and regions discussed in Chapter 16.*

selves about who would take over choice pieces of property owned by Aztec royal families, Chapultepec Park foremost among them. Fittingly, the hill and its surroundings became the property of the viceroys, the king of Spain's highest representatives in New Spain. Chapultepec continued to play a key role in the history of the nation of Mexico – the palace built there by the viceroys was taken over by Emperor Maximilian, then became a military school when he was deposed in 1867, and finally became a modern public park. Today, it is the most extensive green space within the largest city in the Americas.

The story of Chapultepec is based upon a mixture of sources: ancient legend, ethnohistorically documented experiences, archaeological remains, and modern facts. It is a microcosm of the transformation of Mesoamerica, and our knowledge about Mesoamerica, through the latter centuries of the Postclassic period and into the present. Thus it covers the same period of time as do the final five chapters of this book. During the period from AD 1200 to 1520, much of Mesoamerica was transformed into a set of polities whose actions came to be defined by their relations with the Mexica Aztecs of Tenochtitlan. The conquest of the Aztec empire by Spain in 1521 was followed by the steady and rapid expansion of Spanish political domination throughout Mesoamerica. Spanish cultural ascendancy was expressed through the substitution of Spaniards for the native ruling elite, along with an imposition of European styles of architecture and dress, the use of the Spanish language, and suppression of important features of native culture such as religion. Because so many indigenous cultural symbols had religious meaning, material objects like sculpture and painted books were destroyed in order to abolish devil-worship.

Many of the intellectual and artistic masterpieces of Mesoamerica were lost to deliberate destruction, sometimes for the reuse of valuable materials, for example, gold. Places that were already in ruins at the time of conquest were regarded as investment opportunities of the same calibre as, say, mines – speculators would purchase looting rights, and tunnel into pyramids looking for treasure in tombs and caches. Yet, even in the darkest days of cultural destruction, some individuals worked to save native manuscripts and objects of interest. And, in time, Western intellectual traditions embraced an interest in the development of non-Western cultures. Today, through the research efforts of modern archaeologists, ethnohistorians, and art historians, Mesoamerican culture history has been broadly reconstructed, and can be understood in its general processes and in the particulars of events and people.

Middle Postclassic and Late Postclassic

The Postclassic period was ushered in by the transitional Epiclassic period, focused on the precipitous decline of Classic elite Maya traditions – Teotihuacan's great power had been gone for centuries – and the rise of Chichén Itzá, Tula, and other militaristic states of the Early Postclassic period. Some

16.2 *This drawing dates from the 16th century and shows an event that took place about half a century earlier, when the Aztec emperor, Motecuzoma II, posed for his portrait. The image is being carved into the cliff face at Chapultepec, where the Aztec rulers of Tenochtitlan had their pleasure palace, and where they immortalized their images. Motecuzoma II was an Aztec emperor, a Mexica noble, and ruler of the Tenochca. These and other terms describe ethnic, linguistic, and political groups important in the Late Postclassic. They can be distinguished as shown in* **16.13**.

scholars find it useful to divide the last 300 years of Mesoamerican culture history, AD 1200–1521, into Middle Postclassic and Late Postclassic periods, because the rise of the Aztecs is an unprecedented historical phenomenon that dominates the entire culture area.

Thus a "Middle Postclassic" period would begin in about AD 1200 (decline of Chichén and Tula) and extend to the time when the Mexica Aztecs started to influence the dynamics of the larger culture [**16.2**]. While the Mexica had begun their own dynastic line by 1370, they didn't start taking over other states in any effective way until about 1430. It is remarkable that only 90 years later, they would control a tribute empire of 5 to 6 million people (Sanders 1992). Therefore, it makes sense to consider the Mesoamerican world as it was in the period from about 1200 to about 1430, and then follow the growth of Mesoamerica's most sophisticated and extensive political system, and its contemporaries.

Segmentary States of the Middle Postclassic Period

Moving back in time to about 1200, we see that the groups migrating from one part of Mesoamerica to another were, generally, not nomadic hunter-foragers – though later chroniclers sometimes emphasized these elements, taking pride in the vigor of their ancestors. Most migrants were, rather, displaced farmer-artisans, accustomed to life in or near communities that had ruling elites supported by the tributes of the commoners, where monumental structures such as temple-pyramids and ball courts were present, even if on a modest scale, and where there were markets for local distribution of goods. These features are common to complex societies such as advanced chiefdoms and states, and groups like the Mexica were used to life in such settings, and looked toward establishing themselves in a similar situation when they found a place to settle.

Aztec and Other Commonly Used Terms (16.3)	
Aztec	Refers to all ethnic groups who claimed ancestry from the inhabitants of Aztlán, the semi-mythical place of origin for Postclassic migrants from the northwest to the Central Highlands. This is a modern term, and some scholars believe that "Nahua" is more correct, and "Aztec" should not be used at all.
Nahua	Refers to a linguistic subdivision of the great Uto-Aztecan language family (the largest in Mesoamerica); it has two major dialects: Nahuat (spoken in the Gulf lowlands and on the southern Pacific Coast) and Nahuatl. Another dialect, Nahual, is spoken west of the Central Highlands.
Nahuatl	Refers to the dialect of Nahua that was spoken in the Central Highlands of Mexico in the Late Postclassic, and was the lingua franca of trade and politics all over Mesoamerica in that period. Nahuatl was the most important language in use in the Basin of Mexico in AD 1500, and is also known as "Aztec" and "Mexicano."
Mexica	Refers to the Aztec ethnic group that settled on the adjacent islands of Tenochtitlan and Tlatelolco. These were distinct communities, each with its own ruling lineage, but eventually Tenochtitlan overpowered Tlatelolco. The Mexica were so dominant in Mesoamerica in AD 1519 that their name was subsequently applied not only to their capital city, Tenochtitlan-Tlatelolco (Mexico City), but also, in the 19th century, to the whole nation: Mexico.
Tenochca	Refers to the Mexica group that established Tenochtitlan.
Acolhua	Refers to the Aztec ethnic group that occupied the eastern Basin of Mexico, and became the strongest allies of the Mexica. Their capital was at Texcoco.
Tepanec	Refers to the Aztec ethnic group that occupied the western Basin of Mexico, and were overlords of the Mexica before the Tepanec War of *c.* 1430 forced a reversal of political dominance, and they became the Mexica's second most powerful allies. Their capitals were at Tacuba/Tlacopan and Azcapotzalco.
Triple Alliance	Refers to the alliance between the Mexica, the Acolhua, and the Tepanecs.
Aztec Empire	Refers to the territory dominated by the Triple Alliance.

16.3 *The table above lists a set of terms that are used commonly – and sometimes confusingly – to describe the ethnic groups, political factions, and languages of the Postclassic period, particularly in the Central Highlands of Mexico.*

During the Middle Postclassic period, small independent polities were founded or, in some cases, reestablished all over Mesoamerica. These were often city-states, encompassing an urbanized community and its surrounding hinterland with farming villages. In any region, these small states would resemble each other, exploiting the same kinds of resources and having the same kinds of political and social organization. A ruling dynasty with pretensions to elevated status over local commoners was a common feature in these systems, and ruling families in a region tended to intermarry, so they formed an elite class that transcended the political boundaries of their realms.

What is "segmentary" about these small states? The concept refers to their role as segments in a larger regional system, independent pieces that can survive without the other city-states. Social scientists describe such systems as "mechanically-integrated" – a pyramidal pile of oranges, for example, is a mechanically-integrated entity in which each orange's role duplicates that of the others, and the whole pile is held together by proximity and gravitational force. The orange tree, on the other hand, is an "organically-integrated" system, because each part of the tree plays a necessary role in the functioning of the whole organism and the parts are vitally linked together.

Large political systems may be "mechanical" or "organic." An organic system would incorporate diverse regions that together create a vigorous and varied economy and society. A mechanical system would bring together a set of segments that are similar to each other, and impose a kind of ersatz organic integration by assigning the different segments different roles to enhance the desirability and necessity of maintaining the larger system. However, empires built of segmentary states have an inherent fragility, because the component parts do not need the empire to survive. In fact, having an overlord is costly – if independence is feasible, a city-state gains immediate savings in terms of labor and goods that do not have to be sent on to the higher capital.

The Middle Postclassic period shows us many regions where small city-states became established, and then maintained a rough equilibrium of power for decades, if not centuries. In some areas, such as the Basin of Mexico, several city-states became so powerful over the others that they forcibly extracted tribute from them. We have seen how Culhuacan and Xaltocan, as allies of Tula, established this pattern during the Early Postclassic. On this modest foundation were based later tribute empires, political structures wherein paramount states ruled over the other states and lived off them. The most prominent Mesoamerican example was the Aztec empire, headed by Tenochtitlan, but there were others, most notably the Tarascan empire, headed by Tzintzuntzan. Both the Aztec and Tarascan empires achieved a kind of immortality resulting from their rather sudden death by Spanish conquest. Descriptions of the Aztec empire often present a timeless view, as if this realm had enjoyed great extent and complexity for generations. In fact, both the Aztec and Tarascan political systems had grown from small towns to vast regions in fewer than 100 years; what existed at the time of European contact was but a cultural snapshot in a series of rapid changes. Other cities had dominated those regions before Tenochtitlan and Tzintzuntzan, and without Spanish interference, regional cultural evolution would have led to subsequent shifts in the political center.

EAST OF THE ISTHMUS AND THE GULF LOWLANDS

During the Middle Postclassic period, many regions saw the development of small states and in some cases several of these formed alliances with the intent of conquering others. The great Late Classic demographic collapse of the Maya of southern Yucatán permanently depopulated an extensive area, yet even as the tropical forest reclaimed the ruined courtyards and pyramids of Tikal and Caracol, communities in the vicinity of Lake Petén-Itzá formed a focus of settlement for Itzá Maya – their capital at Tayasal, on the lake's island of Flores, was not conquered by the Spanish until 1697 (Jones 1998).

The Maya flourished along Yucatán's long coast, in the northern plains, and in the Guatemala highlands and adjacent Chiapas interior plateau. In these areas, the process of segmentary state formation and growth created a lively landscape of competing polities.

Northern Maya Lowlands: Mayapan's Rise and Fall

Chichén Itzá's florescence was confined to the Early Postclassic – there are even some indications that the site was abandoned during the 13th century. After Chichén declined, the northern Maya lowlands no longer had a major capital, but instead there arose a set of regional states, which will be discussed in greater detail in Chapter 19. Scholars have sometimes called this post-Chichén Postclassic era in the northern lowlands the "Decadent" period, because the transformation from domination by a single massive center to dispersed political power seemed to represent a kind of deterioration of political complexity. By AD 1300, Chichén had regained some population, and, like Teotihuacan, it functioned as a pilgrimage center, its local population serving the needs of those making the trek to a holy site. Thus it would remain throughout the Late Postclassic and into the Colonial period. Political power had moved to nearby Mayapan, but while Mayapan was modeled on Chichén, it was much smaller and shoddier.

Mayapan Traces of occupation dating from as early as the Late Formative period and continuing on underlie Mayapan's Middle Postclassic architecture. Mayapan became powerful in the 13th century, after Chichén Itzá's decline and with the apparent ambition of inheriting Chichén's role as northern Yucatán's strongest city-state. In sharp contrast with Chichén's lavish use of broad plazas, Mayapan's plan [**16.4**] reveals extremely crowded conditions, probably a response to the warfare ongoing among the powerful lineages of northern Yucatán.

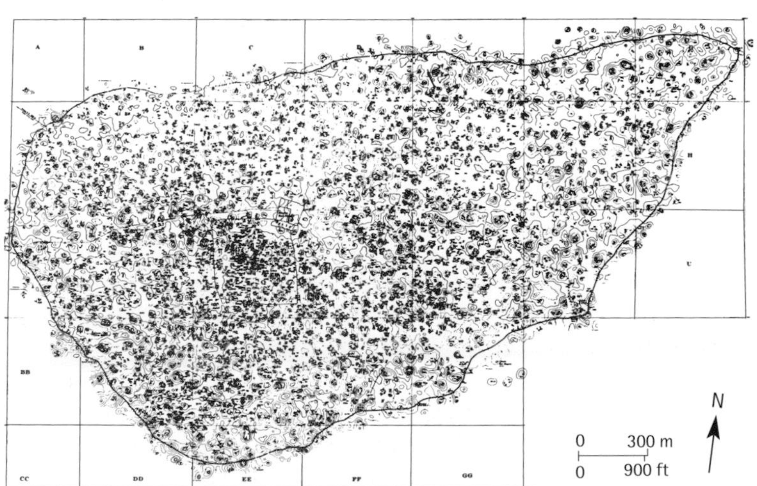

16.4, 16.5 *Mayapan's monumental architecture imitated the Mexicanized part of Chichén, in a crude, miniaturized fashion. "El Castillo" (opposite above) is a much smaller replica of Chichén's great Pyramid of the Feathered Serpent. Mayapan's monumental architecture included elite administrative-residential palaces, but the site did not also have the range of public buildings of its predecessor, lacking ball courts and sweat baths. Within Mayapan's city wall was an area of 4.2 sq. km (1.7 sq. miles) with 4,000 structures (below), nearly 90 percent of them residences (Andrews 1993) – an estimated population of 12,000 living in dense conditions unprecedented among the Maya.*

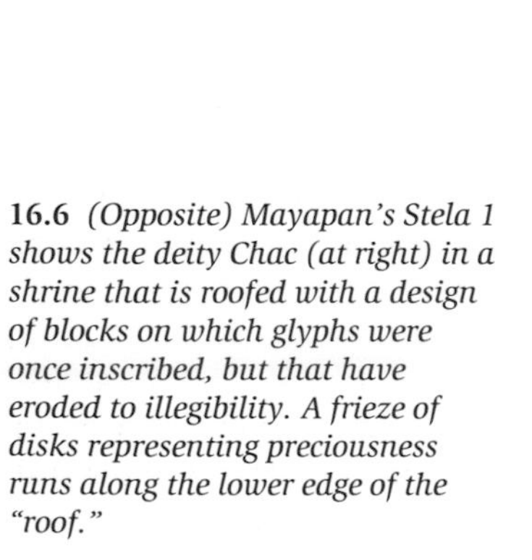

16.6 *(Opposite) Mayapan's Stela 1 shows the deity Chac (at right) in a shrine that is roofed with a design of blocks on which glyphs were once inscribed, but that have eroded to illegibility. A frieze of disks representing preciousness runs along the lower edge of the "roof."*

Mayapan was ruled by a branch of the Itzás, the Cocom family. Evidence from ethnohistoric documents has been interpreted by some scholars to indicate that the Cocoms had a Mul Tepal-style joint rule (discussed in Chapter 14) with the ruling families of the other states, but as practiced at Mayapan, this seems to have amounted to elite hostage-taking. The practice of one dynasty holding captive important members of another dynasty is known from many states, worldwide. Often it involves a seemingly gracious hospitality, such as an extended stay by the heir-apparent of a subordinate dynasty, in order to educate him with the young men of the more powerful ruling family. In fact, this neutralizes the subordinate family's ability to assert itself against their overlords, lest they endanger their own prince.

That the Cocoms were deadly serious about controlling their dynastic rivals is evidenced by the Mexicanized mercenaries from Tabasco that they hired to enforce their tribute-collection policies. Decapitated warriors are depicted in stucco bas-reliefs adorning the façade of the Castillo (Peraza Lope 1999). Cocom intimidation and oppression came to an end in *c.* 1441, when the Cocom rulers were assassinated, apparently in an uprising led by members of the Xiu lineage. Mayapan was destroyed. The Xiu founded Maní, not far from ancient Uxmal, and it became the capital of the largest of northern Yucatán's Late Postclassic kingdoms.

Southeastern Frontier The far eastern boundary of Mesoamerica experienced the same general kinds of changes as were taking place its Northwestern Frontier: isolation from Mesoamerican cultural influence and maintenance of regional polities at a chiefdom level of complexity.

Guatemala Highlands

We noted in Chapter 14 that the collapse of Maya civilization in the southern Yucatán lowlands sent refugees into adjacent regions, including the highlands of Guatemala. Archaeological evidence indicates that this period at the end of the Classic and the start of the Postclassic was not a peaceful one in the highlands. The settlement pattern changed, with valley locations abandoned and hilltop sites becoming established. The hostility that this implies may have had several causes, such as population growth due to intrinsic increase among already-established highlanders, and also the arrival of refugee groups. Another indicator of isolation related to hostility is the divergence of Maya languages, at about AD 1000, into such dialects as Quiché, Cakchiquel, and Tzutujil. Language is, of course, a major component of ethnic identification, and the emergence of regional variants indicates the extent of separation of these populations from each other. These ethnic groups would be among the powerful political forces of this region in the Late Postclassic, to be discussed in greater detail in Chapter 19.

Even more pressure may have been caused by the arrival, in about 1250, of militaristic Putún Itzá Maya (Carmack 1981), with their Mexican-influenced styles in aggression and architecture (boxy stepped pyramids, I-shaped ball courts). In a sense, these would have been refugees from the second "Maya collapse" – after the fall of Chichén, the Putún Itzá pushed south, establishing in the highlands several sites (including Chalchitán and Chuitinamit-Atitlán) that had architectural resemblances to Chichén. Important indigenous documents, such as the Quiché sacred book, *Popol Vuh*, describe the aggression of the invaders, who tried to legitimize their position by tracing Tollan ancestry. As we know "Tollan" was a name applied to several important sites, and in this case it probably refers to Chichén. Scholars do not agree about this literal interpretation of ethnohistoric sources, and some see, in continuities of ceramic types, evidence that the ethnic divisions in the Postclassic period arose from earlier populations in the highlands. The Quiché were one of several Maya groups that claimed territory in the highlands in the Postclassic, in a pattern of segmentary states established on fortifiable hilltops in the 13th century and even earlier.

Southern Pacific Coastal Plain and Isthmus of Tehuantepec

The coastal plain of Guatemala and Chiapas is not well documented for this period, but extrapolating back from the fierce competition for it between the Quiché and the Aztecs in the 15th century, we can assume that cacao production had continued, and that the region saw the development of small polities consisting of a town surrounded by smaller farming villages – these would become the city-states of the Late Postclassic.

Along the Pacific Coast of Tehuantepec, the Middle Postclassic saw the highest population densities that this region achieved, with Saltillo being the largest site, and then the abandonment of the site sometime after

AD 1300. Local populations seem to have reestablished themselves in much smaller settlements as Zapotecs from the Valley of Oaxaca moved in to take over the adjacent Tehuantepec region.

Gulf Lowlands and Southern Central Highlands

Moving north to the southern Gulf lowlands, we find another situation in which the Middle Postclassic is poorly understood from the archaeological record. Again, we can extrapolate from the Late Postclassic ethnohistoric record and assume that during the Middle Postclassic, people living in small polities were farming, fishing, and growing cacao where feasible.

During the early Middle Postclassic, the south-central Gulf lowlands saw radical changes in material culture remains – artifact repertoire and settlement plans – and these indicated influence from the Central Highlands, possibly from the direction of Cholula. Because the archaeological record for this region during the Early Postclassic is not well documented, the reasons for these changes are poorly understood, and may represent local adoption of foreign styles, voluntarily or under the influence of militaristic incursions or, possibly, some sort of collapse of Classic-period culture and population and their replacement by newcomers (Stark 2001).

Other displacements were affecting the north-central Gulf lowlands. It was during the Middle Postclassic that the Totonacs came to dominate the northern part of this region, and the Aztecs named it "Totonacapan" by which they meant "land of food" because of its unfailing abundance. Like the Huastecs, who occupied the northern Gulf lowlands, their language was related to Mayan. The Huastecs themselves may have been pushed south by Early Postclassic droughts, possibly caused by an El Niño event (Wilkerson 2001: 328).

West of the Gulf Lowlands Both the Huasteca and Totonacapan extended west into the Sierra Madre Oriental, the eastern boundary of the Central Highlands. On the western side of the mountains, Puebla and Tlaxcala were undergoing changes, in this "time of important population movements of Mixtec, Otomí, and Huastec along the fringes of the region and abandonment or conquest of Olmeca-Xicalanca centers" in the core of the region (Plunket and Uruñuela 2001: 615). The Tolteca-Chichimeca had established themselves in Cholula, where skeletal evidence indicates a change in the genetics of the population, supporting ethnohistorical documents describing the arrival of the migrants.

To the west, in Morelos, the same migrants from the north were contributing to a resurgence of population, and the establishment of settlements that would become the important centers of the Late Postclassic. Further south, in the Mixteca region, the city-states that were becoming influential in the Early Postclassic continued their growth, and Mixtecs and Zapotecs occupied the Valley of Oaxaca.

WEST MEXICO: THE RISE OF THE TARASCANS OF MICHOACÁN

Far West Mexico was no longer in direct contact with Mesoamerica. The Aztatlán trade routes that had served the Toltecs no longer functioned to move luxury materials toward southwestern North America, where the Great House puebloan systems had fallen into a decline. By the time of European contact, the settlement systems along the Pacific Coast of West Mexico were isolated from the larger events taking place to the east.

West Mexico's interior valleys and basins became the heartland of a new empire developing around Lake Pátzcuaro, as Michoacán emerged as a relatively unified political entity that would mature contemporaneously with, and in opposition to increasing Central Mexican power. By the time of Spanish conquest, the Tarascan empire would control 75,000 sq. km (30,000 sq. miles) and the border between them and the Aztecs would be repeatedly subject to battles between the two. Nonetheless, the Tarascan empire remained stalwartly independent of Aztec incursions, in part because of the distance between them, but Tarascan use of metal in their weaponry must also be considered a factor.

As in Central Mexico, the Colonial-era chroniclers of ancient Michoacán spoke of migrations of Chichimecs, Nahua-speakers, and also the *uacúsecha* (eagles), who were "the ancestors of the Tarascan royal dynasty" (Pollard 1993: 13). The principal deity of the future Tarascan empire-builders was Curicaueri, who represented the sun as well as earthly fire, and as a hunter and a warrior became the patron deity of the Tarascans, and especially of their king [**16.7**]. One sign of the Tarascan region's intellectual independence from Central Mexico is the lack of many basic facets of the Central Mexican belief system. There is no evidence of Central Mexican principles such as duality, or the presence of male and female counterparts of important deities, though there are numerous important goddesses, such as the ethnic *purépecha* goddess Xarátanga, who was worshipped along with Curicaueri at Tzintzuntzan and Ihuatzio. There was no counterpart to Tlaloc (rainfall was in the domain of the Tarascan earth goddess Cuerauáperi) or Quetzalcoatl.

Furthermore, while the Tarascans knew about Central Mexican writing systems, there are no known pre-Columbian Tarascan written records. They did share with other Mesoamericans a calendar of 18 months of 20 days each, and a period of five extra days, to make up a solar vague year, but the most important early 16th-century source on Tarascan culture, the *Relación de Michoacán* (1980 [1541]), reported that the use of named days as a means of divination was not a common Tarascan practice. The Tarascan calendar most closely resembles that of the Matlatzinca, their neighbors to the southeast, in Toluca (Pollard 1993).

Nonetheless, the Tarascans shared many features of Mesoamerican belief systems, including the value of autosacrifice and human sacrifice, veneration of mountains, springs, and caves and also of serpents and butterflies. The ball game was played throughout the Tarascan region, but no ball court has been found at Tzintzuntzan. Tobacco use was an important component

16.7 *The funeral of a Tarascan king (*cazonci*) was celebrated with elaborate rituals, as shown in this illustration from the* Relación de Michoacán *(1980 [1541]). The king's body, topped by royal regalia, is borne by pallbearers, at lower left, while musicians accompany the procession. At lower right, attendants to accompany the dead king to the afterlife are sacrificed.*

of Tarascan rituals, and pipe fragments are found in high frequencies at ceremonial sites.

The Chichimec-Nahua migrations seem to have had much less cultural and demographic impact in Michoacán than they did in Central Mexico, but the migrations during the early part of the Postclassic period resulted in the founding of ruling dynasties of the Late Postclassic. The Tarascan language, sometimes called *purépecha*, is commonly regarded as something of an isolate – some scholars have linked it to Zuni (U.S. Southwest) and Quechua (the language of the Incas) while others have proposed ancient derivation from the Chibchan languages of southern Central America and northern South America.

Archaeological evidence indicates that during the early to middle Postclassic, defensible locations were chosen for settlement. Local elites seem to have competed for territory, and some of the early and important sites were in the Zacapu Basin, just north of Lake Pátzcuaro. Zacapu is the name by which the site of El Palacio-La Crucita is usually known, because it is adjacent to the modern town of that name. It became the Early Postclassic-period capital of the Tarascan empire's earliest rulers, and eventually had a population of 20,000 in an area of 11 sq. km (4.4 sq. miles) (Michelet *et al.* 1989).

By the time of the second Tarascan ruler the capital was established at Uayameo, between Zacapu and Lake Pátzcuaro. This represented a shift in the focus of Tarascan interest to the area around Lake Pátzcuaro. The area around the lake was a very rich environment, with the fertile agricultural land of the alluvial plains, and the fish and game of the lake itself.

The founder of the Late Postclassic dynastic line was Taríacuri, who ruled in the early part of the 14th century. He is regarded as the first unifier of the core region of what would become the Tarascan empire, and his capital was at Pátzcuaro, on the plain south of the lake. Pátzcuaro would remain an

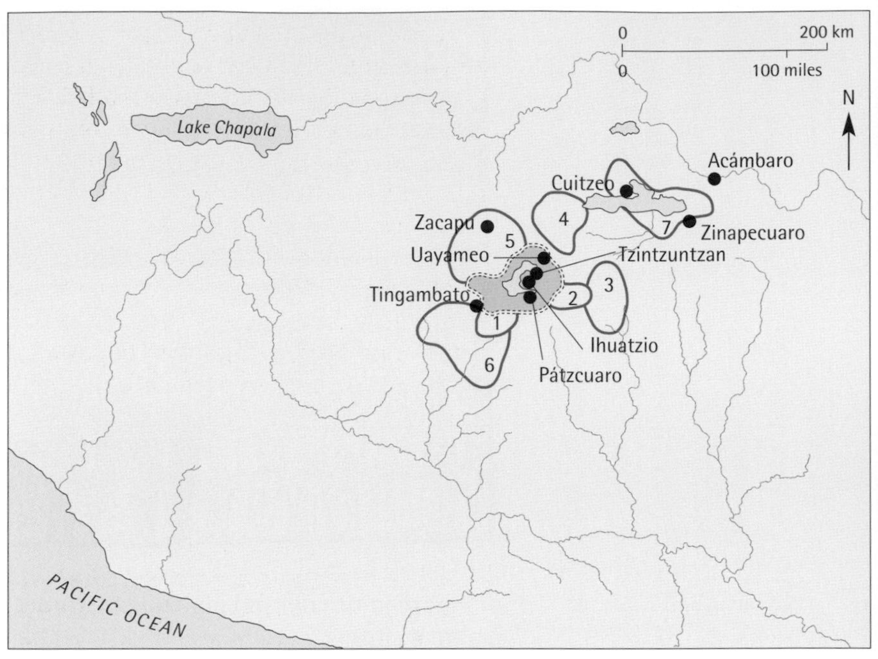

16.8, 16.9 The central part of what would become the Late Postclassic Tarascan empire began to be consolidated in the 14th and early 15th centuries by Taríacuri and his dynasty. This map shows the order in which areas around the lake were subdued, starting with the region southwest of Pátzcuaro and then continuing counterclockwise around the lake basin. Finally, the region around Lake Cuitzeo was attacked. Ihuatzio was one of the capitals of the Tarascan empire. These pyramids at the site were dedicated to Curicaueri and Xarátanga, two of the principal Tarascan deities.

important regional center as the capital shifted north. Upon Taríacuri's death, his lineage controlled the region from three capitals, with Pátzcuaro being ruled by his son, while two of his nephews ruled Ihuatzio and Tzintzuntzan.

Taríacuri and his allies staged a series of conquests that are probably more accurately regarded as looting raids, because true consolidation of the region would not be effected until about 1440. However, there was a method to the staging of the sorties [**16.8**], and by 1440, the military influence of Taríacuri's dynasty extended all around Lake Pátzcuaro and to the northeast, the Cuitzeo region.

The attack on the Cuitzeo region was staged from Ihuatzio [16.9]. This complex center had been occupied during the Early Postclassic, probably by Nahuatl-speaking peoples who had ties with Tula. Ihuatzio's walled core precinct measures about 1,000 m (*c.* 0.6 miles) N–S and 470 m (1,542 ft) E–W, and its interior space is divided further by walls. Among the varied architectural forms found at Ihuatzio are a circular building that possibly functioned as an observatory, and three monumental yácatas. The yácata was a composite architectural form, a huge rectangular platform with a half-round apron projection on the front. This distinctive Tarascan architectural signature is best-known from Tzintzuntzan, which, by the mid-15th century had become the most important Tarascan city. Also, by the mid 1400s, the Tarascans had become the most formidable enemy of the growing Aztec state.

THE BASIN OF MEXICO

At the beginning of this chapter, we found Huemac the Toltec, taking his life at Chapultepec. Huemac, and the Aztecs who also sought refuge at Chapultepec, were speakers of Nahuatl. The migrations that occurred throughout the Postclassic have been understood, to some extent, by changing language patterns. As noted above, language is one of the most important features of shared ethnicity, and the dominance of the Nahuatl-speaking Aztecs during the Late Postclassic can be traced by the increasing area over which there is evidence of the larger Nahua language group. This is part of the Uto-Aztecan language family, the most widely spoken set of indigenous languages in the Americas. Uto-Aztecan languages were – and still are – spoken by native Americans throughout western North America; they are the languages of the Paiute and Shoshone, as well as the Hopi and Pima. Further south, in northwestern Mexico, the Tarahumara, Yaqui, and Huichol speak Uto-Aztecan languages.

Languages of the Nahua group were found throughout the Central Highlands at the time of European contact, and their use extended throughout West Mexico and in more scattered concentrations along the Gulf lowlands and down into Central America. Nahuatl, a dialect within the Nahua group, was the dominant language of the Basin of Mexico in 1519, and was also a *lingua franca* throughout Mesoamerica. All over modern Mexico and Central America are towns with Nahuatl names, often prefixed with a saint's name, and this widespread nomenclature is less a sign of Aztec domination than it is a reflection that Aztec guides often accompanied the Spaniards on their conquests, and translated local names into Nahuatl.

Linguistic historians have long believed that the distribution of the Nahua group of languages in the Central Highlands is related to migration events that took place during the Postclassic period. As we know, the language spoken at Teotihuacan has not been determined. Some scholars believe that the similarities between glyphs found at Teotihuacan and those used in Late

Postclassic Aztec writing indicate continuity in the spoken language, as well. However, analysis of lexical diversity within the language group indicates that Coyotlatelco culture was associated with the spread of Nahua-type languages into the Basin of Mexico and adjacent areas (Kaufman 1976; Luckenbach and Levy 1980), and many scholars believe that the Toltecs were the first great Nahuatl-speaking political power in this region.

Not all the Early Postclassic migrants to the Central Highlands were Nahuatl speakers, and the establishment of different ethnic groups created a mosaic of territorial polities centered upon small towns ruled by lords. We have seen how Tula may have had two allies in the Basin of Mexico, Culhuacan and Xaltocan, the latter a center for speakers of Otomí, a language in the Otomanguean language family. Other ethnic groups that moved through the Basin and contributed to its existing population from the Late Classic and into the Early Postclassic were the Olmeca and Xicalanca from the south, and the Tolteca and Chichimeca from the north.

Aztec Demographics The population of the Basin of Mexico increased dramatically during the Postclassic period due to the combined effects of migration and intrinsic increase. During the Early Postclassic, the population may even have declined somewhat. By about AD 1200, there were fewer than 200,000 people in the Basin; in 1519 there were about 1.6 million (Sanders 1992). Thus the population doubled every 100 years between 1200 and 1500, and a significant proportion of this would have been due to migration. The doubling rate represents an average annual increase of only 0.7 percent, which seems very low by modern standards – our present global population doubling rate is twice that, about 1.4 percent, doubling about every 50 years – but recall that generally, before modern medicine, up to half of all children born did not survive to age five. Even in Mesoamerica, which was relatively free of infectious disease, young children were vulnerable to potentially fatal maladies such as intestinal diseases. And an adult life of hard work, sometimes inadequate diet, and exposure to hazards like warfare meant that the elderly did not form a substantial component of the ancient Mesoamerican population.

Besides, even though this rate of increase sounds low, it is not, ultimately, sustainable. Not too many centuries pass before the limits of the environment's capacity to support the population are exceeded. This happened during the Late Classic in the Maya lowlands, with roughly the same doubling rate, and the ultimate effect was cultural and demographic collapse. As we shall see, by the mid-1450s, famines gripped the Basin's population during a time of subnormal agricultural productivity.

This dramatic increase resulted from intrinsic growth as well as migrations, which pulsed at around AD 1200, judging from a combination of linguistic, ethnohistoric, and archaeological evidence (Smith 1984). Many of the migrants of this pivotal era were from arid lands, and had learned to farm on lands where water was so scarce that daily liquid intake requirements were met with maguey sap. Maguey farming was well-suited to the

16.10 *The Basin of Mexico in about 1200 showed the establishment of the towns that would become important city-state capitals, and the rural farming villages that would spread over the piedmont slopes. Here, the first leaf from the* Codex Xolotl *(1980 [1553–1569]) depicts the travels of the famous migration leader Xolotl, as he established members of his family as rulers in many towns of the Basin of Mexico. In this map, the east is at the top, and the dark squiggle represents the line of mountains that separates the Basin from Tlaxcala and Puebla. Xolotl, draped in animal skins and carrying a bow and arrow, stands on a hill in the lower left section of the map and faces right (south) toward the teardrop-shaped island of Xaltocan, in the northern reaches of the Basin's central lake system. In the upper left are two pyramids that represent Teotihuacan, while Tula is another pyramid behind and below Xolotl.*

unoccupied piedmont slopes above the Basin's northern and eastern alluvial plain, because maguey plants helped maintain terraces where maize and beans and squash could be grown. A maguey farming family, living in a house built among its terraces, got adequate food, drink, and raw materials for weaving and other crafts from its acre or so of land (Evans 1990).

The piedmont sloping down to the fertile alluvial plain had been nearly vacant until the great migrations of around 1200. We reconstruct a circumstance in which groups of farming families arrived in the regions of the Central Highlands and came to the small towns, asking permission of the local lords to settle on the unused land. This was a win-win situation. For the migrants it meant an end to their long journey and a beginning to productive lives as part of a settled landscape. For the lords and their towns, the influx of newcomers swelled the tax base and represented an increase in producers of staple crops and crafts and consumers of all manner of locally made craft items. Small nodes of Toltec-era population became the focal points of extended swathes of terraced farmplots that covered the piedmont by 1519.

Looking in on the Basin at 1200, at the height of the migrations, we would see a skeleton of what would become the Late Postclassic settlement pattern [**16.10, 17.15**]. Among the oldest polities was Otomí-speaking Xaltocan, occupying an island and its marshy hinterland in the northern part of the lake system (Brumfiel *et al.* 1994). Other well-established towns bordered the southern lake system: Culhuacan, Cuitlahuac, Mixquic, Xochimilco, and Chalco. Followers of the great migration leader Xolotl, whose story is told in the set of maps known as the *Codex Xolotl*, settled themselves on the western side of the Basin (the bottom edge of the map shown in **16.10**),

BEING BORN AZTEC

ANCIENT MESOAMERICANS saw time as a set of recurring cycles that can be diagrammed as interlocking cogs, each larger than the next. One of these chronometric cogwheels is the 260-day count of the divinatory almanac (the *tzolkin* or *tonalpahualli*) which may take its length from the human gestation period. Presumably, the birthdate was seen as an echo of the date of conception – perhaps couples preferentially cohabited on auspicious dates of the divinatory almanac. Thus conception, and its calendric echo, birth itself, marked a person's first impression upon time, and the birthdate, from which the individual often took a name, marked that person's life as lucky or unlucky.

In childbirth, the mother was attended by female relatives and by a midwife – or several, if she was wealthy. During pregnancy and then during labor, the mother spent time in the *temascal* sweat bath and was massaged by the midwife to bring the fetus into the proper position (Sahagún 1969: 155, 167).

Labor contractions could be induced by effective medicines made from plant and animal decoctions, but abnormal difficulties in labor were taken as a sign of the mother's infidelities. Should the mother die giving birth, however, her status was elevated to that of a warrior who died in battle, and she became one of the *cihuateteo*, souls who accompanied the sun through each afternoon to sundown [**16.13**].

The healthy new mother was praised as a victorious warrior who had taken a captive – the new baby. The baby's umbilical cord was cut and saved – those of boys would be placed on battlefields by soldiers going into combat, to signify the fate of boys as warriors. Those of

16.11 *Chalchihuitlicue was the water goddess, and the border design on her* quechquémitl *blouse is one of repeated precious disks, the* chalchihuitls *in her name. The pattern of her skirt, however, honors Coatlicue, the snake-skirted earth goddess.*

16.12 *Pity the child born on day 8 Death or 9 Deer; everyone it met would know that 8 Deaths were "evil-tempered...completely perverted and mad...surrounded by vice, sin...dissolute... presumptuous, immodest, brazen..." (Sahagún 1979: 50) – and that's just the start of a long list of unpleasant traits. But there was hope: "the readers of the day signs bettered...the nature of the day sign... They arranged that later, upon Ten Rabbit, he would be bathed and given a name" (Sahagún 1979: 50). But when meeting "10 Rabbit" people might be suspicious, thinking "probably really an 8 Death, trying to pass as 10 Rabbit." The ill-fated signs are depicted as mother and midwife attend to the ill-fated baby.*

girls were buried near the hearth, because a woman's place "was only within the house; it was not necessary for her to go anywhere .... She was to prepare drink ... food, to grind, to spin, to weave" (Sahagún 1969: 173).

Bathing the newborn, the midwife prayed to Chalchihuitlicue [**16.11**], the water goddess who was embodied in lakes and ponds, as well as in the water in the basin in which the baby was ceremonially cleansed. The baby would be bathed again within a few days, in an elaborate ceremony that established its social identity and involved assigning it a name based on the name of the day upon which it was born in the 260-day divinatory almanac, and also a personal name, perhaps that of a grandparent.

But the day name was more than just a standardized way of labeling people, it was destiny. The new baby was brought into life with an identity already formed, not just by the factors that affect any newborn – gender, health, family, and culture – but also by all the character traits embedded in the birth date [**16.12**]. In fact, while each day destined the individual toward certain traits, like thrift or drunkenness, the days had many influences and so destiny was complicated. The name day had several kinds of patron deities, as did its *trecena*, the 13-day period in which it fell (Read 1998: 115). Furthermore, if the birth date was altogether negative, the soothsayer who read the baby's fate could choose a more auspicious date for the official baptismal party, and all these factors would moderate the day sign.

16.13 *This sculpture of a* cihuateotl *depicts a goddess who arose from the body of a woman who died in childbirth. She is adorned with skulls and severed hands, symbols of sacrifice.*

where they founded a capital at Tenayuca and became known as the Tepaneca. Tepanec aggressiveness eventually led to the extinction of the Otomí as a political entity.

Xolotl's followers also settled themselves among old populations on the eastern side of the Basin, founding Texcoco. In time, the Aztecs of the eastern Basin would become known as the Acolhuaque, and they would share power with the Mexica of Tenochtitlan in the last century before European intrusion. This ethnically diverse realm became even more so as other ethnic groups arrived and were settled in *barrios* of Texcoco and elsewhere. Xolotl's great-grandson, Quinatzin, who ruled in the mid 1300s, invited Mixtecans called Tlailotlaque to live in Texcoco. These were literate scribes and artists, and their presence in Texcoco began a long tradition of intellectual sophistication for that city.

By the time these groups settled down, intermarried with existing populations, sometimes becoming subjects and sometimes (sooner or later)

16.15 *(Opposite) The segmentary nature of the Basin of Mexico's political system can be diagrammed as a dendrogram, with each level encompassing the segments below it. At the bottom were the individual households of the farmer artisans, here represented by the Aztec glyph for house. The next level, the local village, is represented by the glyph for* tecpan-calli, *the lord's house. These local lords were low-ranking kin of the city-state rulers, the* tlatoque *(sing.* tlatoani*). At the highest level was the paramount ruler, the* huetlatoani *whose city-state was a capital for the others, thus encompassing a confederation. In the diagram, the* huetlatoani*'s* tecpan *glyph is surmounted by the Aztec glyph for ruler, the* copil *headdress. With Nezahualcoyotl's reorganization in the early 1430s, the* calpixque *steward replaced a* tlatoani *in some cases (see p. 462).*

becoming overlords, all the cultivable regions of the Basin were claimed. So when the last of the migrating groups, the Mexica Aztecs, arrived, they tried to establish themselves upon Chapultepec. But the Mexica, inspired by their tribal god Huitzilopochtli, had become devoted to sacrificial practices that were regarded as threatening by their more settled neighbors. When an estranged Mexica named Copil betrayed their location, the Mexica killed him, throwing his heart in the marshy shallows of western Lake Texcoco. Later, they found on that spot a cactus growing out of a rock, surmounted by an eagle with a snake in its beak – Copil's heart had sprouted what would become the central motif on the modern national flag of Mexico – and this location became the heart of Tenochtitlan [**16.14**].

The city was formally founded as a Mexica settlement in 1325, but occupation on the marshy islands goes back to the 1100s, when it was a small fishing village contemporaneous with the arrival of the Mexica in the Basin. Getting back to the earlier saga of the plucky but unpopular Mexica, we find that, having been driven from Chapultepec, they indentured themselves to Culhuacan, and lived on the barren lava field that had covered Cuicuilco at the end of the Late Formative period. But their sacrifice of the Culhua ruler's daughter was taken amiss by their patrons, and they were evicted, once again on the move and looking for land. The Tepaneca decided to use them as mercenaries and let them settle on the islands in the shallow marshes of western Lake Texcoco, where Copil's heart had taken root. By the 1350s, part of the Mexica group moved to an adjacent island just north of Tenochtitlan, and founded Tlatelolco (Bray 1977).

As Tepanec tributaries and mercenaries, the Mexica were subservient to an aggressive confederation which was building a system of tribute-paying city states that came to encompass much of the central and northern Basin of Mexico by the 1430s. The Tepanec ruler, from about 1380 to the late 1420s, was Tezozomoc of Azcapotzalco, whose "rare and ruthless genius served to form the empire which his Mexica vassals later managed to seize from his successor and then expand" (Davies 1977: 44).

16.14 *This mid-16th-century drawing depicts the cactus that grew out of the heart of Copil, and would become the heart of Tenochtitlan. The cactus-eagle-snake motif adorns the national flag of modern Mexico.*

City-states and Confederations of the Basin of Mexico

The Basin of Mexico's Middle Postclassic population grew around small cities that were supported by farming villages in the adjacent hinterlands. Each of these cities was ruled by a noble family, and each formed a potentially independent segment of the political and ethnic mosaic of the Basin [16.15]. In fact, these city-states were linked by marriage ties among the rulers, by shared ethnicity, and by mutual participation in a marketplace system. They also varied in terms of strength: agricultural and labor potential of the landscape and its farmers, and size of the armies that could be mustered from the local population. The Nahuatl term for the city-state was *altepetl*, literally "water-hill" because the ideal geographical setting would include these two elements (Karttunen 1983:9).

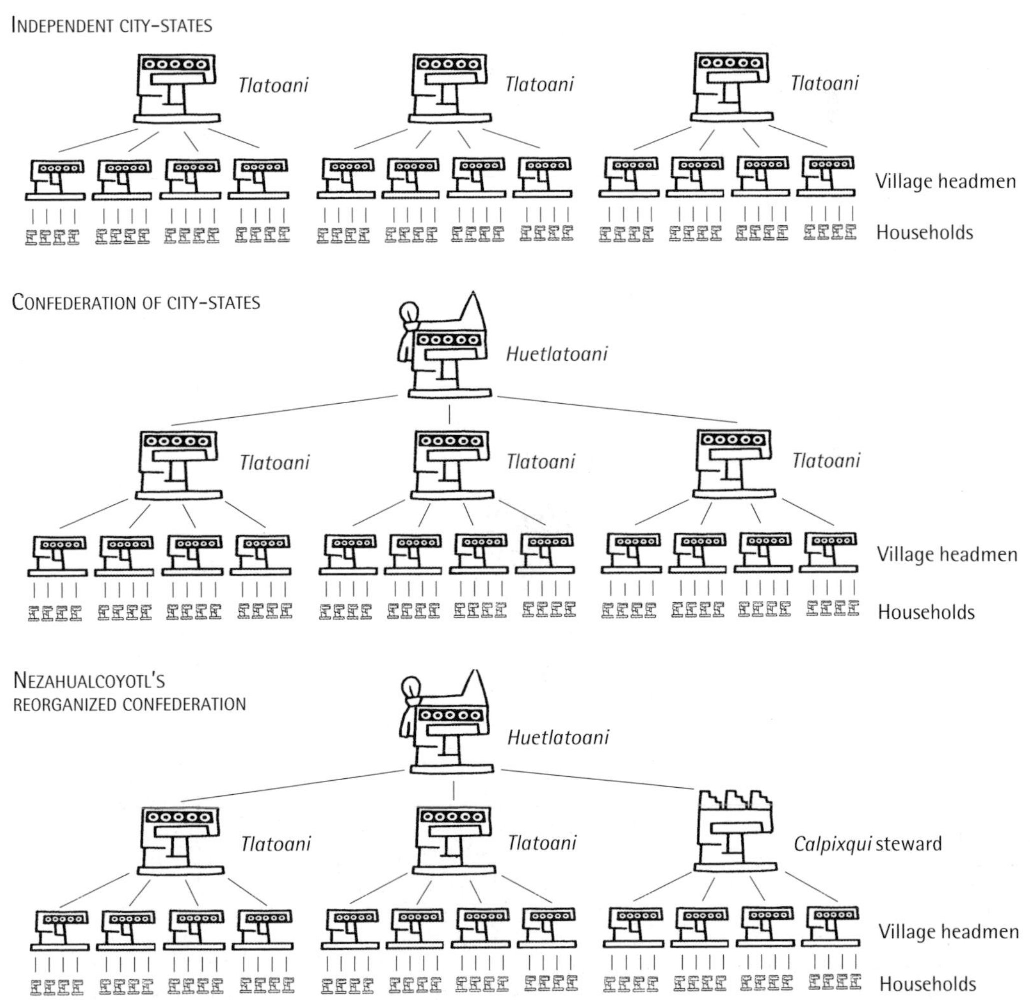

CHINAMPAS

CHINAMPAS were drained fields created by digging relatively deep canals through the muck of swampy fresh water lakes, and piling the muck to form islands between the canals. Thus *chinampas* are a drained-field form of agricultural intensification, and the practice of reclaiming boggy land and transforming it into highly productive farm plots was known all over Mesoamerica, and for many centuries before the Late Postclassic period. The large population of Teotihuacan in the Terminal Formative and Early Classic periods was probably sustained by *chinampa*-style cultivation in the lower Teotihuacan Valley.

Chinampa cultivation in the southern lake system of the Basin of Mexico during the Postclassic period was an important basis for population growth. We have seen how maguey farmers made productive use of the sloping piedmont of the northeastern and eastern Basin, thus converting previously uninhabitable land into farming villages of houses dispersed over terraces. In the swampy shallow lake system, the establishment of *chinampa* plots and canals served the same purpose of transforming unoccupied land into the most productive fields in the Basin, many with houses.

There was a strong feedback process between the development of *chinampas* in the southern Basin's lake system, the growth of Tenochtitlan-Tlatelolco's population, and the political ambitions of the Mexica to control this region. The canals that separated the *chinampa* fields were efficient avenues for canoe traffic that provisioned the growing city of Tenochtitlan-Tlatelolco, which could become more urbanized – more specialized in government, trade, and craft production – because its subsistence needs were supplied by this drained-field hinterland to the south. If Tenochtitlan-Tlatelolco had, in 1520, a population of 100,000 or slightly more, then the city would need about 20,000 tons of grain to supply its basic caloric needs. By that time, the productive capacity of the *chinampas* of the Chalco-Xochimilco district could supply that much (Parsons 1976).

Many maps and drawings of the Early Colonial period illustrate the *chinampas* and their canals (see, for example, Figure **17.14**). Often, in order to stabilize the muck as it was consolidating, pilings were driven along the edges of these islands, or wickerwork fences were embedded there. The wickerwork would serve as a kind of strainer for the muck, permitting the water to drain into the ever-deepening canals, while the soil and organic sediments were trapped, forming the island. Once the island had achieved sufficient height and stability, trees were planted along the edges to further strengthen the *chinampa* [**16.16, 16.17**]. The

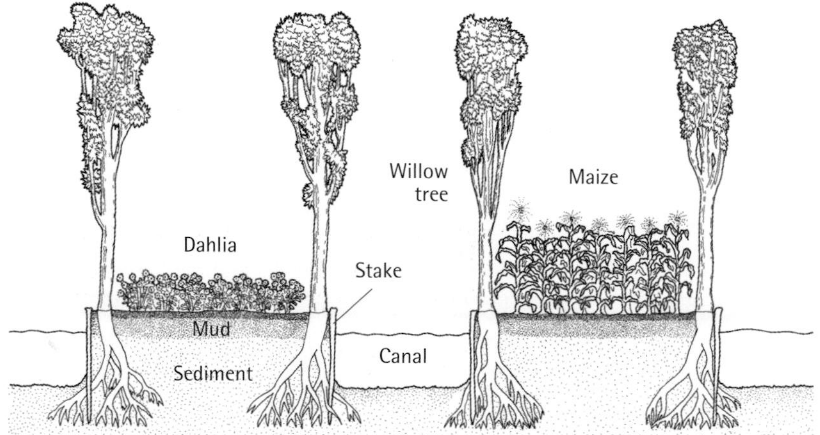

16.16 *The diagram is a cross-section; note how the trees are very tall and slender, securing the soil at the* chinampa *edge while admitting a maximum of sunlight to the plot. Mud scooped from the canals provides nutrients for the soil.*

16.17 *(Opposite)* Chinampas *combine extremely high productivity with the greatest efficiency of transport of goods known in Mesoamerica. The canal systems of the Basin of Mexico's lakes would have been busy thoroughfares, full of canoes supplying Tenochtitlan-Tlatelolco.*

advantages of farming on these islands were important, and included an extremely high crop yield (three crops a year), constant soil moisture, ready supply of soil-enriching lake muck, easy access to fish and other faunal resources of the canals, and efficient transport of crops, by canoe, to market. It may have been the heavily laden canoes that gave rise to the misapprehension that the *chinampas* were "floating gardens." On the contrary, the *chinampa* were deeply rooted, and thus sustained the growth and prosperity of the Basin of Mexico in the Late Postclassic period.

Thus there was a constant ongoing recalculation of alliances and enmities among these polities. They joined together in confederations to protect themselves from takeover by other city-states, but very often one city-state in the confederation would emerge as the most powerful, and thus the institutional framework binding the polities together would develop a higher hierarchical level, and the ruler of the dominant polity would become a paramount ruler whose office would be supported by tributes of labor and goods from the other city-states.

The line between consensual cooperation and extorted submission was sometimes blurry. After all, the most efficient way for a ruler to get rich in such a system would be to make the other rulers his vassals and appropriate a portion of the tributes that would ordinarily go to them. Sometimes the losing dynasty was actually eradicated, but most often, it was kept in place and the ruler was permitted to retain office – but the new overlords took part of the wealth moving up the dendrogram from society's true producers, the farmer artisans. That was why the Tepaneca used the Mexica, in order to increase the territory from which they could draw tributes by having the Mexica terrorize independent city states into subservience.

Such confederations could be readily cobbled together, provided that solidarity could be maintained by incentives or threats, but the segmentary nature of the confederation's component mechanically-integrated parts was its inherent weakness. Because each city-state more-or-less duplicated the organization, functions, and products of the others, independence – or alternative alliances – always presented a desirable option, to be exercised if the overlord weakened.

Tenochtitlan-Tlatelolco, The Atypical City-state of the Mexica

The Mexica, establishing themselves on their islands, represented something of an anomaly because they had no land-based agrarian population. As the last ethnic group to settle in the Basin until the Spaniards arrived, they got last pick of locations, and there were severe limitations on Tenochtitlan as a site. Lack of arable land was one problem, eventually overcome by development of the drained-field cultivation system known as *chinampas*. For another, fresh water was limited to a few small springs, and the Mexica depended on water brought from the Chapultepec springs on the mainland, to which the Tepaneca granted them access. The islands were subject to flooding, a perpetual threat finally dispatched by the Spaniards, who cut a canal through the boundary hills of the Basin in order to drain the lake system (because of this, Mexico City has been sinking ever since).

But consider the advantages. First, islands are defensible. Second, the location was more central than that of any other city-state, given the Basin's layout and topography. The lake offered far greater transport efficiency than did land routes, in terms of movement of goods to and from the city. Once the water supply problem was solved by the construction of a lengthy aqueduct from Chapultepec, and the food supply was guaranteed by the productivity of *chinampas* and provisioning by canoe transport, the location became the strongest in the Basin. So strong, in fact, that Cortés lobbied hard for it to become the capital of New Spain, and thus Tenochtitlan-Tlatelolco became Mexico City, the City of the Mexica.

17 THE AZTECS: AN EMPIRE IS BORN (1325–1440)

17.1, 17.2 *The Postclassic Basin of Mexico's lakeshore alluvial plain was claimed by established city-states, so the Mexica were able to settle on swampy islands near the lake's western edge. Tenochtitlan-Tlatelolco eventually was the Basin's – and Mesoamerica's – largest city, a grid of canals and causeways connecting ritual precincts, palaces, parks, market-places, and the commoners'* barrios.

THE AZTEC EMPIRE IN 1519 consisted of a set of city-states and similar polities that provided tributes or regular gifts to three allied capitals in the Basin of Mexico: Tenochtitlan (which had absorbed Tlatelolco in 1473), Texcoco, and Tacuba/Tlacopan. The rise of the Aztec empire took place in two stages. First was the Middle Postclassic development in the Basin of Mexico of a confederation of city-states [17.1], a hierarchy in which the Mexica of Tenochtitlan-Tlatelolco had a relatively low-level position, and second was the Late Postclassic takeover of the confederation by the Mexica and their allies, and its expansion to a complex tribute-extraction system that reached from coast to coast [18.2, 18.3]. It is a story of the rags-to-riches

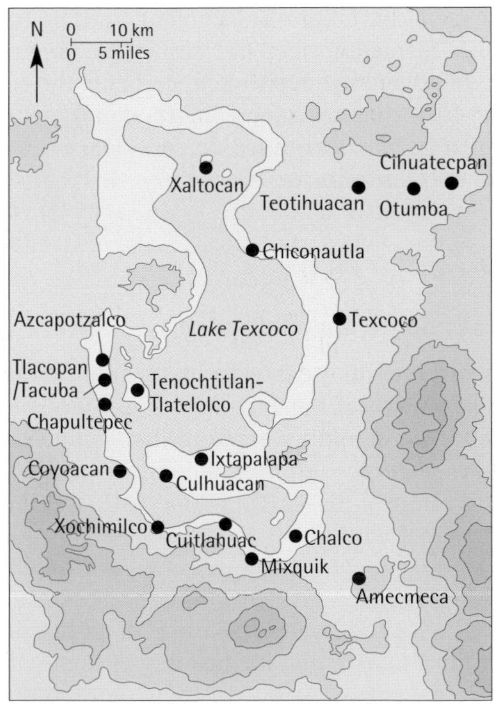

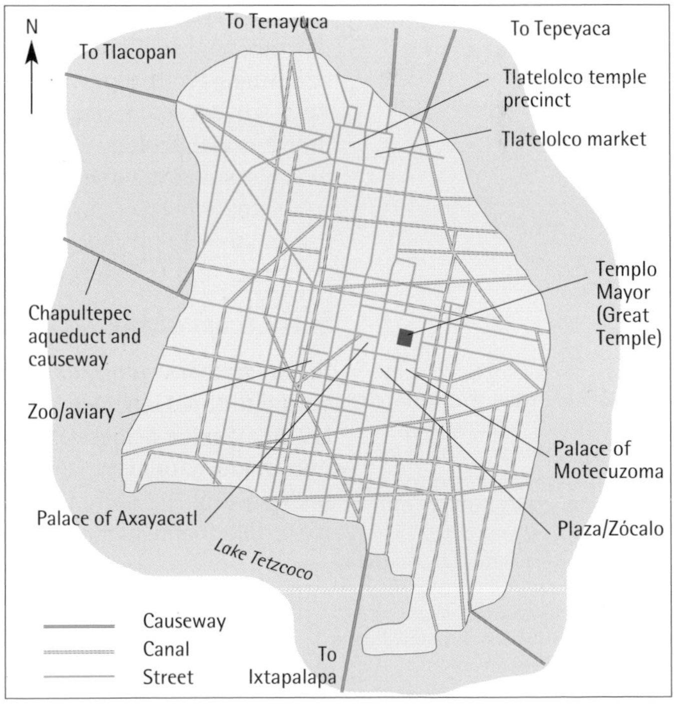

17.3 *(Opposite above) The signature of modern Mexico, an eagle on a cactus springing from a rock, is the central motif of the first illustrated page of the* Codex Mendoza *(1992 [*c. *1541–1542]), describing the foundation of Tenochtitlan (rough meaning: place where the prickly pear cactus grows from a rock). The motif is at the intersection of crisscrossing canals that divided the new city into four quarters. The lower part of the folio shows Mexica warriors conquering Culhuacan (left) and Tenayuca (right) – each town's glyph is next to a drawing of a pyramid topped by a burning temple, an ancient Mesoamerican symbol for political conquest, though at this early stage in their settled history the Mexica were unlikely to have acted independently. The count of years during which these events took place begins at the upper left, with the year 2 House (*c. AD *1325). At lower right, the symbol of the fire drill marks the year of the New Fire Ceremony, which occurred every 52 years, in the year 2 Reed.*

rise of a small but plucky tribe that started life in the Basin of Mexico begging for a spot to camp and, 300 years later, was ensconced in the greatest luxury, dictating policy that affected the lives of millions of people (excellent summaries of Aztec culture and history are available, e.g. Boone 1994, Davies 1977, Smith 1998, Townsend 2000). It is, simultaneously, a story of cultural evolution, of the transformation of local and regional systems of government into a vast machine for funneling goods and labor up to the Aztec lords, and the proliferation of modest social orders into a complicated hierarchy of status positions topped by the ruler of Tenochtitlan.

These two stories – the ethnic history and the case example of cultural evolution – are among the most fascinating in world culture history, and they are preserved in part because of the accident of global interaction that destroyed the Aztec empire. Looking for China, Europeans bumped into the Americas. Finding vast wealth and having military superiority (a modest technological edge in conventional weapons plus bringing, unwittingly, a biological arsenal of devastating diseases), they interrupted indigenous culture history in order to consolidate economic gain. European intrusion destroyed much of Aztec material culture – Colonial towns overlie, and were built from the rubble of, Late Postclassic communities – but many cultural practices and political arrangements were well-documented by the Spanish colonizers for the sake of the Spanish rulers underwriting the colonization process. In this and the next chapter, we examine the processes that brought the Mexica Aztecs of Tenochtitlan and Tlatelolco to the apex of Mesoamerican power, including perspectives on the everyday life of Aztec people. In Chapter 19, we look at the Aztec empire at its height, and the concurrent beginnings of the Spanish intrusion, and, in Chapter 20, we will examine how Europeans overpowered native government, and how the survival of Mesoamerican culture history and its reconstruction through modern archaeology and ethnohistory have permitted us, in modern times, to understand the lives of ancient Mesoamericans.

BASIN OF MEXICO

Early Years of the Mexica at Tenochtitlan-Tlatelolco

17.4 *(Opposite below) By the time the Mexica had become supreme rulers of much of Mesoamerica, they had also developed a taste for luxury and style. This nobleman, depicted in the* Codex Ixtlilxochitl, *folio 105r, wears a long cape, indicating his high status. He holds a floral bouquet and an arrow, symbols of the refined privileges of nobles, and the military prowess by which such privileges were achieved.*

When the Mexica established themselves on the islands that would become Tenochtitlan-Tlatelolco, they were vassals of the Tepanecs of Azcapotzalco [17.2]. Mexica leaders of the early 14th century were not *tlatoque*, but had much more modest status. They were the group's elders in charge of maintaining the sacred ark of their patron deity, Huitzilopochtli, and they were also the heads of groups of related families.

Calpulli Organization Each of these groups formed a basic unit of Aztec society, the *calpulli* (pl. *calpultin*), a Nahuatl word meaning "great house." "*Calpulli*" has no equivalent term in English, and its meaning is somewhat vague. One early chronicler described it as "a barrio [neighborhood] of

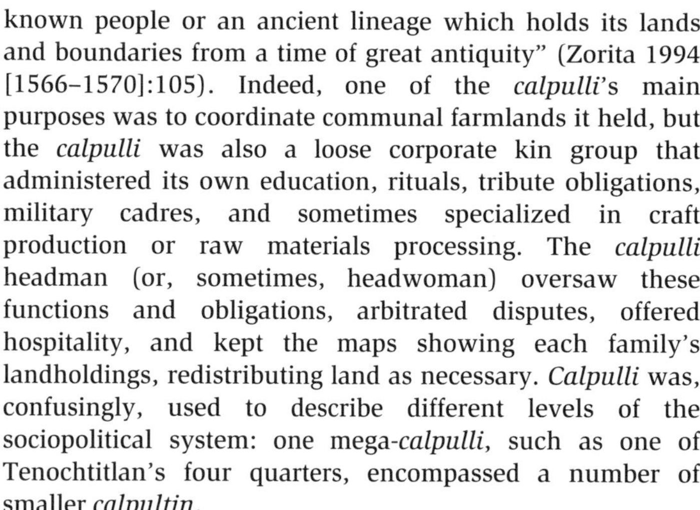

known people or an ancient lineage which holds its lands and boundaries from a time of great antiquity" (Zorita 1994 [1566–1570]:105). Indeed, one of the *calpulli*'s main purposes was to coordinate communal farmlands it held, but the *calpulli* was also a loose corporate kin group that administered its own education, rituals, tribute obligations, military cadres, and sometimes specialized in craft production or raw materials processing. The *calpulli* headman (or, sometimes, headwoman) oversaw these functions and obligations, arbitrated disputes, offered hospitality, and kept the maps showing each family's landholdings, redistributing land as necessary. *Calpulli* was, confusingly, used to describe different levels of the sociopolitical system: one mega-*calpulli*, such as one of Tenochtitlan's four quarters, encompassed a number of smaller *calpultin*.

As we follow Mexica history from its modest beginnings to its imperial pretensions, we find that the *calpulli* plays a diminishing role in the government of Tenochtitlan-Tlatelolco, but it is still an essential basic community unit all over the Central Highlands. In part this is due to the unprecedented urbanization of Tenochtitlan-Tlatelolco, in marked contrast to the rest of the countryside it dominated. Even the other capitals were significantly smaller and less densely settled than the Mexica city, and much more based on extensive land holding. The limited and urbanized land base of the Mexica had important consequences for Aztec social development, because their *calpultin* never had land-holding and food-producing functions to the extent of their rural counterparts, and the rulers saw their own prosperity in trade and tribute from conquest, not from the modest surpluses of a local agrarian economy.

Mexica Noble Rulers: Tlatoque By the late 14th century the Mexica felt themselves ready to have their own noble rulers. In the Basin of Mexico, the ruler's title was *tlatoani* (pl. *tlatoque*), meaning "speaker." This indicates the value of rhetoric and persuasion in government; in order to qualify for office, one must be not only of noble birth, well-versed in ritual if not a high-ranking priest, and successful in war, but also possessed of impressive abilities in the art of argument. While the *tlatoani* and his closest counselors made important decisions, they usually did so by achieving consensus among themselves, and in consultation with their vassal lords, who in turn consulted with their *calpulli* heads. One should not make too much of what might seem to be a nascent democracy – in this society nobles controlled important resources and decided how to use them. The high value placed upon rhetoric and on the role of palaces at all levels as places where lords held court created a system in which lords delivered orations which were displays of memorization of set speeches and imaginative new compositions, but we know from Aztec history that rulers sometimes made and implemented disastrous decisions, against all advice, and this indicates totalitarian rulership, albeit with constraints.

Recognizing the importance of appropriating the prestige of Toltec cultural heritage, the inhabitants of Tenochtitlan-Tlatelolco sought a *tlatoani* from Culhuacan, Tula's ancient ally. Culhuacan's *tlatoani* gave the job to his grandson Acamapichtli, whose mother had married a high-ranking Mexica. Acamapichtli was inaugurated in the 1370s (sources do not agree about the exact date), and ruled until about 1396, founding a dynasty that was only interrupted by the arrival of the Spaniards [17.5]. A few years later

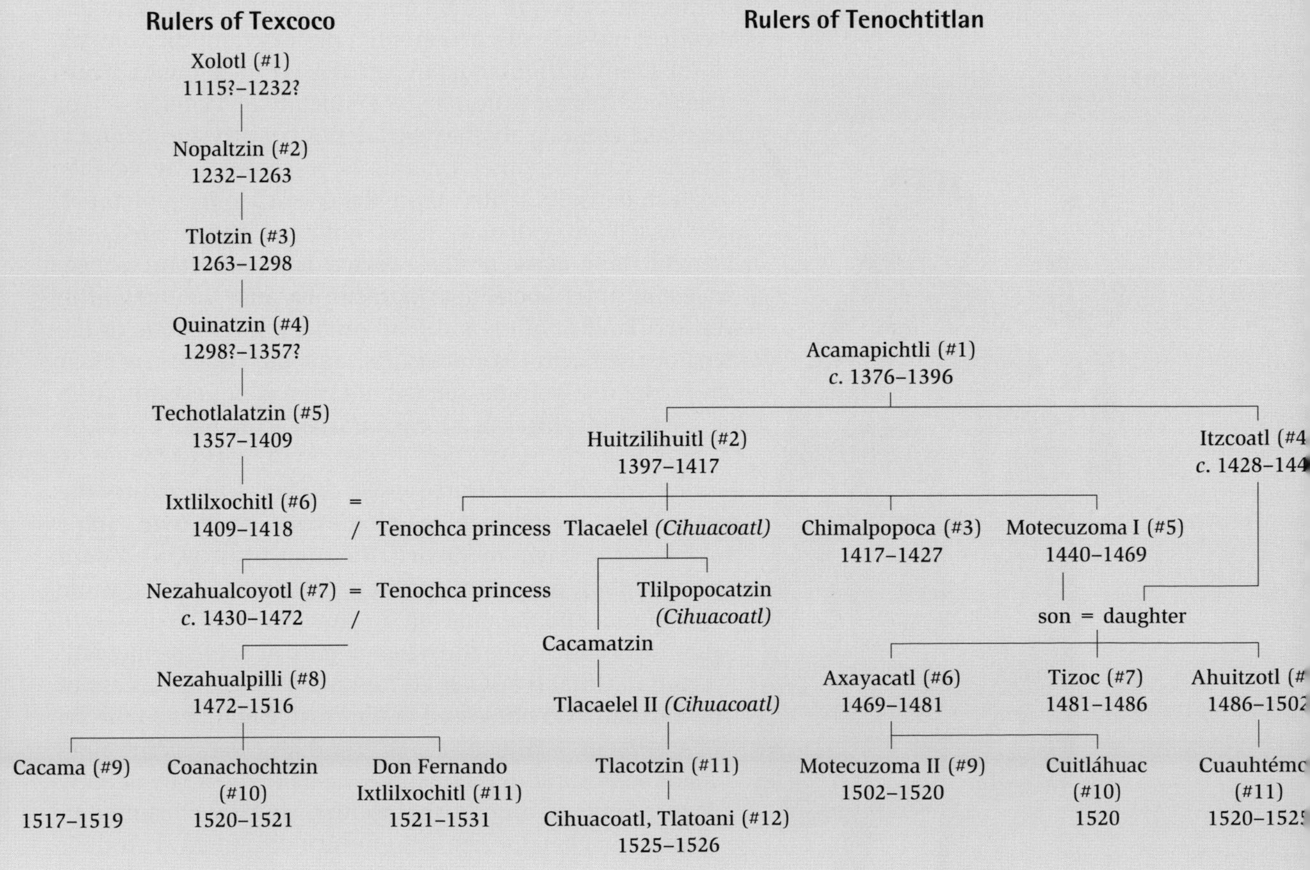

Rulers of Tenochtitlan and Texcoco (17.5)

17.5 *Tenochtitlan's rulers (right side of chart), from inception of the dynasty to Spanish conquest, were all closely related males, but only twice did rulership pass directly from father to son. Instead, sets of brothers dominate the dynastic line, as do links between uncles and nephews. This would seem to indicate that some very important decisions were achieved consensually – at least among the elders of the ruling dynasty – rather than being policy dictated by the ruler.*

Texcoco, Tenochtitlan's leading ally, had a remarkably simple line of succession in comparison to Tenochtitlan's. Their dynastic founder was Xolotl, the pioneering Chichimec tribal leader whose rugged life is purported to have included an impressive 117-year period of rulership, a display of longevity that calls to mind Biblical patriarchs. According to ancient legend, each of Xolotl's descendants ruled for decades. By the time of Quinatzin, the ethnohistoric record was becoming less mythical and more historically sound. Note that Nezahualcoyotl and his son Nezahualpilli successively ruled Texcoco for about 85 years, and in the same period, Tenochtitlan had 6 rulers. Also note that from at least the time of Ixtlilxochitl, Texcocan and Tenochtitlan ruling dynasties were close kin through marriage, and thereafter, by blood.

the Tlatelolcans also sought their own *tlatoani* from the Tepanec ruler, Tezozomoc, who appointed one of his sons to the job. Tezozomoc would have been regarded as a *huetlatoani*, a paramount ruler over the *tlatoque* governing city-states in his confederation.

Under Tezozomoc's late 14th-century leadership, the Tepanecs emerged as nascent empire builders in the Basin of Mexico. Expanding their dominance out of their homeland in the western and northwestern Basin, the Tepanecs began to incorporate territory in regions to the southeast and northeast, and they used the Mexica as mercenary troops. There are some indications that the Mexica began to wage wars of expansion on their own. From 1375–1387, the Mexica harassed the Chalca, who occupied a large, agriculturally rich area of the southeastern Basin.

Flower Wars and Conflicts of Consequence These battles were inconclusive, however, but they may provide early examples of a stylized form of military action called "flower wars" (Hassig 1988). A flower war was a prearranged contest, organized between two rival powers in order to test each other's strength and take captives for sacrifice, not for battlefield carnage: "recreation for the army ... and ... pleasure and food for the gods" (Durán 1994 [1581]: 402). The tradition arose that if officers were captured, they would be exchanged, while the ordinary soldiers would become sacrificial victims.

In the meantime, rather more consequential campaigns were undertaken. In 1383, in conjunction with the Tepanecs, the Mexica attacked and conquered the southern lake cities of Xochimilco, Mixquic, and Cuitlahuac. The southern lakes were loosely connected shallow bodies of fresh water, runoff from the southern rim of the Basin, and draining to the northwest, into saline Lake Texcoco. Their cities sat on islands of high ground, or along the shore, and the actual area of open water was constantly being diminished as *chinampa* systems surrounding the towns increased (see box, pp. 444–445).

The aggressive ambitions of the Mexica increased along with their pride in their island city. In 1390, the original temple of Tenochtitlan was rebuilt for the first time. Visitors to modern Mexico City can see this very temple-pyramid at the Templo Mayor archaeological site – later rebuildings of the pyramid and its temple completely encased this early version, the only one still intact.

Acamapichtli died soon after this first rebuilding, and rulership passed to his son Huitzilihuitl. Huitzilihuitl had married one of Tezozomoc's daughters, and their son, Chimalpopoca, became a great favorite of his Tepanec grandfather. The ruler of Tlatelolco was Tezozomoc's own son, and through these family ties, relations between the Mexica and the Tepanecs became less constrained by formal hierarchy. In fact, Tenochtitlan's tribute to the Tepanecs became largely symbolic. The Mexica continued to help the Tepanecs expand their domain, however, and in 1395 Mexica and Tepanecs conquered Xaltocan, a city-state in the northern Basin of Mexico, ruled by the Otomí. Thus the allies pushed east, toward the confederation of states in the eastern Basin of Mexico, the Acolhua domain.

THE GREAT TEMPLE OF THE AZTECS

THE TEMPLO MAYOR (Great Temple) of the Aztecs at Tenochtitlan was first established when the Tenochca Mexica made the island their home. This earliest version underlies Acamapichtli's rebuilding in 1390, shown as the complete structure (Stage II), which is, itself, encased within later rebuildings. The outermost shell was the one that the Spaniards saw in 1519 [**17.8**].

The west-facing Templo Mayor dominated the central ritual precinct of the city. By 1519, this huge square area measured about 500 m (1,641 ft) on a side, and from it, causeways radiated in the cardinal directions, dividing the city into quarters, and symbolically placing the precinct and its temple at the sacred axis mundi of the secular and supernatural world. The ritual precinct was crowded with temples, dormitories and meeting rooms, a ball court, and an immense skull rack that in 1519 bore 136,000 heads, according to the eyewitness estimate of two of Cortés's men, who counted the poles and multiplied each by the five skulls it carried (Tapia 1963 [*c.* 1534]).

The pyramid and its temples illustrate, from their earliest stages, the architectural signature of Aztec ritual structures: twin staircases leading up to separate temples.

17.6 *Coyolxauhqui schemed against Huitzilopochtli, but he destroyed her, instead. This detail shows that she has been decapitated and her arms have been cut off. Because her image is carved onto a disk, she has sometimes been erroneously called a moon goddess.*

At Tenochtitlan, the temples were shrines to the most important deities, Tlaloc (rain and agricultural fertility) and Huitzilopochtli, the Mexica tribal god who inspired them in their ever-widening campaigns of territorial expansion and blood sacrifice. Thus they honored the two economic bases of Tenochca prosperity, subsistence agriculture and the flow of tribute and long-distance trade goods (Matos 1984).

Aztec rulers regarded the repeated projects of rebuilding and enlarging the Templo Mayor as offerings to the gods. This was their sacred effigy mountain, and behind it, across the Basin, ranged the huge mountains, Popocatépetl (5,469 m; 17,930 ft), Iztaccihuatl (5,234 m; 17,160 ft), and Mount Tlaloc (4,124 m; 13,520 ft). With each rebuilding, precious materials were cached within the structure, offerings to the deities honored by the shrines on top, where the most precious offering of all, living human beings, were sacrificed. Stage IV, for example, was built during a time of drought, and an offering containing the skeletons of children, found on the side dedicated to Tlaloc, may represent a supplication to the rain god – the tears of children on the verge of being sacrificed were thought to be a form of "sympathetic magic" to provoke a response of rainfall. At about the same time, the great round disk depicting the dismembered Coyolxauhqui [**17.6**] was embedded at the foot of the stairs up to the temple dedicated to her brother, Huitzilopochtli, whom she had betrayed. Her symbolic fate was to become a foot wiper for processions glorifying him.

In addition to being a monument to the gods, the Templo Mayor was a monument to Aztec power and to the rulers who organized its construction phases [**17.7**]. With each rebuilding, materials and workers were requisitioned from subject towns in the Basin – yet another reason to control the southern Basin, where stone and wood could be transported directly to the temple by canoe [**17.9, 17.10**]. The pyramid was layers of stone and fill; wood was required for structural timbers for the temples and other buildings in the precinct, and also to use as pilings in an effort to stabilize the area around the pyramid. In time, its

17.7 *These life-size sculptures of standard-bearers were placed against the steps of Stage III as an offering, when Stage IV was built.*

immense weight caused it to sink into the spongy soil of the island, and pilings were driven into the ground and the area around them filled with porous pumice stone to provide strength with less weight.

Dedication ceremonies marking the rebuildings were lavish and costly, especially in terms of human lives – the Stage VI dedication, in the time of Ahuitzotl, is said to have involved 80,400 victims (Durán 1994: 339). Modern scholars believe this to be a gross overstatement, but even if the revised figure is around 20,000 (ibid.: Note 2), it still represents an enormous and bloody spectacle, witnessed by many important guests. Some of these guests were actually the lords of enemy states, brought into the city under cover, and installed in reviewing stands that were hidden from general view, probably to protect them from the hostility of their own people, who would lose faith in rulers so hypocritical as to exhort armies into battle and then partake of the victory feast during which their own soldiers and civilians were put to death.

After the conquest of Tenochtitlan in 1521, the temples were pulled down, and cut stone on the surface was used to build the Early Colonial-period city. Looters tore part of the interior apart, looking for caches of valuable goods. But still, the pyramid loomed over the city, and over the Cathedral, which was built just to the west of the pyramid, in the old ritual precinct. It gradually eroded to a mound about 5 m (16 ft) high, known as the "Hill of the Dogs" because when the city flooded, all the strays took to this, the largest spot of high ground. In time the site was largely leveled and then overbuilt with houses.

In the late 19th century, trenching revealed some of the foundation, but it was not until 1978, when utility workers digging in this

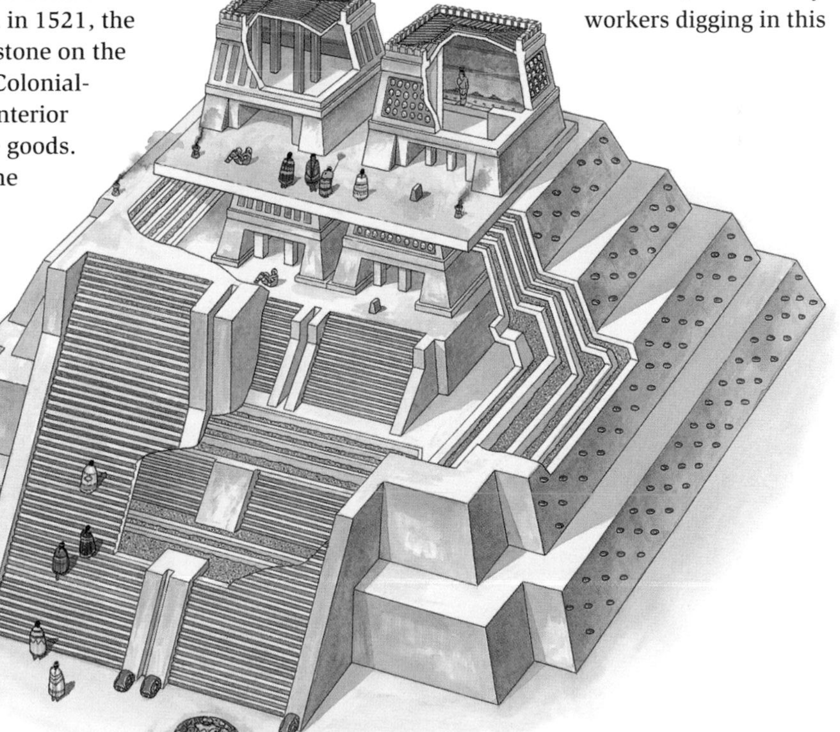

17.8 *The original Templo Mayor is deeply buried under six rebuildings, forming a solid structure which gained dimensions, and grandeur, as Tenochtitlan itself grew to become ancient Mexico's greatest capital.*

area happened upon the massive Coyolxauhqui sculpture, that the Templo Mayor's exact location was revealed (Matos 1994). Since then, the Templo Mayor has been the subject of thorough investigation and has become one of the world's most fascinating archaeological parks, still the heart of the city that was founded upon it.

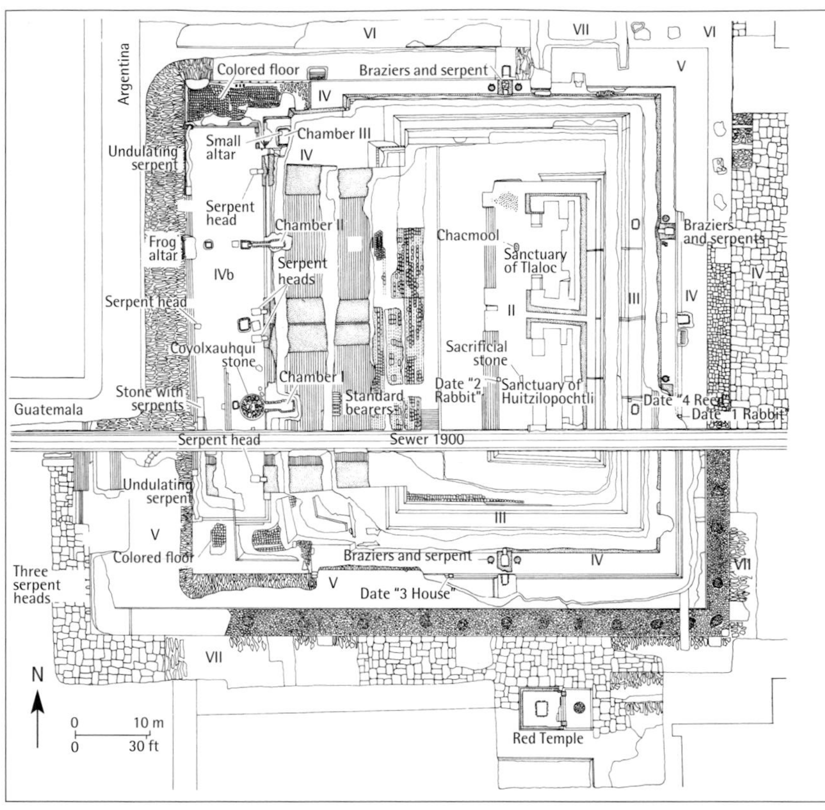

17.9 *The Templo Mayor's seven building episodes took it from a modest shrine in a fishing village to a major monument for an empire. Stage II is the complete pyramid with twin temples that visitors today can see, far inside the surrounding rebuildings. Stage VII was the pyramid at the time of the European intrusion.*

17.10 *Stage III, the first great bid for true monumentality, occurred when the Mexica became independent and acquired some vassal states.*

Great Temple Building and Rebuilding (17.10)

Construction stage	Year	Size	Features
Stage I	At or before AD 1325	Base: significantly less than 17 m E-W, 34 m N-S (56 by 112 ft)	Probably a mud platform with a shrine (or shrines) of perishable material
Stage II	*c.* 1390	Base: 17 m E-W, 34 m N-S (56 by 112 ft)	Stone facing over gravel and lake mud conglomerate
Stage III	*c.* 1431	Base: 40 m E-W, 45 m N-S (131 by 148 ft)	Stone sculptures of standard-bearers recline against the stairs, an offering made when Stage IV was built
Stage IV	*c.* 1454 and *c.* 1469	Base: 55 m E-W, 60 m N-S (180 by 197 ft)	Sculpture of Coyolxauhqui embedded at foot of stairs
Stage V	Early 1480s	Very few remains	
Stage VI	Rededication 1487	Base: 75 m square (246 ft)	
Stage VII	Rebuilding early 1500s	Base: 83.5 m E-W, 76 m N-S (274 by 249 ft); height to summit, 30.7 m (101 ft)	113 steps to a summit platform 44 m (144 ft) across, surmounted by twin temples

The Acolhua Domain

In the conquest of Xaltocan, the Otomí were driven from their capital and became refugees. They were given sanctuary in the upper Teotihuacan Valley, where they were permitted to settle around the town that since that time has been known as Otumba. The Teotihuacan Valley was the northernmost extent of the confederation of the Acolhua, whose capital became Texcoco, across Lake Texcoco from Tenochtitlan. The Acolhua dynasty claimed descent from Xolotl, and only in the late 14th century did Nahuatl become the official language of the court.

The Acolhua domain emerged as the Basin's greatest barrier to Tepanec expansionism, but the Acolhuaque were far from united in their determination to remain independent. Many in the eastern Basin favored incorporation into the Tepanec confederation, especially nobles who were promised that they would replace the existing lords of Acolhua city-states. In 1409, Ixtlilxochitl became Acolhua's king, and established an aggressive stance against the Tepanecs, particularly by claiming himself as the highest-ranking ruler of the old Chichimec line established with Xolotl. Tezozomoc responded by sending quantities of raw cotton to Texcoco with the request that Ixtlilxochitl's Acolhua spin the cotton and weave it into mantles. Ixtlilxochitl complied, but Tezozomoc pressed the point by sending two more shipments of raw cotton, finally provoking Ixtlilxochitl in 1414 to spurn the tribute request and take for himself the grandiose title "Universal Monarch."

Accounts report that around this time the Mexica and Tepanecs harassed the Acolhua and in turn Acolhua forces attacked Azcapotzalco. When Tezozomoc sent spies to determine the strength of support for the Tepanecs among the Acolhua, they asked children seven or younger about the political loyalties of their parents. The spies assumed that such children were incapable of deceit (Alva Ixtlilxóchitl 1985: II: 50), an interesting insight into Aztec attitudes about children (pp. 456–57). Chroniclers describe cities being destroyed, but later events reveal that the "destroyed" cities seem to have remained fully functioning and capable of further aggression against each other. In about 1417 the reign of Chimalpopoca began in Tenochtitlan, and Tezozomoc's relations with the Mexica were close. But one of Chimalpopoca's sisters was married to Ixtlilxochitl, demonstrating the kinship ties binding Aztec lords. In spite of this, Tezozomoc ordered Ixtlilxochitl killed in 1418.

Ixtlilxochitl and his Tenochca wife had a son, a young man of about 17 who witnessed his father's murder and fled into exile. The young man was "Fasting Coyote" – Nezahualcoyotl – "the most interesting personality in the history of ancient Mexico, whose name would be voiced oftener if it were not considered as so unpronounceable" (Nuttall 1925: 459). Nezahualcoyotl (pron. nets-ah-wahl-*coy*-oht) would return, eventually reclaiming the family's throne and enjoying over 40 years of rule, in which he distinguished himself as a statesman, poet, architect, hydraulic engineer, garden designer, patron of education and the arts, and political infighter *par excellence.*

AZTEC CHILDREN AND CHILDRAISING

WHEN TEPANEC SPIES sought the truth from seven-year-olds, they were expressing a commonly-held attitude about how children of different ages would behave. The *Codex Mendoza* (here illustrated, Folios 58 and 60) and other sources tell how children were socialized: what they were taught, and how they were punished if reluctant to learn. Other sources provide further insights about Aztec children and child-raising.

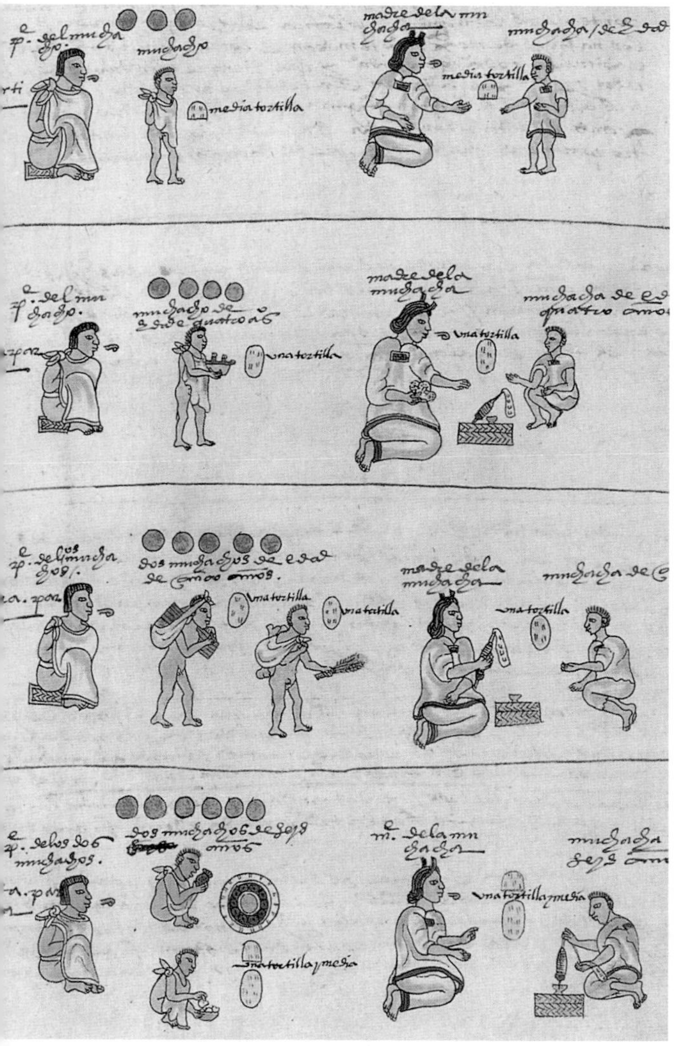

Very young children were trained in tasks that would contribute to the household's well-being and provide their own adult livelihoods [17.11]. Note, in the illustration, that these young children share a close-shorn hair style, but wear a partial version of adult clothes – the boys wear a cloak, but no loincloth, and the girls have a *huipil* blouse, but the youngest do not wear skirts.

Children aged four through seven would have formed a kind of "age-grade" or "age-set" of people who would together participate in certain rites (Clendinnen 1991). Sahagún's informants told of a great festival held every fourth solar year in the year's last month, Izcalli (which corresponded to our January), during which "they lifted by the neck all the small children ... that they might quickly grow tall" (Sahagún 1981: 165–166). Possibly, given the fourth-year timing, this was a kind of leap-year feast, involving a solar calendar correction. In any event, it must have been an exhausting and memorable round of rituals, with special foods, singing and dancing, and general tipsiness as even very young children were given *pulque*. They were also brought to the *calmecac*, a kind of priestly school that trained young people in special skills such as calendrics and rhetoric. There these young children had their ears pierced for the first time. Following this, in ceremonies and parties in the courtyards of the houses of their sponsors, the children were made much of, and danced for the first time in the great Izcalli dances.

Beginning as eight-year-olds, children were subjected to a more rigorous program [17.12] as they were

17.11 *Between ages three and seven, a girl began to learn spinning, and by six years old could spin raw fiber (here, cotton, in her left hand) onto the spindle, which rests in a small spinning cup on a woven mat. The boy of four carries water, five-year-olds hauled loads, using their cloaks as backpacks; at six, the boys scoured the marketplace (large circular symbol) for fallen grains of maize and beans, and at seven they learned to fish with nets. The ovals represent the number of tortillas each received per meal.*

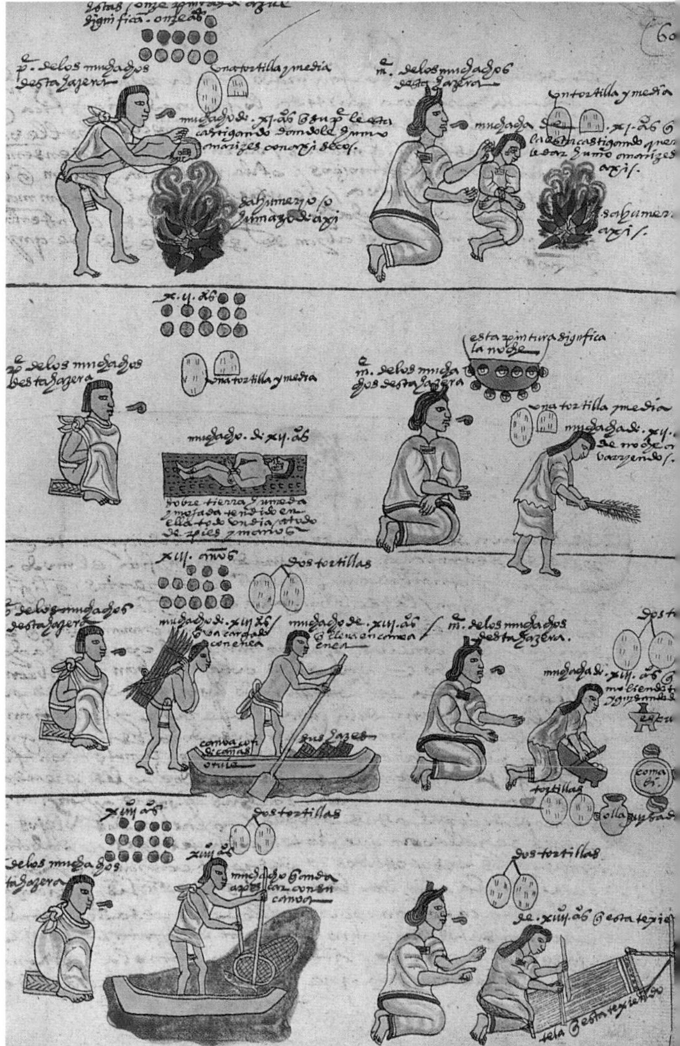

17.12 *Tough love was in store for children aged eight and older who failed to conform to parental expectations of obedience and diligence. These children cried from fear, pain, and/or regret. Needle-ended maguey spikes, often used in auto-sacrifice to draw blood as an expression of piety, were used to administer punishment. Willful 11-year-olds were made to suffer the smoke of burning chiles. Late night events for naughty 12-year-olds include lying bound, naked, on damp bare soil for the boys, while the girls swept under the watchful eyes of the stars. Teenaged girls ground maize and wove cloth, while boys transported loads by tumpline or canoe, and fished.*

socialized into the core Aztec values of moderation, conformance, and steadfast performance of duties to family and rulers. The Aztecs revered moderation in demeanor. They believed that the earth was a "slippery" place (Sahagún 1969: 228) in the sense that one's life was like a path along a ridgetop, with dangers on all sides that could overwhelm anyone losing balance (Burkhart 1989: 58). Immoderate behavior – sloth, gossip, waste, gambling, drunkenness – invited accidents and misfortune, summoned chaos into the life of home, community, and society.

Young people were trained in several different kinds of schools, with somewhat overlapping functions. The commonest was the *telpochcalli*, or "young men's house" where teenaged and young adult men learned to be warriors and did community service of the community. It is likely that every rural village and every city *barrio* had a *telpochcalli* – in the mid 15th century, Motecuzoma I dictated that this pattern should be established to provide adequate military training.

The *calmecac* was more specialized, training boys for the priesthood, and also to become elite artisans such as gold workers and feather workers. The *calmecac* was the institution of choice for nobles, but boys from modest backgrounds were eligible, as well, if they were of good character. Because high-ranking Aztec political officials were often trained in the priesthood as well as in the workings of the civilian bureaucracy, the powerful members of each branch of society would have known each other well. Thus the big-city *calmecac* may have offered similar personal networking opportunities to those presented by some modern prep schools and colleges. However, service to the institution was stressed by both, and novice priests are illustrated in the *Codex Mendoza* as performing a wide range of menial tasks to maintain the temples, and continuing a regimen of corporal punishment for slackers.

Some professions seem to have been restricted to members of particular ethnic groups or lineages, or residents of particular neighborhoods – which may have amounted to the same thing, because, in traditional societies, neighborhoods often have strong ethnic and kin group identities. Sons of feather workers would have learned about that craft from earliest childhood, and sons of *pochteca* merchants would be expected to come into the family business.

Perhaps these great qualities were forged in his character as he waited through the decade between the Tepanec takeover of the Acolhua domain and his return to Texcoco. The Tepanecs awarded Texcoco to the Mexica, which made the Mexica the head of their own confederation while still honoring Tezozomoc as overlord. The Acolhua domain would permanently remain in the shadow of Mexica authority, even after the Tepanecs were overthrown and Nezahualcoyotl was reinstated in Texcoco. Nezahualcoyotl and his successor were careful to reassure the Mexica of Tenochtitlan's unique greatness in the constellation of Mesoamerican politics, and thus the Acolhua were given considerable autonomy.

The Mexica in the 1420s: Preparing for Greatness

In the early 1420s, Nezahualcoyotl was still a young man exiled from his homeland. He had been living in Huexotzingo in the Tlaxcala region, and was permitted by Tezozomoc to return to the Basin of Mexico, where he was put under house arrest in Tenochtitlan. Because he was the grandson of Huitzilihuitl, and the nephew of Chimalpopoca, the "house" in which he was confined was the palace complex, and he apparently had considerable freedom. During this period he began to design the pleasure palace for the Tenochca royal family at Chapultepec, and also began to design an aqueduct to bring water from the springs there to Tenochtitlan. From the heights of Chapultepec, he could look northwest to the city of Tenochtitlan, 5 km (*c.* 3 miles) distant, and beyond Tenochtitlan, in a nearly direct line of sight, saw Texcoco 25 km (15.5 miles) further, and 5 km behind Texcoco, the hill called Texcotzingo, his own family's private retreat that he would eventually redesign as his own pleasure palace. Mesoamericans in general found spiritual value in balanced duality, and thus there was inherent power in the spatial symmetry of the two capital cities and the locales of their dynastic retreats (Evans 2002).

Crisis and Conflict: The Tepanec War

In about 1426, Tezozomoc died, and the confederation he had built had grown so large that the Tepanecs took pains to guard it from takeover. Tezozomoc had chosen one of his sons as heir, and the Mexica had supported this choice, but another son, Maxtla, usurped the throne. Chimalpopoca is said to have advised the legitimate heir to have Maxtla killed. Maxtla managed to turn this plan against his brother, and also against Chimalpopoca and the Tlatelolcan king, who died shortly thereafter. While Chimalpopoca's death may have been at Maxtla's behest, some chroniclers believed that it may have been arranged by his own people, who favored Chimalpopoca's uncle Itzcoatl as a ruler tough enough to deal with the Tepanecs. With the accession of Itzcoatl, Tenochca political organization became more diversified, and a new office was established: the "Cihuacoatl" ("Woman Snake") was the ruler's closest advisor. The first Cihuacoatl was

Tlacaélel, Itzcoatl's nephew, and subsequently the office was held by Tlacaélel's son, grandson, and great-grandson – the last becoming the Mexica *tlatoani* from 1525–1526, in the Early Colonial period [17.5]. In this manner, the Tenochca ruling lineage spawned a double dynastic line.

The enhanced administration was necessary to maintain the ever-growing sister cities of Tenochtitlan and Tlatelolco. Even at this early date, Tlatelolco's merchants were active and their market included elite goods such as plumes and precious stones. With the size of Tenochtitlan outstripping the water supply provided by the island's springs, near the Templo Mayor, the Tenochca pressured the Tepanecs to grant them permanent access to water from Chapultepec springs. This was allowed, but then the Mexica also asked the Tepanecs to provide materials to build the aqueduct, causing the Tepanecs to draw back from accommodating the Tenochca.

The crisis that ensued between the Tepanecs and the Mexica in the late 1420s began with the Tepanecs blockading Tenochtitlan-Tlatelolco. After some diplomatic interchanges, it became clear that the Tepanecs would not accept the greater independence of the Mexica, and thus began the Tepanec War. Crises are often turning points in history, and this was one for the Mexica and their external relations with other states, and for the relationship between the Mexica rulers and commoners. Chroniclers report that the prospect of war frightened the commoners, who were reluctant to see themselves destroyed by the Tepanecs. The elite wanted glory in war and the prizes that the conquest of Azcapotzalco would bring. Itzcoatl is reported to have spoken thus to the commoners:

"If we do not achieve what we intend, we shall place ourselves in your hands so that our flesh becomes your nourishment. In this way you will have your vengeance. You can eat us in cracked and dirty dishes so that we and our flesh are totally degraded." And the people are said to have replied, "if you are victorious we shall serve you and work your lands for you. We shall pay tribute to you, we shall build your houses and be your servants. We shall give you our daughters and sisters and nieces for your pleasure. And when you go to war we shall carry your baggage ... and serve you along the way ... In short, we shall deliver and subject our persons and goods to your service forever" (Durán 1994: 78).

This social contract was, of course, reported long after the fact, and the Mexica had the practice of rewriting history – burning the old books and replacing old accounts with new. Whether or not anything of this sort actually occurred, the placement of this story in the historical record of this period signals an important transformation of Tenochca society. A century earlier, the Mexica were just putting up the first permanent buildings in Tenochtitlan; 50 years earlier, they had received the right to their own Toltec-derived royal dynasty. And now the rulers were actively furthering social stratification, removing themselves and other nobles from accountability to the *calpulli* commoners.

The Tepanec War and the Triple Alliance In about 1428 the Tepanec War broke out, and aligned Tenochtitlan-Tlatelolco with Nezahualcoyotl [**17.13**] and Acolhua loyalists, and also with the Tepanec city Tlacopan (Tacuba) against Maxtla of Azcapotzalco. Cowering in a sweat bath, Maxtla was dragged out to the central plaza and executed. Thus Tenochtitlan, Texcoco, and Tlacopan formed what modern scholars have called the "Triple Alliance" and took over the city-states tributary to the Tepanecs, which included most of the Basin of Mexico. Yet, the spoils – at the end of the Tepanec War and throughout the Late Postclassic – were divided unequally, with Tenochtitlan maintaining leadership, Texcoco taking a lucrative second position, and Tlacopan receiving a smaller portion of the tributes and having no real decision-making power. The Chalcans of the southeastern Basin remained recalcitrant, and it would be another 50 years or so before they were finally subdued. However, acquiring this new Tepanec domain made the Triple Alliance conquerors into imperialists, and the *tlatoani* of each Triple Alliance capital became a *huetlatoani*, promoted up from the ranks of the other city-state rulers. The Triple Alliance would continue to expand its domain for 90 years, when it was taken over by Spain.

17.13 *Nezahualcoyotl is shown here (*Codex Ixtlilxochitl *Fol. 106 r.) dressed for battle, his outer garment entirely embellished with feathers, whose movement would have given an impression of great vitality. Under this he would have worn quilted cotton armor. The weapon in his right hand is a* macuahuitl, *a wooden sword edged with obsidian blades. On his back he carried a drum in order to signal his troops.*

The venture also made the Tenochca rulers, Itzcoatl and Tlacaélel, into major landholders. They took over lands that had supported Azcapotzalco commoners, and from then on, took the rents from them as private income. In another region southwest of Tenochtitlan, the same pattern of larger *chinampas* pertained as was shown in the Maguey Plan [**17.14**], and the plots "were owned by members of the Aztec nobility, who claimed as much as 50 percent of the harvest as rent" (Calnek 1972: 114). Some of the rents from these lands were given to the Tenochca commoners, for support of their *calpulli* temples, but in acquiring extensive properties for their own benefit, the Tenochca rulers seem to have understood and applied the principle of private property.

Private Property In our modern Western world, private property is regarded as a fundamental right of all free people. However, the existence or extent of private property in ancient Mesoamerica has been a matter of scholarly debate. We can assume that people in general "owned" their clothing, and the tools and household goods that they used every day, in the sense that someone else could not casually deprive them of such things without retribution. But a person's access to land was often held communally, and the "ownership" of land and labor in ancient societies is thought to have been strongly embedded within the social structure. That is, an Aztec commoner household had a house and a plot of land, but the land was part of the holdings of their *calpulli*, or was part of the lands associated with a religious or political institution, and farmed for the support of a temple

17.14 *The "Maguey Plan" (1990 [1557–1562]) was, in fact, not drawn on paper made from maguey fiber, but on fig bark paper (Nah.* amatl *or* amate*), and measures 238 by 168 cm (7.8 by 5.5 ft). It is thought to depict an area northwest of Tenochtitlan (Calnek 1973) of plots taken by Tenochtitlan from Azcapotzalco as spoils of the Tepanec War. Six or seven* chinampas *are associated with each house (each with a person's head and name glyph), indicating that this was a farming district, not a plot of city garden* chinampas. *The X is the intersection of two major canals, one, with footsteps, has a causeway alongside the canal.*

or for one or another of the civic offices, such as *tlatoani* or *calpixqui*. When a commoner household ceased to exist, such as when its members had married into or otherwise joined other households, or died, its land was redistributed among other *calpulli* households, but it could not be sold. This practice of selling land defines it as a commodity that can be transferred by a market exchange from one person to another, and economists would say that if land can be treated as a commodity rather than as an unalienable part of the social structure, then one of the essential working parts of capitalism is in place.

Documentary evidence from the Early Colonial period indicates that the Late Postclassic economy was in the process of becoming *capitalized* in that land, labor, and goods were increasingly being regarded as commodities which could be sold for profit. Although a huge proportion of the interchange of these things, particularly goods and labor, still took place at the level of redistribution (as, within a *calpulli*), barter, or marketplace exchange, or gifts and tributes, there are indicators that private ownership of important resources was firmly established. One source stated that land held by a lord (*pillalli*) could be sold if it was not entailed, another cites Nezahualcoyotl's law that one could not sell the same piece of land twice, and Sahagún's informants and Durán both give land as an example of the things an individual could wager (Hicks 1986).

History is full of examples of individuals who made profits on behalf of institutions such as governments, religious organizations, or corporations and then retained some portion of the wealth for themselves. Mesoamerican culture history may also be full of such examples; our best evidence for the emergence of private property as a result of individual opportunism comes from the Aztecs. After the Tepanec War, Tenochca rulers took *calpulli* land to which Azcapotzalco commoners had a socially prescribed relation, and alienated it from them, making it into *pillalli* (noble land) and reducing the status of the former communal landholders to that of sharecroppers. Meanwhile, Tenochca commoners, who could have been given this land as *calpullalli* (*calpulli*-land) continued to develop as a land-poor class of urban artisans and service workers.

Nezahualcoyotl and the Consolidation of the Acolhua Domain

In 1431, with the backing of the Mexica, Nezahualcoyotl established himself in Texcoco. This was a few years after the Triple Alliance victory in the Tepanec War – why did it take so long to install the victorious crown prince of the usurped dynasty? The answer lies in the ethnic and political diversity within the Acolhua domain. This was a hybrid Toltec-Chichimec confederation, with strong Tepanec sympathies and infusions of migrants from the Mixtec regions – it was also a welter of self-interested city-states. That Nezahualcoyotl could forge much of the eastern Basin into a region that remained unified for 85 years indicates that he was a skilled civic engineer as well as having the civil engineering talents that he would demonstrate with hydrological and construction projects. Nezahualcoyotl ingeniously managed to overcome the fragility inherent in the political system of like parts – the confederation of city-states – by several strategies [16.15].

The Acolhua realm [17.15] ran from the northeastern edge of the upper Teotihuacan Valley down to the border with Chalcan city-states on the southeast. Nezahualcoyotl first got rid of individual *tlatoque* that had sided with the Tepanecs, but in most cases he permitted their dynasties to remain in place, which lent stability and encouraged loyalty (Gibson 1971). A number of city-state *tlatoque*, however, were replaced not with other dynastic nobles, but with government stewards, *calpixque*, who were responsible for collecting the tributes from the *calpullis* and sending them along to Nezahualcoyotl in Texcoco. These *calpixqui* towns were along the borders of the Acolhua region, in the upper Teotihuacan Valley and along the border with Chalco. The Teotihuacan Valley had been particularly vexatious with regard to backing the Tepanecs, so Nezahualcoyotl assigned the noble lords of Teotihuacan Valley city-states the tributes of villages that were closer to other capitals than to their own (Gibson 1964). This policy had the effect of interdigitating the region's city-states, preventing any one of them from declaring its independence from the confederation, because it could not depend upon the support of the population of tributary villages in its local tributary hinterland. Thus Nezahualcoyotl forged his confederation into a more stable system than would have been expected given the "mechanical" city-state organization. In fact, the Acolhua domain remained intact for 85 years, until a dynastic fight over succession caused a rift in about 1415.

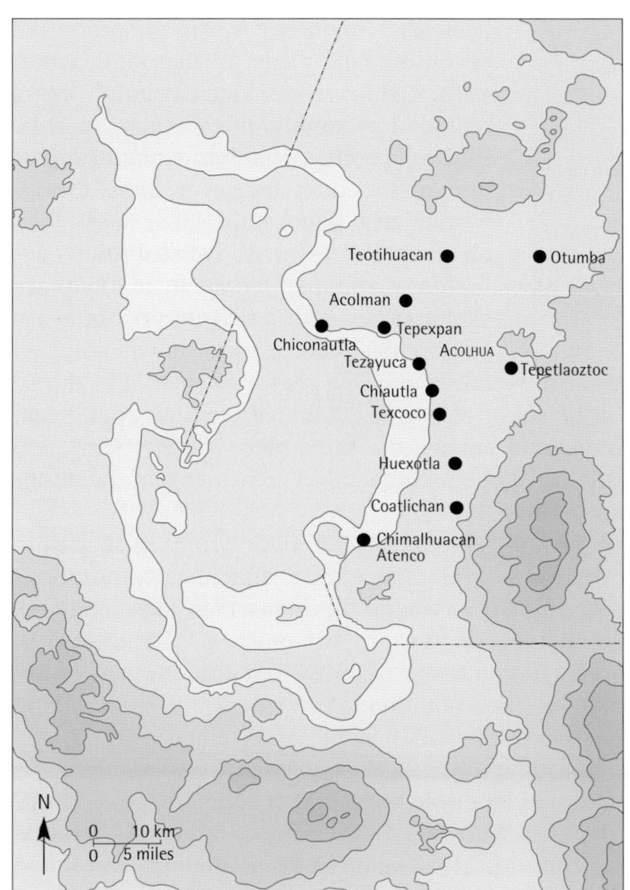

17.15 *The Acolhua domain (within the dashed lines) covered the eastern and northeastern part of the Basin of Mexico. This map shows the Basin's settlement pattern in about 1519.*

Social Strata Among the Aztecs

These actions of the Aztecs rulers are clear examples of social stratification in action. The Late Postclassic period saw the development of the most complex society in Mesoamerica, and the most elaborate and extensive state. Evolutionary processes are plainly demonstrated by the culture historical record both of an expanding Aztec empire and increasingly complicated hierarchy of social statuses, and a growing gap between the nobles and commoners.

Nobles by Birth Aztec society became more stratified, over time, which resulted in a social structure like the one diagrammed in Figure **17.19**. At the highest level, at which all important decisions were made, were the *huetlatoani* and his immediate family. Below that, their more distant kin – the *pipiltin* nobles-by-birth. Below them there was a social gulf between the hereditary nobility and the commoners. This gap was still bridgable during the early-to-mid 15th century, when the Aztec domain was growing fast. Not only could reckless or unlucky hereditary nobles destroy their own position by drunkenness and gambling, but also commoners could gain considerable authority and prestige, as discussed below.

The Political Role of Noblewomen, and Marriage Patterns of the Nobility Political offices were typically held by men; however, women had great influence at all social levels, and had rights to express themselves, including in legal cases, extract themselves from unhappy marriages, and hold property. There is no evidence that any woman ever served as *huetlatoani* in the Late Postclassic period, but among the male candidates for the position, the prestige and family connections of their mothers and wives played an important role, and the women themselves influenced decision-making (Gillespie 1989). Below the imperial level, women sometimes served in administrative positions, their presence becoming more common at the lower levels of the hierarchy. At city-state capitals, there were a few female *tlatoque*, and at the local level, women were listed on census rosters as household heads, the official representatives of their families to the tribute collectors (Williams and Harvey 1997: 201).

Marriage rules in Aztec society were flexible, and this favored the rulers, who could then select their principal wives for solid old-fashioned virtues like wealth and political connections. In fact, men of importance in Aztec society tended to "marry up" – seek out wives of status higher than their own – a situation agreeable to the bride's family, as well. The children of such unions would inherit the highest offices from their father, while also claiming inclusion in the even more prestigious family of their mother. By 1519, several generations of Tenochca noblewomen had become principal wives of other rulers, and thus as their children became rulers they would be tied to Tenochtitlan by bloodlines as well as political subservience (Carrasco 1984). This pattern was repeated down the sociopolitical pyramid, as marriage ties cemented alliances between patrons and their clients.

The Upper Middle Class Two commoner groups achieved important upward social mobility during the 15th century: commoners who were given noble titles by the *huetlatoani*, and *pochteca* merchants. Commoner warriors who distinguished themselves with outstanding military or civil service careers could be named *quauhpipiltin*. They sometimes intermarried with the hereditary nobility, and even achieved the office of *tlatoani*, though in such cases they were preserving a dynastic line by marrying into a lineage that lacked a male heir. When they so served, they had full powers but were denied certain sumptuary perquisites – they couldn't wear crowns, for example. It should be noted that recruiting a commoner male wasn't the only solution to the lack of a male heir, that, as mentioned above, noblewomen also became *tlatoque* on occasion.

More typically, the rulership position given to a noble-by-achievement was *calpixqui*, a steward for the *huetlatoani* who ruled a town that did not have a dynasty, perhaps because the dynasty was abolished when the town had been demoted from city-state status (Schroeder 1991), as happened when Nezahualcoyotl reorganized the Teotihuacan Valley. By the early 16th century, generations of elite polygyny had produced so many hereditary nobles needing jobs that *quauhpipiltin* were more or less abolished by Motecuzoma II, cutting off an important means by which commoners could bridge the social gap between them and the elites.

Other commoners who left their natal huts for permanent life in the palaces were women whose physical

17.16, 17.17 *(Below left and center) Illustrations from the* Florentine Codex *(Sahagún 1959 and 1961 [1569]). (Left) The featherworker and his tools and products, including a shield like the one in 17.13. (Center, top) Hard-working farmers, including one, at right, dressed in European-style clothes. (Center, bottom) The bad farmer and his* coa *at rest.*

17.18 *(Below right) This sculpture from Coxcatlán in the Tehuacán Valley embodies the ideal young man, wearing a cape, loin cloth, and hipcloth. His hands were designed to hold banners or weapons, and his eyes and mouth still bear shell and obsidian inlays, while hair or a headdress would have been attached to the perforations along his hairline.*

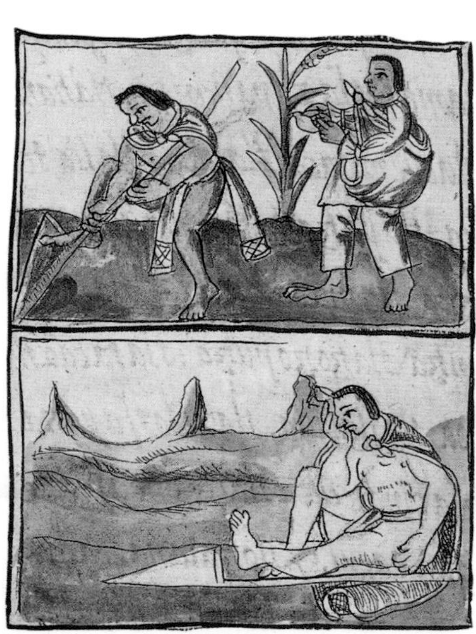

attractiveness or skills in entertainment or artisanship made them eligible for incorporation in the royal and noble households as secondary wives and concubines. Strictly speaking, their social status remained unchanged, but in reality they would have been treated with deference and lived in relative luxury as long as they were held in favor by the household head. The status of their children would depend on many factors, among them the ongoing historical process of increasing social stratification among the Mexica. For example, Itzcoatl's mother was not his father Acamapichtli's principal wife, but a vegetable seller from the Azcapotzalco market. She was definitely one of the king's lesser-status connubial partners, but clearly she and her son managed to attain positions of importance within the palace.

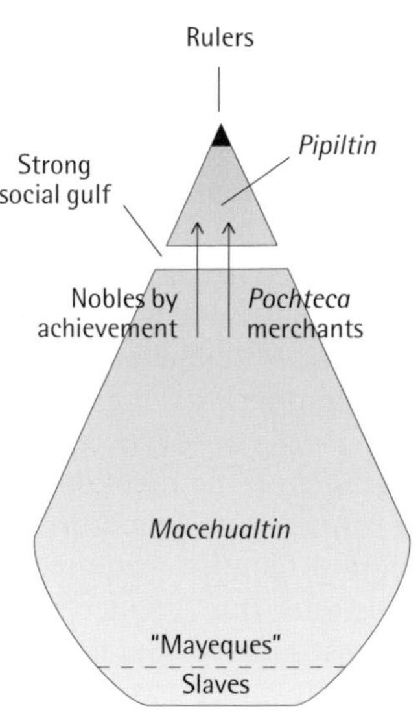

17.19 *This teardrop-shaped model of Aztec social structure expresses how commoners comprised the bulk of the population. They were ruled by a relatively small number of elites, and the bottom of society was occupied by a relatively small number of slaves.*

Itzcoatl's story – of a royal bastard who became one of the great Aztec kings – would seem to inspire the lowly to dream, but it never recurred. Kings still had access to virtually any women they found attractive, but once Itzcoatl secured the foundation for future vast wealth for the Aztec empire, the stakes of rulership became so high that the choice of the heir among the array of legitimate and less-legitimate offspring could not be left to considerations such as merit alone. Royal marriage alliances played a critical role in determining whose offspring would become the next king, and the children of royal concubines had no guarantees of palace patronage.

Pochteca merchants gained and maintained their wealth and authority by controlling long-distance trade, a role that also made them crucial to imperial expansion, because their foreign contacts involved both diplomacy and vanguard militarism. Originally based in Tlatelolco, they kept to themselves in terms of intermarriage and were careful not to excite jealousy by displaying their wealth, while maintaining a critical role in Mexica government (Sahagún 1959 [1569]). Still, their obvious power attracted the vigilant attention of the Tenochca rulers, and the desire of the Tenochca for greater control over the *pochteca* was, no doubt, one of the factors that led to Tenochtitlan's takeover of Tlatelolco in 1473. This rivalry between ambitious, greedy kings and the commoner merchants whose wealth they coveted was a theme in European political history during the same time period as the Late Postclassic.

Working-class Commoners *Macehualtin* were the commoners, typically farmer-artisans, with greater emphasis on artisanship for commoners living in towns and cities. Their membership in *calpullis* was land-based, in the sense that *calpulli* identity was tied to a farming village and its cultivable lands, or to an urban *barrio* neighborhood. In either case, local-level integrative mechanisms included a temple and a young men's house (*telpochcalli*). The *calpulli* headman was either a senior member of one of the *calpulli*'s families, or a nobleman of relatively low position, who would have taken as his principal wife another noble, preferably the daughter of the ruler of the city-state to which his village or *barrio* owed tribute, mimicking the pattern set by city-state kings, wherein a *tlatoani*'s principal wife would, ideally, be the daughter of his overlord, the *huetlatoani*. Good politics would call for rulers to take as lesser wives the daughters of worthy families within their domains, and thus a *tlatoani* would seek secondary wives from families in his city-state, and a village headman would look to daughters of important *calpulli* families. Again, we see a case of sexual penetration of a social barrier, but the issue from such unions would not have been automatically accorded noble status.

Some *macehualtin* may have achieved relatively high status through hard work and good fortune. Urban-dwelling artisans whose work caught the attention of nobles may have thus improved their status. Much depended upon the temper of the times – the state of the economy and the nature of the ruler, himself. Nezahualcoyotl of Texcoco seems to have sought out talented people. Alongside his palace he built a teaching facility for all manner of skills, from rhetoric to crafts. Because it was under his patronage, and his personal talents were so strong and wide-ranging, he may have wanted this complex close to him so that he would be able to work with and learn from the experts, including noble artisans and skilled commoners.

Below the Working Class The status of commoners could be degraded by several circumstances. If a *macehualtin* farming *calpulli* was caught in the middle of warfare between city states, its corporate identity evaporated. When Itzcoatl took over Azcapotzalco's farmlands after the Tepanec War, the property seems to have been privatized, as discussed above, and thus the *macehualtin* no longer had communal rights to it. Their status was reduced, and some scholars use the term "mayeque" to refer to such tenant farmers, but the word was not commonly used in Nahuatl. These tenant farmers would owe a portion of their output as rent to their noble landlords. They held no communal rights to the land, and had no corporate organizations such as a common temple or *telpochcalli*, and presumably had no headman.

At the Bottom of Society Slaves (*tlacotin*) were on the lowest rung, though their lives were not necessarily unpleasant, and some slaves could purchase their freedom if their family's fortunes permitted it. To become enslaved in Aztec society was a matter of personal misfortune rather than class oppression – there was not really a "slave class" but rather a relatively small number of people, at any point in time, who were down on their luck because of criminal activity, debt, or military defeat. In the last case, they would be used to carry loot or tribute from their native region up to Tenochtitlan, and then would die in the next big mass sacrifice.

Slaves were sold in the marketplaces, and the market at Azcapotzalco specialized in them. They were purchased to provide labor, and also as sacrificial victims. A purchaser, or purchasing group, might want to commemorate an event or honor a particular deity by sponsoring a sacrificial rite, and buy a slave for this purpose. Thus if you were a slave between owners, literally "on the market," your life was in jeopardy. The bright side was that if you were physically attractive, you might be purchased to be a deity impersonator and live the life of a god – or goddess – for a full year before being the featured player in the ceremony dedicated to that deity. The end was the same, however: your still-beating heart was ripped from your body and then your right thigh was delicately prepared as the day's special on the menu of the ensuing feast.

The Process of Social Stratification Among the Aztecs

As we have seen in many examples presented in this book, cultural evolutionary processes often resulted in the concentration of power and wealth into the hands of a few people. These rulers then made policy that would concentrate power and wealth even further, distancing the social stratum of the rulers from that of the ruled. Very often, stratification takes place under conditions of social and/or environmental stress. This stress might be demographic growth pushing against the limits of available resources, or intensification of agriculture that requires more complicated mobilization of labor and results in lands that are made much more valuable to their owners. The stress might be warfare, or ethnic conflict, or any of many situations that change the equilibrium of the relations between different factions or classes. In these stressful situations, the material conditions of those already marginal stand to be worsened, and those who are already advantaged can usually benefit further from the desperation of others.

Social and environmental stresses contributed to mechanisms of change (Flannery 1972). Some offices or institutions were "promoted," in that they were elevated to a higher level of the hierarchy, where they exercised more functions than before. An Aztec example would be the promotion of the offices of the Tenochca leader to *tlatoani*, which was achieved with Acamapichtli. While society and political organization became more complex, it was in the interest of the highest rulers to streamline the downward chain of command, and in the Aztec case, the upward flow of tribute. This process of "linearization" streamlined the flow of information or goods by removing intermediaries, as occurred when Tezozomoc ordered the murder of Ixtlilxochitl, the ruler of Texcoco. While another ruler was installed to govern Texcoco, he was not a *huetlatoani* – the city-state rulers reported, and sent tribute, to Tezozomoc.

This was a clearcut case of "meddling," of one government's interference in the affairs of another. Tezozomoc meddled in the autonomous destiny of the Basin of Mexico's last Otomí city-state, Xaltocan, usurping the Xaltocan's dynasty's rights and privilege, and also the land and dwellings of the people of Xaltocan, who were forced to abandon their town and seek refuge elsewhere. These strategies of governmental remodeling and interference in foreign polities resulted in the centralization of decision-making power and the concentration of wealth in fewer hands. This process characterizes Aztec political history from the 1420s to the 1520s, as the Mexica of Tenochtitlan controlled significant proportions of the economic output and political decision-making of more and more polities across Mesoamerica.

At the same time, the Aztec governmental format became more internally diverse. Consider the bureaucratic complexities of levying and keeping track of tribute from conquered provinces that extended over an entire subcontinent: after the difficult business of the conquest itself had been accomplished, and the tame ruler was put in place in the conquered province, then the wealth of the region had to be estimated in order to exact tribute at a significant rate but not one which would destroy the local economy. When the tribute reached Tenochtitlan, it had to be accounted for, stored, maintained, possibly transformed for further use, assigned as royal gifts, used in the royal household – all of which required personnel such as bookkeepers, housekeepers, zookeepers, etc. The recruitment, training, payment, and management of all these people required further managerial personnel.

These processes of stratification and the policies that induced them are evident throughout the culture history recounted thus far in this book, and striking examples will be presented in subsequent chapters. As for their relevance in the modern world, any newspaper's front or business pages will supply examples of each of these phenomena.

Setting the Stage for Empire

With this ongoing process of social stratification, and the political developments of the early 15th century, the Triple Alliance was ready to continue drawing upon the tributes of the Basin, which may have had a population of about 800,000 by this time. In 1431, the Tenochca rebuilt the Templo Mayor again, and at this time enclosed the area that would be the main ritual precinct. This may have coincided with the establishment of a new palace just east of this precinct (see box, pp. 482–483). In the manner of the rich and powerful throughout human history, the Aztec kings sought to award themselves settings of luxury and beauty. Wars, construction projects, and appropriate adornments for these grandiose buildings required large contributions of materials, service crews, and food, both staples to feed the workers and delicacies for elite feasts. This demanded more income, and more conquests.

18 THE AZTEC EMPIRE DEVELOPS (1440–1481)

THE PERIOD ENCOMPASSING the reigns of Motecuzoma I and Axayacatl lasted over 40 years, 1440–1481. During that time the Triple Alliance domain was extended well beyond the Basin of Mexico and became a true tributary empire as Mesoamerica had never seen before. And yet, even as Aztec ambitions grew and their armies marched, it was clear that not all opponents were readily subjugated. To the west, the Tarascans presented an insurmountable barrier to expansion. Other, less formidable enemies needed to be "conquered" repeatedly, refusing to accept their lot as a source of income and sacrificial victims for the great powers of the Basin of Mexico.

THE REIGN OF MOTECUZOMA ILHUICAMINA, 1440–1469

In 1440 Itzcoatl died, and his nephew, the first Motecuzoma, became Tenochca *huetlatoani*. Motecuzoma I's first military campaigns were within the Basin of Mexico, and directed largely at enforcing the established subjugation of the city states around the southern lakes: Xochimilco, Culhuacan, and Coyoacan. There were also more campaigns against the Chalcans, and a fragile peace was achieved. Then the Mexica moved well beyond the Basin of Mexico and began wars of conquest in adjacent regions.

Motecuzoma I (Motecuzoma Ilhuicamina) could be called the founder of the Aztec empire: "If Itzcoatl established the fact of the Aztec empire and its dominion over the Valley of Mexico, his successor ... gave it range." (Boone 1994: 49). Motecuzoma I set a pattern of expansion of the tributary empire that would become standard for the rest of Aztec history. He sent messengers to towns in the Valley of Morelos, and the adjacent eastern Guerrero region to its south, requesting help with monumental building projects in Tenochtitlan. When help was refused, often in the inhospitable form

18.1 *The Teocalli, or Temple Stone, was found in 1831 in Mexico City, in the area of Motecuzoma II's palace, and may have served as his throne. It stands 123 cm (c. 4 ft.) tall and was carved in 1507, a compact mass of dates (as shown flanking the "stairs"), figures, and icons in the form of a temple (Pasztory 1983).*

of killing the messengers, the Aztecs felt justified in sending in their army to conquer the reluctant potential tributaries. Motecuzoma I then headed south, with conquests in the southern Toluca Valley before moving into Morelos and Guerrero.

Mexica conquests tell a somewhat confusing story, because many areas had to be reconquered, and chronicles written in the Early Colonial period sometimes differ as to when, and how definitively, a particular area was conquered. As we know, the Mexica themselves tended to rewrite their own history to glorify particular rulers and their accomplishments, while those of the conquered nations often disputed accounts by the Mexica, because of their desire in the Early Colonial period to emphasize to their new Spanish overlords their own rights and their common cause against the Mexica.

In 1521, the Aztec empire's provinces extended over much of modern Mexico [**18.2, 18.3**]. Scholars have noted the important distinction between those sites listed on the *Codex Mendoza* and in other primary sources, called "tributary provinces," and those with a history of having been conquered, but which do not appear on tribute rolls, called "strategic provinces" (Berdan et al. 1996: 110). The distinction between the two is based on whether or not the province was obliged to provide goods, or did so as a "voluntary" gift (Hicks 1984). Tributary provinces would have sent regular payments of goods and services (labor and military cadres drawn from the *calpullis*). Strategic provinces also sent service cadres, but the goods they sent were defined as "gifts" rather than tribute obligations, and this was thought by the subordinate peoples to be a less onerous form of relationship, perhaps one they voluntarily chose upon seeing the Aztec armies wreak havoc on a neighboring state.

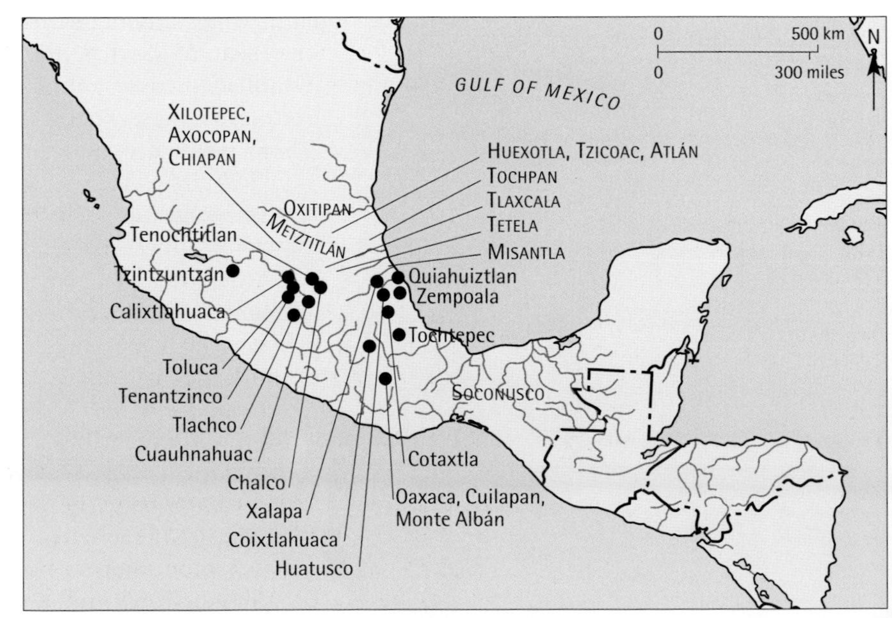

18.2, 18.3 *(Below and opposite) The Aztec empire at its greatest extent, in 1521, was not a continuous sweep of territory, but rather a mosaic of regions brought under control of the Triple Alliance. "Tributary provinces" (starred on the list) made regular payments to the Triple Alliance, while "strategic provinces" provided various kinds of aid to the Triple Alliance, but obligations were regarded as established by mutual consent. In brackets, the emperors during whose reigns the regions were conquered [Itzcoatl, Motecuzoma I, Axayacatl, Tizoc, Ahuitzotl, Motecuzoma II] (based on Gerhard 1993; Hassig 1988; Smith and Berdan 1996). The list below provides a key to* **18.3** *(opposite).*

Acatlan [MI] (37)
Ahuatlan (38)
Atlán [Ax, MII] (51)*
Atotonilco de Pedraza [MI] (2)*
Atotonilco el Grande [MI/Nezahualcoyotl, MII] (50)*
Axocopan [MI] (1)*
Ayotlan (25)
Chiapan [I, MI, Ah] (4)
Chiauhtlan (16)
Cihuatlan [Ah, MII] (23)*
Coixtlahuaca [MI, T, Ah, MII] (33)*
Cotaxtla [MI/Nezahualcoyotl, Ax, Ah] (41)*
Cuahuacan [Ax] (7)*
Cuauhchinanco [MI/Nezahualcoyotl] (49)
Cuauhnahuac [I, MI, Ax] (13)*
Cuilapan [MI, Ah, MII] (32)*
Huatusco [MI/Nezahualcoyotl, Ax, MII] (43)*
Huaxtépec [I, MI] (14)*
Huexotla [Ah, MII] (54)
Ixtepexi [MII] (31)
Ixtlahuaca [Ax] (6)
Malinalco [MI, Ax] (10)*
Miahuatlan [MI?, MII] (28)
Misantla [Ax/Nezahualpilli] (45)
Ocuilan [Ax] (9)*
Ocuituco (15)
Ometepec [Ah] (26)
Oxitipan (55)*
Quiauhteopan [MI] (17)*

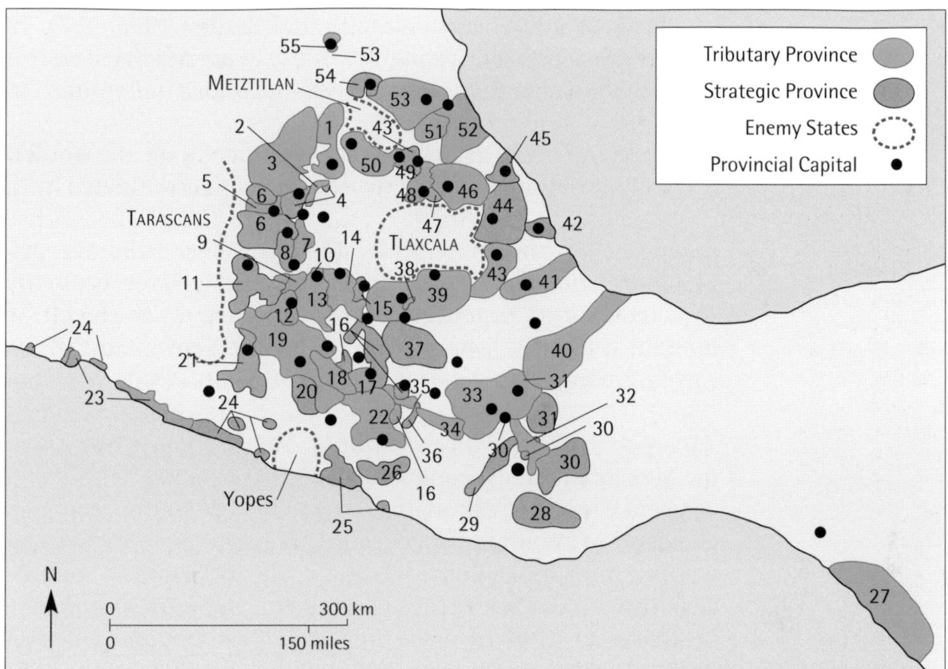

Soconusco [Ah, MII] (27)*
Tecomaixtlahuacan [MII] (36)
Tecpantepec [Ah, MII] (24)
Temazcaltepec [Ax, T, Ah, MII] (11)
Teozacoalco [MII] (29)
Teozapotlán [Ah, MII] (30)
Tepeaca [MI, Ax, T, MII] (39)*
Tepecoacuilco [MI, Ax, Ah, MII] (19)*
Tetela del Río [Ax, Ah] (21)
Tetela (47)
Tlachco [MI, Ax] (12)*
Tlacozauhtitlan [I, MI] (18)*
Tlapacoyan [MI] (48)*
Tlapan [T, Ah, MII] (22)*
Tlatlauhquitepec [MI/Nezahualcoyotl] (46)*
Tlaxiaco [Ah, MII] (34)*
Tochpan [MI/Nezahualcoyotl, Ax, T, MII] (52)*
Tochtepec [MI/Nezahualcoyotl, Ax] (40)*
Toluca [Ax, T, MII] (8)*
Tzicoac [MI/Nezahualcoyotl, Ax, T, Ah, MII] (53)*
Xalapa [Ah, MII] (44)
Xilotepec [MI, Ax, Ah] (3)*
Xocotilan [Ax] (5)*
Yoaltepec [MI] (35)*
Zempoala [MI, MII] (42)
Zompanco (20)

In the following chapters, we depart from the established format of the book, in which we discussed regions as they formed the great geographical subdivisions of Mesoamerica – Isthmus of Tehuantepec and east, and west of the Isthmus. Instead, the history of the expansion of the Aztec empire will guide the regional discussions. Thus we begin with Motecuzoma I's conquests north of the Basin of Mexico, and then move south, into Morelos and eastern Guerrero, east into the Gulf lowlands, and then south again, to the Mixteca regions and the Oaxaca Valley.

The Tula Region and Its Environs

North and northwest of the Basin of Mexico lay high-altitude semi-arid hills and plateaus that linked the Sierra Madre Oriental on the east with the Bajío on the west. The most important culture to arise in this region was that of the Toltec, in the Early Postclassic period. However, in the Late Postclassic there were many city-state capitals, with dependencies scattered throughout the area. These were farmers whose staple products were maguey and nopal.

Chiapan Although Tula had declined precipitously in the 1200s, it remained occupied, and its civic-ceremonial center was an important pilgrimage and pilfering site for the Mexica, who actually removed some of its artistic monuments and installed them in their own sacred precinct in Tenochtitlan. Conquests of Tula began with Itzcoatl and continued under Motecuzoma I, while other Aztec military deployments under Ahuitzotl subdued this province, called "Chiapan" (Smith and Berdan 1996: 267). However, Tula and the other city-state capitals in this area are not listed on tribute rolls, and thus scholars regard this province as "strategic" rather than "tributary."

Atotonilco de Pedraza This small province is on the border between the Basin of Mexico and the Tula region, and it was conquered by Motecuzoma I.

Xilotepec Northwest of Tula, this extensive tributary province was a Chichimec homeland, and some towns may have been tributary to the Tepanecs. Aztec conquests by Motecuzoma I, Axayacatl, and Ahuitzotl brought it into the empire, and it supplied woven cotton textiles and live eagles, among other goods (Smith and Berdan 1996).

Axocopan and Atotonilco el Grande The Axocopan tributary province was the Mezquital Valley, conquered by Motecuzoma I, who also conquered the adjacent province, Atotonilco el Grande. The entire region was fairly cold and dry, but important strategically because these provinces formed a southwestern bulwark against Metztitlán. Metztitlán was a mountainous region consisting of narrow valleys bounded by cliffs. An important gateway from the Basin of Mexico to the northern Gulf lowlands, it was consistently hostile to the Aztec empire, and a policy of containment involved the conquest of a series of provinces surrounding it.

The subjugation of these northern provinces secured a large region with limited but dependable resources. For more exotic tributes, the hot-country products like cotton and cacao that rulers needed to advertise their gloriousness, conquests toward the south and east were necessary.

Late Postclassic Morelos

In Morelos, Late Postclassic-period cultural developments corresponded to those of the Basin of Mexico in many important ways. The dominant ethnic group was Nahuatl-speaking Aztec, and demographic growth was expressed in Morelos, as it was in the Basin, by expansion of rural settlement in a system of virtually continuous terraced farming houselots over the piedmont (Smith and Price 1994), while on the plains irrigation systems intensified cultivation in this *tierra caliente* environment. City-state capitals were densely populated and diverse in terms of their inhabitants' socioeconomic class, ethnic identification, and occupational specialization.

Cuauhnahuac/Cuernavaca Cuauhnahuac (modern Cuernavaca) was founded in the Middle Postclassic, and the pyramid at Teopanzolco, with its typically Aztec twin staircase, represents this early phase. By the early 1400s the city center had shifted to its present location, a new royal palace had been built (later claimed and built over by Cortés), and the city had come to dominate more than 20 other city-states. Cuernavaca is the *tierra caliente* town closest to the Basin of Mexico, a mere 60 km (*c.* 37 miles) south of Tenochtitlan/Mexico City, but 610 m (2,000 ft) lower in elevation, and the gateway to the rich Valley of Morelos, where such products as cotton could be grown. In fact, some accounts cite Huitzilihuitl's earliest incursions in this direction as bringing the Tenochca their first cotton garments, a taste they apparently wished to make into a habit. A more romantic version of the expansionist saga described Huitzilihuitl as a grieving widower after the death of Tezozomoc's daughter, falling in love with a Cuernavacan princess and getting her pregnant (with Motecuzoma I) when she ate a precious jewel he propelled into her courtyard. They were married, one of the usual means by which Aztec rulers secured rights to attractive territories (see box, pp. 474–475). Whether motivated by romance or greed, the Mexica conquered this rich province in 1438.

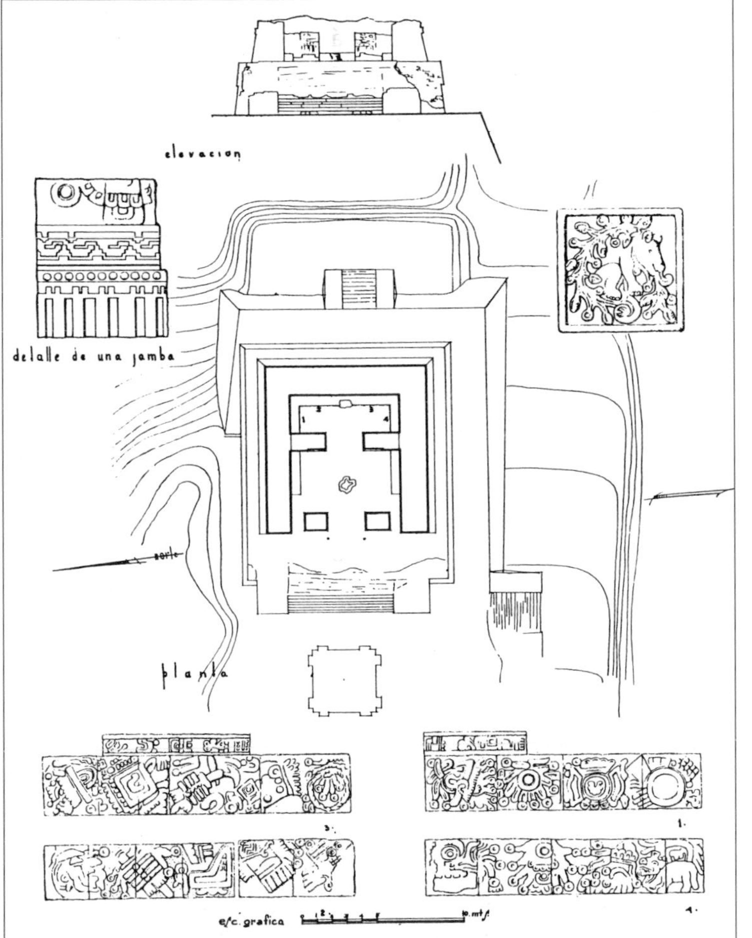

18.4 *High above the Valley of Morelos, the temple of the* pulque *god at Tepoztlán featured banquettes similar to those found at Tula, and, imitating Tula, at some of the exclusive meeting rooms for nobles in Tenochtitlan and other Late Postclassic capitals. This layout was used at ritual feasts held in such rooms, in which* pulque *and other intoxicants were used to induce a transcendent state (front, plan views and bas-relief drawings from Marquina 1999: 217, Lám. 62).*

Huaxtépec Province, and Motecuzoma I's Pleasure Gardens at Huaxtépec

East of Cuauhnahuac was the province of Huaxtépec, which was drawn into the Aztec empire in the reign of Motecuzoma I. It consisted of five separate city-states, most notably Tepoztlán, with its mountainside shrine to the *pulque* god at Tepozteco [**18.4**], Yautepec, and Huaxtépec itself.

Yautepec is notable because it is one of the only Aztec city-states in which archaeological investigation has uncovered not only a portion of the palace, but also several of the city's residences (Smith *et al.* 1999). Founded at the beginning of the Postclassic period (Hare and Smith 1996), Yautepec grew to about 2 sq. km (0.8 sq. miles), with a population of 13,000 by the time of the Spanish conquest. Cotton was grown in the surrounding fields, and another local product was paper made from the bark of the wild fig (*amatl*) tree, which was used not only for writing but also for such ritual purposes as costumes and to blot blood flowing from autosacrificial wounds – the bloodied paper would then be burned as an offering.

One of Yautepec's neighborhoods is thought to have been Molotla, known from a 1540 census which offered a view into patterns of household organization that had persisted since before the Spanish conquest (Carrasco 1976). The

ADULTHOOD, SEX, AND MARRIAGE

AS WE HAVE SEEN, ADULT DUTIES were introduced early into the lives of Aztec children, who were trained, admonished, and disciplined toward useful lives. Boys were trained at home and in special schools; some girls also attended special religious schools. Ritual precincts in major cities included convents where women dedicated their lives to religious service. Most girls were trained in skills that would make them admirable housewives and at the same time would secure their ability to support themselves, because of the importance of textiles in the economy.

A young man was expected to prove himself as an adult by capturing an enemy in battle. This was both a source of private pride and public dignity, because a man could not have an adult male hair cut until this obligation had been met (Joyce 2000). Distinctions in male costume provided a language of ranking much more explicit than our own – from the style and length of a man's cloak, his lip plug and haircut, one knew the number of war captives he had secured. Having achieved adult status, a man was ready to marry.

Marriage For the Aztecs, marriage was the final social stage of the process of becoming adults. Men married at about age 20, and women at about age 15. Marriages between members of ruling dynasties were projects of statecraft, but commoners also took seriously the alliance of one family with another, and matchmakers negotiated the deal. Aztec marriage rules were flexible, and the few prohibitions specified close relatives – these incestuous unions were regarded as extremely sinful (Burkhart 1989: 155). The wedding date was set in consultation with soothsayers and divinatory calendars – even a marriage would have its fate, and it made sense to choose a propitious date to begin the venture.

The wedding was celebrated with a feast held in the home of the bride's parents, and was as festive as they could afford, with wealthier families laying on luxuries like chocolate, flowers, tobacco, and tamales (Sahagún 1969). Guests brought gifts and made speeches to the couple, emphasizing the importance of duty and filial piety. The party then moved to the groom's house, and

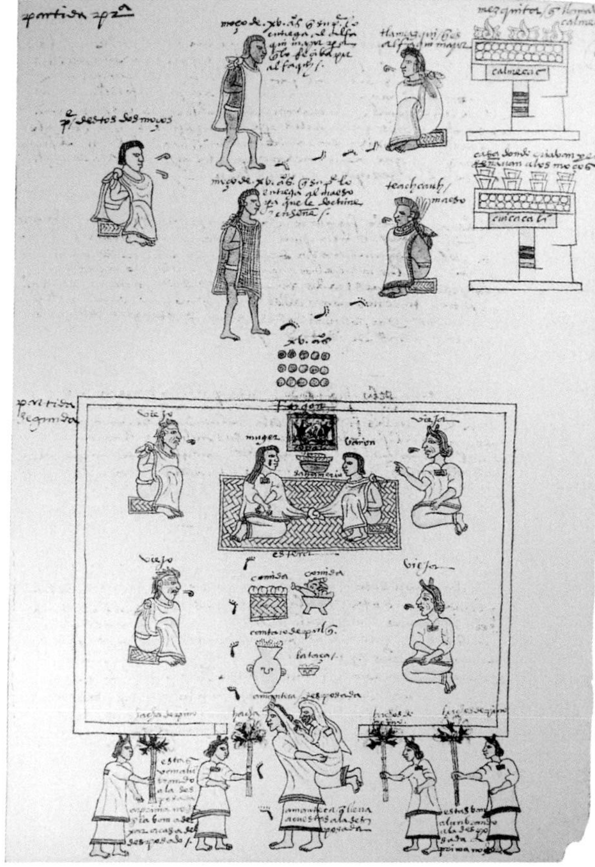

here the knot was tied [18.5]. Until the birth of their first child, the young couple lived with their parents, usually his.

Sex The Aztecs would appreciate this discussion of sex as a subset of marriage, because they believed that lasciviousness was a pathway to perdition, and invoked the death penalty against those guilty of adultery, sodomy, or incest. Young people were supposed to remain chaste, because unmarried teen sex was thought to lead to male impotence and unleash female insatiability (Ortíz de Montellano 1990). Women brought shame on their families if they were not virgins at marriage.

18.5 *(Opposite) "Tying the knot" in Aztec society meant just that: at the wedding, the matchmakers symbolically united the couple by joining his cloak and her skirt* (Codex Mendoza *1992: 4: 127). After receiving gifts of clothing from their new mothers-in-law, the couple retired to a private room for four days, to consummate the marriage, while the matchmakers celebrated by drinking* pulque. *The party resumed on the fifth day, with more feasting, gifts, and speeches. The upper drawing shows a man delivering his 15-year-old sons to their schools.*

Yet, in spite of what seem to be rather heavy penalties for stepping out of line, the Aztecs clearly enjoyed sex. Their attitude could be called "earthy," in part because the Nahuatl word for sex meant "what belongs to the surface of the earth" (López Austin 1993: 67). The pleasure of sex is indicated by the Nahuatl verb *yecoa*, which meant "to taste, sample food or drink; to copulate with someone" (Karttunen 1983: 337). And the association of food and sex is strengthened by the Aztecs' use of aphrodisiacs – to secure someone's affections, serve chocolate to which ground-up "enchanted" maize grains have been added (Ruíz de Alarcón 1984 [1629]). But here two valuable resources, time and cacao beans, are being devoted to pleasure, and this would look like waste to the Aztecs; in Nahuatl many words describing pleasure convey the sense of wasting time as well as enjoying one's self (Karttunen 1983: 8). For the Aztecs, a big problem with eroticism was that it deflected energy that could have been more profitably (and less dangerously) spent on more serious enterprises.

Patron deities watched over sex. Xochiquetzal and Tlazolteotl represented, respectively, woman youthful and fertile, and aging and wise (see box, pp. 404–405). Macuilxochitl/Xochipilli was a patron of palace people, and thus he was patron of such adornments of palace life such as feasting, gambling, flowers, hallucinogens. Sexual abstinence was required during periods honoring him, and if palace people violated this rule, he "visited upon them ... piles, hemorrhoids, suppurating genitals, disease of the groin" (Sahagún 1970: 31).

Some Texcocan sources recount extremely harsh punishments for minor flirtatious infractions — a daughter of Texcocan king Nezahualpilli was condemned to death for talking to a boy, and one of his sons executed for sexual relations with (or possibly only joking with) one of the royal wives [**18.6**]. This is an interesting case of problems with interpreting the ethnohistorical record, because the seemingly independent accounts are cognates of each other, nearly identical variants of the same story. These morality tales may seem to indicate a repressively grim fate for any Aztec who ignored the perils of the slippery slope, but a closer look at the documents reveals not only their repetitive nature but also that they were collected in the mid-to-late 16th century from the last elderly members of a dying Texcocan aristocracy, as they looked back fondly upon what they recalled as the strict morals of the lost empire of their youth (Karttunen and Lockhart 1987: 10).

Thus scholars who generalize from these extreme examples in order to prove that Aztec society was repressively puritanical, or even misogynistic, may miss the overall perspective provided by many graphic and written records from the Early Colonial period that indicate reasonable tolerance of hedonistic behavior, and also free participation by women in public society. However, moderation and circumspection were highly valued, and thus sexual pleasure was best enjoyed by adults, after marriage.

18.6 *Adulterers were dealt with harshly, by being stoned to death* (Codex Mendoza *1992: 4: 147). The stylized glyphs near the couple's heads represent stones. Thieves and some drunkards were also condemned to death by stoning. Elderly people were granted the comfort of intoxication from* pulque, *without fear of punishment.*

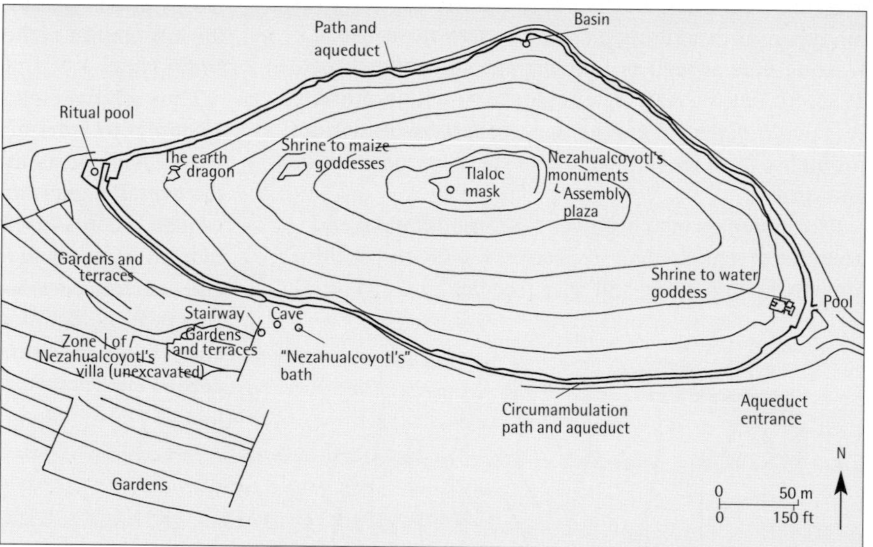

18.7, 18.8 *Texcotzingo was Nezahualcoyotl's royal retreat, an entire hill 5 km east of Texcoco in the Basin of Mexico that was so fabulously designed that Motecuzoma I had no choice but to develop a huge garden at Huaxtépec in the Valley of Morelos in order to keep up appearances. The hill of Texcotzingo (at left in the photo) was remodeled so that facilities for royal visits – residential rooms, meeting rooms, shrines, baths – were cut into its cliffs; some of these are illustrated in the plan. Bas-reliefs sculpted into the cliff faces told a geohistorical story of Nezahualcoyotl's domain and all the living things in it. Then the whole hill-sized sculptural and architectural masterpiece was transformed into a fountain by bringing a stream of water from a spring higher in the mountains to a point near the top of the hill by constructing a solid aqueduct nearly 8 km (nearly 5 miles) long, in places nearly 50 m (c. 150 ft) high. The flow of water rushed down the hill in a set of ingenious channels, forming waterfalls and filling three rock-cut circular baths, watering gardens of exotic plants, and eventually feeding the terraced agricultural fields below.*

census revealed the flexibility of the Aztec co-residential group; of this *barrio*'s 128 multiple-family households (1,056 people in all), most were bound by consanguineal ties among male kin, usually brothers. Only a few of the men were polygynous, and these were nobles with the title *tecuhtli*

(lord) or other high-ranking officials. The value of the multiple-family household as a working unit is demonstrated by Molotla; the land is listed in the household head's name, but all members cooperate to produce the items required by tribute and needed by the families.

Though Huaxtépec gave this province its name, the town's ruler was not a paramount *huetlatoani* for the region. As a city-state capital, Huaxtépec's obligations to the Aztec empire and tributes required were similar to those of other Morelos polities, with one important exception. In the 1460s, Motecuzoma I decided to establish for himself a pleasure garden there. Nezahualcoyotl had dedicated his great dynastic retreat at Texcotzingo in *c.* 1460, so Motecuzoma may have been indulging in a bit of elite status rivalry, combined with conspicuous consumption (Evans 2000). Texcotzingo featured rock-cut round baths with magnificent views of the Basin of Mexico [**18.7, 18.8**], but it was, after all, in the high-altitude environment of the Basin, with attendant limitations upon the kinds of plants that could survive freezing winters.

Huaxtépec and Aztec Gardens Huaxtépec, on the other hand, was tropical, and Motecuzoma could draw upon a much larger range of cultivated plants to develop a garden so beautiful that one of the conquistadores called it "the best that I have ever seen in all my life, and so said ... our Cortés" (Díaz 1956 [1560s]: 375). Aztec gardens were among the most beautiful creations of this culture, and although many were described – and claimed – by the Spaniards, not a single Aztec garden plan remains. We know, from the many gardening and flower terms in Nahuatl, that Aztec interest in horticulture was ardent, and today, decorative plants originally cultivated in Mesoamerica – marigolds, dahlias, cosmos, to name just a few – have become part of the world's supply of beauty.

Aztec lords so valued beautiful plants that sumptuary laws came to embrace them, and commoners were forbidden from cultivating some of them. Professional gardeners were respected artisans with effective techniques. When Motecuzoma I claimed special plants in tribute, the plants were brought to Tenochtitlan "in great quantities, with the earth still about the roots, wrapped in fine cloth" and were then "taken to Huaxtépec and planted around the springs" (Durán 1994: 244–245). Even more important, economically, were medicinal plants. Mesoamericans developed a large and effective pharmacopoeia, formulae for medicines concocted from animals, minerals, and especially plants (Sahagún 1963 [1569]; Cruz 1991 [1552]). The Spaniards recognized the economic importance of these medicines; in 1570, Huaxtépec was visited by the great natural historian Francisco Hernández, sent by Phillip II to study its resources and secure valuable plants (Hernández 1888 [1571]). Aztecs may also be credited with developing the world's first botanical gardens, places designed to display an encyclopedic array of plants. The Old World had many great gardens, but Europe's earliest botanical gardens were established in Italy in the 1540s, probably inspired by Aztec prototypes.

Guerrero

Aztec conquests in eastern Guerrero began with Itzcoatl and were hard fought, because this region was so strategically important as a bulwark against the expanding domain of the Tarascans. Western Guerrero had come under Tarascan control as early as the 1370s. Eastern Guerrero as a region was far more oriented toward the Central Highlands: eastern Guerrero and western Morelos had long had significant cultural interchange – in the Formative period, Teopantecuanitlan and Chalcatzingo had shown signs of affinity.

Guerrero not only had the usual attractive *tierra caliente* products like cotton and cacao, it also had mineral wealth, in ores, finished gold and copper products, and carved stone objects. Mezcala-style masks were among the precious goods cached in Tenochtitlan's Templo Mayor, as its rebuildings progressed. In addition, Guerrero's tribute lists included staple crops such as maize and beans, because some of its provinces were close enough to the Basin of Mexico to supply such basic goods efficiently.

Tlachco, just west of Cuauhnahuac, became a tributary province in Motecuzoma I's time, as did Tepecoacuilco, a large region that included Alahuiztlan, the most important salt-producing town in eastern Guerrero. Further south, Quiauhteopan and Tlacozauhtitlan were conquests of Motecuzoma I and Nezahualcoyotl, respectively. Further to the southeast lay Tlapan, which was subdued after repeated visits by Aztec armies, including in the time of Motecuzoma II (Gutiérrez 2003).

Along the coast of Guerrero, the Aztecs conquered the tributary province of Cihuatlán in the late 15th century, under Ahuitzotl. Salt, gold, and cacao were the important products that drew Aztec interest to this area. Other adjacent regions along the coast were also conquered at this time, but seem to have had a strategic province relationship, in that they were defeated by Ahuitzotl's armies, and regularly supplied various goods and services, but are not listed on tribute rolls.

1450s: Disasters and Development in the Basin of Mexico

Because the Basin's lake system was a bowl into which all runoff drained, chemical salts were concentrated in the largest, deepest part: central Lake Texcoco. This meant that if heavy runoff brought floods, the rising level of the central lake would pollute the surrounding freshwater lakes and marshes, and inundate the marshy islands of Tenochtitlan-Tlatelolco. This happened in 1449, during Motecuzoma I's reign, and the costs were not only in rebuilding the city, but also in reestablishing the *chinampa* systems and then protecting the whole western lagoon – *chinampas*, city, and the many other small towns around it – from another such disaster.

Protection was secured by a system of dikes. The most extensive of these [**19.14**] was designed and built in about 1450 under the supervision of Nezahualcoyotl of Texcoco and Motecuzoma I of Tenochtitlan. It ran for over 14 km (9 miles) north to south, was about 8 m (26 ft) across and 4 m (13 ft) high (Lombardo de Ruiz 1973:116) and closed off all of western Lake Texcoco [**18.9**]. This not only protected the city, but also permitted reclamation of damaged *chinampas* and development of new ones.

Scarcely had the effects of the flood been cleared away when ominous signs of a new disaster appeared, four years of exceptionally cold weather that resulted in insufficient harvests by 1452. The famine grew so severe that 1454, One Rabbit in the Aztec calendar, moved into the Aztec lexicon as a synonym for famine: "the people were one-rabbited ... corn had stopped growing" (Annals of Cuauhtitlan 1992 [*c.* 1570]: 107). The interplay between culture and its ecological setting is always heightened by stress. The steady growth of the population of the Basin during the Late Postclassic owed much to the rise in available food provided by hydrological projects such as *chinampa* development.

Thus the 1450s became a legendary time of famine and sorrow for the Basin of Mexico, as successive years of crop failures left many in the western and southern Basin gripped by ceaseless hunger. Climate conditions in the Basin of Mexico may have been caused, or exacerbated, by very distant volcanic activity, such as the eruption of Arenal in Costa Rica in 1446, and even by the eruptions of Kelut, in Indonesia, in 1450 and 1451 (Gill and Keating 2002). The maguey farmers in the northern and eastern Basin fared better, because maguey will continue to produce its sap regardless of inclement weather. This made for a meager, marginally nutritious diet, but it far exceeded the caloric budgets of the farmers of the southern Basin.

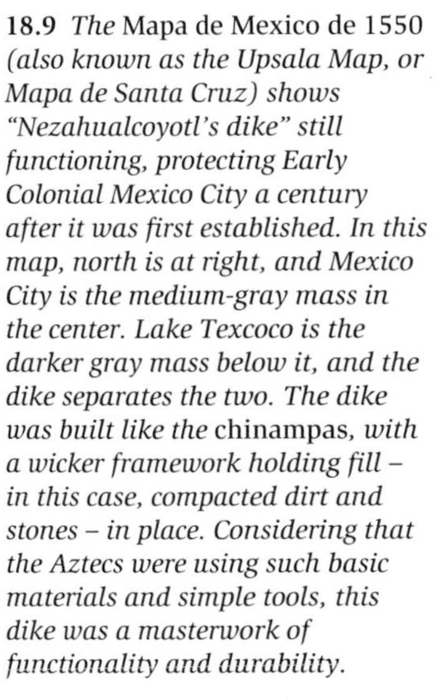

18.9 *The* Mapa de Mexico de 1550 *(also known as the Upsala Map, or Mapa de Santa Cruz) shows "Nezahualcoyotl's dike" still functioning, protecting Early Colonial Mexico City a century after it was first established. In this map, north is at right, and Mexico City is the medium-gray mass in the center. Lake Texcoco is the darker gray mass below it, and the dike separates the two. The dike was built like the* chinampas, *with a wicker framework holding fill – in this case, compacted dirt and stones – in place. Considering that the Aztecs were using such basic materials and simple tools, this dike was a masterwork of functionality and durability.*

Famines are usually caused by a combination of ecological and social factors (Hassig 1986), and in this case the primary cause was environmental: unseasonal frosts killed the crops before they could mature. Kings opened the granaries, but in time, even the emergency supplies were gone. The social factor that contributed to the disaster was pre-Columbian transport technology, which limited the area from which relief supplies could be brought. Those who could not leave the Basin were trapped without food. Those who did leave moved to the Gulf lowlands, Totonacapan, "the land of food" and sold themselves and their families into slavery in order to survive.

The ecological crisis bore several kinds of cultural fruit. The Nahua-speaking population in the Gulf lowlands was increased, adding to the lively ethnic mix of that region. And the Triple Alliance rulers seem to have become determined to avoid another brush with life-threatening food shortages – at least for themselves and their families. The next stage of conquests pushed Aztec hegemony further into *tierra caliente*, especially the Gulf lowlands, securing a refuge in time of need.

It was during this time that Motecuzoma I began several ambitious public works projects, probably with the intention of distributing food from the royal granaries in exchange for labor. One project was the third rebuilding of the Templo Mayor (Stage IV; see box, pp. 462–454), with the sculpture of Coyolxauhqui embedded at the foot of the stairs [**17.6**], and stone sculptures of standard-bearers resting against the Stage III stairs [**17.7**], as an offering buried during the rebuilding. Under Nezahualcoyotl's direction, a new and enlarged aqueduct and causeway was begun to supply Tenochtitlan with water from Chapultepec. Motecuzoma I also directed work at Chapultepec, instituting what would become a regular practice of sculpting portraits of the Tenochca kings on the face of the hill.

Palaces and Government

Another project involved expanding the royal palace. Motecuzoma I lived in a palace complex that had been established by Itzcoatl. It covered a large block west of the Templo Mayor Precinct, *c.* 180 by 190 m (591 by 623 ft), and may have been the first royal residential and administrative establishment that was located outside the temple precinct – the first rulers may have lived in modest buildings around the original temple.

As the wealth and complexity of the tribute empire increased, so did the size and elaboration of the palaces. The Nahuatl word for palace is *tecpan calli* – "lord-place house" – usually shortened to *tecpan*. While the English word "palace" is derived from the Palatine Hill in Rome, where Emperor Augustus lived, the Nahuatl *tecpan* was, literally, the place where the lord was, and the commonest use of the word was in reference to the administrative-residential palace, the seat of local government, and home of the lord and his household. But "*tecpan*" was also used for pleasure palaces, and could even describe the temporary encampments of Aztec kings on military campaigns or on pilgrimages.

The *tecpan* had a distinctive layout that reflected the Aztec style of government. Coming in from the town plaza, you would enter a large courtyard, and across the courtyard would face a raised dais room, open to the courtyard, where the ruler and his closest associates would hold court (see box, pp. 482–483). Nobles and their attendants would gather in the courtyard – one of the privileges of high rank was to go to court every day to converse with other nobles, partake of food and drink, enjoy the entertainments of musicians and acrobats and jesters, and, when governmental issues were on the agenda, listen to speeches and perhaps offer an opinion in an oration.

In 1455, the great hunger over, the Aztecs celebrated their New Fire Ceremony, the Binding of the Years. This event took place every 52 years, counted out in four groups of 13 years, and as year One Rabbit ended, and Two Reed began, the world was at a critical junction, and the continuance of the sun's bounty was dependent upon the piety of the people and the skill of sacrificial priests, such as those atop Cerro de la Estrella near Culhuacan. People everywhere extinguished hearth fires and waited in the dark until the new fire was started by the priests, who fed it immediately with the still-beating heart of a sacrificial victim. Priests lit torches from the new fire and took the fire to the temples and from there it was used to relight all the other hearth fires. The Aztecs could look forward to a new period of prosperity and challenges, but by the time of the next New Fire Ceremony, 1507, alien invaders would be moving into their world.

A New Period of Aztec Expansion: East to the Gulf Lowlands

With the years of famine behind them, the Triple Alliance began extending the tributary empire. They moved toward the northern and north-central Gulf lowlands, and then south, to the Mixteca Alta and Valley of Oaxaca. In both sets of campaigns, the precipitating factor that justified aggression was the murder of Aztec merchants. *Pochteca* traders were constantly ranging over a very large area, and part of their mission was to serve not only as purveyors and securers of goods, but also as diplomatic negotiators, spies, and even advance troops for future Aztec takeovers. These extra-mercantile features of their work must have been common knowledge among the peoples they visited. Thus it is likely that, at times, *pochteca* merchants were killed, though it becomes such a common excuse for Aztec military action that merchants must have worried about being killed by *agents provocateurs* among their own people in order to justify expansion of the tributary empire.

Gulf Lowlands, Central and North

A pass through the mountains northeast of Oaxaca led directly to the south-central Gulf lowlands and the important trading center of Tochtepec. This was the most important town in a densely settled region where cotton, cacao, rubber, and elite goods like gold, greenstones, and feathers were

AZTEC PALACES

ARRIVING IN TENOCHTITLAN for the first time in November 1519, Cortés was installed by Motecuzoma II in the palace once occupied by his great-grandfather, Motecuzoma I: " a very large and beautiful house which had been very well prepared to accommodate us. There he ... led me to a great room facing the courtyard through which we had entered. And he bade me sit on a very rich throne..." (Cortés: 1986 [1519–1526]: 85).

Thus Cortés described the experience of moving through the courtyard to the dais room, where he was invited to occupy the privileged place of an Aztec lord. Motecuzoma then retired to his own *tecpan*-palace, a larger establishment nearby. About these Aztec *huetecpans* ("great palaces") we have relatively little archaeological evidence; they lie buried beneath the modern city, and in fact Motecuzoma II's *huetecpan* now underlies the modern Palacio Nacional of Mexico, on the east side of the Zócalo (main plaza) in Mexico City.

Cortés and his men lived for months as Motecuzoma II's guests in the *huetecpan* that had belonged to Motecuzoma I and then to Axayacatl, and is often referred to as "Axayacatl's palace." Spanish accounts of this and other *tecpans* describe royal residences of great extent and luxury. At "Axayacatl's palace" there were accommodations for the Spaniards, who numbered about 300 men, and many other rooms, including "great oratories for [Motecuzoma II's] idols, and a secret chamber where he kept bars and jewels of gold, which was the treasure that he had inherited from his father Axayaca, and he never disturbed it" (Díaz del Castillo 1956: 194). Motecuzoma should have enjoyed its use while he had it – the Spaniards, seeing the fresh plaster of a recently-sealed door, broke through and looted the treasure soon after their arrival.

Nezahualcoyotl's *huetecpan* in Texcoco may have encompassed nearly 1 sq. km (821.5 by 1,037 m, 2,695 by 3,402 ft [Alva Ixtlilxóchitl 1985: II: 93]). Texcoco was a much less densely populated city than was Tenochtitlan, and the complex apparently included a ball court, and the town marketplace as its largest courtyard. The *Mapa Quinatzin* illustration, dating

18.10, 18.11 *The only complete Aztec* tecpan *to be excavated in the Basin of Mexico is one of the smallest, at the village of Cihuatecpan in the upper Teotihuacan Valley. The plan and reconstruction drawing show the main courtyard surrounded by suites of rooms, with the dais room across from the building's entrance, and service yards in the back.*

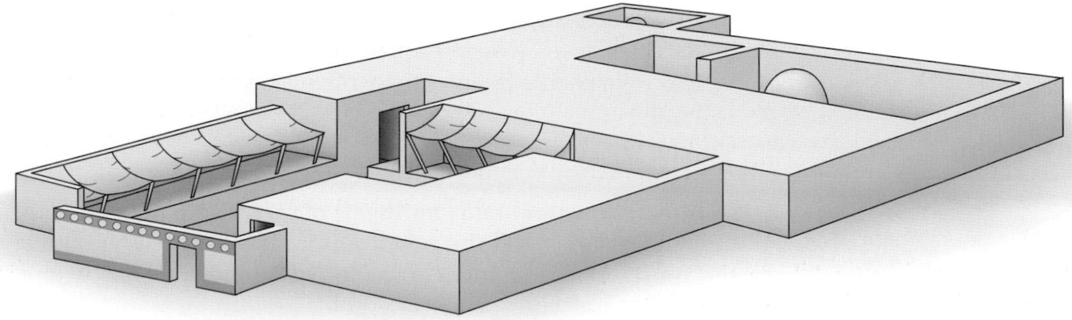

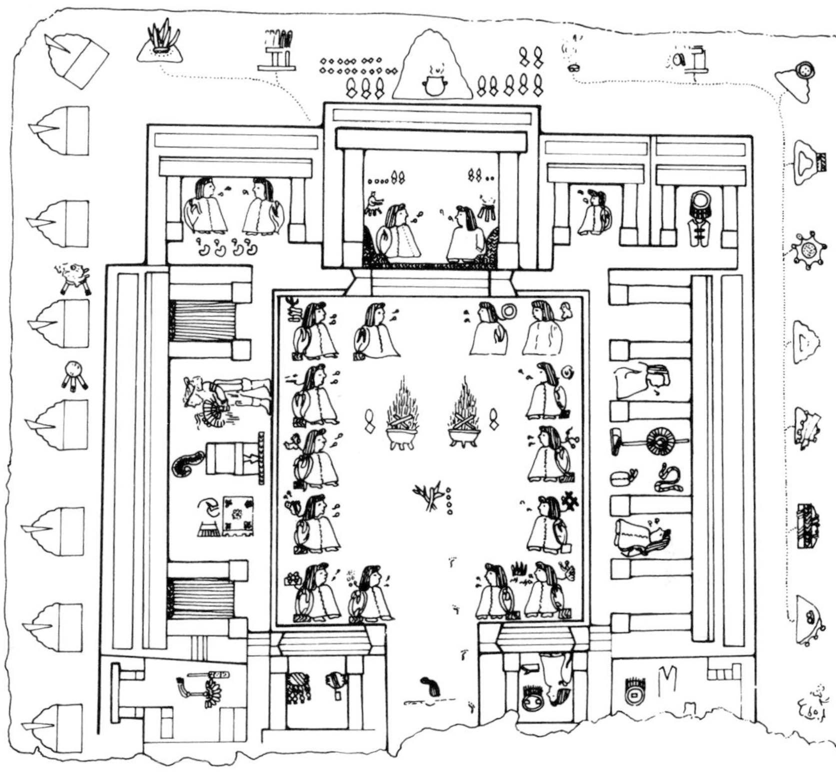

18.12 *At Nezahualcoyotl's* tecpan, *the ruler is in the dais room, facing his son Nezahualpilli (on the left). His lords are in the main courtyard, and the functions of the rooms around it are described in glosses and suggested by symbols, indicating that they are judicial chambers, accommodations for visiting nobles, and store rooms for musical instruments and military equipment.*

from 1541, shows the main courtyard with an assembly of all the tlatoque and calpixqui governors of the city states in Nezahualcoyotl's domain [**18.12**].

The 50 or so *tecpans* in the Basin of Mexico's city-state capitals were much more modest, measuring about 50 m (*c.* 164 ft) on a side, according to limited available archaeological evidence (Evans 2004). An extensive set of residential rooms excavated at Chiconautla in the Teotihuacan Valley is thought to represent part of the *tecpan* (Vaillant and Sanders 2000). In addition, there would have been 300 to 500 smaller *tecpans* in the largest of the Basin's farming villages, and these would provide administration for surrounding smaller villages (Evans 2004). At Cihuatecpan, a maguey-farming village in the upper Teotihuacan Valley, a residence measuring about 25 by 25 m (82 by 82 ft) had a plan conforming to the familiar *tecpan* layout [**18.10, 18.11**]. While it was minuscule compared with big-city *tecpans*, it was three times the size of the next largest house in the village. This size and layout reflect the community-wide functions performed there, and the larger, probably polygynous family of the headman. There are four suites of habitation rooms, plus a small kitchen near the building entrance. Walled yards in the back held two sweat baths, and fragments of figurines of Xochiquetzal found there suggest that the palace women invoked this fertility goddess as they eased labor pains in the sweat baths. Xochiquetzal's other domain, textile arts, was also evidenced by the building's many spindle whorls, for spinning both cotton and maguey (Evans 1991).

Aztec palaces at all levels show remarkable similarities, reflecting the societal value of rhetorical exchange in the course of resolving problems facing the rulers. At each level, the lords met with their constituents in the *tecpan* where the lord's rulership was embedded in the architectural form of the building, in the dais room above the main courtyard. Yet the role of the constituents was also part of the structure, and assembling in the courtyard was clearly essential to their role as "the speaker"'s audience, and, sometimes, as orators themselves.

available and would be demanded in tribute. The conquest of Tochtepec is credited to Nezahualcoyotl by Texcocan chroniclers, and to Motecuzoma I in Tenochca documents.

Another south-central Gulf lowlands province brought into the empire at this time centered upon Cotaxtla, 92 km (57 miles) north of Tochtepec. Again, this seems to have been a victory in which both Texcocan and Tenochca forces played decisive roles. Rebellions there required reconquest by Axayacatl, and Motecuzoma II placed there a *calpixqui* named Teniltzin, who would later meet Cortés. These regions were rich in food – crops and game – and tributes included cotton, cacao, and elite ornaments. Archaeological and ethnohistorical evidence indicates that during the Postclassic period, this landscape was thickly settled (see, e.g., Garraty and Stark 2002), but populations declined drastically in the 16th century as the result of diseases introduced by the European intrusion.

Totonacapan Throughout much of Mesoamerican culture history, the south-central and north-central Gulf lowlands were ethnically distinct from each other, and geographically divided by the Sierra de Chiconquiaco, a spur of mountains that runs from the Sierra Madre Oriental down to the sea. In the Late Postclassic, the Sierra de Chiconquiaco and the Gulf lowlands on either side of it became the region known as Totonacapan, because of the dominance of the Totonac peoples who had occupied it since the beginning of the Early Postclassic.

Totonacapan extends up to the Cazones River in the north, thus encompassing the Late Classic–Early Postclassic area where El Tajín held sway. The southern limits of Totonacapan are less well agreed upon, with some scholars including much of the south-central Gulf lowlands (Medellín Zenil 1960; Solís 1993) and others including only the northern portion, beginning at the Antigua River. Archaeological remains in this whole general area indicate a dense and ethnically diverse population, Totonac ascendancy notwithstanding. The ceramic assemblages are a mix of Totonac styles and those characteristic of Mixteca-Puebla style, the latter reflecting the Postclassic influx of Nahua-speaking migrants from Puebla and Tlaxcala (Daneels 1997).

The south-central Gulf lowlands provinces sent riches to the Aztec empire. A land of abundant local food resources, it also supplied cotton products, feathers, rubber, gold, tobacco, and cacao (Smith and Berdan 1996: 285–287). The region also would have been a source of the tropical plants prized by the Aztec emperors, both for their gardens and as luxury items. Vanilla was first cultivated in the tropical New World, and was not grown elsewhere until the mid-19th century. The Totonacs are credited with learning the secret of producing a perfumed flavoring agent from this, the only fruit-bearing member of the orchid family – fermenting the beans results in the unique taste that is now so widely used.

Zempoala Zempoala was regarded as the most important Totonac center, and at the time of Spanish conquest covered an area of about 8 sq. km (3.2

sq. miles) and had a population of about 30,000 (Solanes and Vela 1993). The site's civic-ceremonial center covered 7.5 hectares (*c.* 19 acres) and was surrounded by a crenellated wall, which enclosed administrative buildings and a large pyramid.

Zempoala was the target of Aztec conquests, first by Motecuzoma I and later by Motecuzoma II. The fact that the province is regarded as "strategic" rather than "tributary" reflects its uneasy relationship with the Aztec empire (Smith and Berdan 1996: 287), which may have been abetted by the Tlaxcalans, foes of the Aztecs. Totonac hostility toward the Aztecs and their demands became apparent to Cortés in his conversations with Zempoala's "Fat Cacique" ("*cacique*" is a Caribbean Arawak term for chief that the Spaniards used; pron. cah*see*kay). This indicated to the Spaniards that they might be able to develop important alliances with some native groups in their confrontation with the Aztecs, and the Totonacs were their first allies.

About 30 km (19 miles) north of Zempoala was one of its dependencies, the fortified site of Quiahuiztlan, in a dramatic hillside setting overlooking the sea. Quiahuiztlan's cultural importance is due to its fortified location, but it is of archaeological interest because of a series of small masonry tombs in the shape of houses, known only from this region. Some scholars believe they date from the Early Colonial period, while others put them in the Late Postclassic.

Misantla Extending over the southern portion of the north-central Gulf lowlands, this province encompassed environmental zones ranging from wooded foothills through rich *tierra caliente* farmlands to the coast. Armies of Nezahualpilli and Axayacatl conquered this region, but its tributes were minimal, not listed on tribute rolls.

Tlatauhquitepec This was another of the provinces that encircled Tlaxcala. Conquered by Nezahualcoyotl and Motecuzoma I, its tributes featured woven cotton goods as well as other products. Unrest in this Totonac province is indicated by the presence, in one of its capitals, of an Aztec military governor.

Tetela Another link in the circum-Tlaxcalan line of provinces, tiny Tetela was high in the mountains of the Sierra Madre Oriental. Its rulers were descended from Chichimecs who arrived in about AD 1200 (Smith and Berdan 1996: 289), and Nahuatl was the dominant language. Tetela seems to have enjoyed relatively friendly relations with the Aztec capitals; the Mexica armed them against the Tlaxcalans, whom the Tetelans regarded as their enemies.

Huatusco About 75 km (47 miles) southwest of Zempoala lay Huatusco, a tributary province on the eastern side of the Sierra Madre Oriental conquered jointly by Texcoco and Tenochtitlan. Again, the tributes featured cotton and cacao. The site of Huatusco was fortified, with a pyramid [**18.13**] and administrative *tecpan* built atop a hill (Medellín Zenil 1952).

18.13 *The Aztec pyramids at Huatusco (above) and Castillo de Teayo [18.14] are among the only remaining structures of this type that are reasonably intact. Huatusco's pyramid was part of an extensive set of architectural remains, platforms and rooms, that may have included an elite residence. The whole complex was surrounded by an enclosing – and fortifying – wall (Umberger 1996: 164).*

Huatusco was another of the series of provinces of the Aztec empire that encircled Tlaxcala, the large region north of the plain of Puebla. Tlaxcala and Puebla will be discussed in greater depth in Chapter 19. Tlaxcala represented the largest and most stubbornly unconquerable area adjacent to the Basin of Mexico, and Aztec control of the Gulf lowlands was that much more costly for having to work around this huge lacuna and also for having to counteract Tlaxcalan efforts to undermine the loyalty, or at least quiescence, of already-conquered provinces.

Xalapa West of Zempoala in the Sierra Madre Oriental, Xalapa was another link in the Aztecs' chain around Tlaxcala, but one which was forged late, not until the time of Ahuitzotl and Motecuzoma II. Ethnically a mixture of Nahuatl-speaking and Totonac populations, Xalapa was one of the empire's "strategic" provinces (Smith and Berdan 1996), acknowledging the authority of the Aztecs and sending them regular gifts, but not listed on the tribute rolls. It extended from the Sierra toward the northwest, into the north-central Gulf lowlands.

Tochpan This tributary province extended from the Sierra down to the coast of the north-central Gulf lowlands, and was largely *tierra caliente*, producing cotton and cacao as well as crops and fish. Woven cotton was an important tribute item, as were greenstones, feathers, and gold. The city of Tochpan was near the coast, and an important market, visited by *pochteca* merchants, was held there. Conquest of the province began under Nezahualcoyotl and Motecuzoma I, and continued with Axayacatl and Motecuzoma II. Unrest in this area is evidenced by the presence of Aztec military governors and garrisons.

In the years of famine in the Basin of Mexico, the Gulf lowlands were a place of refuge for the Aztecs, and some sources indicate that colonies of people from the Basin may have settled there. One likely candidate for such a colony is Castillo de Teayo. This site in the Tochpan province was founded in the early Postclassic, and "is the only place in the empire with a full range of Aztec-related material remains – architecture, sculptures, and, seemingly, ceramics" (Umberger 1996: 178). The many sculptures found here are locally made but of Aztec design, depicting standard-bearers and deities such as the Feathered Serpent and the Flayed Skin God (Xipe Totec).

Atlán This landlocked tributary province on the eastern slopes of the Sierra Madre was ethnically Huastec, with smaller ethnic components of speakers of Otomí, Nahuatl, and Totonac. Conquests by Axayacatl and Motecuzoma II had to be backed up by the establishment of garrisons and military governors.

Tzicoac Another tributary province that extended from the Sierra Madre east into *tierra caliente*, this Huastec region was conquered by Nezahualcoyotl and Motecuzoma I, with follow-up efforts by Axayacatl, Tizoc, Ahuitzotl, and Motecuzoma II. Supplying woven and raw cotton and other goods to the empire, its history of repeated conquests and distance from the Basin of Mexico, from which it was separated by the never-conquered Metztitlan region, indicate relatively weak integration into the empire.

Huexotla The strategic province of Huexotla was on Metztitlan's northern boundary. Another of the provinces that extended down the eastern slope of the Sierras, Huexotla consisted largely of *tierra caliente* suited to growing cotton, some of which was sent to the Aztec empire. The conquest record of this province by the Aztecs is unclear; scholars have identified efforts by Ahuitzotl and Motecuzoma II to keep the province on friendly terms.

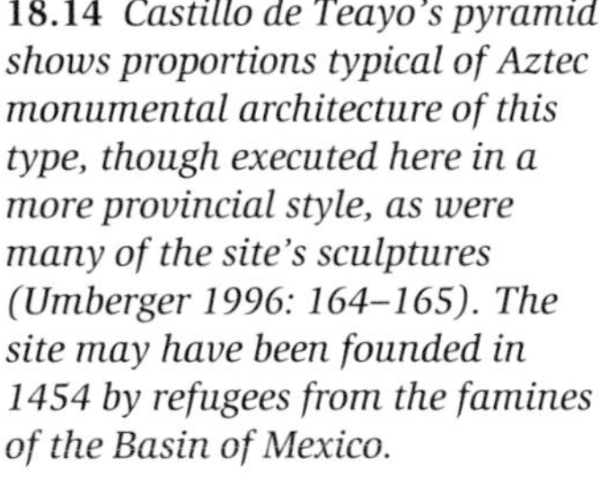

18.14 *Castillo de Teayo's pyramid shows proportions typical of Aztec monumental architecture of this type, though executed here in a more provincial style, as were many of the site's sculptures (Umberger 1996: 164–165). The site may have been founded in 1454 by refugees from the famines of the Basin of Mexico.*

Oxitipan A small isolated region well to the north of Huexotla, Oxitipan was the most northerly outpost of the Aztec empire, a tributary province with a poorly documented record of conquest. It was Huastec, and its tribute included woven cotton and live eagles.

18.15 *This page from the* Codex Mendoza *shows three ways in which relations between the Aztecs and their neighbors could sour. The top row of figures features the central figure of a provincial king having been taken into custody by Mexica soldiers under the authority of their commanding officer, at left. The king's wife and son (at right) are also bound. The center row of figures shows the murder of Aztec merchants (a merchant's pack is just above them) and, at right, the local* cacique *being condemned for permitting this act. At bottom, three archers ask for trouble as they take aim at four Aztec diplomats* (Codex Mendoza *1992: 4: 137).*

The Mixteca and Oaxaca Under Aztec Rule

Motecuzoma's reign encompassed conquests far to the south of the Basin of Mexico, moving into the ancient homelands of the Mixtecs and Zapotecs.

The Mixteca Region In 1458, *pochteca* merchants trading in Coixtlahuaca, a city on the northeastern edge of the Mixteca Alta, were murdered. The Mexica responded by marching south with an army of 200,000 men; they conquered that city, expanding their conquests over a large area to the west in the late 15th and early 16th centuries. Coixtlahuaca was a famous trading center, the gateway to the Mixteca from Puebla and the northern Tehuacán Valley. As the capital of an Aztec tributary province, it was responsible for sending to Tenochtitlan such expensive and labor-intensive items as decorated warriors' costumes, greenstone beads, gold dust, and cochineal dye.

Cochineal is an unprepossessing source of wealth: a scale insect that grows on the nopal cactus, a small smear of white bug on a prickly plant adapted to harsh, arid conditions. Yet the deep red dye that these insects produced was one of the most important products exported to Spain in the Early Colonial period (Donkin 1977). Processing cochineal insects into dye was a very laborious process, and thus cochineal dye, like other products required in tribute, harnessed the labor of the Mixtec population in service to the luxurious tastes of the Aztec rulers.

Mixteca city-states had considerable population to draw upon. Coixtlahuaca and its tributaries comprised about 12,000 people, and Tlaxiaco, Yanhuitlan, and Teposcolula were even larger (Lind 2000). These capitals were generally located on hilltops, and featured large, well-built palaces, temples, and plazas used as marketplaces. The commoners lived in modest houses on terraced slopes below the cities, and probably had local organization similar to the *calpulli*.

As we know from previous discussion, the Mixtec city-states had ancient traditions of kingship. The Spaniards called these kingdoms by the term "cacicazgos" – hispanicizing the Arawak "cacique" into a word for the polity itself (Marcus and Zeitlin 1994). The ruling elite carefully maintained their histories and kept track of calendrics in a set of codices. Some of these surviving books, dating from around AD 1500 and including information going back centuries, are among the only pre-Columbian texts extant today, and include the *Borgia* (1993) and

Nuttall (1975) codices (Kellogg 2001: 241). The genealogical codices were apparently displayed in the palaces, "fastened ... along the length of the rooms of the lords ... valuing and referring to them in assemblies" (Burgoa 1934: 210) and also being used as scripts for theatrical performances before assembled nobles (Pohl 1994a, 1994b).

Mixteca-Puebla style was expressed in codices, ceramics, jewelry, and other products of the Mixtec regions and Puebla, and they represent some of the most sophisticated products of pre-Columbian Mesoamerica, and thus it is not surprising that the Aztecs pursued conquests in the Mixteca regions. Mixtec artisans themselves were prized, and the Texcocans arranged for a group of them to move to Texcoco in order that they might permanently live there, contributing sophistication to Acolhua society and making Texcoco famed as a center of learning. As specialists in writing as well as fine artisanship they were often in charge of scribal duties, highly influential positions because they kept records and interpreted them.

Oaxaca The Mixtecs had established themselves among the Zapotecs in the Valley of Oaxaca 200 years before Motecuzoma I's armies arrived to begin the process of adding this region to their provinces. Military actions by the Aztecs in this region extended into the reign of Motecuzoma II. The Valley of Oaxaca was politically balkanized, and the Mixtecs and Zapotecs, while dominant, were only two of many ethnic groups jostling for territory as population rose in the Late Postclassic (Marcus and Flannery 2000).

Monte Albán was probably the largest city in the Oaxaca Valley, with 14,000 residents (Blanton 2001), but neither it, nor any other center, served as the region's capital. The main acropolis was deserted, unused except for the reuse of Zapotec tombs by Mixtec nobles – such as the rich burial found in Tomb 7. Population ranged down the terraces to the plain.

In the course of their conquests in the region, the Aztecs established a military garrison at the town of Oaxaca after Aztec merchants were killed there. Chroniclers recount that Aztec retribution for these murders was so thorough that the local population was destroyed. Tlacaelel proposed that the city of Oaxaca should be resettled by people from the Basin of Mexico: "people should gather from all the provinces to settle it once more. Let Nezahualcoyotl bring sixty married men and their wives and children from his province" and ordered other local rulers to do the same, offering 600 families from Tenochtitlan, each with "a land grant that will be distributed among them" and they would be ruled by a member of Tenochtitlan's dynasty (Durán 1994: 236). It should be noted that some scholars place this conquest later in the 15th century, in Ahuitzotl's reign, reflecting a lack of agreement in the sources as well as the perpetual rebellions among local populations against Aztec domination, which made repeated conquests necessary.

While Oaxaca was the headquarters for the Aztecs, Cuilapan was the head town of their tributary province, the place of collection for the tribute of woven textiles, some maize and beans, some gold disks, and bags of cochineal dye. Another important town was Teozapotlán (Zaachila); during the Early and Middle Postclassic its ruler was acknowledged by many other rulers in the Oaxaca Valley as a highest authority in the region. However, in the late 15th century the Zapotec ruler there decided to abandon the Oaxaca Valley altogether, and move his court – and thousands of his subjects – down to the town of Tehuantepec, in the Isthmus region near the Pacific Coast (Zeitlin 2001). This migration of Zapotecs pushed local Isthmian ethnic groups (e.g. the Zoque and Mixe) to the margins of the region.

Zaachila, seat of the valley's most prestigious lineage, was a kind of secular palace complex surrounded by the houses and fields of the commoner population. Zaachila's kings used another center, Mitlá, as a place to consult the highest Zapotec priest, resolve disputes among nobles, and as a burial ground. Mitlá is a corruption of the Nahuatl *mictlan*, "place of the

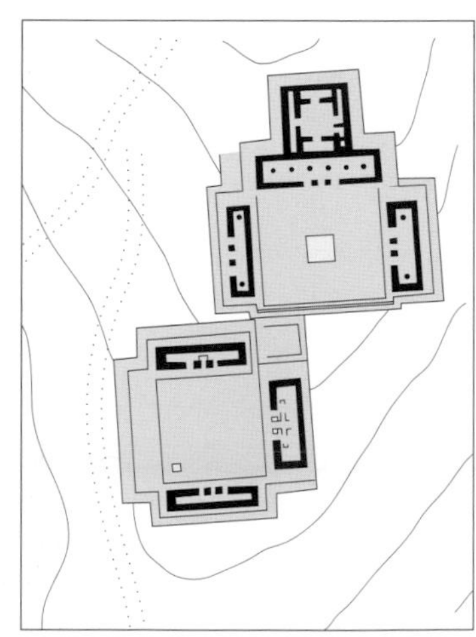

dead," and its Zapotec name has a similar meaning. As we noted in previous discussions of the Zapotecs and Mixtecs, the dead were part of the family, housed in tombs underneath the house. Mitlá's set of five elite residential compounds began to be established in the Classic period, with the Postclassic-period occupation dominating its pre-Columbian cultural sequence. Occupation of the town has continued into the present, and the site is dramatic and accessible [**18.16–18.18**].

THE REIGN OF AXAYACATL, 1469–1481

With the death of Motecuzoma I in 1468, there began a period of nearly 25 years that was dominated by three brothers, Axayacatl, Tizoc, and Ahuitzotl, all grandsons of Motecuzoma I. During Axayacatl's term of office, Tenochtitlan took over its sister city, Tlatelolco, and the revenues from its market and trade systems. Tenochtitlan then turned its attention to the west, and there found in the Tarascans an enemy so formidable that the Aztecs never again provoked a major conflict with them.

18.16–18.18 *The façade of Mitlá's Group of the Columns (opposite above) gives us an idea of what other palaces of the Late Postclassic might have looked like. The stone fretwork decorating it and other compounds at Mitlá is a masterwork of masonry and its panels "emulate weaving patterns, calling attention to the importance of weaving as a form of economic wealth" (Pohl 1999: 184). The plan of the compound (opposite, below right) shows large private courtyards well-suited to feasting, which at Mitlá involved intoxication until the noble participants felt themselves capable of communing with their ancestors, who were buried in tombs under the upper rooms (cross section of building: opposite, below left).*

Picking Fights in the Valley of Toluca in the 1470s

In the 1460s the Tarascans had attacked the town of Toluca, a major center of the Matlatzinca ethnic group. The Tarascans were unsuccessful, but one must consider the logistical handicaps under which they were operating: in direct distance, Toluca is about 200 km (124 miles) from Tzintzuntzan, the Tarascan capital. On the other hand, Toluca is only about 50 km (31 miles) from Tenochtitlan, and the significance of the Tarascan's long distance effort cannot have been lost on the Aztecs.

In the early 1470s, a squabble over tributary rights between Toluca and a neighboring city, Tenantzinco, resulted in the latter's king requesting Axayacatl's help in resolving the dispute. This is a good example of the operation of political "meddling" and "usurpation" as discussed in Chapter 17. The Aztecs were invited to meddle, and ended up usurping local authority and bringing Toluca, Tenantzinco, Calixtlahuaca, Teotenango, and other communities into the empire, reinforcing political centralization of the Central Highlands. A few years earlier, Axayacatl had already exerted certain pressures on the region, such as stepping in to Malinalco's dynastic affairs and appointing the king there (Carrasco 1999: 259).

Calixtlahuaca Among the towns subdued was Calixtlahuaca, which some sources describe as the "cabecera" (the Spanish term for head town) before the Aztecs interfered. Calixtlahuaca had a long period of occupation, beginning in the Formative period, extending through the Classic period and into the Postclassic, when the Matlatzinca are thought to have become established there in about AD 1200 (García Payón 1974, 1979). By the 1470s, when Axayacatl's Aztecs subjugated the area, the site had several impressive

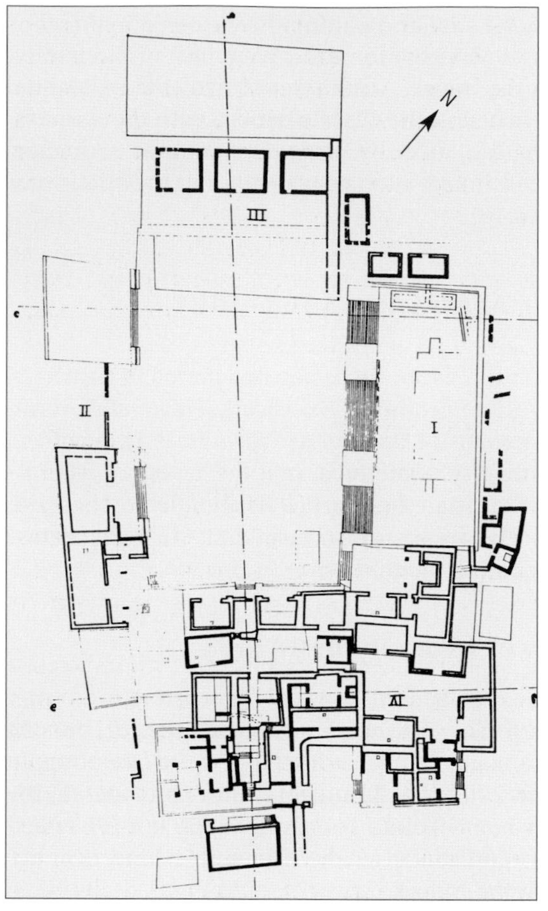

structures [**18.19**]. In addition to the extensive residential compound, there was a circular temple to Quetzalcoatl as Ehécatl, the Wind God [**18.20**].

Palace Scandals and Death in the Basin of Mexico

Axayacatl was quite a young man when he took office, and early in his reign the great Texcocan ruler, Nezahualcoyotl, died. The new Texcocan ruler was only a boy, and while he would grow up to become nearly as influential as his father, there was a void in the balance of political power. Nezahualcoyotl had been a deeply practical strategist, and also a close friend of the ruler of Tlatelolco, Mohquihuix, who had also been a favorite of Motecuzoma I's. The deaths, over a few years, of Motecuzoma I and Nezahualcoyotl coincided with the growing importance of Tlatelolco's long-distance trade system and plans by Mohquihuix to rebel against Tenochtitlan's domination. This would have disturbed Tenochtitlan's access to Tlatelolco's long-distance trade network and distracted Tenochtitlan from its ever-widening wars of tributary conquest. However, Axayacatl's excuse for taking over Tlatelolco focused on the straw issue of "family values" – his sister, Mohquihuix's principal wife, was unhappy in her marriage – Axayacatl (and the Aztec army) stepped in to protect her honor in 1473.

18.21 *(Right) A man caught between two women (as was Mohquihuix) as illustrated here in the* Codex Borgia, *at left, is caught by a modestly dressed respectable woman, while he reaches out to enjoy a nearly-naked object of desire. The couple on the right may be enjoying a more harmonious marriage.*

18.19 *(Opposite left) Calixtlahuaca's largest building is centered upon a large interior patio, with stairs on the northeast side leading up to a platform. The layout of the building corresponds with Late Postclassic palaces, which featured a ruler's dais room overlooking an interior patio, surrounded by other rooms of various sizes. The building is sometimes called a "calmecac" – a priestly school – but such buildings would have been characterized by a more regimented layout.*

18.20 *(Opposite right) From a round temple in Calixtlahuaca, this life-sized statue depicts a young man dressed in* maxtlatl *(loincloth), sandals, and a duck-billed mask, the signature of the deity Quetzalcoatl in the guise of Ehécatl, the Wind God.*

Mohquihuix was accused by his wife and her family of neglecting her sexually, and, what is worse, "doing many bad things with women ... scandalizing the people in many ways" (Annals of Cuauhtitlan. 1992 [*c.* 1570]: 113). It is unclear from the context whether Mohquihuix's crime was that of enjoying his concubines [**18.21**], or by doing so in a public manner in the *tecpan*-palace that was his dynasty's administrative headquarters. One chronicler noted that among the conservative and prudish Aztecs, "death was the penalty for creating a scandal" (Zorita 1994 [1566–1570]: 131). In any event, Axayacatl drove Mohquihuix to suicide and permanently reduced Tlatelolco's status to occupied territory with a military government. Lucrative long-distance trade became Tenochtitlan's asset.

The Tarascan Empire and Tzintzuntzan

In the mid to late 1470s Axayacatl's attention turned west as Aztec military forces went into the Valley of Toluca in 1475–1476, moving from Toluca to the south in the following year and to the north in 1477–1478 (Hassig 1988). The Aztecs perceived that the Tarascans were making a push to the east into the Toluca region, and sought to engage them in battle. It was a disaster for the Aztecs.

To understand how the mighty Aztecs could be so routed, we must consider changes in the Tarascan domain. By the mid 15th century, the major capital of the Tarascans had shifted to Tzintzuntzan [**18.22**, **18.23**], which apparently shared power with Pátzcuaro and Ihuatzio in a kind of triple alliance. Tzintzuntzan would remain the seat of Tarascan kings until 1530, when the Spaniards, who had begun conquest of the region in 1522, murdered the last king, Tangáxuan II. Tzintzuntzan became the location of the modern town, so subsequent construction has obliterated much of the site's area, estimated at nearly 7 sq. km (nearly 3 sq. miles), with about 25,000 to 30,000 residents. The city was situated where a stream running north emptied into Lake Pátzcuaro.

Tzintzuntzan had distinct neighborhoods which were organized into about 40 wards of 25 households each. Most of the population, commoners, lived in small houses and used a modest array of tools and simple vessels. Tarascan commoners farmed, cultivating the same array of crops as was found elsewhere in the highlands – maize, beans, maguey, etc. – and they also produced basic consumer goods in residence-based workshops. The location of the city's marketplace has not been determined, but sources indicate that it met daily, and probably, like Aztec marketplaces, had local and imported goods.

Archaeological survey distinguished between several kinds of elite zones, and the number of elite residents in the city may have been about 5,000. At the top of the social pyramid were the king and his immediate family, their needs attended to by the labor of over 3,000 workers and a dozen artisan groups. The palace complex is thought to underlie the area of the Catholic chapel established in 1525–1526. In addition to serving as the residence of

the king and his household, this complex no doubt served administrative functions, as there seems to have been no separate facility in the city to take care of the bureaucratic chores of maintaining and expanding the Tarascan domain's tribute network and military maneuvers. In the king's personal storehouses were collected feathers and precious metals, while other repositories held items paid in tribute to the state, such as cotton mantles and food items. The king had a menagerie of wild animals and birds, and this was probably near the palace.

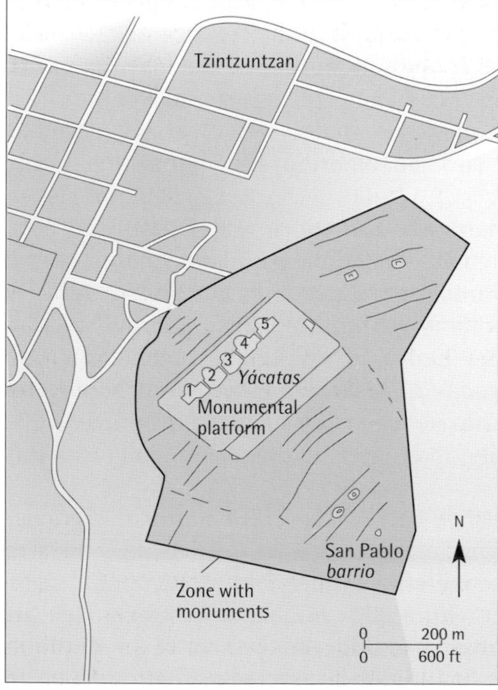

The material culture repertoire associated with elite houses included a much-expanded stock of ceramic vessels, many of them elaborately decorated. In addition, while the commoners used gray obsidian from Michoacán's Zinapécuaro-Ucareo sources, the elites had access to the more unusual varieties in red and green. Their ornaments of personal adornment included ear spools and lip plugs. Metal played a far more important role in Michoacán than it did in the Aztec heartland, and including as an elite status marker (Pollard 1987).

While Sahagún's Aztec informants gave the Tarascans high marks for their artisanship, including cotton weaving and embroidering, and leatherworking, they found among their "faults ... [that] they wore no breech clouts, but went bare, covering themselves only with their ... sleeveless jacket.... The women wore only a skirt, they lacked a shift" (Sahagún 1961: 189).

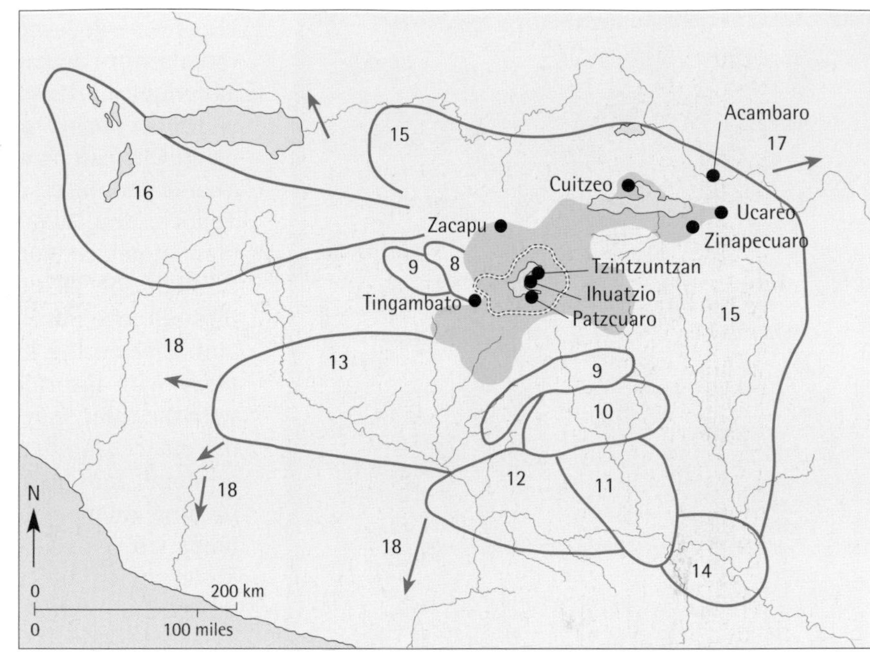

18.24 *The Tarascan empire at* AD *1500 encompassed a vast region, its greatest dimensions being about 350 km E-W by 200 N-S (217 by 124 miles). The shaded area around Lake Pátzcuaro represents early domination by Tarascan military efforts [***16.8***]. Here we see the next stages, starting with areas west of the lake, then moving south and east into the Balsas Drainage and Guerrero. Thereafter, the eastern region toward Toluca was targeted, along with the Lerma Drainage to the north and more westerly valleys. Expansionist efforts continued, pushing toward the northeast and the southwest.*

18.22, 18.23 *(Opposite) Tzintzuntzan is now a major touristic archaeological site, famed for the row of semi-circular* yacátas *that front its main monumental platform. These yácatas were dedicated to Curicaueri, patron sun god of the Tarascan lords, and to his five brothers, who represented the four quarters of the earth – together with Curicaueri, the yácatas thus portrayed "the five directions ... in a manner that made the Lake Pátzcuaro Basin the cosmic center" of the Tarascan world (Pollard 1993: 135). The Tarascan capital faced north on the lake (plan), forming a broad Y shape. The northwest-facing platform with the yácatas measured 450 by 250 m (1,476 by 820 ft), and was used for ceremonies, including the burial of nobles and human sacrifice – a skull rack and sacrificial stones once stood on the platform.*

Nudity always scandalized and fascinated the Aztecs. Military expansion interested them even more, and with the Tarascans they found their "worst enemy" (Durán 1994: 347), possibly because, like the Aztecs, the Tarascans ruled over a huge territory and were aggressively militaristic. We noted in Chapter 16 how the earliest Tarascan kings had staged raids around Lake Pátzcuaro, and then moved up to Lake Cuitzeo. Between 1440 and 1500 they consolidated a huge area [**18.24**].

Making a large part of the Toluca Valley into a conquered province gave the Aztecs a buffer zone and a launching pad against the Tarascans, and in 1478 they moved an army of 24,000 into a border zone and attacked. Unfortunately for the Aztecs, the Tarascans had an army of 40,000, and "the result was the largest pre-Spanish disaster suffered by the Aztec empire" (Smith 1996: 139). Axayacatl led the 2,500 survivors back to the Basin of Mexico, and the Aztecs never directly confronted the Tarascans again. They did, however, maintain control of the Valley of Toluca. Its important cities, Toluca, Teotenango, Tenancingo, and Calixtlahuaca, became tributaries of the Aztecs. Furthermore, lords in Basin of Mexico towns controlled lands in the Toluca Valley.

Back in Tenochtitlan, Axayacatl Consoled Himself with Defeated Chalcans

Defeated by the Tarascans, Axayacatl returned to Tenochtitlan, still the head of a great empire. He was distracted from his political problems by entertainments presented by people from the Chalcan kingdoms in the southeastern Basin of Mexico. It was under his predecessor, his grandfather, Motecuzoma I, that the Chalcans had finally been subdued. All 25 Chalcan

18.25 *The Aztecs danced as part of rituals and festivals, with men and women participating in elaborate line dances such as the one illustrated here.*

kings were deposed (Gibson 1964), and heavy reparations were demanded, including Chalcan women as conquest prizes (Schroeder 1991), and expansion of the Tenochtitlan palace by Chalcan workmen using Chalcan-provided materials. Thus these conquered people, essentially in bondage to the ruler of Tenochtitlan, would have become part of the vast crew of palace workers, and in time some of them, through special talent or luck, would have risen through the ranks of servitude to positions of authority on the household staff, on terms of intimacy with the ruler's wives and concubines, and with the ruler, if he so desired. Axayacatl grew up at the palace, familiar with the huge household, and no doubt indulged by the servants. By the time he became ruler, many of the Chalcan palace concubines would have given birth to children sired by Motecuzoma and other senior nobles. These were the givens of life in royal households of archaic agrarian states.

One day in 1479, Axayacatl was drawn from the interior of his palace to the main courtyard by singing and dancing [**18.25**]. Such activities were fairly common; they entertained the nobles and servants who spent their days in the palace courtyard. This time, however, the singing, by a Chalcan musician, attracted the king's attention, and he joined in, singing and dancing along to the tune of "Song of the [Soldier] Women of Chalco" which celebrated Axayacatl's prowess as a lover, admonishing him to "get it up, make me a woman ... put it in, put it in" (etc.) (Léon-Portilla 1984: 240–243).

The lyrics apparently gently burlesqued the Tenochca conquest of the Chalcans, implying that consummation of military subjugation would be made by Axayacatl, in bed. Axayacatl was so successfully flattered by the song that he invited the Chalcan musician to become part of his household. This did not, however, change Axayacatl's attitude toward Chalco; more land there was appropriated by the Mexica (Hodge 1984), and it was not until the mid-1480s, some years after Axayacatl's death in 1481, that any Chalcan dynasties were restored.

Axayacatl's period of rule had maintained and extended the broad empire his grandfather and Nezahualcoyotl had established. He had also come up against some insurmountable limits, but even more territory would be added by his successors, as the Aztec empire continued to grow.

19 THE AZTEC EMPIRE AT ITS HEIGHT (1481–1519)

AXAYACATL DID WELL to enjoy himself, because he died young. In 1481 he was succeeded by his brother, Tizoc, who ruled for a few years and then was succeeded by another brother, Ahuitzotl, one of the greatest Tenochca kings. Then, in 1502, Axayacatl's son, Motecuzoma Xocoyotzin (Motecuzoma II) took office. The last 20 years of the 15th century brought the Aztec empire to impressive maturity: a vast area supplied the rulers of the Triple Alliance with the tributes of millions of people across Mesoamerica [**19.1**]. Motecuzoma II maintained the empire, but would face a challenge beyond the experience of any of his predecessors: the invasion of Mexico by Europeans.

TIZOC, 1481–1486

Tizoc's formal coronation ceremony in Tenochtitlan conformed to standards of imperial pomp and circumstance. Tizoc was crowned by Nezahualpilli with "a golden diadem set with green stones" and then the Texcocan king further adorned him with jade nose piece and ear spools, golden bracelets

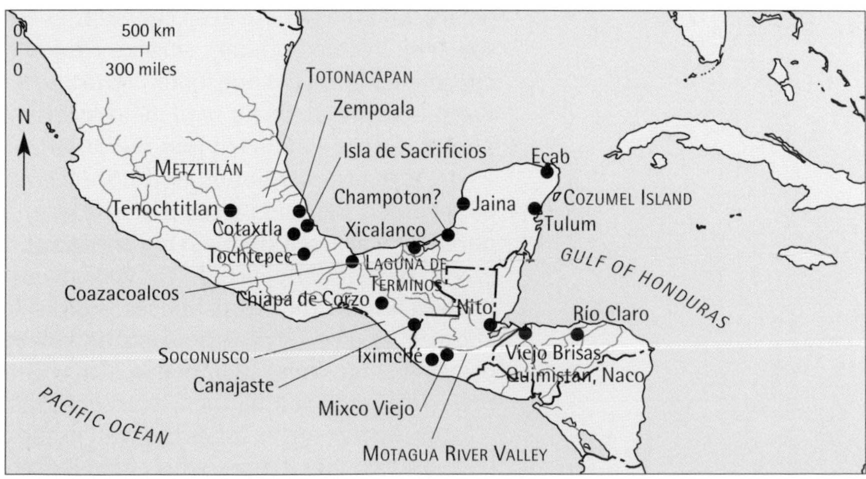

19.1 *Middle America showing Conquest-era and Colonial-period regions and sites.*

and anklets decorated with golden bells, and seated him in a throne called the "'Eagle seat' and ... 'Jaguar seat' ... because it was decorated with eagle feathers and jaguar skins" (Durán 1994: 297). Then Nezahualpilli gave a speech telling Tizoc to honor the gods, help the weak and needy among his people, and especially treat well the "Eagles and Jaguars, the courageous, brave men ... They are the wall around your land, they are its defense" (ibid.: 298).

Eagle Knights, Jaguar Knights

The eagle and jaguar were ancient symbols of militarism, and were adopted as totems for warrior societies. We have noted that in earlier cultures, such as those of Xochicalco, El Tajín, and Tula, eagle and jaguar motifs in particular architectural contexts may have indicated the presence of elite warrior societies like those of the Aztecs.

People everywhere and in all phases of history have advertised their social and economic status through their clothing and ornaments, cosmetics and hairstyles. The Aztecs brought this to a high art, and its greatest refinement is found in the customs and laws regulating how successful war veterans could dress [**19.3**]. Military service was required of all Aztecs, and in fact a man who had not at least helped capture an enemy was required to leave a lock of his hair uncut, from age 15. Such a visible sign of lack of service to the state would no doubt prompt such shame that enthusiasm for battle would be raised simply by the desire of many young men to erase a mark of childhood. Motecuzoma I had instituted *telpochcallis* (young men's houses) in all the *calpullis*, so by the time of the reign of Tizoc, the Aztecs would have had an established program of military training, and ambitious commoners would have regarded military success as a means of enhancing their socioeconomic status.

In addition to specific features of costume and hairstyle, honored warriors were permitted such perquisites as cotton clothing, consumption of human flesh at ritual feasts, public drinking of *pulque*, dining privileges in the palace, and the right to keep concubines (Hassig 1986). In fact, even a king's son who avoided military service could "not receive tobacco, ... not drink chocolate, ... not eat fine foods" (Durán 1971: 42). Commoners could be elevated to noble status for battlefield service, and they and honored hereditary nobles could be inducted into the orders of Eagle and Jaguar Knights [**19.2, 19.4**]. If their contribution to the state was very significant, they could also be awarded the rents from plots of farm land. The commoner elevated to nobility "was freed from paying tribute and taxes and contributions. He was given lands and properties. [He was given] permission to dine as often as he wished within the royal houses, where he was given his ration. He was allowed to dance with the lords whenever dances and celebrations took place. In sum, these men began a new lineage, and their children enjoyed their privileges, calling themselves knights" (Durán 1971: 199–200).

Thus the incentives for doing well in the army were extraordinarily attractive – one could lift one's whole family into the nobility. It is no wonder that the Aztecs expanded their empire so rapidly. However, this strategy held the seeds of its own destruction, because polygynous noble families produced many more offspring than did monogamous commoner couples, and each generation would have a much higher proportion of non-producing nobles to support. By Motecuzoma II's time, the noble class was larger than its environment of productive commoners could support, and it was necessary to limit access to nobility, and even demote some nobles.

Warfare in agrarian societies is generally scheduled for the winter months, so that the farmer artisans who form the bulk of the armies can participate without interrupting the important planting, cultivation, and harvesting tasks that take place from late spring to early fall. In the off season, the commoners trained under the supervision of the warrior-priests in charge of the telpochcallis, and were organized as cadres which together formed the Aztec army. Men went into battle under their local banner, and the organization and discipline of troops in action was based on these localized units. There was no ranked chain of command as has become common in the organization of modern armies — generals decided upon strategy, and valiant warriors were conspicuous on the battlefield for their garb and their bravery – but so formalized was the conduct of conflict that it was virtually impossible for the armies to respond flexibly to tactical challenges.

Nor was the modern goal of killing the enemy on the battlefield valued by the Aztecs, though at times they did so for retribution, and their enemies sometimes destroyed Aztec forces. More generally, the Aztec aim was to take captives for ceremonial sacrifice at a later time. It was this combination of deferred mortality and lack of down-the-line command that favored the Spanish army in battle against the Aztecs, even when the Spaniards were grossly outnumbered. The Spaniards focused on killing the banner carriers and the most gaudily costumed of the fighters, the seasoned veterans. With their banner carriers and lead warriors gone, the rest of the Aztec fighters were baffled as to how to proceed.

Tizoc in Battle It appears that other of the Aztecs' enemies also may have ignored the conventions of captive-oriented warfare, much to the detriment of the Tenochca and their allies. The Tarascans had terribly damaged Aztec armies and their prestige, and Tizoc was not able to achieve decisive and showy victories. His reign began with a lackluster and unproductive campaign to Metztitlán. This was a poor choice. While the region is not far from the Basin of Mexico, the terrain was formidably steep and dissected. Although the local population was small, the people were able to defend themselves in their own territory. Tizoc is reported to have taken fewer captives than the Aztecs lost in casualties.

The Aztec empire could only keep growing if significant conquests were forthcoming. Not only did such conquests increase the empire's territory and tribute base, but also they reduced the probability of insurrection in regions already conquered. It is apparent, from the repetitive nature of the conquest lists, that even when the armies were successful there was a con-

19.3 *(Right) The Aztecs displayed their rank and accomplishments through their clothes and adornments. This was most evident among the military: warriors earned various accoutrements, and even the right to a certain kind of haircut, by distinguishing themselves in battle. At right, Folio 67r from the* Codex Mendoza *shows seasoned warriors and their captives. They carry spears edged with obsidian blades, and distinctive shields. Each has a back device attached to the back of his costume – this highly visible emblem helped cadres of soldiers keep track of where their units were fighting.*

19.4 *(Right) In the Templo Mayor Precinct in Tenochtitlan, the Hall of the Eagle Warriors was the special meeting place for this elite military corps. The stone banquettes lining the rooms were faced with bas-reliefs depicting processions of warriors, identical to those found at Tula's Palacio Quemado (Burned Palace).*

19.2 *(Opposite) At 1.8 m (nearly 6 ft) tall, this ceramic statue of an Eagle Man was one of a pair found standing on one of the banquettes in the Hall of the Eagle Warriors. Features of the statue, and the highly ritualized nature of the functions of this building, together indicate that the statue may represent an anthropomorphized deity – the rising sun – rather than an actual Eagle Warrior (Matos 2002).*

19.5 *The Stone of Tizoc was carved during that* huetlatoani*'s reign, showing that even ineffective rulers can have gaudy monuments – this one is nearly 2.7 m (9 ft) across and features 15 warriors paired with captives representing cities Tizoc battled against. The style of depiction of this processional scene is Mixteca-Pueblan rather than Toltec (Pasztory 1983: 147). The top is a sun disk, and may have served as a platform for human sacrifice.*

stant push on the part of tributary provinces to throw off their obligations and reclaim their independence. A loss of confidence in the Aztec emperor would spread like an epidemic, causing fires of rebellion to start all over the empire, simultaneously demanding the attention of the Aztec armies across a huge area. It seems that the choice was the death of the empire or the death of Tizoc [**19.5**]. His fellow nobles, "angered by his weakness and lack of desire to enlarge and glorify the Aztec nation, hastened his death with something they gave him to eat" (Durán 1994: 307).

AHUITZOTL, 1486–1502

It took a tough man to assume the role of *huetlatoani* of Tenochtitlan, one who knew that mistakes would be fatal and that the termination notice would be delivered by one's own trusted advisers and close kin. The next emperor, Ahuitzotl, met the challenge and succeeded in giving imperial growth new life. He is reported as having been an exceptional military officer, one whose toughness and zeal infected his troops with renewed enthusiasm. While space does not permit a detailed review of his conquests and reconquests, his success in the battlefield is generously evidenced by his ability to maintain and even extend the Aztec empire's holdings. Ahuitzotl made other contributions to Aztec glory; he was apparently keenly interested in Tenochtitlan's development as a dazzling capital, and in 1487 and *c.* 1500 led beautification movements. The first, in 1487, was inspired by the rededication of the Templo Mayor. Twelve years later a serious flood damaged the city, and reconstruction efforts were combined with enhancement of Tenochtitlan's public buildings and gardens.

Rededication of the Templo Mayor: Human Sacrifice and Cannibalism

As we have seen (see box, pp. 452–454), the Templo Mayor in Tenochtitlan was rebuilt six times. The second-to-last rebuilding, Stage VI, substantially enlarged the pyramid, bringing it to a size close to that of Stage VII, which the Spaniards saw in 1519. Stage VI was dedicated in 1487, and the ceremony was no doubt the largest celebration ever staged in Mesoamerica. Rulers of all the tributary provinces – and enemy states like Tlaxcala, Cholula, Metztitlán, and Tarascan Michoacán – came to see the spectacle. All brought gifts that included human beings, slaves or war captives who would be sacrificed to dedicate the newest manifestation of the pyramid and its temples.

Durán gave the number of sacrificial victims as 80,400 (1994: 335) and this has long been disputed as representing a vast inflation of the actual count [**19.9**]. Simply on logistical grounds, accommodating this many slaves awaiting sacrifice, in addition to their guards, and the noble guests contributing them, would tax the resources of the Basin. Durán also says that the victims formed four lines that moved toward the Templo Mayor; each of these lines was a maximum of 5 km (*c.* 3 miles) long. Over a total of 20 km (*c.* 12 miles), the maximum number of individuals walking in single file could not exceed 40,000, and given the cumbersome yokes that slaves wore to prevent escape, may have been far fewer.

Even if a mere 20,000 people (as indicated in the *Codex Telleriano Remensis*, Folio 39r) trudged up the steep, slippery steps of the Templo Mayor to be stretched across sacrificial altars and killed, this is an awesome number of human lives taken in one event [**19.6, 19.7**]. Human sacrifice has a very long history in Mesoamerica, and many of the cultures studied in this book held the belief that humans and their world had been created through the self-sacrifice of the gods. Thus there was a debt that humans could never really repay, but toward which they must make perpetual appropriations so as to express their gratitude and, if possible, put off the inevitable destruction of the present world. As individuals, Mesoamericans included autosacrifice in their regular acts of piety [**19.8**], drawing blood from their arms, legs, earlobes, genitals, tongues, and collecting the blood onto pieces of paper and placing disposable instruments of autosacrifice, such as maguey thorns, into balls of wadded-up grass. These were then burned, an incense as potent as the resinous copal sap that they also offered to their gods.

Deity Impersonation, Human Sacrifice, Transubstantiation, and Cannibalism
In regarding the world around them as infused with powerful living forces, Mesoamericans recognized that such forces were lambent and inhabited different forms. A potent representation of a deity could be a figurine or statue, garbed in the traditional emblems of that deity, or it could be a person, assigned to the role of living embodiment of the deity. Sometimes the individual lived for a full year as the deity, and was given every luxury and privilege until being sacrificed.

19.6, 19.7 *Heart sacrifice, as this illustration from the* Codex Magliabechiano *shows (below), was the means by which thousands died in the 1487 rededication of the Templo Mayor. While priests held the victim by the extremities, the sacrificing priest – and rulers were qualified as priests – sliced through the chest with a large knife of flint or obsidian, and drew out the still-beating heart for presentation to the deity. Sacrificial knives were themselves regarded as sacred, and offerings in the Templo Mayor include flint knives which have been decorated (right).*

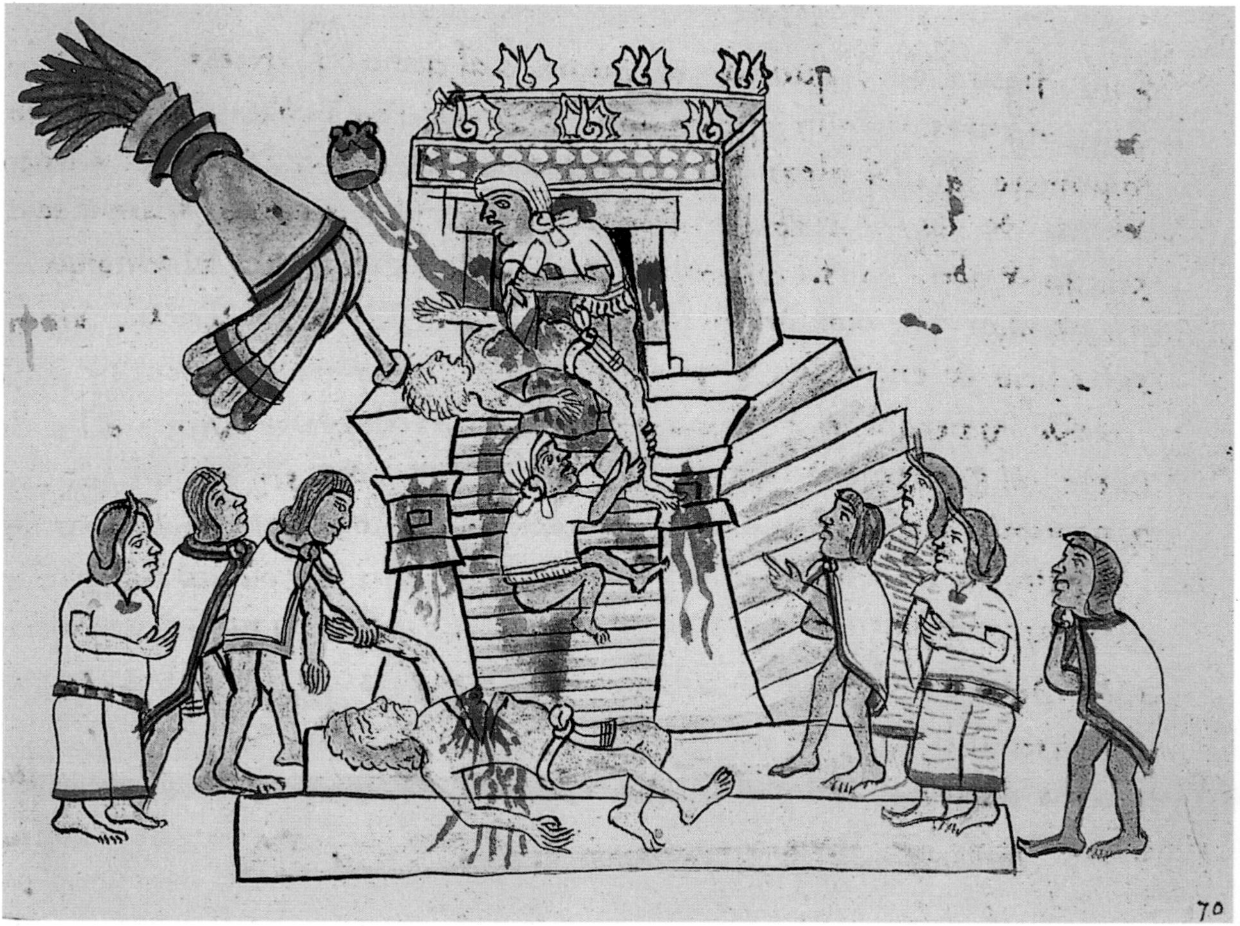

19.8 *This carved panel (21 by 32 cm, c. 8 by 12 inches) was from a stone box used to store instruments of autosacrifice, such as maguey thorns, stingray spines, or, in the case of the warrior depicted drawing blood from his ear, a sharpened human bone. Behind him is a* Xiuhcoatl *(fire serpent), its tail (at right) forming a trapeze-and-ray year sign.*

19.9 *The Templo Mayor precinct had skull racks on which were displayed the remains of sacrificial victims, and also representations of skull racks, like this* tzompantli *sculpted in stone.*

This is a particularly vivid example of the transformation, in the eyes of the onlookers, of a person into a god, and in being sacrificed, the man-god or woman-god then became food for the gods, and, in many cases, food for privileged living humans, as well. The consumption of the flesh of another human being is cannibalism, and there is no doubt that this was practiced among the Aztec elite, and quite probably among other Mesoamerican cultures, as well. However, one did not simply go to the marketplace and purchase a haunch for the family table. Eating the flesh of sacrificial victims was a sacred act, because the dead body had been sanctified by the ritual, if not by having served as a deity impersonator beforehand, and the victim's soul was thought to enter a privileged afterlife. Only nobles could participate in meals involving sacrificial victims, and if the victim was a war captive, the warrior who made the capture was awarded the most valued part of the body, the right thigh (Durán 1971 [1579]: 216). After the feast, the thighbone was wrapped in paper and displayed as a "god-captive" at a celebration the victor held for his friends and family (Sahagún 1981: 60).

19.10, 19.11 *The Soconusco province was the Aztec empire's most distant tributary, and it sent high-value luxury goods up to Tenochtitlan. These are illustrated (opposite, below) on page 47r of the Codex Mendoza (1544), which shows what the Soconusco province paid in tribute every six months. The names of the towns run down the left side of the page, and the tribute items and symbols for quantities fill the page. The flag (extending from each jaguar skin's nose, and from the baskets of cacao beans, next to the jaguars) stands for 20, and the feather (extending from the top of each bunch of feathers) stands for 400.*

*In the sophisticated Aztec economy, everything could be converted to an exchange value, and cotton mantles were a common medium of exchange. The table (based on Gasco and Voorhies 1989: 77) shows how many cotton mantles the Soconusco tribute would bring, if exchanged in the marketplace. The production of a plain cotton mantle (*manta*), from processing the cotton to weaving the four 2.8 sq. m (3.3 sq. yd) panels that comprised the mantle, would have taken roughly 100 person-days of labor, and most of the work was done by women (Hicks 1994: 92).*

Not unexpectedly, the Spaniards found this ritual-culinary practice to be thoroughly repulsive, and were shocked when the Aztecs whom they were trying to convert to Christianity understood too literally some core concepts of the Christian religion. For example, transubstantiation is the ritual conversion, in the context of the eucharist or mass, of bread and wine into the body and blood of Jesus Christ. Sincere participation in holy communion depends upon belief in transubstantiation. With their sophisticated ability to sense supernatural power morphing from one form to another, the Aztecs found the concept of transubstantiation fully understandable, because this was their belief in consuming the body of a sacrificial victim. Some even tried crucifixion as a new innovation in sacrificial techniques, but this zealotry was quickly suppressed.

Aztec Conquests on the Pacific Coast of Guatemala and Chiapas

Ahuitzotl's skill as a military strategist kept the empire he inherited intact, and he managed to extend it in its southernmost direction, to the Pacific Coast of Chiapas and Guatemala. We know that as Aztec *pochteca* merchants extended their range, these coastal regions were prime targets for trade – cacao grown there had been sought since Formative times, and so had important luxuries like quetzal feathers and precious jades that flowed through the coastal plain from their sources in the highlands of Guatemala. It was common practice for Aztec long-distance traders to expect bargains – hard bargaining was one means of sizing up the target province's degree of resistance to incorporation into the Aztec empire. Besides, by the late 15th century, masses of tribute poured into Tenochtitlan, and the emperor's stewards would redistribute it to the *pochteca* to use in trades. Note how the emperor thus skillfully recycled his materials, forcibly demanding an ever-increasing flow of goods, and then flogging off surplus to gain things of high value, confidently expecting to get them cheap.

Soconusco Tribute and Its Exchange Value (19.10)

Material	Amount	Exchange value per item, in cotton mantles		Total annual exchange value, cotton mantles
		every six months	*total for year*	
Cacao beans	200 basket loads	100	200	40,000
Gourd chocolate cups	800	2	4	3,200
Jaguar skins	40	20	40	1,600
Blue-bird skins	160	3	6	960
Quetzal feathers	800 handsful	2	4	3,200
Red feathers	800 handsful	3	6	4,800
Yellow feathers	800 handsful	0.4	0.8	640
Green feathers	800 handsful	0.5	1	800
Blue feathers	800 handsful	*c.* 1.5	*c.* 3	2,400
Chalchihuitl greenstones	2 strings of beads	600	1,200	2,400
Lip plugs, amber and gold	2	25	50	100
Amber chunks, brick size	2	100	200	400
			Total	60,500

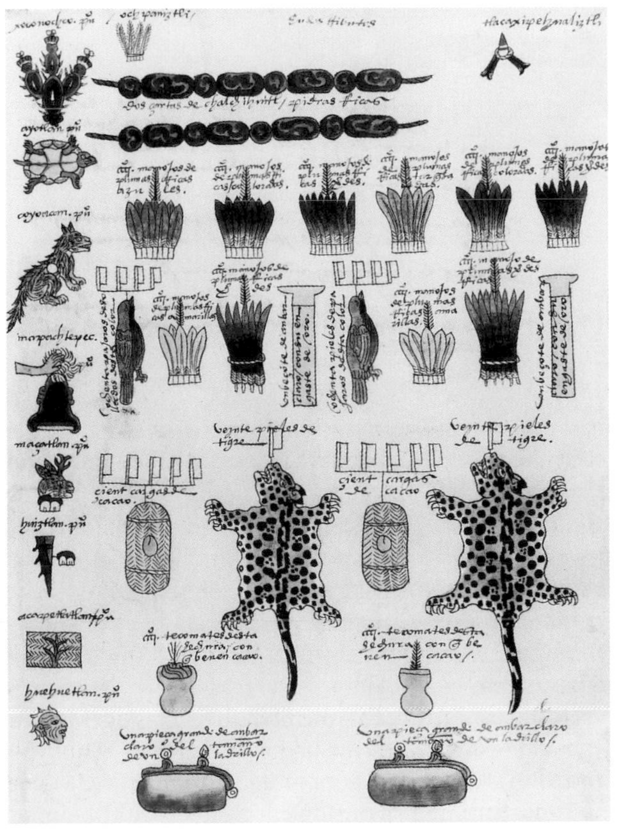

It was only natural that the suppliers of the high-end consumables would resent their end of this unbalanced trading relationship, and along the Chiapas Coast resistance was mounted. This occurred late in Ahuitzotl's reign, probably in *c.* AD 1500. *Pochteca* traders are said to have been embattled in this region, Soconusco, for four years when Aztec armies, led by Ahuitzotl himself, went in and brought this province into the empire [**19.10, 19.11**]. Eight towns along the Soconusco plain became Aztec tributaries, and these were probably capitals of independent polities prior to Aztec conquest (Voorhies 1989). At a distance from Tenochtitlan of about 1,300 km (800 miles) by road, this represents the most distant tributary province of the empire, separated from the rest of the Aztec realm by the unconquered territory. As with so many episodes of conquest in human history, the economic motive of securing valuable products was very powerful, and the value of the tribute may have been enhanced by the porters who carried it, and probably became sacrificial victims.

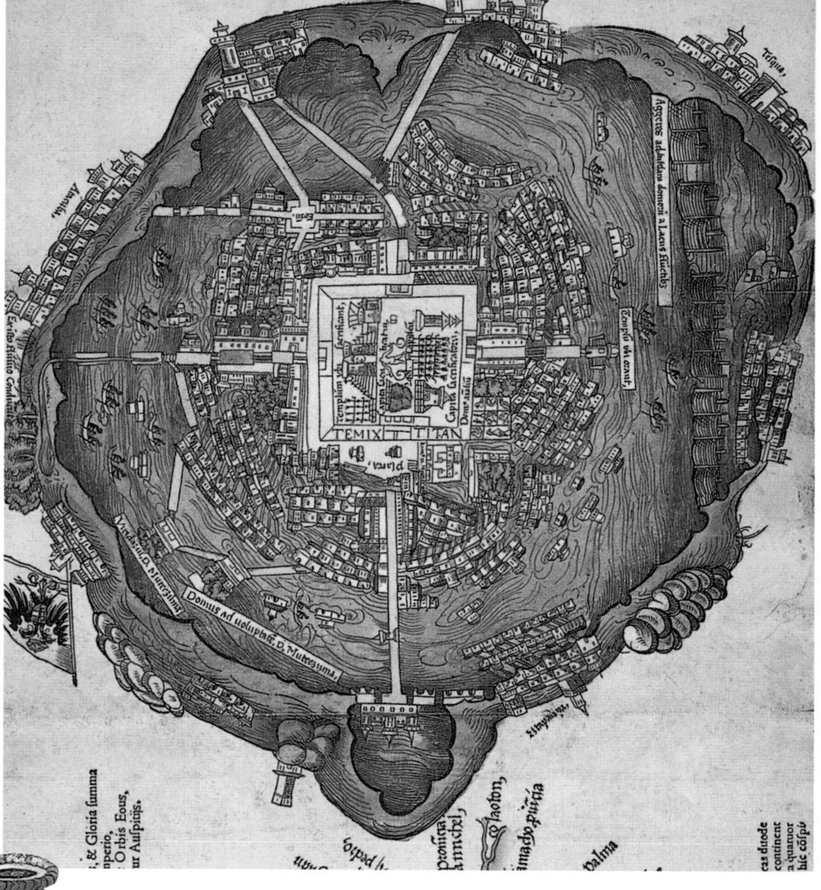

19.12, 19.14 *(Right and opposite) Two maps of Tenochtitlan and environs. Opposite is a modern reconstruction of Tenochtitlan and its surroundings. At near right, the Nuremburg map of 1524, published in Europe along with Cortés's Second Letter. The 1524 map conforms to European conventions of city depiction, including presenting the buildings in a stylized fashion, but the features it shows conform to the layout of the Aztec capital.*

Hydrological Challenges to Tenochtitlan, and Ahuitzotl's Response

Tenochtitlan's islands in the marshy shallows of western Lake Texcoco had been the foundation for what was, by the end of the 15th century, a considerable city. It was criss-crossed with canals and linked to the mainland by causeways, an organized system of roadways and waterways that gave access to all quarters of the city. The water supply from Chapultepec, carried in an aqueduct linked to a causeway, provided the city with sufficient potable water. Yet sometimes in dry years the water level of the surrounding lake sank so low that the canals were barely navigable.

Seeking to solve this problem, Ahuitzotl turned to a classic Mexica response: appropriate the necessary resource from its owner. Thus he instructed the ruler of nearby Coyoacan to cooperate in redirecting water from two springs so that Tenochtitlan's hydrological needs would be met.

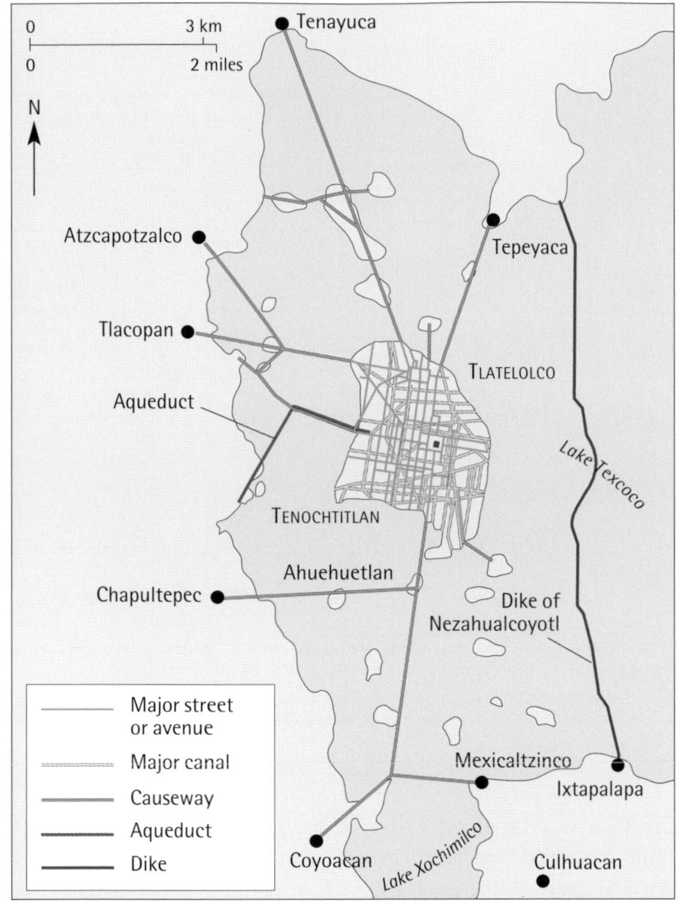

This ruler agreed, but added that he would be remiss if he did not warn Ahuitzotl that the springs were unpredictable and must be handled with care. In cautioning Ahuitzotl, the king of Coyoacan did not, unfortunately, handle the great Mexica *huetlatoani* with sufficient care. Ahuitzotl took umbrage at the warning, and had the king strangled for his impertinence.

Work crews and materials were summoned from the Basin's city-states, and construction of the canals to supply water from the springs began, and was quickly finished. Ahuitzotl ordered the usual round of child sacrifices to the water deities, and the waters began to flow. Tenochtitlan was once again sparkling with canals, its trees verdant with moisture. But the water kept rising, and after 40 days, the *chinampas* around the city suffered damage, and construction crews were called back to try to control the flow that now began to cover the city, requiring evacuation of palaces and commoner houses alike.

Finally, Nezahualpilli of Texcoco intervened, pointing out that Ahuitzotl's pride and bad temper had caused his city to become a deserted ruin that would certainly not build confidence in Aztec invincibility among allies and enemies. Nezahualpilli counseled restoring the springs to their original condition and placating the water goddess with sacrifices and offerings.

Tenochtitlan Renewed Nezahualpilli's plan worked, and Ahuitzotl made amends to his people by paying for the restoration of the city, or at least by ordering tributaries to work on construction projects over the whole city. "In this way Tenochtitlan became well-ordered, attractive, beautifully finished, with large and well-made houses, full of areas for recreation such as pleasing gardens and fine courtyards" (Durán 1994: 373).

The city that Ahuitzotl rebuilt was, in large part, the city that the Spaniards saw and were dazzled by. First, Tenochtitlan in 1519 was larger than any city in Spain [**19.12**]. Estimates as to its population vary, but there were probably about 125,000 residents of urban Tenochtitlan-Tlatelolco, which extended over about 12–15 sq. km (*c.* 5–6 sq. miles). The city was surrounded by dispersed settlement on *chinampas*, and small city-states and farming villages crowded the mainland close to the city.

As a capital city, Tenochtitlan was home to Aztec society's wealthiest fam-

19.13 *(Opposite left) Nezahualpilli ruled Texcoco from 1472 to about 1515. This portrait from the* Codex Ixtlilxochitl *was made in the 1580s, and shows him in courtly garb, his long cape and sandals indicating his high status. In his left hand he carries flowers, as did all noblemen at court, and in his right, a fly whisk made of feathers (Gruzinski 1992).*

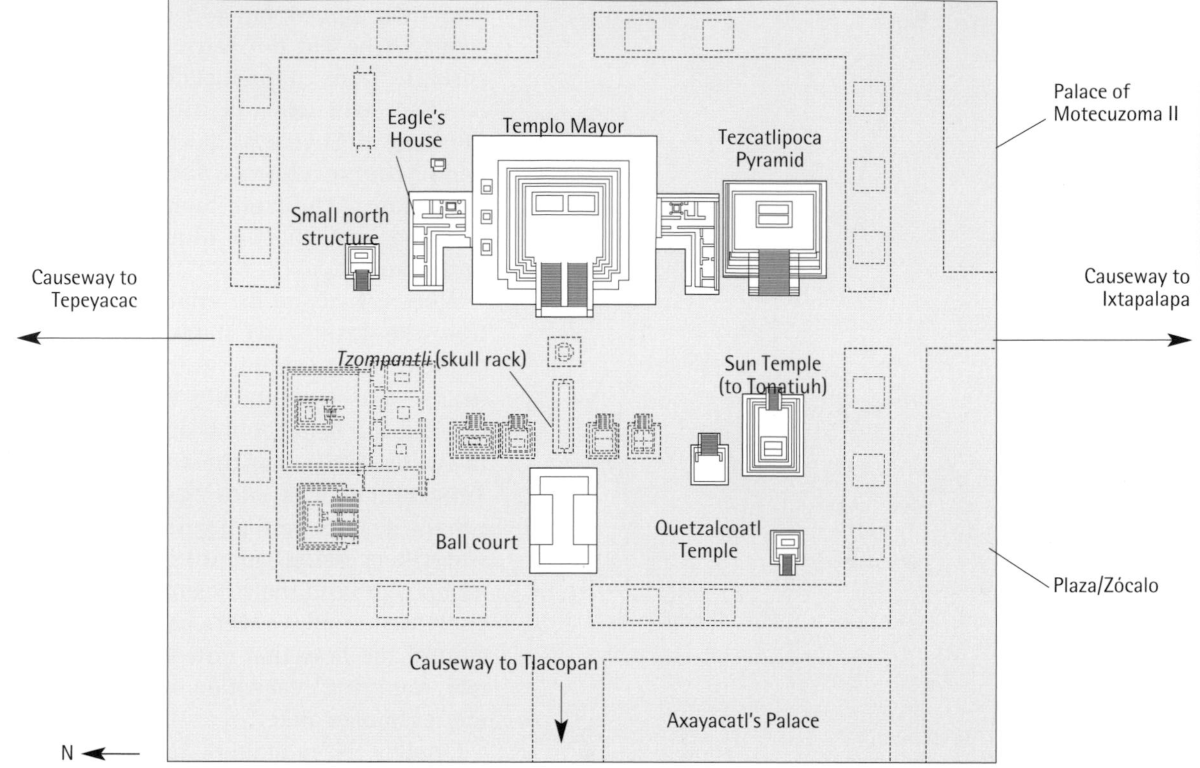

19.15 *In this plan of Tenochtitlan's Templo Mayor precinct, north is at left so that the plan is oriented to the same direction as the drawing from Sahagún's* Primeros Memoriales *[**19.16**]. While the precinct was dominated by the Templo Mayor pyramid, there were, according to Sahagún, over 70 structures within the precinct's boundaries, only a few of which are indicated here. That boundary itself is often called the* coatepantli *(serpent wall) but was a raised platform about 30 m wide, with shrines on top of it (Matos, M. 2003). Thus the design of this platform would be similar to that of the Ciudadela in Teotihuacan, and may have been inspired by it, given that the Aztecs revered Teotihuacan as a holy pilgrimage site.*

ilies, and there were many palaces and mansions, in addition to the royal establishment on the west side of the Templo Mayor precinct, which is known as Axayacatl's palace. Tributary states maintained great houses as embassies, and the many nobles who held high office built themselves fine homes. These were located close to the center of the city, and also along the major canals, which formed impressive green belts. The development of gardens was listed by Sahagún's informants as a highly-regarded elite pastime (Sahagún 1979: 29). A favorite tree was a water-tolerant cypress, a fast-growing relative of the redwood that reached a height of 60 m (*c.* 200 ft). Called *ahuehuetl*, the tree is mentioned in adages as an alter-ego of the king, handsome and protective.

Imagine the city with its canals lined with these huge trees, and the gardens of plaster-washed palaces richly green with *ahuehuetl* and willow. To the Spaniards, many of them from the province of Extremadura, largely deforested for centuries, the sight of this metropolis, centered upon its huge pyramid with canals raying out in all directions into a blue lake and verdant with trees, must indeed have seemed like a fantasy out of one of the contemporary heroic romance novels upon which they all doted. It was a garden city, and in addition to palace gardens, Ahuitzotl and the other *huetlatoque* established for themselves special pleasure parks. Some of these were islands like "Ahuehuetlan" – place of the *ahuehuetl* trees – just to the south-

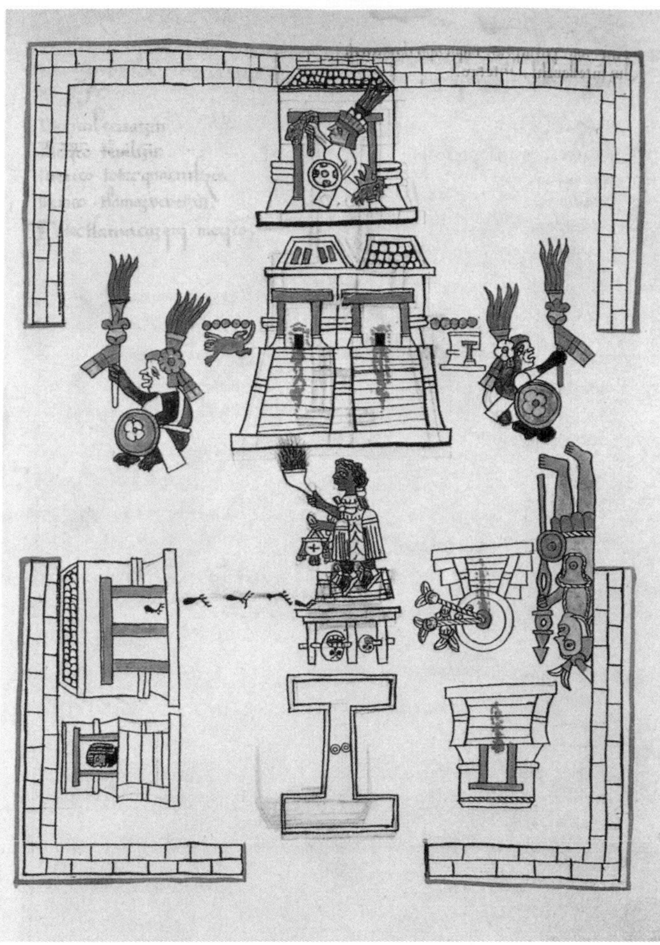

west of the city, marked on the 1524 map as "Domus ad voluptae D. Muteçma" – Motecuzoma's pleasure palace. This must have been wonderfully beautiful in the evening, with torches making rippling shadows across the water, and singing from the king's entertainers drifting out into the night.

The Aztecs invested many projects with spiritual meaning, so it is not surprising that one of the most ambitious pleasure parks developed in Tenochtitlan was a kind of historical theme-park, a zoo where waterfowl were gathered from all over the empire, and comfortably established in natural settings. Many were birds, and "Over each pool for these birds, there were beautifully decorated galleries, and corridors, where Montezuma [Moctecuzoma] came to amuse himself by watching them.... There was also in this house a room in which were kept men, women, and children who had, from birth, white faces and bodies and white, hair, eyebrows and eyelashes" (Cortés 1986: 110). This was clearly an attempt to recreate the Place of Whiteness from which Aztec legends said they had come, and which they had managed to establish here, the capital of their empire.

19.16 *The* Primeros Memoriales *plan (Sahagún 1993 [1559–1561]) is thought to have represented Tenochtitlan's Templo Mayor precinct, and it indicates, in shorthand fashion, some of the many activities that took place there. Directly below the central figure, for example, is a two-head* tzompantli, *and beneath that is an I-shaped ball court with rings in the center.*

MOTECUZOMA XOCOYOTZIN, 1502–1520

Soon after the city had been rebuilt with fine palaces and gardens, Ahuitzotl died. Unbeknownst to him, the isolation of the peoples of the New World since earliest Paleoindian times had already ended with the arrival of Columbus on the Caribbean island of Hispaniola in 1492. Peoples and cultures of the New and Old Worlds would, thereafter, share a common global fate. In the 27 years between this first landfall and the meeting between Cortés and Motecuzoma, European intrusion extended slowly but steadily, and it was inevitable that a sense of the impending cultural collision would reach Tenochtitlan long before the Spaniards did.

In 1502 Motecuzoma Xocoyotzin (Motecuzoma the Younger) became emperor [**19.17**], and in that same year, unsettling portents began to reach the Mexica, evidence that some alien culture had become established on the islands of the Caribbean Sea. There was little culture contact between the peoples of the Caribbean and Mesoamerica, but even the most subtle signs would not be ignored by people alert to the prophetic powers of the world

19.17 *This carved stone is thought to commemorate Motecuzoma II's coronation. The motifs show the five ages of the world, and how they were destroyed (see also pp. 34–35). The central motif is the glyph for the fifth, present age, presumed by the Aztecs to end with an earthquake. At lower right, the first world, which was destroyed by jaguars. At upper right, Ehécatl represents destruction by winds, while the Tlaloc mask at upper left refers to destruction by fiery rain. At lower left, the water goddess's head symbolizes the fourth world's end in floods. Top center, One Alligator may refer to the date of Motecuzoma's coronation ceremony.*

around them. Consider how ocean currents carry trash and flotsam from shipwrecks. Any odd thing washing up on the shores of the Gulf of Mexico would be examined with care, and brought to a local chief and then sent up to Tenochtitlan where the emperor's tribute stewards and divinatory priests would take it to Motecuzoma. One such item was a trunk with clothes and a sword. Motecuzoma shared the contents with his close allies, the rulers of Tacuba and Texcoco, expressing their shared fate in dealing with the aliens.

The early years of the 16th century, when the Spaniards were becoming established in the Caribbean, brought the Aztecs portents as tangible as a wooden trunk, and as ephemeral as the wailing laments of a woman never found, and the visions of men riding on deer – visions seen in a mirror embedded in the forehead of a large bird – who disappeared. A comet appeared in the sky and split into three. Motecuzoma was full of questions, and the soothsayers – including the era's most notable magician,Texcoco's ruler, Nezahualpilli – were full of unpleasant answers. Motecuzoma kept ruling, and the Spaniards kept furthering their explorations, until, on 8 November 1519, they arrived at Tenochtitlan, and Motecuzoma's worst fears began to be realized.

The Intermediate Area as the Spaniards Found It

By 1508 Spanish explorations had only reached the American mainland far to the south of the Aztec empire. In that year, the Spanish government issued contracts for exploration – and exploitation – of the region that would become Panama. The earliest expeditions were disasters, but among the reinforcements sent was Vasco Núñez de Balboa, famed for leading the first Europeans to see the Pacific Ocean from the Americas. Upon Balboa's suggestion the Panamanian site of Darién was selected to be settled, and it became the first permanent European community on the American continent (Parry and Keith 1984: III: 5). Under Balboa's direction the settlement survived and had decent relations with local chiefs, in sharp contrast to Spanish experiences in the Caribbean. No tribute was exacted from the natives, because profits were easily made from local "gold in much quantity" (Balboa 1984 [1513]).

Panama at that time comprised a well-developed system of more than three dozen chiefdoms. Typically, each occupied a river valley that ran from the cordillera spine of the Isthmus of Panama down to the sea, a region that provided a range of resources (Helms 1979). The Panamanians grew some food and also hunted and fished. They were Chibchan speakers, thus linked to South America. Their society was hierarchical, with hereditary nobles, elite warriors, and commoners. The commoners lived in modest, scattered dwellings, and the chiefs had substantial establishments that the Spaniards described as "towns." One of these elite residences measured 73 by 138 m (240 by 450 ft), built of wood and stone and serving not only as habitation but also as a storage facility for food for the local population. Panama in the 16th century AD in certain respects would have much resembled Panama in the 16th century BC – mixed economy, ranked society. And yet there were a few practices that we associate with Mesoamerica, such as using quilted cotton armor in battle, raising domesticated turkeys, and playing a form of the ball game.

Moving northwest, we find a mosaic of Mesoamerican traits interjected into the cultural matrix of lower Central America. Along the Pacific Coast, Mesoamerican traits persisted quite far south, the result of trade and of the establishment of colonies by the Nahuat-speaking Pipil in the Early Postclassic, which was discussed in Chapter 14 with regard to Cihuatán. Cihuatán was abandoned by the Late Postclassic, but other Pipil enclaves survived in what is now El Salvador. This region – eastern Honduras and central and northern Nicaragua – had cultures which were simple and beyond the influence of Mesoamerica. But even further south, in Costa Rica, there are traces of an Aztec colony founded in the late 15th or early 16th century.

As they moved northwest from Panama along the Caribbean Coast, the Spaniards found increasingly strong indicators of even more complex society – the outposts of long-distance trading networks that moved gold out of Panama and toward Mesoamerica. The Caribbean Coast northwest of Panama was a kind of frontier zone, with sites like Río Claro, about 330 km (*c.* 200 miles) east of the Yucatán Peninsula and clearly evidencing contact with Mesoamerica. Río Claro may have been a Pipil Nahuat trading enclave, possibly the "Papayeca" community mentioned by Cortés in 1525. The site is in the Aguan River Valley, a few kilometers inland from the Caribbean, and its center features plazas with platform mounds that are considerably larger than the habitation mounds that surround them. The tallest and most centrally located of these was 7 m (23 ft) high. The site had been made defensible by a ditch, today still an impressive 2.5 m (8 ft) deep (Healy 1992). Río Claro represents a borderlands community, clearly demonstrating complexity in social ranking and public rituals, but with a distinctive local flavor.

Southeastern Mesoamerica

Throughout most of Late Postclassic Honduras, settlements were small towns, probably the seats of local chiefdoms, except in the west, near what had been the Classic Maya region. In the Chamelecón River Valley, the sites of Naco and Viejo Brisas del Valle were substantial communities, about 9 km (*c.* 5.4 miles) apart and politically independent of each other. Naco was well-situated for trade. The Chamelecón River's headwaters were close to the Motagua River drainage at the boundary of the Copán Valley, and Naco was just upstream from a confluence of rivers draining the Ulua Valley, the most important route south to the Pacific. The Naco region was a major cacao-growing area in the contact period, thus a magnet for traders. Naco is also well-known from its visit by Cortés on his trip to Honduras in 1524 and 1525, and by its importance in long-distance trade. The only artifactual substantiation of this comes from objects of copper and obsidian, but influence from Mexico is architecturally evidenced by an I-shaped ball court, part of modest monumental architecture at the site (Henderson *et al.* 1979). Near Naco was another town, Quimistan, and in this vicinity archaeologists found the Quimistan Bell Cave, so-called because of its hoard of 800 cast copper bells, some nearly 7 cm (2 in) in diameter, many of them animal effigies, and a turquoise mosaic mask of Quetzalcoatl as Ehécatl (Stone 1972).

This stash of goods provokes speculation about how trade was carried out, and how traders behaved and were treated – here and in other remote parts of Mesoamerica. Traders carried with them the ideas and styles of all the regions they visited, and the many examples of "Mexicanized" traits that are found throughout the Maya region and locations south and east were not just the result of militarism, or even well-organized Putún or *pochteca* commercial ventures, but also could be credited to repeated contacts by overland traders, a much riskier and rougher enterprise in this part of the world. For traders carrying luxury goods, it was essential to locate a convenient, concealed place to store most of them while the itinerant merchants reconnoitered and negotiated in a nearby town. For some reason, the traders carrying this particular cargo of bells and a deity icon never returned to the cave to reclaim them.

Southeastern Maya of the Late Postclassic

From the eastern highlands of Guatemala, several great valleys drain watercourses in a northeasterly direction toward the Caribbean. The Motagua River Valley, dominated in the Classic period by Quirigua, offered the most direct route up to the Guatemala highlands. North of the Motagua Valley another valley paralleled it, tracing the course of the Polochic River into Guatemala's largest lake, Izabal, which drained into the Caribbean. The decline of the Classic Maya civilization of the southern lowlands seems to have caused an Early Postclassic-period population loss in these valleys, but by the Late Postclassic they had substantial towns, testimony to their enduring importance as conduits of highland luxury goods like jadeite, quetzal feathers, and obsidian as they moved down to trading centers near the Caribbean Sea. Furthermore, cacao was grown in the lower reaches of these valleys, so there was always a valuable product to exchange for exotic goods.

The first contact between Mesoamericans and Spaniards had been in 1502, when Columbus encountered a large trading canoe in the Bay of Honduras [**14.13**]. It may have been based in Nito, the largest town near the Caribbean Coast in this region. Nito, a trading center "where there was extensive trade with all parts" of the country and the Putún Maya merchants from Acalán, on the west coast of the Yucatán Peninsula "had a district of their own" according to one Nito-based Putún merchant interviewed by Hernan Cortés a few decades later (Cortés 1986 [1525]: 383). Nito may have been Quirigua's successor in controlling the luxury goods that moved down from the highlands to this port (Sharer 1984). The Spaniards took over Nito in the 1520s and their violence toward the local population quickly brought an end to the trading networks centered upon this town.

Spaniards and Maya Along the Coast of Yucatán

"When the Spaniards discovered this land, they asked the Indian chief ...'what do you call it?' The Indians, who did not understand, said *uic athan*, which means: 'what are you saying? ... we do not understand you.' And then the Spaniard said, 'they call it *Yucatan*...'" (Ciudad Real (1993 [1586]: II: 320).

In 1508, a Spanish expedition sailing northwest from Panama reached the coastal waters off Yucatán, and then went back toward Spanish bases in the Caribbean. The Spaniards decided to make this new land a target of exploration, but their first attempt, the Valdivia expedition of 1511, was hardly a success, and had bizarre consequences. Shipwrecked off the coast of Yucatán, only 10 men made it to shore. Five, including Valdivia, were sacrificed by the Maya and then served at a feast, three others died of disease, and the last two survived as slaves of the Maya. Both were later to play important and opposing roles in the unfolding drama of the contact period. Geronimo de Aguilar was finally freed when he was purchased out of slavery by Hernan Cortés in Yucatán in 1518. Aguilar had learned to speak Mayan, and could interpret between the Spaniards and the Maya and thus became an important instrument of conquest. When Cortés's ransom arrived, Aguilar bought himself free and went to find the other slave, Gonzalo Guerrero. But Guerrero had become an important man among the Maya and preferred to stay, telling Aguilar "I am married and have three children [the first *mestizos* in the Mesoamerican culture area] ... I have my face tattooed and my ears pierced, what would the Spaniards say should they see me in this guise?" (Díaz 1956: 43). Guerrero, true to his Spanish name meaning warrior, became a Maya war captain, leading attacks against the Spaniards from 1517 – the Córdoba expedition, the second to reach Yucatán – into the 1530s.

The Córdoba expedition was the point in the exploration process at which the Spaniards realized the significance and size of Yucatán (Restall 1998). From the sea, they saw the town of Ecab near the northeast corner of the peninsula, and called it "Gran Cairo" – a flight of romantic fancy, because Cairo in Egypt was, in AD 1500, a city of half a million, while Ecab was probably home to a few thousand. Still, Ecab's plastered buildings gleamed in the sun, and must have seemed to the members of the expedition like a distant vision of the fabled capitals of the east that were going to make them all rich.

Cozumel Island The third Spanish expedition to reach Yucatán was led by Juan de Grijalva, and in 1518 landed on Cozumel Island, which it claimed for Spain. This was probably a perfunctory "conquest" because Cortés also claimed Cozumel for Spain in 1519. Cozumel is 16 km (*c.* 10 miles) offshore from the east coast of Yucatán, with an area of just under 400 sq. km (*c.* 160 sq. miles). It was occupied by the Late Formative period, but its importance grew at the end of the Late Classic period, when the Putún Maya founded a trading station there as they expanded their network of commercial outposts around the Yucatán Coast.

Cozumel flourished in the Late Postclassic period as a commercial center and a major shrine for Ixchel, the Maya goddess of childbirth (Freidel and Sabloff 1984; Sabloff and Rathje 1975). Of the island's 30+ sites, most are coastal shrines that also served as beacon points for signal fires. Trading vessels moving along the coast of the Yucatán Peninsula would have stopped at one of Cozumel's coastal stations, and from there goods were moved along a system of causeways to San Gervasio, the island's largest and most complex Late Postclassic community. Elite residential compounds at San Gervasio resemble those found at Mayapan and Tulum. Ixchel's major shrine was at San Gervasio, and women having trouble conceiving would have visited there to appeal to the goddess. Presumably, commercial and ritual functions coexisted well, with traders able to transport pilgrims, who then may have used their visit as a chance to do a little shopping for unusual things, as pilgrims are known to do, worldwide.

19.18, 19.19 *(Opposite) Overlooking a gloriously scenic Caribbean Coast, Tulum's Castillo is a popular image in promotions for tourism, as this view looking south down the coast shows. The Castillo and other buildings at Tulum are modest in scale and of poor-quality construction. As the plan indicates, the walled rectangular site only measures about 150 by 350 m (492 by 1,148 ft).*

Cozumel's position off the east coast of Yucatán, and its association with each day's return in the east of the life-giving sun, makes it a logical place for shrines to conception and childbirth. Scholars have noted that Cozumel mirrors the position and role of the island of Jaina, the cemetery off Yucatán's west coast. Both were liminal places for the Maya, representing key transitions into the land of the living, and departing from it. With the 16th-century arrival of the Spaniards and the diseases they brought, and disruption of the commercial routes, Cozumel was no longer a center of fertility, but became, like Jaina, a place of the dead.

The Putún Maya traders were at their most powerful in the Late Postclassic, using large dugout canoes to ply the coastal waters from Xicalanco, an Aztec port on the eastern edge of the southern Gulf lowlands, around the Yucatán Peninsula to Nito and beyond. All along, they traded for products brought from inland areas. The standard staple crops were grown in Yucatan to support local populations, and cotton and cacao were also cultivated where conditions permitted, for consumption by local elites and to trade to the long-distance merchants. Salt was produced along the coast, and fish netted offshore were dried to preserve them – both products were widely traded. Valued products of the forest included copal resin, for incense, and a tree bark necessary to the production of *balche'*, a fermented beverage drunk at feasts. The Putún would have maintained warehouses in their regular ports, such as Nito, Cozumel Island, and, on the Yucatán Coast across from Cozumel, Tulum.

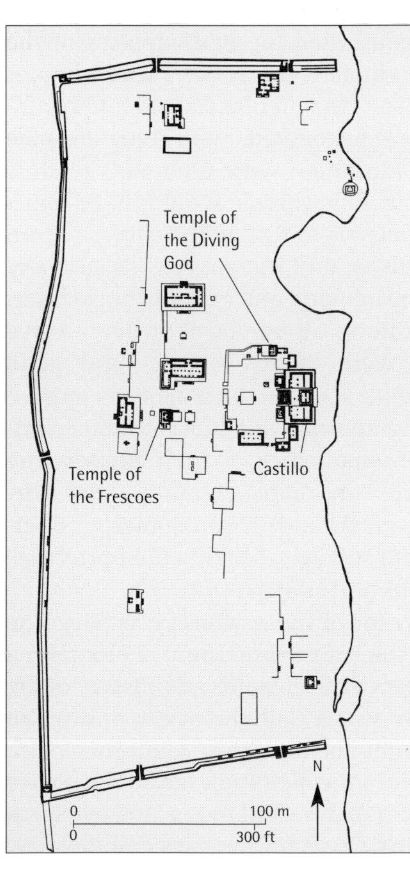

Tulum Many of the Late Postclassic capitals of Yucatán underlie modern towns, so there is little archaeological evidence about their layout and organization. Tulum, a small commercial outpost in the province of Ecab, is exceptional in that the site is reasonably well preserved. Furthermore, because of its proximity to the modern resort, Cancún, Tulum has been recently consolidated and is visited by many tourists [**19.18, 19.19**]. Its situation, on a cliff above the sea, has been made further defensible by its wall. Buildings at the site feature depictions of "diving" gods, so-called because of their descending posture. Frescoed murals also feature Chac, the Maya rain god, and female deities. The style of the murals is most similar to Mixtec codex style, reflecting the active trade in goods, possibly even manuscripts, along the coast. Similar motifs have been found further south, at Santa Rita Corozal, which was probably the Late Postclassic town of Chetumal, on Chetumal Bay (Chase and Chase 1988).

Northern Maya Lowlands

After the fall of Chichén in the 13th century and the subsequent decline of Mayapan by the mid 15th century, no single polity in the northern Maya lowlands controlled the others. Instead, the Late Postclassic period in the Maya lowlands saw the development of a set of about 16 independent provinces [**19.20**]. Some were simply loose confederations of small towns, while others were well-organized city-states, with small communities paying tribute to a capital ruled by a dynasty. For the Maya, the local home community provided a basic orientation to the larger society. This was called the *cah*, and it was a parallel to the Aztec *calpulli* in that it represented the local neighborhood that was also an entity in the larger society, the organizational means through which taxes were paid, land allocated, and disputes mediated. A Mayan word, *cah*'s several meanings include residence and existence itself (Restall 1998).

Kinship ties were essential to mate choice in marriage – one could not marry a person with the same surname – and such ties offer a view of lineage organization. Among the Itzá, an individual had two surnames, the first from the mother and the second from the father, in addition to a day name or given name (Jones 1998). The Maya use of surnames provides insights into social organizational rules that may have been operative among Maya kings in the Classic period. Clearly, patrilineal descent played a leading role in structuring descent rules and inheritance of rulership, but it appears that the matriline was also important in resolving questions about succession to office.

The city-state ruler was known as the *batab* (pl. *batabob*), and among rulers, the most powerful assumed the title *halach uinic* and headed a hierarchy of power, directing the actions of lesser *batabob*. As in Classic times, the lords decided upon political arrangements such as alliances and hostilities between the provinces. They also controlled the marketplaces of the towns, which were smaller and simpler than those of the highlands, and lords probably also negotiated with long-distance traders. Elite men were often polygynous, and their households would have been both expensive to run, with so many wives and children, and lucrative, with so many women producing and embellishing cotton cloth. Among all ranks of society, Maya women were "hard workers and good housekeepers, for on them depends most of the most important and most arduous work for the maintenance of their houses, the education of their children, and the payment of tribute ... sometimes ... cultivating and sowing ... selling their produce" (Landa 1975 [1566]: 91–92).

The writer of these words was Diego de Landa, the most important Colonial-era chronicler of the customs and history of the Maya. He was a Catholic priest, and wrote his account in the 1560s while in Spain, having been recalled from his duties, under accusation that he had too zealously persecuted the natives for heresies and idolatry.

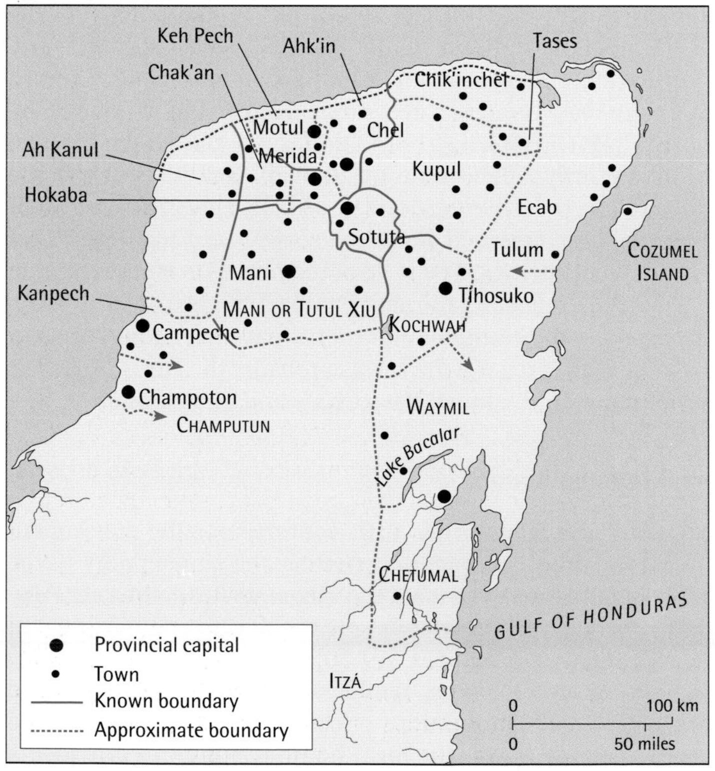

19.20 *The northern Maya lowlands in about 1500 had a population between 600,000 and 1,000,000, distributed among 16 polities.*

19.21 *(Above) Only four pre-Columbian Maya screenfold books survive: the* Paris, Dresden, Grolier, *and* Madrid *(or* Tro-Cortesianus*) codices. "They are thought to have originated in Yucatan, because the language spoken there has proved most useful to study of the hieroglyphic text" (Paxton 2001: 8).* Madrid Codex *page 72, shown here, is part of a divinatory almanac (Bricker 1997).*

In fact, he burned a substantial number of native books – only four Maya codices survive from this era, saved by having been sent to Europe as curiosities. These screenfold books were painted by scribes, high-ranking individuals who served as historians, genealogists, and keepers of calendars and astronomical knowledge [**19.21**].

The Southeastern Highlands of Chiapas and Guatemala

Late Postclassic settlement in the Chiapas Interior Plateau and in the Guatemala highlands was established for clearly defensive purposes, and we see the familiar pattern of small states, internally complex and headed by a ruling dynasty, battling off incursions by their neighbors. Far to the west, Chiapa de Corzo continued to thrive, and after Spanish conquest was made into a Colonial community, and now, as a modern town, has one of the longest continuous histories of settlement in Mesoamerican culture history.

Other settlements in the Chiapas interior were more ephemeral. One of the few sites occupied only during the Late Postclassic was Canajasté, which is quite close to the Guatemala border. Like many sites in the adjacent Guatemala highlands, Canajasté was settled in the 1200s, and featured a defensive wall encircling a 2.5-hectare (6-acre) area, densely packed with a modest ceremonial center and 200 houses (Blake 1984). Artifacts at the site reveal that this region was well integrated into trade routes bringing such exotic items as copper bells and marine shell. However, hostilities are also evidenced: the buildings show signs of having been repeatedly burned, and the community was abandoned before the Spanish arrived in the region.

These are strong suggestions of Late Postclassic violence in Chiapas. For the Guatemala highlands, such patterns are much better documented. Maya from western and northern Yucatán had aggressively established themselves in the Guatemala highlands in the 13th century, and evolved into a welter of loosely related, mutually hostile localized ethnic groups. The Quiché and the Cakchiquel, whose capital, Iximché, fell to Spaniards led by Pedro de Alvarado in 1524, were the most important political powers in the region. Other Maya groups included the Pokomam, with a hilltop capital at Mixco Viejo [**19.22, 19.23**], the Tzutuhil, who built dual-staircase pyramids at their center of Chuitinamit, and the Mam, whose small but impressive center of Zaculeu was at one time overwhelmed by the Quiché, and then surrendered to Alvarado's troops in 1525.

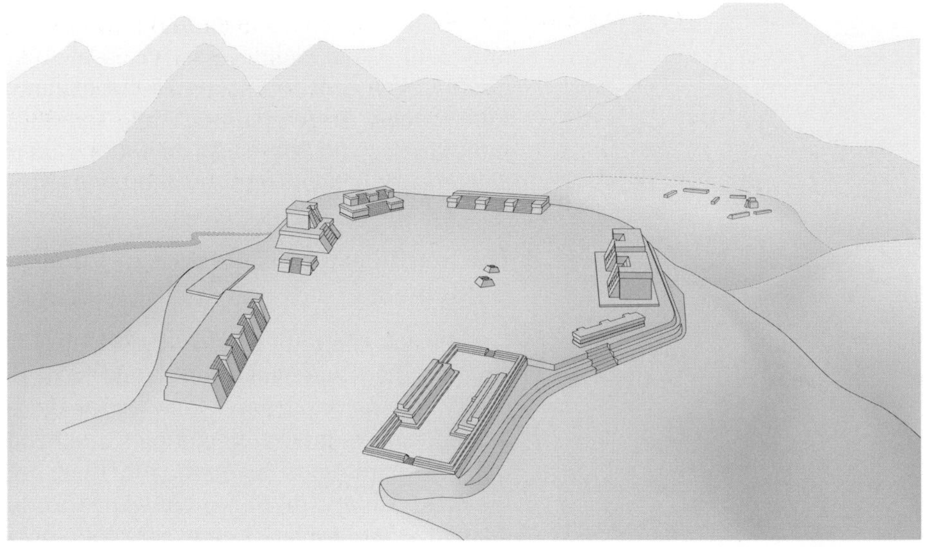

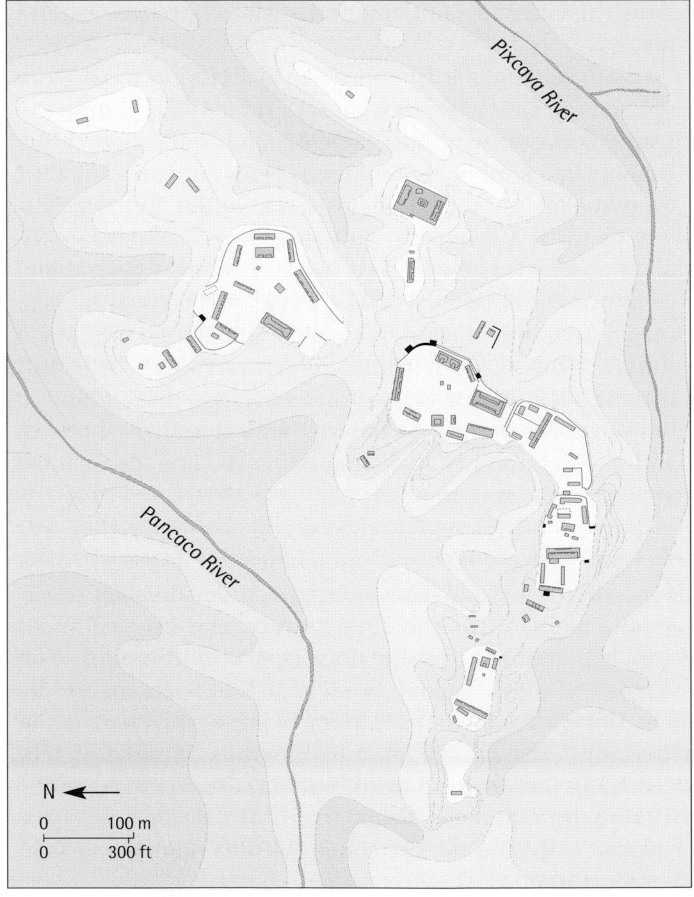

The Quiché were the most aggressive of all. They built their central capital at Utatlan in about 1400 (Carmack 1981). Eventually – by the time the region was conquered by the Spaniards in the 1520s – the male-dominated ruling lineages of the Quiché presided over a system of hierarchically ranked tribute-paying communities, encompassing a population of perhaps 1,000,000. They represent another Late Postclassic-period regional case of cultural evolution parallel to that of the Aztecs, with one city-state intimidating others to support a centralized government with tributes.

The Quiché extended their domain to encompass the Pacific coastal plain of Guatemala. Since Formative times, the coast from the Isthmus of Tehuantepec down into El Salvador had been an important corridor for the movement of goods, migrating populations, and ideas. More importantly, the plain was a rich region in and of itself, the source of some of Mesoamerica's highest-quality cacao. In occupying the Guatemala portion of this plain, the Quiché found themselves having become a buffer state to the Aztec empire, which had moved into the Soconusco region.

Along the Gulf Coast

As the Aztec empire was absorbing Soconusco, drawn to this most distant province by the value of its products and imports, Columbus was just encountering a heavily laden trading canoe in the Gulf of Honduras, and was realizing that the New World held cultures far richer and more complex than those of the Caribbean. It wasn't until the Córdoba and Grijalva expeditions that the Spaniards pushed northwest and then south around the peninsula and found their way to the Gulf of Mexico, and the long curving stretch of the Gulf lowlands that would be their gateway to the Central Highlands. A vivid, firsthand account of the Grijalva expedition was written by Bernal Díaz del Castillo (1956), who then also accompanied Cortés and described the story of the conquest, as did Cortés himself (1986).

Campeche + Tabasco = Acalán

19.22, 19.23 *(Opposite) Mixco Viejo achieved its greatest extent in the Late Postclassic, when it consisted of a set of at least 12 clusters of civic-ceremonial architecture – temples, palaces, ball courts – strung out over hilltops separated by steep ravines. As the reconstruction drawing shows, the setting was dramatic, with plaza groups seeming to float among the peaks of highland Guatemala. The site was first established in the Late Classic. Its Late Postclassic population probably numbered 2,000 or fewer, conquered by the Spanish in 1525.*

On 26 May 1518, the Grijalva expedition landed near Champoton on the west coast of Yucatán. This was another commercial center, and an ancient capital of the Putún Maya (Chapter 14), whose exact location is unknown. Spaniards and Maya skirmished, a few lives were lost on both sides, and the Spaniards pushed off, continuing to move south and west along the coast. At the western base of the Yucatán Peninsula, they came to a huge enclosed bay, the Laguna de Términos, where they saw, but did not approach, Xicalanco, one of the trading centers of the Chontal Maya. They had entered the region of Acalán, homeland of the Toltecized Maya traders who have been variously identified as the Chontal, Putún, and sometimes Putún Itzá. Acalán's ruler was the chief merchant of Itzamkanac (Sharer 1994), about 130 km (*c.* 80 miles) southeast of Xicalanco, along the Candelaría River.

Xicalanco was one of the most distant trading points of Central Mexico's *pochteca* traders, and in about AD 1500 they would have been bringing fine goods for Acalán's rulers. In a strict sense, these trades were not commerce but gift exchange. Emperor Ahuitzotl sent off the *pochteca* with very special clothing items designed for highest rulers, plus gold – not just jewelry, but also "what the princesses required: golden bowls for spindles, and ear plugs of gold and rock crystal" (Sahagún 1959 [1569]: 18). The *pochteca* merchants also carried more utilitarian things, such as obsidian, red dye from the cochineal insect, herbs, and slaves. In return, the merchant "rulers of Anauac [a general term for the coastal hot lands], Xicalanco, Cimatlan, [and] Coatzaqualco reciprocated" (ibid.) and gave the *pochteca* precious greenstones, beautiful shells and feathers, skins of the black jaguar, which they took back to the Aztec emperor. Such trading involved considerable risk for the *pochteca*, because the merchants had to travel through a wide expanse of hostile territory, but the Xicalanco venture is highly reminiscent of preliminary moves upon Soconusco. Given these established patterns of aggression, it would seem that Acalán might have become one of the Aztec empire's next tributary provinces.

Malinche The Grijalva expedition continued along the coast, and less than a year later, the Cortés expedition would retrace its route. West of Xicalanco, Cortés and company stopped along the Tabasco Coast at a town called Potonchan, where the chief gave them a gift of 20 slave women. One of them was the high-born and well-educated Malinalli, also known as Malinche and Marina. Both of her parents were rulers in the Tabasco region, but upon the death of her father, her mother married another ruler and gave birth to a son. Malinalli became an inconvenience in her mother's plans to unite the three domains to be ruled by the new son, so she was sold to Acalán traders and eventually became part of a gesture of hospitality towards the Spaniards. Though technically Cortés's slave, obviously given to him to provide sexual companionship, she quickly became his indispensable partner, because she spoke both Nahuatl and Mayan, and soon learned Spanish. Every interchange between the Aztecs and Spaniards went through her.

Malinalli's family history offers insights into the cultural situation during the Late Postclassic. There is little archaeological evidence from this period for the southern Gulf lowlands, and because the region was never incorporated into the Aztec empire, features of cultural organization have not been well documented. However, details such as Malinalli's story indicate that there was probably a political system of small, loosely allied city-states. Spanish expeditions report seeing numerous towns along the coast and they describe cacao as a major crop. Coatzacoalco, on the coast at the delta of the Coatzacoalcos-Uxpanapa river system, was an important trading center, and had gone to war against the nearest Aztec empire province, Tochtepec in the south-central Gulf lowlands.

South-central Gulf Lowlands

This region covered the stretch of coast between the Tuxtla Mountains on the south and the Sierra de Chiconquiaco on the north – the Aztec empire controlled large areas of the region, the provinces of Tochtepec and Cotaxtla. In the middle lies the present-day city of Veracruz, one of modern Mexico's most important. During the Grijalva expedition, in 1518, the Spaniards disembarked on an island offshore from the location of modern Veracruz. They called it "Isla de Sacrificios" because they found several temples. Ascending the steps, they saw altars with "idols with evil looking bodies, and that very night five Indians had been sacrificed before them; their chests had been cut open, and the arms and thighs had been cut off and the walls were covered with blood" (Díaz 1956 [1560s]: 26). Isla de Sacrificios, only 4 hectares (10 acres) in size, was an important ceremonial site. Like Jaina, it was a cemetery island, and here, as the Spaniards found, sacrificial rituals were performed. Excavations have revealed that the island was occupied throughout the Postclassic period, and had stuccoed buildings that were dedicated to the Feathered Serpent (Medellín Zenil 1955).

The Cortés expedition landed near the present location of the city of Veracruz in Easter week 1519, beginning an inland venture that would bring them the great prize, the Aztec empire. In this vicinity, the Spaniards first encountered a province of the Aztec empire, Cotaxtla (they had sailed past the coast of the province of Tochtepec). With each encounter with the natives, the Spaniards used a combination of appeasement, in the form of gifts, and intimidation, ranging from displays of horsemanship and firearms, to actual military engagement in sorties that sometimes resulted in loss of life on both sides. The Spaniards quickly learned that the Mesoamericans prized greenstones above all, and made glass beads a feature of their gifts. They also repeatedly emphasized to the natives that gold was what they wanted, and were sometimes disappointed when they were brought an alloy of copper made to look like gold.

Cortés was welcomed by the ruler of the town of Cotaxtla, Motecuzoma II's *calpixqui* steward, named Teniltzin, who "brought with him some clever painters ... and ordered them to make pictures true to the nature of the face and body of Cortés and all his captains ... ships, sails and horses ... and he carried the pictures to his master [Motecuzoma]" (Díaz 1956: 72). As noted above, the Aztecs had first conquered Cotaxtla in the reigns of Motecuzoma I and Nezahualcoyotl, and at that time its towns were governed by *tlatoque*, but thereafter, rebellion required reconquest and the installation of military governors and *calpixque*, like Teniltzin, sent from Tenochtitlan. Teniltzin was a welcoming host, and after about a week, a delegation from Tenochtitlan arrived, 100 porters bearing gifts such as a huge embossed disk of solid gold, and another of solid silver, plus other fine worked adornments and 30 loads of cotton textiles.

The Spaniards moved onto Zempoala and met the "Fat Cacique" – "he was so fat that I shall call him by this name" (Díaz 1956: 88). Quite possibly, this portliness was a sign of high status, particularly in the Gulf lowlands where it might have served as a representation of the richness of this land of food. Throughout Mesoamerica there occurred images of an obese male whom archaeologists have dubbed the "Fat God" though there is little evidence of an organized cult venerating such a deity. In the modern U.S., obesity has become a national health problem and occurs much more prevalently among the poor than it does among the rich. This reflects the ready access to cheap, high-calorie food in developed nations, and we must recall that in pre-modern times, starvation was, at least intermittently, a severe problem, as the Aztecs had found in the mid 1450s, and thus obesity expressed access to unlimited riches.

Fat, the *cacique* was, but jolly he was not. He "complained bitterly of the great Montezuma and his governors saying that he had recently been brought under his yoke; that all his golden jewels had been carried off, and he and his people were so grievously oppressed, that they dared do nothing without Montezuma's orders" (Díaz 1956: 88). As if to illustrate this, several days later some natives rushed into Zempoala to warn of the arrival of the Mexica tax collectors. Hurriedly, rooms and food were prepared for them, "and cacao, which is the best thing they have to drink" (Díaz 1956:

88). The five richly dressed tax collectors and their attendants "came to the place where we were assembled ... and approaching us with the utmost assurance and arrogance without speaking to Cortés, or to any of us, they passed us by" (Díaz 1956: 89). You have to admire the self-assurance of these Mexica, among the first of their people to come in contact with alien invaders, and able to act massively unimpressed. Of course, they then hustled the Fat Cacique into conference and dressed him down for entertaining the Spaniards without consulting Motecuzoma first. They demanded 20 sacrificial victims in order to perform the proper rites to overcome the invaders, and assured the *cacique* that the Spaniards would become Mexica slaves.

Cortés's response to this situation set the tone for the rest of the conquest. He imprisoned the tax collectors, but then took two of them aside and assured them of the Spaniards' friendly intent toward the Mexica, a message he wished them to take back to Motecuzoma. He had them escorted beyond Zempoala's borders, and set them free. The other three were also well treated and released. All this was done without the knowledge of the Zempoalans, to whom Cortés gave assurances that the Spaniards were their allies against Motecuzoma, whom they no longer should regard as their king. This was the first of many diplomatic maneuvers that would undermine Motecuzoma's empire, and bring onto the Spanish side hundreds of thousands of allies, without whom the conquest could not have been successful.

20 THE CONQUEST OF MEXICO AND ITS AFTERMATH

"FORTUNE FAVORS THE BOLD" was one of Cortés's favorite mottos, and in this spirit he and his troops began the long march to the Aztec capital, leaving Zempoala in mid-August, 1519. Motecuzoma was the perfect Aztec emperor for the Spaniards to contact. As news of the Spaniards' activities reached him, he became fatalistic and morose, and as the omens began to collect, his response was despair rather than resistance. In Ahuitzotl, the Spaniards would have faced more formidable opposition.

The legend persists that the Mexicans regarded Cortés as the returning god Quetzalcoatl, or even as Huitzilopochtli. Actual references to this in first-hand sources such as Cortés's letters are vague, and the story seems to have arisen in the mid-16th century, when chroniclers such as Motolinía and Sahagún recorded it (Thomas 1995). Certainly the Mexicans regarded the Spaniards as possessing strengths that had to be respected, and Cortés was prepared to exploit every coincidence that identified him with powers that intimidated the Aztecs. The Aztecs, in turn, were predisposed to look for signs of spiritual potency in these unknown adversaries, because they perpetually understood the world in terms of such interpretations. However, they were also practical, and in the range of their responses to the approach of the Spaniards we can perceive the divisions among Tenochca political leaders that was to contribute to the Aztec downfall. Motecuzoma kept sending messengers who would bring gifts, but tell the Spaniards not to come to Tenochtitlan, not to trust the "allies" who told tales of Mexica power and cruelty. When other Tenochcan and Texcocan leaders advocated eliminating the invaders, their sharp protests against appeasement and accurate predictions of disaster had no effect on Motecuzoma.

THE SPANIARDS COLLECT ALLIES

As the Spaniards pressed toward Tenochtitlan, they passed through two important regions, Tlaxcala and Puebla [**20.1**]. Parts of Puebla had become provinces of the Aztec empire, but the region's most important city, Cholula, was not, and had maintained independence from the Triple

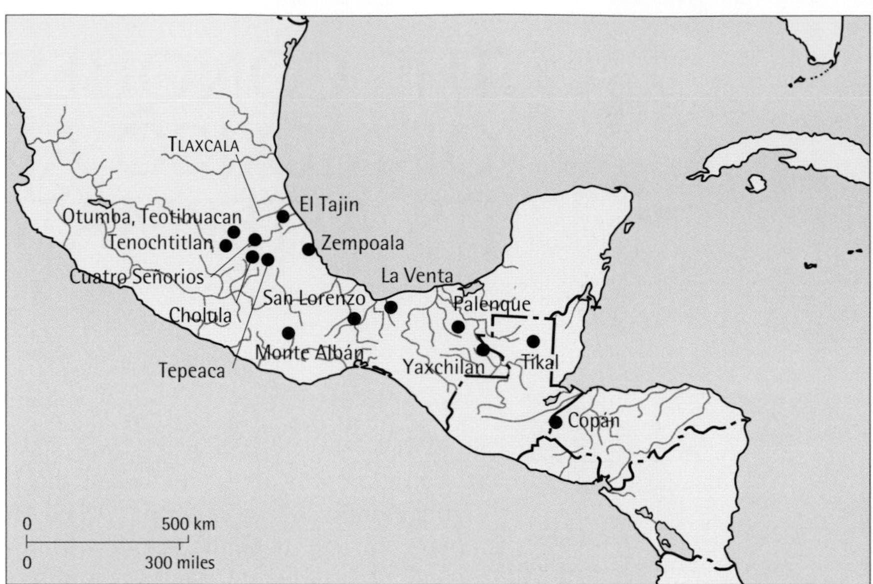

20.1 *Middle America showing sites and regions mentioned in this chapter.*

Alliance without actually incurring enmity. Farther to the north, Tlaxcala was fiercely antagonistic to the Mexica, and its landlocked position, surrounded by Aztec provinces, had resulted in embargos of some basic goods as well as promoting culture isolation and a state of constant readiness for war on its borders. With Tlaxcala the Spaniards made common cause.

Tlaxcala

Tlaxcala was connected to the northern Basin of Mexico by the Plain of Apam, and these adjacent regions shared a high, cool, dry environment. Furthermore, their Postclassic Nahuatl- and Otomí-speaking populations were similarly distributed, with maguey-farming families dispersed over terraced hillsides and small city-states on the alluvial plain (García Cook 1981; Snow 1996), which was "all cultivated and harvested, leaving no place untilled" (Cortés 1986: 68). In contrast to most other regions, where the city-states were distanced from each other, in Tlaxcala the four main capitals (the "Cuatro Señorios") were clustered together, their territories radiating out behind them. These centers, Tepeticpac, Quiahuiztlan, Ocotelulco, and Tizatlan, were so close that the Spaniards thought them to be one city, "so big and remarkable ... much larger than Granada and very much stronger ... and very much supplied with the produce of the land" (Cortés 1986: 67). Cortés also described a large market that drew 30,000 people daily and provided a wide range of goods and services.

For all this seeming unity, there were tensions between the four dynasties, and even between generations within the same dynasty. These problems had the usual sources: greed, sexual jealousy, and ongoing vendettas that had acquired their own momentum. The Tlaxcalan nobles provide an inter-

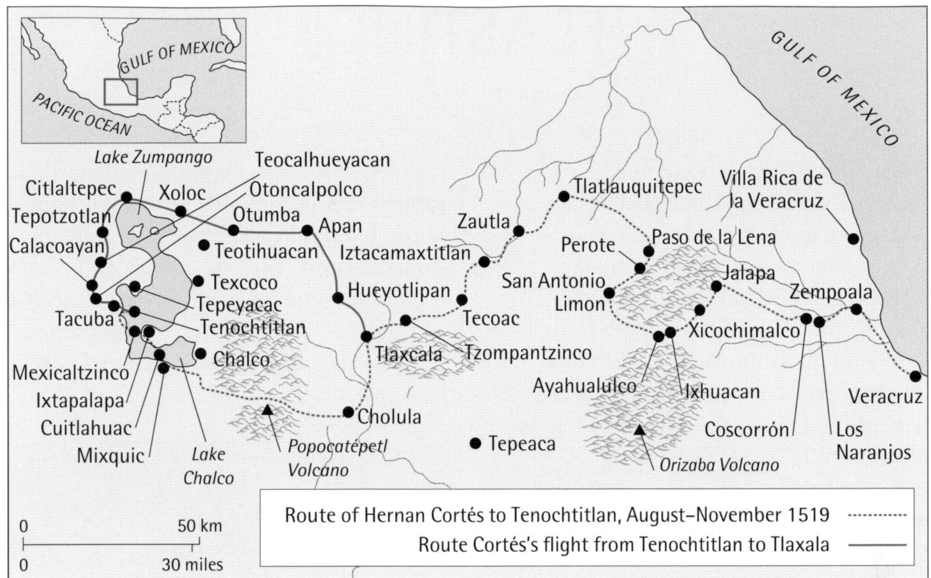

20.2 *Cortés's routes and sites along the way.*

esting case of the use of feasting to relieve these tensions, or, given the circumstances, to channel them differently, because Tlaxcalan feasts involved intoxication and often ended in violence (Motolinía 1950).

The reasons for ingesting hallucinogens until homicidal rage ensued had to do with contacting the spirits of dead ancestors, which was thought to be facilitated by achieving a transcendent state (Pohl 1998). This practice of inducing visions in order to contact the dead is revealed by the motifs decorating the feasting rooms themselves. Archaeological investigation has uncovered part of the palace of Xicotencatl the Elder, the *tlatoani* of Tizatlan, and the highest-ranking among the rulers of the Cuatro Señorios. One of the rooms in his palace has polychromed decorations in Mixteca-Puebla style, depicting such malevolent deities as the Tzitzime and Tezcatlipoca, as well as skulls, hearts, and other themes of death and destruction.

The Tlaxcalan-Spanish Alliance The Spaniards reached the Cuatro Señorios in September of 1519 with some difficulty, because they were ambushed by troops led by Xicotencatl the Younger. But both sides put this skirmish behind them at the peace-making intervention of his father, the elder Xicotencatl, who welcomed the Spaniards and in fact sent them off toward Cholula with porters to carry the cannons. The two Xicotencatls were to quarrel again over the Spaniards nearly a year later, when Cortés and his troops escaped the Basin of Mexico with their lives and sought refuge in Tlaxcala on their way to their base on the Gulf Coast. The younger man suggested that the Tlaxcalans should kill the Spaniards and steal their possessions; his father flew into a rage at this idea, and "ordered his son to be killed when he knew of his plots and treason" (Díaz 1956: 325), and the Spaniards were given sanctuary.

FEASTING

AS WE HAVE SEEN, feasts were an essential component of social life throughout Mesoamerican culture history. Just like modern parties, feasts in ancient societies provided important occasions for demonstrations of social solidarity, for exchanging information and gifts, and for showing off the hosts' ability to command and distribute high quality food and party decorations and favors. Feasts were also occasions where the participants could transcend their everyday lives and (one hopes) enjoy themselves.

With all these motivating factors, it is obvious that feasts would range from spectacular events staged in the main courtyards of the great imperial palaces, with casts of hundreds (guests and servers), to the other end of the power-and-wealth spectrum, where a few poor people would modestly honor an important rite with the best of their limited resources. Sources such as the *Florentine Codex* and *The History of the Indies of New Spain* (Durán 1994 [1581]) offer many descriptions of the most elaborate feasts, in the palaces and in the compounds of the *pochteca* merchants.

The baptismal feast description from the *Florentine Codex* (Sahagún 1979: 117–119), "which telleth how a feast was held," offers a view of a fairly modest event, one which most people would have been likely to have participated in from time to time. When the guests arrived there was a period of settling down in their proper places. As soon as the guests were seated, tobacco was served and smoked, and then flower servers distributed crowns and garlands. In wealthy houses, there were also gifts – tobacco, flowers, and clothing – and then the food was served.

Food preparation was the domain of the women of the house, and they would have spent considerable time planning the menu and readying the dishes. Tamales (steamed dumplings of corn meal with seasonings and fillings) were mainstays of festivals among many groups in Mesoamerica, in ancient times and today. Stews featured turkey and dog meat in a sauce of tomatoes and other vegetables and chiles. Accompanying these entrees were tortillas and sauces not unlike the chile-spiced tomato *salsa* that in the modern U.S. has become the most popular ready-made condiment.

20.3 *At Aztec feasts, guests were presented with flowers, cylindrical pipes full of tobacco, and food, as these illustrations from the* Florentine Codex *show. Dancing and music were highlights of a good party.*

Before dining, each guest "said grace" by dropping a bit of food onto the ground as an offering to Tlaltecuhtli, the earth god (Coe 1994: 77). If the hosts were rich, chocolate was served after dinner. Cacao beans had to be imported from *tierra caliente* regions along the Gulf lowlands and Pacific Coast (Coe and Coe 1996). They were sold whole in city markets, and one could also buy a cup of the prepared beverage, which was made by mixing the ground beans with water, and, if desired, adding such seasonings as chile or honey or vanilla.

Chocolate consumption was restricted both because of the cost and because it was thought to be too stimulating for the inexperienced. The Tenochca emperor drank chocolate every day, and many people probably only had a few cups in a lifetime, but it is likely that most adults had tasted chocolate, because it was customary for kitchen workers to get the leftovers of a feast, and in many noble houses the servants were people from rural farming villages who were working a labor tribute shift.

20.4 *At this* pulque *feast (*Codex Magliabechiano*), the* pulque-*god impersonator drinks through a straw. He faces a woman whose speech scroll is only a series of dots, probably reflecting the drunken disintegration of her verbal skills.*

While chocolate's high cost and stimulating properties made it a status symbol, *pulque*, maguey sap beer, was eschewed by the elite not only because it was abundant and common, but also because it made people drunk. Not that all intoxicants were regarded with distaste: Axayacatl commanded hallucinogenic mushrooms in tribute (de la Garza 1990: 63), and lords and wealthy merchants ate them at their feasts, after which they "ate no more food; they only drank chocolate through the night" while they danced and had visions (Sahagún 1959: 39). This kind of party intoxication was justified by its higher purpose – an avenue to the future, to seeing one's fate – while common drunkenness was despicable, and made the common drunkard a vehicle for forces of chaos that could bring ruin to whole families.

Strong condemnations of the effects of *pulque* drinking seem to have served as constant warnings to a large population of regular drinkers. Maguey was grown everywhere in the Central Highlands, and farming families used fresh sap as potable beverage. Fresh sap ferments within a few days – it would be impossible for families *not* to have a ready supply of crude beer if they wanted it. And *pulque* was highly valued for its medicinal qualities and was used as a base for many other medicines. So almost anyone feeling tired or achy at the end of a long day of work might ease the chill with a bowl of *pulque*, and its use was the reward of old age.

In spite of abhorrence of public drunkenness, the Aztecs well understood that drinking alcohol livened up a party. At a baptismal feast if the *pulque* server "saw that those who he gave wine did not become intoxicated ... but only sat staring and grimacing" he served everyone all over again. Once under the influence, people began singing, and then exchanging sentimental greetings. The mood became so festive that people turned to "laughing and making witty remarks, making others burst into laughter ... [until they] sat exhausted with mirth" (Sahagún 1979: 119). Many feasts featured instrumental music and dancing, as well.

Some parties went all night – the Aztecs seemed to value nearly constant moderation, but when they decided to become immoderate, they wished to savor the experience fully. In fact, if anyone did not have a good time at a party, it was customary for the host to welcome them back the next day, restaging hospitality toward a happier ending.

Alliance with the Tlaxcalans would be crucial to the conquest of the Mexica, and the visit in 1519 gave the partnership a reasonably good start. Xicotencatl described Tenochtitlan and how the Tenochca could seal it off from invasion by partially dismantling the causeways, and how the houses were defensible, with their interior courtyards and high outer walls. The Tlaxcalans urged the Spaniards to travel to Tenochtitlan via Huexotzingo, an independent city-state bitterly opposed to the Mexica. But Cortés chose to travel to Cholula in spite of Xicotencatl's warnings that its "inhabitants were most treacherous" (Díaz 1956: 157).

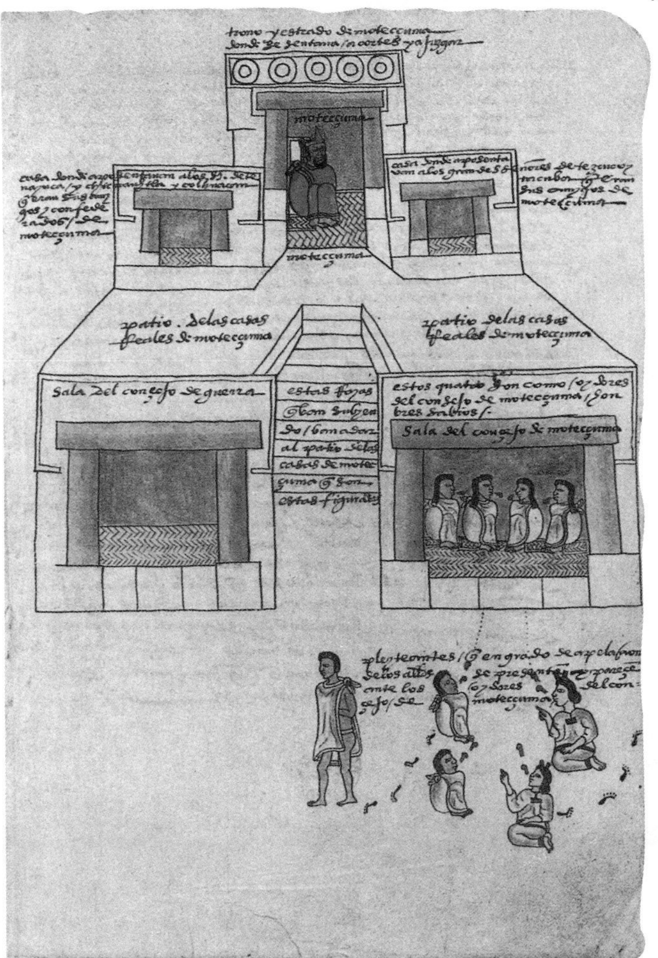

20.5 *Our most complete depiction of Motecuzoma II's palace in Tenochtitlan is this view from the* Codex Mendoza. *The* huetlatoani *is in his upper chamber, probably his dais room, while members of his court are shown in a lower room. Outside, in the courtyard, two men and two women are all talking, arguing about a legal question that the king's judges will decide upon.*

Puebla

The plains of Puebla extend from their northern boundary, with Tlaxcala, down to the edge of the Mixteca Alta and the Tehuacán Valley system. In 1519, the southern part of this region was controlled by the Aztec empire, with the tiny strategic province of Ahuatlan surrounded by the huge tributary province, Tepeaca, which extended from Morelos on the west to Cotaxtla on the east. Tepeaca province had been subdued by a series of conquests going back to the time of Motecuzoma I, and the town of Tepeaca had ongoing conflicts with the Tlaxcalans, Huexotzingans, and Cholulans (Smith and Berdan 1996: 285).

Cholula's relations with its neighbors and with the Aztec empire were complicated, as alliances materialized and then evaporated, old grudges were nursed along and then ignored. According to the Tlaxcalans, the Cholulans had only recently ended their enmity with the Aztec empire, and thus according to the rules of *realpolitik* had become the enemies of the Tlaxcalans.

Cholula was situated amidst fertile and well-irrigated farm land, and Cortés noted that this region was the first place in Mexico that the Spaniards had seen that would be suitable for cattle. As cattle ranching was to become one of the most important industries of Early Colonial New Spain, finding appropriate land was an essential piece of information. The city of Cholula itself prompted other comparisons with the Old World. It was a great pilgrimage center, and Motolinía called it "another Rome, with numerous temples of the demon" – there were at least 300 temple-pyramids – and "every province has its halls and apartments to serve as lodgings during the feasts that were held" (Motolinía 1951: 123). During the Late Postclassic period, Cholula was Mesoamerica's major cult center for the veneration of the Feathered Serpent, whose pyramid was subsequently completely destroyed. The Great Pyramid, still the largest in Mesoamerica, was in ruins in the Late Postclassic period.

Cortés estimated that there were 20,000 houses in Cholula, so its population might have been around 100,000. It had a large marketplace, renowned for the Mixteca-Puebla style pottery sold there – Motecuzoma himself used it in his palace [**20.5**]. They also found something that is a diagnostic of urban life in complex societies: abject poverty. Cortés noted that "there are so many people living in these parts that not one foot of land is uncultivated ...yet in many places they suffer hardships for lack of bread. And there are many poor people who beg from the rich in the streets as the poor do in Spain, and in other civilized places" (Cortés 1986: 75).

Beggars and People of Reason The juxtaposition, in Cortés's thoughts, of the presence of beggars with a high level of social complexity prompts us to ask how Cortés phrased the concept "civilized" in his original Spanish text. His term was "gente de razón" – people of reason, those whose culture was, in many ways, like his own – and not like the cultures of the Caribbean islands. In terms of the cultural evolutionary changes in social structure that we have reviewed in this book, this phrase might have the meaning "people who make rational economic decisions." Egalitarian and even ranked societies are bound by customs that give priority to kin relations as a basis of governance and economic distribution, and there are rather strict limits on the extent to which any family or individual can accumulate a disproportionate amount of wealth. But while stratified societies still depend upon family ties for many basic functions, their large size makes it impossible to depend upon kinship for regulation of relations between groups of people. Limits on the disproportional acquisition of wealth are usually determined by the wealthy themselves, who are typically reluctant to disadvantage themselves, being, after all, people of reason.

Hence the juxtaposition of poverty and societal complexity, of beggars in a land of wealth – features that convinced Cortés that in ancient Mexico he had found important parallels with his own Spain. This was the kind of society he had grown up in, with powerful kings and scheming courtiers and bean-counting bureaucrats, tax-paying peasants and impoverished beggars. There were big cities with busy and complex marketplaces and lots of religious buildings. It is true that Mesoamerica had no metal-dependent technology, and there were no large draft animals to lend impetus to the development of wheeled transport, but these differences only highlighted the similarities in societal structure. Cultural evolution is far from being a simple lockstep process motivated by technological advances. The circumstances under which "gente de razón" emerge from the ranks of kin-based societies are complicated, but they depend on certain preconditions (pp. 24–25), and when these occur, so, worldwide, will beggars and kings.

Cholulan Intrigues Though initially welcomed into the city, the Spaniards began to feel uneasy after a few days. Their hosts were no longer supplying them with food, and seemed reluctant to talk with them. Streets were being barricaded, and on the housetops piles of rocks accumulated. Finally someone told them of a plot to capture them and present them as a gift to Motecuzoma. The Spaniards and their Tlaxcalan supporters turned on the Cholulans – several thousand were massacred, others were taken prisoner and marched to Tlaxcala, probably bound for sacrifice. Cholula was looted and parts of it were burned. After several days of mayhem, Cortés decided to spare the city's lords on promise of future cooperation.

Meanwhile, Motecuzoma had sent a continuous flow of gifts to Cortés, accompanied by strongly-worded messages of discouragement, all of which said: "don't come to Tenochtitlan." The emperor was ill. The roads were impassable. There was no food. The wild animals in the zoo would eat the Spaniards. Like other appeasement policies known from other historical contexts, this one only fed the appetite of the aggressor. In early November, 1519, Cortés and his entourage moved out of Cholula and over the high pass between Iztaccihuatl and Popocatépetl, and down into the Basin of Mexico.

MOTECUZOMA, PRISONER OF FEAR

Motecuzoma II was a man fate chose to bear the unhappy fame of overseeing the downfall of his empire. No matter what the achievements of his 18-year reign (1502–1520), nor the reputation for military excellence and rhetorical skills that gained him the rulership in the first place, nor even the inevitability of European intrusion and cultural domination, Motecuzoma's last few months marked him permanently as weak and vacillating, unable to summon the courage to die fighting, as so many Tenochca would, in the siege of their city in the summer of 1521.

Instead, he now shifted his approach toward the Spaniards. After they entered the Basin of Mexico, he saw to it that they were accommodated and welcomed in their journey. The Spaniards numbered at least 300 (accounts differ as to the exact number) and they were accompanied by about 1,000 Tlaxcalans. In Chalco, Cortés spoke "with the lord and some of the nobles ... who said they were vassals of Moctezuma. In secret they complained to him... saying he committed many grave abuses in ... tribute" (Tapia 1963 [*c.* 1534]: 37). This had become a familiar theme, and Cortés was all too willing to exploit it.

As Cortés and his entourage neared Tenochtitlan, they perceived the size and beauty of the great capital in the distance. Immediately before arriving at Tenochtitlan, the company stayed in a set of nearly completed palaces in the town of Ixtapalapa. These were the property of Motecuzoma's brother Cuitlahuac, who would succeed him as *huetlatoani* of Tenochtitlan in 1520, and then succumb to smallpox, one of the diseases introduced to the New World by Europeans. At this moment in early November, 1519, Cuitlahuac was proudly putting the finishing touches on his new home, "... as good as the best in Spain; that is, in respect of size and workmanship both in their masonry and woodwork and their floors, and furnishings for every sort of household task .... They have many upper and lower rooms and cool gardens, with many trees and sweet-smelling flowers; likewise there are pools of fresh water, very well made and with steps leading down to the bottom. There is a very large kitchen garden next to his house and overlooking it a gallery with very beautiful corridors and rooms, and, in the garden a large reservoir of fresh water, well built with fine stonework, around which runs a well-tiled pavement so wide that four people can walk there abreast. It is four hundred paces square, which is sixteen hundred paces around the edge. Beyond the pavement, toward the wall of the garden, there is a latticework of canes, behind which are all manner of shrubs and scented herbs. Within the pool there are many fish and birds..." (Cortés 1986: 82–83). Díaz was equally impressed, noting that "great canoes were able to pass into the garden from the lake through an opening that had been made so that there was no need for their occupants to land. ... I say again that I stood looking at it and thought that never in the world would there be discovered other lands such as these... Of all these wonders that I then beheld to-day all is overthrown and lost, nothing left standing" (Díaz 1956 [1560s]: 191).

It is worth quoting Cortés and Díaz at length here, not only because their descriptions of Cuitlahuac's palace are among their most extensive, but also because of the complexity of organization indicated by their descriptions. While the beautifully landscaped freshwater ponds must have been striking in their juxtaposition to the expanse of Lake Texcoco beyond, we also see that this was in the service of the state, at several levels. Labor crews performing tribute obligations built the place, dug the ponds, plastered them, brought the stone and timbers and plants – all of this magnificence was paid for by the Aztec empire. And the design of the palace reveals how Aztec potentates were kept in contact with affairs of state – canals brought canoes directly to the palaces (Motecuzoma's new palace in Tenochtitlan was also served by a special canal) just as limousines and helicopters today ferry executive officers of business and government from one important meeting to another.

The next day, 8 November 1519, Cortés and company moved up the causeway and were met by Motecuzoma II [**20.6**]. Hundreds of Aztec lords

20.6 *Cortés, with Marina behind him, meets Motecuzoma II, who is backed by his lords. The drawing is from the* Lienzo de Tlaxcala *(1979 [c. 1550]), which was originally produced in 1550 by the Tlaxcalans to remind the Spaniards of Tlaxcala's important role in the conquest. The artist uses a mixture of native and European styles, with the use of perspective and Western-style posture, and anachronistic details, such as the European chairs in which the principals are seated.*

came forward to greet Cortés. He and Motecuzoma exchanged gifts, and then Motecuzoma led Cortés to Axayacatl's palace, which had been prepared for the Spaniards. This was the scene in which Motecuzoma sat Cortés on the throne of the dais room, and then presented him with even more gifts.

About a week later, Cortés told Motecuzoma that he had learned of a skirmish between Spaniards and Aztec forces down on the Gulf Coast and was so shocked that he felt compelled to take Motecuzoma under protective custody "until the truth were known and he [Motecuzoma] was shown to be blameless" (Cortés 1986: 89). Motecuzoma was finally convinced of the wisdom of this, and moved, with his servants, into Axayacatl's palace. When the perpetrator of the coastal disturbance was brought up to Tenochtitlan to be executed, Cortés had Motecuzoma put in irons, too, but then set him free.

Cortés's actions during this period reveal him to be a master of psychological management: he flattered, frightened, disoriented Motecuzoma. He kept Motecuzoma safe and well tended, needing this tame *huetlatoani* to shield Spanish interests as they undermined and took over the Aztec empire. Cortés insisted that "many times I offered him his liberty ... and each time he told me that he ... did not wish to go" (Cortés 1986: 91), in large part because he did not want to have to deal with lords who would try to convince him to resist the Spaniards.

Meanwhile, the weeks passed rather pleasantly for Motecuzoma and Cortés. Between November 1519 and the beginning of May, 1520, the Spaniards and Mexicans shared a courtly life that was familiar to both groups, with time spent feasting, enjoying women, going on hunting expeditions, gambling. Motecuzoma was generous with gifts, and good-humored in the face of Spanish greed. Playing at a game of chance, Pedro Alvarado consistently cheated when keeping track of Cortés's score, and Motecuzoma made a joke of it, and paid up (Díaz 1956: 235). The Spaniards toured Tenochtitlan-Tlatelolco, admiring the great Tlatelolco market that drew 60,000 buyers and sellers daily to exchange goods from all over Mexico.

Cortés and his men climbed to the top of the highest pyramids, revulsed by the stench of blood that coated the temples. They lectured Motecuzoma about the evils of human sacrifice, but he answered them sharply, and they did not press the point, aware that many Mexican nobles wanted the Spaniards dead. From the tops of pyramids the Spaniards could see the city surrounded by the lake, and its interconnections by canals and bridges. It is obvious from later events that during this time the Spaniards were assessing the city's defenses and planning the best way to launch an attack. It is also clear, from the speed at which Cortés and other Spaniards registered claims to various pieces of property, as soon as the conquest was completed, that they had been praising Motecuzoma's pleasure palaces with an eye toward owning them.

Cortés decided that Tenochtitlan could only be taken from the lake, and

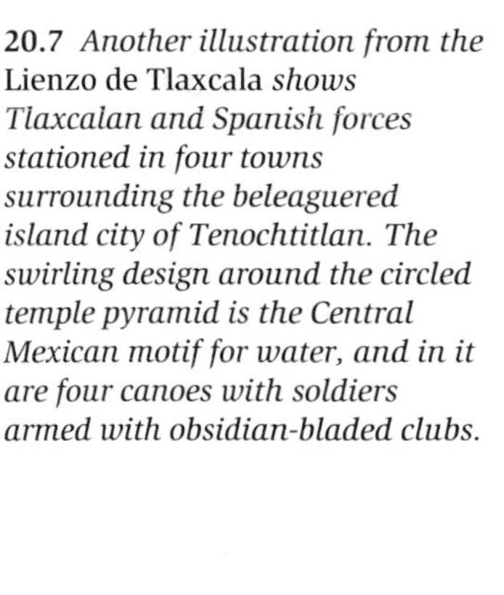
20.7 *Another illustration from the* Lienzo de Tlaxcala *shows Tlaxcalan and Spanish forces stationed in four towns surrounding the beleaguered island city of Tenochtitlan. The swirling design around the circled temple pyramid is the Central Mexican motif for water, and in it are four canoes with soldiers armed with obsidian-bladed clubs.*

thus sailboats must be built in preparation. He sent to the Spaniards on the Gulf Coast for blacksmiths and materials and soon two sloops were ready for testing. Motecuzoma heard about the maiden voyage, and suggested that the boats be used to transport him and his lords to his hunting preserve on the island of Tepepulco, near Ixtapalapa. They soon arrived at Tepepulco, and "Montezuma killed all the game he wanted, deer and hares and rabbits, and returned very contented to the city" (Díaz 1956: 239).

Peace Breaks Down The idyll could not last. Word got out that the Spaniards had broken into the treasury, and Aztec resistance to Motecuzoma's house arrest began to build. Furthermore, Motecuzoma established a secret communication with the Spaniards on the Gulf Coast – Cortés's deputy, Narváez, sent messages to Motecuzoma telling him that Cortés and the others "were bad men and thieves who had fled from Castile without the permission of ... the King" (Díaz 1956: 257) and that once Narváez got permission, he would rescue Motecuzoma and imprison Cortés. Of course, Narváez's intent was to secure for himself the position of chief conquistador, but the behind-the-scenes connivance on both sides indicates the challenges of operating within this welter of plots.

20.8 *Motecuzoma may have been killed by his own people when he tried to calm the Aztecs' anger after Alvarado's massacre of the Aztec lords. The Spaniards took his body and that of another noble outside Axayacatl's palace, and from there the Aztecs carried him off and cremated him. As his body burned, his former subjects regarded him "only with fury, no longer with much of the people's good will ... they said 'This blockhead! He terrorized the world ... This man! If anyone offended him only a little, he at once disposed of him.'" (Sahagún 1975: 66).*

Cortés heard of Narvaez's insubordination, and took some of the Spaniards back to the coast, leaving Alvarado in charge. The deteriorating relations between the Mexica and the captors of their king broke down altogether over the festival of Toxcatl, an important celebration honoring Huitzilopochtli. Alvarado gave permission for the festival to take place, but forbade human sacrifice. Accounts of the events of this last great Tenochca celebration differ, with Alvarado claiming that the Spaniards' food supply had been cut off, that Motecuzoma and his attendants were armed to overthrow the Spaniards, and that the Mexicans fully intended to sacrifice humans, including the Spaniards.

"And when dawn broke, when it was already the feast day ... already began

20.9 *These two scenes from the* Codex Azcatitlan *(late 16th century) show, on the left, Cortés and Marina approaching Tenochtitlan, leading a procession of Spaniards in armor carrying the banner of the Holy Ghost, and on the far left, some of their native porters. In the scene on the right, Motecuzoma is dead, face down on the stairs, while other Aztecs play drums and one bears the banner with the Holy Ghost.*

the singing, the winding dance" (Sahagún 1975: 53) performed by hundreds of Tenochca noblemen in the ritual precinct. Alvarado and his men blocked the exits and massacred hundreds of Aztec lords, the leaders of government and war. The Spaniards went back to Axayacatl's palace, killed some of the Aztec lords attending Motecuzoma, and fortified the palace. They sent Motecuzoma out to urge calm on his people, but the *huetlatoani* no longer commanded the respect of the Tenochca. Meanwhile, the city was in mourning, and fury against the Spaniards was mounting; Aztecs destroyed the sailboats the Spaniards had built, and began readying the city for war.

This was the scene Cortés returned to. Firing their guns and trying to appear confident, Cortés and his men rode across the short causeway from Tacuba to Tenochtitlan, rather than make themselves more vulnerable on the long Ixtapalapa causeway. The city was utterly silent, and Cortés reached Axayacatl's palace unharmed. Yet whenever the Spaniards would show themselves, a shower of rocks hurled from adjacent buildings would drive them to cover, and attempts to leave the palace were doomed. In late June, Cortés ordered the construction of a moveable wooden fortress that would permit the Spaniards to secure the area around the palace. But in the meantime, there was evidence that the Mexica had elected a new *huetlatoani*, and it was Cuitlahuac, Motecuzoma's brother. When Motecuzoma went out onto the roof to address the Tenochca, he was hit by stones and died soon thereafter. The Spaniards killed the several dozen lords who still attended him, and the bodies were pushed outside the palace. Motecuzoma, on whose whim had rested the fate of millions, was cremated without ceremony [**20.8**].

20.10 *(Opposite) Upon arriving in Tenochtitlan, the Spaniards showed off their cannon, as depicted in this illustration from the* Florentine Codex *(top). Unfortunately, they lost such armaments in their hasty retreat on La Noche Triste (second from top), and at the Battle of Otumba had to fight the Aztecs with swords and spears (second from bottom). Scholars have argued about the extent to which Western technology – metal tools and weapons, mechanical devices such as cannons and guns – advantaged the Spaniards over the Aztecs. The overwhelming numbers of the Aztecs, and their adaptability, meant that "most of this technology was not decisive" (Hassig 1992: 164). Horses intimidated the Mexicans, but were soon discovered to be vulnerable to attack. War dogs were a savagely effective menace. But the top prize for a force that effected the conquest goes to diseases such as smallpox (bottom). Infectious disease was not deliberately employed as a weapon, but it killed off far more natives than could any conventional method.*

The Sad Night and the Decisive Battle With their food running low, little potable water, and an increasingly angry populace outside their increasingly damaged walls, the Spaniards prepared to abandon the great capital that Cortés had hoped to deliver unharmed to the Spanish king, Charles V. Cortés's astrologer told him that to stay one more day would bring death to them all. The Spaniards decided to leave at night, because the Aztecs avoided fighting then, so at midnight, 1 July 1520, the Spaniards and their horses moved toward Tacuba. But they were spotted, and soon the war drums atop the pyramids were booming, and the Tenochca were rushing to intercept the fleeing Spaniards.

Considering the war canoes that soon filled the lake, and the ease with which the causeways were broken, it is a wonder that so many Spaniards survived, though several hundred are thought to have perished in the rout that has come to be known as La Noche Triste (the sad night). They had laden their horses with Motecuzoma's gold, and little of this reached the mainland, nor did their firearms and ammunition. The ragged group of survivors, still accompanied by their Tlaxcalan allies, made its way toward the northeast corner of the Basin of Mexico, toward the border with Tlaxcala, and, they hoped, sanctuary.

In the upper Teotihuacan Valley, near the town of Otumba, massed Aztec armies engaged the escaping Spaniards, who numbered about 440 men and 20 horses (Davies 1977), plus their Tlaxcalan allies. It was in the Battle of Otumba that formal Aztec methods of warfare were shown to terrible disadvantage [**20.10**]. The Spaniards cut down the banner carriers and the most gaudily arrayed of the warriors, and thus Aztec battlefield organization dissolved. To be fair to the Aztecs, they had lost nearly 1,000 of their top-ranking lords just days before, in the Toxcatl massacre, and so the armies they were fielding at Otumba were operating under constrained circumstances.

Nonetheless, the Spaniards managed to move east, into Tlaxcala, where their old friend Xicotencatl the Elder gave them sanctuary. In the meantime, more Spaniards were arriving all the time, new gold-seekers who had heard of Motecuzoma's great wealth. For the next nine months Cortés established himself in Tepeaca and readied his troops for the next assault on Tenochtitlan. Because this would be a siege from the lake, Cortés's shipwright supervised the construction of pre-fabricated brigantines in Tlaxcala for transport up to the Basin of Mexico.

The Mexicans, meanwhile, refurbished their city, sacrificed those Spaniards and Tlaxcalans who had fallen into their hands alive, and rejoiced that the enemy had retreated and the threat was over. But by the end of summer, the Spaniards' viral emissary, smallpox, had reached Chalco, and was cutting through Tenochtitlan by late October (Thomas 1995). When Cuitlahuac died of it, the Tenochca elected Ahuitzotl's son, Cuauhtemoc, as *huetlatoani*.

The smallpox epidemics that moved through Mexico at this time began a radical process of population reduction that would continue throughout the

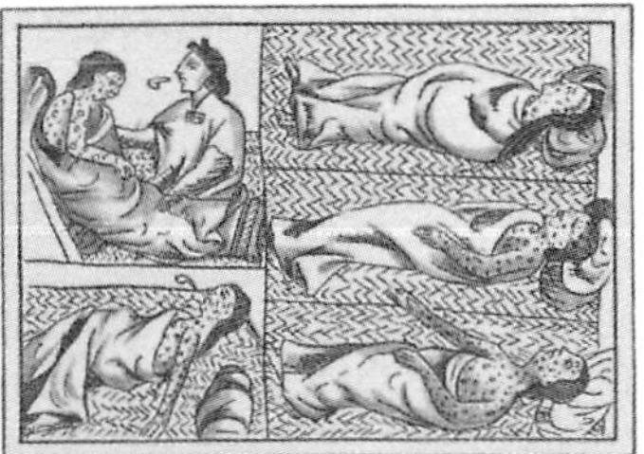

16th century, as one Old World disease after another swept through peoples who lacked any resistance, being without the immunity conferred by having a mild case of the disease in childhood, or resistance on the level of population genetics, by being a member of a group that has survived coexistence with the disease for many generations. Not only did newly introduced infectious diseases strike all ages at once, community by community, thus leaving no one to care for the sick, but the psychological effect was devastating, as well. These were people who watched their world vigilantly for any sign of the mood of the forces around them, and it must have seemed as though in the wake of the Spanish intrusion, the old gods had visited disaster upon their people.

Cortés used these catastrophes to his own advantage. He brought an increasingly large area into alliance with Spain, often in cooperation with the Tlaxcalans as they settled old grudges. Cortés promised the Tlaxcalans incredible prizes if they continued to aid the Spaniards against the Mexica, essentially offering a tax-free partnership in the post-conquest rulership of Mexico. Spain would never permit any such thing, of course, but in the meantime the Tlaxcalans saved Cortés's venture and made it a success. As disease disrupted one region after another, it disrupted political organization, as well, and Cortés made sure that new rulers were his allies. Thus well before Tenochtitlan capitulated to the Spaniards, Cortés had insinuated himself – and Spanish authority – into the Mexican power hierarchy.

Siege of Tenochtitlan The Spaniards returned to the Basin of Mexico early in 1521. They had formed new alliances, such as with the Tenochca's traditional close partner, Texcoco, and that city became their first base of operations in the Basin. Spanish preparations for the assault on Tenochtitlan reveal a combination of European and Mexican methods of provisioning and preparation. The brigantines were a European idea, built by Spaniards and Tlaxcalans under the direction of a Spaniard, and the shaped parts were carried over the mountains from Tlaxcala to Texcoco by 8,000 Tlaxcalan porters, plus another 2,000 carrying food – a line 9.7 km (6 miles) long that arrived in Texcoco on 15 February (Thomas 1995). More labor was required to dig channels from Texcoco to the lake, in order to launch the ships.

The Mexica made desperate attempts to woo allies, but memories of their demanding arrogance were too fresh, and few polities supported them. The Spaniards made forays around the perimeter of the lake; most cities were evacuated at the approach of Cortés and his troops, but at times Mexica army units engaged them in skirmishes. By early summer, 1521, Tenochtitlan would have been sensing the costs of its disintegrating empire, not just in loss of tribute but in disruption of normal food supplies. Cuauhtemoc prepared for war, but was unable to anticipate that the Spaniards would use methods outside Mexica experience, for example, launching an attack in summer, the agricultural season, rather than winter, the war season.

The Spanish forces numbered nearly 1,000 horsemen and infantry, and their native allies numbered in the tens of thousands – some sources esti-

20.11 *Spaniards watched from a distance as their captured comrades were "carried by force up the steps [of a pyramid]...we saw them place plumes on the heads of many of them and they forced them to dance and after they had danced they immediately placed them on their backs and with stone knives they sawed open their chests and drew out their palpitating hearts and offered them to the idols and they kicked the bodies down the steps" (Díaz 1956: 436). The heads of Spaniards and their horses were displayed on the skull rack.*

mate 200,000 or even 500,000 but these are surely exaggerations of what was an impressively substantial number of auxiliary troops. On 1 June, the 12 brigantines were launched from Texcoco, moving to surround Tenochtitlan. It soon became apparent that a negotiated peace was out of the question, and that the city would fall only when the Tenochca were so debilitated by war and starvation that they could no longer fight, and when the buildings were destroyed so that there was no place to defend [**20.11**].

This was a painfully gradual process. In addition to defending their city, house by house, during the day, the Aztecs worked through the nights creating barriers and clearing out the canals as the Spaniards filled them in. The descriptions recounted by Cortés, Díaz del Castillo, and the elite Aztec informants of Sahagún all stress the tenacity of the Tenochca in defending the city. Abandoned by their former allies, the Tenochca must have drawn strength from their great sense of destiny as they struggled onward under siege, even when their only water was brackish, and their only food was grass. On 13 August 1521, the Aztecs gave up their city and their empire, both much damaged by the onslaught of Cortés and the Spaniards. The city, in fact, was mostly leveled. Cuauhtemoc had survived, and surrendered.

EARLY COLONIAL NEW SPAIN

It would take the Spaniards decades to complete their conquest of Mesoamerica – Tayasal (Flores), on an island in Lake Petén Itzá, in the northern lowlands of Guatemala, was the last stronghold of the Itzá Maya, finally conquered by the Spanish in 1697. But in effective terms, Spain had become an empire, and Mesoamerica was the first great civilization it absorbed.

Far beyond the Spaniards' wildest plans of subduing Mexico, diseases cleared the land and simplified the complicated political and ethnic situation. The population of the Basin of Mexico declined from approximately 1.6 million in 1519 to about 250,000 by 1610 (Sanders 1992: 179, see also Lovell 1992, Whitmore 1992), the size of the population at the start of the Postclassic period. Elsewhere in New Spain, the situation was even worse, with whole areas of the Gulf lowlands becoming depopulated. In the Early Colonial period, the Spaniards left the political hierarchy of the Aztec empire largely intact and installed themselves at the top. Aztec society as a whole was demoted, "and whereas for lower classes this entails only a further degradation, for ruling classes the change is absolute, from a dominant to a subordinate rank" (Gibson 1960:169). Conditions worsened as the Spaniards attempted to extract maximum tribute amounts from a population that was a fraction of its former size, not only because of disease but also from enslavement during the conquest and forced labor in mines and rebuilding projects thereafter.

Depopulation made easier the imposition of Spanish practices. In many parts of the Central Highlands, the family farm was an essential component of the economy – its terraced maize fields neatly edged with maguey, its productivity a result of the well-integrated labor efforts of the farming household. As population declined and cattle were introduced, these small holdings were overrun by grazing animals, and eventually abandoned by the families who worked them. The Spaniards imposed abandonment of rural villages in many regions by ordering the "congregation" of dispersed populations into the surviving larger towns. Plantations and ranches spread over former farmland, and bovine demography charted an opposite path to that of the native humans: "herds nearly doubled in fifteen months; insufficiently guarded, they overran the countryside and destroyed all the Indians' maize" (Chevalier 1970: 93).

All of these effects helped the Spaniards to eradicate devil-worshipping native culture while recasting Middle America into a likeness of Spain. When we focus on access to important resources, we find ample evidence of the importance of transferring as much wealth back to Europe as quickly as possible. Yet in addition to the conquistadors and their agenda of violence and greed, there were the missionaries, appalled but undaunted by the extent of soul-saving necessitated by the huge indigenous population and their deeply held beliefs. The task before the missionaries was to convert the native people to Catholic Christianity as quickly as possible. It is obvious that most of these conversions were accomplished at mass meetings that few of the converts would have understood.

20.12 *The proselytizing Spanish clergy attempted to conceptualize Christianity in forms sacred to the Aztecs. Featherwork was among the most valued of native art forms, and this depiction of Christ in featherwork was a fusion of native culture and European values. The script is Cyrillic, an antiquated form of the writing of Russia, and the message here has not been deciphered.*

The longer-term task of conversion required explaining Christianity so that individuals understood and with free will accepted the new faith. This method was applied to converting young Aztec noblemen, with the idea that these would be the opinion leaders of the next generation. This process began soon after the conquest, and was spearheaded by Franciscan missionaries such as Fray Pedro de Gante, a humanist who espoused the tactic of contextualizing the new faith in some of the forms of the old. Thus the native population attended services in "open-air chapels" which were large courtyards attached to European-style churches (McAndrew 1965). Churches themselves were often built upon the leveled-off platforms of native pyramids, and the ritual precinct west of the pyramid/church base became the open-air chapel. Much of public ritual in Mesoamerican culture had always been conducted outdoors, in the courtyards of temple precincts and rulers' houses, and using this architectural form suited the established native habits of listening to sermons in palace courtyards or in the plazas at the base of pyramids.

There were natural points of convergence between native and Christian religions. Each had a formal priesthood, and formalized litanies of prayer. Both celebrated important passages in the lives of individuals with sacred rites celebrating birth, coming of age, marriage, confession of sins, and death. Each belief system honored the body and blood of a sacrificial victim as its most basic sacrament. These parallels made the new religion understandable, while also increasing the possibility that devil-worship could hide behind its structurally similar forms.

Music, poetry, and dance were other native ceremonial practices that the missionaries used as contexts for the new religion. And yet these efforts to syncretize Christianity and the native belief system met with criticism from the more conservative Catholic clergy, who argued for complete eradication of indigenous religion. Given what we know of how the Mesoamericans viewed their lives and world as drenched with spiritual meaning, it is obvious that removing all traces of the indigenous belief system would be impossible. Of course, the showier aspects of Mesoamerican religion – the priesthood, temple precincts, practices such as human sacrifice, the display of books, statuary and amulets – were too visible to survive the vigilance of the missionaries. For those reluctant to convert, there were the more rigorous methods developed by the Spanish Inquisition, whose gruesome punishments for heresy rivaled any sacrificial rites of the natives for pain inflicted in the cause of spiritual betterment.

But how do you eradicate a deeply rooted belief system? Or the spiritual associations of important landscape features, such as the mountains that serve as a horizon calendar? How do you convince a subjugated population that the new god loves them, when they are dying in great numbers from diseases introduced by their conquerors, while their farmlands are overrun by cattle and sheep imported from Spain? How do you convince them that they have no need of talismans like figurines of Tlaloc and Xochiquetzal? An important part of the process of forging the new *mestizo* culture involved the gradual substitution of Christian imagery and significance for that of the old gods [**12.12**]. Patron deities were replaced by patron saints with similar characteristics, and new icons provided comfort as the old idols were destroyed.

World of Wonders

The Age of Discovery that brought the Spaniards to the New World was part of the European Renaissance, and the reports of explorations fueled an ongoing transformation of the Western world view. While the importation of luxury goods like silk from Asia had for centuries been part of European commercial enterprises, the discovery of the Americas, and more important, the discovery of the civilizations of the Americas had the effect of creating a globally shared economy and political system. The modern age began during this time, and modern problems and attitudes have their roots in the Age of Discovery's nationalistic, entrepreneurial spirit and its appropriation of the resources of the world outside Europe to serve the ends of Europe's rulers and capitalistic investors.

In fact, the conflict between rulers – the heirs to ancient dynasties, jealous of their powers – and capitalists was being played out in many nations of Europe. In the Netherlands and England, the entrepreneurial spirit was allowed to serve the government, with the overall effect that private investors were willing to take considerable risks in the business of exploration and exploitation, and this emphasis on the rights of the individual was part of the humanistic emphasis of the Renaissance that would eventually give rise to modern republics such as the United States.

Spain's pioneering role in exploring and laying claim to much of the New World brought incalculable fortune to her rulers, and effectively thwarted her development as a modern nation. But Spain's kings could counter that they had succeeded where other European nations had failed: they had maintained a powerful monarchy in the face of rising republicanism, they had sustained the true Catholic faith at a time that saw the spread of the Reformation, which they regarded as religious heresy, and they had conquered great civilizations and been remarkably successful in destroying indigenous traditions of intellectual achievement.

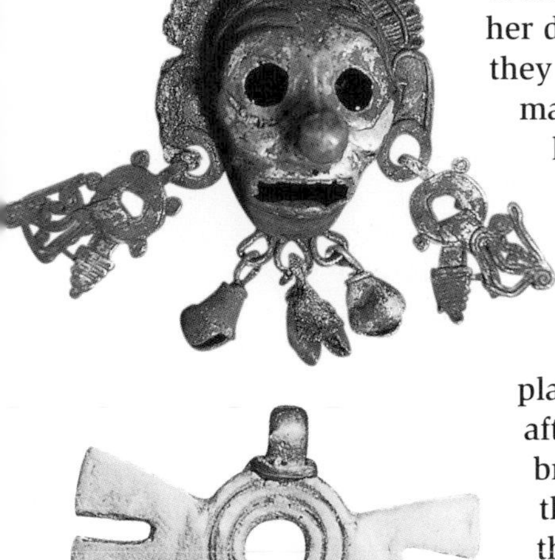

20.13, 20.14 *Under the floor of the shrine to Huitzilopochtli in Stage II of the Templo Mayor was a funerary urn carved out of obsidian. In addition to cremated human bones and incense, it contained these tiny amulets. The silver monkey head wears earrings in the shape of serpents, while the gold bell bears a top ornament signifying "movement."*

These attitudes are demonstrated in the fate of the marvelous objects that Cortés sent back to Spain. The earliest examples were displayed, and it is remarkable that in August of 1520, only nine months after the Spaniards arrived in Tenochtitlan, Albrecht Dürer, the celebrated German painter and engraver, wrote in his diary that he had seen the luxury objects from Mexico. "The things which have been brought to the King from the new golden land ... All the days of my life I have seen nothing that has gladdened my heart so much as these things, for I saw among them wonderful works of art, and I marvelled at the subtle ingenia of men in foreign lands" (quoted in Honour 1975: 28).

Unfortunately for ancient Mexico's cultural heritage, Charles V was more impressed by the gold than the goldworking skill, and reduced the treasures of the New World to negotiable ingots as quickly as possible (Braun 1993: 22). The few items that are today the prizes of Europe's national museums were largely gifts from the Spanish king to his royal relatives in other European capitals. Other kings, more influenced by humanism and its nurturing of intellectual curiosity, established collections of exotic works, "cabinets of curiosities" that were the germinal forms of museums of natural history and art [**20.15**].

This interest in oddities was an important basis for antiquarianism, the study of antiquity through examination of collections of exotic and ancient artifacts and sites. Antiquarianism was itself the outgrowth of the interest in the Classical world of ancient Rome and Greece that had been a major intellectual theme of the Renaissance (Bernal 1980; Willey and Sabloff 1974). It was also the consequence of changes in the way people saw themselves and the earth, relative to the universe. While the early 16th century brought the discovery of Aztec and Inca civilizations, 1543 brought Copernicus's theory that the solar system centered on the Sun – that Earth was not the center of the cosmos. Contributions in the 17th century by Galileo, Kepler, and

20.15 *This Aztec royal headdress features the long iridescent green quetzal feathers associated with Mesoamerican rulership since the Formative period. Now in the Vienna Völkerkunde Museum, it is a rare surviving example of the treasures sent from Mexico in the early 1500s.*

Newton and countless other observers and inventors transformed the Bible-based view of planetary history into one in which humans played a subsidiary role. This growing realization that the literal interpretation of the world through the Bible was at odds with the common sense of experience shook Europeans out of centuries of habitual conformance with the dictates of clergy and kings, as they realized the substance behind challenges to totalitarianism in religion and politics.

The discovery of the Americas and other previously unknown inhabited places also challenged the Bible's explanation of the history and diversity of humankind. The thorny question about these newly discovered peoples was whether or not they *were* human. If native Americans were not human, one could simply treat them like domestic animals and use them for labor and slaughter them at will – a definite economic benefit for the government. But if they were human, then they had souls and one had to convert them to the true faith of Catholicism and away from devil worship. This was the argument of Bartholomé de Las Casas, who had served as Bishop of Chiapa [sic] and who, in 1551, came before Charles V's Council of the Indies to defend the humanity of the native Americans.

"For the Creator of every being has not so despised the peoples of the New World that he willed them to lack reason and made them like brute animals ... On the contrary, they are of such gentleness and decency that they are, more than the other nations of the entire world, supremely fitted and prepared to abandon the worship of idols and to accept ... the word of God" (de Las Casas 1974 [1550]: 28).

Las Casas's arguments won the day, though natives still were not treated as the spiritual equals of the Spaniards – native men could not be ordained as priests, for example. However, the humanism of Las Casas and many others would take its toll on blind faith, because if the world was full of different kinds of humans, then how could the Bible, strictly interpreted, be accurate? These questions, and the efforts to answer them in a systematic way, would eventually, in the 17th and 18th centuries, develop into the scientific perspective of inquiry so essential to modern technological innovation.

Science and Religion, Science and Art Science and religious conviction are both belief systems, but they are based on opposing premises. Religion is grounded in faith, and refers questions back to dogma said to be god-given truth. Science is fueled by doubt, by questions that can be framed into testable hypotheses. Science demands that the experiments performed by one investigator be replicable, that is, repeatable by any other investigator under the same experimental conditions.

This characteristic of scientific findings, that they must be verifiable, sets science in opposition not only to religion, but to art, as well. Great works of scientific insight and great works of artistic expression may both derive from creative and skilled masters of their fields, but the modern value of a work of art lies in its power as a statement of indubitable individual genius. In fact, when any doubt is cast upon an artistic work's authenticity as the product of a respected artist, its value drops.

In Europe of the Middle Ages, virtually all art was in the service of religion, and everyone averred faith in the dogma of the established – institutionalized – religion, Christianity. Culture was holistic (possessed a wholeness) in ways that would have seemed familiar to the Aztecs and other Mesoamericans. To doubt the beliefs held sacred in the society was to declare one's self mad, and to be treated accordingly. Insofar as rulers enjoyed luxuries, they earned them through their special relationship with sanctity ("divine right of kings" was a principle common to Medieval Europe and to ancient Mesoamerica) and their putative role as stewards of their people and their society's resources.

The changes that were taking place in Europe of the Renaissance and the Age of Discovery would particularize Western society until, by the 21st century, the individual's right to choose a way of life is regarded as an essential freedom to be defended by force of arms. In the United States, few individuals live out their whole lives within a community of consanguineal and affinal kin who share work and religious faith. For most of us, our relations with each other are particularized, and there are few overlaps between the people we know from school, work, participation in religion, leisure time activities, military service, and our families. When we consider the holistic societies that characterized all the world of 500 years ago, and still persist in many regions, modern Westerners are likely to see them as oppressive and invasive, denying individuals their rights to choose their life's work, their marriage partner, and the privacy of making such choices without community comment.

The contrast between today's world and that of 500 years ago is useful; it contextualizes the changes that have taken place since. These changes affected New Spain much less than they did New England, because Spanish kings clung to the most conservative kind of royal overlordship of their dominions, and their subjects were either of Spanish descent and beholden to the system that assured them a good living in the colonies, or they were of native or *mestizo* descent, and lacked a choice in the matter.

Indigenous Utopia: The Franciscan Perspective

The unremitting bleakness of the 16th century for the native population was relieved, to some degree, by the stroke of fate that, from 1524 to 1564, the task of converting the populace to Christianity was put in the hands of the Franciscan order. The Franciscans were idealistic, seeing their mission in New Spain as the creation of new utopia among a population unspoiled by the corruption of European life. The Franciscans gained the trust of the natives because of their adherence to their vows of poverty, and their unmistakable devotion to the welfare of the people and ceaseless labor on their behalf – traits in sharp contrast to attitudes of the Spanish conquistadors and colonists, whose unbounded greed was matched by their pretension toward an aristocratic life of ease (Baudot 1995: 87).

The Franciscans began educating the Aztecs right after the conquest, with schools begun by Pedro de Gante in Texcoco in 1523 and in Tenochtitlan in 1525. De Gante lived in the royal palace in Texcoco and saw that the courtyards were the contexts of learning there and in the *calmecac* schools. De Gante began teaching in Texcoco, and then designed the Franciscan school in Tenochtitlan after the architectural pattern of the Aztec palace. The opening, in 1536, of the Colegio de Santa Cruz in Tlatelolco as an institution of higher education for native youth was the Franciscans' strong statement of faith in the abilities of indigenous peoples to contribute to New Spain. Classes covered many basic topics, and were taught in Latin and Nahuatl.

Their works bore important fruit – the Colegio became a workshop in the production of texts and pictures documenting native culture. Sahagún's great work, the *Florentine Codex*, was also known as the *The General History of the Things of New Spain*. The students at the Colegio were the informants for the twelve-volume work, which has been called the world's first ethnography, and which followed a Renaissance-style format of beginning with descriptions of the supernatural (gods, omens), then moving down the Great Chain of Being to earthly lords and wealthy merchants, then describing the common people, plants and animals. Other chroniclers of this period contributed information about regions (e.g., Landa [1975], who burned many Maya books but catalogued their culture). In the late 16th century the Spanish government sponsored an ambitious survey of its holdings, and the results, the *Relaciones Geográficas* ("Geographical Accounts," see Moreno 1968, Mundy 1996) are among the most important sources of information about pre-conquest and early Colonial Mesoamerica.

20.16 *Chichén Itzá's Castillo pyramid, as depicted by Frederick Catherwood, who traveled through the Maya region with John Lloyd Stephens in the 1830s. Their publications were instrumental in publicizing the ancient cultures of Mesoamerica.*

In addition to the documentation of native practices, interest began to arise in ancient ruins and the cultures that had produced them. In the late 16th century, Copán was described, and in the 17th century Tikal and Yaxchilan were discovered, and Teotihuacan was explored by Carlos de Sigüenza y Góngora (1645–1700), an important pioneer in the preservation of ancient Mexican manuscripts. Early Colonial New Spain was isolated by Spain from contact with the rest of the world, but by the 18th century the European intellectual climate of inquiry had begun to affect even the Spaniards. Soon after Pompeii was discovered, near Naples (Italy) in 1748, Charles III ordered that Palenque be explored.

Independence and the Rediscovery of Indigenous Culture In 1803 Alexander von Humboldt arrived in New Spain – his visit coincided with expansion of natural history interest among intellectuals in Europe and the Americas. His book, *Vues des cordillères et monuments,* was published in 1810, the same year that Mexico's struggle for independence began. There was a mutually reinforcing coincidence of the ongoing efforts of Mexico and the Central American nations toward freedom from Spain, and great public interest in the pre-Columbian past. This was an age of well-illustrated travel books, and Stephens and Catherwood's *Incidents of Travel in Central America, Chiapas and Yucatan* (1843) inspired interest in the Maya [**20.16**].

The late 19th century saw the dawn of modern archaeology, with exploration of the Maya region by Alfred Maudslay (Graham 1998), while Leopoldo Batres started excavations at Teotihuacan. These were efforts to explore sites systematically so as to recover information with all possible care. Archaeology was becoming professionalized; in Mexico the government instituted a special agency and laws to inspect and conserve its heritage.

In 1911, a new war of independence was being waged in Mexico, and democratic nationalism in Mexico and Central America brought propagandistic harkening back to indigenous roots of power. Centenary celebration of the Mexican revolution was the impetus for the excavation and reconstruction of the Pyramid of the Sun at Teotihuacan. We can see how effectively this promotion of native culture was accomplished in the Mexican cultural renaissance of the 1920s, 30s, and 40s, which created new appreciation for indigenous imagery and sympathy for the conquered ones in the murals of David Siquieros, José Clemente Orozco, and Diego Rivera, while Frida Kahlo made use of native ethnographic icons in her work. Mexico at this time applied vigorous energy toward universal public education. While this publicized the knowledge of the ancient past and promoted identification with the nation as a whole, there was a loss of indigenous culture, in that education demanded fluency in Spanish, which led to a loss of fluency in native languages and surviving cultural practices.

The 1920s to 1940s saw the discovery of many important sites, such as those of Olmec culture (La Venta, San Lorenzo) which in the 1940s was accepted by many scholars as being the first great complex society in Mesoamerica, predating the Maya. Farther north in the Gulf lowlands, El Tajín and other sites were explored in the 1930s and 1940s, and in the Valley of Oaxaca, Monte Albán began to be excavated in 1931. Research continued in the Maya lowlands, and was initiated along the West Mexico Coast and Northwestern Frontier. In the Basin of Mexico, Archaic and Early Formative sites were discovered in the 1920s through the 1950s, and the Cuicuilco pyramid was uncovered in the mid 1920s.

The Late 20th Century In the 1950s the study of the past was revolutionized by the discovery of radiocarbon dating. While other methods of establishing the actual elapsed time since an object was made or used have been developed before and since radiocarbon dating, none had its versatility or reliability. Chronology is the backbone of all historical description and interpretation, and the ability to place objects, sites, and cultures in chronological order transformed archaeology's power to describe and understand the past (Freter 2001).

The first great goal of the new chronological era was to put things in order, the second was to discern the great processes of change that had taken place, and explain why they had taken place. These goals have occupied archaeologists, ethnohistorians, and art historians working with the material and documentary evidence of ancient Mesoamerican culture for the last 50

20.17 *Visitors to Mesoamerican archaeological sites seek an understanding of ancient cultures, and sometimes also seek ancient wisdom. The spring equinox brings hundreds of thousands of visitors to Chichén Itzá to watch the serpentine shadow form on the balustrade of the Castillo pyramid. These visitors may also to gain spiritual strength from participation in what has become a yearly ritual for a New Age.*

years, and continue to provide focus for ongoing research. At the same time that descriptions of many archaeological cultures have been published, artifacts may be seen at dozens of museums (Gonlin 2001), and many archaeological sites in Mexico and Central America have been made into archaeological parks, among the most spectacular and interesting tourist destinations in the world [**20.17**].

The Living Past

The culture history described in this book has been drawn from the work of scholars who have uncovered sites, charted settlement patterns over vast regions, analyzed skeletons and material culture remains, and deciphered ancient writing and other symbolic systems. We now have a rich set of sources for understanding cultural evolution in Mesoamerica, and can appreciate the lives and work of the ancient peoples who inhabited Middle America, their ingenuity in developing sophisticated cultural solutions to basic human challenges, and the sense of beauty that marked their greatest works. Their history is, once again, as alive as the landscape they dwelt within.

REFERENCE MAPS

1 Northern Arid Zone

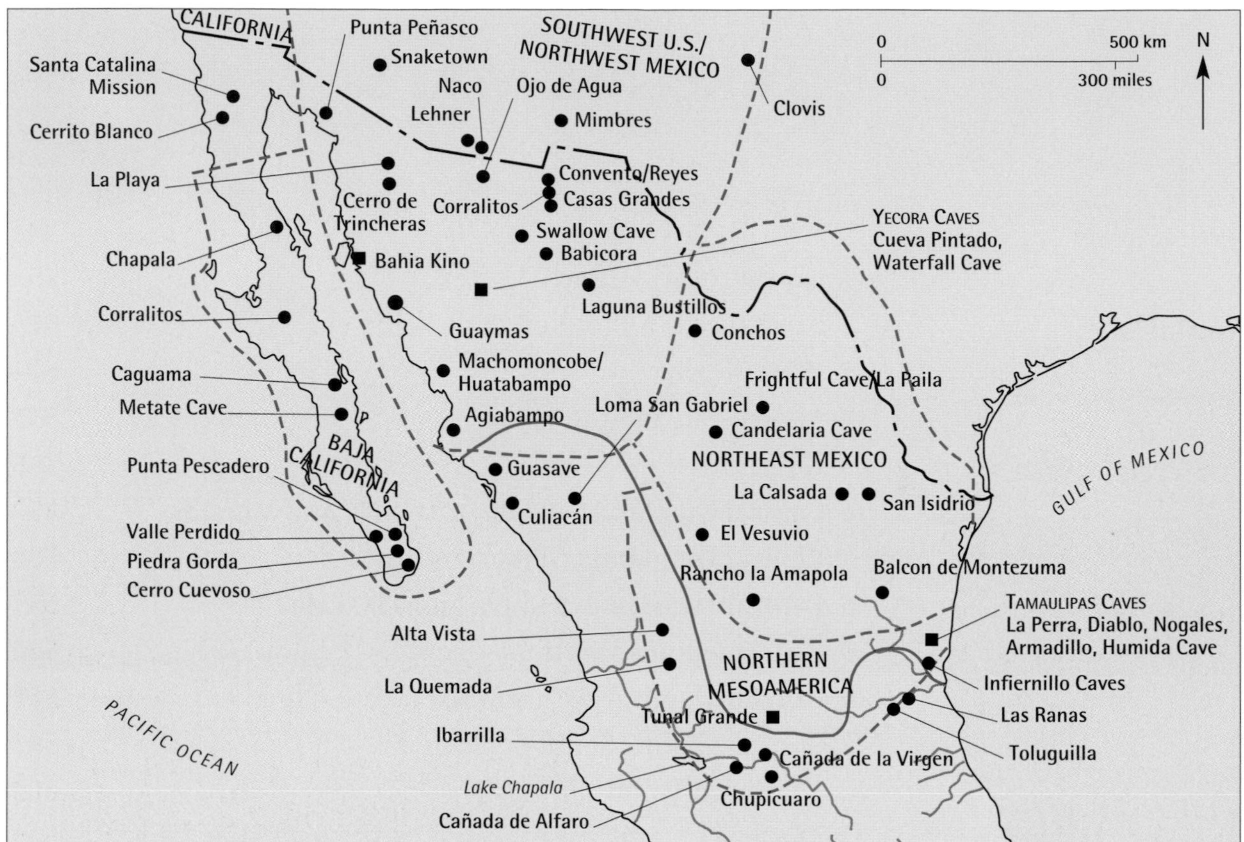

Terrain (natural vegetation) *Hilly plateaus comprising the Sonoran and Chihuahuan deserts (steppe, thicket, and scrub desert), framed by Mexico's two great mountain ranges, Sierra Madre Oriental and Sierra Madre Occidental (montane species at higher altitudes, dry evergreen species in eastern mountains, tropical rainforest along east coast, thorny woodland, scrub, and desert along west coast).*

Climate for cultivation *Arid* tierra fría*; where cultivation is possible, irrigation is required.*

Hazards *Largely too arid and rainfall is too undependable for cultivation; few geophysical hazards (significant earthquakes in Baja California); the southern portion is subject to significant electrical storm activity.*

Modern political identity *United States, parts of Arizona, New Mexico, California, and Texas; Mexico, all or part of states of Baja California, Sonora, Chihuahua, Sinaloa, Durango, Coahuila, Nuevo Leon, Tamaulipas, San Luis Potosí, Querétaro, Guanajuato, Aguascalientes, Zacatecas.*

2 Northwestern Frontier

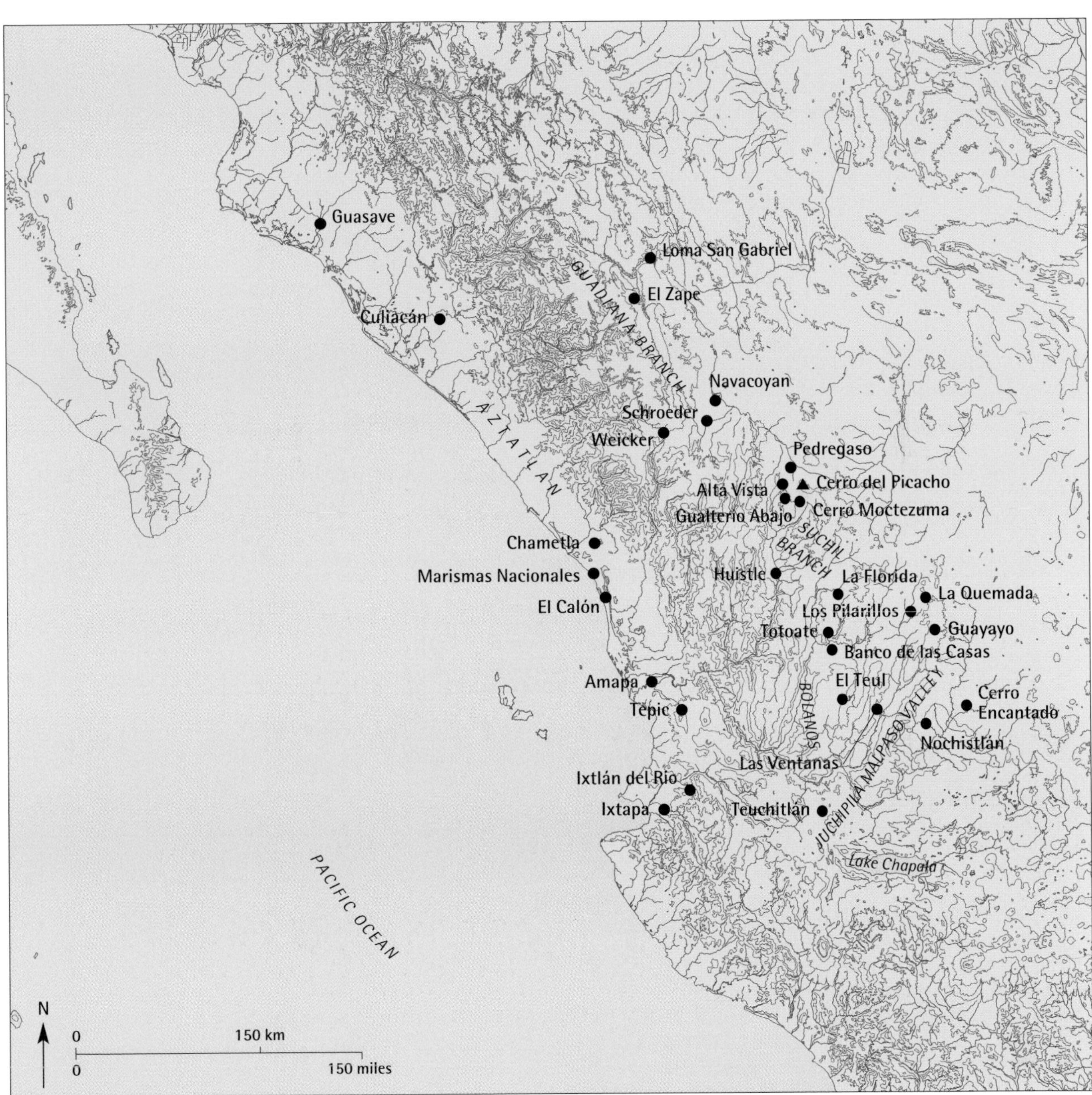

Terrain (natural vegetation) *Sierra Madre Occidental (montane species) and its adjacent Pacific coast (thorny woodland, scrub, and desert; swamplands).*

Climate for cultivation *Subhumid* tierra templada.

Hazards *Low annual rainfall, many electrical storms, frequent hurricanes along the coast.*

Modern political identity *Mexico, all or part of states of Sinaloa, Nayarit, Durango, Zacatecas, Jalisco.*

3 West Mexico

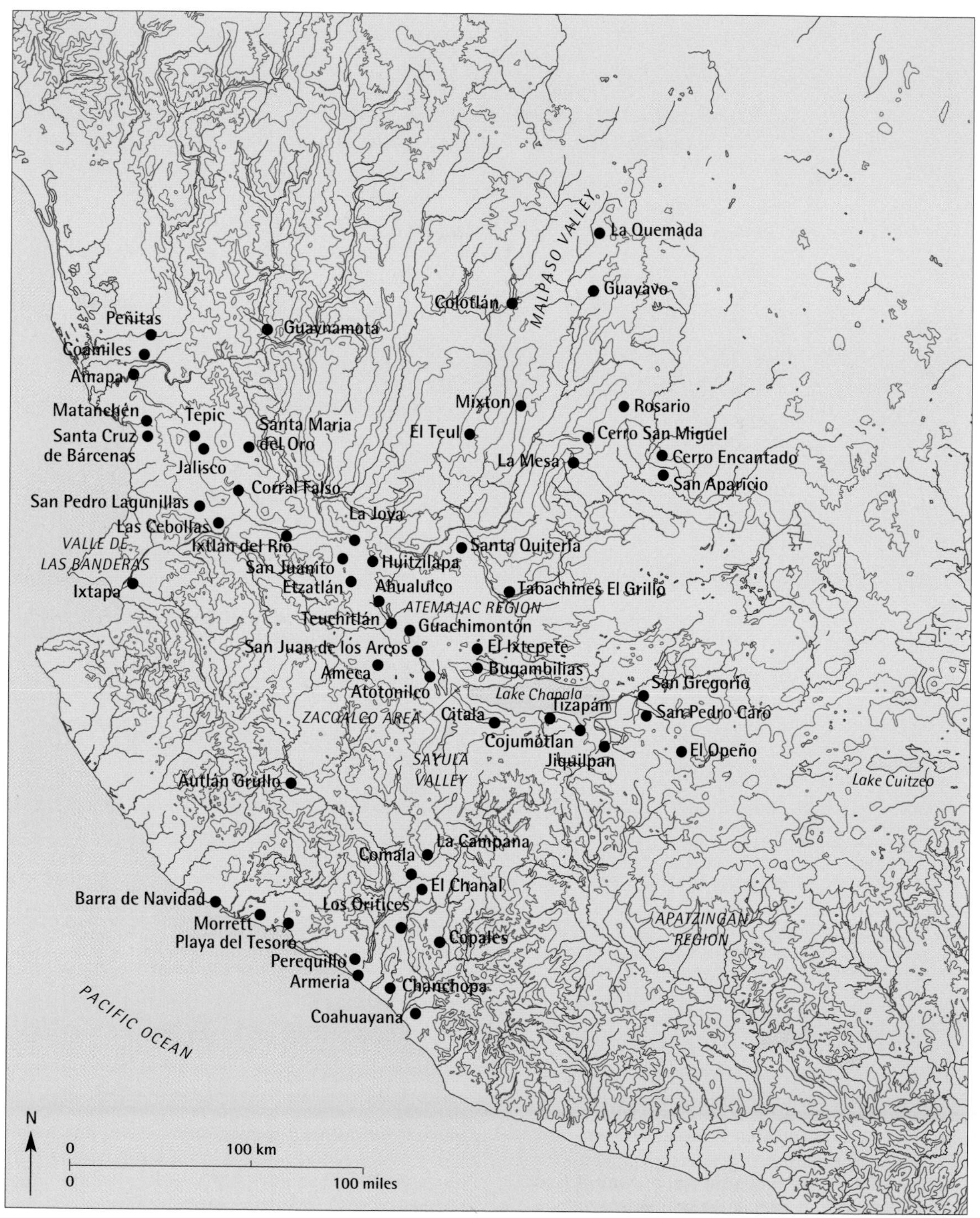

4 Michoacán and the Bajío

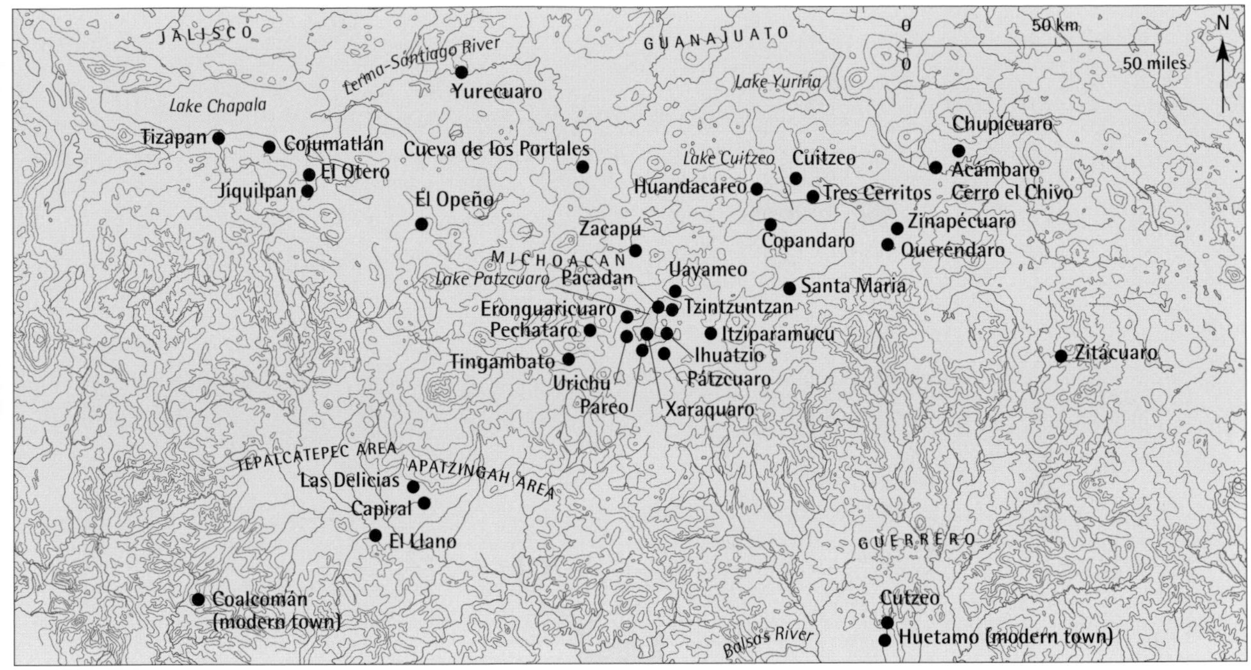

ABOVE **Terrain (natural vegetation)** *Broad, lake-centered valleys (montane species, grasslands).*

Climate for cultivation *Subhumid* tierra templada.

Hazards *Low annual rainfall, frequent electrical storms, some earthquakes and volcanic activity.*

Modern political identity *Mexico, all or part of states of Michoacan, Guanajuato, Jalisco, Querétaro.*

OPPOSITE **Terrain (natural vegetation)** *Mountain valleys (montane species), coastal plains (deciduous woodland and scrub).*

Climate for cultivation *Subhumid* tierra templada.

Hazards *Low annual rainfall, frequent electrical storms, some hurricanes, many earthquakes, and significant volcanic activity.*

Modern political identity *Mexico, all or part of states of Jalisco, Aguascalientes, Nayarit, Colima, Zacatecas, Michoacan.*

5 Guerrero

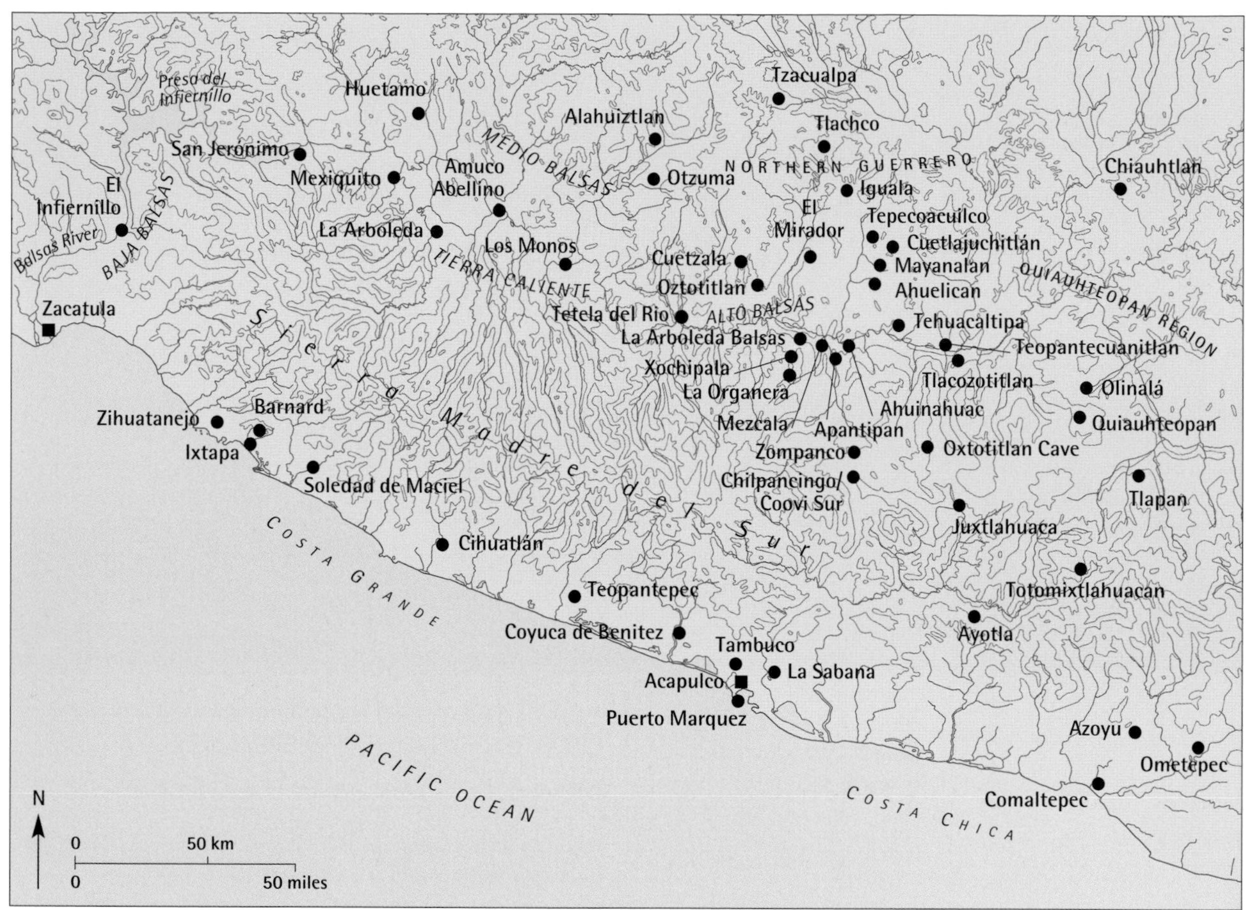

Terrain (natural vegetation) *Mountains of Sierra Madre del Sur (montane species); small valleys, coastal plain (thorny woodland, scrub, and desert; swamplands).*

Climate for cultivation *Humid coast and interior valleys, subhumid mountains with interior arid area – mostly* tierra caliente *and* tierra templada.

Hazards *Many earthquakes, some volcanic activity, low annual rainfall, many electrical storms.*

Modern political identity *Mexico, all or part of states of Guerrero, Michoacan.*

6 Central Highlands, Basin of Mexico and Morelos

Basin of Mexico

Terrain (natural vegetation) *Valley with central lake system (grasslands with thorny woodland, scrub at upper elevations, swamplands around lake), surrounded by mountains (montane species) and hills.*

Climate for cultivation *Subhumid to arid (*tierra templada *and* tierra fría*).*

Hazards *Some earthquakes, volcanic activity, electrical storms, low rainfall.*

Modern political identity *Mexico, part of state of Mexico and all of the Federal District.*

Morelos (inset)

Terrain (natural vegetation) *Broad valley (grasslands) with high mountains to the north and west, hills to south and east (montane species, deciduous woodland).*

Climate for cultivation *Semi-humid to humid (*tierra templada *and* tierra caliente*).*

Hazards *Some earthquake, volcanic activity, electrical storms, low annual rainfall.*

Modern political identity *Mexico, state of Morelos.*

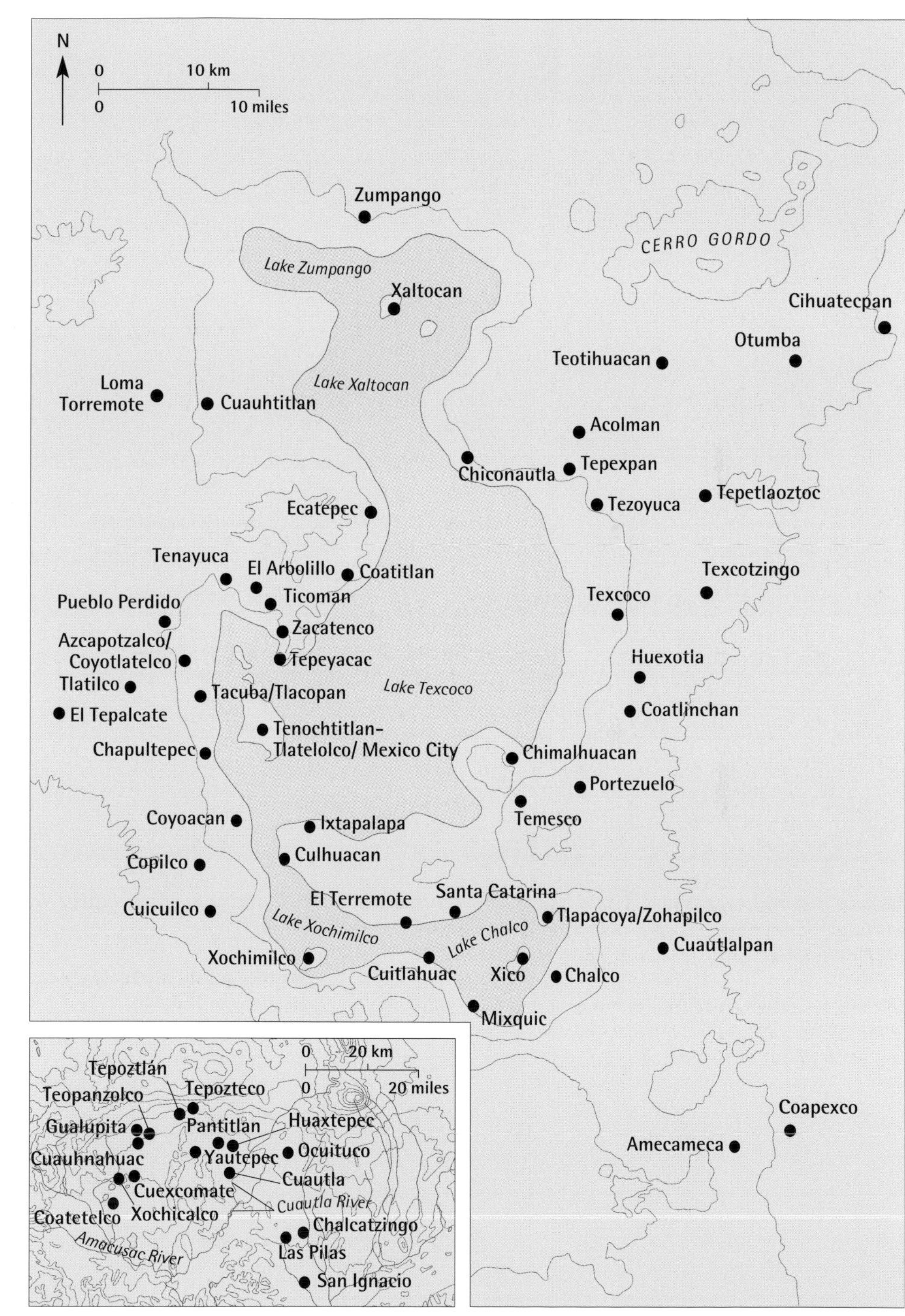

7 Central Highlands, Toluca and Tula

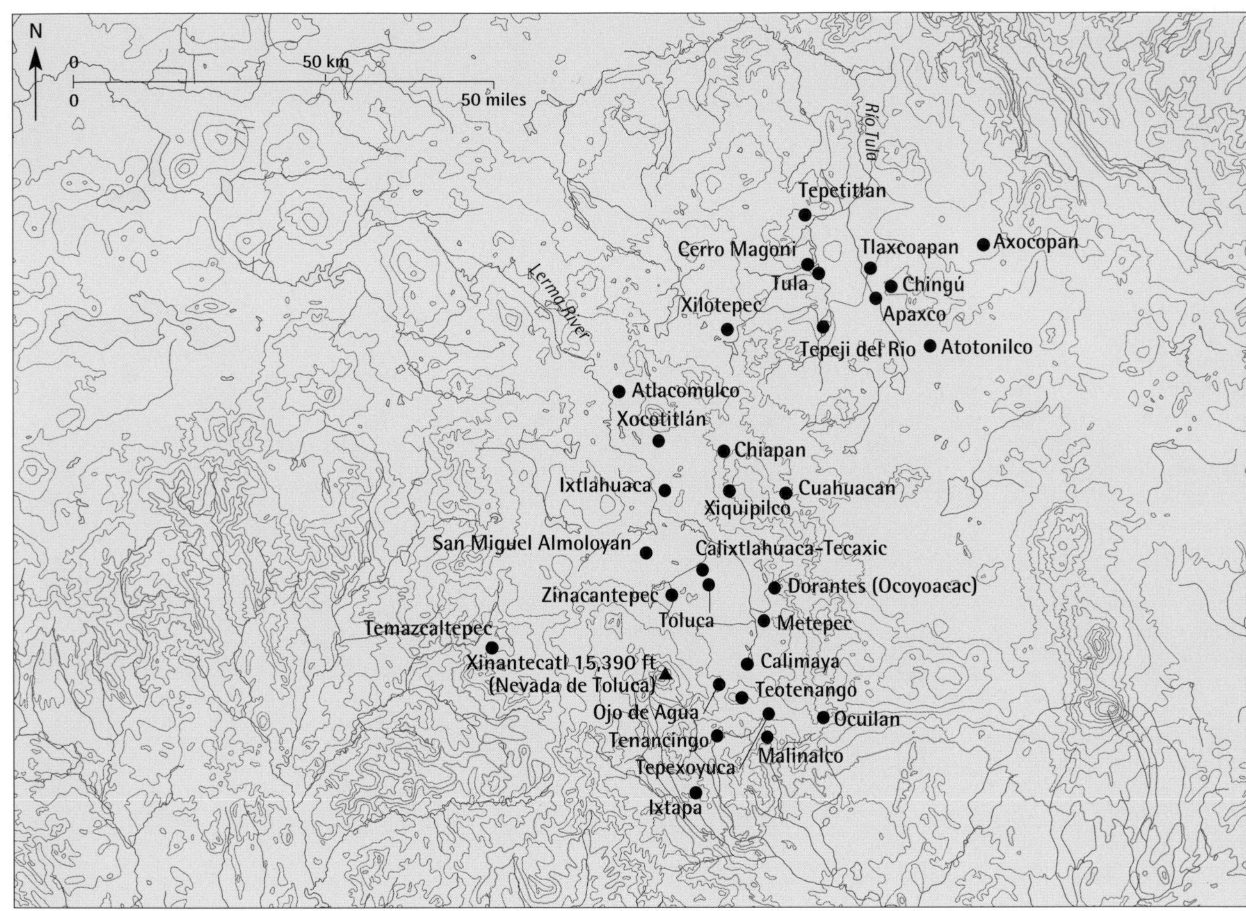

Terrain (natural vegetation) *Broad hilly valleys (grasslands with thorny woodland, scrub), bordered by mountains (montane species).*

Climate for cultivation *Subhumid to arid (*tierra templada *and* tierra fría*).*

Hazards *Some earthquakes, frequent electrical storms, low rainfall.*

Modern political identity *Mexico, all or part of states of Mexico and Hidalgo.*

8 Central Highlands, Puebla and Tlaxcala

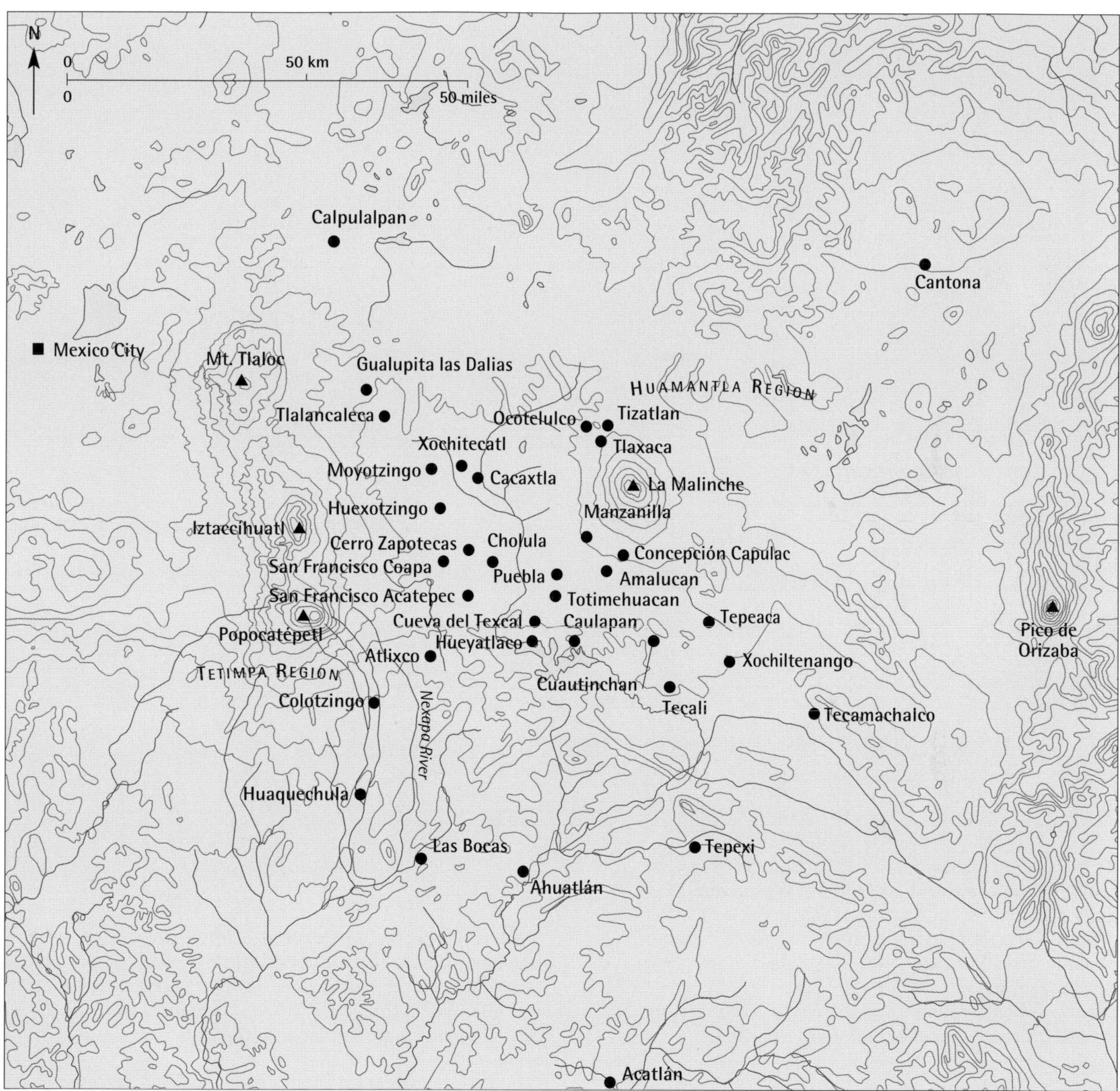

Terrain (natural vegetation) *Broad hilly valleys (grasslands with thorny woodland, scrub at upper elevations) bordered by mountains (montane species).*

Climate for cultivation *Subhumid to arid (*tierra templada *and* tierra fría*).*

Hazards *Some earthquakes, volcanic activity, electrical storms, low annual rainfall.*

Modern political identity *Mexico, part of state of Puebla and all of the state of Tlaxcala.*

9 Gulf Lowlands, North

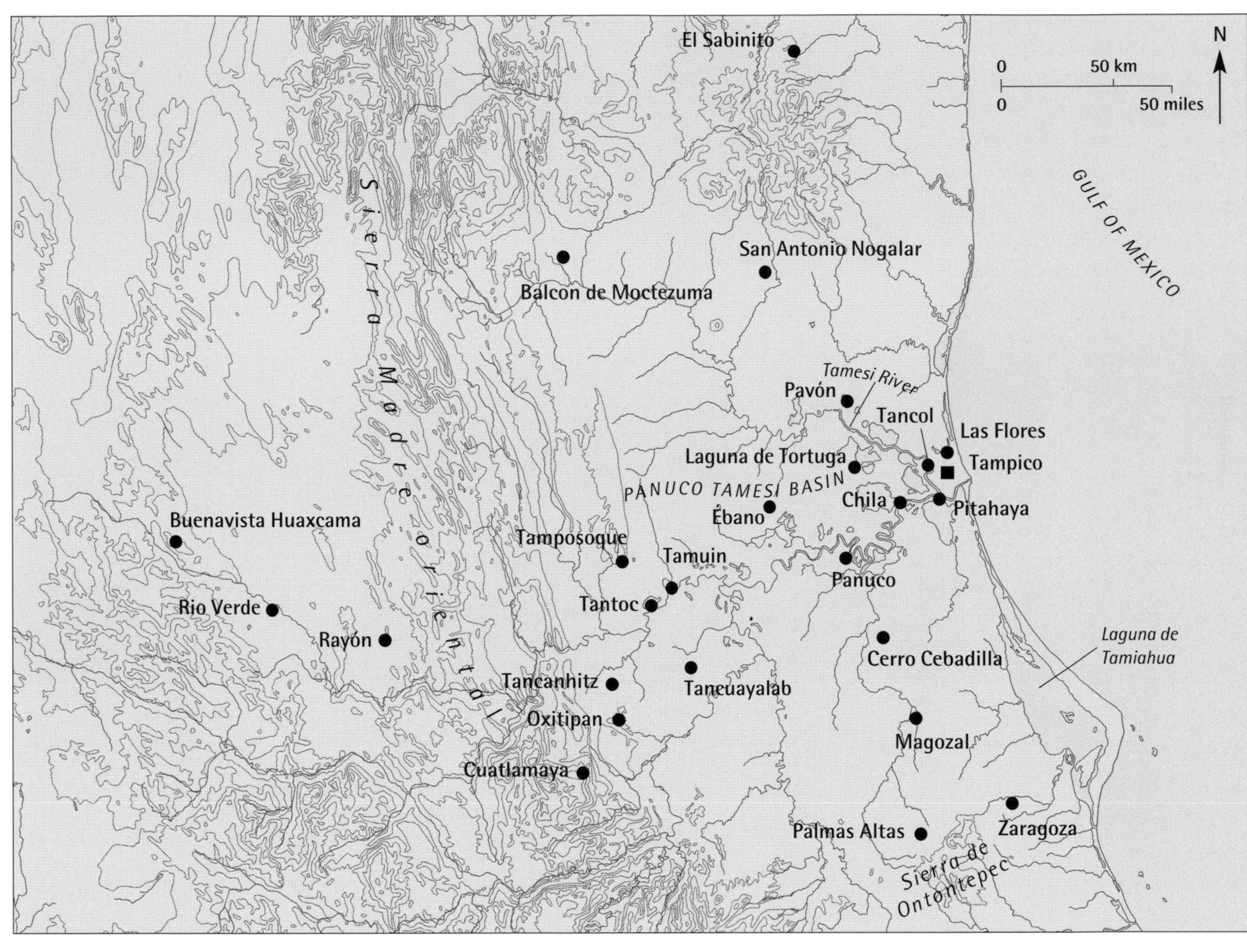

ABOVE **Terrain (natural vegetation)** *Coastal plain (mostly tropical rainforest) and adjacent Sierra Madre Oriental (dry evergreen species in north, montane species at higher elevations).*

Climate for cultivation *Humid lowlands with subhumid mountains (*tierra caliente *and* tierra templada*).*

Hazards *Many hurricanes; electrical storms, flooding, low annual rainfall.*

Modern political identity *Mexico, part of states of Veracruz, San Luis Potosí, Hidalgo.*

OPPOSITE **Terrain (natural vegetation)** *Coastal plain (mostly tropical rainforest with some areas of dry evergreen species) and adjacent Sierra Madre Oriental (montane species); Sierra de Chiconquiaco (montane species) to the south.*

Climate for cultivation *Humid lowlands with subhumid mountains (*tierra caliente *and* tierra templada*).*

Hazards *Many hurricanes, flooding; electrical storms, low annual rainfall.*

Modern political identity *Mexico, part of states of Veracruz and Puebla.*

10 Gulf Lowlands, North-central

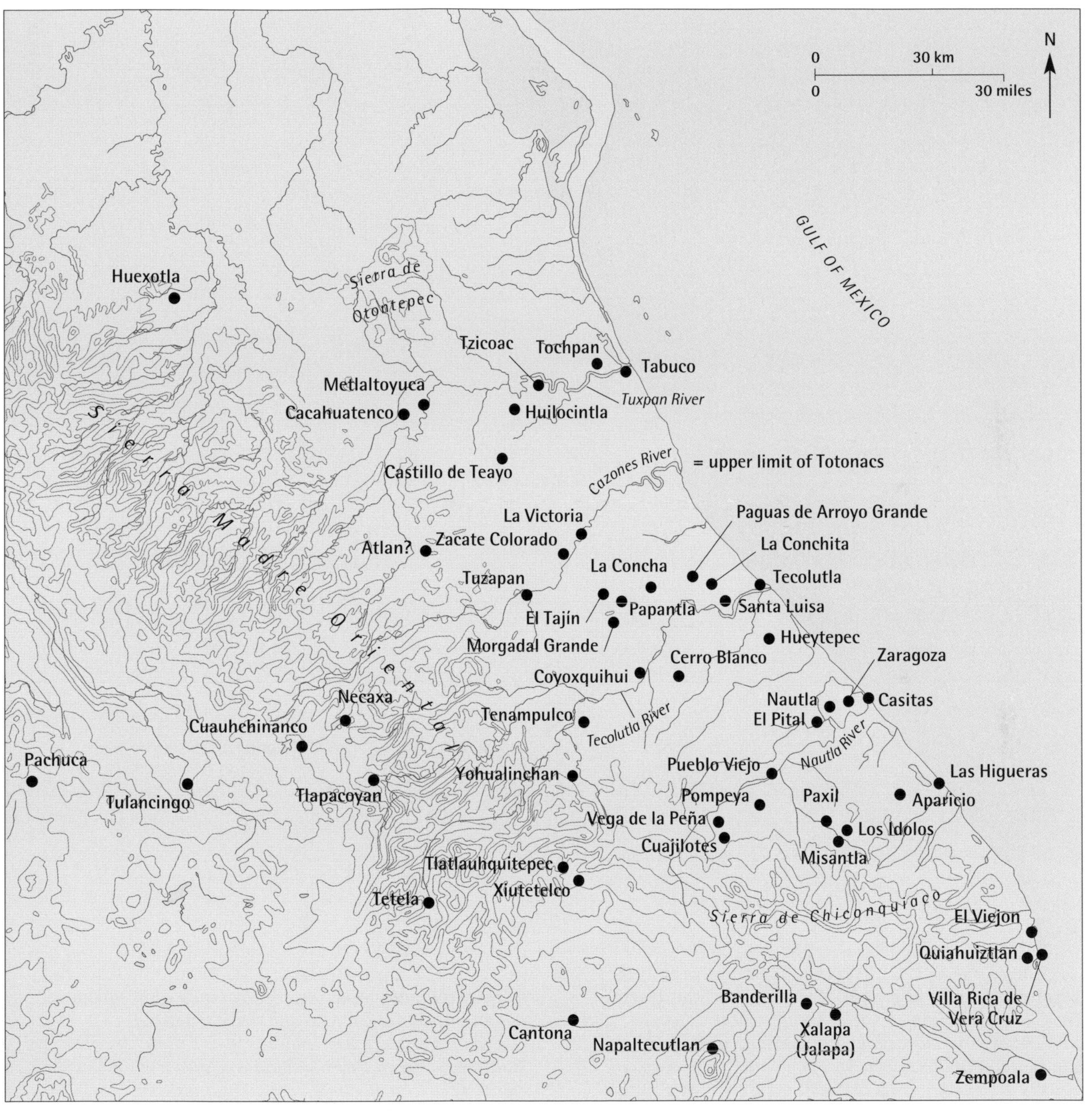

11 Gulf Lowlands, South-central

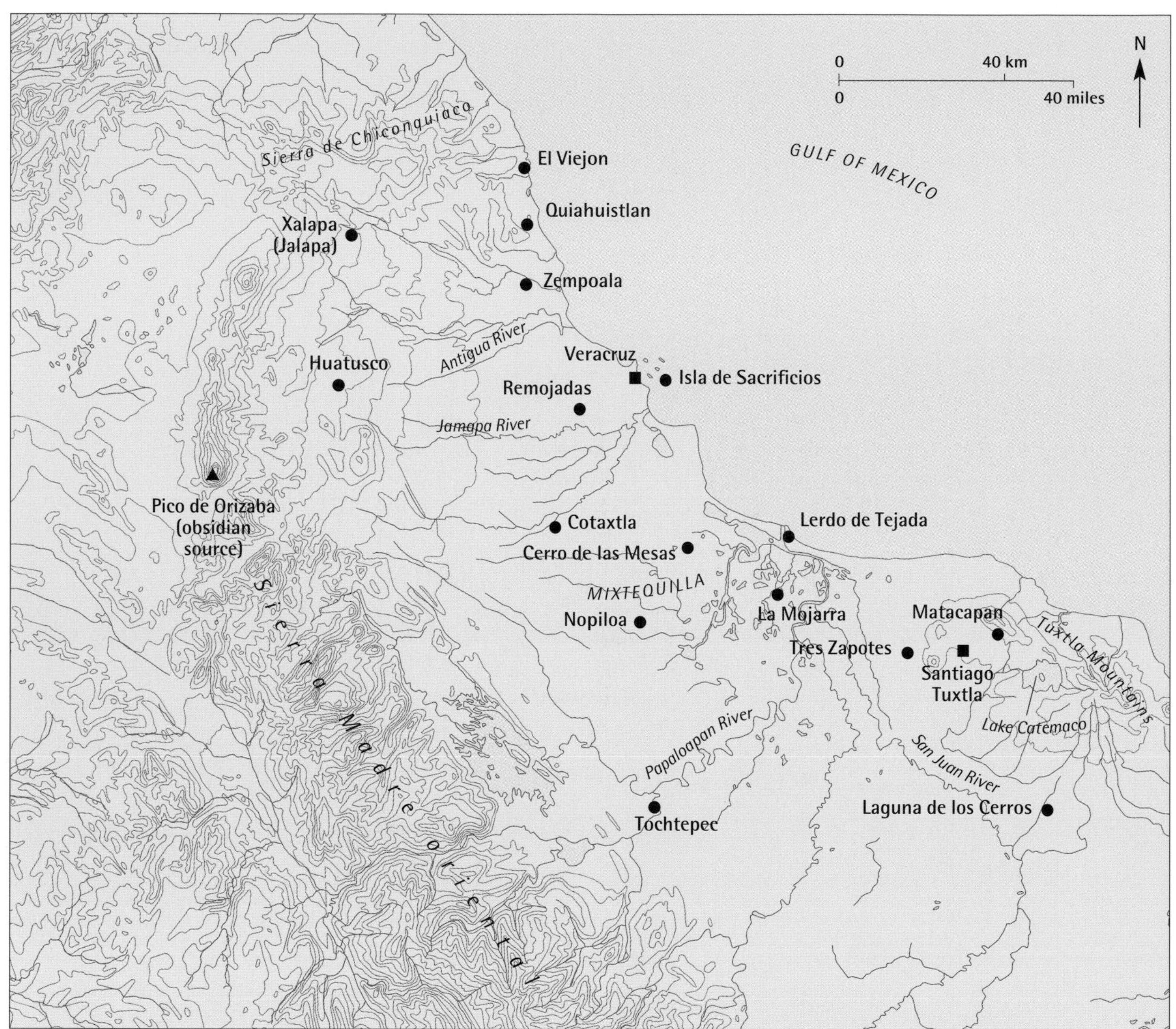

Terrain (natural vegetation) *Coastal plain (mostly dry evergreen species with some areas of tropical rainforest) and adjacent Sierra Madre Oriental (montane species); Sierra de Chiconquiaco to the north, Tuxtla mountains to the south (mostly dry evergreen species with some areas of tropical rainforest).*

Climate for cultivation *Humid lowlands with subhumid mountains (*tierra caliente *and* tierra templada*).*

Hazards *Some earthquakes and volcanic activity; hurricanes; electrical storms, flooding, low annual rainfall.*

Modern political identity *Mexico, part of states of Veracruz, Puebla, and Oaxaca.*

12 Tehuacán Valley

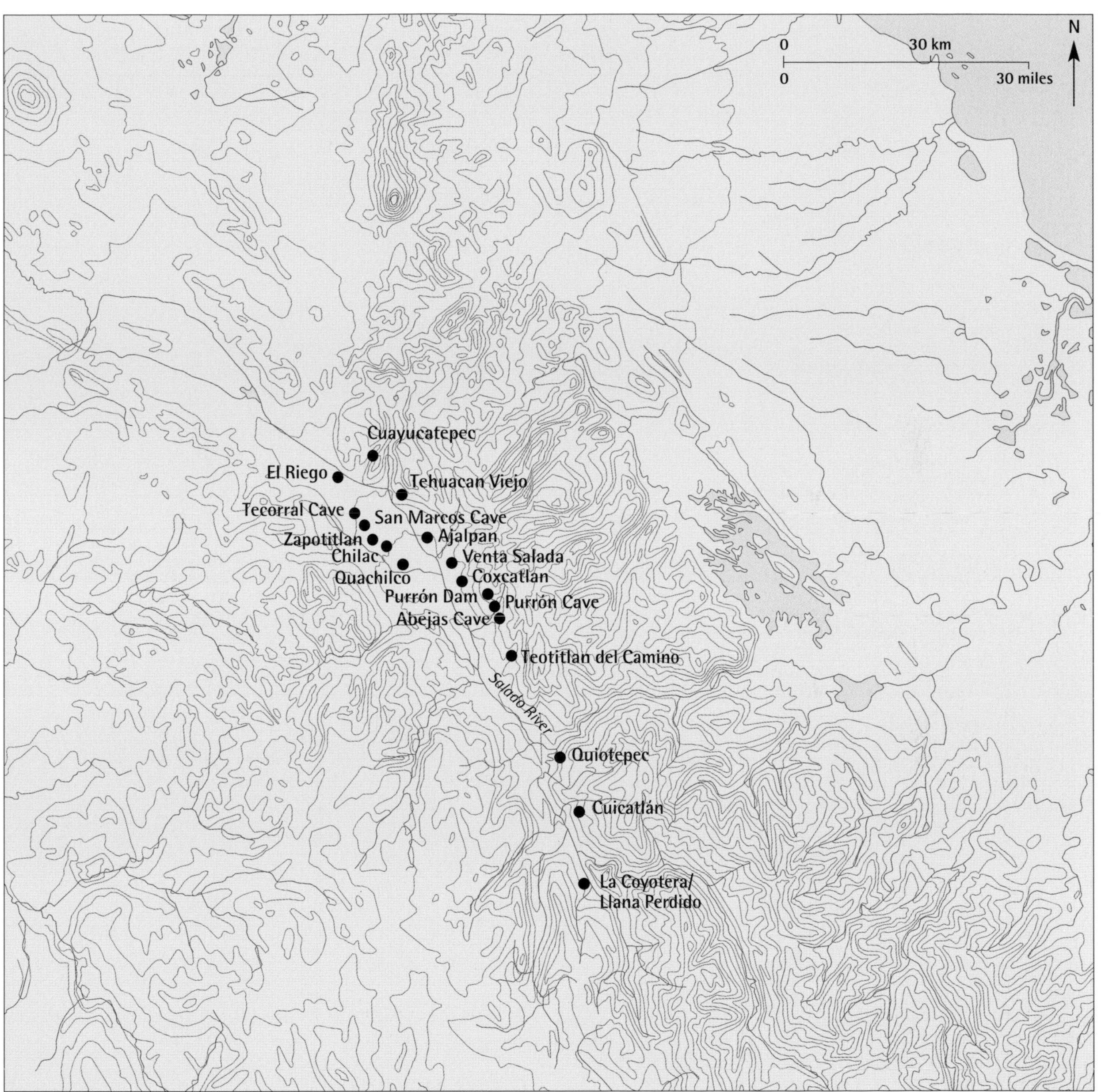

Terrain (natural vegetation) *Narrow, steep-sided valley (grasslands with thorny woodland, scrub) with rugged mountains (montane species).*

Climate for cultivation *Arid* tierra fría; *where cultivation is possible, irrigation is required.*

Hazards *Some earthquakes; low annual rainfall.*

Modern political identity *Mexico, part of state of Puebla.*

13 Mixteca

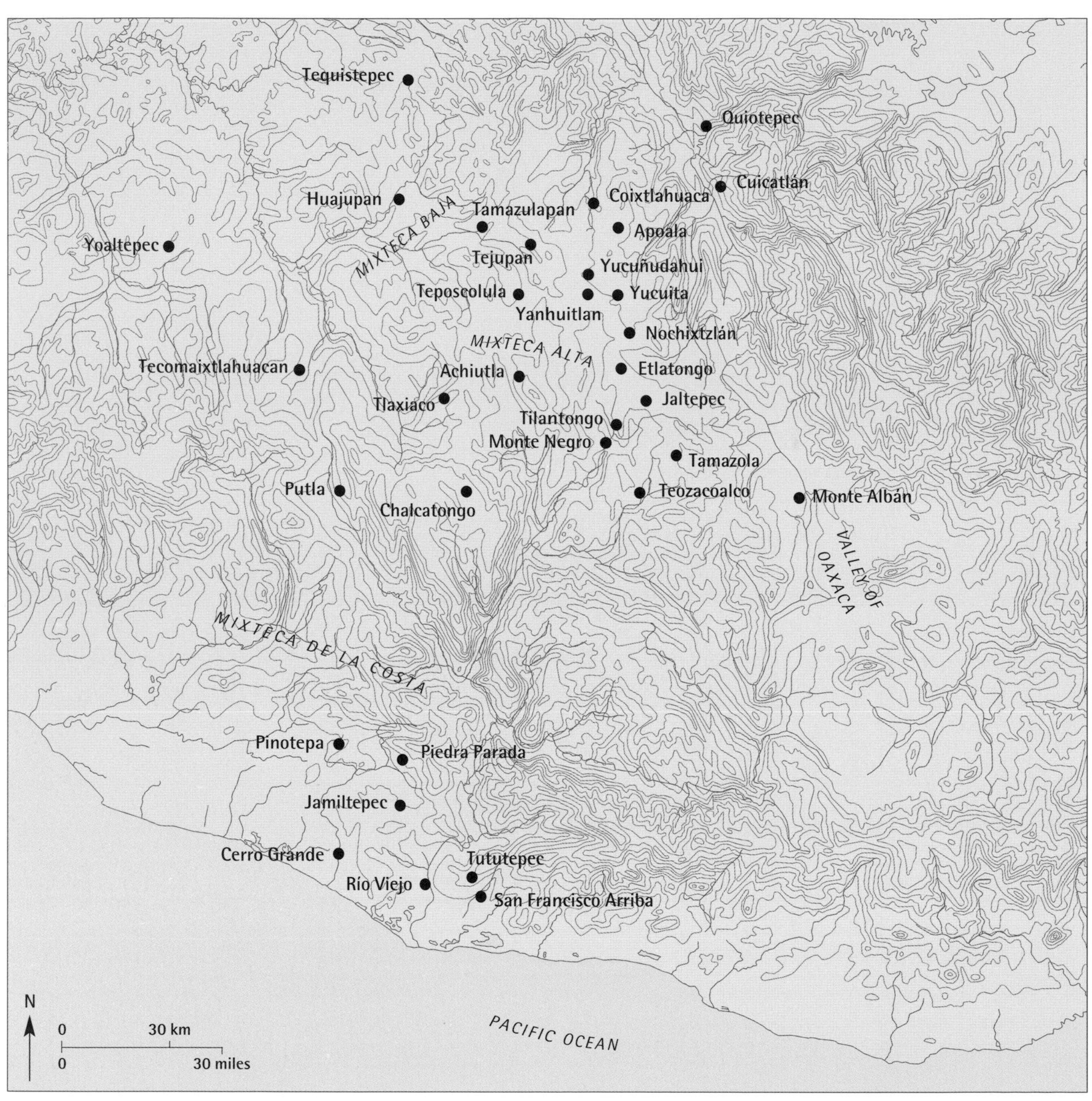

Terrain (natural vegetation) *valleys in mountainous terrain, narrow coastal plain (grasslands with thorny woodland, scrub; montane species).*

Climate for cultivation *humid coast, subhumid mountains (*tierra caliente *and* tierra templada*).*

Hazards *earthquakes; low annual rainfall.*

Modern political identity *Mexico, part of state of Oaxaca.*

14 Valley of Oaxaca

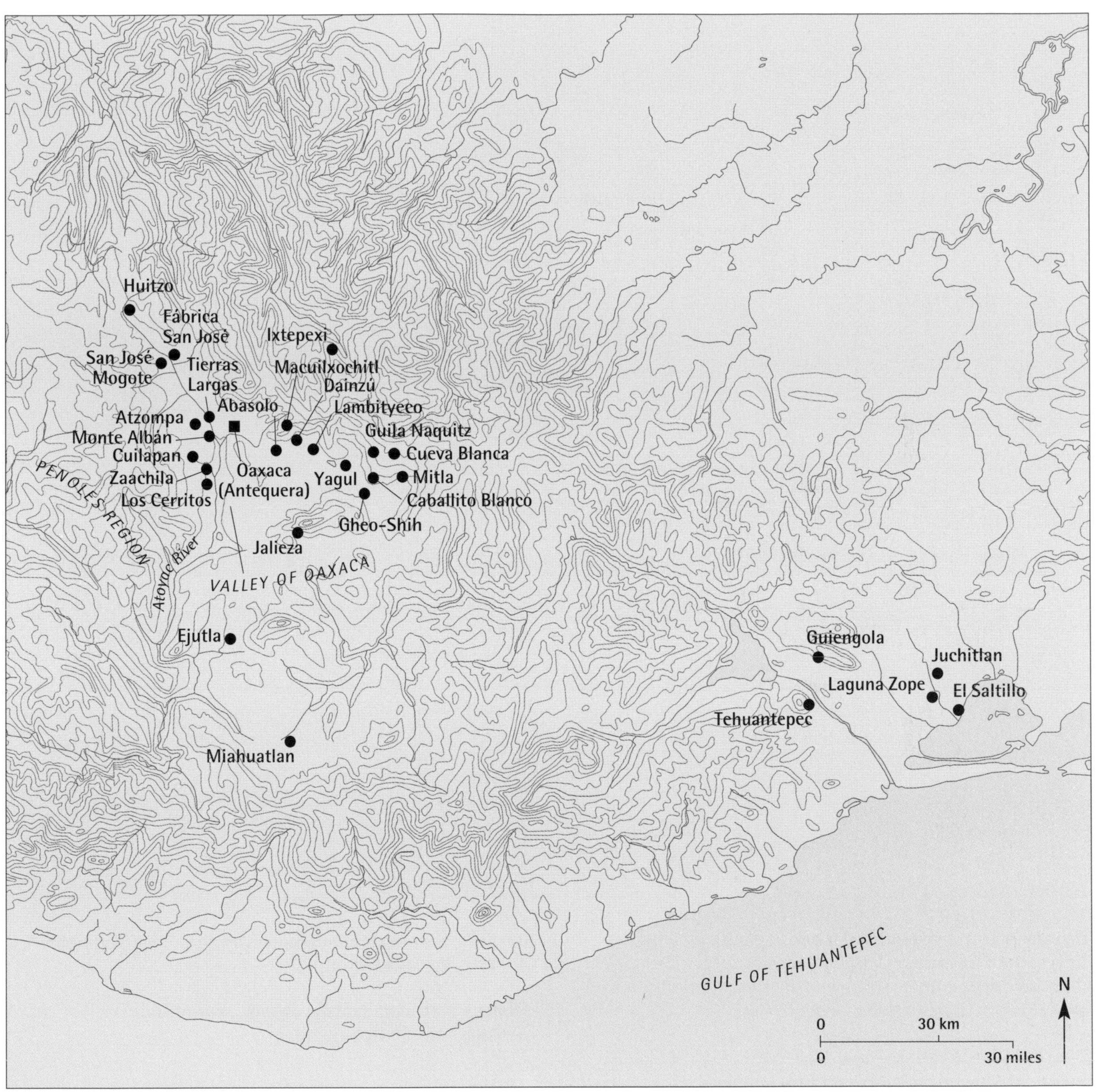

Terrain (natural vegetation) *Broad valley ringed by rugged mountains (grasslands with thorny woodland, scrub; montane species).*

Climate for cultivation *Subhumid (*tierra templada*).*

Hazards *Earthquakes; low annual rainfall.*

Modern political identity *Mexico, part of state of Oaxaca.*

15 Gulf Lowlands, South

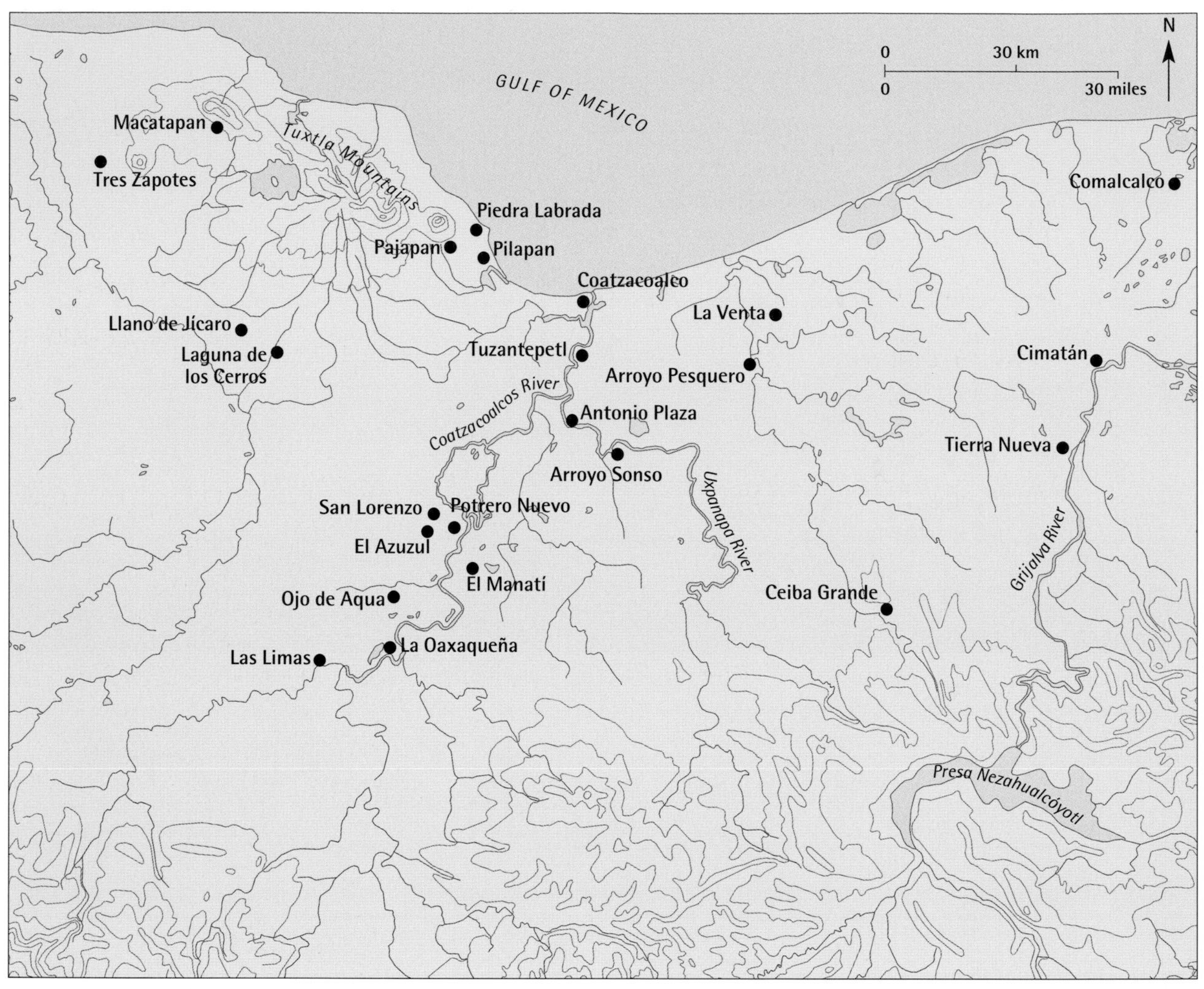

Terrain (natural vegetation) *Coastal plain and adjacent Sierra Madre Oriental; Tuxtla mountains to the northwest, Chontalpa region to the east (mostly tropical rainforest with some areas of dry evergreen species).*

Climate for cultivation *Humid lowlands with subhumid mountains (*tierra caliente *and* tierra templada*).*

Hazards *Some earthquakes and volcanic activity; hurricanes, flooding, low annual rainfall.*

Modern political identity *Mexico, part of states of Veracruz, Tabasco, and Chiapas.*

16 Chiapas Coast and Interior Plateau

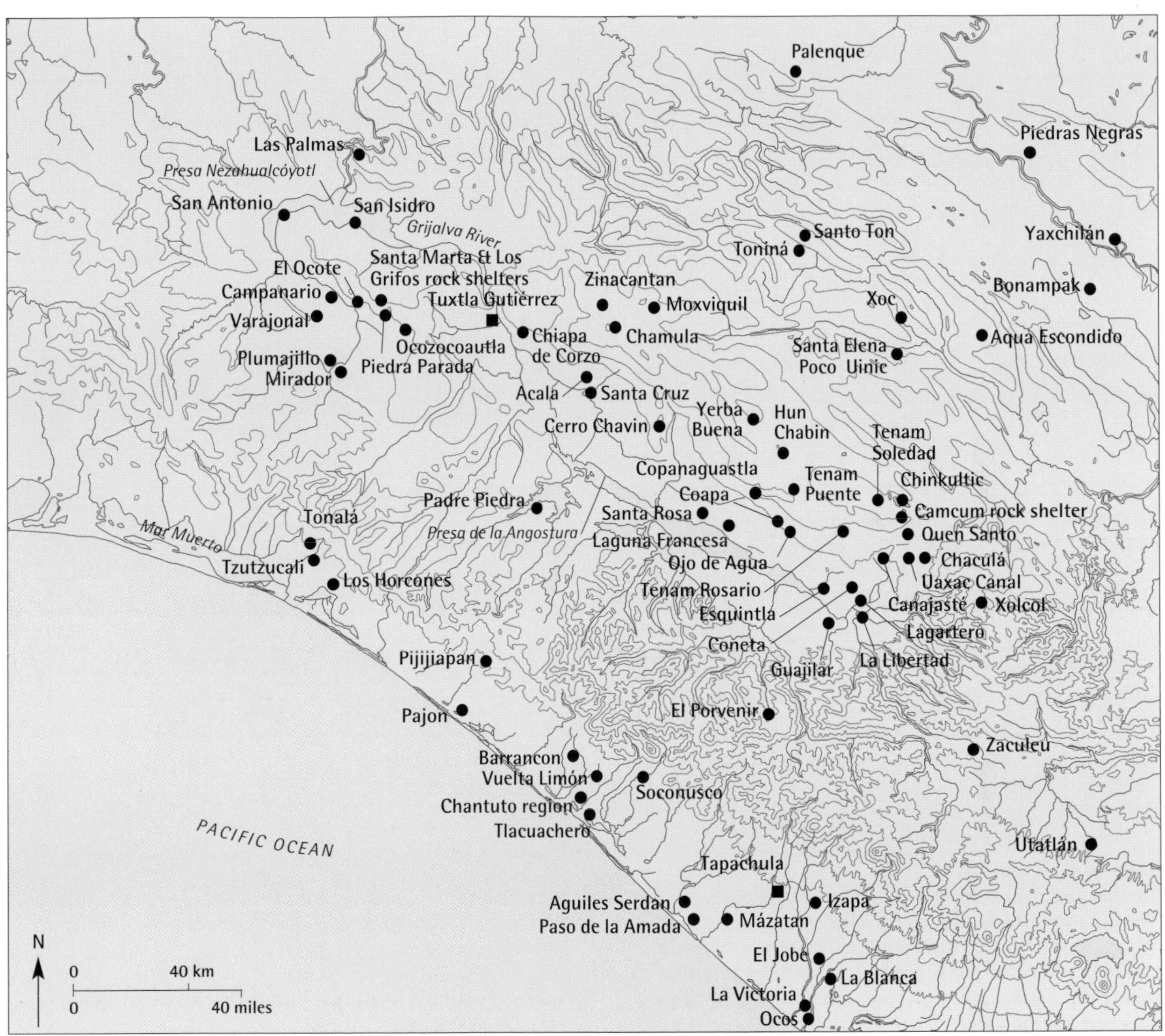

Terrain (natural vegetation) *Gently sloping piedmont (mostly tropical rainforest with some areas of deciduous species), marshy coast (seasonal swampland); Chiapas interior plateau is a set of broad, high valleys surrounded by hills (deciduous, montane species).*

Climate for cultivation *Coast: humid lowlands (*tierra caliente*); interior: semi-humid (*tierra templada*).*

Hazards *Coast: some earthquake activity; electrical storms; interior: severe earthquakes, low annual rainfall.*

Modern political identity *Mexico, part of state of Chiapas.*

17 Guatemala Coast and Highlands

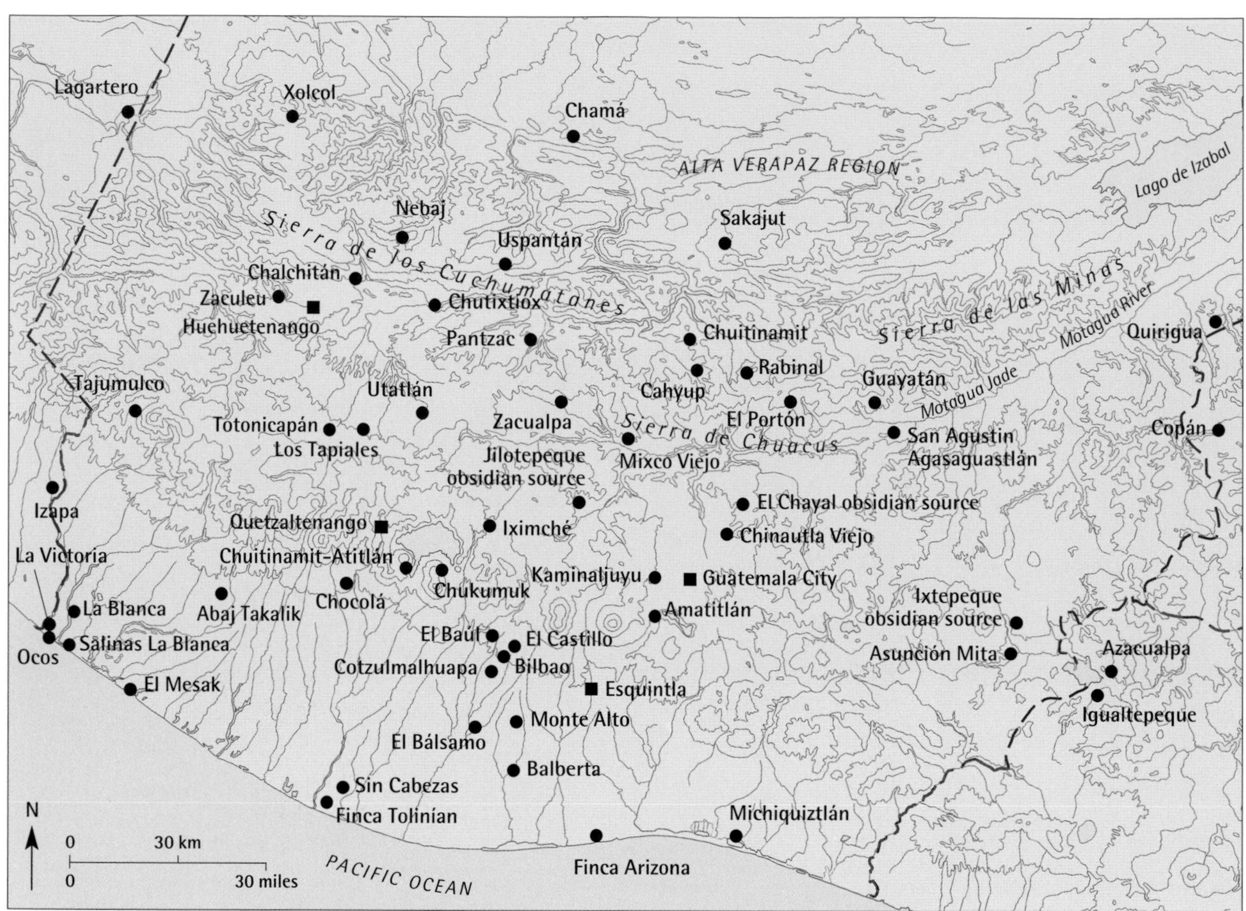

Terrain (natural vegetation) *Gently sloping piedmont (mostly tropical rainforest with some areas of deciduous species), marshy coast (seasonal swampland); Guatemala highlands encompass volcanoes and mountain ranges surrounding substantial valleys (montane species, some seasonal swamplands).*

Climate for cultivation *Coast: humid lowlands (*tierra caliente*); interior: semi-humid (*tierra templada*).*

Hazards *Coast: some earthquake activity, electrical storms; highlands: severe earthquakes, volcanic activity, electrical storms.*

Modern political identity *Guatemala, southern portion, western El Salvador.*

18 Maya Lowlands, North

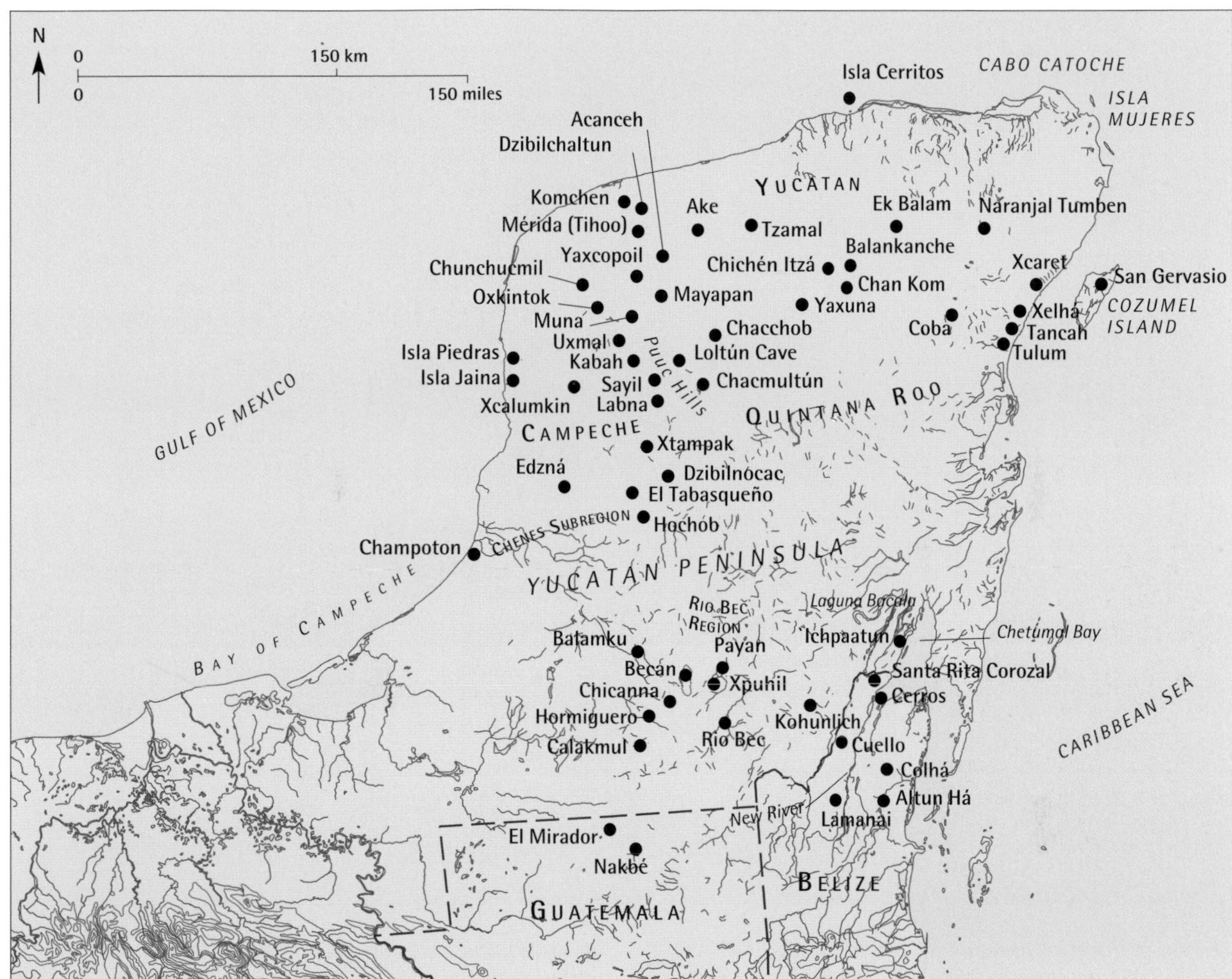

19 Terrain (natural vegetation) *Relatively flat plain with low hills, karstic/limestone terrain (dry evergreen scrub vegetation grading to tropical forest in the south).*

Climate for cultivation *Humid* (tierra caliente)*, with arid conditions in northwest corner.*

Hazards *Some earthquake, volcanic activity in far west; little surface water, low annual rainfall in the north; hurricanes; electrical storms.*

Modern political identity *Mexico, all of state of Yucatan, part of states of Campeche and Quintana Roo.*

19 Maya Lowlands, South

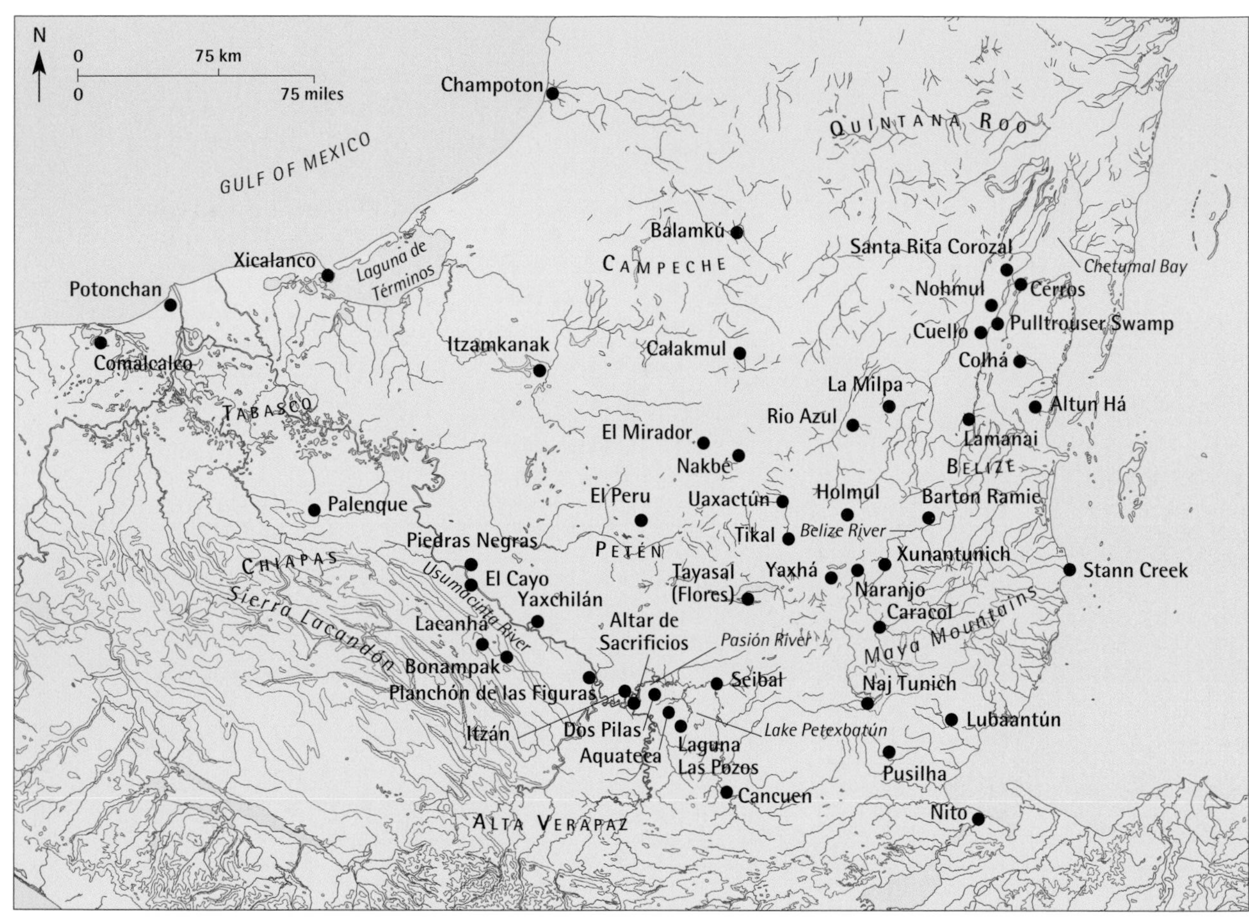

Terrain (natural vegetation) *Relatively flat plain with low hills, karstic/limestone terrain (mostly tropical forest with some pockets of dry evergreen scrub vegetation).*

Climate for cultivation *Humid (*tierra caliente*).*

Hazards *Some earthquake activity; electrical storms; limited surface water.*

Modern political identity *Mexico, part of states of Campeche, Tabasco, Chiapas, and Quintana Roo; northern Guatemala; all of Belize (British Honduras); Motagua Maya in Guatemala and western Honduras.*

20 Southeastern Mesoamerica

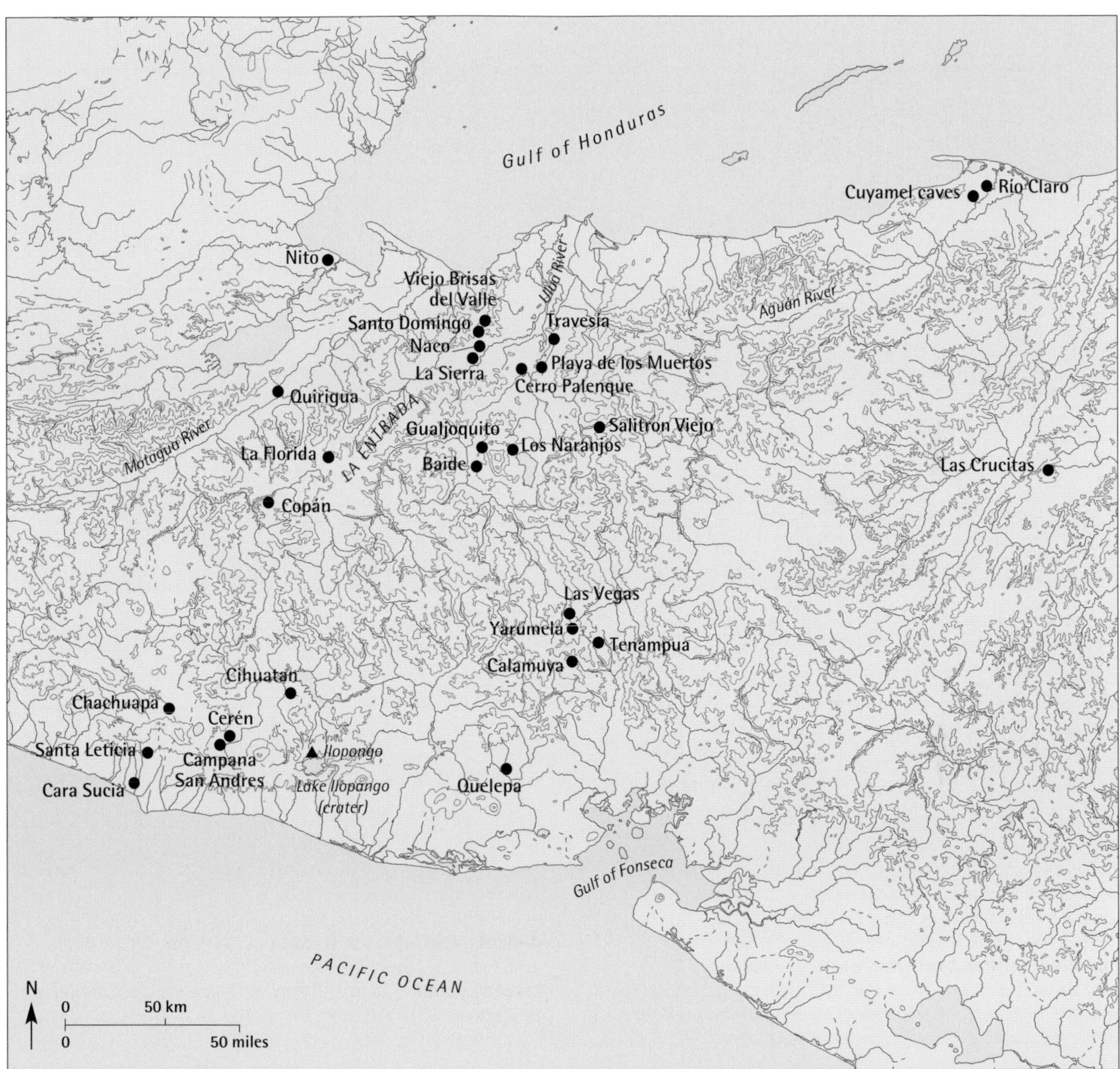

Terrain (natural vegetation) *Mountainous, highly dissected, with some substantial river valleys and small coastal plains (tropical forest, seasonal swampland, montane species, a few pockets of dry evergreen scrub vegetation).*

Climate for cultivation *Semi-humid to humid (*tierra templada *and* tierra caliente*).*

Hazards *Severe earthquakes, active volcanoes; hurricanes, electrical storms.*

Modern political identity *Part of Honduras, El Salvador, Nicaragua, and Costa Rica.*

21 Intermediate Area

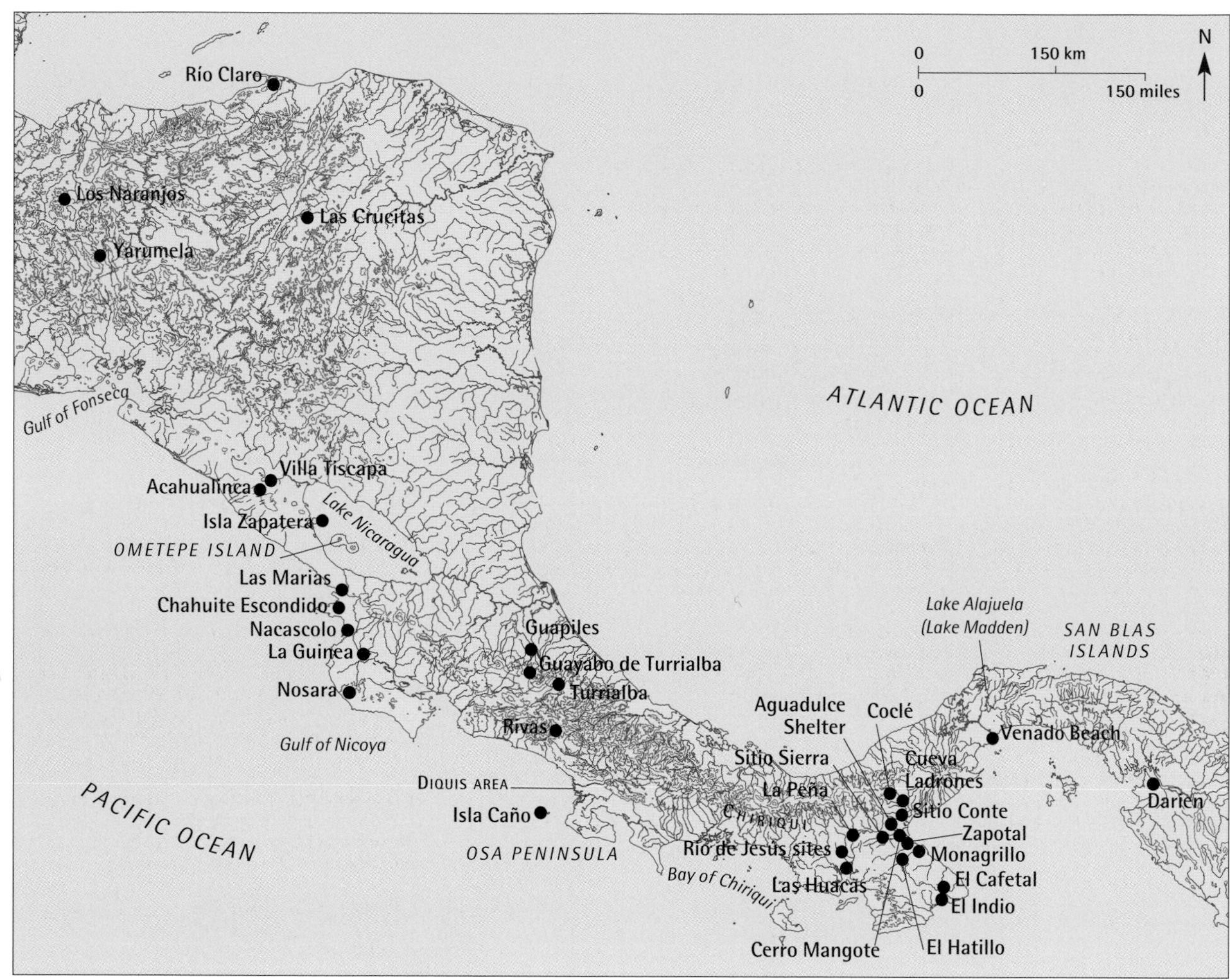

Terrain (natural vegetation) *Highly dissected, some mountainous areas, other regions with extensive swamplands; some substantial river valleys and small coastal plains (tropical forest, seasonal swampland, montane species, a few pockets of dry evergreen scrub vegetation).*

Climate for cultivation *Semi-humid to humid (*tierra templada *and* tierra caliente*).*

Hazards *Earthquakes, volcanic activity, electrical storms.*

Modern political identity *Part of Honduras, Nicaragua, and Costa Rica, all of Panama.*

FURTHER READING AND BIBLIOGRAPHY

These are articles and books that pertain to the subjects of particular chapters, and may be of further interest.

Chapter 1 Ancient Mesoamerica, the Civilization and Its Antecedents
Adams and MacLeod (eds.) 2000 [encyclopedia]; Carrasco (ed.). 2001 [encyclopedia]; Evans and Webster (eds.) 2001 [encyclopedia]; Kirchhoff 1981 (1943) [classic work: defined Mesoamerican culture trait list]; Heyden and Gendrop 1980 [overview: Mesoamerican monumental architecture]; Sanders and Price 1968 [classic overview]; Wolf 1959 [classic overview]

Chapter 2 Ecology and Culture: Mesoamerican Beginnings
Blake (ed.) 1999 [anthology: Pacific Coast Archaic and Formative]; Flannery (ed.) 1986 [anthology: Guilá Naquitz]; Flannery 1972 [classic study of evolution]; West and Augelli 1989 [overview: Middle American geography]; Vitebsky 1995 [overview: shamanism]; Vivó Escoto 1964 [Middle America's climate]; Wagner 1964 [Middle America's plants]; Williams 1992 [regional expression of shamanism]

Chapter 3 Archaic Foragers, Collectors, and Farmers (8000–2000 BC)
Benz 1990 [overview: maize]; Cobean 2002 [overview: obsidian]; Hard and Marrill 1992 [study of cultivation and sedentism]; Parsons and Parsons 1990 [overview: maguey]; Smith 1995 [overview: domestication of plants]; Stark 1981 [overview: rise of sedentism]; Zeitlin and Zeitlin 2000 [overview: Paleoindian and Archaic periods]

Chapter 4 The Initial Formative (*c.* 2000–1200 BC)
Beekman 2000 [overview: West Mexico early development]; Lesure 2000 [figurine use]; Rice 1987 [comprehensive treatment: pottery]; Stark and Arnold (eds.) 1997 [anthology: Gulf lowlands south-central and south]

Chapter 5 The Olmecs: Early Formative (*c.* 1200–900/800 BC)
Benson and de la Fuente (eds.) 1996 [anthology: Olmecs]; Blomster 2004 [site report: Etlatongo]; Coe *et al.* 1995 [anthology: Olmecs]; Clark and Pye (eds.) 2000 [anthology: Olmecs]; Marcus and Flannery 2000 [overview: Zapotec civilization and Oaxaca]

Chapter 6 The Olmecs: Middle Formative (*c.* 900–600 BC)
Fowler (ed.) 1991 [anthology, Pacific coastal plain]; García Cook 1981 [overview: Tlaxcala]; Grove (ed.). 1987 [anthology, Chalcatzingo]; Grove and Joyce (eds.) 1999 [anthology: social patterns]; Plunket (ed.) 2002 [anthology, domestic rituals]; Robin 1989 [Cuello mortuary patterns]

Chapter 7 Middle to Late Formative Cultures (*c.* 600/500–300 BC)
Grove and Joyce (eds.) 1999 [anthology: social patterns]; Flannery and Marcus (eds.) 1983 [overview: Oaxaca]; Miller 1996 [overview: art]

Chapter 8 The Emergence of States in the Late Formative (300 BC–AD 1)
González Licón 1994 [overview: Zapotec and Mixtec culture history]; Marcus and Flannery 1996 [overview: Oaxaca]

Chapter 9 The Terminal Formative (AD 1–300)
Chase and Chase (eds.) 1992 [overview: elites]; Graham 1994 [regional study: Belize]; Grube (ed.) 2001 [anthology: Maya]; Pasztory 1997 [overview: Teotihuacan]

Chapter 10 Teotihuacan and Its International Influence (AD 250/300–600)
Berrin and Pasztory (eds.) 1993 [anthology: Teotihuacan]; Braswell (ed.) [anthology: Classic to Postclassic]; Carrasco, Jones, and Sessions (eds.) 2001 [anthology: Classic to Postclassic Central Mexico]; Middleton *et al.* 1998 [Zapotec mortuary practices]; Sempowski and Spence 1994 [Teotihuacan mortuary practices]

Chapter 11 The Maya in the Early Classic (AD 250–600)
Coe and Kerr 1998 [overview: Maya scribes]; Coe and van Stone 2001 [overview: Maya writing]; Estrada Belli 2001 [Maya site: Holmul]; Fedick (ed.) 1996 [anthology: agriculture]; Marcus 2003; Jones 1989 [Tikal study]; Masson and Freidel (eds.) 2002 [anthology: Maya]; Sabloff (ed.) 2003 [anthology: Tikal]; Sheets (ed.) 2002 [anthology: Cerén]; Traxler 2001 [Copán courtly life]; Urban and Schortman (eds.) 1986 [anthology: Southeastern Mesoamerica]

Chapter 12 The Lowland Maya: Apogee and Collapse (AD 600–900)
Ardren (ed.) 2002 [anthology: Maya gender]; Becker 1979 [overview: Maya elite and sites]; Christie 2003 [anthology: Maya palaces]; Fash 1992 [Copán sculpture]; Gustafson and Trevelyan (eds.) 2002 [anthology: Maya gender]; Newsome 2001 [Copán iconography]; Taube 1992b [overview: Maya deities]; Webster 2001 [overview: Maya collapse]; Wingard 1996 [Copán Maya collapse]

Chapter 13 The Late Classic and Epiclassic in the West (AD 600–1000/1100)
Diehl and Berlo (eds.) 1989 [anthology: Epiclassic]; Finsten 1995 [Jalieza site study]; Hirth (ed.) 2000 [anthology: Xochicalco]; Hosler 1994 [overview: metal use]

Chapter 14 The Maya in the Terminal Classic and Early Postclassic (AD 800–1200)
Bey *et al.* 1997 [site report: Maya transition Classic to Postclassic]; Coe and Coe 1996 [overview: chocolate]; Coe 1994 [overview: cuisine]; Fowler (ed.) 1991 [anthology: Southeastern Mesoamerica]; Smith and Berdan (eds.) 2003 [anthology: Postclassic]; Zeitlin, J. 1993 [ball game cult, coastal Oaxaca]

Chapter 15 The Rise of Tula and Other Epiclassic Transformations (AD 900–1200)
Byland and Pohl 1994 [Mixtec overview]; Davies 1977b [overview: Toltec history]; Mastache, Cobean and Healan 2002 [overview: Tula]

Chapter 16 The Middle Postclassic (1200s–1430)
Chase and Rice (eds.) 1985 [anthology: Maya lowlands]; Nichols and Charlton (eds.) 1997 [anthology: city-states]

Chapter 17 The Aztecs: An Empire is Born (1325–1440)
Bray 1987 [overview: Aztec history]; Burkhart 1989 [Aztec morals and values]; Clendinnen 1991 [overview: Aztec culture]; Davies 1977a [overview: Aztec history]; Durán 1994 (1581) [overview: Aztec history, by 16th-century chronicler]

Chapter 18 The Aztec Empire Develops (1440–1481)
Biskowski 2000 [Aztec maize use]; Gerhard 1993 [review of sources, Aztec empire]; Marcus and Zeitlin (eds.) 1994 [anthology Oaxaca and Mixteca]; McKeever Furst 1995 [overview: religion]; Silverstein 2001 [Aztec imperial defense, Guerrero]

Chapter 19 The Aztec Empire at Its Height (1481–1519)
Carrasco 1999 [development of the Aztec empire]; Chase and Chase 1988 [site report: Corozal]; Codex Borgia 1993 (*c.* 1500) [Mixtec screenfold book, in affordable paperback]; Graham (ed.) 1993 [anthology: Intermediate Area]; Lange (ed.) 1996 [anthology: Intermediate Area]; López Lújan 1994 [site focus: Aztec Templo Mayor]; Parry and Keith (eds.) 1984 [anthology: eyewitness accounts of Age of Discovery]

Chapter 20 The Conquest of Mexico and Its Aftermath Braun 1993 [influence of pre-Columbian forms on modern art]; Chance 1989 [post-contact Oaxaca regional overview]; Charlton 2003 [post-contact transformation of land use]; Cortés 1986 (1519–1526) [eyewitness account of the contact era]; Díaz del Castillo 1956 [1560s) [eyewitness account of the contact era]; Edgerton and Pérez de Lara 2001 [cultural transformation: religion]; Gibson 1964 [overview: transformation of Aztec life]; Ford 1999 [archaeology and biosphere preservation]; Grusinski 1993 [overview: conquest]; Robinson 1997 [cultural transition in Guatemala highlands].

ABBREVIATIONS USED

AA American Antiquity
AAnthro American Anthropologist
AAMCA Archaeology of Ancient Mexico and Central America: An Encyclopedia (Evans and Webster 2001).
AncM Ancient Mesoamerica
ArqM Arqueología Mexicana
CA Current Anthropology
DOSPCAA Dumbarton Oaks Studies in Pre-Columbian Art and Archaeology, Washington DC.
HMAI Handbook of Middle American Indians
INAH Instituto Nacional de Antropología e Historia, Mexico City.
JAA Journal of Anthropological Archaeology
JAR Journal of Archaeological Research
JFA Journal of Field Archaeology
JWP Journal of World Prehistory
LAA Latin American Antiquity
MARI Middle American Research Institute, Tulane University, New Orleans.
MAUM Museum of Anthropology, U. of Michigan, Ann Arbor.
PNWAF Papers of the New World Archaeological Foundation, Brigham Young University, Provo.
UNAM Universidad Nacional Autónoma de México, Mexico City.
VUPA Vanderbilt University Publications in Anthropology, Nashville.
WA World Archaeology

Abascal, Rafael, Patricio Dávila, Peter Schmidt, and Diana Z. de Dávila. 1976. *La Arqueología del Sur-Oeste de Tlaxcala. Comunicaciones Proyecto Puebla-Tlaxcala, Suplemento II.* Fundación Alemana para la Investigación Científica, Puebla, Mexico.

Abrams, Elliot. 1994. *How the Maya Built Their World: Energetics and Ancient Architecture.* U. of Texas Press, Austin.

Acosta, Jorge. 1965. Preclassic and Classic architecture of Oaxaca. *HMAI* 3: 2: 814–836.

Adams, Richard E. W. 1991. *Prehistoric Mesoamerica.* U. of Oklahoma Press, Norman.

Adams, Richard E. W., and Murdo J. MacLeod (eds.). 2000. *Mesoamerica. The Cambridge History of the Native Peoples of the Americas*, Volume II, Part 1. Cambridge U. Press, Cambridge.

Aguilera, Carmen. 1974. La Estela (Elemento 7) de Tlalancaleca. *Comunicaciones* 10: 1–4. Fundación Alemana para la Investigación Científica, Puebla, Mexico.

Agurcia, Ricardo and William Fash. 1991. Maya artistry unearthed. *National Geographic* 180 (3): 94–105.

Aimers, James J., Terry Powis, and Jaime Awe. 2000. Formative Period Round Structures of the Upper Belize River Valley. *LAA* 11: 71–86.

Alva Ixtlilxóchitl, Fernando de. 1985 [1600–1640]. *Obras Históricas.* UNAM.

Anawalt, Patricia Rieff. 1981. *Indian Clothing Before Cortés.* U. of Oklahoma Press, Norman.

—. 1993. Rabbits, *Pulque*, and Drunkenness. In *Current Topics in Aztec Studies*, A. Cordy-Collins and D. Sharon (eds.): 17–38. San Diego Museum Papers 30.

Andrews, Anthony P. 1993. Late postclassic Maya lowland archaeology. *JWP* 7: 35–69.

Andrews, Anthony P. and Fernando Robles C. 1985. Chichén Itzá and Cobá. In *The Lowland Maya Postclassic*, A. F. Chase and P. M. Rice (eds.): 62–72. U. of Texas Press, Austin.

Andrews V, E. Wyllys. 1976. *The Archaeology of Quelepa, El Salvador.* MARI Publication 42.

—. 1990. The Early Ceramic History of the Lowland Maya. In Clancy and Harrison (eds.): 1–19.

Angulo V., Jorge. 1987. Iconographic Analysis of Reliefs. In Grove (ed.): 132–158.

Annals of Cuauhtitlan. 1992 [c. 1570]. *History and Mythology of the Aztecs: The Codex Chimalpopoca. Annals of Cuauhtitlan and Legend of the Suns.* John Bierhorst (ed. and transl.). U. of Arizona Press, Tucson.

Arana, Raul Martín. 1987. Classic and Postclassic Chalcatzingo. In Grove (ed.): 387–399.

Ardren, Traci (ed.). 2002. *Ancient Maya Women.* AltaMira Press, Walnut Creek, CA.

Armillas, Pedro. 1964. Condiciones ambietales y movimientos de pueblos en la frontera septentrional de Mesoamerica. In *Homenaje a Fernando Márquez-Miranda*: 62–82. Publicaciones del Seminario de Estudios Americanistas y el Seminario de Anthropología Americana, Universidades de Madrid y Sevilla, Madrid.

Arnold, Philip J. 2000. Sociopolitical complexity and the gulf Olmecs: A View from the Tuxtla Mountains, Veracruz, Mexico. In Clark and Pye (eds.): 116–135.

Ashmore, W., E. M. Schortman, P. A. Urban, J. C. Benyo, J. M. Weeks, and S. M. Smith. 1987. Ancient society in Santa Bárbara, Honduras. *National Geographic Research* 3: 232–254.

Aveleyra, Luis. 1964. The primitive hunters. *HMAI* I: 384–412.

Aveni, Anthony. 1989. *Empires of Time: Calendars, Clocks, and Cultures.* Basic Books, Inc., New York.

—. 1993. *Ancient Astronomers.* St. Remy Press, Montreal, and Smithsonian Books, Washington, D.C.

Aveni, Anthony F., Anne S. Dowd, and Benjamin Vining. 2003. A statistical approach to the astronomical efficacy of Group E-type structures. *LAA* 14: 159–178.

Awe, Jaime, and Paul F. Healy. 1994. Flakes to Blades? Middle Formative Development Obsidian Artifacts in the Upper Belize Valley. *LAA* 5: 193–205.

Balboa, Vasco Nuñez de. 1984 [1513]. Letter to the King describing his expedition up the Atrato and his hope of finding the other sea. In Parry and Keith (eds.), III: 26–35.

Ball, Joseph W. 2001. Maya lowlands: north. *AAMCA*: 433–441.

Ball, Joseph W., and Jennifer T. Taschek. 1989. Teotihuacan's Fall and the Rise of the Itza. In Diehl and Berlo (eds.): 187–200.

Barbour, Warren. 1976. *The Figurines and Figurine Chronology of Ancient Teotihuacan, Mexico.* Ph.D. dissertation (Anthropology), U. of Rochester. U. Microfilms, Ann Arbor.

Baudot, Georges. 1995. *Utopia and History in Mexico: The First Chroniclers of Mexican Civilization (1520–1569).* U. Press of Colorado, Niwot, CO.

Beadle, George. 1939. Teosinte and the origin of maize. *The Journal of Heredity* 30: 245–247.

Becker, Marshall. 1979. *Theories of Ancient Maya Social Structure; Priests, Peasants, and Ceremonial Centers in Historical Perspective.* U. of Northern Colorado, Museum of Anthropology Occasional Publications in Mesoamerican Anthropology 12.

Beekman, Christopher S. 2000. The correspondence of regional patterns and local strategies in Formative to Classic period West Mexico. *JAA* 19: 385–412.

Bennetzen, Jeff, Edward Buckler, Vicki Chandler, John Dobley, Jane Dorweiler, Brandon Gaut, Michael Freeling, Sarah Hake, Elizabeth Kellogg, R. Scott Poethig, Virginia Walbot, and Susan Wessler. 2001. Genetic evidence and the origin of maize. *LAA* 12: 84–86.

Benson, Elizabeth P. 1997. *Birds and Beasts of Ancient Latin America.* U. Press of Florida, Gainesville.

—. 1998. The lord, the ruler: Jaguar symbolism in the Americas. In Saunders (ed.): 53–76.

—. (ed.). 1981. *The Olmec and Their Neighbors.* Dumbarton Oaks, Washington, D.C.

Benson, Elizabeth P. and Beatriz de la Fuente (eds.). 1996. *Olmec Art of Ancient Mexico.* National Gallery of Art, Washington D.C.

Benz, Bruce F. 1990. Maize: origin, domestication, and development. In Carrasco (ed.): 147–150.

Benz, Bruce F., and Hugh H. Iltis. 1990. Studies in archaeological maize I: The "wild maize" from San Marcos restudied. *AA* 55: 500–511.

Berdan, Frances F. 1992. Annual tribute in Codex Mendoza Part 2. Appendix B in *The Codex Mendoza, V. I: Interpretation*, Frances F. Berdan and Patricia Rieff Anawalt (eds.): 154–156. U. of California Press, Berkeley.

Berdan, Frances F., Richard E. Blanton, Elizabeth Hill Boone, Mary G. Hodge, Michael E. Smith, and Emily Umberger. 1996. *Aztec Imperial Strategies.* Dumbarton Oaks Research Library and Collection, Washington, D.C.

Berdan, Frances F., Richard E. Blanton, Elizabeth Hill Boone, Mary G. Hodge, Michael E. Smith, and Emily Umberger. 1996. Introduction to Part II. In Berdan *et al.*: 109–113.

Berlin, Heinrich. 1958. El glifo 'emblema' en las inscripciones Mayas. *Journal de la Société des Américanistes*, n.s. 47: 111–120.

Berlo, Janet Catherine. 1989. Art historical approaches to the study of Teotihuacan-related ceramics from Escuintla, Guatemala. In Bové and Heller (eds.): 147–166.

—. (ed.). 1992. *Art, Ideology, and the City of Teotihuacan.* Dumbarton Oaks, Washington, D.C.

Bernal, Ignacio. 1973. Stone reliefs in the Dainzú area. In *The Iconography of Middle American Sculpture*, texts by Ignacio Bernal and others: 13–23. Metropolitan Museum of Art, New York.

—. 1980. *A History of Mexican Archaeology.* Thames & Hudson, London.

Berrin, Kathleen, and Esther Pasztory (eds.). 1993. *Teotihuacan, Art from the City of the Gods.* The Fine Arts Museum of San Francisco. Thames & Hudson, New York.

Bey, George, Craig A. Hanson, and William M. Ringle. 1997. Classic to Postclassic at Ek Balam, Yucatan: architectural and ceramic evidence for defining the transition. *LAA* 8: 237–254.

Bishop, Ronald L. 2001. Jade. *AAMCA*: 381–382.

Bishop, Ronald L., and Frederick W. Lange. 1993. Sources of Maya and Central American Jadeitites. In *Precolumbian Jade: New Geological and Cultural Interpretations*, F.W. Lange (ed.): 125–130. U. of Utah Press, Salt Lake City.

Biskowski, Martin. 2000. Maize preparation and the Aztec subsistence economy. *AncM* 11: 293–306.

Blake, Michael. 1984. The Postclassic Maya of Canajasté, Chiapas, Mexico. *Masterkey* 58: 9–17.

—. 1991. An emerging Early Formative chiefdom at Paso de la Amada, Chiapas, Mexico. In Fowler (ed.): 27–46.

—. 2001. Mazatan region. *AAMCA*: 451–453.

—. (ed.). 1999. *Pacific Latin America in Prehistory: The Evolution of Archaic and Formative Cultures.* WSU Press, Pullman WA.

Blanton, Richard E. 2001. Monte Albán. *AAMCA*: 483–486.

Blanton, Richard E., Stephen A. Kowalewski, Gary M. Feinman, and Laura A. Finsten. 1993 *Ancient Mesoamerica: A Comparison of Change in Three Regions.* Cambridge U. Press, Cambridge.

Blomster, Jeffrey P. 1998. Context, cult, and early Formative period public ritual in the Mixteca Alta: analysis of a hollow-baby figurine from Etlatongo, Oaxaca. *AncM* 9: 309–326.

—. 2004. *Etlatongo: Social Complexity, Interaction, and Village Life in the Mixteca Alta of Oaxaca, Mexico.* Wadsworth/Thomson, Belmont, CA.

Boone, Elizabeth H. 1983. *The Codex Magliabechiano and the Lost Prototype of the Magliabechiano Group.* U. of California Press, Berkeley.

—. 1994. *The Aztec World.* St. Remy Press, Montreal, and Smithsonian Books, Washington, D.C.

—. 2000. *Stories in Red and Black: Pictorial Histories of the Aztecs and Mixtecs.* U. of Texas Press, Austin.

Borhegyi, Stephan F. de. 1965. Archaeological synthesis of the Guatemalan Highlands. *HMAI* 2: 1: 3–58.

Bové, Frederick J. 1989. Dedicated to the Costeños: Introduction and new insights. In Bové and Heller (eds.): 1–13.

Bové, Frederick J. 1989. Settlement classification procedures in Formative Escuintla, Guatemala. In Bové and Heller (eds.): 65–101.

Bové, Frederick J., and L. Heller (eds.). 1989. New Frontiers in the Archaeology of the Pacific Coast of Southern Mesoamerica. *Anthropological Research Papers* 39, Arizona State U., Tempe.

Brady, James E., George Hasemann, and John H. Fogarty. 1995. Harvest of skulls and bones: Ritual cave burial in Honduras. *Archaeology* May/June: 36–40.

Brambila Paz, Rosa. 2001. Bajío region. *AAMCA*: 65–66.

Braniff C., Beatriz. 1998. Morales, Guanajuato y la tradición Chupícuaro. *Instituto Nacional de Antropología e Historia, Colección científica* 373. México, D.F.

—. 2000. El juego de pelota en el lejano noroeste. *ArqM* 8: 44: 48–49.

Braswell, Geoffrey (ed.). 2003. *The Maya and Teotihuacan.* U. of Texas Press, Austin

Braudel, Fernand 1972. *The Mediterranean and the Mediterranean World in the Age of Philip II, V. I.* Harper and Row, New York.

Braun, Barbara. 1993. *Pre-Columbian Art and the Post-Columbian World: Ancient American Sources of Modern Art.* Harry N. Abrams, Inc., New York.

Bray, Warwick. 1977. Civilizing the Aztecs. In *The Evolution of Social Systems*, J. Friedman and M.J. Rowlands (eds.): 373–398. Duckworth, London.

—. 1987. *Everyday Life of the Aztecs.* Hippocrene Books. New York.

Bricker, Victoria R. 1997. The "Calendar-Round" Almanac in the Madrid Codex. In *Papers on the Madrid Codex*, Victoria R. Bricker and Gabrielle Vail (eds.): 169–185. MARI 64.

Brown, Kenneth L. 1984. Hallucinogenic mushrooms, jade, obsidian, and the Guatemalan Highlands: What did the Olmecs really want? In Hirth (ed.): 215–234.

Brown, Linda. 2000. From discard to divination: Demarcating the scared through the collection and curation of discarded objects. *LAA* 11: 319–333.

Brown, R. B. 1994. Paquimé. *ArqM* 1: 6: 22–29.

Bruhns, Karen Olsen. 1980. *Cihuatan: An Early Postclassic Town of El Salvador: The 1977–1978 Excavations. U. of Missouri Monographs in Anthropology,* No. 5. Columbia, Missouri.

Brumfiel, Elizabeth M. 1989. Factional competition in complex society. In *Domination and Resistance*, D. Miller, M. Rowlands, and C. Tilley (eds.): 127–139. Unwin Hyman, London.

—. (ed.). 1986. Factional Competition in Complex Society. *Comparative Studies in the Development of Complex Societies, Papers from the World Archaeological Congress.* Department of Archaeology, U. of Southampton, Southampton.

Brumfiel, Elizabeth M., Tamara Salcedo, and David K. Schafer. 1994. The lip plugs of Xaltocan: function and meaning in Aztec archaeology. In *Economies and Polities in the Aztec Realm*, M.G. Hodge and M.E. Smith (eds.): 113–131. Studies in Culture and Society 6. Institute for Mesoamerican Studies, SUNY Albany, and U. of Texas Press, Austin.

Burgoa, Fr. Francisco de. 1934 [1670]. *Palestra Historial.* Vol 24. Publicaciones. del Archivo General de la Nación. Talleres Gráficos de la Nación, Mexico.

Burkhart, Louise M. 1989. *The Slippery Earth: Nahua-Christian Moral Dialogue in Sixteenth-Century Mexico.* The U. of Arizona Press, Tucson.

Byland, Bruce E. 1993. Introduction and commentary. In *The Codex Borgia*: xiii–xxxii. Dover Publications, Inc., New York.

Byland, Bruce E. and John M. D. Pohl. 1994. *In the Realm of 8 Deer. The Archaeology of the Mixtec Codices.* U. of Oklahoma Press, Norman.

Cabrera Castro, Rubén. 1993. Human sacrifice at the Temple of the Feathered Serpent: Recent discoveries at Teotihuacan. In Berrin and Pasztory (eds.): 100–115.

—. 1996. Figuras glíficas de La Ventilla, Teotihuacan. *Arqueología* 15: 27–40.

Cabrera Castro, Rubén and George L. Cowgill. 1993. El Templo de Quetzalcóatl. *ArqM* 1: 1: 21–26.

Cabrero García, María Teresa. 1989. *Civilización en el norte de México.* UNAM.

Calnek, Edward E. 1972. Settlement Pattern and Chinampa Agriculture at Tenochtitlan. *AA* 37:104–115.

—. 1973. The Localization of the Sixteenth Century Map Called the Maguey Plan. *AA* 38:190–195.
—. 1992. The Ethnographic Context of the Third Part of the Codex Mendoza. *The Codex Mendoza. V.1: Interpretation*: 81–91. U. of California Press, Berkeley.
Campbell, Lyle R., and T. Kaufman. 1976. A linguistic look at the Olmecs. *AA* 41: 80–89
Carlson, John B. 1981. Olmec concave iron-ore mirrors. In Benson (ed.): 117 – 147.
—. 1993. Rise and fall of the City of the Gods. *Archaeology* 46: 6: 58–69.
Carmack, Robert M. 1981. *The Quiché Mayas of Utatlán*. U. of Oklahoma Press, Norman.
Carmack, Robert M., Janine Gasco, and Gary Gossen. 1996. *The Legacy of Mesoamerica: History and Culture of a Native American Civilization*. Prentice Hall, Upper Saddle River, NJ.
Carmean, Kelli. 1991. Architectural labor investment and social stratification at Sayil, Yucatán, Mexico. *LAA* 2: 151–165.
Carneiro, Robert L. 1998. What happened at the flashpoint? Conjectures on chiefdom formation at the very moment of conception. In *Chiefdoms and Chieftaincy in the Americas*, Elsa M. Redmond (ed.) 18–42. University Press of Florida, Gainesville.
Carrasco, David (ed.). 2001. *The Oxford Encyclopedia of Mesoamerican Cultures: The Civilizations of Mexico and Central America*. Oxford U. Press, Oxford, England.
Carrasco, David, Lindsay Jones, and Scott Sessions (eds.). 2001. *Mesoamerica's Classic Heritage: from Teotihuacan to the Aztecs*. U. Press of Colorado, Boulder.
Carrasco, Pedro. 1964. Family structure of sixteenth century Tepoztlan. In *Process and Pattern in Culture*, R.A. Manners (ed.): 185–210. Aldine, Chicago.
—. 1971. The Peoples of Central Mexico and Their Historical Traditions. *HMAI* 11: 2: 459–473.
—. 1976. The joint family in ancient Mexico: The case of Molotla. In *Essays on Mexican Kinship*, H.C. Nutini, P. Carrasco, and J. Taggart (eds.): 45–64. U. of Pittsburgh Press, Pittsburgh.
—. 1984. Royal Marriages in Ancient Mexico. In Harvey and Prem (eds.): 41–81.
—. 1999. *The Tenochca Empire of Ancient Mexico: The Triple Alliance of Tenochtitlan, Tetzcoco, and Tlacopan*. U. of Oklahoma Press, Norman.
Carrasco Vargas, Ramón. 2000. El cuchcabal de la Cabeza de Serpiente. *AncM* 7: 42: 12–21.
Caso, Alfonso. 1965. Mixtec writing and calendar. *HMAI* 3: 2: 948–961.
Chagnon, Napoleon A. 1997. *Yanomamo*. Harcourt Brace College Publishers, Fort Worth.
Chance, John K. 1989. *Conquest of the Sierra: Spaniards and Indians in Colonial Oaxaca*. U. of Oklahoma Press, Norman.
Charlton, Thomas H. 2003. On agrarian landholdings in post-conquest rural Mesoamerica. *Ethnohistory* 50: 221–230.
Chase, Arlen F., and Diane Z. Chase. 2001. The royal court of Caracol, Belize: its palaces and people. In Inomata and Houston (eds.): II: 102–137.
Chase, Arlen F., and Prudence M. Rice (eds.). 1985. *The Lowland Maya Postclassic*. U. of Texas Press, Austin.
Chase, Diane Z., and Arlen Chase. 1988. A Postclassic Perspective: Excavations at the Maya Site of Santa Rita Corozal, Belize. *Pre-Columbian Art Research Institute Monograph* 4, San Francisco.
—. and —. (eds.). 1992. *Mesoamerican Elites: An Archaeological Assessment*. U. of Oklahoma Press, Norman.
Chevalier, F. 1970. *Land and Society in Colonial Mexico: The Great Hacienda*. U. of California Press, Berkeley.
Chimalpahin Cuauhtlehuanitzin, Domingo Francisco de San Antón Muñón. 1965 [early 1600s]. *Relaciones Originales de Chalco Amaquemecan*. S. Rendón (ed.). Fondo de Cultural Económica, Mexico.
Christie, Jessica (ed.). 2003. *Maya Palaces and Elite Residences*. U. of Texas Press, Austin
Ciudad Real, Antonio de. 1993 [1586]. *Tratado Curioso y Docto de las Grandezas de la Nueva España*. UNAM.
Clancy, Flora S. and Peter D. Harrison (eds.). 1990. *Vision and Revision in Maya Studies*. U. of New Mexico Press, Albuquerque.
Clark, John E. 1991. The beginnings of Mesoamerica: Apologia for the Soconusco Early Formative. In Fowler (ed.): 13–26.
—. 2001a. Chiapas interior plateau. *AAMCA*: 123–127.
—. 2001b. Formative period. *AAMCA*: 278–283.
—. 2001c. Gulf lowlands: South region. *AAMCA*: 340–344.
Clark, John E., and Michael Blake. 1994. The power of prestige: competitive generosity and the emergence of rank societies in lowland Mesoamerica. In *Factional Competition and Political Development in the New World*, E. Brumfiel and J. Fox (eds.): 17–30. Cambridge U. Press, Cambridge.
Clark, John E., and Mary E. Pye. 2000. The Pacific coast and the Olmec question. In Clark and Pye (eds.): 216–251.
—. and —. (eds.). 2000. *Olmec Art and Archaeology in Mesoamerica*. National Gallery of Art, Washington, D.C. and Yale U. Press, New Haven, NJ.
Clark, John E., and Tamara Salcedo. 1989. Ocos obsidian distribution in Chiapas, Mexico. In Bové and Heller (eds.): 15–24.
Clendinnen, Inga. 1991. *Aztecs: an Interpretation*. Cambridge U. Press, Cambridge.
Cobean, Robert H. 2002. *A World of Obsidian: The Mining and Trade of a Volcanic Glass in Ancient Mexico*. U. of Pittsburgh Press and INAH, Pittsburgh and Mexico City.
Cobean, Robert H., and Alba Guadalupe Mastache Flores. 2001. Coyotlatelco. *AAMCA*: 187–189.
Cobos, Rafael. 2001. Chichén Itzá. In Carrasco (ed.): 183–187.
Codex Borgia. 1993 [*c*. 1500]. *The Codex Borgia*. Dover Publications, Inc., New York.
Codex Boturini (Tira de la Peregrinación). 1975. *Códice Boturini (Tira de la Peregrinación)*. Secretaria de Educación Pública, Mexico City.
Codex Magliabechiano. 1983 [mid 1500s]. *Codex Magliabechiano*. U. of California, Berkeley.
Codex Mendoza. 1992 [*c*. 1541–1542]. *Codex Mendoza. Volume 3: A Facsimile Reproduction of Codex Mendoza*. (F. F. Berdan and P. R. Anawalt eds.). U. of California Press, Berkeley.
Codex Mendoza. 1992 [*c*. 1541–1542]. *Codex Mendoza. Volume 4: Translation*. (F. F. Berdan and P. R. Anawalt eds.). U. of California Press, Berkeley.
Codex Nuttall. 1975 [preconquest]. *Codex Nuttall*. Dover Publications, New York.
Codex Telleriano-Remensis. 1995 [1563]. *Codex Telleriano-Remensis, Manuscrit Mexicain 385, Bibliothèque Nationale of Paris*. Facsimile reproduction, Part I of *Codex Telleriano-Remensis: Ritual, Divination, and History in a Pictorial Aztec Manuscript*, by E. Quiñones Keber: 1–104. U. of Texas Press, Austin.
Codex Xolotl. 1980 [1553–1569]. *Códice Xolotl*. Charles E. Dibble (ed.). UNAM, Instituto de Investigaciones Históricas, Serie Amoxtli: 1. Mexico.
Coe, Andrew. 2001. *Archaeological Mexico: A Traveler's Guide to Ancient Cities and Sacred Sites*. Avalon Travel, Emeryville, CA.
Coe, Michael D. 1961. *La Victoria: An Early Site on the Pacific Coast of Guatemala*. Peabody Museum of Archaeology and Ethnology, Harvard U., Papers 53.
—. 1981. San Lorenzo Tenochtitlan. In Sabloff (ed.): 117–146.
—. 1999. *The Maya*. Sixth edition. Thames & Hudson, London and New York.
Coe, Michael D., and Sophie D. Coe. 1996. *The True History of Chocolate*. Thames & Hudson, London and New York.
Coe, Michael D., Richard A. Diehl, David A. Freidel, Peter T. Furst, F. Kent Reilly, III, Linda Schele, Carolyn E. Tate, and Karl A. Taube. 1995. *The Olmec World: Ritual and Rulership*. The Art Museum, Princeton U.
Coe, Michael D., and Kent V. Flannery. 1964. Microenvironments and Mesoamerican prehistory. *Science* 143: 650–654.
Coe, Michael D., and Justin Kerr. 1998. *Art of the Maya Scribe*. Thames & Hudson, London, and Harry N. Abrams, New York.
Coe, Michael D., and Rex Koontz. 2002. *Mexico*. Fifth edition. Thames & Hudson, London and New York.
Coe, Michael D., and Mark van Stone. 2001. *Reading the Maya Glyphs*. Thames & Hudson, London and New York.

Coe, Sophie D. 1994. *America's First Cuisines.* U. of Texas Press, Austin.
Coe, William R. 1967. *Tikal, A Handbook of the Ancient Maya Ruins.* The University Museum, U. of Pennsylvania, Philadelphia.
—. 1990. *Excavations in the Great Plaza, North Terrace, and North Acropolis of Tikal.* 5 vols. University Museum, U. of Pennsylvania, Tikal Reports 14.
Coggins, Clemency Chase. 1993. The Age of Teotihuacan and Its Mission Abroad. In Berrin and Pasztory (eds.): 140–155.
Coggins, Clemency Chase, and O.C. Shane (eds.). 1984. *Cenote of Sacrifice.* U. of Texas Press, Austin.
Columbus, Hernando. 1984 [1502–1503]. Account of the Fourth Voyage (1502–1503). In Parry and Keith (eds.), II: 120–145.
Cortés, Hernan. 1986 [1519–1526]. *Letters from Mexico.* Yale U. Press, New Haven.
Covarrubias, Miguel. 1957. *Indian Art of Mexico and Central America.* Knopf, New York.
—. 1986 [1946]. *Mexico South.* KPI, London.
Cowgill, George L. 1983. Rulership and the Ciudadela: Political inferences from Teotihuacan architecture. In *Civilization in the Ancient Americas,* R. Leventhal and A. Kolata (eds.): 313–343. U. of New Mexico and Harvard U., Cambridge.
—. 1993. What we still don't know about Teotihuacan. In Berrin and Pasztory (eds.): 116–125.
Crespo Oviedo, Ana María, and Alba Guadalupe Mastache de E. 1981. La presencia en el área de Tula, Hidalgo, de grupos relacionados con el barrio de Oaxaca en Teotihuacan. In *Interacción Cultural en México Central,* Evelyn C. Rattray, Jaime Litvak K., and Clara Diaz O. (coord.): 99–106. UNAM.
Cruz, Martin de la. 1991 [1552]. *Libellus de medicinalibus indorum herbis. Manuscrito azteca de 1552.* Fondo de Cultúra Económica, Instituto Mexicano del Seguro Social. Mexico.
Cyphers, Ann. 1996. Reconstructing Olmec life at San Lorenzo. In Benson and de la Fuente (eds.): 60–71.
—. 2000. Cultural identity and interregional interaction during the Gobernador Phase: A ceramic perspective. In Hirth (ed.): II: 11–16.
Cyphers Guillén, Anne. 1984. The possible role of a woman in Formative exchange. In Hirth (ed.): 115–123.
Dahlin, Bruce. 2000. The barricade and abandonment of Chunchucmil: Implications for northern Maya warfare. *Latin American Antiquity* 11: 283–298.
Daneels, Annick. 1997. Settlement history in the lower Cotaxtla Basin. In Stark and Arnold (eds.): 206–252.
Davies, Nigel. 1977a. *The Aztecs.* Abacus, London.
—. 1977b. *The Toltecs: Until the Fall of Tula.* U. of Oklahoma Press, Norman.
Day, Jane Stevenson. 1991. Remnants of the shaman. In *To Change Place,* D. Carrasco (ed.): 246–247. U. Press of Colorado, Niwot.
—. 1998. The West Mexican ballgame. In Townsend (ed.): 150–167.
de la Fuente, Beatriz. 1995. La pintura mural prehispánica en México. *ArqM* 3: 16: 5–15.
de la Fuente, Beatriz and Leticia Staines Cicero. 2001. Mural painting. *AAMCA*: 491–494.
de la Garza, Mercedes. 1990. *Sueño y alucinación en el mundo náhualt y maya.* UNAM.
—. 1992. *Palenque.* INAH, Chiapas.
—. 1995. Chaac: El dios que sabe muchas caminos. *ArqM* 2: 11: 38–43.
de Las Casas, Bartolomé. 1974 [1552 ms]. *In Defense of the Indians.* Northern Illinois U. Press, DeKalb.
de Montmollin, Olivier. 1995. *Settlement and Politics in Three Classic Maya Polities. Monographs in World Archaeology, no. 24.* Prehistory Press, Madison.
Demarest, Arthur A. 1993. The violent saga of a Maya kingdom. *National Geographic* 183 (2): 94–111.
Demarest, Arthur A., Matt O'Mansky, Claudia Wolley, Dirk Van Tuerenhout, Takeshi Inomata, Joel Palka, and Hector Escobedo. 1997. Classic Maya defensive systems and warfare in the Petexbatun Region. *AncM* 8: 229–253.
DeTerra, Helmut. 1957. *Man and Mammoth in Mexico.* Hutchinson & Co., London.
Di Peso, Charles C., John B. Rinaldo, and G. Fenner. 1974. *Casas Grandes.* Amerind Foundation, Dragoon, and Northland Press, Flagstaff.
Diamond, Jared. 1999. *Guns, Germs, and Steel.* W.W. Norton, New York and London.
Díaz del Castillo, Bernal. 1956 [1560s]. *The Discovery and Conquest of Mexico.* Farrar, Straus, and Cudahy, New York.
Díaz Oyarzábal, Clara Luz. 1981. La presencia en el área de Tula, Hidalgo, de grupos relacionados con el barrio de Oaxaca en Teotihuacan. In *Interacción Cultural en México Central,* Evelyn C. Rattray, Jaime Litvak K., and Clara Diaz O. (coord.): 107–113. UNAM.
Diehl, Richard A. 1983. *Tula: The Toltec Capital of Ancient Mexico.* Thames & Hudson, London and New York.
—. 1993. The Toltec Horizon in Mesoamerica: New Perspectives on an Old Issue. In Rice (ed.): 263–294.
—. 2000. The Precolumbian cultures of the Gulf Coast. In Adams and MacLeod (eds.): 156–196.
Diehl, Richard A. and J.C. Berlo (eds.). 1989. *Mesoamerica after the Collapse of Teotihuacan.* Dumbarton Oaks, Washington, D.C.
Diehl, Richard A., and Michael D. Coe. 1995. Olmec archaeology. In Coe *et al.*: 10–25.
Diehl, Richard A., and Margaret D. Mandeville. 1987. Tula, and Wheeled Animal Effigies in Mesoamerica. *Antiquity* 61: 239–246.
Dillehay, Tom D. 1991. Disease ecology and initial human migration. In *The First Americans: Search and Research,* Tom D. Dillehay, and David J. Meltzer (eds.): 231–263. CRC Press, Boca Raton.
—. 2000. *The Settlement of the Americas: A New Prehistory.* Basic Books, New York.
Dixon, Boyd, L.R.V. Joesink–Mandeville, N. Hasebe, M. Mucio, W. Vincent, D. James, and K. Petersen. 1994. Formative-period architecture at the site of Yarumela, central Honduras. *LAA* 5: 70–87.
Doebley, John, Adrian Stec, Jon Wendel, and Marlin Edwards. 1990. Genetic and morphological analysis of a maize-teosinte F2 population: Implications for the origin of maize. *Proceedings of the National Academy of Sciences* 87: 9888–9892.
Donkin, R. A. 1977. Spanish Red: An Ethnogeographical Study of Cochineal and the Opuntia Cactus. *Transactions of the American Philosophical Society.* 67.
Drennan, Robert D. 1976a. *Fábrica San José and Middle Formative Society in the Valley of Oaxaca.* MAUM Memoir No. 8.
—. 1976b. Religion and social evolution in Formative Mesoamerica. In Flannery (ed.): 345–368.
—. 1978. Excavations at Quachilco: A Report on the 1977 Season of the Palo Blanco Project in the Tehuacán Valley. *MAUM Technical Report* 7.
—. 1979. Excavations at Cuayucatepec (Ts281): A preliminary report. *MAUM Technical Report* 11: 169–199.
Dull, Robert A., John R. Southon, and Payson Sheets. 2001. Volcanism, ecology and culture: A reassessment of the Volcán Ilopango TBJ eruption in the Southern Maya Realm. *LAA* 12: 25–44.
Dunbar, Robin. 1996. *Gossip, Grooming, and the Evolution of Language.* Harvard U. Press, Cambridge.
Durán, Fray Diego. 1971 [1574–79]. *Book of the Gods and Rites and The Ancient Calendar.* U. of Oklahoma Press, Norman.
—. 1994 [1581]. *The History of the Indies of New Spain.* Translated, annotated, and introduced by Doris Heyden. U. of Oklahoma Press, Norman.
Edgerton, Samuel, and Jorge Pérez de Lara. 2001. *Theaters of Conversion: Religious Architecture and Indian Artisans in Colonial Mexico.* U. of New Mexico Press, Albuquerque.
Edmonson, Munro S. 1988. *The Book of the Year: Middle American Calendrical Systems.* U. of Utah Press, Salt Lake City.
Ekholm, Gordon F. 1946. Wheeled toys in Mexico. *AA* 11: 222–228.
Ekholm, S.M. 1969. Mound 30a and the Early Preclassic Ceramic Sequence of Izapa, Chiapas, Mexico. *PNWAF* 25.
Eliade, Mircea. 1964. *Shamanism, Archaic Techniques of Ecstasy.* Routledge & Kegan Paul, London.
Emery, Kitty. 2001. Fauna. *AAMCA*: 255–265.
Ensminger, Audrey *et al.*1994. *Foods and Nutrition Encyclopedia.* 2 volumes. CRC Press, Boca Raton.
Estrada Belli, Francisco. 2001. Maya kingship at Holmul,

Guatemala. *Antiquity* 75(290): 685–686

Evans, Susan Toby. 1991. Architecture and authority in an Aztec village: form and function of the Tecpan. In *Land and Politics in the Valley of Mexico*, H. Harvey (ed.): 63–92. U. of New Mexico Press, Albuquerque.

— 1992. The productivity of maguey terrace agriculture in Central Mexico during the Aztec period. In Killion (ed.): 92–115.

—. 2000. Aztec royal pleasure parks: conspicuous consumption and elite status rivalry. *Studies in the History of Gardens and Designed Landscapes* 20: 206–228.

—. 2001. Aztec Noble Courts. In Inomata and Houston (eds.): I: 237–273.

—. 2004. Aztec palaces. In *Palaces of the Ancient New World*, Susan Toby Evans, and Joanne Pillsbury (eds.). Dumbarton Oaks, Washington, D.C.

Evans, Susan T. and Elliot M. Abrams. 1988. Archaeology at the Aztec Period Village of Cihuatecpan, Mexico. In *Excavations at Cihuatecpan*, S. T. Evans (ed.): 50–234. VUPA 36.

Evans, Susan T., and Janet Catherine Berlo. 1992. Teotihuacan: an introduction. In Berlo (ed.): 1–26.

Evans, Susan T., and Peter Gould 1982 Settlement Models in Archaeology. *JAA* 1: 275–304.

Evans, Susan Toby, and David L. Webster (eds.). 2001. *Archaeology of Ancient Mexico and Central America: An Encyclopedia*. Garland Publishing, New York.

Fash, Barbara W. 1992. Late Classic architectural sculpture themes in Copán. *Ancient Mesoamerica* 3: 89–104.

Fash, William. 1991. *Scribes, Warriors, and Kings: The City of Copán and the Ancient Maya*. Thames & Hudson, London and New York.

Fedick, Scott L. (ed.). 1996. *The Managed Mosaic: Ancient Maya Agriculture and Resource Use*. U. of Utah Press, Salt Lake City.

Feinman, Gary M., Richard E. Blanton and Stephen A. Kowalewski. 1984. Market system development in the prehispanic Valley of Oaxaca, Mexico. In Hirth (ed.): 157–178.

Feinman, G.M. and L. Nicholas. 1992. Pre-Hispanic Interregional Interaction in Southern Mexico: The Valley of Oaxaca and the Ejutla Valley. In *Resources, Power, and Interregional Interaction*, E.M. Schortman, and P.A. Urban (eds.): 75–116. Plenum Press, New York.

Finsten, Laura. 1995. *Jalieza, Oaxaca: Activity Specialization at a Hilltop Center.* VUPA 47.

—. 2001. Peñoles region. *AAMCA*: 585–587.

Fitzsimmons, James L. 1998. Classic Maya mortuary rituals at Piedras Negras, Guatemala. *AM* 9: 271–278.

Flannery, Kent V. 1968. Archeological systems theory and early Mesoamerica. In *Anthropological Archaeology in the Americas*, B. Meggers (ed.): 67–87. Anthropological Society of Washington, Washington, D.C.

—. 1972. The Cultural Evolution of Civilization. *Annual Review of Ecology and Systematics* 3: 399–426.

—. 1976. The Early Mesoamerican house. In Flannery (ed.): 16–24.

—. (ed.). 1976. *The Early Mesoamerican Village*. Academic Press, New York.

—. (ed.). 1986. *Guilá Naquitz: Archaic Foraging and Early Agriculture in Oaxaca, Mexico.* Academic Press, New York.

Flannery, Kent V., Anne V.T. Kirkby, Michael J. Kirkby, and Aubrey W. Williams. 1967. Farming systems and political growth in ancient Oaxaca. *Science* 158: 445–453.

Flannery, Kent V., and Joyce Marcus (eds.) 1983. *The Cloud People: Divergent Evolutions of the Zapotec and Mixtec Civilizations*. Academic Press, New York.

—. and —. 2000. Formative Mexican chiefdoms and the myth of the "Mother Culture." *JAA* 19: 1–37.

Flannery, Kent V., and Ronald Spores. 1983. Excavated sites of the Oaxaca preceramic. In *The Cloud People*, Kent V. Flannery, and Joyce Marcus (eds.): 21–26. Academic Press, New York.

Flannery, Kent V. and Marcus C. Winter. 1976. Analyzing Household Activities. In Flannery (ed.): 34–47.

Fletcher, Laraine. 2001. Nicaragua: North Central and Pacific Regions. *AAMCA*: 513–517.

Florance, Charles A. 1985. Recent Work in the Chupícuaro Region. In *The Archaeology of West and Northwest Mesoamerica*, Michael S. Foster, and Phil C. Weigand (eds.): 9–45. Westview Press, Boulder.

Foias, Antonia E. 2002. At the crossroads: the economic basis of political power in the Petexbatun region. In Masson and Freidel (eds.): 223–248.

Folan, William J., Ellen R. Kintz, and Laraine Fletcher. 1983. *Cobá: A Classic Maya Metropolis*. Academic Press, New York.

Ford, Anabel. 1999. Using the past to preserve the future: Maya ruins are the heart of a bold economic plan. *Discovering Archaeology* 1(5): 98–101

Foster, Michael S. 2001. Shaft tombs. *AAMCA*: 661–662.

Fowler, Melvin L. 1968. Un Sistema Preclásico de Distribución de Agua en la Zona Arqueológica de Amalucan, Puebla. *Instituto Poblano de Antropología e Historia, Publication 2*. Puebla, Mexico.

Fowler, William R. 1989. *The Cultural Evolution of Ancient Nahua Civilizations: The Pipil-Nicarao of Central America.* U. of Oklahoma Press, Norman.

—. (ed.). 1991.*The Formation of complex society in southeastern Mesoamerica.* CRC Press, Boca Raton.

Fox, John Gerard. 1996. Playing with power: Ballcourts and political ritual in southern Mesoamerica. *CA* 7: 483–509.

Freidel, David A., and Jeremy A. Sabloff. 1984. *Cozumel: Late Maya Settlement Patterns.* Academic Press, Orlando.

Freidel, David A., and Linda Schele. 1989. Late Preclassic Maya kingship. *AAnthro* 90: 547–567.

Freidel, David A., Linda Schele, and Joy Parker. 1993. *Maya Cosmos: Three Thousand Years on the Shaman's Path.* William Morrow, New York.

Freter, AnnCorinne. 2001. Dating Methods. *AAMCA*: 202–208.

Furst, Jill L., See McKeever Furst, Jill L.

Furst, Peter T. 1995. Shamanism, Transformation, and Olmec Art. In Coe *et al.*: 68–81.

—. 1974. Morning Glory and Mother Goddess at Tepantitla, Teotihuacan. In Hammond (ed.): 187–215.

—. 2001. Intoxicants and intoxication. *AAMCA*: 371–375.

Galván Villegas, Luis Javier, and Christopher S. Beekman. 2001. Atemajac region. *AAMCA*: 54–56.

Garber, James F. 2001. Ground stone tools. *AAMCA*: 300–303.

García Cook, Angel. 1981. The Historical Importance of Tlaxcala in the Cultural Development of the Central Highlands. *HMAI Supplement* I: 244–276.

—. 2001. Cacaxtla. *AAMCA*: 87.

García Cook, Angel, and Beatriz Leonor Merino Carrión. 1998. Cantona: Urbe prehispánica en México. *LAA* 9: 191–216.

García Cook, Angel, and Felipe Rodriguez. 1975. Excavaciones arqueológicos en "Gualupita las Dalias", Puebla. *Comunicaciones* 12: 1–8. Fundación Alemana para la Investigación Científica, Puebla.

García Moll, Roberto. 1996. Yaxchilán, Chiapas. La ciudad en la selva. *AM* 4: 22: 36–45.

García Payón, José. 1974 and 1979. *La Zona Arqueológica de Tecaxic-Calixtlahuaca y los Matlatzincas*. 2 parts. Biblioteca Enciclopédica del Estado de México, Mexico.

Garraty, Christopher P., and Barbara L. Stark. 2002. Imperial and social relations in Postclassic South-central Veracruz, Mexico. *LAA* 13: 3–33.

Gasco, Janine, and Barbara Voorhies. 1989. The ultimate tribute: The role of the Soconusco as an Aztec tributary. In Voorhies (ed.): 48–94.

Gerhard, Peter. 1993. *A Guide to the Historical Geography of New Spain.* U. of Oklahoma Press, Norman.

Gibson, Charles. 1960. The Aztec aristocracy in Colonial Mexico. *Comparative Studies in Society and History* 2: 169–96.

—. 1964. *The Aztecs Under Spanish Rule*. Stanford U. Press, Stanford.

—. 1971. Structure of the Aztec Empire. *HMAI* 10:376–394.

Gibson, Charles, and John Glass. 1975. A census of Middle American prose manuscripts in the native historical tradition. *HMAI* 15: 4: 322–400.

Gifford, James C. 1960. The type-variety method of ceramic classification as an indicator of cultural phenomena. *AA* 25: 341–347.

Gill, Richardson B., and Jerome P. Keating. 2002. Volcanism and

Mesoamerican archaeology. *AncM* 13: 125–140.
Gill, Richardson Benedict. 2000. *The Great Maya Droughts: Water, Life, and Death.* U. of New Mexico Press, Albuquerque.
Gillespie, Susan D. 1989. *The Aztec Kings: The Construction of Rulership in Mexica History*. Tucson, U. of Arizona Press.
—. 1991. Ballgames and boundaries. In Scarborough and Wilcox (eds.): 317–345.
Gonlin, Nancy. 2001. Museums, archives, and libraries. *AAMCA*: 494–504.
González Lauck, Rebecca. 1996. La Venta: An Olmec Capital. In Benson and de la Fuente (eds.): 72–81.
González Licón, Ernesto. 1994. *Los Zapotecs y Mixtecos: Tres Mil Años de Civilización Precolombina.* Jaca Book and Consejo Nacional para la Cultura y las Artes, Mexico City.
Gorenstein, Shirley. 1985. *Acámbaro: Frontier Settlement on the Tarascan Aztec Border.* VUPA 32.
Graham, Elizabeth A. 1994. *The Highlands of the Lowlands: Environment and Archaeology in the Stann Creek District, Belize, Central America.* Prehistory Press, Madison.
Graham, Ian. 1998. A brief history of archaeological exploration. In *Maya*, Peter Schmidt, Mercedes de la Garza, and Enrique Nalda (eds.): 28–37. Rizzoli International, New York.
Graham, Mark M. (ed.). 1993. *Reinterpreting Prehistory of Central America.* U. Press of Colorado, Niwot.
Greenberg, Joseph H., Christy G. Turner II, and Stephen L. Zegura. 1986. The settlement of the Americas: A comparison of the linguistic, dental, and genetic evidence. *CA* 27: 477–497.
Greene Robertson, M. 1983–1991. *The Sculpture of Palenque.* 4 vol. Princeton U. Press, Princeton.
Grove, David C. 1981. The Formative period and the evolution of complex culture. In *HMAI* Supplement I: 373–391.
—. 1987. Other Ceramic and Miscellaneous Artifacts. In Grove (ed.): 271–294.
—. 1996. Archaeological contexts of Olmec art outside of the Gulf Coast. In Benson and de la Fuente (eds.): 104–117.
—. 2001. Chalcatzingo. *AAMCA*: 117–119.
—. (ed.). 1987. *Ancient Chalcatzingo.* U. of Texas Press, Austin.
Grove, David C., and Anne Cyphers Guillén. 1987. The excavations. In Grove (ed.): 21–55.
Grove, David C., and Jorge Angulo V. 1987. A catalog and description of Chalcatzingo's monuments. In Grove (ed.): 21–131.
Grove, David C., and Rosemary A. Joyce (eds.) 1999. *Social Patterns in Pre-Classic Mesoamerica.* Dumbarton Oaks Research Library and Collections, Washington DC.
Grube, Nikolai (ed.). 2001. *Maya : Divine Kings of the Rain Forest.* Kónemann, Kóhn.
Gruzinski, Serge. 1992. *Painting the Conquest.* Unesco/Flammarion, Paris.
—. 1993. *The Conquest of Mexico.* Polity Press, Cambridge.
Gustafson, Lowell S. and Amelia M. Trevelyan (eds.). 2002. *Ancient Maya Gender Identity and Relations.* Bergin & Garvey, Westport, CT.
Gutiérrez Mendoza, Gerardo. 2003. Territorial structure and urbanism in Mesoamerica: The Huaxtec and Mixtec-Tlapanec-Nahua cases. In Sanders *et al.*(eds.): 85–118.
Hall, Grant D., S.T. Tarka Jr., W.J. Hurst, D. Stuart, and R.E.W. Adams. 1990. Cacao residues in ancient Maya vessels from Rio Azul, Guatemala. *AA* 55: 138–143.
Hammond, Norman (ed.). 1974. *Mesoamerican Archaeology.* U. of Texas Press, Austin.
— (ed.). 1991. *Cuello: An Early Maya Community in Belize.* Cambridge U. Press, Cambridge.
Hammond, Norman, and Jeremy R. Bauer. 2001. A Preclassic Maya sweatbath at Cuello, Belize. *Antiquity* 75: 683–684.
Hansen, Richard D. 1998. Continuity and disjunction: The Pre-Classic antecedents of Classic Maya Architecture. In Houston (ed.): 49–122.
Hard, Robert J., and William L. Marrill. 1992. Mobile agriculturalists and the emergence of sedentism: perspectives from northern Mexico. *AAnthro* 94: 601–620.
Hare, Timothy S., and Michael E. Smith. 1996. A new Postclassic chronology for Yautepec, Morelos. *AncM* 7: 281–297.
Harrison, Peter D. 1999. *The Lords of Tikal. Rulers of an Ancient Maya City.* Thames & Hudson, London and New York.
Harvey, Herbert R. 1986. Household and family structure in Early Colonial Tepetlaoztoc. *Estudios de Cultura Nahuatl* 18: 275–294.
Harvey, Herbert R., and H. J. Prem (eds.). 1984. *Explorations in Ethnohistory.* U. of New Mexico Press, Albuquerque.
Hassig, Ross. 1986. Famine and Scarcity in the Valley of Mexico. *Research in Economic Anthropology*, Supplement 2: 303–317. JAI Press, Greenwich, CT.
—. 1988. *Aztec Warfare: Imperial Expansion and Political Control.* U. of Oklahoma Press, Norman.
—. 1992. *War and Society in Ancient Mesoamerica.* U. of California Press, Berkeley.
Hatch, Marion Popenoe de. 1989. An analysis of the Santa Lucía Cotzumalguapa sculptures. In Bové and Heller (eds.): 167–194.
—. 2001. Kaminaljuyu. *AAMCA*: 387–390.
Hawkes, Jacquetta Hopkins (ed.). 1974. *Atlas of Ancient Archaeology.* McGraw-Hill, New York.
Headrick, Annabeth. 1999. The Street of the Dead ... it really was. Mortuary bundles at Teotihuacan. *AncM* 10: 69–85.
Healan, Dan M. 1977. Architectural Implications of Daily Life in Ancient Tollan, Hidalgo, Mexico. *WA* 9: 140–156.
—. 2001. Tula de Hidalgo. *AAMCA*: 774–777.
Healy, Paul F. 1992. Ancient Honduras: Power, wealth, and rank in early chiefdoms. In *Power and Wealth in the Intermediate Area*, Frederick W. Lange (ed.): 85–108. Dumbarton Oaks, Washington, D.C.
Heilbroner, Robert L. 1975 *The Making of Economic Society*. Prentice Hall, Englewood Cliffs.
Heller, Lynette, and Barbara L. Stark. 1989. Economic organization and social context of a Preclassic center on the Pacific coast of Guatemala: El Bálsamo. In Bové and Heller (eds.): 43–64.
Helms, Mary W. 1976. Introduction. In *Frontier Adaptations in Lower Central America*, M.W. Helms and F.O. Loveland (eds.): 1–22. Institute for the Study of Human Issues, Philadelphia.
—. 1979. *Ancient Panama.* U. Texas Press, Austin.
Henderson, John S., I. Sterns, A. Wonderley, and P. A. Urban. 1979. Archaeological investigations in the Valle de Naco, northwestern Honduras: a preliminary report. *JFA* 6: 169–192.
Hendon, Julia A. 2002. Household and state in pre-Hispanic Maya society: gender, identity, and practice. In Gustafson and Trevelyan (eds.): 75–92.
Hernández, Francisco. 1888 [1571]. *Cuatro Libros de la Naturaleza y Virtudes Medicinales de las Plantas y Animales de la Nueva España.* A. León (ed). Escuela de Artes, Morelia.
Hers, Marie Areti. 1989. *Los Toltecas en tierras Chichimecas.* UNAM.
—. 2002. Chicomóztoc: Un mito revisado. *AM* 10: 56: 48–53.
Hester, Thomas R. 2001. Paleoindian period. *AAMCA*: 577–581.
Heyden, Doris and Paul Gendrop. 1980. *Pre-Columbian Architecture of Mesoamerica.* Electa/Rizzoli, New York.
Hicks, Frederic. 1984. La posición de Temascalapan en La Triple Alianza. *Estudios de Cultural Nahuatl* 17: 235–260.
—. 1986. Prehispanic Background of Colonial Political and Economic Organization in Central Mexico. *HMAI* Supplement 4: 35–54.
—. 1994. Cloth in the political economy of the Aztec state. In *Economies and Polities in the Aztec Realm*, M.G. Hodge and M.E. Smith (eds.): 89–111. Studies in Culture and Society 6. Institute for Mesoamerican Studies, SUNY Albany, and U. of Texas Press, Austin.
Hill, Warren D. and John E. Clark. 2001. Sports, gambling, and government: America's first social compact? *AAnthro* 103: 331–345.
Hill, Warren D., Michael Blake and John E. Clark. 1998. Ball court design dates back 3,400 years. *Nature* 392: 878–879.
Hirth, Kenneth G. 1980. Eastern Morelos and Teotihuacan: A Settlement Survey. VUPA 25.
—. 1984a. Early exchange in Mesoamerica: An introduction. In Hirth (ed.): 1–15.
—. 1984b. Trade and Society in Late Formative Morelos. In Hirth (ed.): 125–146.
—. 1989. Militarism and Social Organization at Xochicalco, Morelos. In Diehl and Berlo (eds.): 69–81.
—. (ed.). 1984. Trade and Exchange in Early Mesoamerica. U. of New

Mexico Press, Albuquerque.
—. (ed.). 2000. *Archaeological Research at Xochicalco*. 2 vols. The U. of Utah Press, Salt Lake City.
Hirth, K.G., G. Lara, and G. Hasemann. 1989. *Archaeological Research in the El Cajon Region*. Volume 1, Prehistoric Cultural Ecology. U. of Pittsburgh Memoirs in Latin American Archaeology No. 1. U. of Pittsburgh and Instituto Hondureño de Antropologia e Historia, Pittsburgh and Tegucigalpa.
Historia Tolteca-Chichimeca. 1989 [1545–1565]. *Historia Tolteca-Chichimeca*. CISINAH and INAH-SEP, Mexico City.
Hodge, Mary G. 1984. *Aztec City-States*. MAUM Memoir 18.
Honour, Hugh. 1975. *The New Golden Land*. Pantheon Books, New York.
Hoopes, John W. 1991. The Isthmian alternative. In Fowler (ed.): 171–192.
Hosler, Dorothy. 1994. *The Sounds and Colors of Power: The Sacred Metallurgical Technology of Ancient West Mexico*. Massachusetts Institute of Technology Press, Cambridge.
Hosler, Dorothy, and A. Macfarlane. 1996. Copper sources, metal production and metals trade in Late Postclassic Mesoamerica. *Science* 273: 1819–1824.
Houston, Stephen D. (ed.). 1998. *Function and Meaning in Classic Maya Architecture*. Dumbarton Oaks, Washington, D.C.
Houston, Stephen D. 2000. Into the minds of ancients: Advances in Maya glyph studies. *JWP* 14: 121–201.
—. 2001. Maya lowlands: South. *AAMCA*: 441–447.
Houston, Stephen D., Oswaldo Chinchilla Mazariegos and David Stuart (eds.). 2001. *The Decipherment of Ancient Maya Writing*. U. of Oklahoma Press, Norman.
Houston, Stephen D., and David Stuart. 2001. Peopling the Classic Maya court. In Inomata and Houston (eds.): I: 54–83.
Huchim Herrera, José, and Lourdes Toscano Hernández. 1999. El Cuadrángulo de los Pájaros de Uxmal. *AM* 7: 37: 18–23.
Humboldt, Alexander von. 1810. *Vues des cordillères, et monumens des peoples indigènes de l'Amèrique*. F. Schoell, Paris.
Hymes, D.H. 1960. Lexicostatistics so far. *CA* 1: 3–44.
Inomata, Takeshi, and Stephen D. Houston (eds.). 2001. *Royal Courts of the Ancient Maya*. 2 vols. Westview Press, Boulder, CO.
—. and —. 2001. Opening the royal Maya court. In Inomata and Houston (eds.): I: 3–23.
Jarquín Pacheco, Ana María, and Enrique Martínez Vargas. 1996. La Campana, Colima. *AM* 3: 18: 69–72.
Jiménez García, Elizabeth, Guadalupe Martínez Donjuán, and Aarón Arboleyda Castro 1998. *Historia General de Guerrero*. Vol. 1. INAH.
Johnson, Frederick, and Richard S. MacNeish. 1972. Chronometric dating. In MacNeish (ed.): 4: 3–55.
Johnston, Kevin J. 2001. Broken fingers: Classic Maya scribe capture and polity consolidation. *Antiquity* 75: 373–381.
Jones, Christopher. 1989. Builders of Tikal: archaeology and history. In *Word and Image in Maya Culture*, William F. Hanks and Don S. Rice (eds.): 255–259. U. of Utah Press, Salt Lake City.
Jones, Grant D. 1998. *The Conquest of the Last Maya Kingdom*. Stanford U. Press, Stanford.
Joralemon, Peter David. 1971. *A Study of Olmec Iconography*. Studies in Pre-Columbian Art and Archaeology No. 7. Dumbarton Oaks, Washington, D.C.
Joyce, Arthur A. 1991. Formative Period social change in the lower Río Verde Valley, Oaxaca, Mexico. *LAA* 2: 126–150.
—. 1993. Interregional interaction and social development on the Oaxaca coast. *AncM* 4: 67–84.
Joyce, Rosemary A. 1991. *Cerro Palenque: Power and Identity on the Maya Periphery*. U. of Texas Press, Austin.
—. 2000. Girling the girl and boying the boy: The production of adulthood in ancient Mesoamerica. *WA* 31: 473–483.
Joyce, Rosemary A., and John S. Henderson. 2001. Beginnings of village life in eastern Mesoamerica. *LAA* 12: 5–24.
Justeson, John S., and T. Kaufman. 1993. A decipherment of Epi-Olmec hieroglyphic writing. *Science* 259: 1703–1711.
—. and —. 1997. A newly discovered column in the hieroglyphic text on La Mojarra Stela I: A test of the Epi-Olmec decipherment. *Science* 277: 207–210.
Kaplan, Jonathon. 2002. From under the volcanoes: Some aspects of the ideology of rulership at Late Preclassic Kaminaljuyu. In *Incidents of Archaeology in Central America and Yucatán*, Michael Love, Marion Popenoe de Hatch, and Hector Escobedo (eds.): 311–358. U. Press of America, Lanham.
Karttunen, Frances. 1983. *An Analytical Dictionary of Nahuatl*. U. of Texas Press, Austin.
Karttunen, Frances, and James Lockhart (eds.). 1987 [1570–1580]. *The Art of Nahuatl Speech: The Bancroft Dialogues*. UCLA Latin American Center Publications, U. of California, Los Angeles.
Kaufman, Terence. 1976. Archaeological and linguistic correlations in Mayaland and associated areas of Mesoamerica. *WA* 8: 101–118.
Kelley, J. Charles. 1986. The Mobile Merchants of Molino. In *Ripples in the Chichimec Sea*, F. J. Mathien and R. H. McGuire (eds.): 81–104. Southern Illinois U. Press, Carbondale and Edwardsville.
—. 1995. Trade goods, traders, and status in northwestern Greater Mesoamerica. In *The Gran Chichimeca*, Jonathan E. Reyman (eds.): 102–145. Avebury, Aldershot, UK.
Kellogg, Susan M. 1993. The social organization of households among the Tenochca Mexica before and after conquest. In Santley and Hirth (eds.): 207–224.
—. 2001. Ethnohistorical sources and methods. *AAMCA*: 240–248.
Kelly, Isabel T. 1980. *Ceramic Sequence in Colima: Capacha, an Early Phase*. Anthropological Papers of the U. of Arizona Number 37.
Kelly, Joyce. 1982. *The Complete Visitor's Guide to Mesoamerican Ruins*. U. of Oklahoma Press, Norman.
Kepecs, Susan. 2003. Salt sources and production. In Smith and Berdan (eds.): 126–130.
Keys, David. 1999. *Catastrophe, An Investigation into the Origins of the Modern World*. Century, London.
Kidder, A.V., J.D. Jennings, and E.M. Shook. 1946. *Excavations at Kaminaljuyu, Guatemala*. Carnegie Institution of Washington.
Killion, Thomas W. (ed.). 1992. *Gardens of Prehistory: The Archaeology of Settlement Agriculture in Greater Mesoamerica*. U. of Alabama Press, Tuscaloosa,
Kirchhoff, Paul. 1981 [1943]. Mesoamerica: Its Geographic Limits, Ethnic Composition and Cultural Characteristics. In *Ancient Mesoamerica*, John Graham (ed.): 1–10. (Reprinted from Acta Americana 1: 92–107.) Peek Publications, Palo Alto.
Kirkby, Anne. 1973. *The Use of Land and Water Resources in the Past and Present, Valley of Oaxaca, Mexico*. MAUM Memoir 5.
Klein, Cecelia F. 1987. The ideology of autosacrifice at the Templo Mayor. In *The Aztec Templo Mayor*, Elizabeth H. Boone (ed.): 293–370. Dumbarton Oaks, Washington DC.
—. 2000. The devil and the skirt: An iconographic inquiry into the pre-Hispanic nature of the Tzitzimime. *AncM* 11: 1–26.
Klein, Cecelia F., Eulogio Guzmán, Elisa C. Mandell, and Maya Stanfield-Mazzi. 2002. The role of shamanism in Mesoamerican art. *CA* 43: 383–419.
Knozorov, Yuri. 2001 [1956]. New data on the Maya written language. In Houston *et al.* (eds.): 144–152.
Koontz, Rex A., Kathryn Reese-Taylor, and Annabeth Headrick (eds.). 2001. *Landscape and Power in Ancient Mesoamerica*. Westview, Boulder.
Kowalewski, Stephen A., Gary Feinman, Laura Finsten, and Richard Blanton. 1991. Pre-Hispanic ballcourts from the Valley of Oaxaca, Mexico. In Scarborough and Wilcox (eds.): 25–44.
Kowalski, Jeff Karl. 1987. *The House of the Governor: A Maya Palace at Uxmal, Yucatan, Mexico*. U. of Oklahoma Press, Norman.
—. 1989. Who Am I among the Itza?: Links between Northern Yucatan and the Western Maya Lowlands and Highlands. In Diehl and Berlo (eds.): 173–185.
Kristan-Graham, Cynthia. 1993. The business of narrative at Tula. *LAA* 4: 3–21.
—. 2001. A sense of place at Chichén Itzá. In Koontz *et al.* (eds.): 317–369.
La Barre, W. 1970. Old and New World narcotics. *Economic Botany* 24: 368–373.
Landa, Friar Diego de. 1975 [1566]. *The Maya: Diego de Landa's*

Account of the Affairs of Yucatán. J. Philip O'Hara, Inc., Chicago.
—. 1978 [1566]. *Yucatán Before and After the Conquest.* Dover, New York.
Lange, Frederick W. (ed.). 1996. *Paths to Central American Prehistory.* U. Press of Colorado, Niwot.
Lange, Frederick W., and Doris Z. Stone (eds.). 1984. *The Archaeology of Lower Central America.* U. of New Mexico Press, Albuquerque.
Laporte, Juan Pedro, and Vilma Fialco C. 1990. New perspectives on old problems: dynastic references for the Early Classic at Tikal. In Clancy and Harrison (eds.): 33–66.
LeCount, Lisa J., Jason Yaeger, Richard M. Leventhal, and Wendy Ashmore. 2002. Dating the rise and fall of Xunantunich, Belize: A Late and Terminal Classic lowland Maya regional center. *AncM* 13: 41–63.
Lee, Thomas A. 1969. The artifacts of Chiapa de Corzo, Chiapas, Mexico. *PNWAF* 26.
—. 1974. The Middle Grijalva regional chronology and ceramic relations. In Hammond (ed.): 1–20.
León-Portilla, Miguel. 1984. The Chalca cihuacuicatl of Aquiauhtzin. Erotic poetry of the Nahuas. *New Scholar* 5: 235–262.
León-Portilla, Miguel, and Carmen Aguilera. 1986. *Mapa de México Tenochtitlan y sus Contornos hacia 1550.* Celanese Mexicana S.A., Mexico.
Lesure, Richard C. 2000. Animal imagery, cultural unities, and ideologies of inequality in early formative Mesoamerica. In Clark and Pye (eds.): 192–215.
Levi-Strauss, Claude. 1983. *The Way of the Masks.* Jonathan Cape, London.
Lienzo of Tlaxcala. 1979 [*c.* 1550]. *Lienzo de Tlaxcalla.* Editorial Cosmos, Mexico.
Lind, Michael D. 2000. Mixtec city-states and Mixtec city-state culture. In *A Comparative Study of Thirty City-State Cultures*, Mogens Herman Hansen (ed.): 567–580. The Royal Danish Academy of Sciences and Letters, Copenhagen.
Lind, Michael, and Javier Urcid. 1983. The lords of Lambityeco and their nearest neighbors. *Notas Americanas* 9: 78–111.
Linné, Sigvald. 2003 [1934]. *Archaeological Researches at Teotihuacan, Mexico.* The U. of Alabama Press, Tuscaloosa.
Lombardo de Ruiz, Sonia. 1973. *Desarrollo Urbano de México-Tenochtitlan Segun las Fuentes Históricas.* SEP-INAH, Mexico.
Long, Austin, Bruce F. Benz, D. J. Donahue, A. J. T. Jull, and L. J. Toolin. 1989. First direct AMS dates on early maize from Tehuacán, Mexico. *Radiocarbon* 31: 1035–1040.
López Austin, Alfredo. 1993. *The Myths of the Opossum: Pathways of Mesoamerican Mythology.* U. of New Mexico Press, Albuquerque.
—. 1997. *Tamoanchan, Tlalocan: Places of Mist.* U. Press of Colorado, Niwot CO.
López Lujan, Leonardo. 1994. *The Offerings of the Templo Mayor of Tenochtitlan.* U. of Colorado Press, Niwot.
López Mestas Camberos, Lorenza, and Jorge Ramos de la Vega. 1998. Excavating the tomb at Huitzilapa. In Townsend (ed.): 52–69.
Lorenzo, José Luis, and Lorena Mirambell. 1986. Preliminary report on archaeological and paleoenvironmental studies in the area of El Cedral, San Luis Potosí, Mexico 1977–1980. In *New Evidence for the Pleistocene Peopling of the Americas*, Alan Lyle Bryan (ed.): 107–112. Center for the Study of Early Man, U. of Maine, Orono.
Love, Michael W. 1991. Style and social complexity in formative Mesoamerica. In Fowler (ed.): 47–76.
Lovell, W. George. 1992. 'Heavy shadows and black night': disease and depopulation in colonial Spanish America. *Annals of the Association of American Geographers* 82: 426–443.
Lowe, Gareth W. 1981. Olmec Horizons defined in Mound 20, San Isidro, Chiapas. In Benson (ed.): 231–255.
Lucero, Lisa J. 2002. Collapse of the Classic Maya: a case for the role of water control. *AAnthro* 104: 814–826.
Luckenbach, Alvin H., and Richard S. Levy. 1980. The implications of Nahua (Aztecan) lexical diversity for Mesoamerican culture-history. *AA* 45: 455–461.
McAnany, Patricia A. 1990. Water Storage in the Puuc Region of the Northern Maya Lowlands. In *Precolumbian Population History in the Maya Lowlands*, T. Patrick Culbert and Don S. Rice (eds.): 263–284. U. of New Mexico Press, Albuquerque.
—. 1995. *Living with the Ancestors: Kinship and Kingship in Ancient Maya Society.* U. of Texas Press, Austin.
McAndrew, John. 1965. *The Open-Air Churches of Sixteenth-Century Mexico.* Harvard U. Press, Cambridge.
McBride, Harold W. 1969. The extent of the Chupícuaro tradition. In *The Natalie Wood Collection of Pre-Columbian Ceramics from Chupícuaro, Guanajuato, Mexico at UCLA*, Jay D. Frierman (ed.): 31–49. U. of California, Los Angeles Museum and Laboratories of Ethnic Arts and Technology.
McCafferty, Geoffrey G. 2000. Tollan ChololIan and the legacy of legitimacy during the Classic-Postclassic transition. In Carrasco *et al.*(eds.): 341–366.
—. 2001a. Cholula. *AAMCA*: 138–142.
—. 2001b. Mountain of heaven, mountain of earth: the Great Pyramid of Cholula as sacred landscape. In Koontz *et al.* (eds.): 279–316.
McGuire, Randall H. 1989. The greater Southwest as a periphery of Mesoamerica. In *Centre and Periphery*, T.C. Champion (ed.): 40–66. Unwin Hyman, London.
—. 2001. Northern Arid Zone. *AAMCA*: 522–528.
McKeever Furst, Jill L. 1995. *Natural History of the Soul in Ancient Mexico.* Yale U. Press, New Haven.
McKillop, Heather I. 2002. *Salt: White Gold of the Ancient Maya.* U. Press of Florida, Gainesville.
MacNeish, Richard S. 1964. Ancient Mesoamerican civilization. *Science* 143: 531–537.
—. 2001. Tehuacán region. *AAMCA*: 705–710.
—. (gen. ed.). 1967–1972. The Prehistory of the Tehuacan Valley. Published for the Robert S. Peabody Foundation, Phillips Academy, Andover MA by the U. of Texas Press, Austin.
Madrid codex. 1967. *Codex Madrid (Codex Tro-Cortesianus).* Museo América, Madrid (F. Anders, ed.). Akademische Druck- u. Verlagsanstalt, Graz.
Maguey plan. 1990 [c. 1557–1562]. Plano en papel de maguey. In *Arquitectura Prehispánica* by Ignacio Marquina, p. 182, Fot. 59. Memorias del Instituto Nacional de Antropología e Historia, N. 1. SEP/INAH, Mexico.
Manzanilla, Linda (coord.). 1993a. *Anatomía de un Conjunto Residencial Teotihuacano en Oztoyahualco.* 2 vols. UNAM, Instituto de Investigaciones Antropológicas, Mexico.
—. 1993b. Daily life in the Teotihuacan apartment compounds. In Berrin and Pasztory (eds.): 90–99.
—. 2001. Cobá. *AAMCA*: 433–441.
Manzanilla López, Rubén and Arturo Talavera González. 1993. El sitio arqueológico de Cuetlajuchitlan. In *A propósito del Formativo*, M.T. Castillo Mangas (ed.): 105–116. INAH, Mexico.
Mapa Quinatzin. 1959 [c. 1542]. In *Mexican Manuscript Painting of the Early Colonial Period* by Donald Robertson, Plates 13, 46–47: 135–40. Yale U. Press, New Haven.
Marcus, Joyce. 2001. Zapotec culture and religion. *AAMCA*: 846–847.
—. 2003. Recent advances in Maya archaeology. *JAR* 11: 71–148.
Marcus, Joyce, and Kent V. Flannery. 1996. *Zapotec Civilization.* Thames & Hudson, London and New York.
—. and —. 2000. Cultural evolution in Oaxaca: the origins of the Zapotec and Mixtec civilizations. In Adams and MacLeod (eds.): 358–406.
Marcus, Joyce, and Judith Francis Zeitlin (eds.). 1994. *Caciques and Their People: A Volume in Honor of Ronald Spores.* MAUM Anthropological Paper 89.
Marquina, Ignacio. 1999 [1951]. *Arquitectura Prehispánica.* Facsimile of the first edition. Memorias del Instituto Nacional de Antropología e Historia, N. 1. SEP/INAH, Mexico.
Martin, Simon. 1996. Calakmul y el enigma del glifo Cabeza de Serpiente. *AM* 3: 18: 42–51.
Martin, Simon, and Nikolai Grube. 2000. *Chronicle of the Maya Kings and Queens: Deciphering the Dynasties of the Ancient Maya.* Thames & Hudson, London and New York.
Martínez Donjuán, Guadalupe. 1995. Teopantecuanitlán. *AM* 2: 12: 58–62.

Masson, Marilyn A., and David A. Freidel (eds.). 2002. *Ancient Maya Political Economics*. AltaMira Press, Walnut Creek, CA.

Mastache, Alba Guadalupe, and Robert H. Cobean. 2001. Ancient Tollan. *RES* 38: 101–133.

—. and —. 2001. Tula region. AAMCA: 777–783.

Mastache, Alba Guadalupe, Robert H. Cobean, and Dan M. Healan. 2002. *Ancient Tollan: Tula and the Toltec Heartland*. U. Press of Colorado, Niwot.

Matheny, R.T., D.L. Gurr, D.W. Forsyth, and F.R. Hauck. 1980–1983. Investigations at Edzná, Campeche, Mexico. *PNWAF* 46.

Matos Moctezuma, Eduardo. 1984. The Templo Mayor of Tenochtitlan: Economics and Ideology. In *Ritual Human Sacrifice in Mesoamerica*, E.H. Boone (ed.): 133–164. Dumbarton Oaks, Washington, D.C.

—. 1994. *The Great Temple of the Aztecs*. Thames & Hudson, London and New York.

—. 2002. Eagle Man. In Matos M. and Solís O. (eds.): 456.

—. 2003. Buildings in the sacred precinct of Tenochtitlan. In Sanders *et al.* (eds.): 119–147.

Matos Moctezuma, Eduardo, and Felipe Solís Olguin (eds.). 2002. *Aztecs*. Royal Academy of Arts, London.

Medellín Zenil, Alfonso. 1952. *Exploraciones en Quauhtochco*. Gobierno del Estado de Veracruz and INAH, Jalapa.

—. 1955. *Exploraciones en la Isla de Sacrificios*. Gobierno del Estado de Veracruz, Jalapa.

—. 1960. *Ceramicas del Totonacapan*. Universidad Veracruzana, Xalapa.

—. 1965. La escultura de Las Limas. *Boletín del INAH* 21: 5–8.

Messenger, Lewis C. 1990. Ancient winds of change: Climatic settings and prehistoric social complexity in Mesoamerica. *AncM* 1: 21–40.

Michaels, George, and Barbara Voorhies. 1999. Late Archaic period coastal collectors in southern Mesoamerica: The Chantuto people revisited. In *Pacific Latin America in Prehistory: The Evolution of Archaic and Formative Cultures*, Michael Blake (ed.): 39–54. WSU Press, Pullman, WA.

Michelet, Dominique, M.C. Arnauld, and M.-F. Fauvet Berthelot. 1989. El proyecto del CEMCA en Michoacan. Etapa I: Un balance. *Trace* 16: 70–87.

Middleton, William D., Gary M. Feinman, and Guillermo Molina. 1998. Tomb use and reuse in Oaxaca, Mexico. *AncM* 9: 297–308.

Milbrath, Susan. 2000. Xochiquetzal and the lunar cult of Central Mexico. In *In Chalchihuitl in Quetzalli*, Eloise Quiñones Keber (ed.): 31–54. Labyrinthos, Lancaster, CA.

Miller, Arthur G. 1973. *The Mural Painting of Teotihuacan*. Dumbarton Oaks, Washington, D.C.

Miller, Mary E. 1986. *The Murals of Bonampak*. Princeton U. Press, Princeton.

—. 2001. *The Art of Mesoamerica*. Third edition. Thames & Hudson, London and New York.

Miller, Mary Ellen, and Marco Samayoa. 1998. Jade, chacmools, and the Maize God. *RES* 33: 55–72.

Miller, Mary, and Karl Taube. 1993. *The Gods and Symbols of Ancient Mexico and the Maya*. Thames & Hudson, London and New York.

Miller, Virginia E. 1991. *The Frieze of the Palace of the Stuccoes, Acanceh, Yucatan, Mexico*. Dumbarton Oaks, Washington, D.C.

—. 1999. The skull rack in Mesoamerica. In *Mesoamerican Architecture as a Cultural Symbol*, Jeff Karl Kowalski (ed.): 340–360. Oxford U. Press, New York.

Millon, René. 1981. Teotihuacan: city, state, and civilization. In *HMAI* Supplement I: 198–243.

—. 1992. Teotihuacan studies: From 1950 to 1990 and beyond. In Berlo (ed.): 339–419.

—. 1993. The Place Where Time Began. In Berrin and Pasztory (eds.): 17–43.

Millon, René, Bruce Drewitt, and George Cowgill. 1973. *Urbanization at Teotihuacan, Mexico. Vol. 1, The Teotihuacan Map*. Part 2: Maps. U. of Texas Press, Austin.

Minc, Leah D. 2001. Pottery. *AAMCA*: 603–610.

Monaghan, John. 1995. *The Covenant with Earth and Rain: Exchange, Sacrifice and Revelation in Mixtec Sociality*. U. of Oklahoma Press, Norman.

—. 2001. Mixtec history, culture, and religion. *AAMCA*: 476–480.

Morelos García, Noel. 1993. *Proceso de Producción de Espacios y Estructuras en Teotihuacan*. Mexico City: INAH Colección Científica.

Moreno Toscano, Alejandra. 1968. *Geografía Económica de México (Siglo XVI)*. El Colegio de México Centro de Estudios Históricos Nueva Serie 2.

Motolinía (Fray Toribio de Benavente). 1950 [1541]. *History of the Indians of New Spain*. Documents and Narratives Concerning the Discovery and Conquest of Latin America, n.s. No. 4, The Cortes Society, Berkeley.

Mountjoy, Joseph B. 1998. The evolution of complex societies in West Mexico: A comparative perspective. In Townsend (ed.): 250–265.

—. 2001. Capacha. *AAMCA*: 95–96.

—. 2001. Rock art. *AAMCA*: 635.

Mountjoy, Joseph, and David Peterson. 1973. *Man and Land at Prehispanic Cholula*. Vanderbilt U. Publications in Anthropology No. 4., Nashville.

Mountjoy, Joseph B., R.E. Taylor, and L. Feldman. 1972. Matanchen Complex. *Science* 175: 1242–1243.

Muller, Florencia. 1985. *La Cerámica de Cuicuilco B*. INAH Serie Arqueología, Mexico.

Mundy, Barbara E. 1996. *The Mapping of New Spain: Indigenous Cartography and the Maps of the Relaciones Geográficas*. U. of Chicago Press, Chicago.

Neff, Hector, and Ronald L. Bishop. 1988. Plumbate Origins and Development. *AA* 53: 505–522.

Nelson, Ben A. 1993. Outposts of Mesoamerican empire and domestic patterning at La Quemada, Zacatecas, Mexico. In *Culture and Contact: Charles C. DiPeso's Gran Chichimeca*, A. I. Woosley and J. C. Ravensloot (eds.): 173–189. U. of New Mexico Press, Albuquerque.

—. 1995. Complexity, hierarchy, and scale: A controlled comparison between Chaco Canyon, New Mexico, and La Quemada, Zacatecas, Mexico. *AA* 60: 597–618.

Nelson, Ben A., J. Andrew Darling, and David A. Kice. 1992. Mortuary practices and the social order at La Quemada, Zacatecas, Mexico. *LAA* 3: 298–315.

Netting, Robert McC. 1989. Smallholders, householders, freeholders: why the family farm works well worldwide. In *The Household Economy*, Richard R. Wilk (ed.): 221–244. Westview Press, Boulder.

Newsome, Elizabeth A. 2001. *Trees of Paradise and Pillars of the World: The Serial Stela Cycle of 18-Rabbit-God K, King of Copán*. U. of Texas Press, Austin.

Nichols, Deborah L. 1982. A Middle Formative Irrigation System near Santa Clara Coatitlan in the Basin of Mexico. *AA* 47: 133–144.

—. 1987. Risk, Uncertainty, and Prehispanic Agricultural Intensification in the Northern Basin of Mexico. *AAnthro* 89: 596–616.

Nichols, Deborah L., and Thomas H. Charlton (eds.). 1997. *The Archaeology of City-States*. Smithsonian Institution Press, Washington, D.C.

Nicholson, Henry B. 1966. The Mixteca-Puebla concept in Mesoamerican archaeology: A reexamination. In *Ancient Mesoamerica*, John Graham (ed): 258–263. Peek Publications, Palo Alto.

—. 1971. Religion in Pre-Hispanic Central Mexico. *HMAI* 10: 1: 395–446.

—. 2001. *Topiltzin Quetzalcoatl: The Once and Future Lord of the Toltecs*. U. Press of Colorado, Boulder.

Nicholson, H. B., and Frederic Hicks. 1961. A brief progress report on the excavations at Cerro Portezuelo, Valley of Mexico. *AA* 27: 106–108.

Niederberger, Christine. 1987. *Paléopaysages et Archéologie Pré-Urbaine du Bassin de Mexico*. Études Mésoaméricaines V. XI, Tomes 1 and 2. Centre d'Études Méxicaines et Centraméricaines, Mexico.

Noble, Sandra B. 1998. Maya dedications of authority. In *The Sowing and the Dawning: Termination, Dedication, and Transformation in the Archaeological and Ethnographic Record of Mesoamerica*, Shirley B. Mock (ed.): 65–79. U. of New Mexico Press, Albuquerque.

Nuttall, Zelia. 1925. The gardens of ancient Mexico. *Annual Report of the Board of Regents of the Smithsonian Institution*, 1923: 453–464. Government Printing Office, Washington, D.C.

O'Mack, Scott. 1991. Yacateuctli and Ehecatl-Quetzalcoatl: Earth-Divers in Aztec Central Mexico. *Ethnohistory* 38: 1–33.
Ochoa, Lorenzo. 2000. La civilización huasteca. *AM* 8: 43: 58–63.
Offner, Jerome A. 1984. Household organization in the Texcocan heartland. In Harvey and Prem (eds.): 127–146.
Oliveros, Arturo. 1989. Las tumbas más antiguas de Michoacán. In *Historia general de Michoacán*, E. Florescano (ed.): 123–134. Instituto de Cultura de Michoacán, Morelia, Mexico.
—. 1995. The Precolumbian image of hurricanes. In *Olmecs, a special edition of AncM*: 60–63.
Ortiz de Montellano, Bernard R. 1990. *Aztec Medicine, Health, and Nutrition*. Rutgers U. Press, New Brunswick.
Ortíz, Ponciano, and María del Carmen Rodríguez. 2000. The sacred hill of El Manati. In Clark and Pye (eds.): 75–93.
Palka, Joel. 2001. Ancient Maya defensive barricades, warfare, and site abandonment. *LAA* 12: 427–430.
Paradis, Louise I. 2001. Guerrero region. *AAMCA*: 311–321.
Parry, John H., and Robert G. Keith (eds.). 1984. *New Iberian World. Volume III: Central America and Mexico*. Times Books, New York.
Parry, William J. 2001. Production and exchange of obsidian tools in late Aztec city-states. *AncM* 12: 101–111.
Parsons, Jeffrey R. 1976. The Role of Chinampa Agriculture in the Food Supply of Aztec Tenochtitlan. In *Cultural Change and Continuity*, C. Cleland (ed.): 233–257. Academic Press, New York.
Parsons, Jeffrey R. and Mary H. Parsons. 1990. *Maguey Utilization in Highland Central Mexico*. MAUM Anthropological Paper 82.
Parsons, Lee A. 1986. *The Origins of Maya Art: Monumental Stone Sculpture of Kaminaljuyú, Guatemala, and the Southern Pacific Coast*. DOSPCAA 28.
Pasztory, Esther. 1983. *Aztec Art*. Harry N. Abrams, Inc., New York.
—. 1993 Teotihuacan unmasked: A view through art. In Berrin and Pasztory (eds.): 44–63.
—. 1997. *Teotihuacan: An Experiment in Living*. U. of Oklahoma Press, Norman.
Paxton, Merideth. 2001. *The Cosmos of the Yucatec Maya: Cycles and Steps from the Madrid Codex*. U. of New Mexico Press, Albuquerque.
Pendergast, David M. 1979–1990. *Excavations at Altun Ha, Belize, 1964–1970*. 3 vol. Royal Ontario Museum, Toronto.
Pennington, Jean A.T., and Helen Nichols Church. 1985. *Food Values of Portions Commonly Used*. Harper & Row, New York.
Peraza Lope, Carlos Alberto. 1999. Mayapán, ciudad-capital del Posclásico. *AM* 7: 37: 48–53.
Pérez, Ventura R. 2002. La Quemada tool-induced bone alterations. *Archaeology Southwest* 16: 10.
Pillsbury, Joanne. 1996. The Thorny Oyster and the Origins of Empire. *LAA* 7: 313–340.
Piña Chan, Román. 1975. *Teotenango: El Antiguo Lugar de la Muralla*. 2 vols. Dirección de Turismo, Gobierno del Estado de México, Mexico City.
—. 1992. *El Lenguaje de las Piedras*. Universidad Autónoma de Campeche, Campeche, Mexico.
—. 2000. Teotenango. *AM* 8: 43: 38–43.
Piperno, D.R., and K.V. Flannery. 2001. The earliest archaeological maize (Zea mays L.) from highland Mexico: New accelerator mass spectrometry dates and their implications. *Proceedings of the National Academy of Sciences* 98: 2101–2103.
Plunket, Patricia (ed.). 2002. *Domestic Ritual in Ancient Mesoamerica*. Monograph, 46. U. of California, Los Angeles, Cotsen Institute of Archaeology Los Angeles.
Plunket, Patricia, and Gabriela Uruñuela. 1998a. Appeasing the volcano gods: Ancient altars attest a 2000-year-old veneration of Mexico's smoldering Popocatepetl. *Archaeology* 51: 4: 36–43.
—. and —. 1998b. Preclassic household patterns preserved under volcanic ash at Tetimpa, Puebla, Mexico. *LAA* 9: 287–309.
Plunket, Patricia, and Gabriela Urunuela. 2001. Puebla-Tlaxcala region. *AAMCA*: 611–617.
Pohl, John M.D. 1994a. Mexican codices, maps, and lienzos as social contracts. In *Writing Without Words*, Elizabeth Hill Boone and Walter D. Mignolo (eds.): 137–160. Duke U. Press, Durham and London.
—. 1994b. Weaving and gift exchange in the Mixtec codices. In *Cloth and Curing: Continuity and Change in Oaxaca*, Grace Johnson and Douglas Sharon (eds.): 3–13. San Diego Museum Papers No. 32.
—. 1998. Themes of drunkenness, violence, and factionalism in Tlaxcalan altar paintings. *RES* 33: 183–207.
—. 1999. *Exploring Mesoamerica*. Oxford U. Press, New York.
Pohl, John M. D., and Bruce E. Byland. 1994. The Mixteca-Puebla Style and Early Postclassic socio-political interaction. In *Mixteca-Puebla: Discoveries and Research in Mesoamerican Art and Archaeology*, H.B. Nicholson and Eloise Quiñones Keber (eds.): 189–199. Labyrinthos, Lancaster CA.
Pohl, Mary D., *et al.* 1996. Early agriculture in the Maya lowlands. *LAA* 7: 355–372.
Pollard, Helen Perlstein. 1987. The political economy of prehispanic Tarascan metallurgy. *American Antiquity* 52: 741–752.
—. 1993. *Taríacuri's Legacy: The Prehispanic Tarascan State*. U. of Oklahoma Press, Norman.
—. 2001. Michoacán region. *AAMCA*: 458–464.
Pollock, H. E. D. 1936. *Round Structures of Aboriginal Middle America*. Carnegie Institution of Washington Publication No. 471.
Pool, Christopher A. 2000. From Olmec to epi-Olmec at Tres Zapotes, Veracruz, Mexico. In Clark and Pye (eds.): 136–153.
Popul Vuh. 1985. *Popul Vuh: The Definitive Edition of the Mayan Book of the Dawn of Life and the Glories of Gods and Kings*. Dennis Tedlock (ed.). Simon and Schuster, New York.
Porter [Weaver], Muriel Noë. 1953. *Tlatilco and the Preclassic Cultures of the New World*. Viking Fund Publications in Anthropology No. 19, New York.
Porter, Muriel Noë. 1956. Excavations at Chupícuaro, Guanajuato, Mexico. *Transactions of the American Philosophical Society*, No. 46, pt. 5.
Potter, Stephen. 1962. *One-Upsmanship*. Penguin Books, New York.
Powis, Terry G., Fred Valdez, Jr., Thomas R. Hester, W. Jeffrey Hurst, and Stanley M. Tarka, Jr. 2002. Spouted vessels and cacao use among the Preclassic Maya. *LAA* 13: 85–106.
Price, Barbara J. 1980. The truth is not in accounts but in account books: On the epistemological status of history. In *Beyond the Myths of Culture*, E. B. Ross (ed.): 155–180. Academic Press, New York.
Proskouriakoff, Tatiana. 1960. Historical implications of a pattern of dates at Piedras Negras, Guatemala. *AA* 25: 454–475.
—. 1963. *An Album of Maya Architecture*. U. of Oklahoma Press, Norman.
Pyburn, K. Anne. 1996. The political economy of ancient Maya land use: the road to ruin. In Fedick (ed.): 236–247.
Pye, Mary E., and Arthur A. Demarest. 1991. The evolution of complex societies in Southeastern Mesoamerica: New evidence from El Mesak, Guatemala. In Fowler (ed.): 77–100.
Quilter, Jeffrey. 2004. *Rivas*. U. of Iowa Press, Iowa City.
Rabinowitz, A. 1986. *Jaguar*. Arbor House, New York.
Rafinesque-Schmaltz, Constantine Samuel. 2001 [1832]. First letter to Mr. Champollion, on the graphic systems of America, and the glyphs of Otolum or Palenque, in Central America. In Houston *et al.* (eds.): 45–47.
Rathje, William L. 1974. The garbage project: A new way of looking at the problems of archaeology. *Archaeology* 27: 236–241.
Rathje, William L., and Michael B. Schiffer. 1982. *Archaeology*. Harcourt Brace Jovanovich, Inc., New York.
Rattray, Evelyn Childs. 1987. Los barrios foráneos de Teotihuacan. In *Teotihuacan*, Emily McClung de Tapia and Evelyn Childs Rattray (eds.): 243–274. UNAM.
Rattray, Evelyn. 1990. New Findings on the Origins of Thin Orange Ceramics. *AncM* 1: 181–195.
—. 1996. A regional perspective on the Epiclassic period in Central Mexico. In *Arqueología Mesoamericana: Homenaje a William Sanders*, coordinated by A. G. Mastache, J. R. Parsons, R. S. Santley, and M. C. Sera: 213–231. INAH, Mexico.
Read, Kay Almere. 1998. *Time and Sacrifice in the Aztec Cosmos*. Indiana U. Press, Bloomington and Indianapolis.
Reents-Budet, Dorie. 1994. *Painting the Maya Universe: Royal Ceramics of the Classic Period*. Duke U. Press, Durham.
Reilly III, F. Kent. 1995. Art, ritual, and rulership in the Olmec world. In

Coe *et al.*: 26–45.

—. 2001. Tlacozotitlán. *AAMCA*: 756.

Relación de Michoacán. 1980 [1541]. *La Relación de Michoacán.* Estudios Michoacanos V. Fimax, Morelia, Michoacán, Mexico.

Renfrew, Colin. 2001. Production and consumption in a sacred economy: The material correlates of high devotional expression at Chaco Canyon. *AA* 66: 14–25.

Restall, Matthew. 1998. *The Maya World: Yucatec Culture and Society, 1550–1850.* Stanford U. Press, Stanford.

Rice, Don S. (ed.) 1993. *Latin American Horizons.* Dumbarton Oaks, Washington D.C.

Rice, Prudence M. 1987. *Pottery Analysis: A Sourcebook.* U. of Chicago Press, Chicago.

—. 1996. Recent Ceramic Analysis. *Journal of Archaeological Research* 4: 133–163 (Pt. 1, Function, Style, and Origins) and 4: 165–202 (Pt. 2, Composition, Production, and Theory).

Ringle, William M., Tomás Gallareta Negrón and George J. Bey III. 1998. The return of Quetzalcoatl: Evidence for the spread of a world religion during the Epiclassic period. *AncM* 9: 183–232.

Robelo, Cecilio A. 1980. *Diccionario de mitología Nahuatl.* 2 vols. Editorial Innovación, Mexico.

Robin, Cynthia. 1989. *Preclassic Maya Burials at Cuello, Belize.* British Archaeological Reports, International Series 480.

Robinson, Eugenia A. 1997. Protohistoric to colonial settlement transition in the Antigua Valley, Guatemala. In *Approaches to the Historical Archaeology of Mexico, Central and South America*, Janine Gasco, Greg C. Smith and Patricia Fournier-García (eds.): 59–70 Monograph, 38. U. of California, Los Angeles, Institute of Archaeology Los Angeles.

Romano, Arturo. 1967. Tlatilco. *Boletín del INAH* 30: 38–42.

Romero, Javier. 1970. Dental mutilation, trephination, and cranial deformation. *HMAI* 9: 50–67.

Rue, David J. 1989. Archaic Middle American agriculture and settlement. *JFA* 16: 177–184.

Ruiz de Alarcón, Hernando. 1984 [1629]. *Treatise on the Heathen Superstitions That Today Live Among the Indians Native to This New Spain, 1629.* U. of Oklahoma Press, Norman.

Ruiz Gordillo, J. Omar. 1999. *Paxil: La Conservación en una Zona Arqueológica de la Región de Misantla, Veracruz.* INAH, Mexico City.

Sabloff, Jeremy A. (ed.). 2003. *Tikal: Dynasties, Foreigners, & Affairs of State.* School of American Research, Santa Fe.

Sabloff, Jeremy A. and W. L. Rathje. 1975. *A Study of Changing Pre-Columbian Commericial Systems: The 1972–1973 Seasons at Cozumel, Mexico: A Preliminary Report.* Peabody Museum of Archaeology and Ethnology, Harvard U., Monographs 3.

Sahagún, Fray Bernardino de. 1950–82 [1569]. *General History of the Things of New Spain (Florentine Codex).* 13 vol. Translated and with notes by A. Anderson and C. Dibble. The School of American Research and the U. of Utah., Santa Fe.

—. 1959 [1569]. *The Merchants. Book 9 of the Florentine Codex.* Translated and with notes by C. E. Dibble and A. J. O. Anderson. The School of American Research and The U. of Utah, Santa Fe.

—. 1961 [1569]. *The People. Book 10 of the Florentine Codex.* Translated and with notes by C. E. Dibble and A. J. O. Anderson. The School of American Research and The U. of Utah, Santa Fe.

—. 1963 [1569]. *Earthly Things. Book 11 of the Florentine Codex.* Translated and with notes by C. E. Dibble and A. J. O. Anderson. The School of American Research and The U. of Utah, Santa Fe.

—. 1969 [1569]. *Rhetoric and Moral Philosophy. Book 6 of the Florentine Codex.* Translated and with notes by C. E. Dibble and A. J. O. Anderson. The School of American Research and The U. of Utah, Santa Fe.

—. 1970 [1569]. *The Gods. Book 1 of the Florentine Codex.* Translated and with notes by A. J. O. Anderson and C. E. Dibble. The School of American Research and The U. of Utah, Santa Fe.

—. 1975 [1569]. *The Conquest of Mexico. Book 12 of the Florentine Codex.* Translated and with notes by A. J. O. Anderson and C. E. Dibble. The School of American Research and The U. of Utah, Santa Fe.

—. 1978 [1569]. *The Origin of the Gods. Book 3 of the Florentine Codex.* Translated and with notes by A. J. O. Anderson and C. E. Dibble. The School of American Research and The U. of Utah, Santa Fe.

—. 1979 [1569]. *Kings and Lords. Book 8 of the Florentine Codex.* Translated and with notes by A. J. O. Anderson and C. E. Dibble. The School of American Research and The U. of Utah, Santa Fe.

—. 1979 [1569]. *The Soothsayers. Book 4 of the Florentine Codex.* Translated and with notes by C. E. Dibble and A. J. O. Anderson. The School of American Research and The U. of Utah, Santa Fe.

—. 1981 [1569]. *The Ceremonies. Book 2 of the Florentine Codex.* Translated and with notes by A. J. O. Anderson and C. E. Dibble. The School of American Research and The U. of Utah, Santa Fe.

—. 1993 [1559–1561]. *Primeros Memoriales. Facsimile edition.* U. of Oklahoma Press, Norman, OK., in cooperation with the Patrimonio Nacional and the Real Academia de la Historia, Madrid.

Sánchez Correa, Sergio Arturo. 1993. El Formative en la región norcentral de Mesoamérica. In *A propósito del Formativo*, María Teresa Castillo Mangas (ed.): 99–103. INAH, Mexico.

Sanders, William T. 1974. Chiefdom to state: Political evolution at Kaminaljuyu, Guatemala. In *Reconstructing Complex Societies*, Charlotte B. Moore (ed.): 97–113. Supplement to the Bulletin of the American Schools of Oriental Research No. 20.

—. 1976. The Agricultural History of the Basin of Mexico. In *The Valley of Mexico*, Eric Wolf (ed.): 101–159. U. of New Mexico Press, Albuquerque.

—. 1981. Ecological Adaptation in the Basin of Mexico: 23,000 B.C. to the Present. In *HMAI* Supplement 1: 147–197.

—. 1992. Ecology and cultural syncretism in 16th-century Mesoamerica. *Antiquity* 66: 172–190.

Sanders, William T., Alba Guadalupe Mastache, and Robert H. Cobean (eds.). 2003. *Urbanism in Mesoamerica Vol. 1.* INAH and The Pennsylvania State U., Mexico City, Mexico, and University Park, PA.

Sanders, William T., Jeffrey R. Parsons, and Robert Santley. 1979. *The Basin of Mexico.* Academic Press, New York.

Sanders, William T., and Barbara Price. 1968. *Mesoamerica: The Evolution of a Civilization.* Random House, New York.

Sanders, William T., and David L. Webster. 1988. The Mesoamerican urban tradition. *AAnthro* 90: 521–546.

Santley, Robert S. 1993. Late Formative period society at Loma Torremote. In Santley and Hirth (eds.): 67–86.

—. 1994. The Economy of Ancient Matacapan. *AncM* 5: 243–266.

Santley, Robert S., Michael J. Berman, and Rani T. Alexander. 1991. The politicization of the Mesoamerican ballgame and its implications for the interpretation of the distribution of ballcourts in Central Mexico. In Scarborough and Wilcox (eds.): 3–24.

Santley, Robert S., and Kenneth Hirth (eds.). 1993. *Prehispanic Domestic Units in Western Mesoamerica.* CRC Press, Boca Raton.

Sarro, Patricia Joan. 2001. The form of power: the architectural meaning of Building A of El Tajín. In Koontz *et al.* (eds.): 231–256.

Saunders, Nicholas J. 1998. Architecture of symbolism: The feline image. In Saunders (ed.): 12–52.

—. (ed.). 1998. *Icons of Power: Feline Symbolism in the Americas.* Routledge, London and New York.

Scarborough, Vernon L. 1994. Maya water management. *National Geographic Research and Exploration* 10: 92: 184–199.

Scarborough, Vernon L., and David Wilcox (eds.). 1991. *The Mesoamerican Ballgame.* U. of Arizona Press, Tucson.

Schaafsma, Curtis F., and Carroll Riley (eds.). 1999. *The Casas Grandes World.* U. of Utah Press, Salt Lake City.

Schele, Linda, and David Freidel. 1990. *A Forest of Kings.* Wm. Morrow and Co., New York.

Schiavetti, Vincent W. 1994. La minería prehispánica de Chalchihuites. *AncM* Vol. 1, No. 6: 48–51.

Schoeninger, Margaret J. 1979. *Dietary Reconstruction at Chalcatzingo, a Formative Period Site in Morelos, Mexico.* MAUM Technical Report 9.

Scholes, France V., and Ralph L. Roys. 1948. *The Maya Chontal Indians of Acalan-Tixchel.* Carnegie Institution of Washington, Publication No. 560.

Schortman, Edward M., Patricia A. Urban, and Marne Ausec. 2001. Politics with Style: Identity Formation in Prehispanic Southeastern Mesoamerica. *AAnthro* 103: 312–330.

Schroeder, Susan. 1991. *Chimalpahin and the Kingdoms of Chalco.* U. of Arizona Press, Tucson.

Schwartz, Marion. 1997. *A History of Dogs in the Early Americas.* Yale U. Press, New Haven.

Scott, Sue. 1993. *Teotihuacan Mazapan Figurines and the Xipe Totec Status: A Link Between the Basin of Mexico and the Valley of Oaxaca.* VUPA 44.

Seitz, Russell, George E. Harlow, V. B. Sisson, and Karl E. Taube. 2001. Formative jades and expanded jade sources in Guatemala. *Antiquity* 75: 687–688

Séjourné, Laurette. 1962. *El Universo de Quetzalcóatl.* Fondo de Cultura Económica, Mexico.

—. 1984 [1966]. *Arqueología de Teotihuacan: La Cerámica.* Fondo de Cultura Económica, Mexico.

Seler, Eduard. 1991 [1894]. Where was Aztlan, the home of the Aztecs? In *Collected Works in Mesoamerican Linguistics and Archaeology* by Eduard Seler, Vol. 2: 18–27. Labyrinthos, Culver City, CA.

—. 1991 [1904]. On the words Anauac and Nauatl. In *Collected Works in Mesoamerican Linguistics and Archaeology* by Eduard Seler, Vol. 2: 28–42. Labyrinthos, Culver City, CA.

Sempowski, Martha L., and Michael W. Spence. 1994. *Mortuary practices and skeletal remains at Teotihuacan, with an addendum by Rebecca Storey.* U. of Utah Press, Salt Lake City.

Shafer, Harry J., and Thomas R. Hester. 1983. Ancient Maya chert workshops in northern Belize, Central America. *American Antiquity* 48: 519–543.

Sharer, Robert J. 1984. Lower Central America as seen from Mesoamerica. In Lange and Stone (eds.): 63–84.

—. 1994. The Ancient Maya. Fifth edition. Stanford U. Press, Stanford.

—. (ed.). 1978. *The Prehistory of Chalchuapa, El Salvador.* 3 vols. U. Museum Monograph 36. U. of Pennsylvania Press, Philadelphia.

Sharer, Robert, Loa B. Traxler, David W. Sedat, E. Bell, M. Canuto, and C. Powell. 1999. Early Classic architecture beneath the Copán Acropolis. *AncM* 10: 3–23.

Shaw, Leslie C. 1999. Social and ecological aspects of Preclassic Maya meat consumption at Colha, Belize. In White (ed.): 83–100.

Sheets, Payson. 1992. *The Ceren Site.* Harcourt Brace Jovanovich College Publishers, Fort Worth.

—. 2000. The Southeast Frontiers of Mesoamerica. In Adams and MacLeod (eds.): 407–448.

—. 2001. Cerén. *AAMCA*: 110–112.

—. (ed.). 2002. *Before the Volcano Erupted: The Ancient Ceren Village in Central America.* U. of Texas Press, Austin.

Shepard, A. O. 1948. *Plumbate: A Mesoamerican Tradeware.* Carnegie Institution of Washington, Publication No. 573, Washington, D.C.

Shook, Edwin M., and A. V. Kidder. 1952. Mound E-III-3, Kaminaljuyú, Guatemala. *Carnegie Institution of Washington, Contributions to American Anthropology and History* 53: 33–127.

Sidrys, Raymond, and Rainer Berger. 1979. Lowland Maya radiocarbon dates and the classic Maya collapse. *Nature* 277: 269–274.

Siller, Juan Antonio. 1984. Presencia de elementos arquitectónicos teotihuacanoides en occident: Tingambato, Michoacán. *Cuadernos de Arquitectura Mesoamérica* No. 2: 60–61.

Silverstein, Jay. 2001. Aztec imperialism at Oztumba, Guerrero: Aztec-colonial relations during the late Postclassic and early colonial periods. *AM* 12: 31–48.

Smith, A. Ledyard. 1965. Architecture of the Guatemalan Highlands. *HMAI* 2: I: 76–94.

Smith, Bruce D. 1995. *The Emergence of Agriculture.* Scientific American Library, New York.

Smith, Mary Elizabeth. 1973. *Picture Writing from Ancient Southern Mexico: Mixtec Place Signs and Maps.* U. of Oklahoma Press, Norman.

Smith, Michael E. 1984. The Aztlan Migrations of the Nahuatl Chronicles: Myth or History? *Ethnohistory* 31: 153–186.

—. 1996. The strategic provinces. In *Aztec Imperial Strategies*, by F. F. Berdan, R. E. Blanton *et al.*: 137–150. Dumbarton Oaks, Washington, D.C.

Smith, Michael E. 1998. *The Aztecs.* Blackwell Publishers, Oxford.

Smith, Michael E. and Frances F. Berdan. 1996. Appendix 4: Province descriptions. In *Aztec Imperial Strategies*, by F. F. Berdan, R. E. Blanton *et al.*: 265–349. Dumbarton Oaks, Washington, D.C.

—. and — (eds.). 2003. *The Postclassic Mesoamerican World.* U. of Utah Press Salt Lake City.

Smith, Michael E., Cynthia Heath-Smith, and Lisa Montiel. 1999. Excavations of Aztec urban houses at Yautepec, Mexico. *LAA* 10: 133–150.

Smith, Michael E. and T. Jeffrey Price. 1994. Aztec-Period Agricultural Terraces in Morelos, Mexico. *JFA* 21: 169–179.

Smith, Virginia G. 1984. *Izapa Relief Carving: Form, Content, Rules for Design, and Role in Mesoamerican Art History and Archaeology.* DOSPCAA 27.

—. 2000. The iconography of power at Xochicalco: The Pyramid of the Plumed Serpents. In Hirth (ed.): II: 57–82. The U. of Utah Press, Salt Lake City.

Smyth, Michael P. 2001. Uxmal. *AAMCA*: 793–796.

Smyth, M. P., C. D. Dore, and N. P. Dunning. 1995. Interpreting prehistoric settlement patterns: lessons from the Maya center of Sayil, Yucatan. *Journal of Field Archaeology* 22: 321–347.

Smyth, M. P., J. Ligorred P., D. Ortegon Z., and P. Farrell. 1998. An Early Classic Center in the Puuc Region: New Data from Chac II, Yucatan, Mexico. *AncM* 9: 233–257.

Snow, Dean R. 1996. Ceramic sequences and settlement location in prehispanic Tlaxcala. In *Antología de Tlaxcala*, Vol. 1: 131–159. INAH, Mexico City.

Solanes, María del Carmen, and Enrique Vela. 1993. Archaeological zones. In *The Huastec and Totonac World*, María Teresa Franco y González Salas (eds.): 148–165. Editorial Jilguero, Mexico City.

Solís, Felipe. 1993. Huastec country. In *The Huastec and Totonac World*, María Teresa Franco y González Salas (eds.): 42–61. Jilguero, Mexico City.

—. 1993. Peoples and cultures in the Totonacapan region. In *The Huastec and Totonac World*, María Teresa Franco y González Salas (eds.): 64–85. Editorial Jilguero, Mexico City.

Spence, Michael W. 1974. Residential Practices and the Distribution of Skeletal Traits in Teotihuacan, Mexico. *Man* 9: 262–273.

Spencer, Charles. 1982. *The Cuicatlán Cañada and Monte Albán: A Study of Primary State Formation.* Academic Press, New York.

Spencer, Charles, and Elsa Redmond. 1997. *Archaeology of the Cañada de Cuicatlán.* Anthropological Papers of the American Museum of Natural History, No. 80.

—. and —. 2001. Multilevel selection and political evolution in the Valley of Oaxaca, 500–100 B. C. *JAA* 20: 195–229.

Spores, Ronald. 1984. *The Mixtecs in Ancient and Colonial Times.* U. of Oklahoma Press, Norman.

Stark, Barbara L. 1981. The rise of sedentary life. In *Handbook of Middle American Indians, Supplement: Archaeology*: 345–372. U. of Texas Press, Austin.

—. 1997. Gulf lowland ceramic styles and political geography in ancient Veracruz. In Stark and Arnold (eds.): 278–309.

—. 2001. Gulf lowlands: South central region. *AAMCA*: 334–340.

—. (ed.). 1991. *Settlement Archaeology of Cerro de las Mesas, Veracruz, Mexico.* Monograph 34, Institute of Archaeology, U. of California, Los Angeles.

Stark, Barbara L., and Philip J. Arnold III (eds.). 1997. *Olmec to Aztec: Settlement Patterns in the Ancient Gulf Lowlands.* U. of Arizona Press, Tucson.

—. and —. 1997. Introduction to the archaeology of the Gulf lowlands. In Stark and Arnold (eds.): 3–32.

Stark, Barbara L., Lynette Heller, and Michael A. Ohnersorgen. 1998. People with cloth: Mesoamerican economic change from the perspective of cotton in South-Central Veracruz. *LAA* 9: 7–36.

Stephens, John Lloyd. 1969 [1841]. *Incidents of Travel in Central America, Chiapas and Yucatan.* 2 vols. Dover, New York.

—. 1991 [1841]. *Incidents of Travel in Yucatan.* Editorial San Fernando,

Mérida, Mexico.
Steward, Julian H. 1955. *Theory of Culture Change*. U. of Illinois Press, Urbana.
Stirling, Matthew. 1943. Stone Monuments of Southern Veracruz. *Bureau of American Ethnology*, Bulletin No. 138.
Stirling, Matthew W., and Marion Stirling. 1942. Finding Jewels of Jade in the Mexican Swamp. *National Geographic* 82: 635–661.
Stone, Andrea. 2002. Spirals, ropes and feathers: The iconography of rubber balls in Mesoamerican art. *AncM* 13: 21–39.
Stone, Doris. 1972 and 1976. *Pre-Columbian Man Finds Central America*. Peabody Museum Press, Cambridge.
Storey, Rebecca. 1992. *Life and Death in the Ancient City of Teotihuacan: A Paleodemographic Synthesis*. The U. of Alabama Press, Tuscaloosa.
Stresser-Péan, Guy. 1977. *San Antonio Nogalar*. Etudes Mesoamericaines III, Mission Archeologique et Etnologique Française au Mexique, Mexico City.
Stuart, David. 2000. 'The arrival of strangers': Teotihuacan and Tollan in Classic Maya History. In Carrasco *et al.* (eds.): 465–513.
Stuart, George E. 1992. Mural masterpieces of ancient Cacaxtla. National Geographic 182 (3): 120–136.
—. 1993. New light on the Olmec. *National Geographic* 184: 88–115.
Sugiura Yamamoto, Yoko. 2000. Cultural lacustre y sociedad del valle de Toluca. *AncM* Vol. 7, No. 43: 32–37.
Sugiura, Yoko. 2001. Toluca region. *AAMCA*: 763–766.
Sugiyama, Saburo. 1992. Rulership, warfare, and human sacrifice at the Ciudadela: An iconographic study of Feathered Serpent representations. In Berlo (ed.): 205–230.
—. 1993. Worldview Materialized in Teotihuacan, Mexico. *LAA* 4: 103–129.
—. 1998. Termination programs and prehispanic looting at the Feathered Serpent Pyramid in Teotihuacan, Mexico. In *The Sowing and the Dawning. Termination, Dedication, and Transformation in the Archaeological and Ethnographic Record of Mesoamerica*, Shirley B. Mock (eds.): 147–164. U. of New Mexico Press, Albuquerque.
Suhler, Charles, Traci Ardren, and David Johnstone. 1998. The chronology of Yaxuna: evidence from excavation and ceramics. *AncM* 9: 167–182.
Sullivan, Thelma D. 1982. Tlazolteotl-Ixcuina: The Great Spinner and Weaver. In *The Art and Iconography of Late Post-Classic Central Mexico*, Elizabeth H. Boone (ed.): 7–35. Dumbarton Oaks, Washington, D.C.
Symonds, Stacey. 2000. The ancient landscape at San Lorenzo Tenochtitlan, Veracruz, Mexico: settlement and nature. In Clark and Pye (eds.): 54–73.
Taladoire, Eric. 1994. El juego de pelota precolombino. *AncM* 2: 9: 6–15.
Tapia, Andrés de. 1963 [c. 1534]. The chronicle of Andrés de Tapia. In *The Conquistadores*, Patricia de Fuentes (ed. and trans.): 19–48. The Orion Press, New York.
Tarkanian, Michael J., and Dorothy Hosler. 2000. La elaboración de hule en Mesoamérica. *AncM* 8: 44: 54–57.
Tate, Carolyn E. 1992. *Yaxchilan: The Design of a Maya Ceremonial City*. U. of Texas Press, Austin.
—. 1999. Patrons of shamanic power: La Venta's supernatural entities in light of Mixe beliefs. *AncM* 10: 169–188.
Taube, Karl A. 1992a. The iconography of mirrors at Teotihuacan. In Berlo (ed.): 169–204.
—. 1992b. The Major Gods of Ancient Yucatán. Dumbarton Oaks Studies in Pre-Columbian Art & Archaeology Number 32. Dumbarton Oaks, Washington, D.C.
—. 1995. The Rainmakers: The Olmec and their contribution to Mesoamerican belief and ritual. In Coe *et al.*: 82–103.
—. 2000. *The Writing System of Ancient Teotihuacan*. Ancient America 1. Center for Ancient American Studies, Barnardsville, N.C., and Washington, D.C.
—. 2002. La serpiente emplumada en Teotihuacan. *AncM* 9: 53: 36–41.
Thomas, Hugh. 1995. *Conquest: Montezuma, Cortés, and the Fall of Old Mexico.* Simon and Schuster, New York.
Thompson, J. Eric S. 1970. *Maya History and Religion*. U. of Oklahoma Press, Norman.
Tichy, Franz. 1976. Orientación de las Pirámides e Iglesias en el Altiplano Mexicano. *Comunicaciones Proyecto Puebla-Tlaxcala*, Suplemento IV. Fundación Alemana para la Investigación Científica, Puebla, Mexico.
Tolstoy, Paul. 1989. Coapexco and Tlatilco: sites with Olmec materials in the Basin of Mexico. In *Regional Perspectives on the Olmec*, Robert J. Sharer and David C. Grove (eds.): 85–121. Cambridge U. Press, New York.
Tolstoy, Paul, and Suzanne K. Fish. 1975. Surface and Subsurface Evidence for Community Size at Coapexco, Mexico. *Journal of Field Archaeology* 2: 97–104.
—. 1978. Western Mesoamerica before A.D. 900. In *Chronologies in New World Archaeology*, R. E. Taylor and C. W. Meighan (eds.): 241–284. Academic Press, New York.
Tolstoy, P., S. K. Fish, M. W. Boksenbaum, K. B. Vaughn, and C. E. Smith. 1977. Early Sedentary Communities of the Basin of Mexico. *Journal of Field Archaeology* 4: 91–107.
Tourtellot, G., and J. A. Sabloff. 1994. Puuc Development as seen from Sayil. In *Hidden Among the Hills: Maya Archaeology of the Northwest Yucatan Peninsula*, H. J. Prem (ed.): 71–92. Verlag von Flemming, Mockmuhl.
Townsend, Richard F. (ed.). 1998. *Ancient West Mexico: Art and Archaeology of the Unknown Past*. The Art Institute of Chicago, Chicago.
—. 2000. *The Aztecs*. Thames & Hudson, London and New York.
Tozzer, Alfred M. 1921. Excavation of a site at Santiago Ahuitzotla, D.F. Mexico. *Smithsonian Institution Bureau of American Ethnology* Bulletin 74.
Traxler, Loa P. 2001. Royal court of Early Classic Copán. In Inomata and Houston (eds.): 46–73.
Turner, Christy G. II and Jacqueline A. Turner. 1999. Man Corn: Cannibalism and Violence in the Prehistoric American Southwest. U. of Utah Press, Salt Lake City.
Umberger, Emily. 1996. Aztec presence and material remains in the outer provinces. In *Aztec Imperial Strategies*, by F. F. Berdan, R. E. Blanton *et al.*: 151–179. Dumbarton Oaks, Washington, D.C.
Urban, P. A., and E. M. Schortman (eds.) *The Southeast Maya Periphery*. U. of Texas Press, Austin.
Urcid, Javier. 2001. Zapotec Hieroglyphic Writing. *Studies in Pre-Columbian Art & Archaeology* No. 34. Dumbarton Oaks, Washington, D.C.
Vaillant, George C. 1931. Excavations at Ticoman. *American Museum of Natural History, Anthropological Papers* 32 No. 2.
Vaillant, George C., and William T. Sanders. 2000. Excavations at Chiconautla. In *The Teotihuacan Valley Project Final Report Volume 5 The Aztec Period Occupation of the Valley Part 2 – Excavations at T.A. 40 and Related Projects*, William T. Sanders and Susan Toby Evans (eds.): 757–787. Occasional Papers in Anthropology Number 26. Department of Anthropology, The Pennsylvania State U., University Park.
Vaillant, Suzannah B., and George C. Vaillant. 1934. Excavations at Gualupita. *American Museum of Natural History, Anthropological Papers* 35 No. 1.
Valadez Azúa, Raúl, Blanca Paredes Gudiño, and Bernardo Rodríguez Galicia. 1999. Entierros de perros descubiertos en la antigua ciudad de Tula. *LAA* 10: 180–200.
Veblen, Thorstein. 1953. *The Theory of the Leisure Class*. New American Library, New York.
Velázquez Morlet, Adriana. 2000. El juego de pelota de Chichén Itzá. *AncM* 8: 44: 46–47.
Vitebsky, Piers. 1995. *The Shaman*. 1st American ed. Little, Brown, Boston.
Vivó Escoto, Jorge A. 1964. Weather and Climate of Mexico and Central America. *HMAI* 1: 187–215.
von Nagy, Christopher. 1997. The geoarchaeology of settlement in the Grijalva delta. In Stark and Arnold (eds.): 253–277.
von Winning, Hasso. 1960. Further examples of figurines on wheels

from Mexico. *Ethnos* 1–2: 63–72.

Voorhies, Barbara. 1989a. A Model of the Pre-Aztec Political System of the Soconusco. In *Ancient Trade and Tribute: Economies of the Soconusco Region of Mesoamerica*, Barbara Voorhies (ed.): 95–129. U. of Utah Press, Salt Lake City.

—. 1989b. Settlement patterns in the western Soconusco: Methods of site recovery and dating results. In Bové and Heller (eds.): 103–124.

—. (ed.). 1989. *Ancient Trade and Tribute: Economies of the Soconusco Region of Mesoamerica*. U. of Utah Press, Salt Lake City.

Wagner, Philip L. 1964. Natural Vegetation of Middle America. In *HMAI* I: 216–264.

Weaver, Muriel Porter. 1993. *The Aztecs, Maya, and Their Predecessors*. Academic Press, New York.

Webster, David L. 1976. *Defensive Earthworks at Becan, Campeche, Mexico, Implications for Maya Warfare*. Middle American Research Institute, Publication 41. Tulane U., New Orleans.

—. 1977. Warfare and the Evolution of Maya Civilization. In *The Origins of Maya Civilization*, R.E.W. Adams (ed.): 335–372. U. of New Mexico Press, Albuquerque.

Webster, David L. 1998. Classic Maya Architecture: Implications and comparisons. In Houston (ed.): 5–47.

—. 2001. Spatial dimensions of Maya courtly life. In Inomata and Houston (eds.): I: 130–167.

—. 2002. *The Fall of the Ancient Maya*. Thames & Hudson, London and New York.

Webster, David, AnnCorinne Freter, and Nancy Gonlin. 2000. *Copán: The Rise and Fall of an Ancient Maya Civilization*. Harcourt College Publishers, Ft. Worth.

Webster, David L., Susan Toby Evans, and William T. Sanders. 1993. *Out of the Past: An Introduction to Archaeology*. Mayfield Publishing Co., Mountain View.

Weigand, Phil C. 1996. The architecture of the Teuchitlán tradition of the Occidente of Mesoamerica. *AncM* 7: 91–101.

—. 2001. West Mexico. *AAMCA*: 818–824.

Weigand, Phil C., and Christopher S. Beekman. 1998. The Teuchitlán Tradition. Rise of a statelike society. In Townsend (ed.): 34–51.

West, Robert C., and John P. Augelli. 1989. *Middle America: Its Land and Peoples*. Prentice Hall, Englewood Cliffs.

Whalen, Michael E., and Paul E. Minnis. 1996. Ball courts and political centralization in the Casas Grandes region. *American Antiquity* 61: 732–746.

Wheeler Pires-Ferreira, Jane. 1976. Shell and iron-ore mirror exchange in Formative Mesoamerica, with comments on other commodities. In Flannery (ed.): 311–328.

White, Christine D. (ed.). 1999. *Reconstructing Ancient Maya Diet*. U. of Utah Press, Salt Lake City.

Whitley, David S., and Marilyn P. Beaudry. 1989. Chiefs on the coast: Developing chiefdoms in the Tiquisate Region in ethnographic perspective. In Bové and Heller (eds.): 101–119.

Whitmore, Thomas M. 1992. Disease and Death in Early Colonial Mexico: Simulating Amerindian Depopulation. *Dellplain Latin American Studies*, No. 28. Westview, Boulder.

Widmer, Randolph J., and Rebecca Storey. 1993. Social organization and household structure of a Teotihuacan apartment compound: S3 W 1:33 of the Tlajinga Barrio. In Santley and Hirth (eds.): 87–104.

Wilkerson, S. Jeffrey K. 1973. An archaeological sequence from Santa Luisa, Veracruz, Mexico. *Contributions of the U. of California Archaeological Research Facility* 13: 37–50.

—. 1983. So green and like a garden. In *Drained Field Agriculture in Central and South America*, J. P. Darch (ed.). BAR International Series 189, Oxford.

—. 1987. *El Tajín. A Guide for Visitors*. Universidad Veracruzana, Xalapa.

—. 1994. The garden city of El Pital. *National Geographic Research and Exploration* 10: 56–71.

—. 2001a. El Tajín: Art and artifacts, chronology, and religion and ideology. *AAMCA*: 693–698.

—. 2001b. Gulf lowlands: north central region. *AAMCA*: 324–329.

—. 2001c. Gulf lowlands: north region. *AAMCA*: 329–334.

—. 2001d. Las Higueras. *AAMCA*: 345–346.

Willey, Gordon R. 1984. A Summary of the Archaeology of Lower Central America. In *The Archaeology of Lower Central America*, Frederick W. Lange and Doris Z. Stone (eds.): 341–378. U. of New Mexico Press, Albuquerque.

—. 1966. *An Introduction to American Archaeology, Volume 1, North and Middle America*. Prentice Hall, Englewood Cliffs, NJ.

Willey, Gordon R., and Philip Phillips. 1958. *Method and Theory in American Archaeology*. U. of Chicago Press, Chicago.

Willey, Gordon R., and Jeremy A. Sabloff. 1974. *A History of American Archaeology*. W.H. Freeman and Co., San Francisco.

Williams, Barbara J., and H. R. Harvey. 1988. Content, Provenience, and Significance of the Codex Vergara and the Códice de Santa María Asunción. *American Antiquity* 53: 337–351.

—. and —. *The Códice de Santa María Asunción. Facsimile and Commentary: Households and Lands in Sixteeth-Century Tepetlaoztoc*. U. of Utah Press, Salt Lake City.

Williams, Eduardo. 1992. Sacred stones: Shamanism and sculpture in ancient West Mexico. In *Ancient America: Contributions to New World Archaeology*, N.J. Saunders (ed.): 65–73. Oxford, Oxbow Monograph 24.

Wingard, John D. 1996. Interactions between demographic processes and soil resources in the Copán Valley, Honduras. In Fedick (ed.): 207–223.

Winter, Marcus. 1976a. Differential patterns of community growth in Oaxaca. In Flannery (ed.): 227–234.

—. 1976b. The archaeological household cluster in the Valley of Oaxaca. In Flannery (ed.): 25–31.

—. 1984. Exchange in Formative highland Oaxaca. In Hirth (ed.): 179–214.

Witmore, Christopher L. 1998. Sacred sun centers. In Townsend (ed.): 136–149.

Wolf, Eric. 1959. *Sons of the Shaking Earth*. U. of Chicago Press, Chicago.

Wolfman, Dan. 1990. Mesoamerican chronology and archaeomagnetic dating, A.D. 1—1200. In *Archaeomagnetic Dating*, J. L. Eighmy and R. S. Sternberg (eds.): 261–308. The U. of Arizona Press, Tucson.

Wonderley, Anthony W. 1991. The Late Preclassic Sula Plain, Honduras. In Fowler (ed.): 143–169.

Woodbury, Richard B., and James A. Neely. 1972. Water control systems of the Tehuacán Valley. In *The Prehistory of the Tehuacán Valley, Vol 4: Chronology and Irrigation*, F. Johnson (ed.): 81–153. U. of Texas Press, Austin.

Woot-Tsuen, Wu Leung, with the cooperation of Felix Busson and Claude Jardin. 1968. Food composition table for use in Africa. U.S. Dept. of Health, Education, and Welfare, Nutrition Program, and Food Consumption and Planning Branch, Food and Agriculture Organization of the United Nations.

Woot-Tsuen, Wu Leung, with the cooperation of M. Flores. 1961. Food Composition Table for Use in Latin America. Interdepartmental Committee on Nutrition for National Defense and The Institute of Nutrition of Central America and Panama, Bethesda, Maryland, and Guatemala City.

Wright, H. E. 1991. Environmental conditions for Paleoindian immigrations. In *The First Americans*, Tom D. Dillehay and David J. Meltzer (eds.): 113–135. CRC Press, Boca Raton.

Zeitlin, Judith F. 1993. The politics of Classic-period ritual interaction: iconography of the ballgame cult in coastal Oaxaca. *AncM* 4: 121–140.

Zeitlin, Robert N. 1993. Pacific coastal Laguna Zope. A regional center in the Terminal Formative hinterlands of Monte Albán. *AncM* 4: 85–101.

—. 2001. Oaxaca and Tehuantepec regions. *AAMCA*: 537–546.

Zeitlin, Robert N., and Judith Francis Zeitlin. 2000. The Paleoindian and Archaic cultures of Mesoamerica. In Adams and MacLeod (eds.): 45–121.

Zorita, Alonso de. 1994 [1566–1570]. *Life and Labor in Ancient Mexico: the Brief and Summary Relations of the Lords of New Spain*. Translated and with an introduction by Benjamin Keen. U. of Oklahoma Press, Norman.

SOURCES OF ILLUSTRATIONS

Frontispiece David Drew. **1.1** Marquina 1951. **1.2** Drawing ML Design. **1.3** Drawing ML Design. **1.4** *clockwise from top* Baghdad Museum, Iraq. Photo Hirmer; Qin Terra-cotta Museum, Lintong, Shaanxi Province, China; Museum of Pakistan, Karachi; Agyptisches Museum und Papyrussammlung, Berlin; Museum fur Volkerkunde, Munich; Photo David Webster. **1.5** Drawing Frederick Catherwood. **1.6** Table based on Webster, Evans, and Sanders 1993: 160–161. **1.7** Photo Joyce Marcus and Kent V. Flannery. **1.8** Drawing Courtesy New World Archaeological Foundation. Illustration Ayax Moreno. **1.9** Table based on Nicholson 1971 and Ortiz de Montellano 1990: 40–41. **1.10** Museo Nacional de Antropología, Mexico. **1.11** American Museum of Natural History, New York. **1.12** Photo Jorge Pérez de Lara. **1.13** Photo ffotograff © N. C Turner. **1.14** Drawing René Millon. **1.15** Museo Arqueologico de Teotihuacan. **1.16** Photo Mary Ellen Miller. 1.17 Photo David Drew. **1.18** Photo Irmgard Groth-Kimball © Thames & Hudson Ltd, London. **1.19** Great Temple Project. **1.20** Great Temple Project. **1.21** Great Temple Project. **2.1** Drawing ML Design after West and Augelli Fig. 2.11. **2.2** Museo Nacional de Antropología, Mexico. **2.3** Drawing ML Design. **2.4** Diagram Susan Toby Evans. **2.5** Drawing Susan Toby Evans. **2.6** Drawing ML Design. **2.7** Drawing Drazen Tomic after Patrick F. Gallagher in Wolf 1959: 7. **2.8** Table Susan Toby Evans. **2.9** Dumbarton Oaks Research Library and Collections, Washington, D.C. **2.10** Drawing after J. D. Jennings, 1968. **2.11** Photo The Art Archive/National Anthropological Museum, Mexico/Dagli Orti. **2.12** Photo Irmgard Groth-Kimball © Thames & Hudson Ltd, London. **3.1** Drawing ML Design. **3.2** Drawing Drazen Tomic after Garber 2001: 302; and after Webster *et al.* 1993: 42. **3.3** After Ensminger 1994, V. 1; Pennington and Church 1985; Woot-Tsuen and Busson and Jardin 1968; Woot-Tsuen and Flores 1961. **3.4** *Codex Magliabechiano*. **3.5** Photo Susan Toby Evans. **3.6** *Codex Florentine*. **3.7** Photo Joyce Marcus and Kent V. Flannery. **3.8** Drawing Joyce Marcus and Kent V. Flannery. **3.9** Drawing Drazen Tomic after Coe and Flannery 1964. **3.10** Drawing ML Design after Rathje and Schiffer 1982: 23, Fig. 2–3; MacNeish 1967, Fig. 186. **3.11** Robert S. Peabody Foundation for Archaeology, Phillips Academy, Andover, Massachusetts. **3.12** Photo Christine Niederberger. **3.13** Photo Joyce Marcus and Kent V. Flannery. **3.14** Drawing Drazen Tomic after Michaels and Voorhies 1999: 41, Fig. 3. **3.15** Drawing after Stone 1972. **4.1** Drawing ML Design. **4.2** Anonymous loan to The Art Museum, Princeton University. **4.3** Courtesy New World Archaeological Foundation. Drawing Ayax Moreno. **4.4** Drawing after Kidder, Jennings, and Shook 1946. **4.5** Drawing Drazen Tomic after Clark 1991: 24, Fig. 8. **4.6** Drawing Joyce Marcus and Kent V. Flannery. **4.7** Courtesy New World Archaeological Foundation. Drawing Ayax Moreno. **4.8** After Clark 2001. **4.9** Photo Napoleon A. Chagnon. **4.10** Drawing Drazen Tomic after Clark and Salcedo 1989: 16, Fig. 1.1. **4.11** Drawing after Hill et al 1998. **4.12** Photo Michael Tarkanian. **4.13** *Codex Florentine*. **4.14** Drawing Drazen Tomic after Minc 2001; Frierman 1969: 80; Sempowski and Spence 1994: 453; Weaver 1993. **4.15** Drawing Drazen Tomic after Marcus and Flannery 1996. **4.16** Drawing Joyce Marcus and Kent V. Flannery. **4.17** Drawing Joyce Marcus and Kent V. Flannery. **4.18** Drawing Drazen Tomic. **5.1** Drawing ML Design. **5.2** Peabody Museum of Archaeology and Ethnology, Harvard University. **5.3** Museo Nacional de Antropología, Mexico City. **5.4** Museo Nacional de Antropología, Mexico City. **5.5** Photo Irmgard Groth-Kimball © Thames & Hudson Ltd, London. **5.6** Photo Michel Zabé. **5.7** Drawing ML Design after Diehl and Coe 1996: 13, Fig. 5. **5.8** Photo Ann Cyphers. **5.9** Museo de Antropología de Xalapa, Universidad Veracruzana. Photo Adrian Mendieta Pérez. **5.10** Photo Kenneth Garrett/National Geographic Image Collection. **5.11** Photo Kenneth Garrett. **5.12** Photo Irmgard Groth-Kimball © Thames & Hudson Ltd, London. **5.13** Drawing David S. Merrill and Drazen Tomic. **5.14** Drawing Felipe Dávalos Gonzalez/National Geographic Image Collection. **5.15** Drawing Drazen Tomic after Marcus and Flannery 1996. **5.16** Photo Joyce Marcus and Kent V. Flannery. **5.17** Drawing Joyce Marcus and Kent V. Flannery. **5.18** Drawing Joyce Marcus and Kent V. Flannery. **5.19** Drawing Joyce Marcus and Kent V. Flannery. **5.20** Drawing Drazen Tomic after Renfrew and Bahn, 3rd edition 2000: 379. **5.21** The Metropolitan Museum of Art, The Michael C. Rockefeller Memorial Collection, Bequest of Nelson A. Rockefeller, 1979. (1979.206.1134). **5.22** Photo Michael D.Coe. **5.23** Drawing from M. N. Porter Tlatilco and the Pre-Classic Cultures of the New World. **5.24** Drawing Miguel Covarrubias. **5.25** Photo Michel Zabé. **5.26** Photo Irmgard Groth-Kimball © Thames & Hudson Ltd, London. **5.27** Museo Nacional de Antropología, Mexico. **5.28** British Museum, London. **5.29** Drawing Drazen Tomic after Gigi Bayliss in Weigand and Beekman 1998: 36, Fig. 2. **5.30** Drawing Gigi Bayliss. **5.31** Drawing Drazen Tomic after Martínez DonJuán 1995. **5.32** Drawing Drazen Tomic. **6.1** Drawing ML Design. **6.2** Dallas Museum of Art, Dallas Art Association Purchase. **6.3** The Art Museum, Princeton University, Museum purchase. **6.4** The Metropolitan Museum of Art, Anonymous loan. **6.5** Drawing Christine Niederberger. **6.6** Photo Leonard Lee Rule III. **6.7** Courtesy New World Archaeological Foundation. Drawing Ayax Moreno. **6.8** Drawing Dumbarton Oaks Research Library and Collections, Washington, D.C. **6.9** Photo Courtesy New World Archaeological Foundation. **6.10** Photo David C. Grove. **6.11** Drawing after Michael D. Coe The Jaguar's Children: Pre-Classic Central Mexico. **6.12** Photo Michel Zabé. **6.13** Drawing Joyce Marcus and Kent V. Flannery. **6.14** Drawing Drazen Tomic after Michael Love 1991: 58, Fig. 6. **6.15** Drawing Drazen Tomic after Rebecca González Lauck in González Lauck 1996: 74, Fig. 1. **6.16** Drawing Richard Cavallin-Cosma. **6.17** Drawing Muriel Porter Weaver 1993. **6.18** Drawing Felipe Dávalos/National Geographic Image Collection. **6.19** Photo Jorge Pérez de Lara. **6.20** Photo Courtesy New World Archaeological Foundation. **6.21** Drawing Courtesy Dr Norman Hammond. **6.22** Playa de Los Muertos figurine. **6.23** Drawing Drazen Tomic after Dixon *et al.* 1994. **7.1** Drawing Stanley H. Boggs. **7.2** Drawing Barbara W. Fash, after Grove 1996. **7.3** Drawing ML Design. **7.4** Drawing Joyce Marcus and Kent V. Flannery. **7.5** Drawing Drazen Tomic after Marcus and Flannery 1996. **7.6** Drawing Drazen Tomic after Marcus and Flannery 1996. **7.7** Table based on Adams 1997: 302; Marcus and Flannery 1996: 20. **7.8** Photo Irmgard Groth-Kimball © Thames & Hudson Ltd, London. **7.9** Danzante sculpture. **7.10** Danzante sculpture. **7.11** *Florentine Codex*. **7.12** *Florentine Codex*. **7.13** Drawing Susan Toby Evans. **7.14** Drawing ML Design after Bové 1989: Figs 4.6, 4.7, 4.9, 4.11. **7.15** After Stone 1976. **7.16** After Stone 1976. **7.17** Drawing after Shook and Kidder 1952. **8.1** Drawing ML Design after McBride 1969. **8.2** Drawing Drazen Tomic. **8.3** Drawing Susan Toby Evans after Marquina 1951. **8.4** Matson Museum of Anthropology, Pennsylvania State University. **8.5** Dumbarton Oaks Research Library and Collections, Washington, D.C. **8.6** Drawing courtesy Beatriz C. Braniff. **8.7** Drawing ML Design after Porter 1956: 524, Map 3. **8.8** Drawing from Porter 1956. **8.9** *Florentine Codex*. **8.10** Drawing Drazen Tomic after Fowler 1968. **8.11** Drawing Angel García Cook 1973. **8.12** Drawing Angel García Cook 1973. **8.13** After Drennan, 1978. **8.14** After Spencer and Redmond 1997. **8.15** Spencer 1982. **8.16** Drawing Drazen Tomic after Acosta 1965. **8.17** Courtesy New World Archaeological Foundation. Drawing Ayax Moreno. **8.18** Drawing Stirling 1943. **8.19** Drawing ML Design. **8.20** After Lowe 1962. **8.21** Drawing from Sharer 1994. **8.22** Photo Marion Hatch. **8.23** Photo Michael D.Coe. **8.24** Drawing from Sharer 1994. **8.25** Drawing T. W. Rutledge. **8.26** Drawing from Sharer 1994. **8.27** Drawing T. W. Rutledge. **8.28** Drawing by Linda Schele, © David Schele, courtesy Foundation for the Advancement of Mesoamerican Studies, Inc. **8.29** Drawing Drazen Tomic after Scarborough 1994: 190. **9.1** Drawing ML Design. **9.2** Drawing Drazen Tomic after Sharer 1994:

183, Fig. 4.27. **9.3** Drawing George Stuart. **9.4** Drawing Joyce Marcus and Kent V. Flannery. **9.5** Drawing Drazen Tomic after Marcus and Flannery 1996: 176–177, Fig. 199. **9.6** Drawing Drazen Tomic after Manzanilla López and Talavera González 1993: 109. **9.7** Drawing Drazen Tomic after Weigand and Beekman 1998: 45, Fig. 16. **9.8** Drawing Drazen Tomic after Gabriela Ulloa. **9.9** Drawing Gabriela Ulloa. **9.10** Drawing Gabriela Ulloa. **9.11** Photo Richard Townsend. **9.12** Photo Huitzilapa Project. **9.13** Yale University Art Gallery. **9.14** Photo Patricia Plunket. **9.15** Marquina 1951. **9.16** Drawing Drazen Tomic after Marquina 1999 (1951): 121, Lám: 36. **9.17** Drawing Drazen Tomic after Wilkerson 1994: 62, Fig. 9. **9.18** Drawing Drazen Tomic. **9.19** After G. Kubler. **9.20** Photo Susan Toby Evans. **9.21** Proyecto Templo de Quetzalcoatl 1988–1989. Drawn by Oralia Cabrera. **9.22** Façade of the temple, Pyramid of the Feathered Serpent. **9.23** Drawing Drazen Tomic after Magda Juarez. **9.24** Dumbarton Oaks Library and Collections, Washington D. C. **10.1** Drawing ML Design. **10.2** Drawing René Millon 1972. **10.3** CNCA-INAH-MEX, Centro de Investigaciones Arqueologicas de Teotihuacan. **10.4** Drawing Oralia Cabrera, modified from Plan 104 of the Proyecto Arqueologico de Teotihuacan 1980–1982. **10.5** View of Teotihuacan looking north. **10.6** Drawing ML Design after Morelos García 1993, Plan p.5. **10.7** Drawing Susan Toby Evans after Oralia Cabrera, modified from Plan 104 of the Proyecto Arqueolgico Teotihuacan 1980–1982. **10.8** Drawing René Millon 1972. **10.9** Museo Nacional de Antropología, Mexico City. **10.10** Fine Arts Museum of San Francisco/ Gift of Jack Tanzer, 1986.74, San Francisco, CA. **10.11** Photo Whitestar. **10.12** Drawing Drazen Tomic. **10.13** From Webster *et al.* 1993: 275, Fig. 8.8. **10.14** From Webster *et al.* 1993: 275, Fig. 8.7. **10.15** Photo Michel Zabé. **10.16** Photo Michel Zabé. **10.17** The Saint Louis Art Museum, Gift of Mr and Mrs George K Conant, Jr. **10.18** Drawing Drazen Tomic after Cabrera Castro 1996: Fig. 8. **10.19** Drawing Ruben Cabrera Castro. **10.20** Photo Whitestar. **10.21** Photo Whitestar. 10.22 Photo Whitestar. **10.23** Drawing Michael Alexander Guran, project architect. **10.24** Photo Jorge Pérez de Lara. 10.25 Drawing Covarrubias 1961. **10.26** Drawing Joyce Marcus and Kent V. Flannery. **10.27** Drawing Joyce Marcus and Kent V. Flannery. **10.28** Drawing Joyce Marcus and Kent V. Flannery. **10.29** Drawing Joyce Marcus and Kent V. Flannery. **10.30** Photo Jorge Pérez de Lara. **10.31** Séjourné 1984. **10.32** Photo Michel Zabé. **11.1** Drawing ML Design. **11.2** Drawing Drazen Tomic. **11.3** University of Pennsylvania Museum. **11.4** Table Susan Toby Evans. **11.5** Table based on Martin and Grube 2000. **11.6** From Martin and Grube 2000. **11.7** Drawing by Linda Schele, © David Schele, courtesy Foundation for the Advancement of Mesoamerican Studies, Inc. **11.8** Photo David Drew. **11.9** Drawing G. Kubler adapted from drawings by Tatania Prouskouriakoff. **11.10** Table based on Martin and Grube 2000. **11.11** Table based on Martin and Grube 2000. **11.12** Drawing Philip Winton after Ian Graham. **11.13** Table based on Martin and Grube 2000. **11.14** Drawing Michael D. Coe. **11.15** Rollout photograph K1185 © Justin Kerr. **11.16** Table based on Martin and Grube 2000. **11.17** British Museum, London. **11.18** Photo Simon Martin. **11.19** Drawing Drazen Tomic after Dull, Southon, and Sheets 2001: 33–34. **11.20** Drawing Drazen Tomic after Sheets 2001: 111. **11.21** Peabody Museum, Harvard University. **11.22** Drawing Drazen Tomic after Smith 1965. **11.23** Table based on Martin and Grube 2000. **12.1** Drawing ML Design. **12.2** Drawing Philip Winton after Carr and Hazard. **12.3** Drawing Philip Winton after Simon Martin. **12.4** Photo Nicholas Hellmuth. **12.5** Photo Henri Stierlin. **12.6** Drawing Christopher A. Klein/National Geographic Image Collection. **12.7** Photo Henri Stierlin. **12.8** Photo Rebecca Storey. **12.9** Drawing Drazen Tomic after Romero 1970. **12.10** Drawing H. Tom Hall/National Geographic Image Collection. **12.11** Rollout photograph K5456 © Justin Kerr. **12.12** Rollout photograph K5824 © Justin Kerr. **12.13** Map: Drazen Tomic; Glyphs: Courtesy Simon Martin and Michael D. Coe. **12.14** Photo Jorge Pérez de Lara. **12.15** Copyright Merle Greene Robertson, 1976. **12.16** Drawing Philip Winton. **12.17** Photo David Drew. **12.18** Photo Whitestar. **12.19** Drawing Philip Winton after Barnhart. **12.20** Table based on Martin and Grube 2000. **12.21** Table based on Martin and Grube 2000. **12.22** Table based on Martin and Grube 2000. **12.23** British Museum, London. **12.24** British Museum, London. **12.25** Drawing Richard Schlecht/ National Geographic Image Collection. **12.26** Table based on Martin and Grube 2000. **12.27** Drawing Philip Winton after Barbara Fash and Refugio Murcia. **12.28** Photo David Drew. **12.29** Drawing Frederick Catherwood. **12.30** Table based on Martin and Grube 2000. **12.31** Table based on Martin and Grube 2000. **12.32** Drawing H. Tom Hall/National Geographic Image Collection. **12.33** Drawing by Linda Schele, © David Schele, courtesy Foundation for the Advancement of Mesoamerican Studies, Inc. **12.34** Drawing Drazen Tomic after Marqina 1999 (1951): 71, Lám. 12 and Evans 1999 (Teotihuacan); Heyden and Gendrop 1980: 107, Fig. 141 (Palenque). **12.35** Table Susan Toby Evans. **12.36** Table based on Martin and Grube 2000. **12.37** David Webster. **12.38** Photo Jorge Pérez de Lara. **12.39** Drawing Tatiana Prouskouriakoff. **12.40** Drawing Virginia Miller after Adela Breton. **12.41** Marquina 1951. **12.42** Photo Filmteam Int. **13.1** Drawing ML Design. **13.2** Chacmool from Chichén Itzá. **13.3** Drawing Karl Taube. **13.4** Drawing E. Contreras S. **13.5** *Codex Magliabechiano.* **13.6** Instituto Nacional de Antropología e Historia. **13.7** Photo Eduardo Williams. **13.8** Drawing ML Design after César Fernández in Jarquín Pacheco and Martínez Vargas 1996: 72. **13.9** Drawing Susan Toby Evans after Malena Juarez. **13.10** *Florentine Codex.* **13.11** Drawing Drazen Tomic. **13.12** Hosler 1997. **13.13** *Codex Mendoza.* **13.14** Drawing courtesy of Dr S. Jeffrey K. Wilkerson. **13.15** Drawing Drazen Tomic after García Paytón in Wilkerson 1987: 46–47. **13.16** Photo Mary Ellen Miller. **13.17** Drawing Drazen Tomic after William H. Bond in Stuart 1992: 122–123. **13.18** Drawing Ken Hirth. **13.19** Photo Whitestar. **13.20** Drawing Smith 2000. **13.21** Drawing ML Design. **13.22** Photo ffotograff © Jill Ranford. **13.23** Photo Joyce Kelly. **14.1** Drawing ML Design. **14.2** Drawing Elia Sánchez. **14.3** Photo Irmgard Groth-Kimball © Thames & Hudson Ltd, London. **14.4** Photo Whitestar. **14.5** From Pohl 1999: 115. **14.6** Drawing Drazen Tomic after A. Coe, 2001. **14.7** Photo Jorge Pérez de Lara. **14.8** Drawing ML Design after Arturo Valle Ucan in Huchim Herrera and Toscano Hernández 1999: 22–23. **14.9** Photo Whitestar. **14.10** Drawing Drazen Tomic after Folan *et al.* 1983, Fig. 1.2. **14.11** Photo Colin McEwan. **14.12** *Codex Mendoza.* **14.13** Photo David Drew. **14.14** Drawing Jean Blackburn. **14.15** Drawing Tatiana Prouskouriakoff. **14.16** Photo Irmgard Groth Kimball © Thames & Hudson Ltd, London. **14.17** Hudson Museum, University of Maine, William P. Palmer III Collection. HM 646. **14.18** Drawing Drazen Tomic after Scarborough in Evans and Webster (eds.) 2001. **14.19** Instituto de Investagaciones Esthésticas, UNAM, Mexico. **14.20** Photo Jeremy A. Sabloff. **14.21** Drawing Drazen Tomic after Sharer 1994. **14.22** Photo Mary Ellen Miller. **14.23** Museo Nacional de Antropología, Mexico. **14.24** American Museum of Natural History, New York. **15.1** Drawing ML Design. **15.2** Museo Nacional de Antropología, Mexico. **15.3** Drawing Drazen Tomic after Fernando Getino in Mastache and Cobean 2000: 103, Fig. 2. **15.4** Photo Jeremy A. Sabloff. **15.5** *Codex Magliabechiano.* **15.6** Drawings Richard Diehl. **15.7** Drawing Richard Diehl. **15.8** Drawing Richard Diehl. **15.9** Museo Nacional de Antropología, Mexico. **15.10** Kunsthistorisches Museum mit MVK und OTM, Vienna. **15.11** Drawing ML Design after Kelley 1986. **15.12** Above, Kelley 1986; below, Courtesy of the American Musuem of Natural History, New York. **15.13** Amy Elizabeth Grey after Di Peso, Rinaldo and Fenner 1974. **15.14** Photo Michael Calderwood. **15.15** Photos Jorge Pérez de Lara. **15.16** *Codex Borgia.* **15.17** Historia Tolteca-Chichimeca. **15.18** *Codex Boturini.* **15.19** *Codex Nuttall.* **15.20** Drawing ML Design after Pohl and Byland 1994: Map 3. **16.1** Drawing ML Design. **16.2** Biblioteca Nacional, Madrid. **16.3** Table Susan Toby Evans. 16.4 Sharer 1994 after map in Jones 1952. **16.5** Photo Jeremy A. Sabloff. **16.6** Drawing Tatania Proskouriakoff. **16.7** Relacíon de Michoacan. **16.8** Drawing ML Design after Pollard 1993. **16.9** Photo Jorge Pérez de Lara. **16.10** *Codex Xolotl.* **16.11** Photo Michel Zabé. **16.12** *Florentine Codex.* **16.13** Photo Jorge Pérez de Lara. **16.14** *Codex Duran.* **16.15** Diagram Susan Toby Evans. **16.16** Drawing ML Design, after Coè. **16.17** Photo Richard Townsend. **17.1** Drawing Drazen Tomic. **17.2** Drawing ML Design after Susan Toby Evans. **17.3** *Codex Mendoza.* **17.4** *Codex Ixtlilxochitl.* **17.5** Diagram Susan Toby Evans. **17.6** Great Temple Project. **17.7** Great Temple Project. **17.8** Drawing Philip Winton. **17.9** Drawing Great Temple Project. **17.10** Table Susan Toby Evans. **17.11** *Codex Mendoza.* **17.12** *Codex Mendoza.* **17.13** *Codex Ixtlilxochitl.* **17.14** Bristol Museums and Art Gallery. **17.15**

Drawing Drazen Tomic. **17.16** *Florentine Codex*. **17.17** *Florentine Codex*. **17.18** Photo Jorge Pérez de Lara. **17.19** Drawing Drazen Tomic. **18.1** Great Temple Project. **18.2** Drawing ML Design. **18.3** Drawing ML Design after Berdan *et al.* 1996: Fig. II-I. **18.4** From Marquina 1999: 217, Lám. 62. **18.5** *Codex Mendoza*. **18.6** After *Codex Mendoza*. **18.7** Photo Richard Townsend. **18.8** Annick Petersen; after Matthew Pietryka. **18.9** University Library of Uppsala. **18.10** Drawing Drazen Tomic after Susan Toby Evans. **18.11** Drawing Drazen Tomic after Susan Toby Evans. **18.12** Mapa Quinatzin. **18.13** Instituto Nacional de Antropología e Historia. **18.14** Photo Joyce Kelly. **18.15** *Codex Mendoza*. **18.16** Photo Mary Ellen Miller. **18.17** Drawing Drazen Tomic after González Licón 1994. **18.18** Drawing Drazen Tomic after González Licón 1994. **18.19** Marquina 1951. **18.20** Photo Michel Zabé. **18.21** *Codex Borgia*. **18.22** Photo Jorge Pérez de Lara. **18.23** Drawing Drazen Tomic after Pollard 19903: 36. **18.24** Drawing ML Design after Pollard 1993: 89. **18.25** After *Codex Duran*. **19.1** Drawing ML Design. **19.2** Great Temple Project. 19.3 *Codex Mendoza*. 19.4 Great Temple Project. **19.5** Museo Nacional de Antropología, Mexico. **19.6** *Codex Magliabechiano*. **19.7** Great Temple Project. **19.8** Photo Michel Zabé. **19.9** Great Temple Project. **19.10** Table based on Gasco and Voorhies 1989: 77; Berdan and Anawalt 1997. **19.11** *Codex Mendoza*. **19.12** Newberry Library, Chicago. **19.13** *Codex Ixtlilxochitl*. **19.14** Drawing ML Design. **19.15** Drawing ML Design. **19.16** Patrimonio Nacional, Palacio Real, Madrid. **19.17** The Art Institute of Chicago, Major Acquisitions Fund, 1990.21. **19.18** Photo Whitestar/Massimo Borchi. **19.19** Lothrop 1924. **19.20** Drawing ML Design after Jean Zallinger and Peter Zallinger. **19.21** *Codex Madrid*. **19.22** Drawing Drazen Tomic. **19.23** Drawing Drazen Tomic. **20.1** Drawing ML Design. **20.2** Drawing ML Design. **20.3** *Florentine Codex*. **20.4** *Codex Magliabechiano*. **20.5** *Codex Mendoza*. **20.6** from Lienzo of Tlaxcala, Courtesy American Museum of Natural History, New York. **20.7** Museo Nacional de Antropología, Mexico. **20.8** *Florentine Codex*. **20.9** *Codex Azcatitlan*. **20.10** *Florentine Codex*. **20.11** *Florentine Codex*. **20.12** Museo Nacional del Virreinato, Tepotzotlan. **20.13** Great Temple Project. **20.14** Great Temple Project. **20.15** Volkerkunde Museum, Vienna. **20.16** Drawing Frederick Catherwood. **20.17** Photo George T. Keene. **Reference maps** Copyright 2001 from Evans and Webster (eds.) 2001. Reproduced by permission of Routledge/Taylor & Francis Books, Inc.

INDEX